Environmental Ethics

Readings in Theory and Application

SIXTH EDITION

LOUIS P. POJMAN
Late of the United States Military Academy, West Point

PAUL POJMAN
Towson University

WADSWORTH
CENGAGE Learning™

Australia • Brazil • Japan • Korea • Mexico • Singapore • Spain • United Kingdom • United States

WADSWORTH
CENGAGE Learning

Environmental Ethics: Readings in Theory and Application, Sixth Edition

Louis P. Pojman, Paul Pojman

Publisher: Clark Baxter

Sr. Sponsoring Editor: Joann Kozyrev

Assistant Editor: Joshua Duncan

Editorial Assistant: Marri Straton

Media Editor: Kimberly Apfelbaum

Marketing Manager: Mark T. Haynes

Marketing Coordinator: Josh Hendrick

Marketing Communications Manager: Laura Localio

Content Project Management: PreMediaGlobal

Senior Art Director: Jennifer Wahi

Print Buyer: Mary Beth Hennebury

Senior Image Acquisition Rights Specialist: Jennifer Meyer Dare

Senior Rights Acquisition Specialist, Text: Katie Huha

Production Service: PreMediaGlobal

Cover Designer: Michelle DiMercurio

Cover Image: Shutterstock Image

Compositor: PreMediaGlobal

For product information and technology assistance, contact us at **Cengage Learning Customer & Sales Support, 1-800-354-9706**

For permission to use material from this text or product, submit all requests online at **www.cengage.com/permissions.** Further permissions questions can be emailed to **permissionrequest@cengage.com.**

Library of Congress Control Number: 2010936474

ISBN-13: 978-0-538-45284-7

ISBN-10: 0-538-45284-6

Wadsworth
20 Channel Center Street
Boston, MA 02210
USA

Cengage Learning is a leading provider of customized learning solutions with office locations around the globe, including Singapore, the United Kingdom, Australia, Mexico, Brazil and Japan. Locate your local office at **international.cengage.com/region.**

Cengage Learning products are represented in Canada by Nelson Education, Ltd.

For your course and learning solutions, visit **www.cengage.com.**

Purchase any of our products at your local college store or at our preferred online store **www.cengagebrain.com.**

Instructors: Please visit **login.cengage.com** and log in to access instructor-specific resources.

Printed in the United States of America
1 2 3 4 5 6 7 14 13 12 11 10

To the people of Kuna Yala: may your voices be heard.

Contents

PREFACE   xi
INTRODUCTION   1
WHAT IS ETHICS?   4

PART I   **Theory 9**

Chapter 1   Introduction   10

1   *An Overview of Environmental Ethics   10*
Clare Palmer

2   *Ideals of Human Excellence and Preserving Natural Environments   36*
Thomas E. Hill, Jr.

3   *Global Environment and International Inequality   47*
Henry Shue

Chapter 2   Animal Rights   58

4   *Rational Beings Alone Have Moral Worth   60*
Immanuel Kant

5   *The Green Kant: Kant's Treatment of Animals   62*
Holly L. Wilson

6   *A Utilitarian Defense of Animal Liberation*   71
Peter Singer

7   *The Radical Egalitarian Case for Animal Rights*   81
Tom Regan

8   *A Critique of Regan's Animal Rights Theory*   89
Mary Anne Warren

9   *Against Zoos*   96
Dale Jamieson

Chapter 3   Value in Nature Itself   104

10   *Naturalizing Values: Organisms and Species*   105
Holmes Rolston, III

11   *Comments on Holmes Rolston's "Naturalizing Values"*   119
Ned Hettinger

12   *Nature*   122
John Stuart Mill

13   *The Shallow and the Deep, Long-Range Ecological Movement*   129
Arne Naess

14   *Ecosophy T: Deep Versus Shallow Ecology*   133
Arne Naess

15   *Deep Ecology*   143
Bill Devall and George Sessions

16   *Deep Ecology: A New Philosophy of Our Time?*   149
Warwick Fox

17   *A Critique of Anti-Anthropocentric Ethics*   156
Richard Watson

18   *Social Ecology Versus Deep Ecology*   165
Murray Bookchin

19   *Radical Environmentalism and Wilderness Preservation: A Third World Critique*   176
Ramachandra Guha

Chapter 4 Ecological Ethics 185

20 *Biodiversity: The Key to Saving Life on Earth* 187
Donella H. Meadows

21 *Why Do Species Matter?* 190
Lilly-Marlene Russow

22 *Reverence for Life* 198
Albert Schweitzer

23 *Biocentric Egalitarianism* 205
Paul Taylor

24 *Ecocentric Ethics: The Land Ethic* 222
Aldo Leopold

25 *The Conceptual Foundations of the Land Ethic* 232
J. Baird Callicott

26 *Should Trees Have Standing? Toward Legal Rights for Natural Objects* 246
Christopher D. Stone

Chapter 5 Population and Consumption 258

27 *A Special Moment in History: The Challenge of Overpopulation and Overconsumption* 260
Bill McKibben

28 *The Tragedy of the Commons* 272
Garrett Hardin

29 *The Unjust War against Population* 282
Jacqueline Kasun

30 *Lifeboat Ethics* 296
Garrett Hardin

31 *Population and Food: A Critique of Lifeboat Ethics* 306
William W. Murdoch and Allan Oaten

Chapter 6 Pollution: Soil Air Water 312

32 *You Are What You Breathe* 314
Hilary French

33 *We All Live in Bhopal   322*
George Bradford

34 *People or Penguins: The Case for Optimal Pollution   327*
William F. Baxter

35 *Is* Silent Spring *Behind Us?   332*
David Pimentel

PART II   **Practice   339**

Chapter 7   Food Ethics   340

36 *Hunger, Duty, and Ecology: On What
We Owe Starving Humans   341*
Mylan Engel, Jr.

37 *The World Food Supply: The Damage Done by
Cattle-Raising   360*
Tristram Coffin

38 *Vegetarianism and Treading Lightly on the Earth   364*
Michael Allen Fox

39 *Can Frankenfood Save the Planet?   371*
Jonathan Rauch

40 *The Unholy Alliance   378*
Mae-Wan Ho

41 *The ETC Report: The Poor Can Feed Themselves   389*

Chapter 8   Climate Change and Energy Policy   412

42 *Understanding the Causes of Global Climate Change   413*
Pew Center on Global Climate Change

43 *Livestock's Role in Climate Change and Air Pollution   417*
UN Report: Climate Change and Livestock

44 *Ethics and Global Climate Change   437*
Stephen M. Gardiner

45 *The Denial Industry   458*
    George Monbiot

46 *Hoodwinked in the Hothouse: False Solutions to
    Climate Change   471*

47 *Climate Justice: The Emerging Movement against Green
    Capitalism   481*
    Ashley Dawson

48 *Sustainability and Technology Solutions in the Climate
    Policy Debate: The Case of Geologic Carbon Sequestration   497*
    Evelyn Wright and Paul Pojman

49 *War and Climate Change   505*
    Barry Sanders

Chapter 9   Race, Class, Gender: Environmental Justice, Ecofeminism, and Indigenous Rights   512

50 *Overcoming Racism in Environmental Decision Making   513*
    Robert D. Bullard

51 *Just Garbage: The Problem of Environmental Racism   530*
    Peter S. Wenz

52 *Deceiving the Third World: The Myth of Catching-Up
    Development   539*
    Maria Mies

53 *Environmental Risks, Rights, and the Failure of Liberal
    Democracy: Some Possible Remedies   547*
    Laura Westra

54 *All Our Relations: Native Struggles for Land and Life   565*
    Winona Laduke

55 *Indigenous Knowledge and Technology: Creating Environmental
    Justice in the Twenty-First Century   569*
    Linda Robyn

56 *Earth Democracy   584*
    Vandana Shiva

57 *The Power and the Promise of Ecological Feminism*   *589*
Karen J. Warren

58 *The Earth Charter: From Global Ethics to International Law
Instrument*   *606*
Introduction by Laura Westra

Chapter 10   The Greening of Spirituality   614

59 *Genesis 1–3*   *615*

60 *Jewish Tradition, the Traditional Jew and the Environment*   *618*
Barry Freundel

61 *The Judeo-Christian Stewardship Attitude to Nature*   *628*
Patrick Dobel

62 *Islamic Environmental Ethics, Law, and Society*   *633*
Mawil Y. Izzi Deen (Samarrai)

63 Satyagraha *for Conservation: A Hindu View*   *640*
O. P. Dwivedi

64 *The Buddhist Attitude Towards Nature*   *650*
Lily De Silva

65 *Pagan Environmentalism: Principles of Unity*   *655*
Starhawk

Chapter 11   The New Green Capitalist Order: Economics, Sustainability, and Response   659

66 *Sustainable Development: Economic Myths and Global
Realities*   *661*
William E. Rees

67 *At the Shrine of Our Lady of Fàtima, or Why Political Questions
Are Not All Economic*   *669*
Mark Sagoff

68 *Toward a Just and Sustainable Economic Order*   *678*
John B. Cobb, Jr.

69 *What Every Environmentalist Needs to Know About Capitalism*   691
Fred Magdoff and John Bellamy Foster

70 *Is Sustainable Capitalism an Oxymoron?*   712
David Schweickart

71 *An Ecological Critique of Global Advertising*   727
Alan Thein Durning

72 *The Challenge of the Future: Private Property, the City, the Globe, and a Sustainable Society*   735
Louis P. Pojman

73 *Strategic Monkeywrenching*   747
Dave Foreman

74 *Ecosabotage and Civil Disobedience*   751
Michael Martin

75 *The Coming Insurrection: Sixth Circle: "The Environment Is an Industrial Challenge"*   766
The Invisible Committee

Preface

ENVIRONMENTAL Philosophy is grounded in the oldest academic tradition (Philosophy), as well as one of the youngest (post-industrial Environmental thinking), and is spread out over fields as diverse as biology, economics, chemistry, geology, and political theory to name a few. It is also one of the fastest changing fields. Enormous amounts of scientific research increasing our understanding of our environment, but also research into technologies which impact, weather negatively or positively, the environment. Policy debates are ongoing, at all levels of government and international organizations.

The text is divided into two sections, Part One Theory and Part Two Practice. It would be simple if the Theory section contained topics that were independent of time and place, concerns of universal importance to all peoples. In pure ethics, indeed, this is what Theory might mean. In as much as this is a text in applied ethics, however, even the theory has ground in practice. Thus while our moral questions about, for instance, other animals, can be asked theoretically (do they have consciousness, are they worthy of moral treatment, rights, etc.), there is also the immediate practical question of 'should we eat them?', or 'should we mass slaughter them in factory farms?'. Nonetheless, the question of animal rights is more of a theory question than say Genetically Modified Foods or Environmental Racism issues clearly grounded in human practice.

I see the Theory side as those issues that change slowly, debates that may develop over time with new ideas but not new facts. On the practice side, the issues change with new developments, with new facts. A cataclysmic drop in human population (dues to war, mass famine, or disease, etc) would make irrelevant Garret Hardin's *Life Boat Ethics*, and perhaps might inspire new theories about how the remaining humans ought to view nature, but not render it irrelevant. It is no surprise then that it is the Practice side that must be updated more frequently, and indeed significant changes have taken place in this regard.

The text is slightly shorter than text in the 5th edition; twenty-five old, often outdated, essays have been removed and nineteen new essays put in their place, reflecting the changes in the field. A new introductory section begins the text with essays by Clare Palmer, "An Overview of Environmental Ethics" and a seminal essay on environmental virtue ethics by Thomas E. Hill, Jr., "Ideals of Human Excellence and Preserving Natural Environments," as well as Henry Shue's "Global Environment and International Inequality." The old sections on Philosophical Theories of Nature have been regrouped and up-dated under the headings Nature and Value, and Ecological Ethics. The Food Ethics section has been updated with a remarkable essay, "The ETC Report: The Poor Can Feed Themselves." Chapter 8 has been renamed "Climate Change and Energy Policy" and has six new essays to reflect what is arguably the single most important field in environmental philosophy and policy. Chap-ter 9 has been reconceived as "Race, Class, Gender: Environmental Justice, Ecofeminism, and Indigenous Rights" and includes essays taken from the old sections of Environmental Justice and non-Western Voices as well as three new essays from indigenous and developing world perspectives. Chapter 10, "The Greening of Spirituality," looks at important trends and issues at the inter-section of spirituality and environmentalism. Most of these essays existed in various places in the 5th edition, but also include two new essays, on Jewish perspectives as well as Paganism. Finally, Chapter 11, "The New Green Capital-ist Order: Economics, Sustainability, and Response" include old essays from the Economics section as well as four new essays centered on the critical debates over the new Green Capitalism.

The debate over whether we are going to turn the solutions of environmen-tal problems over to capitalism are some of the most important issues we face, especially where they intersect with climate and energy policy.

Global Environmental Ethics Watch

Supplement the readings in this book with the latest information on Environ-mental Ethics with access to the Global Environmental Ethics Watch. You and your students will have access to the latest information on key environmental ethics issues from trusted academic journals, news outlets, and magazines. You also will receive access to statistics, primary sources, case studies, podcasts, and much more!

- Videos are also available to spark classroom discussion or enhance the cov-erage outside of class.

- Portals within the site focus on specific topics in environmental ethics, in-cluding animal welfare, deep ecology, ecofeminism, environmental justice, food ethics, and more.

- Current case studies encourage critical thinking and problem solving.

To preview the Global Environmental Ethics Watch, contact your Cengage Learning representative. You can order student copies of this book with access to the site using this ISBN: 9781111875220.

Acknowledgments

The text is dedicated to the Kuna, an indigenous group living on small islands off the Caribbean coast of Panama. Their struggles for freedom and environmental integrity, their resistance to exploitation by global capitalism, and their search for autonomous integration into the global society mirror the struggles of the world. As I write in the Introduction, the Kuna are currently being threatened by numerous environmental issues not of their own making, including plastic garbage washing up in their shores and rising waters and storm surges due to climate change. It is voices such as theirs that must be heard and I thank the people of Ogobsucun, and the environmental organization Earth Train, for providing me with an opportunity to stay with them.

I wish to thank the reviewers who contributed many useful suggestions and gave insight into the ways of using the book: Ben Bradley, Syracuse University; Craig Duncan, Ithaca College; Judith A. Little, SUNY Potsdam; and Mark Sheldon, Northwestern University.

A special thanks to the Cengage, Wadsworth Editorial team including Joann Kozyrev, Sr. Sponsoring Editor; Mark T. Haynes, Marketing Manager; Nathan Gamache, Assistant Editor; and Katie Huha and Karyn Morrison for help with the permissions process as well as the production editors at PreMedia Global, Rathi Thirumalai and Sini Sivaraman.

Louis Pojman, the editor for the first four editions of this anthology, remains the primary editor; two editions later, the majority of essays are still ones he chose. He is the inspiration for the anthology as well as the single greatest influence upon my own environmental thinking. I especially thank Evelyn Wright for her intellectual partnership and continuing inspiration. I would also like to acknowledge my students at Towson University for their inspiring commitment to a value-driven life.

Paul Pojman
Towson University, 2010
Environmental Ethics

Introduction

ENVIRONMENTAL ETHICS, as presented in this text, concerns our religions, our economies, our politics, our future on this planet, and our health. It includes problems of race, class, gender, and globalization. It is not separate from our conception of what it means to be human, of our relationship to nature and technology. It is an interdisciplinary field that is of vital concern to us all.

Human beings have lived on Earth for about 100,000 years, a very short time in relation to the age of the universe (15 billion years) or even to the life of our planet (4.6 billion years). Humans started domesticating animals and growing crops about 10,000 years ago. If we compacted the history of Earth into a movie lasting 1 year, running 146 years per second, life would not appear until March, multicellular organisms not until November, dinosaurs not until December 13 (lasting until the 26th), mammals not until December 15, *Homo sapiens* (our species) not until 11 minutes to midnight on December 25, and civilization not until 1 minute to midnight on December 31. Yet in a very short time, since the Industrial Revolution began 250 years ago, humans—a mere .000002% of Earth's life—have become capable of seriously altering the entire biosphere.

With the Industrial Revolution, a vast acceleration of forest cutting, mining, land development, and fishing began. Industrialized societies saw forests disappearing to fuel the factories, mass migrations of people moving to cities to work in factories, and clouds of pollution hanging over the cities. Many voices lamented this, including most notably Henry David Thoreau (who published *Walden* in 1848), and John Muir (who started the Sierra Club in 1892). Their concerns were echoed in poetry and novels, by unionizers and workplace reformers, as well as by other disparate thinkers and movements. Further complicating matters was the increasing exploitation of newly colonized or conquered societies. The environment was turned into a site of economic competition between the various industrialized nations, continuing up through the twentieth century.

The early twentieth century saw the industrialized nations in the midst of war and economic depression, leaving little time for ideas of environmental awareness. It is notable that the folk singer Woody Guthrie, arguably one of the most passionate voices for social reform the United States has ever heard, saw the environment simply as a source of economics. Dam up the rivers and cut down the forests just give people jobs.

Post World War II, with the economy in the United Sates booming, people finally had a chance to examine where hundreds of years of unrestrained economic development had left us. Aldo Leopold published *A Sand County Almanac* in 1949, arguing for the need to extend our ethical sensibilities beyond the human to include nature. Then in 1962, Rachel Carson's book *Silent Spring*, documenting the poisoning of the environment with DDT, achieved national attention. DDT was banned and the environmental movement was in a sense born.

Since the early 1960s the environmental movement has changed the United States. It is arguably one of the most successful social movements in human history. Of course some may argue that this success has been harmful to humans (especially to economic development), and others may argue that the success is too little too late, but nonetheless it has changed the consciousness and the laws in those places where it has taken root. Our children are being taught recycling in schools, environmental science and studies programs abound at colleges and universities, numerous state and federal governmental agencies have been formed, organic food is available in grocery stores (going from nonexistent, to small time, to one of the most profitable sectors of the food industry), and thousands of laws regulate pollution and development. Undeveloped land cannot be developed without an environmental impact study. Endangered species are protected under law, factories and power plants are regulated, streams are sampled, new chemicals are tested, and in every sector of human interaction with the environment there has been at least discussion if not legislation. No one, not even polluting businesses or apparently anti-environment politicians, can get away without paying lip service to environmentalism. Since the last edition of this text we have seen climate change finally be taken up as a political issue. In fact, we are about to embark on a global venture of a "new green economy," an economy where environmental values form the ideological core.

But on at least two fronts there is new reason for concern. First, globally, the global south and poor in general still suffer a disproportionate impact of environmental problems though contributing less to them and having fewer resources to adequately respond to them. We see this already with the impacts of climate change, and this will only increase as global temperature changes further disrupt ecologies, weather patterns, and ocean conditions. Second, even if the industrial world re-tools to lessen the use of fossil fuels and nonrenewable resources, it remains to be seen if this "new green economy" leads to a more just and sustainable world or if it becomes simply a new way to justify the exploitative practices of global capitalism.

There is thus an urgent need for the rich and powerful to start listening, and for previously marginalized or quiet voices to start being heard. While indigenous peoples and others outside of the global economy have also engaged in unsustainable environmental practices, they also often have a better understanding of such matters than colonial and capitalist powers; increasingly groups around the world are networking and speaking up. One such example is the Kuna.

The Kuna people moved to the archipelago off of Panama's Caribbean coast hundreds of years ago to escape disease and interference from others. They have faced constant threats, including oppression from colonial rulers. Yet they have survived with a remarkably intact culture. They still produce much of their own food through fishing and preindustrial methods of agriculture on the mainland which they paddle to in dugout canoes. Communities meet regularly in large halls to debate and discuss social issues as they have done for generations. They of course face numerous social problems, including the migration of many Kuna to Panama City and the resultant cultural clashes, and increasing dependence on imported goods and technologies with the subsequent need for cash. One of their leaders recently said that for the first time the major threat to the Kuna comes from within.

Yet they are also facing three environmental threats which, although all the world is facing them, the Kuna confront with a particular vulnerability and urgency: global capitalism, plastic garbage and other toxic pollutants, and climate change. Importantly, the Kuna are providing leadership in their responses to them.

In response to global capitalism, the Kuna have enacted laws preventing outside ownership of their land, recognizing that without these protections their islands would be turned into yet another Caribbean resort center, with mega hotels owned by large corporate chains transforming every aspect of the Kuna's identity. The promises of increased wealth, which global capitalism makes to the regions it enters, have been at best mistakes and at worst malicious lies. Rather, the standard of living increases for a few while the rest have their social systems upturned, networks of local production disrupted, and land prices skyrocket beyond the affordability of the people living there. In the words of a Kuna elder, paradoxically, 'money causes hunger'. The Kuna are one of the few indigenous groups able to so protect themselves.

The Kuna used to have a convenient garbage disposal system; their coconut husks, plantain peels, fish bones, as well as human waste could be dumped in the surrounding ocean with minimal impact. But disposable plastics have entered the islands in the forms of bottles, wrappers, and bags. The coast lines are now often encrusted with debris, both from the Kuna themselves as well as from large cruise ships which dump their garbage out at sea. In response, the Kuna have recently passed a resolution working towards the banning of disposable plastics. This is a momentous event in global environmental history. I believe this to be the first

governmental resolution of its kind; some cities have banned some plastics, but this is the first comprehensive resolution recognizing the totality of the problem.

In one sense the Kuna are themselves largely responsible for the garbage on their shores, but when we realize that virtually every region of this planet has been so affected by the onslaught of plastic debris, that there is a garbage patch twice the size of France in the Pacific Ocean, we begin to realize that there is a global pattern here.

The third area of environmental concern the Kuna are facing especially acutely is climate change. Their islands are often only a half meter above sea level. Already storm surges are increasing, and the IPCC reports predict a 5-mm ocean rise per year for the next hundred years (http://www.ipcc.ch/ipccreports/tar/wg2/pdf/wg2TARchap17.pdf). The Kuna themselves have a low carbon footprint, but as is the case all over the world, the people who have contributed the least to global warming are being impacted the most.

They are still discussing their response. Kuna youth are active in global climate change activism, and some are beginning to prepare to move off the islands to the lowland hills on the mainland. They are fortunate to have a land to move to; many other peoples in coastal regions will simply lose everything.

I invite you, as you think about the various issues raised in this text and the enormous challenges we face ahead as we try to move toward a more social just and environmentally sustainable future, to ask, "What would the Kuna do?"; at the very least it is voices such as theirs, which may provide the leadership we need.

What Is Ethics?

We are discussing no small matter, but how we ought to live.
SOCRATES IN PLATO'S REPUBLIC

WHAT IS IT TO BE a moral person? What is the nature of morality, and why do we need it? What is the good, and how will I know it? Are moral principles absolute or simply relative to social groups or individual decision? Is it in my interest to be moral? Is it sometimes in my best interest to act immorally? What is the relationship between morality and religion? What is the relationship between morality and law? What is the relationship between morality and etiquette?

These are some of the questions that we will be examining in this chapter. We want to know how we should live.

The terms *moral* and *ethics* come from Latin and Greek, respectively (*mores* and *ethos*), deriving their meaning from the idea of custom. Although philosophers sometimes distinguish these terms—*morality* referring to the customs, principles, and practices of a people or culture, and *ethics* referring to the whole domain of morality and moral philosophy—I shall use them interchangeably in this book, using the context to make any differences clear.

Moral philosophy refers to the systematic endeavor to understand moral concepts and justify moral principles and theories. It undertakes to analyze such concepts as "right," "wrong," "permissible," "ought," "good," and "evil" in their moral contexts. Moral philosophy seeks to establish principles of right behavior that may serve as action guides for individuals and groups. It investigates which values and virtues are paramount to the worthwhile life or society. It builds and scrutinizes arguments in ethical theories, and it seeks to discover valid principles (e.g., "Never kill innocent human beings") and the relationship between those principles (e.g., "Does saving a life in some situations constitute a valid reason for breaking a promise?").

But it is not obvious that this project of finding principles upon which to base our lives and actions is the best way to proceed. We can reasonably ask whether there are such principles, and even if there are, why they should have hold on us. At the very least our moral instinct precedes our reading of

4

philosophers' ideas on why we ought to be moral. Nonetheless, such ideas can help challenge our preconceptions, help us refine our moral compass, and perhaps help us understand the perspectives of those who we disagree with.

MORALITY AS COMPARED WITH OTHER NORMATIVE SUBJECTS

Moral precepts are concerned with norms—not with what is but with what *ought* to be. How should I live? What is the right thing to do in this situation? Should one always tell the truth? Do I have a duty to report a student whom I have seen cheating in class or a co-worker whom I have seen stealing office supplies? Should I tell my friend that his spouse is having an affair? Ought a woman ever to have an abortion? Should we permit the cloning of human beings? Morality has a distinct action guiding or *normative* aspect, an aspect it shares with other practical institutions, such as religion, law, and etiquette.

Moral behavior, as defined by a given religion, is often held to be essential to the practice of that religion. But neither the practices nor precepts of morality should be identified with religion. The practice of morality need not be motivated by religious considerations. And moral precepts need not be grounded in revelation or divine authority—as religious teachings invariably are. The most salient characteristic of ethics—by which I mean both philosophical morality (or morality, as I will simply refer to it) and moral philosophy—is that it is grounded in reason and human experience.

To use a spatial metaphor, secular ethics is horizontal, omitting a vertical or transcendental dimension. Religious ethics has a vertical dimension, being grounded in revelation or divine authority, though generally using reason to supplement or complement revelation. These two differing orientations will often generate different moral principles and standards of evaluation, but they need not. Some versions of religious ethics that posit God's revelation of the moral law in nature or conscience hold that reason can discover what is right or wrong even apart from divine revelation.

Morality is also closely related to law, and some people equate the two practices. Many laws are instituted to promote well-being (i.e., resolve conflicts of interest and/or promote social harmony), just as morality does, but ethics may judge that some laws are immoral without denying that they are valid laws. For example, laws may permit slavery or irrelevant discrimination against people on the basis of race or sex. An antiabortion advocate may believe that the laws permitting abortion are immoral.

In the television series *Ethics in America* (PBS, 1989), James Neal, a trial lawyer, was asked what he would do if he discovered that his client had committed a murder for which another man had been convicted and would soon be executed. Mr. Neal said that he had a legal obligation to keep this information confidential and that if he divulged it, he would be disbarred. It is arguable that he has a moral obligation that overrides his legal obligation and that demands he take action to protect the innocent man from being executed.

Furthermore, there are some aspects of morality that are not covered by law. For example, it is generally agreed that lying is usually immoral, but there is no general law against it (except under special conditions, such as in cases of perjury or falsifying income tax returns). Sometimes college newspapers publish advertisements for "research assistance," where it is known in advance that the companies will aid and abet plagiarism. The publishing of such research paper ads is legal, but it is doubtful whether it is morally correct. In 1963, 39 people in Queens, New York, watched from their apartments for some forty-five minutes as a man beat and stabbed to death a woman, Kitty Genovese, and did nothing to intervene, not even call the police. These people broke no law, but they were very likely morally culpable for not calling the police.

There is one other major difference between law and morality. In 1351, King Edward of England promulgated a law against treason that made it a crime merely to think homicidal thoughts about the king. But, alas, the law could not be enforced, for no tribunal can search the heart and fathom the intentions of the mind. It is true that *intention*, such as malice aforethought, plays a role in the legal process in determining the legal character of the act, once the act has been committed. But preemptive punishment for people presumed to have bad intentions is illegal. If malicious intentions (called in law *mens rea*) were criminally illegal, would we not all deserve imprisonment? Even if it were possible to detect intentions, when should the punishment be administered? As soon as the subject has the intention? But how do we know that he will not change his mind? Furthermore, is there not a continuum between imagining some harm to X, wishing a harm to X, desiring a harm to X, and intending a harm to X?

Although it is impractical to have laws against bad intentions, these intentions are still bad, still morally wrong. Suppose I plan to push Uncle Charlie off a 1000-foot cliff when we next hike together in order to inherit his wealth but never have a chance to do it (e.g., Uncle Charlie breaks his leg and forswears hiking). Although I have not committed a crime, I have committed a moral wrong. Law generally aims at setting an important but minimal framework in a society of plural values.

Finally, law differs from morality in that there are physical and financial sanctions (e.g., imprisonment and fines) enforcing the law but only the sanctions of conscience and reputation enforcing morality.

Morality also differs from etiquette, which concerns form and style rather than the essence of social existence. Etiquette determines what is polite behavior rather than what is right behavior in a deeper sense. It represents society's decisions about how we are to dress, greet one another, eat, celebrate festivals, dispose of the dead, express gratitude and appreciation, and, in general, carry out social transactions. Whether we greet each other with a handshake, a bow, a hug, or a kiss on the cheek will differ in different social systems; none of these rituals has any moral superiority. People in England hold their forks in their left hands when they eat, whereas people in other countries hold them in their right hand or in whichever hand a person feels like holding them; people in India typically eat without forks at all, using their right hands to eat.

At the same time, it can be immoral to disregard or flout etiquette. Whether to shake hands when greeting a person for the first time or put one's hands together and forward as one bows, as people in India do, is a matter of cultural decision; but once the custom is adopted, the practice takes on the importance of a moral rule, subsumed under the wider principle of Show Respect to People. Similarly, there is no moral necessity of wearing clothes, but many cultures have adopted the custom partly for warmth and partly out of social control of sexuality. But there is nothing wrong with nudists who decide to live together in nudist colonies. But it may well be the case that people running nude in classrooms, stores, and along the road would constitute offensive, or morally insensitive, behavior. Recently, there was a scandal on the beaches of South India where American tourists swam in bikinis, shocking the more modest Indians. There was nothing immoral in itself about wearing bikinis, but given the cultural context, the Americans, in willfully violating etiquette, were guilty of moral impropriety.

Law, etiquette, and religion are all important institutions, but each has limitations. The limitation of the law is that you can't have a law against every social malady nor can you enforce every desirable rule. The limitation of etiquette is that it doesn't get to the heart of what is of vital importance for personal and social existence. Whether one eats with one's fingers pales in significance compared with the importance of being honest or trustworthy or just. Etiquette is a cultural invention, but morality claims to be a discovery.

The limitation of the religious injunction is that it rests on authority, and we are not always sure of or in agreement about the credentials of the authority, nor on how the authority would rule in ambiguous or new cases. Since religion is not founded on reason but on revelation, you cannot use reason to convince someone who does not share your religious views that your view is the right one. I hasten to add that, when moral differences are caused by fundamental moral principles, it is unlikely that philosophical reasoning will settle the matter. Often, however, our moral differences turn out to be rooted in worldviews, not moral principles. For example, whether you believe in killing animals may hinge on your metaphysical view on animals and

TABLE 1   The Relationship Between Ethics, Religion, Etiquette, and Law

Subject	Normative Disjuncts	Sanctions
Ethics	Right, wrong, or permissible—as defined by conscience or reason	Conscience; Praise and blame; Reputation
Religion	Right, wrong, or permissible—as defined by spiritual understanding	Conscience: Eternal; Reward and punishment often linked to supernatural agent or force
Law	Legal and illegal—as defined by a judicial body	Punishments determined by the legislative body
Etiquette	Proper and improper—as defined by culture	Social disapproval

humans. If you do not believe animals experience pain, you probably have little reason not to eat them.

Table 1 may characterize the relationship between ethics, religion, etiquette, and law.

In summary, morality distinguishes itself from law and etiquette by going deeper into the essence of rational existence. It distinguishes itself from religion in that it seeks reasons, rather than authority, to justify its principles. The central purpose of moral philosophy is to secure valid principles of conduct and values that can be instrumental in guiding human actions and producing good character. As such, it is the most important activity known to humans, because it has to do with how we are to live.

STUDY QUESTIONS

1. Illustrate the difference between ethics, law, religion, and etiquette. How are these concepts related? Do you think any one of law, religion, or etiquette is more important than morality in guiding human action? Explain your answer.

2. Based on what you know now, do you think that environmental concerns force us to radically revise our understanding of morality, to merely extend it, or neither?

3. Is it possible to have a religious/spiritual tradition which provides ethical guidance but without being authorization?

FOR FURTHER READING

Frankena, William. *Ethics* (Englewood Cliffs, NJ: Prentice-Hall, 1973).

Kagan, Shelly. *Normative Ethics* (Boulder, CO: Westview Press, 1997).

Mackie, J. L. *Ethics: Inventing Right and Wrong* (New York: Penguin, 1977).

Pojman, Louis. *Ethics: Discovering Right and Wrong*, 3rd ed. (Belmont, CA: Wadsworth, 1989).

Pojman, Louis, ed., *Ethical Theory*, 4th ed. (Belmont, CA: Wadsworth, 2002).

Rachels, James. *Elements of Moral Philosophy* (New York: McGraw-Hill, 1993).

Singer, Peter. *The Expanding Circle: Ethics and Sociobiology* (Oxford: Oxford University Press, 1983).

Taylor, Richard. *Good and Evil* (Buffalo, NY: Prometheus, 1970).

Williams, Bernard. *Morality* (New York: Harper, 1972).

Wilson, James Q. *The Moral Sense* (New York: Free Press, 1993).

PART I

Theory

Chapter 1 Introduction

Chapter 2 Animal Rights

Chapter 3 Value in Nature Itself

Chapter 4 Ecological Ethics

Chapter 5 Population and Consumption

Chapter 6 Pollution: Soil Air Water

Chapter 1

Introduction

THE THREE ESSAYS in this introductory chapter provide, firstly, a bibliographic account on the field of environmental ethics, which can be used to think about potential paper topics; secondly, a challenge to us individually to reconsider what kind of relationship we ourselves wish to have with environmental values; and thirdly, a preliminary look at environmental issues from a global perspective.

1

An Overview of Environmental Ethics

CLARE PALMER

Clare Palmer is professor of philosophy at Washington University, St. Louis. This historiography of a half-century or so of environmental ethics offers an introduction to the field as well as a bibliographic resource for research. Many of the articles referred to are contained in this anthology.

INTRODUCTION

Questions concerning the ways in which human beings can and should interact with the nonhuman natural world can hardly be said to be new.

Throughout recorded human history prescriptions concerning human behavior towards the nonhuman world have existed. Although with reference to restricted periods of time and restricted geographical locations, attempts have been made to categorize such

"A Bibliographic Essay on Environmental Ethics," *Studies in Christian Ethics,* Vol. 7 (1994), T & T Clark Ltd, Edinburgh.

prescriptions and to consider the attitudes that underlie them, to attempt a comprehensive survey would be an enormous task.[1] This chapter concerns a much smaller, more manageable area, and even within this area, I will not attempt to provide a detailed historical survey.[2] I will be sketching, primarily, approaches to what has become known as "environmental ethics" found in the English-speaking Western world, that is to say, the UK, the USA and Australia, during the last thirty years.[3] (A further area which, while relevant, will not be explicitly covered in this paper is the range of positions on exclusively "animal rights" or "animal liberation" issues.)[4] Any sketch such as this cannot avoid emphasizing some areas at the expense of others, and simplifying that which is complex and contested. It also reflects what might be considered "mainstream" philosophical environmental ethics; and thus is open to the range of criticisms which can be or have been made of such environmental ethics by feminists, environmental policy-makers, activists and those interested in urban studies, to name but a few. Despite such criticisms, this overview is intended to provide a helpful context in which to read the chapters gathered in this collection.

A BRIEF HISTORICAL SKETCH

The publications of Rachel Carson's *Silent Spring* in 1962, warning of the dangers to humans and to wildlife from toxic pesticide residues, is widely regarded as the spark which kindled the environmental movement as it is known today. It was not until some time after this, however, that serious philosophical reflection about ethical issues raised by human action in the nonhuman natural world commenced, in the early 1970s.[5] In 1971 the first conference on environmental philosophy was held at the University of Georgia USA;[6] and in 1973 Richard Sylvan (then Routley) gave the paper "Is There Need for a New, an Environmental, Ethic?"—a question which he answered positively. In the same year Scandinavian philosopher Arne Naess published, in *Inquiry*, his article "The Shallow and the Deep, Long-Range Ecology Movements," destined to be of peculiar importance in its popular appeal as the

founding statement of what later became known as deep ecology.[7] In the field of environmental law, Christopher Stone produced and later published an essay entitled "Should Trees Have Standing?" arguing that "environmental issues should be litigated before federal agencies or federal courts in the name of the inanimate objects about to be despoiled … and where inquiry is the subject of public outrage."[8] Stone's paper, while not in itself contributing substantially to the later philosophical debate, helped to make the application of the language of "rights" and "standing" to nonhuman natural objects and areas more familiar, despite its origin in a legal rather than a philosophical context. The year 1974 also saw the publication of John Passmore's philosophical monograph *Man's Responsibility for Nature*.[9]

By 1975, ethical questions concerning the treatment of nonhumans had begun to become more significant on the philosophical agenda. Peter Singer's *Animal Liberation*, developing a utilitarian approach to the treatment of sentient animals, was published. With the publication of this book, and the subsequent proliferation of philosophical work on this topic, ethical questions concerning the treatment of nonhuman animals were well on the way to achieving philosophical respectability. In the environmental field also, by 1979, there was enough ethical interest in environmental issues for Eugene Hargrove to begin producing the journal *Environmental Ethics*, now indisputably the most significant journal in the field. Shortly after this, in the early 1980s, new and influential collections of essays on environmental philosophy were published, most notably a volume from the Australian National University, *Environmental Philosophy* and another collection, also of Australian origin, sharing the same name.[10] By this time, book length studies of environmental ethics had begun to appear.[11]

From the mid-1980s to the present time, research, publication and teaching in environmental ethics has rapidly expanded. Ethical positions first mooted in articles in *Environmental Ethics* in the early 1980s crystallized into densely argued books; most notable amongst these Holmes Rolston's *Environmental Ethics* and Paul Taylor's *Respect for Nature* (to both of which I shall return).[12] In 1989, the International Society for Environmental Ethics

(ISEE) was founded. Several American universities began both undergraduate and graduate courses in environmental ethics, most notably Colorado State University and the University of North Texas in the USA; while Lancaster University in the UK began to offer a taught MA course in Values and the Environmental. New journals relevant to environmental ethics were also founded during the 1990s: in the UK *Environmental Values* in 1992, *Worldviews: Environmental, Culture, Religion* in 1997, and *Ethics, Place and Environmental* in 1998; in the US *Ethics and the Environmental* in 1996 and *Philosophy and Geography* in 1997. By the end of the twentieth century, environmental ethics was a widely studied and hotly debated subject.

CENTRAL QUESTIONS IN ENVIRONMENTAL ETHICS

A wide spectrum of ethical positions is covered by the umbrella term "environmental ethics." These positions draw on a variety of ethical traditions, from Plato and Aristotle to Mill and Moore. As one might expect, a vigorous debate is being conducted between those advocating such diverse approaches. Certain key questions lie at its heart.

One central area of debate concerns value theory in environmental ethics. What is considered to be valuable, and from where does such value come? A number of differing issues and concerns are raised by this question. It is helpful to begin by noting the commonly drawn distinction in environmental ethics between *instrumental* and *non-instrumental* value. Instrumental value is value assigned to something because of its usefulness, as a means to an end. Water, for instance, is of instrumental value to humans because it helps in achieving another goal—that is, remaining alive. But this does not seem to be the case with all kinds of value—for instance, being alive itself. We do not value our lives for any reason beyond themselves; we do not (usually) regard preserving our life as a means to an end, but rather as an end in itself. Value of this sort is non-instrumental value—often called *intrinsic* value

(although as O'Neill's useful chapter "The Varieties of Intrinsic Value" in this book points out intrinsic value is an expression which can be used in a variety of ways in environmental ethics).

This discussion of intrinsic value, however, inevitably raises a second question about the origin of such value. Is it created by human beings, or is it something already in existence in the world, which human beings recognize rather than bring into being? Again, this is a subject of great debate amongst environmental ethicists, sometimes called the dispute between value *subjectivists* and value *objectivists*. Value subjectivists argue that intrinsic value is something which humans create and attach to their own lives, the lives of other people and/or to particular states of affairs (such as pleasure or the avoidance of suffering) or perhaps to qualities such as harmony. Value objectivists, on the other hand, think that non-instrumental value is not something which humans create, but something already in the world. From this perspective, valuing nature intrinsically is not *creating* or *projecting* value but rather *recognizing* value already present. Clearly, such an objectivist view creates difficulties. What kind of "thing" or "quality" is value? Is it a quality possessed by objects or individuals, rather like their color?

A third area of significance, for both subjectivists and objectivists alike, concerns the *location* of such intrinsic value. What actually is of intrinsic value? Here, an even wider array of answers has been advocated. These include attributes of individual living organisms (such as consciousness, sentience, the ability to flourish, or just being alive) and more abstract qualities such as diversity, richness, "naturalness" or balance.

A variety of answers to these questions have been offered by leading environmental ethicists. J. Baird Callicott, some aspects of whose work I will consider later on, argues that all values are *subjective* (human-created, or anthropogenic) but this does not mean they must be human *centered* (anthropocentric). Rather, humans can value the nonhuman world intrinsically, quite apart from its usefulness to humans. Hargrove's chapter "Weak Anthropocentric Intrinsic Value" in this book offers a variant of this view. In contrast, Holmes Rolston (represented in this book by his chapter "Value in Nature and the Value of Nature") argues that value in the natural world is *objective*; it pre-exists human beings, is located in individuals, species, ecosystems and evolutionary processes, and would continue even if humans were to become extinct. For this reason, the natural world objectively contains intrinsic value; and is not only valuable inasmuch as it is useful to humans. Some environmental ethicists have sought to reconcile elements of such arguments. Keekok Lee, for instance, in "Source and Locus of Intrinsic Value: A Reexamination" argues that we need to think of different varieties of intrinsic value: "articulated" intrinsic value, which is created and possessed by humans alone; and "mutely enacted" intrinsic value, which appears in the natural world. The former kind of intrinsic value, she argues, is both subjective and anthropocentric; the latter is objective and located in all living beings.

Another area of debate is more directly ethical. How should human beings act in the nonhuman natural world, given the conclusions of value theory? How does one make ethical decisions where perceived values come into conflict? Should one act in order to preserve some kinds of value over others? Obviously, an environmental ethical edifice must, like any other ethical construction, be built on value theory; the two are, ultimately, inseparable. However, whilst it is only just possible that two philosophers with the same value theory might produce different practical ethical responses, it is quite likely that two philosophers with different underlying value theories might draw similar practical ethical conclusions. Indeed, the possible coincidence of practical ethical conclusions despite underlying *theoretical* differences, is something explored and developed within the work of environmental pragmatism, discussed later in this chapter.

One further distinction remains to be made at this point: that between ethical *monism* and ethical *pluralism*. The central questions at issue here is whether it is possible, within an ethical constituency so large that it could include the entire planet, to arrive at a single governing ethical principle or set of consistent principles to apply to all ethical problems. Ethical monism—the conviction that

such consistency is possible—initially dominated environmental ethics (as indeed, ethics as a whole) and is still championed by some environmental ethicists. More recently, however, some influential figures in environmental ethics have contended that no one ethical principle or set of principles can possibly perform such a comprehensive function. This has led to the advocacy of differing ethical "frameworks" with application to different situations. One might not, for example, expect an ethical framework useful for thinking about a domestic can to be suitable when dealing with the extinction of species. I will explore this discussion in more detail later.

Having thus introduced some of the questions that lie at the heart of the environmental ethical debate, I will now move on to examine, as concisely as possible, some of the key positions presented by different environmental ethicists. These positions, many of which were first proposed in the 1980s, have been foundational for more recent discussions in environmental ethics, some of which I will consider later in this chapter. I will summarize each position, some of its major proponents, different possible forms it might take, and some key criticisms of it.

ANTHROPOCENTRIC APPROACHES TO ENVIRONMENTAL ETHICS

There are a variety of approaches to environmental ethics that can be thought of as being *anthropocentric* or human-centered. Most—but not all—of these approaches maintain that the nonhuman natural world is best considered ethically in terms of its instrumental values to human beings. Such instrumental values may be interpreted very broadly. The natural world can be seen as offering humans a range of physical, aesthetic and spiritual instrumental values, to name but a few. And anthropocentric approaches do not necessarily suggest reckless exploitation of the environment; they may instead maintain that natural resources should be very carefully managed for human benefit including for the benefit of the poor and future human generations (as Barry argues in this volume).[13] Indeed, a broadly anthropocentric approach to environmental values underpins much international environmental policy-making. Most international discussion of central environmental issues—depletion of stratospheric ozone, global warming, marine and atmospheric pollution, treatment of toxic waste, destruction of rainforests—focuses ethically on their effects on human beings. At the level of popular political debate, resource management concerns compose virtually the entire ethical agenda.

Discussion of *sustainable development* also frequently focuses on forms of resource management, with an emphasis on social justice and on the well-being of future generations of humans. Indeed, the most commonly cited definition of sustainable development, taken from the World Commission on Environment and Development (WCED) report *Our Common Future* (1987), is anthropocentric: "sustainable development is development that meets the needs of the present without compromising the ability of future generations to meet their own needs." However, such an understanding of sustainable development is contested in this book. Whilst Cobb in "Toward a Just and Sustainable Economic Order" and Jamieson in "Ethics, Public Policy and Global Warming," worry at various human aspects of sustainable development, Donald Scherer in "Sustainable Resource Ethics" questions the privileging of the human involved in debates about sustainability. He argues that sustainable development needs to take account of "goods other than human well-being and the resources that conduce thereto." Thus Scherer suggests a way in which sustainable development can move beyond the anthropocentric to incorporate a broader understanding of environmental ethics.

Within environmental philosophy, several important thinkers have developed broadly anthropocentric approaches to environmental ethics, though these have taken different forms. John Passmore, for instance, in his early and influential book *Man's Responsibility for Nature* argues—contrary to Routley in the chapter here—that there

is no need for a new environmental ethic.[14] At the root of Passmore's objection to a new environmental ethic—an objection shared by R. G. Frey—is the doubt that there are any rigorous grounds on which intrinsic values in the nonhuman natural world can be based.[15] Values are both human generated and human-focused. Existing Western traditions of environmental management—such as a stewardship tradition—if developed and applied to current ecological problems, can be perfectly adequate.[16]

A rather different, but still anthropocentric, approach to environmental ethics is taken here by Norton in his paper "Environmental Ethics and Weak Anthropocentrism." Norton maintains that environmental ethics need not have recourse to "difficult to justify claims to intrinsic values" in nature. A perfectly sufficient environmental ethic, which can criticize value systems purely exploitative of nature, can be justified on (weakly) anthropocentric grounds alone—which may be the best pragmatic response in a variety of situations where the environment is under threat.[17] From such a perspective, environmental ethics would be principally about "concern for the protection of the resource base through indefinite time."

Such anthropocentric approaches in environmental value have, of course, been attacked from within environmental ethics. Indeed, as reflected by the majority of papers in the collection, one of the central aims of much work in environmental ethics has been to contest an anthropocentric, instrumental valuation of the nonhuman natural world, and to argue that new ways of thinking about and valuing it are needed. The pages of the journal *Environmental Ethics* have reflected such non-anthropocentric views from its early days. Yet outside the academic field of environmental ethics, different kinds of resource management approaches to the nonhuman natural world remain dominant. In recent years, there have been a number of attempts to bring academic environmental ethics and the resource management world of politics and economics together, and to establish shared goals even where the underpinning value approaches may be very different. As I have already suggested, environmental pragmatism is one school of thought in environmental ethics that has adopted this position; I will return to this later in the chapter.

INDIVIDUALS CONSEQUENTIALIST APPROACHES

What I have called "individuals consequentialism" covers a spectrum of positions broadly in the utilitarian tradition of Bentham and Mill. As with all utilitarian positions, the aim of ethical behavior is at the best consequences (however "best" might be interpreted). For individualist consequentialism, the unit of ethical concern is always the individual organism rather than, for instance, the ecosystem or the species. However, it is important to make a distinction here: while the individual organism is the unit of ethical concern, it is the state of affairs within the organism, rather than the organism itself, which generates value. In consequentialist ethical systems, it is always states of affairs, rather than things in themselves that are valuable. I hope this distinction will become clearer as I proceed.[18]

Some important advocates of individualist consequentialism in this context are Peter Singer, Donald VanDeVeer, Robin Attfield, and Gary Varner. Singer's position, first articulated in *Animal Liberation*, is perhaps the closest to traditional utilitarianism. This initial view was later developed in his *Practical Ethics* and his article "Killing Humans and Killing Animals."[19] In *Animal Liberation*, Singer's position is that of a straightforward hedonistic utilitarian—that is to say, value is measured in terms of pleasure and pain. The aim of ethical behavior is to maximize pleasure over pain. Thus to be morally relevant, or "morally considerable," an organism must have the capacity to feel pleasure or pain, or, more fundamentally, to have subjective experience. The capacity to have pleasurable or painful experience means that an organism has "interests": an organism that can feel pain has an interest in avoiding it; an organism which can feel

pleasure has an interest in sustaining or increasing it. Thus where an organism cannot feel pleasure or pain it is not morally considerable, and has no interests. (It is, however, the experience—the state of affairs—that is valuable, not the organism that *has* the experience). This, of course, limits Singer's ethical concerns to sentient animals; in "Not for Humans Only" for instance, he states clearly that trees, for example, do not have interests.

Singer himself recognizes that there are possible difficulties with his position (aside from those which environmental ethicists might identify). One difficulty is that of replaceability: that provided killing is painless, and therefore does not generate painful experience, one organism may be killed and replaced by another, since it is total *experience*, and not the organism, which is valuable. As initially articulated by Singer, replaceability would apply to human beings as well as to nonhuman sentient animals. In order to avoid being seen to uphold this view, in his later articles, Singer "adds-on" to his earlier *hedonistic* utilitarian position what he calls *preference* utilitarianism. He divides the "morally considerable" into two groups: the conscious and the self-conscious. The conscious are organisms which have pleasurable and painful experience, but have no self awareness, no conception of themselves as persisting into the future and hence no preference to go on living. Such organisms are replaceable. However, self-conscious organisms have conceptions of themselves as individuals who endure through time, with desires and preferences about the future, primarily the preference to go on living. These preferences are, for Singer, morally significant, and thus it is worse to kill an animal with a preference to go on living than an animal with no such preference. This allows him to "ring-fence" self-conscious organisms—human beings and a few mammals such as apes and whales—so that they cannot be considered to be replaceable. Singer's position is thus that of a classical utilitarian with preference utilitarianism added on. All non-sentient animals, plants and natural formations are thus morally irrelevant to Singer, except instrumentally in as much as they add pleasurable experience to the lives of sentient animals.

VanDeVeer's position, in his article "Interspecific Justice" is in many respects similar to that of Singer, although he attempts to develop a more discriminating and detailed account.[20] Like Singer, the ability to feel pleasure and pain, and hence to have interests, is the central ethical pillar of his approach. VanDeVeer's particular concern is with decision making where interests conflict (unlike Singer, he does not address the question of replaceability). Instead he develops a two-pronged system of priority principles for the making of ethical decisions. One prong focuses on the psychological complexity of the organism in question: the more complex, the stronger its claim to priority. The second prong concentrates on the importance of the claim for each organism. Is a peripheral or a basic interest at stake in any particular conflict? The more basic the claim, the stronger its priority. The aim of VanDeVeer's principles, as Peter Singer's, is to achieve maximum total utility—the best overall consequences. His account is more meticulous than Singer's, eliding the self-conscious and conscious into one scale of psychological complexity, and also categorizing interests into different degrees of significance. For VanDeVeer, like Singer, non-sentient animals, plants and natural formations, are of no ethical significance, except as instrumentally valuable to those animals which are of direct moral concern.

Robin Attfield acknowledges a considerable debt to Singer and VanDeVeer; a debt which is more obvious in his earlier book *The Ethics of Environmental Concern* than in his later articles and *A Theory of Value and Obligation*.[21] His position contrasts sharply with both Singer and VanDeVeer in that he severs the exclusive link between experience and value, an uncoupling of central importance in environmental ethics. It is not simply the ability to experience, to feel pleasure and pain, which makes an organism morally considerable; it is, rather, its ability to flourish, to exercise the basic capacities of a species. An organism that has the ability to flourish and develop has an interest in

doing so. Thus all organisms, regardless of their sentience, are morally considerable; it is only inanimate objects, which cannot flourish, which are still morally inconsiderable. However, it is important to note, as Attfield is a consequentialist, that *it is the state of affairs of flourishing* which is valuable, rather than the organism itself, and that this leaves him vulnerable to the usual criticisms of individualist consequentialist positions, as will become clear.

This extension of moral considerability makes the need to develop a series of priority principles more pressing, since the greater the number of species admitted to moral consideration, the greater the potential for conflict. In *A Theory of Value and Obligation* Attfield, like VanDeVeer, develops a two-pronged set of priority principles. A sliding scale of psychological complexity, with humans at the top and individual plants at the bottom, forms one prong, while the other is focused around needs, interests, wants, and preferences. Basic and survival needs have priority over wants and preferences; more sophisticated organisms have priority over less sophisticated ones. As with VanDeVeer's priority principles, the aim is to achieve maximum total utility, or the best possible consequences. Attfield works this position out here in the context of sustainability and human hunger in his "Saving Nature, Feeding People and Ethics."

In his 1998 book *In Nature's Interests?* Gary Varner also develops a consequentialist approach to environmental ethics, focusing on the satisfaction of interests, which he argues are possessed by all and only individual living things.[22] Interests, he argues, mean that something "has a welfare or good of its own, that matters from a moral point of view." However, like Attfield and VanDeVeer, Varner creates a value hierarchy; in this instance the hierarchy is based on desires. Some organisms (such as mammals and birds) have desires, and some (such as insects and plants) probably do not. The interests of those organisms who have desires take priority over those organisms who have purely biological interests (such as for water or sunlight) but are not capable of desire. Among those organisms capable of desire, those who have what Varner calls "ground projects" (long-term desires which require satisfaction across a lifetime) take priority over other organisms. With a few possible exceptions, he suggests only humans have this kind of ground project. Thus where human ground projects are at stake, the interests of other organisms are outweighed. However, as Varner insists, this does not mean "anything goes." For instance it is morally important for humans to eat, since this is necessary to continue their ground projects—even though this means the dooming of interests of individuals of other species. However, Varner's hierarchy indicates that it is better to eat (non-desiring) plants than (desiring) animals—so his account of environmental ethics advocates a vegetarian diet (in normal circumstances).

Numerous objections have been leveled at these individualist consequentialist approaches. The identification of value with experience, found in Singer and VanDeVeer, is a particular target of attack from environmental ethicists. John Rodman in his article "The Liberation of Nature" argues that the identification of value with experience is anthropocentric, since it picks a quality paradigmatically possessed by human beings and uses it as a measure by which to judge other species.[23] While Attfield also criticizes the identification of experience with value, a similar criticism can be made of the psychological sliding scale proposed by himself and VanDeVeer. Varner is happy to concede that his account is anthropocentric, inasmuch as some human interests will always trump nonhuman interests.

A second criticism concerns replaceability, a problem which, according to his critics, Singer has not solved by his preference utilitarianism, and which VanDeVeer and Attfield do not acknowledge at all. Both Michael Lockwood in his article "Killing and the Preference for Life" and R. G. Frey in *Rights, Killing and Suffering* raise serious questions over the ethical adequacy of such positions.[24] If, ultimately, it is maximizing a certain state of affairs—be it pleasure, preferences satisfied or flourishing—which is of value, then the possibility of sacrificing any organism if it might lead to the generation of

better states of affairs is always open. From the point of view of ethical deontologists, as I shall move on to consider in the next section, individualist consequentialism thus fails to ascribe enough significance to the organism itself.

A third criticism, leveled both by Rodman and by Tom Regan in *The Case for Animal Rights* is the degree of subjectivity involved in this kind of moral decision making. How can one decide, for instance, whether meat-eating is of basic or peripheral importance? Or whether a bat is more psychologically sophisticated than a cat? How far are such decisions made on the basis of human prejudice?

In contrast with the criticisms of ethical deontologists that individualist consequentialists fail to give enough ethical significance to individual organisms, other holistic environmental ethicists attack the focus on the individual organism altogether. In this important 1980 paper "Animal Liberation: A Triangular Affair," J. Baird Callicott argued that the individual organism was an inappropriate unit on which to focus when working in the field of environmental ethics.[25] In addition, Callicott argues, individualist consequentialism makes it difficult to accept predation (since all killing is regarded as a loss of value) or to support differential ethical treatment of wild and domestic animals. Others, such as Lawrence Johnson in *A Morally Deep World* and Holmes Rolston in *Environmental Ethics,* whilst affirming the value of individual organisms, argue that some value at least should also be assigned to ecological wholes.[26]

Aside from the question whether they are ethically satisfactory in general, it is clear that Singer's and VanDeVeer's positions, which only acknowledge sentient animals as ethically relevant, have difficulty in functioning as *environmental* ethics. Attfield's and Varner's positions, on the other hand, in acknowledging that all living beings can generate value, offer a broader environmental ethic. However, both are still vulnerable to many of the criticisms made above—as indeed are the next group of environmental ethicists I shall consider, the individualist deontologists.

INDIVIDUALIST DEONTOLOGICAL APPROACHES

I have called these approaches to environmental ethics individualist and deontological both because they reject consequentialism, and because their ethical focus is on individuals rather than on wholes. These environmental ethicists consider that individual organisms have value in themselves, value that is not necessarily linked with experience, nor to do with states of affairs within the organism. It is the organism itself which is valuable, not what it is doing.

Kenneth Goodpaster's 1978 article "On Being Morally Considerable" provides an important basis for many individualist deontological positons.[27] Goodpaster considers the question "what makes something morally considerable?" in some detail, arguing that "X's being a living thing is both necessary and sufficient for moral considerability so understood." Tom Regan considers a similar question in his article "The Nature and Possibility of an Environmental Ethic."[28] Here he suggests that all natural objects have "inherent goodness" whether living or not. However, he finds this position difficult to sustain, and later in *The Case for Animal Rights* he retreats from it, concentrating on "rights" that are possessed by those who are "subjects of a life." Regan's concept of mammalian rights is an individualist deontological position; but one with a scope limited to adult mammals.[29]

More developed deontological approaches to environmental ethics is suggested in the work of Albert Schweitzer (albeit in rather vague fashion); and by Paul Taylor in "The Ethics of Respect for Nature" [both in this book] and his influential book *Respect for Nature*. A further version of such a position is proposed by Louis Lombardi in his article "Inherent Worth, Respect and Rights."[30] A consideration of these positions highlights the central divide between deontological individualist environmental ethicists: some suggest that all morally considerable individuals are of equal value, while others argue for a hierarchy of value within the individual deontological framework.

Schweitzer and Taylor fall into the former category, while Lombardi is in the latter.

Schweitzer, of course, was writing long before the general period I am considering: *The Philosophy of Civilization* was published in 1923. However, many of his ideas have been developed in more recent environmental philosophy. Central to Schweitzer's thought is the "will-to-live," an impulse to self-realization found in all living things (and even, according to Schweitzer, in crystals and snowflakes: an assertion which immediately generates problems). Recognition of this will-to-live should engender reverence towards all living things by human beings, who experience and wish to actualize their own will-to-live. On this basis, the taking of any life, however necessary, is wrong, and generates a burden of guilt and responsibility. (Though in contrast, on occasion, Schweitzer also talks about "necessary" harms.) Further, Schweitzer asserts that all wills-to-live are of equal value, and that human beings are not in a position to judge the relative values of different species. (Thus to kill an ant is as bad as to kill an antelope.) However, this perspective stands in tension with another that Schweitzer also seems to hold, where humans are considered to be superior to other species. A parallel tension can be found where Schweitzer hints at the possibility of *restitution*. Restitution in environmental ethics is a kind of ecological compensation: compensating for damage to or death of one individual organism, species or area by good treatment of either the same organism, individual or area at a different time, or of a different organism, species or area. (This raises questions about the possibility of ecological restoration, one of the issues discussed in this volume). Schweitzer, for example, suggests that by helping an insect in difficulties, one is "attempting to cancel out part of man's ever new debt to the animal world."[31] Laying the merits or otherwise of restitution to one side, as a deontologist, Schweitzer cannot consistently advocate restitution, since wrongs cannot be totalled and compensated for (as would be possible for consequentialists).

These tensions are echoed in Paul Taylor's altogether more complex and sophisticated account which urges "respect for nature" rather than "reverence for life." Taylor's background is clearly Aristotelian. He argues that all organisms are teleological centers of life, pursuing their own good in their own way. This telos gives each individual organism *inherent worth*;[32] and this inherent worth is equally possessed by all living organisms, since all have a telos and a good of their own, a good which is as vital to them as a human good is to a human. This forms the basis of his biocentric view, and the scaffolding for his fundamental principle of species impartiality.

Acknowledging the severe difficulties generated by the belief in the inherent worth of every living organism, Taylor devotes much of his book to working out further ethical principles. He argues for four basic principles of duty to the nonhuman natural world: nonmaleficence, noninterference, fidelity, and restitutive justice. In addition to these he suggests five priority principles for resolving situations of conflict: self defense, proportionality, minimum wrong, distribute justice and restitutive justice. While these are too complex to examine in detail here, Taylor considers that careful application of these principles would enable the moral resolution of conflicts between human beings and nonhuman organism.

Both Schweitzer and Taylor claim to be putting forward a view of "biocentric equality"—where all living beings are of equal moral status. Lombardi, however, develops an individualist deontological approach where values of different organisms are graded. Responding to Taylor, Lombardi maintains that the telos possessed by a living thing is, in fact, a capacity, and that inherent worth is assigned on the basis of this capacity. Lombardi then argues that many living beings have additional capacities that increase inherent worth. A plant, for instance, has vegetative capacitive which gives it a little "value-added"; mammals have vegetative capacities, but are also sentient, the added capacity to feel pleasure and pain giving additional value; while human beings, having other additional capacities, such as reflectiveness, have even greater value added. Thus Lombardi constructs a graded individualist deontological environmental ethic built on difference of capacities between species.

Significant criticisms have been made of the individual deontological positions outlined above. Some of these criticisms relate to the very fact that they are deontological. Since this criticism is not confined to environmental ethics, I will not pursue it here. One aspect which is worth nothing, however, is the existence in both Schweitzer and Taylor (where it is particularly significant) of the concept of restitution. As I have already pointed out, such a position cannot be sustained in a deontological system.[33] Indeed, it resembles the much-criticized idea of replaceability, which I considered in the preceding section.

The granting of moral considerability to all living things is also questioned by critics. Both Peter Singer, in his article "The Place of Nonhumans," and W. K. Frankena argue that sentience is necessary for moral considerability.[34] Even more problems are raised by Schweitzer's and Taylor's assertions of the equal value of all living organisms. In actuality, both fail to sustain their positions rigorously. Taylor accepts medical treatment for humans where millions of bacteria may die for one human life; and admits that the infliction of pain makes it worse to kill animals than plants, thus undercutting his egalitarianism. Peter Wenz points out that Taylor also accepts the death and displacement of thousands of organisms to pursue important human projects such as building concert halls.[35] Thus Taylor can be accused of importing a hierarchy by the back door.

The explicit introduction of hierarchy, however as with Lombardi, opens deontological individual thinking to the same criticism as the individualist consequentiality: that of selecting paradigmatic human equalities and judging the value of other organisms by their possession of them. Lombardi's hierarchy would, for instance, fall victim to Rodman's arguments about anthropocentrism.

Further criticisms of deontological individualism in environmental ethics again echo those made of individualist consequentialists. These criticisms largely stem from holistic ethicists, such as J. Baird Callicott, whom I will consider in the following section. Firstly, again, individualist deontologists are unable to ascribe value to ecosystems or species, except inasmuch as their individual members are valuable. Secondly, again, they are unable to distinguish between domestic and wild animals, and different treatments that may be appropriate to these categories. Diversity is also of no value: a field of wheat and a field of wildflowers are of equal worth, since what is important is the telos or will-to-live of each plants, and not the biological context. Questions about how far humans should "interface" in wild nature to protect will-to-live are raised. Indeed, Callicott suggests that such individualist environmental ethics are "fundamentally life-denying," failing to accept as good the vital evolutionary processes of predation and death, by suggesting that all dying is an evil.[36]

HOLISTIC ENVIRONMENTAL ETHICS

In contrast with both the individualist positions considered above, some environmental ethicists focus on ethical consideration of ecological wholes, rather than individuals. By "ecological wholes" I refer to ecosystems and/or species and to the biosphere as a whole, viewed, in thin context, as ethical units. Different language can be used to describe these wholes, community and organism being two of the most popular. These holistic approaches to environmental ethics tend to be consequentialist, rather than deontological, aiming at the good of the whole, even where the scale of the whole and what constitutes good for it are in dispute. A variety of scales and putative goods are suggested by different philosophers, enhanced by different uses of scientific ecology and Darwinian evolutionary theory.

Aldo Leopold's *A Sand County Almanac* is often cited as the foundational work in holistic environmental ethics. This book, a collection of autobiographical and philosophical essays, espouses a land ethic (reproduced in this volume) which "enlarges the boundaries of the community to include soils, waters, plants, and animals, or collectively, the land."[37] Leopold's guiding principle is famously expressed "A thing is right when it tends to preserve the integrity, stability and beauty of the biotic community. It is wrong when it tends otherwise."[38] It is important to note that this is a principle of

extension, not replacement: human ethics are extended to *include* the land; the land ethic does not replace human ethics.

Owing, in part, to the unsystematic nature of Leopold's writing, there has been some discussion amongst environmental ethicists about how best to interpret Leopold's ideas. The essays collected in *A Companion to a Sand County Almanac,* edited by Callicott, emphasize the importance of the holistic, biotic, non anthropocentric approach Leopold adopts.[39] This stress on the importance of the integrity, stability and beauty of the biotic community contrasts strikingly with both individualist deontologists and individualist consequentialists. First, the community, rather than the individual, is the focus of moral significance. For individualist deontologists, the community has moral significance as a collection of morally valuable individuals; while for individualist consequentialists the community is only valuable inasmuch as it contributes to the improvement of individual experience. Secondly, ecological qualities such as integrity and stability are of primary value.[40] Such qualities cannot be valued in either kind of individualist system where individual living organisms or their experiences are the whole locus of value. Other, more recent interpretations of Leopold's thought have suggested that there are senses in which Leopold's work can be regarded as anthropocentric. For instance, Bryan Norton in "The Constancy of Leopold's Land Ethic," argues that whilst Leopold did consider the biotic community to be an organism, he also considered that humans "must and should" manage it; and that ultimately, as parts of the biotic organism, human and biotic interests would coincide.[41]

Several recent environmental ethicists have put forward views advocating a holistic, rather than an individualistic, environmental ethic. Amongst these is Eric Katz's chapter here: "Is There a Place for Animals in the Moral Consideration of Nature?" Katz argues that the well-being of the ecological community as a whole should be the primary ethical goal or principle of an environmental ethic. Individual natural entities do have value; but this value is a "secondary principle." Another significant holistic view—and one deeply influenced by the work of Leopold—is found in Callicott's paper "Animal Liberation: A Triangular Affair." Here, Callicott placed himself in firm opposition to individualist approaches to environmental ethics.

As already noted, Callicott argued that all value is subjective and anthropogenic (contrasting with the views of, for example, Taylor and Attfield, who consider that values exist in nature independently of conscious valuers).[42] Secondly, Callicott accepted a kind of sociobiology, manifesting itself as a belief in the biological origin of ethics in the community. Ethical behavior in human beings is instinctive, having been evolutionarily selected for, since ethical responses by individuals in a biological community makes the species more likely to survive. Thus, Callicott argued, our ethical impulses are triggered when someone is recognized as being part of the community. If the natural world were to be perceived as part of our "community" humans would consider ethical behavior to be appropriate in this context. And from a Darwinian evolutionary perspective, Callicott argued, such a perception would be a correct one; all living things have the same biological origins and do form an interdependent community. Callicott's third point here, which he claimed emerged in the Platonic tradition, is an emphasis on the ethical priority of the community over the individual. Plato, "shrinks from nothing, as long as it seems to him to be in the interests of the community."[43] This holistic approach contrasts very clearly with the individualist focus of the environmental ethicists considered earlier.

Such a holistic perspective led Callicott to argue that to sustain the health of the biological community of which human beings are a part, some individuals may have to be sacrificed for the whole. The most essential species (such as the pollinating honey bee) are more important than, for instance, higher mammals which play a far less vital role in the biological community. This clearly reflects on human beings, who are not only not vital to the system, but who actually destroy it. Indeed, Callicott suggested that the more misanthropy there is in an ethical system, the more ecological it is, and that the human population should

be, in total, about twice that of bears. He also argued that domesticated animals, not being part of the ultimately valuable wild, biotic community, are living artifacts, lacking natural behavior patterns and unable to be "liberated" as some individualist ethicists would claim.

While Leopold and Callicott focus on communities, the "Gaia hypothesis," and the host of metaphysical and ethical questions raised by it, concerns the entire Earth. The "Gaia hypothesis" originated in the work of scientist James Lovelock in his books *Gaia and The Ages of Gaia.*[44] Lovelock contends that the Earth behaves like a single living organism, in that the flora and fauna on Earth act together to regulate the climate and temperature of Earth in order to produce the best conditions for life. Despite scientific criticism, Lovelock argues that this is not a teleological, or purposive process, and dismisses all suggestions that Gaia might be conscious or have a deliberate aim.[45] This point is reinforced in *The Ages of Gaia* by the use of a complex computer model of a fictional world entitled *Daisyworld*. Lovelock himself has not developed "Gaia" into a through-going metaphysical or ethical system, (although periodically, he uses language which suggests this). However, there is no doubt that the Gaia hypothesis can have important ethical implications, although these are dependent on the interpretation of Lovelock's hypothesis which is adopted.

Lovelock himself argues that the Earth is not fragile, and that it has survived many potential crises in the past by adapting to changed conditions. This may mean that the Earth moves to new equilibria, but that life still continues. He suggests that the Earth may have "vital organs" which, while possibly essential for life on Earth to survive at all, are certainly essential for the Earth to continue at its current equilibrium. These vital organs, he suggests, may be the tropical rainforests, deep sea algae, and prokaryotic bacteria. Their destruction could mean that Gaia moves to a new equilibrium; an equilibrium which may support some kind of life, but which would not support human life. With this background, the ethical implications of Gaia are not focused around protecting Gaia herself, but rather on the preservation of human beings from the devastating consequences of a new equilibrium. Therefore, actions that might force Gaia to a new equilibrium—such as global warming by an increase in atmospheric CO2—should be avoided since it may ultimately lead to the destruction of human beings. This is, as Andrew Dobson points out in *Green Political Thought* provides an anthropocentric reason for the protection of Gaia.[46]

Other groups have, however, developed different ethical conclusions, loosely based on the Gaia hypothesis. These highlight the living organismic nature of the Earth, and, in contrast with Lovelock, stress its fragility. This can result in militant ethical stances, such as that put forward by some members of the group Earth First! where the "well-being of the planet" is put before the well-being of individual human beings. A reduction in human population is thus frequently considered to be an ethical necessity. Such plural ethical interpretations make clear the ambiguous position which Lovelock's hypothesis may hold in environmental ethics.

Holistic approaches to environmental ethics have been strongly criticized by individuals, amongst others. Tom Regan, in his chapter "How to Worry about Endangered Species," excerpted from his book *The Case for Animal Rights*, expresses this particularly strongly by describing ethical environmental holism as "environmental fascism" since it includes "the clear prospect that the individual may be sacrificed for the greater biotic good, in the name of the 'stability, integrity and beauty of the biotic community.' " The prioritizing of the whole over the individual, in particular when the whole concerned is the wild biotic community is widely viewed as ethically unacceptable.

RECONCILING POSITIONS

The preceding sections have described a range of different, and sometimes conflicting, positions adopted by those working in environmental ethics——in particular concerning a perceived rift between the individualism of animal liberation positions in contrast with the holism of some environmental ethics. (It

should be remembered, however, that there are individualist environmental ethical positions and that animals are still morally relevant to holistic environmental ethics). In response to some of the problems raised, a number of environmental ethicists have attempted to construct approaches to environmental ethics which take into account elements of both individualist and holistic concerns. This reconciliation between animal liberation and environmental ethics at least can go so far as, in Dale Jamieson's terms, to "have the potential for Hollywood romance"![47] A number of different reconciliatory approaches have been adopted, two of which I will consider below.

Although an important holistic thinker in his earlier work, as we have seen, in later writing, such as "Animal Liberation and Environmental Ethics: Back Together Again" Callicott elaborates a more reconciliatory theory of "nested communities." Here he argues that human beings exist in the center of a series of moral communities which fit, one within the other, as a series of "nests" or concentric circles, with ethical obligations diminishing towards the outside. The major communities Callicott identifies are the human community at the core; the "mixed" community (of human and domestic animals) as the middle "ring"; and the wild or biotic community on the outside. This changes some aspects of Callicott's position in his earlier paper: it allows human concerns to trump those of the wild or biotic community, and it allows for humans to have moral obligations towards animals. (Indeed, his position in this paper has been criticized by Varner as being anthropocentric.[48])

The work of Holmes Rolston represents another key position allowing for both individualist and holistic values. Rolston, whose views are laid out in his systematic work *Environmental Ethics,* is one of the most important figures in the current environmental ethical debate.[49] Like Taylor and Attfield, and unlike Callicott, Rolston argues for objective value in the natural world. The baseline of individual value is the *telos* of each individual organism. Every organism has a good of its own, and is thus a *holder* of value, even if not a *beholder* of it. To this extent, Rolston's views are not dissimilar to those of Taylor. However, Rolston contends that different characteristics—such as sentience or ability for conscious reflection—add value, so that the more sophisticated a living organism, the more valuable it is. Alongside this individualist approach, Rolston also develops an understanding of intrinsic value applicable to ecosystems and species. Species, he argues, provide the normative genetic "set" for the individual, and this genetic set is "as evidently the property of the species as of the individual through whom it passes."[50] A species is a form of life that defends itself and, according to Rolston, thus has value. The ecosystem, and indeed the biosphere as a whole, is a life-creating process. Ethical attention should be not focused on an ecosystem as an individual, but rather as an interconnected matrix within which life evolved and continues to develop. As the womb of life, both producing and nurturing it, the ecosystem is an appropriate unit for moral concern.[51] It would be bizarre, Rolston insists, to value the organisms, the products of the system, without valuing the process which produced them. This wild, systemic value is entirely separate from human culture, exists independently of humans and is increasingly threatened by human development (as well as threatening species and organismic values). Given the extent of this threat, and the significance Rolston considers systemic and species values to have, it is consistent that he should argue in his chapter here "Feeding People versus Saving Nature" that there are occasions when protecting such values takes priority over feeding hungry people. As this book illustrates well, debates over how nature is valued has profound significance for thinking about issues of poverty and sustainability.

RECENT DISCUSSIONS IN ENVIRONMENTAL ETHICS: MONISM AND PLURALISM

This variety of different positions advocated by those working in environmental ethics led to wide-ranging discussion in the 1990s about moral monism and pluralism. Such a diversity of possible objects of moral concern (sentient animals, living organisms, ecosystems, species, the Earth, biodiversity etc.) and so many different approaches to environmental ethics (rights-theories, utilitarianism, virtues theories and so on) were suggested that questions emerged as to whether *any* single ethical approach could be adequate. Moral pluralism, it was suggested by some, might provide a way forward in accommodating so many different approaches and concerns. In the course of this debate, moral monism and pluralism were defined and interpreted in varying ways.[52] Wenz's chapter "Minimal, Moderate, and Extreme Moral Pluralism" is perhaps a good place to start.

Wenz argues that moral pluralism may take different forms, and provides his own three-fold classification, distinguishing extreme, moderate, and minimal moral pluralism. Extreme moral pluralism, in Wenz's classification, is characterized by "alternations between different ethical theories"— theories such as utilitarianism or Kantianism. Moderate moral pluralism is where a single, overarching theory is "pluralistic in the sense that it contains a variety of independent principles, principles that cannot be reduced *to* or derived from a single master principle." Thirdly, minimal moral pluralism refers to a moral theory which "merely lacks a universal algorithmic decision procedure." Indeed, Wenz goes on to argue that all known moral systems are at least this pluralistic (i.e. there are no monistic systems which provide a perfect algorithmic decision making procedure in all circumstances). (Thus approaches we have already considered in this chapter fall into the category of moderate pluralism).

Christopher Stone and Andrew Bennan prefer to use the language of ethical *frameworks* or matrices that can be brought to bear on different situations.[53] Brennan argues that there is no "one set of principles concerning just one form of value that provides ultimate government for our actions."[54] Indeed, he maintains that "an indefinite number of frameworks can be brought to bear. When we restrict our modes of thinking to just one framework, we thereby choose to ignore the perspective supplied by other relevant frameworks."[55] Like Wenz, Brennan notes that pluralism may have different forms: first, the acceptance that different consideration may apply in different cases; and secondly (and more controversially) that in any particular situation, there is no single theoretical lens which provides a privileged set of concepts, principles, and structure. Moral pluralism, Brennan argues, allows for exploration of the complexity of ethical issues rather than the imposition of a single reductionist ethical framework onto a complex situation. Andrew Light, in his "the case for practical Pluralism" (in this volume) reads this debate as concerning the relationship between theory-making and practice. Moral pluralists, he suggests, have been interested in environmental ethics as practice; moral theories are seen as "tools developed in the process of addressing specific policy controversies." Moral monists, on the other hand, he considered to be theoretical purists, who start with theories and apply them to complex situations. This analysis allows Light to link moral pluralism with environmental pragmatism, which we shall consider later.

Attractive as some pluralist positions sound, difficulties are generated by them—many of which are discussed by Callicott in his "The Case Against Moral Pluralism." With Stone's work in mind, Callicott asks questions such as: how can one make moral decisions when two frameworks deliver conflicting ethical responses? Would unscrupulous moral agents switch between frameworks in order to make personal gains? Does this all lead to a kind of ethical "musical chairs"? In his 1994 paper "Moral Monism in Environmental Ethics Defended" Callicott argues that the sensitivity to complexity and different contexts highlighted by pluralists such as Stone and Brennan can be achieved within a monistic framework without the need to resort to pluralism.[56]

Pursuing this question would open up an extensive moral debate. It is clear that the moral pluralisms developed (in differing ways) by Wenz, Brennan, and Stone do generate difficulties. However, pluralist approaches to environmental ethics of this sort are context-sensitive, open-ended, and prepared to engage with the profound complexities

of making ethical decisions. They acknowledge the impossibility of producing clear-cut answers in many ethical situations—especially when considering the difficult ethical questions engendered by human relations with the nonhuman world.

RECENT DISCUSSION IN ENVIRONMENTAL ETHICS: WILDERNESS AND ECOLOGICAL RESTORATION

A number of environmentally significant issues—for instance hunting, biodiversity, agriculture—have been debated within environmental ethics. Two of the most significant and hotly debated issues, however, have been the idea of wilderness and the question of the restoration of land after human use. Both these discussions are of considerable importance, illustrating as they do the significance of debates in environmental ethics for thinking about practical policy-making.

Wilderness

In 1964, the US Wilderness Act designated wilderness as "an area where the earth and its community of life are untrammeled by man, where man himself is a visitor who does not remain." This designation reflected the view that wildernesses are untouched, pristine parts of the natural world, formed without human agency and to be protected from permanent human presence. In this pristine condition, wildernesses could be seen as the location of special human values for recreation, hunting, psychological and spiritual refreshment, scientific study, medicinal possibility, aesthetic wonder—and, for some, a location of intrinsic value. However, during the 1980s and 1990s, this idea of wilderness was challenged for a variety of reasons (many of the key papers relating to this discussion are collected in Callicott and Michael Nelson's edited volume, *The Great New Wilderness Debate*).[57] One key challenge stemmed from Ramachandra Guha's paper "Radical American Environmentalism and Wilderness Preservation: A

Third World Critique."[58] This paper maintained that the idea of wilderness was harmful when exported to developing countries. Many of these countries were densely populated; the creation of wilderness areas from which people were excluded ignored the needs of local people; and inasmuch as such areas become tourist sites for rich visitors, transferred resources from the poor to the rich. Indeed, the whole idea of "setting aside" supposedly pristine areas of land, Guha argues, represents a new, American, imperialist project (both physically and intellectually/spiritually).

Discussion about the idea of wilderness also grew within the US itself, most significantly in a debate between J. Baird Callicott and Holmes Rolston in *The Environmental Professional* in 1991.[59] Callicott contests the idea of wilderness on several grounds. It relies, he suggests, on the idea that humans are separate from nature, and that the wilderness is an "Other" to humans. But this ignores evolutionary theory; humans are "natural." The idea of "preserving" wildernesses also suggests a kind of denial of evolution, and a "freeze-framing" of ecology. In addition, Callicott argues, in the US the wilderness idea is ethnocentric; it depends on the fallacy that when Europeans arrived in the New World it was in "wilderness condition." Yet this either ignores the existence of aboriginal inhabitants, or else it suggests that they are not human beings, so their management of ecosystems can be discounted. Finally, Callicott maintains that the "wilderness idea" is an inappropriate way of dealing with current environmental problems. It can lead to the protection of a few conscience-saving "odds and ends" of remote country whilst outside such locations the environment is devastated. It is better to integrate humans into the natural world and to develop harmonious living than to work with an idea of wild nature as entirely separate from human culture.

Rolston responds by arguing that wild nature *is* radically different from human culture, and (as we have already seen) that it carries nonhuman intrinsic values that should be respected, and that Callicott's arguments do not recognize. This radical culture/nature difference does not mean "freeze-framing"

ecology; it rather means that biological changes in wilderness areas should be driven by evolutionary and ecological processes, not humans. Neither is the view that there is wilderness "untrammeled by man" in the US ethnocentric: Rolston argues that native Americans did not modify the landscape profoundly, did not use high, rough or arid land, and that although they used fire, fire would have occurred anyway.[60] And, overall, the protection of wilderness does not mean that people can do what they like elsewhere; that some places are set aside for wilderness does not mean that in other places greater human/nature harmonious integration should not be an ideal.

This debate continues in different forms amongst environmental ethicists. Reed Noss's chapter for instance maintains, like Rolston, that wildernesses carry intrinsic values, that "huge wild areas are valuable for their own sake." Indeed, to operate healthily with ecosystems containing big predators like wolves, wildernesses may need to be very large; and Noss recommends that about 50 percent of the US should be returned to a wilderness condition to enable the maintenance of biodiversity. What is at stake here are questions about how far humans are viewed as a part of or apart from nature and whether wild nature is thought to be carrying special kinds of intrinsic values. These questions recur with equal force in the debate over restoring nature.

Ecological Restoration

A related central debate in environmental ethics concerns the question whether nature "restored" by humans carries the same value as "wild" nature, understood as nature unmodified by human activity. This issue has been implicit in much work in environmental ethics (as we have seen, restitution was raised in the work of Schweitzer and Taylor, and advocated by Wenz [1988]; and the idea of replaceability in Singer's work raises similar issues). However, environmental ethicists are by no means agreed that restitution or restoration is a principle that should be accepted. Robert Elliott's 1982 paper "Faking Nature" importantly raised the profile of this issue. In "Faking Nature" Elliot explores the implications of what he calls "The Restoration Thesis": that the destruction of what has value is compensated for by the later creation (recreation) of something of equal value. (He is particularly concerned where this restoration thesis is used to legitimate environmental harm on the ground that it may later be made good). Elliot argues that part of the reason why humans might value a natural area is its "specific genesis and history." Creating a replica, with a different origin, creates something less valuable, in the same way that faked paintings, however good, are not as valuable as original paintings. As Elliott argues "we value the forest and river in part because they are representative of the world outside our dominion, because this existence is independent of us." This thesis was developed and revised in a book of the same title (1997) which contains a detailed explanation of Elliott's subjectivist understanding of intrinsic value, restates Elliott's commitment to the value of "naturalness of origin," and distinguishes between different *kinds* of restoration, including benign restorations.[61]

Eric Katz, in a series of papers on restoration, including "The Big Lie," develops Elliott's argument. Working with a definition of "natural" as essentially "independent of the actions of humanity," Katz argues that restored nature is not a forgery, but rather an artifact. It is not autonomous and free like wild nature; it is, instead, anthropocentric, and created for human purposes. And such creation, Katz maintains, is an act of human domination of nature. Thus where nature has been harmed (for instance in an oil spill) those responsible should attempt to clean up, this does not amount to a *restoration* of nature, because nature is not the kind of thing humans can restore.

Whilst no one writing in environmental ethics has endorsed the idea that polices of restoration should be used to justify environmental harm, a number of ethicists have disagreed with the premises of Katz's and Elliott's arguments, and with some of their conclusions. This debate has centered around the kind of relationship envisaged for humans to have with the natural world. Both

Andrew Light and Y. S. Lo explore this question by using analogies from inter-human relationships.[62] Light, for instance, opens up issues about human/nature relationships, suggesting that restoration can be viewed as an attempt to heal relationships between humans and nature, even freeing nature from constraints (such as pollution) that had prevented it from pursuing its autonomy. Engaging in restoration projects may also help humans to understand the natural world better and thus to be more willing to defend it against future harms. Lo questions whether a restored nature is a human artifact, any more than a person who been healed by human medicine should be regarded as an artifact. She argues that to suggest a nature touched or oppressed by human is of less value than "free, autonomous" nature is akin to saying that oppressed humans are worth less than free ones (and thus legitimating further domination). Respect for nature may mean assisting dominated nature to become free again—by restoration; and this restoration, though anthropo*genic* need not be anthropo*centric,* but may be aimed at benefiting the nonhuman world.

As the preceding sections have suggested, debates in environmental ethics about intrinsic value, valuing wholes and/or individuals, monism and pluralism and issues such as the concept of wilderness and the value of nature restoration continue. However, these are not the only voices in discussions about such questions.

RESPONSES TO MAINSTREAM ENVIRONMENTAL ETHICS

There are a number of important responses to the more mainstream environmental ethics approaches outlined above. Here I want to consider three broad schools of thought: deep ecology, ecofeminism, and environmental pragmatism. These "schools" are far from homogeneous; they contain considerable inner diversity and debate. I will conclude by looking, briefly, at ways in which ideas about the social construction have begun to enter debates in environmental ethics.

Deep Ecology

The expression "deep ecology" was first used by Arne Naess in his article "The Shallow and the Deep, Long Range Ecology Movements: A Summary."[63] In this article, Naess suggested that the ecology movement had two strands: the shallow, concerned with pollution and resource depletion; and the deep, which he characterized metaphysically, ethically, and politically. Metaphysically, Naess maintained that deep ecologists reject the idea of humans as separate from their environment, and stress the complex relatedness of all that is. Ethically, deep ecologists espouse biocentric equality in principle (although recognizing that all realistic praxis will require some killing and exploitation) and the equal right of all right of all living organisms to blossom and flourish (an egalitarian, deontological attitude resembling that Schweitzer and Taylor). Politically, deep ecologists favor diversity and decentralization—also political action to relate their principles to practice.

Naess's article was the catalyst for a still continuing debate around these issues, which in a variety of ways engages with the environmental ethics questions explored above. Since Naess's article was published, he himself has developed and revised his views, and a number of other significant voices have joined in the discussion. It is only possible to consider a few of these developments here.

The idea of biocentric equality in principle, outlined by Naess in 1973, has been one of the areas of most discussion, obviously linking closely to other debates in environmental ethics. Difficulty in upholding this principle led Naess, and other deep ecologists, to reformulate this idea; some adopted a hierarchical approach.[64] Although the question of biocentric *equality* has been much debated, affirmation of intrinsic value in nature was widely accepted by deep ecologists, including Naess. This affirmation was most powerfully captured in what has become known as the Deep Ecology Platform, a series of eight principles agreed by Naess and a fellow deep

ecologist George Sessions in 1984, and published (in slightly varying forms) in a variety of places including Naess's article "The Deep Ecological Movement: Some Philosophical Aspects" in this volume.[65] The first of these principles affirms: "The well-being and flourishing of human and nonhuman life on earth have value in themselves (synonyms: intrinsic value, inherent worth). These values are independent of the usefulness of the nonhuman world for human purposes. "The Deep Ecology Platform—maintaining that the flourishing of nonhuman life should be protected by changes in policy and human lifestyles—lies, as it were, in the middle stage of deep ecological thinking. Underpinning the Deep Ecology Platform, Naess suggests, may lie different metaphysical positions or what Naess calls "ecosophies" (hence Light's argument in "The Case for Practical Pluralism" that Naess may be regarded as in some senses a pluralist) and, resting upon it, a range of political and practical responses and strategies in different situations.

It is the metaphysical underpinning of deep ecology, based on developing and revising Naess's work, which has been of particular significance in deep ecological thinking, even having the effect of making deep ecological thinking, even having the effect of making deep ecology seem more like a consciousness movement than an ethical one.[66] This change of consciousness focuses around two key concepts: *holism* and *the extension and realization of the self*. Holism, as used by deep ecologists, is usually based on the claim that everything is fundamentally one. Nothing can be separated from the whole; indeed there are no isolated "things" but an interlocking web of relations in a constant state of flux. Individuals are "knots in a web" or "centers of interaction"—constituted by their relationships. Warwick Fox, in his chapter "Deep Ecology: A New Philosophy of Our Time?" maintains that this holism, the absence of "a firm ontological divide in the field of existence" is "the central intuition of deep ecology." The concept of the extension and realization of the self is closely related to this holism. If everything is fundamentally one, then the distinction between what is self and what is not-self can no longer be simply sustained. Deep ecologists argue that this is true on a physical level since the physical body cannot exist in isolation from its surroundings (a view which deep ecologists reinforce by citing quantum physics and scientific ecology). With the knowledge, human beings can extend their self-identification beyond the confines of their body to include others. Once the factual impossibility of the separation of self from world is recognized, the necessity to extend one's understanding of what constitutes one's self is revealed. If everything is part of one's self, and one is aiming at self-realization (which deep ecologists argue to be the case) then the clear conclusion to be drawn is that the realization of all (living) organisms is necessary for one's own full self-realization.

Politically, deep ecology—both at the metaphysical and the ethical level—has proved an inspiration to a variety of political environmental movements. Many of the members of radical environmental groups such as Earth First! in the US have been influenced by deep ecological thinking.[67] Some deep ecologists, especially in the US, engaged in political activities extending to civil disobedience and sabotage or "monkeywrenching" in order to defend environments threatened by various kinds of harm (such as deforestation or the construction of roads).

At all levels, deep ecology has been severely attacked; most systematically by Richard Sylvan in his "A Critique of Deep Ecology."[68] Ethically, obviously a number of the difficulties associated with affirmation of intrinsic value and egalitarianism in environmental ethics more generally manifest themselves in deep ecology. Metaphysically, the "consciousness-shifting" side of deep ecology has been criticized even more intensely. First, the of scientific ecology and modern physics has been challenged.[69] Secondly, the philosophical acceptability of the form of holism which Naess appears to be advocating has been subject to philosophical criticism for many years.[70] Being dependent on such holism, the deep ecological concept of the extended self is exposed; and this is not the only difficulty with such an idea. Val Plumwood in *Feminism and the Mastery of Nature* argues that the idea of the extended self in deep ecology suggests that the whole world

becomes a kind of extended individual ego incorporating everything that is.[71] It thus fails to acknowledge in any real sense the "otherness" of what is in the world; since everything is viewed as being part of oneself, there is no space for difference. Indeed, ecofeminists such as Plumwood make a variety of criticisms of deep ecology in particular, and of the prevailing debates in environmental ethics in general, as the next section illustrates.

Ecofeminism

Ecofeminism is a term that covers a variety of responses to environmental problems and to theorizing about them. What all these responses have in common is the making of a link between what are often called the "twin oppressions" of women and nature. As Karen Warren and Jim Cheney express it in their chapter "Ecological Feminism and Ecosystem Ecology": "ecofeminists acknowledge up front their basic value commitments: the twin dominations of women and nature exist, are wrong, and ought to be eliminated." However, the nature of the link between these twin oppressions has been understood in many different ways (as Greta Gaard and Lori Gruen explain in their chapter) and consequently the best way of eliminating these twin oppressions is also contested. Here, I am primarily interested in the ways in which ecofeminists have engaged with debates in environmental ethics, and have attempted to reframe some of the terms of the discussion to counter what Val Plumwood calls "the heavily masculine presence which has inhabited most accounts of environmental philosophy, including those of many deep ecologists."[72]

Many of the approaches to environmental ethics considered above have attempted to develop abstract, theoretical, and universally applicable environmental ethical theories. These approaches—such as the deontological egalitarian theory proposed by Paul Taylor—emphasize the importance of human reason, rather than emotion, in constructing and universalizing ethical theory. Ecofeminist ethicists have tended to reject this abstract, rational, and universalist approach to ethical thinking. Such accounts, ecofeminists argue, assume a single, dominant, detached way of viewing the world at all times and places. In contrast, ecofeminists maintain that there are no such value-neutral, universally applicable, unbiased points of view. Rather, all ethical views, however presented, are products of particular worldviews, contexts, and locations. Many ecofeminists also suggest that environmental ethics, rather than being based on a particular universalizing understanding of reason, can instead be built on relationships of *care* between humans and the nonhumans and particular environments in which they are located.[73] This does not mean that reason should be abandoned altogether; but rather that as Plumwood argues, reason should "find a form which encourages sensitivity to the conditions under which we exist on the earth … and enables us to acknowledge our debt to the sustaining others of the earth."[74] Warren also urges that a "felt sensitivity" should become part of environmental ethics, a sensitivity that recognizes the fundamental, essential nature of human relationship with others.[75] The language of relationship resists the kind of incorporation into the extended self for which ecofeminists criticize deep ecology; it allows for the existence of difference. Simultaneously, it makes *relationships*, rather than separate isolated individuals manifesting particular valuable qualities central to ethical decision making. Warren and Cheney argue that ecofeminist ethics grow out of "defining relationships"—relationships that are fundamental in defining who one is.

Ecofeminist approaches to environmental ethics have—as have all the other approaches—been subject to controversy and critique. One difficulty raised concerns the contextual, non-universalist nature of ecofeminist ethics: does this mean that there are no absolutes, that "anything goes"? Ecofeminists have resisted this interpretation by suggesting a series of "boundary conditions" which must be met if an ethic is to be described as "feminist" at all. Warren and Cheney argue that those "boundary conditions" exclude oppressive and patriarchal conceptual frameworks; relationships of an oppressive nature, even where they are defining, cannot be part of ecofeminism. Other

questions have been raised about care as the basis for ethics: does it make sense to talk about a relationship of care with the non-living (such as rocks, as Warren does in her article "The Power and Promise of Ecological Feminism")?[76] How does one care for something that has no state that is better or worse for it? And others have defended more traditional approaches, such as an animal rights perspective, against the charges that such systems are abstract, generalizing and insensitive to difference by maintaining that different individuals *can* have the same morally-relevant features.[77]

This brief consideration of deep ecology and ecofeminism, and their engagement with debates in environmental ethics, has provided a glimpse of just how diverse views about environmental ethics might be. The last area of thought I want to consider here, environmental pragmatism, represents in part at least, an attempt to bring some of these diverse ideas together.

Environmental Pragmatism

The term "pragmatism" has two widely acknowledged uses: a general use referring to the adoption of practical strategies to deal with specific situations; and a philosophical use referring to the thought of the classical American philosophers, in particular Dewey and Peirce. The expression "environmental pragmatism" was first advocated by Andrew Light in 1992 at a conference in Budapest, Hungary (although work advocating pragmatic approaches to environmental ethics had already been published).[78] As with the term pragmatism in general, environmental pragmatism has two strands: a more general, methodological or metaphilosophical approach, represented in the work of Light and Weston; and more specific, philosophical approaches drawing on the work of classic American pragmatic philosophers. These strands are not necessarily in conflict; indeed, some methodological environmental pragmatism has drawn on the ideas of classical philosophical pragmatism. Both strands are represented in Andrew Light and Eric Katz's 1996 edited volume *Environmental Pragmatism.*[79]

The starting point for environmental pragmatism, as argued by Light and Katz, is that debates in environmental ethics—of the kind outlined above—have had little impact on environmental policy-making. Such discussions are philosophers talking to one another, fiddling whilst the environment (in some cases literally!) burns. But as Light and Katz argue "pragmatists cannot tolerate theoretical delays to the contribution that philosophy may make to environmental questions."[80] Environmental pragmatism, then, is concerned to develop strategies by which environmental ethics can contribute to the resolution of practical environmental problems.

Methodologically, this means acceptance of moral pluralism. As with the ecofeminist approaches considered above, environmental pragmatists (such as Weston in "Beyond Intrinsic Value") may argue that environmental ethics is plural and contextual, growing out of the complexity of particular situations and relating to whole webs of needs and desires. This moves environmental ethics debates away from a theoretical search for a single, source of intrinsic value towards working in particular, concrete situations. Environmental pragmatists may also seek ways in which those with different theoretical and practical perspectives can converge in practice with policy-makers and environmental activists (an approach Bryan Norton develops) or argue for a kind of political compatiblism.[81]

Philosophically, the work of classical American pragmatists has also contributed substantially to thinking about environmental pragmatism as Minteer and Manning bear witness in their chapter. In particular, Dewey's work has influenced this, more classical, strand of environmental pragmatism. Dewey's arguments for anti-foundationalism and "denial of the existence of a priori or self justifying "truths" or "moral absolutes," as well as his arguments for democratic, public conversations about social values, have been central to philosophical environment pragmatism (and also to methodological environmental pragmatism).

A number of criticisms can be made of environmental pragmatism: inasmuch as, methodologically, it adopts moral pluralism, it is rejected by moral monists on grounds of consistency; in as much as it is contextualist, those who criticize ecofeminist ethics would also critique environmental pragmatists. Some (although not all) of those who argue for forms of intrinsic value in nature consider that environmental pragmatism is not able to give such non-anthropocentric values proper consideration.[82] Others have argued that policy convergence between those with very different ethical perspectives (anthropocentric and non-anthropocentric, or individualist and holist, for instance) is not as common as might be thought, and that different meta-ethical and ethical positions may issue in conflicting environmental policies.[83] Despite these difficulties, however, the work of environmental pragmatists has been important in bringing together philosophical thinking about the environment with practical environmental issues and problems.

THE SOCIAL CONSTRUCTION OF NATURE

A further response to environmental ethics has been suggested by work which might broadly be called social constructivist and may take a variety of weaker and stronger forms.[84] Weaker forms of constructivism argue that "nature" and "the environment" have been interpreted in a variety of different ways at different times; and that "nature" is inescapably viewed through a cultural lens. What is called nature in one culture at one time may be viewed very differently in a different culture influenced by different political, historical, and social factors. Ideas about "nature" or "the environment" are thus inevitably changing and culturally relative. This view does not, however, mean that there is no "real" nature out there, even though our *knowledge* of it may be mediated and partial (in both senses of the word). But stronger versions of social constructivism seem to go further by apparently contesting the idea that there is a "real" nature at all, working with premises such as: "there is no singular 'nature' as such, only a diversity of contested natures; and … each such nature is constituted through a variety of socio-cultural processes from which such natures cannot be plausibly separated."[85] Here, "nature" or "the environment" is viewed as something socially, culturally, and politically produced in a variety of human discourses and practices. (Even so, not all such claims are intended to be *ontological*—denying that there is any such thing as a "nature" independent of humans—they may rather be *epistemological,* relating to the cultural dependence of all knowledge about nature.)

Such views, especially in stronger forms, raise questions for environmental ethics. If there is no "real" nature independent of human beings, or we can't know about it, what sense can be made of "nature conservation" or "environmental protection"? What could it mean to say that nature (or aspects of it) has (or have) intrinsic value—and what is the political and cultural origin of such claims? If "nature" is a human construction, is it possible to discriminate between more or less "natural" human behavior with respect to it? Strong social constructivism may thus appear to threaten much work in environmental ethics. In response, it has been argued that strong social constructivism is anthropocentrism emerging in new forms—in its most extreme versions now going so far as to maintain that nature has no existence independent of humans.[86] Opponents of strong constructivist claims have argued for forms of realism which insist that humans do have access to meaningful knowledge about nature. Holmes Rolston, for instance, argues that, as organisms, humans do have access to what is "really there" through their senses.[87] Others, accepting weak, or mediated, constructivism, maintain that with this in mind forms of environmental ethics can still be developed.[88] Debates about broadly postmodern thinking in relation to environmental ethics look certain to continue as a location of much future work in environmental ethics.

IN CONCLUSION

The variety of approaches to environmental ethics described in this chapter indicates the diversity

and complexity of the current debate. All the approaches to ethics found in current general ethical theory have been applied within environmental ethics. In addition, considering the possible ethical significance of groupings such as ecosystems and of ideas such as diversity, has led to the development of largely new ethical approaches such as that suggested by Callicott or developed out of the Gaia hypothesis. The environmental problems of the present have drawn attention to the insight that ethical questions are raised by human behavior towards not only nonhuman individuals, but towards ecosystems, species, and the biosphere itself. Deciding what sort of ethical response is appropriate to such questions is the task of environmental ethics. The importance of such responses is beyond doubt.

Work in environmental ethics over the past three decades has focused, to a considerable degree, on how humans should think about wild environments, and what values they might carry. But it seems likely that in future ethical interest in other kinds of environment will grow. There are a number of obvious reasons for this. Wildernesses are declining, both in size and number. Urbanization is expanding. Most people in the world rarely or never enter wild areas, living and working in urban or rural agricultural areas. Environmental ethicists are now turning to think about such urban and agricultural areas, which raise ethical questions just as much as the wilderness environments which have for so long been the focus of environmental ethics.[89] Thus in the future, debates about environmental ethics are likely to expand to consider ever wider kinds of environments and the ethical issues which these environments raise.

ACKNOWLEDGMENTS

I would like to thank Andrew Light and Holmes Rolston for their assistance in rewriting this paper, developed from a much earlier version published in 1994.

NOTES

1. Probably the nearest to a comprehensive survey could be found in J. Baird Callicott, *Earth's Insights* (Berkeley: University of California Press, 1996).

2. The closest to a historical survey, though now a little out of date, is Roderick Nash, *The Rights of Nature* (Madison: University of Wisconsin Press, 1989).

3. The expression "environmental ethics" is used here as an umbrella term to cover all kinds of moral debate concerning human attitudes toward, and treatment of, the nonhuman natural world. It is in itself a contentious term, since it could be argued that the every use of the term "environment" separates human beings from the natural world and suggests that the significance of the natural world is as something which surrounds human beings. For this reason, the term "ecological ethics" has been preferred by some ethicists. This has its own difficulties, since it can be interpreted as referring to posited ecological relationships within ecosystems, or with reading ethical approaches out of ecosystems. In this chapter I have elected to use the term "environmental ethics," since it is widely used and less open to misinterpretation than ecological ethics; but its use is not intended to prejudice questions concerning the relationship of humans with the nonhuman natural world.

4. See E. S. Turner, *All Heaven in a Rage* (London: Michael Joseph, 1964); for a collection of readings from various periods, see Tom Regan and Peter Singer (eds.) *Animal Rights and Human Obligations* (New Jersey: Prentice Hall, 1976). The two main approaches to the moral status of animals— utilitarian and "rights" based—are put forward most coherently in Peter Singer's *Animal Liberation* (St. Albinos Paladin, 1975) and Tom Regan's *The case for Animal Rights* (London: Routledge, 1984).

5. Although there were isolated but significant philosophical considerations of these questions much earlier—most particularly in the work of Albert Schweitzer, and in Aldo Leopold's *A Sand County Almanac* (Oxford: Oxford University Press, 1949, 1987) both of whose work will be considered in this essay.

6. The conference, Philosophy and Environmental Crisis, was held at the University of Georgia, February 18–20, 1971. Proceedings were published in William Blackstone (ed.), *Philosophy and Environmental Crisis* (Athens, GA: University of Georgia Press, 1974).

7. Arne Naess, "The Shallow and the Deep, Long Range Ecology Movements," *Inquiry* 16 (1973): 95–100.

8. Christopher Stone, "Should Trees Have Standing?" *Southern California Law Review* 45, no.4 (1972): 462.

9. John Passmore, *Man's Responsibility for Nature* (London: Duckworth, 1974).

10. Don Mannison, Michael McRobbie, and Richard Routley (eds.), *Environmental Philosophy* (Canberra: Research School of Social Sciences, Australian National University, 1980); Robert Elliot and Arran Gare (eds.), *Environmental Philosophy: A Collection of Readings* (University Park, PA: University of Pennsylvania, 1983).

11. Robin Attfield, *The Ethics of Environmental Concern* (Oxford: Basil Blackwell, 1983).

12. Holmes Rolston III, *Environmental Ethics: Duties to and Values in the Natural World* (Philadelphia: Temple University Press, 1988); Paul Taylor, *Respect for Nature* (Princeton: Princeton University Press, 1986).

13. There is a significant philosophical literature on the moral standing of future generations of humans. See for instance: Derek Parfit, *Reasons and Persons* (Oxford: Clarendon Press, 1984); Robin Attfield, *A Theory of Value and Obligation* (London: Croom Helm, 1987), Avner de-Shalit, *Why Posterity Matters* (London: Routledge, 1995), as well as Andrew Dobson (ed.), *Fairness and Futurity* (Oxford: Oxford University Press, 1999), the original source for the piece by Brian Barry in this volume.

14. Passmore, *Man's Responsibility for Nature.*

15. R. G. Frey, *Rights, Killing and Suffering* (Oxford: Basil Blackwell, 1983).

16. Although it is worth noticing that in later publications, Passmore has been more sympathetic towards a more thoroughgoing environmental ethic. See for instance Passmore's "Attitudes to Nature" in *Nature and Conduct* (Royal Institute of Philosophy, 1975).

17. Norton is an environmental pragmatist, a group of positions discussed later in this chapter, and his approach to value coheres with his pragmatism.

18. I am indebted for the clarity of this distinction to Bernard Williams in J. C. C. Smart and Bernard Williams, *Utilitarianism: For and Against* (Cambridge: Cambridge University Press, 1973), p. 83.

19. Singer, *Animal Liberation; Practical Ethics* (Oxford: Oxford University Press, 1979); and "Killing Humans and Killing Animals," *Inquiry* 21 (1978).

20. Donald VanDeVeer, "Interspecific Justice," *Inquiry* (1979): 55–79.

21. For both Attfield volumes see notes 11 and 13.

22. Gary Varner, *In Nature's Interests?* (New York: Oxford University Press, 1998).

23. John Rodman, "The Liberation of Nature," *Inquiry* 20 (1977).

24. Michael Lockwood, "Killing and the Preference for Life," *Inquiry* 22 (1979).

25. J. Baird Callicott, "Animal Liberation: A Triangular Affair," *Environmental Ethics* 2 (1980): 311–38.

26. Lawrence Johnson, *A Morally Deep World* (Cambridge: Cambridge University Press, 1991); Rolston, *Environmental Ethics*.

27. Kenneth Goodpaster, "On Being Morally Considerable," *Journal of Philosophy* 75 (1978): 308–25.

28. Tom Regan, "The Nature and Possibility of an Environmental Ethic," *Environmental Ethics* 3 (1981): 19–34.

29. Though it should be noted, as Varner (in this volume) points out, that Regan is only arguing that his case applies most clearly to those animals, not that others are necessarily excluded.

30. Taylor, *Respect for Nature*; Louis Lombardi, "Inherent Worth, Respect and Rights," *Environmental Ethics* 5 (1983): 257–70.

31. Albert Schweitzer, *Philosophy of Civilization* (Buffalo, New York: Prometheus Books, 1923, 1987), p. 318.

32. This may sound as if Taylor is straightforwardly equating an "is" with an "ought." In fact, he is most careful not to do this; but it is impossible in a background essay such as this to explain more fully. See Taylor, *Respect for Nature,* p. 71.

33. This same point is made by Peter Wenz in *Environmental Justice* (New York: SUNY Press, 1988).

34. Peter Singer, "The Place of Nonhumans" in K. M. Sayre and K. E. Goodpaster (eds.), *Ethics and Problems of the 21st Century* (Notre Dame: University of Notre Dame Press, 1979), pp. 191–206; W. K. Frankena, "Ethics and the Environment," also in *Ethics and Problems of the 21st Century*, pp. 3–20.

35. Peter Wenz, *Environmental Justice*, p. 286.

36. J. Baird Callicott, "Non-Anthropocentric Value Theory and Environmental Ethics," *American Philosophical Quarterly* 21 (1988): 301.

37. Aldo Leopold, *A Sand County Almanac*, p. 204.

38. Ibid., p. 224.

39. J. Baird Callicott (ed.), *A Companion to a Sand County Almanac* (Wisconsin: University of Wisconsin Press, 1987).

40. Although, as some ecologists have pointed out, neither of these are any longer thought of as necessary qualities of ecological systems.

41. See Bryan Norton, "The Constancy of Leopold's Land Ethic" in Andrew Light and Eric Katz (eds.), *Environmental Pragmatism* (London: Routledge, 1996), pp. 84–102.

42. More recently he has accepted that value may be vertabragenic, generated by all animals with spinal cords; broadly, animals which are conscious (J. Baird Callicott, "Rolston on Intrinsic Values: A Deconstruction," *Environmental Ethics* 14 [1992]: 129–43).

43. Callicott, "Animal Liberation: A Triangular Affair," p. 66.

44. James Lovelock, *Gaia* (Oxford: Oxford University Press, 1979) and *The Ages of Gaia* (Oxford: Oxford University Press, 1982).

45. For the scientific criticism of Gaia, see Richard Dawkins, *The Extended Phenotype* (Oxford: Oxford University Press, 1982), and some *of* the papers in Stephen H. Schneider and Penelope J. Boston (eds.), *Scientists on Gaia* (MIT Press, 1991).

46. Andrew Dobson, *Green Political Thought* (London: Unwin Hyman, 1990), p. 45.

47. Dale Jamieson, "Animal Liberation is an Environmental Ethic," *Environmental Values* 7, no. 1 (1998).

48. Gary Verner "No Holism Without Pluralism," *Environmental Ethics* 13 (1991) 175–9.

49. Rolston, *Environmental Ethics*.

50. Ibid., p. 149

51. Ibid., p 176.

52. See in particular Christopher Stone, *Earth and Other Ethics* (New York: Harper and Row, 1987) and "Moral Pluralism and the Course of Environmental Ethics" (in this volume); Andrew Brennan, *Thinking About Nature* (London: Routledge, 1988) and "Moral Pluralism and the Environment," *Environmental Values* 1, no. 1 (1992), and other articles in this section on moral pluralism in this volume.

53. See Brennan, *Thinking About Nature* and also Brennan "Environmental Awareness and Liberal Education" in this volume.

54. Brennan, "Moral Pluralism and the Environment," p. 6.

55. Brennan, *Thinking About Nature*, p. 3.

56. J. Baird Callicott, "Moral Monism in Environmental Ethics Defended," *Journal of Philosophical Research* 19 (1994).

57. J. Baird Callicott and Michael Nelson (eds.), *The Great New Wilderness Debate* (Athens, GA: University of Georgia Press, 1998).

58. Ramachandra Guha, "Radical American Environmentalism and Wilderness Preservation: A Third World Critique," *Environmental Ethics* 11 (1989): 71–83.

59. Some of Calicott's arguments are reproduced in "A Critique of and an Alternative to the Wilderness Idea"; the full debate is reproduced in *The Great New Wilderness Debate*, pp. 337–93.

60. This discussion about American Indians forms a small part of a much larger debate about the impacts of American Indians on their environment. See for example Shepart Krech, *The Ecological Indian* (New York: W. W. Norton and Company, 1999) and Vine Deloria's review article on Krech in *Worldview; Environment, Culture Religion* 4, no. 3 (2000).

61. Robert Elliot, *Faking Nature: The Ethics of Environmental Restoration* (London: Routledge, 1997).

62. Y. S. Lo. "Natural and Artifactual: Restored Nature as Subject," *Environmental Ethics* 21 (1999): 247–66. For more on Light's position on restoration see his "Restoration, the Value of Participation and the risks of Professionalization" in Paul Gobster and Bruce Hull (eds.), *Restoring Nature: Perspectives from the Social Sciences and Humanities* (Washington, DC: Island Press, 2000), pp. 49–70 and "Restoring Ecological Citizenship" in Ben Minteer and Bob Pepperman-Taylor (eds.), *Democracy and the Claims of Nature* (Lanham, MD: Rowman & Little Field, 2002).

63. Much of Natee's work, and a wide range of responses to it, has been collected in Nina Witozek and Andrew Brennan (eds.), *Philosophical Dialogues: Arne Naess and the Development of Erophilosphy* (Lanham: Rowman and Littlefield, 1999).

64. By 1984, Naees had, for instance, argued that living things could be treated differently without different grades of value being ascribed to them (Arne Naess, "Intuition Intrinsic Value and Deep Ecology" *The Ecologist* 14, no. 5–6 [1984]). By 1992, he accepted the terminology of value hierarchy in nature (personal communication). Other deep ecologists also accepted this. Warwick suggested a value hierarchy based on complexity of experience.

65. Most prominently in Bill Devall and George Sessions (eds.), *Deep Ecology* (Salt Like City: Peregrine Smith, 1985), p.70; and in Witozsek and Brennan, *Philosophical Dialogues*, p. 8.

66. Indeed, in his 1987 Schumacher Lecture, Naess himself comments that "moralizing is not a great force in the world" while Warwick Fox goes so far as to say deep ecology "renders ethics superfluous." Warwick Fox, *Towards a Transpersonal Ecology* (New York: Shambhala, 1991) p. 225.

67. In particular by Devall and Sessions, *Deep Ecology*.

68. Richard Sylvan "A Critique of Deep Ecology," *Radical Philosophy* 40/41 (1986).

69. See Brennan, *Thinking About Nature*.

70. See for instance D. C. Phillip, *Holistic Thought in Social Sciences* (Stanford: Stanford University Press, 1976).

71. Val Plumwood, *Feminism and the Mastery of Nature* (London: Routledge, 1993).

72. Ibid., p. 2.

73. The importance of values associated with particular cherished places is emphasized by Norton and Hannon in this volume.

74. Plumwood, *Feminism and the Mastery of Nature*, p. 196.

75. Karen Warren, "The Power and Promise of Ecological Feminism," *Environmental Ethics* 12 (1990): 125–46.

76. Ibid.

77. See for instance Johnson and Johnson "The Limits of Partiality," in Karen Warren (ed.), *Ecological Feminism* (London: Routledge, 1994).

78. Light's paper was published later as "Materialists, Ontologists, and Environmental Pragmatists," *Social Theory and Practice*, 21 (1995) 315–33.

79. Light and Katz, *Environmental Pragmatism*.

80. Ibid., p. 4.

81. Bryan Norton, *Towards Unity Amongst Environmentalists* (Oxford: Oxford University Press, 1991) and Norton, "Convergence and Contextualism: Some Clarifications and a Reply to Stephenson," *Environmental Ethics* 19 (1997): 87–100; Andrew Light "Compatiblism in Political Ecology" in Light and Katz, *Environmental pragmatism*, pp. 161–84, and Light, "Taking Environmental Ethics Public" in David Schmidtz and Elizabeth Willott (eds.), *Environmental Ethics: What Really Matters? What Really Works?* (Oxford: Oxford University Press, 2001).

82. See for instance Eric Katz "Searching for Intrinsic Value" in Light and Katz, *Environmental Pragmatism*, pp.307–18. As the next note suggests, however, Katz views on environmental pragmatism in some contexts have changed.

83. This latter point need not be an argument against methodological environmental pragmatism. See Eric Katz, "A Pragmatic Reconsideration of Anthropocentrism," *Environmental Ethics* 21 (1999): 377–90.

84. See Anna Peterson, "Environmental Ethics and the Social Construction of Nature" and Mick Smith, "To Speak of Trees," both in *Environmental Ethics* 12, no.4 (1999), for more detailed discussion of this debate in the context of environmental ethics.

85. First sentence of Phil Macnaghten and John Urry, *Contested Natures* (London: Sage, 1998). Similar views are put forward in the context of critical theory in Steven Vogel, *Against Nature* (New York: SUNY Press, 1996). The constructivist/realist debate about nature is interestingly discussed in Kate Soper, *What is Nature?* (Oxford: Blackwell, 1995).

86. See Michael Soulé and Gary Lease (eds.), *Reinventing Nature? Responses to Postmodern Deconstruction* (Washington: Island Press, 1995).

87. See Rolston's article "Nature for Real: Is Nature a Social Construct?" in Tim Chappell (ed.), *The Philosophy of the Environment* (Edinburgh: Edinburgh University Press, 1997).

88. See, for instance, Mick Smith, *An Ethics of Place: Radical Ecology, Postmodernity and Social Theory* (New York: SUNY Press, 2001).

89. See for instance Paul Thompson, *Sprit of the Soil* (London: Routledge, 1994); Peter Wenz, "Pragmatism in Practice: The Efficiency of Sustainable Agriculture," *Environmental Ethics* 21 (1999): 391–410; and Andrew Light, "The Urban Blind Spot in Environmental Ethics," *Environmental Politics* 10 (2001): 7–35.

STUDY QUESTIONS

1. Make a list of the essays mentioned in this article that can be found in this text, and that cannot. Pick one of them of interest and familiarize yourself a bit more with the ideas.

2. In a paragraph, respond to one of the traditions or issues mentioned.

2

Ideals of Human Excellence and Preserving Natural Environments

THOMAS E. HILL, JR.

Thomas Hill is professor of philosophy at University of North Carolina, Chapel Hill.

The moral significance of preserving natural environments is not entirely an issue of rights and social utility, for a person's attitude toward nature may be importantly connected with virtues or human excellences. The question is, "What sort of person would destroy the natural environment—Or even see its value solely in cost/benefit terms?" The answer I suggest is that willingness to do so may well reveal the absence of traits which are a natural basis for a proper humility, self-acceptance, gratitude, and appreciation of the good in others.

I

A wealthy eccentric bought a house in a neighborhood I know. The house was surrounded by a beautiful display of grass, plants, and flowers, and it was shaded by a huge old avocado tree. But the grass required cutting, the flowers needed tending, and the man wanted more sun. So he cut the whole lot down and covered the yard with asphalt. After all it was his property and he was not fond of plants.

It was a small operation, but it reminded me of the strip mining of large sections of the Appalachians. In both cases, of course, there were reasons for the destruction, and property rights could be cited as justification. But I could not help but wonder, "What sort of person would do a thing like that?"

Many Californians had a similar reaction when a recent governor defended the leveling of ancient redwood groves, reportedly saying, "If you have seen one redwood, you have seen them all."

Incidents like these arouse the indignation of ardent environmentalists and leave even apolitical observers with some degree of moral discomfort. The reasons for these reactions are mostly obvious. Uprooting the natural environment robs both present and future generations of much potential use and enjoyment. Animals too depend on the environment; and even if one does not value animals for their own sakes, their potential utility for us is incalculable. Plants are needed, of course, to replenish the atmosphere quite aside from their aesthetic value. These reasons for hesitating to destroy forests and gardens are not only the most obvious ones, but also the most persuasive for practical purposes. But, one wonders, is there nothing more behind our discomfort? Are we concerned solely about the potential use and enjoyment of forests etc., for ourselves, later generations, and perhaps animals? Is there not something else which disturbs us when we witness the destructions or even listen to those who would defend it in terms of cost/benefit analysis?

Thomas E. Hill, Jr., "Ideals of Human Excellence and Preserving Natural Environments," *Environmental Ethics*, Vol. 5 (1983), pp. 211–24. Reprinted by permission.

Imagine that in each of our examples those who would destroy the environment argue elaborately that, even considering future generations of human beings and animals, there are benefits in "replacing" the natural environment which outweigh the negative utilities which environmentalists cite.[1] No doubt we could press the argument on the facts, trying to show that the destruction is shortsighted and that its defenders have underestimated its potential harm or ignored some pertinent rights or interests. But is this all we could say? Suppose we grant, for a moment, that the utility of destroying the redwoods, forests, and gardens is equal to their potential for use and enjoyment by nature lovers and animals. Suppose, further, that we even grant that the pertinent human rights and animal rights, if any, are evenly divided for and against destruction. Imagine that we also concede, for argument's sake, that the forests contain no potentially useful endangered species of animals and plants. Must we then conclude that there is no further cause for moral concern? Should we then feel morally indifferent when we see the natural environment uprooted?

II

Suppose we feel that the answer to these questions should be negative. Suppose, in other words, we feel that our moral discomfort when we confront the destroyers of nature is not fully explained by our belief that they have miscalculated the best use of natural resources or violated rights in exploiting them. Suppose, in particular, we sense that part of the problem is that the natural environment is being viewed exclusively as a natural *resource*. What could be the ground of such a feeling? That is, what is there in our system of normative principles and values that could account for our remaining moral dissatisfaction?[2]

Some may be tempted to seek an explanation by appeal to the interests, or even the rights, of plants. After all, they may argue, we only gradually came to acknowledge the moral importance of all human beings, and it is even more recently that consciences have been aroused to give full weight to the welfare (and rights?) of animals. The next logical step, it may be argued, is to acknowledge a moral requirement to take into account the interests (and rights?) of plants. The problem with the strip miners, redwood cutters, and the like, on this view, is not just that they ignore the welfare and rights of people and animals, they also fail to give due weight to the survival and health of the plants themselves.

The temptation to make such a reply is understandable if one assumes that all moral questions are exclusively concerned with whether *acts* are right or wrong, and that this, in turn, is determined entirely by how the acts impinge on the rights and interests of those directly affected. On this assumption, if there is a cause for moral concern, some right or interest has been neglected; and if the rights and interests of human beings and animals have already been taken into account, then there must be some other pertinent interests, for example, those of plants. A little reflection will show that the assumption is mistaken; but, in all any case, the conclusion that plants have rights or morally relevant interests is surely untenable. We do speak of what is "good for" plants, and they can "thrive" and also be "killed." But this does not imply that they have "interests" in any morally relevant sense. Some people apparently believe that plants grow better if we talk to them, but the idea that the plants suffer and enjoy, desire and dislike, etc., is clearly outside the range of both common sense and scientific belief. The notion that the forests should be preserved to avoid *hurting* the trees or because they have a *right* to life is not part of a widely shared moral consciousness, and for good reason.[3]

Another way of trying to explain our moral discomfort is to appeal to certain religious beliefs. If one believes that all living things were created by a God who cares for them and entrusted us with the use of plants and animals only for limited purposes, then one has a reason to avoid careless destruction of the forests, etc., quite aside from their future utility. Again, if one believes that a divine force is immanent in all nature, then too one might have reason to care for more than sentient things. But such arguments require strong and controversial premises, and, I suspect, they will always have a restricted audience.

Early in this century, due largely to the influence of G.E. Moore, another point of view developed which some may find promising.[4] Moore introduced, or at least made popular, the idea that certain states of affairs are intrinsically valuable—not just valued, but valuable, and not necessarily because of their effects on sentient beings. Admittedly Moore came to believe that in fact the only intrinsically valuable things were conscious experiences of various sorts,[5] but this restriction was not inherent in the idea of intrinsic value. The intrinsic goodness of something, he thought, was an objective, nonrelational property of the thing, like its texture or color, but not a property perceivable by sense perception or detectable by scientific instruments. In theory at least, a single tree thriving alone in a universe without sentient beings, and even without God, could be intrinsically valuable. Since, according to Moore, our duty is to maximize intrinsic value, his theory could obviously be used to argue that we have reason not to destroy natural environments independently of how they affect human beings and animals. The survival of a forest might have worth beyond its worth *to* sentient beings.

This approach, like the religious one, may appeal to some but is infested with problems. There are, first, the familiar objections to intuitionism, on which the theory depends. Metaphysical and epistemological doubts about nonnatural, intuited properties are hard to suppress, and many have argued that the theory rests on a misunderstanding of the words *good, valuable,* and the like.[6] Second, even if we try to set aside these objections and think in Moore's terms, it is far from obvious that everyone would agree that the existence of forests, etc., is intrinsically valuable. The test, says Moore, is what we would say when we imagine a universe with just the thing in question, without any effects or accompaniments, and then we ask, "Would its existences be better than its nonexistence?" Be careful, Moore would remind us, not to construe this question as, "Would you *prefer* the existence of that universe to its nonexistence?" The

question is, "would its existence have the objective non relational property, intrinsic goodness?"

Now even among those who have no worries about whether this really makes sense, we might well get a diversity of answers. Those prone to destroy natural environments will doubtless give one answer, and nature lovers will likely give another. When an issue is a controversial as the one at hand, intuition is a poor arbiter.

The problem, then, in this. We want to understand what underlies our moral uneasiness at the destruction of the redwoods, forests, etc., even part from the loss of these as resources for human beings and animals. But I find no adequate answer by pursuing the questions, "Are rights or interest of plants neglected?" "What is God's will on the matter?" and "What is the intrinsic value of the existence of a tree or forest?" My suggestion, which is in fact the main point on this paper, is that we look at the problem from a different perspective. That is, let us turn for a while from the effort to find reasons why certain acts destructive of natural environments are morally wrong to the ancient task of articulating our ideals of human excellence. Rather than argue directly with destroyers of the environment who say, "Show me why what I am doing is *immoral*" I want to ask, "What sort of person would want to do what they propose?" The point is not to skirt the issue with an ad hominem, but to raise a different moral question, for even if there is no convincing way to show that the destructive acts are wrong (independently of human and animal use and enjoyment), we may find that the willingness to indulge in them reflects the absence of human traits that we admire and regard morally important.

This strategy of shifting questions may seem more promising if one reflects on certain analogous situations. Consider, for example, the Nazi who asks, in all seriousness, "Why is it wrong for me to make lampshades out of human skin—provided, of course, I did not myself kill the victims to get the skins?" We would react more with shock and disgust than with indignation, I suspect, because it is even more evident that the question reveals a defect in the questioner than that the proposed act is itself immoral. Sometimes we may not regard an act wrong at all though we see it as reflecting something objectionable about the person who does it. Imagine, for example, one who laughs spontaneously to himself when he reads a newspaper account of a plane crash that kills hundreds. Or, again, consider an obsequious grandson who, having waited for his grandmother's inheritance with mock devotion, then secretly spits on her grave when at last she dies. Spitting on the grave may have no adverse consequences and perhaps it violates no rights. The moral uneasiness which it arouses is explained more by our view of the agent than by any conviction that what he did was immoral. Had he hesitated and asked, "Why shouldn't I slip on her grave?" it seems more fitting to ask him to reflect on the sort of person he is than to try to offer reasons why he should refrain from spitting.

III

What sort of person, then, would cover his garden with asphalt, strip mine a wooded mountain, or level an irreplaceable redwood groove? Two sorts of answers, though initially appealing, must be ruled out. The first is that persons who would destroy the environment in these ways are either shortsighted, underestimating the harm they do, or else are too little concerned for the well-being of other people. Perhaps too they have insufficient regard for animal life. But these considerations have been set aside in order to refine the controversy. Another tempting response might be that we count it a moral virtue, or at least a human ideal, to love nature. Those who value the environment only for its utility must not really love nature and so in this way fall short of an ideal. But such an answer is hardly satisfying in the present context, for what is at issue is *why* we feel moral discomfort at the activities of those who admittedly value nature only for its utility. That it is ideal to care for nonsentient nature beyond its possible use is really just another way of expressing the general point which is under controversy.

What is needed is some way of showing that this ideal is connected with other virtues, or human excellences, not in question. To do so it is difficult and my suggestions, accordingly, will be tentative and subject to qualification. The main idea is that, though indifference to nonsentient nature does not *necessarily* reflect the absence of virtues, it often signals the absence of certain traits which we want to encourage because they are, in most cases, a natural basis for the development of certain values. It is often thought, for example, that those who would destroy the natural environment must lack a proper appreciation of their place in the natural order, and so must either be ignorant or have too little humility. Though I would argue that this is not necessarily so, I suggest that, given certain plausible empirical assumptions, their attitude may well be rooted in ignorance, a narrow perspective, inability to see things as important apart from themselves and the limited groups they associate with, or reluctance to accept themselves as natural beings. Overcoming these deficiencies will not guarantee a proper more humility, but for most of us it is probably an important psychological preliminary. Later I suggest, more briefly, that indifference to nonsentient nature typically reveals absence of either aesthetic sensibility or a disposition to cherish what has enriched one's life and that these, though not themselves moral virtues, are a natural basis for appreciation of the good in others and gratitude?[7]

Consider first the suggestion that destroyers of the environment lack an appreciation of their place in the universe.[8] Their attention, it seems, must be focused on parochial matters, on what is, relatively speaking, close in space and time. They seem not to understand that we are a speck on the cosmic scene, a brief stage in the evolutionary process, only one among millions of species on Earth, and an episode in the course of human history. Of course, they know that there are stars, fossils, insects, and ancient ruins; but do not they have any idea of the complexity of the processes that led to the natural world as we find it? Are they aware how much the forces at work within their own bodies are like those which govern all living things and even how much they have in common with inanimate bodies? Admittedly scientific knowledge is limited and no one can master it all; but could one who had a broad and deep understanding of his place in nature really be indifferent to the destruction of the natural environment?

This first suggestion, however, may well provoke a protest from a sophisticated anti-environmentalist.[9] "Perhaps *some* may be indifferent to nature from ignorance," the critic may object, "but *I* have studied astronomy, geology, biology, and biochemistry, and I still unashamedly regard the nonsentient environment as simply a resource for our use. It should not be wasted, of course, but what should be preserved is decidable by weighing longterm costs and benefits." "Besides," our critic may continue, "as philosophers you should know the old Humean formula, 'You cannot derive an *ought* from an *is*.' All the facts of biology, biochemistry, etc., do not entail that I ought to love nature or want to preserve it. What one understands is one thing; what one values is something else. Just as nature lovers are not necessarily scientists, those indifferent to nature are not necessarily ignorant."

Although the environmentalist may concede the critic's logical point, he may well argue that, as a matter of fact, increased understanding of nature tends to heighten people's concern for its preservation. If so, despite the objection, the suspicion that the destroyers of the environment lack deep understanding of nature is not, in most cases, unwarranted, but the argument need not rest here.

The environmentalist might amplify his original idea as follows: "When I said the destroyers of nature do not appreciate their place in the universe, I was not speaking of intellectual understanding alone, for, after all, a person can *know* a catalog of facts without ever putting them together and seeing vividly the whole picture which they form. To see oneself as just one part of nature is to look at oneself and the world from a certain perspective which is quite different from being able to recite detailed information from the natural sciences. What the destroyers of nature lack is this perspective, not particular information."

Again our critic may object, though only after making some concessions: "All right," he may say,

"*some* who are indifferent to nature may lack the cosmic perspective of which you speak, but again there is no *necessary* connection between this failing, if it is one, and any particular evaluative attitude toward nature. In fact, different people respond quite differently when they move to a wider perspective. When *I* try to picture myself vividly as a brief transitory episode in the course of nature, I simply get depressed. Far from inspiring me with a love of nature, the exercise makes me sad and hostile. You romantics think only of poets like Wordsworth and artists like Turner, but you should consider how differently Omkar Khayám responded when he took your wider perspective. His reaction, when looking at his life from a cosmic viewpoint, was 'Drink up, for tomorrow we die.' Others respond in an almost opposite manner with a joyless Stoic resignation, exemplified by the poet who pictures the wise man, at the height of personal triumph, being served a magnificent banquet, and then consummating his marriage to his beloved, all the while reminding himself, 'Even this shall pass away.' "[10] In sum, the critic may object, "Even if one should try to see oneself as one small transitory part of nature, doing so does not dictate any particular normative attitude. Some may come to love nature, but others are moved to live for the moment; some sink into sad resignation; others get depressed or angry. So indifference to nature is not necessarily a sign that a person fails to look at himself from the larger perspective."

The environmentalist might respond to this objection in several ways. He might, for example, argue that even though some people who see themselves as part of the natural order remain indifferent to nonsentient nature, this is not a common reaction. Typically, it may be argued, as we become more and more aware that we are parts of the larger whole we come to value the whole independently of its effects on ourselves. Thus, despite the possibilities the critic raises, indifference to nonsentient nature is still in most cases a sign that a person fails to see himself as part of the natural order.

If someone challenges the empirical assumption here, the environmentalist might develop the argument along a quite different line. The initial idea, he may remind us, was that those who would destroy the natural environment fail to *appreciate* their place in the natural order. "Appreciating one's place" is not simply an intellectual appreciation. It is also an attitude, reflecting what one values as well as what one knows. When we say, for example, that both the servile and the arrogant person fails to *appreciate* their place in a society of equals, we do not mean simply that they are ignorant of certain empirical facts, but rather that they have certain objectionable attitudes about their importance relative to other people. Similarly, to fail to appreciate one's place in nature is not merely to lack knowledge or breadth of perspective, but to take a certain attitude about what matters. A person who *understands* his place in nature but still views nonsentient nature merely as a resource takes the attitude that nothing is *important* but human beings and animals. Despite first appearance, he is not so much like the pre-Copernican astronomers who made the intellectual error of treating the Earth as the "center of the universe" when they made their calculation. He is more like the racist who, though well aware of other races, treats all races but his own as insignificant.

So construed, the argument appeals to the common idea that awareness of nature typically has, and should have, a humbling effect. The Alps, a storm at sea, the Grand Canyon, towering redwoods, and "the starry heavens above" move many a person to remarks on the comparative insignificance of our daily concerns and even of our species, and this is generally taken to be a quite fitting response.[11] What seems to be missing, then, in those who understand nature but remain unmoved is a proper humility.[12] Absence of proper humility is not the same as a selfishness or egoism, for one can be devoted to self-interest while still viewing one's own pleasures and projects as trivial and unimportant.[13] And one can have an exaggerated view of one's own importance while grandly sacrificing for those one views as inferior. Nor is the lack of humility identical with belief that one has power and influence, for a person can be quite puffed up about himself while believing that the foolish world will never acknowledge him. The

humility we miss seems not so much a belief about one's relative effectiveness and recognition as an attitude which measures the importance of things independently of their relation to oneself or to some narrow group with which one identifies. A paradigm of a person who lacks humility is the self-important emperor who grants status to his family because it is *his,* subordinates because *he* appointed them, and to his country because he chooses to glorify it. Less extreme but still lacking proper humility is the elitist who counts events significant solely in proportion to how they affect his class. The suspicion about those who would destroy the environment, then, is that what they count important is too narrowly confined in so far as it encompasses only what affects beings who, like us, are capable of feeling.

This idea that proper humility requires recognition of the importance of nonsentient nature is similar to the thought of those who charge meat eaters with "species-ism." In both cases it is felt that people too narrowly confine their concerns to the sorts of being that are most like them. But, however intuitively appealing, the idea will surely arouse objections from our nonenvironmentalist critic. "Why," he will ask, "do you suppose that the sort of humility I *should* have requires me to acknowledge the importance of nonsentient nature aside from its utility? You cannot, by your own admission, argue that nonsentient nature is important, appealing to religious or intuitionist grounds. And simply to assert, without further argument, that an ideal humility requires us to view nonsentient nature as important for its own sake begs the question at issue. If proper humility is acknowledging the relative importance of things as one should, then to show that I must lack this you must first establish that one *should* acknowledge the importance of nonsentient nature."

Though some may wish to accept this challenge, there are other ways to pursue the connection between humility and response to nonsentient nature. For example, suppose we grant that proper humility requires only acknowledging a due status to sentient beings. We must admit, then, that it is logically possible for a person to be properly humble even though he viewed all nonsentient nature simply as a resource. But this logical possibility may be a psychological rarity. It may be that, given the sort of beings we are, we would never learn humility before persons without developing the general capacity to cherish, and regard important, many things for their own sakes. The major obstacle to humility before persons is self-importance, a tendency to measure the significance of everything by its relation to oneself and those with whom one identifies. The processes by which we overcome self-importance are doubtless many and complex, but it seems unlikely that they are exclusively concerned with how we relate to other people and animals. Learning humility requires learning to feel that something matters besides what will affect oneself and one's circle of associates. What leads a child to care about what happens to a lost hamster or a stray dog he will not see again is likely also to generate concern for a lost toy or a favorite tree where he used to live.[14] Learning to value things for their own sake, and to count what affects them important aside from their utility, is not the same as judging them to have some intuited objective property, but it is necessary to the development of humility and it seems likely to take place in experiences with nonsentient nature as well as with people and animals. If a person views all nonsentient nature merely as a resource, then it seems unlikely that he has developed the capacity needed to overcome self-importance.

IV

This last argument, unfortunately, has its limits. It presupposes an empirical connection between experiencing nature and overcoming self-importance, and this may be challenged. Even if experiencing nature promotes humility before others, there may be other ways people can develop such humility in a world of concrete, glass, and plastic. If not, perhaps all that is needed is limited experience of nature in one's early, developing years; mature adults, having overcome youthful self-importance, may live well enough in artificial surroundings. More importantly, the argument does not fully capture the spirit of the intuition that an ideal person stands humbly before nature. That idea is not simply that experiencing nature tends to foster proper humility before other people; it is, in part, that natural surroundings encourage and are appropriate to an ideal sense of oneself as part of the natural world. Standing alone in the forest, after months in the city, is not merely good as a means of curbing one's arrogance before others; it reinforces and fittingly expresses one's acceptance of oneself as a natural being.

Previously we considered only one aspect of proper humility, namely, a sense of one's relative importance with respect to other human beings. Another aspect, I think, is a kind of *self-acceptance*. This involves acknowledging, in more than a merely intellectual way, that we are the sort of creatures that we are. Whether one is self-accepting is not so much a matter of how one attributes *importance* comparatively to oneself, other people, animals, plants, and other things as it is a matter of understanding, facing squarely, and responding appropriately to who and what one is, e.g., one's powers and limits, one's affinities with other beings and differences from them, one's unalterable nature and one's freedom to change. Self-acceptance is not merely intellectual awareness, for one can be intellectually aware that one is growing old and will eventually die while nevertheless behaving in a thousand foolish ways that reflect a refusal to acknowledge these facts. On the other hand, self-acceptance is not passive resignation, for refusal to pursue what one truly wants within one's limits is a failure to accept the freedom and power one has. Particular behaviors, like dying one's gray hair and dressing like those twenty years younger, do not *necessarily* imply lack of self-acceptances, for there could be reasons for acting in these ways other than the wish to hide from oneself what one really is. One fails to accept oneself when the patterns of behavior and emotion are rooted in a desire to disown and deny features of oneself, to pretend to oneself that they are not there. This is not to say that a self accepting persons makes no value judgments about himself, that he likes all facts about himself, wants equally to develop and display them; he can, and should feel remorse for his past misdeeds and strive to change his current vices. The point is that he does not disown them, pretend that they do not exist or are facts something other than himself. Such pretense is incompatible with proper humility because it is seeing oneself as better than one is.

Self-acceptance of this sort has long been considered a human excellence, under various names, but what has it to do with preserving nature? There is, I think, the following connection. As human beings we are part of nature, living, growing, declining, and dying by natural laws similar to those governing other living beings; despite our awesomely distinctive human powers, we share many of the needs, limits, and liabilities of animals and plants. These facts are neither good nor bad in themselves, aside from personal preference and varying conventional values. To say this is to utter a truism which few will deny, but to accept these facts, as facts about oneself, is not so easy—or so common. Much of what naturalists deplore about our increasingly artificial world reflects, and encourages, a denial of these facts, an unwillingness to avow them with equanimity.

Like the Victorian Lady who refuses to look at her own nude body, some would like to create a world of less transitory stuff, reminding us only of our intellectual and social nature, never calling to mind our affinities with "lower" living creatures. The "denial of death," to which psychiatrists call attention,[15] reveals an attitude incompatible with the sort of self-acceptance which philosophers, from the ancients to Spinoza and on, have admired as a human excellence. My suggestion is not merely that experiencing nature causally promotes such self-acceptance, but also that those who fully accept themselves as part of the natural world lack the common drive to disassociate themselves from nature by replacing natural environments with artificial ones. A storm in the wilds helps us to appreciate our animal vulnerability, but equally important,

the reluctance to experience it may *reflect* an unwillingness to accept this aspect of ourselves. The person who is too ready to destroy the ancient redwoods may lack humility, not so much in the sense that he exaggerates his importance relative to others, but rather in the sense that he tries to avoid seeing himself as one among many natural creatures.

V

My suggestion so far has been that, though indifference to nonsentient nature is not itself a moral vice, it is likely to reflect either ignorance, a self-importance, or a lack of self-acceptance which we must overcome to have proper humility. A similar idea might be developed connecting attitudes toward nonsentient nature with other human excellences. For example, one might argue that indifference to nature reveals a lack of either an aesthetic sense or some of the natural roots of gratitude.

When we see a hillside that has been gutted by strip miners or the garden replaced by asphalt, our first reaction is probably, "How Ugly!" The scenes assault our aesthetic sensibilities. We suspect that no one with a keen sense of beauty could have left such a sight. Admittedly not everything in nature strikes us as beautiful, or even aesthetically interesting, and sometimes a natural scene is replaced with a more impressive architectural masterpiece. But this is not usually the situation in the problem cases which environmentalists are most concerned about. More often beauty is replaced with ugliness.

At this point our critic may well object that, even if he does lack a sense of beauty, this is no moral vice. His cost/benefit calculations take into account the pleasure others may derive from seeing the forests, etc., and so why should he be faulted?

Some might reply that, despite contrary philosophical traditions, aesthetics and morality are not so distinct as commonly supposed. Appreciation of beauty, they may argue, is a human excellence which morally ideal persons should try to develop.

But, setting aside this controversial position, there still may be cause for moral concern about those who have no aesthetic response to nature. Even if aesthetic sensibility is not itself a moral virtue, many of the capacities of mind and heart which it presupposes may be ones which are also needed for an appreciation of other people. Consider, for example, curiosity, a mind open to novelty, the ability to look at things from unfamiliar perspectives, empathetic imagination, interest in details, variety and order, and emotional freedom from the immediate and the practical. All these, and more, seem necessary to aesthetic sensibility, but they are also traits which a person needs to be fully sensitive of people of all sorts. The point is not that a moral person must be able to distinguish beautiful from ugly people; the point is rather that unresponsiveness to what is beautiful, awesome, dainty, dumpy, and otherwise aesthetically interesting in nature probably reflects a lack of the openness of mind and spirit necessary to appreciate the best in human beings.

The anti-environmentalist, however, may refuse to accept the charge that he lacks aesthetic sensibility. If he claims to appreciate-seventeenth century miniature portraits, but to abhor natural wildernesses, he will hardly be convincing. Tastes vary, but aesthetic sense is not *that* selective. He may, instead, insist that he *does* appreciate natural beauty. He spends his vacations, let us suppose, hiking in the Sierras, photographing wildflowers, and so on. He might press his arguments as follows: "I enjoy natural beauty as much as anyone, but I fail to see what this has to do with preserving the environment independently of human enjoyment and use. Nonsentient nature is a resource, but one of its best uses is to give us a pleasure. I take this into account when I calculate the costs and benefits of preserving a park, planting a garden, and so on. But the problem you raised explicitly set aside the desire to preserve nature as a means to enjoyment. I say, let us enjoy nature fully while we can, but if at all sentient beings were to die tomorrow we might as well blow up all plant life as well. A redwood groove that no one can use or enjoy is utterly worthless."

The attitude expressed here, I suspect, is not a common one, but it represents a philosophical challenge. The beginnings of a reply may be found in the following. When a person takes joy in some thing, it is a common (and perhaps natural) response is come to cherish it. To cherish something is not simply to be happy with it at the moment, but to care for it for its own sake. This is not to say that one necessarily sees it as having feelings and so wants it to feel good; nor does it imply that one judges the thing to have Moore's intrinsic value. One simply wants the thing to survive and (when appropriate) to thrive, and not simply for its utility. We see this attitude repeatedly regarding mementos. They are not simply valued as a means to remind us of happy occasions; they come to be valued for their own sake. Thus, if someone really took joy in the natural environment, but was prepared to blow it up as soon as sentient life ended, he would lack this common human tendency to cherish what enriches our lives. While this response is not itself a moral virtue, it may be a natural basis of the virtue we call "gratitude." People who have no tendency to cherish things that give them pleasure may be poorly disposed to respond gratefully to persons who are good to them. Again the connection is not one of logical necessity, but it may nevertheless be important. A nonreligious person unable to "thank" anyone for the beauties of nature may nevertheless feel "grateful" in a sense; and I suspect that the person who feels no such "gratitude" toward nature is unlikely to show proper gratitude towards people.

Suppose these conjectures prove to be true. One may wonder what is the point of considering them. Is it to disparage all those who view nature merely as a resource? To do so, it seems, would be unfair, for, even if this attitude typically stems from deficiencies which affect one's attitudes toward sentient beings, there may be exceptions and we have not shown that their view of nonsentient nature is itself blameworthy. But when we set aside questions of blame and inquire what sorts of human traits we want to encourage, our reflections become relevant in a more positive way. The point is not to insinuate that all anti-environmentalists are defective, but to see that those whose value such traits as humility, gratitude, and sensitivity to others have reason to promote the love of nature.

NOTES

1. When I use the expression "the natural environment," I have in mind the sort of examples with which I began. For some purposes it is important to distinguish cultivated gardens from forests, virgin forest from replenished ones, irreplaceable natural phenomena from the replaceable, and so on; but these distinctions, I think, do not affect my main point here. There is also a broad sense, as Hume and Mill noted, in which all that occurs, miracles aside, is "natural." In this sense, of course, strip mining is as natural as a beaver cutting trees for his dam, and, as parts of nature, we cannot destroy the "natural" environment but only alter it. As will be evident, I shall use *natural* in a narrower, more familiar sense.

2. This paper is intended as a preliminary discussion in *normative* ethical theory (as opposed to *metaethics*). The task, accordingly, is the limited, though still difficult, one of articulating the possible basis in our beliefs and values for certain particular moral judgments. Questions of ultimate justification are not set aside. What makes the task difficult and challenging is not that conclusive proofs from the foundation of morality are attempted; it is rather that the particular judgments to be explained seem at first not to fall under the most familiar moral principles (e.g., utilitarianism, respect for rights).

3. I assume here that having a right presupposes having interests in a sense which in turn presupposes a capacity to desire, suffer, etc. Since my main concern lies in another direction, I do not argue the point, but merely note that some regard it as debatable. See, for example, W. Murray Hunt, "Are *Mere Things* Morally Considerable?" *Environmental Ethics* 2 (1980): 59–65; Kenneth E. Goodpaster, "On Stopping at Everything," *Environmental Ethics* 2 (1980): 288–294; Joel Feinberg, "The Rights of Animals and Unborn Generations," in William Blackstone, ed., *Philosophy and Environmental Crisis* (Athens: University of Georgia Press, 1974), pp. 43–68; Tom Regan, "Feinberg on What Sorts of Beings Can Have Rights," *Southern Journal of philosophy* (1976): 485–498; Robert Elliot, "Regan on the Sort of Beings that Can have Rights," *Southern Journal of Philosophy* (1978): 701–705; Scott Lehmann, "Do Wildernesses Have Rights?" *Environmental Ethics* 2 (1981): 129–146.

4. G. E. Moore, *Principles Ethica* (Cambridge: Cambridge University Press, 1903); *Ethics* (London: H. Holt, 1912).

5. G. E. Moore, "Is Goodness a Quality?" *Philosophical Papers* (London: George Allen and Unwin, 1959), pp. 95–97.

6. See, for example, P. H. Nowell-Smith, *Ethics* (New York: Penguin Books, 1954).

7. The issues I raise here, though perhaps not the details of my remarks, are in line with Aristotle's view of moral philosophy, a view revitalized recently by Philippa Foot's *Virtue and Vice* (Berkeley: University of California Press, 1979), Alasdair McIntyre's *After Virtue* (Notre Dame: Notre Dame Press, 1981), and James Wallace's *Virtues and Vices* (Ithaca and London: Cornell University Press, 1978), and other works. For other reflections on relationships between character and natural environments, see John Rodman, "The Liberation of Nature," *Inquiry* (1976): 83–131 and L. Reinhardt, "Some Gaps in Moral Space: Reflections on Forests and Feelings," in Mannison, McRobbie, and Routley, eds., *Environments Philosophy* (Canberra: Australian University Research School of Social Sciences, 1980).

8. Though for simplicity I focus upon those who do strip mining, etc., the argument is also applicable to those whose utilitarian calculations lead them to preserve the redwoods, mountains, etc., but who care for only sentient nature for its own sake. Similarly the phrase "indifferent to nature" is meant to encompass those who are indifferent

except when considering its benefits to people and animals.

9. For convenience I use the labels *environmentalist* and *anti-environmentalist* (or *critic*) for the opening sides in the rather special controversy I have raised. Thus, for example, my "environmentalist" not only favors conserving the forests, etc., but finds something objectionable in wanting to destroy them even aside from the costs to human beings and animals. My "anti-environmentalist" is not simply one who wants to destroy the environment; he is a person who has no qualms about doing so independent of adverse effects on human beings and animals.

10. "Even this shall pass away," by Theodore Tildon, in *The Best Loved Poems of the American People*, ed. Hazel Felleman (Garden City, N.Y.: Doubleday & Co., 1936).

11. An exception, apparently, was Kant, who thought "the starry heavens" sublime and compared them with "the Moral law within," but did not for all that see our species as comparatively insignificant.

12. By "proper humility" I mean that sort and degree of humility that is a morally admirable character trait. How precisely to define this is, of course, a controversial matter, but the point for present purposes is just to set aside obsequiousness, false modesty, underestimation of one's abilities, and the like.

13. I take this point from some of Philippa Foot's remarks.

14. The causal history of this concern may well depend upon the object (tree, toy) having given the child pleasure, but this does not mean that the object is then valued only for further pleasure it may bring.

15. See, for example, Ernest Becker, *The Denial of Death* (New York: Free Press, 1973).

STUDY QUESTIONS

1. What question does Hill raise as being central to an environmental ethic?

2. How is this different than asking "Why it is immoral to harm natural environments"?

3. Hill seems to focus primarily upon the preservation of (relatively) unspoiled ecosystems. Does his analysis also apply to more mundane but also ecologically destructive activities such as burning driving cars, coal fired power plants, etc. If so, what are the implications for us?

3

Global Environment and International Inequality

HENRY SHUE

Henry Shue is a Research Fellow in Politics and International Relations at Merton College, Oxford. Shue has done influential work on torture, global poverty, as well as environmental issues, including climate change.

My aim is to establish that three commonsense principles of fairness, none of them dependent upon controversial philosophical theories of justice, give rise to the same conclusion about the allocation of the costs of protecting the environment.

Poor states and rich states have long dealt with each other primarily upon unequal terms. The imposition of unequal terms has been relatively easy for the rich states because they have rarely needed to ask for the voluntary cooperation of the less powerful poor states. Now the rich countries have realized that their own industrial activity has been destroying the ozone in the earth's atmosphere and has been making far and away the greatest contribution to global warming. They would like the poor states to avoid adopting the same form of industrialization by which they themselves became rich. It is increasingly clear that if poor states pursue their own economic development with the same disregard for the natural environment and the economic welfare of other states that rich states displayed in the past during their development, everyone will continue to suffer the effects of environmental destruction. Consequently, it is at least conceivable that rich states might now be willing to consider dealing cooperatively on equitable terms with poor states in a manner that gives due weight to both the economic development of poor states and the preservation of the natural environment.

If we are to have any hope of pursuing equitable cooperation, we must try to arrive at a consensus about what equity means. And we need to define equity, not as a vague abstraction, but concretely and specifically in the context of both development of the economy in poor states and preservation of the environment everywhere.

FUNDAMENTAL FAIRNESS AND ACCEPTABLE INEQUALITY

What diplomats and lawyers call equity incorporates important aspects of what ordinary people everywhere call fairness. The concept of fairness is neither Eastern nor Western, Northern nor Southern, but universal.[1] People everywhere understand what it means to ask whether an arrangement is fair or biased towards some parties over other parties. If you own the land but I supply the labour, or you own the seed but I own the ox, or you are old but I am young, or you are female but I am male, or you have an education and I do not, or you worked long and hard but I was lazy—in situation after situation it makes perfectly good sense to ask whether a particular division of something among two or more parties is fair to all the parties, in light of this or that difference between them. All people understand the question, even where they have been taught not to ask it. What would be fair? Or, as the lawyers and diplomats would put it, which arrangement would be equitable?

Naturally, it is also possible to ask other kinds of questions about the same arrangements. One can always ask economic questions, for instance, in addition to ethical questions concerning equity: would it increase total output if, say, women were paid less and men were paid more? Would it be more efficient? Sometimes the most efficient arrangement happens also to be fair to all parties, but often it is unfair. Then a choice has to be made between efficiency and fairness. Before it is possible to discuss such choices, however, we need to know the meaning of equity: what are the standards of equity and how do they matter?

Complete egalitarianism—the belief that all good things ought to be shared equally among all people—can be a powerfully attractive view, and it is much more difficult to argue against than many of its opponents seem to think. I shall, nevertheless, assume here that complete egalitarianism is unacceptable. If it were the appropriate view to adopt, our inquiry into equity could end now. The answer to the question, "what is an equitable arrangement?" would always be the same: an equal distribution. Only equality would ever provide equity.

While I do assume that it may be equitable for some good things to be distributed unequally, I also assume that other things must be kept equal—most importantly, dignity and respect. It is part of the current international consensus that every person is entitled to equal dignity and equal respect. In traditional societies in both hemispheres, even the equality of dignity and respect was denied in theory as well as practice. Now, although principles of equality are still widely violated in practice, inequality of dignity and of respect have relatively few public advocates even among those who practice them. If it is equitable for some other human

goods to be distributed unequally, but it is not equitable for dignity or respect to be unequal, the central questions become: "which inequalities in which other human goods are compatible with equal human dignity and equal human respect?" and "which inequalities in other goods ought to be eliminated, reduced or prevented from being increased?"

When one is beginning from an existing inequality, like the current inequality in wealth between North and South, three critical kinds of justification are: justifications of unequal burdens intended to reduce or eliminate the existing inequality by removing an unfair advantage of those at the top; justifications of unequal burdens intended to prevent the existing inequality from becoming worse through any infliction of an unfair additional disadvantage upon those at the bottom; and justifications of a guaranteed minimum intended to prevent the existing inequality from becoming worse through any infliction of an unfair additional disadvantage upon those at the bottom. The second justification for unequal burdens and the justification for a guaranteed minimum are the same: two different mechanisms are being used to achieve fundamentally the same purpose. I shall look at these two forms of justification for unequal burdens and then at the justification for a guaranteed minimum.

UNEQUAL BURDENS

Greater Contribution to the Problem

All over the world parents teach their children to clean up their own mess. This simple rule makes good sense from the point of view of incentive: if one learns that one will not be allowed to get away with simply walking away from whatever messes one creates, one is given a strong negative incentive against making messes in the first place. Whoever makes the mess presumably does so in the process of pursuing some benefit—for a child, the benefit may simply be the pleasure of playing with the objects that constitute the mess. If one learns that whoever reaps the benefit of making the mess must also be the one who pays the cost of cleaning up the mess, one learns at the very least not to make messes with costs that are greater than their benefits.

Economists have glorified this simple rule as the "internalization of externalities." If the basis for the price of a product does not incorporate the costs of cleaning up the mess made in the process of producing the product, the costs are being externalized, that is, dumped upon other parties. Incorporating into the basis of the price of the product the costs that had been coercively socialized is called internalizing an externality.

At least as important as the consideration of incentives, however, is the consideration of fairness or equity. If whoever makes a mess receives the benefits and does not pay the costs, not only does he have no incentive to avoid making as many messes as he likes, but he is also unfair to whoever does pay the costs. He is inflicting costs upon other people, contrary to their interests and, presumably, without their consent. By making himself better off in ways that make others worse off, he is creating an expanding inequality.

Once such an inequality has been created unilaterally by someone's imposing costs upon other people, we are justified in reversing the inequality by imposing extra burdens upon the producer of the inequality. There are two separate points here. First, we are justified in assigning additional burdens to the party who has been inflicting costs upon us. Second, the minimum extent of the compensatory burden we are justified in assigning is enough to correct the inequality previously unilaterally imposed. The purpose of the extra burden is to restore an equality that was disrupted unilaterally and arbitrarily (or to reduce an inequality that was enlarged unilaterally and arbitrarily). In order to accomplish that purpose, the extra burden assigned must be at least equal to the unfair advantage previously taken. This yields us our first principle of equity:

> When a party has in the past taken an
> unfair advantage of others by imposing
> costs upon them without their consent,
> those who have been unilaterally put at a

disadvantage are entitled to demand that in the future the offending party shoulder burdens that are unequal at least to the extent of the unfair advantage previously taken, in order to restore equality.[2]

In the area of development and the environment, the clearest cases that fall under this first principle of equity are the partial destruction of the ozone layer and the initiation of global warming by the process of industrialization that has enriched the North but not the South. Unilateral initiatives by the so-called developed countries (DCs) have made them rich, while leaving the less developed countries (LDCs) poor. In the process the industrial activities and accompanying lifestyles of the DCs have inflicted major global damage upon the earth's atmosphere. Both kinds of damage are harmful to those who did not benefit from Northern industrialization as well as to those who did. Those societies whose activities have damaged the atmosphere ought, according to the first principle of equity, to bear sufficiently unequal burdens henceforth to correct the inequality that they have imposed. In this case, everyone is bearing costs—because the damage was universal—but the benefits have been overwhelmingly skewed towards those who have become rich in the process.

This principle of equity should be distinguished from the considerably weaker—because entirely forward-looking—"polluter pays principle" (PPP), which requires only that all future costs of pollution (in production or consumption) be henceforth internalized into prices. Even the OECD formally adopted the PPP in 1974, to govern relations among rich states.[3]

Spokespeople for the rich countries make at least three kinds of counter-arguments to this first principle of equity. These are:

1. The LDCs have also benefited, it is said, from the enrichment of the DCs. Usually it is conceded that the industrial countries have benefited more than the non-industrialized. Yet it is maintained that, for example, medicines and technologies made possible by the lifestyles of the rich countries have also reached the poor countries,

bringing benefits that the poor countries could not have produced as soon for themselves.

Quite a bit of breath and ink has been spent in arguments over how much LDCs have benefited from the technologies and other advances made by the DCs, compared to the benefits enjoyed by the DCs themselves. Yet this dispute does not need to be settled in order to decide questions of equity. Whatever benefits LDCs have received, they have mostly been charged for. No doubt some improvements have been widespread. Yet, except for a relative trickle of aid, all transfers have been charged to the recipients, who have in fact been left with an enormous burden of debt, much of it incurred precisely in the effort to purchase the good things produced by industrialization.

Overall, poor countries have been charged for any benefits that they have received by someone in the rich countries, evening that account. Much greater additional benefits have gone to the rich countries themselves, including a major contribution to the very process of their becoming so much richer than the poor countries. Meanwhile, the environmental damage caused by the process has been incurred by everyone. The rich countries have profited to the extent of the excess of the benefits gained by them over the costs incurred by everyone through environmental damage done by them, and ought in future to bear extra burdens in dealing with the damage they have done.

2. Whatever environmental damage has been done, it is said, was unintentional. Now we know all sorts of things about CFCs and the ozone layer, and about carbon dioxide and the greenhouse effect, that no one dreamed of when CFCs were created or when industrialization fed with fossil fuels began. People cannot be held responsible, it is maintained, for harmful effects that they could not have foreseen. The philosopher Immanuel Kant is often quoted in the West for having said, "Ought presupposes can"—it can be true that one ought to have done something only if one actually could have done it. Therefore, it is allegedly not fair to hold people responsible for effects they could not have avoided because the effects could not have been predicted.

This objection rests upon a confusion between punishment and responsibility. It is not fair to punish someone for producing effects that could not have been avoided, but it is common to hold people responsible for effects that were unforeseen and unavoidable.

We noted earlier that, in order to be justifiable, an inequality in something between two or more parties must be compatible with an equality of dignity and respect between the parties. If there were an equality between two groups of people such that members of the first group could create problems and then expect members of the second group to deal with the problems, that inequality would be incompatible with equal respect and equal dignity. For the members of the second group would in fact be functioning as servants for the first group. If I said to you, "I broke it, but I want you to clean it up," then I would be your master and you would be my servant. If I thought that you should do my bidding, I could hardly respect you as my equal.

It is true, then, that the owners of many coal-burning factories could not possibly have known the bad effects of the carbon dioxide they were releasing into the atmosphere, and therefore could not possibly have intended to contribute to harming it. It would, therefore, be unfair to punish them—by, for example, demanding that they pay double or triple damages. It is not in the least unfair, however, simply to hold them responsible for the damage that they have in fact done. This naturally leads to the third objection.

3. Even if it is fair to hold a person responsible for damage done unintentionally, it will be said, it is not fair to hold the person responsible for damage he did not do himself. It would not be fair, for example, to hold a grandson responsible for damage done by his grandfather. Yet it is claimed this is exactly what is being done when the current generation is held responsible for carbon dioxide emissions produced in the nineteenth century. Perhaps Europeans living today are responsible for atmosphere-damaging gases emitted today, but it is not fair to hold people responsible for deeds done long before they were born.

This objection appeals to a reasonable principle, namely that one person ought not to be held responsible for what is done by another person who is completely unrelated. "Completely unrelated" is, however, a critical portion of the principle. To assume that the facts about the industrial North's contribution to global warming straightforwardly fall under this principle is to assume that they are considerably simpler than they actually are.

First, and undeniably, the industrial states' contributions to global warming have continued unabated long since it became impossible to plead ignorance. It would have been conceivable that as soon as evidence began to accumulate that industrial activity was having a dangerous environmental effect, the industrial states would have adopted a conservative or even cautious policy of cutting back greenhouse-gas emissions or at least slowing their rate of increase. For the most part this has not happened.

Second, today's generation in the industrial states is far from completely unrelated to the earlier generations going back all the way to the beginning of the Industrial Revolution. What is the difference between being born in 1975 in Belgium and being born in 1975 in Bangladesh? Clearly one of the most fundamental differences is that the Belgian infant is born into an industrial society and the Bangladeshi infant is not. Even the medical setting for the birth itself, not to mention the level of prenatal care available to the expectant mother, is almost certainly vastly more favourable for the Belgian than the Bangladeshi. Childhood nutrition, educational opportunities and life-long standards of living are likely to differ enormously because of the difference between an industrialized and a non-industrialized economy. In such respects current generations are, and future generations probably will be, continuing beneficiaries of earlier industrial activity.

Nothing is wrong with the principle invoked in the third objection. It is indeed not fair to hold someone responsible for what has been done by someone else. Yet that principle is largely irrelevant to the case at hand, because one generation of a rich industrial society is not unrelated to other generations past and future. All are participants in enduring economic structures. Benefits and costs, and rights and responsibilities, carry across generations.

We turn now to a second, quite different kind of justification of the same mechanism of assigning unequal burdens. This first justification has rested in part upon the unfairness of the existing inequality. The second justification neither assumes nor argues that the initial inequality is unfair.

Greater Ability to Pay

The second principle of equity is widely accepted as a requirement of simple fairness. It states:

> Among a number of parties, all of whom are bound to contribute to some common endeavour, the parties who have the most resources normally should contribute the most to the endeavour.

This principle of paying in accordance with ability to pay, if stated strictly, would specify what is often called a progressive rate of payment: insofar as a party's assets are greater, the rate at which the party should contribute to the enterprise in question also becomes greater. The progressivity can be strictly proportional—those with double the base amount of assets contribute at twice the rate at which those with the base amount contribute, those with triple the base amount of assets contribute at three times the rate at which those with the base amount contribute, and so on. More typically, the progressivity is not strictly proportional—the more a party has, the higher the rate at which it is expected to contribute, but the rate does not increase in strict proportion to increases in assets.

The general principle itself is sufficiently fundamental that it is not necessary, and perhaps not possible, to justify it by deriving it from considerations that are more fundamental still. Nevertheless, it is possible to explain its appeal to some extent more fully. The basic appeal of payment in accordance with ability to pay as a principle of fairness is easiest to see by contrast with a flat rate of contribution, that is, the same rate of contribution by every party irrespective of different parties' differing assets. At first thought, the same rate for everyone seems obviously the fairest imaginable arrangement. What could possibly be fairer, one is initially inclined to think, than absolutely equal treatment for everyone? Surely, it seems, if everyone pays an equal rate, everyone is treated the same and therefore fairly? This, however, is an exceedingly abstract approach, which pays no attention at all to the actual concrete circumstances of the contributing parties. In addition, it focuses exclusively upon the contribution process and ignores the position in which, as a result of the process, the parties end up. Contribution according to ability to pay is much more sensitive both to concrete circumstance and to final outcome.

Suppose that Party A has 90 units of something, Party B has 30 units, and Party C has 9 units. In order to accomplish their missions, it is proposed that everyone should contribute at a flat rate of one-third. This may seem fair in that everyone is treated equally: the same rate is applied to everyone, regardless of circumstances. When it is considered that A's contribution will be 30 and B's will be 10, while C's will be only 3, the flat rate may appear more than fair to C who contributes only one-tenth as much as A does. However, suppose that these units represent $100 per year in income and that where C lives it is possible to survive on $750 per year but on no less. If C must contribute 3 units—$300—he will fall below the minimum for survival. While the flat rate of one-third would require A to contribute far more ($3,000) than C, and B to contribute considerably more ($1,000) than C, both A (with $6,000 left) and B (with $2,000 left) would remain safely above subsistence level. A and B can afford to contribute at the rate of one-third because they are left with more than enough while C is unable to contribute at that rate and survive.

While flat rates appear misleadingly fair in the abstract, they do so largely because they look at only the first part of the story and ignore how things turn out in the end. The great strength of progressive rates, by contrast, is that they tend to accommodate final outcomes and take account of whether the contributors can in fact afford their respective contributions.

A single objection is usually raised against progressive rates of contribution: disincentive effects. If those who have more are going to lose what they have at a greater rate than those who have less, the incentive to come to have more in the first place will, it is said, be much less than it would have been with a flat rate of contribution. Why should I take more risks, display more imagination, or expend more effort in order to gain more resources if the result will only be that, whenever something must be paid for, I will have to contribute not merely a larger absolute amount (which would happen even with a flat rate) but a larger percentage? I might as well not be productive if much of anything extra I produce will be taken away from me, leaving me little better off than those who produced far less.

Three points need to be noticed regarding this objection. First, of course, being fair and providing incentives are two different matters, and there is certainly no guarantee in the abstract that whatever arrangement would provide the greatest incentives would also be fair.

Second, concerns about incentives often arise when it is assumed that maximum production and limitless growth are the best goal. It is increasingly clear that many current forms of production and growth are unsustainable and that the last thing we should do is to give people self-interested reasons to consume as many resources as they can, even where the resources are consumed productively. These issues cannot be settled in the abstract either, but it is certainly an open question—and one that should be asked very seriously—whether in a particular situation it is desirable to stimulate people by means of incentives to maximum production. Sometimes it is desirable, and sometimes it is not. This is an issue about ends.

Third, there is a question about means. Assuming that it had been demonstrated that the best goal to have in a specific set of circumstances involved stimulating more production of something, one would then have to ask: how much incentive is needed to stimulate that much production? Those who are preoccupied with incentives often speculate groundlessly that unlimited incentives are virtually always required. Certainly it is true that it is generally necessary to provide some additional incentive in order to stimulate additional production. Some people are altruistic and are therefore sometimes willing to contribute more to the welfare of others even if they do not thereby improve their own welfare. It would be completely unrealistic, however, to try to operate an economy on the assumption that people generally would produce more irrespective of whether doing so was in their own interest—they need instead to be provided with some incentive. However, some incentive does not mean unlimited incentive.

It is certainly not necessary to offer unlimited incentives in order to stimulate (limited) additional production by some people (and not others). Whether people respond or not depends upon individual personalities and individual circumstances. It is a factual matter, not something to be decreed in the abstract, how much incentive is enough: for these people in these circumstances to produce this much more, how much incentive is enough? What is clearly mistaken is the frequent assumption that nothing less than the maximum incentive is ever enough.

In conclusion, insofar as the objection based on disincentive effects is intended to be a decisive refutation of the second principle of equity, the objection fails. It is not always a mistake to offer less than the maximum possible incentive, even when the goal of thereby increasing production has itself been justified. There is no evidence that anything less than the maximum is even generally a mistake. Psychological effects must be determined case by case.

On the other hand, the objection based on disincentive effects may be intended—much more modestly—simply as a warning that one of the possible costs of restraining inequalities by means of progressive rates of contribution, in the effort of being fair, may (or may not) be a reduction in incentive effects. As a caution rather than a (failed) refutation, the objection points to one sensible consideration that needs to be taken into account when specifying which variation upon the general second principle of equity is the best version to adopt in a specific case. One would have to consider how much greater the incentive effect would be if the rate of contribution were less progressive, in light of how unfair the results of a less progressive rate would be.

This conclusion that disincentive effects deserve to be considered, although they are not always decisive, partly explains why the second principle of equity is stated, not as an absolute, but as a general principle. It says: "...the parties who have the most resources *normally* should contribute the most..."—not always, but normally. One reason why the rate of contribution might not be progressive, or might not be as progressive as possible, is the potential disincentive effects of more progressive rates. It would need to be shown case by case that an important goal was served by having some incentive and that the goal in question would not be served by the weaker incentive compatible with a more progressive rate of contribution.

We have so far examined two quite different kinds of justifications of unequal burdens: to reduce or eliminate an existing inequality by removing an unfair advantage of those at the top and to prevent the existing inequality from becoming worse through any infliction of an unfair additional disadvantage upon those at the bottom. The first justification rests in part upon explaining why the initial inequality is unfair and ought to be removed or reduced. The second justification applies irrespective of whether the initial inequality is fair. Now we turn to a different mechanism that—much more directly—serves the second purpose of avoiding making those who are already the worst-off yet worse off.

GUARANTEED MINIMUM

We noted earlier that issues of equity or fairness can arise only if there is something that must be divided among different parties. The existence of the following circumstances can be taken as grounds for thinking that certain parties have a legitimate claim to some of the available resources: (a) the aggregate total of resources is sufficient for all parties to have more than enough; (b) some parties do in fact have more than enough, some of them much more than enough; and (c) other parties have less than enough. American philosopher Thomas Nagel has called such circumstances radical inequality.[4] Such an inequality is radical in part because the total of available resources is so great that there is no need to reduce the best-off people to anywhere near the minimum level in order to bring the worst-off people up to the minimum: the existing degree of inequality is utterly unnecessary and easily reduced, in light of the total resources already at hand. In other words, one could preserve considerable inequality—in order, for instance, to provide incentives, if incentives were needed for some important purpose—while arranging for those with less than enough to have at least enough.

Enough for what? The answer could of course be given in considerable detail, and some of the details would be controversial (and some, although not all, would vary across societies). The basic idea, however, is of enough for a decent chance for a reasonably healthy and active life of more or less normal length, barring tragic accidents and interventions. "Enough" means the essentials for at least a bit more than mere physical survival—for at least a distinctively human, if modest, life. For example, having enough means owning not merely clothing adequate for substantial protection against the elements but clothing adequate in appearance to avoid embarrassment, by local standards, when being seen in public, as Adam Smith noted.

In a situation of radical inequality—a situation with the three features outlined above—fairness demands that those people with less than enough for a decent human life be provided with enough. This yields the third principle of equity, which states:

> When some people have less than enough
> for a decent human life, other people have
> far more than enough, and the total
> resources available are so great that
> everyone could have at least enough
> without preventing some people from still

retaining considerably more than others have, it is unfair not to guarantee everyone at least an adequate minimum.[5]

Clearly, provisions to guarantee an adequate minimum can be of many different kinds, and, concerning many of the choices, equity has little or nothing to say. The arrangements to provide the minimum can be local, regional, national, international or, more likely, some complex mixture of all, with secondary arrangements at one level providing a backstop for primary arrangements at another level.[6] Similarly, particular arrangements might assign initial responsibility for maintaining the minimum to families or other intimate groups, to larger voluntary associations like religious groups or to a state bureau. Consideration of equity might have no implications for many of the choices about arrangements, and some of the choices might vary among societies, provided the minimum was in fact guaranteed.

Children, it is worth emphasizing, are the main beneficiaries of this principle of equity. When a family drops below the minimum required to maintain all its members, the children are the most vulnerable. Even if the adults choose to allocate their own share of an insufficient supply to the children, it is still quite likely that the children will have less resistance to disease and less resilience in general. And of course not all adults will sacrifice their own share to their children. Or, in quite a few cultures, adults will sacrifice on behalf of male children but not on behalf of female children. All in all, when essentials are scarce, the proportion of children dying is far greater than their proportion in the population, which in poorer countries is already high—in quite a few poor countries, more than half the population is under the age of 15.

One of the most common objections to this third principle of equity flows precisely from this point about the survival of children. It is what might be called the over-population objection. I consider this objection to be ethically outrageous and factually groundless, as explained elsewhere.[7]

The other most common objection is that while it may be only fair for each society to have a guaranteed minimum for its own members, it is not fair to expect members of one society to help to maintain a guarantee of a minimum for members of another society.[8] This objection sometimes rests on the assumption that state borders—national political boundaries—have so much moral significance that citizens of one state cannot be morally required, even by considerations of elemental fairness, to concern themselves with the welfare of citizens of a different political jurisdiction. A variation on this theme is the contention that across state political boundaries moral mandates can only be negative requirements not to harm and cannot be positive requirements to help. I am unconvinced that, in general, state political borders and national citizenship are markers of such extraordinary and over-riding moral significance. Whatever may be the case in general, this second objection is especially unpersuasive if raised on behalf of citizens of the industrialized wealthy states in the context of international cooperation to deal with environmental problems primarily caused by their own states and of greatest concern in the medium term to those states.

To help to maintain a guarantee of a minimum could mean either of two things: a weaker requirement (a) not to interfere with others' ability to maintain a minimum for themselves; or a stronger requirement (b) to provide assistance to others in maintaining a minimum for themselves. If everyone has a general obligation, even towards strangers in other states and societies, not to inflict harm on other persons, the weaker requirement would follow, provided only that interfering with people's ability to maintain a minimum for themselves counted as a serious harm, as it certainly would seem to. Accordingly, persons with no other bonds to each other would still be obliged not to hinder the others' efforts to provide a minimum for themselves.

One could not, for example, demand as one of the terms of an agreement that someone make sacrifices that would leave the person without necessities. This means that any agreement to cooperate made between people having more than enough and people not having enough cannot justifiably require those who start out without enough

to make any sacrifices. Those who lack essentials will still have to agree to act cooperatively, if there is in fact to be cooperation, but they should not bear the costs of even their own cooperation. Because a demand that those lacking essentials should make a sacrifice would harm them, making such a demand is unfair.

That (a), the weaker requirement, holds, seems perfectly clear. When, if ever, would (b), the stronger requirement to provide assistance to others in maintaining a minimum for themselves, hold? Consider the case at hand. Wealthy states, which are wealthy in large part because they are operating industrial processes, ask the poor states, which are poor in large part because they have not industrialized, to cooperate in controlling the bad effects of these same industrial processes, like the destruction of atmospheric ozone and the creation of global warming. Assume that the citizens of the wealthy states have no general obligation, which holds prior to and independently of any agreement to work together on environmental problems, to contribute to the provision of a guaranteed minimum for the citizens of the poor states. The citizens of the poor states certainly have no general obligation, which holds prior to and independently of any agreement, to assist the wealthy states in dealing with the environmental problems that the wealthy states' own industrial processes are producing. It may ultimately be in the interest of the poor states to see ozone depletion and global warming stopped, but in the medium term the citizens of the poor states have far more urgent and serious problems—like lack of food, lack of clean water and lack of jobs to provide minimal support for themselves and their families. If the wealthy states say to the poor states, in effect, "our most urgent request of you is that you act in ways that will avoid worsening the ozone depletion and global warming that we have started," the poor states could reasonably respond, "our most urgent request of you is assistance in guaranteeing the fulfillment of the essential needs of our citizens."

In other words, if the wealthy have no general obligation to help the poor, the poor certainly have no general obligation to help the wealthy. If this assumed absence of general obligations means that matters are to be determined by national interest rather than international obligation, then surely the poor states are as fully at liberty to specify their own top priority as the wealthy states are. The poor states are under no general prior obligation to be helpful to the wealthy states in dealing with whatever happens to be the top priority of the wealthy states. This is all the more so as long as the wealthy states remain content to watch hundreds of thousands of children die each year in the poor states for lack of material necessities, which the total resources in the world could remedy many times over. If the wealthy states are content to allow radical inequalities to persist and worsen, it is difficult to see why the poor states should divert their attention from their own worst problems in order to help out with problems that for them are far less immediate and deadly. It is as if I am starving to death, and you want me to agree to stop searching for food and instead to help repair a leak in the roof of your house without your promising me any food. Why should I turn my attention away from my own more severe problem to your less severe one, when I have no guarantee that if I help you with your problem you will help me with mine? If any arrangement would ever be unfair, that one would.

Radical human inequalities cannot be tolerated and ought to be eliminated, irrespective of whether their elimination involves the movement of resources across national political boundaries: resources move across national boundaries all the time for all sorts of reasons. I have not argued here for this judgement about radical inequality, however.[9] The conclusion for which I have provided a rationale is even more compelling: when radical inequalities exist, it is unfair for people in states with far more than enough to expect people in states with less than enough to turn their attention away from their own problems in order to cooperate with the much better-off in solving their problems (and all the more unfair—in light of the first principle of equity—when the problems that concern the much better-off were created by the much better-off themselves in the very process of becoming as well off as they are). The least that

those below the minimum can reasonably demand in reciprocity for their attention to the problems that concern the best-off is that their own most vital problems be attended to: that they be guaranteed means of fulfilling their minimum needs. Any lesser guarantee is too little to be fair, which is to say that any international agreement that attempts to leave radical inequality across national states untouched while asking effort from the worst-off to assist the best-off is grossly unfair.

OVERVIEW

I have emphasized that the reasons for the second and third principles of equity are fundamentally the same, namely, avoiding making those who are already the worst-off yet worst off. The second principle serves this end by requiring that when contributions must be made, they should be made more heavily by the better-off, irrespective of whether the existing inequality is justifiable. The third principle serves this end by requiring that no contributions be made by those below the minimum unless they are guaranteed ways to bring themselves up at least to the minimum, which assumes that radical inequalities are unjustified. Together, the second and third principles require that if any contributions to a common effort are to be expected of people whose minimum needs have not been guaranteed so far, guarantees must be provided; and the guarantees must be provided most heavily by the best-off.

The reason for the first principle was different from the reason for the second principle, in that the reason for the first rests on the assumption that an existing inequality is already unjustified. The reason for the third principle rests on the same assumption. The first and third principles apply, however, to inequalities that are, respectively, unjustified for different kinds of reasons. Inequalities to which the first principle applies are unjustified because of how they arose, namely some people have been benefiting unfairly by dumping the costs of their own advances upon other people. Inequalities to which the third principle applies are unjustified independently of how they arose and simply because they are radical, that is, so extreme in circumstances in which it would be very easy to make them less extreme.

What stands out is that in spite of the different content of these three principles of equity, and in spite of the different kinds of grounds upon which they rest, they all converge upon the same practical conclusion: whatever needs to be done by wealthy industrialized states or by poor non-industrialized states about global environmental problems like ozone destruction and global warming, the costs should initially be borne by the wealthy industrialized states.

NOTES

1. Or so I believe. I would be intensely interested in any evidence of a culture that seems to lack a concept of fairness, as distinguished from evidence about two cultures whose specific conceptions of fairness differ in some respects.

2. A preliminary presentation of these principles at New York University Law School has been helpfully commented upon in Thomas M. Franck, *Fairness in international law and institutions* (Oxford: Clarendon, 1997), pp. 390–91.

3. OECD Council, 14 November 1974C (1974), 223 (Paris: OECD).

4. See Thomas Nagel, "Poverty and food: why charity is not enough," in Peter G. Brown and Henry Shue, eds., *Food policy: the responsibility of the United States in the life and death choices* (New York: Free Press, 1977), pp. 54–62. In an important recent and synthetic discussion Thomas W. Pogge has suggested adding two further features to the characterization of a radical inequality, as well as a different view about its moral status—see Thomas W. Pogge, "A global resources dividend," in David A. Crocker and Toby Linden, eds., *Ethics of consumption: the good life, justice and global stewardship,* in the series Philosophy and the global context (Lanham, MD, Oxford: Row man & Littlefield,

1998), pp. 501–36. On radical inequality, see pp. 502–503.

5. This third principle of equity is closely related to what I called the argument from vital interests in Henry Shue, "The unavoidability of justice," in Andrew Hurrell and Benedict Kingsbury, eds., *The international politics of the environment* (Oxford: Oxford University Press, 1992), pp. 373–97. It is the satisfaction of vital interests that constitutes the minimum everyone needs to have guaranteed. In the formulation here the connection with limits on inequality is made explicit.

6. On the importance of backstop arrangements, or the allocation of default duties, see "Afterword" in Henry Shue, *Basic rights: subsistence, affluence, and US foreign policy,* 2nd ed (Princeton, NJ: Princeton University Press, 1996).

7. *Basic rights*, ch. 4.

8. This objection has recently been provided with a powerful and sophisticated Kantian formulation that deserves much more attention than space here allows—see Richard W. Miller, "Cosmopolitan respect and patriotic concern." *Philosophy & Public Affairs* 27: 3, Summer 1998, pp. 202–24.

9. And for the argument to the contrary see Miller, "Cosmopolitan respect and patriotic concern."

STUDY QUESTIONS

1. What are Shue's principles of fairness?

2. What are the implications of his argument?

Chapter 2

Animal Rights

WHAT SORT OF BEINGS are deserving of moral regard? Only human beings? Or nonhuman animals as well? How ought we to treat animals? Do they have moral rights? Is their suffering to be equated with human suffering? Should experimentation on animals cease? Should large-scale commercial ("factory") farms be abolished because they tend to cause animals great suffering? Do we have a moral duty to become vegetarians? What exactly is the moral status of animals?

In 1975, a book that opened with the following words appeared: "This book is about the tyranny of human over nonhuman animals. This tyranny has caused and today is still causing an amount of pain and suffering that can only be compared with that which resulted from the centuries of tyranny by white humans over black humans." Thus, Peter Singer began his epoch-making *Animal Liberation*, which launched the modern animal rights movement.

Before the 1970s, vegetarianism was restricted to Hindus, Buddhists, and small numbers of other people with relevant moral or spiritual convictions. Today, hundreds of millions more are vegetarians. Exact numbers are, of course, hard to locate, but various polls indicate that 20% to 30% of the people in the United States lean toward vegetarianism (that is, they look for vegetarian food on restaurant menus or at least generally prefer it). The number of strict vegetarians is probably around 5%. There are of course other reasons to be vegetarian other than concern for animals. For some, the belief that a vegetarian diet is healthier suffices, and increasingly, the environmental impact of meat eating is being raised as a reason in itself. For instance, meat eating contributes more to global climate change than transportation. These issues will be discussed in Chapter 8 on Food Ethics; in this chapter, we focus on the question of the moral status of nonhuman animals.

There are two separate defenses of the moral status (or rights) of animals: the utilitarian and the deontological[1] arguments. Peter Singer is the main representative of the utilitarian argument. Utilitarians follow Jeremy Bentham in asserting that what makes beings morally considerable is not reason but *sentience*. All sentient creatures have the ability to suffer and, as such, have interests. The frustration of those interests leads to suffering. Utilitarianism seeks to maximize the satisfaction of interests whether they be those of humans or animals. In some cases, human interests will make special claims on us; for example, humans but not mice or pigs will need schools and books. But if a pig and a child are in pain and you only have one pain reliever, you may have a moral dilemma as to who should receive the pain reliever. Utilitarians will generally allow some animal experimentation; for example, if experimenting on chimpanzees promises to help us find a cure for AIDS, it's probably justified, but a utilitarian animal liberationist like Singer would also be willing to experiment on retarded children if it maximized utility.

The second type of defense of animal rights is the deontological *rights* position, of which Tom Regan is the foremost proponent. The equal-rights position on animal rights contends that the same essential psychological properties—desires, memory, intelligence, and so on—link all animals and the human animal and thereby give us equal intrinsic value upon which equal rights are founded. These rights are inalienable and cannot be forfeited. Contrary to Singer's position, we have no right to experiment on chimpanzees in order to maximize the satisfaction of interests— that's exploitation. Animals like people are "ends in themselves," so utility is not sufficient to override these rights. Regan is thus more radical than Singer. He calls not for reform but for the total dissolution of commercial animal farming, the total elimination of hunting and trapping, and the total abolition of animal experiments. Just as we would condemn a scientist who took children and performed dangerous experiments on them for the good of others, so we must condemn the institutions that use coercion on animals.

Both utilitarian and deontological animal rights proponents have been attacked on their own grounds. R. G. Frey, for example, has argued that utilitarianism does not justify the sweeping indictments or proposals that Singer advocates. He says that because of the greater complexity of the human psyche and its social system, utility will be maximized by exploiting animals. What is needed is an amelioration of existing large-scale farms and safeguards in animal experimentation to ensure against unnecessary suffering.

In our readings, Mary Anne Warren attacks Regan's deontological position for failing to see important differences between human beings and animals (even other primates), especially our ability to reason. Warren—who agrees that we do have duties to be kind to animals, not to kill them without good reason, and to do what we can to make their lives enjoyable—points out that Regan's notion of inherent value is obscure.

We begin our readings with Kant's view that because animals are not self-conscious rational agents capable of forming the moral law, they are not directly morally considerable, followed by Holly Wilson. She examines Kant's argument over animal egalitarianism (whether all animals are equal).

NOTE

1. *Utilitarianism* is the view that the morally right act is the one that maximizes utility. It aims at producing the best overall consequences. *Deontological* ethics holds that certain features in the moral act itself have intrinsic value regardless of the consequences. It is wrong to kill innocent people even to procure good consequences. Some utilitarians deny animals have rights but argue that we should seek to procure their welfare.

4

Rational Beings Alone Have Moral Worth

IMMANUEL KANT

Immanuel Kant (1724–1804) was born into a deeply pietistic Lutheran family in Königsberg, Germany, and was a professor of philosophy at the University of Königsberg. He is a premier philosopher in the Western tradition, setting forth major works in metaphysics, philosophy of religion, ethics, epistemology, political theory, and philosophy of science.

Here, Kant first argues that rational beings are ends in themselves and must never be used as mere means. Only they have intrinsic moral worth. Animals are not persons because they are not rational, self-conscious beings capable of grasping the moral law. Since they are not part of the kingdom of moral legislators, we who are members of that "kingdom" do not owe them anything. But we should be kind to them since that will help develop good character in us and help us treat our fellow human beings with greater consideration. That is, our duties to animals are simply indirect duties to other human beings. See the next reading for further interpretation.

I. SECOND FORMULATION OF THE CATEGORICAL IMPERATIVE: HUMANITY AS AN END IN ITSELF

The will is conceived as a faculty of determining oneself to action in *accordance with the conception of certain laws*. And such a faculty can be found only in rational beings. Now that which serves the will as the objective ground of its self-determination is the *end*, and if this is assigned by reason alone, it must hold for all rational beings. On the other hand, that which merely contains the ground of possibility of the action of which the effect is the end, this is called the *means*. The subjective ground of the desire is the *spring*, the objective ground of the volition is the *motive*; hence the distinction between subjective ends which rest on springs, and objective ends which depend on motives valid for every rational being. Practical principles are *formal* when they abstract from all subjective ends; they are *material* when they assume these, and therefore particular springs of action. The ends which a rational being proposes to himself at pleasure as *effects* of his actions (material ends) are all only relative, for it is only their relation to the particular desires of the subject that gives them their worth, which therefore cannot furnish principles universal and necessary for all rational beings and for every volition, that is to say practical laws. Hence all these relative ends can give rise only to hypothetical imperatives.

Supposing, however, that there were something *whose existence* has *in itself* an absolute worth, something which, being *an end in itself*, could be a source of definite laws, then in this and this alone would lie the source of a possible categorical imperative, *i.e.* a practical law.

The first section is from Kant's *Foundations of the Metaphysics of Morals* (1873), trans. by T. K. Abbott. The second section is from Kant's *Lectures on Ethics*, trans. by Louis Infield (New York: Harper & Row, 1963).

Now I say: man and generally any rational being *exists* as an end in himself, *not merely as a means* to be arbitrarily used by this or that will, but in all his actions, whether they concern himself or other rational beings, must be always regarded at the same time as an end. All objects of the inclinations have only a conditional worth; for if the inclinations and the wants founded on them did not exist, then their object would be without value. But the inclinations themselves being sources of want are so far from having an absolute worth for which they should be desired, that, on the contrary, it must be the universal wish of every rational being to be wholly free from them. Thus the worth of any object which is *to be acquired* by our action is always conditional. Beings whose existence depends not on our will but on nature's, have nevertheless, if they are nonrational beings, only a relative value as means, and are therefore called *things*; rational beings, on the contrary, are called *persons*, because their very nature points them out as ends in themselves, that is as something which must not be used merely as means, and so far therefore restricts freedom of action (and is an object of respect). These, therefore, are not merely subjective ends whose existence has a worth *for us* as an effect of our action, but *objective ends*, that is things whose existence is an end in itself: an end moreover for which no other can be substituted, which they should subserve *merely* as means, for otherwise nothing whatever would possess *absolute worth*; but if all worth were conditioned and therefore contingent, then there would be no supreme practical principle of reason whatever.

If then there is a supreme practical principle or, in respect of the human will, a categorical imperative, it must be one which, being drawn from the conception of that which is necessarily an end for everyone because it is an *end in itself*, constitutes an *objective* principle of will, and can therefore serve as a universal practical law. The foundation of this principle is: *rational nature exists as an end in itself*. Man necessarily conceives his own existence as being so: so far then this is a *subjective* principle of human actions. But every other rational being regards its existence similarly, just on the same rational principle that holds for me: so that it is at the same time an objective principle, from which as a supreme

practical law all laws of the will must be capable of being deduced. Accordingly the practical imperative will be as follows: *So act as to treat humanity, whether in thine own person or in that of any other, in every case as an end-withal, never as means only.* We will now inquire whether this can be practically carried out.

II.

Baumgarten speaks of duties towards beings which are beneath us and beings which are above us. But so far as animals are concerned, we have no direct duties. Animals are not self-conscious and are there merely as a means to an end. That end is man. We can ask, "Why do animals exist?" But to ask, "Why does man exist?" is a meaningless question. *Our duties towards animals are merely indirect duties towards humanity.* Animal nature has analogies to human nature, and by doing our duties to animals in respect of manifestations of human nature, we indirectly do our duty towards humanity. Thus, if a dog has served his master long and faithfully, his service, on the analogy of human service, deserves reward, and when the dog has grown too old to serve, his master ought to keep him until he dies. Such action helps to support us in our duties towards human beings, where they are bounden duties. If then any acts of animals are analogous to human acts and spring from the same principles, we have duties towards the animals because thus we cultivate the corresponding duties towards human beings. If a man shoots his dog because the animal is no longer capable of service, he does not fail in his duty to the dog, for the dog cannot judge, but his *act is inhuman and damages in himself that humanity which it is his duty to show towards mankind.* If he is not to stifle his human feelings, he must practise kindness towards animals, for he who is cruel to animals becomes hard also in his dealing with men. We can judge the heart of a man by his treatment of animals. Hogarth depicts this in his engravings. He shows how cruelty grows and develops. He shows the child's cruelty to animals, pinch the tail of a dog or a cat; he then depicts the grown man in his cart running over a child; and lastly, the culmination of cruelty in murder. He thus brings home to us in a terrible fashion the rewards of cruelty, and this should be an impressive lesson to children. The more we come in contact with animals and observe their behaviour, the more we love them, for we see how great is their care for their young. It is then difficult for us to be cruel in thought even to a wolf. Leibnitz used a tiny worm for purposes of observation, and then carefully replaced it with its leaf on the tree so that it should not come to harm through any act of his. He would have been sorry—a natural feeling for a humane man—to destroy such a creature for no reason. Tender feelings towards dumb animals develop humane feelings towards mankind. In England butchers and doctors do not sit on a jury because they are accustomed to the sight of death and hardened. Vivisectionists, who use living animals for their experiments, certainly act cruelly, although their aim is praiseworthy, and they can justify their cruelty, since animals must be regarded as man's instruments; but any such cruelty for sport cannot be justified. A master who turns out his ass or his dog because the animal can no longer earn its keep manifests a small mind. The Greeks' ideas in this respect were highminded, as can be seen from the fable of the ass and the bell of ingratitude. Our duties towards animals, then, are indirect duties towards mankind.

STUDY QUESTIONS

1. According to Kant, do animals have rights? What capacity do they lack that deprives them of rights?

2. Why should we be kind to animals? Do you agree with Kant? How would an opponent respond to Kant's arguments?

5

The Green Kant: Kant's Treatment of Animals

HOLLY L. WILSON

Holly Wilson is the author of Kant's Pragmatic Anthropology. *Here she argues that the central reason Kant gave animals lower moral status is that raising the status of animals would diminish the status of humans. She further points out that Kant is thus naturally able to address the problem of animal egalitarianism and that Kant should no longer be seen as in opposition to environmental thinking.*

Some environmental theorists want to give animals rights and in so doing raise their moral status. None of these theorists seem at all concerned that this move may lower the moral status of human beings. It is simply assumed that human status will remain unaffected when the status of some or all animals is

The Green Kant: Kant's Treatment of Animals by Holly L. Wilson. Printed by permission of the author.

raised. Kant, on the other hand, was very concerned about maintaining the moral status and dignity of human beings, and for him that meant that animals cannot have rights and must be conceived of as being "mere means" to the end of humanity. It is important to note that he did not mean that they have the same status as things when he says "mere means"; but they also do not have the same status as human beings because they are not ends-in-themselves. Kant spent a lot of time distinguishing between humans and animals ontologically, and in doing so it appears that he did not want human status to decline to that of animals. For him, human dignity depended on human beings distancing themselves from their animality.

Although Kant is criticized for holding that animals are "mere means," none of the interpreters understand correctly what he meant by "mere means" or why he thought that characterization is important. I will show that Kant, by using teleological judgment, does not mean that animals have no moral status and are no more than things. I will also show that his use of teleological judgment has a lot to offer environmental philosophy. I will hold that his position on humans is able to deal with some of the problems environmental philosophers are struggling with, while sidestepping the problems these philosophers ascribe to Kant. Kant's views on animals are consistent with green concerns and are more positive than is usually assumed.

KANT'S VIEWS ON ANIMALS

Kant holds that animals have souls because they move. This is already an ontological distinction between things and animals. In a *Metaphysics* lecture note Kant writes,

> Animals are not mere machines or just matter, for they do have souls, and they do so because everything in nature is either inanimate or animate. When, e.g., we see a mote on a paper, we look to see whether it moves. If it doesn't we'll take it as inanimate matter but as soon as it moves, we'll look to see whether it does so

voluntarily. If we see *that* in the mote, we'll see that it is **animate**, an animal. So an animal is animated matter, for life is the power to determine oneself from an inner principle. Matter as such lacks an inner principle of spontaneity of motion while all matter that is animate has it, as an object of inner sense. Thus: all matter that lives is alive because of a principle of life…. And to the extent it is animated, to that extent it is besouled.[1]

Animals, in contrast to matter, have an inner principle that gives rise to spontaneous movement. Here is a clear and significant difference between things and animals. Such a distinction gives rise to the presumption that animals should be treated differently from things. Yet, at the same time, having a soul does not mean that an animal is an end-in-itself. To further determine the nature of animals, we turn to the *Critique of Teleological Judgment* where Kant makes the distinction between organized beings and things.

Our teleological judgment recognizes that there is a distinction between organized beings and artifacts and other natural realities. Kant holds that organized beings (living beings) have intrinsic purposiveness.[2] By this he means that we judge the inner organization of an organized being to be constituted by parts (organs), which are means to the ends of the organism and also means to each other's ends. There is a kind of organization that one does not find in a watch, for example. The inner organs of the organized being are mutually means and ends for each other, whereas this is not the case in a watch.[3] In a body the blood is the means of distributing oxygen to the brain; the brain is the means for keeping the blood supplied with nutrients (through eating, for instance). In a watch, one part may make the other part move, but that part is not the productive cause of the other part. The watch does not produce other watches, nor does it produce new parts when old ones malfunction. Even a tree is an organized being for Kant, and hence differs from things. The tree produces itself (maintains itself), reproduces, and its parts are teleological wholes in their own right insofar as a branch can be taken from a tree and grafted onto another tree.[4] Organized beings have formative forces [*Bildungstrieb*]; things do not.[5] Organized beings have intrinsic purposiveness; things do not. Again we find an important distinction between animals and plants, and things.

The distinction extends even further. Kant contrasts natural things like rivers and mountains with organized beings. Here too we find a significant difference between natural objects. Organized beings do not have only intrinsic purposiveness; they are also things for which other things can be extrinsically purposive.[6] Kant writes that the sandy soil "enabled extensive spruce forests to establish themselves, for which unreasonable destruction we often blame our ancestors."[7] The sandy soil was extrinsically purposive for the forests, but the forests were not extrinsically purposive for the soil. When we make such purposive judgments it is with regard to beings that are themselves intrinsically purposive. Hence, animals and plants are intrinsically purposive and things for which other things are extrinsically purposive.[8] We make such judgments whenever we characterize an ecosystem as something in which organized beings find a "habitat." That habitat is purposive for the organized being, and that organized being may well be purposive for other organized beings, but the spotted owl is not purposive for the natural objects like dirt or stones or any other objects in the ecosystem.

Hence, organized beings (animals and plants) have another distinction from things. They can be beings for which other things are purposive, which means that they are ends for the sake of which means exist. That they are intrinsically purposive already means that they are ends for which the means of their parts exist, but we can go even further and now say they are ends for which other things and beings exist. Things don't have this kind of distinction.

There is a qualified sense in which one can say that animals have inherent worth, according to Kant, because they are intrinsically and extrinsically purposive. With respect to human beings as natural beings, we are no different from other organized beings in terms of intrinsic and extrinsic purposiveness. We too are intrinsically purposive, we too may be beings for which other beings and things are purposive, and we too may well be means to another organized being's ends (especially for the ends of bacteria and viruses). Several times Kant exclaims that there is no reason why a human being needs to exist as far as ecosystems are concerned.[9] As natural beings we too have the qualified sense of inherent worth, but as natural animals we certainly are not ends-in-ourselves according to Kant. In this limited sense we are no better than animals. However, he makes an argument that it is only as "beings under moral laws" that we have a status of being ends-in-ourselves.[10] Because animals are not capable of 'being under moral laws,' they do not have this same status. In this human beings distinguish themselves from animals.

There is an additional way in which animals distinguish themselves from things and also may be compared to human beings. Namely, animals have a will [*Willkür*]. A will, Kant writes in the *Critique of Pure Reason,* "is purely *animal (arbitrium brutum)*, which cannot be determined save through sensuous impulses, that is, pathologically."[11] These wills are not determined by the concept of a law but rather by forces that are impelled from outside.[12] For instance, a lion may well choose between this zebra and that antelope in the hunt, and hence it exhibits freedom of choice (*arbitrium brutum*). Yet, the lion does not have the freedom not to hunt. It is heteronomously impelled by the presentation of the prey and reacts compelled by its instincts. The prey triggers the impulse to pursue and kill and hence the motive of the pursuit is heteronomous. The lion does not have the autonomy to choose not to be a predator, and hence it does not have a free will (*Wille*), only the freedom of choice (*Willkür*). Animals, as distinct from human beings, do not have the capacity to resist their inclinations (instincts or impulses) based on the concept of a law (for instance, a maxim that would say "refrain from killing animals"). In contrast, a human being may well choose to be a vegetarian based on the concept that killing animals is wrong. Human beings then have the possibility of autonomous action based on the free will (*Wille*).[13] As a result, human beings can act contrary to sensuously determined carnivorous inclinations. Kant assumes animals are driven by instincts rather than by concepts of laws and in this way, animals, though like human beings, are different from human beings.

KANT'S VIEWS ON HUMAN BEINGS

There is another way in which animals differ from human beings. Human beings are capable of the idea of "I." The fact, Kant claims,

> that man can have the idea "I" raises him infinitely above all other beings living on earth. By this he is a person; and by virtue of his unity of consciousness through all the changes he may undergo, he is one and the same person.[14]

Animals are indeed conscious, have presentations,[15] and also reflect,[16] but they are not self-conscious and do not have an "I." As a student from Kant's anthropology class notes, "If a horse could grasp the idea of I, then I would dismount and regard it as my society."[17] If animals don't have an "I," then they are not our equals.

Kant does a curious thing at this point in the *Anthropology*. Right after the preceding quote he goes on to say that a human being is "altogether different in rank and dignity from things, such as irrational animals, which we can dispose of as we please." First of all, he makes it a point to say that animals are things [*Sachen*], and from this he concludes that they do not have the same rank and dignity that human beings have. He emphasizes that we may dispose of animals as we please, just like we may dispose of things as we please. But why is it so important for him now (1798) to equate animals and things after he has made it so clear that animals are not things in his earlier writings? Systematically and ontologically, Kant has established a distinction between things and animals, but now he equates them and claims we may treat them the same way. Is this a considered position, or is there another reason why Kant is taking pains to distance animals from human beings?

I think we can find a clue to unravel this mystery within Kant's essay *The Speculative Beginning of Human History* (1786). Kant acknowledges he is writing a speculative flight of fancy about the beginnings of human freedom and the departure from animality. It is about the first appearance of reason in the human species. In the experience of reason, human beings are raised "beyond any community with animals."[18] A human being (Adam) views himself for the first time as the "true end of nature" because "nothing living on earth can compete with him." He says to the sheep,

> 'the pelt you bear was given to you by nature not for yourself, but for me'; the first time he took that pelt off the sheep and put it on himself (Gen. 3:21); at that same time he saw within himself a privilege by virtue of which his nature surpassed that of all animals, which he now no longer regarded as his fellows in creation, but as subject to his will as means and tools for achieving his own chosen objectives.[19]

This story of using a sheepskin is not about how we ought to relate to animals but rather about how we can indeed use animals as mere means, because we are superior in our ability to compete with animals. It is an account of how human beings, through skills, are able to use animals as means toward human's arbitrarily chosen ends. Kant is right: In the struggle for survival, human beings have clearly outperformed other animals. Our success means that nonhuman animals are no longer our equals, our fellows, or our society.

Yet this experience entails even more. Human beings draw the conclusion that they are not only the last end of nature (*letzter Zweck*), but that they, unlike animals, are ends-in-themselves (*Endzweck*) and that no fellow human being ought to be used "merely as a means to any other end." In other words, human beings are "the equal of all rational beings." Kant ties the moment of recognition of our human dignity to the moment we are able to recognize our ability to use animals as mere means.[20] This association of the two insights is exactly what he is doing in the *Anthropology*. Our dignity as humans is in part determined by our ability to distance ourselves from animals, by using them as means to our ends. This distancing is not just from animals, but also from our own animality because we no longer identify with animal society. The very capacity to turn animals into mere means is one way in which we distance ourselves from our own animality. Is it possible to come to this recognition without having to see animals are mere means? Could we have come to this recognition of our dignity with the use of tools?

Kant seems to think that before we used reason we were animals and that our society was with other animals. Thus, the earliest use of reason required our distancing ourselves not only from other animals but also from our own animality. That distancing doesn't seem to be something we could accomplish just by becoming aware of the possibility of using tools because we are not like tools. We are like animals. For Kant we are animals that have the capacity for reason (*animal rationabilis*).[21] One use of reason is found in our technical predisposition, that is, our capacity for skills that are capable of manipulating things "in any way whatsoever."[22] It is because of this predisposition that we are capable of turning animals into "mere means." We have the capacity to develop skills for survival nonspecific ends, or, as Kant puts it in the *Critique of Teleological Judgment*, for arbitrary ends.[23] Kant goes on to say that the culture of skill is "not adequate to assist the will in the determination and selection of its purposes...."[24] Nothing about our technical predisposition and technical skills specifies only worthy ends, and hence there is nothing about these skills that would keep us from turning animals into mere means.

But our technical predisposition is only one of reason's expressions. We also have a pragmatic predisposition and a moral predisposition. These two present necessary ends for reason. The pragmatic predisposition is expressed in the skill of prudence, which aims at our happiness, a necessary end. Prudence is the capacity we have for using other human beings as means to our own ends. The moral predisposition is expressed in our capacity for limiting and refusing specific technical and pragmatic ends for moral reasons.[25] Treating animals as mere

means may well have a detrimental effect on our happiness, and we may hence put a limit on how we relate to animals. Many people love animals, become friends with them, and as a result treat them very well, sometimes even like children, because it brings them happiness to do so. This treatment is the result of our pragmatic predisposition, because we are limiting our use of animals in order to allow them to bring us happiness. Some people refuse to eat animals because they are saddened by the way animals are farm-raised and slaughtered. This refusal too is a result of our pragmatic predisposition. Others want to protect animals from cruelty because they believe that animals are like us (feel pain and pleasure) and that it is ethically wrong to cause them suffering. This protection is possible using moral reasoning. Still others want to limit our ability to treat animals as mere means by even stronger measures. They want to accord animals rights to ensure their safety and well-being. They do not want our limits to be based on internal measures, mere subjective feelings for animals (as in the pragmatic predisposition), or even benevolence and good will (as in the moral predisposition). They want external coercive juridical forces to come to the aid of animals. They believe that granting animal rights would ensure to a greater extent the well-being of animals and that it would raise the status of animals to that of humans because we would no longer be able to treat animals as mere means.

CAN ANIMALS HAVE RIGHTS?

For Kant, a lot would be at stake if we did move toward according animals rights. First of all, it would entail that we could never use animals, even as we use human beings, because we could never gain their informed consent. According to the third formulation of the categorical imperative we may never treat the humanity in ourselves or in others as means only. This formulation means we may never use human beings as means only. Yet we use people all the time, and our pragmatic predisposition is precisely for that purpose. Kant says in the *Lectures on Ethics*, "A person can, indeed, serve as a means for others, by his work, for example, but in such a way that he does not cease to exist as a person and an end."[26] The reason we can use others without turning them into mere means is because we have the other's consent or free choice.[27] I use students as students, and they use me as a professor. What makes it morally permissible to use another human being is the informed consent she gives ahead of time, which is why students register for their classes themselves and I give out a syllabus at the start of every semester. They are consenting to take the class, and I am giving them the information they need to make an informed decision about whether to permit me to evaluate them. It is impossible to gain the informed consent from animals, however, because we would need to convey information regarding the means used and the possible consequences, and we would need to procure a sure sign of their consent. Such a rigorous requirement would make it impossible for me to take my cat to the vet. She doesn't consent to being in the cat carrier, in the car, at the vet's, and she certainly doesn't consent to the vaccine shots. Having to gain animals' informed consent can be a hindrance to helping them as well as making it impossible to treat them as means. Clearly, by treating animals as "mere means" Kant means *inter alia* that we do not have to gain their consent to use them or take care of them, although, for the most part, it is preferable to treat a pet in a way it wants to be treated whenever possible.

This position, however, raises the marginal case of humans for whom we also cannot gain informed consent (children, the mentally handicapped, and those who are comatose). If we include these marginal cases as persons, why can we not also include animals, or at least animals that exhibit some rationality? Why should animals who exhibit some form of rationality be denied moral personhood while human beings not exhibiting rationality are accorded moral personhood? Kant's answer would be that it is not important for each member of the human species to exhibit all features of rationality; it is enough that the species exhibits all forms. That view is implicit in his formulation of the human species as the *animal rationabilis*, rather than the rational animal.[28]

Human beings are the animals who have the capacity for reason. Each human being, as a member of the species, has the potential for rationality even if she never exhibits it. This potential entails that we must still treat humans who do not exhibit rationality as ends-in-themselves. When it is impossible to gain their consent, it does not inhibit our ability to help them.

What is crucial here is that Kant does not want to isolate an individual human being and evaluate whether that particular individual has the capacity for reason. His position is that human nature is intrinsically communal, and hence the capacity for reason is something we share as a species rather than as individuals. Human beings are defined as the animals capable of developing reason (*animal rationabilis*), so that whether any one individual human being does or does not exhibit reason will not affect one's status and nature. Our natural predispositions, which define human nature for Kant, relate us to all other members of the human species.[29] Hence, to treat any one human being as less than an end-in-herself is already to call into question the status of all other human beings. Nonetheless, Kant's definition of human nature as *animal rationabilis* does not exclude other animals as being "like human beings" in that they exhibit "reason-like" capacities.

So, what about those cases in which animals exhibit primitive forms of rationality? Shouldn't they be granted moral personhood? How would Kant deal with animals who are very much like us? That animals are like us is relevant to moral consideration of them. In the very same section, "Of Duties to Animals and Spirits" in the *Lectures on Ethics*, where Kant grants us permission to use animals as mere means, he also claims we have indirect duties with regard to dogs that serve us and wolves that, like us, care for their young.[30] First, he makes it clear that they are like us (analogues of us), and then he claims that our mistreatment of them (animals like us) would result in diminishing our humanity. The duty is then only indirect because it is contingent upon whether our humanity is furthered or diminished. We have a direct duty to our own humanity, but Kant is equally convinced that our treatment of animals matters because they are like us. By implication one could draw the conclusion that the more like us they are, the more consideration they deserve. This conclusion makes Kantian sense of the problem of marginal cases. Animals who exhibit rudimentary rationality certainly deserve more consideration than flies, because they are more like us. Kant's position also solves the obvious problem with animal egalitarianism, which outrageously implies that all animate beings deserve equal consideration. The less like human beings an animate being is, the less it deserves consideration. The more like us they are, the more consideration they deserve. And Kant does not have to be taken as implying that animals are like us only insofar as they exhibit reasonlike capacities. Dogs are like us in that they exhibit loyalty. Wolves are like us in that they care for their young. Thus animals can be like us in many different ways, not only in that they can suffer pain and pleasure or have capacities for reason.

Kant is also right to give human beings only indirect duties to nonhuman animals because they do not have moral rationality. They are not capable of acting on the conception of a law. They do exhibit cooperation and social behaviors, but these traits appear to be a result of survival mechanisms and conditioned inclinations and not a result of acting on the concept of treating animality as an end and never as a means only. Their behaviors do exhibit order and uniformity, but this display is due to the natural organization in their instincts and to socialized learned behavior, not due to considered reflection on whether every chimp could act on that maxim. Human beings exhibit order and character only when they submit their maxims to the moral law. Humans are held to higher standards morally because there are ontological differences between human beings and animals. We have the capacity for technical and pragmatic reason, and we need morality to limit these ends to morally permissible and worthy ends.

What about the position that would say, 'granted, animals cannot give informed consent, develop character, and act on the conception of the law, but that is just the case with children'? We have the authority to make children do what is in their own best interest, while according them rights not to be mistreated. Why not treat animals

the same way? But are there no ontological differences between animals and children? Children have the potential to develop reason. Should this not inform their treatment? Children should be raised rather than trained. They need to be taught in a way that develops their free will. They need to be given alternatives and to be encouraged to evaluate consequences for their actions. Eventually, they also need to be encouraged to deliberate and reflect on possible actions and on the reasons and motives for those actions. Animals, on the other hand, should be trained. They can be trained to associate reward and punishment with certain behaviors. We cannot reason with them and encourage them to choose between alternative behaviors. Would we be blurring the distinction between children and animals if we were to treat animals like children?

The blurring of the distinction between human beings and nonhuman animals is already occurring in evolutionary psychology, evolutionary ethics, and behaviorism. Human behavior is being understood on the animal model of behaviors. Focus is being put on behavior rather than action. More concern is attached to explaining and controlling behavior than developing ways to teach and instill the importance of making choices and taking responsibility for those choices. A Kantian ought to be concerned about this, and I think Kant would be were he here today.

Clearly humans need to be treated differently from animals because they are different, and animals need to be treated differently from humans. Animals should not be treated as things, but they should also not be treated as humans. The locus of our treatment of animals should be ethical rather than juridical. Cruelty to animals should be against the law, not only because it harms animals but also because it harms our humanity and makes us more likely to be cruel to humans. We can and are able to treat animals humanely without giving animals rights. We ought not to treat animal nature as an end-in-itself, as Christine Korsgaard proposes, however, because animal nature is pursued by animals heteronomously, pathologically, and reactively. To treat animal nature as an end-in-itself would mean having to cooperate in the ends that animal nature pursues, and that would make our actions hetero-nomously motivated.

IN CONCLUSION

Human beings, for Kant, are under moral laws and animals are not. We find ourselves obligated not by the needs of animals but by the moral law. Animals do not find themselves obligated by the moral law nor by us and hence they cannot directly obligate us. Nevertheless, animals, in their vulnerabilities and needs, present reasons for taking them into consideration and reasons for refraining from harming them. Insofar as I have a maxim of benevolence toward human beings who have needs, and I can see those same needs in animals, then out of care for the humanity in myself, I can feel obligated to care about animals, but always by virtue of my concern for the state of my own humanity. Kant is asking us to value the best in ourselves, our humanity, and out of that to find motivation for caring for animals. When we do so it solves the problem of the apparent conflict between doing what is good for us and doing what is good for animals. Taking care of animals and not being cruel to them is good for us. Finding our care for animals in our care for our humanity does not preclude legislating against cruel or arbitrary treatment of animals, but rather gives us reason to legislate against such treatment. We can do this without considering animals to be ends-in-themselves, and thereby lowering the worth of human beings and blurring the ontological and moral lines between human life and animal life.

For Kant, animals, like human beings, are organic beings and do have a sense of inherent worth insofar as they are intrinsically and extrinsically purposive. Animals can be ends for which our actions are means, and we treat them as ends when we treat animals kindly, with benevolence, and when we refrain from harming them and their habitats. What is at stake for Kant is the motive for not treating animals cruelly. Animal rights theorists want people to be coercively motivated to keep them from treating animals cruelly by giving animals rights. If animals have a right not to be treated cruelly, then human beings can be punished if they do treat them cruelly. Kant wants us to be motivated out of respect for our own humanity to keep us from treating animals cruelly, because he knows that our dignity as human beings is always at stake in our treatment of animals. Kant holds that we preserve our moral and inherent dignity by treating animals kindly because in so doing we take our humanity as an end-in-itself since animals are like us. It would be like treating our own humanity as a mere means if we were to be arbitrarily cruel to animals like us. Kant wants us not only to treat animals well but also to learn to respect our own humanity and dignity. And for that we have to distinguish between animals and humans.

NOTES

1. Immanuel Kant, *Metaphysik L1,* in KGS 28:275 (1776), translation by Martin Schönfeld.

2. Immanuel Kant, KU, KGS V:372–76; pp. 251–56.

3. Immanuel Kant, KU, KGS V:373; p. 252.

4. Immanuel Kant, KU, KGS V:371; pp. 249–250.

5. Immanuel Kant, KU, KGS V:374; p. 253.

6. Immanuel Kant, KU, KGS V:367–68; p. 245.

7. Immanuel Kant, Ibid.

8. Immanuel Kant, KU, KGS V:369; p. 246.

9. Immanuel Kant, KU, KGS V:369; p. 247; KU, KGS V:378; p. 258.

10. Immanuel Kant, KU, KGS 435; p. 323.

11. Immanuel Kant, *Critique of Pure Reason* [A802/B830].

12. Immanuel Kant, LoE, KGS 27:344; p. 125. Friedländer, KGS 25 (2,1):577.

13. Immanuel Kant, GR, KGS IV:412; p. 23.

14. Immanuel Kant, Anth, KGS VII:127; p. 9.

15. Immanuel Kant, KU, KGS V:464n; p. 356n.

16. Immanuel Kant, First Intro, KGS, XX:211; p. 400.

17. Immanuel Kant, Menschenkunde, KGS 25(2): 859.

18. Immanuel Kant, Mut, KGS VIII:114; p. 52.

19. Immanuel Kant, Mut, KGS VIII:114; p. 52–3.

20. Immanuel Kant, Ibid.

21. Immanuel Kant, Anth, KGS VII:321; p. 183.

22. Immanuel Kant, Anth, KGS VII:323; p. 184.

23. Immanuel Kant, KU, KGS V:430; p. 317.

24. Immanuel Kant, KU, KGS V:432; p. 319.

25. Immanuel Kant, Anth, KGS VII:323–24; p. 185.

26. Immanuel Kant, LoE, KGS 27:343; p. 124.

27. Immanuel Kant, LoE, KGS 27:384; p. 155.

28. Immanuel Kant, Anth, KGS VI:321; p. 183.

29. Holly L. Wilson, *Kant's Pragmatic Anthropology,* Chapter 3.

30. Immanuel Kant, LoE, KGS 27:459; p. 212.

STUDY QUESTIONS

1. According to Kant, what are the differences among humans, nonhuman animals, and plants?

2. What does it mean to treat an entity as an 'end-in-itself'? Why is it problematic to treat animals this way?

3. Animal egalitarianism claims that all animals deserve equal moral consideration. Discuss this view and Kant's account of why this is wrong.

BIBLIOGRAPHY

Citations from Immanuel Kant are from, *Kant's Gesammelte Schriften*, edited by the Königlich Preußische [now Deutsche] Akademie der Wissenschaft, vols. 1–29 (Berlin: G. Reimer [now de Gruyter], 1902–) [KGS].

Immanuel Kant, *Kritik der Urteilskraft*, in KGS V; *Critique of Judgment*, trans. by Werner S. Pluhar (Indianapolis: Hackett Publishing Co., 1987) [KU].

Immanuel Kant, "Erste Einleitung in die Kritik der Urteilskraft" in KGS XX; "First Introduction to the Critique of Judgment" in *Critique of Judgment*, trans. by Werner S. Pluhar (Indianapolis: Hackett Publishing Co., 1987) [First Intro].

Immanuel Kant, *Critique of Pure Reason*, trans. by Normen Kemp Smith (New York: St. Martin's Press, 1965) [A/B].

Immanuel Kant, *Lectures on Ethics*, in KGS, 27, trans. by Peter Heath (Cambridge: Cambridge University Press, 1997) [LoE].

Immanuel Kant, *Grundlegung zur Metaphysik der Sitten*, in KGS IV; Grounding for the Metaphysics of Morals, trans. by James W. Ellington (Indianapolis: Hackett Publishing Co., Inc., 1981) [GR].

Immanuel Kant, *Anthropologie im pragmatischer Hinsicht*, in KGS, VII; *Anthropology from a Pragmatic Point of View*, trans. by Mary Gregor (The Hague: Maritinus Nijhoff, 1974).

Immanuel Kant, *Menschenkunde*, in KGS, XXV(2) [Menschenkunde].

Immanuel Kant, "Muthmaßlicher Anfang der Menschengeschichte" in KGS VIII; "Speculative Beginning of Human History" in *Perpetual Peace and other Essays on Politics, History, and Morals*, trans. by Ted Humphrey (Indianapolis: Hackett Publishing Co., 1983) [Mut].

Christine M. Korsgaard, "Fellow Creatures: Kantian Ethics and Our Duties to Animals" in *The Tanner Lectures on Human Values*, Volume 25/26, ed. by Grethe B. Peterson. Salt Lake City: Utah University Press, 2004.

Holly L. Wilson, *Kant's Pragmatic Anthropology: Its Origin, Meaning, and Critical Significance* (New York: State University of New York Press, 2006).

6

A Utilitarian Defense of Animal Liberation

PETER SINGER

Peter Singer, professor of philosophy at Princeton University, was included in Time *magazine's 2005 list of the world's most influential people. His book* Animal Liberation *(1975), from which the following selection is taken, is the most influential book written on the subject, having in a sense started the animal rights movement. Singer argues that animal liberation today is analogous to racial and gender injustice in the past. Just as people once thought it incredible that women or blacks should be treated as equal to white men, so now speciesists mock the idea that all animals should be given equal consideration. Singer defines* speciesism *(a term devised by Richard Ryder) as the prejudice (unjustified bias) that favors one's own species over every other. What equalizes all sentient beings is our ability to suffer. In that, we and animals are equal and deserving equal consideration of interests. Singer's argument is a utilitarian one, having as its goal the maximization of interest satisfaction.*

In recent years a number of oppressed groups have campaigned vigorously for equality. The classic instance is the Black Liberation movement, which demands an end to the prejudice and discrimination that has made blacks second-class citizens. The immediate appeal of the black liberation movement and its initial, if limited, success made it a model for other oppressed groups to follow. We became familiar with liberation movements for Spanish-Americans, gay people, and a variety of other minorities. When a majority group—women—began their campaign, some thought we had come to the end of the road. Discrimination on the basis of sex, it has been said, is the last universally accepted form of discrimination, practiced without secrecy or pretense even in those liberal circles that have long prided themselves on their freedom from prejudice against racial minorities.

One should always be wary of talking of "the last remaining form of discrimination." If we have learnt anything from the liberation movements, we should have learnt how difficult it is to be aware of latent prejudice in our attitudes to particular groups until this prejudice is forcefully pointed out.

A liberation movement demands an expansion of our moral horizons and an extension or reinterpretation of the basic moral principle of equality. Practices that were previously regarded as natural and inevitable come to be seen as the result of an unjustifiable prejudice. Who can say with confidence that all his or her attitudes and practices are beyond criticism? If we wish to avoid being numbered amongst the oppressors, we must be prepared to re-think even our most fundamental attitudes. We need to consider them from the point of view of those most disadvantaged by our attitudes, and the practices that follow from these attitudes. If we can make this unaccustomed mental switch we may discover a pattern in our attitudes and practices that consistently operates so as to benefit one

Reprinted from *Animal Rights and Human Obligations* (Englewood Cliffs, N.J.: Prentice Hall, 1976) by permission of Peter Singer.

group—usually the one to which we ourselves belong—at the expense of another. In this way we may come to see that there is a case for a new liberation movement. My aim is to advocate that we make this mental switch in respect of our attitudes and practices towards a very large group of beings: members of species other than our own—or, as we popularly though misleadingly call them, animals. In other words, I am urging that we extend to other species the basic principle of equality that most of us recognize should be extended to all members of our own species.

All this may sound a little far-fetched, more like a parody of other liberation movements than a serious objective. In fact, in the past the idea of "The Rights of Animals" really has been used to parody the case for women's rights. When Mary Wollstonecroft, a forerunner of later feminists, published her *Vindication of the Rights of Women* in 1792, her ideas were widely regarded as absurd, and they were satirized in an anonymous publication entitled *A Vindication of the Rights of Brutes*. The author of this satire (actually Thomas Taylor, a distinguished Cambridge philosopher) tried to refute Wollstonecroft's reasonings by showing that they could be carried one stage further. If sound when applied to women, why should the arguments not be applied to dogs, cats, and horses? They seemed to hold equally well for these "brutes"; yet to hold that brutes had rights was manifestly absurd; therefore the reasoning by which this conclusion had been reached must be unsound, and if unsound when applied to brutes, it must also be unsound when applied to women, since the very same arguments had been used in each case.

One way in which we might reply to this argument is by saying that the case for equality between men and women cannot validly be extended to nonhuman animals. Women have a right to vote, for instance, because they are just as capable of making rational decisions as men are; dogs, on the other hand, are incapable of understanding the significance of voting, so they cannot have the right to vote. There are many other obvious ways in which men and women resemble each other closely, while humans and other animals differ

greatly. So, it might be said, men and women are similar beings, and should have equal rights, while humans and nonhumans are different and should not have equal rights.

The thought behind this reply to Taylor's analogy is correct up to a point, but it does not go far enough. There *are* important differences between humans and other animals, and these differences must give rise to *some* differences in the rights that each have. Recognizing this obvious fact, however, is no barrier to the case for extending the basic principle of equality to nonhuman animals. The differences that exist between men and women are equally undeniable, and the supporters of Women's Liberation are aware that these differences may give rise to different rights. Many feminists hold that women have the right to an abortion on request. It does not follow that since these same people are campaigning for equality between men and women they must support the right of men to have abortions too. Since a man cannot have an abortion, it is meaningless to talk of his right to have one. Since a pig can't vote, it is meaningless to talk of its right to vote. There is no reason why either Women's Liberation or Animal Liberation should get involved in such nonsense. The extension of the basic principle of equality from one group to another does not imply that we must treat both groups in exactly the same way, or grant exactly the same rights to both groups. Whether we should do so will depend on the nature of the members of the two groups. The basic principle of equality, I shall argue, is equality of consideration; and equal consideration for different beings may lead to different treatment and different rights.

So there is a different way of replying to Taylor's attempt to parody Wollstonecroft's arguments, a way which does not deny the differences between humans and nonhumans, but goes more deeply into the question of equality, and concludes by finding nothing absurd in the idea that the basic principle of equality applies to so called "brutes." I believe that we reach this conclusion if we examine the basis on which our opposition to discrimination on grounds of race or sex ultimately rests. We will then see that we would be on shaky ground if we were to demand equality for blacks, women, and other groups of oppressed humans while denying equal consideration to nonhumans.

When we say that all human beings, whatever their race, creed or sex, are equal, what is it that we are asserting? Those who wish to defend a hierarchical, inegalitarian society have often pointed out that by whatever test we choose, it simply is not true that all humans are equal. Like it or not, we must face the fact that humans come in different shapes and sizes; they come with differing moral capacities, differing intellectual abilities, differing amounts of benevolent feeling and sensitivity to the needs of others, differing abilities to communicate effectively, and differing capacities to experience pleasure and pain. In short, if the demand for equality were based on the actual equality of all human beings, we would have to stop demanding equality. It would be an unjustifiable demand.

Still, one might cling to the view that the demand for equality among human beings is based on the actual equality of the different races and sexes. Although humans differ as individuals in various ways, there are no differences between the races and sexes *as such*. From the mere fact that a person is black, or a woman, we cannot infer anything else about that person. This, it may be said, is what is wrong with racism and sexism. The white racist claims that whites are superior to blacks, but this is false—although there are differences between individuals, some blacks are superior to some whites in all of the capacities and abilities that could conceivably be relevant. The opponent of sexism would say the same: a person's sex is no guide to his or her abilities, and this is why it is unjustifiable to discriminate on the basis of sex.

This is a possible line of objection to racial and sexual discrimination. It is not, however, the way that someone really concerned about equality would choose, because taking this line could, in some circumstances, force one to accept a most inegalitarian society. The fact that humans differ as individuals, rather than as races or sexes, is a valid reply to someone who defends a hierarchical society like, say, South Africa, in which all whites are superior in status to all blacks. The existence of individual variations that cut across the lines of race or sex, however, provides us with no defence at all against a more sophisticated opponent of equality, one who proposes that, say, the interests of those with I.Q. ratings above 100 be preferred to the interests of those with I.Q.s below 100. Would a hierarchical society of this sort really be so much better than one based on race or sex? I think not. But if we tie the moral principle of equality to the factual equality of the different races or sexes, taken as a whole, our opposition to racism and sexism does not provide us with any basis for objecting to this kind of inegalitarianism.

There is a second important reason why we ought not to base our opposition to racism and sexism on any kind of factual equality, even the limited kind which asserts that variations in capacities and abilities are spread evenly between the different races and sexes: we can have no absolute guarantee that these abilities and capacities really are distributed evenly, without regard to race or sex, among human beings. So far as actual abilities are concerned, there do seem to be certain measurable differences between both races and sexes. These differences do not, of course, appear in each case, but only when averages are taken. More important still, we do not yet know how much of these differences is really due to the different genetic endowments of the various races and sexes, and how much is due to environmental differences that are the result of past and continuing discrimination. Perhaps all of the important differences will eventually prove to be environmental rather than genetic. Anyone opposed to racism and sexism will certainly hope that this will be so, for it will make the task of ending discrimination a lot easier; nevertheless it would be dangerous to rest the case against racism and sexism on the belief that all significant differences are environmental in origin. The opponent of, say, racism who takes this line will be unable to avoid conceding that if differences in ability did after all prove to have some generic connection with race, racism would in some way be defensible.

It would be folly for the opponent of racism to stake his whole case on a dogmatic commitment to one particular outcome of a difficult scientific issue which is still a long way from being settled. While attempts to prove that differences in certain selected abilities between races and sexes are primarily genetic in origin have certainly not been conclusive, the same must be said of attempts to prove that these differences are largely the result of environment. At this stage of the investigation we cannot be certain which view is correct, however much we may hope it is the latter.

Fortunately, there is no need to pin the case for equality to one particular outcome of this scientific investigation. The appropriate response to those who claim to have found evidence of genetically based differences in ability between the races or sexes is not to stick to the belief that the genetic explanation must be wrong, whatever evidence to the contrary may turn up: instead we should make it quite clear that the claim to equality does not depend on intelligence, moral capacity, physical strength, or similar matters of fact. Equality is a moral ideal, not a simple assertion of fact. There is no logically compelling reason for assuming that a factual difference in ability between two people justifies any *difference in the amount of consideration we give to satisfying their needs and interests*. The principle of the equality of human beings is not a description of an alleged actual equality among humans: it is a prescription of how we should treat humans.

Jeremy Bentham incorporated the essential basis of moral equality into his utilitarian system of ethics in the formula: "Each to count for one and none for more than one." In other words, the interests of every being affected by an action are to be taken into account and given the same weight as the like interests of any other being. A later utilitarian, Henry Sidgwick, put the point in this way: "The good of any one individual is of no more importance, from the point of view (if I may say so) of the Universe, than the good of any other."[1] More recently, the leading figures in contemporary moral philosophy have shown a great deal of agreement in specifying as a fundamental presupposition of their moral theories some similar requirement which operates so as to give everyone's interests equal consideration—although they cannot agree on how this requirement is best formulated.[2]

It is an implication of this principle of equality that our concern for others ought not to depend on what they are like, or what abilities they possess—although precisely what this concern requires us to do may vary according to the characteristics of those affected by what we do. It is on this basis that the case against racism and the case against sexism must both ultimately rest; and it is in accordance with this principle that speciesism is also to be condemned. If possessing a higher degree of intelligence does not entitle one human to use another for his own ends, how can it entitle humans to exploit nonhumans?

Many philosophers have proposed the principle of equal consideration of interests, in some form or other, as a basic moral principle; but, as we shall see in more detail shortly, not many of them have recognized that this principle applies to members of other species as well as to our own. Bentham was one of the few who did realize this. In a forward-looking passage, written at a time when black slaves in British dominions were still being treated much as we now treat nonhuman animals, Bentham wrote:

> The day **may** come when the rest of the animal creation may acquire those rights which never could have been witholden from them but by the hand of tyranny. The French have already discovered that the blackness of the skin is no reason why a human being should be abandoned without redress to the caprice of a tormentor. It may one day come to be recognized that the number of the legs, the villoscity of the skin, or the termination of the **os sacrum**, are reasons equally insufficient for abandoning a sensitive being to the same fate. What else is it that should trace the insuperable line? Is it the faculty of reason, or perhaps the faculty of discourse? But a full grown horse or dog is beyond comparison a more rational, as well as a more conversable animal, than an infant of a day, or a week, or even a month, old. But suppose they were otherwise, what would it avail?

The question is not, Can they reason? nor Can they **talk**? but, **Can they suffer**?[3]

In this passage Bentham points to the capacity for suffering as the vital characteristic that gives a being the *right* to equal consideration. The capacity for suffering—or more strictly, for suffering and/or enjoyment or happiness—is not just another characteristic like the capacity for language, or for higher mathematics. Bentham is not saying that those who try to mark the "insuperable line" that determines whether the interests of a being should be considered happen to have selected the wrong characteristic. The capacity for suffering and enjoying things is a prerequisite for having interests at all, a condition that must be satisfied before we can speak of interests in any meaningful way. It would be nonsense to say that it was not in the interests of a stone to be kicked along the road by a schoolboy. A stone does not have interests because it cannot suffer. Nothing that we can do to it could possibly make any difference to its welfare. A mouse, on the other hand, does have an interest in not being tormented, because it will suffer if it is.

If a being suffers, there can be no moral justification for refusing to take that suffering into consideration. No matter what the nature of the being, the principle of equality requires that its suffering be counted equally with the like suffering—in so far as rough comparisons can be made—of any other being. If a being is not capable of suffering, or of experiencing enjoyment or happiness, there is nothing to be taken into account. This is why the limit of sentience (using the term as a convenient, if not strictly accurate, shorthand for the capacity to suffer or experience enjoyment or happiness) is the only defensible boundary of concern for the interests of others. To mark this boundary by some characteristic like intelligence or rationality would be to mark it in an arbitrary way. Why not choose some other characteristic, like skin color?

The racist violates the principle of equality by giving greater weight to the interests of members of his own race, when there is a clash between their interests and the interests of those of another race. Similarly the speciesist allows the interests of his own species to override the greater interests of members of other species.[4] The pattern is the same in each case. Most human beings are speciesists. I shall now very briefly describe some of the practices that show this.

For the great majority of human beings, especially in urban, industrialized societies, the most direct form of contact with members of other species is at mealtimes: we eat them. In doing so we treat them purely as means to our ends. We regard their life and well-being as subordinate to our taste for a particular kind of dish. I say "taste" deliberately—this is purely a matter of pleasing our palate. There can be no defence of eating flesh in terms of satisfying nutritional needs, since it has been established beyond doubt that we could satisfy our need for protein and other essential nutrients far more efficiently with a diet that replaced animal flesh by soy beans, or products derived from soy beans, and other high-protein vegetable products.[5]

It is not merely the act of killing that indicates what we are ready to do to other species in order to gratify our tastes. The suffering we inflict on the animals while they are alive is perhaps an even clearer indication of our speciesism than the fact that we are prepared to kill them. In order to have meat on the table at a price that people can afford, our society tolerates methods of meat production that confine sentient animals in cramped, unsuitable conditions for the entire durations of their lives. Animals are treated like machines that convert fodder into flesh, and any innovation that results in a higher "conversion ratio" is liable to be adopted. As one authority on the subject has said, "cruelty is acknowledged only when profitability ceases."[6] ...

Since, as I have said, none of these practices cater for anything more than our pleasures of taste, our practice of rearing and killing other animals in order to eat them is a clear instance of the sacrifice of the most important interests of other beings in order to satisfy trivial interests of our own. To avoid speciesism we must stop this practice, and each of us has a moral obligation to cease supporting the practice. Our custom is all the support that the meat-industry needs. The decision to cease giving it that support may be difficult, but it is no more difficult than it would have been for a white South-erner to go against the traditions of his society and free his slaves: if we do not change our dietary ha-bits, how can we censure those slaveholders who would not change their own way of living?

The same form of discrimination may be ob-served in the widespread practice of experimenting on other species in order to see if certain substances are safe for human beings, or to test some psycho-logical theory about the effect of severe punishment on learning, or to try out various new compounds just in case something turns up....

In the past, argument about vivisection has of-ten missed this point, because it has been put in absolutist terms: Would the abolitionist be prepared to let thousands die if they could be saved by ex-perimenting on a single animal? The way to reply to this purely hypothetical question is to pose an-other: *Would the experimenter be prepared to perform his experiment on an orphaned human infant, if that were the only way to save many lives?* (I say "orphan" to avoid the complication of parental feelings, although in doing so I am being overfair to the experimenter, since the nonhuman subjects of experiments are not orphans.) If the experimenter is not prepared to use an orphaned human infant, then his readiness to use nonhumans is simple discrimination, since adult apes, cats, mice and other mammals are more aware of what is happening to them, more self-directing and, so far as we can tell, at least as sensitive to pain, as any human infant. There seems to be no relevant characteristic that human infants possess that adult mammals do not have to the same or a higher de-gree. (Someone might try to argue that what makes it wrong to experiment on a human infant is that the infant will, in time and if left alone, develop into more than the nonhuman, but one would then, to be consistent, have to oppose abortion, since the fetus has the same potential as the infant—indeed, even contraception and abstinence might be wrong on this ground, since the egg and sperm, considered jointly, also have the same potential. In any case, this argument still gives us no reason for selecting a nonhuman, rather than a human with severe and irreversible brain damage, as the subject for our experiments.)

The experimenter, then, shows a bias in favor of his own species whenever he carries out an experiment on a nonhuman for a purpose that he would not think justified him in using a human being at an equal or lower level of sentience, awareness, ability to be self-directing, etc. No one familiar with the kind of results yielded by most experiments on animals can have the slightest doubt that if this bias were eliminated the number of ex-periments performed would be a minute fraction of the number performed today.

Experimenting on animals, and eating their flesh, are perhaps the two major forms of speciesism in our society. By comparison, the third and last form of speciesism is so minor as to be insignificant, but it is perhaps of some special interest to those for whom this article was written. I am referring to speciesism in contemporary philosophy.

Philosophy ought to question the basic as-sumptions of the age. Thinking through, critically and carefully, what most people take for granted is, I believe, the chief task of philosophy, and it is this task that makes philosophy a worthwhile activity. Regrettably, philosophy does not always live up to its historic role. Philosophers are human beings and they are subject to all the preconceptions of the society to which they belong. Sometimes they suc-ceed in breaking free of the prevailing ideology: more often they become its most sophisticated de-fenders. So, in this case, philosophy as practiced in the universities today does not challenge anyone's preconceptions about our relations with other spe-cies. By their writings, those philosophers who tackle problems that touch upon the issue reveal that they make the same unquestioned assumptions as most other humans, and what they say tends to confirm the reader in his or her comfortable specie-sist habits.

I could illustrate this claim by referring to the writings of philosophers in various fields—for in-stance, the attempts that have been made by those interested in rights to draw the boundary of the sphere of rights so that it runs parallel to the bio-logical boundaries of the species *homo sapiens,* in-cluding infants and even mental defectives, but excluding those other beings of equal or greater capacity who are so useful to us at mealtimes and in our laboratories. I think it would be a more appropriate conclusion to this article, however, if I concentrated on the problem with which we have been centrally concerned, the problem of equality.

It is significant that the problem of *equality*, in moral and political philosophy, is invariably formulated in terms of human equality. The effect of this is that the question of the equality of other animals does not confront the philosopher, or student, as an issue itself—and this is already an indication of the failure of philosophy to challenge accepted beliefs. Still, philosophers have found it difficult to discuss the issue of human equality without raising, in a paragraph or two, the question of the status of other animals. The reason for this, which should be apparent from what I have said already, is that if humans are to be regarded as equal to one another, we need some sense of "equal" that does not require any actual, descriptive equality of capacities, talents or other qualities. If equality is to be related to any actual characteristics of humans, these characteristics must be some lowest common denominator, pitched so low that no human lacks them—but then the philosopher comes up against the catch that any such set of characteristics which covers *all* humans will not be possessed *only by humans*. In other words, it turns out that in the only sense in which we can truly say, as an assertion of fact, that all humans are equal, at least some members of other species are also equal—equal, that is, to each other and to humans. If, on the other hand, we regard the statement "All humans are equal" in some non-factual way, perhaps as a prescription, then, as I have already argued, it is even more difficult to exclude nonhumans from the sphere of equality.

This result is not what the egalitarian philosopher originally intended to assert. Instead of accepting the radical outcome to which their own reasonings naturally point, however, most philosophers try to reconcile their beliefs in human equality and animal inequality by arguments that can only be described as devious.

As a first example, I take William Frankena's well-known article "The Concept of Social Justice." Frankena opposes the idea of basing justice on merit, because he sees that this could lead to highly inegalitarian results. Instead he proposes the principle that

> ... all men are to be treated as equals, not because they are equal, in any respect, but *simply because they are human*. They are human because they have *emotions* and *desires*, and are able to *think*, and hence are capable of enjoying a good life in a sense in which other animals are not.[7]

But what is this capacity to enjoy the good life which all humans have, but no other animals? Other animals have emotions and desires, and appear to be capable of enjoying a good life. We may doubt that they can think—although the behavior of some apes, dolphins and even dogs suggests that some of them can—*but what is the relevance of thinking?* Frankena goes on to admit that by "the good life" he means "not so much the morally good life as the happy or satisfactory life," so thought would appear to be unnecessary for enjoying the good life; in fact to emphasize the need for thought would make difficulties for the egalitarian since only some people are capable of leading intellectually satisfying lives, or morally good lives. This makes it difficult to see what Frankena's principle of equality has to do with simply being *human*. Surely every sentient being is capable of leading a life that is happier or less miserable than some alternative life, and hence has a claim to be taken into account. In this respect the distinction between humans and nonhumans is not a sharp division, but rather a continuum along which we move gradually, and with overlaps between the species, from simple capacities for enjoyment and satisfaction, or pain and suffering, to more complex ones.

Faced with a situation in which they see a need for some basis for the moral gulf that is commonly thought to separate humans and animals, but finding no concrete difference that will do the job without undermining the equality of humans, philosophers tend to waffle. They resort to high-sounding phrases like "the intrinsic dignity of the human individual";[8] they talk of the "intrinsic worth of all men" as if men (humans?) had some worth that other beings did not,[9] or they say that

contradicts kant

humans, and only humans, are "ends in themselves," while "everything other than a person can only have value for a person."[10]

This idea of a distinctive human dignity and worth has a long history; it can be traced back directly to the Renaissance humanists, for instance to Pico della Mirandola's *Oration on the Dignity of Man*. Pico and other humanists based their estimate of human dignity on the idea that man possessed the central, pivotal position in the "Great Chain of Being" that led from the lowliest forms of matter to God himself; this view of the universe, in turn, goes back to both classical and Judeo-Christian doctrines. Contemporary philosophers have cast off these metaphysical and religious shackles and freely invoke the dignity of mankind without needing to justify the idea at all. Why should we not attribute "intrinsic dignity" or "intrinsic worth" to ourselves? Fellow-humans are unlikely to reject the accolades we so generously bestow on them, and those to whom we deny the honor are unable to object. Indeed, when one thinks only of humans, it can be very liberal, very progressive, to talk of the dignity of all human beings. In so doing, we implicitly condemn slavery, racism, and other violations of human rights. We admit that we ourselves are in some fundamental sense on a par with the poorest, most ignorant members of our own species. It is only when we think of humans as no more than a small subgroup of all the beings that inhabit our planet that we may realize that in elevating our own species we are at the same time lowering the relative status of all other species.

The truth is that the appeal to the intrinsic dignity of human beings appears to solve the egalitarian's problems only as long as it goes unchallenged. Once we ask *why* it should be that all humans—including infants, mental defectives, psychopaths, Hitler, Stalin and the rest—have some kind of dignity or worth that no elephant, pig, or chimpanzee can ever achieve, we see that this question is as difficult to answer as our original request for some relevant fact that justifies the inequality of humans and other animals. In fact, these two questions are really one: talk of intrinsic dignity or moral worth only takes the problem back one step, because any satisfactory defence of the claim that all and only humans have intrinsic

dignity would need to refer to some relevant capacities or characteristics that all and only humans possess. Philosophers frequently introduce ideas of dignity, respect and worth at the point at which other reasons appear to be lacking, but this is hardly good enough. Fine phrases are the last resource of those who have run out of arguments.

In case there are those who still think it may be possible to find some relevant characteristic that distinguishes all humans from all members of other species, I shall refer again, before I conclude, to the existence of some humans who quite clearly are below the level of awareness, self-consciousness, intelligence, and sentience, of many nonhumans. I am thinking of humans with severe and irreparable brain damage, and also of infant humans. To avoid the complication of the relevance of a being's potential, however, I shall henceforth concentrate on permanently retarded humans.

Philosophers who set out to find a characteristic that will distinguish humans from other animals rarely take the course of abandoning these groups of humans by lumping them in with the other animals. It is easy to see why they do not. To take this line without re-thinking our attitudes to other animals would entail that we have the right to perform painful experiments on retarded humans for trivial reasons; similarly it would follow that we had the right to rear and kill these humans for food. To most philosophers these consequences are as unacceptable as the view that we should stop treating nonhumans in this way.

Of course, when discussing the problem of equality it is possible to ignore the problem of mental defectives, or brush it aside as if somehow insignificant.[11] This is the easiest way out. What else remains? My final example of speciesism in contemporary philosophy has been selected to show what happens when a writer is prepared to face the question of human equality and animal equality without ignoring the existence of mental defectives, and without resorting to obscurantist mumbo-jumbo. Stanley Benn's clear and honest article "Egalitarianism and Equal Consideration of Interests"[12] fits this description.

Benn, after noting the usual "evident human inequalities" argues, correctly I think, for equality of consideration as the only possible basis for egalitarianism. Yet Benn, like other writers, is thinking only of "equal consideration of human interests." Benn is quite open in his defence of this restriction of equal consideration:

> ... not to possess human shape *is* a disqualifying condition. However faithful or intelligent a dog may be, it would be a monstrous sentimentality to attribute to him interests that could be weighed in an equal balance with those of human beings ... if, for instance, one had to decide between feeding a hungry baby or a hungry dog, anyone who chose the dog would generally be reckoned morally defective, unable to recognize a fundamental inequality of claims.
>
> This is what distinguishes our attitude to animals from our attitude to imbeciles. It would be odd to say that we ought to respect equally the dignity or personality of the imbecile and of the rational man ... but there is nothing odd about saying that we should respect their interests equally, that is, that we should give to the interests of each the same serious consideration as claims to considerations necessary for some standard of well-being that we can recognize and endorse.

Benn's statement of the basis of the consideration we should have for imbeciles seems to me correct, but why should there be any fundamental inequality of claims between a dog and a human imbecile? Benn sees that if equal consideration depended on rationality, no reason could be given against using imbeciles for research purposes, as we now use dogs and guinea pigs. This will not do: "But of course we do distinguish imbeciles from animals in this regard," he says. That the common distinction is justifiable is something Benn does not question; his problem is how it is to be justified. The answer he gives is this:

> ... we respect the interests of men and give them priority over dogs not *insofar* as they

are rational, but because rationality is the human norm. We say it is ***unfair*** to exploit the deficiencies of the imbecile who falls short of the norm, just as it would be unfair, and not just ordinarily dishonest, to steal from a blind man. If we do not think in this way about dogs, it is because we do not see the irrationality of the dog as a deficiency or a handicap, but as normal for the species. The characteristics, therefore, that distinguish the normal man from the normal dog make it intelligible for us to talk of other men having interests and capacities, and therefore claims, of precisely the same kind as we make on our own behalf. But although these characteristics may provide the point of the distinction between men and other species, they are ***not*** in fact the qualifying conditions for membership, or the distinguishing criteria of the class of morally considerable persons; ***and this is precisely because a man does not become a member of a different species, with its own standards of normality, by reason of not possessing these characteristics***.

The final sentence of this passage gives the argument away. An imbecile, Benn concedes, may have no characteristics superior to those of a dog; nevertheless this does not make the imbecile a member of "a different species" as the dog is. *Therefore* it would be "unfair" to use the imbecile for medical research as we use the dog. But why? That the imbecile is not rational is just the way things have worked out, and the same is true of the dog—neither is any more responsible for their mental level. If it is unfair to take advantage of an isolated defect, why is it fair to take advantage of a more general limitation? I find it hard to see anything in this argument except a defence of preferring the interests of members of our own species because they are members of our own species. To those who think there might be more to it, I suggest the following mental exercise. Assume that it has been proven that there is a difference in the average, or normal, intelligence quotient for two different races, say whites and blacks. Then substitute the term "white" for every occurrence of "men" and "black" for every occurrence of "dog" in the passage quoted; and substitute "high I.Q." for "rationality" and when Benn talks of "imbeciles" replace this term by "dumb whites"—that is, whites who fall well below the normal white I.Q. score. Finally, change "species" to "race." Now re-read the passage. It has become a defence of a rigid, no-exceptions division between whites and blacks, based on I.Q. scores, *not withstanding an admitted overlap* between whites and blacks in this

respect. The revised passage is, of course, outrageous, and this is not only because we have made fictitious assumptions in our substitutions. The point is that in the original passage Benn was defending a rigid division in the amount of consideration due to members of different species, despite admitted cases of overlap. If the original did not, at first reading strike us as being as outrageous as the revised version does, this is largely because although we are not racists ourselves, most of us are speciesists. Like the other articles, Benn's stands as a warning of the ease with which the best minds can fall victim to a prevailing ideology.

NOTES

1. *The Methods of Ethics* (7th Ed.), p. 382.

2. For example, R. M. Hare, *Freedom and Reason* (Oxford, 1963); and J. Rawls, *A Theory of Justice* (Harvard, 1972). For a brief account of the essential agreement on this issue between these and other positions, see R. M. Hare, "Rules of War and Moral Reasoning," *Philosophy and Public Affairs*, vol. 1, no. 2 (1972).

3. *Introduction to the Principles of Morals and Legislation*, ch. XVII.

4. I owe the term "speciesism" to Richard Ryder.

5. In order to produce 1 lb. of protein in the form of beef or veal, we must feed 21 lbs. of protein to the animal. Other forms of livestock are slightly less inefficient, but the average ratio in the U.S. is still 1:8. It has been estimated that the amount of protein lost to humans in this way is equivalent to 90% of the annual world protein deficit. For a brief account, see Frances Moore Lappé, *Diet for a Small Planet* (Friends of The Earth/Ballantine, New York, 1971), pp. 4–11.

6. Ruth Harrison, *Animal Machines* (Stuart, London, 1964). For an account of farming conditions, see my *Animal Liberation* (New York Review Company, 1975).

7. In R. Brandt (ed.), *Social Justice* (Prentice-Hall, Englewood Cliffs, 1962), p. 19.

8. Frankena, *Op. cit.*, p. 23.

9. H. A. Bedau, "Egalitarianism and the Idea of Equality" in *Nomos IX: Equality*, ed. J. R. Pennock and J. W. Chapman (Atherton Press, New York, 1967).

10. G. Vlastos, "Justice and Equality" in Brandt, *Social Justice*, p. 48.

11. For example, Bernard Williams, "The Idea of Equality," in *Philosophy, Politics and Society* (second series), ed. P. Laslett and W. Runciman (Blackwell, Oxford, 1962), p. 118; J. Rawls, *A Theory of Justice*, pp. 509–10.

12. *Nomos IX: Equality;* the passages quoted are on p. 62ff.

STUDY QUESTIONS

1. According to Singer, what is the relationship between civil rights movements and the animal rights movement?

2. What is *speciesism*? Why is it bad, according to Singer? Do you agree?

3. Are all humans equal, according to Singer? In what way are all sentient beings equal?

4. How does Singer apply the notion of equal consideration of interests?

7

The Radical Egalitarian Case for Animal Rights

TOM REGAN

Professor of philosophy at North Carolina State University and a leading animal rights advocate in the United States, Tom Regan is the author of several articles and books on moral philosophy, including The Case for Animal Rights *(1983).*

Regan disagrees with Singer's utilitarian program for animal liberation, for he rejects utilitarianism as lacking a notion of intrinsic worth. Regan's position is that animals and humans all have equal intrinsic value on which their right to life and concern are based. Regan is revolutionary. He calls for not reform but the total abolition of the use of animals in science, the total dissolution of the commercial animal agriculture system, and the total elimination of commercial and sport hunting and trapping. "The fundamental wrong is the system that allows us to view animals as our resources.... Lab animals are not our tasters; we are not their kings."

I regard myself as an advocate of animal rights—as a part of the animal rights movement. That movement, as I conceive it, is committed to a number of goals, including:

1. the total abolition of the use of animals in science
2. the total dissolution of commercial animal agriculture
3. and the total elimination of commercial and sport hunting and trapping.

There are, I know, people who profess to believe in animal rights who do not avow these goals. Factory farming they say, is wrong—violates animals' rights—but traditional animal agriculture is all right. Toxicity tests of cosmetics on animals violate their rights; but not important medical research—cancer research, for example. The clubbing of baby seals is abhorrent; but not the harvesting of adult seals. I used to think I understood this reasoning. Not any more. You don't change unjust institutions by tidying them up.

What's wrong—what's fundamentally wrong—with the way animals are treated isn't the details that vary from case to case. It's the whole system. The forlornness of the veal calf is pathetic—heart wrenching; the pulsing pain of the chimp with electrodes planted deep in her brain is repulsive; the slow, torturous death of the raccoon caught in the leg hold trap, agonizing. But what is fundamentally wrong isn't the pain, isn't the suffering, isn't the deprivation. These compound what's wrong. Sometimes—often—they make it much worse. But they are not the fundamental wrong.

The fundamental wrong is the system that allows us to view animals as our resources, here for us—to be eaten, or surgically manipulated, or put in our cross hairs for sport or money. Once we accept this view of animals—as our resources—the rest is as predictable as it is regrettable. Why worry about their

From *In Defense of Animals*, ed. Peter Singer (Oxford: Basil Blackwell, 1985). Reprinted by permission of Blackwell Publishers.

loneliness, their pain, their death? Since animals exist for us, here to benefit us in one way or another, what harms them really doesn't matter—or matters only if it starts to bother us, makes us feel a trifle uneasy when we eat our veal scampi, for example. So, yes, let us get veal calves out of solitary confinement, give them more space, a little straw, a few companions. But let us keep our veal scampi.

But a little straw, more space, and a few companions don't eliminate—don't even touch—the fundamental wrong, the wrong that attaches to our viewing and treating these animals as our resources. A veal calf killed to be eaten after living in close confinement is viewed and treated in this way: but so, too, is another who is raised (as they say) "more humanely." To right the fundamental wrong of our treatment of farm animals requires more than making rearing methods "more human"—requires something quite different—requires the *total dissolution of commercial animal agriculture.*

How we do this—whether we do this, or as in the case of animals in science, whether and how we abolish their use—these are to a large extent political questions. People must change their beliefs before they change their habits. Enough people, especially those elected to public office, must believe in change—must want it—before we will have laws that protect the rights of animals. This process of change is very complicated, very demanding, very exhausting, calling for the efforts of many hands—in education, publicity, political organization and activity, down to the licking of envelopes and stamps. As a trained and practicing philosopher the sort of contribution I can make is limited, but I like to think, important. The currency of philosophy is ideas—their meaning and rational foundation—not the nuts and bolts of the legislative process say, or the mechanics of community organization. That's what I have been exploring over the past ten years or so in my essays and talks and, more recently, in my book, *The Case for Animal Rights.*[1] I believe the major conclusions I reach in that book are true because they are supported by the weight of the *best arguments.* I believe the idea of animal rights has reason, not just emotion, on its side.

In the space I have at my disposal here I can only sketch, in the barest outlines, some of the main features of the book. Its main themes—and we should not be surprised by this—involve asking and answering deep foundational moral questions, questions about what morality is, how it should be understood, what is the best moral theory all considered. I hope I can convey something of the shape I think this theory is. The attempt to do this will be—to use a word a friendly critic once used to describe my work—cerebral. In fact I was told by this person that my work is "too cerebral." But this is misleading. My feelings about how animals sometimes are treated are just as deep and just as strong as those of my more volatile compatriots. Philosophers do—to use the jargon of the day—have a right side to their brains. If it's the left side we contribute or mainly should—that's because what talents we have reside there.

How to proceed? We begin by asking how the moral status of animals has been understood by thinkers who deny that animals have rights. Then we test the mettle of their ideas by seeing how well they stand up under the heat of fair criticism. If we start our thinking in this way we soon find that some people believe that we have no duties directly to animals—that we owe nothing *to them*—that we can do nothing that *wrongs them.* Rather, we can do wrong acts that involve animals, and so we have duties regarding them, though none to them. Such views may be called indirect duty views. By way of illustration:

Suppose your neighbor kicks your dog. Then your neighbor has done something wrong. But not to your dog. The wrong that has been done is a wrong to you. After all, it is wrong to upset people, and your neighbor's kicking your dog upsets you. So you are the one who is wronged, not your dog. Or again: by kicking your dog your neighbor damages your property. And since it is wrong to damage another person's property, your neighbor has done something wrong—to you, of course, not to your dog. Your neighbor no more wrongs your dog than your car would be wronged if the windshield were smashed. Your neighbor's duties involving your dog are indirect duties to you. More generally, all of our duties regarding animals are indirect duties to one another—to humanity.

How could someone try to justify such a view? One could say that your dog doesn't feel anything and so isn't hurt by your neighbor's kick, doesn't care about the pain since none is felt, is as unaware of anything as your windshield. Someone could say this but no rational person will since, among other considerations, such a view will commit one who holds it to the position that no human being feels pain either—that human beings also don't care about what happens to them. A second possibility is that though both humans and your dog are hurt when kicked, it is only human pain that matters. But, again, no rational person can believe this. Pain is pain wheresoever it occurs. If your neighbor's causing you pain is wrong because of the pain that is caused, we cannot rationally ignore or dismiss the moral relevance of the pain your dog feels.

Philosophers who hold indirect duty views—and many still do—have come to understand that they must avoid the two defects just noted—avoid, that is, both the view that animals don't feel anything as well as the idea that only human pain can be morally relevant. Among such thinkers the sort of view now favored is one or another form of what is called *contractarianism.*

Here, very crudely, is the root idea: morality consists of a set of rules that individuals voluntarily agree to abide by—as we do when we sign a contract (hence the name: contractarianism). Those who understand and accept the terms of the contract are covered directly—have rights created by, and recognized and protected in, the contract. And these contractors can also have protection spelled out for others who, though they lack the ability to understand morality and so cannot sign the contract themselves, are loved or cherished by those who can. Thus young children, for example, are unable to sign and lack rights. But they are protected by the contract nonetheless because of the sentimental interests of others, most notably their parents. So we have, then, duties involving these children, duties regarding them, but no duties to them. Our duties in their case are indirect duties to other human beings, usually their parents.

As for animals, since they cannot understand the contract, they obviously cannot sign; and since they cannot sign; they have no rights. Like children, however, some animals are the objects of the sentimental interest of others. You, for example, love your dog ... or cat. So these animals—those enough people care about: companion animals, whales, baby seals, the American bald eagle—these animals, though they lack rights themselves, will be protected because of the sentimental interests of people. I have, then, according to contractarianism, no duty directly to your dog or any other animal, not even the duty not to cause them pain or suffering; my duty not to hurt them is a duty I have to those people who care about what happens to them. As for other animals, where no or little sentimental interest is present—farm animals, for example, or laboratory rats—what duties we have grow weaker and weaker, perhaps to the vanishing point. The pain and death they endure, though real, are not wrong if no one cares about them.

Contractarianism could be a hard view to refute when it comes to the moral status of animals if it was an adequate theoretical approach to the moral status of human beings. It is not adequate in this latter respect, however, which makes the question of its adequacy in the former—regarding animals—utterly moot. For consider: morality, according to the (crude) contractarian position before us, consists of rules people agree to abide by. What people? Well, enough to make a difference—enough, that is, so that collectively they have the power to enforce the rules that are drawn up in the contract. That is very well and good for the signatories—but not so good for anyone who is not asked to sign. And there is nothing in contractarianism of the sort we are discussing that guarantees or requires that everyone will have a chance to participate equitably in framing the rules of morality. The result is that this approach to ethics could sanction the most blatant forms of social, economic, moral, and political injustice, ranging from a repressive caste system to systematic racial or sexual discrimination. Might, on this theory, does make right. Let those who are the victims of injustice suffer as they will. It matters not so long as no one else—no contractor, or too few of them—cares about it. Such a theory takes one's moral breath away ... as if, for example, there is nothing wrong with apartheid in South Africa if too few white South Africans are upset by it. A theory with so little to recommend it at the level of the ethics of our treatment of our fellow humans cannot have anything more to recommend it when it comes to the ethics of how we treat our fellow animals.

The version of contractarianism just examined is, as I have noted, a crude variety, and in fairness to those of a contractarian persuasion it must be noted that much more refined, subtle, and ingenious varieties are possible. For example, John Rawls, in his *A Theory of Justice*, sets forth a version of contractarianism that forces the contractors to ignore the accidental features of being a human being—for example, whether one is white or black, male or female, a genius or of modest intellect. Only by ignoring such features, Rawls believes, can we insure that the principles of justice contractors would agree upon are not based on bias or prejudice. Despite the improvement a view such as Rawls's shows over the cruder forms of contractarianism, it remains deficient: it systematically denies that we have direct duties to those human beings who do not have a sense of justice—young children, for instance, and many mentally retarded humans. And yet it seems reasonably certain that, were we to torture a young child or a retarded elder, we would be doing something that wrongs them, not something that is wrong if (and only if) other humans with a sense of justice are upset. And since this is true in the case of these humans, we cannot rationally deny the same in the case of animals.

Indirect duty views, then, including the best among them, fail to command our rational assent. Whatever ethical theory we rationally should accept, therefore, it must at least recognize that we have some duties directly to animals, just as we have some duties directly to each other. The next two theories I'll sketch attempt to meet this requirement.

The first I call the *cruelty-kindness* view. Simply stated, this view says that we have a direct duty to be kind to animals and a direct duty not to be cruel

to them. Despite the familiar, reassuring ring of these ideas, I do not believe this view offers an adequate theory. To make this clearer, consider kindness. A kind person acts from a certain kind of motive—compassion or concern, for example. And that is a virtue. But there is no guarantee that a kind act is a right act. If I am a generous racist, for example, I will be inclined to act kindly toward members of my own race, favoring their interests above others. My kindness would be real and, so far as it goes, good. But I trust it is too obvious to require comment that my kind acts may not be above moral reproach—may, in fact, be positively wrong because rooted in injustice. So kindness, not withstanding its status as a virtue to be encouraged, simply will not cancel the weight of a theory of right action.

Cruelty fares no better. People or their acts are cruel if they display either a lack of sympathy for or, worse, the presence of enjoyment in, seeing another suffer. Cruelty in all its guises *is* a bad thing—*is* a tragic human failing. But just as a person's being motivated by kindness does not guarantee that they do what is right, so the absence of cruelty does not assure that they avoid doing what is wrong. Many people who perform abortions, for example, are not cruel, sadistic people. But that fact about their character and motivation does not settle the terribly difficult question about the morality of abortion. The case is no different when we examine the ethics of our treatment of animals. So, yes, let us be for kindness and against cruelty. But let us not suppose that being for the one and against the other answers questions about moral right and wrong.

Some people think the theory we are looking for is *utilitarianism*. A utilitarian accepts two moral principles. The first is a principle of *equality: everyone's interests count, and similar interests must be counted as having similar weight or importance.* White or black, male or female, American or Iranian, human or animal: everyone's pain or frustration matter and matter equally with the like pain or frustration of anyone else. The second principle a utilitarian accepts is the principle of *utility: do that act that will bring about the best balance of satisfaction over frustration for everyone affected by the outcome.*

As a utilitarian, then, here is how I am to approach the task of deciding what I morally ought to do: I must ask who will be affected if I choose to do one thing rather than another, how much each individual will be affected, and where the best results are most likely to lie—which option, in other words, is most likely to bring about the best results, the best balance of satisfaction over frustration. That option, whatever it may be, is the one I ought to choose. That is where my moral duty lies.

The great appeal of utilitarianism rests with its uncompromising *egalitarianism:* everyone's interests count and count equally with the like interests of everyone else. The kind of odious discrimination some forms of contractarianism can justify—discrimination based on race or sex, for example—seems disallowed in principle by utilitarianism, as is speciesism—systematic discrimination based on species membership.

The sort of equality we find in utilitarianism, however, is not the sort an advocate of animal or human rights should have in mind. Utilitarianism has no room for the *equal moral rights of different individuals because it has no room for their equal inherent value or worth.* What has value for the utilitarian is the satisfaction of an individual's interests, not the individual whose interests they are. A universe in which you satisfy your desire for water, food, and warmth, is, other things being equal, better than a universe in which these desires are frustrated. And the same is true in the case of an animal with similar desires. But neither you nor the animal have any value in your own right. *Only your feelings do.*

Here is an analogy to help make the philosophical point clearer: a cup contains different liquids—sometimes sweet, sometimes bitter, sometimes a mix of the two. What has value are the liquids: the sweeter the better, the bitter the worse. The cup—the container—has no value. It's what goes into it, not what they go into, that has value. For the utilitarian, you and I are like the cup; we have no value as individuals and thus no equal value. What has value is what goes into us, what we serve as receptacles for; our feelings of satisfaction have positive value, our feelings of frustration have negative value.

Serious problems arise for utilitarianism when we remind ourselves that it enjoins us to bring about the best consequences. What does this mean? It doesn't mean the best consequences for me alone, or for my family or friends, or any other person taken individually. No, what we must do is, roughly, as follows: we must add up—somehow!—the separate satisfactions and frustrations of everyone likely to be affected by our choice, the satisfactions in one column, the frustrations in the other. We must total each column for each of the opinions before us. That is what it means to say the theory is aggregative. And then we must choose that option which is most likely to bring about the best balance of totaled satisfactions over totaled frustrations. Whatever act would lead to this outcome is the one we morally ought to perform—is where our moral duty lies. And that act quite clearly might not be the same one that would bring about the best results for me personally, or my family or friends, or a lab animal. The best aggregated consequences for everyone concerned are not necessarily the best for each individual.

That utilitarianism is an aggregative theory—that different individuals' satisfactions or frustrations are added, or summed, or totaled—is the key objection to this theory. My Aunt Bea is old, inactive, a cranky, sour person, though not physically ill. She prefers to go on living. She is also rather rich. I could make a fortune if I could get my hands on her money, money she intends to give me in any event, after she dies, but which she refuses to give me now. In order to avoid a huge tax bite, I plan to donate a handsome sum of my profits to a local children's hospital. Many, many children will benefit from my generosity, and much joy will be brought to their parents, relatives, and friends. If I don't get the money rather soon, all these ambitions will come to naught. The once-in-a-lifetime-opportunity to make a real killing will be gone. Why, then, not really kill my Aunt Bea? Oh, of course I *might* get caught. But I'm no fool and, besides, her doctor can be counted on to cooperate (he has an eye for the same investment and I happen to know a good deal about his shady past). The deed can be done … professionally, shall we say. There is *very* little chance of getting caught. And as for my conscience being guilt ridden, I am a resourceful sort of fellow and will take more than sufficient comfort—as I lie on the beach at Acapulco—in contemplating the joy and health I have brought to so many others.

Suppose Aunt Bea is killed and the rest of the story comes out as told. Would I have done anything wrong? Anything immoral? One would have thought that I had. But not according to utilitarianism. Since what I did brought about the best balance of totaled satisfaction over frustration for all those affected by the outcome, what I did was not wrong. Indeed, in killing Aunt Bea the physician and I did what duty required.

This same kind of argument can be repeated in all sorts of cases, illustrating time after time, how the utilitarian's position leads to results that impartial people find morally callous. It is wrong to kill my Aunt Bea in the name of bringing about the best results for others. A good end does not justify an evil means. Any adequate moral theory will have to explain why this is so. Utilitarianism fails in this respect and so cannot be the theory we seek.

What to do? Where to begin anew? The place to begin, I think, is with the utilitarian's view of the value of the individual—or, rather, lack of value. In its place suppose we consider that you and I, for example, do have value as individuals—what we'll call *inherent value*. To say we have such value is to say that we are something more than, something different from, mere receptacles. Moreover, to insure that we do not pave the way for such injustices as slavery or sexual discrimination, we must believe that all who have inherent value have it equally, regardless of their sex, race, religion, birthplace, and so on. Similarly to be discarded as irrelevant are one's talents or skills, intelligence and wealth, personality or pathology, whether one is loved and admired—or despised and loathed. The genius and the retarded child, the prince and the pauper, the brain surgeon and the fruit vendor, Mother Theresa and the most unscrupulous used car salesman—all have inherent value, all possess it *equally*, and *all have an equal right to be treated with respect*, to be treated in ways that do not reduce them to the status of

things, as if they exist as resources for others. My value as an individual is independent of my usefulness to you. Yours is not dependent on your usefulness to me. For either of us to treat the other in ways that fail to show respect for the other's independent value is to act immorally—is to violate the individual's rights.

Some of the rational virtues of this view—what I call the rights view—should be evident. Unlike (crude) contractarianism, for example, the rights view *in principle* denies the moral tolerability of any and all forms of racial, sexual, or social discrimination; and unlike utilitarianism, this view *in principle* denies that we can justify good results by using evil means that violate an individual's rights—denies, for example, that it could be moral to kill my Aunt Bea to harvest beneficial consequences for others. That would be to sanction the disrespectful treatment of the individual in the name of the social good, something the rights view will not—categorically will not—ever allow.

The rights view—or so I believe—is rationally the most satisfactory moral theory. It surpasses all other theories in the degree to which it illuminates and explains the foundation of our duties to one another—the domain of human morality. On this score, it has the best reasons, the best arguments, on its side. Of course, if it were possible to show that only human beings are included within its scope, then a person like myself, who believes in animal rights, would be obliged to look elsewhere than to the rights view.

But attempts to limit its scope to humans only can be shown to be rationally defective. Animals, it is true, lack many of the abilities humans possess. They can't read, do higher mathematics, build a bookcase, or make *baba ghanoush*. Neither can many human beings, however, and yet we don't say—and shouldn't say—that they (these humans) therefore have less inherent value, less of a right to be treated with respect, than do others. It is the similarities between those human beings who most clearly, most noncontroversially have such value—the people reading this, for example—it is our similarities, not our differences, that matter most. And the really crucial, the basic similarity is simply this; *we are each of us the experiencing subject of a life, each of us a conscious creature having an individual welfare that has importance to us whatever our usefulness to others.* We want and prefer things; believe and feel things; recall and expect things. And all these dimensions of our life, including our pleasure and pain, our enjoyment and suffering, our satisfaction and frustration, our continued existence or our untimely death—all make a difference to the quality of our life as lived, as experienced by us as individuals. As the same is true of those animals who concern us (those who are eaten and trapped, for example), they, too, must be viewed as the experiencing subjects of a life with inherent value of their own.

There are some who resist the idea that animals have inherent value. "Only humans have such value," they profess. How might this narrow view be defended? Shall we say that only humans have the requisite intelligence, or autonomy, or reason? But there are many, many humans who will fail to meet these standards and yet who are reasonably viewed as having value above and beyond their usefulness to others. Shall we claim that only humans belong to the right species—the species *Homo sapiens*? But this is blatant speciesism. Will it be said, then, that all—and only—humans have immortal souls? Then our opponents more than have their work cut out for them. I am myself not ill-disposed to there being immortal souls. Personally, I profoundly hope I have one. But I would not want to rest my position on a controversial, ethical issue on the even more controversial question about who or what has an immortal soul. That is to dig one's hole deeper, not climb out. Rationally, it is better to resolve moral issues without making more controversial assumptions than are needed. The question of who has inherent value is such a question, one that is more rationally resolved without the introduction of the idea of immortal souls than by its use.

Well, perhaps some will say that animals have some inherent value, only *less* than we do. Once again, however, attempts to defend this view can be shown to lack rational justification. What could be the basis of our having more inherent value than animals? Will it be their lack of reason, or autonomy, or intellect? Only if we are willing to make the same judgment in the case of humans who are similarly deficient. But it is not true that such humans—the retarded child, for example, or the mentally deranged—have less inherent value than you or I. Neither, then, can we rationally sustain the view that animals like them in being the experiencing subjects of a life have less inherent value. *All who have inherent value have it equally, whether they be human animals or not.*

Inherent value, then, belongs equally to those who are the experiencing subjects of a life. Whether it belongs to others—to rocks and rivers, trees and glaciers, for example—we do not know. And may never know. But neither do we need to know, if we are to make the case for animal rights. We do not need to know how many people, for example, are eligible to vote in the next presidential election before we can know whether I am. Similarly, we do not need to know *how many* individuals have inherent value before we can know that some do. When it comes to the case for animal rights, then what we need to know is whether the animals who, in our culture are routinely eaten, hunted, and used in our laboratories, for example, are like us in being subjects of a life. And we *do* know this. We do *know* that many—literally, billions and billions—of these animals are subjects of a life in the sense explained and so have inherent value if we do. And since, in order to have the best theory of our duties to one another, we must recognize our equal inherent value, as individuals, *reason*—not sentiment, not emotion—*reason compels us to recognize the equal inherent value of these animals.* And, with this, their equal right to be treated with respect.

That, *very* roughly, is the shape and feel of the case for animal rights. Most of the details of the supporting argument are missing. They are to be found in the book I alluded to earlier. Here, the details go begging and I must in closing, limit myself to four final points.

The first is how the theory that underlies the case for animal rights shows that the animal rights movement is a part of, not antagonistic to, the human rights movement. The theory that rationally grounds the rights of animals also grounds the rights of humans. Thus are those involved in the animal rights movement partners in the struggle to secure respect for human rights—the rights of women, for example, or minorities and workers. The animal rights movement is cut from the same moral cloth as these.

Second, having set out the broad outlines of the rights view, I can now say why its *implications for farming and science*, for example, are both clear and uncompromising. In the case of using animals in science, the rights view is categorically abolitionist. *Lab animals are not our tasters; we are not their kings.* Because these animals are treated—routinely, systematically— as if their value is reducible to their usefulness to others, they are routinely systematically treated with a lack of respect, and thus their rights routinely, systematically violated. This is just as true when they are used in trivial, duplicative, unnecessary or unwise research as it is when they are used in studies that hold out real promise of human benefits. We can't justify harming or killing a human being (my Aunt Bea, for example) just for these sorts of reasons. Neither can we do so even in the case of so lowly a creature as a laboratory rat. It is not just refinement or reduction that are called for, not just larger, cleaner cages, not just more generous use of anesthetic or the elimination of multiple surgery, not just tidying up the system. It is replacement— completely. The best we can do when it comes to using animals in science is—not to use them. That is where our duty lies, according to the rights view.

As for commercial animal agriculture, the rights view takes a similar abolitionist position. The fundamental moral wrong here is not that animals are kept in stressful close confinement, or in isolation, or that they have their pain and suffering, their needs and preferences ignored or discounted. *All* these *are* wrong, of course, but they are not the fundamental wrong. They are symptoms and effects of the deeper, systematic wrong that allows these animals to be viewed and treated as lacking independent value, as resources for us—as, indeed, a renewable resource. Giving farm animals more space, more natural environments, more companions does not right the fundamental wrong, any more than giving lab animals more anesthesia or bigger, cleaner cages would right the fundamental wrong in their case. Nothing less than the total dissolution of commercial animal agriculture will do this, just as, for

similar reasons I won't develop at length here, morality requires nothing less than the total elimination of commercial and sport hunting and trapping. The rights view's implications, then, as I have said, are clear—and are uncompromising.

My last two points are about philosophy—my profession. It is most obviously, no substitute for political action. The words I have written here and in other places by themselves don't change a thing. It is what we do with the thoughts the words express—our acts, our deeds—that change things. All that philosophy can do, and all I have attempted, is to offer a vision of what our deeds could aim at. And the why. But not the how.

Finally, I am reminded of my thoughtful critic, the one I mentioned earlier, who chastised me for being "too cerebral." Well, cerebral I have been: indirect duty views, utilitarianism, contractarianism—hardly the stuff deep passions are made of. I am also reminded, however, of the image another friend once set before me—the image of the ballerina as expressive of disciplined passion. Long hours of sweat and toil, of loneliness and practice, of doubt and fatigue; that is the discipline of her craft. But the passion is there, too: the fierce drive to excel, to speak through her body, to do it right, to pierce our minds. That is the image of philosophy I would leave with you; not "too cerebral," but *disciplined passion*. Of the discipline, enough has been seen. As for the passion:

There are times, and these are not infrequent, when tears come to my eyes when I see, or read, or hear of the wretched plight of animals in the hands of humans. Their pain, their suffering, their loneliness, their innocence, their death. Anger. Rage. Pity. Sorrow. Disgust. The whole creation groans under the weight of the evil we humans visit upon these mute, powerless creatures. It *is* our heart, not just our head, that calls for an end, that demands of us that we overcome, for them, the habits and forces behind their systematic oppression. All great movements, it is written, go through three stages: ridicule, discussion, adoption. It is the realization of this third stage—adoption—that demands both our passion and our discipline, our heart and our head. *The fate of animals is in our hands. God grant we are equal to the task.*

NOTE

1. Tom Regan, *The Case for Animal Rights* (Berkeley: University of California Press, 1983).

STUDY QUESTIONS

1. How is Regan's position on animal rights different from Singer's? Explain.

2. What are Regan's reasons for granting animals equal moral rights?

3. Does Regan allow for experimentation on animals? If we have to test a dangerous AIDS vaccine, on whom should we test it?

8

A Critique of Regan's Animal Rights Theory

MARY ANNE WARREN

The author of many articles in moral philosophy, Mary Anne Warren teaches philosophy at San Francisco State University.

   Warren reconstructs Regan's argument for animal rights and criticizes it for depending on the obscure notion of inherent value. She then argues that all rational human beings are equally part of the moral community since we can reason with each other about our behavior, whereas we cannot so reason with an animal. She puts forth a "weak animal rights theory," which asserts that we ought not to be cruel to animals or kill them without good reason.

Tom Regan has produced what is perhaps the definitive defense of the view that the basic moral rights of at least some non-human animals are in no way inferior to our own. In *The Case for Animal Rights*, he argues that all normal mammals over a year of age have the same basic moral rights.[1] Non-human mammals have essentially the same right not to be harmed or killed as we do. I shall call this "the strong animal rights position," although it is weaker than the claims made by some animal liberationists in that it ascribes rights to only some sentient animals.[2]

   I will argue that Regan's case for the strong animal rights position is unpersuasive and that this

Reprinted from *Between the Species*, Vol. 2, No. 4 (Fall 1987) by permission of Mary Anne Warren.

position entails consequences which a reasonable person cannot accept. I do not deny that some non-human animals have moral rights; indeed, I would extend the scope of the rights claim to include all sentient animals, that is, all those capable of having experiences, including experiences of pleasure or satisfaction and pain, suffering, or frustration.[3] However, I do not think that the moral rights of most non-human animals are identical in strength to those of persons.[4] The rights of most non-human animals may be overridden in circumstances which would not justify overriding the rights of persons. There are, for instance, compelling realities which sometimes require that we kill animals for reasons which could not justify the killing of persons. I will call this view "the weak animal rights" position, even though it ascribes rights to a wider range of animals than does the strong animal rights position.

I will begin by summarizing Regan's case for the strong animal rights position and noting two problems with it. Next, I will explore some consequences of the strong animal rights position which I think are unacceptable. Finally, I will outline the case for the weak animal rights position.

REGAN'S CASE

Regan's argument moves through three stages. First, he argues that normal, mature mammals are not only sentient but have other mental capacities as well. These include the capacities for emotion, memory, belief, desire, the use of general concepts, intentional action, a sense of the future, and some degree of self-awareness. Creatures with such capacities are said to be subjects-of-a-life. They are not only alive in the biological sense but have a psychological identity over time and an existence which can go better or worse for them. Thus, they can be harmed or benefited. These are plausible claims, and well defended. One of the strongest parts of the book is the rebuttal of philosophers, such as R. G. Frey, who object to the application of such mentalistic terms to creatures that do not use a human-style

language.[5] The second and third stages of the argument are more problematic.

In the second stage, Regan argues that subjects-of-a-life have inherent value. His concept of inherent value grows out of his opposition to utilitarianism. Utilitarian moral theory, he says, treats individuals as "mere receptacles" for morally significant value, in that harm to one individual may be justified by the production of a greater net benefit to other individuals. In opposition to this, he holds that subjects-of-a-life have a value independent of both the value they may place upon their lives or experiences and the value others may place upon them.

Inherent value, Regan argues, does not come in degrees. To hold that some individuals have more inherent value than others is to adopt a "perfectionist" theory, i.e., one which assigns different moral worth to individuals according to how well they are thought to exemplify some virtue(s), such as intelligence or moral autonomy. Perfectionist theories have been used, at least since the time of Aristotle, to rationalize such injustices as slavery and male domination, as well as the unrestrained exploitation of animals. Regan argues that if we reject these injustices, then we must also reject perfectionism and conclude that all subjects-of-a-life have equal inherent value. Moral agents have no more inherent value than moral patients, i.e., subjects-of-a-life who are not morally responsible for their actions.

In the third phase of the argument, Regan uses the thesis of equal inherent value to derive strong moral rights for all subjects-of-a-life. This thesis underlies the Respect Principle, which forbids us to treat beings who have inherent value as mere receptacles, i.e., mere means to the production of the greatest overall good. This principle, in turn, underlies the Harm Principle, which says that we have a direct *prima facie* duty not to harm beings who have inherent value. Together, these principles give rise to moral rights. Rights are defined as valid claims, claims to certain goods and against certain beings, i.e., moral agents. Moral rights generate duties not only to refrain from inflicting harm upon beings with inherent value but also to come to their aid when they are threatened by other moral agents. Rights are not absolute but may be overridden in certain circumstances. Just what these circumstances are we will consider later. But first, let's look at some difficulties in the theory as thus far presented.

THE MYSTERY OF INHERENT VALUE

Inherent value is a key concept in Regan's theory. It is the bridge between the plausible claim that all normal, mature mammals—human or otherwise—are subjects-of-a-life and the more debatable claim that they all have basic moral rights of the same strength. But it is a highly obscure concept, and its obscurity makes it ill-suited to play this crucial role.

Inherent value is defined almost entirely in negative terms. It is not dependent upon the value which either the inherently valuable individual or anyone else may place upon that individual's life or experiences. It is not (necessarily) a function of sentience or any other mental capacity, because, Regan says, some entities which are not sentient (e.g., trees, rivers, or rocks) may, nevertheless, have inherent value (p. 246). It cannot attach to anything other than an individual; species, ecosystems, and the like cannot have inherent value.

These are some of the things which inherent value is not. But what is it? Unfortunately, we are not told. Inherent value appears as a mysterious non-natural property which we must take on faith. Regan says that it is a *postulate* that subjects-of-a-life have inherent value, a postulate justified by the fact that it avoids certain absurdities which he thinks follow from a purely utilitarian theory (p. 247). But why is it a postulate that *subjects-of-a-life* have inherent value? If the inherent value of a being is completely independent of the value that it or anyone else places upon its experiences, then why does the fact that it has certain sorts of experiences constitute evidence that it has inherent value? If the reason is that subjects-of-a-life have an existence which can go better or worse for them, then why isn't the appropriate conclusion that all sentient beings have inherent value, since they would all seem to meet that condition? Sentient but mentally unsophisticated beings may have a less extensive range of possible satisfactions and frustrations, but

why should it follow that they have—or may have—no inherent value at all?

In the absence of a positive account of inherent value, it is also difficult to grasp the connection between being inherently valuable and having moral rights. Intuitively, it seems that value is one thing, and rights are another. It does not seem incoherent to say that some things (e.g., mountains, rivers, redwood trees) are inherently valuable and yet are not the sorts of things which can have moral rights. Nor does it seem incoherent to ascribe inherent value to some things which are not individuals, e.g., plant or animal species, though it may well be incoherent to ascribe moral rights to such things.

In short, the concept of inherent value seems to create at least as many problems as it solves. If inherent value is based on some natural property, then why not try to identify that property and explain its moral significance, without appealing to inherent value? And if it is not based on any natural property, then why should we believe in it? That it may enable us to avoid some of the problems faced by the utilitarian is not a sufficient reason, if it creates other problems which are just as serious.

IS THERE A SHARP LINE?

Perhaps the most serious problems are those that arise when we try to apply the strong animal rights position to animals other than normal, mature mammals. Regan's theory requires us to divide all living things into two categories: those which have the same inherent value and the same basic moral rights that we do, and those which have no inherent value and presumably no moral rights. But wherever we try to draw the line, such a sharp division is implausible.

It would surely be arbitrary to draw such a sharp line between normal, mature mammals and all other living things. Some birds (e.g., crows, magpies, parrots, mynahs) appear to be just as mentally sophisticated as most mammals and thus are equally strong candidates for inclusion under the subject-of-a-life criterion. Regan is not in fact advocating that we draw the line here. His claim is only that normal mature mammals are clear cases, while other cases are less clear. Yet, on his theory, there must be such a sharp line *somewhere,* since there are no degrees of inherent value. But why should we believe that there is a sharp line between creatures that are subjects-of-a-life and creatures that are not? Isn't it more likely that "subjecthood" comes in degrees, that some creatures have only a little self-awareness, and only a little capacity to anticipate the future, while some have a little more, and some a good deal more?

Should we, for instance, regard fish, amphibians, and reptiles as subjects-of-a-life? A simple yes-or-no answer seems inadequate. On the one hand, some of their behavior is difficult to explain without the assumption that they have sensations, beliefs, desires, emotions, and memories; on the other hand, they do not seem to exhibit very much self-awareness or very much conscious anticipation of future events. Do they have enough mental sophistication to count as subjects-of-a-life? Exactly how much is enough?

It is still more unclear what we should say about insects, spiders, octopi, and other invertebrate animals which have brains and sensory organs but whose minds (if they have minds) are even more alien to us than those of fish or reptiles. Such creatures are probably sentient. Some people doubt that they can feel pain, since they lack certain neurological structures which are crucial to the processing of pain impulses in vertebrate animals. But this argument is inconclusive, since their nervous systems might process pain in ways different from ours. When injured, they sometimes act as if they are in pain. On evolutionary grounds, it seems unlikely that highly mobile creatures with complex sensory systems would not have developed a capacity for pain (and pleasure), since such a capacity has obvious survival value. It must, however, be admitted that we do not *know* whether spiders can feel pain (or something very like it), let alone whether they have emotions, memories, beliefs, desires, self-awareness, or a sense of the future.

Even more mysterious are the mental capacities (if any) of mobile microfauna. The brisk and efficient way that paramecia move about in their incessant search for food *might* indicate some kind of sentience, in spite of their lack of eyes, ears, brains, and other organs associated with sentience in more complex organisms. It is conceivable—though not very probable—that they, too, are subjects-of-a-life.

The existence of a few unclear cases need not pose a serious problem for a moral theory, but in this case, the unclear cases constitute most of those with which an adequate theory of animal rights would need to deal. The subject-of-a-life criterion can provide us with little or no moral guidance in our interactions with the vast majority of animals. That might be acceptable if it could be supplemented with additional principles which would provide such guidance. However, the radical dualism of the theory precludes supplementing it in this way. We are forced to say that either a spider has the same right to life as you and I do, or it has no right to life whatever—and that only the gods know which of these alternatives is true.

Regan's suggestion for dealing with such unclear cases is to apply the "benefit of the doubt" principle. That is, when dealing with beings that may or may not be subjects-of-a-life, we should act as if they are.[6] But if we try to apply this principle to the entire range of doubtful cases, we will find ourselves with moral obligations which we cannot possibly fulfill. In many climates, it is virtually impossible to live without swatting mosquitoes and exterminating cockroaches, and not all of us can afford to hire someone to sweep the path before we walk, in order to make sure that we do not step on ants. Thus, we are still faced with the daunting task of drawing a sharp line somewhere on the continuum of life forms—this time, a line demarcating the limits of the benefit of the doubt principle.

The weak animal rights theory provides a more plausible way of dealing with this range of cases, in that it allows the rights of animals of different kinds to vary in strength....

WHY ARE ANIMAL RIGHTS WEAKER THAN HUMAN RIGHTS?

How can we justify regarding the rights of persons as generally stronger than those of sentient beings which are not persons? There are a plethora of bad justifications, based on religious premises or false or unprovable claims about the differences between human and non-human nature. But there is one difference which has a clear moral relevance: people are at least sometimes capable of being moved to action or inaction by the force of reasoned argument. Rationality rests upon other mental capacities, notably those which Regan cites as criteria for being a subject-of-a-life. We share these capacities with many other animals. But it is not just because we are subjects-of-a-life that we are both able and morally compelled to recognize one another as beings with equal basic moral rights. It is also because we are able to "listen to reason" in order to settle our conflicts and cooperate in shared projects. This capacity, unlike the others, may require something like a human language.

Why is rationality morally relevant? It does not make us "better" than other animals or more "perfect." It does not even automatically make us more intelligent. (Bad reasoning reduces our effective intelligence rather than increasing it.) But it is morally relevant insofar as it provides greater possibilities for cooperation and for the nonviolent resolution of problems. It also makes us more dangerous than non-rational beings can ever be. Because we are potentially more dangerous and less predictable than wolves, we need an articulated system of morality to regulate our conduct. Any human morality, to be workable in the long run, must recognize the equal moral status of all persons, whether through the postulate of equal basic moral rights or in some other way. The recognition of the moral equality of other persons is the price we must each pay for their recognition of our moral equality. Without this mutual recognition of moral equality, human society can exist only in a state of chronic and bitter conflict. The war between the sexes will persist so long as there is sexism and male domination; racial conflict will never be eliminated so long as there are racist laws and practices. But, to the extent that we achieve a mutual recognition of equality, we can hope to live together, perhaps as peacefully as wolves, achieving (in part) through explicit moral principles what they do not seem to need explicit moral principles to achieve.

Why not extend this recognition of moral equality to other creatures, even though they cannot do the same for us? The answer is that we cannot. Because we cannot reason with most non-human animals, we cannot always solve the problems which they may cause without harming them—although we are always obligated to try. We cannot negotiate a treaty with the feral cats and foxes, requiring them to stop preying on endangered native species in return for suitable concessions on our part.

> If rats invade our houses … we cannot reason with them, hoping to persuade them of the injustice they do us. We can only attempt to get rid of them.[7]

Aristotle was not wrong in claiming that the capacity to alter one's behavior on the basis of reasoned argument is relevant to the full moral status which he accorded to free men. Of course, he was wrong in his other premise, that women and slaves by nature cannot reason well enough to function as autonomous moral agents. Had that premise been true, so would his conclusion that women and slaves are not quite the moral equals of free men. In the case of most nonhuman animals, the corresponding premise is true. If, on the other hand, there are animals with whom we can learn to reason, then we are obligated to do this and to regard them as our moral equals.

Thus, to distinguish between the rights of persons and those of most other animals on the grounds that only people can alter their behavior on the basis of reasoned argument does not commit us to a perfectionist theory of the sort Aristotle endorsed. There is no excuse for refusing to recognize the moral equality of some people on the grounds that we don't regard them as quite as rational as we are, since it is perfectly clear that most people can reason well enough to determine how to act so as to respect the basic rights of others (if they choose to), and that is enough for moral equality.

But what about people who are clearly not rational? It is often argued that sophisticated mental capacities such as rationality cannot be essential for the possession of equal basic moral rights, since nearly everyone agrees that human infants and mentally incompetent persons have such rights, even though they may lack those sophisticated mental capacities. But this argument is inconclusive, because there are powerful practical and emotional reasons for protecting non-rational human beings, reasons which are absent in the case of most non-human animals. Infancy and mental incompetence are human conditions which all of us either have experienced or are likely to experience at some time. We also protect babies and mentally incompetent people because we care for them. We don't normally care for animals in the same way, and when we do—e.g., in the case of much-loved pets—we may regard them as having special rights by virtue of their relationship to us. We protect them not only for their sake but also for our own, lest we be hurt by harm done to them. Regan holds that such "side-effects" are irrelevant to moral rights, and perhaps they are. But in ordinary usage, there is no sharp line between moral rights and those moral protections which are not rights. The extension of strong moral protections to infants and the mentally impaired in no way proves that non-human animals have the same basic moral rights as people.

WHY SPEAK OF "ANIMAL RIGHTS" AT ALL?

If, as I have argued, reality precludes our treating all animals as our moral equals, then why should we still ascribe rights to them? Everyone agrees that animals are entitled to some protection against human abuse, but why speak of animal *rights* if we are not prepared to accept most animals as our moral equals? The weak animal rights position may seem an unstable compromise between the bold claim that animals have the same basic moral rights that we do and the more common view that animals have no rights at all.

It is probably impossible to either prove or disprove the thesis that animals have moral rights by producing an analysis of the concept of a moral right and checking to see if some or all animals satisfy the conditions for having rights. The concept of a moral right is complex, and it is not clear which of its strands are essential. Paradigm rights holders, i.e., mature and mentally competent persons, are *both* rational and morally autonomous beings and sentient subjects-of-a-life. Opponents of animal rights claim that rationality and moral autonomy are essential for the possession of rights, while defenders of animal rights claim that they are not. The ordinary concept of a moral right is probably not precise enough to enable us to determine who is right on purely definitional grounds.

If logical analysis will not answer the question of whether animals have moral rights, practical considerations may, nevertheless incline us to say that they do. The most plausible alternative to the view that animals have moral rights is that, while they do not have *rights*, we are, nevertheless, obligated not to be cruel to them. Regan argues persuasively that the injunction to avoid being cruel to animals is inadequate to express our obligations towards animals, because it focuses on the mental states of those who cause animal suffering, rather than on the harm done to the animals themselves (p. 158). Cruelty is inflicting pain or suffering and either taking pleasure in that pain or suffering or being more or less indifferent to it. Thus, to express the demand for the decent treatment of animals in terms of the rejection of cruelty is to invite the too easy response that those who subject animals to suffering are not being cruel because they regret the suffering they cause but sincerely believe that what they do is justified. The injunction to avoid cruelty is also inadequate in that it does not preclude the killing of animals—for any reason, however trivial—so long as it is done relatively painlessly.

The inadequacy of the anti-cruelty view provides one practical reason for speaking of animal rights. Another practical reason is that this is an age in which nearly all significant moral claims tend to be expressed in terms of rights. Thus, the denial that animals have rights, however carefully qualified, is likely to be taken to mean that we may do whatever we like to them, provided that we do not violate any human rights. In such a context, speaking of the rights of animals may be the only way to persuade many people to take seriously protests against the abuse of animals.

Why not extend this line of argument and speak of the rights of trees, mountains, oceans, or anything else which we may wish to see protected from destruction? Some environmentalists have not hesitated to speak in this way, and, given the importance of protecting such elements of the natural world, they cannot be blamed for using this rhetorical device. But, I would argue that moral rights can meaningfully be ascribed only to entities which have some capacity for sentience. This is because moral rights are protections designed to protect rights holders from harms or to provide them with benefits which matter *to them*. Only beings capable of sentience can be harmed or benefited in ways which matter to them, for only such beings can like or dislike what happens to them or prefer some conditions to others. Thus, sentient animals, unlike mountains, rivers, or species, are at least logically possible candidates for moral rights. This fact together with the need to end current abuses of animals—e.g., in scientific research ... —provides a plausible case for speaking of animal rights.

CONCLUSION

I have argued that Regan's case for ascribing strong moral rights to all normal, mature mammals is unpersuasive because (1) it rests upon the obscure concept of inherent value, which is defined only in negative terms, and (2) it seems to preclude any plausible answer to questions about the moral status of the vast majority of sentient animals....

The weak animal rights theory asserts that (1) any creature whose natural mode of life includes the pursuit of certain satisfactions has the right not to be forced to exist without the opportunity to pursue those satisfactions; (2) that any creature which is capable of pain, suffering, or frustration has the right that such experiences not be deliberately inflicted upon it without some compelling reason; and (3) that no sentient being should be killed without good reason. However, moral rights are not an all-or-nothing affair. The strength of the reasons required to override the rights of a non-human organism varies, depending upon—among other things—the probability that it is sentient and (if it is clearly sentient) its probable degree of mental sophistication....

NOTES

1. Tom Regan, *The Case for Animal Rights* (Berkeley: University of California Press, 1983). All page references are to this edition.

2. For instance, Peter Singer, although he does not like to speak of rights, includes all sentient beings under the protection of his basic utilitarian principle of equal respect for like interests. (*Animal Liberation* [New York: Avon Books, 1975], p. 3.)

3. The capacity for sentience like all of the mental capacities mentioned in what follows is a disposition. Dispositions do not disappear whenever they are not currently manifested. Thus, sleeping or temporarily unconscious persons or nonhuman animals are still sentient in the relevant sense (i.e., still capable of sentience), so long as they still have the neurological mechanisms necessary for the occurrence of experiences.

4. It is possible, perhaps probable that some nonhuman animals—such as cetaceans and anthropoid apes—should be regarded as persons. If so, then the weak animal rights position holds that these animals have the same basic moral rights as human persons.

5. See R. G. Frey, *Interests and Rights: The Case Against Animals* (Oxford: Oxford University Press, 1980).

6. See, for instance, p. 319, where Regan appeals to the benefit of the doubt principle when dealing with infanticide and late-term abortion.

7. Bonnie Steinbock, "Speciesism and the Idea of Equality," *Philosophy* 53 (1978):253.

STUDY QUESTIONS

1. Examine Warren's critique of Regan's position. What is her main criticism? How strong is her criticism?

2. What is the basis for granting human beings moral rights that we do not grant animals? Do you agree with Warren's arguments?

3. What is the weak animal rights position? What is Warren's argument for it?

9

Against Zoos

DALE JAMIESON

Dale Jamieson is professor of environmental studies and philosophy at New York University.

In this controversial essay, which has been greeted with some hostility, Jamieson first details a brief history of public uses of animals up until the time of our present zoological parks. He inquires whether there is any justification for zoos, examining four possible reasons for them: amusement, education, scientific research, and preserving species. While these have some merit, it is not sufficient to justify zoos, which deprive animals of their freedom and a chance to develop their potential. No doubt this is impossible and/or impractical now, but should we not aim at more humane treatment of animals, including the abolition or lessening of violence?

ZOOS AND THEIR HISTORY

We can start with a rough-and-ready definition of zoos: they are public parks which display animals, primarily for the purposes of recreation or education. Although large collections of animals were maintained in antiquity, they were not zoos in this sense. Typically these ancient collections were not exhibited in public parks, or they were maintained for purposes other than recreation or education.

The Romans, for example, kept animals in order to have living fodder for the games. Their enthusiasm for the games was so great that even the

---

Reprinted from Dale Jamieson, "Against Zoos," *In Defense of Animals*, ed. Peter Singer (Oxford: Basil Blackwell, 1985). Reprinted by permission of the author.

first tigers brought to Rome, gifts to Caesar Augustus from an Indian ruler, wound up in the arena. The emperor Trajan staged 123 consecutive days of games in order to celebrate his conquest of Dacia. Eleven thousand animals were slaughtered, including lions, tigers, elephants, rhinoceroses, hippopotami, giraffes, bulls, stags, crocodiles and serpents. The games were popular in all parts of the Empire. Nearly every city had an arena and a collection of animals to stock it. In fifth-century France there were twenty-six such arenas, and they continued to thrive until at least the eighth century.

In antiquity rulers also kept large collections of animals as a sign of their power, which they would demonstrate on occasion by destroying their entire collections. This happened as late as 1719 when Elector Augustus II of Dresden personally slaughtered his entire menagerie, which included tigers, lions, bulls, bears and boars.

The first modern zoos were founded in Vienna, Madrid and Paris in the eighteenth century and in London and Berlin in the nineteenth. The first American zoos were established in Philadelphia and Cincinnati in the 1870s. Today in the United States alone there are hundreds of zoos, and they are visited by millions of people every year. They range from roadside menageries run by hucksters, to elaborate zoological parks staffed by trained scientists.

The Roman games no longer exist, though bullfights and rodeos follow in their tradition. Nowadays the power of our leaders is amply demonstrated by their command of nuclear weapons. Yet we still have zoos. Why?

ANIMALS AND LIBERTY

Before we consider the reasons that are usually given for the survival of zoos, we should see that there is a moral presumption against keeping wild animals in captivity. What this involves, after all, is taking animals out of their native habitats, transporting them great distances and keeping them in alien environments in which their liberty is severely restricted. It is surely true that in being taken from the wild and confined in zoos, animals are deprived of a great many goods. For the most part they are prevented from gathering their own food, developing their own social orders and generally behaving in ways that are natural to them. These activities all require significantly more liberty than most animals are permitted in zoos. If we are justified in keeping animals in zoos, it must be because there are some important benefits that can be obtained only by doing so.

This conclusion is not the property of some particular moral theory; it follows from most reasonable moral theories. Either we have duties to animals or we do not. If we do have duties to animals, surely they include respecting those interests which are most important to them, so long as this does not conflict with other, more stringent duties that we may have. Since an interest in not being taken from the wild and kept confined is very important for most animals, it follows that if everything else is equal, we should respect this interest.

Suppose, on the other hand, that we do not have duties to animals. There are two further possibilities: either we have duties to people that sometimes concern animals, or what we do to animals is utterly without moral import. The latter view is quite implausible, and I shall not consider it further. People who have held the former view, that we have duties to people that concern animals, have sometimes thought that such duties arise because we can "judge the heart of a man by his treatment of animals," as Kant remarked in "Duties to Animals." It is for this reason that he condemns the man who shoots a faithful dog who has become too old to serve. If we accept Kant's premise, it is surely plausible to say that someone who, for no good reason, removes wild animals from their natural habitats and denies them liberty is someone whose heart deserves to be judged harshly. If this is so, then even if we believe that we do not have duties to animals but only duties concerning them, we may still hold that there is a presumption against keeping wild animals in captivity. If this presumption is to be overcome, it must be shown that there are important benefits that can be obtained only by keeping animals in zoos.

ARGUMENTS FOR ZOOS

What might some of these important benefits be? Four are commonly cited: amusement, education, opportunities for scientific research and help in preserving species.

Amusement was certainly an important reason for the establishment of the early zoos, and it remains an important function of contemporary zoos as well. Most people visit zoos in order to be entertained, and any zoo that wishes to remain financially sound must cater to this desire. Even highly regarded zoos, like the San Diego Zoo, have their share of dancing bears and trained birds of prey. But although providing amusement for people is viewed by the general public as a very important function of zoos, it is hard to see how providing such amusement could possibly justify keeping wild animals in captivity.

Most curators and administrators reject the idea that the primary purpose of zoos is to provide entertainment. Indeed, many agree that the pleasure we take in viewing wild animals is not in itself a good enough reason to keep them in captivity. Some curators see baby elephant walks, for example, as a necessary evil, or defend such amusements because of their role in educating people, especially children, about animals. It is sometimes said that people must be interested in what they are seeing if they are to be educated about it, and entertainments keep people interested, thus making education possible.

This brings us to a second reason for having zoos: their role in education. This reason has been cited as long as zoos have existed. For example, in 1898 the New York Zoological Society resolved to take "measures to inform the public of the great decrease in animal life, to stimulate sentiment in favor of better protection, and to cooperate with other scientific bodies … [in] efforts calculated to secure the perpetual preservation of our higher vertebrates." Despite the pious platitudes that are often uttered about the educational efforts of zoos, however, there is little evidence that zoos are very successful in educating people about animals. Stephen Kellert's paper "Zoological Parks in American Society," delivered at the annual meeting of the American Association of Zoological Parks and Aquariums in 1979, indicates that zoo-goers are much less knowledgeable about animals than backpackers, hunters, fishermen and others who claim an interest in animals, and only slightly more knowledgeable than those who claim no interest in animals at all. Even more disturbing, zoo-goers express the usual prejudices about animals; 73 per cent say they dislike rattlesnakes, 52 per cent vultures and only 4 per cent elephants. One reason why some zoos have not done a better job in educating people is that many of them make no real effort at education. In the case of others the problem is an apathetic and unappreciative public.

Edward G. Ludwig's study of the zoo in Buffalo, New York, in the *International Journal for the Study of Animal Problems* for 1981, revealed a surprising amount of dissatisfaction on the part of young, scientifically inclined zoo employees. Much of this dissatisfaction stemmed from the almost complete indifference of the public to the zoo's educational efforts. Ludwig's study indicated that most animals are viewed only briefly as people move quickly past cages. The typical zoo-goer stops only to watch baby animals or those who are begging, feeding or making sounds. Ludwig reported that the most common expressions used to describe animals are "cute," "funny-looking," "lazy," "dirty," "weird" and "strange."

Of course, it is undeniable that some education occurs in some zoos. But this very fact raises other issues. What is it that we want people to learn from visiting zoos? Facts about the physiology and behaviour of various animals? Attitudes towards the survival of endangered species? Compassion for the fate of all animals? To what degree does education require keeping wild animals in captivity? Couldn't most of the educational benefits of zoos be obtained by presenting films, slides, lectures and so forth? Indeed, couldn't most of the important educational objectives better be achieved by exhibiting empty cages with explanations of why they are empty?

A third reason for having zoos is that they support scientific research. This, too, is a benefit that was pointed out long ago. Sir Humphrey Davy, one of the founders of the Zoological Society of London, wrote in 1825: "It would become Britain to offer another, and a very different series of exhibitions to the population of her metropolis; namely, animals brought from every part of the globe to be applied either to some useful purpose, or as objects of scientific research—not of vulgar admiration!" Zoos support scientific research in at least three ways: they fund field research by scientists not affiliated with zoos; they employ other scientists as members of zoo staffs; and they make otherwise inaccessible animals available for study.

The first point we should note is that very few zoos support any real scientific research. Fewer still have staff scientists with full-time research appointments. Among those that do, it is common for their scientists to study animals in the wild rather than those in zoo collections. Much of this research, as well as other field research that is supported by zoos, could just as well be funded in a different way—say, by a government agency. The question of whether there should be zoos does not turn on the funding for field research which zoos currently provide. The significance of the research that is actually conducted in zoos is a more important consideration.

Research that is conducted in zoos can be divided into two categories: studies in behaviour and studies in anatomy and pathology.

Behavioural research conducted on zoo animals is very controversial. Some have argued that nothing can be learned by studying animals that are kept in the unnatural conditions that obtain in most zoos. Others have argued that captive animals are more interesting research subjects than are wild animals: since captive animals are free from predation, they exhibit a wider range of physical and behavioural traits than animals in the wild, thus permitting researchers to view the full range of their genetic possibilities. Both of these positions are surely extreme. Conditions in some zoos are natural enough to permit some interesting research possibilities. But the claim that captive animals are more interesting research subjects than those in the wild is not very plausible. Environments trigger

behaviours. No doubt a predation-free environment triggers behaviours different from those of an animal's natural habitat, but there is no reason to believe that better, fuller or more accurate data can be obtained in predation-free environments than in natural habitats.

Studies in anatomy and pathology are the most common forms of zoo research. Such research has three main purposes: to improve zoo conditions so that captive animals will live longer, be happier and breed more frequently; to contribute to human health by providing animal models for human ailments; and to increase our knowledge of wild animals for its own sake.

The first of these aims is surely laudable, if we concede that there should be zoos in the first place. But the fact that zoo research contributes to improving conditions in zoos is not a reason for having them. If there were no zoos, there would be no need to improve them.

The second aim, to contribute to human health by providing animal models for human ailments, appears to justify zoos to some extent, but in practice this consideration is not as important as one might think. There are very severe constraints on the experiments that may be conducted on zoo animals. In an article entitled "A Search for Animal Models at Zoos," published in *ILAR News* in 1982, Richard Montali and Mitchell Bush drew the following conclusion:

> Despite the great potential of a zoo as a resource for models, there are many limitations and, of necessity, some restrictions for use. There is little opportunity to conduct overly manipulative or invasive research procedures—probably less than would be allowed in clinical research trials involving human beings. Many of the species are difficult to work with or are difficult to breed, so that the numbers of animals available for study are limited. In fact, it is safe to say that over the past years, humans have served more as "animal models" for zoo species than is true of the reverse.

Whether for this reason or others, much of what has been done in using zoo animals as models for humans seems redundant or trivial. For example, the article cited above reports that zoo animals provide good models for studying lead toxicity in humans, since it is common for zoo animals to develop lead poisoning from chewing paint and inhaling polluted city air. There are available for study plenty of humans who suffer from lead poisoning for the same reasons. That zoos make available some additional non-human subjects for this kind of research seems at best unimportant and at worst deplorable.

Finally, there is the goal of obtaining knowledge about animals for its own sake. Knowledge is certainly something which is good and, everything being equal, we should encourage people to seek it for its own sake. But everything is not equal in this case. There is a moral presumption against keeping animals in captivity. This presumption can be overcome only by demonstrating that there are important benefits that must be obtained in this way if they are to be obtained at all. It is clear that this is not the case with knowledge for its own sake. There are other channels for our intellectual curiosity, ones that do not exact such a high moral price. Although our quest for knowledge for its own sake is important, it is not important enough to overcome the moral presumption against keeping animals in captivity.

In assessing the significance of research as a reason for having zoos, it is important to remember that very few zoos do any research at all. Whatever benefits result from zoo research could just as well be obtained by having a few zoos instead of the hundreds which now exist. The most this argument could establish is that we are justified in having a few very good zoos. It does not provide a defence of the vast majority of zoos which now exist.

A fourth reason for having zoos is that they preserve species that would otherwise become extinct. As the destruction of habitat accelerates and as breeding programmes become increasingly successful, this rationale for zoos gains in popularity. There is some reason for questioning the commitment of zoos to preservation: it can be argued that they continue to remove more animals from the wild than they return. Still, zoo breeding programmes have had some notable successes: without them the Père David Deer, the Mongolian Wild Horse and the European Bison would all now be extinct. Recently, however, some problems have begun to be noticed.

A 1979 study by Katherine Ralls, Kristin Brugger and Jonathan Ballou, which was reported in *Science,* convincingly argues that lack of genetic diversity among captive animals is a serious problem for zoo breeding programmes. In some species the infant mortality rate among inbred animals is six or seven times that among non-inbred animals. In other species the infant mortality rate among inbred animals is 100 per cent. What is most disturbing is that zoo curators have been largely unaware of the problems caused by inbreeding because adequate breeding and health records have not been kept. It is hard to believe that zoos are serious about their role in preserving endangered species when all too often they do not take even this minimal step.

In addition to these problems, the lack of genetic diversity among captive animals also means that surviving members of endangered species have traits very different from their con-specifics in the wild. This should make us wonder what is really being preserved in zoos. Are captive Mongolian Wild Horses really Mongolian Wild Horses in any but the thinnest biological sense?

There is another problem with zoo breeding programmes: they create many unwanted animals. In some species (lions, tigers and zebras, for example) a few males can service an entire herd. Extra males are unnecessary to the programme and are a financial burden. Some of these animals are sold and wind up in the hands of individuals and institutions which lack proper facilities. Others are shot and killed by Great White Hunters in private hunting camps. In order to avoid these problems, some zoos have been considering proposals to "recycle" excess animals: a euphemism for killing them and feeding their bodies to other zoo animals. Many people are surprised when they hear of zoos killing animals. They should not be. Zoos have limited capacities. They want to maintain diverse collections. This can be done only by careful management of their "stock."

Even if breeding programmes were run in the best possible way, there are limits to what can be done to save endangered species. For many large mammals a breeding herd of at least a hundred animals, half of them born in captivity, is required if they are to survive in zoos. As of 1971 only eight mammal species satisfied these conditions. Paul and Anne Ehrlich estimate in their book *Extinction* that under the best possible conditions American zoos could preserve only about a hundred species of mammals—and only at a very high price: maintaining a breeding herd of herbivores costs between $75,000 and $250,000 per year.

There are further questions one might ask about preserving endangered species in zoos. Is it really better to confine a few hapless Mountain Gorillas in a zoo than to permit the species to become extinct? To most environmentalists the answer is obvious: the species must be preserved at all costs. But this smacks of sacrificing the lower-case gorilla for the upper-case Gorilla. In doing this, aren't we using animals as mere vehicles for their genes? Aren't we preserving genetic material at the expense of the animals themselves? If it is true that we are inevitably moving towards a world in which Mountain Gorillas can survive only in zoos, then we must ask whether it is really better for them to live in artificial environments of our design than not to be born at all.

Even if all of these difficulties are overlooked, the importance of preserving endangered species does not provide much support for the existing system of zoos. Most zoos do very little breeding or breed only species which are not endangered. Many of the major breeding programmes are run in special facilities which have been established for that purpose. They are often located in remote places, far from the attention of zoo-goers. (For example, the Bronx Zoo operates its Rare Animal Survival Center on St Catherine's Island off the coast of Georgia, and the National Zoo runs its Conservation and Research Center in the Shenandoah Valley of Virginia.) If our main concern is to do what we can to preserve endangered species, we should support such large-scale breeding centres rather than conventional zoos, most of which have neither the staff nor the facilities to run successful breeding programmes.

The four reasons for having zoos which I have surveyed carry some weight. But different reasons provide support for different kinds of zoos. Preservation and perhaps research are better carried out in large-scale animal preserves, but these provide few opportunities for amusement and education. Amusement and perhaps education are better provided in urban zoos, but they offer few opportunities for research and preservation. Moreover, whatever benefits are obtained from any kind of zoo must confront the moral presumption against keeping wild animals in captivity. Which way do the scales tip? There are two further considerations which, in my view, tip the scales against zoos.

First, captivity does not just deny animals liberty but is often detrimental to them in other respects as well. The history of chimpanzees in the zoos of Europe and America is a good example.

Chimpanzees first entered the zoo world in about 1640 when a Dutch prince, Frederick Henry of Nassau, obtained one for his castle menagerie. The chimpanzee didn't last very long. In 1835 the London Zoo obtained its first chimpanzee; he died immediately. Another was obtained in 1845; she lived six months. All through the nineteenth and early twentieth centuries zoos obtained chimpanzees who promptly died within nine months. It wasn't until the 1930s that it was discovered that chimpanzees are extremely vulnerable to human respiratory diseases, and that special steps must be taken to protect them. But for nearly a century zoos removed them from the wild and subjected them to almost certain death. Problems remain today. When chimpanzees are taken from the wild the usual procedure is to shoot the mother and kidnap the child. The rule of thumb among trappers is that ten chimpanzees die for every one that is delivered alive to the United States or Europe. On arrival many of these animals are confined under abysmal conditions.

Chimpanzees are not the only animals to suffer in zoos. In 1974 Peter Batten, former director of the San Jose Zoological Gardens, undertook an exhaustive study of two hundred American zoos. In his book *Living Trophies* he documented large numbers of neurotic, overweight animals kept in cramped, cold cells and fed unpalatable synthetic food. Many had deformed feet and appendages caused by unsuitable floor surfaces. Almost every zoo studied had excessive mortality rates, resulting from preventable factors ranging from vandalism to inadequate husbandry practices. Battan's conclusion was: "The majority of American zoos are badly run, their direction incompetent, and animal husbandry inept and in some cases nonexistent."

Many of these same conditions and others are documented in *Pathology of Zoo Animals,* a review of necropsies conducted by Lynn Griner over the last fourteen years at the San Diego Zoo. This zoo may well be the best in the country, and its staff is clearly well-trained and well-intentioned. Yet this study documents widespread malnutrition among zoo animals; high mortality rates from the use of anaesthetics and tranquillizers; serious injuries and deaths sustained in transport; and frequent occurrences of cannibalism, infanticide and fighting almost certainly caused by overcrowded conditions. Although the zoo has learned from its mistakes, it is still unable to keep many wild animals in captivity without killing or injuring them, directly or indirectly. If this is true of the San Diego Zoo, it is certainly true, to an even greater extent, at most other zoos.

The second consideration is more difficult to articulate but is, to my mind, even more important. Zoos teach us a false sense of our place in the natural order. The means of confinement mark a difference between humans and animals. They are there at our pleasure, to be used for our purposes. Morality and perhaps our very survival require that we learn to live as one species among many rather than as one species over many. To do this, we must forget what we learn at zoos. Because what zoos teach us is false and dangerous, both humans and animals will be better off when they are abolished.

STUDY QUESTIONS

1. Examine the four reasons for zoos. Can you improve on them? Examine Jamieson's reasons for rejecting them as sufficient to justify zoos. Do you agree with him? Are zoos immoral?

2. Can Jamieson's arguments against zoos be applied to owning pets? Why or why not?

3. How would Jamieson (or you) respond to the objection that since we have duties toward animal welfare, we ought to protect weaker animals from their predators, so that zoos could help play a role in promoting their welfare? And just as we want to eliminate gratuitous violence by humans, should we not work to eliminate it in animals—perhaps developing meat substitutes for them, as well as human carnivores?

FOR FURTHER READING

Finsen, Lawrence, and Susan Finsen. *The Animal Rights Movement in America.* New York: Twayne Publishers, 1994.

Frey, R. G. *Rights, Killing, and Suffering.* Oxford: Basil Blackwell, 1983.

Midgley, Mary. *Animals and Why They Matter.* London: Routledge, 1983.

Rachels, James. *Created from Animals: The Moral Implications of Darwinism.* Oxford: Oxford University Press, 1990.

Regan, Tom. *The Case for Animal Rights.* Berkeley: University of California, 1983. The most comprehensive philosophical treatise in favor of animal rights.

Regan, Tom, and Peter Singer, eds. *Animal Rights and Human Obligations*. Englewood Cliffs, NJ: Prentice-Hall, 1976.

Robbins, John. *Diet for a New America: How Your Food Choices Affect Your Health, Happiness, and the Future of Life on Earth*. Walpole, NH: Stillpoint, 1987.
A strong case for vegetarianism.

Rohr, Janelle, ed. *Animal Rights: Opposing Viewpoints*. San Diego: Greenhaven Press, 1989.

Sapontzis, S. F. *Morals, Reason, and Animals*. Philadelphia: Temple University Press, 1987.

Singer, Peter. *Animal Liberation*, 2d ed. New York: New York Review of Books, 1990.

Chapter 3

Value in Nature Itself

IN THIS CHAPTER, we consider the wide-ranging debates over why humans should value nature. There are three general reasons for humans to value nature. First, nature can be valued simply as a source of economics. We derive our food, water, air, clothing, building materials, etc., from nature. We mine its ores, cut its trees, harvest its fish, and develop its land. We value it for the material products it provides. Second, we value nature as a source not just of economic resource but also of aesthetics. Forests, streams, and mountains are beautiful and uplifting. Nature is seen as pure, uncorrupted by humans, and a place of moral and spiritual rejuvenation. As with the first, we here value nature for what nature offers us. Even though we are valuing nature in a less exploitative way, some still argue we need to go further. Thus the third way is to value nature simply for nature's sake, not for what nature offers us. In other words, nature has intrinsic value. Many nature-centered spiritual systems indeed hold this view (for instance, some varieties of Pagans and Wiccans). Many people with green leanings are sympathetic to this position, but as we shall see, it is hard to defend intellectually. At the same time, its pull is strong, and one of the central challenges to environmental thinking is whether to base an environmental ethic on human needs or upon nature itself.

We begin with Holmes Rolston's defense of the thesis that nature has intrinsic and objective value. Nature is good in itself or has a good, so even if there were no sentient beings, it would still have a good. Rolston argues that not only sentient beings but also biological systems have intrinsic value. But not everything in nature has objective value. It occurs only where there is positive creativity. Next Ned Hettinger comments on and critically develops Rolston's theory, pointing out its strengths and weaknesses. John Stuart Mill takes a very different position, contending that nature is wild and destructive and that it ought to be corrected by moral beings.

Next we turn to the most radical of the main environmental theories, deep ecology, first set forth by the Norwegian philosopher Arne Naess and elaborated by Bill Devall and George Sessions. Drawing on Eastern thought, especially Vedantic Hinduism and Buddhism, deep ecology holds that all of us—humans, nonhumans, and biotic communities—are intrinsically related to one another.

Underlying all is an essential unity of being so that, in some sense, no one can realize his, her, or its deepest potential without everyone realizing it. Deep ecology is egalitarian in that everyone and everything is equally valuable as part of the whole. This transpersonal ecology calls on us to go beyond class, gender, and species and find our deepest fulfillment in harmony with nature. In its eightfold path (see Devall and Sessions's article), deep ecology calls for the promotion and greater protection of biodiversity and a reduction of human population. We must also learn to live more simply. Its motto is "Simple in Means, Rich in Ends," signifying an antimaterialist perspective.

The next four articles offer critiques and clarifications on deep ecology. Richard Watson criticizes many of the above-mentioned ecophilosophies for being antianthropocentric—that is, opposing the place of human beings at the center of things; similarly, Murray Bookchin offers a Marxist and anarchist critique of deep ecology, accusing it of being dehumanizing, and Ramachandra Guha offers a third world critique of overly idealistic Western environmentalists.

10

Naturalizing Values: Organisms and Species

HOLMES ROLSTON, III

Holmes Rolston, III, is emeritus professor of philosophy at Colorado State University. He is the author of numerous works on environmental ethics, including Philosophy Gone Wild: Essays in Environmental Ethics *(1986) and* Environmental Ethics: Duties to and Values in the Natural World *(1988).*

In this essay, Rolston examines the fact/value problem as it applies to nature. He argues that values are objective in nature and that just as philosophers are naturalizing ethics, epistemology, and metaphysics, they should naturalize values.

In an age of naturalism, philosophers seem as yet unable to naturalize values. They are naturalizing ethics, epistemology, and metaphysics. They have connected human ethical behavior to Darwinian reciprocity, kin selection, genetic fitness, and so on. They analyze human capacities for epistemology with care to notice how our human perceptions, our sense organs, have an evolutionary history. Our mind and its cognitive capacities are pragmatic ways of functioning in the world. They interpret ideologies and metaphysical views as means of coping, worldviews that enable humans in their societies to cohere and to outcompete other societies. Ethics, epistemology, and metaphysics are survival tools, whatever else they may also become.

But philosophers are slow to naturalize axiology. If they do, they try to demonstrate the biological roots of human values. They show that our values root in our biological needs—for food, shelter, security, resources, self-defense, offspring, stability, and status in our societies. Beyond that, philosophers do not naturalize values in any deeper sense. They cannot disconnect nature from humans so that anything else in nature can have any intrinsic value on its own. That is disconcerting. Nature comes to have value only when humans take it up into their experience. This, they may think, is a naturalized account of value; but, I shall argue here, such analysis has not yet come within reach of a biologically based account of values. Somewhat curiously, the more obvious kind of naturalizing—showing that our values are framed by our evolutionary embodiment in the world—blinds us to the deeper kind of naturalizing—recognizing an evolutionary world in which values, some of which we share, are pervasively embodied in the nonhuman world.

The debate is complex and multi-leveled. We touch the nerve of it here by focusing on value as this is present in living organisms and their species lines. Let's start by looking over the shoulders of some recent scientists and their discoveries.

1. DRAGONFLIES, LEAF STOMATA, BACTERIAL CLOCKS, AND GENOMES

Studies of dragonflies in the Carboniferous show that their wings "are proving to be spectacular examples of microengineering" giving them "the agile, versatile flight necessary to catch prey in flight." They are "adapted for high-performance flight" (Wootton et al., 1998). "To execute these aerobatic maneuvers, the insects come equipped with highly engineered wings that automatically change their flight shape in response to airflow, putting the designers of the latest jet fighters to shame" (Vogel, 1998). Dragonflies have to change their wing shape in flight without benefit of muscles (as in birds and

bats), so they use a flexible aerofoil with veins that enables the wing surface to twist in direct response to aerodynamic loading when suddenly changing directions or shifting from upstroke to downstroke. A hind-wing base mechanism is especially impressive in the way it mixes flexibility and rigidity. "The 'smart' wing-base mechanism is best interpreted as an elegant means of maintaining downstroke efficiency in the presence of these adaptations to improve upstroke usefulness" (Wootton et al., 1998).

Botanists report studies in what they call "a plant's dilemma." Plants need to photosynthesize to gain energy from the sun, which requires access to carbon dioxide in the atmosphere. They also need to conserve water, vital to their metabolism, and access to atmosphere which evaporates water. This forces a trade-off in leaves between too much and too little exposure to atmosphere. The problem is solved by stomata on the undersides of leaves, which can open and close, letting in or shutting out the air. "The stomatal aperture is controlled by osmotic adjustment in the surrounding cells. In a sophisticated regulatory mechanism, light, the carbon dioxide required for photosynthesis, and the water status of the plant are integrated to regulate stomatal aperture for optimization of the plant's growth and performance" (Grill and Ziegler, 1998). The details of such "plant strategies" vary in different species but are quite complex, integrating multiple environmental and metabolic variables—water availability, drought, heat, cold, sunlight, water stress, and energy needs in the plant—for sophisticated solutions to the plant's dilemma.

Even the cyanobacteria, blue-green algae, which are relatively primitive single-celled organisms, can track day and night with molecular clocks built with a genetic oscillator rather similar to those in more advanced organisms. Discovering this, Marcia Barinaga says, "Keeping track of day-night cycles is apparently so essential, perhaps because it helps organisms prepare for the special physiological needs they will have at various times during the daily cycle, that clocks seem to have arisen multiple times, recreating the same design each time" (1998).

Reporting a June 1998 conference on "Molecular Strategies in Evolution," geneticists have found so many examples of "how the genome readies itself for evolution" that they are making a "paradigm shift." Abandoning the idea that genetic mutation is entirely blind and random, and that genetic errors are suppressed to minimize change, geneticists are impressed with the innovative, creative capacities in the genome. These "new findings are persuading them that the most successful genomes may be those that have evolved to be able to change quickly and substantially if necessary" (Pennisi, 1998). Genes do this by using transposons—gene segments, mobile elements—that they can use rapidly to alter DNA and the resulting protein structures and metabolisms in time of stress. "Chance favors the prepared genome," says Lynn Caporale, a biotechnology geneticist. James Shapiro, a bacterial geneticist at the University of Chicago, comments: "The capability of cells has gone far beyond what we had imagined." "Cells engineer their own genomes" (quoted in Pennisi, 1998).

The genome in vertebrates, for example, has evolved quite successful capacities to resist diseases. Transposons turn out to be especially useful in the acquired immune system, which is not present in invertebrates, but which was discovered and elaborated in vertebrates. "The immune system is a wonderful example of how a mobile piece of DNA can have an astounding impact on evolution," says David Schatz of Yale University (quoted in Pennisi, 1998). Innate immunity, which is present in vertebrates, is coded in the genes and "remembers" what has happened in the organism's evolutionary past. But acquired immunity "remembers" what has come along during the organism's biographical past. An organism gets the disease; then its body remembers, forms antigens, and does not get the disease a second time.

One has to use language with care; we should guard against overly cognitive language. But scientists do have to describe what is going on; and there is a kind of acquired learning in immunity, mechanical though the system also is. Immunologists use a term here that philosophers will find revealing. When stem cells from the bone marrow mature in the thymus (T cells), this is called "thymic education" (Abbas et al., 1991, p. 169). Once such an

educated T cell meets an alien microbe, it not only triggers defenses, it triggers a memory. What immunologists call "memory cells" are made; these are both long-lived and reproduce themselves, so that acquired immunity can continue for decades, even a lifetime. The body can remember what sorts of organisms it has met before and be ready for their return. From a philosophical perspective, we may wish to be circumspect about "memory" cells, as we are about "remembering"; and yet the vocabulary is widespread in immunology and seems equally legitimate, say, to the use of "memory" in computer science. Additionally, in organisms—as it is not in computers—this is vital to life. Such capacity is much smarter than mere genetics; the body has defensive capacities far in excess of anything that could have been coded for in the genes.

The immune system has a complex task. A host of metabolically and structurally different cells have to be choreographed in organic unity. Further, invader cells, myriads of kinds of them, and insider cells gone wrong in many different ways—all these must be seen and eliminated. This has to be done at microscopic and molecular ranges with careful regulation, which involves complement molecules that work in a cascade reaction—15–20 different molecules, and 10 or more inhibitors, a total of some 30–40 molecules. Such a cascade might seem overly complex, but it is really a sophisticated form of regulation; there are amplification circuits and stabilizing loops, shut-down provisions and backup pathways. This is, of course, a causal system, but it is more than that; the system is protecting an organismic self.

Complement can be quite destructive and that is a good thing when it provides immunity for the organism, but it is also a bad thing if it goes out of control. So complement requires tight, fail-safe regulation. Immunologists use here the language of a fine-tuned mechanism: "Because of these regulatory mechanisms, a delicate balance of activation and inhibition of the complement cascades is achieved which prevents damage to autologous [self] cells and tissues but promotes the effective destruction of foreign organisms" (Abbas et al., 1991, p. 268). "The consequences of complement activation are so significant and potentially dangerous that the system must be very carefully regulated" (Tizard, 1992, p. 200). Some threats and achievements here seem to be "significant," "dangerous," "effective," and "damaging"; something vital is at stake.

Can you see that philosophers, looking over the shoulders of these scientists with their descriptions of what is going on, have some value questions to ask? The immune system is a sophisticated means of preserving biological identity at a high level of idiographic organismic diversity. All this is going on spontaneously, autonomously, without any animal awareness, much less any humans thinking about it.

There is praise for those dragonfly wings in the Carboniferous, coming from the scientists who study them. What is a philosopher to say? "Well, those are interesting wings to the scientists who study them, but they were of no value to the dragonflies." That seems implausible. Perhaps one can go part way and say: "Well, those wings did have value to the individual dragonflies who owned them. Instrumentally, the dragonflies found them useful. But a dragonfly is incapable of intrinsically valuing anything. Much less do these wings represent anything of value to the species line. Similar engineering features persist, Wootton and his associates add, in present-day dragonflies, living 320 million years later than the fossil dragonflies they studied in Argentina. That does sound like something that has been useful for quite a long time. Could that be of value to the species line?

The repeated discovery of molecular clocks in those cyanobacteria is important in fulfilling the organisms' "needs," and that seems pretty much fact of the matter. After that, do we want to insist that nevertheless this has no "value" to these organisms or their species lines, who have several times discovered how these internal clocks, similarly "designed," increase their adapted fit?

Studying those immune systems, a cell biologist finds something "wonderful." But, you will insist, this is only "wonderful" when cell biologists get there to wonder about it. Perhaps nothing is "astounding" until a human being comes around to be astounded. We do not think that the genomes are astounded. Still, the biological achievements are

there long before we get let in on them. Set aside the wonder. In the objective facts—leaf stomata, genome evolution, bacterial clocks—is there anything there of value?

2. ANTHROPIC VALUERS AND THEIR VALUES

Most philosophers insist there is not. Values in nature are always "anthropocentric," human-centered, or at least "anthropogenic" (generated by humans). Bryan G. Norton concludes: "Moralists among environmental ethicists have erred in looking for a value in living things that is *independent* of human valuing. They have therefore forgotten a most elementary point about valuing anything. Valuing always occurs from the viewpoint of a conscious valuer.... Only the humans are valuing agents" (1991, p. 251). Norton, of course, believes in an objective world that he is anxious to conserve. Walking along a beach, he values, for example, the sand dollars *(Mellita quinquiesperforata)* he finds there. He has respect for life (1991, pp. 3–13). He chose a sand dollar to picture on the cover of his book. Such encounters make him a better person, give him an enlarged sense of his place in the world, and increase his wonder over the world he lives in. So he celebrates "the character-building transformative value of interactions with nature" (1987, pp. 10–11). He gets a lot of good out of respecting sand dollars.

But Norton does not want any epistemological "foundationalism" or "metaphysical realism," as though humans (whether scientists or philosophers) could actually know anything out there in nature independently of ourselves, much less that there are values intrinsic to some of these nonhuman organisms out there. There is no getting out of our epistemological bondage, no getting past "interactions"; it is naive for humans to claim to know objective value in sand dollars. Norton regrets that I, when I claim to know more than "interactions," have fallen into the "devastating legacy" of "outmoded" Cartesian dualism, "a bewitchment of ossified language" (1992, pp. 216–218, 224).

J. Baird Callicott, equally zealous for the conservation of nature, is equally clear about our unique human value-ability. All intrinsic value attached to nature is "grounded in human feelings" but is "projected" onto the natural objects that "excites" the value. "Intrinsic value ultimately depends upon human valuers." "Value depends upon human sentiments" (1984, p. 305). We humans can and ought *place* such value on natural things, at times, but there is no value already *in place* before we come. Intrinsic value is our construct, interactively with nature, but not something discovered which was there before we came. "There can be no value apart from an evaluator, ... all value is as it were in the eye of the beholder [and] ... therefore, is humanly dependent" (1989, p. 26). Such value is "anthropogenic" (1992, p. 132).

> The source of all value is human consciousness, but it by no means follows that the locus of all value is consciousness itself.... An intrinsically valuable thing on this reading is valuable for its own sake, for itself, but it is not valuable in itself, that is, completely independently of any consciousness, since no value can, in principle,... be altogether independent of a valuing consciousness.... Value is, as it were, projected onto natural objects or events by the subjective feelings of observers. If all consciousness were annihilated at a stroke, there would be no good and evil, no beauty and ugliness, no right and wrong; only impassive phenomena would remain. (1989, pp. 133–134, 147)

What that means, of course, is that the dragonfly wings were no "good" to them, or at least of no "value" to them. Though insects, sand dollars, bacteria, and plants may engineer their own genomes, there is nothing valuable about any of these activities, much less right or beautiful. Take our evaluating consciousness away, and there remain only impassive phenomena.

These philosophers have to conclude so because according to classical value theory only humans produce value; wild nature is intrinsically valueless.

That seems to be a metaphysical claim in Callicott. We can know what is there without us: impassive phenomena; we can know what is not there: intrinsic value. Or if not so ontological, this is at least an epistemological claim, as with Norton: we are unable to know what is there without us. All we can know is that some things in nature, before we get there, have the potential to be evaluated by humans. We know this because if and when we humans appear, we may incline, sometimes, to value nature in noninstrumental ways, as when we project intrinsic value onto sequoia trees while hiking through the forest, or have transformative experiences encountering sand dollars on a beach.

The best we can do is to give a dispositional twist to value. To say that *n* is valuable means that *n* (some object in *n*ature) is able to be valued, if and when human valuers, *H*'s (some *H*umans), come along, although *n* has these properties whether or not humans arrive. The object plays its necessary part, though this is not sufficient without the subject. Nature contains "a range of *potential* values in nature actualizable upon interaction with consciousness" (Callicott, 1992, p. 129). By this account there is no actual value ownership autonomous to the dragonflies, bacteria, plants, or genome lines—none at least that we can know about. When cellular biologists arrive with their wonder and resolve to admire and perhaps also to conserve these things, there is value ignition. Intrinsic value in the realized sense emerges relationally with the appearance of the subject-generator. This is something like opening the door of a refrigerator, when things previously in the dark light up. But axiologically speaking, nature is always in the dark—unless and until humans come.

Perhaps you can begin to see why I am disconcerted that philosophers can be so naturalistic one moment and so separatist the next. Naturalists wish to claim that we humans are not metaphysically different from the rest of nature, whether in substance or process. Human activities and those in wild nature are equally natural. Humans are completely natural in their physiologies and in their evolutionary histories. We are a part of nature and not apart from nature. Still, they still practice value apartheid. They resolutely find humans quite axiologically different, with this unique valuing capacity. That does set us apart from the rest of nature.

At the same time that they set us humans apart so surely, they may also find us so epistemologically ignorant that we cannot really know what we might share with the nonhuman lives we encounter. In these values that arise when we interact with nature we are unable to discover anything more than these values that arise within us, based on some potential nature has for us. But humans are sealed off from making any further claims about the objective world. This too is value apartheid.

The anthropogenic view values nature only in association with human participation. This leaves us with an uneasy concern that, however generously we may come to care for some nonhuman others, since it is only *we* who can place value anywhere, since it is only our own values that we can attend to or know about, humans really do remain at the center of concern. Their concern is central to having any value at all. Their concern is all that matters, and it is not always going to be easy to get up concern for animals, plants, species, or ecosystems that really don't matter in themselves, not at least so far as anybody knows.

We are likely to be concerned only if they matter to and for us, and that is going to place humans right back at the center. Nature is actually valuable only when it pleases us, as well as serves us. That seems to be the ultimate truth, even though we penultimately have placed intrinsic value on nature, and take our pleasure enjoying these natural things for what they are in themselves. Without us there is no such pleasure taken in anything. What is value-able, able to value things, is people; nature is able to be valued only if there are such able people there to do such valuing. Nature is not value-able—able to generate values—on its own, nor do plants and animals have any such value-ability.

3. SENTIENT VALUERS AND THEIR VALUES

Peter Singer offers a more expansive account. It is not just humans but the higher animals that can value. We have to move from an anthropocentric to a "sentiocentric" view. Or, better, from an anthropogenic to a "sentiogenic" view. (Please pardon the nonce words.) Animals can value on their own, provided that they have preferences that can be satisfied or frustrated. A mother free-tailed bat, a mammal like ourselves, can, using sonar, wend her way out of Bracken Cave, in Texas, in total darkness, catch 500–1000 insects each hour on the wing, and return to find and nurse her own young. That gives evidence of bat-valuing; she values the insects and the pup.

Now, it seems absurd to say that there are no valuers until humans arrive. There is no better evidence of nonhuman values and valuers than spontaneous wildlife, born free and on its own. Animals hunt and howl; find shelter; seek out their habitats and mates; care for their young; flee from threats; grow hungry, thirsty, hot, tired, excited, sleepy. They suffer injury and lick their wounds. Here we are quite convinced that value is nonanthropogenic, to say nothing of anthropocentric.

These wild animals defend their own lives because they have a good of their own. There is somebody there behind the fur or feathers. Our gaze is returned by an animal that itself has a concerned outlook. Here is value right before our eyes, right behind those eyes. Animals are valuable, able to value things in their world. But we may still want to say that value exists only where a subject has an object of interest. Callicott modifies his position and says that value is not always "anthropogenic"; it may sometimes be "vertebragenic, since nonhuman animals, all vertebrates at the very least, are conscious and therefore may be said, in the widest sense of the term, to value things" (1992, pp. 132, 138).[1]

Well, that's a help, since at least the fellow vertebrates share in our ability to value things. They value things instrumentally, no doubt, since they seek other animals, plants, and insects for food. They value water to drink, dens for shelter, and so on.

Do they value anything intrinsically? Callicott does not address this question, but perhaps he would say (and I would agree) that a vertebrate animal values its own life intrinsically. The deer defends its life as a good of its own. Such life is valued without further contributory reference, even if wolves in turn make use of deer for food. Perhaps the mother wolf can value her young intrinsically, since she puts herself at risk to bear young. Perhaps, unawares, she values the ongoing species line.

Nevertheless, for both Singer and Callicott, when we run out of psychological experience, value is over. Callicott's vertebragenic value still leaves most of the world valueless, since the vertebrates are only about 4 percent of the described species. Indeed, since the numbers of individuals in vertebrate species is typically much lower than the numbers of individuals in invertebrate or plant species, real valuers form only some minuscule fraction of the living organisms on Earth. Nearly everything on Earth is still quite valueless, unless and until these humans come along and place intrinsic value there. As Callicott insists, until humans do this, "there simply is no inherent or intrinsic value in nature" (1989, p. 160). Singer is more generous than Callicott to the invertebrates. Still he claims that we must stop "somewhere between a shrimp and an oyster" (1990, p. 174). Beyond that, he insists, "there is nothing to be taken into account" (1990, p. 8). With Singer, too, most of the biological world has yet to be taken into account.

Moving any further is impossible on a sentience-based theory. Value, like a tickle or remorse, must be felt to be there. Its *esse* is *percipi*. Nonsensed value is nonsense. Only beings with "insides" to them have value. There is no unexperienced value, no value without an experiencing valuer. According to the classical paradigm, so long dominant that to Norton and Callicott it seems elementary, there is no value without an experiencing valuer, just as there are no thoughts without a thinker, no percepts without a perceiver, no deeds without a doer, no targets without an aimer. Valuing is felt preferring by human choosers. Extending this paradigm, sentient animals may also value. Nothing else.

But the problem with the "no value without a valuer" axiom is that it is too subjectivist; it looks for some center of value located in a subjective self. And we nowhere wish to deny that such valuers are sufficient for value. But that is not the whole account of value. Perhaps there can be no doing science without a scientist, no religion without a believer, no tickle without somebody tickled. But there can be law without a lawgiver, history without a historian; there is biology without biologists, physics without physicists, creativity without creators, achievement without conscious achievers—and value without experiencing valuers.

A sentient valuer is not necessary for value. Another way is for there to be a value-generating system able to generate value, such as a plant or a genome. If you like, that is another meaning of value-er; any *x* is a valuer if *x* is value-able, able to produce values.

No, comes the protest, naturalizing value has to be kept close into our human embodiment. We simply do not have the cognitive capacities to know all this about other valuers out there. Metaphysics, epistemology, and ethics can and ought to be naturalized, but that does not mean there are any metaphysicians, epistemologists, or ethicists among the dragonflies, the bacteria, or the plants; we only mean that when humans do these activities, they do so using their naturally evolved capacities. Similarly with axiology, which can and ought to be naturalized, that is interpreted in terms of our naturally evolved capacities. But there are no philosophical axiologists in wild nature, any more than there are metaphysicians, epistemologists, or ethicists.

Maybe we can extend feelings into the higher animals, because evolution does teach their kinship with us. So vertebragenic axiology is a possibility. We can and ought to defer to animals who are close enough kin to us to share some of our cognitive and perceptual abilities. Beyond that, value is over.

Social philosophers are likely to be quite sure about this, and quite uncomfortable with the idea of natural values apart from human persons in their society. Milton Rokeach defines a value this way: "I consider a value to be a type of belief, centrally located within one's belief system, about how one ought or ought not to behave, or about some end-state of existence worth or not worth obtaining." These belief systems are culturally constructed and transmitted; they are personally endorsed, enjoyed, and critiqued. Values have to be thought about, chosen from among options, persistently held, and to satisfy felt preferences (Rokeach, 1968, p. 124). If so, ipso facto, there are none in mere organisms which have no such capacities. So much for the dragonflies and their wings, sand dollars, plants with their leaf stomata, bacteria with their clocks, and those genomes getting ready for evolution.

4. ORGANISMS AND THEIR BIOCENTRIC VALUES

Maybe the problem is that we have let ourselves get imprisoned in our own felt experiences. There is an epistemological problem, but look at it another way. We do have blinders on, psychological and philosophical blinders, that leave us unable to detect anything but experientially based valuers and their felt values. So we are unable to accept a biologically based value account that is otherwise staring us in the face. Let's take another look at organisms and their biocentric values, focusing on plants, to make sure we are not hoping for minimal neural experience.

A plant is not an experiencing subject, but neither is it an inanimate object, like a stone. Nor is it a geomorphological process, like a river. Plants are quite alive. Plants, like all other organisms, are self-actualizing. Plants are unified entities of the botanical though not of the zoological kind; that is, they are not unitary organisms highly integrated with centered neural control, but they are modular organisms, with a meristem that can repeatedly and indefinitely produce new vegetative modules, additional stem nodes, and leaves when there is available space and resources, as well as new reproductive modules, fruits, and seeds.

Plants repair injuries and move water, nutrients, and photosynthate from cell to cell; they store sugars; they make tannin and other toxins and regulate their levels in defense against grazers; they make nectars and emit pheromones to influence the behavior of pollinating insects and the responses of other plants; they emit allelopathic agents to suppress invaders; they make thorns, trap insects, and so on. They can reject genetically incompatible grafts. They have engineered those remarkable stomata.

A plant is a spontaneous, self-maintaining system, sustaining and reproducing itself, executing its program, making a way through the world, checking against performance by means of responsive capacities with which to measure success. Something more than merely physical causes, even when less than sentience, is operating within every organism. There is *information* superintending the causes; without it the organism would collapse into a sand heap. The information is used to preserve the plant identity. This information is recorded in the genes, and such information, unlike matter and energy, can be created and destroyed. That is what worries environmentalists about extinction, for example. In such information lies the secret of life.

Values are like color, the traditionalists say. Both arise in interaction. Trees are no more valuable than they are green on their own. This account seems plausible if one is asking about certain kinds of values, such as the fall colors we enjoy. But consider rather the information that makes photosynthesis possible. Photosynthesis is rather more objective than greenness. What is good for a tree (nitrogen, carbon dioxide, water) is observer-independent. But is not the good of the tree (whether it is injured or healthy) equally observer-independent? The tree's coping based on DNA coding is quite objective (even if, no doubt, there is some observer construction in the theories and instruments by which all this is known). The sequoia tree has, after all, been there two thousand years, whether or not any green-experiencing humans were around. *Sequoia sempervirens*, the species line, has been around several million years, with each of its individual sequoia trees defending a good of their kind.

The tree is value-able ("able-to-value") itself. If we cannot say this, then we will have to ask, as an open question, "Well, the tree has a good of its own, but is there anything of value to it?" "This tree was injured when the elk rubbed its velvet off its antlers, and the tannin secreted there is killing the invading bacteria. But is this valuable to the tree?" Botanists say that the tree is irritable in the biological sense; it responds with the repair of injury. Such capacities can be "vital." These are observations of value in nature with just as much certainty as they are biological facts; that is what they are: facts about value relationships in nature.

We are really quite certain that organisms use their resources, and one is overinstructed in philosophy who denies that such resources are of value to organisms instrumentally. But then, why is the tree not defending its own life just as much fact of the matter as its use of nitrogen and photosynthesis to do so?

But nothing "matters" to a tree; a plant is without minimally sentient awareness—so Callicott, Norton, and Singer protest. By contrast, things do matter to a vertebrate. True, things do not matter *to* trees; still, a great deal matters *for* them. We ask, of a failing tree, What's the matter *with* that tree? If it is lacking sunshine and soil nutrients, and we arrange for these, we say, the tree is benefiting from them; and *benefit* is—everywhere else we encounter it—a value word. Every organism has a *good-of-its-kind;* it defends its own kind as a *good kind.* In this sense, the genome is a set of conservation molecules. To say that the plant has a good of its own seems the plain fact of the matter. The flexible wings did "matter" to the Carboniferous dragonflies. Being prepared for rapid evolution under stress does "matter" to species lines. Biologists regularly speak of the "selective value" or "adaptive value" of genetic variations (Ayala, 1982, p. 88; Tamarin, 1996, p. 558). Plant activities have "survival value," such as the seeds they disperse or the thorns they make.

Natural selection picks out whatever traits an organism has that are valuable to it, relative to its survival. When natural selection has been at work gathering these traits into an organism, that organism is able to value on the basis of those traits. It is a valuing organism, even if the organism is not a sentient valuer, much less a vertebrate, much less a human evaluator. And those traits, though picked out by natural selection, are innate in the organism.

It is difficult to dissociate the idea of value from natural selection.

Any sentigenic, psychogenic, vertebragenic, or anthropogenic theory of value has got to argue away all such natural selection as not dealing with "real" value at all, but mere function. Those arguments are, in the end, more likely to be stipulations than real arguments. If you stipulate that valuing must be felt valuing, that there must be some subject of a life, then trees are not able to value, their leaves and thorns are no good to them, and that is so by your definition. But we wish to examine whether that definition, faced with the facts of biology, is plausible. The sentientist definition covers correctly but narrowly certain kinds of higher animal valuing—namely, that done by humans and their vertebrate relatives—and omits all the rest.

5. SMART GENES, INTELLIGENT SPECIES

These organisms are found in species lines, and next we must evaluate species lines and the genetic creativity that makes speciation possible. As noticed earlier, contemporary geneticists are insisting that thinking of this process as being entirely "blind" misperceives it.[2] Genes have substantial solution-generating capacities. Though not deliberated in the conscious sense, the process is cognitive, somewhat like computers, which, likewise without felt experience, can run problem-solving programs. For these genes in organisms, much is vital, as nothing is in a computer. The genome, getting ready to evolve, has a vast array of sophisticated enzymes to cut, splice, digest, rearrange, mutate, reiterate, edit, correct, translocate, invert, and truncate particular gene sequences. There is much redundancy (multiple and variant copies of a gene in multigene families) that shields the species from accidental loss of a beneficial gene, provides flexibility—both overlapping backup and unique detail—on which these enzymes can work.

John H. Campbell, a molecular geneticist, writes, "Cells are richly provided with special enzymes to tamper with DNA structure," enzymes that biologists are extracting and using for genetic engineering. But this "engineering" is already going on in spontaneous nature:

> Gene-processing enzymes also engineer comparable changes in genes in vivo.... We have discovered enzymes and enzyme pathways for almost every conceivable change in the structure of genes. The scope for self-engineering of multigene families seems to be limited only by the ingenuity of control systems for regulating these pathways. (1983, pp. 408–409)

These pathways may have "governors" that are "extraordinarily sophisticated." "Self-governed genes are 'smart' machines in the current vernacular sense. Smart genes suggest smart cells and smart evolution. It is the promise of radically new genetic and evolutionary principles that are motivating today's study..." (1983, p. 410, 414).

In a study of whether species as historical lines can be considered "intelligent," Jonathan Schull concludes:

> Plant and animal species are information-processing entities of such complexity, integration, and adaptive competence that it may be scientifically fruitful to consider them intelligent.... Plant and animal species process information via multiple nested levels of variation and selection in a manner that is surprisingly similar to what must go on in intelligent animals. As biological entities, and as processors of information, plant and animal species are no less complicated than, say, monkeys. Their adaptive achievements (the brilliant design and exquisite production of biological organisms) are no less impressive, and certainly rival those of the animal and electronic systems to which the term

"intelligence" is routinely (and perhaps validly) applied today. (1990, p. 63)

Analogies with artificial intelligence in computers are particularly striking. Such cognitive processing is not conscious, but that does not mean it is not intelligent, where there are clever means of problem solving in a phyletic lineage. Schull continues:

> Gene pools in evolving populations acquire, store, transmit, transform, and use vast amounts of fitness-relative information.... The information-processing capacities of these massively parallel distributed processing systems surpasses that of even the most sophisticated man-made systems.... It seems likely that an evolving species is a better simulation of "real" intelligence than even the best computer program likely to be produced by cognitive scientists for many years. (1990, pp. 64, 74)

The result, according to David S. Thaler, is "the evolution of genetic intelligence" (1994). So it seems that if we recognize that there are smart computers, we must also recognize that there are even smarter genes. Smarter, and more vital.

Leslie E. Orgel, summarizing the origin of life on Earth, says "Life emerged only after self-reproducing molecules appeared.... Such molecules yielded a biology based on ribonucleic acids. The RNA system then invented proteins. As the RNA system evolved, proteins became the main workers in cells, and DNA became the prime repository of genetic information." "The emergence of catalytic RNA was a crucial early step" (1994, p. 4). That is interesting, because here is "a crucial early step" among Callicott's mere "impassive phenomena."

Not only does such problem solving take place early on, and continuously thereafter, but the genes, over the millennia, get better at it. Past achievements are recapitulated in the present, with variations; and these results get tested today and then folded into the future. Christopher Wills concludes,

There is an accumulated wisdom of the genes that actually makes them better at evolving (and sometimes makes them better at not evolving) than were the genes of our distant ancestors.... This wisdom consists both of the ways that genes have become organized in the course of evolution and the ways in which the factors that change the genes have actually become better at their task. (1989, pp. 6–8)

At least we seem to be getting better and better impassive phenomena.

Donald J. Cram, accepting the Nobel prize for his work deciphering how complex and unique biological molecules recognize each other and interlock, concludes: "Few scientists acquainted with the chemistry of biological systems at the molecular level can avoid being inspired. Evolution has produced chemical compounds that are exquisitely organized to accomplish the most complicated and delicate of tasks." Organic chemists can hardly "dream of designing and synthesizing" such "marvels" (1988, p. 760). Marvels they may be, but not until we get there, Norton must say, and experience their "transformative value."

Talk of a genetic "strategy" has become commonplace among biologists, not thereby implying consciousness, but strongly suggesting a problem-solving skill. A marine snail has evolved a "strategy for rapid immobilization of prey" and can "capture prey with remarkable efficiency and speed" (Teriau et al., 1998). Well, maybe "strategy" is a metaphor, but what the facts that underlie the metaphor still force is the question whether these snails "know how" to capture the fish they catch. And this is only one instance of information pervasively present as needed for an organism's competence in its ecological niche. All biology is cybernetic; the information storage in DNA, the know-how for life, is the principal difference between biology and chemistry or physics.

Is a philosopher still going to insist: Well, all this inventiveness, strategy, remarkable efficiency, wisdom of the genes, exquisite organization to accomplish delicate tasks, and crucial discoveries in evolution to the contrary, there is nothing of value here? Maybe it is time to face up to a crisis?

6. AN EPISTEMIC CRISIS? AN AXIOLOGICAL CRISIS?

The cell biologists, we were saying, have been finding something "wonderful" in genome strategies, but it did seem that this was only "wonderful" when cell biologists got there to wonder about it. Or at least that nothing was "astounding" until a human being came around to be astounded. We do not think that the genomes have a sense of wonder or are astounded. Still, the biological achievements are there long before we get let in on them. Facing up to these facts, which are quite as certain as that we humans are valuers in the world, it can seem "astounding" arrogance to say that, in our ignorance of these events, before we arrived there was nothing of value there.

No, my critics will reply. Rolston has not yet faced up to his epistemological naiveté; he persists in his ontological realism, unaware of how contemporary philosophy has made any scientific knowing of any objective nature out there impossible, much less any realism about natural values. Rolston needs to get his Cartesian epistemology and metaphysics naturalized. He will have to realize how scientists are exporting human experiences and overlaying nature with them when they set up these frameworks of understanding. We need to recognize the metaphors we are projecting onto nature— not so much to strip them all away and see nature without metaphor, as to realize that all of our knowing of nature is metaphorical. That will take care of his plant "dilemmas," of things that "matter" to plants, of genome "engineering," and dragonfly "strategies." Whatever values Rolston is finding in nature are being projected there by these metaphors. He is not naturalizing values at all.

I agree that sometimes we do need to strip off the metaphors that scientists may use. When the comet Shoemaker-Levy crashed into Jupiter in July 1994, astronomers watched with interest; some of them even got ecstatic about the size of the explosive impact. Was this event of any value, or disvalue? Let us grant that nothing matters to Jupiter, nothing matters on Jupiter. The swirls in the planetary winds were disrupted by this outside comet crashing in, but the fierce winds soon mixed up the debris and the flow patterns, after about a month, returned to their pre-impact formations, the effect of the gigantic impact fading. A headline in *Science* put it this way: "A Giant Licks Its Wounds" (Kerr, 1994). John Horgan in *Scientific American* noted that scientists were interested in watching "how bruises left by Shoemaker-Levy disperse" (Horgan, 1994). "Wounds" and "bruises" are only journalistic metaphor, even in science journals, when applied to Jupiter. The excited scientists were observing impassive phenomena.

But what do we say when a wolf, injured in a territorial fight, licks its wounds and limps from a bruised leg? Is that still journalistic metaphor? Or that the elk, rubbing the velvet off its antlers, has "bruised" the tree, and that the tannin is secreted to protect this "injury"? Hard-nosed functionalists can no doubt strip away ideas such as "getting ready," "being prepared," also words such as "engineer" and "information," if such words require conscious deliberation. But even after this stripping down, there remains something here that demands value language. Maybe you can sanitize the language if you have strong enough detergent. But you well may be washing out something important that is going on. In a Darwinian world, where survival is ever at stake, the question of value has a way of dirtying up the cleanest humanistic value theory.

We philosophers may protest that we know how to use words with precision, and scientists can be rather careless with them. That is what has dirtied up otherwise perfectly good value theory. Though unsophisticated biologists have used "value" regarding plants, careful analysis will put that kind of "value" in scare quotes. This so-called value is not a value, really, not one of interest to philosophers because it is not a value with interest in itself. Even if we found such interest-taking value, as we do in the higher animals, we humans would still have to evaluate any such animal values before we knew whether any "real" values were present.

True, the female wolf takes an interest in the deer she slays and the pups she feeds. So one can say, biologically speaking, that she values the deer and her pups. But we do not yet know whether there is any "philosophical" value here. There could in fact be disvalue—a big bad killer wolf, rearing more such killers in the world. Jack the Ripper was a good killer, good of his kind, but a very bad person in the world. We humans have to evaluate what is going on out there, before we can say whether there is any positive value there.

Otherwise we will commit the naturalistic fallacy. We find what biologically *is* in nature and conclude that something valuable is there, something which we may say we *ought* to protect. Considered as normative organismic systems organisms might have goods of their kind and still they might be bad kinds taken for what they are in themselves, or considered in the roles they play. There is a radical gap between finding that these organisms and species have goods of their kinds and in concluding, in a philosophical worldview, that these are good kinds. The gap is between finding animals and plants that have values defended on their own, a biological description, and finding that these animals and plants have intrinsic value worthy of philosophical consideration, which ought to be preserved. That latter step requires philosophical analysis past any biological description.

Man is the measure of things, said Protagoras. Humans are the measurers, the valuers of things, even when we measure what they are in themselves. So humans are the only evaluators who can reflect about what is going on at this global scale, who can deliberate about what they ought to do conserving it. When humans do this, they must set up the scales; and humans are the measurers of things. Animals, organisms, species, ecosystems, Earth cannot teach us how to do this evaluating. Perhaps not, but still they can and do display what it is that is to be evaluated. The axiological scales we construct do not constitute the value any more than the scientific scales we erect create what we thereby measure.

What are we evaluating? Among much else, we are appraising organisms in species lines with their adaptive fits. In this evaluation, we do consider our options, and adopt attitudes toward nature with conscious reflection (such as whether we choose and why to save endangered species) that may result in the values we humans choose. But in the biological world which we have under consideration, such capacities drop out. The plants and animals are not so capable. But that does not mean that value disappears, only that it shifts to the biological level.

An organism cannot survive without situated environmental fitness. There organisms do mostly unconsciously (and sometimes consciously) defend their lives and their kinds. Might they be bad kinds? The cautious philosophical critic will say that, even though an organism evolves to have a situated environmental fitness, not all such situations are necessarily good arrangements; some can be clumsy or bad. They could involve bad organisms in bad evolutionary patterns—perhaps those efficient and venomous snails, destroying those fish, or dragonflies so efficient in flight that they devastate their prey and upset previously stable ecosystems. Perhaps, at times. But with rare exceptions, organisms are well adapted to the niches they fill, and remain so as the co-evolutionary process goes on. By natural selection their ecosystemic roles must mesh with the kinds of goods to which they are genetically programmed. At least we ought to put the burden of proof on a human evaluator to say why any natural kind is a bad kind and ought not to call forth admiring respect.

The world is a field of the contest of values. We can hardly deny that, even if we suppose that those are bad snails killing those fish, or that pest insects come along, eat plant leaves, and capture the stored energy that plants would have otherwise used to preserve their own good kinds. When we recognize how the ecosystem is a perpetual contest of goods in dialectic and exchange, it will become difficult to say that all or even any of the organisms in it are bad kinds, ill-situated in their niches. The misfits are extinct, or soon will be. Rather it seems that many of them, maybe even all of them, will have to be respected for the skills and achievements by which they survive over the millennia. At least we will have to recognize the possibility of intrinsic value in nature, and it will seem arrogant to retreat into a human-centered environmental ethics. This is true no matter how much the anti-foundationalists and the anti-realists protest that we humans cannot know enough about what these animals and plants are like in themselves to escape our own blinders.

Does it not rather seem that when we are describing what benefits the dragonflies or the snails, the plants with their leaf stomata, or the bacteria with their clocks, such value is pretty much fact of the matter. If we refuse to recognize such values as objectively there, have we committed some fallacy? Rather, the danger is the other way round. We commit the subjectivist fallacy if we think all values lie in subjective experience, and, worse still, the anthropocentrist fallacy if we think all values lie in human options and preferences. These plants and animals do not make man the measure of things at all.

Humans are not so much lighting up value in a merely potentially valuable world, as they are psychologically joining ongoing planetary natural history in which there is value wherever there is positive creativity. While such creativity can be present in subjects with their interests and preferences, it can also be present objectively in living organisms with their lives defended, and in species that defend an identity over time, and in systems that are self-organizing and that project storied achievements. The valuing human subject in an otherwise valueless world is an insufficient premise for the experienced conclusions of those who value natural history.

Conversion to a biological and geological view seems truer to world experience and more logically compelling. This too is a perspective, but ecologically better informed; we know our place on a home planet, which is not only our home but that for five or ten million other species. From this more objective viewpoint, there is something subjective, something philosophically naive, and even something hazardous in a time of ecological crisis, about living in a reference frame where one species takes itself as absolute and values every thing else in nature relative to its potential to produce value for itself.

NOTES

1. Callicott recognized this possibility from the start, despite his insistence that humans project all the value present in nature (1989, p. 26).

2. See further analysis and sources in Rolston, 1999, pp. 23–37.

REFERENCES

Abbas, Abul K., Andrew H. Lichtman, and Jordan S. Pober. 1991. *Cellular and Molecular Immunology*. Philadelphia: W. B. Saunders.

Ayala, Francisco J. 1982. *Population and Evolutionary Genetics: A Primer*. Menlo Park, CA: Benjamin/Cummings.

Barinaga, Marcia. 1998. "New Timepiece Has a Familiar Ring," *Science* 281 (4 September): 1429–1431.

Callicott, J. Baird. 1984. "Non-anthropocentric Value Theory and Environmental Ethics," *American Philosophical Quarterly* 21: 299–309.

——— 1989. *In Defense of the Land Ethic*. Albany, NY: State University of New York Press.

——— 1992. "Rolston on Intrinsic Value: A Deconstruction," *Environmental Ethics* 14: 129–143.

Campbell, John H. 1983. "Evolving Concepts of Multigene Families," *Isozymes: Current Topics in Biological and Medical Research, Volume 10: Genetics and Evolution*, 401–417.

Cram, Donald J. 1988. "The Design of Molecular Hosts, Guests, and Their Complexes," *Science* 240 (6 May): 760–767.

Grill, Erwin, and Hubert Ziegler. 1998. "A Plant's Dilemma," *Science* 282 (9 October): 252–254.

Horgan, John. 1994. "By Jove!" *Scientific American* 271 (no. 4, October): 16–20.

Kerr, Richard A. 1994. "A Giant Licks Its Wounds," *Science* 266 (7 October): 31.

Norton, Bryan G. 1987. *Why Preserve Natural Variety?* Princeton, NJ: Princeton University Press.

——— 1991. *Toward Unity Among Environmentalists*. New York: Oxford University Press.

——— 1992. "Epistemology and Environmental Values," *The Monist* 75: 208–226.

Orgel, Leslie E. 1994. "The Origin of Life on the Earth," *Scientific American* 271 (no. 4, October): 76–83 and abstract p. 4.

Pennisi, Elizabeth. 1998. "How the Genome Readies Itself for Evolution," *Science* 281 (21 August): 1131–1134.

Rokeach, Milton. 1968. *Beliefs, Attitudes, and Values*. San Francisco: Jossey-Bass.

Rolston, Holmes, III. 1999. *Genes, Genesis, and God*. New York: Cambridge University Press.

Schull, Jonathan. 1990. "Are Species Intelligent?" *Behavioral and Brain Sciences* 13: 63–75.

Singer, Peter. 1990. *Animal Liberation*, 2nd ed. New York: New York Review Book.

Tamarin, Robert H. 1996. *Principles of Genetics*, 5th ed. Dubuque, IA: William C. Brown.

Teriau, Heinrich, et al. 1998. "Strategy for Rapid Immobilization of Prey by a Fish-hunting Marine Snail," *Nature* 381 (9 May): 148–151.

Thaler, David S. 1994. "The Evolution of Genetic Intelligence," *Science* 264 (8 April): 224–225.

Tizard, Ian R. 1992. *Immunology: An Introduction*, 3rd ed. Fort Worth, TX: Saunders College Publishing.

Vogel, Gretchen. 1998. "Insect Wings Point to Early Sophistication," *Science* 282 (23 October): 599–601.

Wills, Christopher. 1989. *The Wisdom of the Genes: New Pathways in Evolution*. New York: Basic Books.

Wootton, R. J., J. Kuikalová, D. J. S. Newman, and J. Muzón. 1998. "Smart Engineering in the MidCarboniferous: How Well Could Palaeozoic Dragonflies Fly?" *Science* 282 (23 October): 749–751.

STUDY QUESTIONS

1. What does Rolston mean by *naturalizing value?* How does he make a case for this thesis?

2. What is Rolston's objection to subjectivism in values, the idea that all values arise by sentient beings' valuing objects? In another place he calls this the refrigerator-light theory of values. The refrigerator light does not come on until someone opens the door. Similarly, the subjectivist says that values come into existence only when humans or conscious valuers value states of affairs.

3. Discuss the arguments for and against the thesis that nature has objective value—that is, it has value whether or not conscious beings value nature.

11

Comments on Holmes Rolston's "Naturalizing Values"

NED HETTINGER

Ned Hettinger is professor of philosophy at the College of Charleston and author of several works in environmental ethics.

Holmes Rolston has been forcefully defending the value of nature for over twenty-five years. He does so again here today with his characteristic mix of deep biological and philosophical insight. It is a pleasure to help us think about the ideas and arguments of this most able philosophical defender of nature.

Professor Rolston has argued that much natural value is nonanthropocentric; that is, that nature is valuable independently of its use to humans. Humans valuing nature as an end and not simply as a means is an example of such nonanthropocentric value. For instance, people who value the existence of the Arctic National Wildlife Refuge—even though they have no intentions of ever visiting it— value the Refuge for reasons other than its utility to them. Such noninstrumental valuing of nature, though not anthropocentric, is nonetheless *anthropogenic.* Rolston argues that much natural value is also not generated by humans and that it is not dependent on humans in any way. Nature's usefulness to nonhuman sentient animals clearly illustrates these human-independent values. Deer are instrumentally valuable to wolves, whether or not these animals

---

"A Response to Holmes Rolston III," © 1998 Ned Hettinger, was first delivered at the North American Society for Social Philosophy in Washington, D.C., in December 1998, and appears here. It appeared in the previous edition of this work for the first time. It is reprinted by permission of the author.

benefit humans or are noninstrumentally valued by them.

Sentient animals may also demonstrate another of Rolston's claims: that there is nonanthropogenic *intrinsic value* in nature. I don't know whether a mother wolf can intrinsically value her young as Rolston suggests; wolves may not have the cognitive equipment such judgments of value about others may require. Nevertheless, wolves would seem to value the experience of pleasure in their lives, immediately and for itself. The presence of such intrinsic valuing in nonhuman nature has nothing to do with human utility or valuing.

Rolston's defense of natural value independent of humans goes well beyond the existence of instrumental value for *sentient* animals or their possible intrinsic valuings. Rolston argues that instrumental value permeates the biological world. The dragonfly's wings are useful to it, and sunlight, carbon dioxide, and water are instrumentally valuable for plants, even though these organisms do not take a conscious interest in what benefits them. I think Rolston is right that only a philosopher in the grip of a theory would deny that there are instrumental goods for all living beings, including insentient ones. Rolston suggests that biological descriptions about what is good for organisms are factual statements about values in the natural world. Here, he suggests, there is no gap between facts and values. Biological description alone, however, will not allow us to conclude that water is good for plants in a way that oil is not also good for machines. As Rolston knows, we need an argument to show that what is good for machines is only good because machines are useful to humans, while living beings have goods of their own that do not require such further contributory reference.

Rolston also argues that human-independent natural value exists in species and ecosystems, because they too are the beneficiaries of instrumental value. Particular genes are good or bad for species and certain species are beneficial or destructive for self-organizing natural systems. Rolston avoids the potentially problematic position that value is everywhere in nature, theorizing instead that value is present wherever there is positive creativity. Thus, nothing matters on Jupiter; which is to say, I think, that there is no value there, because there is not enough "positive creativity" in the processes of that planet. Rolston has said similar things about the lack of value of clouds and dust devils here on Earth. But he has also suggested that some *abiotic* features of the earth are remarkable, valuable achievements that ought to call forth our admiring respect. Work remains in explaining why, for example, building roads to the top of fourteen-thousand-foot mountains destroys value in these geological marvels, while nothing humans could do to Jupiter would destroy any value there.

Rolston is known for his defense of "objective" value in nature, and we again get such a defense today. By "objective value," I mean value that is not dependent on a valuing subject. Rolston rejects the psychological account of value that allows value only where there are mental states. Value on this subjectivist view is conscious valuing. Rolston points out that instrumental goods for insentient organisms are clear examples of nonpsychological, objective values in nature. Insentient organisms are not subjects; they have no experiential life and thus do not consciously value anything; yet much is good or bad for them. Such biological goods strongly support objectivism about value.

Interestingly, when Rolston finds value in nature, he tends to posit some valuing of that value. He suggests, for example, that because water is good for trees, trees value water, though they obviously do not do so consciously or psychologically. Thus, Rolston rejects that value requires a *conscious* valuer, but he clings to the idea that value requires a valuer of some sort. I suggest he drop this second connection as well. Once we reject a mental state theory of value, we'd do better to drop the assumed necessary connection between value and valuing entirely. Claiming that insentient organisms are valuing entities stretches our concept of valuing in a way that is not helpful, nor needed. That something is good for a being does not imply that the being values it. A suicidal person may not value food, but the food is nonetheless good for her. A vegetarian-fed cat may have a vitamin deficiency but not value the supplements she needs. Why think a tree needs to value water in order for water to be good for it?

Rolston argues for both objective instrumental and objective intrinsic value in nature. The pleasures of sentient animals mentioned above demonstrate only *subjective* intrinsic value or intrinsic *valuing* in nature, not objective intrinsic value. On one standard view of the relation between instrumental and intrinsic values, we can infer the existence of intrinsic goods from the instrumental goods of insentient organisms. If instrumental goods are good only insofar as they are a means to some other good, and if we rule out an endless series or loop of instrumental values (as some pragmatists would allow), then objective instrumental goods for insentient organisms entail the existence of objective intrinsic goods. If water is instrumentally good for trees without further contributory reference, then the flourishing of trees must be good-in-itself.

The question remains, however, whether we humans should value such goods and additionally whether we have obligations to morally consider them. That some being has a good of its own or that some entity is flourishing does not automatically mean we should value that good or flourishing. That bureaucracies are flourishing does not require us to approve of this situation, and, as Rolston suggests, the happiness of Jack the Ripper is not a good we ought to value. I agree with Rolston, however, that the burden is very much on those who suggest that the goods of natural organisms, species, and ecosystems are *bad* goods of this sort. Unless there is some consideration to the contrary, that something is flourishing or has a good of its own presents a prima facie reason for valuing it. There remains, however, the further question about our obligation to promote some acknowledged good. Some theories of right action do not connect obligation with promotion of the good. Some account is needed as to why we humans ought to preserve, protect, and restore these goods in nonhuman nature. Here and elsewhere, Rolston's compelling descriptions of the remarkable characteristics of natural organisms and systems and the story he tells about humans' place in nature goes a long way to providing such an account.

One of the most intuitively powerful arguments Rolston presents for nonanthropogenic value in nature is that it is arrogant to think that for hundreds of millions of years flourishing nature on Earth was actually valueless and then became valuable when humans arrived to bestow value on it. If all value depends on conscious human valuing,

Rolston suggests we would not be able to say that the earth in the age of the early dragonflies was of any *actual* value. And this is something that most of us want to say. However, those who think all value is a function of valuing subjects argue that they can say this. Even if humans are the source of all value that does not preclude humans from assigning value to a world where they do not exist. Subjectivists argue that because humans are here now and intrinsically value those earlier epochs, we can truthfully say that the world of the dragonflies was valuable back then. There is no requirement that the valued thing be contemporaneous with the valuer.

Still, a subjectivist's account of value might seem committed to the view that a world in which valuers never exist is one in which the flourishing earth is *never* valued and thus lacks actual value. To use Rolston's analogy, the refrigerator door in such a world will never be opened, and thus the light of value will never shine on the flourishing earth in that world. However, an ideal observer version of subjectivism about value seems able to handle this problem. If what is of value is what ideal observers would value, and if we assume that such ideal valuers would find the flourishing nonhuman earth valuable, then the actual value of the earth is guaranteed even if humans or other real valuers never arrive on the scene. On this version of subjectivism, the possibility of such idealized valuers is sufficient to actualize value. Thus, I think a version of subjectivism can avoid this problem Rolston has identified.

Finally, I'd like to consider Rolston's suggestion that there is "something hazardous in a time of ecological crisis" about theories of natural value that do no find values in nature but rather in the human response to nature. Is it important for environmental policy that our theory of nature's value be nonanthropocentric and nonanthropogenic? Although anthropocentric values are of crucial importance in environmental policy, I believe it is dangerous to limit our defense of nature to arguments based on its usefulness to us. This is especially true if what one wants to defend is a wild, autonomous nature. Humans often find a technologically enhanced and controlled nature of most use to them.

I am much less confident that it makes a pragmatic difference whether we view nature's noninstrumental value as objective or as the result of human intrinsic valuing. Is our defense of nature more powerful, compelling, and effective if nature is seen to have intrinsic value on its own, rather than having intrinsic value bestowed on it by humans who value it for its own sake? One worry is that a subjectivist account of nature's value would be open to the charge that we are foisting an idiosyncratic value onto those who don't appreciate nature in this way. But wouldn't the objectivist defender of nature be open to a similar charge that she wants us to act to protect values whose existence others don't acknowledge? I do think that a certain conception of the objective value of nature would allow for a response to a liberal critic

of environmental policies that is not available to subjectivists. For the liberal, liberty-limiting laws are only justifiable when they prevent harm to others or unjust treatment of them. If we conceive of nature as having its own good that we can harm and as a valuable other that we must treat justly, then laws and policies that protect nature will pass the liberal's test for justifiable constraints on human liberty. A subjectivist who claims that we ought to value nature for its own sake will not be able to make the case that those whose actions disregard such values are harming nonhuman others, treating them unjustly, and thus that they may be justifiably constrained from such acts by society.

STUDY QUESTIONS

1. Does Hettinger completely agree with Rolston on the objective value of nature? If not, where does he differ?

2. How, according to Hettinger, could a subjectivist respond to Rolston's theory? A subjectivist on values holds that without conscious valuers, no values exist.

3. What is the difference between value that is anthropocentric and value that is

anthropogenic? Give an example of an anthropogenic value that is not anthropocentric.

4. Explain why Hettinger thinks that a certain account of nature's value as objective can provide a response to a liberal critic of environmental laws that is not possible on a subjectivist account of nature's value. Do you think he is right?

12

Nature

JOHN STUART MILL

John Stuart Mill (1806–1873), one of the most important British philosophers of the nineteenth century, is a founder of utilitarianism (See Peter Singer in Chapter 2). He wrote On Liberty *(1859), one of the classic texts of libertarian-orientated philosophies, as well as* The Subjection of Women *(1861), an impassioned argument for woman's liberation.*

In his essay "Nature" Mill first argues that the term nature is used to mean three different things: (1) the aggregate of objects and processes in the universe; (2) that which is not artificial; and (3) that which ought to be the case, the ethical sense (what is sometimes referred to as "Natural Law"). Mill argues that this third sense is not a valid sense of the word at all. Mill then goes on to criticize those who would emulate nature or see it as the proper model for moral action. He argues that given any crime that humans commit— murder, stealing, harming sentient beings—nature commits it in far greater amounts and with impunity. So we should not copy nature or imitate her but correct and improve her.

Nature, Natural, and the group of words derived from them, or allied to them in etymology, have at all times filled a great place in the thoughts and taken a strong hold on the feelings of mankind. That they should have done so is not surprising, when we consider what the words, in their primitive and most obvious signification, represent; but it is unfortunate that a set of terms which play so great a part in moral and metaphysical speculation should have acquired many meanings different from the primary one, yet sufficiently allied to it to admit of confusion. The words have thus become entangled in so many foreign associations, mostly of a very powerful and tenacious character, that they have come to excite, and to be the symbols of, feelings which their original meaning will by no means justify; and which have made them one of the most copious sources of false taste, false philosophy, false morality, and even bad law....

As the nature of any given thing is the aggregate of its powers and properties, so Nature in the abstract is the aggregate of the powers and properties of all things. Nature means the sum of all phenomena, together with the causes which produce them; including not only all that happens, but all that is capable of happening; the unused capabilities of causes being as much a part of the idea of Nature, as those which take effect. Since all phenomena which have been sufficiently examined are found to take place with regularity, each having certain fixed conditions, positive and negative, on the occurrence of which it invariably happens; mankind have been able to ascertain, either by direct observation or by reasoning processes grounded on it, the conditions of the occurrence of many phenomena; and the progress of science mainly consists in ascertaining those conditions. When discovered they

can be expressed in general propositions, which are called laws of the particular phenomenon, and also, more generally, Laws of Nature. Thus, the truth that all material objects tend towards one another with a force directly as their masses and inversely as the square of their distance, is a law of Nature. The proposition that air and food are necessary to animal life, if it be as we have good reason to believe, true without exception, is also a law of nature, though the phenomenon of which it is the law is special, and not, like gravitation, universal.

Nature, then, in this its simplest acceptation, is a collective name for all facts, actual and possible: or (to speak more accurately) a name for the mode, partly known to us and partly unknown, in which all things take place. For the word suggests, not so much the multitudinous detail of the phenomena, as the conception which might be formed of their manner of existence as a mental whole, by a mind possessing a complete knowledge of them: to which conception it is the aim of science to raise itself, by successive steps of generalization from experience.

Such, then, is a correct definition of the word Nature. But this definition corresponds only to one of the senses of that ambiguous term. It is evidently inapplicable to some of the modes in which the word is familiarly employed. For example, it entirely conflicts with the common form of speech by which Nature is opposed to Art, and natural to artificial. For in the sense of the word Nature which has just been defined, and which is the true scientific sense, Art is as much Nature as anything else; and everything which is artificial is natural—Art has no independent powers of its own: Art is but the employment of the powers of Nature for an end. Phenomena produced by human agency, no less than those which as far as we are concerned are spontaneous, depend on the properties of the elementary forces, or of the elementary substances and their compounds. The united powers of the whole human race could not create a new property of matter in general, or of any one of its species. We can only take advantage for our purposes of the properties which we find. A ship floats by the same laws of specific gravity and equilibrium, as a tree uprooted by the wind and blown into the water. The corn which men raise for food grows and produces its grain by the same laws of vegetation by which the wild rose and the mountain strawberry bring forth their flowers and fruit. A house stands and holds together by the natural properties, the weight and cohesion of the materials which compose it: a steam engine works by the natural expansive force of steam, exerting a pressure upon one part of a system of arrangements, which pressure, by the mechanical properties of the lever, is transferred from that to another part where it raises the weight or removes the obstacle brought into connexion with it. In these and all other artificial operations the office of man is, as has often been remarked, a very limited one; it consists in moving things into certain places. We move objects, and by doing this, bring some things into contact which were separate, or separate others which were in contact: and by this simple change of place, natural forces previously dormant are called into action, and produce the desired effect. Even the volition which designs, the intelligence which contrives, and the muscular force which executes these movements are themselves powers of Nature.

It thus appears that we must recognize at least two principal meanings in the word Nature. In one sense, it means all the powers existing in either the outer or the inner world and everything which takes place by means of those powers. In another sense, it means, not everything which happens, but only what takes place without the agency, or without the voluntary and intentional agency, of man. This distinction is far from exhausting the ambiguities of the word; but it is the key to most of those on which important consequences depend.

Such, then, being the two principal senses of the word Nature; in which of these is it taken, or is

it taken in either, when the word and its derivatives are used to convey ideas of commendation, approval, and even moral obligation?

In the second, it is a name for everything which is of itself, without voluntary human intervention. But the employment of the word Nature as a term of ethics seems to disclose a third meaning, in which Nature does not stand for what is, but for what ought to be; or for the rule or standard of what ought to be. A little consideration, however, will show that this is not a case of ambiguity; there is not here a third sense of the word. Those who set up Nature as a standard of action do not intend a merely verbal proposition; they do not mean that the standard, whatever it be, should be *called* Nature; they think they are giving some information as to what the standard of action really is. Those who say that we ought to act according to Nature do not mean the mere identical proposition that we ought to do what we ought to do. They think that the word Nature affords some external criterion of what we should do; and if they lay down as a rule for what ought to be, a word which in its proper signification denotes what is, they do so because they have a notion, either clearly or confusedly, that what is, constitutes the rule and standard of what ought to be.

The examination of this notion is the object of the present Essay. It is proposed to inquire into the truth of the doctrines which make Nature a test of right and wrong, good and evil, or which in any mode or degree attach merit or approval to following, imitating, or obeying Nature. To this inquiry the foregoing discussion respecting the meaning of terms was an indispensable introduction. Language is as it were the atmosphere of philosophical investigation, which must be made transparent before anything can be seen through it in the true figure and position. In the present case it is necessary to guard against a further ambiguity, which though abundantly obvious has sometimes misled even sagacious minds, and of which it is well to take distinct note before proceeding further. No word is more commonly associated with the word Nature, than Law; and this last word has distinctly two meanings, in one of which it denotes some definite portion of what is, in the other, of what ought to be. We speak of the law of gravitation, the three laws of motion, the law of definite proportions in chemical combination, the vital laws of organized beings. All these are portions of what is. We also speak of the criminal law, the civil law, the law of honour, the law of veracity, the law of justice; all of which are portions of what ought to be, or of somebody's suppositions, feelings, or commands respecting what ought to be. The first kind of laws, such as the laws of motion and of gravitation, are neither more nor less than the observed uniformities in the occurrence of phenomena: partly uniformities of antecedence and sequence, partly of concomitance. These are what, in science, and even in ordinary parlance, are meant by laws of nature. Laws in the other sense are the laws of the land, the law of nations, or moral laws; among which, as already noticed, is dragged in, by jurists and publicists, something which they think proper to call the Law of Nature. Of the liability of these two meanings of the word to be confounded there can be no better example than the first chapter of Montesquieu; where he remarks, that the material world has its laws, the inferior animals have their laws, and man has his laws; and calls attention to the much greater strictness with which the first two sets of laws are observed, than the last; as if it were an inconsistency, and a paradox, that things always are what they are, but men not always what they ought to be…. The conception which the ethical use of the word Nature implies, of a close relation if not absolute identity between what is and what ought to be, certainly derives part of its hold on the mind from the custom of designating what is by the expression "laws of nature," while the same word Law is also used, and even more familiarly and emphatically, to express what ought to be.

When it is asserted, or implied, that Nature, or the laws of Nature, should be conformed to, is the Nature which is meant, Nature in the first sense of the term, meaning all which is—the powers and properties of all things? But in this signification, there is no need of a recommendation to act according to nature, since it is what nobody can possibly help doing, and equally whether he acts well or ill. There is no mode of acting which is not conformable to Nature in this sense of the term, and all modes of acting are so in exactly the same degree. Every action is the exertion of some natural power, and its effects of all sorts are so many phenomena of nature, produced by the powers and properties of some of the objects of nature, in exact obedience to some law or laws of nature. When I voluntarily use my organs to take in food, the act and its consequences take place according to laws of nature: if instead of food I swallow poison, the case is exactly the same. To bid people conform to the laws of nature when they have no power but what the laws of nature give them—when it is a physical impossibility for them to do the smallest thing otherwise than through some law of nature, is an absurdity. The thing they need to be told is what particular law of nature they should make use of in a particular case. When, for example, a person is crossing a river by a narrow bridge to which there is no parapet, he will do well to regulate his proceedings by the laws of equilibrium in moving bodies, instead of conforming only to the law of gravitation, and falling into the river.

Yet, idle as it is to exhort people to do what they cannot avoid doing, and absurd as it is to prescribe as a rule of right conduct what agrees exactly as well with wrong; nevertheless a rational rule of conduct *may* be constructed out of the relation which it ought to bear to the laws of nature in this widest acceptation of the term. Man necessarily obeys the laws of nature, or in other words the properties of things, but he does not necessarily *guide* himself by them…. Though we cannot emancipate ourselves from the laws of nature as a whole, we can escape from any particular law of nature, if we are able to withdraw ourselves from the circumstances in which it acts. Though we can do nothing except through laws of nature, we can use one law to counteract another. According to Bacon's maxim, we can obey nature in such a manner as to command it. Every alteration of circumstances alters more or less the laws of nature under which we act; and by every choice which we make either of ends or of means, we place ourselves to a greater or less extent under one set of laws of nature instead of another. If, therefore, the useless precept to follow nature were changed into a precept to study nature; to know and take heed of the properties of the things we have to deal with, so far as these properties are capable of forwarding or obstructing any given purpose; we should have arrived at the first principle of all intelligent action, or rather at the definition of intelligent action itself. And a confused notion of this true principle, is, I doubt not, in the minds of many of those who set up the unmeaning doctrine which superficially resembles it. They perceive that the essential difference between wise and foolish conduct consists in attending, or not attending, to the particular laws of nature on which some important result depends. And they think, that a person who attends to a law of nature in order to shape his conduct by it, may be said to obey it, while a person who practically disregards it, and acts as if no such law existed, may be said to disobey it: the circumstance being overlooked, that what is thus called disobedience to a law of nature is obedience to some other or perhaps to the very law itself. For example, a person who goes into a powder magazine either not knowing, or carelessly omitting to think of, the explosive force of gunpowder, is likely to do some act which will cause him to be blown to atoms in obedience to the very law which he has disregarded.

…But the maxim of obedience to Nature, or conformity to Nature, is held up not as a simply prudential but as an ethical maxim; and by those who talk of *jus naturæ*, even as a law, fit to be administered by tribunals and enforced by sanctions. Right action, must mean something more and other than merely intelligent action: yet no precept beyond this last, can be connected with the word Nature in the wider and more philosophical of its acceptations. We must try it therefore in the other sense, that in which Nature stands distinguished from Art, and denotes, not the whole course of the phenomena which come under our observation, but only their spontaneous course….

… If the artificial is not better than the natural, to what end are all the arts of life? To dig, to plough, to build, to wear clothes, are direct infringements of the injunction to follow nature.

Accordingly it would be said by every one, even of those most under the influence of the feelings which prompt the injunction, that to apply it to such cases as those just spoken of would be to push it too far. Everybody professes to approve and admire many great triumphs of Art over Nature: the junction by bridges of shores which Nature had made separate, the draining of Nature's marshes, the excavation of her wells, the dragging to light of what she has buried at immense depths in the earth; the turning away of her thunderbolts by lightning rods, of her inundations by embankments, of her ocean by breakwaters. But to commend these and similar feats is to acknowledge that the ways of Nature are to be conquered, not obeyed….

… No one, indeed, asserts it to be the intention of the Creator that the spontaneous order of the creation should not be altered, or even that it should not be altered in any new way. But there still exists a vague notion that though it is very proper to control this or the other natural phenomenon, the general scheme of nature is a model for us to imitate: that with more or less liberty in details, we should on the whole be guided by the spirit and general conception of nature's own ways: that they are God's work, and as such perfect; that man cannot rival their unapproachable excellence, and can best show his skill and piety by attempting, in however imperfect a way, to reproduce their likeness; and that if not the whole, yet some particular parts of the spontaneous order of nature, selected according to the speaker's predilections, are in a peculiar sense, manifestations of the Creator's will….

If this notion of imitating the ways of Providence as manifested in Nature is seldom expressed plainly and downrightly as a maxim of general application, it also is seldom directly contradicted. Those who find it on their path prefer to turn the obstacle rather than to attack it, being often themselves not free from the feeling, and in any case afraid of incurring the charge of impiety by saying anything which might be held to disparage the works of the Creator's power. They therefore, for the most part, rather endeavour to show that they have as much right to the religious argument as their opponents, and that if the course they recommend seems to conflict with some part of the ways of Providence, there is some other part with which it agrees better than what is contended for on the other side. In this mode of dealing with the great *à priori* fallacies, the progress of improvement clears away particular errors while the causes of errors are still left standing, and very little weakened by each conflict: yet by a long series of such partial victories precedents are accumulated, to which an appeal may be made against these powerful pre-possessions, and which afford a growing hope that the misplaced feeling, after having so often learnt to recede, may some day be compelled to an unconditional surrender. For however offensive the proposition may appear to many religious persons, they should be willing to look in the face the undeniable fact, that the order of nature, in so far as unmodified by man, is such as no being, whose attributes are justice and benevolence, would have made, with the intention that his rational creatures should follow it as an example. If made wholly by such a Being, and not partly by beings of very different qualities, it could only be as a designedly imperfect work, which man, in his limited sphere, is to exercise justice and benevolence in amending.

[MILL CONSIDERS THE THESIS THAT WE OUGHT TO IMITATE NATURE]

The best persons have always held it to be the essence of religion, that the paramount duty of man upon earth is to amend himself: but all except monkish quietists have annexed to this in their inmost minds (though seldom willing to enunciate the obligation with the same clearness) the additional religious duty of amending the world, and not solely the human part of it but the material; the order of physical nature.

In considering this subject it is necessary to divest ourselves of certain preconceptions which may justly be called natural prejudices, being grounded on feelings which, in themselves natural and inevitable, intrude into matters with which they ought to have no concern. One of these feelings is the astonishment, rising into awe, which is inspired (even independently of all religious sentiment) by any of the greater natural phenomena. A hurricane; a mountain precipice; the desert; the ocean, either agitated or at rest; the solar system, and the great cosmic forces which hold it together; the boundless firmament, and to an educated mind any single star; excite feelings which make all human enterprises and powers appear so insignificant, that to a mind thus occupied it seems insufferable presumption in so puny a creature as man to look critically on things so far above him, or dare to measure himself against the grandeur of the universe. But a little interrogation of our own consciousness will suffice to convince us, that what makes these phenomena so impressive is simply their vastness. The enormous extension in space and time, or the enormous power they exemplify, constitutes their sublimity; a feeling in all cases, more allied to terror than to any moral emotion. And though the vast scale of these phenomena may well excite wonder, and sets at defiance all idea of rivalry, the feeling it inspires is of a totally different character from admiration of excellence. Those in whom awe produces admiration may be aesthetically developed, but they are morally uncultivated. It is one of the endowments of the imaginative part of our mental nature that conceptions of greatness and power, vividly realized, produce a feeling which though in its higher degrees closely bordering on pain, we prefer to most of what are accounted pleasures. But we are quite equally capable of experiencing this feeling towards maleficent power; and we never experience it so strongly towards most of the powers of the universe, as when we have most present to our consciousness a vivid sense of their capacity of inflicting evil. Because these natural powers have what we cannot imitate, enormous might, and overawe us by that one attribute, it would be a great error to infer that their other attributes are such as we ought to emulate, or that we should be justified in using our small powers after the example which Nature sets us with her vast forces.

For, how stands the fact? That next to the greatness of these cosmic forces, the quality which most forcibly strikes every one who does not avert his eyes from it, is their perfect and absolute recklessness. They go straight to their end, without regarding what or whom they crush on the road. Optimists, in their attempts to prove that "whatever is, is right," are obliged to maintain, not that Nature ever turns one step from her path to avoid trampling us into destruction, but that it would be very unreasonable in us to expect that she should. Pope's "Shall gravitation cease when you go by?" may be a just rebuke to anyone who should be so silly as to expect common human morality from nature. But if the question were between two men, instead of between a man and a natural phenomenon, that triumphant apostrophe would be thought a rare piece of impudence. A man who should persist in hurling stones or firing cannon when another man "goes by," and having killed him should urge a similar plea in exculpation, would very deservedly be found guilty of murder.

In sober truth, nearly all the things for which men are hanged or imprisoned for doing to one another are nature's every day performances. Killing, the most criminal act recognized by human laws, Nature does once to every being that lives; and in a large proportion of cases, after protracted tortures such as only the greatest monsters of whom we read of ever purposely inflicted on their living fellow-creatures. If, by an arbitrary reservation, we refuse to account anything murder but what abridges a certain term supposed to be allotted to human life, nature also does this to all but a small percentage of lives, and does it in all the modes, violent or insidious, in which the worst human beings take the lives of one another. Nature impales men, breaks them as if on the wheel, casts them to be devoured by wild beasts, burns them to death, crushes them with stones like the first Christian martyr, starves them with hunger, freezes them with cold, poisons them by the quick or slow venom of her exhalations, and has hundreds of other hideous deaths in reserve, such as the ingenious cruelty of a Nabis or a Domitian never surpassed. All this, Nature does with the most supercilious disregard both of mercy and of justice, emptying her shafts upon the best and noblest indifferently with the meanest and worst; upon those who are engaged in the highest and worthiest enterprises, and often as the direct consequence of the noblest acts; and it might almost be imagined as a punishment for them. She mows down those

on whose existence hangs the well-being of a whole people, perhaps the prospects of the human race for generations to come, with as little compunction as those whose death is a relief to themselves, or a blessing to those under their noxious influence. Such are Nature's dealings with life. Even when she does not intend to kill, she inflicts the same tortures in apparent wantonness. In the clumsy provision which she has made for that perpetual renewal of animal life, rendered necessary by the prompt termination she puts to it in every individual instance, no human being ever comes into the world but another human being is literally stretched on the rack for hours or days, not unfrequently issuing in death. Next to taking life (equal to it according to a high authority) is taking the means by which we live; and Nature does this too on the largest scale and with the most callous indifference. A single hurricane destroys the hopes of a season; a flight of locusts, or an inundation, desolates a district; a trifling chemical change in an edible root starves a million of people. The waves of the sea, like banditti, seize and appropriate the wealth of the rich and the little all of the poor with the same accompaniments of stripping, wounding, and killing as their human antitypes. Everything in short which the worst men commit either against life or property is perpetrated on a larger scale by natural agents. Nature has Noyades[1] more fatal than those of Carrier; her explosions of fire damp are as destructive as human artillery; her plague and cholera far surpass the poison cups of the Borgias. Even the love of "order" which is thought to be a following of the ways of Nature, is in fact a contradiction of them. All which people are accustomed to deprecate as "disorder" and its consequences is precisely a counterpart of Nature's ways. Anarchy and the Reign of Terror are over-matched in injustice, ruin, and death, by a hurricane and a pestilence.

But, it is said, all these things are for wise and good ends. On this I must first remark that whether they are so or not is altogether beside the point. Supposing it true that contrary to appearances these horrors when perpetrated by Nature promote good ends, still as no one believes that good ends would be promoted by our following the example, the course of Nature cannot be a proper model for us to imitate. Either it is right that we should kill because nature kills; torture because nature tortures; ruin and devastate because nature does the like; or we ought not to consider at all what nature does, but what it is good to do. If there is such a thing as a *reductio ad absurdum*, this surely amounts to one....

NOTE

1. Carrier was a French revolutionary who executed large numbers of prisoners by drowning in 1794. The practice is referred to as Noyades. [Ed.]

STUDY QUESTIONS

1. Do you agree with Mill's assessment that the term *nature* is ambiguous? What are the three meanings he gives? Do you agree with his analysis?

2. Is Mill correct in his analysis of Natural Law? Should we follow nature and imitate her ways?

3. Mill says we should correct nature, not imitate her. How would we go about improving or correcting nature?

4. Compare Mill's views with Rolston's and others who would preserve the wilderness intact.

DEEP ECOLOGY

13

The Shallow and the Deep, Long-Range Ecological Movement

ARNE NAESS

Arne Naess (b.1912) was for many years the head of the philosophy department of the University of Oslo, Norway, and founder of the modern theory of deep ecology.

"Deep ecology" (or "ecosophy" = ecological wisdom) is a movement calling for a deeper questioning and a deeper set of answers to our environmental concerns. Specifically, it calls

Reprinted from *Inquiry*, Vol. 16 (Spring 1973) by permission.

into question some of the major assumptions about consumerism and materialism, challenging us to live more simply. Its motto is "Simple in Means, Rich in Ends." It seeks self-realization through oneness with all things. The following is Naess's now classic summary of his lecture at the 3rd World Future Research Conference, Bucharest, September 3, 1972. Naess included the following abstract:

Ecologically responsible policies are concerned only in part with pollution and resource depletion. There are deeper concerns which touch upon principles of diversity, complexity, autonomy, decentralization, symbiosis, egalitarianism, and classlessness.

The emergence of ecologists from their former relative obscurity marks a turning-point in our scientific communities. But their message is twisted and misused. A shallow, but presently rather powerful movement, and a deep, but less influential movement, compete for our attention. I shall make an effort to characterize the two.

1. The Shallow Ecology movement: Fight against pollution and resource depletion. Central objective: the health and affluence of people in the developed countries.

2. The Deep Ecology movement: (1) Rejection of the man-in-environment image in favour of the *relational, total-field image.* Organisms as knots in the biospherical net or field of intrinsic relations. An intrinsic relation between two things *A* and *B* is such that the relation belongs to the definitions or basic constitutions of *A* and *B*, so that without the relation, *A* and *B* are no longer the same things. The total-field model dissolves not only the man-in-environment concept, but every compact thing-in-milieu concept—except when talking at a superficial or preliminary level of communication.

(2) *Biospherical egalitarianism*—in principle. The "in principle" clause is inserted because any realistic praxis necessitates some killing, exploitation, and suppression. The ecological field-worker acquires a deep-seated respect, or even veneration, for ways and forms of life. He reaches an understanding from within, a kind of understanding that others reserve for fellow men and for a narrow section of ways and forms of life. To the ecological field-worker, *the equal right to live and blossom* is an intuitively clear and obvious value axiom. Its restriction to humans is an anthropocentrism with detrimental effects upon the life quality of humans themselves. This quality depends in part upon the deep pleasure and satisfaction we receive from close partnership with other forms of life. The attempt to ignore our dependence and to establish a master–slave role has contributed to the alienation of man from himself.

Ecological egalitarianism implies the reinterpretation of the future-research variable, "level of crowding," so that *general* mammalian crowding and loss of life-equality is taken seriously, not only human crowding. (Research on the high requirements of free space of certain mammals has, incidentally, suggested that theorists of human urbanism have largely underestimated human life-space requirements. Behavioural crowding symptoms [neuroses, aggressiveness, loss of traditions …] are largely the same among mammals.)

(3) *Principles of diversity and symbiosis.* Diversity enhances the potentialities of survival, the chances of new modes of life, the richness of forms. And the so-called struggle of life, and survival of the fittest, should be interpreted in the sense of ability to co-exist and cooperate in complex relationships, rather than ability to kill, exploit, and suppress. "Live and let live" is a more powerful ecological principle than "Either you or me."

The latter tends to reduce the multiplicity of kinds of forms of life, and also to create destruction within the communities of the same species. Ecologically inspired attitudes therefore favour diversity of human ways of life, of cultures, of occupations, of economies. They support the fight against economic and cultural, as much as military, invasion and domination, and they are opposed to the annihilation of seals and whales as much as to that of human tribes or cultures.

(4) *Anti-class posture*. Diversity of human ways of life is in part due to (intended or unintended) exploitation and suppression on the part of certain groups. The exploiter lives differently from the exploited, but both are adversely affected in their potentialities of self-realization. The principle of diversity does not cover differences due merely to certain attitudes or behaviours forcibly blocked or restrained. The principles of ecological egalitarianism and of symbiosis support the same anti-class posture. The ecological attitude favours the extension of all three principles to any group conflicts, including those of today between developing and developed nations. The three principles also favour extreme caution towards any over-all plans for the future, except those consistent with wide and widening classless diversity.

(5) Fight against *pollution and resource depletion*. In this fight ecologists have found powerful supporters, but sometimes to the detriment of their total stand. This happens when attention is focused on pollution and resource depletion rather than on the other points, or when projects are implemented which reduce pollution but increase evils of the other kinds. Thus, if prices of life necessities increase because of the installation of anti-pollution devices, class differences increase too. An ethics of responsibility implies that ecologists do not serve the shallow, but the deep ecological movement. That is, not only point (5), but all seven points must be considered together.

Ecologists are irreplaceable informants in any society, whatever their political contour. If well organized, they have the power to reject jobs in which they submit themselves to institutions or to planners with limited ecological perspectives. As it is now, ecologists sometimes serve masters who deliberately ignore the wider perspectives.

(6) *Complexity, not complication*. The theory of ecosystems contains an important distinction between what is complicated without any Gestalt or unifying principles—we may think of finding our way through a chaotic city—and what is complex. A multiplicity of more or less lawful, interacting factors may operate together to form a unity, a system. We make a shoe or use a map or integrate a

variety of activities into a workaday pattern. Organisms, ways of life, and interactions in the biosphere in general, exhibit complexity of such an astoundingly high level as to colour the general outlook of ecologists. Such complexity makes thinking in terms of vast systems inevitable. It also makes for a keen, steady perception of the profound *human ignorance* of biospherical relationships and therefore of the effect of disturbances.

Applied to humans, the complexity-not-complication principle favours division of labour, *not fragmentation of labour*. It favours integrated actions in which the whole person is active, not mere reactions. It favours complex economies, an integrated variety of means of living. (Combinations of industrial and agricultural activity, of intellectual and manual work, of specialized and non-specialized occupations, of urban and non-urban activity, of work in city and recreation in nature with recreation in city and work in nature …)

It favours soft technique and "soft future-research," less prognosis, more clarification of possibilities. More sensitivity towards continuity and live traditions, and—most importantly—towards our state of ignorance.

The implementation of ecologically responsible policies requires in this century an exponential growth of technical skill and invention—but in new directions, directions which today are not consistently and liberally supported by the research policy organs of our nation-states.

(7) *Local autonomy and decentralization*. The vulnerability of a form of life is roughly proportional to the weight of influences from afar, from outside the local region in which that form has obtained an ecological equilibrium. This lends support to our efforts to strengthen local self-government and material and mental self-sufficiency. But these efforts presuppose an impetus towards decentralization. Pollution problems, including those of thermal pollution and recirculation of materials, also lead us in this direction, because increased local autonomy, if we are able to keep other factors constant, reduces energy consumption. (Compare an approximately self-sufficient locality with one requiring the importation of foodstuff, materials for

house construction, fuel and skilled labour from other continents. The former may use only five per cent of the energy used by the latter.) Local autonomy is strengthened by a reduction in the number of links in the hierarchical chains of decision. (For example, a chain consisting of local board, municipal council, highest sub-national decision-maker, a state-wide institution in a state federation, a federal national government institution, a coalition of nations, and of institutions, e.g., E.E.C.[1] top levels, and a global institution, can be reduced to one made up of local board, nation-wide institution, and global institution.) Even if a decision follows majority rules at each step, many local interests may be dropped along the line, if it is too long.

Summing up, then, it should, first of all, be borne in mind that the norms and tendencies of the Deep Ecology movement are not derived from ecology by logic or induction. Ecological knowledge and the life-style of the ecological field-worker have *suggested, inspired, and fortified* the perspectives of the Deep Ecology movement. Many of the formulations in the above seven-point survey are rather vague generalizations, only tenable if made more precise in certain directions. But all over the world the inspiration from ecology has shown remarkable convergencies. The survey does not pretend to be more than one of the possible condensed codifications of these convergencies.

Secondly, it should be fully appreciated that the significant tenets of the Deep Ecology movement are clearly and forcefully *normative*. They express a value priority system only in part based on results (or lack of results, cf. point [6]) of scientific research. Today, ecologists try to influence policy-making bodies largely through threats, through predictions concerning pollutants and resource depletion, knowing that policy-makers accept at least certain minimum *norms* concerning health and just distribution. But it is clear that there are a vast number of people in all countries, and even a considerable number of people in power, who accept as valid the wider norms and values characteristic of the Deep Ecology movement. There are political potentials in this movement which should not be overlooked and

which have little to do with pollution and resource depletion. In plotting possible futures, the norms should be freely used and elaborated.

Thirdly, in so far as ecology movements deserve our attention, they are *ecophilosophical* rather than ecological. Ecology is *limited* science which makes *use* of scientific methods. Philosophy is the most general forum of debate on fundamentals, descriptive as well as prescriptive, and political philosophy is one of its subsections. By an *ecosophy* I mean a philosophy of ecological harmony or equilibrium. A philosophy as a kind of *sofia* wisdom, is openly normative, it contains *both* norms, rules, postulates, value priority announcements *and* hypotheses concerning the state of affairs in our universe. Wisdom is policy wisdom, prescription, not only scientific description and prediction.

The details of an ecosophy will show many variations due to significant differences concerning not only "facts" of pollution, resources, population, etc., but also value priorities. Today, however, the seven points listed provide one unified framework for ecosophical systems.

In general system theory, systems are mostly conceived in terms of causally or functionally interacting or interrelated items. An ecosophy, however, is more like a system of the kind constructed by Aristotle or Spinoza. It is expressed verbally as a set of sentences with a variety of functions, descriptive and prescriptive. The basic relation is that between subsets of premises and subsets of conclusions, that is, the relation of derivability.

The relevant notions of derivability may be classed according to rigour, with logical and mathematical deductions topping the list, but also according to how much is implicitly taken for granted. An exposition of an ecosophy must necessarily be only moderately precise considering the vast scope of relevant ecological and normative (social, political, ethical) material. At the moment, ecosophy might profitably use models of systems, rough approximations of global systematizations. It is the global character, not preciseness in detail, which distinguishes an ecosophy. It articulates and integrates the efforts of an ideal ecological team, a team comprising not only scientists from an extreme variety of disciplines, but also students of politics and active policy-makers.

Under the name of *ecologism*, various deviations from the deep movement have been championed—primarily with a one-sided stress on pollution and resource depletion, but also with a neglect of the great differences between under- and over-developed countries in favour of a vague global approach. The global approach is essential, but regional differences must largely determine policies in the coming years.

NOTE

1. E.E.C. stands for European Economic Community.

STUDY QUESTIONS

1. Is *deep ecology* a good name for Naess's theory? Does it incorporate positive value unwarrantedly? If not, what should it be called?

2. Are the seven principles of the deep ecology movement good ones? Examine each one, compare them with the corresponding principles of shallow ecology, and comment on their validity.

3. Compare Naess's deep ecology with biocentrism and ecocentrism.

14

Ecosophy T: Deep Versus Shallow Ecology

ARNE NAESS

In this 1985 essay, Naess develops the philosophical implications of deep ecology, which he calls "Ecosophy." He calls his version of ecosophy "Ecosophy T." Naess develops his theory of wider self-realization through identifying one's self with individuals, species, ecosystems, and landscapes.

Reprinted by permission from Arne Naess, "Identification as a Source of Deep Ecological Attitudes" ed. Michael Tobias, in *Deep Ecology* (Santa Monica, C.A.: IMT Productions, 1985).

THE SHALLOW AND THE DEEP ECOLOGICAL MOVEMENT

In the 1960s two convergent trends made headway: a deep ecological concern and a concern for saving deep cultural diversity. These may be put under the general heading "deep ecology" if we view human ecology as a genuine part of general ecology. For each species of living beings there is a corresponding ecology. In what follows I adopt this terminology which I introduced in 1973 (Naess 1973).

The term *deep* is supposed to suggest explication of fundamental presuppositions of valuation as well as of facts and hypotheses. Deep ecology, therefore, transcends the limit of any particular science of today, including systems theory and scientific ecology. *Deepness of normative and descriptive premises questioned* characterize the movement....

Deep ecological argumentation questions both the left-hand and the right-hand slogans. But tentative conclusions are in terms of the latter.

The shallow ecological argument carries today much heavier weight in political life than the deep. It is therefore often necessary for tactical reasons to hide our deeper attitudes and argue strictly homocentrically. This colors the indispensible publication, *World Conservation Strategy*.[1]

As an academic philosopher raised within analytic traditions it has been natural for me to pose the questions: How can departments of philosophy, our establishment of professionals, be made interested in the matter? What are the philosophical problems explicitly and implicitly raised or answered in the deep ecological movement? Can they be formulated so to be of academic interest?

My answer is that the movement is rich in philosophical implications. There has, however, been only moderately eager response in philosophical institutions.

The deep ecological movement is furthered by people and groups with much in common. Roughly speaking, what they have in common concerns ways of experiencing nature and diversity of cultures. Furthermore, many share priorities of life style, such as those of "voluntary simplicity." They wish to live "lightly" in nature. There are

of course differences, but until now the conflicts of philosophically relevant opinion and of recommended policies have, to a surprisingly small degree, disturbed the growth of the movement.

In what follows I introduce some sections of a philosophy inspired by the deep ecological movement. Some people in the movement feel at home with that philosophy or at least approximately such a philosophy, others feel that they, at one or more points, clearly have different value priorities, attitudes or opinions. To avoid unfruitful polemics, I call my philosophy "Ecosophy T," using the character *T* just to emphasize that other people in the movement would, if motivated to formulate their world view and general value priorities, arrive at different ecosophies: Ecosophy "A," "B," ..., "T," ..., "Z."

By an "ecosophy" I here mean a philosophy inspired by the deep ecological movement. The ending *-sophy* stresses that what we modestly try to realize is wisdom rather than science or information. A philosophy, as articulated wisdom, has to be a synthesis of theory and practice. It must not shun concrete policy recommendations but has to base them on fundamental priorities of value and basic views concerning the development of our societies.[2]

Which societies? The movement started in the richest industrial societies, and the words used by its academic supporters inevitably reflect the cultural provinciality of those societies. The way I am going to say things perhaps reflects a bias in favor of analytic philosophy intimately related to social science, including academic psychology. It shows itself in my acceptance in Ecosophy T of the theory of thinking in terms of "gestalts." But this provinciality and narrowness of training does not imply criticism of contributions in terms of trends or traditions of wisdom with which I am not at home, and it does not imply an underestimation of the immense value of what artists in many countries have contributed to the movement.

SELECTED ECOSOPHICAL TOPICS

The themes of Ecosophy T which will be introduced are the following:

The narrow self (ego) and the comprehensive Self (written with capital *S*) Self-realization as the realization of the comprehensive Self, not the cultivation of the ego
The process of identification as the basic tool of widening the self and as a natural consequence of increased maturity Strong identification with the whole of nature in its diversity and interdependence of parts as a source of active participation in the deep ecological movement Identification as a source of belief in intrinsic values. The question of "objective" validity.[3]

SELF-REALIZATION, YES, BUT WHICH SELF?

When asked about *where* their self, their "I," or their ego is, some people place it in the neighborhood of the *larynx*. When thinking, we can sometimes perceive movement in that area. Others find it near their eyes. Many tend to feel that their ego, somehow, is inside their body, or identical with the whole of it, or with its functioning. Some call their ego spiritual or immaterial and not within space. This has interesting consequences. A Bedouin in Yemen would not have an ego nearer the equator than a whale-hunting eskimo. "Nearer" implies space.

William James (1890: Chapter 10) offers an excellent introduction to the problems concerning the constitution and the limits of the self.

The Empirical Self of each of us is all that he is tempted to call by the name of *me*. But it is clear that between what a man calls *me* and what he simply calls *mine* the line is difficult to draw. We feel and act about certain things that are ours very much as we feel and act about ourselves. Our fame, our children, the work of our hands, may be as dear to us as our bodies are, and arouse the same feelings and the same acts of reprisal if attacked. And our

bodies, themselves, are they simply ours, or are they *us*?

The body is the innermost part of *the material Self* in each of us; and certain parts of the body seem more intimately ours than the rest. The clothes come next.... Next, our immediate family is a part of ourselves. Our father and mother, our wife and babes, are bone of our bone and flesh of our flesh. When they die, a part of our very selves is gone. If they do anything wrong, it is our shame. If they are insulted, our anger flashes forth as readily as if we stood in their place. Our *home* comes next. Its scenes are part of our life; its aspects awaken the tenderest feelings of affection.

One of his conclusions is of importance to the concepts of self-realization: "We see then that we are dealing with a fluctuating material. The same object being sometimes treated as a part of me, at other times is simply mine, and then again as if I had nothing to do with it all."

If the term *self-realization* is applied, it should be kept in mind that "I," "me," "ego," and "self" have shifting denotations. Nothing is evident and indisputable. Even *that* we are is debatable if we make the question dependent upon answering *what* we are.

One of the central terms in Indian philosophy is *ātman*. Until this century it was mostly translated with "spirit," but it is now generally recognized that "self" is more appropriate. It is a term with similar connotations and ambiguities as those of "self"—analyzed by William James and other Western philosophers and psychologists. Gandhi represented a *maha-ātman*, a *mahatma*, a great (and certainly very wide) self. As a term for a kind of metaphysical maximum self we find *ātman* in *The Bhagavadgita*.

Verse 29 of Chapter 6 is characteristic of the truly great *ātman*. The Sanskrit of this verse is not overwhelmingly difficult and deserves quotation ahead of translations.

sarvabhūtastham ātmānam
sarvabhutāni cā'tmani
Itsate yogayuktātmā
sarvatra samadarśanah

Radhakrishnan: "He whose self is harmonized by yoga seeth the Self abiding in all beings and all beings in Self; everywhere he sees the same."

Eliot Deutsch: "He whose self is disciplined by yoga sees the Self abiding in all beings and all beings in the Self; he sees the same in all beings."

Juan Mascaró: "He sees himself in the heart of all beings and he sees all beings in his heart. This is the vision of the Yogi of harmony, a vision which is ever one."

Gandhi: "The man equipped with *yoga* looks on all with an impartial eye, seeing *Atman* in all beings and all beings in *Atman*."

Self-realization in its absolute maximum is, as I see it, the mature experience of oneness in diversity as depicted in the above verse. The minimum is the self-realization by more or less consistent egotism— by the narrowest experience of what constitutes one's self and a maximum of alienation. As empirical beings we dwell somewhere in between, but increased maturity involves increase of the wideness of the self.

The self-realization maximum should not necessarily be conceived as a mystical or meditational state. "By meditation some perceive the Self in the self by the self; others by the path of knowledge and still others by the path of works (*karma-yoga*)" [*Gita*: Chapter 13, verse 24]. Gandhi was a *karma-yogi*, realizing himself through social and political action.

The terms *mystical union* and *mysticism* are avoided here for three reasons: First, strong mystical traditions stress the dissolution of individual selves into a nondiversified supreme whole. Both from cultural and ecological points of view diversity and individuality are essential. Second, there is a strong terminological trend within scientific communities to associate mysticism with vagueness and confusion.[4] Third, mystics tend to agree that mystical consciousness is rarely sustained under normal, everyday conditions. But strong, wide identification *can* color experience under such conditions.

Gandhi was only marginally concerned with "nature." In his *ashram* poisonous snakes were permitted to live inside and outside human dwellings. Anti-poison medicines were frowned upon.

Gandhi insisted that trust awakens trust, and that snakes have the same right to live and blossom as the humans (Naess, 1974).

THE PROCESS OF IDENTIFICATION

How do we develop a wider self? What kind of process makes it possible? One way of answering these questions: There is a process of ever-widening identification and ever-narrowing alienation which widens the self. The self is as comprehensive as the totality of our identifications. Or, more succinctly: Our Self is that with which we identify. The question then reads: How do we widen identifications?

Identification is a spontaneous, non-rational, but not irrational, process through which *the interest or interests of another being are reacted to as our own interest or interests*. The emotional tone of gratification or frustration is a consequence carried over from the other to oneself: joy elicits joy, sorrow sorrow. Intense identification obliterates the experience of a distinction between *ego* and *alter*, between me and the sufferer. But only momentarily or intermittently: If my fellow being tries to vomit, I do not, or at least not persistently, try to vomit. I recognize that we are different individuals.

The term *identification, in the sense used here*, is rather technical, but there are today scarcely any alternatives. "Solidarity" and a corresponding adjective in German, "solidarisch," and the corresponding words in Scandinavian languages are very common and useful. But genuine and spontaneous solidarity with others already presupposes a process of identification. Without identification, no solidarity. Thus, the latter term cannot quite replace the former.

The same holds true of empathy and sympathy. It is a necessary, but not sufficient, condition of empathy and sympathy that one "sees" or experiences something similar or identical with oneself.[5]

A high level of identification does not eliminate conflicts of interest: Our vital interests, if we are not plants, imply killing at least some other living beings. A culture of hunters, where identification with hunted animals reaches a remarkably high level, does not prohibit killing for food. But a great variety of ceremonies and rituals have the function to express the gravity of the alienating incident and restore the identification.

Identification with individuals, species, ecosystems and landscapes results in difficult problems of priority. What should be the relation of ecosystem ethics to other parts of general ethics?

There are no definite limits to the broadness and intensity of identification. Mammals and birds sometimes show remarkable, often rather touching, intraspecies and cross-species identification. Konrad Lorenz tells of how one of his bird friends tried to seduce him, trying to push him into its little home. This presupposes a deep identification between bird and man (but also an alarming mistake of size). In certain forms of mysticism, there is an experience of identification with every life form, using this term in a wide sense. Within the deep ecological movement, poetical and philosophical expressions of such experiences are not uncommon. In the shallow ecological movement, intense and wide identification is described and explained psychologically. In the deep movement this philosophy is at least taken seriously: reality consists of wholes which we cut down rather than of isolated items which we put together. In other words: there is not, strictly speaking, a primordial causal process of identification, but one of largely unconscious alienation which is overcome in experiences of identity. To some "environmental" philosophers such thoughts seem to be irrational, even "rubbish."[6] This is, as far as I can judge, due to a too narrow conception of irrationality.

The opposite of *identification* is *alienation*, if we use these ambiguous terms in one of their basic meanings.[7]

The alienated son does perhaps what is required of a son toward his parents, but as performance of moral duties and as a burden, not spontaneously, out of joy. If one loves and respects oneself, identification will be positive, and, in what follows, the term covers this case. Self-hatred or dislike of certain of one's traits induces hatred and dislike of the beings with which one identifies.

Identification is not limited to beings which can reciprocate: Any animal, plant, mountain, ocean may induce such processes. In poetry this is articulated most impressively, but ordinary language testifies to its power as a universal human trait.

Through identification, higher level unity is experienced: from identifying with "one's nearest," higher unities are created through circles of friends, local communities, tribes, compatriots, races, humanity, life, and, ultimately, as articulated by religious and philosophic leaders, unity with the supreme whole, the "world" in a broader and deeper sense than the usual. I prefer a terminology such that the largest units are not said to comprise life *and* "the not living." One may broaden the sense of "living" so that any natural whole, however large, is a living whole.

This way of thinking and feeling at its maximum corresponds to that of the enlightened, or yogi, who sees "the same," the ātman, and who is not alienated from anything.

The process of identification is sometimes expressed in terms of loss of self and gain of Self through "self-less" action. Each new sort of identification corresponds to a widening of the self, and strengthens the urge to further widening, furthering Self-seeking. This urge is in the system of Spinoza called *conatus in suo esse perseverare*, striving to persevere in oneself or one's being (*in se, in suo esse*). It is not a mere urge to survive, but to increase the level of *acting out* (ex) *one's own nature or essence*, and is not different from the urge toward higher levels of "freedom" (*libertas*). Under favorable circumstances, this involves wide identification.

In Western social science, self-realization is the term most often used for the competitive development of a person's talents and the pursuit of an individual's specific interests (Maslow and others). A conflict is foreseen between giving self-realization high priority and cultivation of social bonds, friends, family, nation, nature. Such unfortunate notions have narrow concepts of self as a point of departure. They go together with the egoism-altruism distinction. Altruism is, according to this, a moral quality developed through suppression of selfishness, through sacrifice of one's "own" interests in favor of those of others. Thus, alienation is taken to be the normal state. Identification precludes sacrifice, but not devotion. The moral of self-sacrifice presupposes immaturity. Its relative importance is clear, in so far as we all are more or less immature.

WIDENESS AND DEPTH OF IDENTIFICATION AS A CONSEQUENCE OF INCREASED MATURITY

Against the belief in fundamental ego-alter conflict, the psychology and philosophy of the (comprehensive) Self insist that the gradual maturing of a person *inevitably* widens and deepens the self through the process of identification. There is no need for altruism toward those with whom we identify. The pursuit of self-realization conceived as actualization and development of the Self takes care of what altruism is supposed to accomplish. Thus, the distinction egoism-altruism is transcended.

The notion of maturing has to do with getting out what is latent in the nature of a being. Some learning is presupposed, but thinking of present conditions of competition in industrial, economic growth societies, specialized learning may inhibit the process of maturing. A competitive cult of talents does not favor Self-realization. As a consequence of the imperfect conditions for maturing as persons, there is much pessimism or disbelief in relation to the widening of the Self, and more stress on developing altruism and moral pressure.

The conditions under which the self is widened are experienced as positive and are basically joyful. The constant exposure to life in the poorest countries through television and other media contributes to the spread of the voluntary simplicity movement (Elgin, 1981). But people laugh: What does it help the hungry that you renounce the luxuries of your own country? But identification makes the efforts of simplicity joyful and there is not a feeling of moral compulsion. The widening of the self implies widening perspectives, deepening experiences, and reaching higher levels of activeness (in Spinoza's sense, not as just being busy). Joy and activeness make the appeal to Self-realization stronger than appeal to altruism. The state of alienation is not joyful, and is often connected with feelings of being threatened and narrowed. The "rights" of other living beings are felt to threaten our "own" interests.

The close connection between trends of alienation and putting duty and altruism as a highest value is exemplified in the philosophy of Kant. Acting morally, we should not abstain from maltreating animals because of their sufferings, but because of its bad effect on us. Animals were to Kant, essentially, so different from human beings, that he felt we should not have any moral obligations toward them. Their unnecessary sufferings are morally indifferent and norms of altruism do not apply in our relations to them. When we decide ethically to be kind to them, it should be because of the favorable effect of kindness of us—a strange doctrine.

Suffering is perhaps the most potent source of identification. Only special social conditions are able to make people inhibit their normal spontaneous reaction toward suffering. If we alleviate suffering because of a spontaneous urge to do so, Kant would be willing to call the act "beautiful," but not moral. And his greatest admiration was, as we all know, for stars and the moral imperative, not spontaneous goodness. The history of cruelty inflicted in the name of morals has convinced me that increase of identification might achieve what moralizing cannot: beautiful actions.

RELEVANCE OF THE ABOVE FOR DEEP ECOLOGY

This perhaps rather lengthy philosophical discourse serves as a preliminary for the understanding of two things: first, the powerful indignation of Rachel Carson and others who, with great courage and stubborn determination, challenged authorities in the early 1960s, and triggered the international ecological movement. Second, the radical shift (see Sahlins, 1972) toward more positive appreciation of nonindustrial cultures and minorities—also in the 1960s, and expressing itself in efforts to "save" such cultures and in a new social anthropology.

The second movement reflects identification with threatened cultures. Both reactions were made possible by doubt that the industrial societies are as uniquely progressive as they usually had been supposed to be. Former haughtiness gave way to humility or at least willingness to look for deep changes both socially and in relation to nature.

Ecological information about the intimate dependency of humanity upon decent behavior toward the natural environment offered a much needed rational and economic justification for processes of identification which many people already had more or less completed. Their relative high degree of identification with animals, plants, landscapes, was seen to correspond to *factual relations* between themselves and nature. "Not man apart" was transformed from a romantic norm to a statement of fact. The distinction between man and environment, as applied within the shallow ecological movement, was seen to be illusory. Your Self crosses the boundaries.

When it was made known that the penguins of the Antarctic might die out because of the effects of DDT upon the toughness of their eggs, there was a widespread, *spontaneous* reaction of indignation and sorrow. People who never see penguins and who would never think of such animals as "useful" in any way, insisted that they had a right to live and flourish, and that it was our obligation not to interfere. But we must admit that even the mere appearance of penguins makes intense identification easy.

Thus, ecology helped many to know more *about themselves*. We are living beings. Penguins are too. We are all expressions of life. The fateful dependencies and interrelations which were brought to light, thanks to ecologists, made it easier for people to admit and even to cultivate their deep concern for nature, and to express their latent hostility toward the excesses of the economic growth of societies.

LIVING BEINGS HAVE INTRINSIC VALUE AND A RIGHT TO LIVE AND FLOURISH

How can these attitudes be talked about? What are the most helpful conceptualizations and slogans?

One important attitude might be thus expressed: "Every living being has a *right* to live." One way of answering the question is to insist upon the value in themselves, the autotelic value, of every living being. This opposes the notion that one may be justified in treating any living being as just a means to an end. It also generalizes the rightly famous dictum of Kant "never use a person solely as a means." Identification tells me: if *I* have a right to live, *you* have the same right.

Insofar as we consider ourselves and our family and friends to have an intrinsic value, the widening identification inevitably leads to the attribution of intrinsic value to others. The metaphysical maximum will then involve the attribution of intrinsic value to all living beings. The right to live is only a different way of expressing this evaluation.

THE END OF THE WHY'S

But why has *any* living being autotelic value? Faced with the ever returning question of "why?" we have to stop somewhere. Here is a place where we well might stop. We shall admit that the value in itself is something shown in intuition. We attribute intrinsic value to ourselves and our nearest, and the validity of further identification can be contested, and *is* contested by many. The negation may, however, also be attacked through series of "whys?" Ultimately, we are in the same human predicament of having to start somewhere, at least for the moment. We must stop somewhere and treat where we then stand as a foundation.

The use of "Every living being has a value in itself" as a fundamental norm or principle does not rule out other fundamentals. On the contrary, the normal situation will be one in which several, in part conflicting, fundamental norms are relevant. And some consequences of fundamental norms *seem* compatible, but in fact are not.

The designation "fundamental" does not need to mean more than "not based on something deeper," which in practice often is indistinguishable from "not derived logically from deeper premises." It must be considered a rare case, if some body is able to stick to one and only one fundamental norm. (I have made an attempt to work with a *model* with only one, Self-realization, in Ecosophy T.)

THE RIGHT TO LIVE IS ONE AND THE SAME, BUT VITAL INTERESTS OF OUR NEAREST HAVE PRIORITY OF DEFENSE

Under symbiotic conditions, there are rules which manifest two important factors operating when interests are conflicting: vitalness and nearness. The more vital interest has priority over the less vital. The nearer has priority over the more remote—in space, time, culture, species. Nearness derives its priority from our special responsibilities, obligations and insights.

The terms used in these rules are of course vague and ambiguous. But even so, the rules point toward ways of thinking and acting which do not leave us quite helpless in the many inevitable conflicts of norms. The vast increase of consequences for life in general, which industrialization and the population explosion have brought about, necessitates new guidelines.

Examples: The use of threatened species for food or clothing (fur) may be more or less vital for certain poor, nonindustrial, human communities. For the less poor, such use is clearly ecologically irresponsible. Considering the fabulous possibilities open to the richest industrial societies, it is their responsibility to assist the poor communities in such a way that undue exploitation of threatened species, populations, and ecosystems is avoided.

It may be of vital interest to a family of poisonous snakes to remain in a small area where small children play, but it is also of vital interest to children and parents that there are no accidents. The priority rule of nearness makes it justifiable for the parents to remove the snakes. But the priority of vital interest of snakes is important when deciding where to establish the playgrounds.

The importance of nearness is, to a large degree, dependent upon vital interests of communities rather than individuals. The obligations with the family keep the family together, the obligations within a nation keep it from disintegration. But if the nonvital interests of a nation, or a species, conflict with the vital interests of another nation, or of other species, the rules give priority to the "alien nation" or "alien species."

How these conflicts may be straightened out is of course much too large a subject to be treated even cursorily in this connection. What is said only points toward the existence of rules of some help. (For further discussion, see Naess [1979].)

INTRINSIC VALUES

The term "objectivism" may have undesirable associations, but value pronouncements within the deep ecological movement imply what in philosophy is often termed "value objectivism" as opposed to value subjectivism, for instance, "the emotive theory of value." At the time of Nietzsche there was in Europe a profound movement toward separation of value as a genuine aspect of reality on a par with scientific, "factual" descriptions. Value tended to be conceived as something projected by man into a completely value-neutral reality. The *Tractatus Philosophico-Logicus* of the early Wittgenstein expresses a well-known variant of this attitude. It represents a unique trend of *alienation of value* if we compare this attitude with those of cultures other than our technological-industrial society.

The professional philosophical debate on value objectivism, which in different senses—according to different versions, posits positive and negative values independent of value for human subjects—is of course very intricate. Here I shall only point out some kinds of statements within the deep ecological movement which imply value objectivism in the sense of intrinsic value:

> Animals have value in themselves, not only as resources for humans.
> Animals have a right to live even if of no use to humans. We have no right to destroy the natural features of this planet.

Nature does not belong to man.
Nature is worth defending, whatever the
fate of humans.
A wilderness area has a value independent
of whether humans have access to it.

In these statements, something *A* is said to
have a value independent of whether *A* has a value
for something else, *B*. The value of *A* must therefore
be said to have a value inherent in *A*. *A* has *intrinsic
value*. This does not imply that *A* has value *for B*.
Thus *A* may have, and usually does have, both intrinsic and extrinsic value.

Subjectivistic arguments tend to take for
granted that a subject is somehow implied. There
"must be" somebody who performs the valuation
process. For this subject, something may have value.

The burden of proof lies with the subjectivists
insofar as naive attitudes lack the clear-cut separation of value from reality and the conception of
value as something projected by man into reality
or the neutral facts by a subject.

The most promising way of defending intrinsic
values today is, in my view, to take gestalt thinking
seriously. "Objects" will then be defined in terms of
gestalts, rather than in terms of heaps of things with
external relations and dominated by forces. This
undermines the subject–object dualism essential for
value subjectivism.

OUTLOOK FOR THE FUTURE

What is the outlook for growth of ecological, relevant identification and of policies in harmony with
a high level of identification?

A major nuclear war will involve a setback of
tremendous dimensions. Words need not be wasted
in support of that conclusion. But continued militarization is a threat: It means further domination of
technology and centralization.

Continued population growth makes benevolent policies still more difficult to pursue than they
already are. Poor people in megacities do not have
the opportunity to meet nature, and shortsighted
policies which favor increasing the number of
poor are destructive. Even a small population
growth in rich nations is scarcely less destructive.

The economic policy of growth (as conceived
today in the richest nations of all times) is increasingly destructive. It does not *prevent* growth of
identification but makes it politically powerless.
This reminds us of the possibility of significant
growth of identification in the near future.

The increasing destruction plus increasing information about the destruction is apt to elicit
strong feelings of sorrow, despair, desperate actions
and tireless efforts to save what is left. With the
forecast that more than a million species will die
out before the year 2000 and most cultures be
done away with, identification may grow rapidly
among a minority.

At the present about 10% to 15% of the populace of some European countries are in favor of
strong policies in harmony with the attitudes of
identification. But this percentage may increase
without major changes of policies. So far as I can
see, the most probable course of events is continued
devastation of conditions of life on this planet,
combined with a powerless upsurge of sorrow and
lamentation.

What actually happens is often wildly "improbable," and perhaps the strong anthropocentric
arguments and wise recommendations of *World
Conservation Strategy* (1980) will, after all, make
a significant effect.

NOTES

1. Commissioned by The United Nations Environmental Programme (UNEP) which worked
together with the World Wildlife Fund (WWF).
Published 1980. Copies available through IUNC,
1196 Gland, Switzerland. In India: Department of
Environment.

2. This aim implies a synthesis of views developed in the different branches of philosophy—ontology, epistemology, logic, methodology, theory of value, ethics, philosophy of history, and politics. As a philosopher the deep ecologist is a "generalist."

3. For comprehensive treatment of Ecosophy T, see Naess (1981, Chapter 7).

4. See Passmore (1980). For a reasonable, unemotional approach to "mysticism," see Stahl (1975).

5. For deeper study more distinctions have to be taken into account. See, for instance, Scheler (1954) and Mercer (1972).

6. See, for instance, the chapter "Removing the Rubbish" in Passmore (1980).

7. The diverse uses of the term *alienation (Entfremdung)* have an interesting and complicated history from the time of Rousseau. Rousseau himself offers interesting observations of how social conditions through the process of alienation make *amour de soi* change into *amour propre*. I would say: How the process of maturing is hindered and self-love hardens into egotism instead of softening and widening into Self-realization.

REFERENCES

Elgin, Duane. 1981. *Voluntary Simplicity*. New York: William Morrow.

James, William. 1890. *The Principles of Psychology*. New York, Chapter 10: The Consciousness of Self.

Mercer, Philip. 1972. *Sympathy and Ethics*. Oxford: The Clarendon Press. Discusses forms of identification.

Naess, Arne. 1973. "The Shadow and the Deep, Long-Range Ecology Movement," *Inquiry* 16: 95–100.

———. 1974. *Gandhi and Group Conflict*. 1981, Oslo: Universitetsforlaget.

———. 1979. "Self-realization in Mixed Communities of Humans, Bears, Sheep and Wolves," *Inquiry* 22: 231–241.

———. 1981. *Ekologi, samhälle och livsstil. Utkast til en ekosofi*. Stockholm: LTs förlag.

Passmore, John. 1980. *Man's Responsibility for Nature*. 2nd ed., London: Duckworth.

Sahlins, Marshall. 1972. *Stone Age Economics*. Chicago: Aldine.

Scheler, Max. 1954. *The Nature of Sympathy*. London: Routledge & Keegan Paul.

STUDY QUESTIONS

1. What does Naess mean by *Ecosophy*? What does the ending *-sophy* refer to?

2. What are the basic tenets of Ecosophy T?

3. What does Naess mean by *Self-realization*? Analyze the quotations from Radhakrishnan, Eliot Deutsch, Juan Mascaró, and Gandhi. What do they tell us about Self-realization?

4. How do we develop a wider Self?

5. Explain Naess's idea of *identification*. Is it mystical? How can we identify with "individuals, species, ecosystems, and landscapes"?

6. What is Naess saying about *value objectivism*? Critically discuss this issue.

15

Deep Ecology

BILL DEVALL AND GEORGE SESSIONS

Bill Devall teaches in the sociology department at Humboldt State University in Arcata, California, and George Sessions teaches philosophy at Sierra College in Rocklin, California. Together they have authored Deep Ecology: Living as If Nature Mattered *(1985) from which the present selection is taken.*

This essay sets forth a more recent version of deep ecology than Naess's 1972 summary version, linking it to Zen Buddhism, Taoism, Native American rituals, and Christianity. They contrast deep ecology with the dominant worldview and set forth the eight principles of deep ecology.

The term *deep ecology* was coined by Arne Naess in his 1973 article, "The Shallow and the Deep, Long-Range Ecology Movements." Naess was attempting to describe the deeper, more spiritual approach to Nature exemplified in the writings of Aldo Leopold and Rachel Carson. He thought that this deeper approach resulted from a more sensitive openness to ourselves and nonhuman life around us. The essence of deep ecology is to keep asking more searching questions about human life, society, and Nature as in the Western philosophical tradition of Socrates. As examples of this deep questioning, Naess points out "that we ask why and how, where others do not. For instance, ecology as a science does not ask what kind of a society would be the best for maintaining a particular ecosystem—that is considered a question for value theory, for politics, for ethics." Thus deep ecology goes beyond the so-called factual scientific level to the level of self and Earth wisdom.

Deep ecology goes beyond a limited piecemeal shallow approach to environmental problems and attempts to articulate a comprehensive religious and philosophical worldview. The foundations of deep ecology are the basic intuitions and experiencing of ourselves and Nature which comprise ecological consciousness. Certain outlooks on politics and public policy flow naturally from this consciousness. And in the context of this book, we discuss the minority tradition as the type of community most conducive both to cultivating ecological consciousness and to asking the basic questions of values and ethics addressed in these pages.

Many of these questions are perennial philosophical and religious questions faced by humans in all cultures over the ages. What does it mean to be a unique human individual? How can the individual self maintain and increase its uniqueness while also being an inseparable aspect of the whole system wherein there are no sharp breaks between self and the *other*? An ecological perspective, in this deeper sense, results in what Theodore Roszak calls "an awakening of wholes greater than the sum of their parts. In spirit, the discipline is contemplative and therapeutic."

Reprinted from *Deep Ecology: Living as if Nature Mattered* (Salt Lake City: Peregrine Smith Book, 1985), by permission. Footnotes deleted.

Ecological consciousness and deep ecology are in sharp contrast with the dominant world-view of technocratic–industrial societies which regard humans as isolated and fundamentally separate from the rest of Nature, as superior to, and in charge of, the rest of creation. But the view of humans as separate and superior to the rest of Nature is only part of larger cultural patterns. For thousands of years, Western culture has become increasingly obsessed with the idea of *dominance*: with dominance of humans over nonhuman Nature, masculine over the feminine, wealthy and powerful over the poor, with the dominance of the West over non-Western cultures. Deep ecological consciousness allows us to see through these erroneous and dangerous illusions.

For deep ecology, the study of our place in the Earth household includes the study of ourselves as part of the organic whole. Going beyond a narrowly materialist scientific understanding of reality, the spiritual and the material aspects of reality fuse together. While the leading intellectuals of the dominant worldview have tended to view religion as "just superstition," and have looked upon ancient spiritual practice and enlightenment, such as found in Zen Buddhism, as essentially subjective, the search for deep ecological consciousness is the search for a more objective consciousness and state of being through an active deep questioning and meditative process and way of life.

Many people have asked these deeper questions and cultivated ecological consciousness within the context of different spiritual traditions—Christianity, Taoism, Buddhism, and Native American rituals, for example. While differing greatly in other regards, many in these traditions agree with the basic principles of deep ecology.

Warwick Fox, an Australian philosopher, has succinctly expressed the central intuition of deep ecology: "It is the idea that we can make no firm ontological divide in the field of existence: That there is no bifurcation in reality between the human and the non-human realms … to the extent that we perceive boundaries, we fall short of deep ecological consciousness."

From this most basic insight or characteristic of deep ecological consciousness, Arne Naess has developed two *ultimate norms* or intuitions which are themselves not derivable from other principles or intuitions. They are arrived at by the deep questioning process and reveal the importance of moving to the philosophical and religious level of wisdom. They cannot be validated, of course, by the methodology of modern science based on its usual mechanistic assumptions and its very narrow definition of data. These ultimate norms are *self-realization* and *biocentric equality*.

I. SELF-REALIZATION

In keeping with the spiritual traditions of many of the world's religions, the deep ecology norm of self-realization goes beyond the modern Western *self* which is defined as an isolated ego striving primarily for hedonistic gratification or for a narrow sense of individual salvation in this life or the next. This socially programmed sense of the narrow self or social self dislocates us, and leaves us prey to whatever fad or fashion is prevalent in our society or social reference group. We are thus robbed of beginning the search for our unique spiritual/biological personhood. Spiritual growth, or unfolding, begins when we cease to understand or see ourselves as isolated and narrow competing egos and begin to identify with other humans from our family and friends to, eventually, our species. But the deep ecology sense of self requires a further maturity and growth, an identification which goes beyond humanity to include the nonhuman world. We must see beyond our narrow contemporary cultural assumptions and values, and the conventional wisdom of our time and place, and this is best achieved by the meditative deep questioning process. Only in this way can we hope to attain full mature personhood and uniqueness.

A nurturing nondominating society can help in the "real work" of becoming a whole person. The "real work" can be summarized symbolically as the realization of "self-in-Self" where "Self" stands for organic wholeness. This process of the full unfolding of the self can also be summarized by the phrase, "No one is saved until we are all saved," where the phrase "one" includes not only me, an individual human, but all humans, whales, grizzly bears, whole rain forest ecosystems, mountains and rivers, the tiniest microbes in the soil, and so on.

II. BIOCENTRIC EQUALITY

The intuition of biocentric equality is that all things in the biosphere have an equal right to live and blossom and to reach their own individual forms of unfolding and self-realization within the larger Self-realization. This basic intuition is that all or-ganisms and entities in the ecosphere, as parts of the interrelated whole, are equal in intrinsic worth. Naess suggests that biocentric equality as an intui-tion is true in principle, although in the process of living, all species use each other as food, shelter, etc. Mutual predation is a biological fact of life, and many of the world's religions have struggled with the spiritual implications of this. Some animal lib-erationists who attempt to side-step this problem by advocating vegetarianism are forced to say that the entire plant kingdom including rain forests have no right to their own existence. This evasion flies in the face of the basic intuition of equality. Aldo Leopold expressed this intuition when he said hu-mans are "plain citizens" of the biotic community, not lord and master over all other species.

Biocentric equality is intimately related to the all-inclusive Self-realization in the sense that if we harm the rest of Nature then we are harming our-selves. There are no boundaries and everything is interrelated. But insofar as we perceive things as individual organisms or entities, the insight draws us to respect all human and nonhuman individuals in their own right as parts of the whole without feeling the need to set up hierarchies of species with humans at the top.

The practical implications of this intuition or norm suggest that we should live with minimum rather than maximum impact on other species and on the Earth in general. Thus we see another aspect of our guiding principle: "simple in means, rich in ends."

A fuller discussion of the biocentric norm as it unfolds itself in practice begins with the realization that we, as individual humans, and as communities of humans, have vital needs which go beyond such basics as food, water, and shelter to include love, play, creative expression, intimate relationships with a particular landscape (or Nature taken in its entirety) as well as intimate relationships with other humans, and the vital need for spiritual growth, for becoming a mature human being.

Our vital material needs are probably more simple than many realize. In technocratic-industrial societies there is overwhelming propaganda and advertising which encourages false needs and destructive desires designed to foster increased production and consump-tion of goods. Most of this actually diverts us from facing reality in an objective way and from beginning the "real work" of spiritual growth and maturity.

Many people who do not see themselves as supporters of deep ecology nevertheless recognize an overriding vital human need for a healthy and high-quality natural environment for humans, if not for all life, with minimum intrusion of toxic waste, nuclear radiation from human enterprises, minimum acid rain and smog, and enough free flowing wilderness so humans can get in touch with their sources, the natural rhythms and the flow of time and place.

Drawing from the minority tradition and from the wisdom of many who have offered the insight of interconnectedness, we recognize that deep ecol-ogists can offer suggestions for gaining maturity and encouraging the processes of harmony with Nature, but that there is no grand solution which is guaran-teed to save us from ourselves.

The ultimate norms of deep ecology suggest a view of the nature of reality and our place as an individual (many in the one) in the larger scheme of things. They cannot be fully grasped intellectu-ally but are ultimately experiential. We encourage readers to consider our further discussion of the psychological, social and ecological implications of these norms in later chapters.

As a brief summary of our position thus far, Figure 1 summarizes the contrast between the dominant worldview and deep ecology.

Dominant Worldview	Deep Ecology
Dominance over Nature	Harmony with Nature
Natural environment as resource for humans	All nature has intrinsic worth/biospecies equality
Material/economic growth for growing human population	Elegantly simple material needs (material goals serving the larger goal or self-realization)
Relief in ample resource reserves	Earth "supplies" limited
High technological progress and solutions	Appropriate technology; nondominating science
Consumerism	Doing with enough/recycling
National/centralized community	Minority tradition/bioregion

FIGURE 1 The present carbon cycle.

III. BASIC PRINCIPLES OF DEEP ECOLOGY

In April 1984, during the advent of spring and John Muir's birthday, George Sessions and Arne Naess summarized fifteen years of thinking on the principles of deep ecology while camping in Death Valley, California. In this great and special place, they articulated these principles in a literal, somewhat neutral way, hoping that they would be understood and accepted by persons coming from different philosophical and religious positions.

Readers are encouraged to elaborate their own versions of deep ecology, clarify key concepts and think through the consequences of acting from these principles.

Basic Principles

1. The well-being and flourishing of human and nonhuman Life on Earth have value in themselves (synonyms: intrinsic value, inherent value). These values are independent of the usefulness of the nonhuman world for human purposes.

2. Richness and diversity of life forms contribute to the realization of these values and are also values in themselves.

3. Humans have no right to reduce this richness and diversity except to satisfy *vital* needs.

4. The flourishing of human life and cultures is compatible with a substantial decrease of the human population. The flourishing of nonhuman life requires such a decrease.

5. Present human interference with the nonhuman world is excessive, and the situation is rapidly worsening.

6. Policies must therefore be changed. These policies affect basic economic, technological, and ideological structures. The resulting state of affairs will be deeply different from the present.

7. The ideological change is mainly that of appreciating *life quality* (dwelling in situations of inherent value) rather than adhering to an increasingly higher standard of living. There will be a profound awareness of the difference between big and great.

8. Those who subscribe to the foregoing points have an obligation directly or indirectly to try to implement the necessary changes.

Naess and Sessions Provide Comments on the Basic Principles

RE (1). This formulation refers to the biosphere, or more accurately, to the ecosphere as a whole. This includes individuals, species, populations, habitat, as well as human and nonhuman cultures. From our current knowledge of all-pervasive intimate relationships, this implies a fundamental deep concern and respect. Ecological processes of the planet should, on the whole, remain intact. "The world environment should remain 'natural'" (Gary Snyder).

The term "life" is used here in a more comprehensive nontechnical way to refer also to what biologists classify as "nonliving"; rivers (watersheds), landscapes, ecosystems. For supporters of deep ecology, slogans such as "Let the river live" illustrate this broader usage so common in most cultures.

Inherent value as used in (1) is common in deep ecology literature ("The presence of inherent value in a natural object is independent of any awareness, interest, or appreciation of it by a conscious being.")

RE (2). More technically, this is a formulation concerning diversity and complexity. From an ecological standpoint, complexity and symbiosis are conditions for maximizing diversity. So-called simple, lower, or primitive species of plants and animals contribute essentially to the richness and diversity of life. They have value in themselves and are not merely steps toward the so-called higher or rational life forms. The second principle presupposes that life itself, as a process over evolutionary time, implies an increase of diversity and richness. The refusal to acknowledge that some life forms have greater or lesser intrinsic value than others (see points 1 and 2) runs counter to the formulations of some ecological philosophers and New Age writers.

Complexity, as referred to here, is different from complication. Urban life may be more complicated than life in a natural setting without being more complex in the sense of multifaceted quality.

RE (3). The term "vital need" is left deliberately vague to allow for considerable latitude in judgment. Differences in climate and related factors, together with differences in the structures of societies as they now exist, need to be considered (for some Eskimos, snowmobiles are necessary today to satisfy vital needs).

People in the materially richest countries cannot be expected to reduce their excessive interference with the nonhuman world to a moderate level overnight. The stabilization and reduction of the human population will take time. Interim strategies need to be developed. But this in no way excuses the present complacency—the extreme seriousness of our current situation must first be realized. But the longer we wait the more drastic will be the measures needed. Until deep changes are made, substantial decreases in richness and diversity are liable to occur: the rate of extinction of species will be ten to one hundred times greater than any other period of earth history.

RE (4). The United Nations Fund for Population Activities in their State of World Population Report (1984) said that high human population growth rates (over 2.0 percent annum) in many developing countries "were diminishing the quality of life for many millions of people." During the decade 1974–1984, the world population grew by nearly 800 million—more than the size of India. "And we will be adding about one Bangladesh (population 93 million) per annum between now and the year 2000."

The report noted that "The growth rate of the human population has declined for the first time in human history. But at the same time, the number of people being added to the human population is bigger than at any time in history because the population base is larger."

Most of the nations in the developing world (including India and China) have as their official government policy the goal of reducing the rate of human population increase, but there are debates over the types of measures to take (contraception, abortion, etc.) consistent with human rights and feasibility.

The report concludes that if all governments set specific population targets as public policy to help alleviate poverty and advance the quality of life, the current situation could be improved.

As many ecologists have pointed out, it is also absolutely crucial to curb population growth in the so-called developed (i.e., overdeveloped) industrial societies. Given the tremendous rate of consumption and waste production of individuals in these societies, they represent a much greater threat and impact on the biosphere per capita than individuals in Second and Third World countries.

RE (5). This formulation is mild. For a realistic assessment of the situation, see the unabbreviated version of the I.U.C.N.'s *World Conservation Strategy.* There are other works to be highly recommended, such as Gerald Barney's *Global 2000 Report to the President of the United States.*

The slogan of "noninterference" does not imply that humans should not modify some ecosystems as do other species. Humans have modified the earth and will probably continue to do so. At issue is the nature and extent of such interference.

The fight to preserve and extend areas of wilderness or near-wilderness should continue and should focus on the general ecological functions of these areas (one such function: large wilderness areas are required in the biosphere to allow for continued evolutionary speciation of animals and plants). Most present designated wilderness areas and game preserves are not large enough to allow for such speciation.

RE (6). Economic growth as conceived and implemented today by the industrial states is incompatible with (1)–(5). There is only a faint resemblance between ideal sustainable forms of economic growth and present policies of the industrial societies. And "sustainable" still means "sustainable in relation to humans."

Present ideology tends to value things because they are scarce and because they have a commodity value. There is prestige in vast consumption and waste (to mention only several relevant factors).

Whereas "self-determination," "local community," and "think globally, act locally," will remain key terms in the ecology of human societies, nevertheless the implementation of deep changes requires increasingly global action—action across borders.

Governments in Third World countries (with the exception of Costa Rica and a few others) are uninterested in deep ecological issues. When the governments of industrial societies try to promote ecological measures through Third World governments, practically nothing is accomplished (e.g., with problems of desertification). Given this situation, support for global action through nongovernmental international organizations becomes increasingly important. Many of these organizations are able to act globally "from grassroots to grassroots," thus avoiding negative governmental interference.

Cultural diversity today requires advanced technology, that is, techniques that advance the basic goals of each culture. So-called soft, intermediate, and alternative technologies are steps in this direction.

RE (7). Some economists criticize the term "quality of life" because it is supposed to be vague. But on closer inspection, what they consider to be vague is actually the nonquantitative nature of the term. One cannot quantify adequately what is important for the quality of life as discussed here, and there is no need to do so.

RE (8). There is ample room for different opinions about priorities: what should be done first, what next? What is most urgent? What is clearly necessary as opposed to what is highly desirable but not absolutely pressing?

STUDY QUESTIONS

1. Analyze the eight principles of deep ecology. What problems, if any, do you find with them? Do you accept the first principle that natural objects have inherent value? What things do you think have inherent value and why?

2. What are the implications of Principle 4? If people do not voluntarily curb their population, how would a deep ecologist solve this problem?

3. Is deep ecology workable? Why, or why not?

16

Deep Ecology: A New Philosophy of Our Time?

WARWICK FOX

Warrick Fox is professor of philosophy at University of Central Lancashire. In this essay he offers an overview of the development of deep ecology, examines its relationship to various mystical traditions, and attempts to clarify potential problems.

The Australian philosopher William Godfrey-Smith has remarked that "deep ecology … has an unfortunate tendency to discuss everything at once. Thus a social critique of deep ecology may be backed by such disparate authorities as Ginsberg, Castenada, Thoreau, Spinoza, Buddhist visionaries, and Taoist physics. With a cast of prima donnas like this on stage it is very hard to follow the script." In this paper, I shall try not to "discuss everything at once" by confining my attention mainly to what I take to be the central intuition of deep ecology, and to some considerations related to that intuition. Even so, I shall still be making reference to "Buddhist visionaries and Taoist physics" for at least one compelling reason: not to refer to the parallels between deep ecology, the mystical traditions, and the so-called "new physics" (i.e., post 1920s physics) might well indicate that one had *missed* the central intuition of deep ecology since, fundamentally, each of these fields of understanding subscribes to a similar structure of reality, a similar cosmology. Deep ecology's "disparate authorities" turn out to be not as disparate as they at first appear. Moreover, comparison with these other fields can, I believe, be fruitful in clarifying some of deep ecology's vaguer or more contradictory aspects.

The distinction between 'shallow' and 'deep' ecology was made in 1972 (and published the following year) by the distinguished Norwegian philosopher Arne Naess, and has subsequently been developed by a number of thinkers (most notably, Bill Devall and George Sessions) to the point where we may now reasonably refer to an intellectual 'deep ecology movement.' The shallow/deep ecology distinction has generated so much discussion that it has become difficult to distil to any simple essence but, for the sake of brevity, it could be characterized by the following three points.

First, shallow ecology views humans as separate from their environment. Figure/ground boundaries are sharply drawn such that humans are perceived as the significant figures against a ground that only assumes significance in so far as it enhances humans' images of themselves *qua* important figures. Shallow ecology thus views humans as the source of all value and ascribes only instrumental (or use) value to the nonhuman world. It is, in short, anthropocentric, representing that attitude to conservation that says: "We ought to preserve the environment (i.e., what lies outside the boundary) not for its own sake but because of its value to us (i.e., what lies inside the boundary)." Deep ecology, on the other hand, rejects "the (human)-in-environment image in favour of the relational, total-field image." Organisms and then viewed rather "as knots in the biospherical net or field of

"Deep Ecology: A New Philosophy for Our Time" from *The Ecologist,* Vol. 14 (1984) by Warrick Fox. Reprinted by permission.

intrinsic relations." Figure/ground boundaries are replaced by a holistic or gestalt view where, in Devall's words, "the person is not above or outside of nature … (but) … is part of creation on-going." This 'total-field' conception dissolves not only the notion of humans as septum from their environment but the very notion of the world as composed of discrete, compact, separate 'things'. When we do talk about the world as if it were a collection of discrete, isolable 'things' we are, in Naess's view, "*talking at a superficial or preliminary level of communication.*" Deep ecology thus strives to be non-anthropocentric by viewing humans as just one constituency among others in the biotic community, just one particular strand in the web of life, just one kind of knot in the bio-spherical net. The intrinsic value of the nonhuman members of the biotic community is recognized and the right of these members to pursue their own evolutionary destinies is taken as "an intuitively clear and obvious value axiom." In contrast, the idea that humans are the source or ground of all value ('the measure of all things') is viewed as the arrogant conceit of those who dwell in the moral equivalent of a Ptolemaic universe. Deep ecologists are concerned to move heaven and earth in this universe in order to effect a 'paradigm shift' of comparable significance to that associated with Copernicus.

Second (and directly related to the above), in its acceptance of what Sessions refers to as 'discrete entity metaphysics' shallow ecology accepts by default or positively endorses the dominant metaphysics of mechanistic materialism. Viewing knowledge, too, as amenable to discrete compartmentalization, the shallow approach considers ethics in isolation from metaphysics with the consequence that the dominant metaphysics is usually implicitly assumed. Deep ecology, however, is concerned to criticize mechanistic materialism and to replace it with a better 'code for reading nature.' This code can be generally described as one of 'unity in process.' By this is indicated both the idea that all 'things' are fundamentally (i.e., internally) related and the idea that these interrelationships are in constant flux (i.e., they are characterized by process/dynamism/instability/novelty/creativity, etc). This conception of the world lends itself far more readily to organismic rather than mechanical metaphors, and thus to panpsychic or pantheistic rather than inert, dead-matter conceptions of the nonhuman world. Among Western philosophers, Spinoza, Whitehead and Heidegger are most often invoked for the purposes of articulating this vision of the world or, particularly in the case of Heidegger, for the purposes of articulating the 'letting be' mode of being most appropriate to such a deep ecological understanding of the world. Deep ecology also has an enormous respect for many non-Western views since 'unity in process' and panpsychic conceptions of the world have received sophisticated elaboration in Eastern spiritual traditions and in the mythological systems of other non-Western peoples. This respect also extends to the entire sensibility or mode of being-in-the-world of some of these traditions since this often accords with the non-power-seeking sensibility of deep ecology. In stressing the interconnection between ethics and metaphysics, deep ecology recognizes that an ecologically effective ethics can only arise within the context of a more persuasive and more enchanting cosmology than that of mechanistic materialism.

Third, in terms of its social, political and economic project, shallow ecology tends to accept by default or positively endorse the ideology of economic growth which characterizes industrial and developing societies of all political complexions. It is thus often referred to as the 'Resource Management' or 'Resource Conservation and Development' approach. As such, it is content to operate in a reformist fashion within the 'dominant social paradigm' and, often, to accept the economic reduction (i.e., the reduction of all values to economic terms) for the purposes of decision making. Deep ecology on the other hand is concerned to address existing social, political and economic arrangements and to replace the ideology of economic growth with the ideology of ecological sustainability. It is insisted that economics (etymologically: 'management of the household') must be seen as subsidiary to ecology ('study of the household'), and the economic reduction of values is thus firmly resisted. Key ideas in deep ecology's social, political and economic project include those of a just and sustainable society, carrying capacity, frugality (or 'voluntary simplicity'), dwelling in place, cultural and biological diversity, local autonomy and decentralization, soft energy paths, appropriate technology, reinhabitation, and bioregionalism. These last two perhaps require some elaboration. Reinhabitation refers to the process of relearning how to live in place, how to establish a 'sense of place', how to dwell in and care for a place. Some people are attempting to cultivate consciously this sense, under the most difficult of circumstances, by moving into areas that have been degraded by industrial 'development' and participating in the re-establishment of a rich and diverse ecosystem. Bioregions refer to areas possessing common characteristics of soils, watersheds, plants and animals (e.g., the Amazon jungle). It is argued that bioregions should replace nation-states as the fundamental geographical unit in terms of which humans think and live. The human carrying capacity for each bioregion should be determined in terms of the number of humans that can be supported living at a level of resource use that is adequate for their needs but minimally intrusive on their environment. Here, of course, lie a multitude of difficult questions for the political agenda of deep ecology. However, these questions have, in various forms, been addressed by numerous societies in the past (including a minority tradition in Western society) and are now being taken up by increasing numbers of thinkers in highly industrialized societies.

It should be clear from this summary that many writers whose work falls within the ambit of deep ecology do not necessarily describe themselves as 'deep ecologists'. A good example is Theodore Roszak who, in his 1972 book *Where the Wasteland Ends*, pointed to the same kind of distinction as Naess:

> Ecology stands at a critical cross-roads. Is it, too, to become another anthropocentric technique of efficient manipulation, a matter of enlightened self-interest and expert, long-range resource budgeting? Or will it meet the nature mystics on their own terms and so recognize that we are to embrace nature as if indeed it were a beloved person in whom, as in ourselves, something sacred dwells? …
> The question remains open: which will ecology be, the last of the old sciences or the first of the new?

However, despite this and other attempts by philosophers, historians and sociologists to distinguish between various streams of environmentalism, Naess's twelve year old shallow/deep ecology terminology seems to have stuck as the most economical and striking way of referring to the major division within contemporary environmental thought. The conceptualization of this division clearly constitutes a powerful organizing idea in terms of providing a focal point from which to view the relationships between a number of otherwise very diffuse strands of ecologically oriented thought.

THE INTUITION OF DEEP ECOLOGY

It should be clear from my brief outline of the shallow/deep ecology distinction that many of the views held by deep ecologists go well beyond the data of ecology conceived as an empiric-analytic science. As Arne Naess said when introducing the shallow/deep ecology distinction: "… the norms and tendencies of the Deep Ecology movement are not derived from ecology by logic or induction. Ecological knowledge and the life-style of the ecological field-worker have *suggested, inspired, and fortified* the perspectives of the Deep Ecology movement." Deep ecologists have, therefore, taken the point made by Donald Worster in his study of the history of ecological ideas from the eighteenth century to the early 1970s:

> In the case of the ecological ethic … one might say that its proponents picked out their values first and only afterward came to science for its stamp of approval. It might have been the better part of honesty if they had come out and announced that, for some reason or by some personal standard of value, they were constrained to promote a deeper sense of integration between (humans) and nature, a more-than-economic relatedness – and to let all the appended scientific arguments go. 'Ought' might then be its own justification, its own defence, its own persuasion, regardless of what 'is.'

That more straightforward stance has now and again been adopted by a few intuitionists, mystics, and transcendentalists. Most people, however, have not been so willing to trust their inner voices, perhaps due to lack of self-confidence or out of fear that such wholly individual exercise of choice will lead to the general disintegration of the moral community.

Deep ecologists *are* 'willing to trust their inner voices' in the hope that the dominant social paradigm (within which the moral community is situated) *will* disintegrate—although in a creative rather than a destructive manner. Again, Arne Naess is quite explicit on these points in a recent interview in *The Ten Directions*, a magazine published by the Zen Centre of Los Angeles:

Ten Directions: This brings us back to the question of information versus intuition. Your feeling is that we can't expect to have an ideal amount of information but must somehow act on what we know?

Naess: Yes. It's easier for deep ecologists than for others because we have certain fundamental values, a fundamental view of what's meaningful in life, what's worth maintaining, which makes it completely clear that we are opposed to further development for the sake of increased domination and an increased standard of living. The material standard of living should be drastically reduced and the quality of life, in the sense of basic satisfaction in the depths of one's heart or soul, should be maintained or increased. This view is intuitive, as are all important views, in the sense that it can't be proven. As Aristotle said, it shows a lack of education to try to prove everything because you have to have a starting point. You can't prove the methodology of science, you can't prove logic, because logic presupposes fundamental premises.

However, the *central* intuition of deep ecology, the one from which Naess's views on practice flow, is the first point I made in my summary of the shallow/deep ecology distinction. This is the idea that there is no firm ontological divide in the field of existence. In other words, the world simply is not divided up into independently existing subjects and objects, nor is there any bifurcation in reality between the human and non-human realms. Rather all entities are constituted by their relationships. To the extent that we perceive boundaries, we fall short of a deep ecological consciousness. In Devall's words: "Deep ecology begins with unity rather than dualism which has been the dominant theme of Western philosophy."

THE INTUITION OF DEEP ECOLOGY AND CROSS-DISCIPLINARY PARALLELS

The central intuition of deep ecology finds a profound resonance in both the mystical traditions and the 'new physics'. For example, the 'perennial philosophy' tells us, and the meditative process is claimed to reveal, that 'Thou art That'. In other words, it is claimed that by subtracting your own self-centered and self-serving thoughts from the world you come to realize that "the other is none other than yourself: that the fundamental delusion of humanity is to suppose I am here and you are out there." This understanding permeates the mystical traditions and is exemplified in the Taoist advice to "identify yourself with non-distinction." Likewise, the Zen teacher Chü-chih would answer any question he was asked by holding up one finger, while the contemporary Zen roshi Robert Aitken says that "we save all beings by including them." The mystical traditions are simply full of differing illustrations of this same point. Ken Wilber, editor of the journal *Revision* and perhaps the most significant recent integrator of Eastern and Western worldviews, expresses the mystical understanding in these terms: "We fall from Heaven in this moment and this moment and this, every time we embrace boundaries and live as a separate self sense." Just so, adds the deep ecologist, do we fall short of a *deep* ecological consciousness.

It is now becoming commonplace to point to the fundamentally similar cosmologies embodied in the mystical traditions on the one hand and the 'new physics' on the other. What is *structurally* similar about these cosmologies is that they reveal a 'seamless web' view of the universe. As David Bohm, the distinguished Professor of Theoretical Physics at Birbeck College, University of London, has said in an interview with the philosopher Renée Weber:

Bohm: ... the present state of theoretical physics implies that empty space has all this energy and matter is a slight increase of the energy, and therefore matter is like a small ripple on this tremendous ocean of energy, having some relative stability, and being manifest. (Thus, my suggestion of an 'implicate order') implies a reality immensely beyond what we call matter. Matter itself is merely a ripple in this background... in this ocean of energy...

Weber: This view is of course very beautiful, breath taking in fact, but would a physicist who pressed you on this ... find some kind of basis *in physics* for allowing such a vision to be postulated?

Bohm: Well, I should think it's what physics directly implies.

Both the mystical traditions and the 'new physics' serve to generate, *inter alia*, what we might now call 'ecological awareness', that is, awareness of the fundamental interrelatedness of all things or, more accurately, all events. The theoretical physicist Fritjof Capra has been quite explicit about this: "I think what physics can do is help to generate ecological awareness. You see, in my view now the Western version of mystical awareness, our version of Buddhism or Taoism, will be ecological awareness." When the physicist, the mystic, and the deep ecologist (as philosopher) differ is in their *means* of arriving at an 'ecological awareness'. In terms of Wilber's typology of modes of inquiry, we could say that the physicist (like the 'scientific' ecologist) emphasizes 'empiric-analytic inquiry' (i.e., analysis of measurements), the mystic emphasizes 'transcendental inquiry' (i.e., contemplation), and the deep ecologist (as philosopher) emphasizes 'mental-phenomenological inquiry' (i.e., analysis of meaning: here we include such things as reflection on personal experience, the analysis of valuational arguments, and the meaning of knowledge furnished by the other two modes of inquiry).

However, all three modes of inquiry lead to a similar conception of the underlying structure of reality. Like the mystic and the 'new physicist', the deep ecologist is drawn to a cosmology of (in David Bohm's words) "unbroken wholeness which denies the classical idea of the analyzability of the world into separately and independently existing parts."

A NEW COSMOLOGY

While I refer to this view as the central *intuition* of deep ecology, I do not in any way mean that it is irrational or ungrounded. The deep ecologist who is pressed to say whether there is a basis *in ecology* for "allowing such a vision to be postulated" can reply, in the manner of David Bohm, that this cosmology is what ecology directly implies. Moreover, the deep ecologist can argue that if there is substance to the "hypothesis of emerging cross-disciplinary parallels" advocated by the neurophysiologist Roger Walsh, then the parallels between the structures of reality advanced by deep ecology, the mystical traditions and the 'new physics' are enormously significant rather than trivial coincidences or accidents of language. Briefly, Walsh's hypothesis is that we can enhance our perceptual sensitivity by the augmentation of normal sensory perception (as in science), by intellectual conceptual analysis (as in philosophy), or by direct perceptual training (as in meditation), and that:

> no matter how it is obtained, (perceptual) enhancement of sufficient degree may reveal a different order or reality from that to which we are accustomed. Furthermore, the properties so revealed will be essentially more fundamental and veridical than the usual, and will display a greater degree of commonality across disciplines. Thus as empirical disciplines evolve and become more sensitive, they might be expected to uncover phenomena and properties which point toward underlying commonalities and parallels between disciplines and across levels.

existence—as transient as that may be in terms of evolutionary time.

In pursuing their central intuition of 'unity' (i.e., of no boundaries in the biospherical field), deep ecologists have possibly lost sight of the significance of the 'in process' aspect of their 'unity in process' metaphysics. Attention to this latter aspect suggests that any process continuously produces impermanent, uneven distributions (i.e., different values) of various attributes (and in the process of the world these attributes may be money, information, complexity of relations, and so on). If this were not so then we would have no process but a perfectly uniform, homogenous and, therefore, lifeless field. The only universe where value is spread evenly across the field is a dead universe. Recognizing this, we should be clear that the central intuition of deep ecology does not entail the view that intrinsic value is spread evenly across the membership of the biotic community. Moreover, in situations of genuine value conflict, justice is better served by *not* subscribing to the view of ecological egalitarianism. Cows do scream louder than carrots. As Charles Birch and John Cobb have remarked: "Justice does not require equality. It does require that we share one another's fate." There is, however, a shallow and a deep sense of sharing one another's fate. The shallow sense is simply that of being subject to the same forces. It does not involve caring. The deep sense, intended by Birch and Cobb, involves love and compassion. It involves the *enlargement of one's sphere of identification*. The lesson of ecology is that we do share one another's fate in the shallow sense since we all share the fate of the earth. The message of deep ecology is that we ought to care as deeply and as compassionately as possible about that fate—not because it *affects* us but because it *is* us.

STUDY QUESTIONS

1. How Does Deep Ecology relate to Taoism and physics?

2. For Fox, what are the important contributions of the deep ecological perspective?

17

A Critique of Anti-Anthropocentric Ethics

RICHARD WATSON

Richard Watson is professor of philosophy at Washington University in St. Louis and author of several works in philosophy. Here is his abstract:

Arne Naess, John Rodman, George Sessions, and others designated herein as ecosophers, propose an egalitarian anti-anthropocentric biocentrism as a basis for a new

Reprinted from *Environmental Ethics*, Vol. 5 (Fall 1983) by permission. Notes edited.

environmental ethic. I outline their "hands-off-nature" position and show it to be based on setting man apart. The ecosophic position is thus neither egalitarian nor fully biocentric. A fully egalitarian biocentric ethic would place no more restrictions on the behavior of human beings than on the behavior of any other animals. Uncontrolled human behavior might lead to the destruction of the environment and thus to the extinction of human beings. I thus conclude that human interest in survival is the best ground on which to argue for an ecological balance which is good both for human beings and for the whole biological community.

Anthropocentric is defined specifically as the position "that considers man as the central fact, or final aim, of the universe" and generally "conceiv[es] of everything in the universe in terms of human values."[1] In the literature of environmental ethics, anti-anthropocentric biocentrism is the position that human needs, goals, and desires should not be taken as privileged or overriding in considering the needs, desires, interests, and goals of all members of all biological species taken together, and in general that the Earth as a whole should not be interpreted or managed from a human standpoint. According to this position, birds, trees, and the land itself considered as the biosphere have a right to be and to live out their individual and species' potentials, and that members of the human species have no right to disturb, perturb, or destroy the ecological balance of the planet.

An often quoted statement of this right of natural objects to continue to be as they are found to be occurs in John Rodman's "The Liberation of Nature?":

> To affirm that "natural objects" have "rights" is symbolically to affirm that ALL NATURAL ENTITIES (INCLUDING HUMANS) HAVE INTRINSIC WORTH SIMPLY BY VIRTUE OF BEING AND BEING WHAT THEY ARE.[2]

In "On the Nature and Possibility of an Environmental Ethic," Tom Regan follows an implication of this view by presenting a "preservation principle":

> By the "preservation principle" I mean a principle of nondestruction, noninterference, and, generally, nonmeddling. By characterizing this in terms of a principle, moreover, I am

emphasizing that preservation (letting-be) be regarded as a moral imperative.[3]

Support for this hands-off-nature approach is provided by George Sessions in his "Spinoza, Perennial Philosophy, and Deep Ecology," where, among other things, he describes how Aldo Leopold moved from a position considering humans as stewards or managers of nature to one considering humans as "plain members" of the total biotic community.[4] As Leopold himself puts it:

> A thing is right when it tends to preserve the integrity, stability, and beauty of the biotic community. It is wrong when it tends otherwise.[5]

According to Sessions, Leopold reached this position in part as a result of his dawning realization that ecological communities are internally integrated and highly complex. He saw how human activities have disrupted many ecological communities and was himself involved in some unsuccessful attempts to manage communities of animals in the wild. These failures led Leopold to conclude that "the biotic mechanism is so complex that its workings may never be fully understood."[6]

Like many other environmentalists, Sessions associates Leopold's position with Barry Commoner's first law of ecology: "Everything is connected to everything else,"[7] according to which "any major man-made change in a natural system is likely to be *detrimental* to that system." This view, which considers all environmental managers who try to alter the environment to be suffering from scientific hubris, leads to an almost biblical statement of nescience. In this connection, Sessions quotes the ecologist Frank Egler as saying that "Nature is not only more complex than we think, but it is more complex than we can ever think." The attitude of humble acquiescence to the ways of nature which follows from this view, Sessions says, is summed up in Commoner's third law, "Nature knows best."

The position is presented at length by G. Tyler Miller, in another quotation cited by Sessions:

One of the purposes of this Book [*Replenish the Earth*] is to show the bankruptcy of the term "spaceship earth." ... This is an upside-down view of reality and is yet another manifestation of our arrogance toward nature.... Our task is not to learn how to pilot spaceship earth. It is not to learn how—as Teilhard de Chardin would have it—"to seize the tiller of the world": Our task is to give up our fantasies of omnipotence. In other words, *we must stop trying to steer* [my italics]. The solution to our present dilemma does not lie in attempting to extend our technical and managerial skills into every sphere of existence. Thus, *from a human standpoint our environmental crisis is the result* of our arrogance towards nature [Miller's italics]. Somehow we must tune our senses again to the beat of existence, sensing in nature fundamental rhythms we can trust even though we may never fully understand them. We must learn anew that it is we who belong to earth and not the earth to us. Thus rediscovery of our finitude is fundamental to any genuinely human future.[8]

Sessions, at least, is not naive about some of the problems that arise from these pronouncements. He says that if an environmental ethic is to be derived from ecological principles and concepts, this raises

the old problem of attempting to derive moral principles and imperatives from supposedly empirical fact (the "is-ought problem"). The attempt to justify ecosystem ethics on conventional utilitarian or "rights and obligations" grounds presents formidable obstacles. And, so far, little headway has been made in finding other acceptable grounds for an ecosystem ethics

other than a growing intuitive ecological awareness that *it is right.*[9]

The anti-anthropocentric biocentrists have sought a metaphysical foundation for a holistic environmental ethic in Spinoza. The clearest statement of this appears in Arne Naess's "Spinoza and Ecology." Naess expands from Spinoza in sixteen points, several of which are crucial to my discussion of anti-anthropocentric biocentrism:

1. The nature conceived by field ecologists is not the passive, dead, value-neutral nature of mechanistic science, but akin to the *Deus sive Natura* of Spinoza. All-inclusive, creative (as *natura naturans*), infinitely diverse, and alive in the broad sense of pan-psychism, but also manifesting a structure, the so-called laws of nature. There are always causes to be found, but extremely complex and difficult to unearth. Nature with a capital N is intuitively conceived as perfect in a sense that Spinoza and outdoor ecologists have more or less in common: it is not narrowly moral, utilitarian, or aesthetic perfection. Nature is perfect "in itself."

Perfection can only mean completeness of some sort when applied in general, and not to specifically human achievements....

2. ... The two aspects of Nature, those of extension and thought (better: non-extension), are both complete aspects of one single reality, and *perfection characterizes both*....

3. ... As an *absolutely* all-embracing reality, Nature has no purpose, aim, or goal....

4. There is no established moral world-order. Human justice is not a law of nature. There are, on the other hand, no natural laws limiting the endeavour to extend the realm of justice as conceived in a society of free human beings....

5. Good and evil must be defined in relation to beings for which something is good or evil, useful or detrimental. The terms are meaningless when not thus related....

6. Every thing is connected with every other.... Intimate interconnectedness in the sense of internal rather than external relations characterizes ecological ontology....

7. If one insists upon using the term "rights," every being may be said to have the right to do

what is in its power. It is "right" to express its own nature as clearly and extensively as natural conditions permit.

That right which they [the animals] have in relation to us, we have in relation to them (*Ethics*, Part IV, first scholium to proposition 37).

That rights are a part of a separate moral world order is fiction.

Field ecologists tend to accept a general "right to live and blossom." Humans have no special right to kill and injure. Nature does not belong to them.[10]

Spinoza has also been cited for the general position that the ultimate goal, good, and joy of human beings is understanding which amounts to contemplation of Nature. In "Spinoza and Jeffers on Man in Nature," Sessions says:

> Spinoza's purpose in philosophizing, then, is to break free from the bonds of desire and ignorance which captivate and frustrate most men, thus standing in the way of what real happiness is available to them, and to attain a higher Self which is aligned with a *correct* [my italics] understanding of God/Nature.[11]

The position, however, is not restricted to Spinoza, for, as Sessions notes elsewhere, the best-known statement of this view is probably found in Aldous Huxley's *Perennial Philosophy*:

> Happiness and moral progress depend, it is [mistakenly] thought [today], on bigger and better gadgets and a higher standard of living…. In all the historic formulations of the Perennial Philosophy it is axiomatic that the end of human life is contemplation, or the direct and intuitive awareness of God; that action is the means to that end; that a society is good to the extent that it renders contemplation possible for its members.[12]

A difficult question that arises for advocates of this position is whether or not humans can be activists. For example, near-total passivism seems to be suggested by Michael Zimmerman in his approving summation of what he takes to be Heidegger's admonition to the Western World:

> Only Western man's thinking has ended up by viewing the world as a storehouse of raw material for the enhancement of man's Power…. [A] new kind of thinking must … pass beyond the subjectivistic thinking of philosophy-science-technology…. Heidegger indicates that the new way must "let beings be," i.e., it must let them manifest themselves in their own presence and worth, and not merely as objects for the all-powerful Subject.[13]

On the other hand, Naess is an activist; he and others think that civil disobedience is appropriate to thwart human "misuse" of the environment. And although Naess stresses what he calls the "biospherical egalitarianism" of all biological species on earth," he says in "Environmental Ethics and Spinoza":

> Animals cannot be citizens [i.e., members of a human moral community]. But animals may, as far as I can understand, be members of *life communities* on a par with babies, lunatics, and others who do not cooperate as citizens but are cared for in part for their own good.

This is consistent with Naess's Spinozistic approach, but the more general implication of the species egalitarian approach seems to be inactivism.

In summary, advocates of anti-anthropocentric biocentrism such as Sessions speak of the Judeo-Christian-Platonic-Aristotelian tradition as leading to

> an extreme subjectivist anthropocentrism in which the whole of non-human nature is viewed as a resource for man. By way of a long and convoluted intellectual history, we have managed to subvert completely the organic ecological world view of the hunter and gatherer.

Sessions goes on to deplore "the demise of pantheism and the desacralization of Nature." He then makes a statement highly typical of anti-anthropomorphic biocentrists:

> Part of the genius of Bacon and Descartes was to realize, contrary to the conservatism of the Church authorities, that a new

science was needed to consummate the goal of Judeo-Christian-Platonic-Aristotelian domination of nature. The Enlightenment retained the Christian idea of man's perpetual progress (now defined as increasing scientific-technological control and mastery over nature), thus setting the stage for, and passing its unbridled optimism on to, its twentieth-century successors, Marxism and American pragmatism. The flood-gates had been opened. The Pythagorean theory of the cosmos and the whole idea of a meaningful perennial philosophy were swept away in a deluge of secularism, the fragmentation of knowledge, pronouncements that God was dead and the universe and life of man meaningless, industrialization, the quest for material happiness, and the consequent destruction of the environment. The emphasis was no longer upon either God or Nature, but Man.

Sessions by no means advocates or thinks possible a simple return to pre-Socratic religion or pantheism. But what, on the basis of ecological principles and concepts, is the underlying motif or guiding ideal today for "a correct understanding of God/Nature"? According to Naess, the proper position is an *ecosophy* defined as "a philosophy of ecological harmony or equilibrium." Thus, while deploring the Greek contribution to the present desacralization of nature, these ecosophers do acknowledge the Stoic and Epicurean contributions to the philosophy of balance, harmony, and equilibrium. They present a holistic vision of the Earth circling in dynamic ecological equilibrium as the preferred and proper contemplative object of right-thinking environmental man.

In pursuing a statement of anti-anthropomorphic biocentrism, then, I have exposed five principles of the movement:

1. The needs, desires, interests, and goals of humans are not privileged.

2. The human species should not change the ecology of the planet.

3. The world ecological system is too complex for human beings ever to understand.

4. The ultimate goal, good, and joy of human-kind is contemplative understanding of Nature.

5. Nature is a holistic system of parts (of which ' man is merely one among many equals) all of which are internally interrelated in dynamic, harmonious, ecological equilibrium.

The moral imperative derived from this "eco-sophy" is that human beings do not have the right to, and should not, alter the equilibrium.

II

I do not intend to challenge the controversial naturalistic assumption that some such environmental ethic can be derived from ecological principles and concepts. Whatever the logical problems of deriving value from fact, it is not (and probably never has been) a practical problem for large numbers of people who base their moral convictions on factual premises.

Nevertheless, it must be obvious to most careful readers that the general position characterized in section 1 suffers from serious internal contradictions. I think they are so serious that the position must be abandoned. In what follows I detail the problems that arise in the system, and then offer an alternative to the call for developing a new ecosophic ethic.

To go immediately to the heart of the matter, I take anti-anthropocentrism more seriously than do any of the ecosophers I have quoted or read. If man is a part of nature, if he is a "plain citizen," if he is just one nonprivileged member of a "biospherical egalitarianism," then the human species should be treated in no way different from any other species. However, the entire tone of the position outlined in section 1 is to set man apart from nature and above all other living species. Naess says that nonhuman animals should be "cared for in part for their own good." Sessions says that humans should curb their technological enthusiasms to preserve ecological equilibrium. Rodman says flatly that man should let nature be.

Now, the posing of man against nature in any way is anthropocentric. Man is a part of nature. Human ways—human culture—and human actions are as natural as are the ways in which any other species of animals behaves. But if we view the state of nature or Nature as being natural, undisturbed, and unperturbed only when human beings are *not* present, or only when human beings are curbing their natural behavior, then we are assuming that human beings are apart from, separate from, different from, removed from, or above nature. It is obvious that the ecosophy described above is based on this position of setting man apart from or above nature. (Do I mean even "sordid" and "perverted" human behavior? Yes, that is natural, too.)

To avoid this separation of man from nature, this special treatment of human beings as other than nature, we must stress that man's works (yes, including H-bombs and gas chambers) are as natural as those of bower birds and beavers.

But civilized man wreaks havoc on the environment. We disrupt the ecology of the planet, cause the extinction of myriad other species of living things, and even alter the climate of the Earth. Should we not attempt to curb our behavior to avoid these results? Indeed we should as a matter of prudence if we want to preserve our habitat and guarantee the survival of our species. But this is anthropocentric thinking.

Only if we are thinking anthropocentrically will we set the human species apart as *the* species that is to be thwarted in its natural behavior. Anti-anthropocentric biocentrists suggest that other species are to be allowed to manifest themselves naturally. They are to be allowed to live out their evolutionary potential in interaction with one another. But man is different. Man is *too* powerful, *too* destructive of the environment and other species, *too* successful in reproducing, and so on. What a phenomenon is man! Man is so wonderfully bad that he is not to be allowed to live out his evolutionary potential in egalitarian interaction with all other species.

Why not? The only reason is anthropocentric. We are not treating man as a plain member of the biotic community. We are not treating the human species as an equal among other species. We think

of man as being better than other animals, or worse, as the case may be, because man is so powerful.

One reason we think this is that we think in terms of an anthropocentric moral community. All other species are viewed as morally neutral; their behavior is neither good nor bad. But we evaluate human behavior morally. And this sets man apart. If we are to treat man as a part of nature on egalitarian terms with other species, then man's behavior must be treated as morally neutral, too. It is absurd, of course, to suggest the opposite alternative, that we evaluate the behavior of nonhuman animals morally.

Bluntly, if we think there is nothing morally wrong with one species taking over the habitat of another and eventually causing the extinction of the dispossessed species—as has happened millions of times in the history of the Earth—then we should not think that there is anything morally or ecosophically wrong with the human species dispossessing and causing the extinction of other species.

Man's nature, his role, his forte, his glory and ambition has been to propagate and thrive at the expense of many other species and to the disruption—or, neutrally, to the change—of the planet's ecology. I do not want to engage in speculation about the religion of preliterate peoples, or in debates about the interpretation of documented non-Judeo-Christian-Platonic-Aristotelian religions. I am skeptical, however, of the panegyrics about pantheism and harmonious integration with sacred Nature. But these speculations do not matter. The fact is that for about 50,000 years human beings (*Homo sapiens*) have been advancing like wildfire (to use an inflammatory metaphor) to occupy more and more of the planet. A peak of low-energy technology was reached about 35,000 years ago at which time man wiped out many species of large animals. About 10,000 years ago man domesticated plants and animals and started changing the face of the Earth with grazing, farming, deforestation, and desertification. About 200 years ago man started burning fossil fuels with results that will probably change the climate of the planet (at least temporarily) and that have already resulted in the extinction of many species of living things that perhaps might otherwise have survived. In 1945 man entered an atomic age and we now have the ability to desertify large portions of the Earth and perhaps to cause the extinction of most of the higher forms of life.

Human beings do alter things. They cause the extinction of many species, and they change the Earth's ecology. This is what humans do. This is their destiny. If they destroy many other species and themselves in the process, they do no more than has been done by many another species. The human species should be allowed—if any species can be said to have a right—to live out its evolutionary potential, to its own destruction if that is the end result. It is nature's way.

This is not a popular view. But most alternative anti-anthropocentric biocentric arguments for preserving nature are self-contradictory. Man is a part of nature. The only way man will survive is if he uses his brains to save himself. One reason why we should curb human behavior that is destructive of other species and the environment is because in the end it is destructive of the human species as well.

I hope it is human nature to survive because we are smart. But those who appeal for a new ethic or religion or ecosophy based on an intuitive belief that they know what is right not only for other people, but also for the planet as a whole, exhibit the hubris that they themselves say got us in such a mess in the first place. If the ecosphere is so complicated that we may never understand its workings, how is it that so many ecosophers are so sure that they know what is right for us to do now? Beyond the issue of man's right to do whatever he can according to the power-makes-right ecosophic ethic outlined by Naess, we may simply be wrong about what is "good" for the planet. Large numbers of species have been wiped out before, e.g., at the time the dinosaurs became extinct. Perhaps wiping out and renewal is just the way things go. Of course, a lot of genetic material is lost, but presumably all the species that ever existed came out of the same primordial soup, and could again. In situations where genetic material was limited, as in the Galapagos Islands or Australia, evolutionary radiation filled the niches. Even on the basis of our present knowledge about evolution and ecology, we have little ground to worry about the proliferation

of life on Earth even if man manages to wipe out most of the species now living. Such a clearing out might be just the thing to allow for variety and diversity. And why is it that we harp about genetic banks today anyway? For one thing, we are worried that disease might wipe out our domesticated grain crops. Then where would *man* be? est. pref.

Another obvious anthropocentric element in ecosophic thinking is the predilection for ecological communities of great internal variety and complexity. But the barren limestone plateaus that surround the Mediterranean now are just as much in ecological balance as were the forests that grew there before man cut them down. And "dead" Lake Erie is just as much in ecological balance with the life on the land that surrounds it as it was in pre-Columbian times. The notion of a climax situation in ecology is a human invention, based on anthropocentric ideas of variety, completion, wholeness, and balance. A preference for equilibrium rather than change, for forests over deserts, for complexity and variety over simplicity and monoculture, all of these are matters of human economics and aesthetics. What *would* it be, after all, to think like a mountain as Aldo Leopold is said to have recommended? It would be anthropocentric because mountains do not think, but also because mountains are imagined to be thinking about which human interests in their preservation or development they prefer. The anthropocentrism of ecosophers is most obvious in their pronouncements about what is normal and natural. Perhaps it is not natural to remain in equilibrium, to be in ecological balance.

As far as that goes, most of the universe is apparently dead—or at least inanimate—anyway. And as far as we know, the movement of things is toward entropy. By simplifying things, man is on the side of the universe. → ° of disordering System

And as for making a mess of things, destroying things, disrupting and breaking down things, the best information we have about the origin of the universe is that it is the result of an explosion. If we are going to derive an ethic from our knowledge of nature, is it wrong to suggest that high-technology man might be doing the right thing? Naess does try to meet this objection with his tenth principle:

10 There is nothing in human nature or essence, according to Spinoza, which can *only* manifest or express itself through injury to others. That is, the striving for expression of one's nature does not inevitably imply an attitude of hostile domination over other beings, human or non-human. Violence, in the sense of violent activity, is not the same as violence as injury to others.[14]

But "injury" is a human moral concept. There is no injury to others in neutral nature. Naess and Spinoza are still bound by Judeo-Christian-Platonic-Aristotelian notions of human goodness. But to call for curbing man is like trying to make vegetarians of pet cats. And

I have often been puzzled about why so many environmental philosophers insist on harking to Spinoza as a ground for environmental ethics. It is perfectly plain as Curley and Lloyd point out that Spinoza's moral views are humanistic. They show how difficult it is to reconcile Spinoza's sense of freedom as the recognition of necessity with any notion of autonomy of self that is required to make moral imperatives or morality itself meaningful. That is, to recognize and accept what one is determined to do—even if this recognition and acceptance were not itself determined—is not the same as choosing between two equally possible (undetermined) courses of action. Moral action depends on free choice among undetermined alternatives.

III

There are anthropocentric foundations in most environmental and ecosophical literature. In particular, most ecosophers say outright or openly imply that human individuals and the human species would be better off if we were required to live in ecological balance with nature. Few ecosophers really think that man is just one part of nature among others. Man is privileged—or cursed—at least by having a moral sensibility that as far as we can tell no other entities have. But it is pretty clear (as I argue in "Self-Consciousness and the Rights of Nonhuman Animals and Nature") that on this planet at least only human beings are (so far) full members of a moral community. We ought to be kinder to nonhuman animals, but I do not think that this is because they have any intrinsic rights. As far as that goes, human beings have no intrinsic rights either (as Naess and Spinoza agree). We have to earn our rights as cooperating citizens in a moral community.

Because, unlike many ecosophers, I do not believe that we can return to religion, or that given what we know about the world today we can believe in pantheism or panpsychism, I think it is a mistake to strive for a new environmental ethic based on religious or mystical grounds. And I trust that I have demonstrated both how difficult it is to be fully biocentric, and also how the results of anti-anthropocentric biocentrism go far beyond the limits that ecosophers have drawn. Ecosophers obviously want to avoid the direct implications of treating the human species in the egalitarian and hands-off way they say other species should be treated. It is nice that human survival is compatible with the preservation of a rich planetary ecology, but I think it is a mistake to try to cover up the fact that human survival and the good life for man is some part of what we are interested in. There is very good reason for thinking ecologically, and for encouraging human beings to act in such a way as to preserve a rich and balanced planetary ecology: human survival depends on it.

NOTES

1. *Webster's New World Dictionary*, 2nd ed. (Cleveland, Ohio: William Collins and World Publishing Co., 1976), p. 59.

2. John Rodman, "The Liberation of Nature?" *Inquiry* 20 (1977): 108 (quoted with emphasis in capitals by George Sessions in *Ecophilosophy III*, p. 5a).

3. Tom Regan, "The Nature and Possibility of an Environmental Ethic," *Environmental Ethics* 3 (1981): 31–32.

4. George Sessions, "Spinoza, Perennial Philosophy, and Deep Ecology," unpublished, p. 15.

5. Aldo Leopold, *A Sand County Almanac* (Oxford: Oxford University Press, 1966), p. 240 (quoted by George Sessions in "Spinoza, Perennial Philosophy, and Deep Ecology," unpublished, p. 15).

6. Ibid.

7. Barry Commoner, *The Closing Circle: Nature, Man, and Technology* (New York: Alfred A. Knopf, 1971), p. 33 (quoted by George Sessions in "Panpsychism versus Modern Materialism: Some Implications for an Ecological Ethics," unpublished, p. 35).

8. G. Tyler Miller, *Replenish the Earth* (Belmont, CA.: Wadsworth, 1972), p. 53 (quoted by George Sessions in "Shallow and Deep Ecology: A Review of the Philosophical Literature," unpublished, pp. 44–45).

9. George Sessions, "Shallow and Deep Ecology: A Review of the Philosophical Literature," unpublished, p. 16.

10. Arne Naess, "Spinoza and Ecology," in Sigfried Hessing, ed., *Speculum Spinozanum 1677–1977* (London: Routledge & Kegan Paul, 1977), pp. 419–21.

11. George Sessions, "Spinoza and Jeffers on Man and Nature," *Inquiry* 20 (1977): 494–95.

12. Aldous Huxley, *Perennial Philosophy* (New York: Harper's, 1945), pp. 159–60 (quoted by George Sessions in "Shallow and Deep Ecology: A Review of the Philosophical Literature," unpublished, p. 47).

13. Michael Zimmerman, "Technological Change and the End of Philosophy," unpublished, (quoted by George Sessions in "Spinoza and Jeffers on Man and Nature," *Inquiry* 20 [1977]: 489).

14. Arne Naess, "Spinoza and Ecology," in Sigfried Hessing, ed., *Speculum Spinozanum 1677–1977* (London: Routledge & Kegan Paul, 1977, p. 421).

STUDY QUESTIONS

1. What is *anthropocentrism* according to Watson? How does it differ from *biocentrism*?

2. Carefully compare Watson's criticism with the articles by Taylor, Leopold, Callicott, Naess, and Sessions. Which of these writers does he attack most directly? Do any escape his critique? Are his critical objections sound?

3. Is Watson's version of environmental anthropocentrism plausible? Explain your answer.

18

Social Ecology Versus Deep Ecology

MURRAY BOOKCHIN

Murray Bookchin (1921–2006) has been a leading anarchist and utopian political theorist, especially regarding the philosophy of nature. He is the cofounder and director emeritus of the Institute for Social Ecology. His many books include Toward an Ecological Society, The Ecology of Freedom, *and* The Philosophy of Social Ecology.

Social ecology, which Bookchin develops in this essay, is an egalitarian system that has its roots in Marxist and anarchistic thought, though he disagrees with both at crucial points. Against Marx, Bookchin rejects economic determinism and the dictatorship of the proletariat. He rejects anarchist analysis that identifies the modern nation-state as the primary cause of social domination. Bookchin's primary attack is on social domination, and he shows how it is connected to ecology. In The Ecology of Freedom, *he writes:*

> The cultural, traditional and psychological systems of obedience and command are not merely the economic and political systems to which the terms class and State most appropriately refer. Accordingly, hierarchy and domination could easily continue to exist in a "classless" or "State-less" society. I refer to the domination of the young by the old, of women by men, of one ethnic group by another, of "masses" by bureaucrats who profess to speak of "higher social interests," of countryside by town, and in a more subtle psychological sense, of body by mind, of spirit by a shallow instrumental rationality.

> Bookchin promotes an organic view of social theory, wherein the individual finds meaning only in community that he helps create and of which he is a creation. In this essay, Bookchin opposes social ecology to deep ecology.

BEYOND "ENVIRONMENTALISM"

The environmental movement has travelled a long way beyond those annual "Earth Day" festivals when millions of school kids were ritualistically mobilized to clean up streets and their parents were scolded by Arthur Godfrey, Barry Commoner, and Paul Ehrlich. The movement has gone beyond a naive belief that patchwork reforms and solemn vows by EPA bureaucrats will seriously arrest the insane pace at which we are tearing down the planet. This shopworn "Earth Day" approach toward "engineering" nature so that we can ravage the Earth with minimal effects on ourselves—an approach that I called "environmentalism"—has shown signs of giving way to a more

From *Socialist Review*, Vol. 88, No. 3 (1988): 11–29. Reprinted with permission of the publisher.

searching and radical mentality. Today, the new word in vogue is "ecology"—be it "deep ecology," "human ecology," "biocentric ecology," "anti-humanist ecology," or, to use a term uniquely rich in meaning, "*social* ecology."

Happily, the new relevance of the word "ecology" reveals a growing dissatisfaction with attempts to use our vast ecological problems for cheaply spectacular and politically manipulative ends. Our forests disappear due to mindless cutting and increasing acid rain; the ozone layer thins out from widespread use of fluorocarbons; toxic dumps multiply all over the planet; highly dangerous, often radioactive pollutants enter into our air, water, and food chains. These innumerable hazards threaten the integrity of life itself, raising far more basic issues than can be resolved by "Earth Day" cleanups and fainthearted changes in environmental laws.

For good reason, more and more people are trying to go beyond the vapid "environmentalism" of the early 1970s and toward an *ecological* approach: one that is rooted in an ecological philosophy, ethics, sensibility, image of nature, and, ultimately, an ecological movement that will transform our domineering market society into a nonhierarchical cooperative one that will live in harmony with nature, because its members live in harmony with each other. They are beginning to sense that there is a tie-in between the way people deal with each other as social beings—men with women, old with young, rich with poor, white with people of color, first world with third, elites with "masses"—and the way they deal with nature.

The questions that now face us are: what do we really mean by an *ecological* approach? What is a *coherent* ecological philosophy, ethics, and movement? How can the answers to these questions and many others *fit together* so that they form a meaningful and creative whole? If we are not to repeat all the mistakes of the early seventies with their hoopla about "population control," their latent anti-feminism, elitism, arrogance, and ugly authoritarian tendencies, so we must honestly and seriously appraise the new tendencies that today go under the name of one or another form of "ecology."

TWO CONFLICTING TENDENCIES

Let us agree from the outset that the word "ecology" is no magic term that unlocks the real secret of our abuse of nature. It is a word that can be as easily abused, distorted, and tainted as words like "democracy" and "freedom." Nor does the word "ecology" put us all—whoever "we" may be—in the same boat against environmentalists who are simply trying to make a rotten society work by dressing it in green leaves and colorful flowers, while ignoring the deep-seated *roots* of our ecological problems.

It is time to face the fact that there are differences within the so-called "ecology movement" of the present time that are as serious as those between the "environmentalism" and "ecologism" of the early seventies. There are barely disguised racists, survivalists, macho Daniel Boones, and outright social reactionaries who use the word "ecology" to express their views, just as there are deeply concerned naturalists, communitarians, social radicals, and feminists who use the word "ecology" to express theirs.

The differences between these two tendencies in the so-called "ecology movement" consist not only in quarrels over theory, sensibility, and ethics. They have far-reaching *practical* and *political* consequences on the way we view nature, "humanity," and ecology. Most significantly, they concern how we propose to *change* society and by what *means*.

The greatest differences that are emerging within the so-called "ecology movement" of our day are between a vague, formless, often self-contradictory ideology called "deep ecology" and a socially oriented body of ideas best termed "social ecology." Deep ecology has parachuted into our midst quite recently from the Sunbelt's bizarre mix of Hollywood and Disneyland, spiced with homilies from Taoism, Buddhism, spiritualism, reborn Christianity, and, in some cases, eco-fascism. Social ecology, on the other hand, draws its inspiration from such radical decentralist thinkers as Peter Kropotkin, William Morris, and Paul Goodman, among many others who have challenged society's vast hierarchical, sexist, class-ruled, statist, and militaristic apparatus.

Bluntly speaking, deep ecology, despite all its social rhetoric, has no real sense that our ecological problems have their roots in society and in social problems. It preaches a gospel of a kind of "original sin" that accuses a vague species called "humanity"—as though people of color were equatable with whites, women with men, the third world with the first, the poor with the rich, and the exploited with their exploiters. This vague, undifferentiated humanity is seen as an ugly "anthropocentric" thing—presumably a malignant product of natural evolution—that is "overpopulating" the planet, "devouring" its resources, destroying its wildlife and the biosphere. It assumes that some vague domain called "nature" stands opposed to a constellation of non-natural things called "human beings," with their "technology," "minds," "society," and so on. Formulated largely by privileged white male academics, deep ecology has brought sincere naturalists like Paul Shepard into the same company with patently anti-humanist and macho mountain-men like David Foreman, who writes in *Earth First!*—a Tucson-based journal that styles itself as the voice of a wilderness-oriented movement of the same name—that "humanity" is a cancer in the world of life.

It is easy to forget that this same kind of crude eco-brutalism led Hitler to fashion theories of blood and soil that led to the transport of millions of people to murder camps like Auschwitz. The same eco-brutalism now reappears a half-century later among self-professed deep ecologists who believe that famines are nature's "population control" and immigration into the US should be restricted in order to preserve "our" ecological resources.

Simply Living, an Australian periodical, published this sort of eco-brutalism as part of a laudatory interview of David Foreman by Professor Bill Devall, co-author of *Deep Ecology*, the manifesto of the deep ecology movement. Foreman, who exuberantly expressed his commitment to deep ecology, frankly informs Devall that

> When I tell people how the worst thing we could do in Ethiopia is to give aid—the best thing would be to just let nature seek its own balance, to let the people there just starve—they think this is monstrous....
> Likewise, letting the USA be an overflow

valve for problems in Latin America is not solving a thing. It's just putting more pressure on the resources we have in the USA.

One could reasonably ask what it means for "nature to seek its own balance" in a part of the world where agribusiness, colonialism, and exploitation have ravaged a once culturally and ecologically stable area like East Africa. And who is this all-American "our" that owns the "resources we have in the USA"? Is it the ordinary people who are driven by sheer need to cut timber, mine ores, operate nuclear power plants? Or are they the giant corporations that are not only wrecking the good old USA, but have produced the main problems in Latin America that are sending Indian folk across the Rio Grande? As an ex-Washington lobbyist and political huckster, David Foreman need not be expected to answer these subtle questions in a radical way. But what is truly surprising is the reaction—more precisely, the *lack* of any reaction—which marked Professor Devall's behavior. Indeed, the interview was notable for his almost reverential introduction and description of Foreman.

WHAT IS "DEEP ECOLOGY"?

Deep ecology is enough of a "black hole" of half-digested and ill-formed ideas that a man like Foreman can easily express utterly vicious notions and still sound like a fiery pro-ecology radical. The very words "deep ecology" clue us into the fact that we are not dealing with a body of clear ideas, but with an ideological toxic dump. Does it make sense, for example, to counterpose "deep ecology" with "superficial ecology" as though the word "ecology" were applicable to *everything* that involves environmental issues? Does it not completely degrade the rich meaning of the word "ecology" to append words like "shallow" and "deep" to it? Arne Naess, the pontiff of deep ecology—who, together with George Sessions and Bill Devall, inflicted this vocabulary upon us—has taken a pregnant word—ecology—and stripped it of any inner meaning and integrity by designating the most pedestrian environmentalists as "ecologists," albeit "shallow" ones, in contrast to their notion of "deep."

This is not an example of mere wordplay. It tells us something about the mindset that exists among these "deep" thinkers. To parody the word "shallow" and "deep ecology" is to show not only the absurdity of this terminology but to reveal the superficiality of its inventors. In fact, this kind of absurdity tells us more than we realize about the confusion Naess-Sessions-Devall, not to mention eco-brutalists like Foreman, have introduced into the current ecology movement. Indeed, this trio relies very heavily on the ease with which people forget the history of the ecology movement, the way in which the wheel is reinvented every few years by newly arrived individuals who, well-meaning as they may be, often accept a crude version of highly developed ideas that appeared earlier in a richer context and tradition of ideas. At worst, they shatter such contexts and traditions, picking out tasty pieces that become utterly distorted in a new, utterly alien framework. No regard is paid by such "deep thinkers" to the fact that *the new context in which an idea is placed may utterly change the meaning of the idea itself.* German "National Socialism" was militantly "anti-capitalist." But its "anti-capitalism" was placed in a strongly racist, imperialist, and seemingly "naturalist" context which extolled wilderness, a crude biologism, and anti-rationalism—features one finds in latent or explicit form in Sessions' and Devall's *Deep Ecology.*[1]

Neither Naess, Sessions, nor Devall have written a single line about decentralization, a nonhierarchical society, democracy, small-scale communities, local autonomy, mutual aid, communalism, and tolerance that was not already conceived in painstaking detail and brilliant contextualization by Peter Kropotkin a century ago. But what the boys from Ecotopia do is to totally recontextualize the framework of these ideas, bringing in personalities and notions that basically change their radical libertarian thrust. *Deep Ecology* mingles Woody Guthrie, a Communist Party centralist who no more believed in decentralization than Stalin, with Paul Goodman, an anarchist who would have been mortified to be placed in the same tradition with Guthrie. In philosophy, the book also

intermingles Spinoza, a Jew in spirit if not in religious commitment, with Heidegger, a former member of the Nazi party in spirit as well as ideological affiliation—all in the name of a vague word called "process philosophy." Almost opportunistic in their use of catch words and what Orwell called "doublespeak," "process philosophy" makes it possible for Sessions-Devall to add Alfred North White-head to their list of ideological ancestors because he called his ideas "processual."

One could go on indefinitely describing this sloppy admixture of "ancestors," philosophical traditions, social pedigrees, and religions that often have nothing in common with each other and, properly conceived, are commonly in sharp opposition with each other. Thus, a reactionary like Thomas Malthus and the tradition he spawned is celebrated with the same enthusiasm in *Deep Ecology* as Henry Thoreau, a radical libertarian who fostered a highly humanistic tradition. Eclecticism would be too mild a word for this kind of hodge-podge, one that seems shrewdly calculated to embrace everyone under the rubric of deep ecology who is prepared to reduce ecology to a religion rather than a systematic and critical body of ideas. This kind of "ecological" thinking surfaces in an appendix to the Devall-Sessions book, called *Ecosophy T*, by Arne Naess, who regales us with flow diagrams and corporate-type tables of organization that have more in common with logical positivist forms of exposition (Naess, in fact, was an acolyte of this school of thought for years) than anything that could be truly called organic philosophy.

If we look beyond the spiritual eco-babble and examine the *context* in which demands like decentralization, small-scale communities, local autonomy, mutual aid, communalism, and tolerance are placed, the blurred images that Sessions and Devall create come into clearer focus. These demands are not intrinsically ecological or emancipatory. Few societies were more decentralized than European feudalism, which was structured around small-scale communities, mutual aid, and the communal use of land. Local autonomy was highly prized, and autarchy formed the economic key to feudal communities. Yet few societies were more hierarchical. The manorial economy of the Middle Ages placed a high premium on autarchy or "self-sufficiency" and spirituality. Yet oppression was often intolerable and the great mass of people who belonged to that society lived in utter subjugation by their "betters" and the nobility.

If "nature worship," with its bouquet of wood sprites, animistic fetishes, fertility rites and other such ceremonies, paves the way to an ecological sensibility and society, then it would be hard to understand how ancient Egypt, with its animal deities and all-presiding goddesses, managed to become one of the most hierarchical and oppressive societies in the ancient world. The Nile River, which provided the "life-giving" waters of the valley, was used in a highly ecological manner. Yet the entire society was structured around the oppression of millions of serfs by opulent nobles, such that one wonders how notions of spirituality can be given priority over the need for a critical evaluation of social structures.

Even if one grants the need for a new sensibility and outlook—a point that has been made repeatedly in the literature of social ecology—one can look behind even this limited context of deep ecology to a still broader context. The love affair of deep ecology with Malthusian doctrines, a spirituality that emphasizes self-effacement, a flirtation with a *super*naturalism that stands in flat contradiction to the refreshing naturalism that ecology has introduced into social theory, a crude positivism in the spirit of Naess— all work against a truly organic dialectic so needed to understand *development*. We shall see that all the bumper-sticker demands like decentralization, small-scale communities, local autonomy, mutual aid, communalism, tolerance, and even an avowed opposition to hierarchy, go awry when we place them in the larger context of anti-humanism and "biocentrism" that mark the authentic ideological infrastructure of deep ecology.

THE ART OF EVADING SOCIETY

The seeming ideological "tolerance" and pluralism which deep ecology celebrates has a sinister function of its own. It not only reduces richly nuanced ideas and conflicting traditions to their lowest common denominator; it legitimates extremely primitivistic and reactionary notions in the company of authentically radical contexts and traditions.

Deep ecology reduces people from social beings to a simple species—to zoological entities that are interchangeable with bears, bisons, deer, or, for that matter, fruit flies and microbes. The fact that people can consciously change themselves and society, indeed enhance that natural world in a free ecological society, is dismissed as "humanism." Deep ecology essentially ignores the social nature of humanity and the social origins of the ecological crises.

This "zoologization" of human beings and of society yields sinister results. The role of capitalism with its competitive "grow or die" market economy—an economy that would devour the biosphere whether there were 10 billion people on the planet or 10 million—is simply vaporized into a vapid spiritualism. Taoist and Buddhist pieties replace the need for social and economic analysis, and self-indulgent encounter groups replace the need for political organization and action. Above all, deep ecologists explain the destruction of human beings in terms of the same "natural laws" that are said to govern the population vicissitudes of lemmings. The fact that major reductions of populations would not diminish levels of production and the destruction of the biosphere in a capitalist economy totally eludes Devall, Sessions, and their followers.

In failing to emphasize the unique characteristics of human societies and to give full due to the self-reflective role of human consciousness, deep ecologists essentially evade the *social* roots of the ecological crisis. Deep ecology contains no history of the emergence of society out of nature, a crucial development that brings social theory into organic contact with ecological theory. It presents no explanation of—indeed, it reveals no interest in—the emergence of hierarchy out of society, of classes out of hierarchy, of the state out of classes—in short, the highly graded social as well as ideological developments which are at the roots of the ecological problem.

Instead, we not only lose sight of the social differences that fragment "humanity" into a host of human beings—men and women, ethnic groups, oppressors and oppressed—we lose sight of the individual self in an unending flow of eco-babble that preaches the "realization of self-in-Self where the 'Self' stands for organic wholeness." More of the same cosmic eco-babble appears when we are informed that the "phrase 'one' includes not only men, an individual human, but all humans, grizzly bears, whole rain forest ecosystems, mountains and rivers, the tiniest microbes in the soil, and so on."

ON SELFHOOD AND VIRUSES

Such flippant abstractions of human individuality are extremely dangerous. Historically, a "Self" that absorbs all real existential selves has been used from time immemorial to absorb individual uniqueness and freedom into a supreme "Individual" who heads the state, churches of various sorts, adoring congregations, and spellbound constituencies. The purpose is the same, no matter how much such a "Self" is dressed up in ecological, naturalistic, and "biocentric" attributes. The Paleolithic shaman, in reindeer skins and horns, is the predecessor of the Pharaoh, the Buddha, and, in more recent times, of Hitler, Stalin, and Mussolini.

That the egotistical, greedy, and soloist bourgeois "self" has always been a repellent being goes without saying, and deep ecology as put forth by Devall and Sessions makes the most of it. But is there not a free, independently minded, ecologically concerned, idealistic self with a unique personality that can think of itself as different from "whales, grizzly bears, whole rain forest ecosystems (no less!), mountains and rivers, the tiniest microbes in the soil, and so on"? Is it not indispensable, in fact, for the individual self to disengage itself from a Pharonic "Self," discover its own capacities and uniqueness, and acquire a sense of personality, of self-control and self-direction—all traits indispensable for the achievement of *freedom*? Here, one can imagine Heidegger grimacing with satisfaction at the sight of this self-effacing and passive personality so yielding that it can easily be shaped, distorted, and manipulated by a new "ecological" state machinery with a supreme "Self" at its head. And this all in the name of a "biocentric equality" that is slowly reworked as it has been so often in history, into a social hierarchy. From Shaman to Monarch, from Priest or Priestess to Dictator, our warped social development has been marked by "nature worshippers" and their ritual Supreme Ones who produced unfinished individuals at best or deindividuated the "self-in-Self" at worst, often in the name of the "Great Connected Whole" (to use *exactly* the language of the Chinese ruling classes who kept their peasantry in abject servitude, as Leon E. Stover points out in his *The Cultural Ecology of Chinese Civilization*).

What makes this eco-babble especially dangerous today is that we are already living in a period of massive de-individuation. This is not because deep ecology or Taoism is making any serious in-roads into our own cultural ecology, but because the mass media, the commodity culture, and a market society are "reconnecting" us into an increasingly depersonalized "whole" whose essence is passivity and a chronic vulnerability to economic and political manipulation. It is not an excess of "selfhood" from which we are suffering, but rather the surrender of personality to the security and control of corporations, centralized government, and the military. If "selfhood" is identified with a grasping, "anthropocentric," and devouring personality, these traits are to be found not so much among ordinary people, who basically sense they have no control over their destinies, but among the giant corporations and state leaders who are not only plundering the planet, but also robbing from women, people of color, and the underprivileged. It is not deindividuation that the oppressed of the world require, but *re*individuation that will transform them into active agents in the task of remaking society and arresting the growing totalitarianism that threatens to homogenize us all into a Western version of the "Great Connected Whole."

We are also confronted with the delicious "and so on" that follows the "tiniest microbes in the soil" with which our deep ecologists identify the "Self." Taking their argument to its logical extreme, one might ask: why stop with the "tiniest microbes in the soil" and ignore the leprosy microbe, the viruses that give us smallpox, polio, and, more recently, AIDS? Are they, too, not part of "all organisms and entities in the eco-sphere-of the interrelated whole ... equal in intrinsic worth ...,"as Devall and Sessions remind us in their effluvium of eco-babble? Naess, Devall, and Sessions rescue themselves by introducing a number of highly debatable qualifiers:

> The slogan of "noninterference" does not
> imply that humans should not modify
> some ecosystems as do other species.
> Humans have modified the Earth and will
> probably continue to do so. At issue is the
> nature and extent of such interference.

One does not leave the muck of deep ecology without having mud all over one's feet. Exactly *who* is to decide the "nature" of human "interference" in nature and the "extent" to which it can be done? What are "some" of the ecosystems we can modify and which ones are not subject to human "interference"? Here, again, we encounter the key problem that deep ecology poses for serious, ecologically concerned people: the *social* bases of our ecological problems and the role of the human species in the evolutionary scheme of things.

Implicit in deep ecology is the notion that a "Humanity" exists that accurses the natural world; that individual selfhood must be transformed into a cosmic "Selfhood" that essentially transcends the person and his or her uniqueness. Even nature is not spared from a kind of static, prepositional logic that is cultivated by the logical positivists. "Nature," in deep ecology and David Foreman's interpretation of it, becomes a kind of scenic view, a spectacle to be admired around the campfire. It is not viewed as an *evolutionary* development that is cumulative and *includes* the human species.

The problems deep ecology and biocentricity raise have not gone unnoticed in the more thoughtful press in England. During a discussion of "biocentric ethics" in *The New Scientist* 69 (1976), for example, Bernard Dixon observed that no "logical line can be drawn" between the conservation of whales, gentians, and flamingoes on the one hand and the extinction of pathogenic microbes like the smallpox virus. At which point David Ehrenfeld, in his *Arrogance of Humanism*[2]— a work that is so selective and tendentious in its use of quotations that it should validly be renamed "The Arrogance of Ignorance"—cutely observes that the smallpox virus is "an endangered species." One wonders what to do about the AIDS virus if a vaccine or therapy should threaten its "survival"? Further, given the passion for perpetuating the "ecosystem" of every species, one wonders how smallpox and AIDS viruses should be preserved? In test tubes? Laboratory cultures? Or, to be truly "ecological" in their "native habitat," the human body? In which case, idealistic acolytes of deep ecology should be invited to offer their own bloodstreams in the interests of "biocentric equality." Certainly, "if nature should be permitted to take its course"—as Foreman advises for Ethiopians and Indian peasants—plagues, famines, suffering, wars, and perhaps even lethal asteroids of the kind that exterminated the great reptiles of the Mesozoic should not be kept from defacing the purity of "first nature" by the intervention of human ingenuity and—yes!—*technology*. With so much absurdity to unscramble, one can indeed get heady, almost dizzy, with a sense of polemical intoxication.

At root, the eclecticism which turns deep ecology into a goulash of notions and moods is insufferably reformist and surprisingly environmentalist—all its condemnations of "superficial ecology" aside. Are you, perhaps, a mild-mannered liberal? Then do not fear: Devall and Sessions give a patronizing nod to "reform legislation," "coalitions," "protests," the "women's movement" (this earns all of ten lines in their "Minority Tradition and Direct Action" essay), "working in the Christian tradition" "questioning technology" (a hammering remark, if there ever was one), "working in Green politics" (which faction, the "fundies" or the "realos"?). In short, everything can be expected in so "cosmic" a philosophy. Anything seems to pass through deep ecology's donut hole: anarchism at one extreme and eco-fascism at the other. Like the fast food emporiums that make up our culture, deep ecology is the fast food of quasi-radical environmentalists.

Despite its pretense of "radicality," deep ecology is more "New Age" and "Aquarian" than the environmentalist movements it denounces under those names. Indeed, the extent to which deep ecology accommodates itself to some of the worst features of the "dominant view" it professes to reject is seen with extraordinary clarity in one of its most fundamental and repeatedly asserted demands—namely, that the world's population must be drastically reduced, according to one of its devotees, to 500 million. If deep ecologists have even the faintest knowledge of the "population theorists" Devall and Sessions invoke with admiration—notably, Thomas Malthus, William Vogt, and Paul Ehrlich—then they would be obliged to add: by measures that are virtually eco-fascist. This specter clearly looms before us in Devall's and Sessions' sinister remark: "… the longer we wait [for population control], the more drastic will be the measures needed."

THE "DEEP" MALTHUSIANS

Devall and Sessions often write with smug assurance on issues they know virtually nothing about. This is most notably the case in the so-called "population debate," a debate that has raged for over two hundred years and more and involves explosive political and social issues that have pitted the most reactionary elements in English and American society against authentic radicals. In fact, the eco-babble which Devall and Sessions dump on us in only two paragraphs would require a full-sized volume of careful analysis to unravel.

Devall and Sessions hail Thomas Malthus (1766–1854) as a prophet whose warning "that human population growth would exponentially outstrip food production … was ignored by the rising tide of industrial/technological optimism." First of all, Thomas Malthus was not a prophet; he was an apologist for the misery that the Industrial Revolution was inflicting on the English peasantry and working classes. His utterly fallacious argument

that population increases exponentially while food supplies increase arithmetically was not ignored by England's ruling classes; it was taken to heart and even incorporated into social Darwinism as an explanation of why oppression was a necessary feature of society and why the rich, the white imperialists, and the privileged were the "fittest" who were equipped to "survive"—needless to say, at the expense of the impoverished many. Written and directed in great part as an attack upon the liberatory vision of William Godwin, Malthus' mean-spirited *Essay on the Principle of Population* tried to demonstrate that hunger, poverty, disease, and premature death are *inevitable* precisely because population and food supply increase at different rates. Hence war, famines, and plagues (Malthus later added "moral restraint") were necessary to keep population down—needless to say, among the "lower orders of society," whom he singles out as the chief offenders of his inexorable population "laws."[3] Malthus, in effect, became the ideologue par excellence for the land-grabbing English nobility in its effort to dispossess the peasantry of their traditional common lands and for the English capitalists to work children, women, and men to death in the newly emergent "industrial/technological" factory system.

Malthusianism contributed in great part to that meanness of spirit that Charles Dickens captured in his famous novels, *Oliver Twist* and *Hard Times*. The doctrine, its author, and its overstuffed wealthy beneficiaries were bitterly fought by the great English anarchist, William Godwin, the pioneering socialist, Robert Owen, and the emerging Chartist movement of English workers in the early 19th century. However, Malthusianism was naively picked up by Charles Darwin to explain his theory of "natural selection." It then became the bedrock theory for the new *social* Darwinism, so very much in vogue in the late nineteenth and early twentieth centuries, which saw society as a "jungle" in which only the "fit" (usually, the rich and white) could "survive" at the expense of the "unfit" (usually, the poor and people of color). Malthus, in effect, had provided an ideology that justified class domination, racism, the degradation of women, and, ultimately, British imperialism.

Malthusianism was not only revived in Hitler's Third Reich; it also reemerged in the late 1940s, following the discoveries of antibiotics to control infectious diseases. Riding on the tide of the new Pax Americana after World War II, William F. Vogt and a whole bouquet of neo-Malthusians were to challenge the use of the new antibiotic discoveries to control disease and prevent death—as usual, mainly in Asia, Africa, and Latin America. Again, a new "population debate" erupted, with the Rockefeller interests and large corporate sharks aligning themselves with the neo-Malthusians, and caring people of every sort aligning themselves with third world theorists like Josua de Castro, who wrote damning, highly informed critiques of this new version of misanthropy.

Zero Population Growth fanatics in the early seventies literally polluted the environmental movement with demands for a government bureau to "control" population, advancing the infamous "triage" ethic, according to which various "under-developed" countries would be granted or refused aid on the basis of their compliance to population control measures. In *Food First*, Francis Moore Lappe and Joseph Collins have done a superb job in showing how hunger has its origins not in "natural" shortages of food or population growth, but in social and cultural dislocations. (It is notable that Devall and Sessions do *not* list this excellent book in their bibliography.) The book has to be read to understand the reactionary implications of deep ecology's demographic positions.

Demography is a highly ambiguous and ideo-logically charged social discipline that cannot be reduced to a mere numbers game in biological re-production. Human beings are not fruit flies (the species which the neo-Malthusians love to cite). Their reproductive behavior is profoundly conditioned by cultural values, standards of living, social traditions, gender relations, religious beliefs, socio-political conflicts, and various socio-political expectations. Smash up a stable, precapitalist culture and throw its people off the land into city slums, and, due to demoralization, population may soar rather than decline. As Gandhi told the British, imperialism left India's wretched poor and homeless with

little more in life than the immediate gratification provided by sex and an understandably numbed sense of personal, much less social, responsibility. Reduce women to mere reproductive factories and population rates will explode.

Conversely, provide people with decent lives, education, a sense of creative meaning in life, and, above all, expand the role of women in society—and population growth begins to stabilize and population rates even reverse their direction. Nothing more clearly reveals deep ecology's crude, often reactionary, and certainly superficial ideological framework—all its decentralist, anti-hierarchical, and "radical" rhetoric aside—than its suffocating "biological" treatment of the population issue and its inclusion of Malthus, Vogt, and Ehrlich in its firmament of prophets.

Not surprisingly, the *Earth First!* newsletter, whose editor professes to be an enthusiastic deep ecologist, carried an article titled "Population and AIDS" which advanced the obscene argument that AIDS is desirable as a means of population control. This was no spoof. It was earnestly argued and carefully reasoned in a Paleolithic sort of way. Not only will AIDS claim large numbers of lives, asserts the author (who hides under the pseudonym of "Miss Ann Thropy," a form of black humor that could also pass as an example of macho-male arrogance), but it "may cause a breakdown in technology (read: human food supply) and its export which could also decrease human population." These people feed on human disasters, suffering, and misery, preferably in third world countries where AIDS is by far a more monstrous problem than elsewhere.

We have little reason to doubt that this mentality is perfectly consistent with the "more drastic ... measures" Devall and Sessions believe we will have to explore. Nor is it inconsistent with Malthus and Vogt that we should make no effort to find a cure for this disease which may do so much to depopulate the world. "Biocentric democracy," I assume, should call for nothing less than a "hands-off" policy on the AIDS virus and perhaps equally lethal pathogens that appear in the human species.

WHAT IS SOCIAL ECOLOGY?

Social ecology is neither "deep," "tall," "fat," nor "thick." It is *social*. It does not fall back on incantations, sutras, flow diagrams or spiritual vagaries. It is avowedly *rational*. It does not try to regale metaphorical forms of spiritual mechanism and crude biologism with Taoist, Buddhist, Christian, or shamanistic eco-babble. It is a coherent form of *naturalism* that looks to *evolution* and the *biosphere*, not to deities in the sky or under the earth for quasi-religious and supernaturalistic explanations of natural and social phenomena.

Philosophically, social ecology stems from a solid organismic tradition in Western philosophy, beginning with Heraclitus, the near-evolutionary dialectic of Aristotle and Hegel, and the critical approach of the famous Frankfurt School—particularly its devastating critique of logical positivism (which surfaces in Naess repeatedly) and the primitivistic mysticism of Heidegger (which pops up all over the place in deep ecology's literature).

Socially, it is revolutionary, not merely "radical." It critically unmasks the entire evolution of hierarchy in all its forms, including neo-Malthusian elitism, the eco-brutalism of David Foreman, the anti-humanism of David Ehrenfeld and "Miss Ann Thropy," and the latent racism, first-world arrogance, and Yuppie nihilism of post-modernistic spiritualism. It is noted in the profound eco-anarchistic analyses of Peter Kropotkin, the radical economic insights of Karl Marx, the emancipatory promise of the revolutionary Enlightenment as articulated by the great encyclopedist, Denis Diderot, the *Enrages* of the French Revolution, the revolutionary feminist ideals of Louise Michel and Emma Goldman, the communitarian visions of Paul Goodman and E. A. Gutkind, and the various eco-revolutionary manifestoes of the early 1960s.

Politically, it is *green*—radically green. It takes its stand with the left-wing tendencies in the German Greens and extra-parliamentary street movements of European cities; with the American radical ecofeminist movement; with the demands for a new politics based on citizens' initiatives, neighborhood assemblies, and New England's tradition of town-meetings; with non-aligned anti-imperialist movements at home and abroad; with the struggle by people of color for complete freedom from the domination of privileged whites and from the superpowers.

Morally, it is *humanistic* in the high Renaissance meaning of the term, not the degraded meaning of "humanism" that has been imparted to the world by David Foreman, David Ehrenfeld, and a salad of academic deep ecologists. Humanism from its inception has meant a shift in vision from the skies to the earth, from superstition to reason, from deities to people—who are no less products of natural evolution than grizzly bears and whales. Social ecology accepts neither a "biocentricity" that essentially denies or degrades the uniqueness of human beings, human subjectivity, rationality, aesthetic sensibility, and the ethical potentiality of humanity, nor an "anthropocentricity" that confers on the privileged few the right to plunder the world of life, including human life. Indeed, it opposes "centricity" of *any* kind as a new word for hierarchy and domination—be it that of nature by a mystical "Man" or the domination of people by an equally mystical "Nature." It firmly denies that nature is a static, scenic view which Mountain Men like a Foreman survey from a peak in Nevada or a picture window that spoiled yuppies view from their ticky-tacky country homes. To social ecology, nature *is* natural *evolution*, not a cosmic arrangement of beings frozen in a moment of eternity to be abjectly revered, adored, and worshipped like Gods and Goddesses in a realm of "*super*nature." Natural evolution is nature in the very real sense that it is composed of atoms, molecules that have evolved into amino acids, proteins, unicellular organisms, genetic codes, invertebrates and vertebrates, amphibia, reptiles, mammals, primates, and human beings—all, in a cumulative thrust toward ever-greater complexity, ever-greater subjectivity, and finally, an ever-greater capacity for conceptual thought, symbolic communication, and self-consciousness.

This marvel we call "Nature" has produced a marvel we call homo sapiens—"thinking man"—and, more significantly for the development of society, "thinking woman," whose primeval domestic domain provided the arena for the origins of a caring society, human empathy, love, and idealistic commitment. The human species, in effect, is no less a product of natural evolution and differentiation than blue-green algae. To degrade the human species in the name of "anti-humanism," to deny people their uniqueness as thinking beings with an unprecedented gift for conceptual thought, is to deny the rich fecundity of natural evolution itself. To separate human beings and society from nature is to dualize and truncate nature itself, to diminish the meaning and thrust of natural evolution in the name of a "biocentricity" that spends more time disporting itself with mantras, deities, and supernature than with the realities of the biosphere and the role of society in ecological problems.

Accordingly, social ecology does not try to hide its critical and reconstructive thrust in metaphors. It calls "technological/industrial" society *capitalism*—a word which places the onus for our ecological problems on the *living* sources and *social* relationships that produce them, not on a cutesy "Third Wave" abstraction which buries these sources in technics, a technical "mentality," or perhaps the technicians who work on machines. It sees the domination of women not simply as a "spiritual" problem that can be resolved by rituals, incantations, and shamannesses, important as ritual may be in solidarizing women into a unique community of people, but in the long, highly graded, and subtly nuanced development of hierarchy, which long preceded the development of classes. Nor does it ignore class, ethnic differences, imperialism, and oppression by creating a grab-bag called "Humanity" that is placed in opposition to a mystified "Nature," divested of all development.

All of which brings us as social ecologists to an issue that seems to be totally alien to the crude concerns of deep ecology: natural evolution has conferred on human beings the capacity to form a "second" or cultural nature out of "first" or primeval nature. Natural evolution has not only provided humans with the *ability*, but also the *necessity* to be purposive interveners into "first nature," to consciously *change* "first nature" by means of a highly institutionalized form of community we call "society." It is not alien to natural evolution that a species called human beings have emerged over the billions of years who are capable of thinking in a sophisticated way. Nor is it

alien for human beings to develop a highly sophisticated form of symbolic communication which a new kind of community—institutionalized, guided by thought rather than by instinct alone, and ever-changing—has emerged called "society."

Taken together, all of these human traits—intellectual, communicative, and social—have not only emerged from natural evolution and are inherently human; they can also be placed at the *service* of natural evolution to consciously increase biotic diversity, diminish suffering, foster the further evolution of new and ecologically valuable life-forms, reduce the impact of disastrous accidents or the harsh effects of mere change.

Whether this species, gifted by the creativity of natural evolution, can play the role of a nature rendered self-conscious or cut against the grain of natural evolution by simplifying the biosphere, polluting it, and undermining the cumulative results of organic evolution is above all a *social* problem. The primary question ecology faces today is whether an ecologically oriented society can be created out of the present anti-ecological one.

Unless there is a resolute attempt to fully anchor ecological dislocations in social dislocations; to challenge the vested corporate and political interests we should properly call *capitalism;* to analyze, explore, and attack hierarchy as a *reality*, not only as a sensibility; to recognize the material needs of the poor and of third world people; to function politically, and not simply as a religious cult; to give the human species and mind their due in natural evolution, rather than regard them as cancers in the biosphere; to examine economies as well as "souls," and freedom instead of scholastic arguments about the "rights" of pathogenic viruses—unless, in short, North American Greens and the ecology movement shift their focus toward a *social ecology* and let deep ecology sink into the pit it has created for us, the ecology movement will become another ugly wart on the skin of society.

What we must do, today, is return to *nature*, conceived in all its fecundity, richness of potentialities, and subjectivity—not to *super*nature with its shamans, priests, priestesses, and fanciful deities that are merely anthropomorphic extensions and distortions of the "Human" as all-embracing divinities. And what we must "enchant" is not only an abstract image of "Nature" *that often reflects our own systems of* power, *hierarchy, and domination*—but rather human beings, the human mind, the human spirit.

NOTES

1. Unless otherwise indicated, all future references and quotes come from Bills Devall and George Sessions, *Deep Ecology* (Layton, UT: Gibbs M. Smith, 1985), a book which has essentially become the bible of the "movement" that bears its name.

2. David Ehrenfeld, *The Arrogance of Humanism* (New York: The Modern Library, 1978), pp. 207–211.

3. Chapter Five of his *Essay*, which, for all its "concern" over the misery of the "lower classes," inveighs against the poor laws and argues that the "pressures of distress on this part of the community is an evil so deeply seated that no human ingenuity can reach it." Thomas Malthus, *On Population* (New York: The Modern Library), p. 34.

STUDY QUESTIONS

1. Examine Bookchin's attack on deep ecology. What are his reasons for opposing it? Are his epithets "eco-brutalism," "eco-babble," and so forth, justified? Does Bookchin make a good case for rejecting deep ecology? Or are his attacks incomplete, rhetorical, and ad hominem?

2. What are Bookchin's major assumptions in this essay? Are they defended? Are they defensible?

3. What is *social ecology*? What are its main features? How well does Bookchin defend it?

19

Radical Environmentalism and Wilderness Preservation: A Third World Critique

RAMACHANDRA GUHA

Ramachandra Guha is a sociologist and historian at the Centre for Ecological Sciences, Indian Institute for Science, Bangalore, India. He has written extensively on the historical

Reprinted from *Environmental Ethics*, Vol. 11 (Spring 1989) by permission. Notes deleted.

roots of ecological conflict in the East and West. The following is the original abstract he wrote for this article.

I present a Third World critique of the trend in American environmentalism known as deep ecology, analyzing each of deep ecology's central tenets: the distinction between anthropocentrism and biocentrism, the focus on wilderness preservation, the invocation of Eastern traditions, and the belief that it represents the most radical trend within environmentalism. I argue that the anthropocentrism/biocentrism distinction is of little use in understanding the dynamics of environmental degradation, that the implementation of the wilderness agenda is causing serious deprivation in the Third World, that the deep ecologist's interpretation of Eastern tradition is highly selective, and that in other cultural contexts (e.g., West Germany and India) radical environmentalism manifests itself quite differently, with a far greater emphasis on equity and the integration of ecological concerns with livelihood and work. I conclude that despite its claims to universality, deep ecology is firmly rooted in American environmental and cultural history and is inappropriate when applied to the Third World.

Even God dare not appear to the poor man except in the form of bread.
MAHATMA GANDHI

I. INTRODUCTION

The respected radical journalist Kirkpatrick Sale recently celebrated "the passion of a new and growing movement that has become disenchanted with the environmental establishment and has in recent years mounted a serious and sweeping attack on it—style, substance, systems, sensibilities and all." The vision of those whom Sale calls the "New Ecologists"—and what I refer to in this article as deep ecology—is a compelling one. Decrying the narrowly economic goals of mainstream environmentalism, this new movement aims at nothing less than a philosophical and cultural revolution in human attitudes toward nature. In contrast to the conventional lobbying efforts of environmental professionals based in Washington, it proposes a militant defence of "Mother Earth," an unflinching opposition to human attacks on undisturbed wilderness. With their goals ranging from the spiritual to the political, the adherents of deep ecology span a wide spectrum of the American environmental movement. As Sale correctly notes, this emerging strand has in a matter of a few years made its presence felt in a number of fields: from an academic philosophy (as in the journal *Environmental Ethics*) to popular environmentalism (for example, the group Earth First!).

In this article I develop a critique of deep ecology from the perspective of a sympathetic outsider. I critique deep ecology not as a general (or even a foot soldier) in the continuing struggle between the ghosts of Gifford Pinchot and John Muir over control of the U.S. environmental movement, but as an outsider to these battles. I speak admittedly as a partisan, but of the environmental movement in India, a country with an ecological diversity comparable to the U.S., but with a radically dissimilar cultural and social history.

My treatment of deep ecology is primarily historical and sociological, rather than philosophical, in nature. Specifically, I examine the cultural rootedness of a philosophy that likes to present itself in universalistic terms. I make two main arguments: first, that deep ecology is uniquely American, and despite superficial similarities in rhetorical style, the social and political goals of radical environmentalism in other cultural contexts (e.g., West Germany and India) are quite different; second, that the social consequences of putting deep ecology into practice on a worldwide basis (what its practitioners are aiming for) are very grave indeed.

II. THE TENETS OF DEEP ECOLOGY

While I am aware that the term *deep ecology* was coined by the Norwegian philosopher Arne Naess, this article refers specifically to the American variant. Adherents of the deep ecological perspective in this country, while arguing intensely among themselves over its political and philosophical implications, share some fundamental premises about human-nature interactions. As I see it, the defining characteristics of deep ecology are fourfold:

First, deep ecology argues that the environmental movement must shift from an "anthropocentric" to a "biocentric" perspective. In many respects, an acceptance of the primacy of this distinction constitutes the litmus test of deep ecology. A considerable effort is expended by deep ecologists in showing that the dominant motif in Western philosophy has been anthropocentric— i.e., the belief that man and his works are the center of the universe—and conversely, in identifying those lonely thinkers (Leopold, Thoreau, Muir, Aldous Huxley, Santayana, etc.) who, in assigning man a more humble place in the natural order, anticipated deep ecological thinking. In the political realm, meanwhile, establishment environmentalism (shallow ecology) is chided for casting its arguments in human-centered terms. Preserving nature, the deep ecologists say, has an intrinsic worth quite apart from any benefits preservation may convey to future human generations. The anthropocentric-biocentric distinction is accepted as axiomatic by deep ecologists, it structures their discourse, and much of the present discussion remains mired within it.

The second characteristic of deep ecology is its focus on the preservation of unspoilt wilderness—and the restoration of degraded areas to a more pristine condition—to the relative (and sometimes absolute) neglect of other issues on the environmental agenda. I later identify the cultural roots and portentous consequences of this obsession with wilderness. For the moment, let me indicate three distinct sources from which it springs. Historically, it represents a playing out of the preservationist (read *radical*) and utilitarian (read *reformist*) dichotomy that has plagued American environmentalism since the turn of the century. Morally, it is an imperative that follows from the biocentric perspective; other species of plants and animals, and nature itself, have an intrinsic right to exist. And finally, the preservation of wilderness also turns on a scientific argument—viz., the value of biological diversity in stabilizing ecological regimes and in retaining a gene pool for future generations. Truly radical policy proposals have been put forward by deep ecologists on the basis of these arguments. The influential poet Gary Snyder, for example, would like to see a 90 percent reduction in human populations to allow a restoration of pristine environments, while others have argued forcefully that a large portion of the globe must be immediately cordoned off from human beings.

Third, there is a widespread invocation of Eastern spiritual traditions as forerunners of deep ecology. Deep ecology, it is suggested, was practiced both by major religious traditions and at a more popular level by "primal" peoples in non-Western settings. This complements the search for an authentic lineage in Western thought. At one level, the task is to recover those dissenting voices within the Judeo-Christian tradition; at another, to suggest that religious traditions in other cultures are, in contrast, dominantly if not exclusively "biocentric" in their orientation. This coupling of (ancient) Eastern and (modern) ecological wisdom seemingly helps consolidate the claim that deep ecology is a philosophy of universal significance.

Fourth, deep ecologists, whatever their internal differences, share the belief that they are the "leading edge" of the environmental movement. As the polarity of the shallow/deep and anthropocentric/biocentric distinctions makes clear, they see themselves as the spiritual, philosophical, and political vanguard of American and world environmentalism.

III. TOWARD A CRITIQUE

Although I analyze each of these tenets independently, it is important to recognize, as deep ecologists are fond of remarking in reference to nature, the interconnectedness and unity of these individual themes.

(1) Insofar as it has begun to act as a check on man's arrogance and ecological hubris, the transition from an anthropocentric (human-centered) to a biocentric (humans as only one element in the ecosystem) view in both religious and scientific traditions is only to be welcomed. What is unacceptable are the radical conclusions drawn by deep ecology, in particular, that intervention in nature should be guided primarily by the need to preserve biotic integrity rather than by the needs of humans. The latter for deep ecologists is anthropocentric, the former biocentric. This dichotomy is, however, of very little use in understanding the dynamics of environmental degradation. The two fundamental ecological problems facing the globe are (i) overconsumption by the industrialized world and by urban elites in the Third World and (ii) growing militarization, both in a short-term sense (i.e., ongoing regional wars) and in a long-term sense (i.e., the arms race and the prospect of nuclear annihilation). Neither of these problems has any tangible connection to the anthropocentric-biocentric distinction. Indeed, the agents of these processes would barely comprehend this philosophical dichotomy. The proximate causes of the ecologically wasteful characteristics of industrial society and of militarization are far more mundane: at an aggregate level, the dialectic of economic and political structures, and at a micro-level, the life style choices of individuals. These causes cannot be reduced, whatever the level of analysis, to a deeper anthropocentric attitude toward nature; on the contrary, by constituting a grave threat to human survival, the ecological degradation they cause does not even serve the best interests of human beings! If my identification of the major dangers to the integrity of the natural world is correct, invoking the bogy of anthropocentrism is at best irrelevant and at worst a dangerous obfuscation.

(2) If the above dichotomy is irrelevant, the emphasis on wilderness is positively harmful when applied to the Third World. If in the U.S. the preservationist/utilitarian division is seen as mirroring the conflict between "people" and "interests," in countries such as India the situation is very nearly the reverse. Because India is a long settled and densely populated country in which agrarian populations have a finely balanced relationship with nature, the setting aside of wilderness areas has resulted in a direct transfer of resources from the poor to the rich. Thus, Project Tiger, a network of parks hailed by the international conservation community as an outstanding success, sharply posits the interests of the tiger against those of poor peasants living in and around the reserve. The designation of tiger reserves was made possible only by the physical displacement of existing villages and their inhabitants; their management requires the continuing exclusion of peasants and livestock. The initial impetus for setting up parks for the tiger and other large mammals such as the rhinoceros and elephant came from two social groups, first, a class of ex-hunters turned conservationists belonging mostly to the declining Indian feudal elite and second, representatives of international agencies, such as the World Wildlife Fund (WWF) and the International Union for the Conservation of Nature and Natural Resources (IUCN), seeking to transplant the American system of national parks onto Indian soil. In no case have the needs of the local population been taken into account, and as in many parts of Africa, the designated wildlands are managed primarily for the benefit of rich tourists. Until very recently, wildlands preservation has been identified with environmentalism by the state and the conservation elite; in consequence, environmental problems that impinge far more directly on the lives of the poor—e.g., fuel, fodder, water shortages, soil erosion, and air and water pollution—have not been adequately addressed.

Deep ecology provides, perhaps unwittingly, a justification for the continuation of such narrow and inequitable conservation practices under a newly acquired radical guise. Increasingly, the international conservation elite is using the philosophical, moral, and scientific arguments used by deep ecologists in advancing their wilderness crusade. A striking but by no means atypical example is the recent plea by a prominent American biologist for the takeover of large portions of the globe by the author and his scientific colleagues. Writing in a prestigious scientific forum, the *Annual Review of Ecology and Systematics*, Daniel Janzen argues that only biologists have the competence to decide how the tropical landscape should be used. As "the representatives of the natural world," biologists are "in charge of the future of tropical ecology," and only they have the expertise and mandate to "determine whether the tropical agroscape is to be populated only by humans, their mutualists, commensals, and parasites, or whether it will also contain some islands of the greater nature—the nature that spawned humans, yet has been vanquished by them." Janzen exhorts his colleagues to advance their territorial claims on the tropical world more forcefully, warning that the very existence of these areas is at stake: "if biologists want a tropics in which to biologize, they are going to have to buy it with care, energy, effort, strategy, tactics, time, and cash."

This frankly imperialist manifesto highlights the multiple dangers of the preoccupation with wilderness preservation that is characteristic of deep ecology. As I have suggested, it seriously compounds the neglect by the American movement of far more pressing environmental problems within the Third World. But perhaps more importantly, and in a more insidious fashion, it also provides an impetus to the imperialist yearning of Western biologists and their financial sponsors, organizations such as the WWF and the IUCN. The wholesale transfer of a movement culturally rooted in American conservation history can only result in the social uprooting of human populations in other parts of the globe.

(3) I come now to the persistent invocation of Eastern philosophies as antecedent in point of time but convergent in their structure with deep ecology. Complex and internally differentiated religious traditions—Hinduism, Buddhism, and Taoism—are lumped together as holding a view of nature believed to be quintessentially biocentric. Individual philosophers such as the Taoist Lao Tzu are identified as being forerunners of deep ecology. Even an intensely political, pragmatic, and Christian influenced thinker such as Gandhi has been accorded a wholly undeserved place in the deep ecological pantheon. Thus the Zen teacher Robert Aitken Roshi makes the strange claim that Gandhi's thought was not human-centered and that he practiced an embryonic form of deep ecology which is "traditionally Eastern and is found with differing emphasis in Hinduism, Taoism and in Theravada and Mahayana Buddhism." Moving away from the realm of high philosophy and scriptural religion, deep ecologists make the further claim that at the level of material and spiritual practice "primal" peoples subordinated themselves to the integrity of the biotic universe they inhabited.

I have indicated that this appropriation of Eastern traditions is in part dictated by the need to construct an authentic lineage and in part a desire to present deep ecology as a universalistic philosophy. Indeed, in his substantial and quixotic biography of John Muir, Michael Cohen goes so far as to suggest that Muir was the "Taoist of the [American] West." This reading of Eastern traditions is selective and does not bother to differentiate between alternate (and changing) religious and cultural traditions; as it stands, it does considerable violence to the historical record. Throughout most recorded history the characteristic form of human activity in the "East" has been a finely tuned but nonetheless conscious and dynamic manipulation of nature. Although mystics such as Lao Tzu did reflect on the spiritual essence of human relations with nature, it must be recognized that such ascetics and their reflections were supported by a society of cultivators whose relationship with nature was a far more *active* one. Many agricultural communities do have a sophisticated knowledge of the natural environment that may equal (and sometimes surpass) codified "scientific" knowledge; yet, the elaboration of such traditional ecological knowledge (in both material and spiritual contexts) can hardly be said to rest on a mystical affinity with nature of a deep ecological kind. Nor is such knowledge infallible; as the archaeological record powerfully suggests, modern Western man has no monopoly on ecological disasters.

In a brilliant article, the Chicago historian Ronald Inden points out that this romantic and essentially positive view of the East is a mirror image of the scientific and essentially pejorative view normally upheld by Western scholars of the Orient. In either case, the East constitutes the Other, a body wholly separate and alien from the West; it is defined by a uniquely spiritual and nonrational "essence," even if this essence is valorized quite differently by the two schools. Eastern man exhibits a spiritual dependence with respect to nature—on the one hand, this is symptomatic of his prescientific and backward self, on the other, of his ecological wisdom and deep ecological consciousness. Both views are monolithic, simplistic, and have the characteristic effect—intended in one case, perhaps unintended in the other—of denying agency and reason to the East and making it the privileged orbit of Western thinkers.

The two apparently opposed perspectives have then a common underlying structure of discourse in which the East merely serves as a vehicle for Western projections. Varying images of the East are raw material for political and cultural battles being played out in the West; they tell us far more about the Western commentator and his desires than about the "East." Inden's remarks apply not merely to Western scholarship on India, but to Orientalist constructions of China and Japan as well:

> Although these two views appear to be strongly opposed, they often combine together. Both have a similar interest in sustaining the Otherness of India. The holders of the dominant view, best exemplified in the past in imperial administrative discourse (and today probably by that of "development economics"), would place a traditional, superstition-ridden India in a position of perpetual tutelage to a modern, rational West. The adherents of the romantic view, best exemplified academically in the discourses of Christian liberalism and analytic psychology, concede the realm of the public and impersonal to the positivist. Taking their succour not from governments and big business, but from a plethora of religious foundations and self-help institutes, and from allies in the "consciousness industry," not to mention the important industry of tourism, the romantics insist that India embodies a private realm of the imagination and the religious which modern, western man lacks but needs. They, therefore, like the positivists, but for just one opposite reason, have a vested interest in seeing that the Orien-talist view of India as "spiritual," "mysterious," and "exotic" is perpetuated.

(4) How radical, finally, are the deep ecologists? Notwithstanding their self-image and strident rhetoric (in which the label "shallow ecology" has an opprobrium similar to that reserved for "social democratic" by Marxist-Leninists), even within the American context their radicalism is limited and it manifests itself quite differently elsewhere.

To my mind, deep ecology is best viewed as a radical trend within the wilderness preservation movement. Although advancing philosophical rather than aesthetic arguments and encouraging political militancy rather than negotiation, its practical emphasis—viz., preservation of unspoilt nature—is virtually identical. For the mainstream movement, the function of wilderness is to provide a temporary antidote to modern civilization. As a special institution within an industrialized society, the national park "provides an opportunity for respite, contrast, contemplation, and affirmation of values for those who live most of their lives in the workaday world." Indeed, the rapid increase in visitations to the national parks in postwar America is a direct consequence of economic expansion. The emergence of a popular interest in wilderness sites, the historian Samuel Hays points out, was "not a throwback to the primitive, but an integral part of the modern standard of living as people sought to add new 'amenity' and 'aesthetic' goals and desires to their earlier preoccupation with necessities and conveniences."

Here, the enjoyment of nature is an integral part of the consumer society. The private automobile (and the life style it has spawned) is in many respects the ultimate ecological villain, and an untouched wilderness the prototype of ecological harmony; yet, for most Americans it is perfectly consistent to drive a thousand miles to spend a holiday in a national park. They possess a vast, beautiful, and sparsely populated continent and are also able to draw upon the natural resources of large portions of the globe by virtue of their economic and political dominance. In consequence, America can simultaneously enjoy the material benefits of an expanding economy and the aesthetic benefits of unspoilt nature. The two poles of "wilderness" and "civilization" mutually coexist in an internally coherent whole, and philosophers of both poles are assigned a prominent place in this culture. Paradoxically as it may seem, it is no accident that Star Wars technology and deep ecology both find their fullest expression in that leading sector of Western civilization, California.

Deep ecology runs parallel to the consumer society without seriously questioning its ecological and sociopolitical basis. In its celebration of American wilderness, it also displays an uncomfortable convergence with the prevailing climate of nationalism in the American wilderness movement. For spokesmen such as the historian Roderick Nash, the national park system is America's distinctive cultural contribution to the world, reflective not merely of its economic but of its philosophical and ecological maturity as well. In what Walter Lippman called the American century, the "American invention of national parks" must be exported worldwide. Betraying an economic determinism that would make even a Marxist shudder, Nash believes that environmental preservation is a "full stomach" phenomenon that is confined to the rich, urban, and sophisticated. Nonetheless, he hopes that "the less developed nations may eventually evolve economically and intellectually to the point where nature preservation is more than a business."

The error which Nash makes (and which deep ecology in some respects encourages) is to equate environmental protection with the protection of the wilderness. This is a distinctively American notion, born out of a unique social and environmental history. The archetypal concerns of radical environmentalists in other cultural contexts are in fact quite different. The German Greens, for example, have elaborated a devastating critique of industrial society which turns on the acceptance of environmental limits to growth. Pointing to the intimate links between industrialization, militarization, and conquest, the Greens argue that economic growth in the West has historically rested on the economic and ecological exploitation of the Third World. Rudolf Bahro is characteristically blunt:

> The working class here [in the West] is the richest lower class in the world. And if I look at the problem from the point of view of the whole of humanity, not just from that of Europe, then I must say that the metropolitan working class is the worst exploiting class in history.... What made poverty bearable in eighteenth or nineteenth-century Europe was the prospect of escaping it through exploitation of the periphery. But this is no longer a possibility, and continued industrialism in the Third World will mean poverty for whole generations and hunger for millions.

Here the roots of global ecological problems lie in the disproportionate share of resources consumed by the industrialized countries as a whole *and* the urban elite within the Third World. Since it is impossible to reproduce an industrial mono-culture worldwide, the ecological movement in the West must begin by cleaning up its own act. The Greens advocate the creation of a "no growth" economy, to be achieved by scaling down current (and clearly unsustainable) consumption levels. This radical shift in consumption and production patterns requires the creation of alternate economic and political structures—smaller in scale and more amenable to social participation—but it rests equally on a shift in cultural values. The expansionist character of modern Western man will have to give way to an ethic of renunciation and self-limitation, in which spiritual and communal values play an increasing role in sustaining social life. This revolution in cultural values, however, has as its point of departure an understanding of environmental processes quite different from deep ecology.

Many elements of the Green program find a strong resonance in countries such as India, where a history of Western colonialism and industrial development has benefited only a tiny elite while exacting tremendous social and environmental costs. The ecological battles presently being fought in India have as their epicenter the conflict over nature between the subsistence and largely rural sector and the vastly more powerful commercial-industrial sector. Perhaps the most celebrated of these battles concerns the Chipko (Hug the Tree) movement, a peasant movement against deforestation in the Himalayan foothills. Chipko is only one of several movements that have sharply questioned the non-sustainable demand being placed on the land and vegetative base by urban centers and industry. These include opposition to large dams by displaced peasants, the conflict between small artisan fishing and large-scale trawler fishing for export, the countrywide movements against commercial forest operations, and opposition to industrial pollution among downstream agricultural and fishing communities.

Two features distinguish these environmental movements from their Western counterparts. First, for the sections of society most critically affected by environmental degradation—poor and landless peasants, women, and tribals—it is a question of sheer survival, not of enhancing the quality of life. Second, and as a consequence, the environmental solutions they articulate deeply involve questions of equity as well as economic and political redistribution. Highlighting these differences, a leading Indian environmentalist stresses that "environmental protection per se is of least concern to most of these groups. Their main concern is about the use of the environment and who should benefit from it." They seek to wrest control of nature away from the state and the industrial sector and place it in the hands of rural communities who live within that environment but are increasingly denied access to it. These communities have far more basic needs, their demands on the environment are far less intense, and they can draw upon a reservoir of cooperative social institutions and local ecological knowledge in managing the "commons"—forest, grasslands, and the waters—on a sustainable basis. If colonial and capitalist expansion has both accentuated social inequalities and signaled a precipitous fall in ecological wisdom, an alternate ecology must rest on an alternate society and polity as well.

This brief overview of German and Indian environmentalism has some major implications for deep ecology. Both German and Indian environmental traditions allow for a greater integration of ecological concerns with livelihood and work. They also place a greater emphasis on equity and social justice (both within individual countries and on a global scale) on the grounds that in the absence of social regeneration environmental regeneration has very little chance of succeeding. Finally, and perhaps most significantly, they have escaped the preoccupation with wilderness preservation so characteristic of American cultural and environmental history.

IV. A HOMILY

In 1958, the economist J. K. Galbraith referred to overconsumption as the unasked question of the American conservation movement. There is a marked selectivity, he wrote, "in the conservationist's approach to materials consumption. If we are concerned about our great appetite for materials, it is plausible to seek to increase the supply, to decrease waste, to make better use of the stocks available, and to develop substitutes. But what of the appetite itself? Surely this is the ultimate source of the problem. If it continues its geometric course, will it not one day have to be restrained? Yet in the literature of the resource problem this is the forbidden question. Over it hangs a nearly total silence."

The consumer economy and society have expanded tremendously in the three decades since Galbraith penned these words; yet his criticisms are nearly as valid today. I have said "nearly," for there are some hopeful signs. Within the environmental movement several dispersed groups are working to develop ecologically benign technologies and to encourage less wasteful life styles. Moreover, outside the self-defined boundaries of American environmentalism, opposition to the permanent war economy is being carried on by a peace movement that has a distinguished history and impeccable moral and political credentials.

It is precisely these (to my mind, most hopeful) components of the American social scene that are missing from deep ecology. In their widely noticed book, Bill Devall and George Sessions make no mention of militarization or the movements for peace, while activists whose practical focus is on developing ecologically responsible life styles (e.g., Wendell Berry) are derided as "falling short of deep ecological awareness." A truly radical ecology in the American context ought to work toward a synthesis of the appropriate technology, alternate life style, and peace movements. By making the (largely spurious) anthropocentric-biocentric distinction central to the debate, deep ecologists may have appropriated the moral high ground, but they are at the same time doing a serious disservice to American and global environmentalism.

STUDY QUESTIONS

1. Is Guha's critique of deep ecology sound? How would a full application of deep ecology affect the Third World? Explain.

2. How might deep ecologists like Naess, Devall, or Sessions (Readings 16–18) respond to Guha's criticisms?

3. How might Western environmentalists justify emphasizing quality of life versus sheer survival?

4. Is J. K. Galbraith right that our "appetite for materials" needs to be curbed (or cured)? If so, can you convince your friends?

FOR FURTHER READING

Dwivedi, O. P., and B. N. Tiwari. *Environmental Crisis and Hindu Religion*. New Delhi, India: Gitanjali Publishing House, 1987.

Engel, J. R., and J. G. Engel, eds. *Ethics of Environmental Response*. Tucson: University of Arizona Press, 1990.

Hargrove, Eugene, ed. *Religion and Environmental Crisis*. Athens: University of Georgia Press, 1985.

Johns, David. "Relevance of Deep Ecology to the Third World." *Environmental Ethics* 12 (1990): 233–252.

Noss, John. *Man's Religions*, 7th ed. New York: MacMillan, 1980.

Regan, Tom. *Animal Sacrifices: Religious Perspectives on the Use of Animalism in Science*. Philadelphia: Temple University Press, 1986.

Smart, Ninian. *The Religious Experiences of Mankind*. New York: Scribners, 1969.

Smith, William Cantwell. *Religious Diversity*. New York: Harper & Row, 1976.

Chapter 4

Ecological Ethics

Biodiversity is our most valuable but least appreciated resource
EDWARD O. WILSON, THE DIVERSITY OF LIFE

ACCORDING TO DONELLA MEADOWS, the author of the first reading in this chapter, the total number of species of life is somewhere between 10 million and 30 million, of which only 1.7 million are named and only a small fraction have been studied. Yet we are destroying these species at a record rate. Many types of plants and animals, such as the California condor and the blue whale, are endangered. The majority of the unnamed and unstudied species reside in tropical rain forests in poor countries and are rapidly being destroyed for economic reasons. What should be done about this destruction?

Why should we be concerned with the preservation of species? Why is biodiversity so important that we must make sacrifices to preserve and enhance it? Who cares if the snail darter, a fish of no known use to humans, perishes in the process of building a dam that will develop the economy of the Tennessee Valley? Is biodiversity important in itself? Or do other species of plants and animals have only instrumental value, relative to human need? Do species have intrinsic value?

The philosopher Nicholas Rescher says they do: "When a species vanishes from nature, the world is thereby diminished. Species do not just have an instrumental value ... they have a value in their own right—an intrinsic value." And one of the leading proponents of the land ethic, Baird Callicott, wrote, "[T]he preciousness of individual [animals] ... is inversely proportional to the population of the species." "[T]he human population has become so disproportionate from the biological point of view that if one had to choose between a specimen of *Homo sapiens* and a specimen of a rare even if unattractive species, the choice would be moot."

Donella Meadows argues that three strong reasons should compel us to protect biodiversity: economic value in terms of new drugs and food products produced with the help of these species; their environmental service (without the complex service of microorganisms and other species, life would stop); and their genetic information (vast stores of knowledge are stored in the DNA structure of the living cells of these species). So we have two different kinds of motives: (1) self-interested concern for our survival and flourishing and (2) moral respect for something magnificent that we did not create and do not understand.

In our second reading, Lilly-Marlene Russow asks "Why Do Species Matter?" She argues that we normally ascribe rights to someone because he or she has interests, but species cannot suffer or have interests, since only individual objects can have interests. Since it doesn't make sense to attribute interests to species, it follows that they do not have rights, and so we cannot have obligations to them. She examines three arguments for species preservation and argues that all of them fail. She concludes that individual animals can have aesthetic value, and this is the basis for our obligation to preserve animals of that sort.

Schweitzer's *Civilization and Ethics* in 1923 launched the project of biocentric ethics in post-industrial Eurocentric thought of extending the range of value to include all of life. He called this position "Reverence for Life." Every living thing (every "will-to-live") in nature is endowed with something sacred or intrinsically valuable and should be respected as such:

> Just as in my own will-to-live there is a yearning for more life ... so the same obtains in all the will-to-live around me, equally whether it can express itself to my comprehension or whether it remains unvoiced.
>
> Ethics consists in this, that I experience the necessity of practicing the same reverence for life toward all will-to-live, as toward my own.

Paul Taylor develops Schweitzer's seminal idea. Whereas Schweitzer is not always clear about whether he regards all life-forms as equal—and he sometimes writes as though the will-to-live is embodied in the idea of pleasure and its denial in the idea of pain— Taylor is clearer, self-consciously egalitarian, and separates inherent value from the idea of hedonism (pleasure and pain). For Taylor, all living beings— from amoebas to humans—are of equal inherent value. Each living individual has a goal (what the Greeks called a *telos*), and to have a goal implies a will or desire to attain it. One's goal is one's good, so all living things are inherently good. Kant's notion "end-in-itself," which he applied only to rational beings, is radically expanded by Taylor to cover all living things.

Let us turn to ecocentric ethics. Like biocentric theories, ecocentricism also imputes intrinsic value to nature; whereas biocentric ethics is *individualistic,* ecocentric ethics is *holistic.* It views the biosphere as a totality, including species, populations, land, and ecosystems. The primary source of the modern ecocentric movement is Aldo Leopold's (1887–1948) book *Sand County Almanac* (1949); Leopold, a Wisconsin forest ranger and, later, professor of game management at the University of Wisconsin, attempted to produce a new paradigm to evaluate our conduct. Rather than seeing the environment as merely a resource for human beings, we should view it as the center of value. It is primarily the biotic community that is valuable, and this should guide our moral sensitivities. "A thing is right when it tends to preserve the integrity, stability, and beauty of the biotic community. It is wrong when it tends otherwise." So humans must change their role from conqueror of the land-community to plain member and citizen of it. We must extend our social conscience from people to ecosystems to the land.

Baird Callicott, a disciple of Leopold, attempts to draw out the full picture of the land ethic. Callicott locates the historic sources of Leopold's thought in David Hume, Adam Smith, and Charles Darwin. Hume and Smith made sympathy the basis of moral action, from which altruistic feelings arise. Darwin held that the primeval moral affections centered on the tribe, rather than on its individual members. Leopold, according to Callicott, simply extended this idea to the biotic community. To quote Leopold, "The land ethic simply enlarges the boundaries of the community to include soils, waters, plants, and animals, or collectively: the land. ... It implies respect for ... fellow members and also respect for the community as such."

Callicott holds that intrinsic value is neither purely subjective nor objective but arises when beings like us, with a certain nature, respond to nature. Some philosophers, such as Tom Regan, H. J. McCloskey, and L. W. Sumner, have interpreted Leopold as being antihuman, holding that the biocentric community is the only thing that matters. Sumner calls this "dangerous nonsense" and Regan "environmental fascism." Callicott holds that a more charitable (and accurate) interpretation is to view the land ethic as an extension of our moral consciousness, not canceling out our obligations to other human beings but putting them in a wider ecological context.

We usually seek to protect valuable objects that are threatened by human intervention. While our legal system covers such inanimate objects as corporations and states, it has not widely been extended to cover natural objects. In "Should Trees Have Standing?"—Christopher Stone argues that from both anthropocentric and holistic perspectives, we should assign natural objects (rivers, oceans, trees, the atmosphere, and animals) legal rights. He points out that we already grant such inanimate objects as corporations and municipalities such rights, so why not extend the rights further, using the idea of "legal guardian" to cover these objects?

Stone agrees that the idea of granting natural objects legal standing will seem "unthinkable" to many, but he notes, quoting Darwin on the expanding circle of our moral sentiments, that at one time the idea of granting equal rights to women, blacks, and children was thought to be unthinkable.

20

Biodiversity: The Key to Saving Life on Earth

DONELLA H. MEADOWS

Donella Meadows is an adjunct professor of environmental and policy studies at Dartmouth College and the author of several works in environmental studies, including Limits to Growth. *In this essay, Meadows sets forth three reasons for preserving biodiversity: economic, environmental, and informational. She appeals to both our enlightened self-interest and wider moral sensitivity for nature and its phenomena in calling on us to leave nature alone so that we may not threaten biodiversity.*

The Ozone Hole and the greenhouse effect have entered our public vocabulary, but we have no catchy label for the third great environmental problem of the late 20th century. It's even more diffuse than depletion of the ozone layer or global warming, harder to grasp and summarize. The experts call it "the loss of biodiversity."

Biodiversity obviously has something to do with pandas, tigers and tropical forests. But preserving biodiversity is a much bigger job than

Reprinted from *The Land Steward Letter* (Summer 1990) by permission.

protecting rain forests or charismatic megafauna. It's the job of protecting all life—microscopic creepy-crawlies as well as elephants and condors—and all life's habitats—tundra, prairie and swamp as well as forests.

Why care about tundra, swamp, blue beetles or little blue-stem grasses? Ecologists give three reasons, which boil down to simple self-interest on three levels of escalating importance.

- Biodiversity has both immediate and potential economic value. This is the argument most commonly put forward to defend biodiversity, because it's the one our culture is most ready to hear. It cites the importance of the industries most directly dependent upon nature—fisheries, forestry, tourism, recreation and the harvesting of wild foods, medicines, dyes, rubber and chemicals.

Some ecologists are so tired of this line of reasoning that they refer wearily to the "Madagascar periwinkle argument." That obscure plant yields the drugs vincristine and vinblastine, which have revolutionized the treatment of leukemia. About a third of all modern medicines have derived from molds and plants.

The potential for future discoveries is astounding. The total number of species of life is somewhere between 10 million and 30 million, only 1.7 million of which we have named, only a fraction of which we have tested for usefulness.

The economic value of biodiversity is very real, but ecologists hate the argument because it is both arrogant and trivial. It assumes that the Earth's millions of species are here to serve the economic purposes of just one species. And even if you buy that idea, it misses the larger and more valuable ways that nature serves us.

- Biodiversity performs environmental services beyond price. How would you like the job of pollinating trillions of apple blossoms some sunny afternoon in May? It's conceivable, maybe, that you could invent a machine to do it, but inconceivable that the machine could

work as elegantly and cheaply as the honeybee, much less make honey on the side.

Suppose you were assigned to turn every bit of dead organic matter, from fallen leaves to urban garbage, into nutrients that feed new life. Even if you knew how, what would it cost?

A host of bacteria, molds, mites and worms do it for free. If they ever stopped, all life would stop. We would not last long if green plants stopped turning our exhaled carbon dioxide back into oxygen. Plants would not last long if a few genera of soil bacteria stopped turning nitrogen from the air into nitrate fertilizer.

Human reckoning cannot put a value on the services performed by the ecosystems of Earth. These services include the cleansing of air and water, flood control, drought prevention, pest control, temperature regulation and maintenance of the world's most valuable library—the genes of all living organisms.

- Biodiversity contains the accumulated wisdom of nature and the key to its future. If you ever wanted to destroy a society, you would burn its libraries and kill its intellectuals. You would destroy its knowledge. Nature's knowledge is contained in the DNA within living cells. The variety of that genetic information is the driving engine of evolution, the immune system for life, the source of adaptability—not just the variety of species but also the variety of individuals within each species.

Individuals are never quite alike. Each is genetically unique mostly in subterranean ways that will only appear in future generations. We recognize that is true of human beings. Plant and animal breeders recognize it in dogs, cattle, wheat, roses, apples. The only reason they can bring forth bigger fruits or sweeter smells or disease resistance is that those traits are already present in the genes carried by some individuals.

The amount of information in a single cell is hard to comprehend. A simple one-celled bacterium can carry genes for 1,000 traits, a flowering plant for *wow!*

400,000. Biologist E. O. Wilson says the information in the genes of an ordinary house mouse, if translated into printed letters, would fill all the 15 editions of the Encyclopedia Britannica that have been published since 1768.

The wealth of genetic information has been selected over billions of years to fit the ever-changing necessities of the planet. As Earth's atmosphere filled with oxygen, as land masses drifted apart, as humans invented agriculture and altered the land, there were lurking within individuals pieces of genetic code that allowed them to defend against or take advantage of the changes. These individuals were more fit for the new environment. They bred more successfully. The population began to take on their characteristics. New species came into being.

Biodiversity is the accumulation of all life's past adaptations, and it is the basis for all further adaptations (even those mediated by human gene-splicers).

That's why ecologists value biodiversity as one of Earth's great resources. It's why they take seriously the loss of even the most insignificant species; why they defend not only the preservation of species but the preservation of populations within species, and why they regard the rate of human-induced extinctions as an unparalleled catastrophe.

We don't know how many species we are eliminating, because we don't know how many species there are. It's a fair guess that, at the rate we're destroying habitat, we're pushing to extinction about one species every hour. That doesn't count the species whose populations are being reduced so greatly that diversity within the population is essentially gone. Earth has not seen a spasm of extinctions like this for 65 million years.

Biologists estimate that human beings usurp, directly or indirectly, about 40 percent of each year's total biological production. There is hardly a place on Earth where people do not log, pave,

spray, drain, flood, graze, fish, plow, burn, drill, spill or dump. There is no life zone, with the possible exception of the deep ocean, that we are not degrading.

Besides "loss of diversity," biologists have another name for this problem—"biotic impoverishment." What is impoverished is not just biodiversity, it is also the human economy and human spirit.

Ecologist Paul Ehrlich describes biotic impoverishment this way: "Unless current trends are reversed, Americans will gradually be living in a nation that has fewer warblers and ducks and more starlings and herring gulls, fewer native wildflowers and more noxious weeds, fewer swallowtail butterflies and more cockroaches, smaller herds of elk and bigger herds of rats, less edible seafood, less productive croplands, less dependable supplies of pure fresh water, more desert wastes and dust storms, more frequent floods and more uncomfortable weather."

Biodiversity cannot be maintained by protecting a few species in a zoo, nor by preserving greenbelts or even national parks. To function properly nature needs more room than that. It can maintain itself, however, without human expense, without zookeepers, park rangers, foresters or gene banks. All it needs is to be left alone.

To provide their priceless pollination service, the honeybees ask only that we stop saturating the landscape with poisons, stop paving the meadows where bee-food grows and leave them enough honey to get through the winter.

To maintain our planet, our lives and our future potential, the other species have similar requests, all of which add up to: Control yourselves. Control your numbers. Control your greed. See yourselves as what you are, part of an interdependent biological community—the most intelligent part, though you don't often act that way.

So act that way, either out of a moral respect for something magnificent that you didn't create and do not understand, or out of a practical interest in your own survival.

STUDY QUESTIONS

1. What are Meadows's main reasons for protecting biodiversity? Do her conclusions follow
   from her specific reasons? Explain.

2. Why can't we simply preserve species in zoos
   and national parks?

3. Some species are quite harmful to humans,
   such as the smallpox virus. Shouldn't we
   destroy them altogether?

4. The U.S. Endangered Species Act of 1973
   protects hundreds of species, preventing
   activities that might further threaten these

species. In December 1992, the Bush administration yielded to pressures from environmental
groups and agreed to add 400 species to its list
of endangered (and protected) species over the
next four years, bringing the total to 750 protected species. Business groups complain that
such acts hurt business and threaten jobs.
Should species be protected if such protection
causes unemployment, and is bad for the
economy?

21

Why Do Species Matter?

LILLY-MARLENE RUSSOW

*Lilly-Marlene Russow teaches philosophy at Purdue University and is the author of several
works in philosophy. In this essay, she first examines various test cases to show some of
the complexities involved in any attempt to describe obligations to species. Next, she analyzes
three arguments for obligations to protect endangered species and concludes that not only
do they fail but that there is a conceptual confusion in any attempt to ascribe value to a species.
Whatever duty we do have in this regard must rest on the "value—often aesthetic—of
individual members of certain species."*

I. INTRODUCTION

Consider the following extension of the standard
sort of objection to treating animals differently just
because they are not humans: the fact that a being is
or is not a member of species *S* is not a morally
relevant fact, and does not justify treating that being

differently from members of other species. If so, we
cannot treat a bird differently *just* because it is a
California condor rather than a turkey vulture.
The problem, then, becomes one of determining
what special obligations, if any, a person might
have toward California condors, and what might
account for those obligations in a way that is

Reprinted from *Environmental Ethics*, Vol. 3 (1981) by permission of the author.

generally consistent with the condemnation of speciesism. Since it will turn out that the solution I offer does not admit of a direct and tidy proof, what follows comprises three sections which approach this issue from different directions. The resulting triangulation should serve as justification and motivation for the conclusion sketched in the final section.

II. SPECIES AND INDIVIDUALS

Much of the discussion in the general area of ethics and animals has dealt with the rights of animals, or obligations and duties toward individual animals. The first thing to note is that some, but not all, of the actions normally thought of as obligatory with respect to the protection of vanishing species can be recast as possible duties to individual members of that species. Thus, if it could be shown that we have a *prima facie duty* not to kill a sentient being, it would follow that it would be wrong, other things being equal, to kill a blue whale or a California condor. But it would be wrong for the same reason, and to the same degree, that it would be wrong to kill a turkey vulture or a pilot whale. Similarly, if it is wrong (something which I do not think can be shown) to deprive an individual animal of its natural habitat, it would be wrong, for the same reasons and to the same degree, to do that to a member of an endangered species. And so on. Thus, an appeal to our duties toward individual animals may provide some protection, but they do not justify the claim that we should treat members of a vanishing species with *more* care than members of other species.

More importantly, duties toward individual beings (or the rights of those individuals) will not always account for all the actions that people feel obligated to do for endangered species—e.g., bring into the world as many individuals of that species as possible, protect them from natural predation, or establish separate breeding colonies. In fact, the protection of a species might involve actions that are demonstrably contrary to the interests of some or all of the individual animals: this seems true in cases when we remove all the animals we can from

their natural environment and raise them in zoos, or where we severely restrict the range of a species by hunting all those outside a certain area, as is done in Minnesota to protect the timber wolf. If such efforts are morally correct, our duties to preserve a species cannot be grounded in obligations that we have toward individual animals.

Nor will it be fruitful to treat our obligations to a species as duties toward, or as arising out of the rights of, a species thought of as some special super-entity. It is simply not clear that we can make sense of talk about the interests of a species in the absence of beliefs, desires, purposeful action, etc. Since having interests is generally accepted as at least a necessary condition for having rights, and since many of the duties we have toward animals arise directly out of the animals' interests, arguments which show that animals have rights, or that we have duties towards them, will not apply to species. Since arguments which proceed from interests to rights or from interests to obligations make up a majority of the literature on ethics and animals, it is unlikely that these arguments will serve as a key to possible obligations toward species.

Having eliminated the possibility that our obligations toward species are somehow parallel to, or similar to, our obligation not to cause unwarranted pain to an animal, there seem to be only a few possibilities left. We may find that our duties toward species arise not out of the interests of the species, but are rooted in the general obligation to preserve things of value. Alternatively, our obligations to species may in fact be obligations to individuals (either members of the species or other individuals), but obligations that differ from the ones just discussed in that they are not determined simply by the interests of the individual.

III. SOME TEST CASES

If we are to find some intuitively acceptable foundation for claims about our obligations to protect species, we must start afresh. In order to get clear about what, precisely, we are looking for in this context, what obligations we might think we have toward species, what moral claims we are seeking a foundation for, I turn now to a description of some test cases. An examination of these cases illustrates why the object of our search is not something as straightforward as "Do whatever is possible or necessary to preserve the existence of the species"; a consideration of some of the differences between cases will guide our search for the nature of our obligations and the underlying reasons for those obligations.

Case 1. The snail darter is known to exist only in one part of one river. This stretch of river would be destroyed by the building of the Tellico dam. Defenders of the dam have successfully argued that the dam is nonetheless necessary for the economic development and well-being of the area's population. To my knowledge, no serious or large-scale attempt has been made to breed large numbers of snail darters in captivity (for any reason other than research).

Case 2. The Pére David deer was first discovered by a Western naturalist in 1865, when Pére Armand David found herds of the deer in the Imperial Gardens in Peking: even at that time, they were only known to exist in captivity. Pére David brought several animals back to Europe, where they bred readily enough so that now there are healthy populations in several major zoos. There is no reasonable hope of reintroducing the Pére David deer to its natural habitat; indeed, it is not even definitely known what its natural habitat was.

Case 3. The red wolf (*Canis rufus*) formerly ranged over the southeastern and south-central United States. As with most wolves, they were threatened, and their range curtailed, by trapping, hunting, and the destruction of habitat. However, a more immediate threat to the continued existence of the red wolf is that these changes extended the range of the more adaptable coyote, with whom the red wolf interbreeds very readily; as a result, there are very few "pure" red wolves left. An attempt has been made to capture some pure breeding stock and raise wolves on preserves.

Case 4. The Baltimore oriole and the Bullock's oriole were long recognized and classified as two separate species of birds. As a result of extensive interbreeding between the two species in areas where their ranges overlapped, the American Ornithologists' Union recently declared that there were no longer two separate species; both ex-species are now called "northern orioles."

Case 5. The Appaloosa is a breed of horse with a distinctively spotted coat; the Lewis and Clark expedition discovered that the breed was associated with the Nez Percé Indians. When the Nez Percé tribe was defeated by the U.S. Cavalry in 1877 and forced to move, their horses were scattered and interbred with other horses. The distinctive coat pattern was almost lost; not until the middle of the twentieth century was a concerted effort made to gather together the few remaining specimens and reestablish the breed.

Case 6. Many strains of laboratory rats are bred specifically for a certain type of research. Once the need for a particular variety ceases—once the type of research is completed—the rats are usually killed, with the result that the variety becomes extinct.

Case 7. It is commonly known that several diseases such as sleeping sickness, malaria, and human encephalitis are caused by one variety of mosquito but not by others. Much of the disease control in these cases is aimed at exterminating the disease carrying insect; most people do not find it morally wrong to wipe out the whole species.

Case 8. Suppose that zebras were threatened solely because they were hunted for their distinctive striped coats. Suppose, too, that we could remove this threat by selectively breeding zebras that are not striped, that look exactly like mules, although they are still pure zebras. Have we preserved all that we ought to have preserved?

What does an examination of these test cases reveal? First, that our concept of what a species *is* is not at all unambiguous; at least in part, what counts as a species is a matter of current fashions in taxonomy. Furthermore, it seems that it is not the sheer diversity or number of species that matters: if that were what is valued, moral preference would be given to taxonomic schemes that separated individuals into a larger number of species, a suggestion which seems absurd. The case of the orioles suggests that the decision as to whether to call these things one species or two is not a moral issue at all. Since we are not evidently concerned with the existence or diversity of species in *this* sense, there must be something more at issue than the simple question of whether we have today the same number of species represented as we had yesterday. Confusion sets in, however, when we try to specify another sense in which it is possible to speak of the "existence" of a species. This only serves to emphasize the basic murkiness of our intuitions about what the object of our concern really is.

This murkiness is further revealed by the fact that it is not at all obvious what we are trying to preserve in some of the test cases. Sometimes, as in the case of the Appaloosa or attempts to save a subspecies like the Arctic wolf or the Mexican wolf, it is not a whole species that is in question. But not all genetic subgroups are of interest—witness the case of the laboratory rat—and sometimes the preservation of the species at the cost of one of its externally obvious features (the stripes on a zebra) is not our only concern. This is not a minor puzzle which can be resolved by changing our question from "why do species matter?" to "why do species and/or subspecies matter?" It is rather a serious issue of what makes a group of animals "special" enough or "unique" enough to warrant concern. And of course, the test cases reveal that our intuitions are not always consistent: although the cases of the red wolf and the northern oriole are parallel in important respects, we are more uneasy about simply reclassifying the red wolf and allowing things to continue along their present path.

The final point to be established is that whatever moral weight is finally attached to the preservation of a species (or subspecies), it can be overridden. We apparently have no compunction about wiping out a species of mosquito if the benefits gained by such action are sufficiently important, although many people were unconvinced by similar arguments in favor of the Tellico dam.

The lesson to be drawn from this section can be stated in a somewhat simplistic form: it is not simply the case that we can solve our problems by arguing that there is some value attached to the mere existence of a species. Our final analysis must take account of various features or properties of certain kinds or groups of animals, and it has to recognize that our concern is with the continued existence of individuals that may or may not have some distinctive characteristics.

IV. SOME TRADITIONAL ANSWERS

There are, of course, some standard replies to the question "Why do species matter?" or, more particularly, to the question "Why do we have at least a *prima facie* duty not to cause a species to become extinct, and in some cases, a duty to try actively to preserve species?" With some tolerance for borderline cases, these replies generally fall into three groups: (1) those that appeal to our role as "stewards" or "caretakers," (2) those that claim that species have some extrinsic value (I include in this group those that argue that the species is valuable as part of the ecosystem or as a link in the evolutionary scheme of things), and (3) those that appeal to some intrinsic or inherent value that is supposed to make a species worth preserving. In this section, with the help of the test cases just discussed, I indicate some serious flaws with each of these responses.

The first type of view has been put forward in the philosophical literature by Joel Feinberg, who states that our duty to preserve whole species may be more important than any rights had by individual animals. He argues, first, that this duty does not arise from a right or claim that can properly be attributed to the species as a whole (his reasons are much the same as the ones I cited in Section 2 of this paper), and second, while we have some duty to unborn generations that directs us to preserve species, that duty is much weaker than the actual duty we have to preserve species. The fact that our actual duty extends beyond our duties to future generations is explained by the claim that we have duties of "stewardship" with respect to the world as a whole. Thus, Feinberg notes that his "inclination is to seek an explanation in terms of the requirements of our unique station as rational custodians of the planet we temporarily occupy."

The main objection to this appeal to our role as stewards or caretakers is that it begs the question. The job of a custodian is to protect that which is deserving of protection, that which has some value or worth. But the issue before us now is precisely *whether* species have value, and why. If we justify our obligations of stewardship by reference to the value of that which is cared for, we cannot also explain the value by pointing to the duties of stewardship.

The second type of argument is the one which establishes the value of a species by locating it in the "larger scheme of things." That is, one might try to argue that species matter because they contribute to, or form an essential part of, some other good. This line of defense has several variations.

The first version is completely anthropocentric: it is claimed that vanishing species are of concern to us because their difficulties serve as a warning that we have polluted or altered the environment in a way that is potentially dangerous or undesirable for us. Thus, the California condor whose eggshells are weakened due to the absorption of DDT indicates that something is wrong: presumably we are being affected in subtle ways by the absorption of DDT, and that is bad for us. Alternatively, diminishing numbers of game animals may signal overhunting which, if left unchecked, would leave the sportsman with fewer things to hunt. And, as we become more aware of the benefits that might be obtained from rare varieties of plants and animals (drugs, substitutes for other natural resources, tools for research), we may become reluctant to risk the disappearance of a species that might be of practical use to us in the future.

This line of argument does not carry us very far. In the case of a subspecies, most benefits could be derived from other varieties of the same species. More important, when faced with the loss of a unique variety or species, we may simply decide that, even taking into account the possibility of error, there is not enough reason to think that the species

will ever be of use; we may take a calculated risk and decide that it is not worth it. Finally, the use of a species as a danger signal may apply to species whose decline is due to some subtle and unforeseen change in the environment, but will not justify concern for a species threatened by a known and foreseen event like the building of a dam.

Other attempts to ascribe extrinsic value to a species do not limit themselves to potential human and practical goods. Thus, it is often argued that each species occupies a unique niche in a rich and complex, but delicately balanced, ecosystem. By destroying a single species, we upset the balance of the whole system. On the assumption that the system as a whole should be preserved, the value of a species is determined, at least in part, by its contribution to the whole.

In assessing this argument, it is important to realize that such a justification (a) may lead to odd conclusions about some of the test cases, and (b) allows for changes which do not affect the system, or which result in the substitution of a richer, more complex system for one that is more primitive or less evolved. With regard to the first of these points, species that exist only in zoos would seem to have no special value. In terms of our test cases, the David deer does not exist as part of a system, but only in isolation. Similarly, the Appaloosa horse, a domesticated variety which is neither better suited nor worse than any other sort of horse, would not have any special value. In contrast, the whole cycle of mosquitoes, disease organisms adapted to these hosts, and other beings susceptible to those diseases is quite a complex and marvelous bit of systematic adaptation. Thus, it would seem to be wrong to wipe out the encephalitis-bearing mosquito.

With regard to the second point, we might consider changes effected by white settlers in previously isolated areas such as New Zealand and Australia. The introduction of new species has resulted in a whole new ecosystem, with many of the former indigenous species being replaced by introduced varieties. As long as the new system works, there seems to be no grounds for objections.

The third version of an appeal to extrinsic value is sometimes presented in Darwinian terms: species are important as links in the evolutionary chain. This will get us nowhere, however, because the extinction of one species, the replacement of one by another, is as much a part of evolution as is the development of a new species.

One should also consider a more general concern about all those versions of the argument which focus on the species' role in the natural order of things: all of these arguments presuppose that "the natural order of things" is, in itself, good. As William Blackstone pointed out, this is by no means obvious: "Unless one adheres dogmatically to a position of a 'reverence for all life,' the extinction of some species or forms of life may be seen as quite desirable. (This is parallel to the point often made by philosophers that not all 'customary' or 'natural' behavior is necessarily good.)" Unless we have some other way of ascribing value to a system, and to the animals which actually fulfill a certain function in that system (as opposed to possible replacements), the argument will not get off the ground.

Finally, then, the process of elimination leads us to the set of arguments which point to some *intrinsic value* that a species is supposed to have. The notion that species have an intrinsic value, if established, would allow us to defend much stronger claims about human obligations toward threatened species. Thus, if a species is intrinsically valuable, we should try to preserve it even when it no longer has a place in the natural ecosystem, or when it could be replaced by another species that would occupy the same niche. Most important, we should not ignore a species just because it serves no useful purpose.

Unsurprisingly, the stumbling block is what this intrinsic value might be grounded in. Without an explanation of that, we have no nonarbitrary way of deciding whether subspecies as well as species have intrinsic value or how much intrinsic value a species might have. The last question is meant to bring out issues that will arise in cases of conflict of interests: Is the intrinsic value of a species of mosquito sufficient to outweigh the benefits to be gained by eradicating the means of spreading a disease like encephalitis? Is the intrinsic value of the snail darter sufficient to outweigh the economic hardship that might be alleviated by the

construction of a dam? In short, to say that something has intrinsic value does not tell us *how much value it has*, nor does it allow us to make the sorts of judgments that are often called for in considering the fate of an endangered species.

The attempt to sidestep the difficulties raised by subspecies by broadening the ascription of value to include subspecies opens a whole Pandora's box. It would follow that any genetic variation within a species that results in distinctive characteristics would need separate protection. In the case of forms developed through selective breeding, it is not clear whether we have a situation analogous to natural subspecies, or whether no special value is attached to different breeds.

In order to speak to either of these issues, and in order to lend plausibility to the whole enterprise, it would seem necessary to consider first the justification for ascribing value to whichever groups have such value. If intrinsic value does not spring from anything, if it becomes merely another way of saying that we should protect species, we are going around in circles, without explaining anything. Some further explanation is needed.

Some appeals to intrinsic value are grounded in the intuition that diversity itself is a virtue. If so, it would seem incumbent upon us to create new species wherever possible, even bizarre ones that would have no purpose other than to be different. Something other than diversity must therefore be valued.

The comparison that is often made between species and natural wonders, spectacular landscapes, or even works of art, suggests that species might have some aesthetic value. This seems to accord well with our naive intuitions, provided that *aesthetic value* is interpreted rather loosely; most of us believe that the world would be a poorer place for the loss of bald eagles in the same way that it would be poorer for the loss of the Grand Canyon or a great work of art. In all cases, the experience of seeing these things is an inherently worthwhile experience. And since diversity in some cases is a component in aesthetic appreciation, part of the previous intuition would be preserved. There is also room for degrees of selectivity and concern with superficial changes: the variety of rat that is allowed to become extinct may have no special aesthetic value, and a bird is neither more nor less aesthetically pleasing when we change its name.

There are some drawbacks to this line of argument: there are some species which, by no stretch of the imagination, are aesthetically significant. But aesthetic value can cover a surprising range of things: a tiger may be simply beautiful; a blue whale is awe-inspiring; a bird might be decorative; an Appaloosa is of interest because of its historical significance; and even a drab little plant may inspire admiration for the marvelous way it has been adapted to a special environment. Even so, there may be species such as the snail darter that simply have no aesthetic value. In these cases, lacking any alternative, we may be forced to the conclusion that such species are not worth preserving.

Seen from other angles, once again the appeal to the aesthetic value of species is illuminating. Things that have an aesthetic value may be compared and ranked in some cases, and commitment of resources made accordingly. We believe that diminishing the aesthetic value of a thing for mere economic benefits is immoral, but that aesthetic value is not absolute—that the fact that something has aesthetic value may be overridden by the fact that harming that thing, or destroying it, may result in some greater good. That is, someone who agrees to destroy a piece of Greek statuary for personal gain would be condemned as having done something immoral, but someone who is faced with a choice between saving his children and saving a "priceless" painting would be said to have skewed values if he chose to save the painting. Applying these observations to species, we can see that an appeal to aesthetic value would justify putting more effort into the preservation of one species than the preservation of another; indeed, just as we think that the doodling of a would-be artist may have no merit at all, we may think that the accidental and unfortunate mutation of a species is not worth preserving. Following the analogy, allowing a species to become extinct for *mere* economic gain might be seen as immoral, while the possibility remains open that other (human?) good might outweigh the goods achieved by the preservation of a species.

Although the appeal to aesthetic values has much to recommend it—even when we have taken account of the fact that it does not guarantee that all species matter—there seems to be a fundamental confusion that still affects the cogency of the whole argument and its application to the question of special obligations to endangered species, for if the value of a species is based on its aesthetic value, it is impossible to explain why an endangered species should be more valuable, or more worthy of preservation, than an unendangered species. The appeal to "rarity" will not help, if what we are talking about is species: each species is unique, no more or less rare than any other species: there is in each case one and only one species that we are talking about.

This problem of application seems to arise because the object of aesthetic appreciation, and hence of aesthetic value, has been misidentified, for it is not the case that we perceive, admire, and appreciate a *species*—species construed either as a group or set of similar animals or as a name that we attach to certain kinds of animals in virtue of some classification scheme. What we value is the existence of individuals with certain characteristics. If this is correct, then the whole attempt to explain why species matter by arguing that *they* have aesthetic value needs to be redirected. This is what I try to do in the final section of this paper.

V. VALUING THE INDIVIDUAL

What I propose is that the intuition behind the argument from aesthetic value is correct, but misdirected. The reasons that were given for the value of a species are, in fact, reasons for saying that an individual has value. We do not admire the grace and beauty of the species *Panthera tigris;* rather, we admire the grace and beauty of the individual Bengal tigers that we may encounter. What we value then is the existence of that individual and the existence (present or future) of individuals like that. The ways in which other individuals should be "like that" will depend on why we value that particular sort of individual: the stripes on a zebra do not matter if we value zebras primarily for the way they are adapted to a certain environment, their unique fitness for a certain sort of life. If, on the other hand, we value zebras because their stripes are aesthetically pleasing, the stripes do matter. Since our attitudes toward zebras probably include both of these features, it is not surprising to find that my hypothetical test case produces conflicting intuitions.

The shift of emphasis from species to individuals allows us to make sense of the stronger feelings we have about endangered species in two ways. First, the fact that there are very few members of a species—the fact that we rarely encounter one—itself increases the value of those encounters. I can see turkey vultures almost every day, and I can eat apples almost every day, but seeing a bald eagle or eating wild strawberries are experiences that are much less common, more delightful just for their rarity and unexpectedness. Even snail darters, which, if we encountered them every day would be drab and uninteresting, become more interesting just because we don't—or may not—see them every day. Second, part of our interest in an individual carries over to a desire that there be future opportunities to see these things again (just as when, upon finding a new and beautiful work of art, I will wish to go back and see it again). In the case of animals, unlike works of art, I know that this animal will not live forever, but that other animals like this one will have similar aesthetic value. Thus, because I value possible future encounters, I will also want to do what is needed to ensure the possibility of such encounters—i.e., make sure that enough presently existing individuals of this type will be able to reproduce and survive. This is rather like the duty that we have to support and contribute to museums, or to other efforts to preserve works of art.

To sum up, then: individual animals can have, to a greater or lesser degree, aesthetic value: they are valued for their simple beauty, for their awesomeness, for their intriguing adaptations, for their rarity, and for many other reasons. We have moral obligations to protect things of aesthetic value, and to ensure (in an odd sense) their continued existence; thus we have a duty to protect individual animals (the duty may be weaker or stronger depending on the value of the individual), and to ensure that there will continue to be animals of this sort (this duty will also be weaker or stronger, depending on value).

I began this paper by suggesting that our obligations to vanishing species might appear inconsistent with a general condemnation of speciesism. My proposal is not inconsistent: we value and protect animals because of their aesthetic value, not because they are members of a given species.

STUDY QUESTIONS

1. Do you agree with Russow's rejection of inherent value in species?

2. Is Russow's argument for aesthetic value in individual animals of certain types just another version of anthropocentrism? We get pleasure from beholding certain animals. Does that mean that they are merely resources for our enjoyment?

3. The blue whale is an endangered species, which is valuable for its oil and meat. Supposing its immediate economic value outweighs its aesthetic value, would Russow's arguments conclude that no moral evil would be done in eliminating this species? What do you think?

4. Richard Routley asks the following question to those who see no intrinsic value in other species. Suppose human beings were about to die out. Nothing can be done to save our species. Would it be morally permissible to kill (painlessly, just in case that matters) all other life on Earth before we became extinct? Why, or why not?

22

Reverence for Life

ALBERT SCHWEITZER

Albert Schweitzer (1875–1965) was born in Kaiserberg, Germany, and educated at Strasbourg in Alsace. He was an extraordinarily versatile genius: a concert organist, a musicologist, a theologian, a missionary, a philosopher, and a physician who dedicated his life to the amelioration of suffering and the promotion of life. He built and served in a hospital in Lambarene in French Equatorial Africa (now Gabon). His most famous writings are The Quest for the Historical Jesus *(1906),* Out of My Life and Thought *(1933), and* Civilization and Ethics *(1923) from which the present selection is taken.*

Schweitzer describes his theory of Reverence for Life—the idea that all of life is sacred and that we must live accordingly, treating each living being as an inherently valuable "will-to-live." He was awarded the Nobel Peace Prize in 1952.

Schweitzer relates how the phrase "Reverence for Life" came to him one day in 1915 while he was on a river journey to assist a missionary's sick wife.

At sunset of the third day, near the village of Igendja, we moved along an island in the middle of the wide river. On a sandbank to our left, four hippopotamuses and their young plodded along in our same direction. Just then, in my great tiredness and discouragement, the phrase "Reverence for Life" struck me like a flash. As far as I knew, it was a phrase I had never heard nor ever read. I realized at once that it carried within itself the solution to the problem that had been torturing me. Now I knew a system of values which concerns itself only with our relationship to other people is incomplete and therefore lacking in power for good. Only by means of reverence for life can we establish a spiritual and humane relationship with both people and all living creatures within our reach. Only in this fashion can we avoid harming others, and, within the limits of our capacity, go to their aid whenever they need us.

The following passage is a fuller description of his views. He begins by citing the French philosopher René Descartes (1596–1650) and contrasting that theory of knowledge, which begins with an abstract, isolated self, with the deeper self-awareness that comes from our understanding that all living things (will-to-lives) are sacred and interdependent.

Descartes tells us that philosophizing is based on the judgment: "I think therefore I am." From this meagre and arbitrarily selected beginning it is inevitable that it should wander into the path of the abstract. It does not find the entrance to the ethical realm, and remains held fast in a dead view of the world

Reprinted from *Civilization and Ethics*, trans. A. Naish (London: Black, 1923).

and of life. True philosophy must commence with the most immediate and comprehensive facts of consciousness. And this may be formulated as follows: "I am life which wills to live, and I exist in the midst of life which wills to live." This is no mere excogitated subtlety. Day after day and hour after hour I proceed on my way invested in it. In every moment of reflection it forces itself on me anew. A living world- and life-view, informing all the facts of life, gushes forth from it continually, as from an eternal spring. A mystically ethical oneness with existence grows forth from it unceasingly.

Just as in my own will-to-live there is a yearning for more life, and for that mysterious exaltation of the will-to-live which is called pleasure, and terror in face of annihilation and that injury to the will-to-live which is called pain; so the same obtains in all the will-to-live around me, equally whether it can express itself to my comprehension or whether it remains unvoiced.

Ethics thus consists in this, that I experience the necessity of practising the same reverence for life toward all will-to-live, as toward my own. Therein I have already the needed fundamental principle of morality. It is *good* to maintain and cherish life; it is *evil* to destroy and to check life.

As a matter of fact, everything which in the usual ethical valuation of inter-human relations is looked upon as good can be traced back to the material and spiritual maintenance or enhancement of human life and to the effort to raise it to its highest level of value. And contrariwise everything in human relations which is considered as evil is in the final analysis found to be material or spiritual destruction or checking of human life and slackening of the effort to raise it to its highest value. Individual concepts of good and evil which are widely divergent and apparently unconnected fit into one another like pieces which belong together, the moment they are comprehended and their essential nature is grasped in this general notion.

The fundamental principle of morality which we seek as a necessity for thought is not, however, a matter only of arranging and deepening current views of good and evil, but also of expanding and extending these. A man is really ethical only when he obeys the constraint laid on him to help all life which he is able to succour, and when he goes out of his way to avoid injuring anything living. He does not ask how far this or that life deserves sympathy as valuable in itself, nor how far it is capable of feeling. To him life as such is sacred. He shatters no ice crystal that sparkles in the sun, tears no leaf from its tree, breaks off no flower, and is careful not to crush any insect as he walks. If he works by lamplight on a summer evening, he prefers to keep the window shut and to breathe stifling air, rather than to see insect after insect fall on his table with singed and sinking wings.

If he goes out into the street after a rainstorm and sees a worm which has strayed there, he reflects that it will certainly dry up in the sunshine, if it does not quickly regain the damp soil into which it can creep, and so he helps it back from the deadly paving stones into the lush grass. Should he pass by an insect which has fallen into a pool, he spares the time to reach it a leaf or stalk on which it may clamber and save itself.

He is not afraid of being laughed at as sentimental. It is indeed the fate of every truth to be an object of ridicule when it is first acclaimed. It was once considered foolish to suppose that coloured men were really human beings and ought to be treated as such. What was once foolishness has now become a recognized truth. Today it is considered as exaggeration to proclaim constant respect for every form of life as being the serious demand of a rational ethic. But the time is coming when people will be amazed that the human race was so long before it recognized that thoughtless injury to life is incompatible with real ethics. Ethics is in its unqualified form extended responsibility with regard to everything that has life.

The general idea of ethics as a partaking of the mental atmosphere of reverence for life is not perhaps attractive. But it is the only complete notion possible. Mere sympathy is too narrow a concept to serve as the intellectual expression of the ethical element. It denotes, indeed, only a sharing of the suffering of the will-to-live. But to be ethical is to share the whole experience of all the circumstances and aspirations of the will-to-live, to live with it in its pleasures, in its yearnings, in its struggles toward perfection.

Love is a more inclusive term, since it signifies fellowship in suffering, in joy, and in effort. But it describes the ethical element only as it were by a simile, however natural and profound that simile may be. It places the solidarity created by ethics in analogy to that which nature has caused to come into being in a more or less superficial physical manner, and with a view to the fulfillment of their destiny, between two sexually attracted existences, or between these and their offspring.

Thought must strive to find a formula for the essential nature of the ethical. In so doing it is led to characterize ethics as self-devotion for the sake of life, motived by reverence for life. Although the phrase "reverence for life" may perhaps sound a trifle unreal, yet that which it denotes is something which never lets go its hold of the man in whose thought it has once found a place. Sympathy, love, and, in general, all enthusiastic feeling of real value are summed up in it. It works with restless vitality on the mental nature in which it has found a footing and flings this into the restless activity of a responsibility which never ceases and stops nowhere. Reverence for life drives a man on as the whirling thrashing screw forces a ship through the water.

The ethic of reverence for life, arising as it does out of an inward necessity, is not dependent on the question as to how far or how little it is capable of development into a satisfactory view of life. It does not need to prove that the action of ethical men, as directed to maintaining, enhancing and exalting life, has any significance for the total course of the world-process. Nor is it disturbed by the consideration that the preservation and enhancement of life which it practises are of almost no account at all beside the mighty destruction of life which takes place every moment as the result of natural forces. Determined as it is to act, it is yet able to ignore all the problems raised as to the result of its action. The fact that in the man who has become ethical a will informed by reverence for life and self-sacrifice for the sake of life exists in the world is itself significant for the world.

The universal will-to-live experiences itself in my personal will-to-live otherwise than it does in other phenomena. For here it enters on an individualization, which, so far as I am able to gather in trying to view it from the outside, struggles only to live itself out, and not at all to become one with will-to-live external to itself. The world is indeed the grisly drama of will-to-live at variance with itself. One existence survives at the expense of another of which it yet knows nothing. But in me the will-to-live has become cognizant of the existence of other will-to-live. There is in it a yearning for unity with itself, a longing to become universal.

Why is it that the will-to-live has this experience only in myself? Is it a result of my having become capable of reflection about the totality of existence? Whither will the evolution lead which has thus begun in me?

There is no answer to these questions. It remains a painful enigma how I am to live by the rule of reverence for life in a world ruled by creative will which is at the same time destructive will, and by destructive will which is also creative.

I can do no other than hold on to the fact that the will-to-live appears in me as will-to-live which aims at becoming one with other will-to-live. This fact is the light which shines for me in the darkness. My ignorance regarding the real nature of the objective world no longer troubles me. I am set free from the world. I have been cast by my reverence for life into a state of unrest foreign to the world. By this, too, I am placed in a state of beatitude which the world cannot give. If in the happiness induced by our independence of the world I and another afford each other mutual help in understanding and in forgiveness, when otherwise will would harass other will, then the will-to-live is no longer at variance with itself. If I rescue an insect from a pool of water, then life has given itself for life, and again the self-contradiction of the will-to-live has been removed. Whenever my life has given itself out in any way for other life, my eternal will-to-live experiences union with the eternal, since all life is one. I possess a cordial which secures me from dying of thirst in the desert of life.

Therefore I recognize it as the destiny of my existence to be obedient to the higher revelation of the will-to-live which I find in myself. I choose as my activity the removal of the self-contradiction of the will-to-live, as far as the influence of my own existence extends. Knowing as I do the one thing needful, I am content to offer no opinion about the enigma of the objective world and my own being.

Thought becomes religious when it thinks itself out to the end. The ethic of reverence for life is the ethic of Jesus brought to philosophical expression, extended into cosmical form, and conceived as intellectually necessary.

The surmising and longing of all deeply religious personalities is comprehended and contained in the ethic of reverence for life. This, however, does not build up a world-view as a completed system, but resigns itself to leave the cathedral perforce incomplete. It is only able to finish the choir. Yet in this true piety celebrates a living and continuous divine service....

The ethic of reverence for life also proves its own truth by the way in which it comprehends and includes the most various forms of the ethical impulse. No ethical system has yet proved capable of presenting the effort to attain self-perfection, in which man works on his own being without any action directed externally, on the one hand, and the activist ethic, on the other hand, in connection and interrelation. The ethic of reverence for life accomplishes this, and in such a way that it does not merely solve an academic problem, but brings with it a real deepening of ethical insight.

Ethics is in fact reverence for the will-to-live both within and without my own personality. The immediate product of reverence for the will-to-live which I find in myself is the profound life-affirmation of resignation. I comprehend my will-to-live not only as something which lives itself out in fortunate moments of success, but also as something which is conscious of itself and its own experiences. If I do not allow this experiencing of myself to be dissipated by heedless lack of reflection, but, on the contrary, deliberately pause in it as one who feels its real value, I am rewarded by a disclosure of the secret of spiritual independence. I become a partaker in an unguessed-at freedom amid the destinies of life. At moments when I should otherwise have thought myself to be overwhelmed and crushed, I feel myself uplifted in a state of inexpressible joy, astounding to myself, in which I am conscious of freedom from the world and experience a clarifying of my whole view of life. Resignation is the vestibule through which we pass in entering the palace of ethics. Only he who experiences inner freedom from external events in profound surrender to his own will-to-live is capable of the profound and permanent surrender of himself for the sake of other life.

As I struggle for freedom from the external occurrences of life in reverence for my own will-to-live, so also do I wrestle for freedom from myself. I practise the higher independence not only with regard to that which happens to me personally, but also in respect to the way in which I behave towards the world.

As the result of reverence for my own existence I force myself to be sincere with myself. Anything that I acquire by acting contrary to my convictions is bought too dearly. I am afraid of wounding my will-to-live with poisoned spears by disloyalty to my own personality.

That Kant places sincerity toward oneself in the very centre of his ethical system is a witness to the profoundity of his own ethical perception. But he is unable to grasp the connection between self-sincerity and activist ethics because in his search for the essential nature of the ethical he never gets as far as the idea of reverence for life.

In actual practice the ethic of self-sincerity passes over unconsciously into that of self-sacrifice for others. Sincerity toward myself forces me to acts which appear so much like self-sacrifice that the current ethic derives them from this latter impulse.

Why do I forgive my fellow-man? The current ethic says that it is because I sympathize with him. It presents men as impossibly good when they forgive, and allows them to practise a kind of forgiveness which is really humiliating to the person forgiven. Thus it turns forgiveness into a sort of sweetened triumph of self-sacrifice.

The ethic of reverence for life clears away these obscure and misty notions. All forbearance and forgiveness is for it an act to which it is compelled by sincerity towards itself. I am obliged to exercise unlimited forgiveness because, if I did not forgive, I should be untrue to myself, in that I should thus act as if I were not guilty in the same way as the other has been guilty with regard to me. I must forgive the lies directed against myself, because my own life has been so many times blotted by lies; I must forgive the love-lessness, the hatred, the slander, the fraud, the arrogance which I encounter, since I myself have so often lacked love, hated, slandered, defrauded, and been arrogant. I must forgive without noise or fuss. In general I do not forgive, I do not even get as far as being merely just. And this also is no exaggeration, but a necessary extension and refinement of our usual ethic.

We have to conduct the fight against the evil element which exists in man, not by judging others, but only by judging ourselves. The conflict with our own nature, and sincerity towards ourselves, are the instruments with which we work on others. We move silently into the midst of the struggle for that profound spiritual independence which grows from reverence for our own life. True power makes no noise. It is there, and it produces its effect. True ethic begins where the use of words stops.

The most essential element of activist ethics, even if it does appear as surrender, is thus a product of the impulse to sincerity towards oneself, and in that is contained its real value. The whole ethic of independence from the world only runs as a clear stream when it issues from this source. I am not gentle, peaceable, patient and friendly from a kindly disposition towards others, but because I thus secure the most profound independence. There is an indissoluble connection between the reverence for life with which I face my own existence, and that in which I relate myself to others in acts of self-sacrifice.

It is because the current ethic possesses no fundamental principle of morality that it plunges immediately into the discussion of various conflicting opinions in the ethical realm. The ethic of reverence for life is in no hurry to do this. It takes its own time to think out its fundamental moral principle on all sites. Then, complete in itself, it takes up its own position with regard to these conflicts.

Ethics has to come to an understanding with three opponents; with lack of thought, with egoistic independence, and with the community.

Of the first of these, ethics has not usually taken sufficient account, because it never comes to any open conflict between the two. But, unnoticed, this opponent is constantly on the offensive.

Ethics can take possession of an extensive tract without encountering the troops of egoism. A man can do a great deal of good without being obliged to sacrifice his own interests or desires. Even if he does lose a little bit of his own life in so doing, it is such an insignificant fragment that he misses it no more than he would a single hair or a tiny scale of skin.

To a very large extent the attainment of inner freedom from the world, loyalty to one's own being, existence in distinction from the world, even self-sacrifice for the sake of other life, is only a matter of concentrating attention on this relation. We miss so much of it because we do not keep steadfastly to the point. We do not place ourselves directly under the pressure of the inner impulse to ethical existence. Steam spurts out in all directions from a leaky boiler. The losses of energy on every site are so great in the current ethic because it has at its command no single fundamental moral principle which can act on its thought. It cannot make its boiler steam-tight, nay, it does not even thoroughly inspect it. But reverence for life, which is always present to thought, informs and penetrates, continually and in every direction, a man's observation, reflection and decisions. He can as little resist this process as water can hinder the dyestuff dropped into it from tinting it. The struggle with lack of thought is a conscious process and is always going on.

How does the ethic of reverence for life stand in the conflicts which arise between the inner impulse to self-sacrifice and necessary self-maintenance?

I also am subject to the variance with itself of the will-to-live. My existence is in conflict at a thousand points with that of others. The necessity is laid upon me of destroying and injuring life. If I walk along a lonely road my foot brings annihilation and pain on the tiny beings which people it. In order to maintain my own existence I am obliged to protect it from the existences which would harm it. I become a persecutor of the little mouse which inhabits my dwelling, a destroyer of the insect which desires to breed there, no less than a whole-sale murderer of the bacteria which may endanger my life. I can only secure nourishment for myself by destroying animals and plants. My own good fortune is built on the injuries and hardships of my fellowmen.

How is ethics to exist at all amid the gruesome necessities to which I am a slave because the will-to-live is at variance with itself?

The current ethic seeks for a compromise. It tries to lay down rules as to how much of my own existence and of my own happiness I must give up, and how much I may continue to hold at the expense of the existence and happiness of other life. In so deciding it creates an experimental and relative ethic. That which is actually not ethical at all, but is a hotch-potch of non-ethical necessity and of real ethics, gives itself out as genuinely ethical and normative. Thus a monstrous confusion arises, and thereby a constantly increasing obscuration of the notion of the ethical element.

The ethic of reverence for life recognizes no such thing as a relative ethic. The maintenance and enhancement of life are the only things it counts as being good in themselves. All destruction of and injury to life, from whatever circumstances they may result, are reckoned by it as evil. It does not give place to ready-made accommodations of ethics and necessity which are too eager to occupy the ground. The absolute ethic of reverence makes its own agreements with the individual from moment to moment, agreements always fresh and always original and basic. It does not relieve him of the conflict, but rather forces him to decide for himself in each case how far he can remain ethical and how far he must submit himself to the necessity of destroying and harming life and thus become guilty. Man does not make ethical progress by assimilating instruction with regard to accommodations between the ethical and the necessary, but only by hearing ever more clearly the voice of the ethical element, by being ever more under the control of his own yearning to maintain and to enhance life, and by becoming ever more obstinate in his opposition to the necessity of destroying and injuring life.

In ethical conflicts it is only subjective decisions that a man has to face. No one else can determine for him where lies the utmost limit of the possibility of continuing to maintain and cherish life. He alone has to judge by allowing himself to be led by a sense of responsibility for other lives raised to the highest degree possible. We must never let this sense become dulled and blunted. In effect, however, we are doing so, if we are content to find the conflicts becoming continually more insoluble. The good conscience is an invention of the devil.

What does reverence for life teach us about the relations of man and the non-human animals?

Whenever I injure life of any kind I must be quite clear as to whether this is necessary or not. I ought never to pass the limits of the unavoidable, even in apparently insignificant cases. The countryman who has mowed down a thousand blossoms in his meadow as fodder for his cows should take care that on the way home he does not, in wanton pastime, switch off the head of a single flower growing on the edge of the road, for in so doing he injures life without being forced to do so by necessity.

Those who test operations or drugs on animals, or who inoculate them with diseases so that they may be able to help human beings by means of the results thus obtained, ought never to rest satisfied with the general idea that their dreadful doings are performed in pursuit of a worthy aim. It is their duty to ponder in every separate case whether it is really and truly necessary thus to sacrifice an animal for humanity. They ought to be filled with anxious care to alleviate as much as possible the pain which they cause. How many outrages are committed in this way in scientific institutions where narcotics are often omitted to save time and trouble! How many also when animals are made to suffer agonizing tortures, only in order to demonstrate to students scientific truths which are perfectly well known. The very fact that the animal, as a victim of research, has in his pain rendered such services to suffering men has itself created a new and unique relation of solidarity between him and ourselves. The result is that a fresh obligation is laid on each of us to do as much good as we possibly can to all creatures in all sorts of circumstances. When I help an insect out of his troubles all that I do is to attempt to remove some of the guilt contracted through these crimes against animals.

Wherever any animal is forced into the service of man, the sufferings which it has to bear on that account are the concern of every one of us. No one ought to permit, in so far as he can prevent it, pain or suffering for which he will not take the responsibility. No one ought to rest at ease in the thought that in so doing he would mix himself up in affairs which are not his business. Let no one shirk the burden of his responsibility. When there is so much maltreatment of animals, when the cries of thirsting creatures go up unnoticed from the railway trucks, when there is so much roughness in our slaughterhouses, when in our kitchens so many animals suffer horrible deaths from unskillful hands, when animals endure unheard-of-agonies from heartless men, or are delivered to the dreadful play of children, then we are all guilty and must bear the blame.

We are afraid of shocking or offending by showing too plainly how deeply we are moved by the sufferings which man causes to the nonhuman creatures. We tend to reflect that others are more "rational" than we are, and would consider that which so disturbs us as customary and as a matter of course. And then, suddenly, they let fall some expression which shows us that they, too, are not really satisfied with the situation. Strangers to us hitherto, they are now quite near our own position. The masks, in which we had each concealed ourselves from the other, fall off. We now know that neither of us can cut ourselves free from the horrible necessity which plays ceaselessly around us. What a wonderful thing it is thus to get to know each other!

The ethic of reverence for life forbids any of us to deduce from the silence of our contemporaries that they, or in their case we, have ceased to feel what as thinking men we all cannot but feel. It prompts us to keep a mutual watch in this atmosphere of suffering and endurance, and to speak and act without panic according to the responsibility which we feel. It inspires us to join in a search for opportunities to afford help of some kind or other to the animals, to make up for the great amount of misery which they endure at our hands, and thus to escape for a moment from the inconceivable horrors of existence.

But the ethic of reverence for life also places us in a position of fearful responsibility with regard to our relations to other men.

We find, again, that it offers us no teaching about the bounds of legitimate self-maintenance; it calls us again to come to a separate understanding with the ethic of self-sacrifice in each individual case. According to the sense of responsibility which is my personal experience so I must decide what part of my life, my possessions, my rights, my happiness, my time or my rest, I ought to give up, and what part I ought to keep back.

Regarding the question of property, the ethic of reverence for life is outspokenly individualist in the sense that goods earned or inherited are to be placed at the disposition of the community, not according to any standards whatever laid down by society, but according to the absolutely free decision of the individual. It places all its hopes on the enhancement of the feeling of responsibility in man. It defines possessions as the property of the community, of which the individual is sovereign steward. One serves society by conducting a business from which a certain number of employees draw their means of sustenance; another, by giving away his property in order to help his fellow-men. Each one will decide on his own course somewhere between these two extreme cases according to the sense of responsibility which is determined for him by the particular circumstances of his own life. No one is to judge others. It is a question of individual responsibility; each is to value his possessions as instruments with which he is to work. It makes no difference whether the work is done by keeping and increasing, or by giving up, the property. Possessions must belong to the community in the most various ways, if they are to be used to the best advantage in its service.

Those who have very little that they can call their own are in most danger of becoming purely egoistic. A deep truth lies in the parable of Jesus, which makes the servant who had received the least the least faithful of all.

The ethic of reverence for life does not even allow me to possess my own rights absolutely. It does not allow me to rest in the thought that I, as the more capable, advance at the expense of the less capable. It presents to me as a problem what human law and opinion allow as a matter of course. It prompts me to think of others and to ponder whether I can really allow myself the intrinsic right of plucking all the fruits which my hand is physically able to reach. And then it may occur that following my regard for the existence of others, I do what appears as foolishness to the generality of men. It may, indeed, prove itself to have been actually foolishness so far as my renunciation for the sake of others has really no useful effect. Yet all the same I was right in doing as I did. Reverence for life is the supreme motive. That which it commands has its own meaning, even if it seems foolish or useless. Indeed, we all really seek in one another for that sort of foolishness which shows that we are impelled by the higher responsibility. It is only as we become less rational in the ordinary sense of the word that the ethical disposition works out in us and solves problems previously insoluble.

STUDY QUESTIONS

1. What is Schweitzer's theory of reverence for life? Does it value life itself or a special feature of life?

2. Is Schweitzer an egalitarian? Are all forms of life of equal worth?

3. What does Schweitzer mean in the second paragraph of this selection where he says that the "mysterious exaltation of the will-to-live" is "called pleasure" and "injury to the will-to-live" "pain"? Is this a form of hedonism?

4. Compare Schweitzer's position with Taylor's essay, which follows, as well as with the Hindu and Buddhist views in Chapter 10.

23

Biocentric Egalitarianism

PAUL TAYLOR

Paul Taylor is professor emeritus of philosophy at Brooklyn College, City University of New York, and the author of several works in ethics, including Respect for Nature *(1986), in which he developed the ideas in the following essay.*

Taylor develops Schweitzer's life-centered system of environmental ethics. He argues that each living individual has a "teleological center of life," which pursues its own good in

Reprinted From *Environmental Ethics*, Vol. 3 (Fall 1981) by permission.

its own way, and possesses equal inherent worth. Human beings are no more intrinsically valuable than any other living thing but should see themselves as equal members of Earth's community.

I. HUMAN-CENTERED AND LIFE-CENTERED SYSTEMS OF ENVIRONMENTAL ETHICS

In this paper I show how the taking of a certain ultimate moral attitude toward nature, which I call "respect for nature," has a central place in the foundations of a life-centered system of environmental ethics. I hold that a set of moral norms (both standards of character and rules of conduct) governing human treatment of the natural world is a rationally grounded set if and only if, first, commitment to those norms is a practical entailment of adopting the attitude of respect for nature as an ultimate moral attitude, and second, the adopting of that attitude on the part of all rational agents can itself be justified. When the basic characteristics of the attitude of respect for nature are made clear, it will be seen that a life-centered system of environmental ethics need not be holistic or organicist in its conception of the kinds of entities that are deemed the appropriate objects of moral concern and consideration. Nor does such a system require that the concepts of ecological homeostasis, equilibrium, and integrity provide us with normative principles from which could be derived (with the addition of factual knowledge) our obligations with regard to natural ecosystems. The "balance of nature" is not itself a moral norm, however important may be the role it plays in our general outlook on the natural world that underlies the attitude of respect for nature. I argue that finally it is the good (well-being, welfare) of individual organisms, considered as entities having inherent worth, that determines our moral relations with the Earth's wild communities of life.

In designating the theory to be set forth as life-centered, I intend to contrast it with all anthropocentric views. According to the latter, human actions affecting the natural environment and its nonhuman inhabitants are right (or wrong) by either of two criteria: they have consequences which are favorable (or unfavorable) to human well-being, or they are consistent (or inconsistent) with the system of norms that protect and implement human rights. From this human-centered standpoint it is to humans and only to humans that all duties are ultimately owed. We may have responsibilities *with regard* to the natural ecosystems and biotic communities of our planet, but these responsibilities are in every case based on the contingent fact that our treatment of those ecosystems and communities of life can further the realization of human values and/or human rights. We have no obligation to promote or protect the good of nonhuman living things, independently of this contingent fact.

A life-centered system of environmental ethics is opposed to human-centered ones precisely on this point. From the perspective of a life-centered theory, we have prima facie moral obligations that are owed to wild plants and animals themselves as members of the Earth's biotic community. We are morally bound (other things being equal) to protect or promote their good for *their* sake. Our duties to respect the integrity of natural ecosystems, to preserve endangered species, and to avoid environmental pollution stem from the fact that these are ways in which we can help make it possible for wild species populations to achieve and maintain a healthy existence in a natural state. Such obligations are due to those living things out of recognition of their inherent worth. They are entirely additional to and independent of the obligations we owe to our fellow humans. Although many of the actions that fulfill one set of obligations will also fulfill the other, two different grounds of obligation are involved. Their well-being, as well as human well-being, is something to be realized *as an end in itself.*

If we were to accept a life-centered theory of environmental ethics, a profound reordering of our moral universe would take place. We would begin to look at the whole of the Earth's biosphere in a new light. Our duties with respect to the "world" of nature would be seen as making prima facie claims upon us to be balanced against our duties with respect to the "world" of human civilization. We could no longer simply take the human point of view and consider the effects of our actions exclusively from the perspective of our own good.

II. THE GOOD OF A BEING AND THE CONCEPT OF INHERENT WORTH

What would justify acceptance of a life-centered system of ethical principles? In order to answer this, it is first necessary to make clear the fundamental moral attitude that underlies and makes intelligible the commitment to live by such a system. It is then necessary to examine the considerations that would justify any rational agent's adopting that moral attitude.

Two concepts are essential to the taking of a moral attitude of the sort in question. A being which does not "have" these concepts, that is, which is unable to grasp their meaning and conditions of applicability, cannot be said to have the attitude as part of its moral outlook. These concepts are, first, that of the good (well-being, welfare) of a living thing, and second, the idea of an entity possessing inherent worth. I examine each concept in turn.

1. Every organism, species population, and community of life has a good of its own which moral agents can intentionally further or damage by their actions. To say that an entity has a good of its own is simply to say that, without reference to any *other* entity, it can be benefited or harmed. One can act in its overall interest or contrary to its overall interest, and environmental conditions can be good for it (advantageous to it) or bad for it (disadvantageous to it). What is good for an entity is what "does it good" in the sense of enhancing or preserving its life and well-being. What is bad for an entity is something that is detrimental to its life and well-being.[1]

We can think of the good of an individual nonhuman organism as consisting in the full development of its biological powers. Its good is realized to the extent that it is strong and healthy. It possesses whatever capacities it needs for successfully coping with its environment and so preserving its existence throughout the various stages of the normal life cycle of its species. The good of a population or community of such individuals consists in the population or community maintaining itself from generation to generation as a coherent system of genetically and ecologically related organisms whose average good is at an optimum level for the given environment. Mere *average good* means that the degree of realization of the good of *individual organisms* in the population or community is, on average, greater than would be the case under any other ecologically functioning order of interrelations (among those species populations in the given ecosystem).

The idea of a being having a good of its own, as I understand it, does not entail that the being must have interests or take an interest in what affects its life for better or for worse. We can act in a being's interest or contrary to its interest without its being interested in what we are doing to it in the sense of wanting or not wanting us to do it. It may, indeed, be wholly unaware that favorable and unfavorable events are taking place in its life. I take it that trees, for example, have no knowledge or desires or feelings. Yet it is undoubtedly the case that trees can be harmed or benefited by our actions. We can crush their roots by running a bulldozer too close to them. We can see to it that they get adequate nourishment and moisture by fertilizing and watering the soil around them. Thus we can help or hinder them in the realization of their good. It is the good of trees themselves that is thereby affected. We can similarly act so as to further the good of an entire tree population of a certain species (say, all the redwood trees in a California valley) or the good of a whole community of plant life in a given wilderness area, just as we can do harm to such a population or community.

When construed in this way, the concept of a being's good is not coextensive with sentience or the capacity for feeling pain. William Frankena has argued for a general theory of environmental ethics in which the ground of a creature's being worthy of moral consideration is its sentience. I have offered some criticisms of this view elsewhere, but the full refutation of such a position, it seems to me, finally depends on the positive reasons for accepting a life-centered theory of the kind I am defending in this essay.[2]

It should be noted further that I am leaving open the question of whether machines—in particular, those which are not only goal-directed, but also self-regulating—can properly be said to have a good of their own.[3] Since I am concerned only with human treatment of wild organisms, species populations, and communities of life as they occur in our planet's natural ecosystems, it is to those entities alone that the concept "having a good of its own" will here be applied. I am not denying that other living things, whose genetic origin and environmental conditions have been produced, controlled, and manipulated by humans for human ends, do have a good of their own in the same sense as do wild plants and animals. It is not my purpose in this essay, however, to set out or defend the principles that should guide our conduct with regard to their good. It is only insofar as their production and use by humans have good or ill effects upon natural ecosystems and their wild inhabitants that the ethics of respect for nature comes into play.

2. The second concept essential to the moral attitude of respect for nature is the idea of inherent worth. We take that attitude toward wild living things (individuals, species populations, or whole biotic communities) when and only when we regard them as entities possessing inherent worth. Indeed, it is only because they are conceived in this way that moral agents can think of themselves as having validly binding duties, obligations, and responsibilities that are *owed* to them as their *due*. I am not at this juncture arguing why they *should* be so regarded; I consider it at length below. But so regarding them is a presupposition of our taking the attitude of respect toward them and accordingly understanding ourselves as bearing certain moral relations to them. This can be shown as follows:

What does it mean to regard an entity that has a good of its own as possessing inherent worth?

Two general principles are involved: the principle of moral consideration and the principle of intrinsic value.

According to the principle of moral consideration, wild living things are deserving of the concern and consideration of all moral agents simply in virtue of their being members of the Earth's community of life. From the moral point of view their good must be taken into account whenever it is affected for better or worse by the conduct of rational agents. This holds no matter what species the creature belongs to. The good of each is to be accorded some value and so acknowledged as having some weight in the deliberations of all rational agents. Of course, it may be necessary for such agents to act in ways contrary to the good of this or that particular organism or group of organisms in order to further the good of others, including the good of humans. But the principle of moral consideration prescribes that, with respect to each being an entity having its own good, every individual is deserving of consideration.

The principle of intrinsic value states that, regardless of what kind of entity it is in other respects, if it is a member of the Earth's community of life, the realization of its good is something *intrinsically* valuable. This means that its good is prima facie worthy of being preserved or promoted as an end in itself and for the sake of the entity whose good it is. Insofar as we regard any organism, species population, or life community as an entity having inherent worth, we believe that it must never be treated as if it were a mere object or thing whose entire value lies in being instrumental to the good of some other entity. The well-being of each is judged to have value in and of itself.

Combining these two principles, we can now define what it means for a living thing or group of living things to possess inherent worth. To say that it possesses inherent worth is to say that its good is deserving of the concern and consideration of all moral agents, and that the realization of its good has intrinsic value, to be pursued as an end in itself and for the sake of the entity whose good it is.

The duties owed to wild organisms, species populations, and communities of life in the Earth's natural ecosystems are grounded on their inherent worth. When rational, autonomous agents regard such entities as possessing inherent worth, they place intrinsic value on the realization of their good and so hold themselves responsible for performing actions that will have this effect and for refraining from actions having the contrary effect.

III. THE ATTITUDE OF RESPECT
FOR NATURE

Why should moral agents regard wild living things in the natural world as possessing inherent worth? To answer this question we must first take into account the fact that, when rational, autonomous agents subscribe to the principles of moral consideration and intrinsic value and so conceive of wild living things as having that kind of worth, such agents are *adopting a certain ultimate moral attitude toward the natural world.* This is the attitude I call "respect for nature." It parallels the attitude of respect for persons in human ethics. When we adopt the attitude of respect for persons as the proper (fitting, appropriate) attitude to take toward all persons as persons, we consider the fulfillment of the basic interests of each individual to have intrinsic value. We thereby make a moral commitment to live a certain kind of life in relation to other persons. We place ourselves under the direction of a system of standards and rules that we consider validly binding on all moral agents as such.[4]

Similarly, when we adopt the attitude of respect for nature as an ultimate moral attitude we make a commitment to live by certain normative principles. These principles constitute the rules of conduct and standards of character that are to govern our treatment of the natural world. This is, first, an *ultimate* commitment because it is not derived from any higher norm. The attitude of respect for nature is not grounded on some other, more general, or more fundamental attitude. It sets the total framework for our responsibilities toward the natural world. It can be justified, as I show below, but its justification cannot consist in referring to a more general attitude or a more basic normative principle.

Second, the commitment is a *moral* one because it is understood to be a disinterested matter of principle. It is this feature that distinguishes the attitude of respect for nature from the set of feelings and dispositions that comprise the love of nature. The latter stems from one's personal interest in and response to the natural world. Like the affectionate feelings we have toward certain individual human beings, one's love of nature is nothing more than the particular way one feels about the natural environment and its wild inhabitants. And just as our love for an individual person differs from our respect for all persons as such (whether we happen to love them or not), so love of nature differs from respect for nature. Respect for nature is an attitude we believe all moral agents ought to have simply as moral agents, regardless of whether or not they also love nature. Indeed, we have not truly taken the attitude of respect for nature ourselves unless we believe this. To put it in a Kantian way, to adopt the attitude of respect for nature is to take a stance that one wills it to be a universal law for all rational beings. It is to hold that stance categorically, as being validly applicable to every moral agent without exception, irrespective of whatever personal feelings toward nature such an agent might have or might lack.

Although the attitude of respect for nature is in this sense a disinterested and universalizable attitude, anyone who does adopt it has certain steady, more or less permanent dispositions. These dispositions, which are themselves to be considered disinterested and universalizable, comprise three interlocking sets: dispositions to seek certain ends, dispositions to carry on one's practical reasoning and deliberation in a certain way, and dispositions to have certain feelings. We may accordingly analyze the attitude of respect for nature into the following components. (a) The disposition to aim at, and to take steps to bring about, as final and disinterested ends, the promoting and protecting of the good of organisms, species populations, and life communities in natural ecosystems. (These ends are "final" in not being pursued as means to further ends. They are "disinterested" in being independent of the self-interest of the agent.) (b) The disposition to consider actions that tend to realize those ends to be prima facie obligatory *because* they have that tendency. (c) The disposition to experience positive and negative feelings toward states of affairs in the world *because* they are favorable or unfavorable to the good of organisms, species populations, and life communities in natural ecosystems.

The logical connection between the attitude of respect for nature and the duties of a life-centered system of environmental ethics can now be made clear. Insofar as one sincerely takes that attitude and so has the three sets of dispositions, one will at the same time be disposed to comply with certain rules of duty (such as nonmaleficence and noninterference) and with standards of character (such as fairness and benevolence) that determine the obligations and virtues of moral agents with regard to the Earth's wild living things. We can say that the actions one performs and the character traits one develops in fulfilling these moral requirements are the way one *expresses* or *embodies* the attitude in one's conduct and character. In his famous essay, "Justice as Fairness," John Rawls describes the rules of the duties of human morality (such as fidelity, gratitude, honesty, and justice) as "forms of conduct in which recognition of others as persons is manifested."[5] I hold that the rules of duty governing our treatment of the natural world and its inhabitants are forms of conduct in which the attitude of respect for nature is manifested.

IV. THE JUSTIFIABILITY OF THE ATTITUDE OF RESPECT FOR NATURE

I return to the question posed earlier, which has not yet been answered: why *should* moral agents regard wild living things as possessing inherent worth? I now argue that the only way we can answer this question is by showing how adopting the attitude of respect for nature is justified for all moral agents. Let us suppose that we were able to establish that

there are good reasons for adopting the attitude, reasons which are intersubjectively valid for every rational agent. If there are such reasons, they would justify anyone's having the three sets of dispositions mentioned above as constituting what it means to have the attitude. Since these include the disposition to promote or protect the good of wild living things as a disinterested and ultimate end, as well as the disposition to perform actions for the reason that they tend to realize that end, we see that such dispositions commit a person to the principles of moral consideration and intrinsic value. To be disposed to further, as an end in itself, the good of any entity in nature just because it is that kind of entity is to be disposed to give consideration to *every* such entity and to place intrinsic value on the realization of its good. Insofar as we subscribe to these two principles we regard living things as possessing inherent worth. Subscribing to the principle is what it *means* to so regard them. To justify the attitude of respect for nature, then, is to justify commitment to these principles and thereby to justify regarding wild creatures as possessing inherent worth.

We must keep in mind that inherent worth is not some mysterious sort of objective property belonging to living things that can be discovered by empirical observation or scientific investigation. To ascribe inherent worth to an entity is not to describe it by citing some feature discernible by sense perception or inferable by inductive reasoning. Nor is there a logically necessary connection between the concept of a being having a good of its own and the concept of inherent worth. We do not contradict ourselves by asserting that an entity that has a good of its own lacks inherent worth. In order to show that such an entity "has" inherent worth, we must give good reasons for ascribing that kind of value to it (placing that kind of value upon it, conceiving of it to be valuable in that way). Although it is humans (persons, valuers) who must do the valuing, for the ethics of respect for nature, the value so ascribed is not a human value. That is to say, it is not a value derived from considerations regarding human well-being or human rights. It is a value that is ascribed to nonhuman animals and plants themselves, independently of their relationship to what humans judge to be conducive to their own good.

Whatever reasons, then, justify our taking the attitude of respect for nature as defined above are also reasons that show why we *should* regard the living things of the natural world as possessing inherent worth. We saw earlier that, since the attitude is an ultimate one, it cannot be derived from a more fundamental attitude nor shown to be a special case of a more general one. On what sort of grounds, then, can it be established?

The attitude we take toward living things in the natural world depends on the way we look at them, on what kind of beings we conceive them to be, and on how we understand the relations we bear to them. Underlying and supporting our attitude is a certain *belief system* that constitutes a particular world view or outlook on nature and the place of human life in it. To give good reasons for adopting the attitude of respect for nature, then, we must first articulate the belief system which underlies and supports that attitude. If it appears that the belief system is internally coherent and well-ordered, and if, as far as we can now tell, it is consistent with all known scientific truths relevant to our knowledge of the object of the attitude (which in this case includes the whole set of the Earth's natural ecosystems and their communities of life), then there remains the task of indicating why scientifically informed and rational thinkers with a developed capacity of reality awareness can find it acceptable as a way of conceiving of the natural world and our place in it. To the extent we can do this we provide at least a reasonable argument for accepting the belief system and the ultimate moral attitude it supports.

I do not hold that such a belief system can be *proven* to be true, either inductively or deductively. As we shall see, not all of its components can be stated in the form of empirically verifiable propositions. Nor is its internal order governed by purely logical relationships. But the system as a whole, I contend, constitutes a coherent, unified, and rationally acceptable "picture" or "map" of a total world. By examining each of its main components

and seeing how they fit together, we obtain a scientifically informed and well-ordered conception of nature and the place of humans in it.

This belief system underlying the attitude of respect for nature I call (for want of a better name) "the biocentric outlook on nature." Since it is not wholly analyzable into empirically confirmable assertions, it should not be thought of as simply a compendium of the biological sciences concerning our planet's ecosystems. It might best be described as a philosophical world view, to distinguish it from a scientific theory or explanatory system. However, one of its major tenets is the great lesson we have learned from the science of ecology: the interdependence of all living things in an organically unified order whose balance and stability are necessary conditions for the realization of the good of its constituent biotic communities.

Before turning to an account of the main components of the biocentric outlook, it is convenient here to set forth the overall structure of my theory of environmental ethics as it has now emerged. The ethics of respect for nature is made up of three basic elements: a belief system, an ultimate moral attitude, and a set of rules of duty and standards of character. These elements are connected with each other in the following manner. The belief system provides a certain outlook on nature which supports and makes intelligible an autonomous agent's adopting, as an ultimate moral attitude, the attitude of respect for nature. It supports and makes intelligible the attitude in the sense that, when an autonomous agent understands its moral relations to the natural world in terms of this outlook, it recognizes the attitude of respect to be the only *suitable* or *fitting* attitude to take toward all wild forms of life in the Earth's biosphere. Living things are now viewed as *the appropriate objects of the attitude of respect* and are accordingly regarded as entities possessing inherent worth. One then places intrinsic value on the promotion and protection of their good. As a consequence of this, one makes a moral commitment to abide by a set of rules of duty and to fulfill (as far as one can by one's own efforts) certain standards of good character. Given one's adoption of the attitude of respect, one makes that moral commitment because one considers those rules and standards to be validly binding on all moral agents. They are seen as embodying forms of conduct and character structures in which the attitude of respect for nature is manifested.

This three-part complex which internally orders the ethics of respect for nature is symmetrical with a theory of human ethics grounded on respect for persons. Such a theory includes, first, a conception of oneself and others as persons, that is, as centers of autonomous choice. Second, there is the attitude of respect for persons as persons. When this is adopted as an ultimate moral attitude it involves the disposition to treat every person as having inherent worth or "human dignity." Every human being, just in virtue of her or his humanity, is understood to be worthy of moral consideration, and intrinsic value is placed on the autonomy and well-being of each. This is what Kant meant by conceiving of persons as ends in themselves. Third, there is an ethical system of duties which are acknowledged to be owed by everyone to everyone. These duties are forms of conduct in which public recognition is given to each individual's inherent worth as a person.

This structural framework for a theory of human ethics is meant to leave open the issue of consequentialism (utilitarianism) versus nonconsequentialism (deontology). That issue concerns the particular kind of system of rules defining the duties of moral agents toward persons. Similarly, I am leaving open in this paper the question of what particular kind of system of rules defines our duties with respect to the natural world.

V. THE BIOCENTRIC OUTLOOK
ON NATURE

The biocentric outlook on nature has four main components. (1) Humans are thought of as members of the Earth's community of life, holding that membership on the same terms as apply to all the nonhuman members. (2) The Earth's natural ecosystems as a totality are seen as a complex web of interconnected elements, with the sound biological functioning of each being dependent on the sound biological functioning of the others. (This is the component referred to above as the great lesson that the science of ecology has taught us.) (3) Each individual organism is conceived of as a teleological center of life, pursuing its own good in its own way. (4) Whether we are concerned with standards of merit or with the concept of inherent worth, the claim that humans by their very nature are superior to other species is a groundless claim and, in the light of elements (1), (2), and (3) above, must be rejected as nothing more than an irrational bias in our own favor.

The conjunction of these four ideas constitutes the biocentric outlook on nature. In the remainder of this paper I give a brief account of the first three components, followed by a more detailed analysis of the fourth. I then conclude by indicating how this outlook provides a way of justifying the attitude of respect for nature.

VI. HUMANS AS MEMBERS OF THE
EARTH'S COMMUNITY OF LIFE

We share with other species a common relationship to the Earth. In accepting the biocentric outlook we take the fact of our being an animal species to be a fundamental feature of our existence. We consider it an essential aspect of "the human condition." We do not deny the differences between ourselves and other species, but we keep in the forefront of our consciousness the fact that in relation to our planet's natural ecosystems we are but one species population among many. Thus we acknowledge our origin in the very same evolutionary process that gave rise to all other species and we recognize ourselves to be confronted with similar environmental challenges to those that confront them. The laws of genetics, of natural selection, and of adaptation apply equally to all of us as biological creatures. In this light we consider ourselves as one with them, not set apart from them. We, as well as they, must face certain basic conditions of existence that impose requirements on us for our survival and well-being. Each animal and plant is like us in having a good of its own. Although our human good (what is of true value in human life, including the exercise of individual autonomy in choosing our own particular value systems) is not like the good of a nonhuman animal or plant, it can no more be realized than their good can without the biological necessities for survival and physical health.

When we look at ourselves from the evolutionary point of view, we see that not only are we very recent arrivals on Earth, but that our emergence as a new species on the planet was originally an event of no particular importance to the entire scheme of things. The Earth was teeming with life long before we appeared. Putting the point metaphorically, we are relative newcomers, entering a home that has been the residence of others for hundreds of millions of years, a home that must now be shared by all of us together.

The comparative brevity of human life on Earth may be vividly depicted by imagining the geological time scale in spatial terms. Suppose we start with algae, which have been around for at least 600 million years. (The earliest protozoa actually predated this by several *billion* years.) If the time that algae have been here were represented by the length of a football field (300 feet), then the period during which sharks have been swimming in the world's oceans and spiders have been spinning their webs would occupy three quarters of the length of the field; reptiles would show up at about the center of the field; mammals would cover the last third of the field; hominids (mammals of the family *Hominidae*) the last two feet; and the species *Homo sapiens* the last six inches.

Whether this newcomer is able to survive as long as other species remains to be seen. But there is surely something presumptuous about the way humans look down on the "lower" animals, especially those that have become extinct. We consider the dinosaurs, for example, to be biological failures, though they existed on our planet for 65 million years. One writer has made the point with beautiful simplicity:

> We sometimes speak of the dinosaurs as failures; there will be time enough for that judgment when we have lasted even for one tenth as long....[6]

The possibility of the extinction of the human species, a possibility which starkly confronts us in the contemporary world, makes us aware of another respect in which we should not consider ourselves privileged beings in relation to other species. This is the fact that the well-being of humans is dependent upon the ecological soundness and health of many plant and animal communities, while their soundness and health does not in the least depend upon human well-being. Indeed, from their standpoint the very existence of humans is quite unnecessary. Every last man, woman, and child would disappear from the face of the Earth without any significant detrimental consequence for the good of wild animals and plants. On the contrary, many of them would be greatly benefited. The destruction of their habitats by human "developments" would cease. The poisoning and polluting of their environment would come to an end. The Earth's land, air, and water would no longer be subject to the degradation they are now undergoing as the result of large-scale technology and uncontrolled population growth. Life communities in natural ecosystems would gradually return to their former healthy state. Tropical rain forests, for example, would again be able to make their full contribution to a life-sustaining atmosphere for the whole planet. The rivers, lakes, and oceans of the world would (perhaps) eventually become clean again. Spilled oil, plastic trash, and even radioactive waste might finally, after many centuries, cease doing their terrible work. Ecosystems would return to their proper balance, suffering only the disruptions of natural events such as volcanic eruptions and glaciation. From these the community of life could recover, as it has so often done in the past. But the ecological disasters now perpetrated on it by humans—disasters from which it might never recover—these it would no longer have to endure.

If, then, the total, final, absolute extermination of our species (by our own hands?) should take place and if we should not carry all the others with us into oblivion, not only would the Earth's community of life continue to exist, but in all probability its well-being would be enhanced. Our presence, in short, is not needed. If we were to take the standpoint of the community and give voice to its true interest, the ending of our six-inch epoch would most likely be greeted with a hearty "Good riddance!"

VII. THE NATURAL WORLD AS AN ORGANIC SYSTEM

To accept the biocentric outlook and regard ourselves and our place in the world from its perspective is to see the whole natural order of the Earth's biosphere as a complex but unified web of interconnected organisms, objects, and events. The ecological relationships between any community of living things and their environment form an organic whole of functionally interdependent parts. Each ecosystem is a small universe itself in which the interactions of its various species populations comprise an intricately woven network of cause–effect relations. Such dynamic but at the same time relatively stable structures as food chains, predator–prey relations, and plant succession in a forest are self-regulating, energy-recycling mechanisms that preserve the equilibrium of the whole.

As far as the well-being of wild animals and plants is concerned, this ecological equilibrium must not be destroyed. The same holds true of the well-being of humans. When one views the realm of nature from the perspective of the biocentric outlook, one never forgets that in the long run the integrity of the entire biosphere of our planet is essential to the realization of the good of its constituent communities of life, both human and nonhuman.

Although the importance of this idea cannot be overemphasized, it is by now so familiar and so widely acknowledged that I shall not further elaborate on it here. However, I do wish to point out that this "holistic" view of the Earth's ecological systems does not itself constitute a moral norm. It is a factual aspect of biological reality, to be understood as a set of causal connections in ordinary empirical terms. Its significance for humans is the same as its significance for nonhumans, namely, in setting basic conditions for the realization of the good of living things. Its ethical implications for our treatment of the natural environment lie entirely in the fact that our *knowledge* of these causal connections is an essential *means* to fulfilling the aims we set for ourselves in adopting the attitude of respect for nature. In addition, its theoretical implications for the ethics of respect for nature lie in the fact that it (along with the other elements of the biocentric outlook) makes the adopting of that attitude a rational and intelligible thing to do.

VIII. INDIVIDUAL ORGANISMS AS TELEOLOGICAL CENTERS OF LIFE

As our knowledge of living things increases, as we come to a deeper understanding of their life cycles, their interactions with other organisms, and the manifold ways in which they adjust to the environment, we become more fully aware of how each of them is carrying out its biological functions according to the laws of its species-specific nature. But besides this, our increasing knowledge and understanding also develop in us a sharpened awareness of the uniqueness of each individual organism. Scientists who have made careful studies of particular plants and animals, whether in the field or in laboratories, have often acquired a knowledge of their subjects as identifiable individuals. Close observation over extended periods of time has led them to an appreciation of the unique "personalities" of their subjects. Sometimes a scientist may come to take a special interest in a particular animal or plant, all the while remaining strictly objective in the gathering and recording of data. Non-scientists may likewise experience this development of interest when, as amateur naturalists, they make accurate observations over sustained periods of close acquaintance with an individual organism. As one becomes more and more familiar with the organism and its behavior, one becomes fully sensitive to the particular way it is living out its life cycle. One may become fascinated by it and even experience some involvement with its good and bad fortunes (that is, with the occurrence of environmental conditions favorable or unfavorable to the realization of its good). The organism comes to mean something to one as a unique, irreplaceable individual. The final culmination of this process is the achievement of a genuine understanding of its point of view and, with that understanding, an ability to "take" that point of view. *Conceiving of it as a center of life, one is able to look at the world from its perspective.*

This development from objective knowledge to the recognition of individuality, and from the recognition of individuality to full awareness of an organism's standpoint, is a process of heightening our consciousness of what it means to be an individual living thing. We grasp the particularity of the organism as a teleological center of life, striving to preserve itself and to realize its own good in its own unique way.

It is to be noted that we need not be falsely anthropomorphizing when we conceive of individual plants and animals in this manner. Understanding them as teleological centers of life does not necessitate "reading into" them human characteristics. We need not, for example, consider them to have consciousness. Some of them may be aware of the world around them and others may not. Nor need we deny that different kinds and levels of awareness are exemplified when consciousness in some form is present. But conscious or not, all are equally teleological centers of life in the sense that each is a unified system of goal-oriented activities directed toward their preservation and well-being.

When considered from an ethical point of view, a teleological center of life is an entity whose "world" can be viewed from the perspective of *its* life. In looking at the world from that perspective we recognize objects and events occurring in its life as being beneficent, maleficent, or indifferent. The first are occurrences which increase its powers to preserve its existence and realize its good. The second decrease or

destroy those powers. The third have neither of these effects on the entity. With regard to our human role as moral agents, we can conceive of a teleological center of life as a being whose standpoint we can take in making judgments about what events in the world are good or evil, desirable or undesirable. In making those judgments it is what promotes or protects the being's own good, not what benefits moral agents themselves, that sets the standard of evaluation. Such judgments can be made about anything that happens to the entity which is favorable or unfavorable in relation to its good. As we pointed out earlier, the entity itself need not have any (conscious) *interest* in what is happening to it for such judgments to be meaningful and true.

It is precisely judgments of this sort that we are disposed to make when we take the attitude of respect for nature. In adopting that attitude those judgments are given weight as reasons for action in our practical deliberation. They become morally relevant facts in the guidance of our conduct.

IX. THE DENIAL OF HUMAN SUPERIORITY

The fourth component of the biocentric outlook on nature is the single most important idea in establishing the justifiability of the attitude of respect for nature. Its central role is due to the special relationship it bears to the first three components of the outlook. This relationship will be brought out after the concept of human superiority is examined and analyzed.[7]

In what sense are humans alleged to be superior to other animals? We are different from them in having certain capacities that they lack. But why should these capacities be a mark of superiority? From what point of view are they judged to be signs of superiority and what sense of superiority is meant? After all, various nonhuman species have capacities that humans lack. There is the speed of a cheetah, the vision of an eagle, the agility of a monkey. Why should not these be taken as signs of *their* superiority over humans?

One answer that comes immediately to mind is that these capacities are not as *valuable* as the human capacities that are claimed to make us superior. Such uniquely human characteristics as rational thought, aesthetic creativity, autonomy and self-determination, and moral freedom, it might be held, have a higher value than the capacities found in other species. Yet we must ask: valuable to whom, and on what grounds?

The human characteristics mentioned are all valuable to humans. They are essential to the preservation and enrichment of our civilization and culture. Clearly it is from the human standpoint that they are being judged to be desirable and good. It is not difficult here to recognize a begging of the question. Humans are claiming human superiority from a strictly human point of view, that is, from a point of view in which the good of humans is taken as the standard of judgment. All we need to do is look at the capacities of nonhuman animals (or plants, for that matter) from the standpoint of *their* good to find a contrary judgment of superiority. The speed of the cheetah, for example, is a sign of its superiority to humans when considered from the standpoint of the good of its species. If it were as slow a runner as a human, it would not be able to survive. And so for all the other abilities of nonhumans which further their good but which are lacking in humans. In each case the claim to human superiority would be rejected from a nonhuman standpoint.

When superiority assertions are interpreted in this way, they are based on judgments of *merit*. To judge the merits of a person or an organism one must apply grading or ranking standards to it. (As I show below, this distinguishes judgments of merit from judgments of inherent worth.) Empirical investigation then determines whether it has the "good-making properties" (merits) in virtue of which it fulfills the standards being applied. In the case of humans, merits may be either moral or nonmoral. We can judge one person to be better than (superior to) another from the moral point of view by applying certain standards to their character and conduct. Similarly, we can appeal to nonmoral criteria in judging someone to be an excellent piano player, a fair cook, a poor tennis player, and so on. Different social purposes and roles are implicit in the making of such judgments, providing the frame of reference for the choice of standards by which the nonmoral merits of people are determined. Ultimately such purposes and roles stem from a society's way of life as a whole. Now a society's way of life may be thought of as the cultural form given to the realization of human values. Whether moral or nonmoral standards are being applied, then, all judgments of people's merits finally depend on human values. All are made from an exclusively human standpoint.

The question that naturally arises at this juncture is: Why should standards that are based on human values be assumed to be the only valid criteria of merit and hence the only true signs of superiority? This question is especially pressing when humans are being judged superior in merit to nonhumans. It is true that a human being may be a better mathematician than a monkey, but the monkey may be a better tree climber than a human being. If we humans value mathematics more than tree climbing, that is because our conception of civilized life makes the development of mathematical ability more desirable than the ability to climb trees. But is it not unreasonable to judge nonhumans by the values of human civilization, rather than by values connected with what it is for a member of *that* species to live a good life? If all living things have a good of their own, it at least makes sense to judge the merits of nonhumans by standards derived from *their* good. To use only standards based on human values is already to commit oneself to holding that humans are superior to nonhumans, which is the point in question.

A further logical flaw arises in connection with the widely held conviction that humans are *morally* superior beings because they possess, while others lack, the capacities of a moral agent (free will, accountability, deliberation, judgment, practical reason). This view rests on a conceptual confusion. As far as moral standards are concerned, only beings that have the capacities of a moral agent can properly be judged to be *either* moral (morally good) *or* immoral (morally deficient). Moral standards are simply not applicable to beings that lack such capacities. Animals and plants cannot therefore be said to be morally inferior in merit to humans. Since the only beings that can have moral merits *or be deficient in such merits* are moral agents, it is conceptually incoherent to judge humans as superior to nonhumans on the ground that humans have moral capacities while nonhumans don't.

Up to this point I have been interpreting the claim that humans are superior to other living things as a grading or ranking judgment regarding their comparative merits. There is, however, another way of understanding the idea of human superiority. According to this interpretation, humans are superior to nonhumans not as regards their merits but as regards their inherent worth. Thus the claim of human superiority is to be understood as asserting that all humans, simply in virtue of their humanity, have *a greater inherent worth* than other living things.

The inherent worth of an entity does not depend on its merits.[8] To consider something as possessing inherent worth, we have seen, is to place intrinsic value on the realization of its good. This is done regardless of whatever particular merits it might have or might lack, as judged by a set of grading or ranking standards. In human affairs, we are all familiar with the principle that one's worth as a person does not vary with one's merits or lack of merits. The same can hold true of animals and plants. To regard such entities as possessing inherent worth entails disregarding their merits and deficiencies, whether they are being judged from a human standpoint or from the standpoint of their own species.

The idea of one entity having more merit than another, and so being superior to it in merit, makes perfectly good sense. Merit is a grading or ranking concept, and judgments of comparative merit are based on the different degrees to which things satisfy a given standard. But what can it mean to talk about one thing being superior to another in inherent worth? In order to get at what is being asserted in such a claim, it is helpful first to look at the social origin of the concept of degrees of inherent worth.

The idea that humans can possess different degrees of inherent worth originated in societies having rigid class structures. Before the rise of modern democracies with their egalitarian outlook, one's membership in a hereditary class determined one's social status. People in the upper classes were looked up to, while those in the lower classes were looked down upon. In such a society one's social superiors and social inferiors were clearly defined and easily recognized.

Two aspects of these class-structured societies are especially relevant to the idea of degrees of inherent worth. First, those born into the upper classes were deemed more worthy of respect than those born into the lower orders. Second, the superior worth of upper class people had nothing to do with their merits nor did the inferior worth of those in the lower classes rest on their lack of merits. One's superiority or inferiority entirely derived from a social position one was born into. The modern concept of a meritocracy simply did not apply. One could not advance into a higher class by any sort of moral or nonmoral achievement. Similarly, an aristocrat held his title and all the privileges that went with it just because he was the eldest son of a titled nobleman. Unlike the bestowing of knighthood in contemporary Great Britain, one did not earn membership in the nobility by meritorious conduct.

We who live in modern democracies no longer believe in such hereditary social distinctions. Indeed, we would wholeheartedly condemn them on moral grounds as being fundamentally unjust. We have come to think of class systems as a paradigm of social injustice, it being a central principle of the democratic way of life that among humans there are no superiors and no inferiors. Thus we have rejected the whole conceptual framework in which people are judged to have different degrees of inherent worth. That idea is incompatible with our notion of human equality based on the doctrine that all humans, simply in virtue of their humanity, have the same inherent worth. (The belief in universal human rights is one form that this egalitarianism takes.)

The vast majority of people in modern democracies, however, do not maintain an egalitarian outlook when it comes to comparing human beings with other living things. Most people consider our own species to be superior to all other species and this superiority is understood to be a matter of inherent worth, not merit. There may exist thoroughly vicious and depraved humans who lack all merit. Yet because they are human they are thought to belong to a higher class of entities than any plant or animal. That one is born into the species *Homo sapiens* entitles one to have lordship over those who are one's inferiors, namely, those born into other species. The parallel with hereditary social classes is very close. Implicit in this view is a hierarchical conception of nature according to which an organism has a position of superiority or inferiority in the Earth's community of life simply on the basis of its genetic background. The "lower" orders of life are looked down upon and it is considered perfectly proper that they serve the interests of those belonging to the highest order, namely humans. The intrinsic value we place on the well-being of our fellow humans reflects our recognition of their rightful position as our equals. No such intrinsic value is to be placed on the good of other animals, unless we choose to do so out of fondness or affection for them. But their well-being imposes no moral requirement on us. In this respect there is an absolute difference in moral status between ourselves and them.

This is the structure of concepts and beliefs that people are committed to insofar as they regard humans to be superior in inherent worth to all other species. I now wish to argue that this structure of concepts and beliefs is completely groundless. If we accept the first three components of the biocentric outlook and from that perspective look at the major philosophical traditions which have supported that structure, we find it to be at bottom nothing more than the expression of an irrational bias in our own favor. The philosophical traditions themselves rest on very questionable assumptions or else simply beg the question. I briefly consider three of the main traditions to substantiate the point. These are classical Greek humanism, Cartesian dualism, and the Judeo-Christian concept of the Great Chain of Being.

The inherent superiority of humans over other species was implicit in the Greek definition of man

as a rational animal. Our animal nature was identified with "brute" desires that need the order and restraint of reason to rule them (just as reason is the special virtue of those who rule in the ideal state). Rationality was then seen to be the key to our superiority over animals. It enables us to live on a higher plane and endows us with a nobility and worth that other creatures lack. This familiar way of comparing humans with other species is deeply ingrained in our Western philosophical outlook. The point to consider here is that this view does not actually provide an argument *for* human superiority but rather makes explicit the framework of thought that is implicitly used by those who think of humans as inherently superior to nonhumans. The Greeks who held that humans, in virtue of their rational capacities, have a kind of worth greater than that of any nonrational being never looked at rationality as but one capacity of living things among many others. But when we consider rationality from the standpoint of the first three elements of the ecological outlook, we see that its value lies in its importance for *human* life. Other creatures achieve their species-specific good without the need of rationality, although they often make use of capacities that humans lack. So the humanistic outlook of classical Greek thought does not give us a neutral (non-question-begging) ground on which to construct a scale of degrees of inherent worth possessed by different species of living things.

The second tradition, centering on the Cartesian dualism of soul and body, also fails to justify the claim to human superiority. That superiority is supposed to derive from the fact that we have souls while animals do not. Animals are mere automata and lack the divine element that makes us spiritual beings. I won't go into the now familiar criticisms of this two-substance view. I only add the point that, even if humans are composed of an immaterial, un-extended soul and a material, extended body, this in itself is not a reason to deem them of greater worth than entities that are only bodies. Why is a soul substance a thing that adds value to its possessor? Unless some theological reasoning is offered here (which many, including myself, would find unacceptable on epistemological grounds), no logical connection is evident. An immaterial something which thinks is better than a material something which does not think only if thinking itself has value, either intrinsically or instrumentally. Now it is intrinsically valuable to humans alone, who value it as an end in itself, and it is instrumentally valuable to those who benefit from it, namely humans.

For animals that neither enjoy thinking for its own sake nor need it for living the kind of life for which they are best adapted, it has no value. Even if "thinking" is broadened to include all forms of consciousness, there are still many living things that can do without it and yet live what is for their species a good life. The anthropocentricity underlying the claim to human superiority runs throughout Cartesian dualism.

A third major source of the idea of human superiority is the Judeo-Christian concept of the Great Chain of Being. Humans are superior to animals and plants because their Creator has given them a higher place on the chain. It begins with God at the top, and then moves to the angels, who are lower than God but higher than humans, then to humans, positioned between the angels and the beasts (partaking of the nature of both), and then on down to the lower levels occupied by nonhuman animals, plants, and finally inanimate objects. Humans, being "made in God's image," are inherently superior to animals and plants by virtue of their being closer (in their essential nature) to God.

The metaphysical and epistemological difficulties with this conception of a hierarchy of entities are, in my mind, insuperable. Without entering into this matter here, I only point out that if we are unwilling to accept the metaphysics of traditional Judaism and Christianity, we are again left without good reasons for holding to the claim of inherent human superiority.

The foregoing considerations (and others like them) leave us with but one ground for the assertion that a human being, regardless of merit, is a higher kind of entity than any other living thing. This is the mere fact of the genetic makeup of the species *Homo sapiens*. But this is surely irrational and arbitrary. Why should the arrangement of genes of a certain type be a mark of superior value, especially when this fact about an organism is taken by itself, unrelated to any other aspect of its life? We might just as well refer to any other genetic makeup as a ground of superior value. Clearly we are confronted here with a wholly arbitrary claim that can only be explained as an irrational bias in our own favor.

That the claim is nothing more than a deep-seated prejudice is brought home to us when we look at our relation to other species in the light of the first three elements of the biocentric outlook. Those elements taken conjointly give us a certain overall view of the natural world and of the place of humans in it. When we take this view we come to understand other living things, their environmental conditions, and their ecological relationships in such a way as to awake in us a deep sense of our kinship with them as fellow members of the Earth's community of life. Humans and nonhumans alike are viewed together as integral parts of one unified whole in which all living things are functionally interrelated. Finally, when our awareness focuses on the individual lives of plants and animals, each is seen to share with us the characteristic of being a teleological center of life striving to realize its own good in its own unique way.

As this entire belief system becomes part of the conceptual framework through which we understand and perceive the world, we come to see ourselves as bearing a certain moral relation to nonhuman forms of life. Our ethical role in nature takes on a new significance. We begin to look at other species as we look at ourselves, seeing them as beings which have a good they are striving to realize just as we have a good we are striving to realize. We accordingly develop the disposition to view the world from the standpoint of their good as well as from the standpoint of our own good. Now if the groundlessness of the claim that humans are inherently superior to other species were brought clearly before our minds, we would not remain intellectually neutral toward that claim but would reject it as being fundamentally at variance with our total world outlook. In the absence of any good reasons for holding it, the assertion of human superiority would then appear simply as the expression of an irrational and self-serving prejudice that favors one particular species over several million others.

Rejecting the notion of human superiority entails its positive counterpart: the doctrine of species impartially. One who accepts that doctrine regards all living things as possessing inherent worth—the *same* inherent worth, since no one species has been shown to be either "higher" or "lower" than any other. Now we saw earlier that, insofar as one thinks of a living thing as possessing inherent worth, one considers it to be the appropriate object of the attitude of respect and believes that attitude to be the only fitting or suitable one for all moral agents to take toward it.

Here, then, is the key to understanding how the attitude of respect is rooted in the biocentric outlook on nature. The basic connection is made through the denial of human superiority. Once we reject the claim that humans are superior either in merit or in worth to other living things, we are ready to adopt the attitude of respect. The denial of human superiority is itself the result of taking the perspective on nature built into the first three elements of the biocentric outlook.

Now the first three elements of the biocentric outlook, it seems clear, would be found acceptable to any rational and scientifically informed thinker who is fully "open" to the reality of the lives of nonhuman organisms. Without denying our distinctively human characteristics, such a thinker can acknowledge the fundamental respects in which we are members of the Earth's community of life and in which the biological conditions necessary for the realization of our human values are inextricably linked with the whole system of nature. In addition, the conception of individual living things as teleological centers of life simply articulates how a scientifically informed thinker comes to understand them as the result of increasingly careful and detailed observations. Thus, the biocentric outlook recommends itself as an acceptable system of concepts and beliefs to anyone who is clear-minded, unbiased, and factually enlightened, and who has

a developed capacity of reality awareness with regard to the lives of individual organisms. This, I submit, is as good a reason for making the moral commitment involved in adopting the attitude of respect for nature as any theory of environmental ethics could possibly have.

X. MORAL RIGHTS AND THE MATTER OF COMPETING CLAIMS

I have not asserted anywhere in the foregoing account that animals or plants have moral rights. This omission was deliberate. I do not think that the reference class of the concept, bearer of moral rights, should be extended to include nonhuman living things. My reasons for taking this position, however, go beyond the scope of this paper. I believe I have been able to accomplish many of the same ends which those who ascribe rights to animals or plants wish to accomplish. There is no reason, moreover, why plants and animals, including whole species populations and life communities, cannot be accorded *legal* rights under my theory. To grant them legal protection could be interpreted as giving them legal entitlement to be protected, and this, in fact, would be a means by which a society that subscribed to the ethics of respect for nature could give public recognition to their inherent worth.

There remains the problem of competing claims, even when wild plants and animals are not thought of as bearers of moral rights. If we accept the biocentric outlook and accordingly adopt the attitude of respect for nature as our ultimate moral attitude, how do we resolve conflicts that arise from our respect for persons in the domain of human ethics and our respect for nature in the domain of environmental ethics? This is a question that cannot be adequately dealt with here. My main purpose in this paper has been to try to establish a base point from which we can start working toward a solution to the problem. I have shown why we cannot just begin with an initial presumption in favor of the interests of our own species. It is after all within our power as moral beings to place limits on human population and technology with the deliberate intention of sharing the Earth's bounty with other species. That such sharing is an ideal difficult to realize even in an approximate way does not take away its claim to our deepest moral commitment.

NOTES

1. The conceptual links between an entity *having* a good, something being good *for* it, and events doing good to it are examined by G. H. Von Wright in *The Varieties of Goodness* (New York: Humanities Press, 1963), chaps. 3 and 5.

2. See W. K. Frankena, "Ethics and the Environment," in K. E. Goodpaster and K. M. Sayre, eds. *Ethics and Problems of the 21st Century* (Notre Dame: University of Notre Dame Press, 1979), pp. 3–20. I critically examine Frankena's views in "Frankena on Environmental Ethics," *Monist,* forthcoming.

3. In the light of considerations set forth in Daniel Dennett's *Brain Storms: Philosophical Essays on Mind and Psychology* (Montgomery, Vermont: Bradford Books, 1978), it is advisable to leave this question unsettled at this time. When machines are developed that function in the way our brains do, we may well come to deem them proper subjects of moral consideration.

4. I have analyzed the nature of this commitment of human ethics in "On Taking the Moral Point of View," *Midwest Studies in Philosophy,* vol. 3, *Studies in Ethical Theory* (1978), pp. 35–61.

5. John Rawls, "Justice as Fairness," *Philosophical Review* 67 (1958): 183.

6. Stephen R. L. Clark, *The Moral Status of Animals* (Oxford: Clarendon Press, 1977), p. 112.

7. My criticisms of the dogma of human superiority gain independent support from a carefully reasoned essay by R. and V. Routley showing the many logical weaknesses in arguments for human-centered theories of environmental ethics. R. and V. Routley, "Against the Inevitability of Human Chauvinism," in K. E. Goodpaster and K. M. Sayre, eds., *Ethics and Problems of the 21st Century* (Notre Dame: University of Notre Dame Press, 1979), pp. 36–59.

8. For this way of distinguishing between merit and inherent worth, I am indebted to Gregory Vlastos, "Justice and Equality," in R. Brandt, ed., *Social Justice* (Englewood Cliffs, NJ: Prentice-Hall, 1962), pp. 31–72.

STUDY QUESTIONS

1. Taylor leaves the matter of resolving conflicting claims between humans and nonhumans open in this article. But in his book he lists five principles: self-defense, proportionality, minimum harm, distributive justice, and restitutive justice (restoring ill-gotten gains). The basic needs of humans and nonhumans are to be decided impartially (distributive justice), but those of nonhumans should override the nonbasic needs of humans. Work out implications of these principles.

2. Is Taylor's biocentrism workable? How would it apply to our relationship with viruses, bacteria, ringworms, parasites, and the predatory animals? Would the basic needs of the two weeds or worms override those of one human?

3. Is the notion of objective intrinsic value clear? Is it true? Do we value certain things (e.g., life) because they are intrinsically good, or are they intrinsically good because we value them?

4. What does Taylor say about the relationship between *having a good* and having *inherent worth* or being good? Can something have a good, an interest, without *being* good?

24

Ecocentric Ethics: The Land Ethic

ALDO LEOPOLD

Aldo Leopold (1887–1947) worked for the U.S. Forest Service before becoming the first professor of wildlife management at the University of Wisconsin. He is considered the father of "The Land Ethic." His main work is Sand County Almanac *(1947) from which our selection is taken.*

    Leopold was distressed at the degradation of the environment and argued that we must begin to realize our symbiotic relationship to Earth so that we value "the land" or biotic community for its own sake. We must come to see ourselves, not as conquerors of the land but rather as plain members and citizens of the biotic community.

When god-like Odysseus returned from the wars in Troy, he hanged all on one rope a dozen slave-girls of his household whom he suspected of misbehavior during his absence.

This hanging involved no question of propriety. The girls were property. The disposal of property was then, as now, a matter of expediency, not of right and wrong.

Concepts of right and wrong were not lacking from Odysseus' Greece: witness the fidelity of his wife through the long years before at last his black-prowed galleys clove the wine-dark seas for home. The ethical structure of that day covered wives, but had not yet been extended to human chattels. During the three thousand years which have since elapsed, ethical criteria have been extended to many fields of conduct, with corresponding shrinkages in those judged by expediency only.

THE ETHICAL SEQUENCE

This extension of ethics, so far studied only by philosophers, is actually a process in ecological evolution. Its sequences may be described in ecological as well as in philosophical terms. An ethic, ecologically, is a limitation on freedom of action in the struggle for existence. An ethic, philosophically, is a differentiation of social from anti-social conduct. These are two definitions of one thing. The thing has its origin in the tendency of interdependent individuals or groups to evolve modes of cooperation. The ecologist calls these symbioses. Politics and economics are advanced symbioses in which the original free-for-all competition has been replaced, in part, by cooperative mechanisms with an ethical content.

The complexity of cooperative mechanisms has increased with population density, and with the efficiency of tools. It was simpler, for example, to define the anti-social uses of sticks and stones in the days of the mastodons than of bullets and billboards in the age of motors.

The first ethics dealt with the relation between individuals; the Mosaic Decalogue is an example. Later accretions dealt with the relation between the individual and society. The Golden Rule tries to integrate the individual to society; democracy to integrate social organization to the individual.

There is as yet no ethic dealing with man's relation to land and to the animals and plants which grow upon it. Land, like Odysseus' slave-girls, is still property. The land-relation is still strictly economic, entailing privileges but not obligations.

The extension of ethics to this third element in human environment is, if I read the evidence correctly, an evolutionary possibility and an ecological necessity. It is the third step in a sequence. The first two have already been taken. Individual thinkers since the days of Ezekiel and Isaiah have asserted that the despoliation of land is not only inexpedient but wrong. Society, however, has not yet affirmed their belief. I regard the present conservation movement as the embryo of such an affirmation.

An ethic may be regarded as a mode of guidance for meeting ecological situations so new or intricate, or involving such deferred reactions, that the path of social expediency is not discernible to the average individual. Animal instincts are modes of guidance for the individual in meeting such situations. Ethics are possibly a kind of community instinct in-the-making.

THE COMMUNITY CONCEPT

All ethics so far evolved rest upon a single premise: that the individual is a member of a community of interdependent parts. His instincts prompt him to compete for his place in the community, but his ethics prompt him also to cooperate (perhaps in order that there may be a place to compete for).

The land ethic simply enlarges the boundaries of the community to include soils, waters, plants, and animals, or collectively: the land.

This sounds simple: Do we not already sing our love for and obligation to the land of the free and the home of the brave? Yes, but just what and whom do we love? Certainly not the soil, which we are sending helter-skelter downriver. Certainly not the waters, which we assume have no function except to turn turbines, float barges, and carry off sewage. Certainly not the

plants, of which we exterminate whole communities without batting an eye. Certainly not the animals, of which we have already extirpated many of the largest and most beautiful species. A land ethic of course cannot prevent the alteration, management, and use of these "resources," but it does affirm their right to continued existence, and, at least in spots, their continued existence in a natural state.

In short, a land ethic changes the role of *Homo sapiens* from conqueror of the land-community to plain member and citizen of it. It implies respect for his fellow-members, and also respect for the community as such.

In human history, we have learned (I hope) that the conqueror role is eventually self-defeating. Why? Because it is implicit in such a role that the conqueror knows, *ex cathedra,* just what makes the community clock tick, and just what and who is valuable, and what and who is worthless, in community life. It always turns out that he knows neither, and this is why his conquests eventually defeat themselves.

In the biotic community, a parallel situation exists. Abraham knew exactly what the Land was for: it was to drip milk and honey into Abraham's mouth. At the present moment, the assurance with which we regard this assumption is inverse to the degree of our education.

The ordinary citizen today assumes that science knows what makes the community clock tick; the scientist is equally sure that he does not. He knows that the biotic mechanism is so complex that its workings may never be fully understood.

That man is, in fact, only a member of a biotic team is shown by an ecological interpretation of history. Many historical events, hitherto explained solely in terms of human enterprise, were actually biotic interactions between people and land. The characteristics of the land determined the facts quite as potently as the characteristics of the men who lived on it.

Consider, for example, the settlement of the Mississippi valley. In the years following the Revolution, three groups were contending for its control: the native Indian, the French and English traders, and the American settlers. Historians wonder what would have happened if the English at Detroit had thrown a little more weight into the Indian side of those tipsy scales which decided the outcome of the colonial migration into the cane-lands of Kentucky. It is time now to ponder the fact that the cane-lands, when subjected to the particular mixture of forces represented by the cow, plow, fire, and ax of the pioneer, became bluegrass. What if the plant succession inherent in this dark and bloody ground had, under the impact of these forces, given us some worthless sedge, shrub, or weed? Would Boone and Kenton have held out? Would there have been any overflow into Ohio, Indiana, Illinois, and Missouri? Any Louisiana Purchase? Any transcontinental union of new states? Any Civil War?

Kentucky was one sentence in the drama of history. We are commonly told what the human actors in this drama tried to do, but we are seldom told that their success, or the lack of it, hung in large degree on the reaction of particular soils to the impact of the particular forces exerted by their occupancy. In the case of Kentucky, we do not even know where the bluegrass came from—whether it is a native species, or a stow-away from Europe.

Contrast the cane-lands with what hindsight tells us about the Southwest, where the pioneers were equally brave, resourceful, and persevering. The impact of occupancy here brought no bluegrass, or other plant fitted to withstand the bumps and buffetings of hard use. This region, when grazed by livestock, reverted through a sense of more and more worthless grasses, shrubs, and weeds to a condition of unstable equilibrium. Each recession of plant types bred erosion; each increment to erosion bred a further recession of plants. The result today is a progressive and mutual deterioration, not only of plants and soils, but of the animal community subsisting thereon. The early settlers did not expect this: on the ciénegas of New Mexico some even cut ditches to hasten it. So subtle has been its progress that few residents of the region are aware of it. It is quite invisible to the tourist who finds this wrecked landscape colorful and charming (as indeed it is, but it bears scant resemblance to what it was in 1848).

This same landscape was "developed" once before, but with quite different results. The Pueblo Indians settled the Southwest in pre-Columbian times, but they happened *not* to be equipped with range livestock. Their civilization expired, but not because their land expired.

In India, regions devoid of any sod-forming grass have been settled, apparently without wrecking the land, by the simple expedient of carrying the grass to the cow, rather than vice versa. (Was this the result of some deep wisdom, or was it just good luck? I do not know.)

In short, the plant succession steered the course of history; the pioneer simply demonstrated, for good or ill, what successions inhered in the land. Is history taught in this spirit? It will be, once the concept of land as a community really penetrates our intellectual life.

THE ECOLOGICAL CONSCIENCE

Conservation is a state of harmony between men and land. Despite nearly a century of propaganda, conservation still proceeds at a snail's pace; progress still consists largely of letterhead pieties and convention oratory. On the back forty we still slip two steps backward for each forward stride.

The usual answer to this dilemma is "more conservation education." No one will debate this, but is it certain that only the *volume* of education needs stepping up? Is something lacking in the *content* as well?

It is difficult to give a fair summary of its content in brief form, but, as I understand it, the content is substantially this: obey the law, vote right, join some organizations, and practice what conservation is profitable on your own land; the government will do the rest.

Is not this formula too easy to accomplish anything worthwhile? It defines no right or wrong, assigns no obligation, calls for no sacrifice, implies no change in the current philosophy of values.

In respect of land-use, it urges only enlightened self-interest. Just how far will such education take us? An example will perhaps yield a partial answer.

By 1930 it had become clear to all except the ecologically blind that southwestern Wisconsin's topsoil was slipping seaward. In 1933 the farmers were told that if they would adopt certain remedial practices for five years, the public would donate CCC labor to install them, plus the necessary machinery and materials. The offer was widely accepted, but the practices were widely forgotten when the five-year contract period was up. The farmers continued only those practices that yielded an immediate and visible economic gain for themselves.

This led to the idea that maybe farmers would learn more quickly if they themselves wrote the rules. Accordingly the Wisconsin Legislature in 1937 passed the Soil Conservation District Law. This said to farmers, in effect: *We, the public, will furnish you free technical service and loan you specialized machinery, if you will write your own rules for land-use. Each county may write its own rules, and these will have the force of law.* Nearly all the counties promptly organized to accept the proffered help, but after a decade of operation, *no county has yet written a single rule.* There has been visible progress in such practices as strip-cropping, pasture renovation, and soil liming, but none in fencing wood-lots against grazing, and none in excluding plow and cow from steep slopes. The farmers, in short, have selected those remedial practices which were profitable anyhow, and ignored those which were profitable to the community, but not clearly profitable to themselves.

When one asks why no rules have been written, one is told that the community is not yet ready to support them; education must precede rules. But the education actually in progress makes no mention of obligations to land over and above those dictated by self-interest. The net result is that we have more education but less soil, fewer healthy woods, and as many floods as in 1937.

The puzzling aspect of such situations is that the existence of obligations over and above self-interest is taken for granted in such rural community enterprises

as the betterment of roads, schools, churches, and baseball teams. Their existence is not taken for granted, nor as yet seriously discussed, in bettering the behavior of the water that falls on the land, or in the preserving of the beauty or diversity of the farm landscape. Land-use ethics are still governed wholly by economic self-interest, just as social ethics were a century ago.

To sum up: we asked the farmer to do what he conveniently could to save his soil, and he has done just that, and only that. The farmer who clears the woods off a 75 per cent slope, turns his cows into the clearing, and dumps its rainfall, rocks, and soil into the community creek is still (if otherwise decent) a respected member of society. If he puts lime on his fields and plants his crops on contour, he is still entitled to all the privileges and emoluments of his Soil Conservation District. The District is a beautiful piece of social machinery, but it is coughing along on two cylinders because we have been too timid, and too anxious for quick success, to tell the farmer the true magnitude of his obligations. Obligations have no meaning without conscience, and the problem we face is the extension of the social conscience from people to land.

No important change in ethics was ever accomplished without an internal change in our intellectual emphasis, loyalties, affections, and convictions. The proof that conservation has not yet touched these foundations of conduct lies in the fact that philosophy and religion have not yet heard of it. In our attempt to make conservation easy, we have made it trivial.

SUBSTITUTES FOR A LAND ETHIC

When the logic of history hungers for bread and we hand out a stone, we are at pains to explain how much the stone resembles bread. I now describe some of the stones which serve in lieu of a land ethic.

One basic weakness in a conservation system based wholly on economic motives is that most members of the land community have no economic value. Wildflowers and songbirds are examples.

Of the 22,000 higher plants and animals native to Wisconsin, it is doubtful whether more than 5 per cent can be sold, fed, eaten, or otherwise put to economic use. Yet these creatures are members of the biotic community, and if (as I believe) its stability depends on its integrity, they are entitled to continuance.

When one of these non-economic categories is threatened, and if we happen to love it, we invent subterfuges to give it economic importance. At the beginning of the century songbirds were supposed to be disappearing. Ornithologists jumped to the rescue with some distinctly shaky evidence to the effect that insects would eat us up if birds failed to control them. The evidence had to be economic in order to be valid.

It is painful to read these circumlocutions to-day. We have no land ethic yet, but we have at least drawn nearer the point of admitting that birds should continue as a matter of biotic right, regardless of the presence or absence of economic advantage to us.

A parallel situation exists in respect of predatory mammals, raptorial birds, and fish-eating birds. Time was when biologists somewhat overworked the evidence that these creatures preserve the health of game by killing weaklings, or that they control rodents for the farmer, or that they prey only on "worthless" species. Here again, the evidence had to be economic in order to be valid. It is only in recent years that we hear the more honest argument that predators are members of the community, and that no special interest has the right to exterminate them for the sake of a benefit, real or fancied, to itself. Unfortunately this enlightened view is still in the talk stage. In the field the extermination of predators goes merrily on: witness the impending erasure of the timber wolf by fiat of Congress, the Conservation Bureaus, and many state legislatures.

Some species of trees have been "read out of the party" by economics-minded foresters because they grow too slowly, or have too low a sale value to pay as timber crops: white cedar, tamarack, cypress, beech, and hemlock are examples. In Europe, where forestry is ecologically more advanced, the non-commercial tree species are recognized as members of the native forest community, to be preserved as such, within reason. Moreover some (like beech) have been found to have a valuable function in building up soil fertility. The interdependence of the forest and its constituent tree species, ground flora, and fauna is taken for granted.

Lack of economic value is sometimes a character not only of species or groups, but of entire biotic communities: marshes, bogs, dunes, and "deserts" are examples. Our formula in such cases is to relegate their conservation to government as refuges, monuments, or parks. The difficulty is that these communities are usually interspersed with more valuable private lands; the government cannot possibly own or control such scattered parcels. The net effect is that we have relegated some of them to ultimate extinction over large areas. If the private owner were ecologically minded, he would be proud to be the custodian of a reasonable proportion of such areas, which add diversity and beauty to his farm and to his community.

In some instances, the assumed lack of profit in these "waste" areas has proved to be wrong, but only after most of them had been done away with. The present scramble to reflood muskrat marshes is a case in point.

There is a clear tendency in American conservation to relegate to government all necessary jobs that private landowners fail to perform. Government ownership, operation, subsidy, or regulation is now widely prevalent in forestry, range management, soil and watershed management, park and wilderness conservation, fisheries management, and migratory bird management, with more to come. Most of this growth in governmental conservation is proper and logical, some of it is inevitable. That I imply no disapproval of it is implicit in the fact that I have spent most of my life working for it. Nevertheless the question arises: What is the ultimate magnitude of the enterprise? Will the tax base carry its eventual ramifications? At what point will governmental conservation, like the mastodon, become handicapped by its own dimensions? The answer, if there is any, seems to be in a land ethic, or some other force which assigns more obligation to the private landowner.

Industrial landowners and users, especially lumbermen and stockmen, are inclined to wail long and loudly about the extension of government ownership and regulation to land, but (with notable exceptions) they show little disposition to develop the only visible alternative: the voluntary practice of conservation on their own lands.

When the private landowner is asked to perform some unprofitable act for the good of the community, he today assents only with outstretched palm. If the act costs him cash this is fair and proper, but when it costs only fore-thought, open-mindedness, or time, the issue is at least debatable. The overwhelming growth of land-uses subsidies in recent years must be ascribed, in large part, to the government's own agencies for conservation education: the land bureaus, the agricultural colleges, and the extension services. As far as I can detect, no ethical obligation toward land is taught in these institutions. *interesting*

To sum up: a system of conservation based solely on economic self-interest is hopelessly lopsided. It tends to ignore, and thus eventually to eliminate, many elements in the land community that lack commercial value, but that are (as far as we know) essential to its healthy functioning. It assumes, falsely, I think, that the economic parts of the biotic clock will function without the uneconomic parts. It tends to relegate to government many functions eventually too large, too complex, or too widely dispersed to be performed by government.

An ethical obligation on the part of the private owner is the only visible remedy for these situations.

THE LAND PYRAMID

An ethic to supplement and guide the economic relation to land presupposes the existence of some mental image of land as a biotic mechanism. We can be ethical only in relation to something we can see, feel, understand, love, or otherwise have faith in.

The image commonly employed in conservation education is "the balance of nature." For reasons too lengthy to detail here, this figure of speech fails to describe accurately what little we know about the land mechanism. A much truer image is the one employed in ecology: the biotic pyramid. I shall first sketch the pyramid as a symbol of land, and later develop some of its implications in terms of land-use.

Plants absorb energy from the sun. This energy flows through a circuit called the biota, which may be represented by a pyramid consisting of layers. The bottom layer is the soil. A plant layer rests on the soil, an insect layer on the plants, a bird and rodent layer on the insects, and so on up through various animal groups to the apex layer, which consists of the larger carnivores.

The species of a layer are alike not in where they came from, or in what they look like, but rather in what they eat. Each successive layer depends on those below it for food and often for other services, and each in turn furnishes food and services to those above. Proceeding upward, each successive layer decreases in numerical abundance. Thus, for every carnivore there are hundreds of his prey, thousands of their prey, millions of insects, uncountable plants. The pyramidal form of the system reflects this numerical progression from apex to base. Man shares an intermediate layer with the bears, raccoons, and squirrels which eat both meat and vegetables.

The lines of dependency for food and other services are called food chains. Thus soil-oak-deer-Indian is a chain that has now been largely converted to soil-corn-cow-farmer. Each species, including ourselves, is a link in many chains. The deer eats a hundred plants other than oak, and the cow a hundred plants other than corn. Both, then, are links in a hundred chains. The pyramid is a tangle of chains so complex as to seem disorderly, yet the stability of the system proves it to be a highly organized structure. Its functioning depends on the cooperation and competition of its diverse parts.

In the beginning, the pyramid of life was low and squat; the food chains short and simple. Evolution has added layer after layer, link after link. Man is one of thousands of accretions to the height and complexity of the pyramid. Science has given us many doubts, but it has given us at least one certainty: the trend of evolution is to elaborate and diversify the biota.

Land, then, is not merely soil; it is a fountain of energy flowing through a circuit of soils, plants, and animals. Food chains are the living channels which conduct energy upward; death and decay return it to the soil. The circuit is not closed; some energy is dissipated in decay, some is added by absorption from the air, some is stored in soils, peats, and long-lived forests; but it is a sustained circuit, like a slowly augmented revolving fund of life. There is always a net loss by downhill wash, but this is normally small and offset by the decay of rocks. It is deposited in the ocean and, in the course of geological time, raised to form new lands and new pyramids.

The velocity and character of the upward flow of energy depend on the complex structure of the plant and animal community, much as the upward flow of sap in a tree depends on its complex cellular organization. Without this complexity, normal circulation would presumably not occur. Structure means the characteristic numbers, as well as the characteristic kinds and functions, of the component species. This interdependence between the complex structure of the land and its smooth functioning as an energy unit is one of its basic attributes.

When a change occurs in one part of the circuit, many other parts must adjust themselves to it. Change does not necessarily obstruct or divert the flow of energy; evolution is a long series of self-induced changes, the net result of which has been to elaborate the flow mechanism and to lengthen the circuit. Evolutionary changes, however, are usually slow and local. Man's invention of tools has enabled him to make changes of unprecedented violence, rapidity, and scope.

One change is in the composition of floras and faunas. The larger predators are lopped off the apex of the pyramid; food chains, for the first time in history, become shorter rather than longer. Domesticated species from other lands are substituted for wild ones, and wild ones are moved to new habitats. In this world-wide pooling of faunas and floras, some species get out of bounds as pests and diseases, others are extinguished. Such effects are seldom intended or foreseen; they represent unpredicted and often untraceable readjustments in the structure.

Agricultural science is largely a race between the emergence of new pests and the emergence of new techniques for their control.

Another change touches the flow of energy through plants and animals and its return to the soil. Fertility is the ability of soil to receive, store, and release energy. Agriculture, by overdrafts on the soil, or by too radical a substitution of domestic for native species in the super-structure, may derange the channels of flow or deplete storage. Soils depleted of their storage, or of the organic matter which anchors it, wash away faster than they form. This is erosion.

Waters, like soil, are part of the energy circuit. Industry, by polluting waters or obstructing them with dams, may exclude the plants and animals necessary to keep energy in circulation.

Transportation brings about another basic change: the plants or animals grown in one region are now consumed and returned to the soil in another. Transportation taps the energy stored in rocks, and in the air, and uses it elsewhere; thus we fertilize the garden with nitrogen gleaned by the guano birds from the fishes of seas on the other side of the Equator. Thus the formerly localized and self-contained circuits are pooled on a world-wide scale.

The process of altering the pyramid for human occupation releases stored energy, and this often gives rise, during the pioneering period, to a deceptive exuberance of plant and animal life, both wild and tame. These releases of biotic capital tend to becloud or postpone the penalties of violence.

This thumbnail sketch of land as an energy circuit conveys three basic ideas:

1. That land is not merely soil.
2. That the native plants and animals kept the energy circuit open; others may or may not.
3. That man-made changes are of a different order than evolutionary changes, and have effects more comprehensive than is intended or foreseen.

These ideas, collectively, raise two basic issues: Can the land adjust itself to the new order? Can the desired alterations be accomplished with less violence?

Biotas seem to differ in their capacity to sustain violent conversion. Western Europe, for example, carries a far different pyramid than Caesar found there. Some large animals are lost; swampy forests have become meadows or plowland; many new plants and animals are introduced, some of which escape as pests; the remaining natives are greatly changed in distribution and abundance. Yet the soil is still there and, with the help of imported nutrients, still fertile; and waters flow normally; the new structure seems to function and to persist. There is no visible stoppage or derangement of the circuit.

Western Europe, then, has a resistant biota. Its inner processes are tough, elastic, resistant to strain. No matter how violent the alterations, the pyramid, so far, has developed some new *modus vivendi* which preserves its habitability for man, and for most of the other natives.

Japan seems to present another instance of radical conversion without disorganization.

Most other civilized regions, and some as yet barely touched by civilization, display various stages of disorganization, varying from initial symptoms to advanced wastage. In Asia Minor and North Africa diagnosis is confused by climatic changes, which may have been either the cause or the effect of advanced wastage. In the United States the degree of disorganization varies locally; it is worst in the Southwest, the Ozarks, and parts of the South, and least in New England and the Northwest. Better land-uses may still arrest it in the less advanced regions. In parts of Mexico, South America, South Africa, and Australia a violent and accelerating wastage is in progress, but I cannot assess the prospects.

This almost world-wide display of disorganization in the land seems to be similar to disease in an animal, except that it never culminates in complete disorganization or death. The land recovers, but at some reduced level of complexity, and with a reduced carrying capacity for people, plants, and animals. Many biotas currently regarded as "lands of opportunity" are in fact already subsisting on exploitative agriculture, i.e. they have already exceeded their sustained carrying capacity. Most of South America is overpopulated in this sense.

In arid regions we attempt to offset the process of wastage by reclamation, but it is only too evident that the prospective longevity of reclamation projects is often short. In our own West, the best of them may not last a century.

The combined evidence of history and ecology seems to support one general deduction: the less violent the man-made changes, the greater the probability of successful readjustment in the pyramid. Violence, in turn, varies with human population density; a dense population requires a more violent conversion. In this respect, North America has a better chance for permanence than Europe, if she can contrive to limit her density.

This deduction runs counter to our current philosophy, which assumes that because a small increase in density enriched human life, that an indefinite increase will enrich it indefinitely. Ecology knows of no density relationship that holds for indefinitely wide limits. All gains from density are subject to a law of diminishing returns.

Whatever may be the equation for men and land, it is improbable that we as yet know all its terms. Recent discoveries in mineral and vitamin nutrition reveal unsuspected dependencies in the up-circuit: incredibly minute quantities of certain substances determine the value of soils to plants, of plants to animals. What of the down-circuit? What of the vanishing species, the preservation of which we now regard as an esthetic luxury? They helped build the soil; in what unsuspected ways may they be essential to its maintenance? Professor Weaver proposes that we use prairie flowers to refloculate the wasting soils of the dust bowl; who knows for what purpose cranes and condors, otters and grizzlies may some day be used?

LAND HEALTH AND THE A-B CLEAVAGE

A land ethic, then, reflects the existence of an ecological conscience, and this in turn reflects a conviction of individual responsibility for the health of the land. Health is the capacity of the land for self-renewal. Conservation is our effort to understand and preserve this capacity.

Conservationists are notorious for their dissensions. Superficially these seem to add up to mere confusion, but a more careful scrutiny reveals a single plane of cleavage common to many specialized fields. In each field one group (A) regards the land as soil, and its function as commodity-production; another group (B) regards the land as a biota, and its function as something broader. How much broader is admittedly in a state of doubt and confusion.

In my own field, forestry, group A is quite content to grow trees like cabbages, with cellulose as the basic forest commodity. It feels no inhibition against violence; its ideology is agronomic. Group B, on the other hand, sees forestry as fundamentally different from agronomy because it employs natural species, and manages a natural environment rather than creating an artificial one. Group B prefers natural reproduction on principle. It worries on biotic as well as economic grounds about the loss of species like chestnut, and the threatened loss of the white pines. It worries about a whole series of secondary forest functions: wildlife, recreation, watersheds, wilderness areas. To my mind, Group B feels the stirrings of an ecological conscience.

In the wildlife field, a parallel cleavage exists. For group A the basic commodities are sport and meat; the yardsticks of production are ciphers of take in pheasants and trout. Artificial propagation is acceptable as a permanent as well as a temporary recourse—if its unit costs permit. Group B, on the other hand, worries about a whole series of biotic side-issues. What is the cost in predators of producing a game crop? Should we have further recourse to exotics? How can management restore the shrinking species, like prairie grouse, already hopeless as shootable game? How can management restore the threatened rarities, like trumpeter swan and whooping crane? Can management principles be extended to wildflowers? Here again it is clear to me that we have the same A-B cleavage as in forestry.

In the larger field of agriculture I am less competent to speak, but there seem to be somewhat parallel cleavages. Scientific agriculture was actively developing before ecology was born, hence a slower penetration of ecological concepts might be expected. Moreover the farmer, by the very nature of his techniques, must modify the biota more radically than the forester or the wildlife manager. Nevertheless, there are many discontents in agriculture which seem to add up to a new vision of "biotic farming."

Perhaps the most important of these is the new evidence that poundage or tonnage is no measure of the food-value of farm crops; the products of fertile soil may be qualitatively as well as quantitatively superior. We can bolster poundage from depleted soils by pouring on imported fertility, but we are not necessarily bolstering food-value. The possible ultimate ramifications of this idea are so immense that I must leave their exposition to abler pens.

The discontent that labels itself "organic farming," while bearing some of the earmarks of a cult, is nevertheless biotic in its direction, particularly in its insistence on the importance of soil flora and fauna.

The ecological fundamentals of agriculture are just as poorly known to the public as in other fields of land-use. For example, few educated people realize that the marvelous advances in technique made during recent decades are improvements in the pump, rather than the well. Acre for acre, they have barely sufficed to offset the sinking level of fertility.

In all of these cleavages, we see repeated the same basic paradoxes: man the conqueror *versus* man the biotic citizen; science the sharpener of his sword *versus* science the searchlight on his universe; land the slave and servant *versus* land the collective organism. Robinson's injunction to Tristram may well be applied, at this juncture, to *Homo sapiens* as a species in geological time:

> *Whether you will or not*
> *You are a King, Tristram, for you are one*
>
> *Of the time-tested few that leave the world,*
> *When they are gone, not the same place it was.*
>
> *Mark what you leave.*

THE OUTLOOK

It is inconceivable to me that an ethical relation to land can exist without love, respect, and admiration for land, and a high regard for its value. By value, I of course mean something far broader than mere economic value; I mean value in the philosophical sense.

Perhaps the most serious obstacle impeding the evolution of a land ethic is the fact that our educational and economic system is headed away from, rather than toward, an intense consciousness of land. Your true modern is separated from the land by many middlemen, and by innumerable physical gadgets. He has no vital relation to it; to him it is the space between cities on which crops grow. Turn him loose for a day on the land, and if the spot does not happen to be a golf links or a "scenic" area, he is bored stiff. If crops could be raised by hydroponics instead of farming, it would suit him very well. Synthetic substitutes for wood, leather, wool, and other natural land products suit him better than the originals. In short, land is something he has "outgrown."

Almost equally serious as an obstacle to a land ethic is the attitude of the farmer for whom the land is still an adversary, or a taskmaster that keeps him in slavery. Theoretically, the mechanization of farming ought to cut the farmer's chains, but whether it really does is debatable.

One of the requisites for an ecological comprehension of land is an understanding of ecology, and this is by no means co-extensive with "education"; in fact, much higher education seems deliberately to avoid ecological concepts. An understanding of ecology does not necessarily originate in courses bearing ecological labels; it is quite as likely to be labeled geography, botany, agronomy, history, or economics. This is as it should be, but whatever the label, ecological training is scarce.

The case for a land ethic would appear hopeless but for the minority which is in obvious revolt against these "modern" trends.

The "key-log" which must be moved to release the evolutionary process for an ethic is simply this: quit thinking about decent land-use as solely an economic problem. Examine each question in terms of what is ethically and esthetically right, as well as what is economically expedient. A thing is right when it tends to preserve the integrity, stability, and beauty of the biotic community. It is wrong when it tends otherwise.

It of course goes without saying that economic feasibility limits the tether of what can or cannot be done for land. It always has and it always will. The fallacy the economic determinists have tied around our collective neck, and which we now need to cast off, is the belief that economics determines *all* land-use. This is simply not true. An innumerable host of actions and attitudes, comprising perhaps the bulk of all land relations, is determined by the land-users' tastes and predilections, rather than by his purse. The bulk of all land relations hinges on investments of time, forethought, skill, and faith rather than on investments of cash. As a land-user thinketh, so is he.

I have purposely presented the land ethic as a product of social evolution because nothing so important as an ethic is ever "written." Only the most superficial student of history supposes that Moses "wrote" the Decalogue; it evolved in the minds of a thinking community, and Moses wrote a tentative summary of it for a "seminar." I say tentative because evolution never stops.

The evolution of a land ethic is an intellectual as well as emotional process. Conservation is paved with good intentions which prove to be futile, or even dangerous, because they are devoid of critical understanding either of the land, or of economic land-use. I think it is a truism that as the ethical frontier advances from the individual to the community, its intellectual content increases.

The mechanism of operation is the same for any ethic: social approbation for right actions, social disapproval for wrong actions.

By and large, our present problem is one of attitudes and implements. We are remodeling the Alhambra with a steamshovel, and we are proud of our yardage. We shall hardly relinquish the shovel, which after all has many good points, but we are in need of gentler and more objective criteria for its successful use.

STUDY QUESTIONS

1. Does Leopold make a case for the intrinsic value of the biotic community, or does he only assume this?

2. Analyze Leopold's view of humans and of biotic communities. How do we resolve conflicts between their claims and needs? Which are more important, ecosystems or individuals?

3. Critically discuss the strengths and weaknesses of Leopold's position.

4. Leopold makes two fundamental claims of the American conservation movement. What are they? Has American environmentalism moved in the direction that Leopold advocated?

25

The Conceptual Foundations
of the Land Ethic

J. BAIRD CALLICOTT

J. Baird Callicott (b. 1941) is professor of philosophy and natural resources at the University of North Texas and the author of several works in environmental philosophy, including In Defense of the Land Ethic (1989) from which this essay is taken.

Callicott develops the philosophical implications of Leopold's land ethic. He shows how it is rooted in the eighteenth-century Scottish Sentimentalist School of David Hume and Adam Smith, who said that ethics is based in natural sympathy or sentiments. Leopold, adding a Darwinian dimension to these thoughts, extended the notion of natural sentiments to ecosystems as the locus of value. Callicott argues that Leopold is not claiming that we should sacrifice basic human needs to the environment, but rather that we should see ourselves as members of a wider ecological community.

The two great cultural advances of the past century were the Darwinian theory and the development of geology…. Just as important, however, as the origin of plants, animals, and soil is the question of how they operate as a community. That task has fallen to the new science of ecology, which is daily uncovering a web of interdependencies so intricate as to amaze—were he here—even Darwin himself, who, of all men, should have least cause to tremble before the veil.

ALDO LEOPOLD, FRAGMENT 6B16,
NO. 36, LEOPOLD PAPERS,
UNIVERSITY OF WISCONSIN-
MADISON ARCHIVES

From *Companion to a Sand County Almanac* by J. Baird Callicott. Copyright © 1987. Reprinted by permission of University of Wisconsin Press. Footnotes deleted.

I

As Wallace Stegner observes, *A Sand County Almanac* is considered "almost a holy book in conservation circles," and Aldo Leopold a prophet, "an American Isaiah." And as Curt Meine points out, "The Land Ethic" is the climactic essay of *Sand County*, "the upshot of 'The Upshot.'" One might, therefore, fairly say that the recommendation and justification of moral obligations on the part of people to nature is what the prophetic *A Sand County Almanac* is all about.

But, with few exceptions, "The Land Ethic" has not been favorably received by contemporary academic philosophers. Most have ignored it. Of those who have not, most have been either nonplussed or hostile. Distinguished Australian philosopher John Passmore dismissed it out of hand, in the first book-length academic discussion of the new philosophical subdiscipline called "environmental ethics." In a more recent and more deliberate discussion, the equally distinguished Australian philosopher H. J. McCloskey patronized Aldo Leopold and saddled "The Land Ethic" with various far-fetched "interpretations." He concludes that "there is a real problem in attributing a coherent meaning to Leopold's statements, one that exhibits his land ethic as representing a major advance in ethics rather than a retrogression to a morality of a kind held by various primitive peoples." Echoing McCloskey, English philosopher Robin Attfield went out of his way to impugn the philosophical respectability of "The Land Ethic." And Canadian philosopher L. W. Sumner has called it "dangerous nonsense." Among those philosophers more favorably disposed, "The Land Ethic" has usually been simply quoted, as if it were little more than a noble, but naive, moral plea, altogether lacking a supporting theoretical framework—that is, foundational principles and premises which lead, by compelling argument, to ethical precepts.

The professional neglect, confusion, and (in some cases) contempt for "The Land Ethic" may, in my judgment, be attributed to three things: (1) Leopold's extremely condensed prose style in which an entire conceptual complex may be conveyed in a few sentences, or even in a phrase or two; (2) his departure from the assumptions and paradigms of contemporary philosophical ethics; and (3) the unsettling practical implications to which a land ethic appears to lead. "The Land Ethic," in short, is, from a philosophical point of view, abbreviated, unfamiliar, and radical.

Here I first examine and elaborate the compactly expressed abstract elements of the land ethic and expose the "logic" which binds them into a proper, but revolutionary, moral theory. I then discuss the controversial features of the land ethic and defend them against actual and potential criticism. I hope to show that the land ethic cannot be ignored as merely the groundless emotive exhortations of a moonstruck conservationist or dismissed as entailing wildly untoward practical consequences. It poses, rather, a serious intellectual challenge to business-as-usual moral philosophy.

II

"The Land Ethic" opens with a charming and poetic evocation of Homer's Greece, the point of which is to suggest that today land is just as routinely and remorselessly enslaved as human beings then were. A panoramic glance backward to our most distant cultural origins, Leopold suggests, reveals a slow but steady moral development over three millennia. More of our relationships and activities ("fields of conduct") have fallen under the aegis of moral principles ("ethical criteria") as civilization has grown and matured. If moral growth and development continue, as not only a synoptic review of history, but recent past experience suggest that it will, future generations will censure today's casual and universal environmental bondage as today we censure the casual and universal human bondage of three thousand years ago.

A cynically inclined critic might scoff at Leopold's sanguine portrayal of human history. Slavery survived as an institution in the "civilized" West, more particularly in the morally self-congratulatory United States, until a mere generation before Leopold's own birth. And Western history from imperial Athens and Rome to the Spanish Inquisition and the Third Reich has been a disgraceful series of wars, persecutions, tyrannies, pogroms, and other atrocities.

The history of moral practice, however, is not identical with the history of moral consciousness. Morality is not descriptive; it is prescriptive or normative. In light of this distinction, it is clear that today, despite rising rates of violent crime in the United States and institutional abuses of human rights in Iran, Chile, Ethiopia, Guatemala, South Africa, and many other places, and despite persistent organized social injustice and oppression in still others, moral consciousness is expanding more rapidly now than ever before. Civil rights, human rights, women's liberation, children's liberation, animal liberation, and so forth, all indicate, as expressions of newly emergent moral ideals, that ethical consciousness (as distinct from practice) has if anything recently accelerated—thus confirming Leopold's historical observation.

III

Leopold next points out that "this extension of ethics, so far studied only by philosophers"—and therefore, the implication is clear, not very satisfactorily studied "is actually a process in ecological evolution" (p. 202). What Leopold is saying here, simply, is that we may understand the history of ethics, fancifully alluded to by means of the Odysseus vignette, in biological as well as philosophical terms. From a biological point of view, an ethic is "a limitation on freedom of action in the struggle for existence" (p. 202)....

Let me put the problem in perspective. How, ... did ethics originate and, once in existence, grow in scope and complexity?

The oldest answer in living human memory is theological. God (or the gods) imposes morality on people. And God (or the gods) sanctions it. A most vivid and graphic example of this kind of account occurs in the Bible when Moses goes up on Mount Sinai to receive the Ten Commandments directly from God. That text also clearly illustrates the divine sanctions (plagues, pestilences, droughts,

military defeats, and so forth) for moral disobedience. Ongoing revelation of the divine will, of course, as handily and as simply explains subsequent moral growth and development.

Western philosophy, on the other hand, is almost unanimous in the opinion that the origin of ethics in human experience has somehow to do with human reason. Reason figures centrally and pivotally in the "social contract theory" of the origin and nature of morals in all its ancient, modern, and contemporary expressions from Protagoras, to Hobbes, to Rawls. Reason is the wellspring of virtue, according to both Plato and Aristotle, and of categorical imperatives, according to Kant. In short, the weight of Western philosophy inclines to the view that we are moral beings because we are rational beings. The ongoing sophistication of reason and the progressive illumination it sheds upon the good and the right explain "the ethical sequence," the historical growth and development of morality, noticed by Leopold.

An evolutionary natural historian, however, cannot be satisfied with either of these general accounts of the origin and development of ethics. The idea that God gave morals to man is ruled out in principle—as any supernatural explanation of a natural phenomenon is ruled out in principle in natural science. And while morality might *in principle* be a function of human reason (as, say, mathematical calculation clearly is), to suppose that it is so *in fact* would be to put the cart before the horse. Reason appears to be a delicate, variable, and recently emerged faculty. It cannot, under any circumstances, be supposed to have evolved in the absence of complex linguistic capabilities which depend, in turn, for their evolution upon a highly developed social matrix. But we cannot have become social beings unless we assumed limitations on freedom of action in the struggle for existence. Hence we must have become ethical before we became rational.

Darwin, probably in consequence of reflections somewhat like these, turned to a minority tradition of modern philosophy for a moral psychology consistent with and useful to a general evolutionary account of ethical phenomena. A century earlier, Scottish philosophers David Hume and Adam *more common*

Smith had argued that ethics rest upon feelings or "sentiments"—which, to be sure, may be both amplified and informed by reason. And since in the animal kingdom feelings or sentiments are arguably far more common or widespread than reason, they would be a far more likely starting point for an evolutionary account of the origin and growth of ethics.

Darwin's account, to which Leopold unmistakably (if elliptically) alludes in "The Land Ethic," begins with the parental and filial affections common, perhaps, to all mammals. Bonds of affection and sympathy between parents and offspring permitted the formation of small, closely knit social groups, Darwin argued. Should the parental and familial affections bonding family members chance to extend to less closely related individuals, that would permit an enlargement of the family group. And should the newly extended community more successfully defend itself and/or more efficiently provision itself, the inclusive fitness of its members severally would be increased, Darwin reasoned. Thus the more diffuse familial affections, which Darwin (echoing Hume and Smith) calls the "social sentiments," would be spread throughout a population.

Morality, properly speaking—that is, morality as opposed to mere altruistic instinct—requires, in Darwin's terms, "intellectual powers" sufficient to recall the past and imagine the future, "the power of language" sufficient to express "common opinion," and "habituation" to patterns of behavior deemed, by common opinion, to be socially acceptable and beneficial. Even so, ethics proper, in Darwin's account, remains firmly rooted in moral feelings or social sentiments which were—no less than physical faculties, he expressly avers—naturally selected, by the advantages for survival and especially for successful reproduction, afforded by society.

The protosociobiological perspective on ethical phenomena, to which Leopold as a natural historian was heir, leads him to a generalization which is remarkably explicit in his condensed and often merely resonant rendering of Darwin's more deliberate and extended paradigm: Since "the thing [ethics] has its origin in the tendency of interdependent individuals or groups to evolve modes of co-operation, … all

ethics so far evolved rest upon a single premise: that the individual is a member of a community of interdependent parts" (pp. 202–3).

Hence, we may expect to find that the scope and specific content of ethics will reflect both the perceived boundaries and actual structure or organization of a cooperative community or society. *Ethics and society or community are correlative*. This single, simple principle constitutes a powerful tool for the analysis of moral natural history, for the anticipation of future moral development (including, ultimately, the land ethic), and for systematically deriving the specific precepts, the prescriptions and proscriptions, of an emergent and culturally unprecedented ethic like a land or environmental ethic.

IV

Anthropological studies of ethics reveal that in fact the boundaries of the moral community are generally coextensive with the perceived boundaries of society. And the peculiar (and, from the urbane point of view, sometimes inverted) representation of virtue and vice in tribal society—the virtue, for example, of sharing to the point of personal destitution and the vice of privacy and private property—reflects and fosters the life way of tribal peoples. Darwin, in his leisurely, anecdotal discussion, paints a vivid picture of the intensity, peculiarity, and sharp circumscription of "savage" mores: "A savage will risk his life to save that of a member of the same community, but will be wholly indifferent about a stranger." As Darwin portrays them, tribespeople are at once paragons of virtue "within the limits of the same tribe" and enthusiastic thieves, manslaughterers, and torturers without.

For purposes of more effective defense against common enemies, or because of increased population density, or in response to innovations in subsistence methods and technologies, or for some mix of these or other forces, human societies have grown in extent or scope and changed in form or structure. Nations—like the Iroquois nation or the Sioux nation—came into being upon the merger of previously separate and mutually hostile tribes. Animals and plants were domesticated and erstwhile hunter-gatherers became herders and farmers. Permanent habitations were established. Trade, craft, and (later) industry flourished. With each change in society came corresponding and correlative changes in ethics. The moral community expanded to become co-extensive with the newly drawn boundaries of societies and the representation of virtue and vice, right and wrong, good and evil, changed to accommodate, foster, and preserve the economic and institutional organization of emergent social orders.

Today we are witnessing the painful birth of a human supercommunity, global in scope. Modern transportation and communication technologies, international economic interdependencies, international economic entities, and nuclear arms have brought into being a "global village." It has not yet become fully formed and it is at tension—a very dangerous tension—with its predecessor, the nation-state. Its eventual institutional structure, a global federalism or whatever it may turn out to be, is at this point completely unpredictable. Interestingly, however, a corresponding global human ethic—the "human rights" ethic, as it is popularly called—has been more definitely articulated.

Most educated people today pay lip service at least to the ethical precept that all members of the human species, regardless of race, creed, or national origin, are endowed with certain fundamental rights which it is wrong not to respect. According to the evolutionary scenario set out by Darwin, the contemporary moral ideal of human rights is a response to a perception—however vague and indefinite—that mankind worldwide is united into one society, one community, however indeterminate or yet institutionally unorganized. As Darwin presciently wrote:

> As man advances in civilization, and small tribes are united into larger communities, the simplest reason would tell each individual that he ought to extend his social instincts and sympathies to all the members of the same nation, though

personally unknown to him. This point being once reached, there is only an artificial barrier to prevent his sympathies extending to the men of all nations and races. If, indeed, such men are separated from him by great differences of appearance or habits, experience unfortunately shows us how long it is, before we look at them as our fellow-creatures.

According to Leopold, the next step in this sequence beyond the still incomplete ethic of universal humanity, a step that is clearly discernible on the horizon, is the land ethic. The "community concept" has, so far, propelled the development of ethics from the savage clan to the family of man. "The land ethic simply enlarges the boundary of the community to include soils, water, plants, and animals, or collectively: the land" (p. 204).

As the foreword to *Sand County* makes plain, the overarching thematic principle of the book is the inculcation of the idea—through narrative description, discursive exposition, abstractive generalization, and occasional preachment—"that land is a community" (viii). The community concept is "the basic concept of ecology" (viii). Once land is popularly perceived as a biotic community—as it is professionally perceived in ecology—a correlative land ethic will emerge in the collective cultural consciousness.

V

Although anticipated as far back as the mid-eighteenth century—in the notion of an "economy of nature"—the concept of the biotic community was more fully and deliberately developed as a working model or paradigm for ecology by Charles Elton in the 1920s. The natural world is organized as an intricate corporate society in which plants and animals occupy "niches," or as Elton alternatively called them, "roles" or "professions," in the economy of nature. As in a feudal community, little or no socio-economic mobility (upward or otherwise) exists in the biotic community. One is born to one's trade.

Human society, Leopold argues, is founded, in large part, upon mutual security and economic interdependency and preserved only by limitations on freedom of action in the struggle for existence—that is, by ethical constraints. Since the biotic community exhibits, as modern ecology reveals, an analogous structure, it too can be preserved, given the newly amplified impact of "mechanized man," only by analogous limitations on freedom of action—that is, by a land ethic (viii). A land ethic, furthermore, is not only "an ecological necessity," but an "evolutionary possibility" because a moral response to the natural environment—Darwin's social sympathies, sentiments, and instincts translated and codified into a body of principles and precepts—would be automatically triggered in human beings by ecology's social representation of nature (p. 203).

Therefore, the key to the emergence of a land ethic is, simply, universal ecological literacy.

VI

The land ethic rests upon three scientific cornerstones: (1) evolutionary and (2) ecological biology set in a background of (3) Copernican astronomy. Evolutionary theory provides the conceptual link between ethics and social organization and development. It provides a sense of "kinship with fellow-creatures" as well, "fellow-voyagers" with us in the "odyssey of evolution" (p. 109). It establishes a diachronic link between people and nonhuman nature.

Ecological theory provides a synchronic link—the community concept—a sense of social integration of human and nonhuman nature. Human beings, plants, animals, soils, and waters are "all interlocked in one humming community of cooperations and competitions, one biota." The simplest reason, to paraphrase Darwin, should, therefore, tell each individual that he or she ought to extend his or her social instincts and sympathies to all the members of the biotic community though different from him or her in appearance or habits.

And although Leopold never directly mentions it in *A Sand County Almanac,* the Copernican

perspective, the perception of the earth as "a small planet" in an immense and utterly hostile universe beyond, contributes, perhaps subconsciously, but nevertheless very powerfully, to our sense of kinship, community, and interdependence with fellow denizens of the earth household. It scales the earth down to something like a cozy island paradise in a desert ocean.

Here in outline, then, are the conceptual and logical foundations of the land ethic: Its conceptual elements are a Copernican cosmology, a Darwinian protosociobiological natural history of ethics, Darwinian ties of kinship among all forms of life on earth, and an Eltonian model of the structure of biocenoses all overlaid on a Humean–Smithian moral psychology. Its logic is that natural selection has endowed human beings with an affective moral response to perceived bonds of kinship and community membership and identity; that today the natural environment, the land, is represented as a community, the biotic community; and that, therefore, an environmental or land ethic is both possible—the biopsychological and cognitive conditions are in place—and necessary, since human beings collectively have acquired the power to destroy the integrity, diversity, and stability of the environing and supporting economy of nature. In the remainder of this essay I discuss special features and problems of the land ethic germane to moral philosophy.

The most salient feature of Leopold's land ethic is its provision of what Kenneth Goodpaster has carefully called "moral considerability" for the biotic community per se, not just for fellow members of the biotic community.

> In short, a land ethic changes the role of *Homo sapiens* from conqueror of the land-community to plain member and citizen of it. It implies respect for his fellow-members, *and also respect for the community as such.*
> (p. 204, emphasis added)

The land ethic, thus, has a holistic as well as an individualistic cast.

Indeed, as "The Land Ethic" develops, the focus of moral concern shifts gradually away from plants, animals, soils, and waters severally to the biotic community collectively. Toward the middle, in the subsection called "Substitutes for a Land Ethic," Leopold invokes the "biotic rights" of *species*—as the context indicates—of wildflowers, songbirds, and predators. In "The Out-look," the climactic section of "The Land Ethic," nonhuman natural entities, first appearing as fellow members, then considered in profile as species, are not so much as mentioned in what might be called the "summary moral maxim" of the land ethic: "A thing is right when it tends to preserve the integrity, stability, and beauty of the biotic community. It is wrong when it tends otherwise" (pp. 224–25).

By this measure of right and wrong, not only would it be wrong for a farmer, in the interest of higher profits, to clear the woods off a 75 percent slope, turn his cows into the clearing and dump its rainfall, rocks, and soil into the community creek, it would also be wrong for the federal fish and wildlife agency, in the interest of individual animal welfare, to permit populations of deer, rabbits, feral burros, or whatever to increase unchecked and thus to threaten the integrity, stability, and beauty of the biotic communities of which they are members. The land ethic not only provides moral considerability for the biotic community per se, but ethical consideration of its individual members is preempted by concern for the preservation of the integrity, stability, and beauty of the biotic community. The land ethic, thus, not only has a holistic aspect; it is holistic with a vengeance.

The holism of the land ethic, more than any other feature, sets it apart from the predominant paradigm of modern moral philosophy. It is, therefore, the feature of the land ethic which requires the most patient theoretical analysis and the most sensitive practical interpretation.

VII

As Kenneth Goodpaster pointed out, mainstream modern ethical philosophy has taken egoism as its point of departure and reached a wider circle of moral entitlement by a process of generalization: I am sure that *I*, the enveloped ego, am intrinsically or inherently valuable and thus that *my* interests ought to be considered, taken into account, by "others" when their actions may substantively affect *me*. My own claim to moral consideration, according to the conventional wisdom, ultimately rests upon a psychological capacity—rationality or sentiency were the classical candidates of Kant and Bentham, respectively—which is arguably valuable in itself and which thus qualifies *me* for moral standing. However, then I am forced grudgingly to grant the same moral consideration I demand from others, on this basis, to those others who can also claim to possess the same general psychological characteristic.

A criterion of moral value and consideration is thus identified. Goodpaster convincingly argues that mainstream moral theory is based, when all the learned dust has settled, on this simple paradigm of ethical justification and logic exemplified by the Benthamic and Kantian prototypes. If the criterion of moral values and consideration is pitched low enough—as it is in Bentham's criterion of sentiency—a wide variety of animals are admitted to moral entitlement. If the criterion of moral value and consideration is pushed lower still—as it is in Albert Schweitzer's reverence-for-life ethic—all minimally conative things (plants as well as animals) would be extended moral considerability. The contemporary animal liberation/rights, and reverence-for-life/life-principle ethics are, at bottom, simply direct applications of the modern classical paradigm of moral argument. But this standard modern model of ethical theory provides no possibility whatever for the moral consideration of wholes—of threatened population of animals and plants, or of endemic, rare, or endangered species, or of biotic communities, or most expansively, of the biosphere in its totality—since wholes per se have no psychological experience of any kind. Because mainstream modern moral theory has been "psychocentric," it has been radically and intractably individualistic or "atomistic" in its fundamental theoretical orientation.

Hume, Smith, and Darwin diverged from the prevailing theoretical model by recognizing that altruism is as fundamental and autochthonous in human nature as is egoism. According to their analysis, moral value is not identified with a natural quality objectively present in morally considerable beings—as reason and/or sentiency is objectively present in people and/or animals—it is, as it were, projected by valuing subjects.

Hume and Darwin, furthermore, recognize inborn moral sentiments which have society as such as their natural object. Hume insists that "we must renounce the theory which accounts for every moral sentiment by the principle of self-love. We must adopt a more *publick affection* and allow that the *interests of society* are not, *even on their own account,* entirely indifferent to us." And Darwin, somewhat ironically (since "Darwinian evolution" very often means natural selection operating exclusively with respect to individuals), sometimes writes as if morality had no other object than the commonweal, the welfare of the community as a corporate entity:

> We have now seen that actions are regarded by savages, and were probably so regarded by primeval man, as good or bad, solely as they obviously affect the welfare of the tribe,—not that of the species, nor that of the individual member of the tribe. This conclusion agrees well with the belief that the so called moral sense is aboriginally derived from social instincts, for both relate at first exclusively to the community.

Theoretically then, the biotic community owns what Leopold, in the lead paragraph of "The Outlook," calls "value in the philosophical sense"—that is, direct moral considerability—because it is a newly discovered proper object of a specially evolved "publick affection" or "moral sense" which all psychologically normal human beings have inherited from a long line of ancestral social primates (p. 223).

VIII

In the land ethic, as in all earlier stages of social–ethical evolution, there exists a tension between the good of the community as a whole and the "rights" of its individual members considered severally....

In any case, the conceptual foundations of the land ethic provide a well-informed, self-consistent theoretical basis for including both fellow members of the biotic community and the biotic community itself (considered as a corporate entity) within the purview of morals. The preemptive emphasis, however, on the welfare of the community as a whole, in Leopold's articulation of the land ethic, while certainly consistent with its Humean–Darwinian theoretical foundations, is not determined by them alone. The overriding holism of the land ethic results, rather, more from the way our moral sensibilities are informed by ecology.

IX

Ecological thought, historically, has tended to be holistic in outlook. Ecology is the study of the relationships of organisms to one another and to the elemental environment. These relationships bind the *relata*—plants, animals, soils, and waters—into a seamless fabric. The ontological primacy of objects and the ontological subordination of relationships characteristic of classical Western science is, in fact, reversed in ecology. Ecological relationships determine the nature of organisms rather than the other way around. A species is what it is because it has adapted to a niche in the ecosystem. The whole, the system itself, thus, literally and quite straightforwardly shapes and forms its component species.

Antedating Charles Elton's community model of ecology was F. E. Clements and S. A. Forbes's organism model. Plants and animals, soils and waters, according to this paradigm, are integrated into one superorganism. Species are, as it were, its organs; specimens its cells. Although Elton's community paradigm (later modified, as we shall see, by

Arthur Tansley's ecosystem idea) is the principal and morally fertile ecological concept of "The Land Ethic," the more radically holistic superorganism paradigm of Clements and Forbes resonates in "The Land Ethic" as an audible overtone. In the peroration of "Land Health and the A-B Cleavage," for example, which immediately precedes "The Outlook," Leopold insists that

> in all these cleavages, we see repeated the same basic paradoxes: man the conqueror *versus* man the biotic citizen; science the sharpener of his sword *versus* science the searchlight on his universe; land the slave and servant *versus* land the collective organism. (p. 223)

And on more than one occasion Leopold, in the latter quarter of "The Land Ethic," talks about the "health" and "disease" of the land—terms which are at once descriptive and normative and which, taken literally, characterize only organisms proper.

In an early essay, "Some Fundamentals of Conservation in the Southwest," Leopold speculatively flirted with the intensely holistic superorganism model of the environment as a paradigm pregnant with moral implications....

Had Leopold retained this overall theoretical approach in "The Land Ethic," the land ethic would doubtless have enjoyed more critical attention from philosophers. The moral foundations of a land or, as he might then have called it, "earth" ethic would rest upon the hypothesis that the Earth is alive and ensouled—possessing inherent psychological characteristics, logically parallel to reason and sentiency. This notion of a conative whole earth could plausibly have served as a general criterion of intrinsic worth and moral considerability, in the familiar format of mainstream moral thought.

Part of the reason, therefore, that "The Land Ethic" emphasizes more and more the integrity, stability, and beauty of the environment as a whole, and less and less the biotic right of individual plants and animals to life, liberty, and the pursuit of happiness, is that the superorganism ecological paradigm invites one, much more than

does the community paradigm, to hypostatize, to reify the whole, and to subordinate its individual members.

In any case, as we see, rereading "The Land Ethic" in light of "Some Fundamentals," the whole Earth organism image of nature is vestigially present in Leopold's later thinking. Leopold may have abandoned the "earth ethic" because ecology had abandoned the organism analogy in favor of the community analogy as a working theoretical paradigm. And the community model was more suitably given moral implications by the social/sentimental ethical natural history of Hume and Darwin.

Meanwhile, the biotic community ecological paradigm itself had acquired, by the late thirties and forties, a more holistic cast of its own. In 1935 British ecologist Arthur Tansley pointed out that from the perspective of physics the "currency" of the "economy of nature" is energy. Tansley suggested that Elton's qualitative and descriptive food chains, food webs, trophic niches, and biosocial professions could be quantitatively expressed by means of a thermodynamic flow model. It is Tansley's state-of-the-art thermodynamic paradigm of the environment that Leopold explicitly sets out as a "mental image of land" in relation to which "we can be ethical" (p. 214). And it is the ecosystemic model of land which informs the cardinal practical precepts of the land ethic.

"The Land Pyramid" is the pivotal section of "The Land Ethic"—the section which effects a complete transition from concern for "fellow-members" to the "community as such." It is also its longest and most technical section. A description of the "ecosystem" (Tansley's deliberately nonmetaphorical term) begins with the sun. Solar energy "flows through a circuit called the biota" (p. 215). It enters the biota through the leaves of green plants and courses through plant-eating animals, and then on to omnivores and carnivores. At last the tiny fraction of solar energy converted to biomass by green plants remaining in the corpse of a predator, animal feces, plant detritus, or other dead organic material is garnered by decomposers—worms, fungi, and bacteria. They recycle the participating elements and degrade into entropic equilibrium any remaining energy. According to this paradigm

> land, then, is not merely soil; it is a fountain of energy flowing through a circuit of soils, plants, and animals. Food chains are the living channels which conduct energy upward; death and decay return it to the soil. The circuit is not closed; … but it is a sustained circuit, like a slowly augmented revolving fund of life. (p. 216)

In this exceedingly abstract (albeit poetically expressed) model of nature, process precedes substance and energy is more fundamental than matter. Individual plants and animals become less autonomous beings than ephemeral structures in a patterned flux of energy. According to Yale biophysicist Harold Morowitz,

> viewed from the point of view of modern [ecology], each living thing… is a dissipative structure, that is it does not endure in and of itself but only as a result of the continual flow of energy in the system. An example might be instructive. Consider a vortex in a stream of flowing water. The vortex is a structure made of an ever-changing group of water molecules. It does not exist as an entity in the classical Western sense; it exists only because of the flow of water through the stream. In the same sense, the structures out of which biological entities are made are transient, unstable entities with constantly changing molecules, dependent on a constant flow of energy from food in order to maintain form and structure…. From this point of view the reality of individuals is problematic because they do not exist per se but only as local perturbations in this universal flow.

Though less bluntly stated and made more palatable by the unfailing charm of his prose, Leopold's proffered mental image of land is just as expansive,

systemic, and distanced as Morowitz's. The maintenance of "the complex structure of the land and its smooth functioning as an energy unit" emerges in "The Land Pyramid" as the *summum bonum* of the land ethic (p. 216).

X

From this good Leopold derives several practical principles slightly less general, and therefore more substantive, than the summary moral maxim of the land ethic distilled in "The Outlook." "The trend of evolution [not its "goal," since evolution is ateleological] is to elaborate and diversify the biota" (p. 216). Hence, among our cardinal duties is the duty to preserve what species we can, especially those at the apex of the pyramid—the top carnivores. "In the beginning, the pyramid of life was low and squat; the food chains short and simple. Evolution has added layer after layer, link after link" (pp. 215–16). Human activities today, especially those like systematic deforestation in the tropics, resulting in abrupt massive extinctions of species, are in effect "devolutionary;" they flatten the biotic pyramid; they choke off some of the channels and gorge others (those which terminate in our own species).

The land ethic does not enshrine the ecological status quo and devalue the dynamic dimension of nature. Leopold explains that "evolution is a long series of self-induced changes, the net result of which has been to elaborate the flow mechanism and to lengthen the circuit. Evolutionary changes, however, are usually slow and local. Man's invention of tools has enabled him to make changes of unprecedented violence, rapidity, and scope" (pp. 216–17). "Natural" species extinction, that is, species extinction in the normal course of evolution, occurs when a species is replaced by competitive exclusion or evolves into another form. Normally speciation outpaces extinction. Mankind inherited a richer, more diverse world than had ever existed before in the 3.5 billion-year odyssey of life on Earth. What is wrong with anthropogenic species extirpation and extinction is the *rate* at which it is occurring and the *result:* biological impoverishment instead of enrichment.

Leopold goes on here to condemn, in terms of its impact on the ecosystem, "the world-wide pooling of faunas and floras," that is, the indiscriminate introduction of exotic and domestic species and the dislocation of native and endemic species, mining the soil for its stored biotic energy, leading ultimately to diminished fertility and to erosion; and polluting and damming water courses (p. 217).

According to the land ethic, therefore: Thou shalt not extirpate or render species extinct; thou shalt exercise great caution in introducing exotic and domestic species into local exosystems, in exacting energy from the soil and releasing it into the biota, and in damming or polluting water courses; and thou shalt be especially solicitous of predatory birds and mammals. Here in brief are the express moral precepts of the land ethic. They are all explicitly informed—not to say derived—from the energy circuit model of the environment.

XI

The living channels—food chains—through which energy courses are composed of individual plants and animals. A central, stark fact lies at the heart of ecological processes: Energy, the currency of the economy nature, passes from one organism to another, not from hand to hand, like coined money, but, so to speak, from stomach to stomach. Eating *and being eaten,* living *and dying* are what make the biotic community hum.

The precepts of the land ethic, like those of all previous accretions, reflect and reinforce the structure of the community to which it is correlative. Trophic asymmetries constitute the kernel of the biotic community. It seems unjust, unfair. But that is how the economy of nature is organized (and has been for thousands of millions of years). The land ethic, thus, affirms as good, and strives to preserve, the very inequities in nature whose social counterparts in human communities are condemned as bad and would be eradicated by familiar

social ethics, especially by the more recent Christian and secular egalitarian exemplars. A "right to life" for individual members is not consistent with the structure of the biotic community and hence is not mandated by the land ethic. This disparity between the land ethic and its more familiar social precedents contributes to the apparent devaluation of individual members of the biotic community and augments and reinforces the tendency of the land ethic, driven by the systemic vision of ecology, toward a more holistic or community-per-se orientation.

Of the few moral philosophers who have given the land ethic a moment's serious thought, most have regarded it with horror because of its emphasis on the good of the community and its deemphasis on the welfare of individual members of the community. Not only are other sentient creatures members of the biotic community and subordinate to its integrity, beauty, and stability; so are *we.* Thus, if it is not only morally permissible, from the point of view of the land ethic, but morally required, that members of certain species be abandoned to predation and other vicissitudes of wild life or even deliberately culled (as in the case of alert and sentient whitetail deer) for the sake of the integrity, stability, and beauty of the biotic community, how can we consistently exempt ourselves from a similar draconian regime? We too are only "plain members and citizens" of the biotic community. And our global population is growing unchecked. According to William Aiken, from the point of view of the land ethic, therefore, "massive human diebacks would be good. It is our duty to cause them. It is our species' duty, relative to the whole, to eliminate 90 percent of our numbers." Thus, according to Tom Regan, the land ethic is a clear case of "environmental fascism."

Of course Leopold never intended the land ethic to have either inhumane or antihumanitarian implications or consequences. But whether he intended them or not, a logically consistent deduction from the theoretical premises of the land ethic might force such untoward conclusions. And given their magnitude and monstrosity, these derivations would constitute a *reductio ad absurdum* of the whole land ethic enterprise and entrench and reinforce our current human chauvinism and moral alienation from nature. If this is what membership in the biotic community entails, then all but the most radical misanthropes would surely want to opt out.

XII

The land ethic, happily, implies neither inhumane nor inhuman consequences. That some philosophers think it must follows more from their own theoretical presuppositions than from the theoretical elements of the land ethic itself. Conventional modern ethical theory rests moral entitlement, as I earlier pointed out, on a criterion or qualification. If a candidate meets the criterion—rationality or sentiency are the most commonly posited—he, she, or it is entitled to equal moral standing with others who possess the same qualification in equal degree. Hence, reasoning in this philosophically orthodox way, and forcing Leopold's theory to conform: if human beings are, with other animals, plants, soils, and waters, equally members of the biotic community, and if community membership is the criterion of equal moral consideration, then not only do animals, plants, soils, and waters have equal (highly attenuated) "rights," but human beings are equally subject to the same subordination of individual welfare and rights in respect to the good of the community as a whole.

But the land ethic, as I have been at pains to point out, is heir to a line of moral analysis different from that institutionalized in contemporary moral philosophy. From the biosocial evolutionary analysis of ethics upon which Leopold builds the land ethic, it (the land ethic) neither replaces nor overrides previous accretions. Prior moral sensibilities and obligations attendant upon and correlative to prior strata of social involvement remain operative and preemptive.

Being citizens of the United States, or the United Kingdom, or the Soviet Union, or Venezuela, or some other nation-state, and therefore having national obligations and patriotic duties, does not mean that we are not also members of smaller communities or social groups—cities or townships, neighborhoods, and families—or that we are relieved of the peculiar moral responsibilities attendant upon and correlative to these memberships as well. Similarly, our recognition of the biotic community and our immersion in it does not imply that we do not also remain members of the human community—the "family of man" or "global village"—or that we are relieved of the attendant and correlative moral responsibilities of that membership, among them to respect universal human rights and uphold the principles of individual human worth and dignity. The biosocial development of morality does not grow in extent like an expanding balloon, leaving no trace of its previous boundaries, so much like the circumference of a tree. Each emergent, and larger, social unit is layered over the more primitive, and intimate, ones.

Moreover, as a general rule, the duties correlative to the inner social circles to which we belong eclipse those correlative to the rings farther from the heartwood when conflicts arise. Consider our moral revulsion when zealous ideological nationalists encourage children to turn their parents in to the authorities if their parents dissent from the political or economic doctrines of the ruling party. A zealous environmentalist who advocated visiting war, famine, or pestilence on human populations (those existing somewhere else, of course) in the name of the integrity, beauty, and stability of the biotic community would be similarly perverse. Family obligations in general come before nationalistic duties and humanitarian obligations in general come before environmental duties. The land ethic, therefore, is not draconian or fascist. It does not cancel human morality. The land ethic may, however, as with any new accretion, demand choices which affect, in turn, the demands of the more interior social–ethical circles. Taxes and the military draft may conflict with family-level obligations. While the land ethic, certainly, does not cancel human morality, neither does it leave it unaffected.

Nor is the land ethic inhumane. Nonhuman fellow members of the biotic community have no "human rights," because they are not, by definition, members of the human community. As fellow members of the biotic community, however, they deserve respect.

How exactly to express or manifest respect, while at the same time abandoning our fellow members of the biotic community to their several fates or even actively consuming them for our own needs (and wants), or deliberately making them casualties of wildlife management for ecological integrity, is a difficult and delicate question.

Fortunately, American Indian and other traditional patterns of human–nature interaction provide rich and detailed models. Algonkian woodland peoples, for instance, represented animals, plants, birds, waters, and minerals as other-than-human persons engaged in reciprocal, mutually beneficial socioeconomic intercourse with human beings. Tokens of payment, together with expressions of apology, were routinely offered to the beings whom it was necessary for these Indians to exploit. Care not to waste the usable parts and care in the disposal of unusable animal and plant remains were also an aspect of the respectful, albeit necessarily consumptive, Algonquian relationship with fellow members of the land community. As I have more fully argued elsewhere, the Algonquian portrayal of human–nature relationships is, indeed, although certainly different in specifics, identical in abstract form to that recommended by Leopold in the land ethic…. Is the land ethic prudential or deontological? Is the land ethic, in other words, a matter of enlightened (collective, human) self-interest, or does it genuinely admit nonhuman natural entities and nature as a whole to true moral standing?

The conceptual foundations of the land ethic, as I have here set them out, and much of Leopold's hortatory rhetoric, would certainly indicate that the land ethic is deontological (or duty oriented) rather than prudential. In the section significantly titled "The Ecological Conscience," Leopold complains that the then-current conservation philosophy is inadequate because "it defines no right or wrong, assigns no obligation, calls for no sacrifice, implies no change in the current philosophy of values. In respect of land-use, it urges *only* enlightened self-interest" (pp. 207–8, emphasis

added). Clearly, Leopold himself thinks that the land ethic goes beyond prudence. In this section he disparages mere "self-interest" two more times, and concludes that "obligations have no meaning without conscience, and the problem we face is the extension of the social conscience from people to land" (p. 209).

In the next section, "Substitutes for a Land Ethic," he mentions rights twice—the "biotic right" of birds to continuance and the absence of a right on the part of human special interest to exterminate predators.

Finally, the first sentences of "The Outlook" read: "It is inconceivable to me that an ethical relation to land can exist without love, respect, and admiration for land, and a high regard for its value. By value, I of course mean something far broader than mere economic value; I mean value in the philosophical sense" (p. 223). By "value in the philosophical sense," Leopold can only mean what philosophers more technically call "intrinsic value" or "inherent worth." Something that has intrinsic value or inherent worth is valuable in and of itself, not because of what it can do for us. "Obligation," "sacrifice," "a conscience," "respect," the ascription of rights, and intrinsic value—all of these are consistently opposed to self-interest and seem to indicate decisively that the land ethic is of the deontological type.

Some philosophers, however, have seen it differently. Scott Lehmann, for example, writes,

> Although Leopold claims for communities of plants and animals a "right to continued existence," his argument is homocentric, appealing to the human stake in preservation. Basically it is an argument from enlightened self-interest, where the self in question is not an individual human being but humanity—present and future—as a whole.

Lehmann's claim has some merits, even though it flies in the face of Leopold's express commitments. Leopold does frequently lapse into the language of (collective, long-range, human) self-interest. Early on, for example, he remarks, "in human history, we have learned (I hope) that the conqueror role is eventually *self*-defeating" (p. 204, emphasis added). And later, of the 95 percent of Wisconsin species which cannot be "sold, fed, eaten, or otherwise put to economic use," Leopold reminds us that "these creatures are members of the biotic community, and if (as I believe) its stability depends on its integrity, they are entitled to continuance" (p. 210). The implication is clear: the economic 5 percent cannot survive if a significant portion of the uneconomic 95 percent are extirpated; nor may *we,* it goes without saying, survive without these "resources."

Leopold, in fact, seems to be consciously aware of this moral paradox. Consistent with the biosocial foundations of his theory, he expresses it in sociobiological terms:

> An ethic may be regarded as a mode of guidance for meeting ecological situations so new or intricate, or involving such deferred reactions, that the path of social expediency is not discernible to the average individual. Animal instincts are modes of guidance for the individual in meeting such situations. Ethics are possibly a kind of community instinct in-the-making. (p. 203)

From an objective, descriptive sociobiological point of view, ethics evolve because they contribute to the inclusive fitness of their carriers (or, more reductively still, to the multiplication of their carriers' genes); they are expedient. However, the path to self-interest (or to the self-interest of the selfish gene) is not discernible to the participating individuals (nor, certainly, to their genes). Hence, ethics are grounded in instinctive feeling—love, sympathy, respect—not in self-conscious calculating intelligence. Somewhat like the paradox of hedonism—the notion that one cannot achieve happiness if one directly pursues happiness per se and not other things—one can only secure self-interest by putting the interests of others on a par with one's own (in this case long-range collective human self-interest and the interest of other forms of life and of the biotic community per se).

So, is the land ethic deontological or prudential, after all? It is both—self-consistently both—depending upon one's point of view. From the inside, from the lived, felt point of view of the community member with evolved moral sensibilities, it is deontological. It involves an affective–cognitive posture of genuine love, respect, admiration, obligation, self-sacrifice, conscience, duty, and the ascription of intrinsic value and biotic rights. From the outside, from the objective and analytic scientific point of view, it is prudential. "There is no other way for land to survive the impact of mechanized man," nor, therefore, for mechanized man to survive his own impact upon the land (p. viii).

STUDY QUESTIONS

1. What are the three reasons for the professional neglect, confusion, and neglect of Leopold's "land ethics," according to Callicott?

2. How is the land ethic different from classical and mainstream modern ethical philosophy, such as Kant's and Bentham's systems? Note Goodpaster's criticisms on which Callicott draws.

3. Is Callicott successful in arguing for the natural basis of value in the interaction between valuers (humans) and the environment? Can you see any problems with this view?

4. Leopold wrote "A thing is right when it tends to preserve the integrity, stability, and beauty of the biotic community. It is wrong when it tends otherwise." This passage has been interpreted by some to mean that humans should be sacrificed if they interfere with the good of the biotic community. Callicott tries to modify this statement, removing the misanthropic implications. Go over his defense. Has Callicott strengthened or weakened Leopold's land ethic by modifying it as he does?

26

Should Trees Have Standing? Toward Legal Rights for Natural Objects

CHRISTOPHER D. STONE

Christopher Stone is professor of law at the University of Southern California, Los Angeles, and the author of several works in law and environmental ethics, including Should Trees Have Standing? *from which the present selection is taken.*

Stone argues that a strong case can be made for the "unthinkable idea" of extending legal rights to natural objects. Building on the models of inanimate objects, such as trusts, corporations, nation-states, and municipalities, he proposes that we extend the notion of legal guardian for legal incompetents to cover these natural objects. Note the three main ways that natural objects are denied rights under common law and how Stone's proposal addresses these considerations.

INTRODUCTION: THE UNTHINKABLE

In *Descent of Man,* Darwin observes that the history of man's moral development has been a continual extension in the objects of his "social instincts and sympathies." Originally each man had regard only for himself and those of a very narrow circle about him; later, he came to regard more and more "not only the welfare, but the happiness of all his fellow-men"; then "his sympathies became more tender and widely diffused, extending to men of all races, to the imbecile, maimed, and other useless members of society, and finally to the lower animals...."

The history of the law suggests a parallel development. Perhaps there never was a pure Hobbesian state of nature, in which no "rights" existed except in the vacant sense of each man's "right to self-defense." But it is not unlikely that so far as the earliest "families" (including extended kinship groups and clans) were concerned, everyone outside the family was suspect, alien, rightless. And even within the family, persons we presently regard as the natural holders of at least some rights had none. Take, for example, children. We know something of the early rights-status of children from the widespread practice of infanticide—especially of the deformed and female. (Senicide, as among the North American Indians, was the corresponding rightlessness of the aged.) Maine tells us that as late as the Patria Potestas of the Romans, the father had *jus vitae necisque*—the power of life and death—over his children. A fortiori, Maine writes, he had power of "uncontrolled corporal chastisement; he can modify their personal condition at pleasure; he can give a wife to his son; he can give his daughter in marriage; he can divorce his children of either sex;

he can transfer them to another family by adoption; and he can sell them." The child was less than a person: an object, a thing.

The legal rights of children have long since been recognized in principle, and are still expanding in practice. Witness, just within recent time, *In re Gault,* guaranteeing basic constitutional protections to juvenile defendants, and the Voting Rights Act of 1970. We have been making persons of children although they were not, in law, always so. And we have done the same, albeit imperfectly some would say, with prisoners, aliens, women (especially of the married variety), the insane, Blacks, foetuses, and Indians.

Nor is it only matter in human form that has come to be recognized as the possessor of rights. The world of the lawyer is peopled with inanimate right-holders: trusts, corporations, joint ventures, municipalities, Subchapter R partnerships, and nation-states, to mention just a few. Ships, still re-ferred to by courts in the feminine gender, have long had an independent jural life, often with striking consequences. We have become so accustomed to the idea of a corporation having "its" own rights, and being a "person" and "citizen" for so many stat-utory and constitutional purposes, that we forget how jarring the notion was to early jurists. "That invisible, intangible and artificial being, that mere legal entity" Chief Justice Marshall wrote of the cor-poration in *Bank of the United States v. Deveaux*— could a suit be brought in *its* name? Ten years later, in the *Dartmouth College* case, he was still refusing to let pass unnoticed the wonder of an entity "existing only in contemplation of law." Yet, long before Marshall worried over the personifying of the mod-ern corporation, the best medieval legal scholars had spent hundreds of years struggling with the notion of the legal nature of those great public "corporate bodies," the Church and the State. How could they exist in law, as entities transcend-ing the living Pope and King? It was clear how a king could bind *himself*—on his honor—by a treaty. But when the king died, what was it that was bur-dened with the obligations of, and claimed the rights under, the treaty *his* tangible hand had signed? The medieval mind saw (what we have

lost our capacity to see) how *unthinkable* it was, and worked out the most elaborate conceits and fallacies to serve as anthropomorphic flesh for the Universal Church and the Universal Empire.

It is this note of the *unthinkable* that I want to dwell upon for a moment. Throughout legal history, each successive extension of rights to some new entity has been, theretofore, a bit unthinkable. We are inclined to suppose the rightlessness of rightless "things" to be a decree of Nature, not a legal convention acting in support of some status quo. It is thus that we defer considering the choices involved in all their moral, social, and economic dimensions. And so the United States Supreme Court could straight-facedly tell us in *Dred Scott* that Blacks had been denied the rights of citizenship "as a subordinate and inferior class of beings, who had been subjugated by the dominant race...." In the nineteenth century, the highest court in California explained that Chinese had not the right to testify against white men in criminal matters be-cause they were "a race of people whom nature has marked as inferior, and who are incapable of progress or intellectual development beyond a certain point ... between whom and ourselves nature has placed an impassable difference." The popular conception of the Jew in the 13th Century contributed to a law which treated them as "men *ferae naturae,* protected by a quasi-forest law. Like the roe and the deer, they form an order apart." Recall, too, that it was not so long ago that the foetus was "like the roe and the deer." In an early suit attempting to establish a wrong-ful death action on behalf of a negligently killed foetus (now widely accepted practice), Holmes, then on the Massachusetts Supreme Court, seems to have thought it simply inconceivable "that a man might owe a civil duty and incur a conditional prospective liability in tort to one not yet in being." The first woman in Wisconsin who thought she might have a right to practice law was told that she did not, in the following terms:

> The law of nature destines and qualifies
> the female sex for the bearing and nurture
> of the children of our race and for the
> custody of the homes of the world....
> [A]ll life-long callings of women,

inconsistent with these radical and sacred duties of their sex, as the profession of the law, are departures from the order of nature; and when voluntary, treason against it.... The peculiar qualities of womanhood, its gentle graces, its quick sensibility, its tender susceptibility, its purity, its delicacy, its emotional impulses, its subordination of hard reason to sympathetic feeling, are surely not qualifications for forensic strife. Nature has tempered woman as little for the juridical conflicts of the court room, as for the physical conflicts of the battle field....

The fact is that each time there is a movement to confer rights onto some new "entity," the proposal is bound to sound odd or frightening or laughable. This is partly because until the rightless thing receives its rights, we cannot see it as anything but a *thing* for the use of "us"—those who are holding rights at the time. In this vein, what is striking about the Wisconsin case above is that the court, for all its talk about women, so clearly was never able to see women as they are (and might become). All it could see was the popular "idealized" version of *an object it needed.* Such is the way the slave South looked upon the Black. There is something of a seamless web involved: there will be resistance to giving the thing "rights" until it can be seen and valued for itself; yet, it is hard to see it and value it for itself until we can bring ourselves to give it "rights"—which is almost inevitably going to sound inconceivable to a large group of people.

The reason for this little discourse on the unthinkable, the reader must know by now, if only from the title of the paper. I am quite seriously proposing that we give legal rights to forests, oceans, rivers and other so-called "natural objects" in the environment—indeed, to the natural environment as a whole.

As strange as such a notion may sound, it is neither fanciful nor devoid of operational content. In fact, I do not think it would be a misdescription of recent developments in the law to say that we are already on the verge of assigning some such rights, although we have not faced up to what we are doing in those particular terms. We should do so now, and begin to explore the implications such a notion would hold.

TOWARD RIGHTS FOR THE ENVIRONMENT

Now, to say that the natural environment should have rights is not to say anything as silly as that no one should be allowed to cut down a tree. We say human beings have rights, but—at least as of the time of this writing—they can be executed. Corporations have rights, but they cannot plead the fifth amendment; *In re Gault* gave 15-year-olds certain rights in juvenile proceedings, but it did not give them the right to vote. Thus, to say that the environment should have rights is not to say that it should have every right we can imagine, or even the same body of rights as human beings have. Nor is it to say that everything in the environment should have the same rights as every other thing in the environment.

What the granting of rights does involve has two sides to it. The first involves what might be called the legal-operational aspects; the second, the psychic and socio-psychic aspects. I shall deal with these aspects in turn.

THE LEGAL-OPERATIONAL ASPECTS

What It Means to Be a Holder of Legal Rights

There is, so far as I know, no generally accepted standard for how one ought to use the term "legal rights." Let me indicate how I shall be using it in this piece.

First and most obviously, if the term is to have any content at all, an entity cannot be said to hold a legal right unless and until *some public authoritative body* is prepared to give *some amount of review* to actions that are colorably inconsistent with that "right." For example, if a student can be expelled from a university and cannot get any public official, even a judge or administrative agent at the lowest level, either (i) to require the university to justify its actions (if only to the extent of filling out an affidavit alleging that the expulsion "was not wholly arbitrary and capricious") or (ii) to compel the university to accord the student some procedural safeguards (a hearing, right to counsel, right to have notice of charges), then the minimum requirements for saying that the student has a legal right to his education do not exist.

But for a thing to be *a holder of legal rights,* something more is needed than that some authoritative body will review the actions and processes of those who threaten it. As I shall use the term, "holder of legal rights," each of three additional criteria must be satisfied. All three, one will observe, go toward making a thing *count* jurally—to have a legally recognized worth and dignity in its own right, and not merely to serve as a means to benefit "us" (whoever the contemporary group of rights-holders may be). They are, first, that the thing can institute legal actions *at its behest;* second, that in determining the granting of legal relief, the court must take *injury to it* into account; and, third, that relief must run to the *benefit of it.*

The Rightlessness of Natural Objects at Common Law

Consider, for example, the common law's posture toward the pollution of a stream. True, courts have always been able, in some circumstances, to issue orders that will stop the pollution.... But the stream itself is fundamentally rightless, with implications that deserve careful reconsideration.

The first sense in which the stream is not a rights-holder has to do with standing. The stream itself has none. So far as the common law is concerned, there is in general no way to challenge the polluter's actions save at the behest of a lower *riparian*[*]—another human being—able to show an invasion of *his* rights. This conception of the riparian as the holder of the right to bring suit has more than theoretical interest. The lower riparians may simply not care about the pollution. They themselves may be polluting, and not wish to stir up legal waters. They may be economically dependent on their polluting neighbor. And, of course, when they discount the value of winning by the costs of bringing suit and the chances of success, the action may not seem worth undertaking. Consider, for example, that while the polluter might be injuring 100 downstream riparians $10,000 a year *in the aggregate,* each riparian separately might be suffering injury only to the extent of $100—possibly not enough for any one of them to want to press suit by himself, or even to go to the trouble and cost of securing co-plaintiffs to make it worth everyone's while. This hesitance will be especially likely when the potential plaintiffs consider the burdens the law puts in their way: proving, *e.g.,* specific damages, the "unreasonableness" of defendant's use of the water, the fact that practicable means of abatement exist, and overcoming difficulties raised by issues such as joint causality, right to pollute by prescription, and so forth. Even in states which, like California, sought to overcome these difficulties by empowering the attorney-general to sue for abatement of pollution in limited instances, the power has been sparingly invoked and, when invoked, narrowly construed by the courts.

The second sense in which the common law denies "rights" to natural objects has to do with the way in which the merits are decided in those cases in which someone is competent and willing to establish standing. At its more primitive levels, the system protected the "rights" of the property owning human with minimal weighing of any values: *"Cujus est solum, ejus est usque ad coelum et ad infernos."*[†] Today we have come more and more to make balances—but only such as will adjust the economic best interests of identifiable humans. For example, continuing with the case of streams, there are commentators who speak of a "general rule"

---

[*]Riparian—related to living on the bank of a natural waterway.

[†]To whosoever the soil belongs, he owns also to the sky and to the depths.

that "a riparian owner is legally entitled to have the stream flow by his land with its quality unimpaired" and observe that "an upper owner has, prima facie, no right to pollute the water." Such a doctrine, if strictly invoked, would protect the stream absolutely whenever a suit was brought; but obviously, to look around us, the law does not work that way. Almost everywhere there are doctrinal qualifications on riparian "rights" to an unpolluted stream. Although these rules vary from jurisdiction to jurisdiction, and upon whether one is suing for an equitable injunction or for damages, what they all have in common is some sort of balancing. Whether under language of "reasonable use," "reasonable methods of use," "balance of convenience" or "the public interest doctrine," what the courts are balancing, with varying degrees of directness, are the economic hardships on the upper riparian (or dependent community) of abating the pollution vis-à-vis the economic hardships of continued pollution on the lower riparians. What does not weigh in the balance is the damage to the stream, its fish and turtles and "lower" life. So long as the natural environment itself is rightless, these are not matters for judicial cognizance. Thus, we find the highest court of Pennsylvania refusing to stop a coal company from discharging polluted mine water into a tributary of the Lackawana River because a plaintiff's "grievance is for a mere personal inconvenience; and … mere private personal inconveniences … must yield to the necessities of a great public industry, which although in the hands of a private corporation, subserves a great public interest." The stream itself is lost sight of in "a quantitative compromise between *two* conflicting interests."

The third way in which the common law makes natural objects rightless has to do with who is regarded as the beneficiary of a favorable judgment. Here, too, it makes a considerable difference that it is not the natural object that counts in its own right. To illustrate this point, let me begin by observing that it makes perfectly good sense to speak of, and ascertain, the legal damage to a natural object, if only in the sense of "making it whole" with respect to the most obvious factors. The costs of making a forest whole, for example, would include the costs of reseeding, repairing watersheds, restocking wildlife—the sorts of costs the Forest Service undergoes after a fire. Making a polluted stream whole would include the costs of restocking with fish, water-fowl, and other animal and vegetable life, dredging, washing out impurities, establishing natural and/or artificial aerating agents, and so forth. Now, what is important to note is that, under our present system, even if a plaintiff riparian wins a water pollution suit for damages, no money goes to the benefit of the stream itself to repair *its* damages. This omission has the further effect that, at most, the law confronts a polluter with what it takes to make the plaintiff riparians whole; this may be far less than the damages to the stream, but not so much as to force the polluter to desist. For example, it is easy to imagine a polluter whose activities damage a stream to the extent of $10,000 annually, although the aggregate damage to all the riparian plaintiffs who come into the suit is only $3000. If $3000 is less than the cost to the polluter of shutting down, or making the requisite technological changes, he might prefer to pay off the damages (*i.e.,* the legally cognizable damages) and continue to pollute the stream. Similarly, even if the jurisdiction issues an injunction at the plaintiffs' behest (rather than to order payment of damages), there is nothing to stop the plaintiffs from "selling out" the stream, *i.e.,* agreeing to dissolve or not enforce the injunction at some price (in the example above, somewhere between plaintiffs' damages—$3000— and defendant's next best economic alternative). Indeed, I take it this is exactly what Learned Hand had in mind in an opinion in which, after issuing an anti-pollution injunction, he suggests that the defendant "make its peace with the plaintiff as best it can." What is meant is a peace between *them,* and not amongst them and the river.

I ought to make clear at this point that the common law as it affects streams and rivers, which I have been using as an example so far, is not exactly the same as the law affecting other environmental objects. Indeed, one would be hard pressed to say that there was a "typical" environmental object, so far as its treatment at the hands of the law is concerned. There are some differences in the law applicable to all the various resources that are held in common: rivers, lakes, oceans, dunes, air, streams (surface and subterranean), beaches, and so forth. And there is an even greater difference as between these traditional communal resources on the one hand, and natural objects on traditionally private land, *e.g.,* the pond on the farmer's field, or the stand of trees on the suburbanite's lawn.

On the other hand, although there be these differences which would make it fatuous to generalize about a law of the natural environment, most of these differences simply underscore the points made in the instance of rivers and streams. None of the natural objects, whether held in common or situated on private land, has any of the three criteria of a rights-holder. They have no standing in their own right; their unique damages do not count in determining outcome; and they are not the beneficiaries of awards. In such fashion, these objects have traditionally been regarded by the common law, and even by all but the most recent legislation, as objects for man to conquer and master and use—in such a way as the law once looked upon "man's" relationships to African Negroes. Even where special measures have been taken to conserve them, as by seasons on game and limits on timber cutting, the dominant motive has been to conserve them *for us*—for the greatest good of the greatest number of human beings. Conservationists, so far as I am aware, are generally reluctant to maintain otherwise. As the name implies, they want to conserve and guarantee *our* consumption and *our* enjoyment of these other living things. In their own right, natural objects have counted for little, in law as in popular movements.

As I mentioned at the outset, however, the rightlessness of the natural environment can and should change; it already shows some signs of doing so.

Toward Having Standing in Its Own Right

It is not inevitable, nor is it wise, that natural objects should have no rights to seek redress in their own behalf. It is no answer to say that streams and forests cannot have standing because streams and forest cannot speak. Corporations cannot speak either; nor can states, estates, infants, incompetents, municipalities or universities. Lawyers speak for them, as they customarily do for the ordinary citizen with legal problems. One ought, I think, to handle the legal problems of natural objects as one does the problems of legal incompetents—human beings who have become vegetable. If a human being shows signs of becoming senile and has affairs that he is de jure incompetent to manage, those concerned with his well being make such a showing to the court, and someone is designated by the court with the authority to manage the incompetent's affairs. The guardian (or "conservator" or "committee"—the terminology varies) then represents the incompetent in his legal affairs. Courts make similar appointments when a corporation has become "incompetent"—they appoint a trustee in bankruptcy or reorganization to oversee its affairs and speak for it in court when that becomes necessary.

On a parity of reasoning, we should have a system in which, when a friend of a natural object perceives it to be endangered, he can apply to a court for the creation of a guardianship. Perhaps we already have the machinery to do so. California law, for example, defines an incompetent as "any person, whether insane or not, who by reason of old age, disease, weakness of mind, or other cause, is unable, unassisted, properly to manage and take care of himself or his property, and by reason thereof is likely to be deceived or imposed upon by artful or designing persons." Of course, to urge a court that an endangered river is "a person" under this provision will call for lawyers as bold and imaginative as those who convinced the Supreme Court that a railroad corporation was a "person" under the fourteenth amendment, a constitutional provision theretofore generally thought of as designed to secure the rights of freedmen....

The guardianship approach, however, is apt to raise... [the following objection]: a committee or guardian could not judge the needs of the river or forest in its charge; indeed, the very concept of "needs," it might be said, could be used here only in the most metaphorical way....

... Natural objects *can* communicate their wants (needs) to us, and in ways that are not terribly ambiguous. I am sure I can judge with more certainty and meaningfulness whether and when my lawn wants (needs) water, than the Attorney General can judge whether and when the United States wants (needs) to take an appeal from an adverse judgment by a lower court. The lawn tells me that it wants water by a certain dryness of the blades and soil—immediately obvious to the touch—the appearance of bald spots, yellowing, and a lack of springiness after being walked on; how does "the United States" communicate to the Attorney General? For similar reasons, the guardian-attorney for a smog endangered stand of pines could venture with more confidence that his client wants the smog stopped, than the directors of a corporation can assert that "the corporation" wants dividends declared. We make decisions on behalf of, and in the purported interests of, others every day; these "others" are often creatures whose wants are far less verifiable, and even far more metaphysical in conception, than the wants of rivers, trees, and land....

The argument for "personifying" the environment, from the point of damage calculations, can best be demonstrated from the welfare economics position. Every well-working legal-economic system should be so structured as to confront each of us with the full costs that our activities are imposing on society. Ideally, a paper-mill, in deciding what to produce—and where, and by what methods—ought to be forced to take into account not only the lumber, acid and labor that its production "takes" from other uses in the society, but also what costs alternative production plans will impose on society through pollution. The legal system, through the law of contracts and the criminal law, for example, makes the mill confront the costs of the first group of demands. When, for example, the company's purchasing agent orders 1000 drums of acid from the Z Company, the Z Company can bind the mill to pay for them, and thereby reimburse the society for what the mill is removing from alternative uses.

Unfortunately, so far as the pollution costs are concerned, the allocative ideal begins to break down, because the traditional legal institutions have a more difficult time "catching" and confronting us with the full social costs of our activities. In the lakeside mill example, major riparian interests might bring an action, forcing a court to weigh *their* aggregate losses against the costs to the mill of installing the anti-pollution device. But many other interests—and I am speaking for the moment of recognized homocentric interests—are too fragmented and perhaps "too remote" causally to warrant securing representation and pressing for recovery: the people who own summer homes and motels, the man who sells fishing tackle and bait, the man who rents rowboats. There is no reason not to allow the lake to prove damages to them as the prima facie measure of damages to it. *By doing so, we in effect make the natural object, through its guardian, a jural entity competent to gather up these fragmented and otherwise unrepresented damage claims, and press them before the court even where, for legal or practical reasons, they are not going to be pressed by traditional class action plaintiffs.* Indeed, one way—the homocentric way—to view what I am proposing so far is to view the guardian of the natural object as the guardian of unborn generations, as well as of the otherwise unrepresented, but distantly injured, contemporary humans. By making the lake itself the focus of these damages, and "incorporating" it so to speak, the legal system can effectively take proof upon, and confront the mill with, a larger and more representative measure of the damages its pollution causes.

So far, I do not suppose that my economist friends (unremittent human chauvinists, every one of them!) will have any large quarrel in principle with the concept. Many will view it as a *trompe l'oeil* that comes down, at best, to effectuate the goals of the paragon class action, or the paragon water pollution control district. Where we are apt to part company is here—I propose going beyond gathering up the loose ends of what most people would presently recognize as economically valid damages. The guardian would urge before the court injuries not presently cognizable—the death of eagles and inedible crabs, the suffering of sea lions, the loss from the face of the earth of species of commercially valueless birds, the disappearance of a wilderness area. One might, of course, speak of the damages involved as "damages" to us humans, and indeed, the widespread growth of environmental groups shows that human beings do feel these losses. But they are not, at present, economically measurable losses: How can they have a monetary value for the guardian to prove in court?

The answer for me is simple. Wherever it carves out "property" rights, the legal system is engaged in the process of *creating* monetary worth. One's literary works would have minimal monetary value if anyone could copy them at will. Their economic value to the author is a product of the law of copyright; the person who copies a copyrighted book has to bear a cost to the copyright-holder because the law says he must. Similarly, it is through the law of torts that we have made a "right" of—and guaranteed an economically meaningful value to—privacy. (The value we place on gold—a yellow inanimate dirt—is not simply a function of supply and demand—wilderness areas are scarce and pretty too—but results from the actions of the legal systems of the world, which have institutionalized that value; they have even done a remarkable job of stabilizing the price.) I am proposing we do the same with eagles and wilderness areas as we do with copyrighted works, patented inventions, and privacy: *make* the violation of rights in them to be a cost by declaring the "pirating" of them to be the invasion of a property interest. If we do so, the net social costs the polluter would be confronted with would include not only the extended homocentric costs of his pollution (explained above) but also costs to the environment *per se*.

How, though, would these costs be calculated? When we protect an invention, we can at least speak of a fair market value for it, by reference to which damages can be computed. But the lost environmental "values" of which we are now speaking are by definition over and above those that the market is prepared to bid for: they are priceless.

One possible measure of damages, suggested earlier, would be the cost of making the environment whole, just as, when a man is injured in an automobile accident, we impose upon the responsible party the injured man's medical expenses.

Comparable expenses to a polluted river would be the costs of dredging, restocking with fish, and so forth. It is on the basis of such costs as these, I assume, that we get the figure of $1 billion as the cost of saving Lake Erie. As an ideal, I think this is a good guide applicable in many environmental situations. It is by no means free from difficulties, however.

One problem with computing damages on the basis of making the environment whole is that, if understood most literally, it is tantamount to asking for a "freeze" on environmental quality, even at the costs (and there will be costs) of preserving "useless" objects. Such a "freeze" is not inconceivable to me as a general goal, especially considering that, even by the most immediately discernible homocentric interests, in so many areas we ought to be cleaning up and not merely preserving the environmental status quo. In fact, there is presently strong sentiment in the Congress for a total elimination of all river pollutants by 1985, notwithstanding that such a decision would impose quite large direct and indirect costs on us all. Here one is inclined to recall the instructions of Judge Hays, in remanding Consolidated Edison's Storm King application to the Federal Power Commission in *Scenic Hudson:*

> The Commission's renewed proceedings must include as a basic concern the preservation of natural beauty and of natural history shrines, keeping in mind that, in our affluent society, the cost of a project is only one of several factors to be considered.

Nevertheless, whatever the merits of such a goal in principle, there are many cases in which the social price tag of putting it into effect are going to seem too high to accept. Consider, for example, an oceanside nuclear generator that could produce low-cost electricity for a million homes at a savings of $1 a year per home, spare us the air pollution that comes of burning fossil fuels, but which through a slight heating effect threatened to kill off a rare species of temperature-sensitive sea urchins; suppose further that technological improvements adequate to reduce the temperature to present environmental quality would expend the entire one million dollars in anticipated fuel savings. Are we prepared to tax ourselves $1,000,000 a year on behalf of the sea urchins? In comparable problems under the present law of damages, we work out practicable compromises by abandoning restoration costs and calling upon fair market value. For example, if an automobile is so severely damaged that the cost of bringing the car to its original state by repair is greater than the fair market value, we would allow the responsible tortfeasor to pay the fair market value only. Or if a human being suffers the loss of an arm (as we might conceive of the ocean having irreparably lost the sea urchins), we can fall back on the capitalization of reduced earning power (and pain and suffering) to measure the damages. But what is the fair market value of sea urchins? How can we capitalize their loss to the ocean, independent of any commercial value they may have to someone else?

One answer is that the problem can sometimes be sidestepped quite satisfactorily. In the sea urchin example, one compromise solution would be to impose on the nuclear generator the costs of making the ocean whole somewhere else, in some other way, *e.g.,* reestablishing a sea urchin colony elsewhere, or making a somehow comparable contribution. In the debate over the laying of the trans-Alaskan pipeline, the builders are apparently prepared to meet conservationists' objections halfway by re-establishing wildlife away from the pipeline, so far as is feasible.

But even if damage calculations have to be made, one ought to recognize that the measurement of damages is rarely a simple report of economic facts about "the market," whether we are valuing the loss of a foot, a foetus, or a work of fine art. Decisions of this sort are always hard, but not impossible. We have increasingly taken (human) pain and suffering into account in reckoning damages, not because we think we can ascertain them as objective "facts" about the universe, but because, even in view of all the room for disagreement, we come up with a better society by making rude estimates of them than by ignoring them. We can make such estimates in regard to environmental losses fully aware that what we are really doing is

making implicit normative judgments (as with pain and suffering)—laying down rules as to what the society is going to "value" rather than reporting market evaluations. In making such normative estimates decision-makers would not go wrong if they estimated on the "high side," putting the burden of trimming the figure down on the immediate human interests present. All burdens of proof should reflect common experience; our experience in environmental matters has been a continual discovery that our acts have caused more long-range damage than we were able to appreciate at the outset.

To what extent the decision-maker should factor in costs such as the pain and suffering of animals and other sentient natural objects, I cannot say; although I am prepared to do so in principle.

The Psychic and Socio-psychic Aspects

… The strongest case can be made from the perspective of human advantage for conferring rights on the environment. Scientists have been warning of the crises the earth and all humans on it face if we do not change our ways—radically—and these crises make the lost "recreational use" of rivers seem absolutely trivial. The earth's very atmosphere is threatened with frightening possibilities: absorption of sunlight, upon which the entire life cycle depends, may be diminished; the oceans may warm (increasing the "greenhouse effect" of the atmosphere), melting the polar ice caps, and destroying our great coastal cities; the portion of the atmosphere that shields us from dangerous radiation may be destroyed. Testifying before Congress, sea explorer Jacques Cousteau predicted that the oceans (to which we dreamily look to feed our booming populations) are headed toward their own death: "The cycle of life is intricately tied up with the cycle of water … the water system has to remain alive if we are to remain alive on earth." We are depleting our energy and our food sources at a rate that takes little account of the needs even of humans now living.

These problems will not be solved easily; they very likely can be solved, if at all, only through a willingness to suspend the rate of increase in the standard of living (by present values) of the earth's "advanced" nations, and by stabilizing the total human population. For some of us this will involve forfeiting material comforts; for others it will involve abandoning the hope someday to obtain comforts long envied. For all of us it will involve giving up the right to have as many offspring as we might wish. Such a program is not impossible of realization, however. Many of our so-called "material comforts" are not only in excess of, but are probably in opposition to, basic biological needs. Further, the "costs" to the advanced nations is not as large as would appear from Gross National Product figures. G.N.P. reflects social gain (of a sort) without discounting for the social *cost* of that gain, *e.g.,* the losses through depletion of resources, pollution, and so forth. As has well been shown, as societies become more and more "advanced," their real marginal gains become less and less for each additional dollar of G.N.P. Thus, to give up "human progress" would not be as costly as might appear on first blush.

Nonetheless, such far-reaching social changes are going to involve us in a serious reconsideration of our consciousness toward the environment....

... A few years ago the pollution of streams was thought of only as a problem of smelly, unsightly, unpotable water, *i.e.,* to us. Now we are beginning to discover that pollution is a process that destroys wondrously subtle balances of life within the water, and as between the water and its banks. This heightened awareness enlarges our sense of the dangers to us. But it also enlarges our empathy. We are not only developing the scientific capacity, but we are cultivating the personal capacities *within us* to recognize more and more the ways in which nature—like the woman, the Black, the Indian and the Alien—is like us (and we will also become more able realistically to define, confront, live with and admire the ways in which we are all different).

The time may be on hand when these sentiments, and the early stirrings of the law, can be coalesced into a radical new theory or myth—felt as well as intellectualized—of man's relationships to the rest of nature. I do not mean "myth" in a demeaning sense of the term, but in the sense in which, at different times in history, our social "facts" and relationships have been comprehended and integrated by reference to the "myths" that we are cosigners of a social contract, that the Pope is God's agent, and that all men are created equal. Pantheism, Shinto and Tao all have myths to offer. But they are all, each in its own fashion, quaint, primitive and archaic. What is needed is a myth that can fit our growing body of knowledge of geophysics, biology and the cosmos. In this vein, I do not think it too remote that we may come to regard the Earth, as some have suggested, as one organism, of which Mankind is a functional part—the mind, perhaps: different from the rest of nature, but different as a man's brain is from his lungs....

> ... As I see it, the Earth is only one organized "field" of activities—and so is the **human person**—but these activities take place at various levels, in different "spheres" of being and realms of consciousness. The lithosphere is not the biosphere, and the latter not the ... ionosphere. The Earth is not **only** a material mass. Consciousness is not only "human"; it exists at animal and vegetable levels, and most likely must be latent, or operating in some form, in the molecule and the atom; and all these diverse and in a sense hierarchical modes of activity and consciousness should be seen integrated in and perhaps transcended by an all-encompassing and "eonic" planetary Consciousness.
>
> Mankind's function within the Earth-organism is to extract from the activities of all other operative systems within this organism the type of consciousness which we call "reflective" or "self"-consciousness—or, we may also say to **mentalize** and give meaning, value, and "name" to all that takes place anywhere within the Earth-field....

As radical as such a consciousness may sound today, all the dominant changes we see about us point in its direction. Consider just the impact of space travel, of world-wide mass media, of increasing scientific discoveries about the interrelatedness of all life processes. Is it any wonder that the term "spaceship earth" has so captured the popular imagination? The problems we have to confront are increasingly the world-wide crises of a global organism: not pollution of a stream, but pollution of the atmosphere and of the ocean. Increasingly, the death that occupies each human's imagination is not his own, but that of the entire life cycle of the planet earth, to which each of us is as but a cell to a body.

To shift from such a lofty fancy as the planetarization of consciousness to the operation of our municipal legal system is to come down to earth hard. Before the forces that are at work, our highest court is but a frail and feeble—a distinctly human—institution. Yet, the Court may be at its best not in its work of handing down decrees, but at the very task that is called for: of summoning up from the human spirit the kindest and most generous and worthy ideas that abound there, giving them shape and reality and legitimacy. Witness the School Desegregation Cases which, more importantly than to integrate the schools (assuming they did), awakened us to moral

needs which, when made visible, could not be denied. And so here, too, in the case of the environment, the Supreme Court may find itself in a position to award "rights" in a way that will contribute to a change in popular consciousness. It would be a modest move, to be sure, but one in furtherance of a large goal: the future of the planet as we know it.

How far we are from such a state of affairs, where the law treats "environmental objects" as holders of legal rights, I cannot say. But there is certainly intriguing language in one of Justice Black's last dissents, regarding the Texas Highway Department's plan to run a six-lane expressway through a San Antonio Park. Complaining of the Court's refusal to stay the plan, Black observed that "after today's decision, the people of San Antonio and the birds and animals that make their home in the park will share their quiet retreat with an ugly, smelly stream of traffic.... Trees, shrubs, and flowers will be mowed down." Elsewhere he speaks of the "burial of public parks," of segments of a highway which "devour parkland," and of the park's heartland. Was he, at the end of his great career, on the verge of saying—just saying—that "nature has 'rights' on its own account"? Would it be so hard to do?

STUDY QUESTIONS

1. Is the analogy with extending the circle of moral considerability and rights (from white male adults to women, other races, children, etc.) a good way to view our extending rights to natural objects? Or are there relevant differences? Could the Right to Life Movement use Stone's analogy-argument to institute legislation to protect fetuses?

2. Is Stone's basic argument anthropocentric? That is, underneath the concerns for granting legal standing to natural objects is there really anything more than enlightened self-interest? Or is there something further? (See Garrett Hardin's "Tragedy of the Commons"

[Reading 29] for a way that might reduce Stone's arguments to an antropocentric model.)

3. To which natural objects should we grant rights? If any, we'd probably choose objects traditionally valued by humans, such as the Mississippi River, the Giant Redwoods of California, and the Grand Canyon and Yellowstone National Parks, but how about deer, rats, weeds, ordinary trees, bacteria, lice, and termites? Would they get legal standing? Why, or why not?

4. Sum up the pluses and minuses of Stone's proposal. How would granting legal rights to natural objects be a good thing, and how could it lead to bad consequences?

FOR FURTHER READING

Carlson, Alan. "Appreciation and the Natural Environment." *Journal of Aesthetics and Art* 37 (1979).

Hargrove, Eugene. *Foundations of Environmental Ethics*. Englewood Cliffs, NJ: Prentice-Hall, 1989.

Myers, Norman. *The Sinking Ark*. Oxford: Pergamon Press, 1980.

————. The Primary Source: Tropical Forests and Our Future. New York: Norton, 1984.

Nash, Roderick. *The Rights of Nature*. Madison: University of Wisconsin Press, 1989.

Norton, Bryan G. "Thoreau's Insect Analogies: Or Why Environmentalists Hate Mainstream Economists." *Environmental Ethics* 13:3 (1991).

————. *Why Preserve Natural Variety?* Princeton, NJ: Princeton University Press, 1987.

Shoumatoff, Alex. *The World Is Burning*. Boston: Little, Brown, 1990.

Stone, Christopher D. *Should Trees Have Standing?* Los Altos, CA: Kaufmann, 1974.

Thoreau, Henry David. "Walking." In *The Natural History Essays*. Salt Lake City: Peregrine Smith, 1980.

Wilson, Edward O. *The Diversity of Life*. Cambridge, MA: Harvard University Press, 1992.

————. *Biophilia*. Cambridge, MA: Harvard University Press, 1984.

Wolf, Edward. "Avoiding a Mass Extinction of Species." *State of the World 1988*. Washington, D.C.: Worldwatch Institute, 1988.

Chapter 5

Population and Consumption

THE UNIVERSAL DECLARATION ON HUMAN RIGHTS describes the family as the natural and fundamental unit of society. It follows that any choice and decision with regard to the size of the family must irrevocably rest with the family itself and cannot be made by anyone else.[1]

In evaluating population growth one must keep in mind that such growth increases *exponentially* rather than *linearly*. Linear growth increases by adding 1 unit to the sum: 1, 2, 3, 4, 5, and so forth. Exponential growth increases by a fixed percentage of the whole over a given time. It doubles itself: 1, 2, 4, 8, 16, 32, 64, and so forth.

An ancient Chinese story illustrates this. Once a hero defeated the enemies of his country. The emperor had the hero brought before him and promised the hero anything he wanted. The hero produced a chessboard and asked the Emperor for one grain of rice on the first square, two on the second, four on the third, eight on the fourth, and to continue doubling through all 64 squares. The emperor was astonished. "Is that all you request?" he cried. "You could have had half my kingdom, and all you ask for is a little grain?" But the emperor soon discovered that he could not comply with the hero's request. By the time he had gotten to square 32, he found that on that square alone he owed the hero 8.6 billion grains of rice. By the time he got to square 64, he owed over 10,000,000,000,000,000,000 grains of rice, far more than the entire country produced.

We calculate the doubling time of a given amount by using the *rule of 70*. If a sum increases at 1% per annum, it will double in size in 70 years. If it increases at a 2% rate per annum, it will increase fourfold in 70 years.

About 2,000 years ago, 300 million people existed (about the population of the United States in 2006). It reached a billion in the nineteenth century, and by the end of the twentieth century, it reached 6 billion (about 6.3 billion in 2006). A current estimate is that by 2050, the world's population will be 9.3 billion. How serious is this growth? The more people there are, the more food, water, and energy we need and the more pollution we produce. How many people can Earth reasonably sustain?

As more societies industrialize and achieve middle-class lifestyles, they tend to use more resources and produce more pollution, resulting in more environmental degradation. This use is sometimes referred to as *consumption overpopulation* as opposed to *people overpopulation*. Many countries are rapidly industrializing, including India and China.

For some environmentalists, the picture is quite gloomy; there are simply not enough land resources. Others argue that our problems are moral and political, not demographic. They say we can solve our urban problems if we have the will to live together in equality and harmony. Technology has radically increased our energy and food resources. Enough food exists for all. The real problem is one of just distribution.

Proponents of this view argue that the wealthy nations should moderate their consumptive passions, pointing out that with only 4.5% of the world's population, the United States uses 33% of its resources, 25% of its nonrenewable energy, and produces 33% of its pollution. The average American's negative impact on the environment is about forty or fifty times that of a person in the Third World. In the affluent West, we must reject consumerism and simplify our lives. Those in the poorer developing nations must be allowed to improve their quality of life through education and appropriate technology.

To provide some data, we begin with a reading by Bill McKibben that succinctly sets forth a case for limiting population growth.

Next we turn to Garrett Hardin's classic article, "The Tragedy of the Commons," in which he argues that unless strong social sanctions are enforced, self-interest will lead people to maximize personal utility, which all too often means violating the carrying capacity of the land. With regard to population, he says that unless we have mutually coercive, mutually agreed-on restrictions on procreation, we will not survive, or we will survive with enormous misery.

In our third reading, Jacqueline Kasun takes a diametrically opposite point of view from that of McKibben and Hardin. Citing an impressive array of statistics, Kasun argues that enough food and resources exist to care for a lot more people than presently inhabit Earth and that technology promises to expand our resources efficiently. Population increase, rather than being a liability, is actually a blessing. Such growth stimulates agricultural and economic investment, encourages governments and parents to devote greater resources to education, and inspires both more ideas and the exchange of ideas among people. Contrary to the interests of the ruling elite, we must learn to live creatively with the expanding opportunities that a growing population affords.

Next, Hardin's famous article, "Lifeboat Ethics," argues that affluent societies, like lifeboats, ought to ensure their survival by preserving a safety factor of resources. Giving away its resources to needy nations or admitting needy immigrants is like taking on additional passengers who threaten to capsize the lifeboat. We help neither them nor ourselves. Aiming at perfect distributive justice ends up a perfect catastrophe. Furthermore, we have a duty to our children and grandchildren, which will be compromised if we endeavor to help the poor.

In our final reading, William Murdoch and Allan Oaten take strong issue with Hardin's assessment. They argue that Hardin's arguments rest on misleading metaphors, *lifeboat, commons,* and *ratchet,* and a fuller analysis will reveal that the situation is far more hopeful than Hardin claims. We are responsible for the plight of the poor and must take steps to alleviate their suffering.

NOTE

1. Secretary General of the United Nations U Thant, *International Planned Parenthood News* 168 (February 1968): 3.

27

A Special Moment in History: The Challenge of Overpopulation and Overconsumption

BILL McKIBBEN

Bill McKibben is an environmentalist and writer who lives in the Adirondacks in New York State. In this essay he argues that, because of the environmental crisis we face, we are living in a special time, which could determine the near—and long-term—future of the planet. With the world's population heading for another doubling and with more people consuming more resources and creating more pollutants—and with fewer sinks into which to throw them—the decisions we make in the next few decades may well determine the fate of Earth and prospects for future generations. McKibben's article is valuable for the large amount of data on demographics and global warming (see Chapter 8), which it lucidly sets forth and analyzes.

… We may live in a special time. We may live in the strangest, most thoroughly different moment [of history] since human beings took up farming, 10,000 years ago, and time more or less commenced. Since then time has flowed in one direction—toward *more,* which we have taken to be progress. At first the momentum was gradual, almost imperceptible, checked by wars and the Dark Ages and plagues and taboos; but in recent centuries it has accelerated, the curve of every graph steepening like the Himalayas rising from the Asian steppe. We have climbed quite high. Of course, fifty years ago one could have said the same thing, and fifty years before that, and fifty years before *that.* But in each case it would have been premature. We've increased the population fourfold in that 150 years; the amount of food we grow has gone up faster still; the size of our economy has quite simply exploded.

But now—now may be the special time. So special that in the Western world we might each of us consider, among many other things, having only one child—that is, reproducing at a rate as low as that at which human beings have ever voluntarily reproduced. Is this really necessary? Are we finally running up against some limits?

To try to answer this question, we need to ask another: *How many of us will there be in the near future?* Here is a piece of news that may alter the way we see the planet—an indication that we live at a special moment. At least at first blush the news is hopeful. *New demographic evidence shows that it is at least possible that a child born today will live long enough to see the peak of human population.*

Around the world people are choosing to have fewer and fewer children—not just in China, where the government forces it on them, but in almost every nation outside the poorest parts of Africa. Population growth rates are lower than they have been at any time since the Second World War. In the past three decades the average woman in the developing world, excluding China, has gone from bearing six children to bearing four. Even in Bangladesh the average has fallen from six to fewer than four; even in the mullahs' Iran it has dropped by four children. If this keeps up, the population of the world will not quite double again; United Nations analysts offer as their mid-range projection that it will top out at 10 to 11 billion, up from just under six billion at the moment. The world is still growing, at nearly a record pace—we add a New York City every month, almost a Mexico every year, almost an India every decade. But the rate of growth is slowing; it is no longer "exponential," "unstoppable," "inexorable," "unchecked," "cancerous." If current trends hold, the world's population will all but stop growing before the twenty-first century is out.

And that will be none too soon. There is no way we could keep going as we have been. The *increase* in human population in the 1990s has exceeded the *total* population in 1600. The population has grown more since 1950 than it did during the previous four million years. The reasons for our recent rapid growth are pretty clear. Although the Industrial Revolution speeded historical growth rates considerably, it was really the public-health revolution, and its spread to the Third World at the end of the Second World War, that set us galloping. Vaccines and antibiotics came all at once, and right behind came population. In Sri Lanka in the late 1940s life expectancy was rising at least a year every twelve months. How much difference did this make? Consider the United States: If people died throughout this century at the same rate as they did at its beginning, America's population would be 140 million, not 270 million.

If it is relatively easy to explain why populations grew so fast after the Second World War, it is much harder to explain why the growth is now slowing. Experts confidently supply answers, some of them contradictory: "Development is the best contraceptive"—or education, or the empowerment of women, or hard times that force families to postpone having children. For each example

there is a counterexample. Ninety-seven percent of women in the Arab sheikhdom of Oman know about contraception, and yet they average more than six children apiece. Turks have used contraception at about the same rate as the Japanese, but their birth rate is twice as high. And so on. It is not AIDS that will slow population growth, except in a few African countries. It is not horrors like the civil war in Rwanda, which claimed half a million lives—a loss the planet can make up for in two days. All that matters is how often individual men and women decide that they want to reproduce.

Will the drop continue? It had better. UN midrange projections assume that women in the developing world will soon average two children apiece—the rate at which population growth stabilizes. If fertility remained at current levels, the population would reach the absurd figure of 296 billion in just 150 years. Even if it dropped to 2.5 children per woman and then stopped falling, the population would still reach 28 billion.

But let's trust that this time the demographers have got it right. Let's trust that we have rounded the turn and we're in the home stretch. Let's trust that the planet's population really will double only one more time. Even so, this is a case of good news, bad news. The good news is that we won't grow forever. The bad news is that there are six billion of us already, a number the world strains to support. One more near-doubling—four or five billion more people—will nearly double that strain. Will these be the five billion straws that break the camel's back?

BIG QUESTIONS

We've answered the question *How many of us will there be?* But to figure out how near we are to any limits, we need to ask something else: *How big are we?* This is not so simple. Not only do we vary greatly in how much food and energy and water and minerals we consume, but each of us varies over time. William Catton, who was a sociologist at Washington State University before his retirement, once tried to calculate the amount of energy human beings use each day. In hunter-gatherer times it was about 2,500 calories, all of it food. That is the daily energy intake of a common dolphin. A modern human being uses 31,000 calories a day, most of it in the form of fossil fuel. That is the intake of a pilot whale. And the average American uses six times that—as much as a sperm whale. We have become, in other words, different from the people we used to be. Not kinder or unkinder, not deeper or stupider—our natures seem to have changed little since Homer. We've just gotten bigger. We appear to be the same species, with stomachs of the same size, but we aren't. It's as if each of us were trailing a big Macy's-parade balloon around, feeding it constantly.

So it doesn't do much good to stare idly out the window of your 737 as you fly from New York to Los Angeles and see that there's *plenty* of empty space down there. Sure enough, you could crowd lots more people into the nation or onto the planet. The entire world population could fit into Texas, and each person could have an area equal to the floor space of a typical U.S. home. If people were willing to stand, everyone on earth could fit comfortably into half of Rhode Island. Holland is crowded and is doing just fine.

But this ignores the balloons above our heads, our hungry shadow selves, our sperm-whale appetites. As soon as we started farming, we started setting aside extra land to support ourselves. Now each of us needs not only a little plot of cropland and a little pasture for the meat we eat but also a little forest for timber and paper, a little mine, a little oil well. Giants have big feet. Some scientists in Vancouver tried to calculate one such "footprint" and found that although 1.7 million people lived on a million acres surrounding their city, those people required 21.5 million acres of land to support them—wheat fields in Alberta, oil fields in Saudi Arabia, tomato fields in California. People in Manhattan are as dependent on faraway resources as people on the Mir space station.

Those balloons above our heads can shrink or grow, depending on how we choose to live. All over the earth people who were once tiny are suddenly growing like Alice when she ate the cake. In China per capita income has doubled since the early 1980s. People there, though still Lilliputian in comparison with us, are twice their former size. They eat much higher on the food chain, understandably, than they used to: China slaughters more pigs than any other nation, and it takes four pounds of grain to produce one pound of pork. When, a decade ago, the United Nations examined sustainable development, it issued a report saying that the economies of the developing countries needed to be five to ten times as large to move poor people to an acceptable standard of living—with all that this would mean in terms of demands on oil wells and forests.

That sounds almost impossible. For the moment, though, let's not pass judgment. We're still just doing math. There are going to be lots of us. We're going to be big. But lots of us in relation to what? Big in relation to what? It could be that compared with the world we inhabit, we're still scarce and small. Or not. So now we need to consider a third question.

HOW BIG IS THE EARTH?

Any state wildlife biologist can tell you how many deer a given area can support—how much browse there is for the deer to eat before they begin to suppress the reproduction of trees, before they begin to starve in the winter. He can calculate how many wolves a given area can support too, in part by counting the number of deer. And so on, up and down the food chain. It's not an exact science, but it comes pretty close—at least compared with figuring out the carrying capacity of the earth for human beings, which is an art so dark that anyone with any sense stays away from it.

Consider the difficulties. Human beings, unlike deer, can eat almost anything and live at almost any level they choose. Hunter-gatherers used 2,500 calories of energy a day, whereas modern Americans use seventy-five times that. Human beings, unlike deer, can import what they need from thousands of miles away. And human beings, unlike deer, can figure out new ways to do old things. If, like deer, we needed to browse on conifers to survive, we could crossbreed lush new strains, chop down competing trees, irrigate forests, spray a thousand chemicals, freeze or dry the tender buds at the peak of harvest, genetically engineer new strains—and advertise the merits of maple buds until everyone was ready to switch. The variables are so great that professional demographers rarely even bother trying to figure out carrying capacity. The demographer Joel Cohen, in his potent book *How Many People Can the Earth Support?* (1995), reports that at two recent meetings of the Population Association of America, exactly none of the more than 200 symposia dealt with carrying capacity.

But the difficulty hasn't stopped other thinkers. This is, after all, as big a question as the world offers. Plato, Euripides, and Polybius all worried that we would run out of food if the population kept growing; for centuries a steady stream of economists, environmentalists, and zealots and cranks of all sorts have made it their business to issue estimates either dire or benign. The most famous, of course, came from the Reverend Thomas Malthus. Writing in 1798, he proposed that the growth of population, being "geometric," would soon outstrip the supply of food. Though he changed his mind and rewrote his famous essay, it's the original version that people have remembered—and lambasted—ever since. Few other writers have found critics in as many corners. Not only have conservatives made Malthus's name a byword for ludicrous alarmism, but Karl Marx called his essay "a libel on the human race," Friedrich Engels believed that "we are forever secure from the fear of overpopulation," and even Mao Zedong attacked Malthus by name, adding, "Of all things in the world people are the most precious."

Each new generation of Malthusians has made new predictions that the end was near, and has been proved wrong. The late 1960s saw an upsurge of Malthusian panic. In 1967 William and Paul Paddock published a book called *Famine—1975!*, which contained a triage list: "Egypt: Can't-be-saved.... Tunisia: Should Receive Food.... India: Can't-be-saved." Almost simultaneously

Paul Ehrlich wrote, in his best-selling *The Population Bomb* (1968), "The battle to feed all of humanity is over. In the 1970s, the world will undergo famines—hundreds of millions of people will starve to death." It all seemed so certain, so firmly in keeping with a world soon to be darkened by the first oil crisis.

But that's not how it worked out. India fed herself. The United States still ships surplus grain around the world. As the astute Harvard social scientist Amartya Sen points out, "Not only is food generally much cheaper to buy today, in constant dollars, than it was in Malthus's time, but it also has become cheaper during recent decades." So far, in other words, the world has more or less supported us. Too many people starve (60 percent of children in South Asia are stunted by malnutrition), but both the total number and the percentage have dropped in recent decades, thanks mainly to the successes of the Green Revolution. Food production has tripled since the Second World War, outpacing even population growth. We may be giants, but we are clever giants.

So Malthus was wrong. Over and over again he was wrong. No other prophet has ever been proved wrong so many times. At the moment, his stock is especially low. One group of technological optimists now believes that people will continue to improve their standard of living precisely *because* they increase their numbers. This group's intellectual fountainhead is a brilliant Danish economist named Ester Boserup—a sort of anti-Malthus, who in 1965 argued that the gloomy cleric had it backward. The more people, Boserup said, the more progress. Take agriculture as an example: the first farmers, she pointed out, were slash-and-burn cultivators, who might farm a plot for a year or two and then move on, not returning for maybe two decades. As the population grew, however, they had to return more frequently to the same plot. That meant problems: compacted, depleted, weedy soils. But those new problems meant new solutions: hoes, manure, compost, crop rotation, irrigation. Even in this century, Boserup said, necessity-induced invention has meant that "intensive systems of agriculture replaced extensive systems," accelerating the rate of food production.

Boserup's closely argued examples have inspired a less cautious group of popularizers, who point out that standards of living have risen all over the world even as population has grown. The most important benefit, in fact, that population growth bestows on an economy is to increase the stock of useful knowledge, insisted Julian Simon, the best known of the so-called cornucopians, who died earlier this year. We might run out of copper, but who cares? The mere fact of shortage will lead someone to invent a substitute. "The main fuel to speed our progress is our stock of knowledge, and the brake is our lack of imagination," Simon wrote. "The ultimate resource is people—skilled, spirited, and hopeful people who will exert their wills and imaginations for their own benefit, and so, inevitably, for the benefit of us all."

Simon and his ilk owe their success to this: they have been right so far. The world has behaved as they predicted. India hasn't starved. Food is cheap. But Malthus never goes away. The idea that we might grow too big can be disproved only for the moment—never for good. We might always be on the threshold of a special time, when the mechanisms described by Boserup and Simon stop working. It is true that Malthus was wrong when the population doubled from 750 million to 1.5 billion. It is true that Malthus was wrong when the population doubled from 1.5 billion to three billion. It is true that Malthus was wrong when the population doubled from three billion to six billion. Will Malthus still be wrong fifty years from now?

LOOKING AT LIMITS

The case that the next doubling, the one we're now experiencing, might be the difficult one can begin as readily with the Stanford biologist Peter Vitousek as with anyone else. In 1986 Vitousek decided to calculate how much of the earth's "primary productivity" went to support human beings. He added together the grain we ate, the corn we fed our cows, and the forests we cut for timber and paper; he added the losses in food as we overgrazed grassland and turned it into desert. And when he was finished adding, the number he came up with was 38.8 percent. We use 38.8 percent of everything the world's plants don't need to keep themselves alive; directly or indirectly, we consume 38.8 percent of what it is possible to eat. "That's a relatively large number," Vitousek says. "It should give pause to people who think we are far from any limits." Though he never drops the measured tone of an academic, Vitousek speaks with considerable emphasis: "There's a sense among some economists that we're *so* far from any biophysical limits. I think that's not supported by the evidence."

For another antidote to the good cheer of someone like Julian Simon, sit down with the Cornell biologist David Pimentel. He believes that we're in big trouble. Odd facts stud his conversation—for example, a nice head of iceberg lettuce is 95 percent water and contains just fifty calories of energy, but it takes 400 calories of energy to grow that head of lettuce in California's Central Valley, and another 1,800 to ship it east. ("There's practically no nutrition in the damn stuff anyway," Pimentel says. "Cabbage is a lot better, and we can grow it in upstate New York.") Pimentel has devoted the past three decades to tracking the planet's capacity, and he believes that we're already too crowded—that the earth can support only two billion people over the long run at a middle-class standard of living, and that trying to support more is doing great damage. He has spent considerable time studying soil erosion, for instance. Every raindrop that hits exposed ground is like a small explosion, launching soil particles into the air. On a slope, more than half of the soil contained in those splashes is carried downhill. If crop residue—cornstalks, say—is left in the field after harvest, it helps to shield the soil: the raindrop doesn't hit as hard. But in the developing world, where firewood is scarce, peasants burn those corn-stalks for cooking fuel. About 60 percent of crop residues in China and 90 percent in Bangladesh are removed and burned, Pimentel says. When planting season comes, dry soils simply blow away. "Our measuring stations pick up Chinese soil in the Hawaiian air when ploughing time comes," he says. "Every year in Florida we pick up African soils in the wind when they start to plough."

The very things that made the Green Revolution so stunning—that made the last doubling possible—now cause trouble. Irrigation ditches, for instance, water 17 percent of all arable land and help to produce a third of all crops. But when flooded soils are baked by the sun, the water evaporates and the minerals in the irrigation water are deposited on the land. A hectare (2.47 acres) can accumulate two to five tons of salt annually, and eventually plants won't grow there. Maybe 10 percent of all irrigated land is affected.

Or think about fresh water for human use. Plenty of rain falls on the earth's surface, but most of it evaporates or roars down to the ocean in spring floods. According to Sandra Postel, the director of the Global Water Policy Project, we're left with about 12,500 cubic kilometers of accessible runoff, which would be enough for current demand except that it's not very well distributed around the globe. And we're not exactly conservationists—we use nearly seven times as much water as we used in 1900. Already 20 percent of the world's population lacks access to potable water and fights over water divide in many regions. Already the Colorado River usually dries out in the desert before it reaches the Sea of Cortez, making what the mid-century conservationist Aldo Leopold called a "milk and honey wilderness" into some of the nastiest country in North America. Already the Yellow River can run dry for as much as a third of the year. Already only two percent of the Nile's freshwater flow makes it to the ocean. And we need more water all the time. Producing a ton of grain consumes a thousand tons of water—that's how much the wheat plant breathes out as it grows. "We estimated that biotechnology might cut the amount of water a plant uses by ten percent," Pimentel says. "But plant physiologists tell us that's optimistic—they remind us that water's a pretty important part of photosynthesis. Maybe we can get five percent."…

I said earlier that food production grew even faster than population after the Second World War. Year after year the yield of wheat and corn and rice

rocketed up about three percent annually. It's a favorite statistic of the eternal optimists. In Julian Simon's book *The Ultimate Resource* (1981), charts show just how fast the growth was, and how it continually cut the cost of food. Simon wrote, "The obvious implication of this historical trend toward cheaper food—a trend that probably extends back to the beginning of agriculture—is that real prices for food will continue to drop…. It is a fact that portends more drops in price and even less scarcity in the future."

A few years after Simon's book was published, however, the data curve began to change. That rocketing growth in grain production ceased; now the gains were coming in tiny increments, too small to keep pace with population growth. The world reaped its largest harvest of grain per capita in 1984; since then the amount of corn and wheat and rice per person has fallen by six percent. Grain stockpiles have shrunk to less than two months' supply.

No one knows quite why. The collapse of the Soviet Union contributed to the trend—cooperative farms suddenly found the fertilizer supply shut off and spare parts for the tractor hard to come by. But there were other causes, too, all around the world—the salinization of irrigated fields, the erosion of topsoil, the conversion of prime farmland into residential areas, and all the other things that environmentalists had been warning about for years. It's possible that we'll still turn production around and start it rocketing again. Charles C. Mann, writing in *Science,* quotes experts who believe that in the future a "gigantic, multi-year, multi-billion-dollar scientific effort, a kind of agricultural 'person-on-the-moon project'" might do the trick. The next great hope of the optimists is genetic engineering, and scientists have indeed managed to induce resistance to pests and disease in some plants. To get more yield, though, a cornstalk must be made to put out another ear, and conventional breeding may have exhausted the possibilities. There's a sense that we're running into walls.

We won't start producing *less* food. Wheat is not like oil, whose flow from the spigot will simply slow to a trickle one day. But we may be getting to the point where gains will be small and hard to come by. The spectacular increases may be behind us. One researcher told Mann, "Producing higher yields will no longer be like unveiling a new model of a car. We won't be pulling off the sheet and there it is, a two-fold yield increase." Instead the process will be "incremental, torturous, and slow." And there are five billion more of us to come.

So far we're still fed; gas is cheap at the pump; the supermarket grows ever larger. We've been warned again and again about approaching limits, and we've never quite reached them. So maybe—how tempting to believe it!—they don't really exist. For every Paul Ehrlich there's a man like Lawrence Summers, the former World Bank chief economist and current deputy secretary of the Treasury, who writes, "There are no ... limits to carrying capacity of the Earth that are likely to bind at any time in the foreseeable future." And we are talking about the future—nothing can be *proved*.

But we can calculate risks, figure the odds that each side may be right. Joel Cohen made the most thorough attempt to do so in *How Many People Can the Earth Support?* Cohen collected and examined every estimate of carrying capacity made in recent decades, from that of a Harvard oceanographer who thought in 1976 that we might have food enough for 40 billion people to that of a Brown University researcher who calculated in 1991 that we might be able to sustain 5.9 billion (our present population), but only if we were principally vegetarians. One study proposed that if photosynthesis was the limiting factor, the earth might support a trillion people; an Australian economist proved, in calculations a decade apart, that we could manage populations of 28 billion and 157 billion. None of the studies is wise enough to examine every variable, to reach by itself the "right" number. When Cohen compared the dozens of studies, however, he uncovered something pretty interesting: the median low value for the planet's carrying capacity was 7.7 billion people, and the median high value was 12 billion. That, of course, is just the range that the UN predicts we will inhabit by the middle of the next century. Cohen wrote,

The human population of the Earth now travels in the zone where a substantial fraction of scholars have estimated upper limits on human population size.... The possibility must be considered seriously that the number of people on the Earth has reached, or will reach within half a century, the maximum number the Earth can support in modes of life that we and our children and their children will choose to want.

EARTH2

Throughout the 10,000 years of recorded human history the planet—the physical planet—has been a stable place. In every single year of those 10,000 there have been earthquakes, volcanoes, hurricanes, cyclones, typhoons, floods, forest fires, sandstorms, hailstorms, plagues, crop failures, heat waves, cold spells, blizzards, and droughts. But these have never shaken the basic predictability of the planet as a whole. Some of the earth's land areas—the Mediterranean rim, for instance—have been deforested beyond recovery, but so far these shifts have always been local.

Among other things, this stability has made possible the insurance industry—has underwritten the underwriters. Insurers can analyze the risk in any venture because they know the ground rules. If you want to build a house on the coast of Florida, they can calculate with reasonable accuracy the chance that it will be hit by a hurricane and the speed of the winds circling that hurricane's eye. If they couldn't, they would have no way to set your premium—they'd just be gambling. They're always gambling a little, of course: they don't know if that hurricane is coming next year or next century. But the earth's physical stability is the house edge in this casino. As Julian Simon pointed out, "A prediction based on past data can be sound if it is sensible to assume that the past and the future belong to the same statistical universe."

So what does it mean that alone among the earth's great pools of money and power, insurance companies are beginning to take the idea of global climate change quite seriously? What does it mean that the payout for weather-related damage climbed from $16 billion during the entire 1980s to $48 billion in the years 1990–1994? What does it mean that top European insurance executives have begun consulting with Green-peace about global warming? What does it mean that the insurance giant Swiss Re, which paid out $291.5 million in the wake of Hurricane Andrew, ran an ad in the *Financial Times* showing its corporate logo bent sideways by a storm?

These things mean, I think, that the possibility that we live on a new earth cannot be discounted entirely as a fever dream. Above, I showed attempts to calculate carrying capacity for the world as we have always known it, the world we were born into. But what if, all of a sudden, we live on some other planet? On Earth2?

In 1955 Princeton University held an international symposium on "Man's Role in Changing the Face of the Earth." By this time anthropogenic carbon, sulfur, and nitrogen were pouring into the atmosphere, deforestation was already widespread, and the population was nearing three billion. Still, by comparison with the present, we remained a puny race. Cars were as yet novelties in many places. Tropical forests were still intact, as were much of the ancient woods of the West Coast, Canada, and Siberia. The world's economy was a quarter its present size. By most calculations we have used more natural resources since 1955 than in all of human history to that time.

Another symposium was organized in 1987 by Clark University, in Massachusetts. This time even the title made clear what was happening—not "Man and Nature," not "Man's Role in Changing the Face of the Earth," but "The Earth as Transformed by Human Actions." Attendees were no longer talking about local changes or what would take place in the future. "In our judgment," they said, "the biosphere has accumulated, or is on its way to accumulating, such a magnitude and variety of changes that it may be said to have been transformed."

Many of these changes come from a direction that Malthus didn't consider. He and most of his successors were transfixed by *sources*—by figuring out whether and how we could find enough trees or corn or oil. We're good at finding more stuff; as the price rises, we look harder. The lights never did go out, despite many predictions to the contrary on the first Earth Day. We found more oil, and we still have lots and lots of coal. Meanwhile, we're driving big cars again, and why not? As of this writing, the price of gas has dropped below a dollar a gallon across much of the nation. Who can believe in limits while driving a Suburban? But perhaps, like an audience watching a magician wave his wand, we've been distracted from the real story.

That real story was told in the most recent attempt to calculate our size—a special section in *Science* published last summer. The authors spoke bluntly in the lead article. Forget man "transforming" nature—we live, they concluded, on "a human-dominated planet," where "no ecosystem on Earth's surface is free of pervasive human influence." It's not that we're running out of stuff. What we're running out of is what the scientists call "sinks"—places to put the by-products of our large appetites. Not garbage dumps (we could go on using Pampers till the end of time and still have empty space left to toss them away) but the atmospheric equivalent of garbage dumps.

It wasn't hard to figure out that there were limits on how much coal smoke we could pour into the air of a single city. It took a while longer to figure out that building ever higher smokestacks merely lofted the haze farther afield, raining down acid on whatever mountain range lay to the east. Even that, however, we are slowly fixing, with scrubbers and different mixtures of fuel. We can't so easily repair the new kinds of pollution. These do not come from something going wrong—some engine without a catalytic converter, some waste-water pipe without a filter, some smokestack without a scrubber. New kinds of pollution come instead from things going as they're supposed to go—but at such a high volume that they overwhelm the planet. They come from normal human life—but there are so many of us living those normal lives that something abnormal is happening. And that something is so different from the old forms of pollution that it confuses the issue even to use the word.

Consider nitrogen, for instance. Almost 80 percent of the atmosphere is nitrogen gas. But before plants can absorb it, it must become "fixed"—bonded with carbon, hydrogen, or oxygen. Nature does this trick with certain kinds of algae and soil bacteria, and with lightning. Before human beings began to alter the nitrogen cycle, these mechanisms provided 90–150 million metric tons of nitrogen a year. Now human activity adds 130–150 million more tons. Nitrogen isn't pollution—it's essential. And we are using more of it all the time. Half the industrial nitrogen fertilizer used in human history has been applied since 1984. As a result, coastal waters and estuaries bloom with toxic algae while oxygen concentrations dwindle, killing fish; as a result, nitrous oxide traps solar heat. And once the gas is in the air, it stays there for a century or more.

Or consider methane, which comes out of the back of a cow or the top of a termite mound or the bottom of a rice paddy. As a result of our determination to raise more cattle, cut down more tropical forest (thereby causing termite populations to explode), and grow more rice, methane concentrations in the atmosphere are more than twice as high as they have been for most of the past 160,000 years. And methane traps heat—very efficiently.

Or consider carbon dioxide. In fact, concentrate on carbon dioxide. If we had to pick one problem to obsess about over the next fifty years, we'd do well to make it CO_2—which is not pollution either. Carbon *monoxide* is pollution: it kills you if you breathe enough of it. But carbon *dioxide*, carbon with two oxygen atoms, can't do a blessed thing to you. If you're reading this indoors, you're breathing more CO_2 than you'll ever get outside. For generations, in fact, engineers said that an engine burned clean if it produced only water vapor and carbon dioxide.

Here's the catch: that engine produces a *lot* of CO_2. A gallon of gas weighs about eight pounds.

When it's burned in a car, about five and a half pounds of carbon, in the form of carbon dioxide, come spewing out the back. It doesn't matter if the car is a 1958 Chevy or a 1998 Saab. And no filter can reduce that flow—it's an inevitable by-product of fossil-fuel combustion, which is why CO_2 has been piling up in the atmosphere ever since the Industrial Revolution. Before we started burning oil and coal and gas, the atmosphere contained about 280 parts CO_2 per million. Now the figure is about 360. Unless we do everything we can think of to eliminate fossil fuels from our diet, the air will test out at more than 500 parts per million fifty or sixty years from now, whether it's sampled in the South Bronx or at the South Pole.

This matters because, as we all know by now, the molecular structure of this clean, natural, common element that we are adding to every cubic foot of the atmosphere surrounding us traps heat that would otherwise radiate back out to space. Far more than even methane and nitrous oxide, CO_2 causes global warming—the greenhouse effect—and climate change. Far more than any other single factor, it is turning the earth we were born on into a new planet.

Remember, this is not pollution as we have known it. In the spring of last year the Environmental Protection Agency issued its "Ten-Year Air Quality and Emissions Trends" report. Carbon monoxide was down by 37 percent since 1986, lead was down by 78 percent, and particulate matter had dropped by nearly a quarter. If you lived in the San Fernando Valley, you saw the mountains more often than you had a decade before. The air was *cleaner,* but it was also *different*—richer with CO_2. And its new composition may change almost everything.

Ten years ago I wrote a book called *The End of Nature,* which was the first volume for a general audience about carbon dioxide and climate change, an early attempt to show that human beings now dominate the earth. Even then global warming was only a hypothesis—strong and gaining credibility all the time, but a hypothesis nonetheless. By the late 1990s it has become a fact. For ten years, with heavy funding from governments around the world, scientists launched satellites, monitored weather balloons, and studied clouds. Their work culminated in a long-awaited report from the UN's Intergovernmental Panel on Climate Change, released in the fall of 1995. The panel's 2,000 scientists, from every corner of the globe, summed up their findings in this dry but historic bit of understatement: "The balance of evidence suggests that there is a discernible human influence on global climate." That is to say, we are heating up the planet—substantially. If we don't reduce emissions of carbon dioxide and other gases, the panel warned, temperatures will probably rise 3.6° Fahrenheit by 2100, and perhaps as much as 6.3°.

You may think you've already heard a lot about global warming. But most of our sense of the problem is behind the curve. Here's the current news: the changes are already well under way. When politicians and businessmen talk about "future risks," their rhetoric is outdated. This is not a problem for the distant future, or even for the near future. The planet has already heated up by a degree or more. We are perhaps a quarter of the way into the greenhouse era, and the effects are already being felt. From a new heaven, filled with nitrogen, methane, and carbon, a new earth is being born. If some alien astronomer is watching us, she's doubtless puzzled. This is the most obvious effect of our numbers and our appetites, and the key to understanding why the size of our population suddenly poses such a risk.

STORMY AND WARM

What does this new world feel like? For one thing, it's stormier than the old one. Data analyzed last year by Thomas Karl, of the National Oceanic and Atmospheric Administration, showed that total winter precipitation in the United States had increased by 10 percent since 1900 and that "extreme precipitation events"—rainstorms that dumped more than two inches of water in twenty-four hours and blizzards—had increased by 20 percent. That's because warmer air holds more water vapor than the colder atmosphere of the old earth; more water evaporates from the ocean,

meaning more clouds, more rain, more snow. Engineers designing storm sewers, bridges, and culverts used to plan for what they called the "hundred-year storm." That is, they built to withstand the worst flooding or wind that history led them to expect in the course of a century. Since that history no longer applies, Karl says, "there isn't really a hundred-year event anymore ... we seem to be getting these storms of the century every couple of years." When Grand Forks, North Dakota, disappeared beneath the Red River in the spring of last year, some meteorologists referred to it as "a 500-year flood"—meaning, essentially, that all bets are off. Meaning that these aren't acts of God. "If you look out your window, part of what you see in terms of the weather is produced by ourselves," Karl says. "If you look out the window fifty years from now, we're going to be responsible for more of it."

Twenty percent more bad storms, 10 percent more winter precipitation—these are enormous numbers. It's like opening the newspaper to read that the average American is smarter by 30 IQ points. And the same data showed increases in drought, too. With more water in the atmosphere, there's less in the soil, according to Kevin Trenberth, of the National Center for Atmospheric Research. Those parts of the continent that are normally dry—the eastern sides of mountains, the plains and deserts—are even drier, as the higher average temperatures evaporate more of what rain does fall. "You get wilting plants and eventually drought faster than you would otherwise," Trenberth says. And when the rain does come, it's often so intense that much of it runs off before it can soak into the soil.

So—wetter and drier. *Different.*

In 1958 Charles Keeling, of the Scripps Institution of Oceanography, set up the world's single most significant scientific instrument in a small hut on the slope of Hawaii's Mauna Loa volcano. Forty years later it continues without fail to track the amount of carbon dioxide in the atmosphere. The graphs that it produces show that this most important greenhouse gas has steadily increased for forty years. That's the main news.

It has also shown something else of interest in recent years—a sign that this new atmosphere is changing the planet. Every year CO_2 levels dip in the spring, when plants across the Northern Hemisphere begin to grow, soaking up carbon dioxide. And every year in the fall decaying plants and soils release CO_2 back into the atmosphere. So along with the steady upward trend, there's an annual seesaw, an oscillation that is suddenly growing more pronounced. The size of that yearly tooth on the graph is 20 percent greater than it was in the early 1960s, as Keeling reported in the journal *Nature,* in July of 1996. Or, in the words of Rhys Roth, writing in a newsletter of the Atmosphere Alliance, the earth is "breathing deeper." More vegetation must be growing, stimulated by higher temperatures. And the earth is breathing earlier, too. Spring is starting about a week earlier in the 1990s than it was in the 1970s, Keeling said....

[It's] not clear that the grain belt will have the water it needs as the climate warms. In 1988, a summer of record heat across the rain belt, harvests plummeted, because the very heat that produces more storms also causes extra evaporation. What *is* clear is that fundamental shifts are under way in the operation of the planet. And we are very early yet in the greenhouse era.

The changes are basic. The freezing level in the atmosphere—the height at which the air temperature reaches 32°F—has been gaining altitude since 1970 at the rate of nearly fifteen feet a year. Not surprisingly, tropical and subtropical glaciers are melting at what a team of Ohio State researchers termed "striking" rates. Speaking at a press conference last spring, Ellen Mosley-Thompson, a member of the Ohio State team, was asked if she was sure of her results. She replied, "I don't know quite what to say. I've presented the evidence. I gave you the example of the Quelccaya ice cap. It just comes back to the compilation of what's happening at high elevations: the Lewis glacier on Mount Kenya has lost forty percent of its mass; in the Ruwenzori range all the glaciers are in massive retreat. Everything, virtually, in Patagonia, except for just a few glaciers, is retreating.... We've seen ... that plants are moving up the

mountains.... I frankly don't know what additional evidence you need."

As the glaciers retreat, a crucial source of fresh water in many tropical countries disappears. These areas are "already water-stressed," Mosley-Thompson told the Association of American Geographers last year. Now they may be really desperate.

As with the tropics, so with the poles. According to every computer model, in fact, the polar effects are even more pronounced, because the Arctic and the Antarctic will warm much faster than the Equator as carbon dioxide builds up. Scientists manning a research station at Toolik Lake, Alaska, 170 miles north of the Arctic Circle, have watched average summer temperatures rise by about seven degrees in the past two decades. "Those who remember wearing down-lined summer parkas in the 1970s—before the term 'global warming' existed—have peeled down to T-shirts in recent summers," according to the reporter Wendy Hower, writing in the *Fairbanks Daily News-Miner*. It rained briefly at the American base in McMurdo Sound, in Antarctica, during the southern summer of 1997—as strange as if it had snowed in Saudi Arabia. None of this necessarily means that the ice caps will soon slide into the sea, turning Tennessee into beachfront. It simply demonstrates a radical instability in places that have been stable for many thousands of years. One researcher watched as emperor penguins tried to cope with the early breakup of ice: their chicks had to jump into the water two weeks ahead of schedule, probably guaranteeing an early death. They (like us) evolved on the old earth....

The effects of that warming can be found in the largest phenomena. The oceans that cover most of the planet's surface are clearly rising, both because of melting glaciers and because water expands as it warms. As a result, low-lying Pacific islands already report surges of water washing across the atolls. "It's nice weather and all of a sudden water is pouring into your living room," one Marshall Islands resident told a newspaper reporter. "It's very clear that something is happening in the Pacific, and these islands are feeling it." Global warming will be like a much more powerful version of El Niño that covers the entire globe and lasts forever, or at least until the next big asteroid strikes.

If you want to scare yourself with guesses about what might happen in the near future, there's no shortage of possibilities. Scientists have already observed large-scale shifts in the duration of the El Niño ocean warming, for instance. The Arctic tundra has warmed so much that in some places it now gives off more carbon dioxide than it absorbs—a switch that could trigger a potent feedback loop, making warming ever worse. And researchers studying glacial cores from the Greenland Ice Sheet recently concluded that local climate shifts have occurred with incredible rapidity in the past—188 in one three-year stretch. Other scientists worry that such a shift might be enough to flood the oceans with fresh water and reroute or shut off currents like the Gulf Stream and the North Atlantic, which keep Europe far warmer than it would otherwise be…. In the words of Wallace Broecker, of Columbia University, a pioneer in the field, "Climate is an angry beast, and we are poking it with sticks." But we don't need worst-case scenarios: best-case scenarios make the point. The population of the earth is going to nearly double one more time. That will bring it to a level that even the reliable old earth we were born on would be hard-pressed to support. Just at the moment when we need everything to be working as smoothly as possible, we find ourselves inhabiting a new planet, whose carrying capacity we cannot conceivably estimate. We have no idea how much wheat this planet can grow. We don't know what its politics will be like: not if there are going to be heat waves like the one that killed more than 700 Chicagoans in 1995; not if rising sea levels and other effects of climate change create tens of millions of environmental refugees; not if a 1.58 jump in India's temperature could reduce the country's wheat crop by 10 percent or divert its monsoons….

We have gotten very large and very powerful, and for the foreseeable future we're stuck with the results. The glaciers won't grow back again anytime soon; the oceans won't drop. We've already done deep and systemic damage. To use a human analogy, we've already said the angry and unforgivable words that will haunt our marriage till its end. And yet we can't simply walk out the door. There's no place to go. We have to salvage what we can of our relationship with the earth, to keep things from getting any worse than they have to be.

If we can bring our various emissions quickly and sharply under control, we *can* limit the damage, reduce dramatically the chance of horrible surprises, preserve more of the biology we were born into. But do not underestimate the task. The UN's Intergovernmental Panel on Climate Change projects that an immediate 60 percent reduction in fossil-fuel use is necessary just to stabilize climate at the current level of disruption. Nature may still meet us halfway, but halfway is a long way from where we are now. What's more, we can't delay. If we wait a few decades to get started, we may as well not even begin. It's not like poverty, a concern that's always there for civilizations to address. This is a timed test, like the SAT: two or three decades, and we lay our pencils down. It's *the* test for our generations, and population is a part of the answer….

STUDY QUESTIONS

1. Explain why McKibben thinks we live in a special moment of history. Do you find his arguments cogent and convincing?

2. Doomsdayers have been wrong before in their prediction that the sky is falling. How does McKibben respond to this charge that he and others, like Paul Ehrlich, are unduly pessimistic?

3. What evidence does McKibben bring to bear on the global warming thesis—that humans are responsible for the greenhouse effect, which is having dramatic effects on Earth's climate? How serious is the greenhouse effect?

28

The Tragedy of the Commons

GARRETT HARDIN

Garrett Hardin argues that some social problems have no technical—that is, scientific or technological—solution, but must be addressed by moral and political means. Exponential population growth is one such problem. Hardin calls our attention to a study by the British mathematician William Forster Lloyd (1794–1852), which demonstrates that in nonregulated areas (the "commons") individual rationality and self-interest leads to disaster. Hardin applies Lloyd's study to human population growth and argues that voluntary restriction of population by families is not adequate to deal with this problem, since many will not respond to voluntary procreation limitations. We must have "mutual coercion, mutually agreed upon by the majority of the people affected."

Garrett Hardin (1915–2003) was emeritus professor at the University of California, Santa Barbara, and the author of several works in biology and ethics, including The Limits of Altruism *and* Exploring New Ethics for Survival.

At the end of a thoughtful article on the future of nuclear war, Wiesner and York[1] concluded that: "Both sides in the arms race are … confronted by the dilemma of steadily increasing military power and steadily decreasing national security. *It is our considered professional judgment that this dilemma has no technical solution.* If the great powers continue to look for solutions in the area of science and technology only, the result will be to worsen the situation."

I would like to focus your attention not on the subject of the article (national security in a nuclear world) but on the kind of conclusion they reached, namely that there is no technical solution to the problem. An implicit and almost universal assumption of discussions published in professional and semi-popular scientific journals is that the problem under discussion has a technical solution. A technical solution may be defined as one that requires a change only in the techniques of the natural sciences, demanding little or nothing in the way of change in human values or ideas of morality.

In our day (though not in earlier times) technical solutions are always welcome. Because of previous failures in prophecy, it takes courage to assert that a desired technical solution is not possible. Wiesner and York exhibited this courage; publishing in a science journal, they insisted that the solution to the problem was not to be found in the natural sciences. They cautiously qualified their statement with the phrase, "It is our considered professional judgment…." Whether they were right or not is not the concern of the present article. Rather, the concern here is with the important concept of a class of human problems which can be called "no technical solution problems," and, more specifically, with the identification and discussion of one of these.

Reprinted with permission from *Science*, Vol. 162: 1243–48 (December 1986). Copyright © 1986 by the American Association for the Advancement of Science.

It is easy to show that the class is not a null class. Recall the game of tick-tack-toe. Consider the problem, "How can I win the game of tick-tack-toe?" It is well known that I cannot, if I assume (in keeping with the conventions of game theory) that my opponent understands the game perfectly. Put another way, there is no "technical solution" to the problem. I can win only by giving a radical meaning to the word "win." I can hit my opponent over the head; or I can drug him; or I can falsify the records. Every way in which I "win" involves, in some sense, an abandonment of the game, as we intuitively understand it. (I can also, of course, openly abandon the game—refuse to play it. This is what most adults do.)

The class of "No technical solution problems" has members. My thesis is that the "population problem," as conventionally conceived, is a member of this class. How it is conventionally conceived needs some comment. It is fair to say that most people who anguish over the population problem are trying to find a way to avoid the evils of overpopulation without relinquishing any of the privileges they now enjoy. They think that farming the seas or developing new strains of wheat will solve the problem—technologically. I try to show here that the solution they seek cannot be found. The population problem cannot be solved in a technical way, any more than can the problem of winning the game of tick-tack-toe.

WHAT SHALL WE MAXIMIZE?

Population, as Malthus said, naturally tends to grow "geometrically," or, as we would now say, exponentially. In a finite world this means that the per capita share of the world's goods must steadily decrease. Is ours a finite world?

A fair defense can be put forward for the view that the world is infinite; or that we do not know that it is not. But, in terms of the practical problems that we must face in the next few generations with the foreseeable technology, it is clear that we will greatly increase human misery if we do not, during the immediate future, assume that the world available to the terrestrial human population is finite. "Space" is no escape.[2]

A finite world can support only a finite population; therefore, population growth must eventually equal zero. (The case of perpetual wide fluctuations above and below zero is a trivial variant that need not be discussed.) When this condition is met, what will be the situation of mankind? Specifically, can Bentham's goal of "the greatest good for the greatest number" be realized?

No—for two reasons, each sufficient by itself. The first is a theoretical one. It is not mathematically possible to maximize for two (or more) variables at the same time. This was clearly stated by von Neumann and Morgenstern,[3] but the principle is implicit in the theory of partial differential equations, dating back at least to D'Alembert (1717–1783).

The second reason springs directly from biological facts. To live, any organism must have a source of energy (for example, food). This energy is utilized for two purposes: mere maintenance and work. For man, maintenance of life requires about 1600 kilocalories a day ("maintenance calories"). Anything that he does over and above merely staying alive will be defined as work, and is supported by "work calories" which he takes in. Work calories are used not only for what we call work in common speech; they are also required for all forms of enjoyment, from swimming and automobile racing to playing music and writing poetry. If our goal is to maximize population it is obvious what we must do: We must make the work calories per person approach as close to zero as possible. No gourmet meals, no vacations, no sports, no music, no literature, no art…. I think that everyone will grant, without argument or proof, that maximizing population does not maximize goods. Bentham's goal is impossible.

In reaching this conclusion I have made the usual assumption that it is the acquisition of energy that is the problem. The appearance of atomic energy has led some to question this assumption. However, given an infinite source of energy, population growth still produces an inescapable problem. The problem of the acquisition of energy is replaced by the problem of its dissipation, as J. H. Fremlin has so wittily shown.[4] The arithmetic signs in the analysis are, as it were, reversed; but Bentham's goal is still unobtainable.

The optimum population is, then, less than the maximum. The difficulty of defining the optimum is enormous; so far as I know, no one has seriously tackled this problem. Reaching an acceptable and stable solution will surely require more than one generation of hard analytical work—and much persuasion.

We want the maximum good per person; but what is good? To one person it is wilderness, to another it is ski lodges for thousands. To one it is estuaries to nourish ducks for hunters to shoot; to another it is factory land. Comparing one good with another is, we usually say, impossible because goods are incommensurable. Incommensurables cannot be compared.

Theoretically this may be true; but in real life incommensurables *are* commensurable. Only a criterion of judgment and a system of weighting are needed. In nature the criterion is survival. Is it better for a species to be small and hideable, or large and powerful? Natural selection commensurates the incommensurables. The compromise achieved depends on a natural weighting of the values of the variables.

Man must imitate this process. There is no doubt that in fact he already does, but unconsciously. It is when the hidden decisions are made explicit that the arguments begin. The problem for the years ahead is to work out an acceptable theory of weighting. Synergistic effects, non-linear variation, and difficulties in discounting the future make the intellectual problem difficult, but not (in principle) insoluble.

Has any cultural group solved this practical problem at the present time, even on an intuitive level? One simple fact proves that none has: there is no prosperous population in the world today that has, and has had for some time, a growth rate of zero. Any people that has intuitively identified its optimum point will soon reach it, after which its growth rate becomes and remains zero.

Of course, a positive growth rate might be taken as evidence that a population is below its optimum. However, by any reasonable standards, the most rapidly growing populations on earth today are (in general) the most miserable. This association (which need not be invariable) casts doubt on the optimistic assumption that the positive growth rate of a population is evidence that it has yet to reach its optimum.

We can make little progress in working toward optimum population size until we explicitly exorcize the spirit of Adam Smith in the field of practical demography. In economic affairs, *The Wealth of Nations* (1776) popularized the "invisible hand," the idea that an individual who "intends only his own gain," is, as it were, "led by an invisible hand to promote … the public interest."[5] Adam Smith did not assert that this was invariably true, and perhaps neither did any of his followers. But he contributed to a dominant tendency of thought that has ever since interfered with positive action based on rational analysis, namely, the tendency to assume that decisions reached individually will, in fact, be the best decisions for an entire society. If this assumption is correct, it justifies the continuance of our present policy of laissez-faire in reproduction. If it is correct we can assume that men will control their individual fecundity so as to produce the optimum population. If the assumption is not correct, we need to reexamine our individual freedoms to see which ones are defensible.

TRAGEDY OF FREEDOM
IN A COMMONS

The rebuttal to the invisible hand in population control is to be found in a scenario first sketched in a little-known pamphlet[6] in 1833 by a mathematical amateur named William Forster Lloyd (1794–1852). We may well call it "the tragedy of the commons," using the word "tragedy" as the philosopher Whitehead used it[7]: "The essence of dramatic tragedy is not unhappiness. It resides in the solemnity of the remorseless working of things." He then goes on to say, "This inevitableness of destiny can only be illustrated in terms of human life by incidents which in fact involve unhappiness. For it is only by them that the futility of escape can be made evident in the drama."

The tragedy of the commons develops in this way. Picture a pasture open to all. It is to be expected that each herdsman will try to keep as many cattle as possible on the commons. Such an arrangement may work reasonably satisfactorily for centuries because tribal wars, poaching, and disease keep the numbers of both man and beast well below the carrying capacity of the land. Finally, however, comes the day of reckoning, that is, the day when the long-desired goal of social stability becomes a reality. At this point, the inherent logic of the commons remorselessly generates tragedy.

As a rational being, each herdsman seeks to maximize his gain. Explicitly or implicitly, more or less consciously, he asks, "What is the utility *to me* of adding one more animal to my herd?" This utility has one negative and one positive component.

1. The positive component is a function of the increment of one animal. Since the herdsman receives all the proceeds from the sale of the additional animal, the positive utility is nearly +1.

2. The negative component is a function of the additional overgrazing created by one or more animal. Since, however, the effects of overgrazing are shared by all the herdsmen, the negative utility for any particular decision-making herdsman is only a fraction of −1.

Adding together the component partial utilities, the rational herdsman concludes that the only sensible course for him to pursue is to add another animal to his herd. And another; and another.... But this is the conclusion reached by each and every rational herdsman sharing a commons. Therein is the tragedy. Each man is locked into a system that compels him to increase his herd without limit—in a world that is limited. Ruin is the destination toward which all men rush, each pursuing his own best interest in a society that believes in the freedom of the commons. Freedom in a commons brings ruin to all.

Some would say that this is a platitude. Would that it were! In a sense, it was learned thousands of years ago, but natural selection favors the forces of psychological denial.[8] The individual benefits as an individual from his ability to deny the truth even though society as a whole, of which he is a part, suffers. Education can counteract the natural tendency to do the wrong thing, but the inexorable success of generations requires that the basis for this knowledge be constantly refreshed.

A simple incident that occurred a few years ago in Leominster, Massachusetts, shows how perishable the knowledge is. During the Christmas shopping season the parking meters downtown were covered with plastic bags that bore tags reading: "Do not open until after Christmas. Free parking courtesy of the mayor and city council." In other words, facing the prospect of an increased demand for already scarce space, the city fathers reinstituted the system of the commons. (Cynically, we suspect that they gained more votes than they lost by this retrogressive act.)

In an approximate way, the logic of the commons has been understood for a long time, perhaps since the discovery of agriculture or the invention of private property in real estate. But it is understood mostly only in special cases which are not sufficiently generalized. Even at this late date, cattlemen leasing national land on the western ranges demonstrate no more than an ambivalent understanding, in constantly pressuring federal authorities to increase the head count to the point where overgrazing produces erosion and weed-dominance. Likewise, the oceans of the world continue to suffer from the survival of the philosophy of the commons. Maritime nations still respond automatically to the shibboleth of the "freedom of the seas." Professing to believe in the "inexhaustible resources of the oceans," they bring species after species of fish and whales closer to extinction.[9]

The National Parks present another instance of the working out of the tragedy of the commons. At present they are open to all, without limit. The parks themselves are limited in extent—there is only one Yosemite Valley—whereas population seems to grow without limit. The values that visitors seek in the parks are steadily eroded. Plainly, we must soon cease to treat the parks as commons or they will be of no value to anyone.

What shall we do? We have several options. We might sell them off as private property. We might keep them as public property, but allocate the right to enter them. The allocation might be on the basis of wealth, by the use of an auction system. It might be on the basis of merit, as defined by some agreed-upon standards. It might be by lottery. Or it might be on a first-come, first-served basis, administered to long queues. These, I think, are all the reasonable possibilities. They are all objectionable. But we must choose—or acquiesce in the destruction of the commons that we call our National Parks.

POLLUTION ?

In a reverse way, the tragedy of the commons reappears in problems of pollution. Here it is not a question of taking something out of the commons, but of putting something in—sewage, or chemical, radioactive, and heat wastes into water; noxious and dangerous fumes into the air, and distracting and unpleasant advertising signs into the line of sight. The calculations of utility are much the same as before. The rational man finds that his share of the cost of the wastes he discharges into the commons is less than the cost of purifying his wastes before releasing them. Since this is true for everyone, we are locked into a system of "fouling our own nest," so long as we behave only as independent, rational, free-enterprisers.

The tragedy of the commons as a food basket is averted by private property, or something formally like it. But the air and waters surrounding us cannot readily be fenced, and so the tragedy of the commons as a cesspool must be prevented by different means, by coercive laws or taxing devices that make it cheaper for the polluter to treat his pollutants than to discharge them untreated. We have not progressed as far with the solution of this problem as we have with the first. Indeed, our particular concept of private property, which deters us from exhausting the positive resources of the earth, favors

pollution. The owner of a factory on the bank of a stream—whose property extends to the middle of the stream—often has difficulty seeing why it is not his natural right to muddy the waters flowing past his door. The law, always behind the times, requires elaborate stitching and fitting to adapt it to this newly perceived aspect of the commons.

The pollution problem is a consequence of population. It did not much matter how a lonely American frontiersman disposed of his waste. "Flowing water purifies itself every 10 miles," my grandfather used to say, and the myth was near enough to the truth when he was a boy, for there were not too many people. But as population became denser, the natural chemical and biological recycling processes became overloaded, calling for a redefinition of property rights.

HOW TO LEGISLATE TEMPERANCE?

Analysis of the pollution problem as a function of population density uncovers a not generally recognized principle of morality, namely: *the morality of an act is a function of the state of the system at the time it is performed*.[10] Using the commons as a cesspool does not harm the general public under frontier conditions, because there is no public; the same behavior in a metropolis is unbearable. A hundred and fifty years ago a plainsman could kill an American bison, cut out only the tongue for his dinner, and discard the rest of the animal. He was not in any important sense being wasteful. Today, with only a few thousand bison left, we would be appalled at such behavior.

In passing, it is worth noting that the morality of an act cannot be determined from a photograph. One does not know whether a man killing an elephant or setting fire to the grassland is harming others until one knows the total system in which his act appears. "One picture is worth a thousand words" said an ancient Chinese; but it may take 10,000 words to validate it. It is as tempting to ecologists as it is to reformers in general to try to persuade others by way of the photographic shortcut.

But the essence of an argument cannot be photographed: it must be presented rationally—in words.

That morality is system-sensitive escaped the attention of most codifiers of ethics in the past. "Thou shalt not ..." is the form of traditional ethical directives which make no allowance for particular circumstances. The laws of our society follow the pattern of ancient ethics, and therefore are poorly suited to governing a complex, crowded, changeable world. Our epicyclic solution is to augment statutory law with administrative law. Since it is practically impossible to spell out all the conditions under which it is safe to burn trash in the backyard or to run an automobile without smog-control, by law we delegate the details to bureaus. The result is administrative law, which is rightly feared for an ancient reason—*Quis custodiet ipsos custodes?*—"Who shall watch the watchers themselves?" John Adams said that we must have "a government of laws and not men." Bureau administrators, trying to evaluate the morality of acts in the total system, are singularly liable to corruption, producing a government by men, not laws.

Prohibition is easy to legislate (though not necessarily to enforce); but how do we legislate temperance? Experience indicates that it can be accomplished best through the mediation of administrative law. We limit possibilities unnecessarily if we suppose that the sentiment of *Quis custodiet* denies us the use of administrative law. We should rather retain the phrase as a perpetual reminder of fearful dangers we cannot avoid. The great challenge facing us now is to invent the corrective feedbacks that are needed to keep custodians honest. We must find ways to legitimate the needed authority of both the custodians and the corrective feedbacks.

FREEDOM TO BREED
IS INTOLERABLE

The tragedy of the commons is involved in population problems in another way. In a world governed solely by the principle of "dog eat dog"—if indeed there ever was such a world—how many children a family had would not be a matter of public concern. Parents who bred too exuberantly would leave fewer descendants, not more, because they would be unable to care adequately for their children. David Lack and others have found that such a negative feedback demonstrably controls the fecundity of birds.[11] But men are not birds, and have not acted like them for millenniums, at least.

If each human family were dependent only on its own resources; *if* the children of improvident parents starved to death; *if,* thus, overbreeding brought its own "punishment" to the germ line— *then* there would be no public interest in controlling the breeding of families. But our society is deeply committed to the welfare state,[12] and hence is confronted with another aspect of the tragedy of the commons.

In a welfare state, how shall we deal with the family, the religion, the race, or the class (or indeed any distinguishable and cohesive group) that adopts overbreeding as a policy to secure its own aggrandizement?[13] To couple the concept of freedom to breed with the belief that everyone born has an equal right to the commons is to lock the world into a tragic course of action.

Unfortunately this is just the course of action that is being pursued by the United Nations. In late 1967, some 30 nations agreed to the following[14]:

> The Universal Declaration of Human Rights describes the family as the natural and fundamental unit of society. It follows that any choice and decision with regard to the size of the family must irrevocably rest with the family itself, and cannot be made by anyone else.

It is painful to have to deny categorically the validity of this right; denying it, one feels as uncomfortable as a resident of Salem, Massachusetts, who denied the reality of witches in the 17th century. At the present time, in liberal quarters, something like a taboo acts to inhibit criticism of the United Nations. There is a feeling that the United Nations is "our last and best hope," that we shouldn't find fault with it; we shouldn't play into the hands of the archconservatives. However, let us not forget what Robert Louis Stevenson said: "The truth that is suppressed by friends is the readiest weapon of the enemy." If we love the truth we must openly deny the validity of the Universal Declaration of Human Rights, even though it is promoted by the United Nations. We should also join with Kingsley Davis[15] in attempting to get Planned Parenthood–World Population to see the error of its ways in embracing the same tragic ideal.

CONSCIENCE IS SELF-ELIMINATING

It is a mistake to think that we can control the breeding of mankind in the long run by an appeal to conscience. Charles Galton Darwin made this point when he spoke on the centennial of the publication of his grandfather's great book. The argument is straightforward and Darwinian.

People vary. Confronted with appeals to limit breeding, some people will undoubtedly respond to the plea more than others. Those who have more children will produce a larger fraction of the next generation than those with more susceptible consciences. The difference will be accentuated, generation by generation.

In C. G. Darwin's words: "It may well be that it would take hundreds of generations for the progenitive instinct to develop in this way, but if it should do so, nature would have taken her revenge, and the variety *Homo contracipiens* would become extinct and would be replaced by the variety *Homo progenitivus*."[16]

The argument assumes that conscience or the desire for children (no matter which) is hereditary—but hereditary only in the most general formal sense. The result will be the same whether the attitude is transmitted through germ cells, or exosomatically, to use A. J. Lotka's term. (If one denies the latter possibility as well as the former, then what's the point of education?) The argument has here been stated in the context of the population problem, but it applies equally well to any instance in which society appeals to an individual exploiting a

commons to restrain himself for the general good—by means of his conscience. To make such an appeal is to set up a selective system that works toward the elimination of conscience from the race.

PATHOGENIC EFFECTS OF CONSCIENCE

The long-term disadvantage of an appeal to conscience should be enough to condemn it; it has serious short-term disadvantages as well. If we ask a man who is exploiting a commons to desist "in the name of conscience," what are we saying to him? What does he hear?—not only at the moment but also in the wee small hours of the night when, half asleep, he remembers not merely the words we used but also the nonverbal communication cues we gave him unawares? Sooner or later, consciously or subconsciously, he senses that he has received two communications and that they are contradictory: (i) (intended communication) "If you don't do as we ask, we will openly condemn you for not acting like a responsible citizen"; (ii) (the unintended communication) "If you *do* behave as we ask, we will secretly condemn you for a simpleton who can be shamed into standing aside while the rest of us exploit the commons."

Every man then is caught in what Bateson has called a "double bind." Bateson and his coworkers have made a plausible case for viewing the double bind as an important causative factor in the genesis of schizophrenia.[17] The double bind may not always be so damaging, but it always endangers the mental health of anyone to whom it is applied. "A bad conscience," said Nietzsche, "is a kind of illness."

To conjure up a conscience in others is tempting to anyone who wishes to extend his control beyond the legal limits. Leaders at the highest level succumb to this temptation. Has any President during the past generation failed to call on labor unions to moderate voluntarily their demands for higher wages, or to steel companies to honor voluntary guidelines on prices? I can recall none. The rhetoric used on such occasions is designed to produce feelings of guilt in noncooperators.

For centuries it was assumed without proof that guilt was a valuable, perhaps even indispensable, ingredient of the civilized life. Now, in this post-Freudian world, we doubt it.

Paul Goodman speaks from the modern point of view when he says: "No good has ever come from feeling guilty, neither intelligence, policy, nor compassion. The guilty do not pay attention to the object but only to themselves, and not even to their own interests, which might make sense, but to their anxieties."[18]

One does not have to be a professional psychiatrist to see the consequences of anxiety. We in the Western world are just emerging from a dreadful two-centuries-long Dark Ages of Eros that was sustained partly by prohibition laws, but perhaps more effectively by the anxiety-generating mechanisms of education. Alex Comfort has told the story well in *The Anxiety Makers*[19]; it is not a pretty one.

Since proof is difficult, we may even concede that the results of anxiety may sometimes, from certain points of view, be desirable. The larger question we should ask is whether, as a matter of policy, we should ever encourage the use of a technique the tendency (if not the intention) of which is psychologically pathogenic. We hear much talk these days of responsible parenthood; the coupled words are incorporated into the titles of some organizations devoted to birth control. Some people have proposed massive propaganda campaigns to instill responsibility into the nation's (or the world's) breeders. But what is the meaning of the word responsibility in this context? Is it not merely a synonym for the word conscience? When we use the word responsibility in the absence of substantial sanctions are we not trying to browbeat a free man in a commons into acting against his own interest? Responsibility is a verbal counterfeit for a substantial *quid pro quo*. It is an attempt to get something for nothing.

If the word responsibility is to be used at all, I suggest that it be in the sense Charles Frankel uses it.[20] "Responsibility," says this philosopher, "is the product of definite social arrangements." Notice that Frankel calls for social arrangements—not propaganda.

MUTUAL COERCION MUTUALLY AGREED UPON

The social arrangements that produce responsibility are arrangements that create coercion, of some sort. Consider bank-robbing. The man who takes money from a bank acts as if the bank were a commons. How do we prevent such action? Certainly not by trying to control his behavior solely by a verbal appeal to his sense of responsibility. Rather than rely on propaganda we follow Frankel's lead and insist that a bank is not a commons; we seek the definite social arrangements that will keep it from becoming a commons. That we thereby infringe on the freedom of would-be robbers we neither deny nor regret.

The morality of bank-robbing is particularly easy to understand because we accept complete prohibition of this activity. We are willing to say "Thou shalt not rob banks," without providing for exceptions. But temperance also can be created by coercion. Taxing is a good coercive device. To keep downtown shoppers temperate in their use of parking space we introduce parking meters for short periods, and traffic fines for longer ones. We need not actually forbid a citizen to park as long as he wants to; we need merely make it increasingly expensive for him to do so. Not prohibition, but carefully biased options are what we offer him. A Madison Avenue man might call this persuasion; I prefer the greater candor of the word coercion.

Coercion is a dirty word to most liberals now, but it need not forever be so. As with the four-letter words, its dirtiness can be cleansed away by exposure to light, by saying it over and over without apology or embarrassment. To many, the word coercion implies arbitrary decisions of distant and irresponsible bureaucrats; but this is not a necessary part of its meaning. The only kind of coercion I recommend is mutual coercion, mutually agreed upon by the majority of the people affected.

To say that we mutually agree to coercion is not to say that we are required to enjoy it, or even to pretend we enjoy it. Who enjoys taxes? We all grumble about them. But we accept compulsory taxes because we recognize that voluntary taxes would favor the conscienceless. We institute and (grumblingly) support taxes and other coercive devices to escape the horror of the commons.

An alternative to the commons need not be perfectly just to be preferable. With real estate and other material goods, the alternative we have chosen is the institution of private property coupled with legal inheritance. Is this system perfectly just? As a genetically trained biologist I deny that it is. It seems to me that, if there are to be differences in individual inheritance, legal possession should be perfectly correlated with biological inheritance—that those who are biologically more fit to be the custodians of property and power should legally inherit more. But genetic recombination continually makes a mockery of the doctrine of "like father, like son" implicit in our laws of legal inheritance. An idiot can inherit millions, and a trust fund can keep his estate intact. We must admit that our legal system of private property plus inheritance is unjust—but we put up with it because we are not convinced, at the moment, that anyone has invented a better system. The alternative of the commons is too horrifying to contemplate. Injustice is preferable to total ruin.

It is one of the peculiarities of the warfare between reform and the status quo that it is thoughtlessly governed by a double standard. Whenever a reform measure is proposed it is often defeated when its opponents triumphantly discover a flaw in it. As Kingsley Davis has pointed out,[21] worshippers of the status quo sometimes imply that no reform is possible without unanimous agreement, an implication contrary to historical fact. As nearly as I can make out, automatic rejection of proposed reforms is based on one of two unconscious assumptions: (i) that the status quo is perfect; or (ii) that the choice we face is between reform and no action; if the proposed reform is imperfect, we presumably should take no action at all, while we wait for a perfect proposal.

But we can never do nothing. That which we have done for thousands of years is also action. It also produces evils. Once we are aware that the status quo is action, we can then compare its discoverable advantages and disadvantages with the predicted advantages and disadvantages of the proposed reform, discounting as best we can for our lack of experience. On the basis of such a comparison, we can make a rational decision which will not involve the unworkable assumption that only perfect systems are tolerable.

RECOGNITION OF NECESSITY

Perhaps the simplest summary of this analysis of man's population problems is this: the commons, if justifiable at all, is justifiable only under conditions of low-population density. As the human population has increased, the commons has had to be abandoned in one aspect after another.

First we abandoned the commons in food gathering, enclosing farm land and restricting pastures and hunting and fishing areas. These restrictions are still not complete throughout the world.

Somewhat later we saw that the commons as a place for water disposal would also have to be abandoned. Restrictions on the disposal of domestic sewage are widely accepted in the Western world; we are still struggling to close the commons to pollution by automobiles, factories, insecticide sprayers, fertilizing operations, and atomic energy installations.

In a still more embryonic state is our recognition of the evils of the commons in matters of pleasure. There is almost no restriction on the propagation of sound waves in the public medium. The shopping public is assaulted with mindless music, without its consent. Our government is paying out billions of dollars to create supersonic transport which will disturb 50,000 people for every one person who is whisked from coast to coast 3 hours faster. Advertisers muddy the airwaves of radio and television and pollute the view of travelers. We are a long way from outlawing the commons in matters of pleasure. Is this because our Puritan inheritance makes us view pleasure as something of a sin, and pain (that is, the pollution of advertising) as the sign of virtue?

Every new enclosure of the commons involves the infringement of somebody's personal liberty. Infringements made in the distant past are accepted because no contemporary complains of a loss. It is the newly proposed infringements that we vigorously oppose; cries of "rights" and "freedom" fill the air. But what does "freedom" mean? When men mutually agreed to pass laws against robbing, mankind became more free, not less so. Individuals locked into the logic of the commons are free only to bring on universal ruin; once they see the necessity of mutual coercion, they become free to pursue other goals. I believe it was Hegel who said, "Freedom is the recognition of necessity."

The most important aspect of necessity that we must now recognize is the necessity of abandoning the commons in breeding. No technical solution can rescue us from the misery of overpopulation. Freedom to breed will bring ruin to all. At the moment, to avoid hard decisions many of us are tempted to propagandize for conscience and responsible parenthood. The temptation must be resisted, because an appeal to independently acting consciences selects for the disappearance of all conscience in the long run, and an increase in anxiety in the short.

The only way we can preserve and nurture other and more precious freedoms is by relinquishing the freedom to breed, and that very soon. "Freedom is the recognition of necessity"—and it is the role of education to reveal to all the necessity of abandoning the freedom to breed. Only so, can we put an end to this aspect of the tragedy of the commons.

NOTES

1. J. B. Wiesner and H. F. York, *Sci. Amer.* 211 (No. 44), 27 (1964).

2. G. Hardin, *J. Hered.* 50, 68 (1959); S. von Hoernor, *Science* 137, 18 (1962).

3. J. von Neumann and O. Morgenstern, *Theory of Games and Economic Behavior* (Princeton Univ. Press, Princeton, NJ, 1947), p. 11.

4. J. H. Fremlin, *New Sci.,* No. 415 (1964), p. 285.

5. A. Smith, *The Wealth of Nations* (Modern Library, New York, 1937), p. 423.

6. W. F. Lloyd, *Two Lectures on the Checks to Population* (Oxford Univ. Press, Oxford, England, 1833), reprinted (in part) in *Population, Evolution, and Birth Control,* G. Hardin, Ed. (Freeman, San Francisco, 1964), p. 37.

7. A. N. Whitehead, *Science and the Modern World* (Mentor, New York, 1948), p. 17.

8. G. Hardin, Ed., *Population, Evolution and Birth Control* (Freeman, San Francisco, 1964), p. 56.

9. S. McVay, *Sci. Amer.* 216 (No. 8), 13 (1966).

10. J. Fletcher, *Situation Ethics* (Westminster, Philadelphia, 1966).

11. D. Lack, *The Natural Regulation of Animal Numbers* (Clarendon Press, Oxford, 1954).

12. H. Girvetz, *From Wealth to Welfare* (Stanford Univ. Press, Stanford, Calif., 1950).

13. G. Hardin, *Perspec. Biol. Med.* 6, 366 (1963).

14. U Thant, *Int. Planned Parenthood News,* No. 168 (February 1968), p. 3.

15. K. Davis, *Science,* 158, 730 (1967).

16. S. Tax, Ed., *Evolution After Darwin* (Univ. of Chicago Press, Chicago, 1960), vol. 2, p. 469.

17. G. Bateson, D. D. Jackson, J. Haley, and J. Weakland, *Behav. Sci.* 1, 251 (1956).

18. P. Goodman, *New York Rev. Books* 1968, 10 (8), 22 (23 May 1968).

19. A. Comfort, *The Anxiety Makers* (Nelson, London, 1967).

20. C. Frankel, *The Case for Modern Man* (Harper, New York, 1955), p. 203.

21. J. D. Roslansky, *Genetics and the Future of Man* (Appleton-Century-Crofts, New York, 1966), p. 177.

STUDY QUESTIONS

1. What does Hardin mean when he says that the problem of population growth has no technical solution?

2. Explain the idea of the "tragedy of the commons" as first set forth by William Forster Lloyd. How does it work?

3. What does Hardin mean when he says, "Freedom in a commons brings ruin to all"? How does he define true "freedom" at the end of his essay?

4. How does Hardin apply the tragedy of the commons to human population growth? Do you agree with his analysis? Explain.

5. What does Hardin mean by "conscience is self-eliminating"? What is wrong with appealing to conscience to solve environmental problems?

6. How serious is the current population growth? What do you think should be done about it?

29

The Unjust War against Population

JACQUELINE KASUN

Jacqueline Kasun is professor of economics at Humboldt State University in Arcata, California. Her writings have appeared in The Wall Street Journal, The American Spectator, *and* The Christian Science Monitor. *She is the author of* The War against Population *(1988) from which this selection is taken.*

Kasun argues that Doomsdayers like the Smithsonian Institution and Garrett Hardin are carrying out an irrational campaign against our freedom to propagate. The idea that humanity is multiplying at a horrendous rate is one of the unexamined dogmas of our time. Kasun offers evidence to the contrary and charges the Doomsdayers with bad faith and with attempting to take control of our families, churches, and other voluntary institutions around the globe.

It was a traveling exhibit for schoolchildren. Titled "Population: The Problem Is Us," it toured the country at government expense in the mid-1970s. It consisted of a set of illustrated panels with an accompanying script that stated:

... there are too many people in the world. We are running out of space. We are running out of energy. We are running out of food. And, although too few people seem to realize it, we are running out of time.[1]

Reprinted from *The War Against Population* (San Francisco: Ignatius, 1988) by permission. Notes edited.

It told the children that "the birth rate must decrease and/or the death rate must increase" since resources were all but exhausted and mass starvation loomed. It warned that, "driven by starvation, people have been known to eat dogs, cats, bird droppings, and even their own children," and it featured a picture of a dead rat on a dinner plate as an example of future "food sources." Overpopulation, it threatened, would lead not only to starvation and cannibalism but to civil violence and nuclear war.

The exhibit was created at the Smithsonian Institution, the national museum of the U.S. government, using federal funds provided by the National Science Foundation, an agency of the U.S. government.

Concurrently, other American schoolchildren were also being treated to federally funded "population education," instructing them on "the growing pressures on global resources, food, jobs, and political stability." They read Paul Ehrlich's book, *The Population Bomb*. They were taught, falsely, that "world population is increasing at a rate of 2 percent per year whereas the food supply is increasing at a rate of 1 percent per year," and equally falsely, that "population growth and rising affluence have reduced reserves of the world's minerals." They viewed slides of the "biological catastrophes" that would result from overpopulation and held class discussions on "what responsible individuals in a 'crowded world' should or can do about population growth." They learned that the world is like a spaceship or a crowded lifeboat, to deduce the fate of mankind, which faces a "population crisis." And then, closer to home, they learned that families who have children are adding to the problems of overpopulation, and besides, children are a costly burden who "need attention … 24 hours a day" and spoil marriages by making their fathers "jealous" and rendering their mothers "depleted." They were told to "say good-bye" to numerous wildlife species doomed to extinction as a result of the human population explosion.

This propaganda campaign in the public schools, which indoctrinated a generation of children, was federally funded, despite the fact that no

law had committed the United States to this policy. Nor, indeed, had agreement been reached among informed groups that the problem of "overpopulation" even existed. To the contrary, during the same period the government drive against population was gaining momentum, contrary evidence was proliferating. One of the world's most prominent economic demographers, Colin Clark of Oxford University, published a book titled *Population Growth: The Advantages;* and economists Peter Bauer and Basil Yamey of the London School of Economics discovered that the population scare "relies on misleading statistics … misunderstands the determinants of economic progress … misinterprets the causalities in changes in fertility and changes in income" and "envisages children exclusively as burdens." Moreover, in his major study of The *Economics of Population Growth,* Julian Simon found that population growth was economically beneficial. Other economists joined in differing from the official antinatalist position.

Commenting on this body of economic findings, Paul Ehrlich, the biologist-author of *The Population Bomb,* charged that economists "continue to whisper in the ears of politicians all kinds of nonsense." If not on the side of the angels, Ehrlich certainly found himself on the side of the U.S. government, which since the mid-1960s has become increasingly committed to a worldwide drive to reduce the growth of population. It has absorbed rapidly increasing amounts of public money, as well as the energies of a growing number of public agencies and publicly subsidized private organizations.

The spirit of the propaganda has permeated American life at all levels, from the highest reaches of the federal bureaucracy to the chronic reporting of overpopulation problems by the media and the population education being pushed in public schools. It has become so much a part of daily American life that its presuppositions and implications are scarcely examined; though volumes are regularly published on the subject, they rarely do more than restate the assumptions as a prelude to proposing even "better" methods of population planning.

But even more alarming are some neglected features inherent in the proposed needs and the probable results of population planning. The factual errors are egregious, true, and the alarmists err when they claim that world food output per person and world mineral reserves are decreasing—that, indeed, the human economic prospect has been growing worse rather than more secure and prosperous by all available objective standards. But these are not the most significant claims made by the advocates of government population planning. The most fundamental, which is often tacit rather than explicit, is that the world faces an unprecedented problem of "crisis" proportions that defies all familiar methods of solution.

Specifically, it is implied that the familiar human response to scarcity—that of economizing—is inadequate under the "new" conditions. Thus the economist's traditional reliance on the individual's ability to choose in impersonal markets is disqualified. Occasionally it is posited that the market mechanism will fail due to "externalities," but it is more often said that mankind is entering by a quantum leap into a new age in which all traditional methods and values are inapplicable. Sometimes it is implied that the uniqueness of this new age inheres in its new technology, and at other times that human nature itself is changing in fundamental respects.

Whatever the cause of this leap into an unmapped future, the widely held conclusion is that since all familiar human institutions are failing and will continue to fail in the "new" circumstances, they must be abandoned and replaced. First among these supposedly failing institutions is the market mechanism, that congeries of institutions and activities by which individuals and groups carry out production and make decisions about the allocation of resources and the distribution of income. Not only the market, but democratic political institutions as well are held to be manifestly unsuitable for the "new" circumstances. Even the traditional family is labeled for extinction because of its inability to adapt to the evolving situation. The new school family life and sex education programs, for example, stress the supposed decline of the traditional family—heterosexual marriage, blood or adoptive relationships—and its replacement by new, "optional" forms, such as communes and homosexual partnerships. Unsurprisingly, traditional moral and ethical teachings must be abandoned.

The decision to repudiate the market is of interest not only to economists but to both those capitalists and market socialists who have seen how impersonal markets can mediate the innate conflict between consumer desires and resource scarcity. The most elegant models of socialism have incorporated the market mechanism into their fundamental design. Adam Smith's "invisible hand," which leads men to serve one another and to economize in their use of resources as they pursue their own self-interest, is relied upon to a considerable extent in a number of socialist countries. John Maurice Clark called it "our main safeguard against exploitation" because it performs "the simple miracle whereby each one increases his gains by increasing his services rather than by reducing them," and Walter Eucken said it protects individuals by breaking up the great concentrations of economic power. The common element here is, of course, the realization that individual decision-making leads not to chaos but to social harmony.

This view is denied by the population planners and it is here that the debate is, or should be, joined. Why are the advocates of government population planning so sure that the market mechanism cannot handle population growth? Why are they so sure that the market will not respond as it has in the past to resource scarcities—by raising prices so as to induce consumers to economize and producers to provide substitutes? Why can individual families not be trusted to adjust the number of their children to their incomes and thus to the given availability of resources? Why do the advocates of government population control assume that human beings must "overbreed," both to their own detriment and to that of society?

It is occasionally averred that the reason for this hypothetical failure is that individuals do not bear the full costs of their childbearing decisions but transfer a large part to society and therefore tend to have "too many" children. This is a dubious claim, for it overlooks the fact that individual families do not receive all the benefits generated by their childbearing. The lifetime productivity and social contribution of children flows largely to persons other than their parents, which, it might be argued, leads families to have fewer children than would be in the best interests of society. Which of these "externalities" is the more important, or whether they balance one another, is a question that waits not merely for an answer but for a reasoned study.

Another reason commonly given for the alleged failure of personal decisions is that individuals do not know how to control the size of their families. But a deeper look makes it abundantly clear that the underlying reason is that the population planners do not believe that individuals, even if fully informed, can be relied upon to make the proper choice. The emphasis on "outreach" and the incentives that pervade the United States' domestic and foreign population efforts testify to this, as will be shown in more depth shortly.

More important than these arguments, however, is the claim that new advances in technology are not amenable to control by market forces—a traditional argument in favor of socialism. From the time of Saint Simon to that of Veblen and on to our own age, the argument has been advanced that the market forces of supply-and-demand are incapable of controlling the vast powers of modern technology. At the dawn of the nineteenth century Saint Simon called for the redesigning of human society to cope with the new forces being unleashed by science. Only planned organization and control would suffice, he claimed. "Men of business" and the market forces which they represented would have to be replaced by planning "experts." In the middle of the nineteenth century Marx created a theoretic model of the capitalist market that purported to prove that the new technological developments would burst asunder the forms of private property and capitalist markets. Three-quarters of a century later Veblen spoke for the planning mentality when he wrote in 1921:

> The material welfare of the community is
> unreservedly bound up with the due

working of this industrial system, and therefore with its unreserved control by the engineers, who alone are competent to manage it. To do their work as it should be done these men of the industrial general staff must have a free hand, unhampered by commercial considerations....

In our own time, Heilbroner expresses a similar but even more profound distrust of market forces:

> ... the external challenge of the human
> prospect, with its threats of runaway
> populations, obliterative war, and potential
> environmental collapse, can be seen as an
> extended and growing crisis induced by
> the advent of a command over natural
> processes and forces that far exceeds the
> reach of our present mechanisms of social
> control.

Heilbroner's position is uniquely modern in its pessimism. Unlike Marx and Veblen, who believed that the profit-seeking aspects of supply-and-demand unduly restricted the new technology from fulfilling its *beneficent* potential, Heilbroner sees the market as incapable of controlling an essentially *destructive* technology. Technology, in Heilbroner's view, brings nuclear arms, industrial pollution, and the reduction in death rates that is responsible for the population "explosion"; all of these stubbornly resist control by the market or by benign technological advance. Heilbroner has little hope that pollution-control technology, for example, will be able to offset the bad effects of industrial pollution.

An additional argument is that mankind is rapidly approaching, or has reached, the "limits to growth" or the "carrying capacity" of an earth with "finite" resources. Far from being a new position, it dates back to Thomas Malthus' *Essay on the Principle of Population* (1798), which held that the growth of population must inevitably outrun the growth of food supply. It must be one of the curiosities of our age that though Malthus' forecast has proved mistaken—that, in fact, the living standards of the average person have reached a level probably unsurpassed in history—doom is still pervasively forecast. The modern literature of "limits" is voluminous, including such works as the much-criticized *Limits to Growth* published by the Club of Rome, and the Carter administration's *Global 2000*. In common, these works predict an impending exhaustion of various world economic resources which are assumed to be absolutely fixed in quantity and for which no substitutes can be found. The world is likened to a "spaceship," as in Boulding's and Asimov's writings; or, even more pessimistically, an overloaded "lifeboat," as in Garrett Hardin's articles.

Now, in the first place, as for the common assumption in this literature that the limits are fixed and known (or, as Garrett Hardin puts it, each country's "lifeboat" carries a sign that indicates its "capacity"), no such knowledge does in fact exist—for the earth, or for any individual country, or with regard to any resource. No one knows how much petroleum exists on earth or how many people can earn their living in Illinois. What is known is that the types and quantities of economic resources are continually changing, as is the ability of given areas to support life. In the same territories in which earlier men struggled and starved, much larger populations today support themselves in comfort. The difference, of course, lies in the *knowledge* that human beings bring to the task of discovering and managing resources.

But then, secondly, the literature of limits rules out all such increasing knowledge. Indeed, in adopting the lifeboat or spaceship metaphor, the apostles of limits not only rule out all new knowledge, but the discovery of new resources, and in fact, virtually all production. Clearly, if the world is really a spaceship or a lifeboat, then both technology and resources are absolutely fixed, and beyond a low limit, population growth would be disastrous. Adherents of the view insist that that limit is either being rapidly approached or has been passed, about which more later. Important here is that even this extreme view of the human situation does not rule out the potential of market forces. Most of mankind throughout history has lived under conditions that would be regarded today as extreme, even

desperate, deprivation. And over the millennia private decisions and private transactions have played an important, often a dominant, role in economic life. The historical record clearly shows that human beings can act and cooperate on their own in the best interests of survival, even under very difficult conditions. But history notwithstanding, the claims that emergencies of one kind or another require the centralized direction of economic life have been recurrent, especially during this century, which, ironically, has been the most economically prosperous. Today's advocates of coercion—the proponents of population control—posit the imminent approach of resource exhaustion, a condition wherein human beings will abandon all semblance of rational and civilized behavior.

To ward off their "emergency," the proponents of population control call for the adoption of measures that they admit would not be normally admissible. This is surely ample reason for a thoughtful and thorough examination of measures already being propagated.

Social and economic planning require an administrative bureaucracy with powers of enforcement. Modern economic analysis clearly shows that there are no impersonal, automatic mechanisms in the public sector that can simply and perfectly compensate for private market "failure." The public alternative is fraught with inequity and inefficiency, which can be substantial and exceedingly important. Although the theory of bureaucratic behavior has received less attention than that of private consumer choice, public administrators have also proved subject to greed, which hardly leads to social harmony. Government employees and contractors have the same incentives to avoid competition and form monopolies as private firms. They can increase their incomes by padding their costs and bloating their projects, and excuse it by exaggerating the need for their services and discrediting alternative solutions.

Managers of government projects have no market test to meet since they give away their products, even force them on an unwilling public, while collecting the necessary funds by force through the tax system. They can use their government grants to lobby for still more grants and to finance legal action to increase their power. They can bribe other bureaucrats and grants recipients to back their projects with the promise of reciprocal services. Through intergovernmental grants and "subventions" they can arrange their financial affairs so that apparently no one is accountable for any given decision or program. In short, the record of bureaucratic behavior confirms the statement of the great socialist scholar Oskar Lange, that "the real danger of socialism is that of a bureaucratization of economic life." The danger may well be more serious than we realize—it could be nothing less than totalitarianism.

Finally, proponents of the "population crisis" believe that not only must the *agencies* and *methods* of control be changed under the "new" circumstances but also the *criteria for choice*. Since, they argue, the technological and demographic developments of the modern age render all traditional standards of value and goodness either obsolete or questionable, these must be revised—under the leadership, of course, of those who understand the implications of the new developments.

Above all, they hold that the traditional concept of the value and dignity of the individual human being must be overhauled. The good of the *species,* as understood fully only by the advocates of the new views, must in all cases supersede the good as perceived and sought after by individuals.

Clearly, in the late twentieth century a worldview has emerged that calls into question not only the presuppositions of much of economics, but some basic political and philosophical thought as well. The history of our age may be determined by the outcome of the confrontation between these views.

It must be emphasized that the essential issue is not birth control or family planning. People have throughout history used various means to determine the size of their families, generating a great deal of discussion and debate. But the critical issue raised by recent history, especially in the United States, is whether government has the right or duty to preside over the reproductive process ... for what reasons, to what extent?

Recent official action in the United States has proceeded as if the question had already been answered. The fact is, however, that it has been neither explicitly asked nor discussed, even as we rush toward a future shaped by its affirmative answer. It is this question that must be examined.

SCARCITY OR LIFEBOAT ECONOMICS: WHICH IS RIGHT?

The fact of scarcity is the fundamental concern of economics. As one leading textbook puts it in its opening pages, "wants exceed what is available."[2] It pertains to the rich as well as to the poor, since scarcity is not the same thing as poverty. As another text tells students, "higher production levels seem to bring in their train ever-higher consumption standards. Scarcity remains."[3]

> Yet another explains,
> we are not able to produce all of
> everything that everyone wants free; thus
> we must "economize" our resources, or
> use them as efficiently as possible ...
> human wants, if not infinite, go ... far
> beyond the ability of our productive
> resources to satisfy them....[4]

That scarcity is no less real in affluent societies than in poor ones is explained in more general terms by other economists who stress the need to make *choices* whenever alternatives exist. In the words of McKenzie and Tullock,

> the individual makes **choices** from among
> an array of alternative options ... in each
> choice situation, a person must always
> forgo doing one or more things when
> doing something else. Since **cost** is the
> most highly valued alternative forgone, all
> rational behavior involves a cost.[5]

Clearly, the affluent person or society faces a large list of highly valued alternatives, and is likely to have a difficult choice to make—to be more acutely aware of the scarcity and the need to give up one thing in order to have another. It follows that scarcity does not lessen with affluence but is more likely to increase.

Simply put, economists understand scarcity as the inescapable fact that candy bars and ice cream cannot be made out of the same milk and chocolate. A choice must be made, regardless of how much milk and chocolate there is. And the decision to produce milk and chocolate rather than cheese and coffee is another inescapable choice. And so the list continues, endlessly, constituting the core of economics. How to choose what to produce, for whom, and how, is the very stuff of economics.

It is important to notice how different these traditional economic concepts of scarcity and choice are from the notions of "lifeboat economics." In Garrett Hardin's metaphor, the lifeboat's capacity is written on its side. The doomsday literature of limits is shot through with the conceit of absolute capacity, which is alien to economics. Not the least of the differences is that in economics humanity is viewed not only as the *raison d'être* of other forms of wealth but as one of the sources of wealth; human labor and ingenuity are resources, means for creating wealth. In the lifeboat, human beings are pure burdens, straining the capacity of the boat. Which of these views is closer to reality?

Is the earth rapidly approaching or has it surpassed its capacity to support human life? But before delving into the existence and nature of limits, keep in mind that the notion of a limited carrying capacity is not the only argument for population control. The view of people, or at least of more people, as simply a curse or affliction has its adherents. Thus Kingsley Davis writes of the plague, and Paul Ehrlich speaks with obvious repugnance of "people, people, people, people." Other writers, both old and new, attribute, if not a negative, at least a zero value to people. Thus John D. Rockefeller III, submitting the final report of the Commission on Population Growth and the American Future, wrote:

> in the long run, no substantial benefits
> will result from further growth of the
> Nation's population, rather … the gradual

stabilization of our population would contribute significantly to the Nation's ability to solve its problems. We have looked for, and have not found, any convincing economic argument for continued population growth. The health of our country does not depend on it, nor does the vitality of business nor the welfare of the average person.[6]

The notion embodied in this statement—that, to validate its claim to existence, a human life should justify itself by contributing to such things as the "vitality of business"—is a perfect example of the utilitarian ethic. Though economics has skirted utilitarianism at times, it was never in this sense, but rather in its belief that human beings could be rational in making choices. Economics has been content to value all things in terms of what they mean to individual human beings; it has never valued human beings in terms of supposedly higher values.

The idea that the earth is incapable of continuing to support human life suffuses United States governmental publications. The House Select Committee on Population reported in 1978 that

> the four major biological systems that
> humanity depends upon for food and raw
> materials—ocean fisheries, grasslands,
> forests, and croplands—are being strained
> by rapid population growth to the point
> where, in some cases, they are actually
> losing productive capacity.[7]

The Carter administration's *Global 2000* report, which was much criticized by research experts, predicted:

> With the persistence of human poverty
> and misery, the staggering growth of
> human population, and ever increasing
> human demands, the possibilities of further
> stress and permanent damage to the
> planet's resource base are very real.

Such statements have been duly broadcast by the media despite the facts, which tell a quite different story.

In the first place, world food production has increased considerably faster than population in recent decades. The increase in per capita food output between 1950 and 1977 amounted to either 28 percent or 37 percent, depending on whether United Nations or United States Department of Agriculture figures are used, as Julian Simon has shown. Clearly, this is a very substantial increase. More recent United Nations and U.S. Department of Agriculture data show that world food output has continued to match or outstrip population growth in the years since 1977. Some of the most dramatic increases have occurred in the poorest countries, those designated for "triage" by the apostles of doom. For example, rice and wheat production in India in 1983 was almost three-and-a-half times as great as in 1950. This was considerably more than twice the percentage increase in the population of India in the same period.[8]

In a recent article written at the Harvard Center for Population Studies, Nick Eberstadt calls attention to the great increases in the world food supply in recent decades. He points out that only about 2 percent of the world's population suffers from serious hunger, in contrast to the much larger estimates publicized by the Food and Agricultural Organization of the United Nations in its applications for grants to continue its attempts to "solve" the world hunger problem. Eberstadt notes that the improving world food situation is probably reflected by the fact that "in the past thirty years, life expectancy in the less developed countries, excluding China, has risen by more than a third," and that "in the past twenty years in these same nations, death rates for one-to-four-year-olds, the age group most vulnerable to nutritional setback, have dropped by nearly half."

He points out that the much-decried increase in food imports by some less-developed countries is not a cause for alarm, but actually requires a smaller proportion of their export earnings to finance than in 1960.

In 1980, according to Eberstadt, even the poorest of the less-developed countries had to use less than 10 percent of their export earnings to pay for their food imports. The good news is underscored by the fact that these countries have been able to export their manufactured and other nonfood items so much in recent years that it is profitable—it is the efficient choice—for them to export these products in exchange for food, just as developed countries do.

The recent famine in Africa may seem to belie these optimistic findings. Africa, however, is a continent torn by war; farmers cannot cultivate and reap in battle zones, and enemy troops often seize or burn crops. Collectivist governments, also endemic in Africa, often seize crops and farm animals without regard for farmers' needs. War and socialism are two great destroyers of the food supply in Africa, as they have been in other continents.

The impressive increases in food production that have occurred in recent decades have barely scratched the surface of the available food-raising resources, according to the best authorities. Farmers use less than half of the earth's arable land and only a minute part of the water available for irrigation. Indeed, three-fourths of the world's available cropland requires no irrigation.

How large a population could the world's agricultural resources support using presently known methods of farming? Colin Clark, former director of the Agricultural Economic Institute at Oxford University, classified world land-types by their food-raising capabilities and found that if all farmers were to use the best methods, enough food could be raised to provide an American-type diet for 35.1 billion people, more than seven times the present population. Since the American diet is a very rich one, Clark found that it would be possible to feed three times as many again, or more than twenty-two times as many as now exist, at a Japanese standard of food intake. Clark's estimate assumed that nearly half of the earth's land area would remain in conservation areas, for recreation and the preservation of wildlife.

Roger Revelle, former director of the Harvard Center for Population Studies, estimated that world agricultural resources are capable of providing an adequate diet (2,500 kilocalories per day), as well as fiber, rubber, tobacco, and beverages, for 40 billion people, or eight times the present number.

This, he thought, would require the use of less than one-fourth—compared with one-ninth today—of the earth's ice-free land area. He presumed that average yields would be about one-half those presently produced in the United States Midwest. Clearly, better yields and/or the use of a larger share of the land area would support over 40 billion persons.

Revelle has estimated that the less-developed continents, those whose present food supplies are most precarious, are capable of feeding 18 billion people, or six times their present population. He has estimated that the continent of Africa alone is capable of feeding 10 billion people, which is twice the amount of the present world population and more than twenty times the 1980 population of Africa. He sees "no known physical or biological reason" why agricultural yields in Asia should not be greatly increased. In a similar vein, the Indian economist Raj Krishna has written that

> ... the amount of land in India that can be brought under irrigation can still be doubled ... Even in Punjab, the Indian state where agriculture is most advanced, the yield of wheat can be doubled. In other states it can be raised three to seven times. Rice yields in the monsoon season can be raised three to 13 times, rice yields in the dry season two to three-and-a-half times, jowar (Indian millet) yields two to 11 times, maize yields two to 10 times, groundnut yields three-and-a-half to five-and-a-half times and potato yields one-and-a-half to five-and-a-half times.[9]

What Mr. Krishna is, in fact, saying is that Indian agriculture is potentially capable of feeding not only the people of India but the entire population of the world!

Revelle sums up his conclusions and those of other experts by quoting Dr. David Hopper, another well-known authority on agriculture:

> The world's food problem does not arise from any physical limitation on potential output or any danger of unduly stressing the environment. The limitations on abundance are to be found in the social and political structures of nations and in the economic relations among them. The unexploited global food resource is there, between Cancer and Capricorn. The successful husbandry of that resource depends on the will and actions of men.[10]

Obviously, such great expansions of output would require large inputs of fertilizer, energy, and human labor, as Revelle puts it:

> Most of the required capital facilities can be constructed in densely populated poor countries by human labor, with little modern machinery: in the process much rural unemployment and under-employment can be alleviated.

In other words, as Clark has noted, future generations can and will build their own farms and houses, just as in the past.

> With regard to fertilizer, Clark has pointed out that the world supply of the basic ingredients, potash and sulphates, is adequate for several centuries, while the third major ingredient, nitrogen, is freely available in the atmosphere, though requiring energy for extraction. Since the world's coal supply is adequate for some 2,000 years, this should pose no great problem. Revelle states that in principle ... most—perhaps all—of the energy needed in modern high-yielding agriculture could be provided by the farmers themselves. For every ton of cereal grain there are one to two tons of humanly inedible crop residues with an energy content considerably greater than the food energy in the grain.

Surprisingly, in view of the recurrent alarms about desertification, urban encroachment, and other forces supposedly reducing the amount of world agricultural land, it is actually increasing.

Julian Simon has drawn attention to the data indicating this trend:

> A demographer, Joginder Kumar, found in a study at the University of California at Berkeley that there was 9 percent more total arable land in 1960 than in 1950 in 87 countries for which data were available and which constituted 73 percent of the world's total land area. And United Nations data show a 6 percent rise in the world's arable, permanent cropland from around 1963 to 1977 (the last date for which data are available).[11]

And UN data show a further increase of almost 1 percent between 1977 and 1980. Simon also notes that

> there are a total of 2.3 billion acres in the United States. Urban areas plus highways, nonagricultural roads, railroads, and airports total 61 million acres—just 2.7 percent of the total. Clearly, there is little competition between agriculture and cities and roads.

And that,

> furthermore, between 1.25 million and 1.7 million acres of cropland are being created yearly with irrigation, swamp drainage, and other reclamation techniques. This is a much larger quantity of new farmland than the amount that is converted to cities and highways each year.

Simon's point is significant: a very small share of the total land area is used for urban purposes—less than 3 percent in the United States. This is probably a high percentage by world standards since the United States has a peculiarly sprawling type of development. Doxiadis and Papaioannou have estimated that only three-tenths of 1 percent of the land surface of the earth is used for "human settlements."

Similarly, the biologist Francis P. Felice has shown that all the people in the world could be put into the state of Texas, forming one giant city with a population density less than that of many existing cities, and leaving the rest of the world empty. Each man, woman, and child in the 1984 world population could be given more than 1,500 square feet of land space in such a city (the average home in the United States ranges between 1,400 and 1,800 square feet). If one-third of the space of this city were devoted to parks and one-third to industry, each family could still occupy a single-story dwelling of average U.S. size.

In like vein, R. L. Sassone has calculated that there would be standing room for the entire population of the world within one-quarter of the area of Jacksonville, Florida.

Evidently, if the people of the world are floating in a lifeboat, it is a mammoth one quite capable of carrying many times its present passengers. An observer, in fact, would get the impression that he was looking at an empty boat, since the present occupants take up only a fraction of 1 percent of the boat's space and use less than one-ninth of its ice-free land area to raise their food and other agricultural products. The feeling of the typical air passenger that he is looking down on a mostly empty earth is correct.

On the extremely unlikely assumption that no improvements take place in technology and that population growth continues at its present rate, it will be more than a century and a quarter before world population will approach the limit of the support capacity estimated by Revelle, and almost two centuries before the limit estimated by Clark is reached. And, again on these wild surmises, what will the world be like then? At least one-half of the world's land area will still be in conservation and wildlife areas; and human settlements will occupy no more than 8 percent of the land. In a word, although by our assumptions, average living standards will no longer be able to rise, the boat will still be mostly empty.

Yet despite the optimism for human life in agriculture, and although most of the people in the less-developed world are still engaged in such work, we do live in the industrial age. Among the roughly one-third of the people who live in industrial countries, only a small proportion are farmers. In the

United States, for example, one out of thirty people in the labor force is a farmer.

Even the most superficial view of the industrial economy shows how vastly it differs from the economy of agriculture. It uses a high proportion of fossil fuels and metal inputs; it is relatively independent of climate and seasons; a high proportion of its waste products are "nonbiodegradable"; and it requires clustering rather than dispersal of its productive units, which encourages urbanization. While depending on agriculture for much of its resources, including its initial stock of capital, it has contributed greatly to the productivity and security of agriculture by providing energy, labor-saving machinery, and chemical fertilizers. Above all, perhaps, it has provided agriculture with cheap, fast transportation, so that local crop failures no longer mean famine.

It is generally agreed that industrialization has been important in reducing mortality and hence increasing population. And concerns regarding the limits of industry match those over the capacity of agriculture. How far can we go with the industrial process before we run out of the minerals and energy that are essential to it? How much "disruption" of nature does the industrial system create and how much can the earth and its inhabitants endure?

It is quite evident that, with few exceptions, intellectuals have never much liked the industrial process. Its noise, smoke—its obliteration of natural beauty—have never endeared it to the more genteel classes, or perhaps to anybody. But where its unattractive characteristics were once regarded as an unavoidable cost, given the benefits for human beings, now there is a growing conviction—especially among environmentalists—that these costs are unendurable and could be avoided by simply dispensing with part of the population. This is a simple choice from a set of complex alternatives, which raises much more far-reaching questions than whether we are simply "running out of everything."

First, though, the question: Are we running out of everything? If we are, the industrialization process, as well as all the benefits and problems it creates, will soon be at an end. (For those who dislike industry this should be good news indeed, though they shy away from the argument.)

On this score, the signs are clear. There is very little probability of running out of anything essential to the industrial process at any time in the foreseeable future. Over the past decades there have been recurrent predictions of the imminent exhaustion of all energy and basic metals, none of which has come about. And properly so, because it is a familiar chemical principle that nothing is ever "used up." Materials are merely changed into other forms. Some of these forms make subsequent recycling easier, others less so. It is cheaper to retrieve usable metals from the city dump than from their original ore, but once gasoline has been burned it cannot be reused as gasoline. Economists gauge the availability of basic materials by measuring their price changes over time. A material whose price has risen over time (allowing for changes in the average value of money) is becoming more scarce, while one whose price has fallen is becoming more abundant, relative to the demand for it. Two major economic studies of the availability of basic metals and fuels found no evidence of increasing scarcity over the period 1870–1972. And in 1984 a group of distinguished resource experts reported that the cost trends of non-fuel minerals for the period 1950–1980 "fail to support the increasing scarcity hypothesis."

> Julian Simon has recently noted the trend of decreasing scarcity for all raw materials:
>
> An hour's work in the United States has bought increasingly more of copper, wheat, and oil (representative and important raw materials) from 1800 to the present. And the same trend has almost surely held throughout human history. Calculations of expenditures for raw materials as a proportion of total family budgets make the same point even more strongly. These trends imply that the raw materials have been getting increasingly available and less scarce relative to the most important and most fundamental element of life, human work-time. The prices of

raw materials have even been falling relative to consumer goods and the Consumer Price Index. All the items in the Consumer Price Index have been produced with increasing efficiency in terms of labor and capital over the years, but the decrease in cost of raw materials has been even greater than that of other goods, a very strong demonstration of progressively decreasing scarcity and increasing availability of raw materials.[12]

Simon also noted that the real price of electricity had fallen at the end of the 1970s to about one-third its level in the 1920s.

Even the Carter administration's gloomy *Global 2000* report admitted that "the real price of most mineral commodities has been constant or declining for many years," indicating less scarcity. Yet the report, in the face of all the evidence of a historical decline in industrial resource scarcity, trumpets an imminent reversal of the trend and an abrupt increase in the prices and scarcity of raw materials.

Other analysts disagree. As Ansley Coale points out, metals exist in tremendous quantities at lower concentrations. Geologists know that going from a concentration of 6 percent to 5 percent multiplies the available quantities by factors of ten to a thousand, depending on the metal.

Ridker and Cecelski of Resources for the Future are equally reassuring, concluding, "in the long run, most of our metal needs can be supplied by iron, aluminum, and magnesium, all of which are extractable from essentially inexhaustible sources."[13]

Even should scarcities of such materials develop, the economic impact would be small:

> metals ... are only a small fraction of the cost of finished goods. The same is true with energy.... In the United States, for example, non-fuel minerals account for less than one-half of one percent of the total output of goods and services, and energy costs comprise less than one percent.

In the case of fuels, the United States has currently reduced its own sources of low-cost petroleum. This can hardly be described as a "crisis," since higher-cost petroleum supplies are still available here while large reserves of low-cost petroleum remain and are being discovered in other parts of the world, though cartel influences are presently affecting prices. Extremely large deposits of coal remain in the United States and throughout the world, enough for a thousand years, possibly more than twice that, at foreseeable rates of increase in demand.

Summarizing the conclusions of a group of energy experts in 1984, Simon and Kahn wrote:

> Barring extraordinary political problems, we expect the price of oil to go down ... there is no basis to conclude ... that humankind will ever face a greater shortage of oil in economic terms than it does now; rather, decreasing shortage is the more likely ...

Speaking of all kinds of energy, they concluded:

> The prospect of running out of energy is purely a bogeyman. The availability of energy has been increasing, and the meaningful cost has been decreasing, over the entire span of humankind's history. We expect this benign trend to continue at least until our sun ceases to shine in perhaps 7 billion years....

Furthermore, the United States has tremendous, unexploited opportunities to economize on energy. Because energy has been so cheap, Americans drive their cars more than any other people and, in some parts of the United States, heat their houses without insulation and even with open windows. A reduction in U.S. energy consumption by one-half would put us on a par with the people of western Europe, whose living standards are as high as ours.

Although history teaches that we can expect great technological changes in the future, the nature of these changes is unknown. To attempt, then, to determine the safe capacity of our lifeboat, it seems the better part of wisdom not to anticipate any miraculous rescues, such as breakthroughs in the use of solar or nuclear power. Old-fashioned as it may seem, the coal on board alone will provide us with energy for at least a millennium, to say nothing of the petroleum and natural gas—and solar and nuclear possibilities—all of which remain substantial.

The message is clear. The boat is extremely well stocked. The industrial system will not grind to a halt for lack of supplies.

But what about the disruption (an obscure term, and so all the more dreaded) supposedly created by population growth and/or industrialization? As Heilbroner puts it: "The sheer scale of our intervention into the fragile biosphere is now so great that we are forced to proceed with great caution lest we inadvertently bring about environmental damage of an intolerable sort."

Man has, of course, been intervening in the biosphere for thousands of years. Perhaps the most massive human intervention was the invention of agriculture. It is not certain that modern industry, which is confined to much smaller areas, is having even an equal effect. Both humanity and the rest of the biosphere have apparently survived the agricultural intervention rather well; in fact, well enough so that our present anxiety is whether too many of us have survived.

"Too many for what?" springs to mind. The fact that more people are now living longer, healthier, better-fed, and more comfortable lives, and have been for many decades, rather suggests that the interventions have been the very opposite of intolerable. According to a number of authorities, the best overall index of environmental quality is life expectancy, which has been increasing throughout the world during this century. It is precisely because of this increase that population has grown even though birth rates have fallen. It is possible, of course, that what the population alarmists really mean is that there are too many *other* people for their taste, or for those who prefer solitude, which is quite another thing....

These and other economists have spelled out the case against the assumptions and teachings of the population-bombers: population growth permits the easier acquisition as well as the more efficient use of the economic infrastructure—the modern transportation and communications systems, and the education, electrification, irrigation, and waste disposal systems. Population growth encourages agricultural investment—clearing and draining land, building barns and fences, improving the water supply. Population growth increases the size of the market, encouraging producers to specialize and use cost-saving methods of large-scale production. Population growth encourages governments, as well as parents, philanthropists, and taxpayers, to devote more resources to education. If wisely directed, these efforts can result in higher levels of competence in the labor force. Larger populations not only inspire more ideas but more *exchanges,* or improvements, of ideas among people, in a ratio that is necessarily more than proportional to the number of additional people. (For example, if one person joins an existing couple, the possible number of exchanges does not increase by one-third but triples.) One of the advantages of cities, as well as of large universities, is that they are mentally stimulating, that they foster creativity.

The arguments and evidence that population growth does not lead to resource exhaustion, starvation, and environmental catastrophe fail to persuade the true believers in the population bomb. They have, after all, other rationalizations for their fears of doom. Another recurring theme of the doomsdayers is, in the words of a public affairs statement by the U.S. Department of State, that population growth increases the size of the "politically volatile age group—those 15–24 years," which contributes to political unrest. Ambassador Richard Elliot Benedick, coordinator of population affairs in the U.S. State Department, spelled out the concern for the Senate Foreign Relations Committee in 1980:

> Rapid population growth ... creates a large proportion of youth in the population. Recent experience, in Iran and other countries, shows that this younger age group—frequently unemployed and crowded into urban slums—is particularly susceptible to

extremism, terrorism, and violence as outlets for frustration.[14]

The ambassador went on to enumerate a long list of countries of economic and strategic importance to the United States where, he claimed, population growth was encouraging "political instability." The list included Turkey, Egypt, Iran, Pakistan, Indonesia, Mexico, Venezuela, Nigeria, Bolivia, Brazil, Morocco, the Philippines, Zimbabwe, and Thailand—countries of special importance to the United States because of their "strategic location, provision of military bases or support, and supply of oil or other critical raw materials." While he admitted that it is "difficult to be analytically precise in pinpointing exact causes of a given historical breakdown in domestic or international order," he nevertheless insisted that "unprecedented demographic pressures" were of great significance.

No results of scientific research support Benedick's belief; it is simply another one of those unverified *assumptions* that advocates of population control rely upon to make their case. It may be, of course, that Ambassador Benedick is right: that the young tend to be more revolutionary and that public bureaucracies who want to stay in power would be wise to encourage the aging of the population through lower birth rates. As public bureaucracies increase their power in this age of growth of government, we may see an increasing manipulation of the population so as to ensure an older and more docile citizenry. However, putting aside the ethical implications and the welfare of society, and speaking only of the self-interest of the ruling bureaucracy, the risks are obvious. Such policy could arouse a deep antagonism among those on the check list, especially if they are citizens of countries who perceive the policy as a tool of outside interference in their most intimate national affairs.

The question, then, is resolved in favor of the economic notion of scarcity rather than the lifeboat model of absolute limits being the more nearly correct. While resources are always scarce relative to the demands that human beings place upon them, there is no indication of imminent, absolute limits. The limits are so far beyond the levels of our present use of resources as to be nearly invisible, and are actually receding as new knowledge develops. Ironically, though, the perception of economic scarcity may increase along with increasing wealth and income. There is no evidence whatsoever that slower rates of population growth encourage economic growth or economic welfare; on the contrary, the developing countries with *higher* rates of population growth have had higher average rates of per-capita-output growth in the period since 1950. It may, of course, be in the interests of a ruling bureaucracy to rid itself of those people it finds troublesome, but the policy can hardly promote the general welfare, and it would prove very costly, even to the ruling elites.

NOTES

1. Projectbook for the Exhibition "Population: The Problem Is Us": A Book of Suggestions or Implementing the Exhibition in Your Own Institution (Washington: The Smithsonian Institution, undated, circulated in late 1970s), p. 9.

2. Armen A. Alchian and William R. Allen, *University Economics,* 3rd ed. (Belmont: Wadsworth Publishing Co., 1972), p. 7.

3. Paul A. Samuelson, *Economics,* 11th ed. (New York: McGraw Hill, 1980), p. 17.

4. George Leland Bach, *Economics: An Introduction to Analysis and Policy,* 10th ed. (Englewood Cliffs: Prentice-Hall, Inc., 1980), p. 3.

5. Richard B. McKenzie and Gordon Tullock, *Modern Political Economy* (New York: McGraw-Hill, 1978), p. 18.

6. John D. Rockefeller III, Letter to the President and Congress, transmitting the Final Report on the Commission on Population Growth and the American Future, dated March 27, 1972.

7. Select Committee on Population, Report, "World Population: Myths and Realities," U.S. House of Representatives, 95th Congress, 2nd Session (Washington: U.S. Government Printing Office, 1978), p. 5.

8. *The Global 2000 Report to the President: Global Future: Time to Act,* prepared by the Council on Environmental Quality and the U.S. Department of State (Washington: U.S. Government Printing Office, January 1981), p. ix.

9. Raj Krishna, "The Economic Development of India," *Scientific American,* vol. 243, no. 3. September 1980, pp. 173–174.

10. Revelle, "The World Supply of Agricultural Land," op. cit., p. 184, quoting W. David Hopper, "The Development of Agriculture in Developing Countries," *Scientific American,* September 1976, pp. 197–205.

11. Julian L. Simon, "Worldwide, Land for Agriculture Is Increasing, Actually," *New York Times,* October 7, 1980, p. 23.

12. Simon, "Global Confusion," op. cit., p. 11.

13. Ronald G. Ridker and Elizabeth W. Cecelski, "Resources, Environment, and Population: The Nature of Future Limits," *Population Bulletin,* vol. 34, no. 3, August 1979, p. 29.

14. Richard Elliot Benedick, Statement before the Senate Foreign Relations Committee, April 29, 1980, reprinted in *Department of State Bulletin,* vol. 80, no. 2042, September 1980, p. 58.

STUDY QUESTIONS

1. How strong is Kasun's case that the "Population Control Industry" is misleading us about the dangers of our present population growth?

2. According to Kasun, what is the truth about population growth in relation to scarcity of resources?

3. Compare Kasun's arguments with Hardin's. Which one has the stronger case, and why?

4. Evaluate the anthropocentric viewpoint in Kasun's essay.

5. Do you think Kasun ignores quality-of-life issues?

30

Lifeboat Ethics

GARRETT HARDIN

A biographical sketch of Garrett Hardin is found at the beginning of Reading 28.
He argues that the proper metaphor that characterizes our global ecological situation is not "spaceship" but "lifeboat." The spaceship metaphor is misleading since Earth has no

Reprinted from *Bioscience,* Vol. 24, No. 10: 561–8 (October 1974) by permission.

captain to steer it through its present and future problems. Rather, each rich nation is like a lifeboat in an ocean in which the poor of the world are swimming and in danger of drowning. Hardin argues that affluent societies, like lifeboats, ought to ensure their own survival by preserving a safety factor of resources. For a society to give away its resources to needy nations or to admit needy immigrants is like taking on additional passengers who would threaten to cause the lifeboat to capsize. Under these conditions, it is our moral duty to refrain from aiding the poor. interesting

No generation has viewed the problem of the survival of the human species as seriously as we have. Inevitably, we have entered this world of concern through the door of metaphor. Environmentalists have emphasized the image of the earth as a spaceship—Spaceship Earth. Kenneth Boulding ... is the principal architect of this metaphor. It is time, he says, that we replace the wasteful "cowboy economy" of the past with the frugal "spaceship economy" required for continued survival in the limited world we now see ours to be. The metaphor is notably useful in justifying pollution control measures.

Unfortunately, the image of a spaceship is also used to promote measures that are suicidal. One of these is a generous immigration policy, which is only a particular instance of a class of policies that are in error because they lead to the tragedy of the commons. ... These suicidal policies are attractive because they mesh with what we unthinkably take to be the ideals of "the best people." What is missing in the idealistic view is an insistence that rights and responsibilities must go together. The "generous" attitude of all too many people results in asserting inalienable rights while ignoring or denying matching responsibilities.

For the metaphor of a spaceship to be correct the aggregate of people on board would have to be under unitary sovereign control. ... A true ship always has a captain. It is conceivable that a ship could be run by a committee. But it could not possibly survive if its course were determined by bickering tribes that claimed rights without responsibilities.

What about Spaceship Earth? It certainly has no captain, and no executive committee. The United Nations is a toothless tiger, because the signatories of its charter wanted it that way. The spaceship metaphor is used only to justify spaceship demands on common resources without acknowledging corresponding spaceship responsibilities.

An understandable fear of decisive action leads people to embrace "incrementalism"—moving toward reform by tiny stages. As we shall see, this strategy is counterproductive in the area discussed here if it means accepting rights before responsibilities. Where human survival is at stake, the acceptance of responsibilities is a precondition to the acceptance of rights, if the two cannot be introduced simultaneously.

LIFEBOAT ETHICS

Before taking up certain substantive issues let us look at an alternative metaphor, that of a lifeboat. In developing some relevant examples the following numerical values are assumed. Approximately two-thirds of the world is desperately poor, and only one-third is comparatively rich. The people in poor countries have an average per capita GNP (Gross National Product) of about $200 per year; the rich, of about $3,000. (For the United States it is nearly $5,000 per year.) Metaphorically, each rich nation amounts to a lifeboat full of comparatively rich people. The poor of the world are in New other, much more crowded lifeboats. Continu-Meta. ously, so to speak, the poor fall out of their lifeboats and swim for a while in the water outside, hoping to be admitted to a rich lifeboat, or in some other way to benefit from the "goodies" on board. What should the passengers on a rich lifeboat do? This is the central problem of "the ethics of a lifeboat."

First we must acknowledge that each lifeboat is effectively limited in capacity. The land of every nation has a limited carrying capacity. The exact limit is a matter for argument, but the energy crunch is convincing more people every day that we have already exceeded the carrying capacity of the land. We have been living on "capital"—stored petroleum and coal—and soon we must live on income alone.

Let us look at only one lifeboat—ours. The ethical problem is the same for all, and is as follows. Here we sit, say 50 people in a lifeboat. To be generous, let us assume our boat has a capacity of 10 more, making 60. (This, however, is to violate the engineering principle of the "safety factor." A new plant disease or a bad change in the weather may decimate our population if we don't preserve some excess capacity as a safety factor.)

The 50 of us in the lifeboat see 100 others swimming in the water outside, asking for admission to the boat, or for handouts. How shall we respond to their calls? There are several possibilities.

One. We may be tempted to try to live by the Christian ideal of being "our brother's keeper," or by the Marxian ideal ... of "from each according to his abilities, to each according to his needs." Since the needs of all are the same, we take all the needy into our boat, making a total of 150 in a boat with a capacity of 60. The boat is swamped, and everyone drowns. Complete justice, complete catastrophe.

Two. Since the boat has an unused excess capacity of 10, we admit just 10 more to it. This has the disadvantage of getting rid of the safety factor, for which action we will sooner or later pay dearly. Moreover, *which* 10 do we let in? "First come, first served?" The best 10? The neediest 10? How do we *discriminate*? And what do we say to the 90 who are excluded?

Three. Admit no more to the boat and preserve the small safety factor. Survival of the people in the lifeboat is then possible (though we shall have to be on our guard against boarding parties).

The last solution is abhorrent to many people. It is unjust, they say. Let us grant that it is.

"I feel guilty about my good luck," say some. The reply to this is simple: *Get out and yield your place to others.* Such a selfless action might satisfy the conscience of those who are addicted to guilt but it would not change the ethics of the lifeboat. The needy person to whom a guilt-addict yields his place will not himself feel guilty about his sudden good luck. (If he did he would not climb aboard.) The net result of conscience-stricken people relinquishing their unjustly held positions is the elimination of their kind of conscience from the lifeboat. The lifeboat, as it were, purifies itself of guilt. The ethics of the lifeboat persist, unchanged by such momentary aberrations.

This then is the basic metaphor within which we must work out our solutions. Let us enrich the image step by step with substantive additions from the real world.

REPRODUCTION

The harsh characteristics of lifeboat ethics are heightened by reproduction, particularly by reproductive differences. The people inside the lifeboats of the wealthy nations are doubling in numbers every 87 years; those outside are doubling every 35 years, on the average. And the relative difference in prosperity is becoming greater.

Let us, for a while, think primarily of the U.S. lifeboat. As of 1973 the United States had a population of 210 million people, who were increasing by 0.8% per year, that is, doubling in number every 87 years.

Although the citizens of rich nations are outnumbered two to one by the poor, let us imagine an equal number of poor people outside our lifeboat—a mere 210 million poor people reproducing at a quite different rate. If we imagine these to be the combined populations of Colombia, Venezuela, Ecuador, Morocco, Thailand, Pakistan, and the Philippines, the average rate of increase of the people "outside" is 3.3% per year. The doubling time of this population is 21 years.

Suppose that all these countries, and the United States, agreed to live by the Marxian ideal, "to each according to his needs," the ideal of most Christians as well. Needs, of course, are determined by population size, which is affected by reproduction. Every nation regards its rate of reproduction as a sovereign right. If our lifeboat were big enough in the beginning it might be possible to live *for a while* by Christian-Marxian ideals. *Might.*

Initially, in the model given, the ratio of non-Americans to Americans would be one to one. But consider what the ratio would be 87 years later. By this time Americans would have doubled to a population of 420 million. The other group (doubling every 21 years) would now have swollen to 3,540 million. Each American would have more than eight people to share with. How could the lifeboat possibly keep afloat?

All this involves extrapolation of current trends into the future, and is consequently suspect. Trends may change. Granted: but the change will not necessarily be favorable. If—as seems likely—the rate of population increase falls faster in the ethnic group presently inside the lifeboat than it does among those now outside, the future will turn out to be even worse than mathematics predicts, and sharing will be even more suicidal.

RUIN IN THE COMMONS

The fundamental error of the sharing ethic is that it leads to the tragedy of the commons. Under a system of private property the men (or group of men) who own property recognize their responsibility to care for it, for if they don't they will eventually suffer. A farmer, for instance, if he is intelligent, will allow no more cattle in a pasture than its carrying capacity justifies. If he overloads the pasture, weeds take over, erosion sets in, and the owner loses in the long run.

But if a pasture is run as a commons open to all, the right of each to use it is not matched by an operational responsibility to take care of it. It is no use asking independent herdsmen in a commons

to act responsibly, for they dare not. The considerate herdsman who refrains from overloading the commons suffers more than a selfish one who says his needs are greater. (As Leo Durocher says, "Nice guys finish last.") Christian-Marxian idealism is counterproductive. That it *sounds* nice is no excuse. With distribution systems, as with individual morality, good intentions are no substitute for good performance.

A social system is stable only if it is insensitive to errors. To the Christian-Marxian idealist a selfish person is a sort of "error." Prosperity in the system of the commons cannot survive errors. If *everyone* would only restrain himself, all would be well; but it takes *only one less than everyone* to ruin a system of voluntary restraint. In a crowded world of less than perfect human beings—and we will never know any other—mutual ruin is inevitable in the commons. This is the core of the tragedy of the commons.

WORLD FOOD BANKS

In the international arena we have recently heard a proposal to create a new commons, namely an international depository of food reserves to which nations will contribute according to their abilities, and from which nations may draw according to their needs. Nobel laureate Norman Borlaug has lent the prestige of his name to this proposal.

A world food bank appeals powerfully to our humanitarian impulses. We remember John Donne's celebrated line, "Any man's death diminishes me." But before we rush out to see for whom the bell tolls let us recognize where the greatest political push for international granaries comes from, lest we be disillusioned later. Our experience with Public Law 480 clearly reveals the answer. This was the law that moved billions of dollars worth of U.S. grain to food-short, population-long countries during the past two decades. When P.L. 480 first came into being, a headline in the business magazine *Forbes* ... revealed the power behind it: "Feeding the World's Hungry Millions: How It Will Mean Billions for U.S. Business."

And indeed it did. In the years 1960 and to 1970 a total of $7.9 billion was spent on the "Food for Peace" program as P.L. 480 was called. During the years 1948 to 1970 an additional $49.9 billion were extracted from American taxpayers to pay for other economic aid programs, some of which went for food and food-producing machinery. (This figure does *not* include military aid.) That P.L. 480 was a give-away program was concealed. Recipient countries went through the motions of paying for P.L. 480 food—with IOU's. In December 1973 the charade was brought to an end as far as India was concerned when the United States "forgave" India's $3.2 billion debt.... Public announcement of the cancellation of the debt was delayed for two months: one wonders why.

The search for a rational justification can be short-circuited by interjecting the word "emergency." Borlaug uses this word. We need to look sharply at it. What is an "emergency"? It is surely something like an accident, which is correctly defined as *an event that is certain to happen, though with a low frequency....* A well-run organization prepares for everything that is certain, including accidents and emergencies. It budgets for them. It saves for them. It expects them—and mature decision-makers do not waste time complaining about accidents when they occur.

What happens if some organizations budget for emergencies and others do not? If each organization is solely responsible for its own well-being, poorly managed ones will suffer. But they should be able to learn from experience. They have a chance to mend their ways and learn to budget for infrequent but certain emergencies. The weather, for instance, always varies and periodic crop failures are certain. A wise and competent government saves out of the production of the good years in anticipation of bad years that are sure to come. This is not a new idea. The Bible tells us that Joseph taught this policy to Pharaoh in Egypt more than 2,000 years ago. Yet it is literally true that the vast majority of the governments of the world today have no such policy. They lack either the wisdom or the competence, or

both. Far more difficult than the transfer of wealth from one country to another is the transfer of wisdom between sovereign powers or between generations.

"But it isn't their fault! How can we blame the poor people who are caught in an emergency? Why must we punish them?" The concepts of blame and punishment are irrelevant. The question is, what are the operational consequences of establishing a world food bank? If it is open to every country every time a need develops, slovenly rulers will not be motivated to take Joseph's advice. Why should they? Others will bail them out whenever they are in trouble.

Some countries will make deposits in the world food bank and others will withdraw from it: there will be almost no overlap. Calling such a depository-transfer unit a "bank" is stretching the metaphor of *bank* beyond its elastic limits. The proposers, of course, never call attention to the metaphorical nature of the word they use.

THE RATCHET EFFECT

An "international food bank" is really, then, not a true bank but a disguised one-way transfer device for moving wealth from rich countries to poor. In the absence of such a bank, in a world inhabited by individually responsible sovereign nations, the population of each nation would repeatedly go through a cycle of the sort shown in Figure 1. P_2 is greater than P_1, either in absolute numbers or because a deterioration of the food supply has removed the safety factor and produced a dangerously low ratio of resources to population. P_2 may be said to represent a state of overpopulation, which becomes obvious upon the appearance of an "accident," e.g., a crop failure. If the "emergency" is not met by outside help, the population drops back to the "normal" level—the "carrying capacity" of the environment—or even below. In the absence of population control by a sovereign, sooner or later the population grows to P_2 again and the cycle repeats. The long-term population curve ... is an

[handwritten margin note: govt can expect emer.]

[handwritten note at bottom: *population dieback*]

irregularly fluctuating one, equilibrating more or less about the carrying capacity.

A demographic cycle of this sort obviously involves great suffering in the restrictive phase, but such a cycle is normal to any independent country with inadequate population control. The third-century theologian Tertullian ... expressed what must have been the recognition of many wise men when he wrote: "The scourges of pestilence, famine, wars, and earthquakes have come to be regarded as a blessing to overcrowded nations, since they serve to prune away the luxuriant growth of the human race."

Only under a strong and farsighted sovereign—which theoretically could be the people themselves, democratically organized—can a population equilibrate at some set point below the carrying capacity, thus avoiding the pains normally caused by periodic and unavoidable disasters. For this happy state to be achieved it is necessary that those in power be able to contemplate with equanimity the "waste" of surplus food in times of bountiful harvests. It is essential that those in power resist the temptation to convert extra food into extra babies. On the public relations level it is necessary that the phrase "surplus food" be replaced by "safety factor."

But wise sovereigns seem not to exist in the poor world today. The most anguishing problems are created by poor countries that are governed by rulers insufficiently wise and powerful. If such countries can draw on a world food bank in times of "emergency," the population *cycle* of Figure 1 will be replaced by the population *escalator* of Figure 2. The input of food from a food bank acts as the pawl of a ratchet, preventing the population from retracing its steps to a lower level. Reproduction pushes the population upward, inputs from the world bank prevent its moving downward. Population size escalates, as does the absolute magnitude of "accidents" and "emergencies." The process is brought to an end only by the total collapse of the whole system, producing a catastrophe of scarcely imaginable proportions.

Such are the implications of the well-meant sharing of food in a world of irresponsible reproduction.

All this is terribly obvious once we are acutely aware of the pervasiveness and danger of the commons. But many people still lack this awareness and the euphoria of the "benign demographic transition" ... interferes with the realistic appraisal of pejoristic mechanisms. As concerns public policy, the deductions drawn from the benign demographic transition are these:

1. If the per capita GNP rises the birth rate will fall; hence, the rate of population increase will fall, ultimately producing ZPG (Zero Population Growth).

2. The long-term trend all over the world (including the poor countries) is of a rising per capita GNP (for which no limit is seen).

3. Therefore, all political interference in population matters is unnecessary; all we need to do is

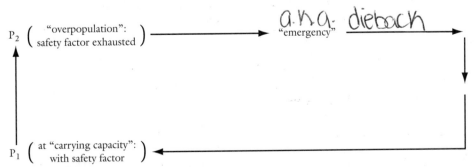

FIGURE 1 The population cycle of a nation that has no effective, conscious population control, and which receives no aid from the outside. P_2 is greater than P_1.

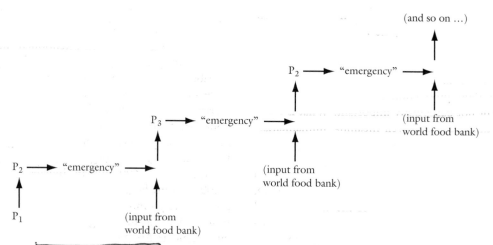

FIGURE 2 The Population Escalator. Note that input from a world food bank acts like the pawl of a ratchet, preventing the normal population cycle shown in Figure 1 from being completed. P_{n+1} is greater than P_n and the absolute magnitude of the "emergencies" escalates. Ultimately the entire system crashes. The crash is not shown, and few can imagine it.

foster economic "development"—*note the metaphor*—and population problems will solve themselves.

Those who believe in the benign demographic transition dismiss the pejoristic mechanism of Figure 2 in the belief that each input of food from the world fosters development within a poor country, thus resulting in a drop in the rate of population increase. Foreign aid has proceeded on this assumption for more than two decades. Unfortunately it has produced no indubitable instance of the asserted effect. It has, however, produced a library of excuses. The air is filled with plaintive calls for more massive foreign aid appropriations so that the hypothetical melioristic process can get started.

The doctrine of demographic laissez-faire implicit in the hypothesis of the benign demographic transition is immensely attractive. Unfortunately there is more evidence against the melioristic system than there is for it.... On the historical side there are many counterexamples. The rise in per capita GNP in France and Ireland during the past century has been accompanied by a rise in population growth. In the 20 years following the Second World War the same positive correlation was noted almost everywhere in the world. Never in world history before

1950 did the worldwide population growth reach 1% per annum. Now the average population growth is over 2% and shows no signs of slackening.

On the theoretical side, the denial of the pejoristic scheme of Figure 2 probably springs from the hidden acceptance of the "cowboy economy" that Boulding castigated. Those who recognize the limitations of a spaceship, if they are unable to achieve population control at a safe and comfortable level, accept the necessity of the corrective feedback of the population cycle shown in Figure 1. No one who knew in his bones that he was living on a true spaceship would countenance political support of the population escalator shown in Figure 2.

ECO-DESTRUCTION VIA THE GREEN REVOLUTION

The demoralizing effect of charity on the recipient has long been known. "Give a man a fish and he will eat for a day: teach him how to fish and he will eat for the rest of his days." So runs an ancient Chinese proverb. Acting on this advice the Rockefeller and Ford Foundations have financed a multipronged program for improving agriculture in the hungry nations. The result, known as the "Green Revolution," has been quite remarkable. "Miracle wheat" and "miracle rice" are splendid technological achievements in the realm of plant genetics.

Whether or not the Green Revolution can increase food production is doubtful ..., but in any event not particularly important. What is missing in this great and well-meaning humanitarian effort is a firm grasp of fundamentals. Considering the importance of the Rockefeller Foundation in this effort it is ironic that the late Alan Gregg, a much-respected vice president of the Foundation, strongly expressed his doubts of the wisdom of all attempts to increase food production some two decades ago. (This was before Borlaug's work— supported by Rockefeller—had resulted in the development of "miracle wheat.") Gregg ... likened the growth and spreading of humanity over the surface of the earth to the metastasis of cancer in the human body, wryly remarking that "Cancerous growths demand food; but, as far as I know, they have never been cured by getting it."

"Man does not live by bread alone"—the scriptural statement has a rich meaning even in the material realm. Every human being born constitutes a draft on all aspects of the environment— food, air, water, unspoiled scenery, occasional and optional solitude, beaches, contact with wild animals, fishing, hunting—the list is long and incompletely known. Food can, perhaps, be significantly increased: but what about clean beaches, unspoiled forests, and solitude? If we satisfy the need for food in a growing population we necessarily decrease the supply of other goods, and thereby increase the difficulty of equitably allocating scarce goods....

The present population of India is 600 million, and it is increasing by 15 million per year. The environmental load of this population is already great. The forests of India are only a small fraction of what they were three centuries ago. Soil erosion, floods, and the psychological costs of crowding are serious. Every one of the net 15 million lives added each year stresses the Indian environment more severely. *Every life saved this year in a poor country diminishes the quality of life for subsequent generations.*

Observant critics have shown how much harm we wealthy nations have already done to poor nations through our well-intentioned but misguided attempts to help them.... Particularly reprehensible is our failure to carry out postaudits of these attempts.... Thus we have shielded our tender consciences from knowledge of the harm we have done. Must we Americans continue to fail to monitor the consequences of our external "dogooding"? If, for instance, we thoughtlessly make it possible for the present 600 million Indians to swell to 1,200 millions by the year 2001—as their present growth rate promises—will posterity in India thank us for facilitating an even greater destruction of *their* environment? Are good intentions ever a sufficient excuse for bad consequences?

IMMIGRATION CREATES A COMMONS

I come now to the final example of a commons in action, one for which the public is least prepared for rational discussion. The topic is at present enveloped by a great silence which reminds me of a comment made by Sherlock Holmes in A. Conan Doyle's story, "Silver Blaze." Inspector Gregory had asked, "Is there any point to which you would wish to draw my attention?" To this Holmes responded:

> "To the curious incident of the dog in the nighttime."
>
> "The dog did nothing in the night-time," said the Inspector.
>
> "That was the curious incident," remarked Sherlock Holmes.

By asking himself what would repress the normal barking instinct of a watchdog Holmes realized that it must be the dog's recognition of his master as the criminal trespasser. In a similar way we should ask ourselves, what repression keeps us from discussing something as important as immigration?

It cannot be that immigration is numerically of no consequence. Our government acknowledges a *net* flow of 400,000 a year. Hard data are understandably lacking on the extent of illegal entries, but a not implausible figure is 600,000 per year.... The natural increase of the resident population is now about 1.7 million per year. This means that the yearly gain from immigration is at least 19%, and may be 37%, of the total increase. It is quite conceivable that educational campaigns like that of Zero Population Growth, Inc., coupled with adverse social and economic factors—inflation, housing shortage, depression, and loss of confidence in national leaders—may lower the fertility of American women to a point at which all of the yearly increase in population would be accounted for by immigration. Should we not at least ask if that is what we want? How curious it is that we so seldom discuss immigration these days!

Curious, but understandable—as one finds out the moment he publicly questions the wisdom of the status quo in immigration. He who does so is promptly charged with *isolationism, bigotry, prejudice, ethnocentrism, chauvinism,* and *selfishness.* These are hard accusations to bear. It is pleasanter to talk about other matters, leaving immigration policy to wallow in the cross-currents of special interests that take no account of the good of the whole—*or of the interests of posterity.*

We Americans have a bad conscience because of things we said in the past about immigrants. Two generations ago the popular press was rife with references to *Dagos, Wops, Pollacks, Japs, Chinks,* and *Krauts*—all pejorative terms which failed to acknowledge our indebtedness to Goya, Leonardo, Copernicus, Hiroshige, Confucius, and Bach. Because the implied inferiority of foreigners was *then* the justification for keeping them out, it is *now* thoughtlessly assumed that restrictive policies can only be based on the assumption of immigrant inferiority. *This is not so.*

Existing immigration laws exclude idiots and known criminals; future laws will almost certainly continue this policy. But should we also consider the quality of the average immigrant, as compared with the quality of the average resident? Perhaps we should, perhaps we shouldn't. (What is "quality" anyway?) But the quality issue is not our concern here.

From this point on, *it will be assumed that immigrants and native-born citizens are of exactly equal quality,* however quality may be defined. The focus is

only on quantity. The conclusions reached depend on nothing else, so all charges of ethnocentrism are irrelevant.

World food banks move food to the people, thus facilitating the exhaustion of the environment of the poor. By contrast, unrestricted immigration moves people to the food, thus speeding up the destruction of the environment in rich countries. Why poor people should want to make this transfer is no mystery: but why should rich hosts encourage it? This transfer, like the reverse one, is supported by both selfish interests and humanitarian impulses.

The principal selfish interest in unimpeded immigration is easy to identify; it is the interest of the employers of cheap labor, particularly that needed for degrading jobs. We have been deceived about the forces of history by the lines of Emma Lazarus inscribed on the Statue of Liberty:

> *Give me your tired, your poor*
> *Your huddled masses yearning to breathe free,*
> *The wretched refuse of your teeming shore,*
> *Send these, the homeless, tempest-tossed, to me:*
> *I lift my lamp beside the golden door.*

The image is one of an infinitely generous earth-mother, passively opening her arms to hordes of immigrants who come here on their own initiative. Such an image may have been adequate for the early days of colonization, but by the time these lines were written (1886) the force for immigration was largely manufactured inside our own borders by factory and mine owners who sought cheap labor not to be found among laborers already here. One group of foreigners after another was thus enticed into the United States to work at wretched jobs for wretched wages.

At present, it is largely the Mexicans who are being so exploited. It is particularly to the advantage of certain employers that there be many illegal immigrants. Illegal immigrant workers dare not complain about their working conditions for fear of being repatriated. Their presence reduces the bargaining power of all Mexican-American laborers. Cesar Chavez has repeatedly pleaded with congressional committees to close the doors to more Mexicans so that those here can negotiate effectively for higher wages and decent working conditions. Chavez understands the ethics of a lifeboat.

The interests of the employers of cheap labor are well served by the silence of the intelligentsia of the country. WASPs—White Anglo-Saxon Protestants—are particularly reluctant to call for a closing of the doors to immigration for fear of being called ethnocentric bigots. It was, therefore, an occasion of pure delight for this particular WASP to be present at a meeting when the points he would like to have made were made better by a non-WASP speaking to other non-WASPS. It was in Hawaii, and most of the people in the room were second-level Hawaiian officials of Japanese ancestry. All Hawaiians are keenly aware of the limits of their environment, and the speaker had asked how it might be practically and constitutionally possible to close the doors to more immigrants to the islands. (To Hawaiians, immigrants from the other 49 states are as much of a threat as those from other nations. There is only so much room in the islands, and the islanders know it. Sophistical arguments that imply otherwise do not impress them.)

Yet the Japanese-Americans of Hawaii have active ties with the land of their origin. This point was raised by a Japanese-American member of the audience who asked the Japanese-American speaker: "But how can we shut the doors now? We have many friends and relations in Japan that we'd like to bring to Hawaii some day so that they can enjoy this beautiful land."

The speaker smiled sympathetically and responded slowly: "Yes, but we have children now and someday we'll have grandchildren. We can bring more people here from Japan only by giving away some of the land that we hope to pass on to our grandchildren some day. What right do we have to do that?"

To be generous with one's own possessions is one thing; to be generous with posterity's is quite another. This, I think, is the point that must be gotten across to those who would, from a commendable love of distributive justice, institute a ruinous system of the commons, either in the form of a world food bank or that of unrestricted immigration. Since every speaker is a member of some ethnic group it is always possible to charge him with ethnocentrism. But even after purging an argument of ethnocentrism the rejection of the commons is still valid and necessary if we are to save at least some parts of the world from environmental ruin. Is it not desirable that at least some of the grandchildren of people now living should have a decent place in which to live?

Plainly many new problems will arise when we consciously face the immigration question and seek rational answers. No workable answers can be found if we ignore population problems. And—if the argument of this essay is correct—so long as there is no true world government to control reproduction everywhere it is impossible to survive in dignity if we are to be guided by Spaceship ethics. Without a world government that is sovereign in reproductive matters mankind lives, in fact, on a number of sovereign lifeboats. For the foreseeable future survival demands that we govern our actions by the ethics of a lifeboat. Posterity will be ill served if we do not.

STUDY QUESTIONS

1. What is Hardin's case against helping poor, needy countries? What is the significance of the lifeboat metaphor?

2. What is the relationship of population policies to world hunger?

3. Explain the "ratchet effect." Is Hardin right that in bringing aid to countries who do not control their population we act immorally?

31

Population and Food: A Critique of Lifeboat Ethics

WILLIAM W. MURDOCH AND ALLAN OATEN

William Murdoch is professor of biological science at the University of California at Santa Barbara and is the author of Environment: Resources, Pollution and Society *(2nd ed., 1975). Allan Oaten is also a biologist who has taught at the University of California at Santa Barbara and specializes in mathematical biology and statistics.*

Murdoch and Oaten begin by attacking Hardin's metaphors of "lifeboat," "commons," and "ratchet" as misleading. They then argue that other factors are needed to understand the population and hunger problem, including parental confidence in the future, low infant mortality rates, literacy, health care, income and employment, and an adequate diet. They claim that once the socioeconomic conditions are attended to, population size will take care of itself. Nonmilitary foreign aid to Third World countries is both just and necessary if we are to prevent global disaster.

MISLEADING METAPHORS

[Hardin's] "Lifeboat" Article actually has two messages. The first is that our immigration policy is too generous. This will not concern us here. The second, and more important, is that by helping poor nations we will bring disaster to rich and poor alike.

> Metaphorically, each rich nation amounts to a lifeboat full of comparatively rich people. The poor of the world are in other, much more crowded lifeboats. Continuously, so to speak, the poor fall out of their lifeboats and swim for a while in the water outside, hoping to be admitted to a rich lifeboat, or in some other way to benefit from the "goodies" on board. What should the passengers on a rich lifeboat do? This is the central problem of "the ethics of a lifeboat." (Hardin)

Among these so-called "goodies" are food supplies and technical aid such as that which led to the Green Revolution. Hardin argues that we should withhold such resources from poor nations on the grounds that they help to maintain high rates of population increase, thereby making the problem worse. He foresees the continued supplying and increasing production of food as a process that will be "brought to an end only by the total collapse of the whole system, producing a catastrophe of scarcely imaginable proportions."

Turning to one particular mechanism for distributing these resources, Hardin claims that a world food bank is a commons—people have more motivation to draw from it than to add to it; it will have a ratchet or escalator effect on population because inputs from it will prevent population declines in over-populated countries. Thus "wealth can be steadily moved in one direction only, from the slowly-breeding rich to the rapidly-breeding poor, the process finally coming to a halt only when all countries are equally and miserably poor." Thus our help will not only bring ultimate disaster to poor countries, but it will also be suicidal for us.

As for the "benign demographic transition" to low birth rates, which some aid supporters have predicted, Hardin states flatly that the weight of evidence is against this possibility.

Finally, Hardin claims that the plight of poor nations is partly their own fault: "wise sovereigns seem not to exist in the poor world today. The most anguishing problems are created by poor countries that are governed by rulers insufficiently wise and powerful." Establishing a world food bank will exacerbate this problem: "slovenly rulers" will escape the consequences of their incompetence—"Others will bail them out whenever they are in trouble"; "Far more difficult than the transfer of wealth from one country to another is the transfer of wisdom between sovereign powers or between generations."

What arguments does Hardin present in support of these opinions? Many involve metaphors: lifeboat, commons, and ratchet or escalator. These metaphors are crucial to his thesis, and it is, therefore, important for us to examine them critically.

The lifeboat is the major metaphor. It seems attractively simple, but it is in fact simplistic and obscures important issues. As soon as we try to use it to compare various policies, we find that most relevant details of the actual situation are either missing or distorted in the lifeboat metaphor. Let us list some of these details.

Most important, perhaps, Hardin's lifeboats barely interact. The rich lifeboats may drop some handouts over the side and perhaps repel a boarding party now and then, but generally they live their own lives. In the real world, nations interact a great deal, in ways that affect food supply and population size and growth, and the effect of rich nations on poor nations has been strong and not always benevolent.

First, by colonization and actual wars of commerce, and through the international marketplace, rich nations have arranged an exchange of goods that has maintained and even increased the economic imbalance between rich and poor nations. Until recently we have taken or otherwise obtained cheap raw material from poor nations and sold them expensive manufactured goods that they cannot make themselves. In the United States, the structure of tariffs and internal subsidies discriminates selectively against poor nations. In poor countries, the concentration on cash crops rather than on food crops, a legacy of colonial times, is now actively encouraged by western multinational corporations.... Indeed, it is claimed that in famine-stricken Sahelian Africa, multinational agribusiness has recently taken land out of food production for cash crops.... Although we often self-righteously take the "blame" for lowering the death rates of poor nations during the 1940s and 1950s, we are less inclined to accept responsibility for the effects of actions that help maintain poverty and hunger. Yet poverty directly contributes to the high birth rates that Hardin views with such alarm.

Second, U.S. foreign policy, including foreign aid programs, has favored "pro-Western" regimes, many of which govern in the interests of a wealthy elite and some of which are savagely repressive. Thus, it has often subsidized a gross maldistribution of income and has supported political leaders who have opposed most of the social changes that can lead to reduced birth rates. In this light, Hardin's pronouncements on the alleged wisdom gap between poor leaders and our own, and the difficulty of filling it, appear as a grim joke: our response to leaders with the power and wisdom Hardin yearns for has often been to try to replace them or their policies as soon as possible. Selective giving and withholding of both military and nonmilitary aid has been an important ingredient of our efforts to maintain political leaders we like and to remove those we do not. Brown ..., after noting that the withholding of U.S. food aid in 1973 contributed to the downfall of the Allende government in

Chile, comments that "although Americans decry the use of petroleum as a political weapon, calling it 'political blackmail,' the United States has been using food aid for political purposes for twenty years—and describing this as 'enlightened diplomacy.'"

Both the quantity and the nature of the supplies on a lifeboat are fixed. In the real world, the quantity has strict limits, but these are far from having been reached (University of California Food Task Force 1974). Nor are we forced to devote fixed proportions of our efforts and energy to automobile travel, pet food, packaging, advertising, corn-fed beef, "defense" and other diversions, many of which cost far more than foreign aid does. The fact is that enough food is now produced to feed the world's population adequately. That people are malnourished is due to distribution and to economics, not to agricultural limits (United Nations Economic and Social Council 1974).

Hardin's lifeboats are divided merely into rich and poor, and it is difficult to talk about birth rates on either. In the real world, however, there are striking differences among the birth rates of the poor countries and even among the birth rates of different parts of single countries. These differences appear to be related to social conditions (also absent from lifeboats) and may guide us to effective aid policies.

Hardin's lifeboat metaphor not only conceals facts, but misleads about the effects of his proposals. The rich lifeboat can raise the ladder and sail away. But in real life, the problem will not necessarily go away just because it is ignored. In the real world, there are armies, raw materials in poor nations, and even outraged domestic dissidents prepared to sacrifice their own and others' lives to oppose policies they regard as immoral.

No doubt there are other objections. But even this list shows the lifeboat metaphor to be dangerously inappropriate for serious policy making because it obscures far more than it reveals. Lifeboats and "lifeboat ethics" may be useful topics for those who are shipwrecked; we believe they are worthless—indeed detrimental—in discussions of food-population questions.

The ratchet metaphor is equally flawed. It, too, ignores complex interactions between birth rates and social conditions (including diets), implying as it does that more food will simply mean more babies. Also, it obscures the fact that the decrease in death rates has been caused at least as much by developments such as DDT, improved sanitation, and medical advances, as by increased food supplies, so that cutting out food aid will not necessarily lead to population declines.

The lifeboat article is strangely inadequate in other ways. For example, it shows an astonishing disregard for recent literature. The claim that we can expect no "benign demographic transition" is based on a review written more than a decade ago. … Yet, events and attitudes are changing rapidly in poor countries: for the first time in history, most poor people live in countries with birth control programs; with few exceptions, poor nations are somewhere on the demographic transition to lower birth rates …; the population-food squeeze is now widely recognized, and governments of poor nations are aware of the relationship. Again, there is a considerable amount of evidence that birth rates can fall rapidly in poor countries given the proper social conditions (as we will discuss later); consequently, crude projections of current populations growth rates are quite inadequate for policy making.

THE TRAGEDY OF THE COMMONS

Throughout the lifeboat article, Hardin bolsters his assertions by reference to the "commons." … The thesis of the commons, therefore, needs critical evaluation.

Suppose several privately owned flocks, comprising 100 sheep altogether, are grazing on a public commons. They bring in an annual income of $1.00 per sheep. Fred, a herdsman, owns only one sheep. He decides to add another. But 101 is too many: the commons is overgrazed and produces less food. The sheep lose quality and income drops to 90¢ per sheep. Total income is now $90.90 instead of $100.00. Adding the sheep has brought an overall loss. But Fred has gained: *his* income is $1.80 instead of $1.00. The gain from the additional sheep, which is his alone, outweighs the loss from overgrazing, which he shares. Thus he promotes his interest at the expense of the community.

This is the problem of the commons, which seems on the way to becoming an archetype. Hardin, in particular, is not inclined to underrate its importance: "One of the major tasks of education today is to create such an awareness of the dangers of the commons that people will be able to recognize its many varieties, however disguised" ... and "All this is terribly obvious once we are acutely aware of the pervasiveness and danger of the commons. But many people still lack this awareness...."

The "commons" affords a handy way of classifying problems: the lifeboat article reveals that sharing, a generous immigration policy, world food banks, air, water, the fish populations of the ocean, and the western range lands are, or produce, a commons. It is also handy to be able to dispose of policies one does not like and "only a particular instance of a class of policies that are in error because they lead to the tragedy of the commons."

But no metaphor, even one as useful as this, should be treated with such awe. Such shorthand can be useful, but it can also mislead by discouraging and obscuring important detail. To dismiss a proposal by suggesting that "all you need to know about this proposal is that it institutes a commons and is, therefore, bad" is to assert that the proposed commons is worse than the original problem. This might be so if the problem of the commons were, indeed, a tragedy—that is, if it were insoluble. But it is not.

Hardin favors private ownership as the solution (either through private property or the selling of pollution rights). But, of course, there are solutions other than private ownership; and private ownership itself is no guarantee of carefully husbanded resources.

One alternative to private ownership of the commons is communal ownership of the sheep—or, in general, of the mechanisms and industries that exploit the resource—combined with communal planning for management. (Note, again, how the metaphor favors one solution: perhaps the "tragedy" lay not in the commons but in the sheep. "The Tragedy of the Privately Owned Sheep" lacks zing, unfortunately.) Public ownership of a commons has been tried in Peru to the benefit of the previously privately owned anchovy fishery.... The communally owned agriculture of China does not seem to have suffered any greater overexploitation than that of other Asian nations.

Another alternative is cooperation combined with regulation. For example, Gulland ... has shown that Antarctic whale stocks (perhaps the epitome of a commons since they are internationally exploited and no one owns them) are now being properly managed, and stocks are increasing. This has been achieved through cooperation in the International Whaling Commission, which has by agreement set limits to the catch of each nation.

In passing, Hardin's private ownership argument is not generally applicable to nonrenewable resources. Given discount rates, technology substitutes, and no more than an average regard for posterity, privately owned nonrenewable resources, like oil, coal and minerals, are mined at rates that produce maximum profits, rather than at those rates that preserve them for future generations....

BIRTH RATES: AN ALTERNATIVE VIEW

Is the food-population spiral inevitable? A more optimistic, if less comfortable, hypothesis, presented by Rich and Brown, is increasingly tenable: contrary to the "ratchet" projection, population growth rates are affected by many complex conditions besides food supply. In particular, a set of socioeconomic conditions can be identified that motivate parents to have fewer children; under these conditions, birth rates can fall quite rapidly, sometimes even before birth control technology is available. Thus, population growth can be controlled more effectively by intelligent human intervention that sets up the appropriate conditions than by doing nothing and trusting to "natural population cycles."

These conditions are parental confidence about the future, an improved status of women, and literacy. They require low infant mortality rates, widely available rudimentary health care, increased income and employment, and an adequate diet above subsistence levels. Expenditure on schools (especially elementary schools), appropriate health services (especially rural para-medical services), and agriculture reform (especially aid to small farmers) will be needed, and foreign aid can help here. It is essential that these improvements be spread across the population; aid can help here, too, by concentrating on the poor nations' poorest people, encouraging necessary institutional and social reforms, and making it easier for poor nations to use their own resources and initiative to help themselves. It is *not* necessary that per capita GNP be very high, certainly not as high as that of the rich countries during their gradual demographic transition. In other words, low birth rates in poor countries are achievable long before the conditions exist that were present in the rich countries in the late 19th and early 20th centuries.

Twenty or thirty years is not long to discover and assess the factors affecting birth rates, but a body of evidence is now accumulating in favor of this hypothesis. Rich and Brown show that at least 10 developing countries have managed to reduce their birth rates by an average of more than one birth per 1,000 population per year for periods of 5 to 16 years. A reduction of one birth per 1,000 per year would bring birth rates in poor countries to a rough replacement level of about 16/1,000 by the turn of the century, though age distribution effects would prevent a smooth population decline. We have listed these countries in Table 1, together with three other nations, including China, that are poor and yet have brought their birth rates down to 30 or less, presumably from rates of over 40 a decade or so ago.

These data show that rapid reduction in birth rates is possible in the developing world. No doubt it can be argued that each of these cases is in some way special. Hong Kong and Singapore are relatively rich; they, Barbados, and Mauritius are also tiny. China is able to exert great social pressure on its citizens; but China is particularly significant. It is enormous; its per capita GNP is almost as low as India's; and it started out in 1949 with a terrible health system. Also, Egypt, Chile, Taiwan, Cuba, South Korea, and Sri Lanka are quite large, and they are poor or very poor (Table 1). In fact, these examples represent an enormous range of religion, political systems, and geography and suggest that such rates of decline in the birth rate can be achieved whenever the appropriate conditions are met. "The common factor in these countries is that the *majority* of the population has shared in the economic and social benefits of significant national progress. ... [M]aking health, education and jobs more broadly available to lower income groups in poor countries contribute[s] significantly toward the motivation for smaller families that is the prerequisite of major reduction in birth rates." ...

The converse is also true. In Latin America, Cuba (annual per capita income $530), Chile ($720), Uruguay ($820), and Argentina ($1,160) have moderate to truly equitable distribution of goods and services and relatively low birth rates (27, 25, 23, and 22, respectively). In contrast, Brazil ($420), Mexico ($670), and Venezuela ($980) have very unequal distribution of goods and services and high birth rates (38, 42, and 41, respectively). Fertility rates in poor and relatively poor nations seem unlikely to fall as long as the bulk of the population does not share in increased benefits....

... As a disillusioning quarter-century of aid giving has shown, the obstacles of getting aid to those segments of the population most in need of it are enormous. Aid has typically benefited a small rich segment of society, partly because of the way aid programs have been designed but also because of human and institutional factors in the poor nations themselves.... With some notable exceptions, the distribution of income and services in poor nations is extremely skewed—much more uneven than in rich countries. Indeed, much of the population is essentially outside the economic system. Breaking this pattern will be extremely difficult. It will require not only aid that is designed specifically to benefit the rural poor, but also important institutional changes such as decentralization of decision making and the development of greater

TABLE 1   **Declining Birth Rates and Per Capita Income in Selected Developing Countries. (These Are Crude Birth Rates, Uncorrected for Age Distribution.)**

Country	Time Span	Average Annual Decline in Crude Birth Rate	Crude Birth Rate 1972	$ Per Capita Per Year 1973
		Births/1,000/year		
Barbados	1960–69	1.5	22	570
Taiwan	1955–71	1.2	24	390
Tunisia	1966–71	1.8	35	250
Mauritius	1961–71	1.5	25	240
Hong Kong	1960–72	1.4	19	970
Singapore	1955–72	1.2	23	920
Costa Rica	1963–72	1.5	32	560
South Korea	1960–70	1.2	29	250
Egypt	1966–70	1.7	37	210
Chile	1963–70	1.2	25	720
China			30	160
Cuba			27	530
Sri Lanka			30	110

autonomy and stronger links to regional and national market for local groups and industries such as cooperative farms.

Thus, two things are being asked of rich nations and of the United States in particular: to increase nonmilitary foreign aid, including food aid, and to give it in ways, and to governments, that will deliver it to the poorest people and will improve their access to national economic institutions. These are not easy tasks, particularly the second, and there is no guarantee that birth rates will come down quickly in all countries. Still, many poor countries have, in varying degrees, begun the process of reform, and recent evidence suggests that aid and reform together can do much to solve the twin problems of high birth rates and economic underdevelopment. The tasks are far from impossible. Based on the evidence, the policies dictated by a sense of decency are also the most realistic and rational.

STUDY QUESTIONS

1. What are the criticisms leveled against Hardin's arguments?

2. What is Murdoch and Oaten's view on the question of population growth? What is the gradual demographic transition theory? Is their view plausible?

3. Compare Hardin's arguments with Murdoch and Oaten's response. Where does the evidence lie?

4. What are the disanalogies between a lifeboat and the United States?

Chapter 6

Pollution: Soil Air Water

IN 1962, Rachel Carson published *Silent Spring* in which she documented the effects of DDT and other pesticides on human health. She charged that these "elixirs of death" were causing widespread cancer and genetic mutations as well as wreaking havoc on birds, fish, and wildlife. Her famous opening words not only mark the beginning of the modern environmental movement but also set its tone.

> There was once a town in the heart of America where all life seemed to live in harmony with its surroundings. The town lay in the midst of a checkerboard of prosperous farms, with fields of grain and hillsides of orchards where, in spring, white clouds of bloom drifted above the green fields. In autumn, oak and maple and birch set up a blaze of color that flamed and flickered across a backdrop of pines. Then foxes barked in the hills and deer silently crossed the fields, half hidden in the mists of the fall mornings....
>
> Then a strange blight crept over the area and everything began to change. Some evil spell had settled on the community: mysterious maladies swept the flocks of chickens; the cattle and sheep sickened and died. Everywhere was a shadow of death. The farmers spoke of much illness among their families. In the town the doctors had become more and more puzzled by new kinds of sickness appearing among their patients. There had been several sudden and unexplained deaths, not only among adults but even among children, who would be stricken suddenly while at play and die within a few hours.

It took ten years before DDT was banned from agricultural use. Meanwhile it was discovered that we were releasing hosts of other toxins into our air, water, and soil. Although governments now regulate toxins, they are still used in enormous quantities in both agriculture and industry.

In 1989, the oil tanker *Exxon Valdez* ran aground off the Alaskan Coast, spilling 1.26 million barrels of oil into Prince William Sound. It was the worst oil spill in history. The pristine beauty of the Alaskan Coast with its wealth of birds, fish, and wildlife was degraded. Five hundred square miles of the Sound were polluted. Millions of fish, birds, and wildlife were killed, and fishermen lost their means of livelihood. The fishing industry, which earns $100 million annually in Prince William Sound, ground to an abrupt halt. The Exxon Corporation was unprepared for an accident of such magnitude. It had only 69 barrels of oil dispersant on hand in Alaska, when nearly 10,000 barrels were needed to clean up the spill. The ship's captain, Joseph Hazelwood, was found guilty of negligence and operating the tanker under the influence of alcohol, and Exxon was fined $100 million. Greenpeace put an ad in newspapers, showing Joseph Hazelwood's face, with the caption: "It wasn't his driving that caused the Alaskan oil spill. It was yours. The spill was caused by a nation drunk on oil. And a government asleep at the wheel."

This spill has just been exceeded by the British Petroleum Deep Water spill in the Gulf of Mexico. An explosion on April 20, 2010, on off shore drilling rig killed eleven workers and triggered a massive leak at the sea bed level. It is still disputed what exactly the series of failures was; BP claims that Halliburton Energy Services, which had installed infrastructure on the sea bed, shares blame. Over 2 million (some estimates reported numbers closer to 2.5 million) gallons of crude oil leaked into the Gulf of Mexico every day for almost 4 months. The spill was capped on July 15, but the ecological consequences, though it is still assessed, are obviously enormous. Mainstream environmentalism has been remarkably passive about this issue, and the story has already mostly dropped out of the media. There are around 3,500 other offshore rigs in the Gulf of Mexico, though only a small number are deep wells.

Pollution may be broadly defined as any unwanted state or change in the properties of air, water, soil, liquid, or food that can have a negative impact on the health, well-being, or survival of human beings or other living organisms. Most pollutants are undesirable chemicals that are produced as by-products when a resource is converted into energy or a commodity. Types of pollution include contaminated water, chemically polluted air (such as smog), toxic waste in the soil, poisoned food, high

levels of radiation, and noise. They also include acid rain and second-hand cigarette smoke because these can have a deleterious effect on our health.

Three factors determine the severity of a pollutant: its chemical nature (how harmful it is to various types of living organisms), its concentration (the amount per volume of air, water, soil, or body weight), and its persistence (how long it remains in the air, water, soil, or body).

A pollutant's persistence can be divided into three types: degradable, slowly degradable, and nondegradable. Degradable pollutants, such as human sewage and contaminated soil, are usually broken down completely or reduced to acceptable levels by natural chemical processes. Slowly degradable pollutants, such as DDT, plastics, aluminum cans, and chlorofluorocarbons (CFCs), often take decades to degrade to acceptable levels. Nondegradable pollutants, such as lead and mercury, are not broken down by natural processes.

We know little about the short- and long-range harmful potential, for people and for the environment, of most of the more than 70,000 synthetic chemicals in commercial use. The Environmental Protection Agency (EPA) estimates that 80% of cancers are caused by pollution. We know that half of our air pollution is caused by the internal combustion engines of motor vehicles and that coal-burning stationary power plants produce unacceptable amounts of sulfur dioxide (SO_2). The World Health Organization (WHO) estimates that about 1 billion urban people (about one-fifth of humanity) are being exposed to health hazards from air pollution and that emphysema, an incurable lung disease, is rampant in our cities. Studies tell us that smog is hazardous to our health and that it has caused thousands of deaths in such cities as London, New York, and Los Angeles.

In the United States, 80% of freshwater aquifers are in danger, so a large percentage (estimates are more than 30%) of the U.S. population is drinking contaminated water. By 1991 the EPA had listed 1211 hazardous waste sites for cleanup, at an estimated cost of $26 million per site. Acid rain is killing our forests and lakes.

In our first reading, Hilary French documents the dire consequences of air pollution. Her essay provides hard data around which rational discussion can take place.

Our second reading contains a sharp indictment of corporate capitalism by George Bradford. Reacting to what he perceived to be a condoning of the tragedy of Bhopal, India (where a Union Carbide factory exploded, killing 3,000 people in 1984) by the *Wall Street Journal,* Bradford lashes out at the whole economic and social philosophy that permitted and is responsible for this and many other threats to humanity. In the Third World, businesses cut costs by having lax safety standards. Chemicals that are banned in the United States and Europe are produced overseas. Even in the United States and Europe, our industrial culture continues to endanger our lives. We must throw "off this Modern Way of Life," argues Bradford, for it only constitutes a "terrible burden" that threatens to crush us all.

Our third reading, "People or Penguins: The Case for Optimal Pollution" by William Baxter, explores the relationship between resources and pollution, showing that we cannot have the good of resource use without the bad of pollution. The point is to decide on the proper balance. Those like Baxter, who take a decidedly anthropocentric point of view, argue that we ought to risk pollution that might endanger other species (as DDT does) if it promotes human advantage.

In our fourth reading, entomologist David Pimentel assesses the progress and problems of pesticide use since *Silent Spring* was written. On the one hand, much progress has been made so that the poisons in pesticides affect humans and wildlife less directly. But unfortunately, pesticide-resistant insects have replaced their less damaging ancestors. Furthermore, pesticides have destroyed some of the natural enemies of certain pests, so more crops are now lost to insects than they were when *Silent Spring* was written. However, because of better overall agricultural techniques and fertilizers, the total picture is positive.

32

You Are What You Breathe

HILARY FRENCH

Hilary French is a staff researcher for the Worldwatch Institute.

In this essay, French provides a detailed, documented account of the devastating global effects of air pollution. Because the wind carries the polluted air from one nation to another, this problem requires international as well as national action and cooperation. If we are to solve the problem, our lifestyles will have to change.

Asked to name the world's top killers, most people wouldn't put air pollution high on their lists.

A nuisance, at best, but not a terribly serious threat to health.

The facts say otherwise. In greater Athens, for example, the number of deaths rises sixfold on heavily polluted days. In Hungary, the government attributes 1 in 17 deaths to air pollution. In Bombay, breathing the air is equivalent to smoking 10 cigarettes a day. And in Beijing, air-pollution-related respiratory distress is so common that it has been dubbed the "Beijing Cough."

Air pollution is truly a global public health emergency. United Nations statistics show that more than one billion people—a fifth of humanity—live in areas where the air is not fit to breathe. Once a local phenomenon primarily affecting city dwellers and people living near factories, air pollution now reaches rural as well as urban dwellers. It's also crossing international borders.

In the United States alone, roughly 150 million people live in areas whose air is considered unhealthy by the Environmental Protection Agency (EPA). According to the American Lung Association, this leads to as many as 120,000 deaths each year.

A century ago, air pollution was caused primarily by the coal burned to fuel the industrial revolution. Since then, the problem and its causes have become more complex and widespread. In some parts of the world, including much of Eastern Europe and China, coal continues to be the main source of pollution. Elsewhere, automobiles and industries are now the primary cause.

Adding to the miasma, industries are emitting pollutants of frightening toxicity. Millions of tons of carcinogens, mutagens, and poisons pour into the air each year and damage health and habitat near their sources and, via the winds, sometimes thousands of miles away. Many regions that have enjoyed partial success combating pollution are finding their efforts overwhelmed as populations and economies grow and bring in more power plants, home furnaces, factories, and motor vehicles.

Meanwhile, global warming has arisen as the preeminent environmental concern; this sometimes conveys the misleading impression that conventional air pollution is yesterday's problem. But air pollutants and greenhouse gases stem largely from fossil fuels burned in energy, transportation, and industrial systems. Having common roots, the two problems can also have common solutions. Unfortunately, policymakers persist in tackling them separately, which runs the risk of lessening one while exacerbating the other.

Air pollution has proven so intractable a phenomenon that a book could be written about the history of efforts to combat it. Law has followed law. As one problem has largely been solved, a new one has frequently emerged to take its place. Even some of the solutions have become part of the problem: The tall smokestacks built in the 1960s and 1970s to disperse emissions from huge coal-burning power plants became conduits to the upper atmosphere for the pollutants that form acid rain.

Turning the corner on air pollution requires moving beyond patchwork, end-of-the-pipe approaches to confront pollution at its sources. This will mean reorienting energy, transportation, and industrial structures toward prevention.

CHEMICAL SOUP

Although air pollution plagues countries on all continents and at all levels of development, it comes in many different varieties. The burning of fossil fuels—predominantly coal—by power plants, industries, and home furnaces was the first pollution problem recognized as a threat to human health. The sulfur dioxide and particulate emissions associated with coal burning—either alone or in combination—can raise the incidence of respiratory diseases such as coughs and colds, asthma, bronchitis, and emphysema. Particulate matter (a general term for a complex and varying mixture of pollutants in minute solid form) can carry toxic metals deep into the lungs.

Pollution from automobiles forms a second front in the battle for clean air. One of the worst auto-related pollutants is ozone, the principal ingredient in urban smog. Formed when sunlight causes hydrocarbons (a by-product of many industrial processes and engines) to react with nitrogen oxides (produced by cars and power plants), ozone can cause serious respiratory distress. Recent U.S. research

T A B L E 1   **Health Effects of Pollutants from Automobiles[1]**

Pollutant	Health Effect
Carbon monoxide	Interferes with blood's ability to absorb oxygen; impairs perception and thinking; slows reflexes; causes drowsiness; and so can cause unconsciousness and death; if inhaled by pregnant women, may threaten growth and mental development of fetus.
Lead	Affects circulatory, reproductive, nervous, and kidney systems; suspected of causing hyperactivity and lowered learning ability in children; hazardous even after exposure ends.
Nitrogen oxides	Can increase susceptibility to viral infections such as influenza. Can also irritate the lungs and cause bronchitis and pneumonia.
Ozone	Irritates mucous membranes of respiratory system; causes coughing, choking, and impaired lung function; reduces resistance to colds and pneumonia; can aggravate chronic heart disease, asthma, bronchitis, and emphysema.
Toxic emissions	Suspected of causing cancer, reproductive problems, and birth defects. Benzene is a known carcinogen.

[1] Automobiles are a primary source, but not the only source, of these pollutants.

SOURCE: National Clean Air Coalition and the U.S. Environmental Protection Agency.

suggests that ground-level ozone causes temporary breathing difficulty and long-term lung damage at lower concentrations than previously believed.

Other dangerous pollutants spewed by automobiles include nitrogen dioxide, carbon monoxide, lead, and such toxic hydrocarbons as benzene, toluene, xylene, and ethylene dibromide (see Table 1).

At elevated levels, nitrogen dioxide can cause lung irritation, bronchitis, pneumonia, and increased susceptibility to viral infections such as influenza. Carbon monoxide can interfere with the blood's ability to absorb oxygen; this impairs perception and thinking, slow reflexes, and causes drowsiness and—in extreme cases—unconsciousness and death. If inhaled by a pregnant woman, carbon monoxide can threaten the fetus's physical and mental development.

Lead affects the circulatory, reproductive, nervous, and kidney systems. It is suspected of causing hyperactivity and lowered learning ability in children. Because it accumulates in bone and tissue, it is hazardous long after exposure ends.

Concern is growing around the world about the health threat posed by less common but extremely harmful airborne toxic chemicals such as benzene, vinyl chloride, and other volatile organic chemicals produced by automobiles and industries. These chemicals can cause a variety of illnesses, such as cancer and genetic and birth defects, yet they have received far less regulatory attention around the world than have "conventional" pollutants.

WHERE THE BREATHING ISN'T EASY

With the aid of pollution control equipment and improvements in energy efficiency, many Western industrialized countries have made significant strides in reducing emissions of sulfur dioxide and particulates. The United States, for example, cut sulfur oxide emissions by 28 percent between 1970 and 1987 and particulates by 62 percent (see Figure 1). In Japan, sulfur dioxide emissions fell by 39 percent from 1973 to 1984.

The same cannot be said for Eastern Europe and the Soviet Union, where hasty industrialization after World War II, powered by abundant high-sulfur brown coal, has led to some of the worst air pollution ever experienced. Pollution control technologies have been virtually nonexistent. And,

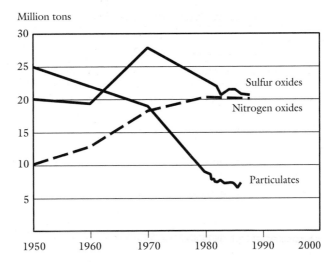

Million tons

FIGURE 1 Emissions of Selected Pollutants in the United States, 1950–1987.
SOURCE: Worldwatch Institute, based on Summers and Heston.

because of heavily subsidized fuel prices and the absence of market forces governing production, these countries never made the impressive gains in energy efficiency registered in the West after the oil shocks of the 1970s.

Many developing countries also confront appalling air pollution problems. The lack of adequate pollution control technologies and regulations, plus plans to expand energy and industrial production, translates into worsening air quality in many cities. Urbanization in much of the Third World means that increasing numbers of people are exposed to polluted city air.

A 1988 report by the United Nations' Environment Program (UNEP) and the World Health Organization (WHO) gives the best picture to date of the global spread of sulfur dioxide and particulate pollution (see Table 2). Of the 54 cities with data available on sulfur dioxide pollution for 1980 to 1984, 27 were on the borderline or in violation of the WHO health standard.

High on the list were Shenyang, Tehran, and Seoul, as well as Milan, Paris, and Madrid; this indicates that sulfur dioxide problems have by no means been cured in industrial countries. Though conditions are gradually improving in most of the

TABLE 2 **Violations of Sulfur Dioxide and Suspended Particulate Matter Standards, Selected Cities[1]**

City	Sulfur Dioxide	Particulates[2]
	(number of days above WHO standard)	
New Delhi	6	294
Xian	71	273
Beijing	68	272
Shenyang	146	219
Tehran	104	174
Bangkok	0	97
Madrid	35	60
Kuala Lampur	0	37
Zagreb	30	34
Sao Paulo	12	31
Paris	46	3
New York	8	0
Milan	66	n.a.
Seoul	87	n.a.

[1] Averages of readings at a variety of monitoring sites from 1980 to 1984.
[2] For Madrid, Sao Paulo, and Paris, the reading is of smoke rather than particulates.
SOURCE: United Nations' Environment Program and World Health Organization, Assessment of Urban Air Quality (Nairobi: Global Environment Monitoring System, 1988).

cities surveyed, several in the Third World reported a worsening trend.

Suspended particulate matter poses an even more pervasive threat, especially in the developing world, where the appropriate control technologies have not been installed and conditions are frequently dusty. Fully 37 of the 41 cities monitored for particulates averaged either borderline or excessive levels. Annual average concentrations were as much as five times the WHO standard in both New Delhi and Beijing.

Ozone pollution, too, has become a seemingly intractable health problem in many parts of the world. In the United States, 1988 ushered in one of the hottest and sunniest years on record, and also one of the worst for ground-level ozone in more than a decade. According to the Natural Resources Defense Council, the air in New York City violated the federal health standard on 34 days—two to three times a week, all summer long. In Los Angeles, ozone levels surged above the federal standard on 172 days. At last count 382 counties, home to more than half of all Americans, were out of compliance with the EPA ozone standard.

Ozone is becoming a problem elsewhere, too. In Mexico City, the relatively lenient government standard of a one-hour ozone peak of 0.11 parts per million not to be exceeded more than once daily is topped more than 300 days a year—nearly twice as often as Los Angeles violates its much stricter standard.

The other automobile-related pollutants also constitute a far-flung health threat. The WHO/UNEP report estimates that 15 to 20 percent of urban residents in North America and Europe are exposed to unacceptably high levels of nitrogen dioxide, 50 percent to unhealthy carbon monoxide concentrations, and a third to excessive lead levels. In a study in Mexico City, lead levels in the blood of 7 out of 10 newborns were found to exceed WHO standards. "The implication for Mexican society, that an entire generation of children will be intellectually stunted, is truly staggering," says Mexican chemist and environmental activist Manuel Guerra.

Airborne toxic chemical emissions present no less of a danger. In the United States, the one country that has begun to tally total emissions, factories

reported 1.3 million tons of hazardous emissions in 1987, including 118,000 tons of carcinogens. According to the EPA, these emissions cause about 2,000 cancer deaths a year.

These deaths fall disproportionately on certain communities. For example, in West Virginia's Kanawha Valley—home to a quarter of a million people and 13 major chemical plants—state health department records show that, between 1968 and 1977, the incidence of respiratory cancer was more than 21 percent above the national average. According to EPA statistics, a lifetime of exposure to the airborne concentrations of butadiene, chloroform, and ethylene oxide in this valley could cause cancer in 1 resident in 1,000.

Unfortunately, data are not so extensive for other countries. Wherever uncontrolled polluting industries such as chemical plants, smelters, and paper mills exist, however, emission levels are undoubtedly high. Measurements of lead and cadmium in the soil of the upper Silesian towns of Olkosz and Slawkow in Poland, for instance, are among the highest recorded anywhere in the world.

The health damage inflicted by air pollution comes at great human cost; it also carries an economic price tag. The American Lung Association estimates that air pollution costs the United States $40 billion annually in health care and lost productivity.

CLEARING THE AIR

In the Western industrial world, the last 20 years has been a period of intense political and scientific activity aimed at restoring clean air. The approaches to date, however, have tended to be technological Band-Aids rather than efforts to address the roots of the problem.

Scrubbers, nitrogen-oxides control technologies, and new cleaner-burning coal technologies can all reduce emissions dramatically, but they are not the ultimate solutions. For one, they can create environmental problems of their own, such as the need to dispose of scrubber ash, a hazardous waste. Second, they do little if anything to reduce carbon dioxide emissions, so make no significant contribution to slowing global warming.

For these reasons, technologies of this kind are best viewed as a bridge to the day when energy-efficient societies are the norm and pollution-free sources such as solar, wind, and water power provide the bulk of the world's electricity.

Improving energy efficiency is a clean air priority. Such measures as more-efficient refrigerators and lighting can markedly and cost-effectively reduce electricity consumption; this will in turn reduce emissions. Equally important, the savings that results from not building power plants because demand has been cut by efficiency can more than offset the additional cost of installing scrubbers at existing plants.

Using conservative assumptions, the Washington, D.C.–based American Council for an Energy Efficient Economy concluded that cutting sulfur dioxide emissions steeply with a scrubbers/conservation combination could actually save consumers in the Midwest up to $8 billion.

Similar rethinking can help reduce auto emissions. To date, modifying car engines and installing catalytic converters have been the primary strategies employed to lower harmful emissions. These devices reduce hydrocarbon emissions by an average of 87 percent, carbon monoxide by an average of 85 percent, and nitrogen oxides by 62 percent over the life of a vehicle. Although catalytic converters are sorely needed in countries that don't require them, they alone are not sufficient. Expanding auto fleets are overwhelming the good they do, even in countries that have mandated their use.

Alternative fuels, such as methanol, ethanol, natural gas, hydrogen, and electricity, are being pushed by many governments as the remedy for the air pollution quagmire. Although these fuels may have some role to play eventually, they can by no means be viewed as a panacea.

Reducing air pollution in cities is likely to require a major shift away from automobiles as the cornerstone of urban transportation systems. As congestion slows traffic to a crawl in many cities, driving to work is becoming unattractive anyway. Convenient public transportation, car pooling, and measures that facilitate bicycle commuting are the cheapest, most effective ways for metropolitan areas to proceed.

Driving restrictions already exist in many of the world's cities. For example, Florence has turned its downtown into a pedestrian mall during daylight hours. Budapest bans motor traffic from all but two streets in the downtown area during particularly polluted spells. In Mexico City and Santiago, one-fifth of all vehicles are kept off the streets each weekday based on their license-plate numbers.

As with power plant and auto emissions, efforts to control airborne toxic chemicals will be most successful if they focus on minimizing waste rather than simply on controlling emissions. Such a strategy also prevents waste from being shifted from one form to another. For instance, control technologies such as scrubbers and filters produce hazardous solid wastes that must be disposed on land.

The Congressional Office of Technology Assessment has concluded it is technically and economically feasible for U.S. industries to lower production of toxic wastes and pollutants by up to 50 percent within the next few years. Similar possibilities exist in other countries.

Freedom of environmental information can also be a powerful regulatory tool. In the United States, "right-to-know" legislation requiring industries to release data on their toxic emissions has been instrumental in raising public awareness of the threat and spurring more responsible industrial behavior. The Monsanto Company, a major chemical producer, was so embarrassed by the enormous pollution figures it was required to release in 1989 that it simultaneously announced its intention to cut back emissions 90 percent by 1992.

Few European countries have released information about emissions from industrial plants, although that may change if the European Economic Community (EEC) issues a directive now in draft form on freedom of information regarding environmental matters. The recent political transformation in Eastern Europe and the Soviet Union are gradually improving the environmental data flow, although much progress in this area remains to be made.

SOLUTION FROM SMOG CITY

In most parts of the world, air pollution is now squarely on the public policy agenda. This is a promising sign. Unfortunately, the public's desire for clean air has not yet been matched with the political leadership needed to provide it. Recent developments at the national and international levels, though constituting steps forward, remain inadequate to the task.

In the United States, for example, recent major amendments to the Clean Air Act of 1970 will cut acid rain emissions in half, tighten emissions standards for automobiles significantly, and require much stricter control of toxic air pollutants.

Almost any legislation would be an improvement. Twenty years after the act became law, 487 counties still are not in compliance. But the legislation fails to address the problem at a fundamental level by not encouraging energy efficiency, waste reduction, and a revamping of transportation systems and urban designs.

Los Angeles—with the worst air quality in the United States—is one of the first regions in the world to really understand that lasting change will not come through mere tinkering. Under a bold new air-quality plan embracing the entire region, the city government will discourage automobile use, boost public transportation, and control household and industrial activities that contribute to smog.

For example, paints and solvents will have to be reformulated to produce fewer ozone-forming fumes; gasoline-powered lawn mowers and lighter fluid will be banned; carpooling will be mandated; and the number of cars per family limited. Even though the plan has been approved by all of the relevant state and federal agencies, implementing it at the local level will be a challenge.

Most of Europe, though quicker than the United States to cut back sharply on the emissions that cause acid rain, has been slower to tackle urban air quality. Non-EEC countries such as Austria, Norway, Sweden, and Switzerland have had strong auto emissions control legislation in place for several years, but until recently the EEC had been unable to agree on its own stringent standards.

This finally changed in June 1989, when the EEC Council of Environmental Ministers ended a nearly four-year debate and approved new standards for small cars. These will be as tough as those now in effect in the United States. To meet them, small cars will have to be equipped with catalytic converters. Although an important step forward, it's somewhat ironic that Europe sees its adoption of U.S. standards as a major victory at the same time the United States realizes these regulations don't go far enough.

In Eastern Europe and the Soviet Union, air pollution emerged as a pressing political issue as *glasnost* and the revolutions of 1989 opened up public debate. Air pollution in much of the region is taking a devastating toll on human health. Fledgling governments in Eastern Europe are under pressure to show some improvements.

A HELPFUL HAND

To make a dent in their pollution, Eastern Europe and the Soviet Union will need Western technologies and a dose of domestic economic and environmental reform. Given current economic conditions in these countries, money for purchasing pollution control, energy efficiency, renewable energy, and waste reduction technologies will have to come in part in the form of environmental aid from the West.

Aid of this kind can be classified as enlightened philanthropy, since stemming pollution in Eastern Europe, where even rudimentary controls are still lacking, can yield a far greater return on the investment than taking further incremental steps at home. To illustrate this point, Sweden receives 89 percent of the sulfur that contributes to the acid rain poisoning its lakes and forests from other countries. Because much of this is of Eastern European origin, anything Sweden does to combat emissions there helps at home.

Air pollution is beginning to emerge on the political agenda in the Third World as well. In Cubatão, Brazil, a notoriously polluted industrial city known as "the Valley of Death," a five-year-old government cleanup campaign is starting to make a dent in the problem. Total emissions of particulates, for instance, were cut from 521,600 pounds a day in 1984 to 156,000 in 1989.

Mexico City, too, is embarking on an ambitious cleanup. With the support of the World Bank, Japan, the United States, and West Germany, the municipal government is introducing a package of measures aimed at cutting automotive pollution dramatically over the next two to three years. As part of the plan, driving will be restricted on certain days. In March 1991, Mexican President Carlos Salinas de Gortari ordered the shutdown of a large oil refinery on the outskirts of Mexico City that has long been a major contributor to the city's pollution problem.

Industrial countries are involved in a variety of efforts to assist developing countries with air pollution problems. The International Environmental Bureau in Switzerland and the World Environment Center in New York City help facilitate transfer of pollution control information and technology to the Third World. The World Bank is exploring ways to step up its air pollution control activities. One proposed project involving the World Bank and the UN Development Program would help Asian governments confront urban air pollution, among other environmental problems.

Legislation passed by the U.S. Congress requires the Agency for International Development to encourage energy efficiency and renewable energy through its programs in the interests of slowing global warming. This step will reduce air pollution at the same time.

While the means are available to clear the air, it will be a difficult task. In the West, powerful businesses such as auto manufacturers and electric utilities will strongly resist measures that appear costly. In Eastern Europe, the Soviet Union, and the developing world, extreme economic problems coupled with shortages of hard currency mean that money for pollution prevention and control is scarce.

Overcoming these barriers will require fundamental modifications of economic systems. As long as air pollution's costs remain external to economic accounting systems, utilities, industries, and individuals will have little incentive to reduce the amount of pollution they generate. Taxes, regulations, and public awareness can all be harnessed to bring the hidden costs of air pollution out into the open.

On the promising side, faced with mounting costs to human health and the environment, people on every continent are beginning to look at pollution prevention through a different economic lens. Rather than a financial burden, they're seeing that it is a sound investment. The old notion that pollution is the price of progress seems finally to be becoming a relic of the past.

STUDY QUESTIONS

1. What conclusions should we come to after reading French's assessment of the hazards of air pollution? What does the data signify for the future?

2. If you were to propose a plan to solve the problem of air pollution, how would you begin? What sort of measures would you take both locally and nationally? How would you deal with other nations who are polluting the atmosphere?

3. Is air pollution an area that the United Nations should be involved in? Explain your reasoning.

33

We All Live in Bhopal

GEORGE BRADFORD

George Bradford is an editor of The Fifth Estate.

In this essay, Bradford argues that in the Third World, as well as in Europe and the United States, industrial capitalism is harming hundreds of thousands of people and imposing a frightful risk on millions more through unsafe practices that pollute our air, water, soil, and food. Taking the tragic explosion of the Union Carbide insecticide plant in Bhopal, India as his point of departure, he recounts a tale of corporate negligence and moral culpability. Calling these large corporations "corporate vampires," Bradford accuses them of turning industrial civilization into "one vast, stinking extermination camp."

Our modern way of life, dependent on dangerous industrial institutions, reeks with harmful pollution. We must rid ourselves of it before we are crushed by it.

The cinders of the funeral pyres at Bhopal are still warm, and the mass graves still fresh, but the media prostitutes of the corporations have already begun their homilies in defense of industrialism and its uncounted horrors. Some 3,000 people were slaughtered in the wake of the deadly gas cloud, and 20,000 will remain permanently disabled. The poison gas left a 25 square mile swath of dead and dying, people and animals, as it drifted southeast away from the Union Carbide factory. "We thought it was a plague," said one victim. Indeed it was: a chemical plague, an *industrial plague*.

Ashes, ashes, all fall down!

A terrible, unfortunate, "accident," we are reassured by the propaganda apparatus for Progress, for History, for "Our Modern Way of Life." A price, of course, has to be paid—since the risks are necessary to ensure a higher Standard of Living, a Better Way of Life.

The *Wall Street Journal,* tribune of the bourgeoisie, editorialized, "It is worthwhile to remember that the Union Carbide insecticide plant and the people surrounding it were where they were for compelling reasons. India's agriculture has been thriving, bringing a better life to millions of rural people, and partly because of the use of modern agricultural technology that includes applications of insect killers." The indisputable fact of life, according to this sermon, is that universal recognition that India, like everyone else, "needs technology. Calcutta-style scenes of human deprivation

George Bradford, "We All Live in Bhopal," in *Fifth Estate* (4632 Second, Detroit, MI 48201) (Winter 1985): Vol. 19, No. 4 (319). Reprinted in J. Zerzan and Alice Carnes, *Questioning Technology* (Santa Cruz, CA: Freedom Press, 1988). Reprinted by permission.

can be replaced as fast as the country imports the benefits of the West's industrial revolution and market economics." So, despite whatever dangers are involved, "the benefits outweigh the costs" (December 13, 1984).

The *Journal* was certainly right in one regard— the reasons for the plant and the people's presence there are certainly compelling: capitalist market relations and technological invasion are as compelling as a hurricane to the small communities from which those people were uprooted. It conveniently failed to note, however, that countries like India do not import the *benefits* of industrial capitalism; those benefits are *exported* in the form of loan repayments to fill the coffers of the bankers and corporate vampires who read the *Wall Street Journal* for the latest news of their investments. The Indians only take the risks and pay the costs; in fact, for them, as for the immiserated masses of people living in the shantytowns of the Third World, there are no risks, only certain hunger and disease, only the certainty of death squad revenge for criticizing the state of things as they are.

GREEN REVOLUTION
A NIGHTMARE

In fact, the Calcutta-style misery is the result of Third World industrialization and the so called industrial "Green Revolution" in agriculture. The Green Revolution, which was to revolutionize agriculture in the "backward" countries and produce greater crop yields, has only been a miracle for the banks, corporations and military dictatorships who defend them. The influx of fertilizers, technology, insecticides and bureaucratic administration exploded millennia-old rural economies based on subsistence farming, creating a class of wealthier farmers dependent upon western technologies to produce cash crops such as coffee, cotton and wheat for export, while the vast majority of farming communities were destroyed by capitalist market competition and sent like refugees into the

growing cities. These victims, paralleling the destroyed peasantry of Europe's Industrial Revolution several hundred years before, joined either the permanent underclass of unemployed and underemployed slumdwellers eking out a survival on the tenuous margins of civilization, or became proletarian fodder in the Bhopals, Sao Paulos and Djakartas of an industrializing world—an industrialization process, like all industrialization in history, paid for by the pillage of nature and human beings in the countryside.

Food production goes up in some cases, of course, because the measure is only quantitative— some foods disappear while others are produced year round, even for export. *But subsistence is destroyed.* Not only does the rural landscape begin to suffer the consequences of constant crop production and use of chemicals, but the masses of people—laborers on the land and in the teeming hovels growing around the industrial plants—go hungrier in a vicious cycle of exploitation, while the wheat goes abroad to buy absurd commodities and weapons.

But subsistence is culture as well: culture is destroyed with subsistence, and people are further trapped in the technological labyrinth. The ideology of progress is there, blared louder than ever by those with something to hide, a cover-up for plunder and murder on levels never before witnessed.

INDUSTRIALIZATION OF
THE THIRD WORLD

The industrialization of the Third World is a story familiar to anyone who takes even a glance at what is occurring. The colonial countries are nothing but a dumping ground and pool of cheap labor for capitalist corporations. Obsolete technology is shipped there along with the production of chemicals, medicines and other products banned in the developed world. Labor is cheap, there are few if any safety standards, and *costs are cut.* But the formula of cost–benefit still stands: the costs are simply borne by others, by the victims of Union Carbide, Dow, and Standard Oil.

Chemicals found to be dangerous and banned in the US and Europe are produced instead overseas—DDT is a well-known example of an enormous number of such products, such as the unregistered pesticide Leptophos exported by the Velsicol Corporation to Egypt which killed and injured many Egyptian farmers in the mid-1970s. Other products are simply dumped on Third World markets, like the mercury-tainted wheat which led to the deaths of as many as 5,000 Iraqis in 1972, wheat which had been imported from the US. Another example was the wanton contamination of Nicaragua's Lake Managua by a chlorine and caustic soda factory owned by Pennwalt Corporation and other investors, which caused a major outbreak of mercury poisoning in a primary source of fish for the people living in Managua.

Union Carbide's plant at Bhopal did not even meet US safety standards according to its own safety inspector, but a UN expert on international corporate behavior told the *New York Times,* "A whole list of factors is not in place to insure adequate industrial safety" throughout the Third World. "Carbide is not very different from any other chemical company in this regard." According to the *Times,* "In a Union Carbide battery plant in Jakarta, Indonesia, more than half the workers had kidney damage from mercury exposure. In an asbestos cement factory owned by the Manville Corporation 200 miles west of Bhopal, workers in 1981 were routinely covered with asbestos dust, a practice that would never be tolerated here." (12/9/84)

Some 22,500 people are killed every year by exposure to insecticides—a much higher percentage of them in the Third World than use of such chemicals would suggest. Many experts decried the lack of an "industrial culture" in the "underdeveloped" countries as a major cause of accidents and contamination. But where an "industrial culture" thrives, is the situation really much better?

INDUSTRIAL CULTURE AND INDUSTRIAL PLAGUE

In the advanced industrial nations an "industrial culture" (and little other) exists. Have such disasters been avoided as the claims of these experts would lead us to believe?

Another event of such mammoth proportions as those of Bhopal would suggest otherwise—in that case, industrial pollution killed some 4,000 people in a large population center. That was London, in 1952, when several days of "normal" pollution accumulated in stagnant air to kill and permanently injure thousands of Britons.

Then there are the disasters closer to home or to memory, for example, the Love Canal (still leaking into the Great Lakes water system), or the massive dioxin contaminations at Seveso, Italy and Times Creek, Missouri, where thousands of residents had to be permanently evacuated. And there is the Berlin and Farro dump at Swartz Creek, Michigan, where C-56 (a pesticide by-product of Love Canal fame), hydrochloric acid and cyanide from Flint auto plants had accumulated. "They think we're not scientists and not even educated," said one enraged resident, "but anyone who's been in high school knows that cyanide and hydrochloric acid is what they mixed to kill the people in the concentration camps."

A powerful image: industrial civilization as one vast, stinking extermination camp. We all live in Bhopal, some closer to the gas chambers and to the mass graves, but all of us close enough to be victims. And Union Carbide is obviously not a fluke—the poisons are vented in the air and water, dumped in rivers, ponds and streams, fed to animals going to market, sprayed on lawns and roadways, sprayed on food crops, every day, everywhere. The result may not be as dramatic as Bhopal (which then almost comes to serve as a *diversion,* a deterrence machine to take our minds off the pervasive reality which Bhopal truly represents), but it is as deadly. When ABC News asked

University of Chicago professor of public health and author of *The Politics of Cancer,* Jason Epstein, if he thought a Bhopal-style disaster could occur in the US, he replied: "I think what we're seeing in America is far more slow—not such large accidental occurrences, but a slow, gradual leakage with the result that you have excess cancers or reproductive abnormalities."

In fact, birth defects have doubled in the last 25 years. And cancer is on the rise. In an interview with the *Guardian,* Hunter College professor David Kotelchuck described the "Cancer Atlas" maps published in 1975 by the Department of Health, Education and Welfare. "Show me a red spot on these maps and I'll show you an industrial center of the US," he said. "There aren't any place names on the maps but you can easily pick out concentrations of industry. See, it's not Pennsylvania that's red it's just Philadelphia, Erie and Pittsburgh. Look at West Virginia here, there's only two red spots, the Kanawha Valley, where there are nine chemical plants including Union Carbide's, and this industrialized stretch of the Ohio River. It's the same story wherever you look."

There are 50,000 toxic waste dumps in the United States. The EPA admits that *ninety per cent* of the 90 billion pounds of toxic waste produced annually by US industry (70 per cent of it by chemical companies) is disposed of "improperly" (although we wonder what they would consider "proper" disposal). These deadly products of industrial civilization—arsenic, mercury, dioxin, cyanide, and many others—are simply dumped, "legally" and "illegally," wherever convenient to industry. Some 66,000 different compounds are used in industry. Nearly a billion tons of pesticides and herbicides comprising 225 different chemicals were produced in the US last year, and an additional 79 million pounds were imported. Some two per cent of chemical compounds have been tested for side effects. There are 15,000 chemical plants in the United States, daily manufacturing mass death.

All of the dumped chemicals are leaching into our water. Some three to four thousand wells, depending on which government agency you ask, are contaminated or closed in the US. In Michigan alone, 24 municipal water systems have been contaminated, and a thousand sites have suffered major contamination. According to the Detroit *Free Press,* "The final toll could be as many as 10,000 sites" in Michigan's "water wonderland" alone (April 15, 1984).

And the coverups go unabated here as in the Third World. One example is that of dioxin; during the proceedings around the Agent Orange investigations, it came out that Dow Chemical had lied all along about the effects of dioxin. Despite research findings that dioxin is "exceptionally toxic" with "a tremendous potential for producing chlor-acne and systemic injury," Dow's top toxicologist, V. K Rowe, wrote in 1965, "We are not in any way attempting to hide our problems under a heap of sand. But we certainly do not want to have any situations arise which will cause the regulatory agencies to become restrictive."

Now Vietnam suffers a liver cancer epidemic and a host of cancers and health problems caused by the massive use of Agent Orange there during the genocidal war waged by the US. The sufferings of the US veterans are only a drop in the bucket. And dioxin is appearing everywhere in our environment as well, in the form of recently discovered "dioxin rain."

GOING TO THE VILLAGE

When the Indian authorities and Union Carbide began to process the remaining gases in the Bhopal plant, thousands of residents fled, despite the reassurances of the authorities. The *New York Times* quoted one old man who said, "They are not believing the scientists or the state government or anybody. They only want to save their lives."

The same reporter wrote that one man had gone to the train station with his goats, "hoping that he could take them with him—anywhere, as long as it was away from Bhopal" (December 14, 1984). The same old man quoted above told the reporter, "All the public has gone to the village."

The reporter explained that "going to the village" is what Indians do when trouble comes.

A wise and age-old strategy for survival by which little communities always renewed themselves when bronze, iron and golden empires with clay feet fell to their ruin. But subsistence has been and is everywhere being destroyed, and with it, culture. What are we to do when there is no village to go to? When we all live in Bhopal, and Bhopal is everywhere? The comments of two women, one a refugee from Times Creek, Missouri, and another from Bhopal, come to mind. The first woman said of her former home, "This was a nice place once. Now we have to bury it." The other woman said, "Life cannot come back. Can the government pay for the lives? Can you bring those people back?"

The corporate vampires are guilty of greed, plunder, murder, slavery, extermination and devastation. And we should avoid any pang of sentimentalism when the time comes for them to pay for their crimes against humanity and the natural world. But we will have to go beyond them, to ourselves: subsistence, and with it culture, has been destroyed. We have to find our way back to the village, out of industrial civilization, out of this exterminist system.

The Union Carbides, the Warren Andersons, the "optimistic experts" and the lying propagandists all must go, but with them must go the pesticides, the herbicides, the chemical factories and the chemical way of life which is nothing but death.

Because this is Bhopal, and it is all we've got. This "once nice place" can't be simply buried for us to move on to another pristine beginning. The empire is collapsing. We must find our way back to the village, or as the North American natives said, "back to the blanket," and we must do this not by trying to save an industrial civilization which is doomed, but in that renewal of life which must take place in its ruin. By throwing off this Modern Way of Life, we won't be "giving things up" or sacrificing, but throwing off a terrible burden. Let us do so soon before we are crushed by it.

STUDY QUESTIONS

1. Does Bradford make his case that Western industrial society is dangerous to humanity and nature and needs to be rejected? What are the implications of Bradford's indictment? What sort of world do you think that he would want us to live in? Is Bradford a "Luddite"? (Luddites were people in England in the early nineteenth century who went around destroying machines because they believed that the Industrial Revolution was evil.)

2. Is the anger that comes through in this article justified? Is modern industrial practice really morally irresponsible? Explain your answer.

3. How might someone in the business community respond to Bradford's essay? Can our industrial practices be defended?

34

People or Penguins:
The Case for Optimal Pollution

WILLIAM F. BAXTER

William Baxter is professor of law at Stanford University and the author of People or
Penguins: The Case for Optimal Pollution *(1974) from which this selection is taken.*

   *In this essay, Baxter aims at clarifying the relationship between resource use and
pollution. They are the opposite sides of the same coin, the privilege and its price, the good
and the bad. Baxter argues that we cannot have a pollution-free society without harming
humans. If we are humanists, committed to promoting the human good above all else, as he
is, we should be willing to allow pollution where it harms animals and trees if overall benefits
accrue to human beings.*

I start with the modest proposition that, in dealing
with pollution, or indeed with any problem, it is
helpful to know what one is attempting to accomplish. Agreement on how and whether to pursue a
particular objective, such as pollution control, is not
possible unless some more general objective has
been identified and stated with reasonable precision. We talk loosely of having clean air and clean
water, of preserving our wilderness areas, and so
forth. But none of these is a sufficiently general
objective: each is more accurately viewed as a
means rather than as an end.

   With regard to clean air, for example, one may
ask, "how clean?" and "what does clean mean?" It
is even reasonable to ask, "why have clean air?"
Each of these questions is an implicit demand that
a more general community goal be stated—a goal
sufficiently general in its scope and enjoying sufficiently general assent among the community of

actors that such "why" questions no longer seem
admissible with respect to that goal.

   If, for example, one states as a goal the proposition that "every person should be free to do whatever he wishes in contexts where his actions do not
interfere with the interests of other human beings,"
the speaker is unlikely to be met with a response of
"why." The goal may be criticized as uncertain in
its implications or difficult to implement, but it is so
basic a tenet of our civilization—it reflects a cultural
value so broadly shared, at least in the abstract—that
the question "why" is seen as impertinent or im-
ponderable or both.

   I do not mean to suggest that everyone would
agree with the "spheres of freedom" objective just
stated. Still less do I mean to suggest that a
society could subscribe to four or five such general
objectives that would be adequate in their coverage
to serve as testing criteria by which all other

Reprinted with permission of Columbia University Press from William F. Baxter, *People or Penguins: The Case for Optimal Pollution* (1974).

disagreements might be measured. One difficulty in the attempt to construct such a list is that each new goal added will conflict, in certain applications, with each prior goal listed; and thus each goal serves as a limited qualification on prior goals.

Without any expectation of obtaining unanimous consent to them, let me set forth four goals that I generally use as ultimate testing criteria in attempting to frame solutions to problems of human organization. My position regarding pollution stems from these four criteria. If the criteria appeal to you and any part of what appears hereafter does not, our disagreement will have a helpful focus: which of us is correct, analytically, in supposing that his position on pollution would better serve these general goals. If the criteria do not seem acceptable to you, then it is to be expected that our more particular judgments will differ, and the task will then be yours to identify the basic set of criteria upon which your particular judgments rest.

My criteria are as follows:

1. The spheres of freedom criterion stated above.

2. Waste is a bad thing. The dominant feature of human existence is scarcity—our available resources, our aggregate labors, and our skill in employing both have always been, and will continue for some time to be, inadequate to yield to every man all the tangible and intangible satisfactions he would like to have. Hence, none of those resources, or labors, or skills, should be wasted—that is, employed so as to yield less than they might yield in human satisfactions.

3. Every human being should be regarded as an end rather than as a means to be used for the betterment of another. Each should be afforded dignity and regarded as having an absolute claim to an evenhanded application of such rules as the community may adopt for its governance.

4. Both the incentive and the opportunity to improve his share of satisfactions should be preserved to every individual. Preservation of

incentive is dictated by the "no-waste" criterion and enjoins against the continuous, totally egalitarian redistribution of satisfactions, or wealth; but subject to that constraint, everyone should receive, by continuous redistribution if necessary, some minimal share of aggregate wealth so as to avoid a level of privation from which the opportunity to improve his situation becomes illusory.

The relationship of these highly general goals to the more specific environmental issues at hand may not be readily apparent, and I am not yet ready to demonstrate their pervasive implications. But let me give one indication of their implications. Recently scientists have informed us that use of DDT in food production is causing damage to the penguin population. For the present purposes let us accept that assertion as an indisputable scientific fact. The scientific fact is often asserted as if the correct implication—that we must stop agricultural use of DDT—followed from the mere statement of the fact of penguin damage. But plainly it does not follow if my criteria are employed.

My criteria are oriented to people, not penguins. Damage to penguins, or sugar pines, or geological marvels is, without more, simply irrelevant. One must go further, by my criteria, and say: Penguins are important because people enjoy seeing them walk about rocks; and furthermore, the well-being of people would be less impaired by halting use of DDT than by giving up penguins. In short, my observations about environmental problems will be people-oriented, as are my criteria. I have no interest in preserving penguins for their own sake.

It may be said by way of objection to this position, that it is very selfish of people to act as if each person represented one unit of importance and nothing else was of any importance. It is undeniably selfish. Nevertheless I think it is the only tenable starting place for analysis for several reasons. First, no other position corresponds to the way most people really think and act—i.e., corresponds to reality.

Second, this attitude does not portend any massive destruction of nonhuman flora and fauna, for people depend on them in many obvious ways, and they will be preserved because and to the degree that humans do depend on them.

Third, what is good for humans is, in many respects, good for penguins and pine trees—clean air for example. So that humans are, in these respects, surrogates for plant and animal life.

Fourth, I do not know how we could administer any other system. Our decisions are either private or collective. Insofar as Mr. Jones is free to act privately, he may give such preferences as he wishes to other forms of life: he may feed birds in winter and do less with himself, and he may even decline to resist an advancing polar bear on the ground that the bear's appetite is more important than those portions of himself that the bear may choose to eat. In short my basic premise does not rule out private altruism to competing life-forms. It does rule out, however, Mr. Jones' inclination to feed Mr. Smith to the bear, however hungry the bear, however despicable Mr. Smith.

Insofar as we act collectively on the other hand, only humans can be afforded an opportunity to participate in the collective decisions. Penguins cannot vote now and are unlikely subjects for the franchise—pine trees more unlikely still. Again each individual is free to cast his vote so as to benefit sugar pines if that is his inclination. But many of the more extreme assertions that one hears from some conservationists amount to tacit assertions that they are specially appointed representatives of sugar pines, and hence that their preferences should be weighted more heavily than the preferences of other humans who do not enjoy equal rapport with "nature." The simplistic assertion that agricultural use of DDT must stop at once because it is harmful to penguins is of that type.

Fifth, if polar bears or pine trees or penguins, like men, are to be regarded as ends rather than means, if they are to count in our calculus of social organization, someone must tell me how much each one counts, and someone must tell me how these life-forms are to be permitted to express their preferences, for I do not know either answer. If the answer is that certain people are to hold their proxies, then I want to know how those proxy-holders are to be selected: self-appointment does not seem workable to me.

Sixth, and by way of summary of all the foregoing, let me point out that the set of environmental issues under discussion—although they raise very complex technical questions of how to achieve any objective—ultimately raise a normative question: what ought we to do. Questions of ought are unique to the human mind and world—they are meaningless as applied to a nonhuman situation.

I reject the proposition that we ought to respect the "balance of nature" or to "preserve the environment" unless the reason for doing so, express or implied, is the benefit of man.

I reject the idea that there is a "right" or "morally correct" state of nature to which we should return. The word "nature" has no normative connotation. Was it "right" or "wrong" for the earth's crust to heave in contortion and create mountains and seas? Was it "right" for the first amphibian to crawl up out of the primordial ooze? Was it "wrong" for plants to reproduce themselves and alter the atmospheric composition in favor of oxygen? For animals to alter the atmosphere in favor of carbon dioxide both by breathing oxygen and eating plants? No answers can be given to these questions because they are meaningless questions.

All this may seem obvious to the point of being tedious, but much of the present controversy over environment and pollution rests on tacit normative assumptions about just such nonnormative phenomena: that it is "wrong" to impair penguins with DDT, but not to slaughter cattle for prime rib roasts. That it is wrong to kill stands of sugar pines with industrial fumes, but not to cut sugar pines and build housing for the poor. Every man is entitled to his own preferred definition of Walden Pond, but there is no definition that has any moral superiority over another, except by reference to the selfish needs of the human race.

From the fact that there is no normative definition of the natural state, it follows that there is no normative definition of clean air or pure water—hence no definition of polluted air—or of pollution—except by reference to the needs of man. The "right" composition of the atmosphere is one which has some dust in it and some lead in it and some hydrogen sulfide in it—just those amounts that attend a sensibly organized society thoughtfully and knowledgeably pursuing the greatest possible satisfaction for its human members.

The first and most fundamental step toward solution of our environmental problems is a clear recognition that our objective is not pure air or water but rather some optimal state of pollution. That step immediately suggests the question: How do we define and attain the level of pollution that will yield the maximum possible amount of human satisfaction?

Low levels of pollution contribute to human satisfaction but so do food and shelter and education and music. To attain ever lower levels of pollution, we must pay the cost of having less of these other things. I contrast that view of the cost of pollution control with the more popular statement that pollution control will "cost" very large numbers of dollars. The popular statement is true in some senses, false in others; sorting out the true and false senses is of some importance. The first step in that sorting process is to achieve a clear understanding of the difference between dollars and resources. Resources are the wealth of our nation; dollars are merely claim checks upon those resources. Resources are of vital importance; dollars are comparatively trivial.

Four categories of resources are sufficient for our purposes: At any given time a nation, or a planet if you prefer, has a stock of labor, of technological skill, of capital goods, and of natural resources (such as mineral deposits, timber, water, land, etc.). These resources can be used in various combinations to yield goods and services of all kinds—in some limited quantity. The quantity will be larger if they are combined efficiently, smaller if combined inefficiently. But in either event the resource stock is limited, the goods and services that they can be made to yield are limited; even the most efficient use of them will yield less than our population, in the aggregate, would like to have.

If one considers building a new dam, it is appropriate to say that it will be costly in the sense that it will require x hours of labor, y tons of steel and concrete, and z amount of capital goods. If

these resources are devoted to the dam, then they cannot be used to build hospitals, fishing rods, schools, or electric can openers. That is the meaningful sense in which the dam is costly.

Quite apart from the very important question of how wisely we can combine our resources to produce goods and services, is the very different question of how they get distributed—who gets how many goods? Dollars constitute the claim checks which are distributed among people and which control their share of national output. Dollars are nearly valueless pieces of paper except to the extent that they do represent claim checks to some fraction of the output of goods and services. Viewed as claim checks, all the dollars outstanding during any period of time are worth, in the aggregate, the goods and services that are available to be claimed with them during that period—neither more nor less.

It is far easier to increase the supply of dollars than to increase the production of goods and services—printing dollars is easy. But printing more dollars doesn't help because each dollar then simply becomes a claim to fewer goods, i.e., becomes worth less.

The point is this: many people fall into error upon hearing the statement that the decision to build a dam, or to clean up a river, will cost $X million. It is regrettably easy to say: "It's only money. This is a wealthy country, and we have lots of money." But you cannot build a dam or clean a river with $X million—unless you also have a match, you can't even make a fire. One builds a dam or cleans a river by diverting labor and steel and trucks and factories from making one kind of goods to making another. The cost in dollars is merely a shorthand way of describing the extent of the diversion necessary. If we build a dam for $X million, then we must recognize that we will have $X million less housing and food and medical care and electric can openers as a result.

Similarly, the costs of controlling pollution are best expressed in terms of the other goods we will have to give up to do the job. This is not to say the job should not be done. Badly as we need more housing, more medical care, and more can openers, and more symphony orchestras, we could do with somewhat less of them, in my judgment at least, in exchange for somewhat cleaner air and rivers. But that is the nature of the trade-off, and analysis of the problem is advanced if that unpleasant reality is kept in mind. Once the trade-off relationship is clearly perceived, it is possible to state in a very general way what the optimal level of pollution is. I would state it as follows:

People enjoy watching penguins. They enjoy relatively clean air and smog-free vistas. Their health is improved by relatively clean water and air. Each of these benefits is a type of good or service. As a society we would be well advised to give up one washing machine if the resources that would have gone into that washing machine can yield greater human satisfaction when diverted into pollution control. We should give up one hospital if the resources thereby freed would yield more human satisfaction when devoted to elimination of noise in our cities. And so on, trade-off by trade-off, we should divert our productive capacities from the production of existing goods and services to the production of a cleaner, quieter, more pastoral nation up to—and no further than—the point at which we value more highly the next washing machine or hospital that we would have to do without than we value the next unit of environmental improvement that the diverted resources would create.

Now this proposition seems to me unassailable but so general and abstract as to be unhelpful—at least unadministerable in the form stated. It assumes we can measure in some way the incremental units of human satisfaction yielded by very different types of goods.... But I insist that the proposition stated describes the result for which we should be striving—and again, that it is always useful to know what your target is even if your weapons are too crude to score a bull's eye.

STUDY QUESTIONS

1. Evaluate the four tenets of Baxter's environmental philosophy.

    a. Which do you agree with, and which do you disagree with? Explain why.

    b. Is human benefit the only morally relevant criterion with regard to our behavior to animals and the environment?

    c. Do penguins and sugar pine trees have intrinsic value? Or is their value entirely instrumental, derived from benefits to humans?

2. Do you agree with Baxter that pollution is just the opposite side of the coin of resource use? Do you also agree that on the principle that "waste is a bad thing" we are led to use resources for human good and thus bring about some level of pollution?

3. Compare Baxter's analysis with those of Bradford and French. What are their similarities and differences? Does Baxter shed any light on the matter?

FOR FURTHER READING

Bernards, Neal, ed. *The Environmental Crisis*. San Diego, CA: Greenhaven Press, 1991.

Bogard, William. The Bhopal Tragedy: Language, Logic and Politics in the Production of a Hazard. Boulder, CO: Westview, 1989.

Brown, Lester. *The Twenty Ninth Day*. New York: Norton, 1978.

———, ed. *The Worldwatch Reader*. Washington, DC: Worldwatch Institute, 1991.

Brown, Michael. *The Toxic Cloud*. New York: Harper & Row, 1987.

Gore, Albert. *Earth in the Balance*. Boston: Houghton Mifflin, 1992.

Keeble, John. *Out of the Channel: The Exxon Valdez Spill.* New York: HarperCollins, 1991.

Lomborg, Bjorn. *The Skeptical Environmentalist.* New York: Routledge, 2001.

McKibben, Bill. *The End of Nature.* New York: Random House, 1989.

Postel, Sandra. *Defusing the Toxic Threat: Controlling Pesticides and Industrial Waste.* Washington, DC: Worldwatch Institute, 1987.

Ray, Dixy Lee, and Lou Guzzo. *Trashing the Planet.* Washington, DC: Regnery Gateway, 1990.

Silver, Cheryl Pollack. *Protecting Life on Earth: Steps to Save the Ozone Layer.* Washington, DC: Worldwatch Institute, 1988.

Simon, Julian. *The Ultimate Resource.* Princeton, NJ: Princeton University Press, 1981.

Wellburn, Alan. *Air Pollution and Acid Rain.* New York: Wiley, 1988.

35

Is *Silent Spring* Behind Us?

DAVID PIMENTEL

David Pimentel is professor of entomology at Cornell University and the author of Ecological Effects of Pesticides on Nontarget Species *(1971).*

In this selection, Pimentel assesses the progress of the pesticide problem since Rachel Carson's Silent Spring. *Assembling an array of information, he details the ways in which the situation has improved and the ways in which it has deteriorated.*

Is *silent spring* behind us? Have environmental problems associated with pesticide use improved? The answer is a qualified "yes."

Rachel Carson's warning in 1962 generated widespread concern, but many years elapsed before action was taken to halt some of the environmental damage being inflicted by pesticides on our sensitive natural biota. More than 20 years later we still have not solved all the pesticide environmental problems, although some real progress has been made.

FEWER PESTICIDE PROBLEMS DURING THE PAST TWO DECADES

Chlorinated insecticides, such as DDT, dieldrin, and toxaphene, are characterized by their spread and persistence in the environment. The widespread use of chlorinated insecticides from 1945 to 1972 significantly reduced the populations of predatory birds such as eagles, peregrine falcons, and ospreys. Trout, salmon, and other fish populations were seriously

Reprinted from *Silent Spring Revisited*, ed. G. J. Marco, R. M. Hollingsworth, and W. Durham (Washington, D.C.: American Chemical Society, 1987) by permission. Notes deleted.

reduced, and their flesh was contaminated with pesticide residues. Snakes and other reptile populations, as well as certain insect and other invertebrate populations that were highly sensitive to the chlorinated insecticides, were reduced.

Since the restriction on the use of chlorinated insecticides went into effect in 1972, the quantities of these residues in humans and in terrestrial and aquatic ecosystems have slowly declined. From 1970 to 1974, for example, DDT residues in human adipose tissue declined by about one-half in Caucasians who were 0–14 years of age (see Table 1). The declines in other Caucasian age groups and in blacks have not been as great. In agricultural soils, DDT residues have declined by about one-half or from 0.015 parts per million (ppm) in 1968 to 0.007 ppm in 1973. The decline of DDT in soil led to a decline in the amount of DDT running into aquatic ecosystems and resulted in a significant decline in DDT residues found in various fish. For example, in lake trout caught in the Canadian waters of eastern Lake Superior, DDT residues declined from 1.04 ppm in 1971 to only 0.05 ppm in 1975. In aquatic birds that feed on fish, DDT residues also declined. For example, DDT residues in brown pelican eggs collected in South

Carolina declined from 0.45 ppm in 1968 to only 0.004 ppm in 1975.

Because DDT and other organochlorine residues in terrestrial ecosystems have declined, various populations of birds, mammals, fishes, and reptiles have started to recover and increase in number. For example, peregrine falcons have been bred in the laboratory and then successfully released in the environment. Limited data do exist on the recoveries of a few animal species, but we do not know the recovery rates for those animal populations that were seriously affected by chlorinated insecticides. Those species with short generation times and high reproductive rates, like insects, have probably recovered best.

New pesticide regulations established in the early 1970s restricted the use of highly persistent pesticides, which include chlorinated insecticides. DDT, toxaphene, and dieldrin, for example, persist in the environment for 10 to 30 years. Two major problems are associated with the use of highly persistent pesticides. Annual applications of chlorinated insecticides add to the total quantity of insecticides in the environment because they degrade slowly. This persistence in the environment increases the chances for the chemicals to move out of the target area into the surrounding environment.

The amount of chlorinated insecticide residues in the environment since most of the chlorinated insecticides were banned has been declining. But because these insecticides are relatively stable, some will persist 30 years or more, and some will be present in the U.S. environment until the end of this century. Fortunately these residues are relatively low, so their effect on most organisms should be minimal.

Persistence of chlorinated insecticides in the environment is only one of the problems created by these chemicals. Their solubility in fats and oils resulted in their accumulation in the fatty tissues of animals, including humans. Thus, bioaccumulation of chlorinated insecticides is a serious environmental problem. Organisms like water fleas and fish, for example, concentrated DDT and other chlorinated insecticides from a dosage of 1 part per billion (ppb) in the environment to

TABLE 1   **Total DDT Equivalent Residues in Human Adipose Tissue from General U.S. Population by Race**

Age (years)	1970	1971	1972	1973	1974
Caucasians					
0–14	4.16	3.32	2.79	2.59	2.15
15–44	6.89	6.56	6.01	5.71	4.91
45 and above	8.01	7.50	7.00	6.63	6.55
Blacks					
0–14	5.54	7.30		4.68	3.16
15–44	10.88	13.92	11.32	9.97	9.18
45 and above	16.56	19.57	15.91	14.11	11.91

Note: All residues are measured in parts per million lipid weight.

levels in their tissues of 100,000 times that. Bioaccumulation continues in the environment with several pesticides (e.g., parathion and 2,4–D), but restricting the use of chlorinated insecticides has reduced this environmental problem.

Movement and magnification of pesticides in the food chain also occurs, but must be carefully documented. Some organisms concentrate pesticides in their bodies 100,000-fold over levels in the ambient environment, and this condition might mistakenly be interpreted as a case of biomagnification in the food chain. Biomagnification in the food chain has been documented with birds like osprey and gulls that feed on fish and has proven to be a serious problem to these predaceous birds.

INCREASED PESTICIDE PROBLEMS DURING THE PAST TWO DECADES

Although restricted use of chlorinated insecticides has relieved some environmental problems, the escalation of pesticide use since 1970 has intensified several other environmental and social problems. Pesticide production and use has increased 2.3-fold since 1970, from around 1.0 to nearly 1.5 billion pounds annually.

Recent research has documented the fact that certain pesticide use may actually increase pest problems. For example, herbicides like 2,4–D used at recommended dosages on corn increased the susceptibility of corn to both insects and plant pathogens. Also the reproduction of certain insects can be stimulated by low dosages of certain insecticides, as occurred in the Colorado potato beetle. For example, sublethal doses of parathion increase egg production by 65%. In addition, most of the insecticides that replaced the chlorinated insecticides are more toxic per unit weight than the chlorinated insecticides.

If one pesticide is more toxic and more biologically active than another, it is not necessarily hazardous to the environment. Risk depends on the dosage and method of application of the specific pesticide. If one pesticide's per-unit weight is more toxic than another, the more toxic chemical is usually applied at a lower dosage that will cause about a 90% kill in the pest population. Thus, a highly toxic material used at a low dosage can achieve about the same mortality as a low-toxicity material. Both high- and low-toxicity pesticides affect pests and nontarget organisms in a similar manner, but the risks to humans handling highly toxic pesticides are far greater than when handling pesticides with a low toxicity. Humans handling highly toxic pesticides like parathion are more likely to be poisoned than those handling pesticides of low toxicity like DDT. If one spills DDT and wipes the pesticide off the skin, no harm is done. However, a similar accident with parathion often leads to poisoning severe enough to require hospitalization.

Human Poisonings

Humans are exposed to pesticides by handling and applying them, by contacting them on treated vegetation, and, to a lesser extent, from their presence in food and water supplies. The number of annual human pesticide poisonings has been estimated at about 45,000; about 3000 of these are sufficiently severe to require hospitalization. The number of annual accidental deaths caused by pesticides is about 50. Accurate data on human pesticide poisonings still are not available 20 years after *Silent Spring*.

Furthermore, detecting the causes of cancer from pesticides is exceedingly difficult because of the long lag time prior to illness and the wide variety of cancer-producing factors that humans are exposed to in their daily activities. No one knows if less human cancer is caused by pesticides now than 20 years ago. Probably less than 1% of human cancers today are caused by pesticides.

We are constantly exposed to pesticides. Despite efforts to keep pesticides out of our food and water, about 50% of U.S. foods sampled by the

Food and Drug Administration (FDA) contain detectable levels of pesticides. Improvements in analytical chemical procedures are helping us detect smaller and smaller quantities of pesticides in food and water. These extremely low dosages should have little or no public health effect.

Domestic Animal Poisonings

Because domestic animals are present on farms and near homes where pesticides are used, many of these animals are poisoned. Dogs and cats are most frequently affected because they often wander freely about the home and farm and have ample opportunity to come in contact with pesticides.

A major loss of livestock products (about $3 million annually) occurs when pesticide residues are found in these products. This problem will probably continue as the quantity of pesticides used continues to rise.

Bee Poisonings

Honeybees and wild bees are essential to the pollination of fruits, vegetables, forage crops, and natural plants. Pesticides kill bees, and the losses to agriculture from bee kills and the related reduction of pollination are estimated to be $135 million each year. Evidence suggests that bee poisonings are probably greater now than in 1962 for several reasons. More highly toxic insecticides are being used, and greater quantities of insecticides are being dispensed. In addition, more pesticide is being applied by aircraft, and aircraft applications are employing ultra low volume (ULV) application equipment. ULV applications require smaller droplets for coverage, and this practice tends to increase pesticide drift problems.

Crop Losses

Although pesticides are employed to protect crops from pests, some crops are damaged as a result of pesticidal treatments. Heavy pesticide use damages crops and causes declines in yields because: (1) herbicide residues that remain in the soil after use on one crop injure chemically sensitive crops planted in rotation, (2) certain desired crops cannot be planted in rotation because of knowledge of potential hazard injury, (3) excessive residues of pesticides remain on the harvested crop and result in its destruction or devaluation, (4) pesticides that are applied improperly or under unfavorable environmental conditions result in drift and other problems, and (5) pesticides drift from a treated crop to nearby crops and destroy natural enemies or the crop itself.

Although an accurate estimate of the negative impact of pesticides on crops in agriculture is extremely difficult to obtain, a conservative estimate is about $70 million annually. The problem is probably worse today than in Carson's time because 7 times more pesticide is being applied today than 20 years ago, and its use is more widespread. This statement is especially true of herbicides.

Reduced Populations of Natural Enemies

In undisturbed environments, most insect and mite populations remain at low densities because a wide array of factors, including natural enemies, control them. When insecticides or other pesticides are applied to crops to control one or more pest species, natural enemy populations are sometimes destroyed, and subsequently pest outbreaks occur.

For example, before the synthetic pesticide era (1945) the major pests of cotton in the United States were the boll weevil and cotton leafworm. When extensive insecticide use began in 1945, several other insect and mite species became serious pests. These include the cotton bollworm, tobacco budworm, looper, cotton aphid, and spider mites. In some regions where pesticides are used to control the boll weevil, as many as five additional treatments have to be made to control bollworms and budworms because their natural enemies have been destroyed. This cycle has meant more pesticide use, more natural enemies destroyed, greater pest populations, and more pesticides used.

Pesticide Resistance

In addition to destroying natural enemies, the widespread use of pesticides often causes pest populations to develop resistance and pass it on to their progeny. More than 420 species of insects and mites and several weed species have developed resistance to pesticides. Pesticide resistance in pests results in additional sprays of some pesticides or the use of alternative and often more expensive pesticides. Again the process of pest control escalates the cycle of pesticide use and the development of resistance.

An estimated $133 million worth of added sprays or more expensive pesticides has been employed to deal with the resistance problem annually. This dollar cost, of course, does not include the side effects apparent in the environment and in public health from using more pesticides and more toxic pesticides.

Fishery Losses

Pesticides in treated cropland often run off and move into aquatic ecosystems. Water-soluble pesticides are easily washed into streams and lakes, whereas other pesticides are carried with soil sediments into aquatic ecosystems. Each year several million tons of soil, and with it, pesticides, are washed into streams and lakes.

At present only a small percentage of fish kills are reported because of the procedures used in reporting fish losses. For example, 20% of the reported fish kills give no estimate of the number of dead fish because fish kills often cannot be investigated quickly enough to determine the primary cause. Also, fast-moving waters rapidly dilute all pollutants, including pesticides, and thus make the cause of the kill difficult to determine. Dead fish are washed away or sink to the bottom, so accurate counts are not possible.

Samples of water recently confirmed a steadily decreasing concentration of pesticides found in surface waters and streams from 1964 to 1978. This reduction is apparently related to the replacement of persistent pesticides with less persistent materials. Despite the reduced pesticide residues in streams, an estimated $800,000 or more in fish is lost annually (each fish was calculated to have a value of 40 cents). This estimate of nearly $1 million probably is several times too low and does not confirm that *Silent Spring* is behind us.

Impacts on Wildlife and Microorganisms

Too little information exists to make even a conservative estimate of the populations of vertebrates, invertebrates, and microorganisms that are adversely affected by pesticides. Most invertebrates and microorganisms perform many essential functions to agriculture, forestry, and other segments of human society; such as preventing the accumulation of water, cleaning water or soil of pollutants, recycling vital chemical elements within the ecosystem, and conserving soil and water. An estimated 200,000 species of plants and animals exist in the United States and, at best, we have information on the effects of pesticides on less than 1000 species. Most of these data are based on "safe concentration" tests conducted in the laboratory. This situation confirms that little is known about pesticide effects on the natural environment. At present evaluation must be based on indicator species.

STATUS OF INTEGRATED PEST MANAGEMENT

Integrated pest management (IPM), introduced more than a decade ago, aimed to reduce pesticide use by monitoring pest populations and using pesticides only when necessary as well as augmenting pest control with alternative nonchemical strategies. What happened? IPM has not been successful, and in fact, more of all kinds of pesticides are being used in the United States and throughout the world than ever before.

The reasons for the poor performance of IPM are complex. First, IPM technology, even if it is simply monitoring pest and natural enemy populations, requires a great deal more basic information than scientists now have. This fact signals the pressing need for basic research on the ecology of pests, their natural enemies, and their environment. Also, the use of this basic information to develop control programs is much more sophisticated than routine application of pesticides. Because this technology is more sophisticated, trained manpower is needed, and often the farmer is not trained and cannot be expected to carry out effective IPM programs.

Pesticides are unquestionably simple and quick to use. They have a significant psychological advantage over IPM and especially over nonchemical controls like biological control. Biological controls gradually bring pest populations under control, but do not give the immediate satisfaction of direct kill like pesticides do. However, as research continues and greater ecological knowledge of pests and agroecosystems increases, IPM has the potential to improve pest control.

WHY ARE LOSSES DUE TO PESTS GREATER TODAY THAN 40 YEARS AGO?

Currently, an estimated 37% of all crops is lost annually to pests (13% to insects, 12% to plant pathogens, and 12% to weeds) in spite of the combined use of pesticidal and nonchemical controls. According to a survey of data collected from 1942 to the present, crop losses from weeds declined slightly from 13.8% to 12% because of a combination of improved herbicidal, mechanical, and cultural weed control practices. During the same period, losses from plant pathogens increased slightly from 10.5% to 12%.

On average, however, crop losses due to insects have increased nearly twofold (from 7% to about 13%) from the 1940s to the present in spite of a 10-fold increase in insecticide use. Thus far the impact of this loss in terms of production has been effectively offset through the use of higher yielding varieties and increased use of fertilizers.

The substantial increase in crop losses caused by insects can be accounted for by some of the major changes that have taken place in U.S. agriculture since the 1940s. These changes include

- planting of crop varieties that are increasingly susceptible to insect pests;

- destruction of natural enemies of certain pests, which in turn creates the need for additional pesticide treatments;

- increase in the development of pesticide resistance in insects;

- reduced crop rotations and crop diversity and an increase in the continuous culture of a single crop;

- reduced FDA tolerance and increased cosmetic standards of processors and retailers for fruits and vegetables;

- reduced field sanitation including less destruction of infected fruit and crop residues;

- reduced tillage, leaving more crop remains on the land surface to harbor pests for subsequent crops;

- culturing crops in climatic regions where they are more susceptible to insect attack;

- use of pesticides that alter the physiology of crop plants and make them more susceptible to insect attack.

CONCLUSION

Progress has been made on pesticide problems, but *Silent Spring* is not entirely behind us. Pesticide use continues, and the quantities of pesticides applied grow annually despite support for IPM control. In future decades, as the world population grows rapidly and agricultural production is stretched to meet food needs, we should not forget Carson's warnings.

Pesticides will continue to be effective pest controls, but the challenge now is to find ways to use them judiciously to avoid many of the environmental hazards and human poisonings that exist today. With this goal for research and development we can achieve effective, relatively safe pest control programs.

STUDY QUESTIONS

1. Go over Pimentel's discussion and describe the ways the pesticide problem has improved and how it has deteriorated.

2. Can you suggest ways to improve our situation still further?

PART II

Practice

Chapter 7 Food Ethics

Chapter 8 Climate Change and Energy Policy

Chapter 9 Race, Class, Gender: Environmental Justice, Ecofeminism, and Indigenous Rights

Chapter 10 The Greening of Spirituality

Chapter 11 The New Green Capitalist Order: Economics, Sustainability, and Response

Chapter 7

Food Ethics

Hunger is a child with shriveled limbs and a swollen belly. It is the grief of parents, or a person gone blind for lack of vitamin A.[1]

   The victim of starvation burns up his own body fats, muscles and tissues for fuel. His body quite literally consumes itself and deteriorates rapidly. The kidneys, liver and endocrine system often cease to function properly. A shortage of carbohydrates, which play a vital role in brain chemistry, affects the mind. Lassitude and confusion set in, so that starvation victims often seem unaware of their plight. The body's defenses drop; disease kills most famine victims before they have time to starve to death. An individual begins to starve when he has lost about a third of his normal body weight. Once this loss exceeds 40%, death is almost inevitable.[2]

TEN THOUSAND PEOPLE starve to death every day, another 2 billion (out of a global population of over 6 billion) are malnourished, and 460 million are permanently hungry. Almost half of these are children. More than one-third of the world goes to bed hungry each night. In recent years, devastating famines have occurred in Bangladesh (1974), Ethiopia (1972–74, 1984), Cambodia (1978), Chad and Sudan (1985), and in many of the other 43 countries making up the sub-Saharan region of Africa throughout the 1970s and 1980s, including the recent famine in Somalia. Since the 1960s conditions have deteriorated in many parts of the world.[3]

   On the other hand, another third of the world lives in affluence. Imagine ten children eating at a table. The three healthiest eat the best food and throw much of it away or give it to their pets. Two other children get just enough to get by on. The other five do not get enough food. Three of them who are weak manage to stave off hunger pangs by eating bread and rice, but the other two are unable to do even that and die of hunger-related diseases, such as pneumonia and dysentery. Such is the plight of children in the world.

In the United States, enough food is thrown into the garbage each day to feed an entire nation, more money is spent on pet food than on aid to the world's starving, and many people are grossly overweight.

Problems of global scarcity, poverty, hunger, and famine are among the most urgent facing us. What is our duty to the hungry in our country and in other lands? What obligations do we have toward the poor abroad? What rights do the starving have against us? To what extent, if any, should hunger relief be tied to population control?

In our first reading, Mylan Engel, Jr. links world hunger with environmental integrity and animal rights and argues that by changing the way we eat, we could save millions of lives and feed the whole world. He argues that even by our present moral values we have a moral duty to become vegetarians. We then examine genetically modified foods, with Jonathon Rauch arguing that they are potentially the solution to world hunger and Mae-Wan Ho presenting evidence that they not only are dangerous for the environment but are also taking autonomy away from individual farmers. Finally, Tristam Coffin and Michael Allen Fox examine the impact of the meat industry upon the world's food supply and the environment.

NOTES

1. Arthur Simon, *Bread for the World* (New York: Paulist Press, 1975).

2. *Time Magazine*, November 11, 1974.

3. Statistics in this introduction come from the U.N. Food and Agriculture Organization. Some of the discussion is based on Arthur Simon, op. cit.

36

Hunger, Duty, and Ecology: On What We Owe Starving Humans

MYLAN ENGEL, JR.

Mylan Engel, Jr. is associate professor of philosophy at Northern Illinois University. His primary areas of interest include epistemology, philosophy of religion, and practical ethics. His current research centers on the following issues: personal and doxastic justification in epistemology; epistemic contextualism, skepticism, and closure; rational belief in the absence of reasons; human obligations toward nonhuman animals; and our duties to those living in absolute poverty. Engel has provided the following abstract of his article.

An argument is advanced for the moral obligatoriness of (O₁) supporting famine relief organizations through financial contributions and (O₂) refraining from squandering food in situations of food scarcity. Unlike other ethical arguments for the obligation to assist the world's absolutely poor, my argument is not predicated on any highly contentious ethical theory which can you reject. Rather, it is predicated on your own beliefs. The argument shows that the things you currently believe already commit you to the obligatoriness of helping to reduce malnutrition and famine-related diseases by sending a nominal percentage of your income to famine-relief organizations and by not squandering food that could be fed to them. Being consistent with your own beliefs implies that to do any less is to be profoundly immoral.

HUNGER, DUTY, AND ECOLOGY: ON WHAT WE OWE STARVING HUMANS

You probably remember many of the tragic events of September 11, 2001. Nineteen terrorists hijacked four commercial airliners, crashing two of them into the World Trade Center towers, one into the Pentagon, and one in a field in Pennsylvania. Approximately 3,200 innocent individuals died needlessly. People around the world stared at their television sets in horror and disbelief as the news media aired clips of the attack 'round the clock. The tragedy immediately roused President Bush to declare "war on terrorism." Volunteers from all across America traveled to New York at their own expense to aid in the rescue and clean-up efforts. Charitable contributions poured into the American Red Cross, which in turn wrote checks totaling $143.4 million in emergency aid (averaging $45,837 per family). The U.S. government put together a $5 billion relief package that will provide $1.6 million to each of the victim's families. The United States has spent billions more on its military efforts to root out Osama bin Laden and his al-Qaeda terrorist network. As the dust from the 9/11 attacks has finally settled, it is safe to say that Americans are now taking terrorism seriously.

Here are some of the tragic events that took place on 9/11 that you probably don't recall. On that infamous day, more than 33,000 innocent children under the age of five died *senseless, needless* deaths—18,000 died from malnutrition and another

15,300 died of untreated poverty-related diseases. It must be stressed that almost all of these deaths were *unnecessary*. They could have *easily been prevented*. The United States alone grows enough grain and soybeans to feed the world's human population several times over. Given this overabundance of food, the lives of those children who starved to death on 9/11 could have easily been saved, had we only diverted a relatively modest portion of this food to them. As for the disease-related deaths, 19% of the 33,000 children who lost their lives on 9/11 died from the dehydrating effects of chronic diarrhea. Almost all of these 6,350 diarrheal dehydration deaths could have been prevented by administering each child a single packet of oral rehydration salts (cost per packet: 15 cents). Another 19% of these children died from acute respiratory infections. Most of them could have been saved with a course of antibiotics (cost: 25 cents). Most of the 2,300 children who died from measles could have been saved with vitamin A therapy (cost per capsule: less than 10 cents). What makes the deaths of these children particularly tragic is that virtually all of them were readily preventable. They occurred only because otherwise good people did nothing to prevent them.

Despite the fact that the number of innocent children who died needlessly on 9/11 was ten times greater than the number of innocent people who lost their lives in the 9/11 terrorist attack, compassionate conservative President Bush did not declare war on hunger or on poverty. The U.S. government did not immediately institute a multibillion dollar relief package for the world's absolutely poor. People did not make out generous checks to famine-relief organizations. The media did not so much as mention the tragedy of so many innocent young lives lost. And, as if 9/11 wasn't enough for us to deal with, on 9/12 another 33,000 innocent children under the age of five died unnecessarily, and another 33,000 on 9/13. In the 22 months that have transpired since the 9/11 tragedy, more than 22 million innocent children under the age of five have died needlessly. By any objective measure, the tragedy of the 9/11 attack pales in comparison with the tragedy of world hunger and famine-related disease. Each year the latter claims 3,800 times more innocent lives than the 9/11 attack. Despite the magnitude of the tragedy of global hunger and childhood malnutrition, the overwhelming majority of affluent and moderately affluent people, including most philosophers, send no money to famine-relief organizations. Of the 4 million people who receive solicitations from UNICEF each year, less than 1% donate anything at all. For most of us, world hunger doesn't even register a blip on our moral radar screens, much less present itself as a serious moral problem requiring action on our part.

My aim in the present paper is an ambitious one. I hope to convince you (and others) to *take hunger seriously*. How? By showing you that your beliefs already commit you to the view that global hunger and *absolute poverty*[1] impose serious moral obligations on moderately affluent people. Starting with your beliefs as premises, I shall argue that affluent and moderately affluent people, like you and me, are morally obligated:

(O$_1$) to provide modest financial support for famine-relief organizations and/or other humanitarian organizations working to reduce the amount of unnecessary pain, suffering, and death in the world, and

(O$_2$) to refrain from squandering food that could be fed to the world's absolutely poor.

1. PRELIMINARIES

The central questions this essay addresses are not new: Is it morally permissible for moderately

affluent people who have the financial means to prevent some innocent children from starving to death to do nothing to reduce the number of children suffering from starvation? Are moderately affluent people morally obligated to send money to famine-relief organizations to help reduce world hunger and absolute poverty? If so, what is the extent of their obligation—i.e., just how much money must they send to these humanitarian organizations if they are to avoid being immoral?

These questions took center stage in the 1970s when a spate of philosophers offered arguments defending the view that affluent and moderately affluent people are morally required to provide financial support to organizations working to alleviate hunger, malnutrition, and absolute poverty around the world. Arguments from practically every theoretical perspective in normative ethics (except for libertarianism, which will be discussed later) were advanced: utilitarian arguments, Kantian arguments, human rights-based arguments, and ideal contractarian arguments. Working backwards, Jan Narveson (1977) rejects the libertarian "Nobody needs to help anybody" stance as unreasonable and, using a Rawlsean approach, he tentatively defends the view that one is free to acquire more property than one's neighbor, but only if one is "willing to contribute a certain amount of one's wealth to those in undeserved misfortune, once one gets beyond a certain minimal amount—a fraction which perhaps increases as one gets more and more." William Aiken (1977) argues that the moral right to be saved from starvation derives from the more general moral right to be saved from preventable death due to deprivation and that this latter right generates a stringent corresponding moral obligation on the part of those in a position to prevent such deaths. As Aiken puts it:

> Until it is true that I cannot help another without putting myself in an equivalent position of need (that is, dying of deprivation), I have a *prima facie* obligation to honor others' right to be saved from preventable death due to deprivation.[2]

The Kantian argument is predicated on Kant's claim that we have an imperfect duty to help those in dire need. As I interpret Kant, the duty is imperfect, since (i) there is no specific person to whom we owe it; (ii) since we owe it to persons generally and because we cannot possibly help *every* person in dire need, we are free to fulfill the duty in various ways as various opportunities to help present themselves; and (iii) the duty is a general duty that is never completely satisfied—i.e., no matter how many people in dire need we help, we are still obligated to help other people in dire need when we can do so. It is not a duty that we should fulfill *only* when some especially salient case presents itself. It is a duty that we should fulfill *whenever* we can, provided that doing so won't prevent us from our doing any of our other overriding duties. Most of us living in affluent nations have relatively few nearby opportunities to help people in dire need (because most of the people we regularly encounter are not in dire need). But there are millions of people elsewhere who are in dire need (of food, medicine, etc.), some of whom we can help by sending money to organizations like OXFAM, and so, on Kantian grounds, we ought to send money to these organizations whenever doing so will not prevent us from carrying out any of our other duties. Emphasizing consequentialist reasoning, Peter Unger (1996) argues that our *primary basic moral values* entail the following Pretty Demanding Dictate:

> (P₁) On pain of living a life that's seriously immoral, a typical well-off person, like you and me, must give away most of her financially valuable assets, and much of her income, directing the funds to lessen efficiently the serious suffering of others.

In his seminal article "Famine, Affluence, and Morality," Peter Singer (1972) offers a utilitarian argument to the effect that we ought to send famine-relief organizations "as much money as possible, that is, at least up to the point at which by giving more one would begin to cause serious suffering for oneself and one's dependents—perhaps even beyond this point to the point of marginal utility." Singer begins his argument with the following much-discussed example:

The Pond: Suppose that on my way to give a lecture I notice that a small child has fallen in [a pond] and is in danger of drowning. Would anyone deny that I ought to wade in and pull the child out? This will mean getting my clothes muddy and either canceling my lecture or delaying it until I can find something dry to change into, but compared with the avoidable death of the child this is insignificant.

The Pond example is supposed to motivate the following principle:

> (P₁) If it is in our power to prevent something very bad from happening, without thereby sacrificing anything of comparable moral significance, we ought to do it.[3]

Singer takes (P₂) to be uncontroversial and thinks it explains why we ought to pull the child from the pond. Given (P₂), Singer reasons as follows: Since absolute poverty is very bad, we ought to prevent as much absolute poverty as we can, without thereby sacrificing anything of comparable moral significance. Since most of the material possessions with which we surround ourselves pale in significance compared to an innocent child's life, we ought to forego such luxuries and save children instead.

These arguments taken together present us with a certain sort of puzzle. First, each of these arguments is initially quite compelling, at least if one accepts the normative framework within which the argument is couched. For example, it seems that any hedonistic or preference act-utilitarian is committed to Singer's principle (P₂), regardless whether The Pond justifies (P₂). Because the other premises in Singer's argument are uncontroversial, it looks as if any hedonistic or preference act-utilitarian must accept Singer's robust conclusion. In short, these arguments provide strong utilitarian, Kantian, rights-based, and contractarian reasons for thinking that we have a moral duty to assist those in absolute poverty. Second, utilitarianism, Kantian ethics, human rights-based ethics, and contractarianism are among the most widely accepted theories in normative ethics. Most philosophers working in ethics today claim to accept some version of one of these theories. Third, with the possible exception of Narveson's view, all of the arguments just considered draw highly demanding conclusions. These arguments (especially Singer's, Unger's, and Aiken's) conclude that we are morally obligated to send sizeable portions of our wealth and income to famine-relief organizations like CARE and that we should continue doing so up to the point where further contributions would reduce us to the same level of need as those we are trying to help. Fourth, few people, philosophers included, contribute anything to CARE, OXFAM, or UNICEF, and almost no people contribute sizeable portions of their income to these organizations, even after they have heard the arguments. What has gone wrong?

Perhaps such highly demanding views are psychologically overwhelming and hence counterproductive. Shelly Kagan considers such an objection. As he puts it:

> [I]f morality demands too much … then when people fall short of its requirements (as doubtless they will do) they will say to themselves that they might as well obey none of morality's requirements at all. Given this all-or-nothing attitude, it is important that morality's requirements not be too severe—for were they severe morality would fall into wide neglect.

Call this objection *Too Much*. According to Too Much, what has gone wrong is that the overly demanding moral principles advocated by Singer, Unger, and Aiken have generated a counterproductive kind of futility thinking: "If I can't live up to the ideal, I shouldn't even try to approximate it." But Too Much is a psychological thesis. Even if true, it has no bearing on what our *actual* moral duties are. It is only concerned with what moral duties and principles we should publicly espouse. In short, Too Much can be restated as follows: "There may be good consequentialist reasons for *understating* the extent of people's *actual* moral obligations, namely, that by doing so people will fulfill

more of their *actual* obligations than they otherwise would have." Such an observation tells us nothing about what our *actual* duties are nor does it do anything to *reduce* or *minimize* those actual duties. Plus, Too Much is probably false. It is highly doubtful that people engage in the sort of all-or-nothing thinking that Too Much predicts, for as Kagan observes:

> Many people disobey the speed limit; few consequently feel free to run down pedestrians. I see no reason why we couldn't teach people to think, "Well, I'm not doing all I should—but only a *monster* would fail to do at least … "

If all-or-nothing futility thinking isn't to blame, then our puzzle remains. Why have such seemingly compelling arguments been so ineffective in evoking behavioral change? I think the answer is more straightforward than Too Much. Moral arguments often tell people that they ought to do things they don't want to do. Typically, when people are presented with an argument telling them that they ought to do *X*—where *X* is something they would rather not do—they look for reasons to reject that argument. One of the most common reasons that I have heard philosophers give for rejecting the arguments of Singer and company runs roughly as follows:

> Singer's preference utilitarianism is irremediably flawed, as are Kant's ethics, Aiken's theory of human rights, and Rawlsean contractarianism. The literature is peppered with devastating objections to these views. Because all of the aforementioned arguments are predicated on flawed ethical theories, all these arguments are also flawed. Until someone can provide me with clear moral reasons grounded in a true moral theory for sending large portions of my income to famine-relief organizations, I will continue to spend my money on what I please.

Such a self-serving reply is both disingenuous and sophistical. It is disingenuous because, as noted earlier, utilitarianism, Kantian ethics, human rights-based ethics, and contractarianism are among the most widely accepted theories in normative ethics. In other contexts, philosophers typically embrace one of these four theoretical approaches to ethics. It is sophistical because a similar reply can be used to "justify" or rationalize virtually any behavior. Because no moral theory to date is immune to objection, one could, for example, "justify" rape on the grounds that all of the arguments against rape are predicated on flawed ethical theories.

The speciousness of such a "justification" of rape is obvious. No one who seriously considers the brutality of rape can think that it is somehow justified/permissible *simply because* all current ethical theories are flawed. But such specious reasoning is often used to "justify" allowing millions of innocent children to starve to death each year. I aim to block this spurious reply by providing an argument for the moral obligatoriness of (O_1) and (O_2), which does not rest on any particular, highly contentious ethical theory. Rather, it rests on beliefs you already hold.[4]

One caveat before we begin. Ethical arguments are often context-dependent, in that they presuppose a specific audience in a certain set of circumstances. Recognizing what that intended audience and context are can prevent confusions about the scope of the ethical claim being made. My argument is context-dependent in precisely this way. It is not aimed at those relatively few people in developed nations who are so impoverished that they couldn't contribute to famine relief without extreme sacrifice. Rather, it is directed at people like you who are relatively well-off and who could easily contribute to famine relief with minimal sacrifice. I intend to show that your beliefs commit you to the view that it is morally wrong not to support famine-relief organizations (or other organizations working to reduce unnecessary suffering) for anyone who is in the circumstances in which you typically find yourself and *a fortiori* that it is morally wrong for you not to support such organizations. Enough by way of preamble, on to your beliefs.

2. THE THINGS YOU BELIEVE

The beliefs attributed to you herein would normally be considered noncontentious. In most contexts, we would take someone who didn't hold these beliefs to be either morally defective or irrational. Of course, in most contexts, people aren't being asked to part with their hard-earned cash. Still, even with that two-week luxury cruise in the Bahamas on the line, you will, I think, readily admit to believing the following propositions:

(B_1) Other things being equal, a world with less (more) pain and suffering is better (worse) than a world with more (less) pain and suffering.

(B_2) A world with less (more) *unnecessary* suffering is better (worse) than a world with more (less) *unnecessary* suffering.[5]

For those who have doubts as to whether or not they really do believe these two propositions, compare our world α as it actually is—where millions of innocent children suffer slow painful deaths from starvation each year—with possible world W_1, where W_1 is like our world in all respects except for two, namely, in W_1 every child has sufficient food to eat and every country has instituted effective population measures that have reduced human population to sustainable levels. W_1 is clearly a better world than α, and you know that it is. After all, unnecessary suffering is intrinsically bad and α contains vastly more unnecessary suffering than W_1.

Unnecessary suffering isn't the only thing you disvalue, as is evidenced by your belief:

(B_3) A world with fewer (more) *unnecessary* childhood deaths is better (worse) than a world with more (fewer) *unnecessary* childhood deaths.

Because you believe (B_3) and also believe that *unnecessary* suffering is intrinsically bad, you no doubt believe both:

(B_4) It is bad when an innocent child under the age of 5 dies instantly in an automobile accident, and

(B$_5$) It is even worse when an innocent child under the age of 5 suffers a slow painful death from starvation.

These beliefs together commit you to the belief:

(B$_6$) Other things being equal, the world would be: (i) better if there were fewer children starving to death, (ii) much better if there were no children starving to death, and (iii) worse if there were more children starving to death.

Having reflected upon Singer's Pond, you surely believe:

(B$_7$) It is wrong to let an innocent child under age 5 *drown when one can easily save that child with no risk and with minimal cost to oneself.*

The fact that you accept (B$_7$) demonstrates that you believe that there are at least some positive duties—i.e., duties to benefit others. So, you probably believe:

(B$_8$) We ought to take steps to make the world a better place, *especially those steps that require little effort and minimal sacrifice on our part.*

But even if you reject (B$_8$) on the grounds that we have no positive duties (or very limited positive duties), you still think there are negative duties to do no harm, and so you believe:

(B$_{8'}$) One ought to avoid making the world a worse place, *at least whenever one can do so with minimal effort and negligible sacrifice.*

You also believe:

(B$_9$) A morally good person will take steps to make the world a better place and even stronger steps to avoid making the world a worse place, and

(B$_{10}$) Even a "minimally decent person"[6] would take steps to help reduce the amount of unnecessary pain, suffering, and death in the world *if s/he could do so with little effort on her/his part.*

You also have beliefs about the sort of person you are. You believe one of the following propositions when the reflexive pronoun is indexed to yourself:

(B$_{11}$) I am a morally good person; or—

(B$_{12}$) I am at least a minimally decent person.

You also believe of yourself:

(B$_{13}$) I am the sort of person who certainly would take steps to help reduce the amount of unnecessary pain, suffering, and death in the world *if I could do so with little effort on my part,* and

(B$_{14}$) I am an intellectually honest individual.

Finally, like most people, you believe:

(B$_{15}$) It is wrong to kill an innocence person unjustly.

And so you believe:

(B$_{16}$) It is wrong to kill innocent children between the ages of 2 and 5 as a means of population control, when equally effective nonlethal means of population control are readily available.

Even where *unjust killing* is not involved, you believe:

(B$_{17}$) Other things being equal, it is better when a person lives out her natural lifespan than when she dies prematurely.

Because you believe (B$_7$), (B$_8$), (B$_{10}$), and (B$_{17}$), presumably you also believe:

(B$_{18}$) Other things being equal, it is wrong to let an innocent person die *when one can prevent that death with minimal effort and negligible sacrifice.*

Because (B$_{18}$) is completely general in its application, it commits you to the following belief as well:

(B$_{19}$) Other things being equal, it is wrong to let an innocent person die as a means of population control *when one can prevent that death with minimal effort and negligible sacrifice* and when equally effective nonlethal means of population control are readily available.

3. WHY YOU ARE COMMITTED TO THE MORAL OBLIGATORINESS OF (O_1)

The burden of the present section is to show that your beliefs (B_1)–(B_{19}) already commit you to obligation (O_1). Using different subsets of [(B_1), (B_2), ..., (B_{19})], I will argue that anyone who believes (B_1)–(B_{19}) is committed to accepting two commonsensical, minimally demanding, normative principles and that these two principles entail that we are morally obligated (O_1) to send a modest portion of our income to famine-relief organizations and/or other organizations working to reduce unnecessary suffering. Because each of these normative principles independently entails obligation (O_1), you don't have to believe all of (B_1)–(B_{19}) for my argument to succeed. However, the more of these propositions you believe, the greater *your* commitment to the obligatoriness of (O_1).

Upon closer inspection, the arguments for demanding dictates like those advocated by Unger and Singer break down. For example, Unger's argument for his Pretty Demanding Dictate is predicated on *The Weak Principle of Ethical Integrity*:

> Other things being even nearly equal, if it's **all right** for you to impose losses on others with the result that there's a significant lessening in the serious losses suffered by others overall, then, if you're to avoid doing what's seriously wrong, *you **can't fail to impose*** much lesser losses on yourself, nor can you fail to accept such lesser losses, when the result's a much more significant lessening of such serious losses overall. (Unger's italics; bold emphasis mine)

But this principle is false. The fact that it would be *permissible* for you to impose certain losses on others does not entail that it is *obligatory* for you to impose lesser losses on yourself. It only entails that it would be *permissible* for you to impose such losses on yourself, and that has never been in doubt. What is at issue is whether or not we are *obligated* to impose such losses on ourselves. Because Unger's argument is predicated on a false normative principle, his argument for Pretty Demanding Dictate is unsound.

In order for Singer's argument for the obligation to assist to be sound, his principle (P_2) must be true, but is (P_2) true? Singer suggests that it is the truth of (P_2) that accounts for the wrongness of letting the child drown. To be sure, (P_2) entails that it is wrong to let the child drown, but so do many other weaker principles. Consider the following highly specific principle:

> (P_3) If one encounters a young child drowning in a shallow pond and one can save the child without personal risk and without ruining more than $400 worth of clothes, then one ought to save the child.

Like (P_2), (P_3) also entails that it is wrong to let the child drown. So, it is not clear that it is (P_2)'s truth that accounts for the wrongfulness of letting the child drown. Perhaps, it is the truth of (P_3) instead. To be sure, one can rightfully object that (P_3) is not couched at the appropriate level of generality for a normative principle. The point of mentioning (P_3) is just to show that there are considerably weaker principles than (P_2) that can account for the wrongness of letting the child drown. Because other weaker principles can account for the wrongfulness of letting the child drown, Singer's example does not show that (P_2) is true. Here is a more plausible principle:

> (P_4) Other things being equal, if you can prevent an innocent person from dying with minimal effort, with no noticeable reduction in your standard of living or the standard of living of your dependents, with no risk to yourself or others, and without thereby failing to fulfill any other more pressing obligation, then you ought to do so.

Unlike (P_3), (P_4) is sufficiently general to provide normative guidance in a wide variety of circumstances. Moreover, (P_4) also entails that it would be wrong of you to let the child drown. Granted, if you wade into the pond, you will ruin your cotton twill pants, your oxford cloth shirt, and your tweed jacket, but being a professor you have several tweed jackets, several pairs of Dockers, and numerous oxford cloth shirts. Even if the clothes you are wearing are completely ruined, there will be no noticeable difference in your standard of living. You will simply wear different clothes that are already hanging in your closet. My modest principle (P_4) has another thing going for it, as well. Anyone, like you, who believes (B_3), (B_8), (B_{10}), (B_{12}), (B_{17}), and (B_{18}) is already committed to (P_4), on pain of inconsistency.

Your beliefs $[(B_1)$, (B_2), (B_8), and $(B_{10})]$ also commit you to another minimalistic principle:

(P_5) If you can help to reduce the amount of unnecessary suffering in the world with minimal effort on your part, with no risk to yourself or others, with no noticeable reduction in your standard of living or the standard of living of your dependents, and without thereby failing to fulfill any other more pressing obligation, then you ought to do so.

Now here's the rub. Any affluent or moderately affluent person who is committed to (P_4) and (P_5) is already committed to the obligatoriness of sending a portion of her income to famine relief organizations and/or other organizations working to reduce unnecessary suffering. Consider the implications of your commitment to (P_4). According to (P_4), you ought to prevent a person from dying if you can do so with minimal effort and no noticeable reduction in your standard of living or that of your dependents, all else being equal. By sending a modest portion of your income to OXFAM, CARE, or UNICEF, you can prevent many innocent children from dying unnecessarily. Plus, you can do so with no noticeable reduction in your or your dependents' standards of living, and your doing so will not prevent you from fulfilling any more pressing

obligation. So, according to (P_4), you ought to do so. It is worth noting that your belief (B_{18})—it is wrong to let an innocent person die *when one can prevent that death with minimal effort and minimal sacrifice on one's part*—entails the same result. By not sending money to famine-relief organizations like those listed above, you are letting numerous innocent children under the age of 5 die when you could have easily prevented their deaths with *little effort* (writing out a check) and *minimal sacrifice* on your part (no noticeable reduction in your standard of living). (B_{18}) entails that it is wrong of you to let these children die. Thus, your beliefs about the intrinsic badness of unnecessary childhood deaths and our duties to help prevent such deaths commit you to the obligatoriness of sending a portion of your income to organizations like OXFAM, CARE, and UNICEF to prevent some of those innocent children from dying.

Your beliefs about the intrinsic badness of unnecessary suffering $[(B_1)$ and $(B_2)]$ and your beliefs about our duties to minimize such suffering $[(B_8)$, (B_{10}), (B_{12}), and $(B_{13})]$ together commit you to the view that you ought to help reduce the amount of unnecessary suffering in the world when you can do so with minimal effort, with no risk to yourself or others, and with no noticeable reduction in your standard of living [i.e., they commit you to (P_5)]. Children living in absolute poverty don't only *die* from starvation. They *suffer* terribly from unrelenting hunger and its attendant diseases, including impaired brain development, measles, chronic diarrhea, chronic fatigue, and wasting. Sending a modest portion of your income to OXFAM, CARE, or UNICEF will enable these organizations to provide food, clean water, and needed medications to numerous malnourished children, thereby alleviating their suffering and greatly reducing their risk of disease. Because you can easily do so (by making out a check) with no risk to yourself or to others, with no noticeable reduction in your standard of living, and without failing to perform any other more serious obligation, your beliefs, together with their concomitant, (P_5), entail that you ought to do so.

Your other beliefs support the same conclusion. You believe (B_9)—a morally good person will take steps to make the world a better place and even stronger steps to avoid making the world a worse place—and (B_{10})—even a "minimally decent person" would take steps to help reduce the amount of unnecessary pain, suffering, and death in the world *if s/he could do so with little effort on her/his part.* You also believe that you are a morally good person [(B_{11})], or at least a minimally decent one [(B_{12})], and that you are the kind of person who would take steps to help reduce the amount of pain, suffering, and death in the world *if you could do so with little effort on your part* [(B_{13})]. As we have already seen, *with minimal effort and negligible sacrifice,* you could take steps to help reduce both the number of unnecessary childhood deaths and the amount of unnecessary suffering experienced by these impoverished children just by writing out a modest check to OXFAM, CARE, UNICEF, or some other humanitarian organization working effectively to reduce the amount of unnecessary suffering in the world. Given (B_{10}), you ought to provide modest support to one (or more) of these organizations. Given (B_{12}) and (B_{13}), if you really are the kind of person you think you are, you will provide such support to one (or more) of these organizations.

We have just seen that consistency with your other beliefs requires that you send a portion of your income to famine-relief organizations and/or other organizations working to reduce unnecessary suffering and prevent unnecessary death. But how much of your money are you obligated to send to such worthy organizations? Here I must appeal to your belief (B_{14}). Because you take yourself to be an intellectually honest individual, you must honestly ask yourself how much can you afford to send to famine relief organizations with no noticeable reduction in your standard of living (or in the standard of living of your dependents). Granted, just how much money you can send without noticeably reducing your standard of living will depend on what stage of life you are in and on the extent of your financial resources. Even so, I submit that, like most moderately affluent people, you could easily divert 2% of your income to such worthy causes as famine relief and global population control without the slightest noticeable change in your current

standard of living. I arrived at this number in the following highly scientific manner. I asked my teaching assistant who makes $9,000 per year if he could send 1% of his income ($90 per year, $7.50 per month) to famine-relief organizations with no noticeable difference in his current standard of living, and he said, "Yes." Almost everyone reading this article, except for students who are being forced to read it for a class, makes considerably more money than my teaching assistant; and although it may be true that you have more financial obligations than my T.A. (your house payment, insurance, college tuition for your children, etc. versus his rent, insurance, student fees, etc.), still, given the law of marginal utility, if he can afford to send 1% of his income with no noticeable reduction in his standard of living, you can almost certainly afford to send 2% of your income without noticeably reducing your standard of living. As overpaid philosophy professors, many of you make $40,000 a year. Two percent of $40,000 is $800/year or $15/week. Sending $15/week to famine-relief organizations would prevent more than 250 innocent children under age 5 from dying annually, and your life wouldn't be worse off in any noticeable way. Did your standard of living change *in any noticeable way* when George "Read My Lips" Bush increased your taxes by 2% (while promising to cut them)? No. So, it is extremely doubtful that you would be able to notice a 2% reduction in your current income level, especially if you have your credit card billed automatically for $60 each month. It would be just another monthly payment that you wouldn't even notice.

Many of you could send an even greater percentage of your income (perhaps as much as 5% of your income) with no noticeable reduction in your standard of living. As I said earlier, this is where intellectual honesty comes in. You must honestly determine what percentage of your income you could send to famine-relief organizations without noticeably reducing your standard of living and without thereby failing to fulfill any other overriding obligations, for, according to your own beliefs, that percentage is the *minimum* amount that you are morally required to send to famine-relief organizations and/or other organizations working to reduce unnecessary suffering.

One thing seems reasonably clear: You could easily send 1% of your income to such worthy organizations as OXFAM, CARE, UNICEF, and IPPF with no noticeable difference in your standard of living or the standard of living of any of your dependents. Because your beliefs commit you to (P_4) and (P_5), your beliefs commit you to contributing at the very least 1% of your income, and probably 2% or more, to such important organizations. To do any less is seriously immoral, *by your own standards.*

What about students? Because students also accept (B_1)–(B_{19}), their beliefs likewise entail that if they can reduce the number of innocent children starving to death *with minimal effort and negligible sacrifice on their part,* then they ought to do so. The question is whether they can do so with minimal effort and sacrifice. If you're a student, money's tight, right? As a student struggling to pay your own bills, can you really be morally obligated to support organizations working to save the lives of innocent impoverished children? The answer will no doubt vary from student to student, but here again, intellectual honesty must play a role. Would your life really be any worse off, say, if you had one less beer ($2.00) or café latté ($2.50) per week, or one less pack of cigarettes ($4.00) per month? Or suppose you bought one less CD ($15.00) every two months. Would that really make your life noticeably worse off? (How many CDs sit unused on your shelf anyway?) If we are honest with ourselves, most of us, *including most students,* have to admit that we make lots of frivolous purchases. Reducing the number of these frivolous purchases ever so slightly won't make any noticeable difference in our quality of life, and, in some cases, reducing the number of these purchases would actually improve both our health and the quality of our lives—e.g., reducing the number of cigarettes one smokes or the number of high-fat café lattés one drinks. By way of illustration, suppose you drank one fewer café lattés per week. As a result, you would save $10 per month. By simply sending the $10 saved each month to OXFAM, you would, over the course of a year, prevent 40 children from dying soon, and your standard of living would remain essentially the same. If you are absolutely crazy about café lattés and feel your life wouldn't be complete

without a latté a day, then you must honestly ask yourself whether you could cut back on some other frivolous purchases without noticeably reducing the quality of your life. Even buying just one fewer CD *per year* and sending that $15.00 to UNICEF would prevent 5 children from dying soon. The point is simply this: By cutting out a frivolous purchase here or there, even students could help to reduce the number of innocent children suffering and dying from absolute poverty and malnutrition *with minimal effort and no noticeable reduction in their standards of living.*

The moral of the present section is clear: Consistency with your own beliefs forces you to admit: (i) that you are morally obligated to send a portion of your income to famine-relief organizations and/or other organizations working to reduce the amount of unnecessary pain, suffering, and death in the world and (ii) that the minimum you are obligated to send is whatever amount you could send with no noticeable reduction in your or your dependents' standards of living and without thereby failing to meet any of your other more stringent obligations. For most of us, that means sending 2% of our income to such organizations (which amounts to around 1.5% of your income after taxes). For most students, it means cutting back on a few frivolous purchases and sending the money saved to one of these organizations. To make fulfilling this obligation as easy and effortless as possible, I have provided the addresses and phone numbers for OXFAM, CARE, UNICEF, and IPPF at the end of this article.

4. WHY YOU ARE COMMITTED TO THE MORAL OBLIGATORINESS OF (O_2)

You have just seen that your beliefs entail that you are obligated:

(O_1) To send a modest portion of our income to humanitarian organizations working to reduce the amount of unnecessary suffering in the world.

But our duties to the world's absolutely poor don't stop with (O$_1$). As we shall presently see, your beliefs also entail that we are obligated:

(O$_2$) To refrain from squandering food that could be fed to the world's absolutely poor, especially when doing so involves no risk to ourselves or others.

A. Malnutrition

When we think of malnutrition, images of poor starving children wasting away in undeveloped nations quickly come to mind. We don't think of the obese people suffering from diabetes, hypertension, and heart disease that are all too common in developed countries. But these latter people are clearly malnourished, as well. The fact is that there are two kinds of malnutrition—undernutrition and overnutrition—and both of them result in preventable disease, unnecessary suffering, and premature death. *Undernutrition* arises when a person consumes insufficient calories and/or insufficient macro- and micro-nutrients to meet the basic energy and nutrient requirements for normal biological and metabolic function. Undernutrition causes a wide variety of deficiency diseases including: tissue wasting (due to protein deficiency); brain underdevelopment (due to inadequate fat consumption prior to age 2); blindness (vitamin A deficiency); scurvy (vitamin C deficiency), beriberi (thiamin deficiency), and pellagra (niacin and protein deficiency); and death from starvation (insufficient calories). These diseases, so common in undeveloped countries, are virtually nonexistent in developed nations. *Overnutrition* arises when one consumes too many calories, excess fat, excess saturated fat, excess protein, excess cholesterol, excess refined sugar, and excess sodium. Overnutrition gives rise to a wide variety of diseases of excess: coronary artery disease, stroke and other arteriosclerotic diseases (excess cholesterol, saturated fat, transfatty acids, and iron); obesity (excess fat and calories); hypertension (excess fat, calories, and sodium), diabetes mellitus (excess fat, calories, and refined sugar), some forms of cancer (excess fat), and osteoporosis (excess protein consumption,

coupled with inactivity). These diseases, rampant in developed countries, are practically unheard of in underdeveloped countries. As we shall see, both forms of malnutrition have the same root cause, a form of agriculture that (i) fosters overnutrition and (ii) systematically requires the overnourished to squander food that could have been made available to the undernourished.

B. Day-Old Bread: Why Squandering Food in a World of Scarcity Is Morally Wrong

Day-Old Bread: Suppose there is a small bakery in my neighborhood that sells its day-old bread at one-third of the regular price. The bakery doesn't want to run out of bread for its full-paying customers, so it typically bakes twelve more loaves of bread than it anticipates needing. Also suppose there is a small homeless shelter for battered women and children in the neighborhood. It can afford to buy only the discounted day-old bread. When there is no day-old bread available, these people go without bread for the day. Suppose, I know all these facts, but I, nevertheless, start buying the remaining twelve loaves of bread (in addition to the loaf I regularly buy) right before the bakery closes each day just because I like the way it makes my kitchen smell. As a result, there is no longer any day-old bread available. Of course, I can't eat that much bread. So, the next day, when that fresh-baked smell is gone, I simply throw all twelve loaves of bread in the garbage. By squandering food in this way, I have knowingly caused the women and children in the shelter to go hungry, and I have done so just to satisfy my trivial desire to have my kitchen smell a certain way. Finally, suppose I keep up my bread-purchasing habit for so long that some of these women and children end up dying from hunger-related diseases.

Have I done anything wrong? Your beliefs entail that I have. You believe that a world with more *unnecessary* suffering is worse than a world with less *unnecessary* suffering [(B$_2$)], and you also believe that we ought to avoid making the world a worse place when we can do so with minimal effort and negligible sacrifice [(B_8·)]. In Day-Old Bread, I have knowingly squandered food that these women and children would have been able to eat and have, thus, knowingly caused them to suffer unnecessarily just so that I could experience a certain olfactory sensation. I have knowingly made the world a worse place by increasing the amount of unnecessary suffering it contains for an entirely trivial reason. Here, I have actively and knowingly made others worse off. One thing I could have easily done to avoid making the world a worse place would have been to purchase only the bread I need, leaving the rest for others to consume. Perhaps, it would not be wrong of me to purchase vastly more bread than I need in a world where everyone's food needs were adequately met, but as your beliefs rightly reveal, it is wrong of me to waste food that could be fed to severely undernourished humans who desperately need that food. Simply put, your beliefs entail that we are obligated to (O_2)—to refrain from squandering food that could be fed to others who desperately need it.

Multi-Squanderer Scenario: Suppose I am not unique in my desire to smell fresh-baked bread. Suppose that there are people in every community in America who enjoy the smell of fresh-baked bread as much as I do and who, like me, buy up all the available bread at their local bakeries just before closing time so that there is no day-old bread available anywhere in the country. And suppose that, as a result, women and children in shelters all across North America are starving to death, just so lots of other North Americans can enjoy the smell of fresh-baked bread. Does the fact that lots of other people are squandering bread in this way make it any less wrong of me to squander the bread from my local bakery? Not one bit. The fact that other people are behaving immorally does not justify my doing so. Given your beliefs, the only difference between Day-Old Bread and Multi-Squanderer Scenario is that in the latter case lots of other people are just as morally culpable as I am.

C. Eating in a World of Scarcity: (O_2)'s Implications

Day-Old Bread illustrates that your beliefs commit you to the moral obligatoriness of not squandering food that could be fed to the world's absolutely poor. You are not alone in this commitment. Anyone who believes (B_1)–(B_{19}), and that includes almost everyone, is committed to the obligatoriness of (O_2). Even without appealing to (B_1)–(B_{19}), almost everyone would agree that it is wrong to knowingly throw away bread that could save other people's lives and that, therefore, we are obligated not to squander food in this way. What most people don't realize is that in order to fulfill obligation (O_2), they must radically change the way they eat.

If you are like most moderately affluent people, you eat meat and lots of it: Bacon or sausage for breakfast, one or two quarter-pound hamburgers for lunch, and steak, pork chops, or chicken for dinner. For most people in affluent nations, eating this way is normal—it's how they were raised to eat—and it seems not only permissible, but downright wholesome. But things are not always as they seem. The burden of the present section is to show that anyone who believes (B_1)–(B_{19}) is already committed, on pain of inconsistency, to the immorality of eating most meat. Elsewhere, I have argued that beliefs like (B_1), (B_2), (B_8), (B_8·), and (B_{10}) commit us to the immorality of eating meat and other animal products because of the enormous amount of unnecessary *animal* suffering modern animal factories generate.[7] Here, I am interested in the untold *human* suffering that such a system of agriculture produces.

The numbers used in Day-Old Bread were not chosen at random. They were chosen because it takes 12.9 pounds of grain to produce one pound of beef. This grain could be fed directly to the world's starving poor, but instead it is fed to intentionally bred cows—cows that would not have existed and, hence, would not have needed to be fed, had we not artificially inseminated their mothers. These cows, in turn, convert that grain to manure. By cycling grain through cattle to produce animal protein, we lose 90% of that grain's protein, 96% of its calories, 100% of its carbohydrates, and 100% of its fiber. By cycling grain through cattle so that affluent people can eat meat, starving *humans* are being deprived of that grain so that *cows* can be fed. As a result, while more than 1 billion humans experience chronic hunger, cows in feedlots never go hungry. Playing off our Day-Old Bread analogy, those 12.9 pounds of grain could have been converted to 12.9 loaves of bread that could have, in turn, been fed to the world's starving poor. Instead, that grain/bread is wasted, just so people in affluent nations can eat meat and other animal products. There is no way around it: Whenever one purchases a pound of beef, one is supporting a system of agriculture that effectively squanders 12.9 pounds of grain for every pound of beef produced.

Although beef production is one of the most inefficient means of food production, all forms of animal agriculture are highly inefficient. Of the 12 million tons of grain protein produced in the United States in 1991, 10 million tons were fed to livestock, leaving only 2 million tons for human consumption. Of the 9.2 million tons of legume protein produced in the United States that year, 9 million tons were fed to livestock, leaving only 0.2 million ton for human consumption. For the 21 million tons of plant protein fed to livestock, we received only 7 million tons of livestock protein in return (a 33% protein-conversion efficiency rate). The end result is a net loss of 14 million tons of protein, protein that could have saved the lives of starving children had it not been squandered on livestock production. And protein isn't the only macronutrient we lose by feeding grain to livestock. We also lose all of that grain's carbohydrates and fiber (meat contains no carbohydrates or fiber) and approximately 90% of its caloric energy. I noted at the outset that the United States grows more than enough grain and soybeans to feed the world's entire human population. Unfortunately, most of that grain is squandered on livestock production. Of the estimated 740 kg of grain grown in the United States per person per year, 663 kg are fed to livestock, leaving only 77 kg for human consumption.[8] Were we to forego foods of animal origin and eat that grain directly, there would be more than enough grain left over to feed the world's starving human population.

The irony is that the same system of agriculture that deprives starving humans of grain, thereby contributing to undernutrition in poor nations, is also one of the primary causes of overnutrition in affluent nations. It is now an established fact that diets high in saturated fat and cholesterol greatly increase the risk of several chronic degenerative diseases, including heart disease, hypertension, obesity, diabetes, and some forms of cancer. We also know that meat and animal products are the principal sources of saturated fat and cholesterol in standard Western diets. The evidence is so compelling that the American Dietetic Association, the leading nutritional organization in the United States, now maintains:

> Scientific data suggest positive relationships between a vegetarian diet and reduced risk for several chronic degenerative diseases and conditions, including obesity, coronary artery disease, hypertension, diabetes mellitus, and some types of cancer. *It is the position of The American Dietetic Association (ADA) that appropriately planned vegetarian diets are healthful, are nutritionally adequate, and provide health benefits in the prevention and treatment of certain diseases.*[9]

The ADA also holds:

> Well-planned vegan and lacto-ovo vegetarian diets are appropriate for all stages of the life cycle, including during pregnancy and lactation. Appropriately planned vegan and lacto-ovo vegetarian diets satisfy nutrient needs of infants, children, and adolescents and promote normal growth.

One result of feeding our children a meat-based diet—childhood obesity—is both ironic and sad. While children in underdeveloped countries are starving to death, more than one-fifth of U.S. children are obese. In addition, the damage to coronary arteries arising from a meat-based diet begins remarkably early. Dr. Spock points out: "Fatty deposits are now typically found in the coronary arteries of children on a typical American diet by the age of three. And by the age of twelve, they are found in 70% of children." As a result, Dr. Spock recommends vegan diets for all children over the age of 2. These last observations demonstrate that our duty not to squander food is not overridden by a biological need to consume meat and animal products. There is no such need. Neither adults nor children need to consume any animal products at all. As the ADA has averred, appropriately planned vegan diets—diets devoid of meat and animal products—are *nutritionally adequate* for all stages of the life cycle. If Dr. Spock is right, appropriately planned vegan diets are *nutritionally superior* to meat-based diets. Either way, we have no need for meat and animal products. We eat them only because we like the way they taste.

Does the desire for a particular taste sensation justify us in squandering food that could be fed to starving children? No. In Day-Old Bread, we saw that your beliefs entail the wrongness of squandering 12 loaves of bread just so one can experience a particular olfactory sensation. By doing so, one not only fails to benefit others, one actively makes others worse off. Of course, by purchasing meat because one likes its taste, one is squandering 12 pounds of grain, just to experience a particular gustatory sensation, and, in so doing, one is actively making others—those in desperate need of that grain—worse off. Surely, the fact that it is a *gustatory* sensation, rather than an *olfactory* sensation, is not morally relevant. Because your beliefs entail that it is wrong to squander bread in Day-Old Bread, your beliefs also entail that it is wrong to squander grain by purchasing meat. Hence, your commitment to the obligatoriness of not squandering grain commits you to the obligatoriness of adopting a predominantly plant-based diet devoid of meat and animal products obtained from grain-fed animals. Because virtually all commercially produced meat (including beef, pork, chicken, turkey, and farm-raised fish), dairy products, and eggs come from grain-fed animals, consistency with your own beliefs requires that you adopt a quasi-vegan diet devoid of beef,

pork, chicken, turkey, farm-raised fish, dairy products, and eggs.[10]

One might object that (O$_2$) does not entail that the obligatoriness of adopting such a diet on the grounds that the difficulty of planning a nutritionally balanced quasi-vegan diet for oneself and one's family simply makes such a diet too risky. Such an objection is entirely unfounded. It is extremely easy to eat a nutritionally balanced vegan diet. No special food combining is necessary. All one need do is eat sufficient calories centered around the Physicians Committee for Responsible Medicine's *new* four food groups: I. Whole Grains (5+ servings/day), II. Vegetables (3+ servings/day), III. Fruits (3+ servings/day), and IV. Legumes (2+ servings/day). Anyone who eats the recommended daily servings from these new four groups will be eating a nutritionally sound plant-based diet. And far from being risky, such a diet will reduce one's risk of heart disease, cancer, stroke, hypertension, obesity, and diabetes.

There is no justification for squandering precious grain reserves in a world of food scarcity. This conclusion is not derived from some highly contentious ethical theory you likely reject, but from beliefs you already hold. Consistency with your own beliefs entails that it's wrong to squander food that could be fed to the world's starving poor for trivial reasons like taste or smell. Because modern meat, dairy, and egg production necessarily squanders grain that could be fed directly to humans, *your own beliefs* entail that it is wrong to consume these products, which, in turn, entails that quasi-vegan diets are obligatory.

5. OBJECTIONS AND REPLIES

A. The Iteration Objection

In Section 3, after showing that Singer's and Unger's attempts to defend highly demanding dictates fail, I argued that your beliefs commit you to two *much less demanding* normative principles (P$_4$) and (P$_5$), which, in turn, entail that you are obligated to (O$_1$)—to send a modest portion of your income to famine-relief organizations and/or other

[handwritten: what about grass fed?]   *[handwritten: womp…]*

organizations working to reduce unnecessary suffering. The present worry is that these two principles will ultimately reduce to the very same highly demanding dictate from which I was aiming to distance myself. Because *standards of living* are vague and lack precise boundaries, there can be a repeated series of non-noticeable reductions in one's standard of living, such that, before long, one is radically worse off than one's original starting position, and noticeably so.

My response is quite simple. Neither (P_4) nor (P_5) is intended to be iterated in this way. In fact, (P_4) and (P_5) are intended to be compatible with gradual increases in one's standard of living so as to enable one to do even more to help reduce the amount of unnecessary suffering down the road. To block the iteration objection and to make explicit the kinds of principles your beliefs clearly commit you to, (P_4) and (P_5)—as they apply to *moderately affluent* people—should be restricted as follows: The principles never require a moderately affluent person to have a standard of living *noticeably* lower than the highest standard of living she has ever enjoyed. Even with this restriction in place, (P_4) and (P_5) still entail that most of us are morally required to send at least 2% of our income to famine-relief organizations and/or other organizations working to reduce unnecessary suffering. The reason is this: Because standards of living typically continue to improve the longer people are in the workforce, most people are currently enjoying their highest standards of living. (P_4) and (P_5) require these people to provide whatever amount of financial assistance they can provide without noticeably lowering their standard of living from its current optimal level.

B. The Libertarian Objection: There Are No Positive Duties

Strict libertarians insist that although we have negative duties to do no harm, we have *no* positive duties to assist others. Thus, on the libertarian view, it would not be wrong of you to let the child drown in Singer's Pond. Libertarians maintain that even though you could save the child with minimal

sacrifice and no risk to yourself, you have absolutely no positive obligation to assist the child in any way. Because they deny the existence of positive duties, libertarians contend that it also would *not* be wrong of you *not* to save the lives of numerous starving children by sending a modest portion of your income to famine-relief organizations. Granted, libertarians do think that it would be *good* of you to wade in and save the child. They also think it would be *good* of you to send money to such worthy causes as famine relief, but these actions would be entirely supererogatory on your part. Thus, the libertarian objection runs as follows: Because there are *no* positive duties, we have *no* obligation to send money to famine-relief organizations, even though that money would save the lives of numerous innocent children.

As noted earlier, Narveson claims that such a libertarian "nobody-needs-to-help-anybody" stance is unreasonable. A variation on the trolley problem suggests that he is right. Suppose that six innocent people are trapped on the tracks and a runaway trolley is barreling down on them. Fortunately, you just happen to be standing right next to a switch which, if flipped, will divert the trolley onto a second track. Even more fortunately, unlike typical trolley problems where three people are trapped on the second track and you have to decide between killing three and letting six die, in the present trolley case, no one is on the other track and so, if the switch is flipped, the train will be diverted to the second track where it will roll safely to a stop with no one being injured. The question is this: Are you morally required to flip the switch and save the six people? Not according to the libertarian. Even though you are standing right next to the switch and can flip the switch with little effort and no sacrifice on your part, with no risk to yourself or others, and without thereby violating any other obligations, the libertarian maintains that it would *not* be wrong of you to let the six die by not flipping the switch.

Such a position strikes most of us as morally outrageous. You *should* flip the switch, and it would be *clearly wrong* of you not to do so. And you, no doubt, agree. Because you believe that one should wade into the pond to save the child [(B₇)], you surely think it would be wrong not to flip the switch. I realize that a die-hard libertarian might remain unconvinced, but you are not a die-hard libertarian. You believe that there are both positive and negative duties. Thus, the libertarian objection under consideration gives *you* absolutely no reason to think that (O₁) is not obligatory.

C. Malthusian Musings

A common reason offered for not sending money to famine-relief organizations is that doing so will just exacerbate the problem. If lots more children under age 5 survive, then when they reach puberty and start having their own children, there will be even more mouths to feed, and as a result, there will be even more human suffering due to starvation. In short, it is better to let 12 million children starve to death each year than to save them and have two or three times that many children starving 15 years from now.

Couched in the more scientific language of ecology, the Malthusian objection runs as follows: Left unchecked, organisms will reproduce until they reach the carrying capacity K of their respective ecosystems. Once they exceed K, there will be a major crash in the population size of that organism. By feeding starving humans, the anti-assistance argument goes, we are simply speeding up the time at which we exceed the Earth's K for humans (hereafter K_h). Better to let 12 million children starve to death each year than to exceed K_h and have an even more devastating population crash.

The first thing to note is that we don't think Malthusian worries about exceeding K_h give us a good reason to let our own children starve. But if we don't let our children starve, then, as adults, they will probably procreate, thereby hastening the time when K_h is exceeded. If ecologically based, global human population concerns give us a reason to let distant children die, they give us an equally good reason to let our own children die. You wouldn't think of letting your own children die to help reduce human population. Thus you

must not find letting children starve to death to be a legitimate way to curb human population growth.

Second, there are other more effective ways of reducing human population growth: improving educational opportunities and employment opportunities *for women* (which drives up the opportunity cost of procreation), improving the economic security of the elderly, providing ready access to birth control, and providing abortion services.[11] Even more draconian policies, like mandatory sterilization after having one child, are preferable to letting children starve to death. Because there are numerous more effective means of curbing population growth than letting innocent children starve, anyone who accepts (B₁₉) must think it wrong to let innocent children starve as a means of population control.

Third, demographic studies repeatedly show that childhood morality rates and birthrates are positively correlated—as childhood mortality rates decline, so do birthrates—and so, supporting famine-relief organizations working to reduce the number of unnecessary childhood deaths is, paradoxically, a way of slowing population growth. But suppose you question the validity of these studies. Suppose you dig in your Malthusian heels and insist that feeding the world's starving children will increase the number of humans suffering from starvation down the road. Such insistence does not absolve you from obligation (O₁); it just means that you are obligated to fulfill it in a different way. Instead of being required to send money to a famine-relief organization, you will be obligated to send money to humanitarian organizations, like the IPPF, that are working to reduce the rate of population growth in underdeveloped countries through effective birth control measures.

Fourth, those who take Malthusian concerns seriously are even more obligated to refrain from consuming meat and other animal products, because intentionally breeding millions of cows and pigs and billions of chickens greatly reduces the world's K_h. Intentionally adding billions of farm animals to the world greatly increases the number of animal mouths that must be fed and, thus, greatly reduces the amount of food available for human consumption.

Appendix

Oxfam America
26 West St.
Boston, MA 02111
1-800-OXFAM US
    [1-800-693-2687].

International Planned
    Parenthood
    Federation (IPPF)
902 Broadway, 10th
    Floor
New York, NY 10010

United Nations
    Children's Fund
333 East 38th St.
New York, NY 10016
UNICEF: 1-800-
    FOR KIDS
    [1-800-367-5437]

CARE
151 Ellis St.
Atlanta, GA 30303
1-800-521-CARE
    [1-800-521-2273]

6. CONCLUSION

The implications of your beliefs are clear. Given your beliefs, it follows that we are morally obligated to (O_1)—to send a modest portion of our income to famine-relief organizations and/or other organizations working to reduce the amount of unnecessary pain, suffering, and death in the world—and to (O_2)—to refrain from squandering food that could be fed to the world's absolutely poor. (O_2), in turn, entails that we are obligated to adopt a quasi-vegan diet, rather than squander grain on a meat-based diet. These conclusions were not derived from some highly contentious ethical theory that you can easily reject, but from your own firmly held beliefs. Consequently, consistency demands that you embrace these obligations and modify your behavior accordingly.

NOTES

1. Following Peter Singer (who borrows the term from Robert McNamara), I use 'absolute poverty' to refer to "a condition of life so characterised by malnutrition, illiteracy, disease, squalid surroundings, high infant mortality and low life expectancy as to be beneath any reasonable definition of human decency" [Singer, *Practical Ethics,* Second Edition (Cambridge: Cambridge University Press, 1993), p. 219.]. Singer reports that, according to the World Watch Institute, as many as 1.2 billion people live in absolute poverty (pp. 219–20).

2. William Aiken, "The Right to Be Saved from Starvation" in *World Hunger and Moral Obligation,* eds. W. Aiken and H. LaFollette (Englewood Cliffs, NJ: Prentice-Hall, 1977), pp. 86 and 93. Aiken argues that one's right to be saved from starvation is claimable against all persons who satisfy three minimal conditions: (i) they must know that the person is starving, (ii) they must have the means necessary to save the person, and (iii) they must be able to save the person without placing themselves in an equally bad or worse situation than the person they are saving (pp. 91–93).

3. By "without sacrificing anything of comparable moral significance" Singer means "without causing anything else comparably bad to happen, or doing something that is wrong in itself, or failing to promote some moral good, comparable in significance to the bad thing that we prevent." ("Famine, Affluence, and Morality," *Philosophy and Public Affairs,* vol. 1, no. 3 [Spring 1972], p. 234).

4. Obviously, if you do not hold these beliefs (or enough of them), my argument will have no force for you, nor is it intended to. It is only aimed at those of you who do hold these widespread commonsense beliefs.

5. By "*unnecessary* suffering" I mean suffering which serves no greater, outweighing justifying good. If some instance of suffering is required to bring about a greater good (e.g., a painful root canal may be the only way to save a person's tooth), then that suffering is *not* unnecessary. Thus, in the case of (B_2), no *ceteris paribus* clause is needed, because if other things are *not* equal such that the suffering in question is justified by an overriding justifying

good that can only be achieved by allowing that suffering, then that suffering is *not* unnecessary.

6. By a "minimally decent person" I mean a person who does the very minimum required by morality and no more. I borrow this terminology from Judith Jarvis Thomson who distinguishes a *good* Samaritan from a *minimally decent* Samaritan. See her "A Defense of Abortion," *Philosophy and Public Affairs* 1 (1971): 62–65.

7. See my "The Immorality of Eating Meat" in *The Moral Life,* ed. Louis Pojman (New York and Oxford: Oxford University Press, 2000), pp. 856–889. There I documented that the routine unanaesthetized mutilations (castration, branding, dehorning, debeaking, dubbing, tail docking, and tooth pulling) and abysmal living conditions which farm animals are forced to endure in factory farms, along with inhumane transportation and slaughter processes, greatly increase the amount of unnecessary suffering in the world; and I argued that because you could easily take steps to help reduce such unnecessary suffering by eating something other than meat, consistency with your beliefs forces you to admit that eating meat is morally wrong.

8. Data on protein production and consumption and grain production and consumption taken from *Food, Energy, and Society,* Revised Edition, eds. David Pimentel and Marcia Pimentel (Niwot, CO: University of Colorado Press, 1996), pp. 77–78.

9. "Position of the American Dietetic Association: Vegetarian Diets," *Journal of the American Dietitic Association* 97 (November 1997): 1317. For those wishing to learn more about sound vegetarian nutrition, the ADA has published this article in its entirety at: www.eatright.org/adap1197.html.

10. (O$_2$) does not entail that it is wrong to eat meat *per se,* e.g. it does *not* entail that eating the flesh of wild animals is wrong. Hence, the use of 'quasi-vegan' in the text. However, (O$_2$) does entail that it is wrong to eat virtually all commercially produced meat and animal products because these products are obtained from grain-fed animals and their production necessarily squanders grain which could have been fed to starving humans.

11. Regardless of one's views on abortion, presumably it would be better to abort a fetus quickly and relatively painlessly than to let that fetus be born only to starve to death slowly and painfully.

STUDY QUESTIONS

1. Examine Engel's arguments for his two main principles. Discuss their premises. Do you see any problems with them?

2. Is Engel correct that virtually all major moral theories contain principles that require us to make some modest sacrifices for the welfare of the absolutely poor?

3. Examine the objections that Engel discusses against his position. Does he defeat them? Are there other objections you can think of?

4. How much should we give to the absolutely poor? Is Engel too lenient, too stringent, or about right?

5. Examine Engel's Day-Old Bread example and discuss its implications.

37

The World Food Supply: The Damage Done by Cattle-Raising

TRISTRAM COFFIN

Tristram Coffin was the editor of The Washington Spectator, *a public concerns newsletter.*

This article from The Washington Spectator *reports on the ecological costs of cattle-raising. For example, in California it takes 5214 gallons of water to produce one edible pound of beef, as compared to 23 gallons for the same amount of tomatoes. In addition, lowering one's meat diet is likely to result in greater health. Coffin calls on us to change our diet, for our own good and the good of humankind, from one heavy in meat to more grains, vegetables, and fruits.*

In this century, the number and impacts of livestock have swelled apace with human population and affluence. Since mid-century human numbers have doubled to [5.8] billion, while the number of four-legged livestock—cattle, pigs, sheep, goats, horses, buffalo and camels—has grown from 2.3 billion to 4 billion. At the same time, the fowl population multiplied from about 3 billion to nearly 11 billion. There are now three times as many domestic animals as people.[1]

"Currently, sufficient land, energy and water exist to feed well over twice the world's population" (*Earth Save Foundation*). But this is not the whole story. The Foundation adds, "Yet half of the world's grain harvest is fed to livestock, while millions of humans go hungry. In 1984 when thousands of Ethiopians were dying from famine, Ethiopia continued growing and shipping millions of dollars worth of livestock to the United States and other European countries."

Worldwatch Institute reports: "Rings of barren earth spread out from wells on the grasslands of Soviet Turkmenia. Heather and lilies wilt in the nature preserves of the southern Netherlands.

"Forests teeming with rare forms of plant and animal life explode in flame in Costa Rica. Water tables fall and fossil fuels are wasted in the U.S. Each of these cases of environmental decline issues from a single source: the global livestock industry."

The simple fact is that the livestock industry is a better paying customer than are hungry human beings. In turn, the industry is supported by the lusty appetite for meat of well-to-do individuals. Since 1985, North Americans have been eating 50% more beef, 280% more poultry and 33% more dairy products. In its tract "Our Food, Our World," the Foundation points out that this is a diet with one-third more fat, one-fifth less carbohydrate, and levels of protein consumption "far exceeding official recommendation."

Reprinted from *The Washington Spectator*, ed. Tristram Coffin, Vol. 19.2 (January 15, 1993).

"This increased demand for animal products has resulted in a vast reallocation of resources, has promoted the degradation of global systems, and has disrupted indigenous cultures. The impact on human health has been equally devastating."

Worldwatch advises: "Feeding the world's current population on an American-style diet would require two and a half times as much grain as the world's farmers produce for all purposes. A future world of 8 to 14 billion people eating the American ration of 220 grams a day can be nothing but a flight of fancy." Why? "In the U.S., over one-third of all raw materials—including fossil fuels—consumed for all purposes are devoted to the production of livestock" [*Earth Save*].

Example: it takes 16 pounds of grain and soy to produce one pound of beef. One half the Earth's land mass is grazed for livestock, as compared to the 2% used for fruits and vegetables.

Growing cattle crops is an "extremely energy-intensive process. Farmers must pump water, plow, cultivate and fertilize the fields, then harvest and transport the crops. The number of calories of fossil fuel expended to produce one calorie of protein from beef is 78, as compared to 2 calories to produce the same one calorie of soybeans." The energy used to produce one pound of grain-fed beef is equal to one gallon of gasoline, according to *Earth Save*.

What about water? "Our Food, Our World" estimates that livestock production accounts for more than half of all water consumed. In California it takes 5214 gallons of water to produce one edible pound of beef, as compared to 23 gallons for the same amount of tomatoes … Water tables, like the Ogallala aquifer under the Great Plains states, are fast being depleted.

Marc Reisner writes in his book *California Desert,* "It offends me that we give three times more water to grow cows than we give to people in California."

The Growth of Deserts—"Our Food, Our World" contends that livestock grazing and overuse of land to grow food crops for cattle have played a major role in the growth of deserts. "Regions most affected by desertification are all cattle-producing areas, including the western half of the U.S., Central and South America, Australia and sub-Saharan Africa.

The main causes of desertification are overgrazing of livestock, overcultivation of land, improper irrigation techniques, deforestation [to clear land for cattle raising as is now occurring in the Brazilian Rain Forest]."

Why? "Under persistent grazing, the bare ground becomes impermeable to rainwater, which then courses off the surface, carrying away topsoil and scouring stream beds into deep gullies. Upstream, water tables fall for lack of replenishment; downstream, flooding occurs more frequently and sediment clogs waterways, dams and estuaries. In drier climates wind sweeps away the destabilized soil."

The U.N. Environment Program estimates that 73% of the world's 3.3 billion hectares of dry rangeland is at least moderately desertified, having lost more than 25% of its carrying capacity. "There is little debate that degradation is occurring in environments where rainfall is more plentiful and regular. The perennial plants that flourish in these zones are easily disrupted by cattle; clay soils are easily compacted and rendered impervious to water; and rains often arrive in strong, sudden downpours, sluicing away soils destabilized by cattle" (Worldwatch Institute).

Philip Fradkin, writing in *Audubon* magazine, says: "The impact of countless hooves and mouths over the years has done more to alter the type of vegetarian and land forms of the West than all the water projects, strip mines, power plants, freeways, and subdivision developments combined."

A few pertinent facts: Each year, an estimated 125,000 square miles of rainforest are destroyed, together with the loss of 1,000 plant and animal species. In Central America cattle ranching has destroyed more rainforests than has any other activity. A quarter of Central American rainforests have been cleared for pasture. This creates a profitable market for cattle sold to the U.S. market.

Livestock production creates other environmental problems—the pollution of the atmosphere by carbon dioxide and methane, of water by animal wastes and pesticides. Worldwatch Institute states: "The millions of tons of animal waste that accumulate at modern production facilities can pollute rivers and groundwater if precautions are not taken. If they get into rivers or open bodies of water, nitrogen and phosphorus in manure overfertilize algae, which grow rapidly, deplete oxygen supplies, and suffocate aquatic ecosystems. From the hundreds of algae-choked Italian lakes to the murky Chesapeake Bay, and from the oxygen-starved Baltic Sea to the polluted Adriatic, animal wastes add to the nutrient loads from fertilizer runoff, human sewage and urban and industrial pollution."

In the Netherlands, the 14 million animals in feeding houses in the southern part of the nation "excrete more nitrogen- and phosphorus-rich manure than the soil can absorb … pushing freshwater ecosystems into decline."

And, "manure nitrogen, mixed with nitrogen from artificial fertilizers, percolates through the soil into the underground water tables as nitrates…. In the U.S., roughly one-fifth of the wells in livestock states, such as Iowa, Kansas and Nebraska, have nitrate levels that exceed health standards. Manure nitrogen also escapes into the air as gaseous ammonia, a pollutant that causes acid rain."

The *Earth Save* study looks at three problems:

- "The metabolic processes of cattle result in the emission of large quantities of methane. Each cow produces 1 pound of methane for every 2 pounds of meat it yields. The amount of methane emitted by the world's cattle annually: 100 million tons." 20% of total world methane emissions comes from cattle.

- Wastes from factory farmers, feedlots and dairies create a buildup of toxins in the land and water. The E.P.A. estimates that almost half the wells and surface streams in the U.S. are "contaminated by agricultural pollutants."

- Chemical pesticides are used so widely and in such large quantities that they "poison the environment and the human food chain. The increase in overall pesticide use since 1945, when petro-chemical based agriculture became popular, is 3,300%."

Loss of Forests—Not only rangeland, but forests, too, suffer from heavy livestock production.

The Worldwatch study reports, "Forests suffer, as branches are cut for fodder or entire stands are leveled to make way for pastures. The roster of impacts from forest clearing includes the loss of watershed protection, loss of plant and animal species, and on a larger scale, substantial contributions of the greenhouse gas carbon dioxide to the atmosphere."

Examples: in Latin America, more than 20 million hectares of moist tropical forests have been cleared for cattle pasture. The U.N. Food and Agricultural Organization says that Central America has lost more than a third of its forest since the early 1960s. Nearly 70% of the deforested land in Panama and Costa Rica is now pasture.

"Eradicating tree cover sets the wheels of land degradation in motion. Shallow, acidic, and nutrient-poor, tropical soils lose critical phosphorus and other nutrients when the forest is converted to pasture…. Most pasture is abandoned within a decade for land newly carved from the forest … Forest destruction for ranching also contributes to climate change. When living plants are cut down and burned, or when they decompose, they release carbon into the atmosphere as the greenhouse gas carbon dioxide. In the atmosphere, carbon dioxide traps the heat of the sun, warming the earth. The expansion of pastures into Latin American forests has released an estimated 1.4 billion tons of carbon into the atmosphere."

Worldwatch points out that methane, a byproduct of cattle-raising, is the second most important greenhouse gas.

Effect on Health—*Earth Save* warns, "Animal products contain large quantities of saturated fat, cholesterol and protein and no dietary fiber. The impact of this diet on human health has been devastating…. Fortunately, by observing a low-fat diet free of animal products, some diseases can be commonly prevented, consistently improved and sometimes cured." Some fats are associated with most of the diseases of affluence that are among the leading causes of death in industrialized countries: heart disease, stroke, breast and colon cancer. The study laments that physicians generally are taught to cure disease, but not how to prevent it. The majority "are taught little about nutrition as a preventative measure," but many are inquiring into this possibility.

"*Great Protein Fiasco*"—The Worldwatch study comments: "The adverse health impacts of excessive meat-eating stem in large part from what nutritionists call the *great protein fiasco*—a mistaken belief by many Westerners that they need to consume large quantities of protein. This myth, propagated as much as a century ago by health officials and governmental dietary guidelines, has resulted in Americans and other members of industrial societies ingesting twice as much protein as they need. Among the affluent, the protein myth is dangerous because of the saturated fats that accompany concentrated protein in meat and dairy products."

Low-fat diets are now recommended by the U.S. Surgeon General, the U.S. National Research Council, the American Heart Association, and the World Health Organization. They recommend lowering fat consumption to no more than 30% of calories, as compared to the U.S. norm of 37%. [Many health specialists recommend lowering the fat consumption to 10 to 15%—ed. note.]

Higher meat consumption among the well-to-do may also create a problem for the poor, "as the share of farmland devoted to feed cultivation expands, reducing production of food staples," says the Worldwatch study. It points out that in Egypt, for example, "over the past quarter-century, corn grown for animal feed has taken over cropland from wheat, rice, sorghum and millet—all staple grains fed to livestock rose from 10 to 36%."

Much the same is true in Mexico, where 30% of the grain is fed to livestock, "although 22% of the country's people suffer from malnutrition." The share of cropland growing animal food and fodder went up from 5% in 1960 to 23% in 1980. A study of agriculture in 23 third world countries showed that in 13 countries, farmers had shifted more than 10% of grain land from food crops to feed crops in the last 25 years. In nine countries, "the demand for meat among the rich was squeezing out staple production for the poor."

The picture in the U.S.: more than a million farms and ranches raise young beef, while four big companies slaughter nearly 60% of them. Since 1962, the number of huge American beef feedlots, capable of holding 16,000 head of cattle, has risen from 23 to 189. At the same time, small feedlots, holding no more than 1,000, have dropped by 117,000.

The big operations have no trouble getting government support, such as guaranteed minimum prices, government storage of surpluses, feed subsidies, import levies and product insurance. The Organization for Economic Cooperation and Development reports that in 1990 government programs in the industrial democracies gave subsidies to animal farmers and feed growers worth $120 billion.

What is the answer? The *Los Angeles Times* states: "The Seeds of Change [a group based in Santa Fe, NM] philosophy holds that adopting a plant-based diet is the best solution for improving individual health and lessening the toll of the human race on our Earth's limited resources." Seeds of Change founder Gabriel Howearth recommends:

> Bush acorn squash and bush buttercup squash, both high in vitamin A and free amino acids. Jerusalem artichokes, a native North American food plant with a varied vitamin balance and useful digestive enzymes. Hopi blue starch corn grown without irrigation in the Southwest and a traditional staple of the Hopi Indians … Okra, containing high amounts of vitamin C and amino acids, good in vegetable soup, stew and gumbo. Amaranth, a high-protein garden grain.

Howearth's goal "is to get all kinds of people, even those who work and have limited leisure time, to grow their own food—in their backyards, on their balconies, or on their rooftops."

This is not a goal everyone can follow. What many can do is change their diet from heavy meats to more vegetables and fruits. They will be less likely to become ill, and they will help save the planet Earth.

NOTE

1. From *The Worldwatch Institute*, quoted in "World Food Supply: The Damage Done by Cattle-Raising." *The Washington Spectator* (Jan. 15, 1993).

STUDY QUESTIONS

1. Go over the figures and damage caused by cattle-raising, mentioned in this essay. Are you convinced by the article that the situation is as bad as it is made out to be? Explain your answer.

2. If the raising of cattle and other livestock is so damaging to the environment and our health, what should we be doing about it?

38

Vegetarianism and Treading Lightly on the Earth

MICHAEL ALLEN FOX

Michael Allen Fox was educated at Cornell University and the University of Toronto, taught philosophy for thirty-nine years at Queen's University in Canada, and is now retired and living in Australia, where he is Adjunct Professor of Social Science at the University of New England. He has published work in such journals as Ethics, Environmental Ethics, Environmental Values, Ethics and the Environment, *and* International Journal of Applied Ethics, *and his most recent books are* Deep Vegetarianism *(also translated into Chinese) and* The Accessible Hegel.

The meat-based diet that is the prevailing choice in affluent, industrialized parts of the world is unhealthy and environmentally unsustainable in a number of ways. These claims are explained and documented in some detail in this essay. The negative effects of meat production on species diversity in particular are illustrated with special reference to rain forest destruction for cattle grazing. Also investigated here is the link between animal agriculture and the manipulative or dominating mindset that encourages viewing animals and ecosystems generally just as resources to be exploited at will. In contrast, it is argued, a vegetarian food system would enable us to take greater responsibility for our actions by minimizing our impact on the planet and help us regain a sense of being part of nature rather than existing apart from it.

Reprinted by permission of the author.

MOVING AWAY FROM MEAT

I begin with a basic assumption: Scientific evidence increasingly reveals that a vegetarian—even a vegan—diet is from a nutritional standpoint, at least as healthy as, and in all probability healthier than, one that features meat (Anonymous 1988a; Anonymous 1988b; U.S. National Research Council 1989; Barnard 1990; Chen 1990; Lappé 1992; White and Frank 1994; Melina and Davis 2003; Rice 2004; Saunders 2003). But beyond this important finding, many people are coming to understand that the amount of meat they consume individually and collectively has a profound effect on the way we use and manage natural resources—forests, land, water, and nonrenewable energy. To put it simply, the greater our dependence on meat and other animal products, the more we overexploit these resources to satisfy our food preferences. And if (as I argue here) the prevailing form of agroindustry significantly abuses and damages the environment, then it follows that the more meat we consume, the more the well-being of the planet, and consequently our own well-being, will suffer. This insight leads to an awareness that the dietary orientation of unhealthy, meat-dependent societies needs to change, not only for the good of each of their members, but also for the benefit of nature as a whole.

Many of us live in societies that encourage individuality, self-reliance, self-development, and the cultivation of personal taste. These are good things, to be sure. However, we are bombarded all the time by messages that encourage us to pursue the construction of selfhood by means of consumer choices—that is, by acting out self-centered desires and fantasies in our role as powerful purchasers within the global market system. We are all conditioned to view what we purchase as consumers simply as an expression of personal freedom, of consequence to ourselves alone. Numerous vested interests energetically promote this outlook: business leaders, industry spokes-persons, the media, politicians, advertisers, and image-makers, to name a few. It therefore takes major effort to develop a contrasting form of awareness, namely, one that acknowledges that what we decide to buy has wider consequences. Many of these

consequences have an impact on the environment. When we begin to appreciate the connections between our purchases and the environment, we start to question our choices and the influences that helped bring them about. Being sensitized by ecological issues, as a growing number of citizens are today, opens our minds to the possibility of change through the formation of new values. The process of becoming a vegetarian is often part of this creative ferment.

THE ENVIRONMENTAL IMPACT OF DIETARY CHOICE

The eco-destructive side of the meat industry's operations has been demonstrated with ample documentation from both government and non-government sources (Robbins 1987; Fiddes 1991; Durning & Brough 1995; Hill 1996; Fox 1999; Rice 2004; Gold 2004; Tudge 2004a, 2004b). These effects include:

- toxic chemical residues in the food chain
- pharmaceutical additives in animal feeds
- polluting chemicals and animal wastes from feedlot runoff in waterways and underground aquifers
- loss of topsoil caused by patterns of relentless grazing
- domestic and foreign deforestation and desertification resulting from the clearing of land for grazing and cultivating animal feed
- threatened habitats of wild species of plants and animals
- intensive exploitation of water and energy supplies
- ozone depletion caused by extensive use of fossil fuels and significant production of methane gas by cattle

A brief case study will help place these complex problems in context and help us comprehend their interconnections.

Canada is a typical Western industrialized country with a population only one-tenth that of the United States. Since the time of white settlement, expanding agriculture has been the major factor in an 85% reduction of wetlands (Government of Canada 1991: 9–9, 9–15). Agricultural acreage has increased fourfold since 1900, and the total area under irrigation more than doubled between 1970 and 1988 (Government of Canada 1991: 26–6, 9–14). We infer that the consumption of meat is a powerful force here, given that in North America some 95% of oats and 80% of corn crops end up as livestock feed (Animal Alliance of Canada 1991; Government of Canada 1991; Agriculture Canada 1994).

Farm animals in Canada produce 322 million liters (85 million U.S. gal) of manure *daily*, an overwhelming proportion of which comes from cattle. Each marketed kilogram (2.2 lb) of edible beef generates at least 40 kg (88 lb) of manure, and each marketed kilogram of pork 15 kg (33 lb). These wastes, plus the runoff of water used to clean farm buildings and equipment and pesticide residues and other agricultural chemicals, are often poorly handled, causing the contamination of waterways and soil, as well as air pollution (Government of Canada 1991: 9–26).

Now consider that to produce each quarter-pound hamburger costs the environment 11,000 L (2,904 gal) of water. This amounts to 96,800 L (25,555 gal) per kilogram. Meanwhile, a kilo of rice or cheese requires 5,000 L (1,320 gal) of water to produce, and a kilo of wheat only 1,000 L (264 gal) (Pearce 2006). Which is a better investment in the earth's future?

Finally, reflect on the accelerating demand for meat worldwide. As an example, whereas annual meat consumption in China averaged 4 kg (8.8 lb) in the 1960s, it is about 60 kg (132 lb) today (Porritt 2006).[1] This trend has prompted the prestigious World Watch Institute to focus attention on global problems of meat production in the latest edition of its *State of the World* report (Starke 2006).

Obviously not all of the environmentally negative effects of today's unsound agricultural practices can be blamed on livestock management. And clearly some of the abuses already listed can be reduced or eliminated by a dedicated approach to recycling animal manure (and even human waste) into fertilizer, the use of natural means of pest control instead of harmful chemicals, and like measures. So it has been argued that the proper target of criticism is not meat production per se, but rather the intensive rearing methods used by contemporary agribusiness. There is some point to this rejoinder, and those who obtain meat from their own or others' free-range, organic, or biodynamic operations surely contribute less to the environmental toll on the planet. But, given the rate at which smaller-scale family farms are being forced out of competition (and out of existence) by larger and larger corporate conglomerates (Berry 1996), the opportunities for obtaining "environmentally friendly" meat are extremely rare. Taking current agricultural trends into account, then, only a tiny fraction of the population can conceivably exercise this option, and an even tinier group desires to do so in the first place. But the bottom line is that vegetarians are able to live more lightly on the land than do meat eaters of any description.

Is there evidence to back up this assertion? The short answer is yes. Consider the following observations.

> Substituting a grass-feeding livestock system (using only ruminant animals) for the current grain and grass system was found to reduce the energy inputs about 60% and land resources about 8%.… [In addition, it] would free up about 300 million tons of grain for export each year. This amount of grain is sufficient to feed a human population of 400 million a vegetarian-type diet for an entire year (Pimentel 1990: 12).
>
> All the grain fed to livestock could feed five times as many people. (*Proponents of intensive animal agriculture claim that we only put animals on land that could not support plant production. But we could grow more than enough plant food for human consumption if we used*

even a fraction of the land that is now used to grow plant food for livestock consumption.) (Animal Alliance of Canada 1991)

Merely making animal agriculture more ecologically efficient would greatly reduce resource depletion and increase global food supplies. Imagine what a gradual and complete conversion of the meat economy to a vegetarian economy worldwide could achieve.

One of the accomplishments of environmental philosophy in its relatively short history is the establishment of ecologically informed ethical thinking. If this phrase stands for anything, it certainly must entail that an overarching goal of human life ought to minimize the harmful impact our existence—as individuals and as collectivities—has upon the biosphere. It follows that we also ought to make lifestyle choices that help secure this objective. Now a diet that relies heavily on meat appears affordable and environmentally sustainable only to those who (a) are unaware of the larger ecological costs of meat production; (b) assume that these costs do not have to be factored into our choices and a calculation of their consequences; or (c) believe that the costs can be passed on to others—people in developing nations, our children, and other future persons. We all have to eat and the earth inevitably has to absorb the impact of our pursuing this natural end, but we should aim to reduce and confine the ecological stresses that are under our species' control. Vegetarianism seems plainly to be the best way to manage the environmental harm and degradation caused by humans' quest for nourishment. Some of the eco-destructive effects of the meat industry listed earlier are not caused by plant-based agriculture, and with respect to other results, the effects are less severe. By enabling us to eat lower down on the food chain, a vegetarian regime makes more efficient use of solar and caloric energy inputs. (For example, by concentrating on plant sources of protein—such as soya, beans, and nuts—we get at it more directly than we do by eating animals that have processed cellulose into protein for us.) As an energy-saving diet,

vegetarianism lightens the exploitative load we place upon the earth's ecosystems.

MEAT PRODUCTION AS A THREAT
TO BIODIVERSITY

We have seen that the global environmental consequences of the meat production system are serious. They are also pervasive. To show this, I want to shift attention now to the effects of animal agriculture on planetary biodiversity and on our attitudes toward nature as a whole.

There are many causes of species extinction, both natural and human. In relation to human factors, no single activity accounts totally for the sort of ecocide that undermines species viability. We should not expect, therefore, that the process whereby the flesh of animals appears on our tables explains by itself why certain ecosystems and the life forms they support are either under threat or beyond recovery.

Let us begin by getting some idea of the scope of species eradication by humans. According to E. O. Wilson, who has conducted one of the most detailed studies of the problem, rain forest extinctions for which our species are responsible occur at between 1,000 and 10,000 times the natural rate (Wilson 1993). Wilson approximates that 27,000 species per year (74 per day, 3 per hour) are perishing at our hands. A more recently completed twenty-year study by the World Conservation Union shows that "at least one in eight plant species in the world—and nearly one in three in the United States—are under threat of extinction" (Stevens 1998). This appalling pace of destruction stems from several major dynamics, including the clearing of foreign and domestic forests for agricultural purposes and development, drainage and filling of wetlands, damming of rivers, use and abuse of coral reefs, and relentless high-tech ocean fishing. Among these, deforestation and overfishing are the most evident areas in which a relationship between human diet and species extinction is to be discovered. I shall focus here on the devastation of the irreplaceable rain forests of Latin America.

Most people who follow the news are conscious that global rain forests perform unique functions within the regulative cycles of the biosphere, helping to maintain global temperature, providing fresh supplies of oxygen and water to the atmosphere, and sheltering the most complex web of life imaginable. It is reported that 40% to 50% of the world's plant and animal species dwell in rain forests (McKisson & MacRae-Campbell 1990). This super-abundance of life forms yields a wide range of raw materials used in the manufacture of all manner of consumer goods and pharmaceuticals, upon which the quality of human life crucially depends. Products of great value include hardwoods, rattan, natural rubber, waxes, essential oils, fruits, and nuts. One-quarter of all drug compounds obtained from pharmacies contain rain forest ingredients, whereas for most of the world's people, traditional medicines extracted from plants are used exclusively to treat ailments (Collins 1990; U.N. Food and Agricultural Organization 1995). Notwithstanding all this, a Smithsonian-sponsored research team found that an area of Amazon-basin rain forest equivalent to seven football fields is being cleared *per minute* for grazing land (Smithsonian Institution 2002). Sadly, "fewer than one percent of tropical rain forest plants have been chemically screened for useful medicinal properties" (Collins 1990: 32). Meanwhile, "studies in Peru, the Brazilian Amazon, the Philippines and Indonesia suggest that harvesting forest products sustainably is at least twice as profitable as clearing [the forests] for timber or to provide land for agriculture" (U.N. Food and Agricultural Organization 1995: 62).

That the rain forests are the earth's principal networks of species diversity seems unarguable. But why does this diversity matter so much? Thomas E. Lovejoy, a conservation biologist, places the matter in perspective:

> Assuming that the [earth's] biota contains ten million species, they then represent ten million successful sets of solutions to a series of biological problems, any one of which could be immensely valuable to us

in a number of ways.... The point ... is not that the "worth" of an obscure species is that it may someday produce a cure for cancer. The point is that the biota as a whole is continually providing us with new ways to improve our biological lot, and that species that may be unimportant on our current assessment of what may be directly useful may be important tomorrow. (Lovejoy 1986:16–17)

Wilson has commented that "biodiversity is our most valuable but least appreciated resource" (Wilson 1993: 281), and Collins remarks that the rain forests comprise a unique "genetic library" of virtually untapped information (Collins 1990: 32).

Solid, human-centered reasons for preserving biological diversity are to be found in these reflections. But might there not be additional good grounds for promoting species diversity? We have no difficulty in valuing other species instrumentally—in terms of what they can do for us. Perhaps we can also value them for their own sake—that is, for having a marvellous way of being that is worthy of celebrating quite independently of any actual or potential use we might make of them, and no matter how remotely related to ourselves they may be.

We are now in a position to consider the role that animal agriculture plays in undermining species diversity on the planet. Former U.S. Vice President Al Gore has written that "at the current rate of deforestation, virtually all of the tropical rain forests will be gone partway through the next century" (Gore 1993: 119)—that is, the century we live in now.[2] It is difficult to establish a precise correlation between animal agriculture and rain forest decimation, but it should be noted that the World Watch Institute has observed that "the human appetite for animal flesh is a driving force behind virtually every major category of environmental damage now threatening the human future" (World Watch Institute 2004). Rain forests are cleared by humans seeking firewood, settlement space, farm plots, monocultural plantations, expanded land holdings, oil, minerals, pastureland for cattle, and, more recently, soybean cultivation.[3]

Hydroelectric projects, roads, and other development schemes also take their toll. Even though these pressures are numerous and diverse, grazing may be identified as a major threat (Greenpeace International 2006a).[4]

Conversion of tropical rain forests to pasture land for cattle has proceeded at a remarkable pace in Central America since the middle of the twentieth century. The inherent nature of rain forests is such that when they are cleared, only poor quality, unsustainable pastureland remains, and this contributes to the dynamics of expanding destruction as new grazing areas are sought to replace older, exhausted ones. Norman Myers contends that from Mexico to Brazil "the number one factor in elimination of Latin America's tropical forests is cattlegrazing" (Myers 1984: 127). Most of the beef produced in this region is exported to the American market, although an increasing portion goes to Western Europe and Japan (Myers 1984; Rifkin 1992). The United States contains only 5% of the world's population, yet it produces, imports, and consumes more beef than any other country (Myers 1984). The beef imported from Latin America ends up as fast food burgers, processed meats, and pet foods.[5] Myers notes that "convenience foods … constitute the fastest-growing part of the entire food industry in the United States"; 50% of all meals are now consumed in either fast food or institutional settings (Myers 1984: 130). These patterns demonstrate forcefully the connection between meat eating and rain forest destruction. We cannot save the forests just by saying no to fast-food hamburgers, but we can help turn things around if enough of us set an example by reducing the meat in our diets and if, in this way, we set an example for others.

MEAT PRODUCTION AND THE DOMINATION OF NATURE

The case of rain forest decimation for cattle grazing is a typical ecological horror story. But viewed through a slightly different prism, what we encounter here is one of the many forms of the human domination and manipulation of nature. I mean to point out here by that the range of our activities starkly display our species' tendency to treat nature and natural biological systems purely as instruments for achieving human and often very narrow, short-sighted objectives.

According to the manipulative mindset, nature or parts of nature (such as members of nonhuman species) merely constitute resources or materials for our use and disposal as we see fit. The slash-and-burn practice that seals the fate of rain forests as obstacles that are "in the way" of profit to be extracted from low-cost meat provides but one example of this mentality at work in the world. Whereas the rain forests are treated as dispensable, the animals subsequently bred on this land are themselves no more than commodities destined for some distant stockyard—just further contents of the organic cash till that is nature.

But the attitude evident here, which permits the ruthless exploitation of cattle from rain forest regions, is in reality no different from that which endorses the widespread practice of animal confinement on factory farms. Animals there have manifestly become machines or artefacts of production and reproduction (Mason & Singer 1990; Rice 2004; Gold 2004). New developments may yield even more ominous scenarios. Researchers have considered or are actively considering the application of genetic techniques to create freakish monster animals and to clone superproductive animals (U.S. Congress, Office of Technology Assessment 1985; British Medical Association 1992; Fox 1992; Spallone 1992). Other scientific fantasies include animals with modified physiologies that experience little or no stress (Mason & Singer 1990), animals with no pain receptors (Rollin 1995), and the manufacture of synthetic meat (Edelman et al. 2005; Reuters 2005). Greed is driving some of these developments; the thinking behind others must be that if the experiments are successful and lead to economical avenues of meat production, then it will be alright to treat the animal artifacts that result as mere things, and hence the major ethical objections to factory farming will simply melt away.[6]

What does all this add up to? The meat industry, itself feeding off human demand for certain types of food, is ushering in an era of activities that are totally lacking in compassion or a sense of connection with nature. Although we seem to be learning to connect to nature on one level—concern over ecological issues—on another level we have become out of touch with what matters most. The vast majority would not wish to visit a slaughterhouse for any reason,[7] and from what people know of modern livestock production processes, they would never want their pet or any animal they cared about to be treated the way food animals routinely are, let alone how they may be treated in the future. But at the same time, the consumers' selection of meat and meat products as foods of choice goes on with apparently little thought. In this manner, we accustom ourselves to accept the domination and manipulation of nature that as sensitive, caring people we ought to be aware of and reject. We thus find ourselves caught in a trap of our own making. We can, however, seek a way out by being reflective and deciding in favor of a lifestyle that does not rest upon the subjugation of the earth and the suffering of nonhuman forms of life. This is the vegetarian option, which is where I started.

CONCLUSION: A VEGETARIAN ETHIC

Vegetarianism encourages us to think of ourselves as *part of* nature rather than *apart from* nature. The vegetarian outlook recognizes the importance of ecologically sustainable human activity and affirms the requirement that we seek to minimize our impact on the planet, and this recognition includes the amount of harm we do in the course of looking after our essential needs. Mindfulness of both short- and long-term consequences of individual choice and collective behavior are hallmarks of a commitment to vegetarianism as a way of life. This choice also entails compassionate cohabitation with other species and respect for the earth to the greatest extent that these precepts can be followed, both in one's personal activities and in social policy and planning. The vegetarian way of life offers us a chance to re-establish contact with the land, eat locally grown foods, and recover connections with nature. Finally, vegetarianism is liberating in the sense that it frees us *from* the exploitation of animals and nature, while it frees us *to* discover who we are in more positive, life-affirming ways that are healthy for both humans and the planet that is our home.

NOTES

1. Also of interest here, it has been reported that nearly 15% of the Chinese population is now overweight, and childhood obesity in China has increased by 28 times over the past decade and a half, the causes of this being cited as greater meat consumption and lack of exercise (Guardian Weekly 2006).

2. See also his acclaimed environmental documentary film *An Inconvenient Truth* (2006).

3. Rain forest destruction for the purpose of creating soya plantations will cause concern among vegetarians, but this process is in fact geared toward supplying feed for livestock animals, not food for humans (Greenpeace International 2006b).

4. The radical transformation and degradation of *American* land by animal agriculture should not be underestimated and likewise presents a tragic story (Berry 1996; University of Washington Students n.d.).

5. Fast-food giants Burger King and McDonald's have pledged to stop using rain-forest-grown beef; others have made no such commitment. Greenpeace has recently charged that McDonald's beef and Kentucky Fried Chicken's chicken are fed on soya grown in cleared Amazon rain forests (Greenpeace International 2006c).

6. The case of synthetic or laboratory-grown meat is represented by smug journalists as a big "problem" for vegetarianism because its ethical position in

regard to meat eating would supposedly be undermined by the prospect of animal flesh being produced without pain, suffering, and killing. But first, this view shows little understanding of what vegetarianism is all about (see the final section of this article and Fox 1999). Second, synthetic meat is merely a possibility today; we are very far from seeing it drive conventional factory farms out of business. And if it did, this would cause as big an economic upheaval as a large-scale transition to vegetarianism. Third, if meat eaters so desperately want meat that they will queue up for fake, laboratory-cultured versions, let them do so and leave the fresh, healthy, naturally grown plants to the rest of us.

7. I have, and it is a profoundly disturbing experience. For readers with strong stomachs who might be willing to "visit" an abattoir through the pages of a book, I recommend Coe (1995) and Eisnetz (1997).

39

Can Frankenfood Save the Planet?

JONATHAN RAUCH

Jonathan Rauch is a writer for the Atlantic Monthly. *In this essay he presents evidence to the effect that genetically engineered food could provide enough nutrition to save future generations from starvation. He argues that environmentalists who oppose genetically modified food are actually working against the best interests of humankind and their pets.*

That genetic engineering may be the most environmentally beneficial technology to have emerged in decades, or possibly centuries, is not immediately obvious. Certainly, at least, it is not obvious to the many U.S. and foreign environmental groups that regard biotechnology as a bête noire. Nor is it necessarily obvious to people who grew up in cities, and who have only an inkling of what happens on a modern farm. Being agriculturally illiterate myself, I set out to look at what may be, if the planet is fortunate, the farming of the future.

It was baking hot that April day. I traveled with two Virginia state soil-and-water-conservation officers and an agricultural-extension agent to an area not far from Richmond. The farmers there are national (and therefore world) leaders in the application of what is known as continuous no-till farming. In plain English, they don't plough. For thousands of years, since the dawn of the agricultural revolution, farmers have ploughed, often several times a year; and with ploughing has come runoff that pollutes rivers and blights aquatic habitat, erosion that wears away the land, and the release into the atmosphere of greenhouse gases stored in the soil. Today, at last, farmers are working out methods that have begun to make ploughing obsolete.

Reprinted from the *Atlantic Monthly* (October 2003) by permission of the author.

At about one-thirty we arrived at a 200-acre patch of farmland known as the Good Luck Tract. No one seemed to know the provenance of the name, but the best guess was that somebody had said something like "You intend to farm this? Good luck!" The land was rolling, rather than flat, and its slopes came together to form natural troughs for rainwater. Ordinarily this highly erodible land would be suitable for cows, not crops. Yet it was dense with wheat—wheat yielding almost twice what could normally be expected, and in soil that had grown richer in organic matter, and thus more nourishing to crops, even as the land was farmed. Perhaps most striking was the almost complete absence of any chemical or soil runoff. Even the beating administered in 1999 by Hurricane Floyd, which lashed the ground with nineteen inches of rain in less than twenty-four hours, produced no significant runoff or erosion. The land simply absorbed the sheets of water before they could course downhill.

At another site, a few miles away, I saw why. On land planted in corn whose shoots had only just broken the surface, Paul Davis, the extension agent, wedged a shovel into the ground and dislodged about eight inches of topsoil. Then he reached down and picked up a clump. Ploughed soil, having been stirred up and turned over again and again, becomes lifeless and homogeneous, but the clump that Davis held out was alive. I immediately noticed three squirming earthworms, one grub, and quantities of tiny white insects that looked very busy. As if in greeting, a worm defecated. "Plant-available food!" a delighted Davis exclaimed.

This soil, like that of the Good Luck Tract, had not been ploughed for years, allowing the underground ecosystem to return. Insects and roots and microorganisms had given the soil an elaborate architecture, which held the earth in place and made it a sponge for water. That was why erosion and runoff had been reduced to practically nil. Crops thrived because worms were doing the ploughing. Crop residue that was left on the ground, rather than ploughed under as usual, provided nourishment for the soil's biota and, as it decayed, enriched the soil. The farmer saved the fuel he would have used driving back and forth with a heavy plough. That saved

money, and of course it also saved energy and reduced pollution. On top of all that, crop yields were better than with conventional methods.

The conservation people in Virginia were full of excitement over no-till farming. Their job was to clean up the James and York Rivers and the rest of the Chesapeake Bay watershed. Most of the sediment that clogs and clouds the rivers, and most of the fertilizer runoff that causes the algae blooms that kill fish, comes from farmland. By all but eliminating agricultural erosion and runoff—so Brian Noyes, the local conservation-district manager, told me—continuous no-till could "revolutionize" the area's water quality.

Even granting that Noyes is an enthusiast, from an environmental point of view no-till farming looks like a dramatic advance. The rub—if it is a rub—is that the widespread elimination of the plough depends on genetically modified crops.

It is only a modest exaggeration to say that as goes agriculture, so goes the planet. Of all the human activities that shape the environment, agriculture is the single most important, and it is well ahead of whatever comes second. Today about 38 percent of the earth's land area is crop land or pasture—a total that has crept upward over the past few decades as global population has grown. The increase has been gradual, only about 0.3 percent a year; but that still translates into an additional Greece or Nicaragua cultivated or grazed every year.

Farming does not go easy on the earth, and never has. To farm is to make war upon millions of plants (weeds, so-called) and animals (pests, so-called) that in the ordinary course of things would crowd out or eat or infest whatever it is a farmer is growing. Crop monocultures, as whole fields of only wheat or corn or any other single plant are called, make poor habitat and are vulnerable to disease and disaster. Although fertilizer runs off and pollutes water, farming without fertilizer will deplete and eventually exhaust the soil. Pesticides can harm the health of human beings and kill desirable or harmless bugs along with pests. Irrigation leaves behind trace elements that can accumulate and poison the soil. And on and on.

The trade-offs are fundamental. Organic farming, for example, uses no artificial fertilizer, but it does use a lot of manure, which can pollute water and contaminate food. Traditional farmers may use less herbicide, but they also do more ploughing, with all the ensuing environmental complications. Low-input agriculture uses fewer chemicals but more land. The point is not that farming is an environmental crime—it is not—but that there is no escaping the pressure it puts on the planet.

In the next half century the pressure will intensify. The United Nations, in its midrange projections, estimates that the earth's human population will grow by more than 40 percent, from 6.3 billion people today to 8.9 billion in 2050. Feeding all those people, and feeding their billion or so hungry pets (a dog or a cat is one of the first things people want once they move beyond a subsistence lifestyle), and providing the increasingly protein-rich diets that an increasingly wealthy world will expect—doing all of that will require food output to at least double, and possibly triple.

But then the story will change. According to the UN's midrange projections (which may, if anything, err somewhat on the high side), around 2050 the world's population will more or less level off. Even if the growth does not stop, it will slow. The crunch will be over. In fact, if in 2050 crop yields are still increasing, if most of the world is economically developed, and if population pressures are declining or even reversing—all of which seems reasonably likely—then the human species may at long last be able to feed itself, year in and year out, without putting any additional net stress on the environment. We might even be able to grow everything we need while *reducing* our agricultural footprint: returning cropland to wilderness, repairing damaged soils, restoring ecosystems, and so on. In other words, human agriculture might be placed on a sustainable footing forever: a breathtaking prospect.

The great problem, then, is to get through the next four or five decades with as little environmental damage as possible. That is where biotechnology comes in.

One day recently I drove down to southern Virginia to visit Dennis Avery and his son, Alex. The older Avery, a man in late middle age with a chinstrap beard, droopy eyes, and an intent, scholarly manner, lives on ninety-seven acres that he shares with horses, chickens, fish, cats, dogs, bluebirds, ducks, transient geese, and assorted other creatures. He is the director of global food issues at the Hudson Institute, a conservative think tank; Alex works with him, and is trained as a plant physiologist. We sat in a sun-room at the back of the house, our afternoon conversation punctuated every so often by dog snores and rooster crows. We talked for a little while about the Green Revolution, a dramatic advance in farm productivity that fed the world's burgeoning population over the past four decades, and then I asked if the challenge of the next four decades could be met.

"Well," Dennis replied, "we have tripled the world's farm output since 1960. And we're feeding twice as many people from the same land. That was a heroic achievement. But we have to do what some think is an even more difficult thing in this next forty years, because the Green Revolution had more land per person and more water per person—"

"—and more potential for increases," Alex added, "because the base that we were starting from was so much lower."

"By and large," Dennis went on, "the world's civilizations have been built around its best farmland. And we have used most of the world's good farmland. Most of the good land is already heavily fertilized. Most of the good land is already being planted with high-yield seeds. [Africa is the important exception.] Most of the good irrigation sites are used. We can't triple yields again with the technologies we're already using. And we might be lucky to get a fifty percent yield increase if we froze our technology short of biotech."

"Biotech" can refer to a number of things, but the relevant application here is genetic modification: the selective transfer of genes from one organism to another. Ordinary breeding can cross related varieties, but it cannot take a gene from a bacterium, for instance, and transfer it to a wheat plant. The organisms resulting from gene transfers are called "transgenic" by scientists—and "Frankenfood" by many greens.

Gene transfer poses risks, unquestionably. So, for that matter, does traditional crossbreeding. But many people worry that transgenic organisms might prove more unpredictable. One possibility is that transgenic crops would spread from fields into forests or other wild lands and there become environmental nuisances, or worse. A further risk is that transgenic plants might cross-pollinate with neighboring wild plants, producing "superweeds" or other invasive or destructive varieties in the wild. Those risks are real enough that even most biotech enthusiasts—including Dennis Avery, for example—favor some government regulation of transgenic crops.

What is much less widely appreciated is biotech's potential to do the environment good. Take as an example continuous no-till farming, which really works best with the help of transgenic crops. Human beings have been ploughing for so long that we tend to forget why we started doing it in the first place. The short answer: weed control. Turning over the soil between plantings smothers weeds and their seeds. If you don't plough, your land becomes a weed garden—unless you use herbicides to kill the weeds. Herbicides, however, are expensive, and can be complicated to apply. And they tend to kill the good with the bad.

In the mid-1990s the agricultural-products company Monsanto introduced a transgenic soybean variety called Roundup Ready. As the name implies, these soybeans tolerate Roundup, an herbicide (also made by Monsanto) that kills many kinds of weeds and then quickly breaks down into harmless ingredients. Equipped with Roundup Ready crops, farmers found that they could retire their ploughs and control weeds with just a few applications of a single, relatively benign herbicide—instead of many applications of a complex and expensive menu of chemicals. More than a third of all U.S. soybeans are now grown without ploughing, mostly owing to the introduction of Roundup Ready varieties. Ploughless cotton farming has likewise received a big boost from the advent of bioengineered varieties. No-till farming without biotech is possible, but it's more difficult and expensive, which is why no-till and biotech are advancing in tandem.

In 2001 a group of scientists announced that they had engineered a transgenic tomato plant able to thrive on salty water—water, in fact, almost half as salty as seawater, and fifty times as salty as tomatoes can ordinary abide. One of the researchers was quoted as saying, "I've already transformed tomato, tobacco, and canola. I believe I can transform any crop with this gene"—just the sort of Frankenstein hubris that makes environmentalists shudder. But consider the environmental implications. Irrigation has for millennia been a cornerstone of agriculture, but it comes at a price. As irrigation water evaporates, it leaves behind traces of salt, which accumulate in the soil and gradually render it infertile. (As any Roman legion knows, to destroy a nation's agricultural base you salt the soil.) Every year the world loses about 25 million acres—an area equivalent to a fifth of California—to salinity; 40 percent of the world's irrigated land, and 25 percent of America's, has been hurt to some degree. For decades traditional plant breeders tried to create salt-tolerant crop plants, and for decades they failed.

Salt-tolerant crops might bring millions of acres of wounded or crippled land back into production. "And it gets better," Alex Avery told me. The transgenic tomato plants take up and sequester in their leaves as much as six or seven percent of their weight in sodium. "Theoretically," Alex said, "you could reclaim a salt-contaminated field by growing enough of these crops to remove the salts from the soil."

His father chimed in: "We've worried about being able to keep these salt-contaminated fields going even for decades. We can now think about *centuries.*"

One of the first biotech crops to reach the market, in the mid-1990s, was a cotton plant that makes its own pesticide. Scientists incorporated into the plant a toxin-producing gene from a soil bacterium known as *Bacillus thuringiensis*. With Bt cotton, as it is called, farmers can spray much less, and the poison contained in the plant is delivered only to bugs that actually eat the crop. As any environmentalist can tell you, insecticide is not very nice stuff—especially if you breathe it, which many Third World farmers do as they walk through their fields with backpack sprayers.

Transgenic cotton reduced pesticide use by more than two million pounds in the United States from 1996 to 2000, and it has reduced pesticide sprayings in parts of China by more than half. Earlier this year the Environmental Protection Agency approved a genetically modified corn that resists a beetle larva known as rootworm. Because rootworm is American corn's most voracious enemy, this new variety has the potential to reduce annual pesticide use in America by more than 14 million pounds. It could reduce or eliminate the spraying of pesticide on 23 million acres of U.S. land.

All of that is the beginning, not the end. Bioengineers are also working, for instance, on crops that tolerate aluminum, another major contaminant of soil, especially in the tropics. Return an acre of farmland to productivity, or double yields on an already productive acre, and, other things being equal, you reduce by an acre the amount of virgin forest or savannah that will be stripped and cultivated. That may be the most important benefit of all.

Of the many people I have interviewed in my twenty years as a journalist, Norman Borlaug must be the one who has saved the most lives. Today he is an unprepossessing eighty-nine-year-old man of middling height, with crystal-bright blue eyes and thinning white hair. He still loves to talk about plant breeding, the discipline that won him the 1970 Nobel Peace Prize: Borlaug led efforts to breed the staples of the Green Revolution. (See "Forgotten Benefactor of Humanity," by Gregg Easterbrook, an article on Borlaug in the January 1997 *Atlantic*.) Yet the renowned plant breeder is quick to mention that he began his career, in the 1930s, in forestry, and that forest conservation has never been far from his thoughts. In the 1960s, while he was working to improve crop yields in India and Pakistan, he made a mental connection. He would create tables detailing acres under cultivation and average yields—and then, in another column, he would estimate how much land had been saved by higher farm productivity. Later, in the 1980s and 1990s, he and others began paying increased attention to what some agricultural economists now call the Borlaug hypothesis: that the Green Revolution has saved not only many human

lives but, by improving the productivity of existing farmland, also millions of acres of tropical forest and other habitat—and so has saved countless animal lives.

From the 1960s through the 1980s, for example, Green Revolution advances saved more than 100 million acres of wild lands in India. More recently, higher yields in rice, coffee, vegetables, and other crops have reduced or in some cases stopped forest-clearing in Honduras, the Philippines, and elsewhere. Dennis Avery estimates that if farming techniques and yields had not improved since 1950, the world would have lost an additional 20 million or so square miles of wildlife habitat, most of it forest. About 16 million square miles of forest exists today. "What I'm saying," Avery said, in response to my puzzled expression, "is that we have saved every square mile of forest on the planet."

Habitat destruction remains a serious environmental problem; in some respects it is the most serious. The savannahs and tropical forests of Central and South America, Asia, and Africa by and large make poor farmland, but they are the earth's store-houses of biodiversity, and the forests are the earth's lungs. Since 1972 about 200,000 square miles of Amazon rain forest have been cleared for crops and pasture; from 1966 to 1994 all but three of the Central American countries cleared more forest than they left standing. Mexico is losing more than 4,000 square miles of forest a year to peasant farms; sub-Saharan Africa is losing more than 19,000.

That is why the great challenge of the next four or five decades is not to feed an additional three billion people (and their pets) but to do so without converting much of the world's prime habitat into second- or third-rate farmland. Now, most agronomists agree that some substantial yield improvements are still to be had from advances in conventional breeding, fertilizers, herbicides, and other Green Revolution standbys. But it seems pretty clear that biotechnology holds more promise—probably much more. Recall that world food output will need to at least double and possibly triple over the next several decades. Even if production could be increased that much using conventional technology, which is doubtful, the required amounts of pesticide and fertilizer and other polluting chemicals would be immense. If properly developed, disseminated, and used, genetically modified crops might well be the best hope the planet has got.

If properly developed, disseminated, and used, that tripartite qualification turns out to be important, and it brings the environmental community squarely, and at the moment rather jarringly, into the picture.

Not long ago I went to see David Sandalow in his office at the World Wildlife Fund, in Washington, D.C. Sandalow, the organization's executive vice-president in charge of conservation programs, is a tall, affable, polished, and slightly reticent man in his forties who holds degrees from Yale and the University of Michigan Law School.

Some weeks earlier, over lunch, I had mentioned Dennis Avery's claim that genetic modification had great environmental potential. I was surprised when Sandalow told me he agreed. Later, in our interview in his office, I asked him to elaborate. "With biotechnology," he said, "there are no simple answers. Biotechnology has huge potential benefits and huge risks, and we need to address both as we move forward. The huge potential benefits include increased productivity of arable land, which could relieve pressure on forests. They include decreased pesticide usage. But the huge risks include severe ecological disruptions—from gene flow and from enhanced invasiveness, which is a very antiseptic word for some very scary stuff."

I asked if he thought that, absent biotechnology, the world could feed everybody over the next forty or fifty years without ploughing down the rain forests. Instead of answering directly he said, "Biotechnology could be part of our arsenal if we can overcome some of the barriers. It will never be a panacea or a magic bullet. But nor should we remove it from our tool kit."

Sandalow is unusual. Very few credentialed greens talk the way he does about biotechnology, at least publicly. They would readily agree with him about the huge risks, but they wouldn't be caught dead speaking of huge potential benefits—a point I will come back to. From an ecological point of view, a very great deal depends on other environmentalists' coming to think more the way Sandalow does.

Biotech companies are in business to make money. That is fitting and proper. But developing and testing new transgenic crops is expensive and commercially risky, to say nothing of politically controversial. When they decide how to invest their research-and-development money, biotech companies will naturally seek products for which farmers and consumers will pay top dollar. Roundup Ready products, for instance, are well suited to U.S. farming, with its high levels of capital spending on such things as herbicides and automated sprayers. Poor farmers in the developing world, or course, have much less buying power. Creating, say, salt-tolerant cassava suitable for growing on hardscrabble African farms might save habitat as well as lives—but commercial enterprises are not likely to fall over one another in a rush to do it.

If earth-friendly transgenics are developed, the next problem is disseminating them. As a number of the farmers and experts I talked to were quick to mention, switching to an unfamiliar new technology—something like no-till—is not easy. It requires capital investment in new seed and equipment, mastery of new skills and methods, a fragile transition period as farmer and ecology readjust, and an often considerable amount of trial and error to find out what works best on any given field. Such problems are only magnified in the Third World, where the learning curve is steeper and capital cushions are thin to nonexistent. Just handing a peasant farmer a bag of newfangled seed is not enough. In many cases peasant farmers will need one-on-one attention. Many will need help to pay for the seed, too.

Finally there is the matter of using biotech in a way that actually benefits the environment. Often the technological blade can cut either way, especially in the short run. A salt-tolerant or drought-resistant rice that allowed farmers to keep land in production might also induce them to plough up virgin land that previously was too salty or too dry to farm. If the effect of improved seed is to make farming more profitable, farmers may respond, at least temporarily, by bringing more land into production. If a farm becomes more productive, it may require fewer workers; and if local labor markets cannot provide jobs for them, displaced workers may move to a nearby patch of rain forest and burn it down to make way for subsistence farming. Such transition problems are solvable, but they need money and attention.

In short, realizing the great—probably unique—environmental potential of biotech will require stewardship. "It's a tool," Sara Scherr, an agricultural economist with the conservation group Forest Trends, told me, "but it's absolutely not going to happen automatically."

So now ask a question: Who is the natural constituency for earth-friendly biotechnology? Who cares enough to lobby governments to underwrite research—frequently unprofitable research—on transgenic crops that might restore soils or cut down on pesticides in poor countries? Who cares enough to teach Asian or African farmers, one by one, how to farm without ploughing? Who cares enough to help poor farmers afford high-tech, earth-friendly seed? Who cares enough to agitate for programs and reforms that might steer displaced peasants and profit-seeking farmers away from sensitive lands? Not politicians, for the most part. Not farmers. Not corporations. Not consumers.

At the World Resources Institute, an environmental think tank in Washington, the molecular biologist Don Doering envisions transgenic crops designed specifically to solve environmental problems: crops that might fertilize the soil, crops that could clean water, crops tailored to remedy the ecological problems of specific places. "Suddenly you might find yourself with a virtually chemical-free agriculture, where your cropland itself is filtering the water, it's protecting the watershed, it's providing habitat," Doering told me. "There is still so little investment in what I call design-for-environment." The natural constituency for such investment is, of course, environmentalists.

But environmentalists are not acting such a constituency today. They are doing the apposite. For example, Greenpeace declares on its Web site: "The introduction of genetically engineered (GE) organisms into the complex ecosystems of our environment is a dangerous global experiment with nature and evolution … GE organisms must not be released into

the environment. They pose unacceptable risks to ecosystems, and have the potential to threaten biodiversity, wildlife and sustainable forms of agriculture."

Other groups argue for what they call the Precautionary Principle, under which no transgenic crop could be used until proven benign in virtually all respects. The Sierra Club says on its Web site,

> In accordance with this Precautionary Principle, we call for a moratorium on the planting of all genetically engineered crops and the release of all GEOs [genetically engineered organisms] into the environment, *including those now approved*. Releases should be delayed until extensive, rigorous research is done which determines the long-term environmental and health impacts of each GEO and there is public debate to ascertain the need for the use of each GEO intended for release into the environment. [italics added]

Under this policy the cleaner water and healthier soil that continuous no-till farming has already brought to the Chesapeake Bay watershed would be undone, and countless tons of polluted runoff and eroded topsoil would accumulate in Virginia rivers and streams while debaters debated and researchers researched. Recall David Sandalow: "Biotechnology has huge potential benefits and huge risks, and we need to address both as we move forward." A lot of environmentalists would say instead, "*before* we move forward." That is an important difference, particularly because the big population squeeze will happen not in the distant future but over the next several decades.

For reasons having more to do with policies than with logic, the modern environmental movement was to a large extent founded on suspicion of markets and artificial substances. Markets exploit the earth; chemicals poison it. Biotech touches both hot buttons. It is being pushed forward by greedy corporations, and it seems to be the very epitome of the unnatural.

Still, I hereby hazard a prediction. In ten years or less, most American environmentalists (European ones are more dogmatic) will regard genetic modification as one of their most powerful tools. In only the past ten years or so, after all, environmentalists have reversed field and embraced market mechanisms—tradable emissions permits and the like—as useful in the fight against pollution. The environmental logic of biotechnology is, if anything, even more compelling. The potential upside of genetic modification is simply too large to ignore—and therefore environmentalists will not ignore it. Biotechnology will transform agriculture, and in doing so will transform American environmentalism.

STUDY QUESTIONS

1. Discuss the promise of genetically modified food. What environmental problems can it solve? How can it help alleviate world hunger?

2. Discuss the risks involved in producing genetically modified food. Why are so many environmentalists against it?

3. How do you think we should proceed with regard to genetically modified food?

40

The Unholy Alliance

MAE-WAN HO

Mae-Wan Ho, trained as a geneticist, is a leading social and environmental activist. She is the author of numerous books and articles, including most recently Genetic Engineering, Dream or Nightmare? *She proposes an immediate moratorium on genetically modified foods until their safety, in all phases, can be properly tested.*

Genetic engineering biotechnology is inherently hazardous. It could lead to disasters far worse than those caused by accidents to nuclear installations. In the words of the author, "genes can replicate indefinitely, spread and recombine." For this reason the release of a genetically engineered micro-organism that is lethal to humans could well spell the end of humanity. Unfortunately the proponents of this terrifying technology share a genetic determinist mindset that leads them to reject the inherently dangerous nature of their work. What is particularly worrying at first sight is the irresistible power of the large corporations which are pushing this technology.

From *The Ecologist*, Vol. 27, No. 4 (July/August 1997). Reprinted by permission of *The Ecologist*, www.theecologist.org.

Suddenly, the brave new world dawns.

Suddenly, as 1997 begins and the millennium is drawing to a close, men and women in the street are waking up to the realization that genetic engineering biotechnology is taking over every aspect of their daily lives. They are caught unprepared for the avalanche of products arriving, or soon to arrive, in their supermarkets: rapeseed oil, soybean, maize, sugar beet, squash, cucumber.… It started as a mere trickle less than three years ago—the BST-milk from cows fed genetically engineered bovine growth hormone to boost milk yield, and the tomato genetically engineered to prolong shelf-life. They had provoked so much debate and opposition, as did indeed the genetic screening tests for an increasing number of diseases. Surely, we wouldn't, and shouldn't, be rushed headlong into the brave new world.

Back then, in order to quell our anxiety, a series of highly publicized "consensus conferences" and "public consultations" were carried out. Committees were set up by many European governments to consider the risks and the ethics, and the debates continued. The public were, however, only dimly aware of critics who deplored "tampering with nature" and "scrambling the genetic code of species" by introducing human genes into animals, and animal genes into vegetables. Warnings of unexpected effects on agriculture and biodiversity, of the dangers of irreversible "genetic pollution," warnings of genetic discrimination and the return of eugenics, as genetic screening and prenatal diagnosis became widely available, were marginalized. So too were condemnations of the immorality of the "patents on life"—transgenic animals, plants and seeds, taken freely by geneticists of developed countries from the Third World, as well as human genes and human cell lines from indigenous peoples.

By and large, the public were lulled into a false sense of security, in the belief that the best scientists and the new breed of "bioethicists" in the country were busy considering the risks associated with the new biotechnology and the ethical issues raised. Simultaneously, glossy information pamphlets and reports, which aimed at promoting "public understanding" of genetic "modification," were widely distributed by the biotech industries and their friends, and endorsed by government scientists. "Genetic modification," we are told, is simply the latest in a "seamless" continuum of biotechnologies practised by human beings since the dawn of civilization, from bread and wine-making, to selective breeding. The significant advantage of genetic modification is that it is much more "precise," as genes can be individually isolated and transferred as desired.

Thus, the possible benefits promised to humankind are limitless. There is something to satisfy everyone. For those morally concerned about inequality and human suffering, it promises to feed the hungry with genetically modified crops able to resist pests and diseases and to increase yields. For those who despair of the present global environmental deterioration, it promises to modify strains of bacteria and higher plants that can degrade toxic wastes or mop up heavy metals (contaminants). For those hankering after sustainable agriculture, it promises to develop Greener, more environmentally friendly transgenic crops that will reduce the use of pesticides, herbicides and fertilizers.

That is not all. It is in the realm of human genetics that the real revolution will be wrought. Plans to uncover the entire genetic blueprint of the human being would, we are told, eventually enable geneticists to diagnose, in advance, all the diseases that an individual will suffer in his or her lifetime, even before the individual is born, or even as the egg is fertilized *in vitro*. A whole gamut of specific drugs tailored to individual genetic needs can be designed to cure all diseases. The possibility of immortality is dangling from the horizons as the "longevity gene" is isolated.

There are problems, of course, as there would be in any technology. The ethical issues have to be decided by the public. (By implication, the science is separate and not open to question.) The risks will be minimized. (Again, by implication, the risks have nothing to do with the science.) After all, nothing in life is without risk. Crossing roads is a risk. The new biotechnology (i.e. genetic engineering biotechnology) is under very strict government regulation, and the government's scientists and other experts will see to it that neither the consumer nor the environment will be unduly harmed.

Then came the relaxation of regulation on genetically modified products, on grounds that over-regulation is compromising the "competitiveness" of the industry, and that hundreds of field trials have demonstrated the new biotechnology to be safe. And, in any case, there is no essential difference between transgenic plants produced by the new biotechnology and those produced by conventional breeding methods. (One prominent spokesperson for the industry even went as far as to refer to the varieties produced by conventional breeding methods, *retrospectively,* as "transgenics.")[1] This was followed, a year later, by the avalanche of products approved, or seeking, approval marketing, for which neither segregation from non-genetically engineered produce nor labelling is required. One is left to wonder why, if the products are as safe and wonderful as claimed, they could not be segregated, as organic produce has been for years, so that consumers are given the choice of buying what they want.

A few days later, as though acting on cue, the Association of British Insurers announced that, in future, people applying for life policies will have to divulge the results of any genetic tests they have taken. This is seen, by many, as a definite move towards open genetic discrimination. A few days later, a scientist of the Roslin Institute near Edinburgh announced that they had successfully "cloned" a sheep from a cell taken from the mammary gland of an adult animal. "Dolly," the cloned lamb, is now seven months old. Of course it took nearly 300 trials to get one success, but no mention is made of the vast majority of the embryos that failed. Is that ethical? If it can be done on sheep, does it mean it can be done for human beings? Are we nearer to cloning human beings? The popular media went wild with heroic enthusiasm at one extreme to the horror of Frankenstein at the other. Why is this work only coming to public attention now, when the research has actually been going on for at least 10 years?[2]

I should, right away, dispel the myth that genetic engineering is just like conventional breeding techniques. It is not. Genetic engineering bypasses conventional breeding by using the artificially constructed vectors to multiply copies of genes, and in many cases, to carry and smuggle genes into cells. Once inside cells, these vectors slot themselves into the host genome. In this way, *transgenic* organisms are made carrying the desired *transgenes*. The insertion of foreign genes into the host genome has long been known to have many harmful and fatal effects including cancer; and this is born out by the low success rate of creating desired transgenic organisms. Typically, a large number of eggs or embryos have to be injected or infected with the vector to obtain a few organisms that successfully express the transgene.

The most common vectors used in genetic engineering biotechnology are a chimaeric recombination of natural genetic parasites from different sources, including viruses causing cancers and other diseases in animals and plants, with their pathogenic functions 'crippled,' and tagged with one or more antibiotic resistance 'marker' genes, so that cells transformed with the vector can be selected. For example, the vector most widely used in plant genetic engineering is derived from a tumour-inducing plasmid carried by the soil bacterium *Agrobacterium tumefaciens.* In animals, vectors are constructed from *retroviruses* causing cancers and other diseases. A vector currently used in fish has a framework from the Moloney marine leukaemic virus, which causes leukaemia in mice, but can infect all mammalian cells. It has bits from the Rous Sarcoma virus, causing sarcomas in chickens, and from the vesicular stomatitis virus, causing oral lesions in cattle, horses, pigs and humans. Such mosaic vectors are particularly hazardous. Unlike natural parasitic genetic elements which have various degrees of host specificity, vectors used in genetic engineering, partly by design and partly on account of their mosaic character, have the ability to overcome species barriers and to infect a wide range of species. Another obstacle to genetic engineering is that all organisms and cells have natural defence mechanisms that enable them to destroy or inactivate foreign genes, and transgene instability is a big problem for the industry. Vectors are now increasingly constructed to overcome those mechanisms that maintain the integrity of species. The result is that the artificially constructed vectors are especially good at carrying out horizontal gene transfer.

Let me summarize why rDNA technology differs radically from conventional breeding techniques.

1. Genetic engineering recombines genetic material in the laboratory between species that do not interbreed in nature.

2. While conventional breeding methods shuffle different forms (alletes) of the same genes, genetic engineering enables completely new (exotic) genes to be introduced with unpredictable effects on the physiology and biochemistry of the resultant transgenic organism.

3. Gene multiplications and a high proportion of gene transfers are mediated by vectors which have the following undesirable characteristics:

   a. Many are derived from disease-causing viruses, plasmids and mobile genetic elements—parasitic DNA that have the ability to invade cells and insert themselves into the cell's genome causing genetic damages.

   b. They are designed to break down species barriers so that they can shuttle genes between a wide range of species. Their wide host range means that they can infect many animals and plants, and in the process pick up genes from viruses of all these species to create new pathogens.

   c. They routinely carry genes for antibiotic resistance, which is already a big health problem.

   d. They are increasingly constructed to overcome the recipient species' defence mechanisms that break down or inactivate foreign DNA.

The public are totally unprepared. They are being plunged headlong, against their will, into the brave new genetically engineered world, in which giant, faceless multinational corporations will control every aspect of their lives, from the food they can eat to the baby they can conceive and give birth to.

Isn't it a bit late in the day to tell us that? you ask. Yes and no. Yes, because I, who should, perhaps, have known better, was caught unprepared like the rest. And no, because there have been so many people warning us of that eventuality, who have campaigned tirelessly on our behalf, some of them going back to the earliest days of genetic engineering in the 1970s—although we have paid them little heed. No, it is not too late, if only because that is precisely what we tend to believe, and are encouraged to believe. A certain climate is created—that of being rapidly overtaken by events—reinforcing the feeling that the tidal wave of progress brought on by the new biotechnology is impossible to stem, so that we may be paralysed into accepting the inevitable. No, because we shall not give up, for the consequence of giving up is the brave new world, and soon after that, there may be no world at all. The gene genie is fast getting out of control. The practitioners of genetic engineering biotechnology, the regulators and the critics alike, have *all* underestimated the risks involved, which are *inherent* to genetic engineering biotechnology, particularly as misguided by an outmoded and erroneous worldview that comes from bad science. The dreams may already be turning into nightmares.

That is why people like myself are calling for an immediate moratorium on further releases and marketing of genetically engineered products, and for an independent public enquiry to be set up to look into the risks and hazards involved, taking into account the most comprehensive, scientific knowledge in addition to the social, moral implications. This would be most timely, as public opposition to genetic engineering biotechnology has been gaining momentum throughout Europe and the USA.

In Austria, a record 1.2 million citizens, representing 20 percent of the electorate, have signed a people's petition to ban genetically engineered foods, as well as deliberate releases of genetically modified organisms and patenting of life. Genetically modified foods were also rejected earlier by a lay people consultation in Norway, and by 95 percent of consumers in Germany, as revealed by a recent survey. The European Parliament has voted by an overwhelming 407 to 2 majority to censure the

Commission's authorization, in December 1996, for imports of Ciba-Geigy's transgenic maize into Europe, and is calling for imports to be suspended while the authorization is re-examined. The European Commission has decided that in the future genetically engineered seeds will be labelled, and is also considering proposals for retroactive labelling. Commissioner Emma Bonino is to set up a new scientific committee to deal with genetically engineered foods, members of which are to be completely independent of the food industry. Meanwhile, Franz Fischler, the European Commissioner on Agriculture, supports a complete segregation and labelling of production lines of genetically modified and non-genetically modified foods.

In June this year, President Clinton imposed a five-year ban on human cloning in the USA, while the UK House of Commons Science and Technology Committee (STC) wants British law to be amended to ensure that human cloning is illegal. The STC, President Chirac of France and German Research Minister Juergen Ruettgers are also calling for an international ban on human cloning.

Like other excellent critics before me,[3] I do not think there is a grand conspiracy afoot, though there are many forces converging to a single terrible end. Susan George comments, "They don't have to conspire if they have the same world-view, aspire to similar goals and take concerted steps to attain them."[4]

I am one of those scientists who have long been highly critical of the reductionist mainstream scientific world-view, and have begun to work towards a radically different approach for understanding nature.[5] But I was unable, for a long time, to see how much science really matters n the affairs of the real world, not just in terms of practical inventions like genetic engineering, but in how that scientific world-view takes hold of people's unconscious, so that they take action, involuntarily, unquestioningly, to shape the world to the detriment of human beings. I was so little aware of how that science is used, without conscious intent, to intimidate and control, to obfuscate, to exploit and oppress; how

that dominant world-view generates a selective blindness to make scientists themselves ignore or misread scientific evidence.

The point, however, is not that *science* is bad—but that there can be *bad science* that ill-serves humanity. Science can often be wrong. The history of science can just as well be written in terms of the mistakes made than as the series of triumphs it is usually made out to be. Science is nothing more, and nothing less, than a system of concepts for understanding nature and for obtaining reliable knowledge that enables us to live sustainably with nature. In that sense, one can ill-afford to give up science, for it is through our proper understanding and knowledge of nature that we can live a satisfying life, that we can ultimately distinguish the good science, which serves humanity, from the bad science that does not. In this view, science is imbued with moral values from the start, and cannot be disentangled from them. Therefore it is bad science that purports to be "neutral" and divorced from moral values, as much as it is bad science that ignores scientific evidence.

It is clear that I part company with perhaps a majority of my scientist colleagues in the mainstream, who believe that science can never be wrong, although it can be misused. Or else they carefully distinguish science, as neutral and value-free, from its application, technology, which can do harm or good.[6] This distinction between science and technology is spurious, especially in the case of an experimental science like genetics, and almost all of biology, where the techniques determine what sorts of question are asked and hence the range of answers that are important, significant and relevant to the science. Where would molecular genetics be without the tools that enable practitioners to recombine and manipulate our destiny? It is an irresistibly heroic view, except that it is totally wrong and misguided.

It is also meaningless, therefore, to set up Ethical Committees which do not question the basic scientific assumptions behind the practice of genetic engineering biotechnology. Their brief is severely limited, often verging on the trivial and banal—such as whether a pork gene transferred to food plants might be counter to certain religious beliefs—in comparison with the much more fundamental questions of eugenics, genetic discrimination and, indeed, whether gene transfers should be carried out at all. They can do nothing more than make the unacceptable acceptable to the public.

The debate on genetic engineering biotechnology is dogged by the artificial separation imposed between "pure" science and the issues it gives rise to. "Ethics" is deemed to be socially determined, and therefore negotiable, while the science is seen to be beyond reproach, as it is the "laws" of nature. The same goes for the distinction between "technology"—the application of science—from the science. Risk assessments are to do with the technology, leaving the science equally untouched. The technology can be bad for your health, but not the science. In this article, I shall show why science cannot be separated from moral values nor from the technology that shapes our society. In other words, bad science is unquestionably bad for one's health and well-being, and should be avoided at all costs. Science is, above all, fallible and negotiable, because we have the choice, to do or not to do. It should be negotiated for the public good. That is the only ethical position one can take with regard to science. Otherwise, we are in danger of turning science into the most fundamentalist of religions that, working hand in hand with corporate interests, will surely usher in the brave new world.

BAD SCIENCE AND BIG BUSINESS

What makes genetic engineering biotechnology dangerous, in the first instance, is that it is an unprecedented, close alliance between two great powers that can make or break the world: science and commerce. Practically all established molecular geneticists have some direct or indirect connection with industry, which will set limits on what the scientists can and will do research on, not to mention the possibility of compromising their integrity as independent scientists.[7]

The worst aspect of the alliance is that it is between the most reductionist science and multinational monopolistic industry at its most aggressive and exploitative. If the truth be told, it is bad science working together with big business for quick profit, aided and abetted by our governments for the banal reason that governments wish to be re-elected to remain in 'power.'[8]

Speaking as a scientist who loves and believes in science, I have to say it is bad science that has let the world down and caused the major problems we now face, not the least among which is by promoting and legitimizing a particular world-view. It is a reductionist, manipulative and exploitative world-view. Reductionist because it sees the world as bits and pieces, and denies there are organic wholes such as organisms, ecosystems, societies and community of nations. Manipulative and exploitative because it regards nature and fellow human beings as objects to be manipulated and exploited for gain, life being a Darwinian struggle for survival of the fittest.

It is by no means coincidental that the economic theory currently dominating the world is rooted in the same *laissez-faire* capitalist ideology that gave rise to Darwinism. It acknowledges no values other than self-interest, competitiveness and the accumulation of wealth, at which the developed nations have been very successful. Already, according to the 1992 United Nations Development Programme Report, the richest fifth of the world's population has amassed 82.7 per cent of the wealth, while the poorest fifth gets a piddling 1.4 per cent. Or, put in another way, there are now 477 billionaires in the world whose combined assets are roughly equal to the combined annual incomes of the poorer half of humanity—2.8 billion people.[9] Do we need to be more "competitive" still to take from the poorest their remaining pittance? That is, in fact, what we are doing.

The governmental representatives of the superpowers are pushing for a "globalized economy" under trade agreements which erase all economic borders. "Together, the processes of deregulation and globalization are undermining the power of both unions and governments and placing the power of global corporations and finance beyond the reach of public accountability."[10] The largest corporations continue to consolidate that power through mergers, acquisitions and strategic alliances. Multinational corporations now comprise 51 of the world's 100 largest economies: only 49 of the latter are nations. By 1993, agricultural biotechnology was being controlled by just 11 giant corporations, and these are now undergoing further mergers. The OECD (Organization for Economic Co-operation and Development) member countries are at this moment working in secret in Paris on the Multilateral Agreements on Investment (MAI), which is written by and for corporations to prohibit any government from establishing performance or accountability standards for foreign investors. European Commissioner, Sir Leon Brittan, is negotiating in the World Trade Organization, on behalf of the European Community, to ensure that no barriers of any kind should remain in the South to dampen exploitation by the North and, at the same time, to protect the deeply unethical "patents of life" through Trade Related Intellectual Property Rights (TRIPS) agreements.[11] So, in addition to gaining complete control of the food supply of the South through exclusive rights to genetically engineered seeds, the big food giants of the North can asset-strip the South's genetic and intellectual resources with impunity, up to and including genes and cell lines of indigenous peoples.

There is no question that the mindset that leads to and validates genetic engineering is *genetic determinism*—the idea that organisms are determined by their genetic makeup, or the totality of their genes. Genetic determinism derives from the marriage of Darwinism and Mendelian genetics. For those imbued with the mindset of genetic determinism, the major problems of the world can be solved simply by identifying and manipulating genes, for genes determine the characters of organisms; so by identifying a gene we can predict a desirable or undesirable trait, by changing a gene we change the trait, by transferring a gene we transfer the corresponding trait.

The Human Genome Project was inspired by the same genetic determinism that locates the "blueprint" for constructing the human being in the human genome. It may have been a brilliant political move to capture research funds and, at the same time, to revive a flagging pharmaceutical industry, but its scientific content was suspect from the first.

Genetic engineering technology promises to work for the benefit of mankind; the reality is something else.

- It displaces and marginalizes all alternative approaches that address the social and environmental causes of malnutrition and ill-health, such as poverty and unemployment, and the need for a sustainable agriculture that could regenerate the environment, guarantee long-term food security and, at the same time, conserve indigenous biodiversity.

- Its purpose is to accommodate problems that reductionist science and industry have created in the first place—widespread environmental deterioration from the intensive, high-input agriculture of the Green Revolution, and accumulation of toxic wastes from chemical industries. What's on offer now is more of the same, except with new problems attached.

- It leads to discriminatory and other unethical practices that are against the moral values of societies and community of nations.

- Worst of all, it is pushing a technology that is untried, and, according to existing knowledge, is inherently hazardous to health and biodiversity.

Let me enlarge on that last point here, as I believe it has been underestimated, if not entirely overlooked by the practitioners, regulators and many critics of genetic engineering biotechnology alike, on account of a certain blindness to concrete scientific evidence, largely as a result of their conscious or unconscious commitment to an old, discredited paradigm. The most immediate hazards are likely to be in public health—which has already reached a global crisis, attesting to the failure of decades of reductionist medical practices —although the hazards to biodiversity will not be far behind.

GENETIC ENGINEERING BIOTECHNOLOGY IS INHERENTLY HAZARDOUS

According to the 1996 World Health Organization Report, at least 30 new diseases, including AIDS, Ebola and Hepatitis C, have emerged over the past 20 years, while old infectious diseases such as tuberculosis, cholera, malaria and diphtheria are coming back worldwide. Almost every month now in the UK we hear reports on fresh outbreaks: *Streptococcus,* meningitis, *E. coli.* Practically all the pathogens are resistant to antibiotics, many to multiple antibiotics. Two strains of *E. coli* isolated in a transplant ward outside Cambridge in 1993 were found to be resistant to 21 out of 22 common antibiotics.[12] A strain of *Staphylococcus* isolated in Australia in 1990 was found to be resistant to 31 different drugs.[13] Infections with these and other strains will very soon become totally invulnerable to treatment. In fact, scientists in Japan have already isolated a strain of *Staphylococcus aureus* that is resistant even to the last resort antibiotic, vancomycin.[14]

Geneticists have now linked the emergence of pathogenic bacteria and of antibiotic resistance to *horizontal gene transfer*—the transfer of genes to unrelated species, by infection through viruses, though pieces of genetic material, DNA, taken up into cells from the environment, or by unusual mating taking place between unrelated species. For example, horizontal gene transfer and subsequent genetic recombination have generated the bacterial strains responsible for the cholera outbreak in India in 1992,[15] and the Streptococcus epidemic in Tayside in 1993.[16] The *E. coli* 157 strain involved in the recent outbreaks in Scotland is believed to have originated from horizontal gene transfer from the pathogen, *Shigella.*[17] Many unrelated bacterial pathogens, causing diseases from bubonic plague to tree blight,

are found to share an entire set of genes for invading cells, which have almost certainly spread by horizontal gene transfer.[18] Similarly, genes for antibiotic resistance have spread horizontally and recombined with one another to generate multiple antibiotic resistance throughout the bacterial populations.[19] Antibiotic resistance genes spread readily by contact between human beings, and from bacteria inhabiting the gut of farm animals to those in human beings.[20] Multiple antibiotic-resistant strains of pathogens have been endemic in many hospitals for years.[21]

What is the connection between horizontal gene transfer and genetic engineering? Genetic engineering is a technology designed specifically to transfer genes horizontally between species that do not interbreed. It is designed to break down species barriers and, increasingly, to overcome the species' defence mechanisms which normally degrade or inactivate foreign genes.[22]

For the purpose of manipulating, replicating and transferring genes, genetic engineers make use of recombined versions of precisely those genetic parasites causing diseases including cancers, and others that carry and spread virulence genes and antibiotic resistance genes. Thus the technology will contribute to an increase in the frequency of horizontal gene transfer of those genes that are responsible for virulence and antibiotic resistance, and allow them to recombine to generate new pathogens.

What is even more disturbing is that geneticists have now found evidence that the presence of antibiotics typically increases the frequency of horizontal gene transfer 100-fold or more, possibly because the antibiotic acts like a sex hormone for the bacteria, enhancing mating and exchange of genes between unrelated species.[23] Thus, antibiotic resistance and multiple antibiotic resistance cannot be overcome simply by making new antibiotics, *for antibiotics create the very conditions to facilitate the spread of resistance.* The continuing profligate use of antibiotics in intensive farming and in medicine, in combination with the commercial-scale practice of genetic engineering, may already be major contributing factors for the accelerated spread of multiple antibiotic resistance among new and old pathogens that the WHO

1996 Report has identified within the past 10 years. For example, there has been a dramatic rise both in terms of incidence and severity of cases of infections by *Salmonella*,[24] with some countries in Europe witnessing a staggering 20-fold increase in incidence since 1980.

That is not all. One by one, those assumptions on which geneticists and regulatory committees have based their assessment of genetically engineered products to be "safe" have fallen by the wayside, especially in the light of evidence emerging within the past three to four years. However, there is still little indication that the new findings are being taken on board. On the contrary, regulatory bodies have succumbed to pressure from the industry to relax already inadequate regulations. Let me list a few more of the relevant findings in genetics.

We have been told that horizontal gene transfer is confined to bacteria. That is not so. It is now known to involve practically all species of animal, plant and fungus. It is possible for any gene in any species to spread to any other species, especially if the gene is carried on genetically engineered gene-transfer vectors. Transgenes and antibiotic resistance marker genes from transgenic plants have been shown to end up in soil fungi and bacteria.[25] The microbial populations in the environment serve as the gene-transfer highway and reservoir, supporting the replication of the genes and allowing them to spread and recombine with other genes to generate new pathogens.[26]

We have been assured that "crippled" laboratory strains of bacteria and viruses do not survive when released into the environment. That is not true. There is now abundant evidence that they can either survive quite well and multiply, or they can go dormant and reappear after having acquired genes from other bacteria to enable them to multiply.[27] Bacteria co-operate much more than they compete. They share their most valuable assets for survival.

We have been told that DNA is easily broken down in the environment. Not so. DNA can remain in the environment where they can be picked up by bacteria and incorporated into their genome.[28]

DNA is, in fact, one of the toughest molecules. Biochemists jumped with joy when they didn't have to work with proteins anymore, which lose their activity very readily. By contrast, DNA survives rigorous boiling, so when they approve processed food on grounds that there can be no DNA left, ask exactly how the processing is done, and whether the appropriate tests for the presence of DNA have been carried out.

The survival of "crippled" laboratory strains of bacteria and viruses and the persistence of DNA in the environment are of particular relevance to the so-called contained users producing transgenic pharmaceuticals, enzymes and food additives. "Tolerated" releases and transgenic wastes from such users may already have released large amounts of transgenic bacteria and viruses as well as DNA into the environment since the early 1980s when commercial genetic engineering biotechnology began.

We are told that DNA is easily digested by enzymes in our gut. Not true. The DNA of a virus has been found to survive passage through the gut of mice. Furthermore, the DNA readily finds its way into the bloodstream, and into all kinds of cell[s] in the body.[29] Once inside the cell, the DNA can insert itself into the cell's genome, and create all manner of genetic disturbances, including cancer.[30]

There are yet further findings pointing to the potential hazards of generating new disease-causing viruses by recombination between artificial viral vectors and vaccines and other viruses in the environment. The viruses generated in this way will have increased host ranges, infecting and causing diseases in more than one species, and hence very difficult to eradicate. *We are already seeing such viruses emerging.*

- Monkeypox, a previously rare and potentially fatal virus caught from rodents, is spreading through central Zaire.[31] Between 1981 and 1986 only 37 cases were known, but there have been at least 163 cases in one eastern province of Zaire alone since July 1995. For the first time, humans are transmitting the disease directly from one to the other.

- An outbreak of hantavirus infection hit southern Argentina in December 1996, the first time the virus was transmitted from person to person.[32] Previously, the virus was spread by breathing in the aerosols from rodent excrement or urine.

- New highly virulent strains of infectious bursal disease virus (IBDV) spread rapidly throughout most of the poultry industry in the Northern Hemisphere, and are now infecting Antarctic penguins, and are suspected of causing mass mortality.[33]

- New strains of distemper and rabies viruses are spilling out from towns and villages to plague some of the world's rarest wild animals in Africa[34]: lions, panthers, wild dogs, giant otter.

None of the plethora of new findings has been taken on board by the regulatory bodies. On the contrary, safety regulations have been relaxed. The public is being used, against its will, as guinea pigs for genetically engineered products, while new

viruses and bacterial pathogens may be created by the technology every passing day.

The present situation is reminiscent of the development of nuclear energy which gave us the atom bomb, and the nuclear power stations that we now know to be hazardous to health and also to be environmentally unsustainable on account of the long-lasting radioactive wastes they produce. Joseph Rotblat, the British physicist who won the 1995 Nobel Prize after years of battling against nuclear weapons, has this to say. "My worry is that other advances in science may result in other means of mass destruction, maybe more readily available even than nuclear weapons. Genetic engineering is quite a possible area, because of these dreadful developments that are taking place there."[35]

The large-scale release of transgenic organisms is much worse than nuclear weapons or radioactive nuclear wastes, as genes can replicate indefinitely, spread and recombine. There may yet be time enough to stop the industry's dreams turning into nightmares if we act now, before the critical genetic "melt-down" is reached.

NOTES

1. The first time I heard the word "transgenic" being used on cultivars resulting from conventional breeding methods was from Henry Miller, a prominent advocate for genetic engineering biotechnology, in a public debate with myself, organized by the Oxford Centre for Environment, Ethics and Society, in Oxford University on February 20, 1997.

2. "Scientists scorn sci-fi fears over sheep clone," *The Guardian*, February 24, 1997, p. 7. Lewis Wolpert, development biologist at University College London was reported as saying, "It's a pretty risky technique with lots of abnormalities." Also report and interview in the Eight O'Clock News, BBC Radio 4, February 24, 1997.

3. As for instance, Spallone, 1992.

4. George, 1988, p. 5.

5. My colleague Peter Saunders and I began working on an alternative approach to neo-Darwinian evolutionary theory in the 1970s. Major collections of multi-author essays appeared in Ho and Saunders, 1984: Pollard, 1981: Ho and Fox, 1988.

6. Lewis Wolpert, who currently heads the Committee for the Public Understanding of Science, argues strenuously for this 'fundamentalist' view of science. See Wolpert, 1996.

7. See Hubbard and Wald, 1993.

8. This was pointed out to me by Martin Khor, during a Course on Globalization and Economics that he gave at Schumacher College, February 3–10, 1997.

9. See Korten, 1997.

10. Korten, 1997, p. 2.

11. See Perlas, 1994; also WTO: New setback for the South, *Third World Resurgence* issue 77/78, 1997, which contains many articles reporting on the WTO meeting held in December 1996 in Singapore.

12. Brown *et al.,* 1993.

13. Udo and Grubb, 1990.

14. "Superbug spectre haunts Japan," Michael Day, *New Scientist* 3 May, 1997, p. 5.

15. See Bik *et al.,* 1995; Prager *et al.,* 1995; Reidl and Makalanos, 1995.

16. Whatmore *et al.,* 1994; Kapur *et al.,* 1995; Schnitzler *et al.,* 1995; Upton *et al.,* 1996.

17. Professor Hugh Pennington, on BBC Radio 4 News, February 1997.

18. Barinaga, 1996.

19. Reviewed by Davies, 1994.

20. Tschape, 1994.

21. See World Health Report, 1996; also Garret, 1995, chapter 13, for an excellent account of the history of antibiotic resistance in pathogens.

22. See Ho and Tappeser, 1997.

23. See Davies, 1994.

24. WHO Fact Sheet No. 139, January 1997.

25. Hoffman *et al.,* 1994; Schluter *et al.,* 1995.

26. See Ho, 1996a.

27. Jager and Tappeser, 1996, have extensively reviewed the literature on the survival of bacteria and DNA released into different environments.

28. See Lorenz and Wackernagel, 1994.

29. See Schubert *et al.,* 1994; also *New Scientist* January 24, p. 24, featured a short report on recent findings of the group that were presented at the International Congress on Cell Biology in San Francisco, December 1996.

30. Wahl *et al.,* 1984; see also relevant entries in Kendrew, 1995, especially "slow transforming retroviruses" and "Transgenic technologies."

31. "Killer virus piles on the misery in Zaire" Debora MacKenzie, *New Scientist* April 19, 1997, p. 12.

32. "Virus gets personal," *New Scientist* April 26, 1997, p. 13.

33. "Poultry virus infection in Antarctic penguins," Heather Gardner, Knowles Kerry and Martin Riddle, *Nature* 387, May 15, 1997, p. 245.

34. See Pain, 1997.

35. Quoted in "The spectre of a human clone" *The Independent,* February 26, 1997, p. 1.

STUDY QUESTIONS

1. What is a 'vector,' and how are vectors used in modifying organisms?

2. What is horizontal gene transfer, and what are the concerns about it?

3. It is often claimed that genetic modification of food is not substantively different from conventional food breeding. Discuss three of Ho's reasons for disputing this claim.

4. We are typically taught that the aim of science is 'knowledge.' Although Ho does not disagree that this is *an* aim of science, she believes that science now more often aims to serve the ends of business. Discuss some of her examples.

41

The ETC Report: The Poor Can Feed Themselves

By 2050, or much sooner, we will be growing food under climatic conditions we've never seen before and learning that "normal" weather is an illusive fiction. Yet, we are told that global land grabs and plantations of agrofuels are a "win-win." The truth is that policy-makers don't know enough about our food supply. We don't know where our food comes from and we don't know who is feeding the hungry today. We have absolutely no idea who will feed us in 2050. This report raises more questions than answers. It begins with a comparison of the likelihood of the industrial food chain and the peasant food web getting us through climate chaos.

THE INDUSTRIAL FOOD CHAIN

Ninety-six percent of all recorded food and agricultural research takes place in industrialized countries, and 80% of that research is on food processing and retailing. Over the last half-century, the industrial food chain has consolidated so that each link in the chain—from seed to soup—is dominated by a handful of multinationals working with an ever-narrower commodity list that has left half of humanity either dangerously malnourished or overweight.

The industrial food chain focuses on far fewer than 100 breeds of five livestock species. Corporate plant breeders work with 150 crops but focus on barely a dozen. Of the 80,000 commercial plant varieties in the market today, well over half are ornamentals. What remains of our declining fish stocks comes from 336 species accounting for almost two-thirds of the aquatic species we consume. Along with the loss of diversity has come a loss of quality. The nutritional content of many of our grains and vegetables has dropped between 5 and 40% so that we have to eat more calories to get the same nutrition.

In the face of climate chaos, the industrial chain is imposing a patent regime that prizes uniformity over diversity and enforces a technological model that costs more and takes more time to breed one genetically engineered variety than it does to breed hundreds of conventional varieties. The industrial food chain doesn't know who the hungry are, where they are, or what they need.

THE PEASANT FOOD WEB

Eighty-five percent of the world's food is grown and consumed if not within the "100 mile diet" within national borders and/or the same eco-regional zone. Most of this food is grown from peasant-bred seed without the industrial chain's synthetic fertilizers. Peasants breed and nurture 40

Reprinted with permission of ETC Group-Action Group on Erosion, Technology and Concentration, 431 Gilmour St, Second Floor Ottawa, ON Canada. As found at www.etcgroup.org.

Peasants?

"The language around us is changing all the time. Historically, we were peasants. Then when that term came to mean 'backward' we became 'farmers.' In these days 'farmer' has the connotation of inefficiency and we are strongly encouraged to be more modern, to see ourselves as managers, business people or entrepreneurs capable of handling increasingly larger pieces of territory. Well, I am a farmer and I am a peasant. I learned that I had much more in common with peasants than I did with some of my agribusiness neighbours. I am reclaiming the term peasant because I believe that small is more efficient, it is socially intelligent, it is community oriented. Being a peasant stands for the kind of agriculture and rural communities we are striving to build."

—Karen Pedersen, past-president, National Farmers Union (Canada)

"This debate in the literature…is a fabrication at a higher level, by those who know more. In the countryside, out there, there is no such debate. We continue being peasants. That's the way it is."

—Emiliano Cerros Nava, an executive commission member of UNORCA in Mexico

---

Peasants currently manage over half of the world's arable land. (See Annex.) From regional data, it is fair to estimate: 17 million peasant farms in Latin America grow between a half to two-thirds of staple foods; Africa's 33 million peasant farms (mostly female-led) account for 80% of farms and most of the domestic food consumption; Asia's 200 million peasant rice farms produce most of its harvest. Although their well-being fluctuates sometimes tragically, and they survive under harsh conditions with little external support, the 1,520 million peasant farm family members mostly feed themselves. The 712 million rural hungry (who can't afford to buy much of their food in the industrial food chain's markets) likely depend on peasants for whatever food they have. There are another 1.1 billion in the rural South who may not be hungry but also have limited access to the industrial chain and who are also likely to rely heavily on peasant surpluses as well as their own hunting, gathering and gardening.

Peasants are also the ones who feed the hungry. Rural peasant production is closest to the 712 million rural people who make up three-quarters of the world's hungry. These people are not only rural but also remote and impoverished or, in other words, of little interest to the industrial chain that prefers middle-class urban markets. Meanwhile, urban peasants grow at least a quarter of the food in the South's cities—the food that is most accessible to the 238 million hungry people who can't afford high food prices. By these estimates, at least 70% of the world's population is fed by peasants.

Policymakers must re-examine the common fallacy that, even when properly supported, the world's peasant food network lacks the bounty, efficiency and resilience to confront the food and climate crises. At the same time, policymakers must deconstruct the mythology surrounding the effectiveness of the industrial food system. The reality is that the world's 3 billion or so indigenous and peasant producers rural and urban, fishers and pastoralists not only feed a majority of the world's people and most of the world's malnourished, they create and conserve most of the world's biodiversity and are humanity's best defense against climate change.

As we prepare for 2050, then, logic suggests the need for policies that will make it possible for rural people to remain rural and for urbanites to grow as much of their own food as possible.

The bottom line for both Rome and Copenhagen is that in the middle of a crisis—do no harm! Do nothing to disrupt the existing sources of food security. This means safeguarding peasant farms, respecting their resource rights, guaranteeing access to uncultivated lands, and protecting/promoting urban gardens.

What do we need to do to ensure food security?

If we can't be sure what will grow well where, and if we are sure that extreme weather events will disrupt the food supply much more than in the past, then the central policy questions for shaping a sound food system become clear:

1. How can we ensure that food production for human consumption is given priority over other consumption demands?

2. How can we increase the species diversity of plants, livestock and aquatic species in order to adjust to changing climatic conditions?

3. How can we protect and improve the genetic diversity within plants, aquatic species and livestock to withstand extreme weather events, new pests and diseases, and changing climates?

4. How can we encourage breeders to reset goals to develop diverse and reliable plants and animals?

5. How can we protect and improve biological controls and soil nutrients to safeguard food and reduce reliance on synthetic chemicals?

6. How can we strengthen local community food production to reduce energy dependence and increase food quality?

7. How can we minimize loss and waste throughout the food system?

8. How do we ensure that food is nutritious, adequate, appropriate, and accessible to all?

9. How do we guarantee that peasant producers have stable and equitable production and marketing arrangements?

QUESTION 1

How Can We Ensure That Food Production for Human Consumption Is Given Priority Over Other Consumption Demands?

Because climate change means that we can't be sure what will grow where or with what consistency, common sense dictates that if we don't know otherwise we have to assume that land and natural resources already support endangered livelihoods and that changes in use should not be permitted in the absence of study and consultation (i.e., if we don't know—don't change it). We must operate on the assumption that marginalized rural populations have a high dependence on non-cultivated biomass (roadsides, forests, savannas, marine and freshwater species, etc.) and that marginalized urban and peri-urban populations have a high food production dependence on all accessible urban soils and water. And, despite our focus on food, we must recognize that both rural and urban peasants also produce other survival essentials such as community fuels, fibres, shelters and medicines.

Climate-Ready Failures. In October 2008, GRAIN first exposed the new "land grab" in the global South, a rush to control overseas farmland, led by corporate investors and governments. Nowhere is this development more foolhardy than in sub-Saharan Africa. A recent report coordinated by Bioversity International warns that climate-induced crop losses in this region could be as high as 50% just 10 years from now. By 2050, the report says, the majority of African countries will be experiencing "novel" growing conditions on most of their crop land. "Novel" doesn't mean good. Overwhelmingly, Africa will be hotter, drier and more exposed to extreme weather events than any time in the past century. The hotter Sahelian countries, the study says, will have climates with few analogs for any crop (meaning that they have no place to look today for the breeding material they will need tomorrow). Nevertheless, some of these countries like Sudan, Cameroon, and Nigeria—major land grab targets—actually have crop areas that are analogs to many future climates. Not only are they unlikely to be able to help themselves but, also, their potentially valuable germplasm is poorly represented in major gene banks. If large areas are sown to uniform export crops, this unique genetic diversity may become extinct before it can be collected. Such land grabs not only threaten national food security but they endanger the future food security of many other (including OECD) countries.

Lamb Grab. Another growing (but reversible) threat to our land-use is from grain-fed livestock production. Forty percent of our global grain supply feeds animals. Forty-seven million hectares are sown annually to fodder grasses and legumes. The protein and calorie loss in feeding crops to cattle, rather than food to people, is massive. UNEP (United Nations Environment Programme) calculates that the loss of calories by feeding cereals to animals instead of using the cereals as human food represents the annual calorie need for more than 3.5 billion people. Despite this, policy-makers are told they must anticipate a 3% per annum rise in meat and dairy consumption. Such a dietary shift is unhealthy and unsustainable as well as unacceptable given the climate changes ahead. The logical policy response is to invest in educational and regulatory initiatives that encourage consumption of more grains, vegetables and fruits.

This is not to suggest that peasant livestock production doesn't have a role. The UN Framework Convention on Climate Change (UNFCCC) sees livestock as a prominent source of greenhouse gas (GHG) emissions while the negotiators addressing the food crisis often look upon peasant livestock keepers and pastoralists as either a disease threat or a barrier to agrofuel production. In reality, peasant livestock systems (mobile or sedentary) can be extremely efficient at enriching biodiversity and in sequestering greenhouse gases. While industrial livestock operations are the leading emitter of nitrous oxide, most extensive livestock systems (i.e., smallholder) are climate friendly. Peasant herds logically occupy the slopes and soils not suitable for crops. These grazing lands cover over 45% of the earth's surface—1.5 times more than forest. While forests may add only about 10% to their biomass each year, savannas can reproduce 150% and tropical savannas have a greater potential to store carbon below ground than any other terrestrial ecosystem. Manure, generated by peasant livestock holds, when deposited on fields and pastures, doesn't produce significant amounts of methane. By contrast, factory farms produce manure in liquid form releasing 18 million tones of methane annually. The peasant web is agro-ecologically sound—the industrial chain is not. The obvious solution to curtail nitrous oxide and methane emissions generated by industrial livestock is to shut down factory farm production.

Agrofuels. Policymakers are frequently told that there is plenty of unused, marginal land to grow biomass crops (for agrofuels, bio-electricity and bio-chemicals) in the global South. This self-serving argument is nonsense—especially when no one knows how our crops and livestock will withstand climate change. Many of the plants now being established for bio-energy production on plantations in Africa, Asia, and Latin America have been sparsely studied and their performance and environmental impact is unknown. *Jatropha curcas*, a small tree native to Latin America, is being planted over large areas of Ethiopia, Mozambique and Tanzania, and each country expects to produce 60,000 tons of agrofuel by 2017. Some of the most commonly introduced fuel/biomass crops, *Jatropha curcas* among them, are believed to have a very narrow genetic base as well as production problems. No matter what plant species is employed, agrofuels/biomass plants compete with food crops for land, water and nutrients. Governments and corporations do not have the right to take this risk. By encouraging biofuel production, governments are failing to meet their obligations on the progressive realization of the right to adequate food.

The absurdity of growing biomass for export (not for local community use) in Africa is overwhelming. Maize is one of Africa's most important and preferred food crops. It is also a major first-generation agrofuel. In parts of East Africa, however, peasants are abandoning maize for crops that are more suited to drier conditions such as sorghum and millet even though stover production—used for either feed or fuel—is substantially lower. Yet European governments in pursuit of climate carbon credits are pressing for greater agrofuel/biomass production in Africa.

Hidden Harvest. So-called underutilized lands are the "commons" from which rural and peri-urban peasants collect and manage medicinal plants, fuel, as well as fish, game, uncultivated vegetables, nuts, fruit, and fungi. The "hidden harvest" not only provides irreplaceable nutrients in their diet, it is also essential for food security. Collection of "wild" and uncultivated materials takes place throughout the year but can become critical for survival in the weeks or months leading up to harvest when family food stocks are lowest. In some areas of Africa, wild resources cover up to 80% of household food needs during staple crop shortages. Even when the annual proportion of the hidden harvest seems low, its availability can mean the difference between life and death. Turning the commons into a global link in the industrial food or fuel chain could massively increase food insecurity.

For example, peasant communities in Borneo routinely gather nourishment from 800 different plants and more than 100 species of ground fauna along with hundreds of bird species. Only a third of their diet comes from cultivated crops. During the rainy season in one region of Kenya, women draw 35% of their plant material (for food, fibre and medicines) from so-called "marginal" lands. Other peasants in Kenya draw a quarter of their annual food supply from the "wild" but their dependence rises to almost half during the dry months. Peasant women in Uttar Pradesh, India, derive almost half their income from forest species. Even middle-class women in the same region obtain a third of their income from the same source. In one semi-arid region in India where common lands have declined between a third and a half since the 1960s, peasants still derive 14–23% of their nourishment from "wild" plants and animals. In drought years, this vital harvest can rise to half of their food intake. The Mende of Sierra Leone take more than half their food from forests, streams and fallow fields. In sum, it is safe to estimate that no less than 15% of the annual food supply of rural peasants in the global South comes from lands and life that the peasants nurture—but don't cultivate and that economists don't calculate. *But the most important reality for rural peoples and policymakers is that the absence of this 15% of the food supply in the weeks before crop harvests could mean mass starvation.*

Urban Harvest. Urban peasant food production may be even more substantial. According to one estimate cited by Canada's International Development Research Centre (IDRC), 25% of the entire global food output is grown in cities. Undertaken before the recent food crisis, it is likely that this figure significantly underestimates the current level of urban food production. History shows that urban agriculture production rises with food prices. Some years ago, UNDP estimated that at least 800 million urbanites produce some of their own food, including at least 200 million urban families that sell some of their produce in local markets. Again, these figures are probably much higher today. Almost 18% of the land in downtown Hanoi is used to grow food. In Quito, about 35% of urban land is used for agriculture and in the Argentinian city of Rosario, 80% of the land grows some food. In Abomey and Bohicon, two cities in Benin, half of the population in the peri-urban area is growing food as their primary activity.

Urban food production is a second "hidden harvest" that is usually overlooked or opposed by city and national administrations but is vital to local food security. As multinational hypermarket chains spread throughout the cities and towns of Latin America, Asia, and now Africa, urban production is seen as competition and the city water and sanitation regulations are sometimes employed to destroy the competitors. Yet, in the middle of a food crisis and with climate change all around, every effort must be made to strengthen city farming. Urban gardening and livestock keeping would benefit from policies that promote sound farming practices and safeguard water and soil quality.

The industrial food chain seems to be unaware that not less than 15% of the food critical to the rural hungry and perhaps 25% of the food critical to the urban hungry lie outside the conventional agricultural system. This being the case, how can they protect food security? How is it that the industrial chain can deny the importance of these unconventional food webs? And, most importantly, how can policy-makers at a time of food and climate crisis safeguard and strengthen this web?

POLICYMAKERS SHOULD CONSIDER:

1. Discouraging industrial-scale meat and dairy production and encouraging diets high in grains, vegetables and fruit. This could liberate 40% of the world's grain production, reduce energy consumption through transportation savings and reduce GHG emissions while improving human nutrition and lowering health costs.

2. Rejecting agrofuels/biomass crops except for locally produced, community-based consumption.

3. Prohibiting land speculation and "land grabs."

4. Strengthening customary use of land and resource rights, while taking special measures to protect women's rights to productive assets.

5. Encouraging urban and peri-urban food production and distribution, again taking into account and supporting the important contribution of women producers.

QUESTION 2

How Can We Increase the Species Diversity of Plants, Aquatic Species and Livestock in Order to Adjust to Changing Climatic Conditions?

The history of the industrial food chain is a history of biological reductionism. Over the latter half of the 20th century, the chain has persistently narrowed our capacity to ensure food security. Can the chain reverse its trendline? Can the chain change?

Field. Global crop production concentrates on 12 plant species (including maize, rice, wheat, soybeans, potatoes, sweet potatoes, bananas and plantains, sorghum, cassava, millets, sunflowers and canola). Only about 150 plant species are grown commercially around the world. Peasants have domesticated at least 5,000 plant species, but the industrial food chain uses only 3% of them.

An estimated 640 million peasant farmers and an additional 190 million pastoralists raise livestock for their own consumption and local markets.

Thanks to the ingenuity of farmers, literally hundreds of local plant species have been shown to have remarkable plasticity (e.g., adaptability, resilience) when confronted with extraordinarily different growing conditions including temperature, altitude, photosensitivity, soil conditions and pests and diseases. In harmony with the reductionist trendline (perhaps, understandably, given limited resources), national and international gene banks have also focused on the major global commercial species and have poor collections of the marginalized species that might feed humanity through the climate crisis. Of the 628,000 documented accessions within the Consultative Group on International Agricultural Research (CGIAR)—the largest international gene bank network—for example, nine crops account for more than half of the total collection and two crops—rice and wheat—account for almost one quarter. This means that public breeders don't have access to the ex situ species diversity they need now to prepare for tomorrow. It also means that only the peasant web maintains this species diversity (*in situ*). But, the important message for everybody is that the species that are absent in the ex situ gene bank collections are exposed to genetic erosion in the *in situ* ("on farm") environment.

Fowl. Although peasants have domesticated 40 livestock species, the industrial food chain has concentrated livestock production on just five species (bovines, chickens, pigs, sheep and goats). This shortsighted industrial approach must be reversed if we are to utilize the best species for different slope and soil conditions and new climatic challenges. Our focus must be on the exploration of the 35 livestock species that are largely outside commerce today.

We must also protect, develop and expand beyond the 60 fodder species important to livestock ruminants. Ninety percent of the world's forage grasses originate in sub-Saharan Africa, for example. Forage legumes such as alfalfa, vetch and clover are nearly universal. We need new pasture species for new conditions. Dependence on a few species increases the risk of food losses in a world of climate chaos.

Fish. Currently, 336 species from 115 families of fish and invertebrates are commercially farmed with 47% of all fish production coming from aquaculture. However, the potential number of edible aquatic species vastly exceeds current use. There are more than 15,200 freshwater species and at least 20,000 marine species. Almost two-thirds of global species consumption (industrial catch) comes from five groups: finfish families (Salmonidae, Cyprinidae and Cichlidae), marine crustaceans and the bivalve mollusks (mussels, clams, scallops, and oysters), which are over-exploited and endangered. Tragically, ocean trawlers discard at least 40% of their annual catch. By contrast, coastal and inland fishers use a vastly greater (although uncounted) range of species and discard very little. Freshwater species play an important role in feeding people but the ecosystems in which they live also provide invaluable ecosystem services important to survive climate change. In terms of goods and services, FAO reports, inland waters contribute more to global economies than all terrestrial ecosystems combined, including forests, grasslands and rangelands. The only group that has demonstrated the capacity to monitor and manage either the food stocks and the ecology of inland waters is the artisanal fishers themselves.

The importance of inland peasant fishponds to food security can't be exaggerated. Asian aquaculture, for example, is mostly on peasant farms of less than 2 hectares (ha). Thai freshwater fish ponds are usually less than 0.3 ha but they produce an average of 2,300 kg/ha. Over 90% of Indian shrimp farms are less than 2 ha. Vietnam's tiny catfish ponds still produce 400,000 kg/ha, and backyard water holes in Bangladesh, amazingly, yield substantial quantities of catfish for household diets and local markets. Not only must the small-scale production be protected, it must also be recognized as the basis for strengthening rural and urban aquaculture.

POLICYMAKERS SHOULD CONSIDER:

1. Supporting farmers, livestock keepers and fishers, especially the role of women, in *in situ* conservation and use of diverse local species.

2. Promoting priority market access for underutilized species (aquatic, crop and livestock) that show climate resilience and disease resistance.

3. Encouraging but only with the approval and oversight of peasants gene banks, sperm banks, etc., to collect and characterize underutilized species as an urgent national and global priority.

QUESTION 3

How Can We Protect and Improve Genetic Diversity within Plants, Aquatic Species and Livestock to Withstand Extreme Weather Events, New Pests and Diseases, and Changing Climates?

The genetic diversity within a species can be as extraordinary as the diversity between species. Faced with uncertain and inconsistent conditions on land and at sea, governments must not only explore underutilized species but also encourage genetic diversity within species. Understandably, prior to the recognition of climate change, government conservation efforts focused on the most important plant, livestock and aquatic species (through gene banks for orthodox seed, *in situ* collections for vegetatively propagated plants; cryogenically preserved eggs and sperm, etc.). Collection efforts within the species also concentrated upon yield and uniformity characteristics to maximize profit and meet industrial processing requirements. The food crisis and climate change require a paradigm shift.

> Now, the key words must be *diversity* and *plasticity*.

Field.   Thanks to the ingenuity of farmers, the world's major food crops have been encouraged to grow at a remarkable range of altitudes and latitudes in a variety of ecosystems. From early in the 20th century and especially since the 1960s, public and private commercial breeding has narrowed the genetic base of the world's top food crops and massively eroded their genetic diversity. Beginning in the 1960s, the Green Revolution's emphasis on wheat, rice and maize and the focus of commercial breeders on soybeans, alfalfa, cotton and canola (oilseed rape) pushed so-called "poor people's crops" to the margins causing genetic erosion even in low-priority species. By the early 1990s it

was roughly estimated that genetic diversity in the world's leading crops was declining by about 2% per annum and that perhaps three-quarters of the germplasm pool for these crops was already extinct. This loss of diversity severely limits the resilience of crops to respond to climate change.

More than the hunger crisis, the climate crisis points to the need to conserve and utilize genetic diversity in both the major food crops and in other crops that show a great potential to be productive while withstanding new pests, diseases and conditions. Who is best able to do this?

Fowl.   The world's dominant five livestock species—along with the handful of commercial breeds that dominate industrial production—can be found on every continent except Antarctica. Reports commissioned by FAO warn that climate change may require the mass movement of livestock breeds and express concern that globalization—especially vertical integration along the food chain and standardization trends among the major food retailers—could further narrow the genetic base of commercial species at a time when diversity is needed most. The report specifically warns that new developments in biotechnology will combine with retail standardization to adversely affect small livestock keepers and their ability to conserve livestock genetic diversity.

The lack of genetic diversity within the five commercial livestock species is astonishing—and the loss is accelerating. While 21% of all livestock breeds are thought to be endangered, not enough is known about another 36% to determine their condition. Ten breeds are becoming extinct every year. Among the five livestock species an average of just five breeds dominate commercial production around the world. Leading the cattle herd is the Holstein-Friesian dairy breed (128 countries). The White Leghorn chicken is found almost everywhere. The Large White pig is farmed in 117 countries. Marino sheep, with derivatives, is probably in more than 60 countries, and the Saanen dairy goat can be found in 81 countries. Artificial insemination in the 1960s, embryo transfer in the 1980s and embryo sexing in the mid-1990s encouraged the overuse of a handful of superior animals for millions of progeny. Although the result has been a major increase in productivity, the consequent genetic uniformity, combined with genetic erosion, could spell disaster down the road.

Who can help us conserve and utilize livestock genetic diversity to meet new climatic challenges? To date, the industrial food model has encouraged uniformity, destroyed diversity and increased vulnerability. Is there any evidence that it can change? Avian influenza and Mexican swine flu (H1N1) are just two recent examples of global pandemics largely provoked by extreme genetic uniformity in commercial breeds raised in confined and crowded conditions. Genetically uniform and intensively raised livestock are much more vulnerable to disease and climate change. Peasant-bred breeds are more diverse and more resilient but because they tolerate diseases that kill their more fragile cousins in the industrial food chain, industry and governments cull (i.e., exterminate) these hardy breeds at the first sign of problems rather than building upon the sturdier stock to withstand new threats.

> To protect those livestock breeds that have been bred weak, we are culling those that have been bred hardy—rendering the genetic traits of the hardy extinct.

A handful of companies control livestock genomics and production. Out front is Tyson Foods (USA), which operates in 90 countries and is the world's largest processor and marketer of chicken, beef and pork. The company—with annual sales of $27 billion—is also one of the four global corporations that control broiler genetics. Among others, EW Gruppe in Germany is the world's top breeder in broilers, chickens and turkeys and provides the genetics for 68% of white egg layers and 17% of brown egg layers. Hendrix Genetics (Netherlands) ranks first in the worldwide supply of brown egg layers, second in turkey genetics, fourth in broilers and number two in pig genetics. The company sells layer hen breeding stock in over 100 countries.

> This level of corporate concentration represents a direct threat to our long-term food security.

What can we hope for from the peasant web? Livestock keepers and pastoralists are breeding all 40 domesticated species and, according to FAO, are currently protecting 7,616 breeds. If we are going to have the kind of livestock we need for the soils and slopes best suited for livestock-keeping, it would be better to work with those who have practical incentive, animal germplasm, ecosystem knowledge, and breeding experience to do the job.

Fish. The world's marine fish stocks are already in rapid decline. Freshwater species are equally suffering from industrial and agricultural pollution and the barriers erected by the world's 45,000 dams. Strains of salmon, shrimp, oyster, carp and tilapia are found almost everywhere. From its possible origins in the Danube River, carp is now harvested in 96 countries. Nile tilapia is native to West Africa and the Nile River but is grown in 61 countries on all continents today. Tiger shrimp are farmed in 23 countries in the Indian and Pacific oceans. Pacific oysters originated in Japan and are now harvested in 31 countries. Atlantic salmon were originally native to both sides of the North Atlantic. Today's Atlantic salmon are grown in at least 19 countries and Chile is one of the world's most important exporters.

Despite their geographic diversity, many commercial species have an extraordinarily narrow and narrowing genetic base. Most experts agree that so-called "wild" carp no longer exist but there is some genetic variability in escapees derived from domesticated varieties. The salmon farmed in 19 countries is based upon a single Norwegian breeding program that has been privatized into a company called Nofima.

So, who will best steward our fisheries through climate change? The industrial food chain that jettisons all but a handful of species and whose breeding programs have increased uniformity and vulnerability? Or, the tens of millions of inshore and freshwater fishers who welcome species diversity and know how to protect fragile ecosystems?

POLICYMAKERS SHOULD CONSIDER:

1. Eliminating industrial farming/fishing subsidies and adopting regulatory systems that encourage genetic diversity among plant, animal and aquatic food species.

2. Supporting the conservation of endangered genetic diversity first through *in situ* collections and, secondarily, *ex situ* collections, with the permission and guidance of peasants.

3. Prioritizing the conservation and enhancement strategies of peasant producers and orienting conservation programs in gene banks etc., to meet their breeding requirements.

QUESTION 4

How Can We Encourage Breeders to Reset Goals to Develop Diverse and Reliable Plants and Animals?

Perhaps it's hard for the industrial food system to be innovative when it is caught up in chains. For all its vaunted research investment, the industrial model has yet to develop and introduce a single new crop or livestock species (although there are at least 80,000 higher-order plants and many hundreds of mammals, birds and aquatic species potentially available). The uncertainties of climate change demand a complete rethink of our research (and especially breeding) priorities. Plant breeders need to nurture species and genetic diversity in the field during the same growing season.

Rights Make a Wrong

The major legacy of the industrial agricultural research chain will be the creation of intellectual property rights over crops, livestock and fish (including their genetic parts and components). Attempts to monopolize plant varieties began in the 1930s but grew into a global force in the 1960s with the formation of an International Convention for the Protection of New Varieties of Plants (UPOV). In order to assert legal ownership over living material, breeders abandoned diversity and marginalized agronomic priorities in order to develop varieties that were "distinct, uniform and stable." These are the mirror opposites of what we need today and tomorrow. Physical distinctiveness may help defend ownership in court, but it is not necessarily beneficial in the field. If it doesn't serve an economic purpose, breeders' efforts to achieve distinctiveness simply means a waste of time and money. The industrial food chain prizes uniformity and stability. But these attributes fight against climate readiness and food security. Today, our crops and livestock desperately need genetic diversity, not uniformity. While we don't want "unstable" varieties and breeds, we do want "plasticity" the genetic capacity of plants and animals to respond rapidly to changing conditions. Replanted seed adapts over generations to local agronomic conditions and offers higher and more reliable yields. Both patents and related regulations are forcing farmers to buy new and, therefore, unadapted seed every season, denying agriculture one of its most important tools. Any restrictions on the right to conduct research using patented breeding material must be struck down since it blocks peasants from their customary breeding activities.

> We need as many breeders and as much diversity as possible. *Intellectual property regulations are a direct attack on global food security.*

Can the industrial chain breed for diverse conditions? In fact, the research food chain isn't even very good at breeding with readily available genetic diversity. In 2007 there were over 72,500 proprietary plant varieties (including ornamentals) ostensibly available in the marketplace. And, over the last 40 years, Green Revolution plant breeders have released 8,000 new crop varieties.

By contrast, since the 1960s peasants have bred far more than 1.9 million plant varieties. We know this because peasants have donated that number of unique farm-bred varieties to the world's gene banks. But, since the gene banks have mostly been looking for the major crop species, some of the most important peasant plant breeding has been ignored. As already discussed, peasants grow thousands of plant species annually and at least 103 of these species each contributes 5% or more of the human calories available in one or more countries. If policymakers are informed by the track record, it is clearly peasant farming systems that are the proven leaders in using genetic diversity to help crops withstand climate change.

Lab Lobotomy? Even if we revoke monopolistic intellectual property regimes, can we reorganize conventional agricultural research to address these new breeding goals? The second legacy of the agricultural genetic-engineering industry will be its fragmentation and privatization of the crop improvement system established one hundred years ago. University training is now oriented to molecular biology and combinatorial technologies designed to identify and transfer genes between species. Graduates have no real understanding of plant breeding or agriculture. Today's institutional plant breeders and taxonomists are yesterday's news—themselves a dying breed. For example, FAO's 2006 assessment of plant breeding capacity in Africa shows less support for plant breeders today than in 1985, noting that "local plant breeding programs are generally poorly funded, including funds for field trials, staff travel, data analysis and infrastructure." In the USA, the number of public sector breeders working on fruit and vegetable crops declined by 43% from 1994 to 2001. At the moment when taxonomy, conventional plant breeding, and a holistic sense of ecosystem adaptation are vital to withstand climate change, the biosciences have given themselves a frontal "labotany."

Since the 1960s peasants have bred far more than 1.9 million plant varieties.

Cash Crunch. Can we afford to make the shift from the industrial breeding strategy toward a more diversified approach? The third legacy of the agbiotech industry is the entrenchment of an extraordinarily slow and expensive research model. Corporate wastefulness at the breeding end of the food chain is already damaging to food security. According to Monsanto, it takes at least 10 years and between $100 and $150 million to introduce a new genetically modified trait into plant varieties. One public researcher reports that it took 16 years to introduce the well-known and well-characterized *Bt* trait into GM crops. This is in contrast to conventional, commercial breeders who rarely spend more than $1 million to breed a plant variety. (DNA marker-assisted breeding technologies can speed the pace of conventional breeding.) In short, for every new biotech variety, conventional breeders can introduce between 100 and 150 standard varieties in less time. Despite this, the world's largest seed companies are working almost exclusively on GM seeds.

Let Them Eat Chrysanthemums? If data from the European Plant Variety Protection Office accurately reflects the orientation of the world's industrial food chain, then the chain is having trouble getting its priorities sorted. Fully 59% of all the plant variety "rights" granted between 1995 and 2009 went to ornamental species (notably roses and chrysanthemums), while only 27% went to agricultural varieties that feed people or livestock and just 14% went to vegetables and fruits over a time period in which the ranks of the hungry swelled by more than 160 million. The UPOV registry of protected plant varieties includes more than 29,000 roses and chrysanthemums—almost exactly the count for wheat, rice and maize combined.

The bottom line critique of industrial plant and livestock breeding is that it focuses on too few species, the wrong species and the wrong breeding goals. It is also too slow, too expensive, and its dependence on intellectual property forces the development of varieties that exacerbate climate vulnerability.

The peasant breeding system creates vastly more varieties of many more species that has as its primary goal ecosystem adaptability and yield reliability. However, this in no way means that the peasant web will manage climate change without consequences. Peasants, too, will experience growing conditions they have never seen before and they will need to work with novel species and breeding material in order to survive.

There is a desperate need to encourage germplasm exchanges between and among peasant organizations around the world, and to insure that they have priority access to whatever gene bank materials they need.

See-Through Systems? Some public (institutional) breeders while acknowledging their situation and limitations can't see how they can get "there" from "here." How is it possible to work with so many species for so many environments? How is it possible to work with peasants? To do so will require a social re-organization of scientific research. However, peasant organizations have never been better prepared to meet these challenges. Communications technologies make it vastly easier to maintain a constant exchange of research information between all the concerned parties. Conventional public researchers and peasant breeders could and should be able to work together.

*In the early 1980s, the seed industry trade group, ASSINSEL, lobbied strenuously for worldwide adoption of plant breeder's rights (patent-like protection for corporate plant breeders). ASSINSEL's booklet, **Feeding the 500 Million,** argued that breeders' rights would be essential to stimulate plant breeding and feed the world's hungry. Thirty years later, corporate breeders have patented more ornamentals than food crops. And the 500 million hungry have more than doubled in number. Let them eat roses and chrysanthemums!*

Today's climate change emergency should also encourage policymakers to consider a "tried-and-true" participatory breeding strategy that brought tremendous plant diversity to a range of new ecosystems in one country. Between the 1860s and 1920s, the U.S. Department of Agriculture annually mailed millions of small packets of experimental seeds to farmers throughout the United States. Farmers in much of the country were breaking sod for the first time and there were few certainties about growing conditions. The initiative was highly successful. Tens of thousands of farmers/plant breeders produced their own varieties, exchanged seed with their neighbors, and turned their country into a breadbasket. *Today, national and international gene banks should follow USDA's example, multiply appropriate seed stocks, and—working with peasant organizations—send small packets of experimental seed to producers around the world.*

POLICYMAKERS SHOULD CONSIDER:

1. Reorienting breeding programs to ensure both seasonal and long-term species and genetic diversity.

2. Promoting "bulk population" breeding strategies for developing materials that can withstand extreme weather events.

3. Eliminating intellectual property regimes or unnecessary phytosanitary regulations that privilege genetic uniformity.

4. Prohibiting any measures—public or private—that constrain the right of peasants to save or exchange food genetic resources.

5. Introducing a seed multiplication program through gene banks to distribute experimental seed packets to peasant organizations for distribution to interested members.

QUESTION 5

How Can We Protect and Improve Biological Controls and Soil Nutrients to Safeguard Food and Reduce Reliance on Synthetic Chemicals?

Peak Oil Meets Peak Soil. As we struggle to feed the world in the decades ahead, we either will not have—or will not be able to afford—fossil carbon to drive farm machinery or to provide synthetic fertilizers and pesticides. Studies suggest, however, that pests and diseases will migrate around the world putting new pressures on productivity. Even in the regions expected to benefit from climate change (northern USA, Canada and much of Western Europe) increased temperatures and CO_2 levels portend a boom in rusts, blight and insects and, most worryingly, a speedup in the pace of disease and insect mutation. Microbes play a crucial role in climate mitigation. Soil organic matter, as FAO points out, is the major global storage reservoir for carbon (not forests). Microbe diversity turns this material into soil nutrients beneficial to crops and contributes to climate regulation and stabilization. An estimated 140–170 million tons of nitrogen, for example, are fixed by microbes worldwide annually—equivalent to US $90 billion worth of nitrogen fertilizers. (By comparison, the big seven fertilizer companies have total annual sales of less than $5 billion.) The use of synthetic fertilizer is a major contributor to emissions of nitrous oxide in agriculture.

Global fertilizer production has risen more than 31% since the World Food Summit of 1996 and is expected to climb further with the expansion of the industrial food chain's promotion of agrofuels and the removal of cellulose fiber from fields. Already, fertilizers account for 1.2% of total GHG emissions equivalent to the total emissions from countries like Indonesia or Brazil.

Monocultures of genetically uniform crops deplete microbial diversity while increasing crop vulnerability. The best way to ensure that beneficial microbe diversity maintains soil nutrients is to promote the species and genetic diversity already discussed.

POLICYMAKERS SHOULD CONSIDER:

1. Expanding public research on the beneficial use of microbes for soil fertility and as biocontrol agents.

2. Working with peasants to monitor beneficial microbe environments as well as the advance of new pests and diseases.

3. Through regulation and education, encourage moves away from dependence on fossil carbons.

QUESTION 6

How Can We Strengthen Local Food Production to Reduce Energy Dependence and Increase Food Quality?

Can the industrial food chain be made more efficient and effective? The total energy in the food system in OECD states is approximately 4 kcal invested to supply 1 kcal of food, while in the global South, the ratio is approximately 1 kcal invested to supply 1 kcal of food.

If you live in an OECD country, there is an almost automatic assumption that the whole world is part of a globalized food chain. This is entirely wrong. It bears repeating that 85% of the world's cultivated food is grown and consumed domestically (i.e., if not within sight of the farm, at least within the same country or eco-region). The percentage of world food sold through the industrial food chain is uncertain but likely includes almost all of the 15% that is exported across national borders and the vast majority of food marketed in OECD countries.

It is equally likely that the majority of the world's food does not depend upon industry-based agricultural inputs. In 1996, for example, FAO estimated that 1.4 billion people depend upon farm-saved seed. That figure roughly equaled the total number of peasant farmers at that time. While peasants may occasionally purchase seed or fertilizer or pesticides, the majority (either by choice or by necessity) produce their food without external inputs. In other words, "conventional" food production is not industrialized while "unconventional" production is dependent upon a globalized industrial system. *The web is much bigger than the chain.*

Setting aside small farm production, at least 15% of the global South's consumed food in rural areas isn't cultivated and at least 25% of its urban food is grown by urban-dwelling peasants who are not associated with the industrial food chain. Conservatively, then, at least 20% of the global South's food supply comes from the uncalculated "hidden harvest" of rural and urban production. This figure must, at the very least, be added to the productivity of peasant farmers and pastoralists. In other words, not less than 70% of the South's food supply is the work of peasants.

POLICYMAKERS SHOULD CONSIDER:

1. Making urban and peri-urban food production a national priority.
2. Developing special breeding initiatives intended to support urban agriculture.
3. Supporting peasant-based food production and facilitating direct peasant-consumer marketing arrangements, with special attention to the role of women.
4. Encouraging organic production.

QUESTION 7

How Can We Minimize Loss and Waste Throughout the Food System?

Waste to Waist. The industrial chain is enormously wasteful. Food spoilage in the industrial food system's markets is higher (+/–30%) because of distance, time, storage, and other wasteful (including consumer) practices. One study estimates that U.S. households throw out 1.28 lbs. of food a day in their trash (14% of all meats, grains, fruits and vegetables coming into the home), the equivalent of $43 billion worth of food. On top of that, commercial retail food establishments (convenience stores, fast-food, groceries) throw away 27 million tons of food annually.

Even recognizing that the majority of the world's hungry live in tropical or sub-tropical areas where food losses—from field to fork—are often devastating, the industrial food chain—mostly in temperate climes with better storage—is unconscionably wasteful. A 2009 industry survey of the most efficient UK food supply chains concluded that on average, 20% of costs in the chain add no value.

> Of the 3,900 calories available to the average U.S. consumer daily, 1,100 calories are wasted.

During the World Food Summit in November 2009, the U.S. National Institute of Diabetes and Digestive and Kidney Diseases reported that, since the previous food crisis of 1974, U.S. food wastage had risen from 28% to 40% of the country's total food supply—an average per capita waste of 1,400 kilocalories a day (nationally, 150 trillion kilocalories a year). This figure does not take into account the calorie loss from turning grain into meat and dairy products or from wasting good food on fat waists. The environmental damage is also substantial: the unnecessary consumption of more than 300 million barrels of oil a year and a quarter of the U.S. freshwater supply to make food that goes uneaten.

As a result of breeding for high yields and factory farming practices, U.S. and UK data show that essential nutrients in the food supply have declined in recent decades, with double-digit percentage declines of iron, zinc, calcium, selenium, etc. A 2009 study reports declines of 5% to 40% or more in some minerals in vegetables and fruits. Fewer nutrients per serving translate into less nutrition per calorie served. Fast-growing plants tend to dilute nutrient concentrations. In addition, high levels of nitrogen fertilizers reduce nutrient density and flavour. Similarly, Green Revolution wheat varieties bred for higher yields contain diminished protein content.

When the industrial food chain moves south, the waste and the expense come along with it. On average, the South's urban consumers spend at least 30% more on food than rural consumers and, still, their average calorie intake is lower. Studies show that poor urbanites spend as much as 60–80% of family income on food—and that their lack of cash translates more directly into food shortages and malnutrition than for their country cousins. It is hard to see how the industrial food chain can shake off its wasteful habits. Eighty percent of all research on food and agriculture concentrates not on farm-based food production but on food processing and retailing. And 96% of this research takes place in OECD countries. Despite industry's attempts to make the chain more efficient and profitable, the losses and abuses are staggering.

POLICYMAKERS SHOULD CONSIDER:

1. Reducing post-harvest losses (including consumer waste) as an important strategy for food security.

2. Recognizing and reversing industrial breeding strategies that diminish essential nutrients of food crops.

QUESTION 8

How Can We Ensure That Food Is Nutritious, Adequate, Appropriate, and Accessible to All?

After decades of consolidation, the world's largest grocery retailers occupy the most powerful position on the agroindustrial food chain. The top 100 global food retailers—with sales of US $1.8 trillion in 2007—account for 35% of all grocery sales worldwide. The top 3 mega-grocery retailers—Wal-Mart, Carrefour and Tesco—account for 50% of the revenues earned by the top 10 companies. In a single decade, Latin American markets saw the same level of supermarket penetration that took five decades in USA and

Europe. The pace of market penetration continues in Asia, and now Africa.

In South Africa, four supermarket chains control 94.5% of the retail food market. The country's 1,700 supermarkets (most of which have been established since 1994) have displaced an estimated 350,000 "spazas" (Mom 'n Pop food shops). Giant grocery retailers also have major impacts on the other end of the food chain—buying or contracting with farmers. Wal-Mart says it will buy from more than one million Chinese farmers by 2011. Retail giants (including Tesco, Metro, Car-refour, Wal-Mart) advise governments on WTO compliance and *codex alimentarius* regulations. The impact of food retailers on diet and obesity is undeniable. In Guatemala, for example, a proudly indigenous country and homeland to global crops like maize and beans, the expansion of supermarket chains has been especially damaging to the nutrition of poor consumers who are pressed to buy cheap, highly processed pastries, cookies and crackers instead of their native staples. A 2007 study found that a 1% increase in supermarket purchases translates into a 41% decline in maize calorie consumption and a 6.5% falloff in bean consumption.

POLICYMAKERS SHOULD CONSIDER:

1. Regulatory incentives to protect and enhance local markets, local production and consumption.

2. Before allowing the entry of global retail food giants: examine the social and economic impacts of oligopolistic retail food markets, including potential impacts on peasant food producers (both rural and urban), the survival of small businesses in the formal and informal sectors, and the nutrition and diets of poor consumers.

3. Insuring that food retailers do not exploit agricultural workers in the global South through labor contracts or procurement standards.

4. Rejecting industry-driven food safety and phytosanitary standards and so-called "sustainable" procurement standards that discriminate against peasant farmers and small-scale businesses.

5. Incorporating the Right to Food in binding law, nationally and internationally.

QUESTION 9

How Can We Be Sure That Peasant Producers Have Equitable and Stable Production and Marketing Arrangements?

Chain Reaction? There is growing recognition and support for peasant farmers and their role in confronting the food and climate crisis. The first-ever independent global assessment of agricultural science and technology, the International Assessment of Agricultural Knowledge, Science & Technology (IAASTD), sponsored by the World Bank, the Food & Agriculture Organization and other U.N. agencies, warns that the world can't rely on technological fixes—such as transgenic crops—to solve systemic problems of persistent hunger, poverty and environmental crises, and affirms the crucial role of small-scale farmers and low-impact farming.

UNEP's February 2009 report, *The Environmental Food Crisis*, calls for a global micro-financing fund to boost small-scale farmer productivity and the development of diversified and resilient eco-agriculture systems that provide critical ecosystem services, as well as adequate food to meet local needs. The *Córdoba Call for Coherence and Action on Food Security and Climate Change* asserts that the interests of peasant producers must be at the center of the food and climate debate and that "excessive reliance on market-based approaches is a mistake." The authors of the Call are food and agriculture specialists and include the first and current UN Special Rapporteurs on the Right to Food.

Peasants must take the lead in developing strategies—including technological strategies—to meet the food and climate crises. This doesn't mean abandoning the potential for conventional science. The Western model of science and technology has developed micro-techniques that can have macro-applications—high-tech advances that are often widely deployed. By contrast, peasant research often develops macro-technologies for micro-environments—that is, wide-tech and complex, integrated strategies that are location specific. Over the last hundred years since the rediscovery of Mendel's law, these two scientific solitudes have rarely been integrated. These strategies can only be brought together appropriately when leadership comes from the peasant organizations that are both closest to the land and closest to the hungry. Food sovereignty—the right of nations and peoples to democratically determine their own food systems—is paramount.

POLICYMAKERS SHOULD CONSIDER:

1. Most international agricultural policies dictated by free trade agreements and international financial institutions work against peasant farming systems. These policies have aggravated hunger and contributed to unsustainable farming practices. The seriousness of today's crises demands that policymakers revoke failed agricultural trade policies.

2. Supporting farmers and small producers to remain on the land and maintain their livelihoods through access to land, water, credit and markets. Respect and uphold resource rights, including the right to save and exchange seed and genetic resources. This includes Farmers' Rights, Livestock Keepers' Rights, and "aquatic rights."

3. Supporting proposals for food sovereignty put forth by the world's largest peasant organizations, fishers, pastoralists and other important small producers, environmentalists and consumer networks, in the Nyeleni World Forum for Food Sovereignty, organized in Mali 2007 (see box, on next page).

CONCLUSION

In the final analysis, there is no reason to be sanguine. We are deeply in trouble and there is no guarantee that humanity will rise to the challenges ahead. Neither the industrial food chain nor the peasant web has all that is necessary to get us through our compounding crises. The industrial food chain—rigid, reductionist and centrally regulated—doesn't have the resilience to respond to the current food crisis or the coming climate chaos. The peasant system—diverse, decentralized, and dynamic—has the natural resources, research capacity and resilience to better meet the challenges ahead. It is not the capacity or competence of the peasant system that we need to worry about, it is the lack of capacity and incompetence of government and science to "scale up" their systems to meet the potential of peasant provisioning.

Annex: Peasants—Counting Up

While statisticians think in terms of 1.5 billion (or so) smallholder farmers, the more realistic figure is probably double that number when full account is taken of the urban gardeners and livestock keepers, nomadic pastoralists, fishers and forest-keepers around the world. Urban gardeners often move back and forth between town and country and fishers often farm as well. Here is a different calculation…

Farmers. Of the 450 million farms, 382 million (85%) have 2 hectares or less and statisticians customarily refer to them as smallholders or peasants. Close to 380 million peasant farms are in the global South, meaning that at least 1.5 billion people per farm) live there. Very significantly, 370 million are indigenous peasants on at least 92 million farms. In total, peasants probably have significantly more than half of the world's cropland. Of the global 1.56 billion hectares in arable and permanent crops (many countries classify "peasants" as holding 5 hectares or less), 764 million hectares could be held by peasants and not less than 225 million are held by big farmers. Mid-size farmers would then hold 571 million hectares (or an average of 36.8 ha). In some definitions, some researchers

---

Six Pillars of Food Sovereignty from Nyeleni 2007

Focuses on Food for People, putting the right to food at the centre of food, agriculture, livestock and fisheries policies; *and rejects* the proposition that food is just another commodity or component for international agri-business.

Values Food Providers and respects their rights; and rejects those policies, actions and programmes that undervalue them, threaten their livelihoods and eliminate them.

Localises Food Systems, bringing food providers and consumers closer together; *and rejects* governance structures, agreements and practices that depend on and promote unsustainable and inequitable international trade and give power to remote and unaccountable corporations.

Puts Control Locally over territory, land, grazing, water, seeds, livestock and fish populations; *and rejects*

the privatisation of natural resources through laws, commercial contracts and intellectual property rights regimes.

Builds Knowledge and Skills that conserve, develop and manage localised food production and harvesting systems; *and rejects* technologies that undermine, threaten or contaminate these, e.g. genetic engineering.

Works with Nature in diverse, agroecological production and harvesting methods that maximise ecosystem functions and improve resilience and adaptation, especially in the face of climate change; *and rejects* energy-intensive industrialised methods which damage the environment and contribute to global warming.

---

tend to incorporate peasant "farms" that have much less than one-tenth of a hectare per person. The inclusion of these almost-landless peasants into productivity calculations grossly distorts the productivity of most peasant farms.

Pastoralists. An estimated 640 million peasant farmers and an additional 190 million pastoralists raise livestock for their own consumption and local markets. Since pastoralists move about and routinely cross national boundaries, they are seldom included in food security calculations.

Fishers. There are about 30-35 million peasant fishers but probably more than 100 million peasants are involved in fishing, processing and distributing what amounts to half the world's fish caught for direct human consumption (or 30 million metric tons). These figures, however, only speak to peasant production for the market and not the fishing and—aquaculture activities of indigenous—peoples or rural and urban peasants outside the market. In total, 2.9 billion people get 15% or more of their protein from ocean or freshwater fish. In the poorest countries, 18.5% of protein

comes from artisanal (small scale and/or subsistence) fishers. Unlike most commercial fisheries and ocean-going fish factories, peasant fishers focus almost exclusively on fish for human consumption as opposed to fishmeal for livestock feed.

Urban Gardeners. Before the current food crisis, an estimated 800 million peasants were involved in urban farming. Of these, 200 million produce food primarily for urban markets and manage to provide full-time employment for about 150 million family members. On average, the world's cities produce about one-third of their own food consumption. In times of high food prices, the amount of urban and peri-urban gardening and livestock-keeping increases significantly.

Hunters and Gatherers. It is not possible to quantify the proportion of the food supply that comes from forests, roadsides, and other "marginal" land. We do know that at least 410 million people live in—or adjacent to—forests and derive much of their food and livelihood from forests. In total, 1.6 billion people get some portion of their food and livelihood from forests around the world.

REFERENCES

Agriculture Canada, Market Information Service. 1994. *Livestock Market Report, 1993*. Ottawa: Agriculture Canada.

Animal Alliance of Canada. 1991. "Enviro Facts about Livestock Production (compiled from World Watch Paper No. 103). Toronto: Animal Alliance of Canada.

Anonymous. 1988a. "Position of the American Dietetic Association: Vegetarian Diets." *Journal of the American Dietetic Association* 3: 351–355.

Anonymous. 1988b. "The Vegetarian Advantage." *Health* 20 (October): 18.

Barnard, Neal D. 1990. *The Power of Your Plate*. Summertown, TN: Book Publishing.

Berry, Wendell. 1996. *The Unsettling of American Culture and Agriculture*. Berkeley: University of California Press.

British Medical Association. 1992. *Our Genetic Future: The Science and Ethics of Genetic Technology*. Oxford: Oxford University Press.

Chen, Junshi. 1990. *Diet, Lifestyle and Mortality in China: A Study of 65 Chinese Counties*. Ithaca, NY: Cornell University Press.

Coe, Sue. 1995. *Dead Meat*. New York: Four Walls Eight Windows.

Collins, Mark, ed. 1990. *The Last Rain Forests: A World Conservation Atlas*. New York: Oxford University Press.

Durning, Alan T. and Brough, Holly B. 1995. "Animal Farming and the Environment." In *Just Environments: Intergenerational, International and Interspecies Issues*. Ed. David E. Cooper and Joy A. Palmer. London: Routledge.

Edelman, P. D. et al. 2005. "*In Vitro*-Cultured Meat Production." *Tissue Engineering* 11, No. 5/6: 659–662.

Eisnetz, Gail. 1997. *Slaughterhouse*. Buffalo: Prometheus Books.

Fiddes, Nick. 1991. *Meat: A Natural Symbol*. London: Routledge.

Fox, Michael Allen. 1999. *Deep Vegetarianism*. Philadelphia: Temple University Press.

Fox, Michael W. 1992. *Superpigs and Wondercorn: The Brave New World of Biotechnology and Where It All May Lead*. New York: Lyons & Burford.

Gold, Mark. 2004. "The Global Benefits of Eating Less Meat" (a 76-page report). Compassion in World Farming Trust. www.cifw.org.uk/education/eat.html

Gore, Albert. 1993. *Earth in the Balance: Ecology and the Human Spirit*. New York: Plume.

Government of Canada. 1991. *The State of Canada's Environment*. Ottawa: Supply and Services Canada.

Greenpeace International. 2006a. *Eating Up the Amazon* (a 64-page report). 6 April.

Greenpeace International. 2006b. "Greenpeace closes Amazon soya facilities in Brazil and Europe." 22 May press release. www.greenpeace.org.uk/forests

Greenpeace International. 2006c. "Greenpeace prevents soya from Amazon rain forest destruction entering Europe." 7 April press release. www.greenpeace.org/international/press/releases/greenpeace-prevents-soya-from-2

Guardian Weekly. 2006. "China's Expanding Girth." 25–31 August: 2.

Hill, John Lawrence. 1996. *The Case for Vegetarianism: Philosophy for a Small Planet*. Lanham, MD: Rowman & Littlefield.

Lappé, Frances Moore. 1992. *Diet for a Small Planet* (20th ed.). New York: Ballantine.

Lovejoy, Thomas E. 1986. "Species Leave the Ark One by One." In *The Preservation of Species: The Value of Biological Diversity*. Ed. Brian G. Norton. Princeton: Princeton University Press.

Mason, Jim and Singer, Peter. 1990. *Animal Factories* (rev. ed.). New York: Harmony Books.

McKisson, Nicki and MacRae-Campbell, Linda. 1990. *The Future of Our Tropical Rainforests*. Tucson: Zephyr Press.

Melina, Vesanto and Davis, Brenda. 2003. *The New Becoming Vegetarian: The Essential Guide to a Healthy Vegetarian Diet* (2nd rev. ed.). Summer-town, TN: Healthy Living Publications.

Myers, Norman. 1984. *The Primary Source: Tropical Forests and Our Future*. New York: Norton.

Pearce, Fred. 2006. "The Parched Planet." *New Scientist*, 26 February: 32–36.

Pimentel, David. 1990. "Environmental and Social Implications of Waste in U.S. Agriculture and

Food Sectors." *Journal of Agricultural Ethics* 3: 5–20.

Porritt, Jonathon. 2006. "Hard facts to swallow." *Guardian Weekly*, 13–19 January: 18.

Reuters. 2005. "Scientists propose growing artificial meat." 7 July dispatch. www.msnbc.msn.com/id/ 8498629/

Rice, Pamela. 2004. *101 Reasons Why I'm a Vegetarian*. New York: Lantern Books.

Rifkin, Jeremy. 1992. *Beyond Beef: The Rise and Fall of the Cattle Culture*. New York: Dutton.

Robbins, John. 1987. *Diet for a New America*. Walpole, NH: Stillpoint.

Rollin, Bernard E. 1995. *The Frankenstein Syndrome: Ethical and Social Issues in The Genetic Engineering of Animals*. New York: Cambridge University Press.

Saunders, Kerrie K. 2003. *The Vegan Diet as Chronic Disease Prevention: Evidence Supporting the New Four Food Groups*. New York: Lantern Books.

Smithsonian Institution. 2002. "Smithsonian researchers show Amazonian deforestation accelerating." *Science Daily Online*, 15 January. www.science-daily.com/ releases/2002/01/020115075118.htm

Spallone, Pat. 1992. *Generation Games: Genetic Engineering and the Future for Our Lives*. Philadelphia: Temple University Press.

Starke, Linda, ed. 2006. *State of the World 2006*. Washington, DC: World Watch Institute.

Stevens, William K. 1998. "Plant Species Threats Cited." *The Globe and Mail* (Toronto), 9 April: A15.

Tudge, Colin. 2004a. "It's a Meat Market." *New Scientist*, 13 March: 19.

———, 2004b. *So Shall We Reap: What's Gone Wrong with the World's Food—and How to Fix It*. Harmondsworth, Middlesex: Penguin.

U.N. Food and Agricultural Organization. 1995. *Dimensions of Need: An Atlas of Food and Agriculture*. Santa Barbara: ABC-CLIO.

University of Washington Students. n.d. "Rape of Mother Earth." www.students.washington.edu/ careuw/rapeofmotherearth.pdf

U.S. Congress, Office of Technology Assessment. 1985. *Technology, Public Policy, and the Changing Structure of American Agriculture: A Special Report for the 1985 Farm Bill*. Washington, DC: US Government Printing Office.

U.S. National Research Council. 1989. *Diet and Health: Implications for Reducing Chronic Disease Risk*. Washington, DC: National Academy Press.

White, Randall and Frank, Erica. 1994. "Health Effects and Prevalence of Vegetarianism." *Western Journal of Medicine* 160: 465–471.

Wilson, Edward O. 1993. *The Diversity of Life*. New York: Norton.

World Watch. 2004. "Is Meat Sustainable?" (editorial). *World Watch Magazine* 17(4), July/August.

STUDY QUESTIONS

1. Fox argues that our food choices have consequences that extend beyond our personal lives and that we should take responsibility for them. What do you think of his argument?

2. If you were convinced that eating meat is morally wrong, would you give it up? Why, or why not?

3. Toward the end of this reading, Fox alleges that humans have a "manipulative mindset" in relation to the natural world. Is animal agriculture part of this mindset? Discuss.

4. What sort of diet, in your opinion, would be consistent with the principle that humans ought to minimize their impact on the biosphere? Explain your answer.

5. If synthetic meat (meat made in laboratories) were widely available, would there remain any moral objection to eating meat? Defend your answer.

FOR FURTHER READING

Aiken, William, and Hugh LaFollette, eds., *World Hunger and Moral Obligation,* 2nd ed., Englewood Cliffs, N. J.: Prentice Hall, 1996. The best collection of readings available, containing four of the readings in this chapter, plus others of great importance.

Ehrlich, Paul. *The Population Bomb.* New York: Ballantine Books, 1971. An important work, warning of the dangers of the population explosion.

Lappé, Francis, and Joseph Collins. *Food First: Beyond the Myth of Scarcity.* New York: Ballantine Books, 1978. An attack on Neo-Malthusians like Hardin in which the authors argue that we have abundant resources to solve the world's hunger problems.

O'Neill, Onora. *Faces of Hunger.* London: Allen & Unwin, 1986. A penetrating Kantian discussion of the principles and problems surrounding world hunger.

Rifkin, Jeremy. *Beyond Beef.* New York: Plume, 1993.

Simon, Arthur. *Bread for the World.* New York: Paulist Press, 1975. A poignant discussion of the problem of world hunger from a Christian perspective with some thoughtful solutions.

Chapter 8

Climate Change and Energy Policy

WHAT IS THE GREENHOUSE EFFECT? Atmospheric gases keep our planet warm in a manner analogous to the glass panes of a greenhouse. The Sun's rays (energy in the form of light) are allowed in through the glass, but the heat that is then generated is trapped by the glass. The same phenomenon occurs when you keep your car windows closed on a sunny day. The heat is trapped inside, so it is warmer in the car than it is outside.

Likewise, the Sun's energy reaches Earth in the form of light, infrared radiation, and small amounts of ultraviolet radiation. Earth's surface absorbs much of this solar energy, some of which is used for photosynthesis, and transforms it to heat energy, which rises back into the troposphere (the innermost layer of the atmosphere, occupying the area about 11 above sea level). But water vapor (mostly in the form of clouds), carbon dioxide (CO_2), methane, and other gases block some of the heat energy from escaping, like the panes of the greenhouse. They absorb the heat and warm Earth. Without this heat-trapping blanket, Earth's surface would cool to about 0°F (−18°C) instead of maintaining an average temperature of 57°F (14°C). Most of our planet would be frozen like Mars.

The problem, then, is not the greenhouse process but its *increased* activity. It's too much of a good thing. For the past 8000 years, Earth's average temperature has never been warmer than 1°C, and the last time it was 2°C warmer was 125,000 years ago. Hansen and others have presented evidence that Earth has begun to get warmer and by current trends the polar ice caps will gradually melt, causing a rise in the ocean's level of anywhere from 6 to 9 feet. Millions of people living on islands and along coastlines would be displaced as their land was flooded by the oceans. While people in northern Canada, northern Russia, and Greenland might rejoice over warmer weather, most of the temperate zones would become much warmer. Air conditioner use would increase, demanding more energy and creating more pollution, which in turn would create a greater greenhouse effect. Weather patterns would change, negatively affecting agriculture and causing global starvation.

In the last few years the issue of climate change has finally received governmental attention. The question now is: what are we going to do? The proposal is to turn over the solution to market forces: on the one hand to offer incentives for "green technologies"; and on the other to create a "cap-and-trade" system, which would cap the total allowable amount of carbon we could release by issuing a fixed number of carbon credits, but would allow these carbon credits to be traded. The environmental movement is fractured as to how to proceed: one branch sees the economic takeover of the environmental movement as a sign of its success; the other sees it as a sell out to large corporations.

The first three essays offer an introduction to the science behind our understanding of climate change as well as the observed and predicted impacts. Together they make the argument that urgent action is needed. But although there is consensus that action is needed, there is vast difference of opinion as to what that action should be. The last four essays examine the growing resistance to proposed technological solutions, examining both the proposals (such as carbon capture and storage, bio-fuels, etc.) and the global social concerns.

42

Understanding the Causes of Global Climate Change

PEW CENTER ON GLOBAL CLIMATE CHANGE

The Pew Center on Global Climate Change is a nonprofit organization dedicated to bringing "together business leaders, policy makers, scientists, and other experts to bring a new approach to a complex and often controversial issue. Our approach is based on sound science, straight talk, and a belief that we can work together to protect the climate while sustaining economic growth." For further up-to-date information, visit their web site (from which this section was taken) at http://www.pewclimate.org.

Average air temperatures at the Earth's surface have increased by approximately 0.6°C (1°F) over the 20th century. Analysis of the various human and natural influences on the global climate indicates that this warming cannot be explained without taking into account human emissions of greenhouse gases (GHGs). Furthermore, current analyses indicate that GHGs have been the dominant force driving temperature increases over the past 50 years.

INTRODUCTION

Recent decades have seen record-high average global surface air temperatures. The years 1998,

2002, and 2003 were the three warmest years recorded in the instrumental record (which dates back to the mid-1800s). In fact, all of the top 10 warmest years on record have occurred since 1990. These record warm years are the result of a century of global warming. Between 1900 and 2000, global surface air temperatures increased by 0.4–0.8°C (0.7–1.4°F). Over the past 30 years, temperatures in the lower atmosphere, or troposphere, have warmed by 0.07–0.1°C (0.1–0.2°F) per decade.

This warming has resulted from numerous factors that influence climate. Some of these factors are natural, such as changes in solar radiation and volcanic activity. Others, particularly emissions of greenhouse gases (GHGs) and land-use changes, are human in origin. Determining their relative contributions to observed climate change is a difficult task. Nevertheless, the current scientific consensus is that, at least over the past 50 years, the major factor driving observed temperature increases has been human emissions of GHGs.

How have scientists arrived at this conclusion? Climate varies considerably over annual to millennial time-scales, and a change in global temperatures alone does not indicate human influence. The attribution of climate change to specific factors requires an analysis of the long-term temperature increases and the factors that could be responsible for those increases.

CLIMATE OVER THE PAST MILLENNIUM

Determining climate patterns over many centuries is difficult because of the absence of instrumental temperature records before the mid-1800s. A number of attempts at reconstructing a temperature record of the northern hemisphere over the past 1000 years have used "proxy" indicators of temperature, such as tree rings, coral reefs, and ice cores.

Despite significant uncertainties, the studies yield consistent results, indicating that the Northern Hemisphere was in a relative warm phase between 1000 and 1400 AD; followed by a prolonged cool phase until the 1800s. These studies also indicate that the last 50 years were probably warmer than

any time period during the previous 1000 years … and recent data suggest that recent temperatures may be unprecedented over the past 2000 years.

THE FACTORS INFLUENCING CLIMATE

Climate varies considerably over time. This variability is a response to climate "forcings"—factors that cause warming or cooling of the atmosphere. Over most of the Earth's history, such forcings have been exclusively natural, and include variability in solar radiation, the Earth's orbit, and the frequency or intensity of volcanic activity. However, since the industrial revolution, human activities have had an increasing influence on the global climate system.

Greenhouse gases. Collectively, GHGs have enhanced the greenhouse effect, contributing to global warming over the past century. Carbon dioxide (CO_2), methane (CH_4), nitrous oxide (N_2O), and tropospheric ozone have all increased well above their pre-industrial concentrations. Various industrial GHGs that were previously absent from the atmosphere have also accumulated.

Land-use changes. Land-use changes have influenced the reflectivity of the Earth's surface, resulting in either a warming or a cooling depending on the change. Deforestation and agricultural activities have a net cooling effect because cleared land surfaces reflect more solar radiation than rough or forested lands. Increased urbanization causes localized warming at the Earth's surface, known as the "Urban Heat Island" (UHI) effect. Despite suggestions that UHIs have contributed significantly to rectent warming, analysis of 20th century temperature observations indicates that they have had a relatively small effect on global warming trends. On a global scale, the net effects of land-use change are believed to have caused a net cooling of global temperatures since the industrial revolution.

Aerosols. Atmospheric particles, or aerosols, from industry and fossil fuel combustion also can cool or heat the Earth's surface and atmosphere. Sulfate aerosols reflect sunlight and contribute to cloud formation, both of which have a cooling effect. Black carbon aerosols (soot) warm the atmosphere by absorbing solar radiation, and have probably contributed significantly to observed global warming. They also shade the Earth's surface, which has a minor cooling effect. Although the exact magnitude of warming caused by black carbon aerosols is uncertain, some scientists have suggested that reductions in black carbon emissions as well as CO_2 may help slow the rate of global warming over the near-term.

Cosmic rays. In recent years, the influence of cosmic rays on the formation of clouds has been considered as a potential factor in long-term climate change. However, trends in cosmic rays and clouds over the 20th century suggest that cosmic rays are not a major factor influencing the climate change that is currently being observed.

Collectively, some of these factors have had an important influence on the global climate over the past 50 years.... [T]he dominant force has been GHGs, which have had a net warming effect. Natural changes in solar radiation have contributed to warming as well, but these are minor relative to the effects of GHGs. Other factors appear to have had a cooling effect, but not large enough to offset warming caused by GHGs.

CLIMATE CHANGE OVER THE 20TH CENTURY

There is uniform consensus that average surface air temperatures over the 20th century increased between 1900–1940, decreased slightly between 1940–1970, and increased again from 1970 to the present, based on the instrumental temperature record. The first step in determining the causes of climate change is to compare this pattern of warming with what is known about the various factors that have influenced climate over the 20th century.

1900–1940. Although the burning of fossil fuels was commonplace as early as the 1700s, CO_2 concentrations were only about 295 parts per million (ppm) by 1900, just 7% higher than pre-industrial levels of 270 ppm. The warming associated with this CO_2 increase is considered to be too small to account for the observed warming. However, natural factors, particularly increases in

solar radiation and a decline in volcanic activity, are well correlated with temperature over this time period, indicating that the warming was predominantly due to these two factors.

1940–1970. The cooling observed between 1940–1970 has been the cause of much speculation, because it is inconsistent with the larger picture of global warming over the 20th century. By 1970, concentrations of CO_2 were approximately 330 ppm, 20% above pre-industrial levels, yet cooling occurred. Again, natural factors appear to have played an important role. Solar radiation decreased between 1940–70, partly explaining the observed cooling. In addition, rapid increases in human emissions of sulfate aerosols probably played a significant role by shading the Earth's surface from solar radiation.

1970–present. Since 1970, atmospheric CO_2 has increased further to ~370 ppm, 30% above pre-industrial levels. By 2000, other GHGs, such as methane and nitrous oxide, were 100% and 15%, respectively, above their pre-industrial levels. The warming caused by this substantial increase in GHGs has exceeded the cooling associated with sulfate aerosols. Sulfur emissions were declining in the United States and Europe by the late 20th century due to air pollution regulations, although global emissions continue to increase. Solar radiation has been relatively stable over the late 20th century, except for the 11-year cycle of sunspot activity, which is not sufficient to account for the observed warming.

SUPPORTING EVIDENCE FROM CLIMATE MODELS

Analysis of the factors that can force climate changes and corresponding temperature changes over the 20th century provide strong evidence of a human influence on climate. Furthermore, statistical analyses detect human influences on climate that are distinct from natural variability. When only natural factors or human factors are included in climate models, results differ significantly from observations during certain time periods. Thus, climate models perform best at reproducing 20th century climate

---

B o x 1   Katrina and Global Warming

Was Katrina's Power a Product of Global Warming?

With a unique confluence of geography, expansive lowlands (particularly in the New Orleans area), wetland loss, deforestation, rapid development, large populations of the poor, and a heavy concentration of industry, the Gulf Coast is extremely vulnerable to hurricanes, with or without global warming. Katrina is not the first category 5 hurricane to hit the Gulf Coast (it actually weakened slightly to category 4 shortly before landfall in Louisiana and Mississippi); in fact, of the three previous similar events, two of them occurred in 1935 and 1969, prior to the period of most of the human-induced global warming that has occurred so far. Clearly, then, global warming is not required for an extremely intense hurricane to strike.

But can science tell us whether Katrina's destructiveness was related to global warming? Not directly: science, as a method, is not good at assigning causation for uncontrolled events, and no single weather event can be linked directly to a long-term driver, such as global warming. This inability to draw a definite conclusion, however, in no sense justifies the conclusion that global warming did not influence Katrina.

What science does offer on this question is a general understanding of the physics of tropical storms that can inform reasonable assessment. Because hurricanes draw strength from heat in ocean surface waters, warming the water should generate more powerful hurricanes, on average. Indeed, sea surface temperature records show that the oceans are more than 1 degree F warmer on average today compared to a century ago. On short time scales (days to months), temperatures fluctuate above and below the long-term average, and the water can be warmer or cooler than the average on any given day. But the higher the average, the more likely the water will be warm enough to produce a strong storm on any given day

during the hurricane season. Case in point: while Katrina was strengthening from a tropical storm to a category 5 hurricane, as it passed between the Florida Keys and the Gulf Coast, the surface waters in the Gulf of Mexico were unusually warm—about 2 degrees F warmer than normal for this time of year. From this "first-principles" perspective, then, it is no surprise that Katrina became a very powerful storm. While there is no method to determine whether global warming played a role, it is reasonable to say it increased the probability that the Gulf surface water would be unusually warm on any given day, as it was on August 29 when Katrina's intensity peaked.

Beyond inferences from our understanding of storm physics, is there evidence that storms are actually becoming more intense, as we would expect? A study published recently in Nature found that since the early 1950s, the average intensity of tropical storms has increased globally, and this trend correlates very well through time with the increase in average sea surface temperatures in the tropics. These data show a real trend that fits expectations from our basic understanding of climate, and a powerful storm like Katrina makes sense in this context.

So, although we cannot be certain global warming intensified Katrina per se, it clearly has created circumstances under which powerful storms are more likely to occur at this point in history (and in the future) than they were in the past. Moreover, it would be scientifically unsound to conclude that Katrina was not intensified by global warming. A reasonable assessment of the science suggests that we will face similar events again and that powerful storms are likely to happen more often than we have been accustomed to in the past.

SOURCE: The Pew Center on Global Climate Change. Used with permission.

---

observations when they include both human and natural factors. Furthermore, despite the importance of both natural and human factors in driving climate, human factors account for the majority of the observed increase in globally averaged surface air temperatures over the past 50 years. Thus, recent trends in surface air temperatures and atmospheric temperatures are the result of a significant human influence, specifically increases in atmospheric GHG concentrations.

CONCLUSIONS

The current state of knowledge regarding 20th century temperature changes is clear. Temperatures of recent decades, at least in the northern hemisphere, are likely warmer than at any point during at least the previous millennium, and the probability that an unknown factor other than GHGs can account for this warming is low. Thus, despite the long-term natural variability of the climate system, current scientific evidence indicates there is a significant human influence on current climate trends. This human contribution to global warming is projected to grow increasingly strong in future decades as human emissions of long-lived GHGs continue to alter the composition of the atmosphere.

STUDY QUESTIONS

1. In a paragraph, summarize the evidence that shows that the observed changes in world climate are due to human activity.

2. Browse The Pew Center on Global Climate Change's website: http://www.pewclimate.org/. What are the dangers of global warming?

3. Go to the above website, and also to http://www.ipcc.ch/, the website of the Intergovernmental Panel on Climate Change (IPCC). What new developments have occurred since the publication of this book?

43

Livestock's Role in Climate Change and Air Pollution

UN REPORT: CLIMATE CHANGE AND LIVESTOCK

This UN sponsored LEAD report argues that, "the livestock sector generates more greenhouse gas emissions as measured in CO_2 equivalent—18 percent—than transport." The essay provides exacting details as well as a careful introduction to climate change; see in particular Figure 1 for a global carbon accounting.

ISSUES AND TRENDS

The atmosphere is fundamental to life on earth. Besides providing the air we breathe it regulates temperature, distributes water, it is a part of key processes such as the carbon, nitrogen and oxygen cycles, and it protects life from harmful radiation. These functions are orchestrated, in a fragile dynamic equilibrium, by a complex physics and chemistry. There is increasing evidence that human activity is altering the mechanisms of the atmosphere.

In the following sections, we will focus on the anthropogenic processes of climate change and air pollution and the role of livestock in those processes

Livestock's Role in Climate Change and Air Pollution UN REPORT ftp://ftp.fao.org/docrep/fao/010/a0701e/a0701e03.pdf

(excluding the ozone hole). The contribution of the livestock sector as a whole to these processes is not well known. At virtually each step of the livestock production process substances contributing to climate change or air pollution are emitted into the atmosphere, or their sequestration in other reservoirs is hampered. Such changes are either the direct effect of livestock rearing, or indirect contributions from other steps on the long road that ends with the marketed animal product. We will analyse the most important processes in their order in the food chain, concluding with an assessment of their cumulative effect. Subsequently a number of options are presented for mitigating the impacts.

CLIMATE CHANGE: TRENDS AND PROSPECTS

Anthropogenic climate change has recently become a well-established fact and the resulting impact on the environment is already being observed. The greenhouse effect is a key mechanism of temperature regulation. Without it, the average temperature of the earth's surface would not be 15°C but −6°C. The earth returns energy received from the sun back to space by reflection of light and by emission of heat. A part of the heat flow is absorbed by so-called greenhouse gases, trapping it in the atmosphere. The principal greenhouse gases involved in this process include carbon dioxide (CO_2), methane (CH_4), nitrous oxide (N_2O) and chlorofluorocarbons. Since the beginning of the industrial period anthropogenic emissions have led to an increase in concentrations of these gases in the atmosphere, resulting in global warming. The average temperature of the earth's surface has risen by 0.6 Use °C. since the late 1800s.

Recent projections suggest that average temperature could increase by another 1.4 to 5.8 °C by 2100. Even under the most optimistic scenario, the increase in average temperatures will be larger than any century-long trend in the last 10 000 years of the present-day interglacial period. Ice-core-based climate records allow comparison of the current situation with that of preceding interglacial periods. The Antarctic Vostok ice core, encapsulating the last 420 000 years of Earth history, shows an overall remarkable correlation between greenhouse gases and climate over the four glacial-interglacial cycles (naturally recurring at intervals of approximately 100 000 years). These findings were recently confirmed by the Antarctic Dome C ice core, the deepest ever drilled, representing some 740 000 years—the longest, continuous, annual climate record extracted from the ice (EPICA, 2004). This confirms that periods of CO_2 build-up have most likely contributed to the major global warming transitions at the earth's surface. The results also show that human activities have resulted in present-day concentrations of CO_2 and CH_4 that are unprecedented over the last 650 000 years of earth history (Siegenthaler et al., 2005).

Global warming is expected to result in changes in weather patterns, including an increase in global precipitation and changes in the severity or frequency of extreme events such as severe storms, floods and droughts.

Climate change is likely to have a significant impact on the environment. In general, the faster the changes, the greater will be the risk of damage exceeding our ability to cope with the consequences. Mean sea level is expected to rise by 9–88 cm by 2100, causing flooding of low-lying areas and other damage. Climatic zones could shift poleward and uphill, disrupting forests, deserts, rangelands and other unmanaged ecosystems. As a result, many ecosystems will decline or become fragmented and individual species could become extinct (IPCC, 2001a).

The levels and impacts of these changes will vary considerably by region. Societies will face new risks and pressures. Food security is unlikely to be threatened at the global level, but some regions are likely to suffer yield declines of major crops and some may experience food shortages and hunger. Water resources will be affected as precipitation and evaporation patterns change around the world. Physical infrastructure will be damaged, particularly by the rise in sea-level and extreme weather events. Economic activities, human settlements, and human health will experience many direct and indirect effects. The poor and disadvantaged and more generally the less advanced countries are the most vulnerable to the negative consequences of climate change because of their weak capacity to develop coping mechanisms.

Global agriculture will face many challenges over the coming decades and climate change will complicate these. A warming of more than 2.5°C could reduce global food supplies and contribute to higher food prices. The impact on crop yields and productivity will vary considerably. Some agricultural regions, especially in the tropics and subtropics, will be threatened by climate change, while others, mainly in temperate or higher latitudes, may benefit.

The livestock sector will also be affected. Livestock products would become costlier if agricultural disruption leads to higher grain prices. In general, intensively managed livestock systems will be easier to adapt to climate change than will crop systems. Pastoral systems may not adapt so readily. Pastoral

communities tend to adopt new methods and technologies more slowly, and livestock depend on the productivity and quality of rangelands, some of which may be adversely affected by climate change. In addition, extensive livestock systems are more susceptible to changes in the severity and distribution of livestock diseases and parasites, which may result from global warming.

As the human origin of the greenhouse effect became clear, and the gas emitting factors were identified, international mechanisms were created to help understand and address the issue. The United Nations Framework Convention on Climate Change (UNFCCC) started a process of international negotiations in 1992 to specifically address the greenhouse effect. Its objective is to stabilize greenhouse gas concentrations in the atmosphere within an ecologically and economically acceptable

---

Box 2   The Kyoto Protocol

In 1995 the UNFCCC member countries began negotiations on a protocol—an international agreement linked to the existing treaty. The text of the so-called Kyoto Protocol was adopted unanimously in 1997; it entered into force on 16 February 2005.

The Protocol's major feature is that it has mandatory targets on greenhouse-gas emissions for those of the world's leading economies that have accepted it. These targets range from 8 percent below to 10 percent above the countries' individual 1990 emissions levels with a view to reducing their overall emissions of such gases by at least 5 percent below existing 1990 levels in the commitment period 2008 to 2012. In almost all cases—even those set at 10 percent above 1990 levels—the limits call for significant reductions in currently projected emissions.

To compensate for the sting of those binding targets, the agreement offers flexibility in how countries may meet their targets. For example, they may partially compensate for their industrial, energy and other emissions by increasing "sinks" such as forests, which remove carbon dioxide from the atmosphere, either on their own territories or in other countries.

Or they may pay foreign projects that result in greenhouse-gas cuts. Several mechanisms have been established for the purpose of emissions trading. The Protocol allows countries that have unused emissions

units to sell their excess capacity to countries that are over their targets. This so-called "carbon market" is both flexible and realistic. Countries not meeting their commitments will be able to buy compliance but the price may be steep. Trades and sales will deal not only with direct greenhouse gas emissions. Countries will get credit for reducing greenhouse gas totals by planting or expanding forests ("removal units") and for carrying out "joint implementation projects" with other developed countries—paying for projects that reduce emissions in other industrialized countries. Credits earned this way may be bought and sold in the emissions market or "banked" for future use.

The Protocol also makes provision for a "clean development mechanism," which allows industrialized countries to pay for projects in poorer nations to cut or avoid emissions. They are then awarded credits that can be applied to meeting their own emissions targets. The recipient countries benefit from free infusions of advanced technology that for example allow their factories or electrical generating plants to operate more efficiently—and hence at lower costs and higher profits. The atmosphere benefits because future emissions are lower than they would have been otherwise.

SOURCE: UNFCCC (2005).

timeframe. It also encourages research and monitoring of other possible environmental impacts, and of atmospheric chemistry. Through its legally binding Kyoto Protocol, the UNFCCC focuses on the direct warming impact of the main anthropogenic emissions (see Box 2). This chapter concentrates on describing the contribution of livestock production to these emissions. Concurrently it provides a critical assessment of mitigation strategies such as emissions reduction measures related to changes in livestock farming practices.

The direct warming impact is highest for carbon dioxide simply because its concentration and the emitted quantities are much higher than that of the other gases. Methane is the second most important greenhouse gas. Once emitted, methane remains in the atmosphere for approximately 9–15 years. Methane is about 21 times more effective in trapping heat in the atmosphere than carbon dioxide over a 100-year period. Atmospheric concentrations of CH_4 have increased by about 150 percent since pre-industrial times (Table 1), although the rate of increase has been declining recently. It is emitted from a variety of natural and human-influenced sources. The latter include landfills, natural gas and petroleum systems, agricultural activities, coal mining, stationary and mobile combustion, wastewater treatment and certain industrial process (US-EPA, 2005). The IPCC has estimated that slightly more than half of the current CH_4 flux to the atmosphere is anthropogenic (IPCC, 2001b). Total global anthropogenic CH_4 is estimated to be 320 million tonnes CH_4/yr, i.e. 240 million

tonnes of carbon per year (van Aardenne et al., 2001). This total is comparable to the total from natural sources (Olivier et al., 2002).

Nitrous oxide, a third greenhouse gas with important direct warming potential, is present in the atmosphere in extremely small amounts. However, it is 296 times more effective than carbon dioxide in trapping heat and has a very long atmospheric lifetime (114 years).

Livestock activities emit considerable amounts of these three gases. Direct emissions from livestock come from the respiratory process of all animals in the form of carbon dioxide. Ruminants, and to a minor extent also monogastrics, emit methane as part of their digestive process, which involves microbial fermentation of fibrous feeds. Animal manure also emits gases such as methane, nitrous oxides, ammonia and carbon dioxide, depending on the way they are produced (solid, liquid) and managed (collection, storage, spreading).

Livestock also affect the carbon balance of land used for pasture or feedcrops, and thus indirectly contribute to releasing large amounts of carbon into the atmosphere. The same happens when forest is cleared for pastures. In addition, greenhouse gases are emitted from fossil fuel used in the production process, from feed production to processing and marketing of livestock products. Some of the indirect effects are difficult to estimate, as land use related emissions vary widely, depending on biophysical factors as soil, vegetation and climate as well as on human-practices.

T A B L E 1   Past and current concentration of important greenhouse gases

Gas	Pre-industrial concentration (1 750)	Current tropospheric	Global warming concentration potential*
Carbon dioxide (CO_2)	277 ppm	382 ppm	1
Methane (CH_4)	600 ppb	1 728 ppb	23
Nitrous oxide (N_2O)	270–290 ppb	318 ppb	296

NOTE: ppm = parts per million; ppb = parts per billion; ppt = parts per trillion; *Direct global warming potential (GWP) relative to CO_2 for a 100 year time horizon. GWPs are a simple way to compare the potency of various greenhouse gases. The GWP of a gas depends not only on the capacity to absorb and reemit radiation but also on how long the effect lasts. Gas molecules gradually dissociate or react with other atmospheric compounds to form new molecules with different radiative properties.
SOURCE: WRI (2005); 2005 CO_2: NOAA (2006); GWPs: IPCC (2001b).

AIR POLLUTION: ACIDIFICATION AND NITROGEN DEPOSITION

Industrial and agricultural activities lead to the emission of many other substances into the atmosphere, many of which degrade the quality of the air for all terrestrial life.[1] Important examples of air pollutants are carbon monoxide, chlorofluorocarbons, ammonia, nitrogen oxides, sulphur dioxide and volatile organic compounds.

In the presence of atmospheric moisture and oxidants, sulphur dioxide and oxides of nitrogen are converted to sulphuric and nitric acids. These airborne acids are noxious to respiratory systems and attack some materials. These air pollutants return to earth in the form of acid rain and snow, and as dry deposited gases and particles, which may damage crops and forests and make lakes and streams unsuitable for fish and other plant and animal life. Though usually more limited in its reach than climate change, air pollutants carried by winds can affect places far (hundreds of kilometres if not further) from the points where they are released.

The stinging smell that sometimes stretches over entire landscapes around livestock facilities is partly due to ammonia emission.[2] Ammonia volatilization (nitrified in the soil after deposition) is among the most important causes of acidifying wet and dry atmospheric deposition, and a large part of it originates from livestock excreta. Nitrogen (N) deposition is higher in northern Europe than elsewhere (Vitousek *et al.*, 1997). Low-level increases in nitrogen deposition associated with air pollution have been implicated in forest productivity increases over large regions. Temperate and boreal forests, which historically have been nitrogen-limited, appear to be most affected. In areas that become nitrogen-saturated, other nutrients are leached from the soil, resulting eventually in forest diebaek—counteracting, or even overwhelming, any growth-enhancing effects of CO_2 enrichment. Research shows that in 7–18 percent of the global area of (semi-) natural ecosystems, N deposition substantially exceeds the critical load, presenting a risk of eutrophication and increased leaching (Bouwman and van Vuuren, 1999) and although knowledge of the impacts of N deposition at the global level is still limited, many biologically valuable areas may be affected (Phoenix *et al.*, 2006). The risk is particularly high in Western Europe, in large parts of which over 90 percent of the vulnerable ecosystems receive more than the critical load of nitrogen. Eastern Europe and North America are subject to medium risk levels. The results suggest that even a number of regions with low population densities, such as Africa and South America, remote regions of Canada and the Russian Federation, may become affected by N eutrophication.

LIVESTOCK IN THE CARBON CYCLE

The element carbon (C) is the basis for all life. It is stored in the major sinks shown in Figure 1 which also shows the relative importance of the main fluxes. The global carbon cycle can be divided into two categories: the geological, which operates over large time scales (millions of years), and the biological/physical, which operates at shorter time scales (days to thousands of years)

Ecosystems gain most of their carbon dioxide from the atmosphere. A number of autotrophic organisms[3] such as plants have specialized mechanisms that allow for absorption of this gas into their cells. Some of the carbon in organic matter produced in plants is passed to the heterotrophic animals that eat them, which then exhale it into the atmosphere in the form of carbon dioxide. The CO_2 passes from there into the ocean by simple diffusion.

Carbon is released from ecosystems as carbon dioxide and methane by the process of respiration that takes place in both plants and animals. Together, respiration and decomposition (respiration mostly by bacteria and fungi that consumes organic matter) return the biologically fixed carbon back to the atmosphere. The amount of carbon taken up by photosynthesis and released back to the atmosphere by respiration each year is 1 000 times greater than the amount of carbon that moves through the geological cycle on an annual basis.

direct use by plants and animals. This shortage of fixed nitrogen has historically posed natural limits to food production and hence to human populations.

However, since the third decade of the twentieth century, the Haber-Bosch process has provided a solution. Using extremely high pressures, plus a catalyst composed mostly of iron and other critical chemicals, it became the primary procedure responsible for the production of chemical fertilizer. Today, the process is used to produce about 100 million tonnes of artificial nitrogenous fertilizer per year. Roughly 1 percent of the world's energy is used for it (Smith, 2002).

A large share of the world's crop production is fed to animals, either directly or as agro-industrial by-products. Mineral N fertilizer is applied to much of the corresponding cropland, especially in the case of high-energy crops such as maize, used in the production of concentrate feed. The gaseous emissions caused by fertilizer manufacturing should, therefore, be considered among the emissions for which the animal food chain is responsible.

About 97 percent of nitrogen fertilizers are derived from synthetically produced ammonia via the Haber-Bosch process. For economic and environmental reasons, natural gas is the fuel of choice in this manufacturing process today. Natural gas is expected to account for about one-third of global energy use in 2020, compared with only one-fifth in the mid-1990s (IFA, 2002). The ammonia industry used about 5 percent of natural gas consumption in the mid-1990s. However, ammonia production can use a wide range of energy sources. When oil and gas supplies eventually dwindle, coal can be used, and coal reserves are sufficient for well over 200 years at current production levels. In fact 60 percent of China's nitrogen fertilizer production is currently based on coal (IFA, 2002). China is an atypical case: not only is its N fertilizer production based on coal, but it is mostly produced in small and medium-sized, relatively energy-inefficient, plants. Here energy consumption per unit of N can run 20 to 25 percent higher than in plants of more recent design. One study conducted by the Chinese government estimated that energy consumption per unit of output for small plants was more than 76 percent higher than for large plants (Price *et al.*, 2000).

On-farm fossil fuel may emit 90 million tones CO_2 per year. The share of energy consumption accounted by the different stages of livestock production varies widely, depending on the intensity of livestock production (Sainz, 2003). In modern production systems the bulk of the energy is spent on production of feed, whether forage for ruminants or concentrate feed for poultry or pigs. As well as the energy used for fertilizer, important amounts of energy are also spent on seed, herbicides/pesticides, diesel for machinery (for land preparation, harvesting, transport) and electricity (irrigation pumps, drying, heating, etc.). On-farm use of fossil fuel by intensive systems produces CO_2 emissions probably even larger than those from chemical N fertilizer for feed. Sainz (2003) estimated that, during the 1980s, a typical farm in the United States spent some 35 megajoules (MJ) of energy per kilogram of carcass for chicken, 46 MJ for pigs and 51 MJ for beef, of which amounts 80 to 87 percent was spent for production.[4] A large share of this is in the form of electricity, producing much lower emissions on an energy equivalent basis than the direct use of fossil sources for energy.

A rough indication of the fossil fuel use related emissions from intensive systems can, nevertheless, be obtained by supposing that the expected lower energy need for feed production at lower latitudes (lower energy need for corn drying for example) and the elsewhere, often lower level of mechanization, are overall compensated by a lower energy use efficiency and a lower share of relatively low CO_2 emitting sources (natural gas and electricity). Minnesota figures can then be combined with global feed production and livestock populations in intensive systems. The resulting estimate for maize only is of a magnitude similar to the emissions from manufacturing N fertilizer for use on feedcrops. As a conservative estimate, we may suggest that CO_2 emissions induced by on-farm fossil fuel use for feed production may be 50 percent higher than that from feed-dedicated N fertilizer production, i.e. some 60 million tonnes CO_2 globally. To this we must add farm emissions related directly to live-stock rearing, which we may estimate at roughly 30 million tonnes of CO_2 (this figure is derived by applying Minnesota's figures to the global total of intensively-man-aged livestock populations, assuming that lower energy use for heating at lower latitudes is counterbalanced by lower energy efficiency and higher ventilation requirements).

On-farm fossil fuel use induced emissions in extensive systems sourcing their feed mainly from natural grasslands or crop residues can be expected to be low or even negligible in comparison to the above estimate. This is confirmed by the fact that there are large areas in developing countries, particularly in Africa and Asia, where animals are an important source of draught power, which could be considered as a CO_2 emission avoiding practice. It has been estimated that animal traction covered about half the total area cultivated in the developing countries in 1992 (Delgado *et al.*, 1999). There are no more recent estimates and it can be assumed that this share is decreasing quickly in areas with rapid mechanization, such as China or parts of India. However, draught animal power remains an important form of energy, substituting for fossil fuel combustion in many parts of the world, and in some areas, notably in West Africa, is on the increase.

Livestock-related land use changes may emit 2.4 billion tonnes of CO_2 per year. Land use in the various parts of the world is continually changing, usually in response to competitive demand between users. Changes in land use have an impact in carbon fluxes, and many of the land-use changes involve livestock, either occupying land (as pasture or arable land for feedcrops) or releasing land for other purposes, when for example, marginal pasture land is converted to forest.

A forest contains more carbon than does a field of annual crops or pasture, and so when forests are harvested, or worse, burned, large amounts of carbon are released from the vegetation and soil to the atmosphere. The net reduction in carbon stocks is not simply equal to the net CO_2 flux from the cleared area. Reality is more complex: forest clearing can produce a complex pattern of net fluxes

that change direction over time (IPCC guidelines). The calculation of carbon fluxes owing to forest conversion is, in many ways, the most complex of the emissions inventory components. Estimates of emissions from forest clearing vary because of multiple uncertainties: annual forest clearing rates, the fate of the cleared land, the amounts of carbon contained in different ecosystems, the modes by which CO_2 is released (e.g., burning or decay), and the amounts of carbon released from soils when they are disturbed.

Responses of biological systems vary over different time-scales. For example, biomass burning occurs within less than one year, while the decomposition of wood may take a decade, and loss of soil carbon may continue for several decades or even centuries. The IPCC (2001b) estimated the average annual flux owing to tropical deforestation for the decade 1980 to 1989 at 1.6 ± 1.0 billion tonnes C as CO_2 (CO_2-C). Only about 50-60 percent of the carbon released from forest conversion in any one year was a result of the conversion and subsequent biomass burning in that year. The remainder were delayed emissions resulting from oxidation of biomass harvested in previous years (Houghton, 1991).

Clearly, estimating CO_2 emissions from land use and land-use change is far less straightforward than those related to fossil fuel combustion. It is even more difficult to attribute these emissions to a particular production sector such as livestock. However, livestock's role in deforestation is of proven importance in Latin America, the continent suffering the largest net loss of forests and resulting carbon fluxes. Latin America is the region where expansion of pasture and arable land for feedcrops is strongest, mostly at the expense of forest area. The LEAD study by Wassenaar *et al.*, (2006) and Chapter 2 showed that most of the cleared area ends up as pasture and identified large areas where livestock ranching is probably a primary motive for clearing. Even if these final land uses were only one reason among many others that led to the forest clearing, animal production is certainly one of the driving forces of deforestation. The conversion of forest into pasture releases considerable amounts of carbon into the atmosphere, particularly when the area is not logged but simply burned. Cleared patches may go through several changes of land-use type. Over the 2000–2010 period, the pasture areas in Latin America are projected to expand into forest by an annual average of 2.4 million hectares—equivalent to some 65 percent of expected deforestation. If we also assume that at least half the cropland expansion into forest in Bolivia and Brazil can be attributed to providing feed for the livestock sector, this results in an additional annual deforestation for livestock of over 0.5 million hectares—giving a total for pastures plus feedcrop land, of some 3 million hectares per year.

In view of this, and of worldwide trends in extensive livestock production and in cropland for feed production, we can realistically estimate that "livestock induced" emissions from deforestation amount to roughly 2.4 billion tonnes of CO_2 per year. This is based on the somewhat simplified assumption that forests are completely converted into climatically equivalent grasslands and croplands (IPCC 2001b, p. 192), combining changes in carbon density of both vegetation and soil[5] in the year of change. Though physically incorrect (it takes well over a year to reach this new status because of the "inherited", i.e. delayed emissions) the resulting emission estimate is correct provided the change process is continuous.

Other possibly important, but un-quantified, livestock-related deforestation as reported from for example Argentina is excluded from this estimate.

In addition to producing CO_2 emissions, the land conversion may also negatively affect other emissions. Mosier *et al.* (2004) for example noted that upon conversion of forest to grazing land, CH_4 oxidation by soil micro-organisms is typically greatly reduced and grazing lands may even become net sources in situations where soil compaction from cattle traffic limits gas diffusion.

Livestock-related releases from cultivated soils may total 28 million tonnes CO_2 per year. Soils are the largest carbon reservoir of the terrestrial carbon cycle. The estimated total amount of carbon stored in soils is about 1 100 to 1 600 billion tonnes (Sundquist, 1993), more than twice the carbon in

living vegetation (560 billion tonnes) or in the atmosphere (750 billion tonnes). Hence even relatively small changes in carbon stored in the soil could make a significant impact on the global carbon balance (Rice, 1999).

Carbon stored in soils is the balance between the input of dead plant material and losses due to decomposition and mineralization processes. Under aerobic conditions, most of the carbon entering the soil is unstable and therefore quickly respired back to the atmosphere. Generally, less than 1 percent of the 55 billion tonnes of C entering the soil each year accumulates in more stable fractions with long mean residence times.

Human disturbance can speed up decomposition and mineralization. On the North American Great Plains, it has been estimated that approximately 50 percent of the soil organic carbon has been lost over the past 50 to 100 years of cultivation, through burning, volatilization, erosion, harvest or grazing (SCOPE 21, 1982). Similar losses have taken place in less than ten years after deforestation in tropical areas (Nye and Greenland, 1964). Most of these losses occur at the original conversion of natural cover into managed land.

Further soil carbon losses can be induced by management practices. Under appropriate management practices (such as zero tillage) agricultural soils can serve as a carbon sink and may increasingly do so in future. Currently, however, their role as carbon sinks is globally insignificant. A very large share of the production of coarse grains and oil crops in temperate regions is destined for feed use.

The vast majority of the corresponding area is under large-scale intensive management, dominated by conventional tillage practices that gradually lower the soil organic carbon content and produce significant CO_2 emissions. Given the complexity of emissions from land use and land-use changes, it is not possible to make a global estimation at an acceptable level of precision. Order-of-magnitude indications can be made by using an average loss rate from soil in a rather temperate climate with moderate to low organic matter content that is somewhere between the loss rate reported for zero and conventional tillage: Assuming an annual loss rate of 100 kg CO_2 per hectare per year (Sauvé et al., 2000: covering temperate brown soil CO_2 loss, and excluding emissions originating from crop residues), the approximately 1.8 million km^2 of arable land cultivated with maize, wheat and soybean for feed would add an annual CO_2 flux of some 18 million tonnes to the livestock balance.

Tropical soils have lower average carbon content (IPCC 2001b, p. 192), and therefore lower emissions. On the other hand, the considerable expansion of large-scale feedcropping, not only into uncultivated areas, but also into previous pastureland or subsistence cropping, may increase CO_2 emission. In addition, practices such as soil liming contribute to emissions. Soil liming is a common practice in more intensively cultivated tropical areas because of soil acidity. Brazil[6] for example estimated its CO_2 emissions owing to soil liming at 8.99 million tonnes in 1994, and these have most probably increased since then. To the extent that these emissions concern cropland for feed production they should be attributed to the livestock sector. Often only crop residues and by-products are used for feeding, in which case a share of emissions corresponding to the value fraction of the commodity[7] (Chapagain and Hoekstra, 2004) should be attributed to livestock. Comparing reported emissions from liming from national communications of various tropical countries to the UNFCCC with the importance of feed production in those countries shows that the global share of liming related emissions attributable to livestock is in the order of magnitude of Brazil's emission (0.01 billion tonnes CO_2).

Another way livestock contributes to gas emissions from cropland is through methane emissions from rice cultivation, globally recognized as an important source of methane. Much of the methane emissions from rice fields are of animal origin, because the soil bacteria are to a large extent "fed" with animal manure, an important fertilizer source (Verburg, Hugo and van der Gon, 2001). Together with the type of flooding management, the type of fertilization is the most important factor controlling methane emissions from rice cultivated areas. Organic fertilizers lead to higher emissions than

mineral fertilizers. Khalil and Shearer (2005) argue that over the last two decades China achieved a substantial reduction of annual methane emissions from rice cultivation—from some 30 million tonnes per year to perhaps less than 10 million tonnes per year—mainly by replacing organic fertilizer with nitrogen-based fertilizers. However, this change can affect other gaseous emissions in the opposite way. As nitrous oxide emissions from rice fields increase, when artificial N fertilizers are used, as do carbon dioxide emissions from China's flourishing charcoal-based nitrogen fertilizer industry (see preceding section). Given that it is impossible to provide even a rough estimate of livestock's contribution to methane emissions from rice cultivation, this is not further considered in the global quantification.

Releases from Livestock-induced desertification of pastures may total 100 million tonnes CO_2 per year. Livestock also play a role in desertification. Where desertification is occurring, degradation often results in reduced productivity or reduced vegetation cover, which produce a change in the carbon and nutrient stocks and cycling of the system. This seems to result in a small reduction in aboveground C stocks and a slight decline in C fixation. Despite the small, sometimes undetectable changes in aboveground biomass, total soil carbon usually declines. A recent study by Asner, Borghi and Ojeda, (2003) in Argentina also found that desertification resulted in little change in woody cover, but there was a 25 to 80 percent decline in soil organic carbon in areas with long-term grazing. Soil erosion accounts for part of this loss, but the majority stems from the non-renewal of decaying organic matter stocks, i.e. there is a significant net emission of CO_2.

Lal (2001) estimated the carbon loss as a result of desertification. Assuming a loss of 8–12 tonnes of soil carbon per hectare (Swift et al., 1994) on a desertified land area of 1 billion hectares (UNEP, 1991), the total historic loss would amount to 8–12 billion tonnes of soil carbon. Similarly, degradation of aboveground vegetation has led to an estimated carbon loss of 10–16 tonnes per hectare—a historic total of 10–16 billion tonnes. Thus, the total C loss

---

B o x 3   The many climatic faces of the burning of tropical savannah

Burning is common in establishing and managing of pastures, tropical rain forests and savannah regions and grasslands worldwide (Crutzen and Andreae, 1990; Reich *et al.*, 2001). Fire removes ungrazed grass, straw and litter, stimulates fresh growth, and can control the density of woody plants (trees and shrubs). As many grass species are more fire-tolerant than tree species (especially seedlings and saplings), burning can determine the balance between grass cover and ligneous vegetation. Fires stimulate the growth of perennial grasses in savannahs and provide nutritious re-growth for livestock. Controlled burning prevents uncontrolled, and possibility, more destructive fires and consumes the combustible tower layer at an appropriate humidity stage. Burning involves little or no cost. It is also used at a small scale to maintain biodiversity (wildlife habitats) in protected areas.

The environmental consequences of rangeland and grassland fires depend on the environmental context and conditions of application. Controlled burning in tropical savannah areas has significant environmental impact, because of the large area concerned and the relatively low level of control. Large areas of savannah in the humid and subhumid tropics are burned every year for rangeland management. In 2000, burning affected some 4 million km^2. More than two-thirds of this occurred in the tropics and sub-tropics (Tansey *et al.*, 2004). Globally about three quarters of this burning took place outside forests. Savannah burning represented some 85 percent of the area burned in Latin American fires 2000, 60 percent in Africa, nearly 80 percent in Australia.

Usually, savannah burning is not considered to result in net CO_2 emissions, since emitted amounts of carbon dioxide released in burning are re-captured in grass re-growth. As well as CO_2, biomass burning releases important amounts of other globally relevant trace gases (NO_x, CO, and CH_4) and aerosols (Crutzen and Andreae, 1990; Scholes and Andreae, 2000). Climate effects include the formation of photochemical smog, hydrocarbons, and NO_x. Many of the emitted elements lead to the production of tropospheric ozone (Vet, 1995; Crutzen and Goldammer, 1993), which is another important greenhouse gas influencing the atmosphere's oxidizing capacity, while bromine, released in significant amounts from savannah fires, decreases stratospheric ozone (Vet, 1995; ADB, 2001).

Smoke plumes may be redistributed locally, transported throughout the lower troposphere, or entrained in large-scale circulation patterns in the mid and upper troposphere. Often fires in convection areas take the elements high into the atmosphere, creating increased potential for climate change. Satellite observations have found large areas with high O_3 and CO levels over Africa, South America and the tropical Atlantic and Indian Oceans (Thompson *et al.*, 2001).

Aerosols produced by the burning of pasture biomass dominate the atmospheric concentration of aerosols over the Amazon basin and Africa (Scholes and Andreae, 2000; Artaxo *et al.*, 2002). Concentrations of aerosol particles are highly seasonal. An obvious peak in the dry (burning) season which contributes to cooling both through increasing atmospheric scattering of incoming light and the supply of cloud condensation nuclei. High concentrations of cloud condensation nuclei from the burning of biomass stimulate rainfall production and affect large-scale climate dynamics (Andreae and Crutzen, 1997).

---

as a consequence of desertification may be 18–28 billion tonnes of carbon (FAO, 2004b). Livestock's contribution to this total is difficult to estimate, but it is undoubtedly high: livestock occupies about two-thirds of the global dry land area, and the rate of desertification has been estimated to be higher under pasture than under other land uses (3.2 million hectares per year against 2.5 million hectares per year for cropland, UNEP, 1991). Considering only soil carbon loss (i.e. about 10 tonnes of carbon per hectare), pasture desertification-induced oxidation of carbon would result in CO_2 emissions in the order of 100 million tonnes of CO_2 per year.

Another, largely unknown, influence on the fate of soil carbon is the feedback effect of climate change. In higher latitude cropland zones, global warming is expected to increase yields by virtue of longer growing seasons and CO_2 fertilization (Cantagallo, Chimenti and Hall, 1997; Travasso *et al.*, 1999). At the same time, however, global warming may also accelerate decomposition of carbon already stored in soils (Jenkinson, 1991; MacDonald, Randlett and Zalc, 1999; Niklinska, Maryanski and Laskowski, 1999; Scholes *et al.*, 1999). Although much work remains to be done in quantifying the CO_2 fertilization effect in cropland, van Ginkel, Whitmore and Gorissen (1999) estimate the magnitude of this effect (at current rates of increase of CO_2 in the atmosphere) at a net absorption of 0.036 tonnes of carbon per hectare per year in temperate grassland, even after the effect of rising temperature on decomposition is deducted. Recent research indicates that the magnitude of the temperature rise on the acceleration of decay may be stronger, with already very significant net losses over the last decades in temperate regions (Bellamy *et al.*, 2005; Schulze and Freibauer, 2005). Both scenarios may prove true, resulting in a shift of carbon from soils to vegetation—i.e. a shift towards more fragile ecosystems, as found currently in more tropical regions.

Carbon emissions from livestock rearing

Respiration by livestock is not a net source of CO_2. Humans and livestock now account for about a quarter of the total terrestrial animal biomass.[8] Based on animal numbers and liveweights, the total livestock biomass amounts to some 0.7 billion tonnes (Table 3; FAO, 2005b).

How much do these animals contribute to greenhouse gas emissions? According to the function established by Muller and Schneider (1985, cited by Ni *et al.*, 1999), applied to standing stocks per country and species (with country specific liveweight), the carbon dioxide from the respiratory process of livestock amount to some 3 billion tonnes of CO_2 (see Table 3) or 0.8 billion tonnes of carbon. In general, because of lower offtake rates and therefore higher inventories, ruminants have higher emissions relative to their output. Cattle alone account for more than half of the total carbon dioxide emissions from respiration.

However, emissions from livestock respiration are part of a rapidly cycling biological system, where the plant matter consumed was itself created through the conversion of atmospheric CO_2 into organic

TABLE 3 **Livestock numbers (2002) and estimated carbon dioxide emissions from respiration**

Species	World total (million head)	Biomass (million tonnes liveweight)	Carbon dioxide emissions (million tonnes CO_2)
Cattle and buffaloes	1496	501	1906
Small ruminants	1784	47.3	514
Camels	19	5.3	18
Horses	55	18.6	71
Pigs	933	92.8	590
Poultry	17437	33.0	61
Total		699	3161

Chicken, ducks, turkey and geese.
Includes also rabbits.
SOURCE: FAO (2006b); own calculations.

compounds. Since the emitted and absorbed quantities are considered to be equivalent, livestock respiration is not considered to be a net source under the Kyoto Protocol. Indeed, since part of the carbon consumed is stored in the live tissue of the growing animal, a growing global herd could even be considered a carbon sink. The standing stock livestock biomass increased significantly over the last decades (from about 428 million tonnes in 1961 to around 699 million tonnes in 2002). This continuing growth could be considered as a carbon sequestration process (roughly estimated at 1 or 2 million tonnes carbon per year). However, this is more than offset by methane emissions which have increased correspondingly.

The equilibrium of the biological cycle is, however, disrupted in the case of overgrazing or bad management of feedcrops. The resulting land degradation is a sign of *decreasing* re-absorption of atmospheric CO_2 by vegetation re-growth. In certain regions the related net CO_2 loss may be significant.

Methane released from enteric fermentation may total 86 million tonnes per year. Globally, livestock are the most important source of anthropogenic methane emissions. Among domesticated livestock, ruminant animals (cattle, buffaloes, sheep, goats and camels) produce significant amounts of methane as part of their normal digestive processes. In the rumen, or large fore-stomach, of these animals, microbial fermentation converts fibrous feed into products that can be digested and utilized by the animal. This microbial fermentation process, referred to as enteric fermentation, produces methane as a by-product, which is exhaled by the animal. Methane is also produced in smaller quantities by the digestive processes of other animals, including humans (US-EPA, 2Qp5).

There are significant spatial variations in methane emissions from enteric fermentation. In Brazil, methane emission from enteric fermentation totalled 9.4 million tonnes in 1994—93 percent of agricultural emissions and 72 percent of the country's total emissions of methane. Over 80 percent of this originated from beef cattle (Ministerio da Ciencia e Tecnologia—EMBRAPA report, 2002). In the United States methane from enteric fermentation totalled 5.5 million tonnes in 2002, again overwhelmingly originating from beef and dairy cattle. This was 71 percent of all agricultural emissions and 19 percent of the country's total emissions (US-EPA, 2004).

This variation reflects the fact that levels of methane emission are determined by the production system and regional characteristics. They are affected by energy intake and several other animal and diet factors (quantity and quality of feed, animal body weight, age and amount of exercise). It varies among animal species and among individuals of the same species. Therefore, assessing methane emission from enteric fermentation in any particular country requires a detailed description of the livestock population (species, age and productivity categories), combined with information on the daily feed intake and the feed's methane conversion rate (IPCC revised guidelines). As many countries do not possess such detailed information, an approach based on standard emission factors is generally used in emission reporting.

Methane emissions from enteric fermentation will change as production systems change and move towards higher feed use and increased productivity. We have attempted a global estimate of total methane emissions from enteric fermentation in the livestock sector. Applying these emission factors to the livestock numbers in each production system gives an estimate for total global emissions of methane from enteric fermentation 86 million tonnes CH_4 annually. This is not far from the global estimate from the United States Environmental Protection Agency (US-EPA, 2005), of about 80 million tonnes of methane annually. Table 4 summarizes these results. The relative global importance of mixed systems compared to grazing systems reflects the fact that about two-thirds of all ruminants are held in mixed systems.

Methane released from animal manure may total 18 million tonnes per year. The anaerobic decomposition of organic material in livestock manure also releases methane. This occurs mostly when manure is managed in liquid form, such as in lagoons or holding tanks. Lagoon systems are typical for most large-scale pig operations over most of the world (except in Europe). These systems are also used in large dairy operations in North America and in some developing countries, for example Brazil. Manure deposited on fields and pastures, or otherwise handled in a dry form, does not produce significant amounts of methane.

Methane emissions from livestock manure are influenced by a number of factors that affect the growth of the bacteria responsible for methane formation, including ambient temperature, moisture and storage time. The amount of methane produced also depends on the energy content of manure, which is determined to a large extent by livestock diet. Not only do greater amounts of manure lead to more CH_4 being emitted, but higher energy feed also produces manure with more volatile solids, increasing the substrate from which CH_4 is produced. However, this impact is somewhat offset by the possibility of achieving higher digestibility in feeds, and thus less wasted energy (USDA, 2004).

Globally, methane emissions from anaerobic decomposition of manure have been estimated to total just over 10 million tonnes, or some 4 percent of global anthropogenic methane emissions (US-EPA, 2005). Although of much lesser magnitude than

T A B L E 4   Global methane emissions from enteric fermentation in 2004

Emissions (million tonnes CH$_4$ per year by source)

Region/country	Dairy cattle	Other cattle	Buffaloes	Sheep and goats	Pigs	Total
Sub-Saharan Africa	2.30	7.47	0.00	1.82	0.02	**11.61**
Asia[*]	0.84	3.83	2.40	0.88	0.07	**8.02**
India	1.70	3.94	5.25	0.91	0.01	**11.82**
China	0.49	5.12	1.25	1.51	0.48	**8.85**
Central and South America	3.36	17.09	0.06	0.58	0.08	**21.17**
West Asia and North Africa	0.98	1.16	0.24	1.20	0.00	**3.58**
North America	1.02	3.85	0.00	0.06	0.11	**5.05**
Western Europe	2.19	2.31	0.01	0.98	0.20	**5.70**
Oceania and Japan	0.71	1.80	0.00	0.73	0.02	**3.26**
Eastern Europe and CIS	1.99	2.96	0.02	0.59	0.10	**5.66**
Other developed	0.11	0.62	0.00	0.18	0.00	**0.91**
Total	**15.69**	**50.16**	**9.23**	**9.44**	**1.11**	85.63
Livestock Production System						
Grazing	4.73	21.89	0.00	2.95	0.00	**29.58**
Mixed	10.96	27.53	9.23	6.50	0.80	**55.02**
Industrial	0.00	0.73	0.00	0.00	0.30	**1.04**

[*]Excludes China and India.

SOURCE: see Annex 3.2, own calculations.

emissions from enteric fermentation, emissions from manure are much higher than those originating from burning residues and similar to the lower estimate of the badly known emissions originating from rice cultivation. The United States has the highest emission from manure (close to 1.9 million tonnes, United States inventory 2004), followed by the EU. As a species, pig production contributes the largest share, followed by dairy. Developing countries such as China and India would not be very far behind, the latter in particular exhibiting a strong increase. The default emission factors currently used in country reporting to the UNFCCC do not reflect such strong changes in the global livestock sector. For example, Brazil's country report to the UNFCCC (Ministry of Science and Technology, 2004) mentions a significant emission from manure of 0.38 million tonnes in 1994, which would originate mainly from dairy and beef cattle. However, Brazil also has a very strong industrial pig production sector, where some 95 percent of manure is held in open tanks for several months before application (EMBRAPA, personal communication).

Table 5 summarizes the results by species, by region and by farming system. The distribution by species and production system is also illustrated in Maps 16, 17, 18 and 19 (Annex 1). China has the largest country-level methane emission from manure in the world, mainly from pigs. At a global level, emissions from pig manure represent almost half of total livestock manure emissions. Just over a quarter of the total methane emission from managed manure originates from industrial systems.

T A B L E 5   Global methane emissions from manure management in 2004

Emissions (million tonnes CH$_4$ per year by source)

Region/country	Dairy cattle	Other cattle	Buffaloes	Sheep and goats	Pigs	Poultry	Total
Sub-Saharan Africa	1.10	0.32	0.00	0.08	0.03	0.04	**0.57**
Asia[*]	0.31	0.08	0.09	0.03	0.50	0.13	**1.14**
India	0.20	0.34	0.19	0.04	0.17	0.01	**0.95**
China	0.08	0.11	0.05	0.05	3.43	0.14	**3.84**
Central and South America	0.10	0.36	0.00	0.02	0.74	0.19	**1.41**
West Asia and North Africa	0.06	0.09	0.01	0.05	0.00	0.11	**0.32**
North America	0.52	1.05	0.00	0.00	1.65	0.16	**3.39**
Western Europe	1.16	1.29	0.00	0.02	1.52	0.09	**4.08**
Oceania and Japan	0.08	0.11	0.00	0.03	0.10	0.03	**0.35**
Eastern Europe and CIS	0.46	0.65	0.00	0.01	0.19	0.06	**1.38**
Other developed	0.01	0.03	0.00	0.01	0.04	0.02	**0.11**
Global Total	**3.08**	**4.41**	**0.34**	**0.34**	**8.38**	**0.97**	**17.52**
Livestock Production System							
Grazing	0.15	0.50	0.00	0.12	0.00	0.00	**0.77**
Mixed	2.93	3.89	0.34	0.23	4.58	0.31	**12.27**
Industrial	0.00	0.02	0.00	0.00	3.80	0.67	**4.48**

*Excludes China and India.
SOURCE: see Annex 3.3, own calculations.

Carbon emissions from livestock processing and refrigerated transport

A number of studies have been conducted to quantify the energy costs of processing animals for meat and other products, and to identify potential areas for energy savings (Sainz, 2003). The variability among enterprises is very wide, so it is difficult to generalize. For example, Ward, Knox and Hobson (1977) reported energy costs of beef processing in Colorado ranging from 0.84 to 5.02 million joules per kilogram of live weight. Sainz (2003) produced indicative values for the energy costs of processing, given in Table 6.

CO$_2$ **emissions from livestock processing may total several tens of million tonnes per year.** To obtain a global estimate of emissions from processing, these indicative energy use factors could be combined with estimates of the world's livestock production from market-oriented intensive systems. However, besides their questionable global validity, it is highly uncertain what the source of this energy is and how this varies throughout the world. Since mostly products from intensive systems are being processed, the above case of Minnesota (Section on *on-farm fossil fuel use*) constitutes an interesting example of energy use for processing, as well as a breakdown into energy sources. Diesel use here is

T A B L E 6   Indicative energy costs for processing

Product	Fossil energy cost	Units	Source
Poultry meat	2.59	MJ-kg-1 live wt	Whitehead and Shupe, 1979
Eggs	6.12	MJ-dozen-1	OECD, 1982
Pork-fresh	3.76	MJ-kg-1 carcass	Singh. 1986
Pork-processed meats	6.30	MJ-kg-1 meat	Singh, 1986
Sheep meat	10.4	MJ-kg-1 carcass	McChesney et al., 1982
Sheep meat-frozen	0.432	MJ-kg-1 meat	Unklesbay and Unklesbay, 1982
Beef	4.37	MJ-kg-1 carcass	Poulsen, 1986
Beef-frozen	0.432	MJ-kg-1 meat	Unklesbay and Unklesbay, 1982
Milk	1.12	MJ-kg-1	Miller, 1986
Cheese, butter, whey powder	1.49	MJ-kg-1	Miller, 1986
Milk powder, butter	2.62	MJ-kg-1	Miller, 1986

SOURCE: Sainz (2003).

mainly for transport of products to the processing facilities. Transport-related emissions for milk are high, owing to large volumes and low utilization of transport capacity. In addition, large amounts of energy are used to pasteurize milk and transform it into cheese and dried milk, making the dairy sector responsible for the second highest CO_2 emissions from food processing in Minnesota. The largest emissions result from soybean processing and are a result of physical and chemical methods to separate the crude soy oil and soybean meal from the raw beans. Considering the value fractions of these two commodities (see Chapagain and Hoekstra, 2004) some two-thirds of these soy-processing emissions can be attributed to the livestock sector. Thus, the majority of CO_2 emissions related to energy consumption from processing Minnesota's agricultural production can be ascribed to the livestock sector.

Minnesota can be considered a "hotspot" because of its CO_2 emissions from livestock processing and cannot, in light of the above remarks on the variability of energy efficiency and sources, be used as a basis for deriving a global estimate. Still, considering also Table 7, it indicates that the total animal product and feed processing related emission of the United States would be in the order of a few million tonnes CO_2. Therefore, the probable order of magnitude for the emission level related to global animal-product processing would be several tens of million tonnes CO_2.

CO_2 emissions from transport of livestock products may exceed 0.8 million tonnes per year. The last element of the food chain to be considered in this review of the carbon cycle is the one that links the elements of the production chain and delivers the product to retailers and consumers, i.e. transport. In many instances transport is over short distances, as in the case of milk collection cited above. Increasingly the steps in the chain are separated over long distances, which makes transport a significant source of greenhouse gas emissions.

Transport occurs mainly at two key stages: delivery of (processed) feed to animal production sites and delivery of animal products to consumer markets. Large amounts of bulky raw ingredients for concentrate feed are shipped around the world. These long-distance flows add significant CO_2 emissions to the livestock balance. One of the most notable long-distance feed trade flows is for soybean, which is also the largest traded volume among feed ingredients, as well as the one with the strongest increase. Among soybean (cake) trade flows the one from Brazil to Europe is of a particularly important

TABLE 7 **Energy use for processing agricultural products in Minnesota, in United States in 1995**

Commodity	Production[1] (10^6 tonnes)	Diesel (1000 m³)	Natural gas (106 m³)	Electricity (106 kWh)	Emitted CO_2 (10³ tonnes)
Corn	22.2	41	54	48	226
Soybeans	6.4	23	278	196	648
Wheat	2.7	19		125	86
Dairy	4.3	36	207	162	537
Swine	0.9	7	21	75	80
Beef	0.7	2.5	15	55	51
Turkeys	0.4	1.8	10	36	34
Sugar beets[2]	7.4	19	125	68	309
Sweet corn/peas	1.0	6	8	29	40

[1]Commodities: unshelled corn ears, milk, live animal weight. 51 percent of milk is made into cheese, 35 percent is dried, and 14 percent is used as liquid for bottling.

[2]Beet processing required an additional 440 thousand tonnes of coal. 1000 m³ diesel—2.65-103 tonnes CO_2; 106 m³ natural gas—1.91-103 tonnes CO_2; 106 kWh—288 tonnes CO_2.

SOURCE: Ryan and Tiffany (1998). Related CO_2 emissions based on efficiency and emission factors from the United States' Common Reporting Format report submitted to the UNFCCC in 2005.

volume. Cederberg and Flysjö (2004) studied the energy cost of shipping soybean cake from the Mato Grosso to Swedish dairy farms: shipping one tonne requires some 2900 MJ, of which 70 percent results from ocean transport. Applying this energy need to the annual soybean cake shipped from Brazil to Europe, combined with the IPCC emission factor for ocean vessel engines, results in an annual emission of some 32 thousand tonnes of CO_2.

While there are a large number of trade flows, we can take pig, poultry and bovine meat to represent the emissions induced by fossil energy use for shipping animal products around the world. The figures presented in Table 15, Annex 2, are the result of combining traded volumes (FAO, accessed December 2005) with respective distances, vessel capacities and speeds, fuel use of main engine and auxiliary power generators for refrigeration, and their respective emission factors (IPCC, 1997).

These flows represent some 60 percent of international meat trade. Annually they produce some 500 thousand tonnes of CO_2. This represents more than 60 percent of total CO_2 emissions

induced by meat-related sea transport, because the trade flow selection is biased towards the long distance exchange. On the other hand, surface transport to and from the harbour has not been considered. Assuming, for simplicity, that the latter two effects compensate each other, the total annual meat transport-induced CO_2 emission would be in the order of 800–850 thousand tonnes of CO_2.

SUMMARY OF LIVESTOCK'S IMPACT

Overall, livestock activities contribute an estimated 18 percent to total anthropogenic greenhouse gas emissions from the five major sectors for greenhouse gas reporting: energy, industry, waste, land use, land use change and forestry (LULUCF) and agriculture.

Considering the last two sectors only, livestock's share is over 50 percent. For the agriculture sector alone, livestock constitute nearly 80 percent of all emissions.

Here we will summarize the impact for the three major greenhouse gases.

Carbon dioxide

Livestock account for 9 percent of global anthropogenic emissions. When deforestation for pasture and feedcrop land, and pasture degradation are taken into account, livestock-related emissions of carbon dioxide are an important component of the global total (some 9 percent). However, as can be seen from the many assumptions made in preceding sections, these totals have a considerable degree of uncertainty. LULUCF sector emissions in particular are extremely difficult to quantify and the values reported to the UNFCCC for this sector are known to be of low reliability. This sector is therefore often omitted in emissions reporting, although its share is thought to be important.

Although small by comparison to LULUCF, the livestock food chain is becoming more fossil fuel intensive, which will increase carbon dioxide emissions from livestock production. As ruminant production (based on traditional local feed resources) shifts to intensive monogastrics (based on food transported over long distances), there is a corresponding shift away from solar energy harnessed by photosynthesis, to fossil fuels.

Methane

Livestock account for 35–40 percent of global anthropogenic emissions. The leading role of livestock, in methane emissions, has long been a well-established fact. Together, enteric fermentation and manure represent some 80 percent of agricultural methane emissions and about 35–40 percent of the total anthropogenic methane emissions.

With the decline of ruminant livestock in relative terms, and the overall trend towards higher productivity in ruminant production, it is unlikely that the importance of enteric fermentation will increase further. However, methane emissions from animal manure, although much

lower in absolute terms, are considerable and growing rapidly.

Nitrous oxide

Livestock account for 65 percent of global anthropogenic emissions. Livestock activities contribute substantially to the emission of nitrous oxide, the most potent of the three major greenhouse gases. They contribute almost two-thirds of all anthropogenic N_2O emissions, and 75–80 percent of agricultural emissions. Current trends suggest that this level will substantially increase over the coming decades.

Ammonia

Livestock account for 64 percent of global anthropogenic emissions. Global anthropogenic atmospheric emission of ammonia has recently been estimated at some 47 million tonnes N (Galloway et al., 2004). Some 94 percent of this is produced by the agricultural sector. The livestock sector contributes about 68 percent of the agriculture share, mainly from deposited and applied manure.

The resulting air and environmental pollution (mainly eutrophication, also odour) is more a local or regional environmental problem than a global one. Indeed, similar levels of N depositions can have substantially different environmental effects depending on the type of ecosystem they affect. The modelled distribution of atmospheric N deposition levels are a better indication of the environmental impact than the global figures. The distribution shows a strong and clear co-incidence with intensive livestock production areas.

The figures presented are estimates for the overall global-level greenhouse gas emissions. However, they do not describe the entire issue of livestock-induced change. To assist decision-making, the level and nature of emissions need to be understood in a local context. In Brazil, for example, carbon dioxide emissions from land-use change (forest conversion and soil organic matter loss) are reported to be much higher than emissions from the energy sector. At the same time, methane emissions from enteric fermentation strongly dominate the country's total methane emission, owing to the extensive beef cattle population. For this same reason pasture soils produce the highest nitrous oxide emissions in Brazil, with an increasing contribution from manure. If livestock's role in land-use change is included, the contribution of the livestock sector to the total greenhouse gas emission of this very large country can be estimated to be as high as 60 percent, i.e. much higher than the 18 percent at world level.

NOTES

1. The addition of substances to the atmosphere that result in direct damage to the environment, human health and quality of life is termed air pollution.

2. Other important odour-producing livestock emissions are volatile organic compounds and hydrogen sulphide. In fact, well over a hundred gases pass into the surroundings of livestock operations (Burton and Turner, 2003; NRC, 2003).

3. Autotrophic organisms are auto-sufficient in energy supply, as distinguished from parasitic and saprophytic; heterotrophic organisms require an external supply of energy contained in complex organic compounds to maintain their existence.

4. As opposed to post-harvest processing, transportation, storage and preparation. Production includes energy use for feed production and transport.

5. The most recent estimates provided by this source are 194 and 122 tonnes of carbon per hectare in tropical forest, respectively for plants and soil, as opposed to 29 and 90 for tropical grassland and 3 and 122 for cropland.

6. Brazil's first national communication to the UNFCCC, 2004.

7. The value fraction of a product is the ratio of the market value of the product to the aggregated market value of all the products obtained from the primary crop.

8. Based on SCOPE 13 (Bolin *et al.*, 1979), with human population updated to today's total of some 6.5 billion.

STUDY QUESTIONS

1. Discuss Figure 1; is anything surprising?

2. What are the contributions of livestock to each of the three major greenhouse gasses (carbon dioxide, methane, and nitrous oxide)?

3. [Note: The text for this can be found at: http://www.fao.org/docrep/010/a0701e/a0701e00.htm. For more information see: http://www.fao.org/ag/portal/index_en/en/]

44

Ethics and Global Climate Change

STEPHEN M. GARDINER

Stephen Gardiner is professor of philosophy at the University of Washington. This article is perhaps the most comprehensive examination of the ethical issues surrounding the complexities of climate change. Gardiner attempts to make climate change more accessible to philosophers and nonexperts and then challenges us to see it as a moral issue.

Very few moral philosophers have written on climate change. This is puzzling, for several reasons. First, many politicians and policy makers claim that climate change is not only the most serious environmental problem currently facing the world, but also one of the most important international problems per se. Second, many of those working in other disciplines describe climate change as fundamentally an ethical issue.

Third, the problem is theoretically challenging, both in itself and in virtue of the wider issues it raises. Indeed, some have even gone so far as to suggest that successfully addressing climate change will require a fundamental paradigm shift in ethics (Jamieson 1992, p. 292.)

Arguably, then, there is a strong presumption that moral philosophers should be taking climate change seriously. So, why the neglect? In my view, the most plausible explanation is that study of climate change is necessarily interdisciplinary, crossing boundaries between (at least) science, economics, law, and international relations.

This fact not only creates an obstacle to philosophical work (since amassing the relevant information is both time-consuming and intellectually demanding) but also makes it tempting to assume that climate change is essentially an issue for others to resolve. Both factors contribute to the current malaise—and not just within philosophy, but in the wider community too.

My aims in this survey, then, will be twofold. First, I will try to overcome the interdisciplinary obstacle to some extent, by making the climate change issue more accessible to both philosophers and non-philosophers alike. Second, by drawing attention to the ethical dimensions of the climate change problem, I will make the case that the temptation to defer to experts in other disciplines should be resisted. Climate change is fundamentally an ethical issue. As such, it should be of serious concern to both moral philosophers and humanity at large.

The interdisciplinary nature of the climate change problem once prompted John Broome to imply that a truly comprehensive survey of the relevant literature would be impossible (Broome 1992, p. viii). I shall not attempt the impossible. Instead, I shall present an overview of the most major and recent work relevant to philosophical discussion. Inevitably, this overview will be to some extent selective and opinionated. Still, I hope that it will help to reduce the interdisciplinary obstacles to philosophical work on climate change, by giving both philosophers and the public more generally some sense of what has been said so far and what might be at stake. In my view, the ethics of global climate change is still very much in its infancy. Hopefully, this small contribution will encourage its development.

I. TERMINOLOGY

While global warming has catastrophic communications attached to it, climate change sounds a more controllable and less emotional challenge.

FRANK LUNTZ

Potential confusion about the climate change problem begins even with the terms used to describe it: from 'greenhouse effect' to 'global warming' to the more recently favored 'climate change.' To begin with, many people spoke of 'the greenhouse effect.' This refers to the basic physical mechanism behind projected changes in the climate system. Some atmospheric gases (called 'greenhouse gases' [GHG]) have asymmetric interactions with radiation of different frequencies: just like glass in a conventional greenhouse, they allow shortwave incoming solar radiation through but reflect some of the Earth's outgoing long-wave radiation back to the surface. This creates "a partial blanketing effect," which causes the temperature at the surface to be higher than would otherwise be the case (Houghton 1997, pp. 11–12). Humans are increasing the atmospheric concentrations of these gases through industrialization. This would, other things being equal, be expected to result in an overall warming effect.

The basic greenhouse mechanism is both well understood and uncontroversial. Still, the term 'greenhouse effect' remains unsatisfactory to describe the problem at hand. There are two reasons. First, there is a purely natural greenhouse effect, without which the earth would be much colder than it is now. Hence, it is not accurate to say that "the greenhouse effect" as such is a problem; in fact, the reverse is true: without some greenhouse effect, the Earth would be much less hospitable for life as we know it. The real problem is the enhanced, human-induced, greenhouse effect. Second, it is not the greenhouse effect in isolation which causes the climate problem. Whether an increase in the concentration of greenhouse gases does in fact cause the warming we would otherwise expect depends on how the immediate effects of an increase in low frequency radiation play out in the overall climate system. But that system is complex, and its details are not very well understood.

For a while, then, the term 'global warming' was favored. This term captures the point that it is the effects of increased levels of greenhouse gases which are of concern. However, it also has its limitations. In particular, it highlights a specific effect, higher temperatures, and thus suggests a one-dimensional problem. But while it is true that rising temperature has been a locus for concern about increasing human emissions of greenhouse gases, it is not true that temperature as such defines either the core problem or even (arguably) its most important aspects. Consider, for example, the following. First, a higher global temperature does not in itself constitute the most important impact of climate change. Indeed, considered in isolation, there might be no particular reason to prefer the world as it is now to one several degrees warmer. However, second, this thought is liable to be misleading. For presumably if one is imagining a warmer world and thinking that it may be appealing, one is envisioning the planet as it might be in a stable, equilibrium state at the higher level, where humans, animals, and plants have harmoniously adapted to higher temperatures. But the problem posed by current human behavior is not of this kind. The primary concern of many scientists is that an enhanced greenhouse effect puts extra energy into the earth's climate system and so creates an imbalance. Hence, most of the concern about present climate change has been brought about because it seems that change is occurring at an unprecedented rate, that any equilibrium position is likely to be thousands, perhaps tens or hundreds of thousands, of years off, and that existing species are unlikely to be able to adapt quickly and easily under such conditions. Third, though it is at present unlikely, it is still possible that temperature might go down as a result of the increase in atmospheric greenhouse gas concentrations. But this does not cast any doubt on the serious nature of the problem. This is partly because a rapid and unprecedented lowering of temperature would have similar kinds of adverse effects on human and nonhuman life and health as a rapid warming, and partly because the effects most likely to cause cooling (such as a shutdown of the thermohaline circulation [THC] which supports the Gulf Stream current to Northern Europe [discussed in the next section]) may well be catastrophic even in relation to the other projected effects of global warming.

For all these reasons, current discussion tends to be carried out under the heading 'climate change.' This term captures the fact that it is interference in the climate system itself which is the crucial issue, not what the particular effects of that interference turn out to be. The fundamental problem is that it is now possible for humans to alter the underlying dynamics of the planet's climate and so the basic life-support system both for themselves and all other forms of life on Earth. Whether the alteration of these dynamics is most conveniently tracked in terms of increasing, declining, or even stable temperatures is of subsidiary interest in comparison to the actual changes in the climate itself and their consequences for human, and nonhuman, life.

II. CLIMATE SCIENCE

Almost no one would deny that in principle our actions and policies should be informed by our best scientific judgments, and it is hard to deny that our best scientific judgments about climate change are expressed in the IPCC reports.

JAMIESON, 1998, P. 116

Recent scientific evidence shows that major and widespread climate changes have occurred with startling speed .... Climate models typically underestimate the size, speed, and extent of those changes .... Climate surprise to be expected.

U.S. NATIONAL RESEARCH COUNCIL, 2002, P. 1

What do we know about climate change? In 1988, the Intergovernmental Panel on Climate Change (IPCC) was jointly established by the World Meteorological Association and the United Nations Environment Program to provide member governments with state of the art assessments of "the science, the impacts, and the economics of—and the options for mitigating and/or adapting to—climate change" (IPCC 2001*b*, p. vii). The IPCC has, accordingly, submitted three comprehensive reports, in 1990, 1995, and 2001. The results have remained fairly consistent across all three reports, though the level of confidence in those results has increased. The main findings of the most recent are as follows.

The IPCC begins with an account of patterns of climate change observed so far. On temperature, they report: "The global average surface temperature has increased over the 20th century by about 0.68C"; "Globally, it is very likely that the 1990s was the warmest decade and 1998 the warmest year in the instrumental record, since 1861"; and "The increase in temperature in the 20th century is likely to have been the largest of any century during the past 1,000 years" (IPCC 2001*b*, p. 152). For other phenomena, they say that snow cover and ice extent have decreased, global average sea level has risen, and ocean heat content has increased. They also cite evidence for increases in the amount of precipitation in some regions; the frequency of heavy precipitation events; cloud cover in some latitudes; and the frequency, persistence, and intensity of El Nino phenomenon.

The IPCC also surveys the literature on relevant human activities. They conclude that since preindustrial times (1750 is the usual benchmark), humans have altered "the atmosphere in ways that are expected to affect the climate" by markedly increasing the concentrations of greenhouse gases (IPCC 2001*b*, p. 154). The main culprit is carbon dioxide, for which "the concentration has increased by 31% since 1750"; "the present CO_2 concentration has not been exceeded during the past 420,000 years and likely not during the past 20 million years"; and "the current rate of increase is unprecedented during at least the past 20,000 years ... at about 1.5 ppm [parts per million] (0.4%) per year"

(IPCC 2001*b*, p. 155). The main anthropogenic sources of CO_2 are the burning of fossil fuels (about 75 percent) and changes in land-use patterns (principally, deforestation). Of secondary importance is methane, where the present atmospheric concentration "has increased by ... 151% since 1750; and has not been exceeded during the past 420,000 years," and "slightly more than half of current ... emissions are anthropogenic (e.g., use of fossil fuels, cattle, rice agriculture and landfills)" (IPCC 2001*b*, pp. 156–57). Molecule for molecule, methane is a more potent greenhouse gas than carbon dioxide. Still, because CO_2 lasts much longer in the atmosphere (about 5–200 years, as opposed to methane's 12 years), it is the more important anthropogenic greenhouse gas.

The IPCC also tries to predict future climate. To do so, it uses computer models to simulate a variety of different possible future scenarios, incorporating different assumptions about economic growth, world population, and technological change. The basic results are as follows. First, carbon dioxide emissions due to the burning of fossil fuels are "virtually certain to be the dominant influence on the trends in atmospheric CO_2 concentration during the 21st century," and by 2100, that concentration should be 90–250 percent above preindustrial levels (of 280 parts per million), at 540–970 parts per million (IPCC 2001*b*, pp. 158–59). Second, if this occurs, the full range of model scenarios predict that surface temperature will increase by 1.4–5.88C over the century. The IPCC states that this is not only a much larger projected rate of warming than that observed during the twentieth century but one "very likely ... without precedent during at least the last 10,000 years." Third, models indicate that "stabilisation of atmospheric CO_2 concentrations at 450, 650 or 1,000 ppm would require global anthropogenic CO_2 emissions to drop below 1990 levels, within a few decades, about a century, or about two centuries, respectively, and continue to decrease steadily thereafter. Eventually CO_2 emissions would need to decline to *a very small fraction* of current emissions" (IPCC 2001*b*, p. 160; emphasis added).

Alarming as the IPCC predictions are, we should also pay attention to the fact that they might be overly optimistic. For some authors argue that the current climate models typically underestimate the potential for nonlinear threshold effects (U.S. National Research Council 2002; Gagosian 2003). One well-known threat of this sort is the potential collapse of the West Antarctic Ice Sheet (WAIS), which would eventually raise global sea levels by 4–6 meters. But the recent literature registers even greater concern about a lesser-known issue: the possibility of a weakening or shutdown of the deep circulation system which drives the world's ocean currents. This system, known as "the Ocean Conveyor," distributes "vast quantities of heat around our planet, and thus plays a fundamental role in governing Earth's climate ... [and] in the distribution of life-sustaining water" (Gagosian 2003, p. 4).

The Ocean Conveyor has been called the climate's "Achilles Heel" (Broecker 1997), because it appears to be a major threshold phenomenon. There are two grounds for concern. First, there is strong evidence that in the past the conveyor has slowed, and slowed very quickly, with significant climatic consequences. One such event, 12,700 years ago, saw a drop in temperatures in the North Atlantic region of around 5 degrees Celsius in a single decade. This apparently caused icebergs to spread as far south as the coast of Portugal and has been linked to widespread global drought. Second, the operation of the conveyor is governed by factors that can be affected by climate change. In particular, the world's currents are driven by the sinking of a large volume of salty water in the North Atlantic region. But this process can be disrupted by an influx of fresh water, which both dilutes the salty water and can also create a lid over it, restricting heat flow to the atmosphere.

The possibility of dramatic climate shifts of this sort complicates the picture of a global warming world in several ways. First, it suggests that gradual warming at the global level could cause, and coexist with, dramatic cooling in some regions. (Among other things, this has serious ramifications for our ability to plan for future changes.) Second, it envisages that the major losers from climate change may not be the usual suspects, the less developed countries (LDCs). For it is the rich countries bordering the North Atlantic that are particularly vulnerable to Conveyor shifts. Climate models predict that "the North Atlantic region would cool 3 to 5 degrees Celsius if conveyor circulation were totally disrupted," producing winters "twice as cold as the worst winters on record in the eastern United States in the past century" for a period of up to a century (Gagosian 2003, p. 7).

The IPCC does not emphasize the problem of the Ocean Conveyor. For one thing, though it acknowledges that most models predict a weakening of the conveyor during the twenty-first century, it emphasizes that such changes are projected to be offset by the more general warming; for another, it suggests that a complete shutdown is unlikely during the twenty-first century (though increasingly likely thereafter) (IPCC 2001*b*, p. 16). Hence, the IPCC's attitude is relatively complacent. Still, it is not clear what justifies such complacency. On the one hand, even if the threshold will not be reached for 100 years, this is still a matter of serious concern for future generations, since once the underlying processes which will breach it are in motion, it will be difficult, if not impossible, to reverse them. On the other hand, the current models of thermohaline circulation are not very robust, primarily because scientists simply do not know where the threshold is. And some models do predict complete shutdown within a range which overlaps with IPCC projections for the twenty-first century (IPCC 2001*b*, p. 440).

III. SCIENTIFIC UNCERTAINTY

Scientists aren't any time soon going to give politicians some magic answer. Policy makers for a long, long time are going to have to deal with a situation where it's not clear what the costs and benefits are, where lots of people disagree about them, and they can't wait until everything is resolved.

ROBERT J. LAMPERT

Should the public come to believe that the scientific issues are settled, their views about global warming

will change accordingly. Therefore, you need to continue to make the lack of scientific certainty a primary issue.

FRANK LUNTZ, IN LEE 2003

It is sometimes argued that the uncertainty of the scientist's predictions is a reason for not acting at present, and that we should wait until some further research has been concluded. This argument is poor economics.

BROOME, 1992, P. 17

Politically, the most common objection raised to action on climate change is that of scientific uncertainty. In this section, I will explain why most writers on the subject believe this objection to be a red herring.

The first thing to note is that, at least in economics, uncertainty is a technical term, to be distinguished from risk. In the technical sense, a risk involves a known, or reliably estimable, probability, whereas an uncertainty arises when such probabilities are not available. So to say that there is scientific uncertainty surrounding global warming is to claim that we do not know, and cannot reliably estimate, the probability that climate change will occur, nor its extent if it does occur.

This distinction is useful, because the first problem with the objection from scientific uncertainty is that the IPCC does not seem to view global warming as uncertain in the technical sense. As we have seen, the 2001 Scientific Assessment explicitly assigns probabilities to its main climate predictions, making the situation one of risk, rather than uncertainty. Furthermore, these probabilities are of considerable magnitude. (For example, the IPCC says that it is "very likely" that in the twenty-first century there will be "higher maximum temperatures and more hot days over nearly all land areas" [IPCC 2001*b*, p. 162], by which they mean a probability of 90–99 percent [IPCC 2001*b*, p. 152, n. 7].) Given that many of the effects assigned high probabilities are associated with significant costs, they would seem to justify some kinds of action.

But perhaps the idea is that the IPCC's probability statements are not reliable, so that we should ignore them, treat the situation as genuinely uncertain, and hence refuse to act. Still, there is a difficulty. For, to an important extent, some kind of uncertainty "is an inherent part of the problem" (Broome 1992, p. 18). Arguably, if we knew exactly what was going to happen, to whom, and whose emissions would cause it, the problem might be more easily addressed; at the very least, it would have a very different shape. Hence, to refuse to act because of uncertainty is either to refuse to accept the global warming problem as it is (insisting that it be turned into a more respectable form of problem before one will address it) or else to endorse the principle that to "do nothing" is the appropriate response to uncertainty. The former is a head-in the-sand approach and clearly unacceptable, but the latter is also dubious and does not fit our usual practice.

The third, and perhaps most crucial, point to make about the problem of uncertainty is that it is important not to overplay it. For one thing, many decisions we have to make in life, including many important decisions, are also subject to considerable uncertainties. For another, all uncertainties are not created equal. On the one hand, the reason I am unable to assign probabilities may be that I know absolutely nothing about the situation, or else that I have only one past instance to go on. But I may also be uncertain in circumstances where I have considerable information.

Now it seems clear that uncertainty in the first kind of case is worse than uncertainty in the second, and potentially more paralyzing. Furthermore, and this is the crucial point, it seems reasonably clear that scientific uncertainty about global warming is of the second kind. As Donald Brown argues: "A lot of climate change science has never been in question, ... many of the elements of global warming are not seriously challenged even by the-scientific skeptics, and ... the issues of scientific certainty most discussed by climate skeptics usually deal with the magnitude and timing of climate change, not with whether global warming is a real threat" (Brown 2002, p. 102). To see this, let us briefly examine a number of sources of uncertainty about global warming.

The first concerns the direct empirical evidence for anthropogenic warming itself. This has two main aspects. First, systematic global temperature records, based on measurements of air temperature on land and surface-water temperature measurements at sea, exist only from 1860, and satellite-based measurements are available only from 1979. The direct evidence for recent warming comes from the former. But skeptics suggest that the satellite measurements do not match the surface readings and do not provide evidence for warming. Second, there is no well-defined baseline from which to measure change. While it is true that the last couple of decades have been the warmest in human history, it is also true that the long-term climate record displays significant short-term variability and that, even accounting for this, climate seems to have been remarkably stable since the end of the last Ice Age 10,000 years ago, as compared with the preceding 100,000 years. Hence, global temperatures have fluctuated considerably over the long-term record, and it is clear that these fluctuations have been naturally caused.

The skeptics are right, then, when they assert that the observational temperature record is a weak data set and that the long-term history of the climate is such that even if the data were more robust, we would be rash to conclude that humans are causing it solely on this basis. Still, it would be a mistake to infer too much from the truth of these claims. For it would be equally rash to dismiss the possibility of warming on these grounds. For, even though it might be true that the empirical evidence is consistent with there being no anthropogenic warming, it is also true that it provides just the kind of record we would expect if there were a real global warming problem.

This paradox is caused by the fact that our epistemological position with respect to climate change is intrinsically very difficult: it may simply be impossible to confirm climate change empirically from this position. This is because our basic situation may be a bit like that of a coach who is asked whether the current performance of a fifteen-year-old athlete shows that she will reach the highest level of her sport. Suppose the coach has the best evidence that she can have. It will still only be evidence for a fifteen-year-old. It will be at most consistent with reaching the highest level. It cannot be taken as a certain prediction. But that does not mean it is no prediction at all, or worthless. It is simply the best prediction she is currently in a position to make.

Fortunately, for the climate change problem, the concern with the empirical record is not the end of the matter. For the temperature record is far from our only evidence for warming. Instead, we also have strong theoretical grounds for concern. First, the basic physical and chemical mechanisms which give rise to a potential global warming effect are well understood. In particular, there is no scientific controversy over the claims (a) that in itself a higher concentration of greenhouse gas molecules in the upper atmosphere would cause more heat to be retained by the earth and less radiated out into the solar system, so that other things being equal, such an increase would cause global temperatures to rise; and (b) that human activities since the industrial revolution have significantly increased the atmospheric concentration of greenhouse gases. Hence, everyone agrees that the basic circumstances are such that a greenhouse effect is to be expected.

Second, the scientific dispute, insofar as there is one, concerns the high level of complexity of the global climate system, given which there are the other mechanisms that might be in play to moderate such an effect. The contentious issue here is whether there might be negative feedbacks that either sharply reduce or negate the effects of higher levels of greenhouse gases, or even reduce the amount of them present in the atmosphere. However, current climate models suggest that most related factors will likely exhibit positive feedbacks (water vapor, snow, and ice), while others have both positive and negative feedbacks whose net effect is unclear (e.g., clouds, ocean currents). Hence, there is genuine scientific uncertainty. But this does not by itself justify a skeptical position about action on climate change. For there may be no more reason to assume that we will be saved by unexpectedly large negative feedbacks than that the warming effect will be much worse than we would otherwise anticipate, due to unexpectedly large positive feedbacks.

This is the basic scientific situation. However, three further aspects of uncertainty are worth mentioning. First, the conclusions about feedback are also open to doubt because considerable uncertainties remain about the performance of the models. In particular, they are not completely reliable against past data. This is to be expected because the climate is a highly complex system which is not very well understood. Still, it clouds the overall picture. Second, as mentioned earlier, the current models tend to assume that atmospheric feedbacks scale linearly with surface warming, and they do not adequately account for possible threshold effects, such as the possible collapse of the West Antarctic Ice Sheet. Hence, they may underestimate the potential risks from global warming. Finally, there is a great deal of uncertainty about the distribution of climate change. Though global rises may seem small, they disguise considerable variation within years and across regions. Furthermore, though it is very difficult to predict which regions will suffer most, and in what ways, such evidence as there is suggests that, at least in the medium term, the impact will be heaviest in the tropical and sub-tropical regions (where most of the LDCs are), and lighter in the temperate regions (where most of the richer countries are).

In conclusion, there are substantial uncertainties surrounding both the direct empirical evidence for warming and our theoretical understanding of the overall climate system. But these uncertainties cut both ways. In particular, while it is certainly conceivable (though, at present, unlikely) that the climate change problem will turn out to be chimerical, it is also possible that global warming will turn out to be much worse than anyone has yet anticipated. More importantly, the really vital issue does not concern the presence of scientific uncertainty, but rather how we decide what to do under such circumstances. To this issue we now turn.

IV. ECONOMICS

Economic analyses clearly show that it will be far more expensive to cut CO_2 emissions radically than to pay the costs of adaptation to the increased temperatures.

LOMBORG, 2001, P. 318

Cost-benefit analysis, when faced with uncertainties as big as these, would simply be self-deception. And in any case, it could not be a successful exercise, because the issue is too poorly understood, and too little accommodated in the current economic theory.

BROOME, 1992, P. 19

As it turns out, many recent skeptics no longer cite scientific uncertainty as their reason for resisting action on climate change. Instead, they claim to accept the reality of human-induced climate change but argue that there is a strong economic rationale for refusing to act. Prevention, they insist, is more expensive than adaptation; hence, both present and future generations would be better off if we simply accepted that there will be climate change and tried to live with it. Furthermore, they assert, money that might be spent on prevention would be better spent helping the world's poor. I will consider the first of these arguments in this section and the second later on.

Several attempts have been made to model the economic implications of climate change. Politically prominent among these is the DICE model proposed by the Yale economist William Nordhaus. The DICE model is an integrated assessment model. Integrated assessment (IA) models combine the essential elements of biophysical and economic systems in an attempt to understand the impact of climate and economic policies on one another. Typically, such models aim to find a climate policy which will maximize the social welfare function. And many give the surprising result that only limited abatement should occur in the next twenty to thirty years, since the costs of current reductions are too high in comparison to the benefits. Hence, proponents of these models argue that, based on economic costs, the developed world (and the United States in particular) should pursue adaptation rather than abatement. This is the argument embraced by Lomborg, who cites Nordhaus's work as his inspiration.

1. The Cost Argument

A full response to Lomborg's proposal requires addressing both the argument about costs and the more general argument for an adaptation, rather than mitigation, strategy. Let us begin with the cost argument.

The first point to make is that, even if Nordhaus's calculations were reliable, the costs of climate change mitigation do not seem unmanageable. As Thomas Schelling puts it:

> The costs in reduced productivity are estimated at two percent of GNP forever. Two percent of GNP seems politically unmanageable in many countries. Still, if one plots the curve of US per capita GNP over the coming century with and without the two percent permanent loss, the difference is about the thickness of a line drawn with a number two pencil, and the doubled per capita income that would have been achieved by 2060 is reached in 2062. If someone could wave a wand and phase in, over a few years, a climate-mitigation program that depressed our GNP by two percent in perpetuity, no one would notice the difference. (Schelling 1997)

Even Lomborg agrees with this. For he not only cites the 2 percent figure with approval but adds, "there is no way that the cost [of stabilizing abatement measures] will send us to the poorhouse" (Lomborg 2001, p. 323).

The second point is that Nordhaus's work is extremely controversial. For one thing, some claim that his model is simplistic, both in itself and, especially, relative to the climate models. Indeed, one commentator goes so far as to say that "the model is extremely simple—so simple that I once, during a debate, dubbed it a toy model" (Gundermann 2002, p. 150). For another others offer rival models which endorse the exact opposite to Nodhaus's conclusion: that action now (in the form of carbon taxes, etc.) would be more beneficial in the long term than waiting, even perhaps if global warming does not actually transpire (e.g., Costanza 1996; De Leo et al. 2001; Woodward and Bishop 1997).

Part of the reason that such disputes arise is because the models embody some very questionable assumptions. Some are specific to Nordhaus (e.g.,

Gundermann 2002, p. 154). But others are the result of two more general kinds of difficulty.

The first is practical. There are severe informational problems involved in any reliable cost-benefit analysis for climate change. In particular, over the timescale relevant for climate change, "society is bound to be radically transformed in ways which are utterly unpredictable to us now," and these changes will themselves be affected by climate (Broome 1992, p. 10; see also Jamieson 1992, pp. 288–89). Hence, Broome, for example, argues that fine-grained cost-benefit analyses are simply not possible for climate change.

The second kind of difficulty, of more interest to ethicists perhaps, is there are some basic philosophical problems inherent in the methods of conventional economic analysis. Here let me mention just two prominent examples.

One concerns the standard economic treatments of intergenerational issues. Economists typically employ a social discount rate (SDR) of 2–10 percent for future costs (Lomborg uses 5 percent; Nordhaus 3–6 percent). But this raises two serious concerns. The first is that, for the short- to medium-term effects of climate change (say, over ten to fifty years), model results can be extremely sensitive to the rate chosen. For example, Shultz and Kasting claim that the choice of SDR makes the rest of the climate change model largely irrelevant in Nordhaus's model, and variations in the SDR make a huge difference to model results more generally (Schultz and Kasting 1997, cited by Gundermann 2002, p. 147). The other concern is that, when the SDR is positive, all but the most catastrophic costs disappear after a number of decades, and even these become minimal over very long time periods. This has serious consequences for the intergenerational ethics of climate change. As John Broome puts it: "It is people who are now children and people who are not yet born who will reap most of the benefits of any project that mitigates the effects of global warming. Most of the benefits of such a project will therefore be ignored by the consumer-price method of project evaluation. It follows that this method is quite useless for assessing such long-term projects. This is my main

reason for rejecting it [for climate change]" (Broome 1992, p. 72).

The second philosophical problem inherent in conventional economic analysis is that it cannot adequately capture all of the relevant costs and benefits. The obvious cases here are costs to nonhumans (such as animals, plants, species, and ecosystems) and noneconomic costs to humans, such as aesthetic costs (Sagoff 1998; Schmidtz 2001). But there is also concern that conventional economic analysis cannot adequately take into account costs with special features, such as irreversible and nonsubstitutable damages, that are especially associated with climate change (Shogren and Toman 2000; Costanza 1996).

We can conclude, then, that there are strong reasons to be skeptical about Lomborg's cost argument in particular and about the reliability of fine-grained economic analyses of climate change more generally. Still, John Broome argues that two things can be said with some confidence: first, the specific effects of climate change "are very uncertain," where (as argued in the previous section) "this by itself has important consequences for the work that needs to be done," and, second, these effects "will certainly be long lived, almost certainly large, probably bad, and possibly disastrous" (Broome 1992, p. 12). To these claims we might add that at 2 percent of world production, the estimated costs of stabilizing emissions do not seem obviously prohibitive.

2. The Adaptation Argument

We can now turn to the more general argument that, instead of reducing emissions, we should pursue a policy of trying to adapt to the effects of climate change. The first thing to note about this argument is that adaptation measures will clearly need to be part of any sensible climate policy, because we are already committed to some warming due to past emissions, and almost all of the proposed abatement strategies envisage that overall global emissions will continue to rise for at least the next few decades, committing us to even more. Hence, the choice cannot be seen as being one between abatement and adaptation, since advocates of abatement generally support a combination of strategies. The real issue is rather whether adaptation should be our only strategy, so that abatement is ignored (Jamieson, forthcoming).

If this is the proposal, several points can be made about it. First, we should beware of making the case for adaptation a self-fulfilling prophesy. For example, it is true that the existing capital stock in the United States made it difficult for America to meet its original Kyoto target for 2008–12. But it is also true that a significant amount of this capital was invested after the United States committed itself to stabilizing emissions at the Rio Earth Summit of 1992. Furthermore, matters will only get worse. The Bush administration's current energy plan calls for the building of 1,300 new power plants in the next twenty years, boosting supply (and thereby emissions) by more than 30 percent.

Second, the comparison between abatement and adaptation costs looks straightforward but is not. In particular, we have to bear in mind the different kinds of economic costs at stake in each case. On the one hand, suppose we allow global warming to continue unchecked. What will we be adapting to? Chances are, we will experience both a range of general gradual climatic changes and an increase in severe weather and climate events. On the other hand, if we go for abatement, we will also be adapting, but this time to increases in tax rates on (or decreases in permits for) carbon emissions. But there is a world of difference between these kinds of adaptation: in the first case, we would be dealing with sudden, unpredictable, large-scale impacts which descend at random on particular individuals, communities, regions, and industries and visit them with pure, unrecoverable costs, whereas, in the second, we would be addressing gradual, predictable, incremental impacts, phased in so as to make adaptation easier. Surely, adaptation in the second kind of case is, other things being equal, preferable to the first.

Third, any reasonable abatement strategy would need to be phased in gradually, and it is well documented that many economically beneficial energy savings could be introduced immediately, using existing technologies. These facts suggest that the adaptation argument is largely irrelevant to what to do now. For the first steps that need to be taken would be economically beneficial, not costly. Yet opponents of action on climate change do not want to do even this much.

V. RISK MANAGEMENT AND THE PRECAUTIONARY PRINCIPLE

The risk assessment process … is as much policy and politics as it is science. A typical risk assessment relies on at least 50 different assumptions about exposure, dose-response, and relationships between animals and humans. The modeling of uncertainty also depends on assumptions. Two risk assessments conducted on the same problem can vary widely in results.

RAFFENSBERGER AND TICKNER, 1999, P. 2

Serious as they are, these largely technical worries about conventional economic analysis are not the only reasons to be wary of any economic solution to the climate change problem. For some writers suggest that exclusive reliance on economic analysis would be problematic even if all of the numbers were in, since the climate problem is ultimately one of values, not efficiency: as Dale Jamieson puts it, its "fundamental questions" concern "how we ought to live, what kinds of societies we want, and how we should relate to nature and other forms of life" (Jamieson 1992, p. 290).

But the problem may not be just that climate change raises issues of value. It may also show that our existing values are insufficient to the task. Jamieson, for example, offers the following argument. First, he asserts that our present values evolved relatively recently, in "low-population-density and low-technology societies, with seemingly unlimited access to land and other resources." Then he claims that these values include as a central component an account of responsibility which "presupposes that harms and their causes are individual, that they can be readily identified, and that they are local in time and space." Third, he argues that problems such as climate change fit none of these criteria.

Hence, he concludes, a new value system is needed (Jamieson 1992, pp. 291–92).

How then should we proceed? Some authors advocate a rethinking of our basic moral practices. For example, Jamieson claims that we must switch our focus away from approaches (such as those of contemporary economics) which concentrate on "calculating probable outcomes" and instead foster and develop a set of "twenty-first century virtues," including "humility, courage, ... moderation," "simplicity and conservatism" (Jamieson 1992, p. 294).

Other climate change theorists, however, are less radical. For example, Henry Shue employs the traditional notions of a "No Harm Principle" and rights to physical security (Shue 1999, p. 43). He points out that even in the absence of certainty about the exact impacts of climate change, there is a real moral problem posed by subjecting future generations to the risk of severe harms. This implies a motive for action in spite of the scientific and economic uncertainties. Similarly, many policy makers appeal to the "precautionary principle," which is now popular in international law and politics and receives one of its canonical statements in the 1992 United Nations Framework Convention on Climate Change (1992). The exact formulation of the precautionary principle is contro-versial; but one standard version is the Wingspread Statement, which reads: "When an activity raises threats of harm to human health or the environment, precautionary measures should be taken even if some cause and effect relationships are not fully established scientifically" (Wingspread Statement 1998).

Both no harm principles and the precautionary principle, are, however, controversial. No harm principles are often criticized for being either obscure or else overly conservative when taken literally; and the precautionary principle generates similar objections: its critics say that it is vacuous, extreme, and irrational. Still, I would argue that, at least in the case of the precautionary principle, many of these initial objections can be overcome (Gardiner 2004a). In particular, a core use of the precautionary principle can be captured by restricting its application to those situations which satisfy John Rawls's criteria for the application of a maximum principle: the parties lack, or have good

reason to doubt, relevant probability information; they care little for potential gains; and they face unacceptable outcomes (Rawls 1999, p. 134). And this core use escapes the initial, standard objections.

More importantly for current purposes, I would also claim that a reasonable case can be made that climate change satisfies the conditions for the core precautionary principle (Gardiner 2004a). First, many of the predicted outcomes from climate change seem severe, and some are catastrophic. Hence, there are grounds for saying there are unacceptable outcomes. Second, as we have seen, for gradual change, either the probabilities of significant damage from climate change are high or else we do not know the probabilities; and for abrupt change the probabilities are unknown. Finally, given widespread endorsement of the view that stabilizing emissions would impose a cost of "only" 2 percent of world production, one might claim that we care little about the potential gains—at least relative to the possibly catastrophic costs.

There is reason to believe, then, that the endorsement by many policy makers of some form of precautionary or no harm approach is reasonable for climate change. But exactly which "precautionary measures" should be taken? One obvious first step is that those changes in present energy consumption which would have short-term, as well as long-term, economic benefits should be made immediately. In addition, we should begin acting on low-cost emissions-saving measures as soon as possible. Beyond that, it is difficult to say exactly how we should strike a balance between the needs of the present and those of the future. Clearly, this is an area where further thought is urgently needed.

Still, it is perhaps worthwhile closing this section with one, speculative, opinion about how we should direct our efforts. By focusing on the possibility of extreme events, and considering the available science, Brian O'Neill and Michael Oppenheimer suggest in a recent article in *Science* that "taking a precautionary approach because of the very large uncertainties, a limit of 2 C above 1990 global average temperature is justified to protect [the West Antarctic Ice Sheet]. To avert shutdown of the [Thermohaline circulation], we define a limit of 3 C warming over 100 years" (O'Neill and Oppenheimer 2002). It is not clear how robust these assertions are. Still, they suggest a reasonable starting point for discussion. For, on the assumption that these outcomes are unacceptable, and given the IPCC projections of a warming of between 1.4 and 5.88C over the century, both claims appear to justify significant immediate action on greenhouse gas stabilization.

VI. RESPONSIBILITY FOR THE PAST

I'll tell you one thing I'm not going to do is I'm not going to let the United States carry the burden for cleaning up the world's air, like the Kyoto Treaty would have done. China and India were exempted from that treaty. I think we need to be more evenhanded.

GEORGE W. BUSH, QUOTED BY SINGER 2002, P. 30

Even in an emergency one pawns the jewellery before selling the blankets .... Whatever justice may positively require, it does not permit that poor nations be told to sell their blankets [compromise their development strategies] in order that the rich nations keep their jewellery [continue their unsustainable lifestyles].

SHUE, 1992, P. 397; QUOTED BY GRUBB 1995, P. 478

To demand that [the developing countries] act first is patently unfair and would not even warrant serious debate were it not the position of a superpower.

HARRIS, 2003

Suppose, then, that action on climate change is morally required. Whose responsibility is it? The core ethical issue concerning global warming is that of how to allocate the costs and benefits of greenhouse gas emissions and abatement. On this issue, there is a surprising convergence of philosophical writers on the subject: they are virtually unanimous in their conclusion that the developed countries should take the lead role in bearing the costs of climate change, while the less developed countries should be allowed to increase emissions for the foreseeable future.

Still, agreement on the fact of responsibility masks some notable differences about its justification, form, and extent; so it is worth assessing the competing accounts in more detail. The first issue to be considered is that of "backward-looking considerations." The facts are that developed countries are responsible for a very large percentage of historical emissions, whereas the costs likely to be imposed by those emissions are expected to be disproportionately visited on the poorer countries (IPCC 1995, p. 94). This suggests two approaches. First, one might invoke historical principles of justice that require that one "clean up one's own mess." This suggests that the industrialized countries should bear the costs imposed by their past emissions. Second, one might characterize the earth's capacity to absorb man-made emissions of carbon dioxide as a common resource, or sink (Traxler 2002, p. 120), and claim that, since this capacity is limited, a question of justice arises in how its use should be allocated (Singer 2002, pp. 31–32). On this approach, the obvious argument to be made is that the developed countries have largely exhausted the capacity in the process of industrializing and so have, in effect, denied other countries the opportunity to use "their shares." On this view, justice seems to require that the developed countries compensate the less developed for this overuse.

It is worth observing two facts about these two approaches. First, they are distinct. On the one hand, the historical principle requires compensation for damage inflicted by one party on another and does not presume that there is a common resource; on the other, the sink consideration crucially relies on the presence of a common resource and does not presume that any (further) damage is caused to the disenfranchised beyond their being deprived of an opportunity for use. Second, they are compatible. One could maintain that a party deprived of its share of a common resource ought to be compensated both for that and for the fact that material harm has been inflicted upon it as a direct result of the deprivation.

Offhand, the backward-looking considerations seem weighty. However, many writers suggest that in practice they should be ignored. One justification that is offered is that, until comparatively recently, the developed countries were ignorant of the effects of their emissions on the climate and so should not be held accountable for past emissions (or at least those prior to 1990, when the IPCC issued its first report). This consideration seems to me far from decisive, because it is not clear how far the ignorance defense extends. On the one hand, in the case of the historical principle, if the harm inflicted on the world's poor is severe, and if they lack the means to defend themselves against it, it seems odd to say that the rich nations have no obligation to assist, especially when they could do so relatively easily and are in such a position largely because of their previous causal role. On the other hand, in the case of the sink consideration, if you deprive me of my share of an important resource, perhaps one necessary to my very survival, it seems odd to say that you have no obligation to assist because you were ignorant of what you were doing at the time. This is especially so if your overuse both effectively denies me the means of extricating myself from the problem you have created and also further reduces the likelihood of fair outcomes on this and other issues (Shue 1992).

A second justification for ignoring past emissions is that taking the past into account is impractical. For example, Martino Traxler claims that any agreement which incorporates backward-looking considerations would require "a prior international agreement on what constitutes international distributive justice and then an agreement on how to translate these considerations into practical allocations" and that, given that "such an agreement is [un]likely in our lifetime," insisting on it "would amount to putting off any implementation concerning climate change indefinitely" (Traxler 2002, p. 128). Furthermore, he asserts that climate change takes the form of a commons problem and so poses a significant problem of defection: "Each nation is (let us hope) genuinely concerned with this problem, but each nation is also aware that it is in its interest not to contribute or do its share, regardless of what other countries do .... In short, in the absence of the appropriate international coercive

muscle, defection, however unjust it may be, is just too tempting" (Traxler 2002, p. 122).

Though rarely spelled out, such pragmatic concerns seem to influence a number of writers. Still, I am not convinced—at least by Traxler's arguments. For one thing, I do not see why a complete background understanding of international justice is required, especially just to get started. For another, I am not sure that defection is quite the problem, or at least has the implications, that Traxler suggests. In particular, Traxler's argument seems to go something like this: since there is no external coercive body, countries must be motivated not to defect from an agreement; but (rich) countries will be motivated to defect if they are asked to carry the costs of their past (mis)behavior; therefore, past behavior cannot be considered, otherwise (rich) countries will defect. But this reasoning is questionable, on several grounds. First, it seems likely that if past behavior is not considered, then the poor countries will defect. Since, in the long run, their cooperation is required, this would suggest that Traxler's proposal is at least as impractical as anyone else's. Second, it is not clear that no external coercive instruments exist. Trade and travel sanctions, for example, are a possibility and have precedents. Third, the need for such sanctions (and indeed, the problem of defection in general) is not brought on purely by including the issue of backward-looking considerations in negotiation, nor is it removed by their absence. So it seems arbitrary to disallow such considerations on this basis. Finally, Traxler's argument seems to assume (first) that the only truly urgent issue that needs to be addressed with respect to climate change is that of future emissions growth, and (second) that this issue is important enough that concerns about (i) the costs of climate change to which we are already committed, and (ii) the problem of inequity in the proceeds from those emissions (e.g., that the rich countries may have, in effect, stolen rights to develop from the poorer countries) can be completely ignored. But such claims seem controversial.

The arguments in favor of ignoring past emissions are then unconvincing. Hence, contrary to many writers on this subject, I conclude that we should not ignore the presumption that past emissions pose an issue of justice which is both practically and theoretically important. Since this has the effect of increasing the obligations of the developed nations, it strengthens the case for saying that these countries bear a special responsibility for dealing with the climate change problem.

VII. ALLOCATING FUTURE EMISSIONS

The central argument for equal per capita rights is that the atmosphere is a global commons, whose use and preservation are essential to human well being.

BAER, 2002, P. 401

Much like self-defense may excuse the commission of an injury or even a murder, so their necessity for our subsistence may excuse our indispensable current emissions and the resulting future infliction of harm they cause.

TRAXLER, 2002, P. 107

Let us now turn to the issue of how to allocate future emissions. Here I cannot survey all the proposals that have been made; but I will consider four prominent suggestions.

1. Equal Per Capita Entitlements

The most obvious initial proposal is that some acceptable overall level of anthropogenic greenhouse emissions should be determined …, and then that this should be divided equally among the world's population, to produce equal per capita entitlements to emissions. This proposal seems intuitive but would have a radical redistributive effect. Consider the following illustration. Singer points out that stabilizing carbon emissions at current levels would give a per capita rate of roughly one tonne per year. But actual emissions in the rich countries are substantially in excess of this: the United States is at more than 5 tonnes per capita (and rising); and Japan, Australia, and Western Europe are all in a range from 1.6 to

4.2 tonnes per capita (with most below 3). India and China, on the other hand, are significantly below their per capita allocation (at 0.29 and 0.76, respectively). Thus, Singer suggests (against the present President Bush's claim at the beginning of the previous section), an "even-handed approach" implies that India and China should be allowed increases in emissions, while the United States should take a massive cut (Singer 2002, pp. 39–40).

Two main concerns have been raised about the per capita proposal. The first is that it might encourage population growth, through giving countries an incentive to maximize their population in order to receive more emissions credits (Jamieson 2001, p. 301). But this concern is easily addressed: most proponents of a per capita entitlement propose indexing population figures for each country to a certain time. For example, Jamieson proposes a 1990 baseline (relevant due to the initial IPCC report), whereas Singer proposes 2050 (to avoid punishing countries with younger populations at present). The second concern is more serious. The per capita proposal does not take into account the fact that emissions may play very different roles in people's lives. In particular, some emissions are used to produce luxury items, whereas others are necessary for most people's survival.

2. Rights to Subsistence Emissions

This concern is the basis for the second proposal on how to allocate emissions rights. Henry Shue argues that people should have inalienable rights to the minimum emissions necessary to their survival or to some minimal quality of life. This proposal has several implications. First, it suggests that there might be moral constraints on the limitation of emissions, so that establishing a global emissions ceiling will not be simply a matter for climatologists or even economists. If some emissions are deemed morally essential then they may have to be guaranteed even if this leads to an overall allocation above the scientific optimum. Traxler is explicit as to why this is the case. Even if subsistence emissions cause harm, they can be morally excusable because "they present their potential emitters with such a hard choice between avoiding a harm today or avoiding a harm in the future" that they are morally akin to self-defense. Second, the proposal suggests that actual emissions entitlements may not be equal for all individuals and may vary over time. For the benefits that can actually be drawn from a given quantity of green-house gas emissions vary with the existing technology, and the necessity of them depends on the available alternatives. But both vary by region, and will no doubt evolve in the future, partly in response to emissions regulation. Third, as Shue says, the guaranteed minimum principle does not imply that allocation of any remaining emissions rights above those necessary for subsistence must be made on a per capita basis. The guaranteed minimum view is distinct from a more robust egalitarian position which demands equality of a good at all levels of its consumption (Shue 1995, pp. 387–88); hence, above the minimum some other criterion might be adopted.

The guaranteed minimum approach has considerable theoretical appeal. However, there are [two] reasons to be cautious about it. First, determining what counts as a "subsistence emission" is a difficult matter, both in theory and in practice. For example, Traxler defines subsistence emissions in terms of physiologically and socially necessary emissions but characterizes social necessity as "what a society needs or finds indispensable in order to survive" (Traxler 2002, p. 106). But this is problematic. For one thing, much depends on how societies define what they find "indispensable." (It is hard not to recall the first President Bush's comment, back in 1992, that "the American way of life is not up for negotiation.") For another, and perhaps more importantly, there is something procedurally odd about the proposal. For it appears to envisage that the climate change problem can be resolved by appealing to some notion of social necessity that is independent of, and not open to, moral assessment. But this seems somehow backwards. After all, several influential writers argue that part of the challenge of climate change is the deep questions it raises about how we should live and what kinds of societies we ought to have

(Jamieson 1992, p. 290; and IPCC 2001a, 1.4; questioned by Lomborg 2001, pp. 318–22).

Second, in practice, the guaranteed approach may not differ from the per capita principle, and yet may lack the practical advantages of that approach. On the first issue, given the foregoing point, it is hard to see individuals agreeing on an equal division of basic emissions entitlements that does anything less than exhaust the maximum permissible on other (climatological and intergenerational) grounds; and easy to see them being tempted to overshoot it. Furthermore, determining an adequate minimum may turn out to be almost the same task as (a) deciding what an appropriate ceiling would be and then (b) assigning per capita rights to the emissions it allows. For a would also require a view about what constitutes an acceptable form of life and how many emissions are necessary to sustain it. On the second issue, the subsistence emissions proposal carries political risks that the per capita proposal does not, or at least not to the same extent. For one thing, the claim that subsistence emissions are nonnegotiable seems problematic given the first point (above) that there is nothing to stop some people claiming that almost any emission is essential to their way of life. For another, the claim that nonsubsistence emissions need not be distributed equally may lead some in developed countries to argue that what is required to satisfy the subsistence constraint is extremely minimal and that emissions above that level should be either grandfathered or else distributed on other terms favorable to those with existing fossil-fuel intensive economies. But this would mean that developing countries might be denied the opportunity to develop, without any compensation.

3. Priority to the Least Well-Off

The third proposal I wish to consider offers a different justification for departing from the per capita principle: namely, that such a departure might maximally (or at least disproportionately) benefit the least well-off. The obvious version of this argument suggests, again, that the rich countries should carry the costs of dealing with global warming, and the LDCs should be offered generous economic assistance. But there are also less obvious versions, some of which may be attributable to some global warming skeptics.

The first is offered by Bjørn Lomborg. Lomborg claims that the climate change problem ultimately reduces to the question of whether to help poor inhabitants of the poor countries now or their richer descendents later. And he argues that the right answer is to help now, since the present poor are both poorer and more easily helped. Kyoto, he says, "will likely cost at least $150 billion a year, and possibly much more," whereas "just $70–80 billion a year could give all Third World inhabitants access to the basics like health, education, water and sanitation" (Lomborg 2001, p. 322).

But this argument is far from compelling. For one thing, it seems falsely to assume that helping the poor now and acting on climate change are mutually exclusive alternatives (Grubb 1995, p. 473, n. 25). For another, it seems to show a giant leap of political optimism. If their past record is anything to go by, the rich countries are even less likely to contribute large sums of money to help the world's poor directly than they are to do so to combat climate change (Singer 2002, pp. 26–27).

A second kind of priority argument may underlie the present President Bush's proposal of a "greenhouse gas intensity approach," which seeks to index emissions to economic activity. Bush has suggested reducing the amount of greenhouse gas per unit of U.S. GDP by 18 percent in ten years, saying "economic growth is the solution, not the problem" and "the United States wants to foster economic growth in the developing world, including the world's poorest nations" (Singer 2002, p. 43). Hence, he seems to appeal to a Rawlsian principle.

Peter Singer, however, claims that there are two serious problems with this argument. First, it faces a considerable burden of proof: it must show that U.S. economic activity not only makes the poor better off, but maximally so. Second, this burden cannot be met: not only do CIA figures show the United States "well above average in emissions per head it produces in proportion to per capita GDP," but "the vast majority of the goods and services that the US produces—89 percent of them—are consumed in the US" (Singer 2002,

pp. 44–45). This, Singer argues, strongly suggests that the world's poor would be better off if the majority of the economic activity the United States undertakes (with its current share of world emissions) occurred elsewhere.

4. Equalizing Marginal Costs

A final proposal superficially resembles the equal intensity principle but is advocated for very different reasons. Martino Traxler proposes a "fair chore division" which equalizes the marginal costs of those aiming to prevent climate change. Such a proposal, he claims, is politically expedient, in that it (*a*) provides each nation in the global commons with "no stronger reasons to defect from doing its (fair) share than it gives any other nation" and so (*a*) places "the most moral pressure possible on each nation to do its part" (Traxler 2002, p. 129).

Unfortunately, it is not clear that Traxler's proposal achieves the ends he sets for it. First, by itself, *a* does not seem a promising way to escape a traditional commons or prisoner's dilemma situation. What is crucial in such situations is the magnitude of the benefits of defecting relative to those of cooperating; whether the relative benefits are equally large for all players is of much less importance. Second, this implies that *b* must be the crucial claim, but *b* is also dubious in this context. For Traxler explicitly rules out backward-looking considerations on practical grounds. But this means ignoring the previous emissions of the rich countries, the extent to which those emissions have effectively denied the LDCs "their share" of fossil-fuel-based development in the future, and the damages which will be disproportionately visited on the LDCs because of those emissions. So, it is hard to see why the LDCs will experience "maximum moral pressure" to comply. Third, equal marginal costs approaches are puzzling for a more theoretical reason. In general, equality of marginal welfare approaches suffer from the intuitive defect that they take no account of the overall level of welfare of each individual. Hence, under certain conditions, they might license taking large amounts from the poor (if they are so badly off anyway that changes for the worse make little difference), while leaving the rich relatively untouched (if they are so used to a life of luxury that they suffer greatly from even small losses). Now, Traxler's own approach does not fall into this trap, but this is because he advocates that costs should be measured not in terms of preferences or economic performance but, rather, in terms of subsistence, near subsistence, and luxury emissions. Thus, his view is that the rich countries should have to give up all of their luxury emissions before anyone else need consider giving up subsistence and near-subsistence emissions. But this raises a new concern. For in practice this means that Traxler's equal burdens proposal actually demands massive action from the rich countries before the poor countries are required to do anything at all (if indeed they ever are). And however laudable, or indeed morally right, such a course of action might be, it is hard to see it as securing the politically stable agreement that Traxler craves, or, at least, it is hard to see it as more likely to do so than the alternatives. So, the equal marginal costs approach seems to undercut its own rationale.

VIII. WHAT HAS THE WORLD DONE?
THE KYOTO DEAL

This has been a disgraceful performance. It is the single worst failure of political leadership that I have seen in my lifetime.

        AL GORE, QUOTED BY HOPGOOD 1998, P. 199

The system is made in America, and the Americans aren't part of it.

                DAVID DONIGER

We have seen that there is a great deal of convergence on the issue of who has primary responsibility to act on climate change. The most defensible accounts of fairness and climate change suggest that the rich countries should bear the brunt, and perhaps even the entirety, of the costs. What, then, has the world done?

The current international effort to combat climate change has come in three main phases. The first came to fruition at the Rio Earth Summit of 1992. There, the countries of the world committed themselves to the Framework Convention on Climate Change (FCCC), which required "stabilization of greenhouse gas concentrations in the atmosphere at a level that would prevent dangerous anthropogenic interference with the climate system" and endorsed a principle of "common but differentiated responsibilities," according to which, the richer, industrialized nations (listed under "Annex I" in the agreement) would take the lead in cutting emissions, while the less developed countries would pursue their own development and take significant action only in the future. In line with the FCCC, many of the rich countries (including the United States, European Union, Japan, Canada, Australia, New Zealand, and Norway) announced that they would voluntarily stabilize their emissions at 1990 levels by 2000.

Unfortunately, it soon became clear that merely voluntary measures were ineffective. For, as it turned out, most of those who had made declarations did nothing meaningful to try to live up to them, and their emissions continued to rise without constraint. Thus, a second phase ensued. Meeting in Berlin in 1995, it was agreed that the parties should accept binding constraints on their emissions, and this was subsequently achieved in Japan in 1997, with the negotiation of the Kyoto Protocol. This agreement initially appeared to be a notable success, in that it required the Annex I countries to reduce emissions to roughly 5 percent below 1990 levels between 2008 and 2012. But it also contained two major compromises on the goal of limiting overall emissions, in that it allowed countries to count forests as sinks and to meet their commitments through buying unused capacity from others, through permit trading.

The promise of Kyoto turned out to be short lived. First, it proved so difficult to thrash out the details that a subsequent meeting, in the Hague in November 2000, broke down amid angry recriminations. Second, in March 2001, the Bush administration withdrew U.S. support, effectively killing the Kyoto agreement. Or so most people thought. For, as it turned out, the U.S. withdrawal did not cause immediate collapse. Instead, during the remainder of 2001, in meetings in Bonn and Marrakesh, a third phase began in which a full agreement was negotiated, with the European Union, Russia, and Japan playing prominent roles, and sent to participating governments for ratification. Many nations swiftly ratified, including the European

Union, Japan, and Canada, so that, at the time of writing, the Kyoto Treaty needs only ratification by Russia to pass into international law.

On the surface, then, the effort to combat global climate change looks a little bruised, but still on track. But this appearance may be deceptive. For there is good reason to think that the Kyoto Treaty is deeply flawed, both in its substance and its background assumptions (Barrett 2003; Gardiner 2004b). Let us begin with two substantive criticisms.

The first is that Kyoto currently does very little to limit emissions. Initial projections suggested that the Bonn-Marrakesh agreement would reduce emissions for participants by roughly 2 percent on 1990 levels, down from the 5 percent initially envisaged by the original Kyoto agreement (Ott 2001). But recent research suggests that such large concessions were made in the period from Kyoto to Marrakesh that (a) even full compliance by its signatories would result in an overall increase in their emissions of 9 percent above 2000 levels by the end of the first commitment period; and (b) if present slow economic growth persists, this would actually match or exceed projected business-as-usual emissions (Babiker et al. 2002). Coupled with emissions growth in the LDCs, this means that there will be another substantial global increase by 2012. This is nothing short of astounding given that by then we will be "celebrating" twenty years since the Earth Summit (Gardiner 2004b).

It is worth pausing to consider potential objections to this criticism. Some would argue that, even if it achieves very little, the current agreement is to be valued either procedurally (as a necessary first step), symbolically (for showing that some kind of agreement is possible), geo-politically (for showing that the rest of the world can act without the United States), or as simply the best that is possible under current conditions (Athanasiou and Baer 2001, 2002, p. 24). There is something to be said for these views. For the current Kyoto Protocol sets targets only for 2008–12, and these targets are intended as only the first of many rounds of abatement measures. Kyoto's enthusiasts anticipate that the level of cuts will be deepened and their coverage expanded (to include the developing countries) as subsequent targets for new periods are negotiated.

Nevertheless, I remain skeptical. This is partly due to the history of climate negotiations in general, and the current U.S. energy policy in particular; and partly because I do not think future generations will see reason to thank us for symbolism rather than action. But the main reason is that there are clear ways in which the world could have done better (Gardiner 2004b).

This leads us to the second substantive criticism of Kyoto: that it contains no effective compliance mechanism. This criticism arises because, although the Bonn-Marrakash agreement allows for reasonably serious punishments for those who fail to reach their targets, these punishments cannot be enforced. For the envisioned treaty has been set up so that countries have several ways to avoid being penalized. On the one hand, enforcement is not binding on any country that fails to ratify the amendment necessary to punish it (Barrett 2003, p. 386). On the other, the penalties take the form of more demanding targets in the next decade's commitment period—but parties can take this into account when negotiating their targets for that commitment period, and in any case a country is free to exit the treaty with one year's notice, three years after the treaty has entered into force for it (FCCC, article 25).

The compliance mechanisms for Kyoto are thus weak. Some would object to this, saying that they are as strong as is possible under current institutions. But I argue that this is both misleading and, to some extent, irrelevant. It is misleading because other agreements have more serious, external sanctions (e.g., the Montreal Protocol on ozone depletion allows for trade sanctions), and also because matters of compliance are notoriously difficult in international relations, leading some to suggest that it is only the easy, and comparatively trivial, agreements that get made. It is somewhat irrelevant because part of what is at stake with climate change is whether we have institutions capable of responding to such global and long-term threats (Gardiner 2004b).

Kyoto is also flawed in its background assumptions. Consider the following three examples. First, the agreement assumes a "two track" approach, whereby an acceptable deal on climate can be made without addressing the wider issue of international justice. But this, Shue argues, represents a compound injustice to the poor nations, whose bargaining power on climate change is reduced by existing injustice (Shue 1992, p. 373). Furthermore, this injustice appears to be manifest, in that the treaty directly addresses only the costs of preventing future climate change and only indirectly (and minimally) addresses the costs of coping with climate change to which we are already committed (Shue 1992, p. 384). Second, the Bonn-Marrakesh deal eschews enforcement mechanisms external to the climate change issue, such as trade sanctions. Given the apparent fragility of such a commitment on the part of the participant countries, this is probably disastrous. Third, Kyoto takes as its priority the issue of cost-effectiveness. As several authors point out, this tends to shift the focus of negotiations away from the important ethical issues and (paradoxically) to tend to make the agreement less, rather than more, practical.

Why is Kyoto such a failure? The reasons are no doubt complex and include the political role of energy interests, confusion about scientific uncertainties and economic costs, and the inadequacies of the international system. But two further factors have also been emphasized in the literature. So, I will just mention them in closing. The first is the role of the United States, which, with 4 percent of the world's population, emits roughly 25 percent of global greenhouse gases. From the early stages, and on the most important issues, the United States effectively molded the agreement to its will, persistently objecting when other countries tried to make it stronger. But then it abandoned the treaty, seemingly repudiating even those parts on which it had previously agreed. This behavior has been heavily criticized for being seriously unethical (e.g., Brown 2002; Harris 2000a). Indeed, Singer even goes so far as to suggest that it is so unethical that the moral case for economic sanctions against the United States (and other countries which have refused to act on climate change) is stronger than it was for apartheid South Africa, since the South African regime, horrible as it was, harmed only its own citizens, whereas the United States harms citizens of other countries.

The second reason behind Kyoto's failure is its intergenerational aspect. Most analyses describe the climate change problem in intragenerational, game theoretic terms, as a prisoner's dilemma (Barrett 2003, p. 368; Danielson 1993, pp. 95–96; Soroos 1997, pp. 260–61) or battle-of-the-sexes problem (Waldron 1990). But I have argued that the more important dimension of climate change may be its intergenerational aspect (Gardiner 2001). Roughly speaking, the point is this. Climate change is caused primarily by fossil fuel use. Burning fossil fuels has two main consequences: on the one hand, it produces substantial benefits through the production of energy; on the other, it exposes humanity to the risk of large, and perhaps catastrophic, costs from climate change. But these costs and benefits accrue to different groups: the benefits arise primarily in the short to medium term and so are received by the present generation, but the costs fall largely in the long term, on future generations. This suggests a worrying scenario. For one thing, so long as high energy use is (or is perceived to be) strongly connected to self-interest, the present generation will have strong egoistic reasons to ignore the worst aspects of climate change. For another, this problem is iterated: it arises anew for each subsequent generation as it gains the power to decide whether or not to act. This suggests that the global warming problem has a seriously tragic structure. I have argued that it is this background fact that most readily explains the Kyoto debacle (Gardiner 2004b).

IX. CONCLUSION

This article has been intended as something of a primer. Its aim is to encourage and facilitate wider engagement by ethicists with the issue of global climate change. At the outset, I offered some general reasons why philosophers should be more interested in climate change. In closing, I would like to offer one more. I have suggested that climate change poses some difficult ethical and philosophical problems. Partly as a consequence of this, the public and political debate surrounding climate change is often simplistic, misleading, and awash with conceptual confusion. Moral philosophers should see this as a call to arms. Philosophical clarity is urgently needed. Given the importance of the problem, let us hope that the call is answered quickly.

REFERENCES

Athanasiou, Tom, and Baer, Paul. 2001. Climate Change after Marrakesh: Should Environmentalists Still Support Kyoto? Earthscape Update, December, http://www.earthscape.org/p1/att02/att02.html.

Athanasiou, Tom, and Baer, Paul. 2002. *Dead Heat: Global Justice and Global Warming.* New York: Seven Stories Press.

Babiker, Mustapha H.; Jacoby, Henry D.; Reilly, John M.; and Reiner, David M. 2002. The Evolution of a Climate Regime: Kyoto to Marrakech and Beyond. *Environmental Science and Policy* 5:195–206.

Baer, Paul. 2002. Equity, Greenhouse Gas Emissions, and Global Common Resources. In *Climate Change Policy: A Survey*, ed. Stephen H. Schneider, Armin Rosencranz, and John O. Niles, pp. 393–408. Washington, D.C.: Island Press.

Barrett, Scott. 2003. *Environment and Statecraft.* Oxford: Oxford University Press.

Broecker, Wallace S. 1997. Thermohaline Circulation, the Achilles' Heel of Our Climate System: Will Man-Made CO_2, Upset the Current Balance? *Science* 278 (November 28):1582–88.

Broome, John. 1992. *Counting the Cost of Global Warming.* Isle of Harris, UK: White Horse Press.

Brown, Donald. 2002. *American Heat: Ethical Problems with the United States' Response to Global Warming.* Lanham, Md.: Rowman & Littlefield.

Costanza, Robert. 1996. Review of *Managing the Commons: The Economics of Climate Change*, by William D. Nordhaus. *Environment and Development Economics* 1:381–84.

Danielson, Peter. 1993. Personal Responsibility. In *Ethics and Climate Change: The Greenhouse Effect*, eds. H. Coward and T. Hurka, pp. 81–98. Waterloo: Wilfred Laurier Press.

De Leo, Giulio; Rizzi, L.; Caizzi, A.; and Gatto, M. 2001. The Economic Benefits of the Kyoto Protocol. *Nature* 413:478–79.

Gagosian, Robert. 2003. Abrupt Climate Change: Should We Be Worried? Woods Hole Oceanographic Institute. Available at http://www.whoi.edu/nstitutes/occi/hottopics_climate-change.html.

Gardiner, Stephen M. 2001. The Real Tragedy of the Commons. *Philosophy & Public Affairs* 30: 387–416.

Gardiner, Stephen M. 2004a. A Core Precautionary Principle. *International Journal of Global Environmental Problems: Special Issue on the Precautionary Principle*, vol. 5, no. 2 (in press).

Gardiner, Stephen M. 2004b. The Global Warming Tragedy and the Dangerous Illusion of the Kyoto Protocol. *Ethics and International Affairs* 18:23–39.

Grubb, Michael. 1995. Seeking Fair Weather: Ethics and the International Debate on Climate Change. *International Affairs* 71:463–96.

Gundermann, Jesper. 2002. Discourse in the Greenhouse. In *Sceptical Questions and Sustainable Answers*, by Danish Ecological Council, pp. 139–64. Copenhagen: Danish Ecological Council.

Harris, Paul, ed. 2000a. *Climate Change and American Foreign Policy.* New York: St. Martin's.

Hopgood, Stephen. 1998. *American Foreign Policy and the Power of the State.* Oxford: Oxford University Press.

IPCC (Intergovernmental Panel on Climate Change). 1995. *Climate Change 1995: Economic and Social Dimensions of Climate Change.* Cambridge: Cambridge University Press.

IPCC. 2001a. *Climate Change 2001: Mitigation.* Cambridge: Cambridge University Press. Available at http://www.ipcc.ch.

IPCC. 2001b. *Climate Change 2001: Synthesis Report.* Cambridge University Press: Cambridge. Available at http://www.ipcc.ch.

Jamieson, Dale. 1990. *Managing the Future: Public Policy, Scientific Uncertainty, and Global Warming.* In *Upstream/Downstream Essays in Environmental Ethics*, ed. D. Scherer, pp. 67–89. Philadelphia: Temple University Press.

Jamieson, Dale. 1992. Ethics, Public Policy and Global Warming. *Science, Technology and Human Values* 17:139–53. Reprinted in Dale Jamieson, *Morality's Progress.* Oxford: Oxford University Press, 2003. References are to the later version.

Jamieson, Dale. 1998. Global Responsibilities: Ethics, Public Health and Global Environmental Change. *Indiana Journal of Global Legal Studies* 5:99–119.

Jamieson, Dale. 2001. Climate Change and Global Environmental Justice. In *Changing the Atmosphere:*

Expert Knowledge and Global Environmental Governance, ed. P. Edwards and C. Miller, pp. 287–307. Cambridge, Mass.: MIT Press.

Lomborg, Bjorn. 2001. Global Warming. In *The Sceptical Environmentalist*, by Bjorn Lomborg, pp. 258–324. Cambridge: Cambridge University Press.

O'Neill, Brian C., and Oppenheimer, Michael. 2002. Dangerous Climate Impacts and the Kyoto Protocol. *Science* 296 (June 14): 1971–72.

Ott, Hermann. 2001. Climate Policy after the Marrakesh Accords: From Legislation to Implementation. Available at http://ww.wupperinst.org-/download/Ott-after-marrakesh.pdf. Published as *Global Climate: Yearbook of International Law*. Oxford: Oxford University Press.

Raffensberger, Carolyn, and Tickner, Joel, eds. 1999. Protecting Public Health and the Environment: Implementing the Precautionary Principle. Washington, D.C.: Island Press.

Rawls, John. 1999. *A Theory of Justice*. Rev. ed. Cambridge, Mass.: Harvard University Press.

Sagoff, Mark. 1988. *The Economy of the Earth*. Cambridge: Cambridge University Press.

Schelling, Thomas. 1997. The Cost of Combating Global Warming: Facing the Tradeoffs. *Foreign Affairs* 76:8–14.

Schmidtz, David. 2001. A Place for Cost-Benefit Analysis. *Noûs* 11, suppl.: 148–71.

Schultz, Peter, and Kasting, James. 1997. Optimal Reductions in CO_2 Emissions. *Energy Policy* 25:491–500.

Shogren, Jason, and Toman, Michael. 2000. Climate Change Policy. Discussion Paper 00–22, Resources for the Future, Washington, D.C., May 14–25, available at http://www.rff.org.

Shue, Henry. 1992. The Unavoidability of Justice. In *The International Politics of the Environment*, ed.

Andrew Hurrell and Benedict Kingsbury, pp. 373–97. Oxford: Oxford University Press.

Shue, Henry, 1995. Avoidable Necessity: Global Warming, International Fairness and Alternative Energy. In *Theory and Practice, NOMOS XXXVII*, ed. Ian Shapiro and Judith Wagner DeCew, pp. 239–64. New York: New York University Press.

Shue, Henry. 1999. Bequeathing Hazards: Security Rights and Property Rights of Future Humans. In *Global Environmental Economics: Equity and the Limits to Markets*, ed. M. Dore and T. Mount, pp. 38–53. Oxford: Blackwell.

Singer, Peter. 2002. One Atmosphere. In *One World: The Ethics of Globalization*, by Peter Singer, chap. 2. New Haven, Conn.: Yale University Press.

Soroos, Marvin S. 1997. *The Endangered Atmosphere: Preserving a Global Commons*. Columbia: University of South Carolina Press.

Traxler, Martino. 2002. Fair Chore Division for Climate Change. *Social Theory and Practice* 28:101–34.

United Nations Framework Convention on Climate Change. 1992. *Framework Convention on Climate Change*. Available at http://www.unfccc.int.

U.S. National Research Council, Committee on Abrupt Climate Change. 2002. *Abrupt Climate Change: Inevitable Surprise*. Washington, D.C.: National Academies Press.

Waldron, Jeremy. 1990. Who Is to Stop Polluting? Different Kinds of Free-Rider Problem. In *Ethical Guidelines for Global Bargains*. Program on Ethics and Public Life. Ithaca, N.Y.: Cornell University.

Wingspread Statement. 1998. Available at http://www.gdrc.org/u-gov/precaution-3.html.

Woodward, Richard, and Bishop, Richard. 1997. How to Decide When Experts Disagree: Uncertainty-Based Choice Rules in Environmental Policy. *Land Economics* 73:492–507.

STUDY QUESTIONS

1. Some people argue that we should not act until there is more scientific certainty about climate change. How does Gardiner address this argument?

2. Is Lomborg correct in saying that mitigation is economically and ethically unwarranted?

3. Should the industrialized nations be excused from moral responsibility for their past emissions because of their ignorance of the possibility of climate change?

4. What four proposals for allocating future emissions does Gardiner consider? Which is the most plausible one? Why?

5. Why does Gardiner believe that the Kyoto Protocol is a failure? Do you think he is correct? Why, or why not?

FOR FURTHER READING

Gore, Al. *An Inconvenient Truth: The Planetary Emergency of Global Warming and What We Can Do About It.* Rodale Press, 2006.

Intergovernmental Panel on Climate Change (IPCC), http://www.ipcc.ch/

Michaels, Patrick J. *Meltdown: The Predictable Distortion of Global Warming by Scientists, Politicians, and the Media.* Cato Institute (November 25, 2004).

Pew Center on Global Climate Change, http://www.pewclimate.org/

Pittock, A. Barrie. *Climate Change: Turning Up the Heat.* Earthscan Press, 2006.

Weart, Spencer. *The Discovery of Global Warming.* Harvard University Press, 2003.

45

The Denial Industry

GEORGE MONBIOT

George Monbiot is a renowned author and journalist, with a weekly column for The Guardian. *This selection, taken from his book,* Heat, *examines the deliberate spreading of misinformation on the human contribution to global warming.*

Look at the canting holy-oilers!

Thus they have snatched from us so many a prize,

With our own weapons they would foil us;

They too are devils, only in disguise.

Faust, *Part II, Act V*

But first I want to examine why we have been so slow to act.

On almost every other serious issue, the professional classes appear to be better informed than the rest of the population. On climate change the reverse seems to be true. The only people I have met over the past three years who haven't the faintest idea what manmade climate change is or how it is caused are university graduates. In 2004, for example, I had to tell a press officer at the British government's Department for Transport what carbon dioxide was. In 2005, I heard an insurer explain that he was failing to persuade the financial markets to take climate change seriously, as the senior managers either hadn't understood it or didn't believe in it. In 2006, I spoke to a journalist of 20 years' standing about the problem of rising carbon emissions, and was asked 'what are carbon emissions and why are they a problem?' But over the same period—and perhaps I don't get out enough—I have never spoken to a shop assistant, taxi driver, bar tender or vagrant who did not possess at least a vague idea of what climate change means and why it is happening.

From this I deduce that the problem is not that people aren't hearing about it, but that they don't want to know. The professional classes have the most freedom to lose and the least to gain from an attempt to restrain it. The effort to tackle climate change suffers from the problem of split incentives: those who are least responsible for it are the most likely to suffer its effects.

Bangladesh and Ethiopia are two of the countries which will be hit hardest. A sea level rise of 1 metre could permanently flood 21 percent of Bangladesh, including its best agricultural land, pushing some 15 million people out of their homes. Storm surges of the kind the country experienced in 1998 are likely to become more common: in that instance, 65 per cent of Bangladesh was temporarily drowned, and its farming and infrastructure ruined. By 2004, half of Bhola, the country's largest island, on which 1.6 million people live, had already been washed away. Climate scientists blamed this on rising sea levels: the erosion rate has accelerated since the 1960s.

Ethiopia has already been suffering a series of droughts linked to climate change. A paper published in the *Philosophical Transactions of the Royal Society* shows that the spring rains have steadily diminished since 1996. It blames the trend on rising sea surface temperatures in the Indian Ocean. In 2005, partly as a result of the droughts caused by the failure of these rains, between 8 and 10 million Ethiopians were at risk of starvation.

Most of the rich countries, being located in temperate latitudes, will, in the initial stages at least, suffer lesser ecological effects. They will also have more money with which to protect their citizens from floods, droughts and extremes of temperature. Within these countries, the richest people, who can buy their way out of trouble, will be harmed last. The blame, as this table suggests, is inversely proportional to the impacts.

Country	Carbon dioxide emissions, 2003 (tonnes per capita)
Luxembourg	24.3
United States	20.0
United Kingdom	9.5
Bangladesh	0.24
Ethiopia	0.06

SOURCE: US Energy Information Administration.

The Ethiopians, on average, emit one 400th of the carbon dioxide produced by the people of Luxembourg, the country which has the highest gross domestic product per person.

So asking wealthy people in the rich nations to act to prevent climate change means asking them to give up many of the things they value—their high-performance cars, their flights to Tuscany and Thailand and Florida—for the benefit of other people.

The problem is compounded by the fact that the connection between cause and effect seems so improbable. By turning on the lights, filling the kettle, taking the children to school, driving to the shops, we are condemning other people to death. We never chose to do this. We do not see ourselves as killers. We perform these acts without passion or intent.

Many of those things we have understood to be good—even morally necessary—must also now be seen as bad. Perhaps the most intractable cause of global warming is 'love miles': the distance you must to travel to visit friends and partners and relatives on the other side of the planet. The world could be destroyed by love.

To make this even more difficult, the early effects of climate change, for those of us who live in the temperate countries of the rich world, are generally pleasant. Our winters are milder, our springs come sooner. We have suffered the occasional flood and drought and heat-wave. But the overwhelming sensation, just when we need to act with the greatest urgency, is that of being blessed by our pollution.

A wealthy society's split incentives are shared by its government. As Tony Blair has remarked, 'there is a mismatch in timing between the environmental and electoral impact.' By the time the decisions he has made come home to roost, he will have been out of office for years. If a government allows the growth of air travel to continue, for example, the effects are delayed, diffuse and hard to blame on any one source. If, by contrast, it restricts or reverses the growth in flights, the effects are immediately attributable to its actions. Everyone knows who is responsible if we may no longer fly to Thailand.

But it is not just a matter of a failure to engage. Assisting our reluctance is an active campaign of dissuasion.

I first became aware of it after reading a series of truly idiotic articles in the British press. In some newspapers, as the following examples suggest, a total absence of scientific knowledge is no barrier to publication.

> George W. Bush is right. The Kyoto Treaty is a silly waste of time. The greenhouse effect probably doesn't exist. There is as yet no evidence for it (Peter Hitchens, *Mail on Sunday*).
>
> And if the climate is indeed overheating, that does not mean that manmade emissions are necessarily to

blame. Indeed, it is extremely unlikely that they would be since carbon dioxide forms a relatively small proportion of the atmosphere, most of which consists of water vapour (Melanie Phillips, *Daily Mail*).

The greenhouse effect, first observed in the middle of the nineteenth century, is the phenomenon which keeps this planet warm enough to sustain life. Peter Hitchens appears to have confused it with manmade climate change. But this did not prevent him from feeling qualified to continue thus:

> Global warming is probably caused by, would you believe it, the sun. The temperature of the atmosphere, measured by NASA, has not risen in the past 22 years. There was global warming between 1870 and 1940, when there were far fewer greenhouse gases than now. The only reason these facts are so little-known is that a self-righteous love of 'the environment' has now replaced religion as the new orthodoxy … Why are we so blinkered to these lies?

If most of the atmosphere consisted of water vapour, we would need gills. But Melanie Phillips is sure enough of her atmospheric physics to allege that

> … the theory that global warming is all the fault of mankind is a massive scam based on flawed computer modelling, bad science and an anti-Western ideology …. The majority of well-meaning opinion in the Western world believes a pack of lies and propaganda.

At first I mistook all this for native idiocy, and doubtless this plays a supporting role. But it was after I investigated another set of assertions that I began to see that these claims did not originate in the newspapers.

Unlike most of those who have maintained in the media that climate change is not happening, David Bellamy is, or was, a scientist, formerly a senior lecturer in botany at the University of Durham. He was also an environmentalist and a famous and rather wonderful television presenter. In the early 2000s, he decided that climate change wasn't happening. Here is what he wrote in an article published in 2004 in the *Daily Mail,* under the title 'Global Warming? What a Load of Poppycock!'

> The link between the burning of fossil fuels and global warming is a myth. It is time the world's leaders, their scientific advisers and many environmental pressure groups woke up to the fact.

In April 2005, I read a letter of his in *New Scientist.*

> Further to your coverage of climate change and melting ice in the Himalayas, it should be pointed out that glaciers in many other parts of the world are not shrinking but in fact are growing …. Indeed, if you take all the evidence that is rarely mentioned by the Kyotoists into consideration, 555 of all the 625 glaciers under observation by the World Glacier Monitoring Service in Zurich, Switzerland, have been growing since 1980.

I was astonished by this claim: it conflicted with everything I had read about 'glacier mass balance'—the degree to which they are advancing or retreating. So I telephoned the World Glacier Monitoring Service and read out Bellamy's letter. 'This,' they told me, 'is complete bullshit.' The latest studies show unequivocally that most of the world's glaciers are retreating.

But Bellamy's figures must have come from somewhere, so I e-mailed him to ask for his source. After several requests, he explained that he had found them on a website called www.iceagenow.com. I urge you to visit it: it is an extraordinary production. But there indeed was all the material Bellamy had cited in his letter, including the figures—or something resembling the figures—he quoted.

> Since 1980, there has been an advance of more than 55 per cent of the 625 mountain glaciers under observation by the World Glacier Monitoring group in Zurich.'*

The source, which Bellamy also cited in his e-mail to me, was given as 'the latest issue of *21st Century Science and Technology'.*

This, I found, is a publication belonging to the American millionaire Lyndon Larouche. Larouche has claimed that the British royal family is running an international drugs syndicate, that Henry Kissinger is a communist agent, that the British government is controlled by Jewish bankers, and that modern science is a conspiracy against human potential. In 1989 he received a fifteen-year sentence for conspiracy, mail fraud and tax-code violations.

21st Century Science and Technology gave no source for its figures; but the same data could be found all over the internet. They were first published online by the 'Science and Environmental Policy Project', which is run by an environmental scientist called Dr S. Fred Singer. After they were posted on his website—www.sepp.org—they were reproduced by several other groups, such as the Competitive Enterprise Institute, the National Center for Public Policy Research and The Advancement of Sound Science Coalition. They had also found their way into the *Washington Post.* But where did they come from? Fred Singer cited half a source:

> a paper published in *Science* in 1989.

> I went through every edition of *Science* published in 1989, both manually and electronically. Not only did it contain nothing resembling those figures; throughout that year there was no paper

---

*You may have noticed that while Bellamy's source claimed that 55 per cent of 625 glaciers are advancing, Bellamy claimed that 555 of them—or 89 per cent—are advancing. This figure seems to have existed nowhere else. But on the standard English keyboard, '5' and '%' occupy the same key. If you try to hit '%', but fail to press shift, you get 555, instead of 55%. This is the only explanation I can produce for his figure. When I challenged him, he admitted that there had been 'a glitch of the electronics'.

published in this journal about glacial advance or retreat. Satisfied that the figures were nonsense, I left it there.

But after I had published these findings in the *Guardian,* one of my readers wrote to Dr S. Fred Singer.

Dear Professor Singer,
How do you answer the statement by George Monbiot, writing in the *Guardian* newspaper on Tuesday, that you cited a non-existent paper in an unspecified 1989 edition of *Science* as the only source for a claim that most of the world's glaciers were advancing?

Singer's response was interesting, and unexpected.

Monbiot is confused—or simply lying … he has a vivid imagination that borders on being slanderous …. I know nothing about a 1989 paper in *Science*. This is the same Monbiot who along with other 'climate campaigners' complained in *Nature* (31 March 2005) that some of us are creating the impression that 'climate scientists are deeply divided' while—acc. to him—there is a 'robust' consensus about anthropogenic global warming. Obviously, he has been smoking something or other.

My correspondent wrote back:

Dear Professor Singer,
Thank you for your quick reply to my query. However, I found your statements very puzzling …. When I did a Google search of www.sepp.org, I did find two pages that made exactly the same claim that Monbiot ascribed to you. It seems that he was neither lying nor confused …. Could you please be specific about this 1989 paper in *Science*? It looks very unlikely that the WGMS would have said what you claim.

This time Singer replied in less aggressive tones: the claim, he said, had been posted on his site by 'former SEPP associate Candace Crandall'. It 'appears to be incorrect and has been updated'. He forgot to add that Candace Crandall was his wife. Almost a year later, when writing this book, I checked his website, and found this paragraph:

The World Glacier Monitoring Service in Zurich, in a paper published in *Science* in 1989, noted that between 1926 and 1960, more than 70 per cent of 625 mountain glaciers in the United States, Soviet Union, Iceland, Switzerland, Austria and Italy were retreating. After 1980, however, 55 per cent of these same glaciers were advancing.

It had not been changed. What I also found, on the SEPP site and the others which had published the glacier figures, were most of the allegations, however daft or misleading, which had later been made in the press by David Bellamy, Peter Hitchens, Melanie Phillips, the novelist Michael Crichtoh and most of the other prominent repudiators of manmade climate change. The groups I've listed appear to have compiled and distributed the facts and figures the writers used. The groups have something else in common: they have all been funded by Exxon.[*]

ExxonMobil is the world's most profitable corporation. In autumn 2005, it reported *quarterly* profits of almost $10 billion, the highest corporate earnings on record. It makes most of this money from oil, and has more to lose than any other company from efforts to tackle climate change. Its approach to the issue could be summed up thus:

Should the public come to believe that the scientific-issues are settled, their views about global warming will change accordingly. Therefore, you need to continue to make the lack of scientific certainty a primary issue in the debate.

---

[*]This is not suggest that Bellamy, Hitchens, Phillips or Crichton have themselves taken any money from Exxon.

These words are not mine. Nor are they Exxon's. They were written for Republican Party activists by a political consultant named Frank Luntz, during the first mid-term election campaign in George W. Bush's presidency. As we will see, there are plenty of places in which Exxon finds itself at home. But in other respects it has difficulties: it must confront a scientific consensus as strong as that which maintains that smoking causes lung cancer or that HIV causes AIDS.

The website www.exxonsecrets.org, using data found in the company's official documents, lists 124 organizations which have taken money, from the company or work closely with those which have. They take a consistent line on climate change: that the science is contradictory, the scientists are split, environmentalists are charlatans, liars or lunatics, and if governments took action to prevent global warming, they would be endangering the global economy for no good reason. The findings these organizations dislike are labelled 'junk science'. The findings they welcome are labelled 'sound science'.

Among the organizations that have been funded by Exxon are some well-known websites and lobby groups, such as TechCentralStation, the Cato Institute and the Heritage Foundation. Some of those on the list have names which make them look like grassroots citizens' organizations or academic bodies: the Center for the Study of Carbon Dioxide and Global Change, for example; the National Wetlands Coalition; the National Environmental Policy Institute; the American Council on Science and Health. One or two of them, such as the Congress of Racial Equality and George Mason University's Law and Economics Center, *are* citizens' organizations or academic bodies, but the line they take on climate change is very much like that of the other sponsored groups. While all these groups are based in the United States of America, their publications are read and cited, and their staff are interviewed and quoted, all over the world.

By funding a large number of organizations, Exxon helps to create the impression that doubt about climate change is widespread. For those who do not understand that scientific findings cannot be trusted if they have not appeared in peer-reviewed journals, the names of these institutes help to suggest that serious researchers are challenging the consensus.

This is not to claim that all the science these groups champion is bogus. On the whole, they use selection, not invention. They will find one contradictory study—such as the discovery of tropospheric cooling I mentioned in the previous chapter and which, in a garbled form, was used by *Peter Hitchens*—and promote it relentlessly. They will continue to do so long after it has been disproved by further work. Though, for example, John Christy, the author of the troposphere paper, admitted in August 2005 that his figures were incorrect, his initial findings are still being circulated and championed by many of these groups, as a quick internet search will show you.

But they do not stop there. The chairman of Fred Singer's Science and Environmental Policy Project (Singer is the president) is a man called *Frederick Seitz*. Seitz is a physicist, who in the 1960s was president of the US National Academy of Sciences. In 1998, he wrote a document, known as the 'Oregon Petition', which has been cited by almost every journalist who claims that climate change is a myth.

The petition reads as follows:

> We urge the United States government to reject the global warming agreement that was written in Kyoto, Japan, in December, 1997, and any other similar proposals. The proposed limits on greenhouse gases would harm the environment, hinder the advance of science and technology, and damage the health and welfare of mankind.
>
> There is no convincing scientific evidence that human release of carbon dioxide, methane, or other greenhouse gasses is causing or will, in the foreseeable future, cause catastrophic heating of the Earth's atmosphere and disruption of the Earth's climate. Moreover, there is substantial scientific evidence that increases in atmospheric carbon dioxide produce

many beneficial effects upon the natural plant and animal environments of the Earth.

Anyone with a degree could sign it. It was attached to a letter written by Seitz, entitled *Research Review of Global Warming Evidence:*

> Below is an eight-page review of inform-ation on the subject of 'global warming', and a petition in the form of a reply card. Please consider these materials carefully.
>
> The United States is very close to adopting an international agreement that would ration the use of energy and of technologies that depend upon coal, oil, and natural gas and some other organic compounds.
>
> This treaty is, in our opinion, based upon flawed ideas. Research data on climate change do not show that human use of hydrocarbons is harmful. To the contrary, there is good evidence that increased at-mospheric carbon dioxide is environmen-tally helpful.
>
> … Frederick Seitz, Past President, Na-tional Academy of Sciences.

The lead author of the 'review' which followed Frederick Seitz's letter is a Christian fundamentalist called Arthur B. Robinson. He has never worked as a climate scientist. It was co-published by Robinson's organization—the Oregon Institute of Science and Medicine—and an outfit called the George C. Marshall Institute, which has received $630,000 from ExxonMobil since 1998. The other three authors were Arthur Robinson's 22-year old son and two employees of the George C. Marshall In-stitute. The chairman of the George C. Marshall Institute was Frederick Seitz.

The paper maintained that

> As coal, oil, and natural gas are used to feed and lift from poverty vast numbers of people across the globe, more carbon dioxide will be released into the atmosphere. This will help to maintain and improve the health, longevity, prosperity, and productivity of all people …. We are living in an increasingly lush environment of plants and animals as a result of the carbon dioxide increase. Our children will enjoy an Earth with far more plant and animal life than that with which we now are blessed. This is a wonderful and unexpected gift from the Industrial Revolution.

It was printed in the font and format of the *Pro-ceedings of the National Academy of Sciences:* the journal of the organization of which Frederick Seitz—as he had just reminded his correspondents—was once president.

Soon after the petition was published, the Na-tional Academy of Sciences released this statement:

> The Council of the National Academy of Sciences is concerned about the confusion caused by a petition being circulated via a letter from a former president of this Academy …. The petition was mailed with an op-ed article from *The Wall Street Journal* and a manuscript in a format that is nearly identical to that of scientific articles published in the *Proceedings of the National Academy of Sciences.* The NAS Council would like to make it clear that this petition has nothing to do with the National Academy of Sciences and that the manuscript was not published in the *Proceedings of the National Academy of Sciences* or in any other peer-reviewed journal. The petition does not reflect the conclusions of expert reports of the Academy.

But it was too late. Seitz, the Oregon Institute and the George C. Marshall Institute had already circulated tens of thousands of copies, and the peti-tion had established a major presence on the inter-net. Some 17,000 graduates signed it, the great majority of whom have no background in climate science. It has been repeatedly cited—by David Bellamy, Melanie Phillips and the rest—as a petition by climate scientists. It is promoted by the Exxon-sponsored sites as evidence that there is no scientific consensus on climate change.

All this is now well-known to climate scientists and environmentalists. But the most, interesting thing I have discovered while researching this issue is that the corporate campaign to deny that man-made climate change is taking place was not initiated by Exxon, or by any other firm directly involved in the fossil fuel industry. It was started by the tobacco company Philip Morris.

In December 1992, the US Environmental Protection Agency published a 500-page report called *Respiratory Health Effects of Passive Smoking*. It found that

> … the widespread exposure to environmental tobacco smoke (ETS) in the United States presents a serious and substantial public health impact.
>
> In adults: ETS is a human lung carcinogen, responsible for approximately 3,000 lung cancer deaths annually in US nonsmokers.
>
> In children: ETS exposure is causally associated with an increased risk of lower respiratory tract infections (LRIs) such as bronchitis and pneumonia. This report estimates that 150,000 to 300,000 cases annually in infants and young children up to 18 months of age are attributable to ETS.

Had it not been for the settlement of a major class action against the tobacco companies in the United States, we would never have been able to see what happened next. But in 1998 they were forced to publish their internal documents and post them on the internet.

Within two months, Philip Morris, the world's biggest tobacco firm, had devised a strategy for dealing with the passive-smoking report. In February 1993 Ellen Merlo, its senior vice president of corporate affairs, sent a letter to William I. Campbell, Philip Morris's chief executive officer and president, explaining her intentions.

> Our overriding objective is to discredit the EPA report …. Concurrently, it is our objective to prevent states and cities, as well as businesses, from passive-smoking bans.
>
> To this end, she had hired a public relations company called APCO. She had

attached the advice it had given her. APCO warned that No matter how strong the arguments, industry spokespeople are, in and of themselves, not always credible or appropriate messengers.

So the fight against a ban on passive smoking had to be associated with other people and other issues. Philip Morris, APCO said, needed to create the impression of a 'grassroots' movement—one that had been formed spontaneously by concerned citizens to fight 'over-regulation'. It should portray the danger of tobacco smoke as just one 'unfounded fear' among others, such as concerns about pesticides and cellphones. APCO proposed to set up

> a national coalition intended to educate the media, public (Officials and the public about the dangers of 'junk science'. Coalition will address credibility of government's scientific studies, risk assessment techniques and misuse of tax dollars …. Upon formation of Coalition, key leaders will begin media outreach, e.g., editorial board tours, opinion articles, arid brief elected officials in selected states.

APCO would found the coalition, write its mission statements, and 'prepare and place opinion articles in key markets.' For this it required $150,000 for its own fees and $75,000 for the coalition's costs.

By May 1993, as another memo from APCO to Philip Morris shows, the fake citizens' group had a name: The Advancement for Sound Science Coalition, or TASSC. It was important, further letters stated, 'to ensure that TASSC has a diverse group of contributes'; to 'link the tobacco issue with other more "politically correct" products'; and to associate scientific studies which cast smoking in a bad light with 'broader questions about government research and regulations', such as

- Global warming
- Nuclear waste disposal
- Biotechnology.

APCO would engage in the

intensive recruitment of high-profile representatives from business and industry, scientists, public officials, and other individuals interested in promoting the use of sound science.

By September 1993, APCO had produced a 'Plan for the Public Launching of TASSC'. The media launch would not take place in

Washington, DC or the top media markets of the country. Rather, we suggest creating a series of aggressive, de-centralized launches in several targeted local and regional markets across the country. This approach: …

- Avoids cynical reporters from major media: less reviewing/challenging of TASSC messages.

The media coverage, the public relations company hoped, would enable TASSC to 'establish an image of a national grassroots coalition'.

In case the media asked hostile questions, APCO circulated a sheet of answers, drafted by Philip Morris. The first question was:

Isn't it true that Philip Morris created TASSC to act as a front group for it?
A: No, not at all. As a large corporation, PM belongs to many national, regional, and state business, public policy, and legislative organizations. PM has contributed to TASSC, as we have with various groups and corporations across the country.

The fifth question was:

What areas of public policy would you like to see TASSC investigate?
A: We are not in a position to suggest that TASSC examine any issue; it's an independent organization and will no doubt proceed as best they determine.

It should already have become clear that there are similarities between the language used and the approaches adopted by Philip Morris and by the organizations funded by Exxon. The two lobbies use the same terms, which appear to have been invented by Philip Morris's consultants. 'Junk science' meant peer-reviewed studies showing that smoking was linked to cancer and other diseases. 'Sound science' meant studies sponsored by the tobacco industry suggesting that the link was inconclusive. Both lobbies recognized that their best chance of avoiding regulation was to challenge the scientific consensus. As a memo from the tobacco company Brown and Williamson noted,

Doubt is our product since it is the best means of competing with the 'body of fact' that exists in the mind of the general public. It is also the means of establishing a controversy.

Both industries also sought to distance themselves from their own campaigns, creating the impression that they were spontaneous movements of professionals or ordinary citizens: the 'grassroots'.

But the connection goes much further than that. TASSC, the 'coalition' created by Philip Morris, was the first and most important of the corporate-funded organizations denying that climate change is taking place. It has done more damage to the campaign to halt it than any other body.

TASSC did as its founders at APCO suggested, and sought funding from other sources. Between 2000 and 2002 it received $30,000 from Exxon. The website it has financed—www.JunkScience. com—has been the main entrepot for almost every kind of climate change denial that has found its way into the mainstream press. While Fred Singer was the first to have posted the glacier figures on the web, it was JunkScience.com that popularized them. In fact you can still find them there today. It equates environmentalists with Nazis, communists and terrorists. It flings at us the accusations which could justifiably be levelled against itself: the website claims, for example, that it is campaigning against 'faulty scientific data and analysis used to advance special and, often, hidden agendas'. I have lost count of the number of correspondents who, while questioning manmade global warming, have pointed me there.

The man who runs it is called Steve Milloy. In 1992, he started working for APCO—Philip Morris's consultants. While he was there, he set up the JunkScience site. In March 1997, the documents show, he was appointed TASSC's executive director. By 1998, as he explained in a memo to the board members, his Junk-Science website was being funded by TASSC. Both he and the 'coalition' continued to receive money from Philip Morris. An internal document dated February 1998 reveals that TASSC took $200,000 from the tobacco company in 1997. Philip Morris's 2001 budget document records a payment to Steven Milloy of $90,000. Altria, Philip Morris's parent company, admits that Milloy was under contract to the tobacco firm until at least the end of 2005.

He has done well. You can find his name attached to letters and articles seeking to discredit passive-smoking studies all over the internet and in the academic databases. He has even managed to reach the *British Medical Journal*: I found a letter from him there which claimed that the studies it had reported 'do not bear out the hypothesis that maternal smoking/passive smoking increases cancer risk among infants'. TASSC paid him $126,000 in 2004 for fifteen hours of work a week. Two other organizations are registered at his address: the Free Enterprise Education Institute and the Free Enterprise Action Institute. They have received $10,000 and $50,000 respectively from Exxon. The secretary of the Free Enterprise Action Institute is a man called Thomas Borelli. Borelli was the Philip Morris executive who oversaw the payments to TASSC.

Milloy also writes a weekly 'Junk Science' column for Fox News. Without declaring his interests, he has used this column to pour scorn on studies documenting the medical effects of second-hand tobacco smoke and showing that climate change is taking place. Even after Fox News was told about the money he had been receiving from Philip Morris and Exxon, it continued to employ him,

without informing its readers about his interests. It still describes him thus:

> Steven Milloy publishes JunkScience.com, CSRWatch.com. He is a junk-science expert, an advocate of free enterprise and an adjunct scholar at the Competitive-Enterprise Institute.

TASSC's headed notepaper names an advisory board of eight people. Three of them are listed by Exxonsecrets.org as working for organizations taking money from Exxon. One of them is Frederick Seitz, the man who wrote the Oregon Petition, and who chairs Fred Singer's Science and Environmental Policy Project.

In 1979, Seitz became a permanent consultant to the tobacco company RJ Reynolds. He worked for the firm until at least 1987, for an annual fee of $65,000. He was in charge of deciding which medical research projects the company should fund, and handed out millions of dollars a year to American universities. The purpose of this funding, a memo from the chairman of RJ Reynolds shows, was to 'refute the criticisms against cigarettes'. An undated note in the Philip Morris archive shows that it was planning a 'Seitz symposium' with the help of TASSC, in which Frederick Seitz would speak to '40-60 regulators'.

S. Fred Singer also had connections with the tobacco industry. In, March 1993, APCO sent a memo to Ellen Merlo, the vice president of Philip Morris who had just commissioned it to fight the Environmental Protection Agency.

> As you know, we have been working with Dr. Fred Singer and Dr. Dwight Lee, who have authored articles on junk science and indoor air quality (IAQ) respectively. Attached you will find copies of the junk science and IAQ articles which have been approved by Drs Singer and Lee .... We discussed with Dr Singer Ellen's suggestion for the junk science article to have a more personal introduction, however he is adamant that this would not be his style. Please review the articles and let us know

as soon as possible whether you have any comments or questions about them.

Singer's article, entitled *Junk Science at the EPA*, claimed that

> The latest 'crisis'—environmental tobacco smoke—has been widely criticized as the most shocking distortion of scientific evidence yet.'

He alleged that the Environmental Protection Agency had had to 'rig the numbers' in its report on passive smoking. This was the report that Philip Morris and APCO had set out to discredit a month before Singer wrote his article.

In another note, APCO reveals that it has discussed with Fred Singer the means of organizing an international movement to support TASSC's aims.

I have no evidence that Fred Singer or his organization have taken money from Philip Morris. But many of the other bodies which have been sponsored by Exxon and have sought to repudiate climate change were also funded by the tobacco company. Among them are some of the world's best-known 'think tanks': the Competitive Enterprise Institute, the Cato Institute, the Heritage Foundation, the Hudson Institute, the Frontiers of Freedom Institute, the Reason Foundation and the Independent Institute, as well as George Mason University's Law and Economics Center. I can't help wondering whether there is any aspect of 'conservative' thought in the United States which has not been formed and funded by the corporations.

Until I came across this material, I believed that the accusations, the insults and the taunts such people had slung at us environmentalists were personal: that they really did hate us, and had found someone who would pay to help them express those feelings. Now I realise that they have simply transferred their skills.

But they are taken seriously throughout the English-speaking media. This is how the BBC introduced an online debate it hosted in July 2004:

> Ask the experts: What does the future hold for climate change? ... Your questions were answered by former Environment Minister Michael Meacher and global climate-change expert Dr S. Fred Singer.

The BBC's debate pitches a non-scientist against a scientist: the authority, in other words, appears to lie with the 'global climate-change expert' Dr Singer, though his publication record over the past twenty years has been sparse. The BBC chose him rather than any of the thousands of environmental scientists with stronger credentials because its editors believed that this was where the debate lay: between those who claimed climate change was happening, and those who claimed it was not. They believed it, despite several reminders to the contrary from the Royal Society, because Fred Singer and Steve Milloy and others had created this impression through their appearances in the media. The story was self-perpetuating.

Until mid 2005, the BBC seemed incapable of hosting a discussion on climate change without bringing in one of the Exxon-sponsored deniers to claim that it was not taking place. On only one occasion did it tell its listeners that the 'expert' it had chosen had been funded by an oil company. It could be argued that, by failing to declare their interests it was providing free, unacknowledged airtime for the corporation. It now appears to have woken up to the extent to which it has been (in the words of one senior executive I spoke to) 'fooled by those people'. But in the United States and Australia, Exxon's experts are still being presented as serious scientists. Steve Milloy, for example, has appeared on CNN, ABC, MSNBC, National Public Radio and most of the major programmes on the Fox News network.

They are also taken seriously by politicians. In 2003, James Inhofe, the Republican senator from Oklahoma, delivered a speech to the Senate called 'The Science of Climate Change'. Here is an extract.

> The claim that global warming is caused by manmade emissions is simply untrue and not based on sound science.
>
> Carbon dioxide does not cause catastrophic disasters—actually it would be beneficial to our environment and our economy.
>
> ... With all of the hysteria, all of the fear, all of the phoney science, could it be

that manmade global warming is the greatest hoax ever perpetrated on the American people? It sure sounds like it.

How did he know? Because he had spoken to 'the nation's top climate scientists', whom he then proceeded to list. The list began with Dr S. Fred Singer. It went on to name Frederick Seitz, the two employees of the George C. Marshall Institute who wrote the 'review' Seitz had circulated, and eight others working with organizations sponsored by Exxon. Alarmingly, Inhofe continues to chair the Senate Committee on Environment and Public Works.

In 2004, *Harper's* magazine published a leaked memo from Myron Ebell of the Competitive Enterprise Institute to Phil Cooney, the chief of staff of the White House Council on Environmental Quality. The Competitive Enterprise Institute has been given over $2m by Exxon. In 1997, the only year for which I have records, it received $125,000 from Philip Morris. Ebell's memo showed that the White House and the Institute had been working together to discredit a report on climate change produced by the Environmental Protection Agency, whose head at the time was Christine Todd Whitman.

Dear Phil,

Thanks for calling and asking for our help .... As I said, we made the decision this morning to do as much as we could to deflect criticism by blaming EPA for freelancing. It seems to me that the folks at EPA are the obvious fall guys, and we would only hope that the fall guy (or gal) should be as high up as possible. I have done several interviews and have stressed that the President needs to get everyone rowing in the same direction. Perhaps tomorrow we will call for Whitman to be fired.

The New York Times later discovered that Phil Cooney, who is a lawyer with no scientific training, had been imported into the White House from the American Petroleum Institute, to control the presentation of climate science. He edited scientific reports, striking out evidence that glaciers were retreating and inserting phrases suggesting that there was serious scientific doubt about global warming. When the revelations were published he resigned and took up a post at Exxon.

The oil company also has direct access to the White House. On 6 February 2001, seventeen days after George W. Bush was sworn in, A. G. (Randy) Randol, ExxonMobil's senior environmental adviser, sent a fax to John Howard, an environmental official at the White House. It began by discussing the role of Robert Watson, the head of the Intergovernmental Panel on Climate Change. It suggested he had a 'personal agenda' and asked

Can Watson be replaced now at the request of the US?

It went on to ask that the United States be represented at the panel's discussions by a Dr Harlan Watson. Both requests were met. One Watson was sacked, the other was appointed, and he continues to wreak havoc at international climate meetings.

While they have been most effective in the United States of America, the impacts of the climate-change deniers sponsored by Exxon and Philip Morris have been felt all over the world—I have seen their arguments endlessly repeated in Australia, Canada, India, Russia and the United Kingdom. By dominating the media debate on climate change during seven or eight critical years in which urgent international talks should have been taking place, by constantly seeding doubt about the science just as it should have been most persuasive, they have justified the money their sponsors spent on them many times over. I think it is fair to say that the professional denial industry has delayed effective global action on climate change by several years.

None of this is to suggest that the science should not be subject to constant scepticism and review, or that environmentalists should not be held to account. It is only through repeated challenges to accepted wisdom that science has progressed. Climate-change campaigners have no greater right to be wrong than anyone else: if we mislead the public, we should expect to be exposed. We also need to know that we are not wasting our time: there is no point in devoting your life to fighting a problem that does not exist.

But the people who have been paid by Exxon are not, as they claim, 'climate sceptics'. They do not fit the usual definition of 'sceptic':

> A seeker after truth; an inquirer who has not yet arrived at definite conclusions.

They are members of a public relations industry, which begins with a conclusion and then devises arguments to support it.

Nor is this to suggest that political resistance to dealing with climate change is entirely the work of these people The US government, for example, doesn't need Exxon's help to sabotage the international climate negotiations. One of the reasons why the professional climate-change deniers have been so successful in penetrating the media is that the story they have to tell is one that people want to hear.

In one respect, almost everyone—including the campaigners—is in denial about climate change. We have chosen to believe that the targets set by some of the more progressive governments provide realistic means of dealing with it. The United Kingdom, for example, intends to cut carbon emissions by 60 per cent by 2050. This is one of the world's most ambitious objectives. It is also, as I hope the previous chapter demonstrated, next to useless. But most of the climate-change reports, produced by the major environmental groups seek to demonstrate that this target can be met without major economic loss. Whether or not it can be met is irrelevant: it is the wrong target. None of them has yet stepped forward to say that we need a cut of the magnitude the science demands.

The British government's chief scientist, Sir David King, has been heroic in drawing attention to the dangers of climate change, and he has taken plenty of flak for it. In a speech in October 2004, he said the following:

> So what is the point at which the Greenland ice sheet will start melting? The latest indication is when the temperature around the Greenland land mass area is 2.7° centigrade above the pre-industrial

level .... What level of carbon dioxide therefore do we need to avoid going beyond in order to avoid testing this theory of melting of the Greenland ice sheet? ... I used to say 550 parts per million, I'm now thinking that that might be pushing it a bit. So we are talking about perhaps 500 parts per million as the level beyond which we shouldn't go.

In September 2005, I attended a conference in London at which Sir David was speaking. He told it that a 'reasonable' target for stabilizing carbon dioxide in the atmosphere was 550 parts per million. This happens to be the target set by the British government. It would be 'politically unrealistic', he said, to demand anything lower. Simon Retallack from the Institute for Public Policy Research stood up and reminded Sir David that as chief scientist his duty is not to represent political reality, but to represent scientific reality. Retallack's own work shows that at 550 parts per million the chances of preventing more than 2° of global warming are just 10–20 per cent. Sir David replied that if he recommended a lower limit, he would lose credibility with the government.

I think many people feel like him: that if they adopted the position determined by science rather than the position determined by politics, no one would take them seriously.

But the thought that worries me most is this. As people in the rich countries—even the professional classes—begin to wake up to what the science is saying, climate-change denial will look as stupid as Holocaust denial, or the insistence that AIDS can be cured with beetroot. But our response will be to demand that the government acts, while hoping that it doesn't. We will wish our governments to pretend to act. We get the moral satisfaction of saying what we know to be right, without the discomfort of doing it.

> My fear is that the political parties in most rich nations have already recognized this. They know that we want tough targets, but that we also want those targets to be missed. They know that we will grumble

about their failure to curb climate change, but that we will not take to the streets. They know that nobody ever rioted for austerity.

This is a gloomy thought. But it does reinforce my belief that we must make the necessary changes as painless as possible.

STUDY QUESTIONS

1. What does Monbiot mean by the "denial industry"?

2. Discuss the parallels between tobacco and energy industries in this regard.

3. What is the boundary between rational and irrational doubts? (Not discussed in this essay)

46

Hoodwinked in the Hothouse: False Solutions to Climate Change

This essay provides an introduction to rationale behind the global Climate Justice Movement.

Rising Tide North America's (RTNA) mission is to phase out fossil fuel usage and make a just transition to sustainable ways of living. RTNA firmly believes that the means by which our society reduces greenhouse gases are as important as the ends of preventing climate change and organizes against climate "solutions" that harm communities or the environment. RTNA strives to bring an earth-centered, global justice analysis to the climate change movement, to support community-based solutions to the climate crisis, and to end corporate control over systems of food and energy production, land management, and other areas that influence climate change. From www.risingtidenorthamerica.org/

HOODWINKED IN THE HOTHOUSE

Only a few years ago, some companies were saying climate change wasn't a problem. Now, as its impacts become apparent, corporations are suddenly scrambling to claim leadership on the issue. Desperate to avoid regulation that may hit their profits, they present a dizzying array of "false solutions," quick fixes that perpetuate inequalities in our society and attempt to cash in on the crisis.

Our fear of change and the unknown, and the widely held belief that technological progress can solve all problems make these techno-fixes and market-based solutions extremely seductive.

In most cases it's an easy sell. Since the 1980's, global politics have been dominated by a model of corporate globalization: An entire generation has grown up in a world in where little has been possible without corporate assent. Economic growth and increased consumption are society's implicit goals and to achieve this, multinational corporations must be given free reign.

Yet upon closer examination, the choices they have presented are false ones, dangerous detours on the road to a just, livable planet, distracting us from the root causes of the crisis.

Meanwhile, climate change is already effecting the planet, and it's the poorest who are hardest hit. Flooding from severe storms, rise in sea levels and melting glaciers affect millions in Asia and Latin America, while sub-Saharan Africa is experiencing sustained droughts. Death and increasing poverty result.

Consider: half the world's annual CO_2 emissions come from the Global North[*], making up only 15% of the global population. The path is clear: for humanity's survival, for justice, and for sustainability, we must reduce our emissions and consumption here at home.

To do so, we must educate ourselves about bogus climate change solutions we are given and act to restructure our relationships to the earth and its peoples to achieve a zero carbon society; short cuts are clearly insufficient.

CLEAN COAL AND CARBON CAPTURE AND STORAGE

Carbon capture and storage (CCS) is a major departure from other climate mitigation strategies. Rather than stopping pollution or replacing a fossil fuel, it allows current activities to continue but captures the carbon emissions and buries them under the ground. This "carbon sequestration" is primarily considered for coal power plants—it's a key component of the "clean coal" myth—although its use for other fossil fuels has also been proposed.

Even proponents recognize that CCS is unlikely to be widely operational until at least 2030, a bit late if we want quick action on climate change! Methods for determining how much carbon can be stored in an underground site or how to indicate technological failure—such as leaking toxic concentrations of CO_2—have yet to be developed. The infrastructure necessary to widely implement CCS would be extraordinary and highly controversial. CSS would demand thousands of miles of pipelines and hundreds of untested underground storage sites. Most troubling, it would require new "CCS-ready" coal-fired power plants, hundreds of which are already on the drawing board despite the embryonic state of the technology.

By far the greatest concern is that CCS legitimates the continued dominance and expansion of tie coal industry under the notion that coal can someday be clean. The impurities flushed from one stage of the coal "cleaning" process are stored behind over 600 earthen-sludge dams throughout the United States. Residents nearby these sites are exposed to heavy metals as the reservoirs leak into drinking water. Dams can rupture from age or poor construction, as was tragically demonstrated by the toxic coal ash spill in Tennessee on Christmas Eve 2008, which buried homes and rivers in more than a billion gallons of sludge.

Coal power plants are responsible for an estimated 24,000+ premature deaths in the United States each year caused by the fine particulate matter they release into the air. In contradiction to the "clean" propaganda, mercury emissions are actually higher in "clean" coal plants than conventional ones.

Even if coal could somehow be prepared and burned safely, there is no way to repair the damage of coal extraction, which has devastated

---

[*]Throughout this booklet, the rich countries, aka the developed world or the First World, are referred to as the "Global North." The poorer countries, aka the developing world or the Third World, are referred to as the "Global South."

communities and ecosystems from Bangladesh to Black Mesa, Arizona. The worst forms of mining—termed "mountain top removal"—can level up to 10 square miles of landscape in a single operation. West Virginia alone has seen well over 500 square miles of mountains and 1,500 miles of rivers destroyed by mountain top removal coal extraction.

Many environmentalists agree that "clean" coal is too dirty for the Global North, but, vacating any notions of global human rights or international solidarity amongst environmental activists, contend that it should be deployed for the Global South's energy needs.

Natural Gas and Liquefied Natural Gas

BY RORY COX

Speaking of fossil fuels masquerading as clean energy, for decades natural gas from North American fields has been touted as a "bridge fuel" to a renewable future. Decades later, we are no closer to the other side of that bridge. Instead, oil and gas multinationals are trying to sell us another bridge: Imported Liquefied Natural Gas (LNG). LNG is simply natural gas super-cooled to a -260 Fahrenheit liquid, which allows it to be shipped overseas on tankers. LNG technology allows natural gas extracted from sources in the Middle East, Russia, and Nigeria to be imported into North America.

While natural gas—which often requires devastating mining operations and thousands of miles of pipelines—is the "least dirty" of the fossil fuels, the process of shipping natural gas overseas adds 15 and 25% to its CO_2 emissions. In some cases, emissions generated from LNG use can be as harmful as emissions generated from the use of coal.

AGROFUELS

Agrofuels (or "biofuels" as they are known by their proponents) rely on industrial scale agriculture, which has long been dependent on deforestation and cheap fossil fuels. In many countries, rainforests are being plowed under for the expansion of agrofuel plantations, destroying carbon stores vital to regulation of ecosystems.

Across the United States and European Union, governments announced steadily increasing targets for the inclusion of agrofuels in the fuel that runs our cars. In response, the agricultural market made a wholly predictable shift toward fuel production, contributing to the skyrocketing price of grain around the world.

Just with these preliminary agrofuel targets, staple foods are becoming less affordable for the poorest people, and thousands have protested in Indonesia, Mexico and in many African countries over price hikes. Agrofuel production inevitably outcompetes food production, since the buying power of rich northern agrofuel consumers is greater than the buying power of poor southern food consumers. For countries with a strong car culture, most arable land would need to be converted to agrofuels to keep the gas flowing. The reality, however, is that most agrofuel consumption in the Global North does not come from domestic industry, but is based on importation from the Global South, just as oil is imported today.

"2nd Generation" Agrofuels

"We are told that corn and sugar ethanol is merely a stepping stone to advanced 'second generation' fuels. This next generation is to be made from the inedible parts of plants, grown on marginal and idle lands and won't compete with food. Unfortunately, all forms of agriculture require land, soil, water and fertilizers—all of "which are dwindling resources. The removal of wastes and residues from agricultural and forested lands for fuel production will deprive soils of organic matter required by healthy ecosystems. Energy demand is too huge to use plants for fuel sustainably and the efficiency of plant growth and conversion to fuels is too poor. The intensifying scramble for land is causing the displacement of people, often violently, from their traditional lands. Stripping the land bare, planting mono-cultures, and using every scrap of plant life for fuel is a clear path to catastrophe."

—RACHEL SMOLKER, PHD, RESEARCH BIOLOGIST

Furthermore, recent scientific reports have suggested that biofuels made from corn, sugar cane and soy are having a worse impact on the climate than burning fossil fuels. Most agrofuels are grown on large mono-culture plantations. Such plantations require large scale deforestation that actually contributes to climate change, as do the nitrous oxide emissions from chemical fertilizers. Emissions from oil are merely shifted to emissions from wasteful agricultural land use.

Agrofuel targets in climate and energy policies have one source: lobbying by companies with investments in agrofuels. The beneficiaries of the rush to agrofuels are neither the climate nor farmers, but multinational agricultural corporations.

Biofuels and Communities

Exploitation of workers on plantations. In the Brazilian sugar-cane industry, cutters receive only a fraction of a dollar per ton of sugar cane cut, and many people have died in sugar cane plants and plantations.

Unemployment and the destruction of the rural economy. Actual employment generated by agrofuel production is very now. The spread of agrofuel plantations weakens rural economies, increases poverty, and pushes people into the cities where they swell the slums.

Human rights violations. In Tanzania, more than 11,000 people have been evicted from one agrofuel plantation alone. Oil palm plantations in Indonesia have been imposed on communities with adverse effects on their livelihoods while agrofuel companies have a history of violations of human rights.

Water stress. In India it takes nearly a thousand gallons of water to produce 4 cups of sugarcane derived ethanol. Scarce water resources could be further depleted.

The Nuclear Option

The nuclear industry has latched onto the climate crisis in a last ditch attempt to survive in the face of long-term public opposition.

Nuclear power is presented as clean energy because no carbon dioxide is emitted during the electricity generation process. Yet huge amounts of energy are required for every other stage in the process, including the mining, milling and transportation of the uranium; the construction and decommissioning of the power plants; and the reprocessing, storage and disposal of nuclear waste. At present, most of this energy comes from fossil fuels.

Uranium is mainly mined in vast open-cast pits. In some hard-to-reach seams uranium is removed through in situ leaching, where sulfuric acid, nitrous acid and ammonia are injected into the seam and pumped up again years later. Typical-grade uranium ore requires a thousand tons of rock to be ground up to produce one ton of useful fuel. The other 999 tons of rock is radioactive indefinitely and is left in the environment where its radioactive products are free to be leached out.

The economics of nuclear power are highly uncertain, particularly with the new generation of "safe" designs. The first of these "third generation" plants is under construction in Finland. In August 2007, after 27 months of construction, the project was declared to be between 24 and 30 months behind schedule and $2,230 million over budget.

Nuclear power plants take far longer to build than almost any other energy source and—when the lifecycle costs are taken into account—are far more expensive then most every other climate solution under consideration. It is only through the tax-payers covering nuclear waste disposal, reprocessing, storage and plant decommissioning costs—and frequently subsidizing the initial construction as well—that nuclear power remains an energy option at all.

CARBON TRADING

Part I: Cap and Trade

The practice of carbon trading was implemented by the Kyoto Protocol as another strategy for tackling climate change, while allowing "business as usual" in many industries that profit most from the use of fossil fuels. Essentially, governments create a market commodity out of carbon pollution by issuing a finite amount of tradable pollution permits each year. As the theory goes, the amount of permits issued would decrease year to year and carbon emissions would be reduced. Because the permits are tradable, and emissions cuts are easier and cheaper for some businesses to make than others, the "invisible hand" of the market will cut overall emissions as efficiently as possible, at the lowest possible cost to the economy.

Established by the Kyoto Protocol, a cap and trade system is up and running in Europe, but it has been an unmitigated failure, beset by fraud and market manipulation. Known as "The European Emissions Trading Scheme" (ETS), the market includes within its scope large industrial plants including power stations and factories—entities that comprise just under half of Europe's total CO_2 emissions. Some power companies were issued the permits free of charge, yet have raised prices to "compensate" for the costs of the scheme, resulting in windfall profits. At the same time, other companies overestimated their emissions upon entering the scheme, miscalculations that lead to bottom-basement prices for the remaining permits and reduced incentives to limit emissions.

Worse, monitoring of emissions is inadequate. The levels of greenhouse gases that individual countries emit cannot be precisely quantified—studies claim the level of uncertainty is as high as 30%—and nearly half the emissions sites that purchase carbon credits in Europe are not satisfactorily monitored. Furthermore, enforcement of penalties for exceeding limits is almost nonexistent.

Is there any wonder that Europe's CO_2 emissions are rising despite their commitments under Kyoto?

Proponents say these problems can be fixed, but there are more fundamental issues. Carbon-trading seeks reductions on the cheap—sometimes you get what you pay for. While short term reductions in carbon emissions may be less expensive in carbon trading markets, there is no incentive toward crucial long term changes and investments that will be necessary to move us into a post-carbon society. Furthermore, as exemplified by the US sulfur dioxide trading market, communities with less political clout—typically low income communities and communities of color—can see increases in pollution under permit trading regimes, as neighborhoods and towns with more political clout demand more rigorous enforcement of pollution limits.

Perhaps the most troubling aspect of cap-and-trade is that it creates an experimental new system of private property rights. Permits are accounted for in corporate balance sheets and recorded in legal statutes the same way as patents or land grants from the government. When property rights are created and given to the most powerful actors in society, their ability to shape future privileges is only further entrenched. The level of the cap and the rules associated with the trading become the product of endless lobbying by companies trying to retain their high allowances, not scientific understandings of ecosystem and biosphere health. This power dynamic also exists on a global level as the countries and companies of the Global North fight to retain their high share of rights to emit.

At a time when poorly understood, experimental markets dominated by powerful interests have thrust millions of households into foreclosure and the world into the worst global recession in decades, do we really want another opaque commodity trading market?

Europe says it intends to fill some of the holes in the ETS—for instance, by auctioning some permits instead of giving them away. But the EU has no intention of removing one of the biggest problems with carbon trading—the fact that carbon credits (popularly referred to as "carbon offsets") can simply be bought from the Global South to substitute for emissions reductions at home.

Carbon Trading Part II: Carbon Offsets

The UN's "Clean Development Mechanism" (CDM) is the largest generator of carbon offset credits. Perversely, factories in India and China have sold offset credits for implementing modest clean ups required by law throughout the Global North, and then have used their "emissions reduction" revenue to expand the same, highly-polluting industries. As a result, local communities have suffered from exposure to pollutants (like arsenic, acid rain, and mercury) while greenhouse gas emissions have continued to rise.

Tragically, environmentally conscious individuals have been hoodwinked by the "carbon neutral" mentality, priming the pump for the global offset industry. We are told that we can "offset" our emissions from a particularly polluting activity for a small fee. The fee is used to plant trees to soak up CO_2, or to help people in the Global South reduce their emissions.

Tree planting has been widely discredited as an offset because the polluting activities take place immediately even though the tree plantations only soak up carbon emissions over a period of decades. Furthermore, release the stored CO_2 back into the atmosphere after they die. The creation of offset tree plantations has frequently stripped communities of control of common lands often used for subsistence agriculture.

Offsetting encourages us to think we can buy our way out of the changes we need to make to the way we live, but the reality is that the vast majority of offset projects are either scientifically dubious or minor tweaks that distract us from the large changes we need to make in our own backyard. In order to tackle climate change we need to support community-led sustainable development in the Global South as well as reductions in CO_2 emissions in the Global North, not instead of them!

SEEING REDD: THE WORLD BANK'S ANTI-SOLUTIONS

BY ALTERECO, THE TRANSNATIONAL INSTITUTE, AND RISING TIDE NORTH AMERICA

Tragically, the World Bank is a central agent for delivering "green" development within the UN's climate treaties. The Bank, a powerful and deeply undemocratic international institution, has a long and controversial history of assisting large corporations in "developing" poor countries.

The Bank manages the massive Prototype Carbon Fund (PCF), a corporate and government investment pool that claims to "pioneer the market for project-based greenhouse gas emission reductions while promoting sustainable development," making the Bank a kingmaker within the offset market.

Despite the stated goal of the PCF, less than a quarter of its offset projects are linked to development and a mere 6% of funds are set aside to promote sustainable development. More than 80% of the funds released have gone to heavily polluting industries in the oil, gas, cement, iron and steel production and industrial gases sectors. Communities living in the wake of these projects have been devastated by their environmental and health impacts.

Will the UN Help Us?

Activists from Climate Justice Now! described the atmosphere during the 2008 UN climate meetings in Poland: "Private investors are circling like vultures, swooping in on every opportunity for creating new profits. Business and corporate lobbyists expanded their influence and monopolized conference space at Poznan. At least 1,500 industry lobbyists were present either as observers or as members of government delegations."

The UN process on climate has been blighted and continually sidetracked by an all-encompassing focus on the inner working of carbon markets. This approach was introduced when the United States, under Al Gore's tenure as lead negotiator, stated it would not ratify the Kyoto protocol without a central role for carbon markets within the plan. More then ten years after weakening the protocol, the US has still declined to sign on.

The Bank's latest scheme, called "Reducing Emissions from Deforestation and Degradation" (REDD) is part of the "Bali Roadmap" established by the UN in 2007, and is slated to be a key component of any post-Kyoto climate treaty. This new plan offers a means for rich countries to avoid responsibility for over-consumption and evade emissions cuts by buying offsets.

The logic underpinning REDD is fairly simple: at present, the short-term economic gains from deforestation outweigh the long-term benefits of forest conservation. The Bank argues that investing up to $10 billion globally per year into saving forests will change the economic balance in favor of conservation. This money would be paid in the form of carbon credits—the more trees a country or company saves or pays to save, the more it earns the right to pollute.

The Bank's record of failed forest conservation projects is worse than its efforts at green development. During the 1980s, human rights activists and environmentalists worldwide campaigned against the Bank's funding of logging projects, megadams and road building programs. Recently, in massive logging and agrofuels projects in the volatile Democratic Republic of Congo, in Indonesia, and in the Amazon Basin, the Bank has been harshly criticized for funding environmental destruction and encouraging social unrest.

Given the Bank's past record, there are other reasons to be concerned as well. In many tropical countries, governments have attempted to legally define remaining forests as leaseable state lands, so that indigenous peoples who have lived in forests for millennia are being evicted from their homes. With the World Bank and their corporate partners' interests in protecting lucrative forest carbon "reservoirs," the risks to forest-dwelling people will surely grow.

MEGADAMS

FROM WRITINGS BY THE WORLD RAINFOREST MOVEMENT AND INTERNATIONAL RIVERS

While hydroelectric dams do not require combustion to generate electricity, they have deep ecological and social footprints and they still produce greenhouse gases. The flooding created by dam construction has forced thousands of people worldwide out of their homes. Protesting communities are often brutalized during violent evictions of villages and cities to make way for dam construction. In the Pacific Northwest, salmon are on the brink of extinction due in large part to dams blocking their annual migration and the higher temperature of stagnant water behind them.

Newly built dams flood thousands of acres of forests, killing trees and starting the decomposition of massive amounts of organic material. This accelerated decomposition releases tons of methane and CO_2 into the atmosphere. One study found that the net release of CO_2 from hydroelectric dams in tropical regions is as high as the greenhouse gas emissions of a coal plant producing an equal amount of electricity.

The CDM (detailed in the "Carbon Offsets" section) is increasing subsidies to hydropower developers while allowing major fossil fuel emitters to carry on polluting. By the beginning of 2008, 654 such projects had received or had applied to receive status as UN sanctioned carbon offsets. Hydro is now the most common technology in the CDM, representing a quarter of all projects.

Like many other offset projects, the great majority of hydroelectric projects in the CDM were in the works long before they applied for carbon credits. Absurdly, more than a third of the dam projects that have been approved for credits by the UN committee in charge of the CDM were built before CDM approval!

The large dams now angling for CDM certification also impose significant environmental and social damage. The massive 880 Megawatt Campos Novos Dam in Brazil (completed in 2005, yet applied for credits in 2007) displaced 3,000 people, many of whom were never granted their promised compensation. In addition to this injustice, local project opponents were subjected to arbitrary arrests and police violence.

Geoengineering

The term geoengineering refers to the large scale manipulation of the environment to bring about specific environmental change, particularly to counteract the undesirable side effects of other human activities. Geoengineering rests on the assumption that humans are masters of the universe and the natural world, and have the ability to control and engineer its systems. Climate change has shown that humans do not and probably never will understand the planet's systems well enough to try to artificially engineer a rebalancing of the scales that over-consumption has tipped.

Once any of these geoengineering schemes is embarked upon, it must be maintained for as long as the carbon dioxide emissions that it aimed to counteract remain in the atmosphere regardless of any negative impact the scheme turns out to have. Some of the very worst and most absurd of these false solutions are described here:

Sulphates in the Stratosphere

When volcanoes erupt they release sulfates which are known to have a cooling effect on global tempera-tures by reflecting solar energy back into space. Some scientists are proposing to increase levels of (banned) sulfate aerosols to simulate this effect. However, a dramatic increase in sulfates would have serious im-pacts on ecosystems, including acid rain and localized climatic disruptions, such as droughts. Nobel prize winner Paul Crutzen, who advocated research into sulfate aerosols as a last ditch solution to global warm-ing, predicted around half a million deaths as a result of increased particulate pollution.

Sunshades to Space

This scheme involves a set of 16 trillion transparent, sunlight-refracting shades installed in space about 1.5 million km from Earth. The project would re-quire 20 launchers each positioning 800,000 screens every five minutes for ten years to initiate and would cost trillions of dollars to deploy.

Genetically Engineered Trees

Some believe we can create unlimited quantities of "renewable" carbon neutral wood energy using ge-netically engineered trees. Some consider burning wood "carbon neutral" due to the notion that the CO % released during burning would have been released anyway as the tree died and decomposed.

Towards that end, companies like Arborgen are de-veloping trees with resistance to drought, freezing, diseases and insects, as well as reduced lignin. (Lig-nin is a structural material that gives trees strength and flexibility but "gets in the way" of industrial processes.) Since trees spread pollen and seeds over hundreds of miles, contamination of native forests by GE trees is virtually inevitable and once it occurs could devastate native forest ecosystems globally.

Ocean Fertilization

This idea centers on encouraging the growth of phytoplankton in the oceans, which take up carbon dioxide as they photosynthesize. In theory, some of this carbon dioxide might not return immediately to the carbon cycle.

Exactly how much carbon dioxide is seques-tered, and for how long, has not been quantified. Ocean scientists have warned that this technology is potentially dangerous to ocean ecosystems, un-likely to sequester much carbon dioxide, and has the potential to increase levels of other dangerous greenhouse gases such as nitrous oxide and methane. In addition, expanding phytoplankton populations could amplify ocean acidification in deep ocean waters and deplete nutrient loading in surface waters (potentially leading to the creation of "dead zones").

Plastic Coated Deserts

In this plan, 67,000 square miles of desert would be coated in shiny plastic each year for 60 years to reflect sunlight. The plastic sheeting would have to be maintained, and periodically replaced, for a century or two. Premature removal would have a rapid global warming effect.

Burning Trees to Cool the Planet

Another strange idea is using charcoal (marketed as "biochar" to make it sound more appealing) to save the planet. The idea is to plant over half a billion hectares of tree plantations and burn them using a pyrolysis (low oxygen) process to make charcoal.

The charcoal is then tilled into the ground, so that the carbon in the charcoal is safely sequestered in soil, away from the atmosphere.

> *"Ladies and gentlemen, I have the answer! Incredible as it might seem, I have stumbled across the single technology which will save us from runaway climate change! From the goodness of my heart I offer it to you for free. No patents, no small print, no hidden clauses. Already this technology, a radical new kind of carbon capture and storage, is causing a stir among scientists. It is cheap, it is efficient and it can be deployed straight away. It is called ... leaving fossil fuels in the ground."*

—GEORGE MONBIOT, COLUMNIST WITH THE GUARDIAN UK

Demanding Climate Justice

> *"The economic logic behind dumping a load of toxic waste in the lowest wage country is impeccable and we should face up to that ... I've always thought that under-populated countries in Africa are vastly UNDER-polluted"*

—LARRY SUMMERS, DIRECTOR OF OBAMA'S NATIONAL ECONOMIC COUNCIL, FORMER CHIEF ECONOMIST AT THE WORLD BANK

Environmental and social justice activists in the Global South are demanding that the world's wealthiest nations assume responsibility for the disaster have created rather than perpetuate carbon colonialism in the developing world. Social movements and grassroots organizations rooted in the Global South have long realized the futility of certain "solutions" and remind us that any old action won't do.

Our Southern allies believe we should respond to climate change through commitments to reduced consumption and by payment of the ecological debt from the Global North to the Global South owed from decades of resource extraction. Investment in community-led renewable energy initiatives and sustainable, small-scale agriculture infrastructure geared to meeting the right of all people to healthy food are supported, corporate development is rejected.

The climate crisis demands that we, as residents of the Global North, ask what kind of world we want to live in, and recognize that the answer is as much a social issue as it is an environmental one. Climate Justice is more than a theoretical goal—it is a practice in the movement against climate chaos. No effort to create a livable climate future will succeed without the empowerment of marginalized communities. No justice will be found without an end to policies long-pursued by the wealthy countries which treat communities—from Iraq's oil fields to Indonesia's palm oil plantations to Appalachia's coal fields—merely as resource colonies.

Real Solutions

An evaluation of climate solutions must start with basic, yet rarely asked, questions: Who owns, controls, and profits from each technology? Who loses? Beyond measuring carbon impact, how does each proposal affect communities and other aspects of ecosystem health?

While technologies—micro-hydro, organic agriculture, public transit, passive solar home heating and many others—will be important in making a just transition to a post-carbon world, it's imperative to recognize that great problems have always been met by great social changes, not merely by technological shifts. Changes in technology are only a fraction of the climate solution, yet they consume nearly the entirety of the policy debate.

Growth of the whole global economy means consumption of an ever-increasing amount of goods, using an ever-increasing amount of energy, mineral, agricultural and forest resources. Replacing "growth" as the main objective of the economy is a fundamental change that must be made to address climate change. Building a new paradigm, rooted in meeting human needs equitably and sustainably, is as big a challenge as climate change itself. But if human society is to survive as we presently know it, the two must be inseparable.

Effective and just solutions to climate change require decision-making that incorporates all who are affected by the results of the decisions—not just deals between those who stand to profit. The hold that corporate interests and centuries-old colonial mindsets have over political decision-making must be broken. Only then can we begin creating a new, more just society in the shell of the old.

> *"If we hold up banners saying climate change kills and we want more government action, the very power groups driving the destruction will cheer and might give us even more carbon finance or agrofuels. Instead, we need to mobilize against the false solutions and for real, meaningful actions that will actually cut emissions and deliver climate justice … The time for marching for global action on climate change' without denouncing the false solutions and the drivers of climate change is over."*

—SIMONE LOVERA, ACTIVIST WITH
FRIENDS OF THE EARTH
PARAGUAY AND THE GLOBAL
FOREST COALITION

> *"Farming communities are more threatened now by the so-called solutions to climate change promoted by corporate interests, G8 countries, the World Trade Organization and the World Bank, than by climate change in itself. Industrial agrofuels, climate-ready seeds, fertilization of oceans and carbon-trading schemes, both deepen and widen the privatization of all natural resources on Earth and thus exclude local communities from access to those resources which where once called the Commons: land, water, seeds and now, perhaps, even the air we breathe."*

—LA VIA CAMPESINA

> *"Not only does the carbon trading mechanism not work, it makes the greedy north feel like they have done something meaningful while we keep drowning. Using the market to solve a problem the market created seems little short of insanity.**—Sandy Gauntlett, Pacific People's Environment Coalition"We are taking away food from poor peoples tables and putting it into rich people's cars."*

—ANNIE SUGRUE, SOUTHERN AFRICAN
SUSTAINABILITY CAMPAIGNER

STUDY QUESTIONS

1. Discuss two proposed "solutions" to climate change and their problems.

2. Discuss two more solutions.

3. What different kinds of problems are discussed—that is, what patterns emerge in critiquing the different technological options (e.g., displacing people from land)? Find at least five and discuss.

47

Climate Justice: The Emerging Movement against Green Capitalism

ASHLEY DAWSON

Ashley Dawson is an activist and associate professor of the English department in the Graduate Center, City University of New York. This essay analyses resistance to capitalist solutions to climate change and provides a context for rethinking the relation of climate change to social justice.

> *This is how one pictures; the angel of history. His face is turned towards the past. Where we perceive a chain of events, he sees one single catastrophe which keeps piling wreckage upon wreckage and hurls it in front of his feet. The angel would like to stay, waken the dead, and make whole what has been smashed. But a storm is blowing from Paradise; it has got caught in his wings with such violence that the Angel can no longer close them. The storm irresistibly propels him into the future to which his back is turned, while the pile of debris before him grows skyward. This storm is what we call progress.*
>
> —WALTER BENJAMIN, THESES ON THE PHILOSOPHY
> OF HISTORY

A specter is haunting the planet—the specter of ecocide. The United States, and with it the rest of the world, is experiencing an unprecedented emergency brought on by three intertwined factors: a credit-fueled financial crisis, wildly gyrating energy prices linked to the peaking of oil supplies, and an accelerating climate crisis. Although the news has been filled over the last two years with reports of the subprime mortgage crisis, food riots, and the melting of the polar ice caps, these alarming phenomena are seldom linked to one another. Moreover, these grave epiphenomena are not often tied to their underlying cause: the planet-consuming rapacity of a capitalist system that must grow incessantly or expire.[1] Yet the more desperately we try to exorcise this specter of ecocide through saccharine exercises in "greenwashing" and politically palatable half measures, the louder the death rattle of the planet becomes.

The current triple crisis signals the collapse of the neoliberal paradigm that has held sway since the last major crisis of accumulation during the 1970s.[2] While there will inevitably be significant continuities between the neoliberal era and what is to come, the triple crisis nevertheless signals the onset of a new phase of capitalism. This new phase, which is most aptly characterized as "green capitalism," will see the emergence of new spaces of accumulation and novel types of regulation.[3] Green capitalism does not seek to and will not

Ashley Dawson, "Climate Justice: The Emerging Movement Against Green Capitalism," *South Atlantic Quarterly*, Vol. 109, No. 2(2010): 313–38. Durham, N.C.: Duke University Press.

solve the underlying ecological contradictions of capital's insatiable appetite for ceaselessly expanding accumulation on a finite environmental base. Instead, green capitalism seeks to profit from the current crisis. In doing so, it remorselessly intensifies the contradictions, the natural destruction, and human suffering associated with ecocide.

The lineaments of green capitalism have been emerging for some time, dating perhaps most clearly back to the creation of the World Bank's Global Environment Facility in 1991.[4] Nevertheless, with the long-delayed conclusion over the debate about whether climate change is actually taking place over the last several years and the coeval crisis of neoliberalism, a truly green capitalist new order is emerging far more clearly. Take the landmark climate change legislation that, at the time of this writing, has barely scraped through the U.S. House of Representatives and is set to come up for negotiation in the Senate. Fred Krupp of the Environmental Defense Fund, one of the biggest green groups in the United States, called the global warming bill "the most important environmental and energy legislation in the history of our country."[5] Yet the bill, seen as a triumph after more than twenty years of congressional inaction on the climate crisis, not only fails to mandate necessary reductions in greenhouse gas emissions, but in addition establishes a market-based cap-and-trade policy that essentially commodifies the atmosphere. In recent years, a scientific consensus has emerged that emissions cuts on the order of 85 to 95 percent will be required to prevent the planet from entering into cycles of cataclysmic, runaway climate change.[6] Yet the new bill, known as the American Clean Energy and Security Act (ACES), measures emissions relative to 2005 rather than the Kyoto-mandated date of 1990.[7] It promises a meager 17 percent reduction by 2020, which translates into only 4 to 5 percent less emissions than the United States produced in 1990. The heavily promoted cap-and-trade provision of ACES promises an even more derisory 1 percent reduction by 2020. In addition, like the European Union's highly flawed Emissions Trading Scheme, the plan is filled with loopholes: at least 85 percent of the allowances for continuing to pollute will be given away for free rather than auctioned, as Barack Obama had pledged during his presidential campaign. While the promised reductions in greenhouse gas emissions may be risible under cap-and-trade, the profits that polluting corporations stand to gain are not. Advocates of the carbon market are looking forward to the emergence of a global trading system ultimately valued at more than $10 trillion per year.[8] With an emerging cadre of brokers set to begin trading in carbon futures using precisely the same financial sleights of hand that led to the current economic crisis, the foundations for green capitalism are clearly now in place.

As the climate crisis intensifies, the contradictions of green capitalism will produce more and more of what Zygmunt Bauman calls "human waste," the population of human beings rendered surplus by the remorseless advance of modernity.[9] On one level, these wasted lives will be the result of worsening environmental instability alone, as climate change leads to desiccation, water shortages, crop failure, and extreme weather events on an unparalleled scale. On another level, however, the practices of carbon offsetting that are an integral part of green capitalism will play a crucial role in mass displacement. Offsets such as those implicit in the Clean Development Mechanism, established by the United Nations Framework Convention on Climate Change (UNFCCC), allow polluters to continue their unsustainable behavior by paying others—typically in the global South—to absorb such pollution. However, by establishing vast plantations of quick-growing eucalyptus trees in countries such as Brazil, for example, these offsets displace huge numbers of subsistence farmers and pollute the groundwater through intensive use of the pesticides necessary to sustain such monocultural developments.[10] In many cases, deforestation simply moves elsewhere, meaning that there is no net diminution of carbon. Offsets and the green capitalist system of which they are an integral part will thus dramatically augment the production of both surplus people and megaslums that has characterized the neoliberal era.[11] In scenarios based on current predictions by the Intergovernmental Panel on Climate Change, for example, 20 percent of the world's population could be rendered homeless by the end of this century.

Green capitalism will necessarily hinge on new forms of authoritarian control over the wasted lives that it ineluctably produces. Global elites are already preparing for this eventuality.[12] Tire U.S. military, for its part, commissioned a report in 2007, *National Security and the Threat of Climate Change,* that frames global warming as a threat multiplier that the security establishment must prepare to face on several fronts.[13] As environmental and political instability grow, the turn to popular authoritarian ideologies and increasingly draconian forms of rule over those marginalized by the prevailing socioeconomic-ecological order will necessarily be ratcheted up.[14] This trend toward heightened authoritarianism is the dark but integral side of green capitalism, which will nevertheless always blame the instability and suffering that are structurally inherent in this mode of accumulation on the "human waste" it produces.

In what follows I sketch the recent birth of a climate justice movement. In the United States, this movement builds on the deep and powerful roots of the environmental justice movement, which in turn draws on the organizing tactics, cultural forms, and ideological stance of the civil rights movements. This emergent climate justice movement will play a pivotal role in challenging green capitalism, both in the United States and internationally. We cannot expect such a challenge to come from the mainstream environmental movement. As the comments of the Environmental Defense Fund's Krupp suggest, many prominent conservation organizations have bought into the new green capitalist order. In addition, although some of them have made significant strides of late, many of these mainstream organizations have failed to incorporate the perspectives of communities most affected by the toxic by-products of unregulated industrial growth. This failure stems not simply from their closeness to procorporate interests but also from a reifying epistemological stance toward nature embodied in the wilderness ethic, one that sees the environment and human beings and their social struggles in antithetical terms. Building on several decades of activism within the environmental justice movement, the emerging movement for climate justice challenges the wilderness ethic, and in so doing strives to organize discussion and militancy around the climate crisis in an engagement with issues of inequality and injustice. The stance of the climate justice movement is, as a result, far more attuned to the issues that drive environmental activism throughout the global South.[15] The movement for climate justice thus promises to be a vehicle for mobilizing the kind of transnational, grassroots alliances that will be decisive in the unfolding fight against ecocide.

Genuine solutions to the climate crisis cannot emerge from climate negotiations, whether on a domestic or an international level, unless significant pressure—pressure that is greater than that of powerful corporate interests—is brought to bear by a globally linked, locally grounded group of social movements mobilizing around the theme of climate justice. This will take genuine organizing—a task that the Left has tended to shy away from.[16] Such organizing is a particularly urgent task on both a practical and a theoretical level, given the predominantly anarchist, antistatist character of the global justice movement in the North. Rather than abdicating engagement with the organs of state power, the crisis of our times requires transformation of these organs through practices of radical democracy. In addition, however, a movement for climate justice needs a theoretical grasp of the economic, political, and ecological stakes at play in the new green capitalist order.

"THERE IS NO SUCH THING AS A NATURAL DISASTER"

When Hurricane Katrina approached New Orleans in late August 2005, it was packing category 5 wands whipped, up by the thermal energy in the warm waters of the Gulf of Mexico. By the time that it touched, land east of the city, however, the hurricane had lost a great deal of its force. After a tense night, residents of the Crescent City who, too stubborn or too poor to leave, had ridden the storm out heaved a collective sigh of relief. The worst, however, was still to come. Katrina shoved a powerful storm surge across the wetlands east of the city and into Lake Pontchartrain, which borders the city to the north. As the storm moved inland, powerful cyclonic winds piled the storm surge up against hurricane protection levees on the city's lakefront and along the Industrial Canal in the eastern portion of the city called the Lower Ninth Ward. These levees eventually ruptured, disgorging toxic floodwaters into the low-lying sections of the city. There was nothing natural about the disaster that ensued.

The work of critical black intellectuals and their allies in the years since Hurricane Katrina has centered on framing the disaster in terms of climate justice.[17] Such analysis forms part of a concerted campaign against dominant views of the disaster—reflected, for example, in the pronouncements of President George W. Bush—as an "act of God," which no one could have foreseen. The points activists made in this context bear reiteration and amplification for a number of reasons. First of all, Katrina and its aftermath illustrated in gruesome detail points that members of the environmental justice movement, which I will discuss in the next section, had been making for more than two decades. In addition, the dynamics of the disaster were perhaps the first clear-cut instance of the toll that climate change may take on domestic soil, revealing with horrible clarity the ways in which increasingly extreme weather events will magnify already-existing inequalities. The fossil fuel industry has spent millions of dollars trying to obscure this connection.[18] But if any lesson can be extracted from the great suffering occasioned by Katrina, it is that the neoliberal order, left to run its course, will create immeasurable human misery and displacement as the climatic instability that it has helped catalyze intensifies. We can look to New Orleans and Katrina, in other words, to learn lessons about how *not* to behave in the future. Finally, it is important to discuss the critique generated by the disaster in New Orleans precisely because, rather than learning from this painful past, the rest of the nation has begun to forget Katrina and the many displaced residents of New Orleans. Memories of the suffering and heroism that unfolded in New Orleans after Katrina struck must be kept alive as an integral part of the movement for climate justice.

As in many other cities around the world, the geography of New Orleans reflects class and racial disparities.[19] The low-lying and hence more vulnerable areas into which the waters of the storm surge flooded were inhabited primarily by low-income people of color, although middle-class black neighborhoods and ethnically mixed areas were also affected. Despite the sweeping devastation wrought by the storm (71 percent of New Orleans's housing stock was damaged), as television coverage in the initial days following the storm showed, it was the city's predominantly poor African American population, trapped in flooded houses, neighborhoods, and the squalid conditions of the Superdome, who suffered the most from the deluge. As geographer Neil Smith puts it, "In every phase and aspect of a disaster—causes, vulnerability, preparedness, results and response, and reconstruction—the contours of disaster and the difference between who lives and who dies is to a greater or lesser extent a social calculus."[20]

Hurricane Katrina stripped away the sly avowals of race blindness and postracialism that have characterized the era after civil rights in general and the Bush administration in particular. In place of such studied mendacity, the disaster revealed the production of what Rob Nixon calls "unimagined communities," populations who find no place in neoliberalism but whose existence is nevertheless an integral part of it.[21] We are living, that is, through a period of new enclosures in which a global assault on various forms of common wealth is taking place with ever-heightened ferocity.[22] As was true of the original enclosures during the early modern period in Britain, these new enclosures separate people from the means of subsistence. They literally produce surplus population, Bauman's "human waste." Dating roughly to the 1970s, when capitalism entered a crisis of overproduction and embarked on a new, savage round of what David Harvey labels "accumulation by dispossession,' the new enclosures are not, however, simply an economic process.[23] As the notion of unimagined communities suggests, this production of a superfluous humanity also depends on representational processes of marginalization, subordination, and scapegoating. This is, in short, a specifically neoliberal mode of biopower that hinges on allotting social death just as much as it depends on guaranteeing the right to live.[24] Yet contrary to the work of critics such as Bauman and Giorgio Agamben, whose notion of *homno sacer* has been widely embraced as a way of accounting for the production of people stripped of human rights in extraterritorial zones such as the Guantánamo Bay detention camp, "human waste" is not a universal category produced by a uniform modernity. Instead, the unimagining of *specific* communities is linked to concatenated processes of race and class formation within particular national and subnational arenas during the neoliberal era.[25] The state, a major target for enclosure in its social mode (e.g., education, health care, welfare, etc.), plays a critical role in this production of unimagined communities.

How did the production of surplus people take place in New Orleans before Katrina? Prior to the neoliberal era, the city's economy depended primarily on three bases: the petrochemical industrial complex, shipping, and tourism.[26] During the 1970s, however, the fossil fuel industry largely left New Orleans to consolidate itself in Houston: at the same time, containerization drastically reduced the labor necessary in shipping. While New Orleans remains an important port, a relatively small segment of the labor force is employed in such well-remunerated work. The majority of the city's residents, absent state intervention to create alternative, high-wage activities, were consigned to the low-paying service sector. As New Orleans's economic base atrophied, significant numbers of whites fled to the suburbs, and the city became predominantly African American. New Orleans also became increasingly anomalous in political terms: in a conservative and increasingly Republican South, the city had a sizable black majority that consistently returned Democrats to power.

These shifts worsened the city's already precarious environmental conditions. Ever since its founding, the city's fortuitous site as a commercial hub at the gateway of the Mississippi River had won out over its perilous position in the midst of a highly mutable delta ecosystem.[27] In the course of the twentieth century, attempts to fortify and expand the city's position through the raising of levees and the draining of swampland following the highly mechanistic protocols of the Army Corps of Engineers ironically further endangered the city since they allowed the settlement of land that was below sea level.[28]

Corruption also played a role in the city's increasingly parlous state. Tax breaks and scant oversight permitted petroleum companies to cut canals into the fragile freshwater estuaries to the east of the city, dramatically accelerating erosion of the marshes that provide a vital buffer between the city and the hungry tides of the Gulf of Mexico.[29] Powerful real estate interests, tied in many cases to Big Oil, successfully lobbied local and federal officials for permission and infrastructural support to drain and develop swampland in areas such as New Orleans East.[30] Developers then conned potential residents, most of whom were African American, into believing that this area, which was surrounded by water on every side, was on higher ground. Naturally enough, as we know, this area suffered catastrophic flooding during the Katrina crisis. Finally, in the years before Katrina, repeated calls to stem wetlands erosion and to fix the failing levee system that protects the city were met with blank indifference by a federal administration more interested in tax cuts for the wealthy and imperial escapades in Iraq than in the South's sole blue state.

In the days following Katrina, the national media, kept so tightly on a leash in its coverage of the war on terror, bore shocked witness to the immense suffering of the heretofore invisible citizens of New Orleans, who went without help for days as the waters rose around them. Against arguments that their abandonment was the product of a mistake in planning by one or another level of officialdom, critical analysis in the wake of Katrina stressed the structural nature of their invisibility highlighting economic and political factors such as the ones I have just detailed. The structural character of the unimagining of African American communities that took place before, during, and after Katrina was also made plain by the abrupt shift in media coverage after the first days of the crisis.[31] In New Orleans's low-income residents had been largely invisible before the crisis, they became hypervisible as the media began covering instances of the "looting" of private property after the storm. As critics such as Michael Eric Dyson and the INCITE! collective have documented, there was a glaring racial disparity between media accounts of white survivors who resorted to urban foraging in the absence of federal and local aid and the coverage accorded to African Americans who did the same thing.[32] The latter were depicted as criminals instead of desperate survivors by the national media. This return to the racialized script of popular authoritarianism that has been so crucial to maintaining hegemony during the neoliberal period had immediate and dramatic results. Within a week of the storm's passage, the city was locked down by members of the National Guard intent on protecting private property, and Louisiana governor Kathleen Blanco was boasting on national television that the troops dispatched to the city had experience killing terrorists in Iraq and would not hesitate to do the same thing in New Orleans.[33]

The production of unimagined communities gathered speed following the storm in what amounts to an undeclared policy of ethnic cleansing of New Orleans. The City essentially became a lab for neoliberal free market experiments in sectors as diverse as housing, education, and policing. While the Federal Emergency Management Agency's criminally bumbling response to the crisis was no doubt partially a result of cronyism within the Bush administration, it was also in the interest of Republican-controlled federal agencies to do nothing since such inactivity would effectively destroy the Democratic power base in the city.[34] The disaster capitalism complex consolidated in Iraq was quickly put into play in New Orleans, with no-bid contracts for the demolition of public housing and urban reconstruction going to many of the same Bush administration—linked multinational corporations that engaged in flagrant war profiteering in Iraq.[35] Displaced residents were shipped off to distant cities and to grim, concentration camp—like, formaldehyde-laced FEMA trailer parks far away from their homes. Above all others, these policies attacked and purged the city's most vulnerable

people: poor black women and their children.[36] With an African American population greater than 70 percent before the flooding, New Orleans is now less than 50 percent black.

Plans for reconstruction of the city have become a particular flash point as neighborhood groups and critical intellectuals have mobilized to challenge the ethnic cleansing of New Orleans in the wake of Katrina. The Urban Land Institute (ULI), a Washington, D.C.–based consulting group drafted by the city's mayor to provide a plan for reconstruction, recognized that much of the city's abusive development in low-lying swampland was likely to be unsustainable in the face of the increasingly extreme weather events the city will no doubt face in the future.[37] But the plan submitted to the mayor's Bring Back New Orleans Commission generated huge controversy since it called for the demolition of all housing in predominantly African American neighborhoods such as New Orleans East, the Lower Ninth Ward, and Broadmoor. These areas were to be turned into urban parkland that would double as a containment zone in the event of future flooding. The ULI plan contained no provision for housing and resettlement of the residents of these areas, despite widespread recognition of the potential for redevelopment of blighted core urban areas built on the higher ground formed by natural levees. A tremendous outcry naturally ensued, and Mayor Ray Nagin rejected the ULI plan for shrinking the city. There was, however, no attempt to frame an alternative plan. Residents of flooded areas were told they could return to their homes, but little was done to rebuild the infrastructure of their neighborhoods. Political expediency has essentially substituted long-term imperilment of these displaced people who are returning to flood zones for the controversial policy of short-term ethnic cleansing of the city.

The vacuum left by federal and local authorities during and after the Katrina disaster has been filled by local grassroots organizations. Neighborhoods such as the Lower Ninth Ward and Broadmoor have united to resist demolition plans and to call for more egalitarian provision of relief funds.[38] Organizations emerging from the neighborhoods have been particularly adept at engaging with powerful planning and relief organizations based outside the city such as Harvard's Department of Urban Planning and Design and Bard Pitt's Make It Right Foundation to generate plans for egalitarian and sustainable redevelopment of these communities. Despite the significant successes achieved by such organizations, however, it is important to note that the flooded areas that have been quickest to redevelop have been ones with mixed-ethnic and mixed-income populations. Many poorer areas of the city simply lack the capital and organizational resources to achieve such successes, despite the attempts of grassroots groups to overcome fragmentation through initiatives such as the Neighborhoods Partnership Network. In addition, many of the successful neighborhood groups have been led by outsiders. The relationship between local activists and well-meaning outsiders has not been without controversy during reconstruction. Groups staffed by predominantly white, middle-class activists such as Common Ground have been accused of marginalizing local African American leadership and organizations, as well as unwittingly aiding the forces of gentrification by bringing thousands of bohemian twentysomethings to live in underpopulated neighborhoods that remain on their knees.[39]

Four years after Hurricanes Katrina and Rita struck the Gulf Coast, residents of New Orleans are terrified that they are once again being forgotten and consigned to invisibility.[40] Although the city has long celebrated its unique character, the danger now is that it will be seen as anomalous and disconnected from the rest of the United States.[41] Federal funding such as the Road Home program, insufficient to start with, is now drying up. There is still no broad plan to deal with the ecological and economic contradictions of the city. The valiant efforts of grassroots groups may have led to impressive reconstruction efforts in particular parts of the city, but such groups cannot engage in the systematic restoration of the wetlands on the city's easterly flank that must be a crucial part of protecting the city against future violent weather events. Despite the commencement of the Obama administration, no significant federal intervention seems likely; indeed,

with Democratic control of Louisiana essentially destroyed, a neoconservative governor is competing with other Republicans to spurn all offers of federal aid.

Notwithstanding these setbacks and obstacles, however, the Katrina tragedy has helped galvanize African American activists and their allies on both a local and a national scale to theorize and organize around climate justice. Katrina, they argue, was not a natural disaster. The horrible toll taken by the storm—nearly three thousand dead, hundreds of thousands displaced—was a result of the systematic production of inequality and invisibility during the neoliberal era. It was also a harbinger of tragedies to come, unless we change course dramatically. Efforts to deal with climate change must hinge on rendering visible and protecting communities made vulnerable by the capitalist system and the climatic instability it is provoking. These credos are central to the movement for climate justice, to which I now turn.

CLIMATE JUSTICE

The climate justice movement is an outgrowth of the struggle for environmental justice. The latter movement was sparked when a largely poor and African American community in rural Warren County, North Carolina, rose up in opposition to the building of a toxic waste landfill there in 1982.[42] This protest inspired studies which demonstrated that race—rather than income or any other variable—was the primary factor associated with the location of toxic waste facilities.[43] As it unfolded during the rest of the 1980s, the environmental justice movement was completely distinct from the mainstream environmental movement. First, it drew on the protest repertoire and cultural forms of the civil rights movement in the South. In addition, unlike most elite national environmental organizations, it was led largely by women and grew from women's concern with the desire to protect family and community.[44] The environmental justice movement also pioneered strategies of participatory democracy in its organizing campaigns.[45]

Unlike mainstream environmental organizations, which became increasingly bureaucratically organized and centered on lobbying inside the Capital Beltway after the 1970s, the environmental justice movement grew out of and was attuned to the needs of poor communities. When concern over toxic waste galvanized the environmental movement following the Love Canal disaster in 1978, for example, many mainstream organizations called for closure of polluting industries. By contrast, the environmental justice movement tended to be aware of the economic needs of working-class communities and hence was less quick to adopt a purely NIMBY-ist attitude toward environmental problems. Environmental justice advocates hence called not just for *freedom from* contamination but also for *access* to environmental and social goods such as safe, well-paying jobs.

Arguably the most significant aspect of the environmental justice movement, however, was its challenge to the wilderness ethic that underlay the efforts of mainstream environmental organizations. Many of these organizations had their roots in the Progressive Era, when the first great wave of industrialization and urbanization in U.S. history created highly insalubrious conditions in many American cities and generated a longing to preserve what were perceived as imperiled "wild" areas. Of course, such areas had been constructed through complex interactions between people and nature long before the arrival of Europeans in the Americas. Yet for early environmental organizations such as the Sierra Club, nature and human beings were seen as at odds, if not antithetical. The idea of an urban environmental movement was consequently a contradiction in terms for these organizations. Yet the environmental justice movement as it developed during the 1980s and 1990s highlighted precisely the manner in which racialized patterns of urban development had exposed African American and other ethnic minority communities to environmental hazards in radically disproportionate numbers.[46] In fighting these conditions, activists and intellectuals in the environmental justice movement also challenged many of the pejorative racial stereotypes that were resurrected by neoconservative scholars like Charles Murray to explain and demonize racialized urban poverty during the neoliberal era.

The Harlem-based organization WE ACT exemplifies many of these broader trends within the environmental justice movement. Shortly after the organization was formed in the late 1980s, a group of its organizers, nicknamed the "Sewage Seven," were arrested while doing civil disobedience to protest toxic fumes emitted by the North River Sewage Treatment Plant, located along the Hudson River in West Harlem.[47] In 2000, WE ACT sued the city's Metropolitan Transportation Authority over its plans to locate a sixth bus terminal in Harlem. As these two cases suggest, one of the primary concerns driving the organization was air quality. New York neighborhoods populated predominantly by ethnic minorities have extremely high rates of asthma; in Harlem, roughly one-quarter of children suffer from the disease. It is hardly a coincidence that the community is also burdened by a disproportionate share of the city's most polluting facilities, including incinerators, diesel bus depots, sewage and sludge treatment plants, solid waste transfer stations, and power plants. Yet despite the apparently intuitive "commonsense" link between such facilities, air quality, and pulmonary diseases, public health authorities have tended to individualize high rates of asthma.[48] Since studies generally found no correlation between individual sources of pollution and disease, medical authorities usually blamed the domiciles (or, to be more specific, the mothers) of sick children for illness-causing poor hygiene. Drawing on the arguments of activist intellectuals such as Robert Bullard and Cynthia Hamilton, groups such as WE ACT rejected such blame-the-victim, individualizing arguments, pointing to the presence of multiple "toxic time bombs" in the city's African American and Latino neighborhoods.[49]

Powered by groups such as WE ACT, the environmental justice movement gained steam during the late 1980s and early 1990s, both through important demonstrations against environmental injustice such as the Great Louisiana Toxics March of 1988 and through the development of an intellectual framework on a national scale in documents such as the United Church of Christ's landmark study *Toxic Waste and Race in the United States.*[50]

Such activism was supported by pathbreaking scholarship such as Robert Bullard's *Dumping in Dixie*.[51] In 1991, at the historic People of Color Environmental Leadership Summit, activists drafted a set of seventeen principles for environmental justice. These core tenets underlined that the movement was not just about environmental issues, but rather that social justice goals such as economic equity, cultural liberation, and the political participation of people of color at all levels of decision making were an integral part of the struggle.[52] In addition, while recognizing that people of color are disproportionately exposed to environmental toxins as a result of conscious and unconscious forms of racism, the documents that emerged from the summit stressed that *no one* should have to cope with such hazards. The environmental justice movement thus stressed that it, like the civil rights movement whose legacy it extends, embodies the inclusive, emancipatory vision articulated in the founding documents of U.S. democracy. In 1994, President Bill Clinton recognized the importance of this vision by issuing Executive Order 12898, which mandated that federal agencies pursue policies of environmental justice. Yet despite its recognition of the movement's goals, Clinton's order was vaguely worded and allowed federal agencies to drag their feet.[53] It took the Environmental Protection Agency six years from the time of Clinton's order to issue instructions to state agencies on how to handle environmental justice claims. Once the Bush administration assumed power, these hesitant moves toward environmental justice were largely discarded. Business groups argued that such measures would dampen economic development, and without any provisions concerning racism and social justice in the foundational environmental legislation of the 1970s, the movement found it had little traction once the relatively sympathetic Clinton regime ended.

Although the Obama administration has adopted a far more responsive position toward the movement that promises significant advances to come, during the Bush years advocates of environmental justice were hardly in hibernation. Sustainable South Bronx (SSBX), for example, which grew out of and carries forward community struggle over polluting solid waste facilities very similar to those tackled by WE ACT, established the Bronx Environmental Stewardship Training (BEST) Academy during the Bush years. BEST provides green job training for youths in a neighborhood burdened not simply with high pollution and asthma rates, but also with some of the highest unemployment levels in New York City.[54] As well as keeping us such exemplary local work, organizations such as SSBX, stymied on the federal level, ramped up their efforts to shape urban, state, and regional policy around the broad framework of environmental justice. Many grassroots environmental justice groups played an active role, for example, in drafting PlaNYC, New York City's blueprint for urban sustainability over the coming century. This level of involvement is a huge victory, one that reflects decades of activism for the inclusion of communities most affected by environmental and social injustices. Nonetheless, even on this local level there have been significant obstacles to realizing the vision of inclusion and participation. The opposition from SSBX to New York City's plans to build a prison in the South Bronx made for thorny relations with the authorities drafting PlaNYC, for example, despite SSBX's pioneering history of jumpstarting urban environmental sustainability projects such as the South Bronx Greenway.[55]

In addition to these multifaceted efforts, the environmental justice movement also began to adopt a far more international frame. This was partially a result of attempts to draw on international treaties and on transnational solidarity to sweep aside the obstacles erected by the Bush administration. Yet this shift toward a broader spatial scale of activism also coincided with, on the one hand, the growing impact of the global justice movement within the United States and, on the other, increasing public awareness of the climate change crisis. A central element of this strategy involved redefining climate change as an environmental justice and human rights issue. Like the Katrina disaster, climate change, the movement argued, is not simply about the environment. In 1999, the San Francisco–based NGO Corporate Watch began working with communities in the United States and internationally to

DOWN AT THE CROSSROADS

It is an ugly and rather terrifying fact that the environment we take for granted as the context for life on the planet is likely to alter radically in the relatively near future as a result of runaway climate change. On June 23, 2008, NASA climate scientist James Hansen appeared before a House of Representatives' select committee twenty years to the day since his history-making public announcement of global warming to Congress. Although he repeated his original assertions concerning anthropogenic climate change, one major difference set off this reappearance: Hansen asserted in the starkest language that the world has almost run out of time to prevent Earth's feedback mechanisms from triggering runaway climate change.[67] According to new research presented by Hansen during his testimony, the atmosphere is far more sensitive to carbon dioxide emissions that the most recent work of the Intragovernmental Panel on Climate Change supposed. As a result, according to Hansen, a safe level of carbon dioxide concentration in the atmosphere would be no more than 350 parts per million. Currently, the carbon dioxide amount is 385 parts per million, with a rise of more than 2 parts per million per year. We need, in other words, not simply to freeze carbon dioxide emissions, but to *remove* significant amounts from the atmosphere through massive projects such as reforestation. A corollary of Hansen's alarming findings is the fact that the now nearly universally accepted target of maintaining warming below two degrees Celsius above preindustrial levels is a recipe for disaster rather than salvation.

Needless to say, policy makers have not absorbed these findings adequately. Indeed, one of the British government's chief scientific advisors recently made headlines by publicly urging ministers to prepare the nation to adapt to four degrees Celsius of warming.[68] While it clearly makes sense to seek to adapt to the intensified climatic instability already triggered by greenhouse gas emissions, what precisely would it mean to try to adapt to four degrees of warming? An answer can be gleaned from recent reports commissioned by tough-minded (and

hardly bleeding-heart liberal) entities such as the Pentagon and the European Council.[69] These agencies increasingly view climate changes in terms of a threat to collective security rather than simply as an environmental or even humanitarian problem.

Given these realities, it is difficult to overstate the importance of our historical moment. In looking back to Hurricane Katrina and in reading it as a harbinger, it's hard not to think of Walter Benjamin's angel of history, who is driven into the future by a storm that gets called progress while watching catastrophe pile up. But perhaps such apocalyptic imagery is dangerous, since it tends to suggest that the fate of human beings lies in the clouds rather than in our own hands.[70] Of course, there will always be significant struggles to be waged to challenge the iniquities of green capitalism. The movement for climate justice, I submit, will grow increasingly important as the need to mitigate the damaging impacts of climate change becomes ever more apparent.

A more judicious and more hopeful image to characterize the present is that of the crossroads, with all its symbolic significance for African diasporic cultures. We inhabit a place in time where two worlds touch, a liminal space potent with possibility and danger. Down one path lies green capitalism. This discussion of Hurricane Katrina strives to make clear the likely results of continuing in this direction. Down the other path lies climate and environmental justice. This path leads away from the climatic contradictions of green capitalism, toward a more egalitarian society framed on principles of social justice. Core tenets of the vision for such a society include a just transition to sustainable energy sources, with the adoption of low-consumption lifestyles, particularly in the global North; a minimum of 60 percent immediate greenhouse gas emissions reductions in the United States, leading to a 90 percent total cut by 2050; repayment of the ecological debt of the North to the South; equal access to and responsibility for common global resources (including the atmosphere) for all peoples; current and future support for refugees of all kinds; and a commitment to allowing those most affected to define the solutions to climate chaos. EJCC's ten principles of climate justice elucidate some of the central steps necessary to realize these elements of climate justice.[71]

Such goals may appear utopian in the percent context. But then, after years of rejecting metanarratives, progressives need a comprehensive positive vision, as well as careful strategic thought about how to realize that vision. Admittedly, there are many obstacles to be overcome. Climate justice still remains relatively peripheral to the mission of most mainstream environmental organizations, although that has begun to change. In additions, as J. Timmons Roberts argues, the movement is characterized by a loose coalition of groups rather than one central organizational base.[72] But what Roberts perceives as a weakness may in fact be a strength: after all, one of the defining features of the global justice movement over the last decade has been the flexibility and radical democracy introduced by a politics of nonhierarchical affiliation.[73] While it is certainly true that the climate justice movement faces a well-funded and powerful opposition that has successfully rolled back many of the progressive features of the Kyoto Protocol and seems set to torpedo its successor agreement in Copenhagen, the potential inherent in the transnational coalitional politics of the movement for climate justice should still not be underestimated. These new forms of affiliation are evident in the movement's mobilizing efforts in the run-up to the Copenhagen conference in December 2009. On the Mobilization for Climate Justice's Web site, for example, policy documents articulating the flaws in the UN's "corporate climate agenda" sit side by side with information about demonstrations against a polluting oil refinery in a low-income neighborhood in California and a statement from the international peasants' organization Via Campesina arguing that the false solutions to climate change adopted by the UNFCCC are at present far more damaging for small-scale, sustainable family farming than climate change itself.[74] Such multiscalar

organizing efforts are a crucial strength of the contemporary movement for climate change.

Intellectuals have an important role to play in this struggle for climate justice. The science involved in climate change is formidably complex and needs to be articulated to the public in clear terms that reverse the creeping apathy that has relegated climate injustice to a relatively minor concern in the minds of many people in the midst of the present economic crisis. Links between climate change and the other aspects of the triple crisis of our times also must be unpacked. The efforts of corporate greenwashing campaigns need to be debunked. Perceptions that the unjust and injurious effects of climate change are a result of God-given natural disasters must be challenged. In all these and many other endeavors to turn the tide against green capitalism, the efforts of activists in the environmental and climate justice movement over the last three decades serve as a map and a beacon to guide us down from the crossroads.

In the course of my research for this paper in New Orleans and New York, I was privileged to speak to an amazing group of activists and intellectuals. What I have written owes an enormous debt to their generosity and insight, although of course all infelicities as well as conclusions are my own. My thanks go in particular to Kathleen Coverick of the Broadmoor Development Corporation in New Orleans, Miquela Craytor of Sustainable South Bronx, Liz Davey of Tulane University, Michael Dorsey of Dartmouth College, Tonya Foster, DeVaney Jackson of the Brooklyn Rescue Mission, Cale Layton, Janet Redman of the Institute for Policy Studies, Brad Richard, Hal Roark of the Broadmoor Development Corporation, Christina Schiavoni of World Hunger Year, Peggy Shepard of WE ACT, Stephen Tremaine of the Bard College Urban Studies in New Orleans Program, and Jennifer Whitney.

NOTES

1. On the ecological or so-called second contradiction of capitalism, see James O'Connor, *Natural*

Causes: Essays in Ecological Marxism (New York: Guilford Press, 1998); and Joel Kovel, *The Enemy of*

Nature: The End of Capitalism or the End of the World? (New York: Zed Books, 2007).

2. Although there are many works on neoliberalism and its contradictions, the ones that I have found most useful are David Harvey, *A Brief History of Neoliberalism* (New York: Oxford University Press, 2007); and Neil Smith, *The Endgame of Globalization* (New York: Routledge, 2005).

3. For a succinct account of this new phase of capital, see Tadzio Mueller and Alexis Passadakis, "20 Theses against Green Capitalism," *Inter Activist,* http://info.interactivist.net/node/u656 (accessed July 20, 2009).

4. See Zoe Young, *A New Green Order? The World Bank and the Politics of the Global Environment Facility* (London: Pluto Press, 2002).

5. Fred Krupp quoted in Brian Tokar, "Politics-as-Usual while the Planet Burns," ZSpace, July 2, 2009, www.zcommunications.org/zspace/commentaries/3913.

6. For a clear explanation of the science behind these figures and a program for achieving the necessary cuts, see George Monbiot, *Heat: How to Stop the Planet from Burning* (Boston, MA: South End Press, 2009).

7. On ACES, see Tokar, "Politics-as-Usual."

8. Ibid.

9. Zygmunt Bauman, *Wasted Lives: Modernity and Its Outcasts* (Malden, MA: Blackwell, 2004), 5.

10. Tim Forsyth and Zoe Young, "Carbon CO_2lonialism," *Climate and Capitalism,* June 5, 2007, http://climateandcapitalism.com/?p=105.

11. On neoliberalism's production of slums, see Mike Davis, *Plant of Slums* (New York: Verso, 2007).

12. According to a report recently presented to European Union heads of state by two senior foreign policy officials, for example, climate change threatens to significantly intensify global political instability. Javier Solana, "Before the Flood," *Guardian,* March 10, 2008. www.guatdian.co.uk/commentisfree/2008/mat/to/beforetheflood.

13. Center for naval Analyses, *National Security and the Threat of Climate Change,* 2007, www.securityandclimae.cna.org/report.

14. The classic and still timely work on popular authoritarianism is Stuart hall et al., *Policing the Crisis: Mugging, the State, and Law and Order* (New York: Macmillan, 1978). For more recent analysis of this dynamic, see Loic Wacquant, *Punishing the Poor: The Neoliberal Government of Social Insecurity* (Durham, NC: Duke University Press, 2009).

15. For a discussion of the disparities in North-South environmental activism, see Ramachandra Guha and Juan Martinez-Alier, *Varieties of Environmentalism: Essays North and South* (New York: Earthscan, 1997).

16. See, for example, Timothy Brennan and Keya Ganguly, "Crude Wars," in *Democracy, states, and the Struggle for Global Justice,* ed. Heath Gautney et al. (New York: Routledge, 2009). 31–44.

17. Obviously, a lot of ink has been spilled about the Katrina disaster. Some of the texts that I have found most useful include Robert D. Bullard and Beverly Wright, *Race, Place, and Environmental Justice after Hurricane Katrina: Struggles to Reclaim, Rebuild, and Revitalize New Orleans and the Gulf Coast* (Boulder, CO: Westview, 2009); Michael Eric Dyson, *Come Hell or High Water: Hurricane Katrina and the Color of Disaster* (New York: Basic Books, 2006); Henry A. Giroux, *Stormy Weather: Katrina and the Politics of Disposability* (Boulder, CO: Paradigm, 2006); Chester W. Hartman and Gregory D. Squires, eds., *There is No Such Thing as a Natural Disaster: Race, Class, and Hurricane Katrina* (New York: Routledge, 2006); Manning Marable and Kristen Clarke, eds., *Seeking Higher Ground: The Hurricane Katrina Crisis, Race, and Public Policy Reader* (New York: Palgrave Macmillan, 2008); South End Press Collective, ed., *What Lies Beneath: Katrina, Race, and the State of the Nation* (Cambridge, MA: South End Press, 2007); and David Dante Troutt, ed., *After the Storm: Black Intellectuals Explore the Meaning of Hurricane Katrina* (New York: New Press, 2006).

18. Ross Gelbspan, "Nature Fights Back," in *What Lies Beneath,* 23.

19. On the geographical history of New Orleans, see Craig E. Colten, *An Unnatural Metropolis: Wresting New Orleans from Nature* (Baton Rouge, LA: Louisiana State University Press, 2005).

20. Neil Smith, "There's No Such Thing as a Natural Disaster," Understanding Katrina, June 11, 2006, http://understandingkatrina.ssrc.org/Smith/.

21. Rob Nixon, "Unimagined Communities: Developmental Refugees, Megadams, and Monumental Modernity," in "New Enclosures," ed. Ashley

Dawson, special issue, *New Formations,* no. 69 (forthcoming).

22. For an extended discussion of this process, see Ashley Dawson, "The New Enclosures," in "New Enclosures," ed. Ashley Dawson, special issue, *New Formations,* no. 69 (forthcoming).

23. On accumulation by dispossession, see David Harvey, *The New Imperialism* (New York: Oxford University Press, 2003).

24. On contemporary black social death, see Cheryl I. Harris and Devon W. Carbado, "Loot of Find: Fact or Frame?" in *After the Storm,* 87–110; and Dylan Rodriguez, "The Meaning of 'Disaster' under the Dominance o White Life," in *What Lies Beneath,* 132–56.

25. This point is made forcefully by Giroux, *Stormy Weather,* 20.

26. Philip E. Steinberg, "What Is a City? Katrina's Answers," in *What Is a City?: Rethinking the Urban after Hurricane Katrina,* ed. Philip E. Steinberg and Rob Shields (Athens, GA: University of Georgia Press, 2008), 12.

27. On the history of New Orleans's precarious site, see Colten, *An Unnatural Metropolis*; and Peirce F. Lewis, *New Orleans: The Making of an Urban Landscape* (Charlottesville, VA: University of Virginia Press, 2003).

28. For a brilliant exposition of the flawed policies of the Army Corps of Engineers in Louisiana, see John McPhee, *The Control of Nature* (New York: Farrar, Straus, and Giroux, 1990).

29. Kalamu Ya Salaam, "Introduction: Below the Water Line," in *What Lies Beneath,* x–xi.

30. Billy Sothern, *Down in New Orleans: Reflections from a Drowned City* (Berkeley: University of California Press, 2007), 213–82.

31. Robert D. Bullard, *Dumping in Dixie: Race, Class, and Environmental Quality* (Boulder, CO: Westview Press, 1990). For a powerful counter-narrative to such corporate news accounts, see Spike Lee, dir., *When the Levees Broke: A Requiem in Four Acts* (New York: HBO Films, 2006).

32. Dyson, *Come Hell or High Water,* 166: and Alisa Bierra, Mayaba Liebenthal, and INCITE! "To Render Ourselves Visible: Women of Color Organizing and Hurricane Katrina," in *What Lies Beneath,* 31–47.

33. Giroux, *Stormy Weather,* 54.

34. John Valery White, "The Persistence of Race Politics," in Troutt, *After the Storm,* 41–62.

35. On disaster capitalism in New Orleans, see Naomi Klein, *The Shock Doctrine: The Rise of Disaster Capitalism* (New York: Metropolitan, 2007), 406–22.

36. See Bierra, Liebenthal, and INCITE! "To Render Ourselves Visible," 39.

37. On this redevelopment plan, see Sothern, *Down in New Orleans,* 215–28; and David Dante Troutt, *"Many Thousands Gone, Again."* in *After the Storm,* 3–28.

38. Kathleen Coverick, interview with author, June 29, 2009; and Stephen Tremaine, interview with author, June 27, 2009. For information on these neighborhood organizations, see Broadmoor Improvement Organization, www.broadmoor improvement.com; and Help Holy Cross, www.helpholycross.org.

39. For a critique of Common Ground and similar organizations, see Bierra, Liebenthal, and INCITE! "To Render Ourselves Visible." 40–41.

40. Brad Richard, interview with author, June 28, 2009.

41. Tremaine, interview.

42. Historical details concerning the environmental justice movement are largely drawn from Melissa Checker, *Polluted Promises: Environmental Racism and the Search for Justice in a Southern Town* (New York: New York University Press, 2005).

43. Ibid., 20.

44. On gender and environmental justice, see Rachel Stein, ed., *New Perspectives on Environmental Justice: Gender, Sexuality, and Activism* (New Brunswick, NJ: Rutgers University Press, 2004).

45. Peggy Shepard, interview with author, April 21, 2009.

46. See, for example, the pathbreaking collection edited by Robert D. Bullard, *Unequal Protection: Environmental Justice and Communities of Color* (San Francisco: Sierra Club Books, 1994).

47. For a timeline of WE ACT's activities and further information about the organization, see the group's Web site, www.weact.org (accessed August 26, 2009).

48. On WE ACT's struggle with public health authorities, see Julie Sze, "Gender, Asthma Politics, and Urban Environmental Justice Activism," in *New Perspectives on Environmental Justice,* 177–90.

49. Bullard and Hamilton cited in ibid., 181.

50. Note that the United Church of Christ recently published a twentieth anniversary follow-up to its landmark report. The new report, which discusses Hurricane Katrina in detail, concludes that although efforts toward environmental justice have gained significant nominal support, ethnic minority communities remain disproportionately affected by environmental injustices. The report is available at www.ejnet.org/ej/twart.pdf (accessed August 26, 2009).

51. Bullard, *Dumping in Dixie.*

52. For more information on the summit, including policy papers that emerged from the meeting, see the *Environmental* Justice Resource Center's Web site. www.ejrc.can.edu/EJSUMMITwelcome.html (accessed August 26, 2009).

53. J. Timmons Roberts, "Globalizing Environmental Justice," in *Environmental Justice and Environmentalism: The Social Justice Challenge to the Environmental Movement,* ed. Ronald Sandler and Phaedra C. Pezzullo (Cambridge, MA: MIT Press, 2007), 287.

54. Miquela Craytor, interview, July 23, 2009. For more information about Sustainable South Bronx, see the group's Web site. www.ssbx.org (accessed August 26, 2009).

55. Craytor, interview.

56. Kenny Bruno, Joshua Karliner, and China Brotsky, *Greenhouse Gangsters vs. Climate Justice* (San Francisco: Transnational Resource and Action Center, 1999), available at www.corpwatch.org/downloads/greenhousegangsters.pdf (accessed August 26, 2009).

57. For a blistering investigation of Big Oil's funding of climate change denial, see Monbiot, *Heat,* 20–42.

58. On new, transnational scales of social justice and activism, see Nancy Fraser, *Scales of Justice: Reimagining Political Space in a Globalizing World* (New York: Columbia University Press, 2008).

59. On Saro-Wiwa and the Ogoni struggle, see Rob Nixon, "Pipe Dreams: Ken Saro-Wiwa, Environmental Justice, and Micro-minority Rights," *Black Renaissance/Renaissance Noire 1* (Fall 1996): 35–95.

60. Bruno, Karliner, and Brotsky, *Greenhouse Gangsters vs. Climate Justice,* 19.

61. Heidi Bachram, "Climate Fraud and Carbon Colonialism: The New Trade in Greenhouse Gases," *Capitalism Nature Socialism* 15.4 (December 2004): 1–16.

62. Ibid., 3.

63. Ibid., 4.

64. Ibid., 9.

65. J. Andrew Hoerner and Nia Robinson, *A Climate of Change: African Americans, Global Warming, and a Just Climate Policy for the U.S.* (Oakland, CA: Environmental Justice and Climate Change Initiative, 2008), available at www.rprogress.org/publications/2008/climateofchange.pdf (accessed August 26, 2009).

66. For further discussion of the climate justice movement's goals, see Michael Dorsey, "Exploring Climate Justice," podcast, February 16, 2009, www.dartmouth.edu/~news/features/podcasts/2009/dorsey.html (accessed July 23, 2009).

67. For a text of Hansen's recent testimony before a House committee, see James Hansen, "The New Testimony before Congress," June 23, 2008, available at http://gristmill.grist.org/story/2008/6/23/164650/123.

68. James Randerson, "Climate Change: Prepare for Global Temperature Rise of 4C. Warns Top Scientist," *Guardian,* August 7, 2008, www.guardian.co.uk/environment/2008/aug/06/climatechange.scienceofclimatechange.

69. On the controversial report to the Pentagon, for example, see Mark Townsend and Paul Harris, "Now the Pentagon Tells Bush: Climate Change Will Destroy Us," *Observer,* February 22, 2004, www.guardian.co.uk/environment/2004/feb/22/usnews.theobserver; and Peter Schwartz and Doug Randall, *An Abrupt Climate Change Scenario and Its Implications for United States national Security* (San Francisco: Global Business Network, 2003), available at www.mindfully.org/Air/2003/Pentagon-Climate-Change10cot03.htm (accessed August 26, 2009).

70. For a fuller discussion of the pitfalls of apocalyptic environmentalism, see Cindy Katz, "Under the Falling Sky: Apocalyptic Environmentalism and the Production of Nature," in *Marxism in the Postmodern Age: Confronting the New World Order,* ed. Antonio Callari, Stephen Cullenberg, and Carole Biewener (New York: Guilford Press, 1995), 276–80.

71. EJCC, "The 10 Principles of Just Climate Change Policies in the U.S." http://ejcc.org/cj/ten_ principles/ (accessed September 29, 2009).

72. Roberts, "Globalizing Environmental Justice," 297.

73. For a discussion of the global justice movement's organizing principles, see Notes from Nowhere, ed., *We Are Everywhere: The Irresistible Rise of Global Anti-Capitalism* (New York: Verso, 2003).

74. Mobilization for Climate Justice, www.actforcli matejustice.org (accessed July 23, 2009).

STUDY QUESTIONS

1. What is the position of Climate Justice Movement?

2. What does the author mean by "Hurricane Katrina was not a natural disaster"?

3. What is the link between Green Capitalism and Climate Change?

48

Sustainability and Technology Solutions in the Climate Policy Debate: The Case of Geologic Carbon Sequestration

EVELYN WRIGHT AND PAUL POJMAN

Evelyn Wright is an energy policy economist teaching at Franklin & Marshall College. Paul Pojman is the coeditor of this anthology (see Introduction). This essay examines the nature of technorationality in dealing with questions of appropriate uses of technology in environmental remediation. We argue that resistance to technological solutions to climate

---

Evaluating Technology Options by Wright and Pojman. Reprinted by permission of the author.

and efficiency but should also include questions of social order, justice and fairness, equity and power. There may well be a 'good' way to implement CCS; designing that solution, though, lays outside the traditional scope of engineering and economics.

STUDY QUESTIONS

1. How is climate change different from other environment concerns?

2. Summarize and respond to the three discussion points.

3. Comment on the author's claim that a commitment to technological progress amounts to an ideology.

REFERENCES

Anderson, S. and R. Newell. "Prospects for Carbon Capture and Storage Technologies," in *Annual Review of the Environment and Resources*, Vol. 29, pp. 109–142, 2004.

Climate Action Network (CAN) Europe. *Final Report of the Climate Technologies Assessment Project,* http://www.climate.org/CTAP/03 CTAP final report 2004.pdf, September, 2004.

Hawkins, D. "Passing Gas: Policy Implications of Leakage from Geologic Carbon Storage Sites," Paper read at Sixth International Conference on Greenhouse Gas Control Technologies, September 30–October 4, at Kyoto, Japan, 2002.

http://www.globalroadsafety.org/documents/index. shtml: accessed Feb. 2010.

Marcuse, H. One-Dimensional Man: Studies in the Ideology of Advanced Industrial Society. Beacon Press: 1964.

Meadows, D. H., D. L. Meadows, J. Randers, and W. W.Behrens III. *The Limits to Growth*, Universe Books, New York: 1972.

Meadows, D. H., D. L. Meadows, and J. Randers, *Beyond the Limits*, Chelsea Green Publishing Company, White River Junction, VT: 1992.

McIntyre, M., Rosenberg, M., Hayes, L., Eds. UN Road Safety Collaboration and Commission of Global Road Safety. Prepared by The Task Force for Child Survival and Development, September 2004.

Muttitt, G. and B. Diss, "Carbon Injection: An Addict's Response to climate Change," in *The Ecologist,* 2001.

Pacala, S. and R. Socolow. "Stabilization Wedges: Solving the climate Problem for the Next 50 Years with Current Technologies," in *Science*, Vol. 305, pp. 968–972, 2004.

Socolow, R., "Living Ethically in a Greenhouse," *Energy and Responsibility: A Conference on Ethics and the Environment*, University of Tennessee, Knoxville, TN, Apr 10–12, 2008.

Winner L. "Do Artifacts Have Politics?" in *Daedalus,* Vol. 109, No. 1, Winter 1980.

STUDY QUESTIONS

1. Briefly outline the technology of Carbon Capture and Storage.

2. The authors cite Marcuse famous quip in the 1960's that the threat of nuclear war keeps in power the very people and systems that perpetuate this threat. How is this related to CCS?

3. What are the strengths and weaknesses of technorationality?

49

War and Climate Change

BARRY SANDERS

Barry Sanders was professor of History of Ideas and English at Pitzer College, retiring in 2005. The reading is Chapter 2 of his acclaimed book, "The Green Zone," which examines the environmental impacts of war. This selection focuses upon fuel use.

I begin this part of the story with the combat vehicles, planes, and helicopters, and then only with a selection of them. The vital statistics for almost all armament—their type and number—remain highly classified. By one count, the United States Armed Forces currently commands the deserts and the neighborhoods of Iraq with about 30,000 vehicles. According to its own figures, the DoD inventory of fleet vehicles worldwide—including passenger cars, buses, light trucks, and so on—totals 187,493, 13 percent of which it houses overseas. The Army and Marine Corps own and operate their own tactical wheeled vehicles, such as 140,000 High-Mobility Multipurpose Wheeled Vehicles (the HMMWV, or HUMVEE). The Army also operates over 4,000 combat vehicles and several hundred fixed wing aircraft. Except for eighty nuclear submarines and aircraft carriers, the entire military fleet runs on oil.

Armor often means the difference between living and dying, and so the Army relies on heavily armored machines like the HMMWV (M1114) and its seventeen variations, including the Guardian Armored Security Vehicle M1117 (popular with MPs), the Cougar HEV Armored Truck, the LAV (light armored vehicle), the ICV (infantry carrier vehicle), the Stryker troop carrier, the High Mobility Multi-Purpose Wheeled Vehicle M1151, the Bradley Fighting Vehicle, the M-1 Abrams tank, and a behemoth called the Mine-Resistant Ambush-Protective vehicle, a thirty-ton armored bus for ferrying VIPs, and popularly known as the Rhino Runner. Military brass covet the Rhino Runner, for it holds the distinction as the most heavily armored, safest vehicle ever manufactured.

I list here but a few of the vehicles in the Army's inventory. The military uses scores of other, more obscure tracked- and wheeled-vehicles as well. As you can imagine, such armored vehicles do not sit lightly on the ground. A United Nations Environment Program report about the first Gulf War points to the damage inflicted by seventy-ton tanks like the M-1 Abrams on the ecology of the desert: "Approximately fifty percent of Kuwait's land area has had its fragile soil surface destroyed as scores of tanks moved out of that country each day and headed for Iraq." Once the surface of the desert has broken apart, the report goes on, the wind has an easier job of eroding even more land mass.

The military—the Army, Navy, and Air force—leads the world, of course, in its wide range of flying machines, including fixed-wing attack jets, transport planes, helicopters, stealth bombers, and much more. Based on data provided by CENTAF; I count forty-three different types of fighter planes,

Barry Sanders, "War and Climate Change," as appeared in Barry Freundel, *Jewish Perspectives*. Used with permission of the author and AK Press.

eleven different kinds of attack planes, thirteen kinds of bombers, sixteen kinds of cargo planes, and nine different kinds of helicopters—all told, ninety-two different kinds of aircraft.

Military brass also operates its own private airline, known as the Air Mobility Command or AMC. The Pentagon prefers to keep these planes, for the most part, off the record. The AMC consists of a fleet of long-range C-17 Globemasters, C-5 Galaxies, C-141 Starlifters, KC-135 Stratotankers, KC-10 Extenders, and C-9 Nightingales. As an additional perk, for generals and admirals, the military has on hand, for their private use, seventy-one Lear jets, thirteen Gulfstream IIIs, and seventeen Cessna Citation luxury jets.

These armored vehicles, planes, and luxury planes consume close to two million reported gallons of oil every day. As I have said, we are using up at an alarming rate the very commodity we have sworn to protect. For Doctor King, recall, oil constitutes the full-time business of America in general. It should make sense to us, then, that the business of the military, both in times of peace and war, likewise, has to be oil itself. In the end, the United States must have access to as much oil as possible—it would love to own it all—to maintain its position as the most prosperous nation in the world. Indeed, since capitalism requires an ever-expanding market, the country must have more and more oil each year. The nation's appetite grows in concert with the market.

Of the Army's top ten gas-guzzlers, only the M-1 Abrams tank and the Apache helicopter are combat vehicles. As for the rest, ironically, the, military needs most of these fuel-famished vehicles-along with a good number of its troops—for re-supplying its vast fleet of fuel-dependent combat vehicles and fighter planes. These support, or non-tactical, vehicles consume over half the fuel in the battlefield. Fuel constitutes the lifeblood of these vehicles, and they require it in astonishing amounts, consume it with astonishing speed, and demand it with astonishing rapidity. To complicate things even more, the military currently uses fourteen different kinds of fuel products, from gasoline and diesel to a range of highly toxic jet fuels, either kerosene or naphtha-derived. Jet fuel—JP-8—accounts for more than fifty percent of total DoD fuel consumption.

No wonder, then, that *The Energy-Bulletin*, a clearing house for information regarding the peak global energy supply, for May 2007, can list the following astonishing facts:

> The US military is the largest consumer of energy in the world.... The DoD's total primary energy consumption in fiscal year 2006 was 1 quadrillion Btu [1,000,000,000,000,000]. It corresponds to only 1 percent of total energy consumption in USA. For those of you who think this is not much … Nigeria, with a population of more than 140 million, consumes as much energy as the US military. The DoD per capita consumption (524 trillion Btu) is 10 times more than per capita energy consumption than China, or 30 times more than that of Africa.

The Energy Bulletin bases its numbers on a total of 1.4 million active duty military and civilian personnel.

The Pentagon is the largest single consumer of petroleum in the world, using enough oil in one year to run all of the transit systems in the United States for the next fourteen to twenty-two years. It is not, of course, just that our own military consumes inconceivable amounts of gasoline. The military also consumes one quarter of the world's jet fuel. A class at the University of Wisconsin, "Iraq and Our Energy Future," taught by Professor Zoltan Grossman, uncovered the following shocking bits of data: The world's militaries combined are responsible for an astonishing two-thirds of the ozone-depleting, greenhouse gas, chlorofluorocarbon, or CFC-113, released into the atmosphere. CFCs are highly persistent and highly toxic, and at one moment tore a hole in the ozone layer as large, in terms of square miles, as the Arctic itself. The Army and Air Force use CFC-113 as a cleaning solvent for tanks and airplanes. Doctor Helen Caldicott, the physician and anti-nuclear activist who started Physicians for Social Responsibility, believes the problem extends far beyond simple cleaning solvents. She indicts the military for releasing chlorofluorocarbons into the atmosphere during the process of enriching uranium for munitions.

The one thing we do know with some certainty about the military is that fuel accounts for more than three-quarters of the Department of Defense's energy consumption. According to *The Energy Bulletin,* the Defense Energy Support Center (DESC), the agency charged with procuring all fuel products for all branches of the military, "purchases more light refined petroleum product that any other single organization or country in the world." It should thus come as no surprise that the military also ranks as the largest single polluter of any single agency or organization in the world. Only three countries consume more oil per capita than the Department of Defense: Gibraltar, Netherland Antilles, and Singapore. For just the first three weeks of combat in Iraq, the Army calculated that its branch alone would require more than 40 million gallons of fuel, an amount of fuel that approximately 80,000 people burn through in an entire year's worth of driving.

For fiscal year 1999, the DESC spent its yearly budget of 3.5 billion dollars for 110 million barrels of petroleum products. That represents such a colossal amount of fuel, I feel compelled to let the DESC boast about its own numbers: "That's enough fuel for 1,000 cars to drive around the world 4,620 times—or 115.5 trillion miles." But, as staggering as that figure might sound, the DoD outdid itself in fiscal 2004. That year, the DESC almost doubled its purchases—by that time, we had two wars to support—spending 8.5 billion dollars for 144 million barrels of petroleum product. Since each barrel yields about 19.5 gallons of fuel, 144 million barrels of petroleum product equals nearly 2.8 billion gallons of gasoline!

The United States Department of Transportation Statistical Records Office places the number of vehicles registered in this country at 62 million. According to the EPA, the average driver goes through 500 gallons of fuel a year, which means that sixty-two million vehicles, collectively, consume approximately 31 billion gallons of fuel for the year. The DoD's 2.8 billion gallons of fuel would keep almost ten percent of those vehicles, 5.6 million of them, running for the entire year.

The DESC's 144 million barrels of oil for the year averages out to about 395,000 barrels per day, almost as much as the daily energy consumption of Greece. But those numbers do not, in the end, mean very much. While researching any military subject presents enormous difficulties for the layperson, the most convoluted and messy one surely must be fuel. Several major factors make it impossible to uncover actual numbers for fuel consumption, so that the number of barrels a day that the military uses—a number deliberately well hidden—has to be good higher than the reported 395,000 barrels a day—much closer to 500,000 barrels per day, and, as I want to show, probably much higher than that—in fact, nearly triple that figure, to one million barrels a day or more.

To begin, the DoD provides no official accounting for the amount of oil the military consumes in garrisons and bases abroad. And that figure may be substantial. Tom Cutler, former head of NATO's Petroleum Planning Committee, says that as much as "one-third of US military consumption occurs outside US territorial boundaries." The Pentagon does not count that fuel in its published figure of 144 million barrels. If Cutler is anywhere near accurate, we need to add at least another 45 or 50 million barrels per year to the total, or around 150,000 barrels a day. That would immediately raise the daily military consumption to around 550,000 barrels a day.

There's more. None of the official Pentagon figures include fuel that the military obtains at no cost overseas. And, again, that number may be fairly substantial. Kuwait has been the largest supplier of such fuel, providing US troops with free fuel from the start of the Gulf War in 2003. According to an article in Agence France-Presse, for March 17, 2000, "Kuwait supplied the United States military with fuel at no cost." But after two years, the Kuwaitis began to rethink their on-going largesse and, when America ousted Saddam Hussein, they decided that they should get paid for their fuel. The London-based pan-Arab newspaper, Al-Hayat, reported that, in March 2005, the Kuwaiti government demanded a payment of 500 million dollars for the fuel it had supplied to the US Army from March 2003 to fall 2005. The Emirate had settled on a preferential price for the United States of twenty-one dollars a barrel.

No matter the discount, then Secretary of Defense, Donald Rumsfeld, wrote an indignant letter back to Kuwaiti's energy minister, Sheik Ahmed Fahd Al Ahmed Sabah. Rumsfeld made it clear that Washington had liberated the Emirate from Iraqi occupation in 1991 and now, because Kuwait enjoys a fiscal surplus, he saw no need for Kuwait to demand any payment for a single drop of that fuel.

If the Kuwaiti numbers are anywhere near correct—and Rumsfeld never disputes those figures in his letter—we need to add an additional 75,000 barrels a day to our running total of 550,000 barrels. The number then grows from the official 395,000 or 400,000 barrels a day, to roughly 625,000 barrels a day, already an increase of over 50 percent. No military source has revealed whether Kuwait is continuing to supply that free fuel or not, or even if it now supplies fuel at a cost, and how much it supplies. One can only wonder. And the chase for answers and accuracy goes on.

For the DoD's numbers also omit fuel consumed by independent contractors, by leased and privatized facilities, and by all the rented and leased fleet vehicles. What shall we add for all those extras to the stated number? Conservatively, perhaps, another 100,000 or 150,000 barrels a day? That would now bring us to 725,000 or more barrels a day. Given that each barrel yields 19.5 gallons, all the branches of the military consume on the order of 14.5 million gallons of fuel every day. At this point, its fuel consumption would rank it with the daily use of nations like Singapore, Australia, Thailand, and the Netherlands. (Australia has a population of 20.5 million people, the Netherlands 26.6 million and Thailand 61.5 million people. Remember, the military has a stated 1.4 or 1.5 million soldiers on active duty.) And I have not yet included the most significant and probably largest omission that prevents anyone from finding out the military's total number of barrels.

The Pentagon employs a different accounting practice for the fuel that the Navy uses when it operates in international waters, adding yet another level of murkiness to an already opaque problem. Indeed, no one outside the Pentagon, and maybe no one inside the Pentagon, can say with any certainty just how much fuel the Navy actually uses. (Some critics of military fuel efficiency say that the Navy's figures

may even be higher than the largest consumer of fuel of all the armed services: the Air Force.) For the Pentagon places the fuel it designates for consumption in international waters—that which the Navy primarily uses in its ships on the open seas—in a separate category called International Bunker Fuel.

International Bunker Fuel—or more accurately called Bunker Oil—remains totally off the record, ghost stuff, as unidentified as the prisoners the United States keeps confined at Guantanamo Bay. I should note that even in the case of civilian commercial shipping, for the purposes of greenhouse emissions inventories, the United States subtracts data about International Bunker Fuel from its national totals. How large, then, is the military Bunker number? Who knows? My figure for the military of 725,000 or more barrels a day, which at the outset may have sounded extreme, could, in fact, turn out to be a quite conservative estimate. The final number might run as high as one million barrels a day, or close to half a billion barrels a year. I settle on that figure of one million as a safe, and even conservative, number.

Again, using the figure of 19.5 gallons of fuel that each barrel of oil yields, at a million barrels a day, the military would wind up using close to 20 million gallons of fuel each and every day. If that indeed turns out to be the case, the United States military would then rank in fuel consumption with countries like Indonesia, Iran, and Spain. Only fourteen countries, including the United States, would exceed those military numbers. It is truly an astonishing accomplishment, especially when one considers, once again, that the military has only about 1.5 million troops on active duty, and Iran has a population of 66 million, Indonesia a whopping 235 million.

The military is thus consuming fossil fuel out of proportion to nations 200 times its size. We have been doing this steadily for years and years. Surely, we do not think that the rest of the world does not notice. We should not be surprised that our country inspires deep feelings of envy, hatred, and even outright aggression. The former president told us that the extremists hate our democratic way of life, I think they hate our imperial way of life.

In the end, however, no military official, and no independent scholar seems to know the answer to what would seem like two straightforward questions:

How much fuel are we, American citizens, purchasing to keep the armed services running at full speed, and thus to keep 300 million Americans safe and secure? And, two, how much are we paying for that fuel? (Of course I am asking, how much greenhouse gases are we willing to pump into the atmosphere, around the world, for that so-called protection?) As for the first question, the most honest conclusion may come from one critical observer, who has followed the intricacies of military fuel consumption very closely, for a fairly long time: "The reality is that even the U.S. Department of Defense (DoD) does not know precisely where and how much energy it consumes."

And for the second, but related, question— "How much do Americans pay for that fuel?"—we can say quite generally that military fuel does not come cheap. In 2002, at something called the Tactical Wheeled Vehicles Conference, General Paul Kern, head of the Army Material command, revealed that the actual cost of fuel, depending on how it got delivered, could range anywhere from a low of 1 dollar to a high of 400 dollars per gallon. The average, he allowed, hovered around an astonishing 300 dollars a gallon.

Military vehicles have utterly no respect for CAFE (Corporate Average Fuel Economy) standards, or fuel standards of any kind. After all, we are at war; fuel economy is a luxury. But war or not, military vehicles exist in a world apart from conservation of any kind. One hears talk these days from military planners about the desire for more fuel efficient vehicles and the need for alternative fuels. Think about what that actually means: a cleaner, more efficient way of killing human beings. As if moving from the single shot rifle to an automatic made for a better society. How bizarre to think about installing "an environmentally sensitive culture" inside the military. We might then boast to the Iraqis: Notice how little fuel we consumed to destroy your homeland. The reasoning is absurd.

The topic is, finally, of little real concern for the Pentagon. Indeed, the military refers to fuel consumption in terms of "gallons per mile," "gallons per minute," and "barrels per hour." One quickly realizes that military "assets," as the Pentagon likes to call its rolling arsenal, have to operate in a world all their own, free of restraints of any kind—both in the fuel they consume and the pollutants they exhaust. For example, the High Mobility Multi-Purpose Wheeled Vehicle, the Humvee, gets four miles per gallon. But that's amazingly fuel efficient compared with the stalwart of all the fighting vehicles, the M-1 Abrams tank, which, according to the military's own spec sheets, gets .2 miles per gallon, or, stated another way, requires five gallons of fuel to cover a single mile. Just firing up the tank's turbine requires ten gallons of fuel. During battle, over ideal terrain, the Abrams can go through roughly 7 barrels, or 252 gallons—usually of JP-8 jet fuel—each and every hour (a barrel of oil yields more gallons of diesel and jet fuel than it does of regular gasoline). It takes nearly 500,000 gallons a day to supply an armored division of 348 tanks. The Army tries to keep entire inventory of Abrams tanks up and running in Iraq—all 1,838 of them.

The Army's principle flying machine, the Apache helicopter, blows through fuel at an astonishing rate. Powered by two General Electric gas-turbine engines, each rated at 1,890-horsepower, the Apache gets about one-half mile to the gallon. Just 1 pair of Apache battalions in a single night's raid will consume about 60,000 gallons of jet fuel.

Feeding the appetites of these voracious machines, with gasoline or diesel or kerosene, requires intricate logistical planning and support from some 2,000 trucks, a battery of computers, another 20,000 GIs, and, according to an Associated Press article for September 2007, as many as 180,000 workers under federal contracts, perhaps more contract workers, in fact, than soldiers. Over thirty private security companies operate in Iraq, including the major ones like Blackwater USA, Triple Canopy; Kellogg, Brown & Root; DynCorp International; and the Vinnell Corporation. The largest of them, however, is not even American, but British, named the Aegis Defense Services. The Department of Defense awarded Aegis with the largest security catch up to that time, May 2004—"a massive $293 million, three-years contract."

Many of the contract workers—especially those employed by Blackwater—served formerly as military Special Forces troops, such as Navy Seals and the Army's Delta Force. The Seals conduct their operations guided by the philosophy of "spray and pray"—shoot first and hope to God that you have hit the right target—a credo that seems to underlie a good deal of the behavior of the mercenaries working fro Blackwater USA. The company's CEO, Erik Prince, left a career appointment in the Seals to start what is now a billion-dollar federal contracting firm, Blackwater USA. After the uproar over some of his men who "sprayed" to death seventeen innocent Iraqis on September 16, 2007 in Baghdad, the *Wall Street Journal* reported that Erik Prince no longer cared about the security business. He intended, instead, to expand into a "full spectrum" defense contractor, the *Journal* went on, offering "one-stop shopping" for anything and everything the military might need, from unmanned planes to tanks and ammunition.

The Navy uses an enormous amount of that fuel. The Navy's battleships consume sixty-eight barrels per hour. No match for its non-nuclear aircraft carriers, which burn approximately 134 barrels per hour. Rear Admiral Eugene Carroll, Jr., retired from the US Navy and now part of the Center for Defense Information, a think-tank based in Washington, DC, served as the commander of the carrier the *USS Independence*. Talking about his ship, Carroll provided a picture of the staggering amounts of fuel that those huge vessels require. Keep in mind that the Independence weighs 81,000 tons fully loaded, and stretches almost 3.5 football fields in length. The ship gets its power from four 70,000 shp steam turbines.

In 1991, Admiral Carroll boasted that,

> while stationed off the coast of Vietnam, the ship [*USS Independence*] consumed 100,000 gallons of fuel a day. Every four days the *Independence* took on a million gallons of new fuel—half of which went to supply the carrier's jet aircraft. Steaming to the Persian Gulf in fourteen days, the Independence would consume more than two million gallons of fuel. Simply "standing by" in the Gulf, the carrier must still consume oil at a voracious pace in order to purify 380,000 gallons of fresh water daily and produce enough electricity to power the equivalent of a city of 40,000 people.

While the Navy decommissioned the forty-year-old *Independence* at the end of September

1998, Carroll's testimony offers some evidence of the almost unimaginable appetites of the Navy's huge aircraft carriers.

According to the US Navy Official Website, as of November 2007, the Navy had 335,000 personnel on active duty, an inventory of 4,000 airplanes and helicopters, and most important, 285 combat and support ships. The DoD keeps classified the number and kinds of vessels stationed in the Gulf. But, we do know that President Bush ordered the *USS Stennis* and the *USS Ronald Reagan* to the Gulf in January 2007 as part of the surge. He also sent a "strike group," led by the nuclear aircraft carrier the *USS Eisenhower*, along with a cruiser, a destroyer, a frigate, a submarine escort, and a supply ship.

Already sitting in the Gulf were ten other "Carrier Task Forces" built around the aircraft carriers *Kitty Hawk, Constellation, Enterprise, John F. Kennedy, Chester W. Nimitz, Carl Vinson, Theodore Roosevelt, George Washington, Harry S. Truman,* and the *Abraham Lincoln*. On the subject of naval build-up, Chalmers Johnson reports that "to dominate the oceans and seas of the world, we are creating some thirteen naval task forces built around aircraft carriers whose names sum up our military heritage—*Kitty Hawk, Constellation, Enterprise, John F. Kennedy, Nimitz, Dwight D. Eisenhower, Carl Vinson, Theodore Roosevelt, Abraham Lincoln, George Washington, John C. Stennis, S. Truman,* and *Ronald Reagan*."

The *USS Abraham Lincoln*—familiar to us as the ship on whose deck President Bush declared to the nation, on May 2, 2003, his famous (or infamous) phrase, "Mission Accomplished"—remains in service, but the military keeps classified all the numbers about its fuel consumption. The *USS Lincoln* helped deliver the opening salvos and air strikes in Operation Iraqi Freedom. From March 2003 until mid-April of that same year, during its deployment in the Gulf, the Navy launched 16,500 sorties from its deck, and fired 1.6 million pounds of ordnance from its guns.

Of all the branches, the Air Force, by every account, uses the most fuel. In 2006, for instance, the Air Force consumed nearly half of the DoD supply, 2.6 billion gallons of jet fuel, the same amount of fuel US planes consumed during World War II from December 1941 to August 1945. Any of the

Air Force's large helicopters—the Sea Stallion, Super Stallion, Sea Dragon, or Pave Low III—suck up five gallons every mile. But that's nothing compared with the fighter planes. The F-4 Phantom Fighter uses 40 barrels of fuel per hour, or more than 1,600 gallons, each and every hour. At peak thrust, the F-15 uses about 25 gallons per minute, or 1,580 gallons per hour; the F-16 Fighter Jet uses a bit more, 28 gallons per minute or 1,680 gallons per hour—as much fuel in that 1 hour as in 3 years of driving for the average American!

Tom Cutler, whom we met earlier as head of NATO's Petroleum Advisory Committee, writing in the *Armed Forces Journal International* (Spring 2004) points out, that to reach supersonic speeds, a pilot must turn on the plane's afterburners, which can triple a jet's speed and increase fuel consumption twenty times. With its afterburners kicked in, for example, "the F-15 torches fuel at the astounding rate off 4 gallons per second—14,400 gallons per hour. And as the military opts for bigger, faster and more sophisticated weapons, fuel efficiency continues to plummet."

As astounding and shocking as that figure may sound—14,400 gallons an hour—the principle gas hog award goes to the B-52 Stratocruiser, which has 8 jet engines, and zips through an astonishing 86 barrels of fuel, or roughly 3,334 gallons per hour. That's with no afterburners. That number represents the plane's standard fuel use, hour after hour. Imagine: 500 gallons per minute! In just ten of those minutes, the B-52 gulps down the same amount of fuel that the average driver consumes over one year of driving.

To keep the B-52 or the F-111 in the air for extended periods of time requires in-flight re-fueling. According to Janet Ginsberg, of *Business Week* magazine,

> the Air Force—the military's largest consumer, at two billion gallons a year—

spends most of its fuel-delivery budget refueling planes in the air, at a cost of $ 17.50 per gallon .... Fuel efficiency has never been a military priority, largely because the Pentagon's accounting system considers fuel purchase costs separately from delivery costs. That may have played a role in a 1997 decision by the Air Force not to install more efficient engines in the B-52H bomber.

The B-52H Bomber, the plane to which Ginsberg refers, is nick-named the Stratofortress by the military. While it holds an enormous 47,975 gallons of fuel, it still requires mid-air refueling. That's the job of the aerial refueling tankers, the KC-135 Stratotanker and the larger KC-10 Extender, which carries twice as much fuel as the Stratotanker—about 356,000 pounds, or close to 60,000 gallons. The Air Force owns both of these flying gas stations. It also owns 94 of those B-52H long-range bombers. Using EPA standards for yearly automobile fuel consumption, the amount of fuel that the KC-10 carries would keep the average family car—which uses, you will recall, on average about 500 gallons a year—running for approximately 118 years—in other words, a couple of lifetimes of driving.

The Pentagon makes public very few statistics about the B-52H and F-117 Stealth fighter planes, except to boast that the B-52H can carry 16 of the 2000-pound laser-guided bombs or 80 of the 500-pound laser-guided bombs. It is remarkable that we even know that the Stealth fighters exist. The number and kinds of vehicles, and planes housed at those 860 American bases in foreign countries, also remain a mystery. We can assume, with confidence, however, that those bases run through a considerable number of barrels of fuel.

STUDY QUESTIONS

1. Based upon Sander's estimates, make an estimate on how much fuel the military uses all together.

2. What are some other environmental impacts of war?

Chapter 9

Race, Class, Gender
Environmental Justice, Ecofeminism, and Indigenous Rights

ENVIRONMENTAL JUSTICE BEGINS with the observed fact that certain groups of people bear a disproportionate burden of environmental problems. That is, polluting factories, lead in water pipes, filthy air, polluted water, toxic soil, etc., are more likely to be found in places where people have less control over decision making—typically, minorities and the poor. There is an active debate as to whether this observed distribution of pollution is due to race or economic class. There is ample evidence that much of the inequitable distribution of pollutants is due to race, but there are also plenty of examples of poor nonminorities having more contact with pollutants than the richer folks.

In 1987, the original study by the United Church of Christ argued that the observed patterns amounted to "environmental racism." Although today the term *environmental justice* is more commonly used so as to broaden the scope of the problem (the Environmental Protection Agency, for instance, has an office of Environmental Justice, not Environmental Racism), the fact that race is a factor is critically important. The United States and many other countries tolerate what is essentially discrimination on the basis of poverty, but they have enacted legislation to combat discrimination on the basis of race. Thus, inasmuch as environmental racism exists, it not only falls afoul of our moral sensibilities but also intersects with civil rights legislation. This merger of environmental concerns with concepts of race and class is arguably the single largest expansion of the environmental movement, ever.

Why? Environmentalism was previously a movement of the middle and upper classes, of people who had sufficient education and leisure time to understand and enjoy nature and what was happening to it. The movement consisted of people whose jobs did not depend on a polluting factory or logging a forest. Thus, in a sense, a split occurred within the left: the old school left, the socialist labor left (the left of Franklin Roosevelt), which sought to put people to work, and the environmentalists who sought to save nature.

This new movement of environmental justice or environmental racism is crossing that gap. The poor and disenfranchised of all types now have something in common with environmentalists, for it is they—the poor and disenfranchised—who bear the greatest burden of environmental degradation.

Ecofeminism addresses a broad set of concerns at the intersection of feminist and ecological analyses. Ecofeminists have pointed out the connections, but in philosophy and in practice, between domination of women and the domination of nature, which is often gendered female. They have also pointed out that ecological devastation often impacts woman especially hard, and that there is a wisdom located within woman's communities that we need to turn to. Contemporary earth-based spiritualities often draw heavily from ecofeminism.

Indigenous environmental understandings intersect both of the above, but add the perspective of the remaining cultures that predate colonization and the creation of the global modern state system. They offer us not only their memories of oppression and exploitation but also ancestral memories which have been largely lost elsewhere. Although they of course are spread across the globe and have different cultures, histories, and perspectives, they are increasingly organizing and presenting a unified "indigenous voice." The rest of the world is starting to listen.

50

Overcoming Racism in Environmental Decision Making

ROBERT D. BULLARD

Robert Bullard is professor of sociology and Director of the Environmental Justice Resource Center at Clark Atlanta University. He is arguably the most visible leader of the environmental justice movement.

Despite the recent attempts by federal agencies to reduce environmental and health threats in the United States, inequities persist.[1] If a community is poor or inhabited largely by people of color, there is a good chance that it receives less protection than a community that is affluent or white.[2] This situation is a result of the country's environmental policies, most of which "distribute the costs in a regressive pattern while providing disproportionate benefits for the educated and wealthy."[3] Even the

Robert D. Bullard, "Overcoming Racism in Environmental Decision Making," *Resources for the Future*, Washington, D.C. Reprinted by permission of Robert D. Bullard.

Environmental Protection Agency (EPA) was not designed to address environmental policies and practices that result in unfair outcomes. The agency has yet to conduct a single piece of disparate impact research using primary data. In fact, the current environmental protection paradigm has institutionalized unequal enforcement; traded human health for profit; placed the burden of proof on the "victims" rather than on the polluting industry; legitimated human exposure to harmful substances; promoted "risky" technologies such as incinerators; exploited the vulnerability of economically and politically disenfranchised communities; subsidized ecological destruction; created an industry around risk assessment; delayed cleanup actions; and failed to develop pollution prevention as the overarching and dominant strategy. As a result, low-income and minority communities continue to bear greater health and environmental burdens, while the more affluent and whites receive the bulk of the benefits.[4]

The geographic distribution of both minorities and the poor has been found to be highly correlated to the distribution of air pollution; municipal landfills and incinerators; abandoned toxic waste dumps; lead poisoning in children; and contaminated fish consumption.[5] Virtually all studies of exposure to outdoor air pollution have found significant differences in exposure by income and race. Moreover, the race correlation is even stronger than the class correlation.[6] The National Wildlife Federation recently reviewed some 64 studies of environmental disparities; in all but one, disparities were found by either race or income, and disparities by race were more numerous than those by income. When race and income were compared for significance, race proved to be the more important factor in 22 out of 30 tests.[7] And researchers at Argonne National Laboratory recently found that

> In 1990, 437 of the 3,109 counties and independent cities failed to meet at least one of the EPA ambient air quality standards. ... 57 percent of whites, 65 percent of African-Americans, and 80 percent of Hispanics live in 437 counties with substandard air quality. Out of the whole population, a total of 33 percent of whiles, 50 percent of African-Americans, and 60 percent of Hispanics live in the 136 counties in which two or more air pollutants exceed standards. The percentage living in the 29 counties designated as nonattainment areas for three or more pollutants are 12 percent of whites, 20 percent of African-Americans, and 31 percent of Hispanics.[8]

The public health community has very little information on the magnitude of many air pollution-related health problems. For example, scientists are at a loss to explain the rising number of deaths from asthma in recent years. However, it is known that persons suffering from asthma are particularly sensitive to the effects of carbon monoxide, sulfur dioxide, particulate matter, ozone, and oxides of nitrogen.[9]

Current environmental decision making operates at the juncture of science, technology, economics, politics, special interests, and ethics and mirrors the larger social milieu where discrimination is institutionalized. Unequal environmental protection undermines three basic types of equity: procedural, geographic, and social.

PROCEDURAL EQUITY

Procedural equity refers to fairness—that is, to the extent that governing rules, regulations, evaluation criteria, and enforcement are applied in a nondiscriminatory way. Unequal protection results from nonscientific and undemocratic decisions, such as exclusionary practices, conflicts of interest, public hearings held in remote locations and at inconvenient times, and use of only English to communicate with and conduct hearings for non-English-speaking communities.

A 1992 study by staff writers from the *National Law Journal* uncovered glaring inequities in the way EPA enforces its Superfund laws:

> There is a racial divide in the way the U.S. government cleans up toxic waste sites and punishes polluters. White communities see

faster action, better results and stiffer penalties than communities where blacks, Hispanics and other minorities live. This unequal protection often occurs whether the community is wealthy or poor.[10]

After examining census data, civil court dockets, and EPA's own record of performance at 1,177 Superfund toxic waste sites, the authors of the *National Law Journal* report revealed the following:

- Penalties applied under hazardous waste laws at sites having the greatest white population were 500 percent higher than penalties at sites with the greatest minority population. Penalties averaged out at $335,566 at sites in white areas but just $55,318 at sites in minority areas.

- The disparity in penalties applied under the toxic waste law correlates with race alone, not income. The average penalty in areas with the lowest median income is $113,491— 3 percent more than the average penalty in areas with the highest median income.

- For all the federal environmental laws aimed at protecting citizens from air, water, and waste pollution, penalties for noncompliance were 46 percent higher in white communities than in minority communities.

- Under the Superfund cleanup program, abandoned hazardous waste sites in minority areas take 20 percent longer to be placed on the National Priority List than do those in white areas.

- In more than half of the 10 autonomous regions that administer EPA programs around the country, action on cleanup at Superfund sites begins from 12 to 42 percent later at minority sites than at white sites.

- For minority sites, EPA chooses "containment," the capping or walling off of a hazardous waste dump site, 7 percent more frequently than the cleanup method preferred under the law: permanent "treatment" to eliminate the waste or rid it of its toxins. For white sites, EPA orders permanent treatment 22 percent more often than containment.[11]

These findings suggest that unequal environmental protection is placing communities of color at risk. The National Law Journal study supplements the findings of several earlier studies and reinforces what grassroots activists have been saying all along. ... Not only are people of color differentially affected by industrial pollution but they can expect different treatment from the government.[12]

GEOGRAPHIC EQUITY

Geographic equity refers to the location and spatial configuration of communities and their proximity to environmental hazards and locally unwanted land uses (LULUs), such as landfills, incinerators, sewage treatment plants, lead smelters, refineries, and other noxious facilities. Hazardous waste incinerators are not randomly scattered across the landscape. Communities with hazardous waste incinerators generally have large minority populations, low incomes, and low property values.[13]

A 1990 Greenpeace report, Playing with Fire, found that communities with existing incinerators have 89 percent more people of color than the national average; communities where incinerators are proposed for construction have minority populations that are 60 percent higher than the national average; the average income in communities with existing incinerators is 15 percent lower than the national average; property values in communities that host incinerators are 38 percent lower than the national average; and average property values are 35 percent lower in communities where incinerators have been proposed.[14]

The industrial encroachment into Chicago's Southside neighborhoods is a classic example of geographic inequity. Chicago is the nation's third largest city and one of the most racially segregated cities in the country. More than 92 percent of the city's 1.1 million African-American residents live in racially segregated areas. The Altgeld Gardens housing project, located on the city's southeast side, is one of these segregated enclaves. The neighborhood is home to 150,000 residents, of whom 70 percent are African-American and 11 percent are Latino.

Altgeld Gardens is encircled by municipal and hazardous waste landfills, toxic waste incinerators, grain elevators, sewage treatment facilities, smelters, steel mills, and a host of other polluting industries.[15] Because of its location, Hazel Johnson, a community organizer in the neighborhood, has dubbed the area a "toxic doughnut." There are 50 active or closed commercial hazardous waste landfills; 100 factories, including 7 chemical plants and 5 steel mills; and 103 abandoned toxic waste dumps.[16]

Currently, health and risk assessment data collected by the state of Illinois and EPA for facility permitting have failed to take into account the cumulative and synergistic effects of having so many "layers" of poisons in one community. Altgeld Gardens residents wonder when the government will declare a moratorium on permitting any new noxious facilities in their neighborhood and when the existing problems will be cleaned up. All of the polluting industries imperil the health of nearby residents and should be factored into future facility-permitting decisions.

In the Los Angeles air basin, 71 percent of African-Americans and 50 percent of Latinos live in areas with the most polluted air, whereas only 34 percent of whites live in highly polluted areas.[17] The "dirtiest" zip code in California (90058) is sandwiched between South-Central Los Angeles and East Los Angeles.[18] The one-square mile area is saturated with abandoned toxic waste sites, freeways, smokestacks, and waste-water pipes from polluting industries. Some 18 industrial firms in 1989 discharged more than 33 million pounds of waste chemicals into the environment.

Unequal protection may result from land-use decisions that determine the location of residential amenities and disamenities. Unincorporated communities of poor African-Americans suffer a "triple" vulnerability to noxious facility siting.[19] For example, Wallace, Louisiana, a small unincorporated African-American community located on the Mississippi River, was rezoned from residential to industrial use by the mostly white officials of St. John the Baptist Parish to allow construction of a Formosa Plastics Corporation plant. The company's plants

have been major sources of pollution in Baton Rouge, Louisiana; Point Comfort, Texas; Delaware City, Delaware; and its home country of Taiwan.[20] Wallace residents have filed a lawsuit challenging the rezoning action as racially motivated.

Environmental justice advocates have sought to persuade federal, state, and local governments to adopt policies that address distributive impacts, concentration, enforcement, and compliance concerns. Some states have tried to use a "fair share" approach to come closer to geographic equity. In 1990, New York City adopted a fair share legislative model designed to ensure that every borough and every community within each borough bears its fair share of noxious facilities. Public hearings have begun to address risk burdens in New York City's boroughs.

Testimony at a hearing on environmental disparities in the Bronx points to concerns raised by African-Americans and Puerto Ricans who see their neighborhoods threatened by garbage transfer stations, salvage yards, and recycling centers:

> On the Hunts Point peninsula alone there are at least thirty private transfer stations, a large-scale Department of Environmental Protection (DEP) sewage treatment plant and a sludge de watering facility, two Department of Sanitation (DOS) marine transfer stations, a citywide private regulated medical waste incinerator, a proposed DOS resource recovery facility and three proposed DEP sludge processing facilities. That all of the facilities listed above are located immediately adjacent to the Hunts Point Food Center, the biggest wholesale food and meat distribution facility of its kind in the United States, and the largest source of employment in the South Bronx, is disconcerting. A policy whereby low-income and minority communities have become the "dumping grounds" for unwanted land uses, works to create an environment of disincentives to community-based development initiatives. It also undermines existing businesses.[21]

Some communities form a special case for environmental justice. For example, Native American reservations are geographic entities but are also quasi-sovereign nations. Because of less stringent environmental regulations than those at the state and federal levels, Native American reservations from New York to California have become prime targets for risky technologies.[22] Indian nations do not fall under state jurisdiction. Similarly, reservations have been described as the "lands the feds forgot."[23] More than 100 industries, ranging from solid waste landfills to hazardous waste incinerators and nuclear waste storage facilities, have targeted reservations.[24]

SOCIAL EQUITY

Social equity refers to the role of sociological factors, such as race, ethnicity, class, culture, lifestyles, and political power, in environmental decision making. Poor people and people of color often work in the most dangerous jobs and live in the most polluted neighborhoods, and their children are exposed to all kinds of environmental toxins on the playgrounds and in their homes and schools.

Some government actions have created and exacerbated environmental inequity. More stringent environmental regulations have driven noxious facilities to follow the path of least resistance toward poor, overburdened communities. Governments have even funded studies that justify targeting economically disenfranchised communities for noxious facilities. Cerrell Associates, Inc., a Los Angeles–based consulting firm, advised the state of California on facility siting and concluded that "ideally ... officials and companies should look for lower socioeconomic neighborhoods that are also in a heavy industrial area with little, if any, commercial activity."[25]

The first state-of-the-art solid waste incinerator slated to be built in Los Angeles was proposed for the South-Central Los Angeles neighborhood. The city-sponsored project was defeated by local residents.[26] The two permits granted by the California Department of Health Services for state-of-the-art toxic waste incinerators were proposed for mostly Latino communities: Vernon, near East Los Angeles, and Kettleman City, a farm worker community in the agriculturally rich Central Valley. Kettleman City has 1,200 residents, of which 95 percent are Latino. It is home to the largest hazardous waste incinerator west of the Mississippi River. The Vernon proposal was defeated, but the Kettleman City proposal is still pending.

PRINCIPLES OF ENVIRONMENTAL JUSTICE

To end unequal environmental protection, governments should adopt five principles of environmental justice: guaranteeing the right to environmental protection, preventing harm before it occurs, shifting the burden of proof to the polluters, obviating proof of intent to discriminate, and redressing existing inequities.

The Right to Protection

Every individual has a right to be protected from environmental degradation. Protecting this right will require enacting a federal "fair environmental protection act." The act could be modeled after the various federal civil rights acts that have promoted nondiscrimination—with the ultimate goal of achieving "zero tolerance"—in such areas as housing, education, and employment. The act ought to address both the intended and unintended effects of public policies and industrial practices that have a disparate impact on racial and ethnic minorities and other vulnerable groups. The precedents for this framework are the Civil Rights Act of 1964, which attempted to address both de jure and de facto school segregation, the Fair Housing Act of 1968, the same act as amended in 1988, and the Voting Rights Act of 1965.

For the first time in the agency's 23-year history, EPA's Office of Civil Rights has begun investigating charges of environmental discrimination under Title VI of the 1964 Civil Rights Act. The cases involve waste facility siting disputes in Michigan, Alabama, Mississippi, and Louisiana. Similarly, in September 1993, the U.S. Civil Rights Commission issued a report entitled *The Battle for Environmental Justice in Louisiana: Government, Industry, and the People.* This report confirmed what most people who live in "Cancer Alley"—the 85-mile stretch along the Mississippi River from Baton Rouge to New Orleans—already knew: African-American communities along the Mississippi River bear disproportionate health burdens from industrial pollution.[27]

A number of bills have been introduced into Congress that address some aspect of environmental justice:

- The "Environmental Justice Act of 1993" (H.R. 2105) would provide the federal government with the statistical documentation and ranking of the top 100 "environmental high impact areas" that warrant attention.

- The "Environmental Equal Rights Act of 1993" (H.R. 1924) seeks to amend the Solid Waste Act and would prevent waste facilities from being sited in "environmentally disadvantaged communities."

- The "Environmental Health Equity Information Act of 1993" (H.R. 1925) seeks to amend the Comprehensive Environmental Response, Compensation, and Liability Act of 1990 (CERCLA) to require the Agency for Toxic Substances and Disease Registry to collect and maintain information on the race, age, gender, ethnic origin, income level, and educational level of persons living in communities adjacent to toxic substance contamination.

- The "Waste Export and Import Prohibition Act" (H.R. 3706) would ban waste exports as of I July 1994 to countries that are not members of the Organization for Economic Cooperation and Development (OECD); the bill would also ban waste exports to and imports from OECD countries as of 1 January 1999.

The states are also beginning to address environmental justice concerns. Arkansas and Louisiana were the first two to enact environmental justice laws. Virginia has passed a legislative resolution on environmental justice. California, Georgia, New York, North Carolina, and South Carolina have pending legislation to address environmental disparities.

Environmental justice groups have succeeded in getting President Clinton to act on the problem of unequal environmental protection, an issue that has been buried for more than three decades. On 11 February 1994, Clinton signed an executive order entitled "Federal Actions to Address Environmental Justice in Minority Populations and Low-Income Populations." This new executive order reinforces what has been law since the passage of the 1964 Civil Rights Act, which prohibits discriminatory practices in programs receiving federal financial assistance.

The executive order also refocuses attention on the National Environmental Policy Act of 1970 (NEPA), which established national policy goals for the protection, maintenance, and enhancement of the environment. The express goal of NEPA is to ensure for all U.S. citizens a safe, healthful, productive, and aesthetically and culturally pleasing environment. NEPA requires federal agencies to prepare detailed statements on the environmental effects of proposed federal actions significantly affecting the quality of human health. Environmental impact statements prepared under NEPA have routinely downplayed the social impacts of federal projects on racial and ethnic minorities and low-income groups.

Under the new executive order, federal agencies and other institutions that receive federal monies have a year to implement an environmental justice strategy. For these strategies to be effective, agencies must move away from the "DAD" (decide, announce, and defend) modus operandi. EPA cannot address all of the environmental injustices alone but must work in concert with other stakeholders, such as state and local governments and private industry. A new interagency approach might include the following:

- Grassroots environmental justice groups and their networks must become full partners, not silent or junior partners, in planning the implementation of the new executive order.

- An advisory commission should include representatives of environmental justice, civil rights, legal, labor, and public health groups, as well as the relevant governmental agencies, to advise on the implementation of the executive order.

- State and regional education, training, and outreach forums and workshops on implementing the executive order should be organized.

- The executive order should become part of the agenda of national conferences and meetings of elected officials, civil rights and environmental groups, public health and medical groups, educators, and other professional organizations.

The executive order comes at an important juncture in this nation's history: Few communities are willing to welcome LULUs or to become dumping grounds for other people's garbage, toxic waste, or industrial pollution. In the real world, however, if a community happens to be poor and inhabited by persons of color, it is likely to suffer from a "double whammy" of unequal protection and elevated health threats. This is unjust and illegal.

The civil rights and environmental laws of the land must be enforced even if it means the loss of a few jobs. This argument was a sound one in the 1860s, when the 13th Amendment to the Constitution, which freed the slaves in the United States, was passed over the opposition of proslavery advocates who posited that the new law would create unemployment (slaves had a zero unemployment rate), drive up wages, and inflict undue hardship on the plantation economy.

Prevention of Harm

Prevention, the elimination of the threat before harm occurs, should be the preferred strategy of governments. For example, to solve the lead problem, the primary focus should be shifted from treating children who have been poisoned to eliminating the threat by removing lead from houses.

Overwhelming scientific evidence exists on the ill effects of lead on the human body. However, very little action has been taken to rid the nation's housing of lead even though lead poisoning is a preventable disease tagged the "number one environmental health threat to children."[28]

Lead began to be phased out of gasoline in the 1970s. It is ironic that the "regulations were initially developed to protect the newly developed catalytic converter in automobiles, a pollution-control device that happens to be rendered inoperative by lead, rather than to safeguard human health."[29] In 1971, a child was not considered "at risk" unless he or she had 40 micrograms of lead per deciliter of blood (μg/dl). Since that time, the amount of lead that is considered safe has continually dropped. In 1991, the U.S. Public Health Service changed the official definition of an unsafe level to 10 μg/dl. Even at that level, a child's IQ can be slightly diminished and physical growth stunted.

Lead poisoning is correlated with both income and race. In 1988, the Agency for Toxic Substances and Disease Registry found that, among families earning less than $6,000, 68 percent of African-American children had lead poisoning, as opposed to 36 percent of white children.[30] In families with incomes exceeding $15,000, more than 38 percent of African-American children suffered from lead poisoning, compared with 12 percent of white children. Thus, even when differences in income are taken into account, middle-class African-American children are three times more likely to be poisoned with lead than are their middle-class white counterparts.

A 1990 report by the Environmental Defense Fund estimated that, under the 1991 standard of 10 μg/dl, 96 percent of African-American children and 80 percent of white children of poor families who live in inner cities have unsafe amounts of lead in their blood—amounts sufficient to reduce IQ somewhat, harm hearing, reduce the ability to concentrate, and stunt physical growth.[31] Even in families with annual incomes greater than $15,000, 85 percent of urban African-American children have unsafe lead levels, compared to 47 percent of white children.

In the spring of 1991, the Bush administration announced an ambitious program to reduce lead exposure of children, including widespread testing of homes, certification of those who remove lead from homes, and medical treatment for affected children. Six months later, the Centers for Disease Control announced that the administration "does not see this as a necessary federal role to legislate or regulate the cleanup of lead poisoning, to require that homes be tested, to require home owners to disclose results once they are known, or to establish standards for those who test or clean up lead hazards."[32]

According to the New York Times, the National Association of Realtors pressured President Bush to drop his lead initiative because they feared that forcing homeowners to eliminate lead hazards would add from $5,000 to $10,000 to the price of those homes, further harming a real estate market already devastated by the aftershocks of Reaganomics.[33] The public debate has pitted real estate and housing interests against public health interests. Right now, the housing interests appear to be winning.

For more than two decades, Congress and the nation's medical and public health establishments have waffled, procrastinated, and shuffled papers while the lead problem steadily grows worse. During the years of President Reagan's "benign neglect," funding dropped very low. Even in the best years, when funding has risen to as much as $50 million per year, it has never reached levels that would make a real dent in the problem.

Much could be done to protect at-risk populations if the current laws were enforced. For example, a lead smelter operated for 50 years in a predominately African-American West Dallas neighborhood, where it caused extreme health problems for nearby residents. Dallas officials were informed as early as 1972 that lead from three lead smelters was finding its way into the bloodstreams of children who lived in two mostly African-American and Latino neighborhoods: West Dallas and East Oak Cliff.[34]

Living near the RSR and Dixie Metals smelters was associated with a 36-percent increase in childhood blood lead levels. The city was urged to restrict the emissions of lead into the atmosphere and to undertake a large screening program to determine the extent of the public health problem. The city failed to take immediate action to protect the residents who lived near the smelters.

In 1980, EPA, informed about possible health risks associated with the Dallas lead smelters,

commissioned another lead-screening study. This study confirmed what was already known a decade earlier: Children living near the Dallas smelters were likely to have greater lead concentrations in their blood than children who did not live near the smelters.[35]

The city only took action after the local newspapers published a series of headline-grabbing stories in 1983 on the "potentially dangerous" lead levels discovered by EPA researchers in 1981.[36] The articles triggered widespread concern, public outrage, several class-action lawsuits, and legal action by the Texas attorney general.

Although EPA was armed with a wealth of scientific data on the West Dallas lead problem, the agency chose to play politics with the community by scrapping a voluntary plan offered by RSR to clean up the "hot spots" in the neighborhood. John Hernandez, EPA's deputy administrator, blocked the cleanup and called for yet another round of tests to be designed by the Centers for Disease Control with EPA and the Dallas Health Department. The results of the new study were released in February 1983. Again, this study established the smelter as the source of elevated lead levels in West Dallas children.[37] Hernandez's delay of cleanup actions in West Dallas was tantamount to waiting for a body count.[38]

After years of delay, the West Dallas plaintiffs negotiated an out-of-court settlement worth more than $45 million. The lawsuit was settled in June 1983 as RSR agreed to pay for cleaning up the soil in West Dallas, a blood-testing program for children and pregnant women, and the installation of new antipollution equipment. The settlement was made on behalf of 370 children—almost all of whom were poor, black residents of the West Dallas public housing project—and 40 property owners. The agreement was one of the largest community lead-contamination settlements ever awarded in the United States.[39] The settlement, however, did not require the smelter to close. Moreover, the pollution equipment for the smelter was never installed.

In May 1984, however, the Dallas Board of Adjustments, a city agency responsible for monitoring land-use violations, asked the city attorney to close the smelter permanently for violating the city's zoning code. The lead smelter had operated in the mostly African-American West Dallas neighborhood for 50 years without having the necessary use permits. Just four months later, the West Dallas smelter was permanently closed. After repeated health citations, fines, and citizens' complaints against the smelter, one has to question the city's lax enforcement of health and land-use regulations in African-American and Latino neighborhoods.

The smelter is now closed. Although an initial cleanup was carried out in 1984, the lead problem has not gone away.[40] On 31 December 1991, EPA crews began a cleanup of the West Dallas neighborhood. It is estimated that the crews will remove between 30,000 and 40,000 cubic yards of lead-contaminated soil from several West Dallas sites, including school property and about 140 private homes. The project will cost EPA from $3 million to $4 million. The lead content of the soil collected from dump sites in the neighborhood ranged from 8,060 to 21,000 parts per million.[41] Under federal standards, levels of 500 to 1,000 parts per million are considered hazardous. In April 1993, the entire West Dallas neighborhood was declared a Superfund site.

There have been a few other signs related to the lead issue that suggest a consensus on environmental justice is growing among coalitions of environmental, social justice, and civil libertarian groups. The Natural Resources Defense Council, the National Association for the Advancement of Colored People Legal Defense and Education Fund, the American Civil Liberties Union, and the Legal Aid Society of Alameda County joined forces and won an out-of-court settlement worth between $15 million and $20 million for a blood-testing program in California. The lawsuit (*Matthews v. Coye*) arose because the state of California was not performing the federally mandated testing of some 557,000 poor children who receive Medicaid. This historic agreement will likely trigger similar actions in other states that have failed to perform federally mandated screening.[42]

Lead screening is important but it is not the solution. New government-mandated lead abatement initiatives are needed. The nation needs a "Lead Superfund" cleanup program. Public health should not be sacrificed even in a sluggish housing market. Surely, if termite inspections (required in both booming and sluggish housing markets) can be mandated to protect individual home investment, a lead free home can be mandated to protect human health. Ultimately, the lead debate—public health (who is affected) versus property rights (who pays for cleanup)—is a value conflict that will not be resolved by the scientific community.

Shift the Burden of Proof

Under the current system, individuals who challenge polluters must prove that they have been harmed, discriminated against, or disproportionately affected. Few poor or minority communities have the resources to hire the lawyers, expert witnesses, and doctors needed to sustain such a challenge. Thus, the burden of proof must be shifted to the polluters who do harm, discriminate, or do not give equal protection to minorities and other overburdened classes.

Environmental justice would require the entities that are applying for operating permits for landfills, incinerators, smelters, refineries, and chemical plants, for example, to prove that their operations are not harmful to human health, will not disproportionately affect minorities or the poor, and are nondiscriminatory.

A case in point is Louisiana Energy Services' proposal to build the nation's first privately owned uranium enrichment plant. The proposed plant would handle about 17 percent of the estimated U.S. requirement for enrichment services in the year 2000. Clearly, the burden of proof should be on Louisiana Energy Services, the state government, and the Nuclear Regulatory Commission to demonstrate that local residents' rights would not be violated in permitting the plant. At present, the burden of proof is on local residents to demonstrate that their health would be endangered and their community adversely affected by the plant.

According to the Nuclear Regulatory Commission's 1993 draft environmental impact statement, the proposed site for the facility is Claiborne Parish, Louisiana, which has a per-capita income of only $5,800 per year—just 45 percent of the national

the federal judge ruled against the plaintiffs on the grounds that "purposeful discrimination" was not demonstrated.

Although the Northwood Manor residents lost their lawsuit, they did influence the way the Houston city government and the state of Texas addressed race and waste facility siting. Acting under intense pressure from the African-American community, the Houston city council passed a resolution in 1980 that prohibited city-owned trucks from dumping at the controversial landfill. In 1981, the Houston city council passed an ordinance restricting the construction of solid waste disposal sites near public facilities such as schools. And the Texas Department of Health updated its requirements of landfill permit applicants to include detailed land use, economic, and socio-demographic data on areas where they proposed to site landfills. Black Houstonians had sent a clear signal to the Texas Department of Health, the city of Houston, and private disposal companies that they would fight any future attempts to place waste disposal facilities in their neighborhoods.

Since *Bean v. Southwestern Waste,* not a single landfill or incinerator has been sited in an African-American neighborhood in Houston. Not until nearly a decade after that suit did environmental discrimination resurface in the courts. A number of recent cases have challenged siting decisions using the environmental discrimination argument: *East Bibb Twiggs Neighborhood Association v. Macon-Bibb County Planning & Zoning Commission* (1989), *Bordeaux Action Committee v. Metro Government of Nashville* (1990), *R.I.S.E. v. Kay* (1991), and *El Pueblo para El Aire y Agua Limpio v. County of Kings* (1991). Unfortunately, these legal challenges are also confronted with the test of demonstrating "purposeful" discrimination.

Redress Inequities

Disproportionate impacts must be redressed by targeting action and resources. Resources should be spent where environmental and health problems are greatest, as determined by some ranking scheme—but one not limited to risk assessment. EPA already has geographic targeting that involves

selecting a physical area, often a naturally defined area such as a watershed; assessing the condition of the natural resources and range of environmental threats, including risks to public health; formulating and implementing integrated, holistic strategies for restoring or protecting living resources and their habitats within that area; and evaluating the progress of those strategies toward their objectives.[57]

Relying solely on proof of a cause-and-effect relationship as defined by traditional epidemiology disguises the exploitative way the polluting industries have operated in some communities and condones a passive acceptance of the status quo.[58] Because it is difficult to establish causation, polluting industries have the upper hand. They can always hide behind "science" and demand "proof" that their activities are harmful to humans or the environment.

A 1992 EPA report, *Securing Our Legacy,* described the agency's geographic initiatives as "protecting what we love."[59] The strategy emphasizes "pollution prevention, multimedia enforcement, research into causes and cures of environmental stress, stopping habitat loss, education, and constituency building."[60] Examples of geographic initiatives under way include the Chesapeake Bay, Great Lakes, Gulf of Mexico, and Mexican Border programs.

Such targeting should channel resources to the hot spots, communities that are burdened with more than their fair share of environmental problems. For example, EPA's Region VI has developed geographic information system and comparative risk methodologies to evaluate environmental equity concerns in the region. The methodology combines susceptibility factors, such as age, pregnancy, race, income, pre-existing disease, and lifestyle, with chemical release data from the Toxic Release Inventory and monitoring information; state health department vital statistics data; and geographic and demographic data—especially from areas around hazardous waste sites—for its regional equity assessment.

Region VI's 1992 Gulf Coast Toxics Initiatives project is an outgrowth of its equity assessment. The project targets facilities on the Texas and Louisiana coast, a "sensitive ... ecoregion where most of the releases in the five-state region occur."[61] Inspectors will spend 38 percent of their time in this "multimedia enforcement effort."[62] It is not clear how this percentage was determined, but, for the project to move beyond the "first-step" phase and begin addressing real inequities, most of its resources (not just inspectors) must be channeled to the areas where most of the problems occur.

A 1993 EPA study of Toxic Release Inventory data from Louisiana's petrochemical corridor found that "populations within two miles of facilities releasing 90% of total industrial corridor air releases feature a higher proportion of minorities than the state average; facilities releasing 88% have a higher proportion than the Industrial Corridor parishes' average.[63]

To no one's surprise, communities in Corpus Christi, neighborhoods that run along the Houston Ship Channel and petrochemical corridor, and many unincorporated communities along the 85-mile stretch of the Mississippi River from Baton Rouge to New Orleans ranked at or near the top in terms of pollution discharges in EPA Region VI's Gulf Coast Toxics Initiatives equity assessment. It is very likely that similar rankings would be achieved using the environmental justice framework. However, the question that remains is one of resource allocation—the level of resources that Region VI will channel into solving the pollution problem in communities that have a disproportionately large share of poor people, working-class people, and people of color.

Health concerns raised by Louisiana's residents and grassroots activists in such communities as Alsen, St. Gabriel, Geismer, Morrisonville, and Lions—all of which are located in close proximity to polluting industries—have not been adequately addressed by local parish supervisors, state environmental and health officials, or the federal and regional offices of EPA.[64]

A few contaminated African-American communities in southeast Louisiana have been bought out or are in the process of being bought out by industries under their "good neighbor" programs. Moving people away from the health threat is only a partial solution, however, as long as damage to the environment continues. For example, Dow Chemical, the state's largest chemical plant, is buying out residents of mostly African-American Morrisonville.[65] The communities of Sun Rise and Reveilletown, which were founded by freed slaves, have already been bought out.

Many of the community buy-out settlements are sealed. The secret nature of the agreements limits public scrutiny, community comparisons, and disclosure of harm or potential harm. Few of the recent settlement agreements allow for health monitoring or surveillance of affected residents once they are dispersed.[66] Some settlements have even required the "victims" to sign waivers that preclude them from bringing any further lawsuits against the polluting industry.

A FRAMEWORK FOR ENVIRONMENTAL JUSTICE

The solution to unequal protection lies in the realm of environmental justice for all people. No community—rich or poor, black or white—should be allowed to become a "sacrifice zone." The lessons from the civil rights struggles around housing, employment, education, and public accommodations over the past four decades suggest that environmental justice requires a legislative foundation. It is not enough to demonstrate the existence of unjust and unfair conditions; the practices that cause the conditions must be made illegal.

The five principles already described—the right to protection, prevention of harm, shifting the burden of proof, obviating proof of intent to discriminate, and targeting resources to redress inequities—constitute a framework for environmental justice. The framework incorporates a legislative strategy, modeled after landmark civil rights mandates, that would make environmental discrimination illegal and costly.

Although enforcing current laws in a nondiscriminatory way would help, a new legislative initiative is needed. Unequal protection must be attacked via a federal "fair environmental protection act" that redefines protection as a right rather than a privilege. Legislative initiatives must also be directed at states because many of the decisions and problems lie with state actions.

Noxious facility siting and cleanup decisions involve very little science and a lot of politics. Institutional discrimination exists in every social arena, including environmental decision making. Burdens and benefits are not randomly distributed. Reliance solely on "objective" science for environmental decision making—in a world shaped largely by power politics and special interests—often masks institutional racism. For example, the assignment of "acceptable" risk and use of "averages" often result from value judgments that serve to legitimate existing inequities. A national environmental justice framework that incorporates the five principles presented above is needed to begin addressing environmental inequities that result from procedural, geographic, and societal imbalances.

The antidiscrimination and enforcement measures called for here are no more regressive than the initiatives undertaken to eliminate slavery and segregation in the United States. Opponents argued at the time that such actions would hurt the slaves by creating unemployment and destroying black institutions, such as businesses and schools. Similar arguments were made in opposition to sanctions against the racist system of apartheid in South Africa. But people of color who live in environmental sacrifice zones"—from migrant farm workers who are exposed to deadly pesticides to the parents of inner-city children threatened by lead poisoning—will welcome any new approaches that will reduce environmental disparities and eliminate the threats to their families' health.

NOTES

1. U.S. Environmental Protection Agency, *Environmental Equity: Reducing Risk for All Communities* (Washington, D.C., 1992); and K. Sexton and Y. Banks Anderson, eds., "Equity in Environmental Health: Research Issues and Needs," *Toxicology and Industrial Health* 9 (September/October 1993).

2. R. D. Bullard, "Solid Waste Sites and the Black Houston Community," *Sociological Inquiry* 53, nos. 2 and 3 (1983): 273–88; idem, *Invisible Houston: The Black Experience in Boom and Bust* (College Station, Tex.: Texas A&M University Press, 1987); idem, *Dumping in Dixie: Race, Class, and Environmental Quality* (Boulder, Colo.: Westview Press, 1990); idem, *Confronting Environmental Racism: Voices from the Grassroots* (Boston, Mass.: South End Press, forth); D. Russell, "Environmental Racism," *Amicus Journal* 11, no. 2 (1989): 22–32; M. Lavelle and M. Coyle, "Unequal Protection," *National Law Journal*, 21 September 1992, 1–2; R. Austin and M. Schill, "Black, Brown, Poor, and Poisoned: Minority Grassroots Environmentalism and the Quest for Eco-Justice," *Kansas Journal of Law and Public Policy* 1 (1991): 69–82; R. Godsil, "Remedying Environmental Racism," *Michigan Law Review* 90 (1991): 394–427; and B. Bryant and P. Mohai, eds., *Race and the Incidence of Environmental Hazards: A Time for Discourse* (Boulder, Colo.: Westview Press, 1992).

3. R. B. Stewart, "Paradoxes of Liberty, Integrity, and Fraternity: The Collective Nature of Environmental Quality and Judicial Review of Administration Action," *Environmental Law* 7, no. 3 (1977): 474–76; M. A. Freeman, "The Distribution of Environmental Quality," in A. V. Kneese and B. F. Bower, eds., *Environmental Quality Analysis* (Baltimore, Md.: Johns Hopkins University Press for Resources for the Future, 1972); W. J. Kruvant, "People, Energy, and Pollution," in D. K. Newman and D. Day, eds., *American Energy Consumer* (Cambridge, Mass.: Ballinger, 1975), 125–67; and L. Gianessi, H. M. Peskin, and E. Wolff, "The Distributional Effects of Uniform Air Pollution Policy in the U.S.," *Quarterly Journal of Economics* 56, no. 1 (1979): 281–301.

4. Freeman, note 3 above; Kruvant, note 3 above; Bullard, 1983 and 1990, note 2 above; P. Asch and J. J. Seneca, "Some Evidence on the Distribution of Air Quality," *Land Economics* 54, no. 3 (1978): 278–97; United Church of Christ Commission for Racial Justice, *Toxic Wastes and Race in the United States: A National Study of the Racial and*

Socioeconomic Characteristics of Communities with Hazardous Waste Sites (New York: United Church of Christ, 1987); Russell, note 2 above; R. D. Bullard and B. H. Wright, "Environmentalism and the Politics of Equity; Emergent Trends in the Black Community," *Mid-American Review of Sociology* 12, no. 2 (1987): 21–37; idem, "The Quest for Environmental Equity: Mobilizing the African American Community for Social Change," *Society and Natural Resources* 3, no. 4 (1990): 301–11; M. Gelobter, "The Distribution of Air Pollution by Income and Race" (paper presented at the Second Symposium on Social Science in Resource management, Urbana, Ill., June 1988); R. D. Bullard and J. R. Feagin, "Racism and the City," in M. Gottdiene, and C. V. Pickvance, eds., *Urban Life in Transition* (Newbury Park, Calif.: Sage, 1991), 55–76; R. D. Bullard, "Urban Infrastructure: Social, Environmental, and Health Risks to African Americans," in B. J. Tidwell, ed., *The State of Black America 1992* (New York: National Urban League, 1992), 183–96; P. Ong and E. Blumenberg, "Race and Environmentalism" (paper prepared for the Graduate School of Architecture and Urban Planning, University of California at Los Angeles, 14 March 1990); and B. H. Wright and R. D. Bullard, "Hazards in the Workplace and Black Health," *National Journal of Sociology* 4, no. 1 (1990): 45–62.

5. Freeman, note 3 above; Gianessi, Peskin, and Wolff, note 3 above; Gelobter, note 4 above; D. R. Wernette and L. A. Nieves, "Breathing Polluted Air," *EPA Journal* 18, no. 1 (1992): 16–17; Bullard, 1983, 1987, and 1990, note 2 above; R. D. Bullard, "Environmental Racism," *Environmental Protection* 2 (June 1991): 25–26; L. A. Nieves, "Not in Whose Backyard? Minority Population Concentrations and Noxious Facility Sites" (paper presented at the Annual Meeting of the American Association for the Advancement of Science, Chicago, 9 February 1992); United Church of Christ, note 4 above; Agency for Toxic Substances and Disease Registry, *The Nature and Extent of Lead Poisoning in Children in the United States: A Report to Congress* (Atlanta, Ga. U.S. Department of Health and Human Services, 1988); K. Florini et al., *Legacy of Lead: America's Continuing Epidemic of Childhood Lead Poisoning* (Washington, D.C.: Environmental Defense Fund, 1990); and P. West, J. M. Fly, F. Larkin, and P. Marans, "Minority Anglers and Toxic Fish Consumption: Evidence of the State-Wide Survey of Michigan," in B. Bryant and P. Mohai, eds., *The Proceedings of the Michigan Conference on Race and the Incidence of Environmental Hazards* (Ann Arbor, Mich.: University of Michigan School of Natural Resources, 1990), 108–22.

6. Gelobter, note 4 above; and M. Gelobter, "Toward a Model of Environmental Discrimination," in Bryant and Mohai, eds., note 5 above, pages 87–107.

7. B. Goldman, *Not Just Prosperity: Achieving Sustainability with Environmental Justice* (Washington, D.C.: National Wildlife Federation Corporate Conservation Council, 1994), 8.

8. Wernette and Nieves, note 5 above, pages 16–17.

9. H. P. Mak, P. Johnson, H. Abbey, and R. C. Talamo, "Prevalence of Asthma and Health Service Utilization of Asthmatic Children in an Inner City," *Journal of Allergy and Clinical Immunology* 70 (1982): 367–72; I. F. Goldstein and A. L. Weinstein, "Air Pollution and Asthma: Effects of Exposure to Short-Term Sulfur Dioxide Peaks," *Environmental Research* 40 (1986): 332–45; J. Schwartz et al., "Predictors of Asthma and Persistent Wheeze in a National Sample of Children in the United States," *American Review of Respiratory Disease* 142 (1990): 555–62; U.S. Environmental Protection Agency, note I above; and E. Mann, L.A.'s *Lethal Air: New Strategies for Policy, Organizing and Action* (Los Angeles: Labor/Community Strategy Center, 1991).

10. Lavelle and Coyle, note 2 above, pages 1–2.

11. Ibid., 2.

12. Bullard, 1983 and 1990, note 2 above; Gelobter, note 4 above; and United Church of Christ, note 4 above.

13. Bullard, 1983 and 1990, note 2 above; P. Costner and J. Thornton, *Playing with Fire* (Washington, D.C.: Greenpeace, 1990); and United Church of Christ, note 4 above.

14. Costner and Thornton, note 13 above.

15. M. H. Brown, *The Toxic Cloud: The Poisoning of America's Air* (New York: Harper and Row, 1987); and J. Summerhays, *Estimation and Evaluation of Cancer Risks Attributable lo Air Pollution in Southeast Chicago* (Washington, D.C.: U.S. Environmental Protection Agency, 1989).

16. *Greenpeace Magazine,* "Home Street, USA: Living with Pollution," October/November/December 1991, 8–13.

17. Mann, note 9 above; and Ong and Blumenberg, note 4 above.

18. Mann, note 9 above; and J. Kay, "Fighting Toxic Racism: L.A.'s Minority Neighborhood Is the 'Dirtiest' in the State," *San Francisco Examiner,* 7 April 199 1, Al.

19. Bullard, 1990, note 2 above.

20. K. C. Colquette and E. A. Henry Robertson, "Environmental Racism: The Causes, Consequences, and Commendations," *Tulane Environmental Law Journal* 5, no. 1 (1991): 153–207.

21. F. Ferrer, "Testimony by the Office of Bronx Borough President," in *Proceedings from the Public Hearing on Minorities and the Environment: An Exploration into the Effects of Environmental Policies, Practices, and Conditions on Minority and Low-Income Communities* (Bronx, N.Y.: Bronx Planning Office, 20 September 1991).

22. B. Angel, *The Toxic Threat to Indian Lands: A Greenpeace Report* (San Francisco, Calif.: Greenpeace, 1992); and J. Kay, "Indian Lands Targeted for Waste Disposal Sites," *San Francisco Examiner,* 10 April 1991, Al.

23. M. Ambler, "The Lands the Feds Forgot," *Sierra,* May/June 1989, 44

24. Angel, note 22 above; C. Beasley, "Of Poverty and Pollution: Deadly Threat on Native Lands," *Buzzworm* 2, no. 5 (1990): 39–45; and R. Tomsho, "Dumping Grounds: Indian Tribes Contend with Some of the Worst of America's Pollution," *Wall Street Journal,* 29 November 1990, A1.

25. Cerrell Associates, Inc., *Political Difficulties Facing Waste-to-Energy Conversion Plant Siting* (Los Angeles: California Waste Management Board, 1984).

26. L. Blumberg and R. Gottlieb, *War on Waste: Can America Win Its Battle with Garbage?* (Washington, D.C.: Island Press, 1989).

27. U.S. Commission on Civil Rights, The Battle for Environmental Justice in Louisiana: Government, Industry, and the People (Kansas City, Mo., 1993).

28. Agency for Toxic Substances and Disease Registry, note 5 above.

29. P. Reich, The Hour of Lead (Washington, D.C.: Environmental Defense Fund, 1992).

30. Agency for Toxic Substances and Disease Registry, note 5 above.

31. Florini et al., note 5 above.

32. P. J. Hilts, "White House Shuns Key Role in Lead Exposure," *New York Times,* 24 August 1991, 14.

33. Ibid.

34. Dallas Alliance Environmental Task Force, *Alliance Final Report* (Dallas, Tex.: Dallas Alliance, 1983).

35. J. Lash, K. Gillman, and D. Sheridan, *A Season of Spoils: The Reagan Administration's Attack on the Environment* (New York: Pantheon Books, 1984), 131–39.

36. D. W. Nauss, "EPA Official: Dallas Lead Study Misleading," *Dallas Times Herald,* 20 March 1983, 1; idem, "The People vs. the Lead Smelter," *Dallas Times Herald,* 17 July 1983, 18; B. Lodge, "EPA Official Faults Dallas Lead Smelter," *Dallas Morning News,* 20 March 1983, A1; and Lash, Gillman, and Sheridan, note 35 above.

37. U.S. Environmental Protection Agency Region VI, *Report of the Dallas Area Lead Assessment Study* (Dallas, Tex., 1983).

38. Lash, Gillman, and Sheridan, note 35 above.

39. Bullard, 1990, note 2 above.

40. S. Scott and R. L. Loftis, "Slag Sites' Health Risks Still Unclear," *Dallas Morning News,* 23 July 1991, A1.

41. Ibid.

42. B. L. Lee, "Environmental Litigation on Behalf of Poor, Minority Children: Matthews v. Coye: A Case Study" (paper presented at the Annual Meeting of the American Association for the Advancement of Science, Chicago, 9 February 1992).

43. Nuclear Regulatory Commission, *Draft Environmental Impact Statement for the Construction and Operation of Claiborne Enrichment Center, Homer, Louisiana* (Washington, D.C., 1993), 3108.

44. See U.S. Census Bureau, *1990 Census of Population General Population Characteristics—Louisiana* (Washington, D.C.: U.S. Government Printing Office, May 1992).

45. Nuclear Regulatory Commission, note 43 above, pages 4–38.

46. Citizens for a Better Environment, *Richmond at Risk* (San Francisco, Calif., 1992).

47. Bay Area Air Quality Management District, *General Chemical Incident of July 26*, 1993 (San Francisco, Calif., 15 September 1993), 1.

48. R. Sanchez, "Health and Environmental Risks of the Maquiladora in Mexicali," *Natural Resources Journal* 30 (Winter 1990): 16386.

49. Center for Investigative Reporting, *Global Dumping Grounds: The International Traffic in Hazardous Waste* (Washington, D.C.: Seven Locks Press, 1989), 59.

50. Working Group on Canada-Mexico Free Trade, "Que Pasa? A Canada-Mexico 'Free' Trade Deal," *New Solutions: A Journal of Environmental and Occupational Health Policy* 2 (1991): 10–25.

51. Bullard, 198 3, note 2 above.

52. Bullard, 1987, note 2 above.

53. Bullard, 1983, 1987, and 1990, note 2 above. The unit of analysis for the Houston waste study was the neighborhood, not the census tract. The concept of neighborhood predates census tract geography, which became available only in 1950. Neighborhood studies date back nearly a century. Neighborhood as used here is defined as "a social/spatial unit of social organization ... larger than a household and smaller than a city." See A. Hunter, "Urban Neighborhoods: Its Analytical and Social Contexts," *Urban Affairs Quarterly* 14 (1979): 270. The neighborhood is part of a city's geography, a place defined by specific physical boundaries and block groups. Similarly, the black neighborhood is a "highly diversified set of interrelated structures and aggregates of people who are held together by forces of white oppression and racism." See J. E. Blackwell, *The Black Community: Diversity and Unity* (New York: Harper & Row, 1985), xiii.

54. Bullard, 1983, 1987, and 1990, note 2 above.

55. Ibid.

56. Ibid.

57. U.S. Environmental Protection Agency, *Strategies and Framework for the Future: Final Report* (Washington, D.C., 1992), 12.

58. K. S. Shrader-Frechette, *Risk and Rationality: Philosophical Foundations for Populist Reform* (Berkeley, Calif.: University of California Press, 1992), 98.

59. U.S. Environmental Protection Agency, "Geographic Initiatives: Protecting What We Love," *Securing Our Legacy: An EPA Progress Report 1989–1991* (Washington, D.C., 1992), 32.

60. Ibid.

61. U.S. Environmental Protection Agency, note 1 above, vol. 2, Supporting Documents, page 60.

62. Ibid.

63. U.S. Environmental Protection Agency, *Toxic Release Inventory & Emission Reduction 1987– 1990 in the Lower Mississippi River Industrial Corridor* (Washington, D.C., 1993), 25.

64. Bullard, 1990, note 2 above; C. Beasley, "Of Pollution and Poverty: Keeping Watch in Cancer Alley," *Buzzworm* 2, no. 4 (1990): 3945; and S. Lewis, B. Keating, and D. Russell, *Inconclusive by Design: Waste, Fraud, and Abuse in Federal Environmental Health Research* (Boston, Mass.: National Toxics Campaign, 1992).

65. J. O'Byrne, "The Death of a Town," *Times Picayune*, 20 February 1991, A1.

66. Bullard, 1990, note 2 above; J. O'Byrne and M. Schleifstein, "Invisible Poisons," *Times Picayune*, 18 February 1991, A1; and Lewis, Keating, and Russell, note 64 above.

STUDY QUESTIONS

1. Bullard argues that "unequal environmental protection undermines three basic types of equity: procedural, geographic, and social." Discuss each of these.

2. Bullard advocates the adoption of five principles to increase (or ensure) environmental justice. Discuss three of them in depth.

3. Discuss the following question: Is the disproportionate distribution of pollutants more due to racial discrimination or to economic class inequalities?

51

Just Garbage: The Problem of Environmental Racism

PETER S. WENZ

Peter S. Wenz is professor of philosophy at the University of Illinois at Springfield and the author of several works in environmental ethics, including his books Environmental Justice *(1988),* Nature's Keeper *(1996), and* Environmental Ethics for Everyone *(2000).*

In this essay, Wenz argues that it is unjust for poor people, whether or not they are predominantly minorities, to be exposed disproportionately to pollution and other locally undesirable land uses (LULUs). He proposes a system whereby all communities must earn equal pollution points that cannot be bought and sold on the market. This would prevent rich people from buying their way out of exposure to environmental degradation and influence decision makers (who come mostly from economically advantaged groups) to reduce overall pollution to protect themselves and their families.

Environmental racism is evident in practices that expose racial minorities in the United States, and people of color around the world, to disproportionate shares of environmental hazards. These include toxic chemicals in factories, toxic herbicides and pesticides in agriculture, radiation from uranium mining, lead from paint on older buildings, toxic wastes illegally dumped, and toxic waster legally stored. In this chapter, which concentrates on issues of toxic waste, both illegally dumped and legally stored, I will examine the justness of current practices as well as the arguments commonly given in their defense. I will then propose an alternative practice that is consistent with prevailing principles of justice.

A DEFENSE OF CURRENT PRACTICES

Defenders often claim that because economic, not racial, considerations account for disproportionate impacts of nonwhites, current practices are neither racist nor morally objectionable. Their reasoning recalls the Doctrine of Double Effect. According to that doctrine, an effect whose production is usually blameworthy becomes blameless when it is incidental to, although predictably conjoined with, the production of another effect whose production is morally justified. The classic case concerns a pregnant woman with uterine cancer.

Reprinted with permission from *Faces of Environmental Racism* by Laura Westra and Peter S. Wentz (Lanham, M.D.: Rowman & Littlefield, 1995). Notes edited.

A common, acceptable treatment for uterine cancer is hysterectomy. This will predictably end the pregnancy, as would an abortion. However, Roman Catholic scholars who usually consider abortion blameworthy consider it blameless in this context because it is merely incidental to hysterectomy, which is morally justified to treat uterine cancer. The hysterectomy would be performed in the absence of pregnancy, so the abortion effect is produced neither as an end-in-itself, nor as a means to reach the desired end, which is the cure of cancer.

Defenders of practices that disproportionately disadvantage nonwhites seem to claim, in keeping with the Doctrine of Double Effect, that racial effects are blameless because they are sought neither as ends-in-themselves nor as means to reach a desired goal. They are merely predictable side effects of economic and political practices that disproportionately expose poor people to toxic substances. The argument is that burial of toxic wastes, and other locally undesirable land uses (LULUs), lower property values. People who can afford to move elsewhere do so. They are replaced by buyers (or renters) who are predominately poor and cannot afford housing in more desirable areas. Law professor Vicki Been puts it this way: "As long as the market allows the existing distribution of wealth to allocate goods and services, it would be surprising indeed if, over the long run, LULUs did not impose a disproportionate burden upon the poor." People of color are disproportionately burdened due primarily to poverty, not racism.[1] This defense against charges of racism is important in the American context because racial discrimination is illegal in the United States in circumstances where economic discrimination is permitted.[2] Thus, legal remedies to disproportionate exposure of nonwhites to toxic wastes are available if racism is the cause, but not if people of color are exposed merely because they are poor.

There is strong evidence against claims of racial neutrality. Professor Been acknowledges that even if there is no racism in the process of siting LULUs, racism plays at least some part in the disproportionate exposure of African Americans to them. She cites evidence that "racial discrimination in the sale and rental of housing relegates people of color

(especially African Americans) to the least desirable neighborhoods, regardless of their income level."[3]

Without acknowledging for a moment, then, that racism plays no part in the disproportionate exposure of nonwhites to toxic waste, I will ignore this issue to display a weakness in the argument that justice is served when economic discrimination alone is influential. I claim that even if the only discrimination is economic, justice requires redress and significant alteration of current practices. Recourse to the Doctrine of Double Effect presupposes that the primary effect, with which a second effect is incidentally conjoined, is morally justifiable. In the classic case, abortion is justified only because hysterectomy is justified as treatment for uterine cancer. I argue that disproportionate impacts on poor people violate principles of distributive justice, and so are not morally justifiable in the first place. Thus, current practices disproportionately exposing nonwhites to toxic substances are not justifiable even if incidental to the exposure of poor people.

Alternate practices that comply with acceptable principles of distributive justice are suggested below. They would largely solve problems of environmental racism (disproportionate impacts on nonwhites) while ameliorating the injustice of disproportionately exposing poor people to toxic hazards. They would also discourage production of toxic substances, thereby reducing humanity's negative impact on the environment.

THE PRINCIPLE OF COMMENSURATE BURDENS AND BENEFIT

We usually assume that, other things being equal, those who derive benefits should sustain commensurate burdens. We typically associate the burden of work with the benefit of receiving money, and the burdens of monetary payment and tort liability with the benefits of ownership.

There are many exceptions. For example, people can inherit money without working, and be given ownership without purchase. Another exception, which dissociates the benefit of ownership from the burden of tort liability, is the use of tax money to protect the public from hazards associated with private property, as in Superfund legislation. Again, the benefit of money is dissociated from the burden of work when governments support people who are unemployed.

The fact that these exceptions require justification, however, indicates an abiding assumption that people who derive benefits should shoulder commensurate burdens. The ability to inherit without work is justified as a benefit owed to those who wish to bequeath their wealth (which someone in the line of inheritance is assumed to have shouldered burdens to acquire). The same reasoning applies to gifts.

Using tax money (public money) to protect the public from dangerous private property is justified as encouraging private industry and commerce, which are supposed to increase public wealth. The system also protects victims in case private owners become bankrupt as, for example, in Times Beach, Missouri, where the government bought homes made worthless due to dioxin pollution. The company responsible for the pollution was bankrupt.

Tax money is used to help people who are out of work to help them find a job, improve their credentials, or feed their children. This promotes economic growth and equal opportunity. These exceptions prove the rule by the fact that justification for any deviation from the commensuration of benefits and burdens is considered necessary.

Further indication of an abiding belief that benefits and burdens should be commensurate is grumbling that, for example, many professional athletes and corporate executives are overpaid. Although the athletes and executives shoulder the burden of work, the complaint is that their benefits are disproportionate to their burdens. People on welfare are sometimes criticized for receiving even modest amounts of taxpayer money without shouldering the burdens of work, hence recurrent calls for "welfare reform." Even though these calls are often justified as means to reducing government budget deficits, the moral issue is more basic than the economic. Welfare expenditures are minor

compared to other programs, and alternatives that require poor people to work are often more expensive than welfare as we know it.

The principle of commensuration between benefits and burdens is not the only moral principle governing distributive justice, and may not be the most important, but it is basic. Practices can be justified by showing them to conform, all things considered, to this principle. Thus, there is no move to "reform" the receipt of moderate pay for ordinary work, because it exemplifies the principle. On the other hand, practices that do not conform are liable to attack and require alternate justification, as we have seen in the cases of inheritance, gifts, Superfund legislation, and welfare.

Applying the principle of commensuration between burdens and benefits to the issue at hand yields the following: In the absence of countervailing considerations, the burdens of ill health associated with toxic hazards should be related to benefits derived from processes and products that create these hazards.

TOXIC HAZARDS AND CONSUMERISM

In order to assess, in light of the principle of commensuration between benefits and burdens, the justice of current distributions of toxic hazards, the benefits of their generation must be considered. Toxic wastes result from many manufacturing processes, including those for a host of common items and materials, such as paint, solvents, plastics, and most petrochemical-based materials. These materials surround us in the paint on our homes, in our refrigerator containers, in our clothing, in our plumbing, in our garbage pails, and elsewhere.

Toxins are released into the environment in greater quantities now than ever before because we now have a consumer-oriented society where the acquisition, use, and disposal of individually owned items is greatly desired. We associate the numerical dollar value of the items at our disposal with our "standard of living," and assume that a higher standard is conducive to, if not identical with, a better life. So toxic wastes needing disposal are produced as by-products of the general pursuit of what our society defines as valuable, that is, the consumption of material goods.

Our economy requires increasing consumer demand to keep people working (to produce what is demanded). This is why there is concern each Christmas season, for example, that shoppers may not buy enough. If demand is insufficient, people may be put out of work. Demand must increase, not merely hold steady, because commercial competition improves labor efficiency in manufacture (and now in the service sector as well), so fewer workers can produce desired items. More items must be desired to forestall labor efficiency-induced unemployment, which is grave in a society where people depend primarily on wages to secure life's necessities.

Demand is kept high largely by convincing people that their lives require improvement, which consumer purchases will effect. When improvements are seen as needed, not merely desired, people purchase more readily. So our culture encourages economic expansion by blurring the distinction between wants and needs.

One way the distinction is blurred is through promotion of worry. If one feels insecure without the desired item or service, and so worries about life without it, then its provision is easily seen as a need. Commercials, and other shapers of social expectations, keep people worried by adjusting downward toward the trivial what people are expected to worry about. People worry about the provision of food, clothing, and housing without much inducement. When these basic needs are satisfied, however, attention shifts to indoor plumbing, for example, then to stylish indoor plumbing. The process continues with need for a second or third bathroom, a kitchen disposal, and a refrigerator attached to the plumbing so that ice is made automatically in the freezer, and cold water can be obtained without even opening the refrigerator door. The same kind of progression results in cars with CD players, cellular phones, and automatic readouts of average fuel consumption per mile.

Abraham Maslow was not accurately describing people in our society when he claimed that after physiological, safety, love, and (self-) esteem needs are met, people work toward self-actualization, becoming increasingly their own unique selves by fully developing their talents. Maslow's Hierarchy of Needs describes people in our society less than Wenz's Lowerarchy of Worry. When one source of worry is put to rest by an appropriate purchase, some matter less inherently or obviously worrisome takes its place as the focus of concern. Such worry-substitution must be amenable to indefinite repetition in order to motivate purchases needed to keep the economy growing without inherent limit. If commercial society is supported by consumer demand, it is worry all the way down. Toxic wastes are produced in this context.

People tend to worry about ill health and early death without much inducement. These concerns are heightened in a society dependent upon the production of worry, so expenditure on health care consumes an increasing percentage of the gross domestic product. As knowledge of health impairment due to toxic substances increases, people are decreasingly tolerant of risks associated with their proximity. Thus, the same mindset of worry that elicits production that generates toxic wastes, exacerbates reaction to their proximity. The result is a desire for their placement elsewhere, hence the NIMBY syndrome—Not In My Back Yard. On this account, NIMBYism is not aberrantly selfish behavior, but integral to the cultural value system required for great volumes of toxic waste to be generated in the first place.

Combined with the principle of Commensurate Burdens and Benefits, that value system indicates who should suffer the burden of proximity to toxic wastes. Other things being equal, those who benefit most from the production of waste should shoulder the greatest share of burdens associated with its disposal. In our society, consumption of goods is valued highly and constitutes the principal benefit associated with the generation of toxic wastes. Such consumption is generally correlated with income and wealth. So other things being equal, justice requires that people's proximity to toxic wastes be related positively to their income and wealth. This is exactly opposite to the predominant tendency in our society, where poor people are more proximate to toxic wastes dumped illegally and stored legally.

REJECTED THEORIES OF JUSTICE

Proponents of some theories of distributive justice may claim that current practices are justified. In this section I will explore such claims.

A widely held view of justice is that all people deserve to have their interests given equal weight. John Rawls's popular thought experiment in which people choose principles of justice while ignorant of their personal identities dramatizes the importance of equal consideration of interests. Even selfish people behind the "veil of ignorance" in Rawls's "original position" would choose to accord equal consideration to everyone's interests because, they reason, they may themselves be the victims of any inequality. Equal consideration is a basic moral premise lacking serious challenge in our culture, so it is presupposed in what follows. Disagreement centers on application of the principle.

LIBERTARIANISM

Libertarians claim that each individual has an equal right to be free of interference from other people. All burdens imposed by other people are unjustified unless part of, or consequent upon, agreement by the party being burdened. So no individual who has not consented should be burdened by burial of toxic wastes (or the emission of air pollutants, or the use of agricultural pesticides, etc.) that may increase risks of disease, disablement, or death. Discussing the effects of air pollution, libertarian Murray Rothbard writes, "The remedy is simply to enjoin anyone from injecting pollutants into the air, and thereby invading the rights of persons and property. Period."[4] Libertarians John Hospers and Tibor R. Machan seem to endorse Rothbard's position.[5]

The problem is that implementation of this theory is impractical and unjust in the context of our civilization. Industrial life as we know it inevitably includes production of pollutants and toxic substances that threaten human life and health. It is impractical to secure the agreement of every individual to the placement, whether on land, in the air, or in water, of every chemical that may adversely affect the life or health of the individuals in question. After being duly informed of the hazard, someone potentially affected is bound to object, making the placement illegitimate by libertarian criteria.

In effect, libertarians give veto power to each individual over the continuation of industrial society. This seems a poor way to accord equal consideration to everyone's interests because the interest in physical safety of any one individual is allowed to override all other interests of all other individuals in the continuation of modern life. Whether or not such life is worth pursuing, it seems unjust to put the decision for everyone in the hands of any one person.

UTILITARIANISM

Utilitarians consider the interests of all individuals equally, and advocate pursuing courses of action that promise to produce results containing the greatest (net) sum of good. However, irrespective of how "good" is defined, problems with utilitarian accounts of justice are many and notorious.

Utilitarianism suffers in part because its direct interest is exclusively in the sum total of good, and in the future. Since the sum of good is all that counts in utilitarianism, there is no guarantee that the good of some will not be sacrificed for the greater good of others. Famous people could receive (justifiably according to utilitarians) particularly harsh sentences for criminal activity to effect general deterrence. Even when fame results from honest pursuits, a famous felon's sentence is likely to attract more attention than sentences in other cases of similar criminal activity. Because potential criminals are more likely to respond to sentences in such cases, harsh punishment is justified for utilitarian reasons on grounds that are unrelated to the crime.

Utilitarianism suffers in cases like this not only from its exclusive attention to the sum total of good, but also from its exclusive preoccupation with future consequences, which makes the relevance of past conduct indirect. This affects not only retribution, but also reciprocity and gratitude, which utilitarians endorse only to produce the greatest sum of future benefits. The direct relevance of past agreements and benefits, which common sense assumes, disappears in utilitarianism. So does direct application of the principle of Commensurate Burdens and Benefits.

The merits of the utilitarian rejection of common sense morality need not be assessed, however, because utilitarianism seems impossible to put into practice. Utilitarian support for any particular conclusion is undermined by the inability of anyone actually to perform the kinds of calculations that utilitarians profess to use. Whether the good is identified with happiness or preference-satisfaction, the two leading contenders at the moment, utilitarians announce the conclusions of their calculations without ever being able to show the calculation itself.

When I was in school, math teachers suspected that students who could never show their work were copying answers from other students. I suspect similarly that utilitarians, whose "calculations" often support conclusions that others reach by recourse to principles of gratitude, retributive justice, commensuration between burdens and benefits, and so forth, reach conclusions on grounds of intuitions influenced predominantly by these very principles.

Utilitarians may claim that, contrary to superficial appearances, these principles are themselves supported by utilitarian calculations. But, again, no one has produced a relevant calculation. Some principles seem *prima facie* opposed to utilitarianism, such as the one prescribing special solicitude of parents for their own children. It would seem that in cold climates more good would be produced if people bought winter coats for needy children, instead of special dress coats and ski attire for their own children. But utilitarians defend the principle of special parental concern. They declare this principle consistent with utilitarianism by appeal to entirely untested, unsubstantiated assumptions about counterfactuals. It is a kind of "Just So" story that explains how good is maximized by adherence to current standards. There is no calculation at all.

Another indication that utilitarians cannot perform the calculations they profess to rely upon concerns principles whose worth are in genuine dispute. Utilitarians offer no calculations that help to settle the matter. For example, many people wonder today whether or not patriotism is a worthy moral principle. Detailed utilitarian calculations play no part in the discussion.

These are some of the reasons why utilitarianism provides no help to those deciding whether or not disproportionate exposure of poor people to toxic wastes is just.

Free Market Approach

Toxic wastes, a burden, could be placed where residents accept them in return for monetary payment, a benefit. Since market transactions often satisfactorily commensurate burdens and benefits, this approach may seem to honor the principle of commensuration between burdens and benefits.

Unlike many market transactions, however, whole communities, acting as corporate bodies, would have to contract with those seeking to bury wastes. Otherwise, any single individual in the community could veto the transaction, resulting in the impasse attending libertarian approaches.[6] Communities could receive money to improve such public facilities as schools, parks, and hospitals, in addition to obtaining tax revenues and jobs that result ordinarily from business expansion.

The major problem with this free market approach is that it fails to accord equal consideration to everyone's interests. Where basic or vital goods and services are at issue, we usually think equal consideration of interests requires ameliorating inequalities of distribution that markets tend to produce. For example, one reason, although not the only reason, for public education is to provide every child with the basic intellectual tools necessary for success in our society. A purely free market approach, by contrast, would result in excellent education for children of wealthy parents and little or no education for children of the nation's poorest residents. Opportunities for children of poor parents would be so inferior that we would say the children's interests had not been given equal consideration.

The reasoning is similar where vital goods are concerned. The United States has the Medicaid program for poor people to supplement market transactions in health care precisely because equal consideration of interests requires that everyone be given access to health care. The 1994 health care debate in the United States was, ostensibly, about how to achieve universal coverage, not about whether or not justice required such coverage. With the exception of South Africa, every other industrialized country already has universal coverage for health care. Where vital needs are concerned, markets are supplemented or avoided in order to give equal consideration to everyone's interests.

Another example concerns military service in time of war. The United States employed conscription during the Civil War, both world wars, the Korean War, and the war in Vietnam. When the national interest requires placing many people in mortal danger, it is considered just that exposure be largely unrelated to income and market transactions.

The United States does not currently provide genuine equality in education or health care, nor did universal conscription (of males) put all men at equal risk in time of war. In all three areas, advantage accrues to those with greater income and wealth. (During the Civil War, paying for a substitute was legal in many cases.) Imperfection in practice, however, should not obscure general agreement in theory that justice requires equal consideration of interests, and that such equal consideration requires rejecting purely free market approaches where basic or vital needs are concerned.

Toxic substances affect basic and vital interests. Lead, arsenic, and cadmium in the vicinity of children's homes can result in mental retardation of the children.[7] Navaho teens exposed to radiation from uranium mine tailings have seventeen times the national average of reproductive organ cancer.[8] Environmental Protection Agency (EPA) officials estimate that toxic air pollution in areas of South Chicago increases cancer risks one hundred to one thousand times.[9] Pollution from Otis Air Force base in Massachusetts is associated with alarming increases in cancer rates.[10] Non-Hodgkin's Lymphoma is related to living near stone, clay, and

glass industry facilities, and leukemia is related to living near chemical and petroleum plants.[11] In general, cancer rates are higher in the United States near industries that use toxic substances and discard them nearby.[12]

In sum, the placement of toxic wastes affects basic and vital interests just as do education, health care, and wartime military service. Exemption from market decisions is required to avoid unjust impositions on the poor, and to respect people's interests equally. A child dying of cancer receives little benefit from the community's new swimming pool.

COST-BENEFIT ANALYSIS (CBA)

CBA is an economist's version of utilitarianism, where the sum to be maximized is society's wealth, as measured in monetary units, instead of happiness or preference satisfaction. Society's wealth is computed by noting (and estimating where necessary) what people are willing to pay for goods and services. The more people are willing to pay for what exists in society, the better off society is, according to CBA.

CBA will characteristically require placement of toxic wastes near poor people. Such placement usually lowers land values (what people are willing to pay for property). Land that is already cheap, where poor people live, will not lose as much value as land that is currently expensive, where wealthier people live, so a smaller loss of social wealth attends placement of toxic wastes near poor people. This is just the opposite of what the Principle of Commensurate Burdens and Benefits requires.

The use of CBA also violates equal consideration of interests, operating much like free market approaches. Where a vital concern is at issue, equal consideration of interests requires that people be considered irrespective of income. The placement of toxic wastes affects vital interests. Yet CBA would have poor people exposed disproportionately to such wastes.[13]

In sum, libertarianism, utilitarianism, free market distribution, and cost-benefit analysis are inadequate principles and methodologies to guide the just distribution of toxic wastes.[13]

LULU POINTS

An approach that avoids these difficulties assigns points to different types of locally undesirable land uses (LULUs) and requires that all communities earn LULU points.[14] In keeping with the Principle of Commensurate Benefits and Burdens, wealthy communities would be required to earn more LULU points than poorer ones. Communities would be identified by currently existing political divisions, such as villages, towns, city wards, cities, and counties.

Toxic waste dumps are only one kind of LULU. Others include prisons, half-way houses, municipal waste sites, low-income housing, and power plants, whether nuclear or coal fired. A large deposit of extremely toxic waste, for example, may be assigned twenty points when properly buried but fifty points when illegally dumped. A much smaller deposit of properly buried toxic waste may be assigned only ten points, as may a coal-fired power plant. A nuclear power plant may be assigned twenty-five points, while municipal waste sites are only five points, and one hundred units of low-income housing are eight points.

These numbers are only speculations. Points would be assigned by considering probable effects of different LULUs on basic needs, and responses to questionnaires investigating people's levels of discomfort with LULUs of various sorts. Once numbers are assigned, the total number of LULU points to be distributed in a given time period could be calculated by considering planned development and needs for prisons, power plants, low-income housing, and so on. One could also calculate points for a community's already existing LULUs. Communities could then be required to host LULUs in proportion to their income or wealth, with new allocation of LULUs (and associated points) correcting for currently existing deviations from the rules of proportionality.

Wherever significant differences of wealth or income exist between two areas, these areas should be considered part of different communities if there is any political division between them. Thus, a county with rich and poor areas would not be considered a single community for purposes of locating LULUs. Instead, villages or towns may be so considered. A city with rich and poor areas may similarly be reduced to its wards. The purpose of segregating areas of different income or wealth from one another is to permit the imposition of greater LULU burdens on wealthier communities. When wealthy and poor areas are considered as one larger community, there is the danger that the community will earn its LULU points by placing hazardous waste near its poorer members. This possibility is reduced when only relatively wealthy people live in a smaller community that must earn LULU points.

PRACTICAL IMPLICATIONS

Political strategy is beyond the scope of this ..., so I will refrain from commenting on problems and prospects for securing passage and implementation of the foregoing proposal. I maintain that the proposal is just. In a society where injustice is common, it is no surprise that proposals for rectifications meet stiff resistance.

Were the LULU points proposal implemented, environmental racism would be reduced enormously. To the extent that poor people exposed to environmental hazards are members of racial minorities, relieving the poor of disproportionate exposure would also relieve people of color.

This is not to say that environmental racism would be ended completely. Implementation of the proposal requires judgment in particular cases. Until racism is itself ended, such judgment will predictably be exercised at times to the disadvantage of minority populations. However, because most people of color currently burdened by environmental racism are relatively poor, implementing the proposal would remove 80 to 90 percent of the effects of environmental racism. While efforts to end racism at all levels should continue, reducing the burdens of racism is generally advantageous to people of color. Such reductions are especially worthy when integral to policies that improve distributive justice generally.

Besides improving distributive justice and reducing the burdens of environmental racism, implementing the LULU points proposal would benefit life on earth generally by reducing the generation of toxic

The question of how the poor in the North, those in the countries of the South, and peasants and women worldwide may attain this "good life" is usually answered in terms of what, since Rostow, can be called the "catching-up development" path. This means that by following the same path of industrialization, technological progress and capital accumulation taken by Europe and the USA and Japan the same goal can be reached. These affluent countries and classes, the dominant sex—the men—the dominant urban centres and lifestyles are then perceived as the realized utopia of liberalism, a utopia still to be attained by those who apparently still lag behind. Undoubtedly the industrialized countries' affluence is the source of great fascination to all who are unable to share in it. The so-called "socialist" countries' explicit aim was to catch up, and even to overtake capitalism. After the breakdown of socialism in Eastern Europe, particularly East Germany, the aim is now to quickly catch up with the lifestyle of the so-called market economies, the prototype of which is seen in the USA or West Germany.

A brief look at the history of the underdeveloped countries and regions of the South but also at present day East Europe and East Germany can teach us that this catching-up development path is a myth: nowhere has it led to the desired goal.

This myth is based on an evolutionary, linear understanding of history. In this concept of history the peak of the evolution has already been reached by some, namely, men generally, white men in particular, industrial countries, urbanites. The "others"—women, brown and black people, "underdeveloped" countries, peasants—will also reach this peak with a little more effort, more education, more "development." Technological progress is seen as the driving force of this evolutionary process. It is usually ignored that, even in the early 1970s, the catching-up development theory was criticized by a number of writers. Andre Gunder Frank, Samir Amin, Johan Galtung, and many others have shown that the poverty of the underdeveloped nations is not as a result of "natural" lagging behind but the direct consequence of the overdevelopment of the rich industrial countries who exploit the so-called periphery in Africa, South America and Asia. In the course of this colonial history, which continues today, these areas were progressively under-developed and made dependent on the so-called metropolis. The relationship between these over-developed centres or metropoles and the under-developed peripheries is a colonial one. Today, a similar colonial relationship exists between Man and Nature, between men and women, between urban and rural areas. We have called these the colonies of White Man. In order to maintain such relationships force and violence are always essential.

But the emotional and cognitive acceptance of the colonized is also necessary to stabilize such relationships. This means that not only the colonizers but also the colonized must accept the lifestyle of "those on top" as the only model of the good life. This process of acceptance of the values, lifestyle and standard of living of "those on top" is invariably accompanied by a devaluation of one's own: one's own culture, work, technology, lifestyle and often also philosophy of life and social institutions. In the beginning this devaluation is often violently enforced by the colonizers and then reinforced by propaganda, educational programmes, a change of laws, and economic dependency, for example, through the debt trap. Finally, this devaluation is often accepted and internalized by the colonized as the "natural" state of affairs. One of the most difficult problems for the colonized (countries, women, peasants) is to develop their own identity after a process of formal decolonization—identity no longer based on the model of the colonizer as the image of the true human being; a problem addressed by Fanon, Memmi, Freire, and Blaise. To survive, wrote Memmi, the colonized must oppress the colonization. But to become a true human being he/she, him/herself, must oppress the colonized which, within themselves, they have become. This means that he/she must overcome the fascination exerted by the colonizer and his lifestyle and re-evaluate what he/she is and does.

To promote the elimination of the colonizers from within the colonized, it is useful to look more closely at the catching-up development myth.

It may be argued that those who have so far paid the price for development also look up to those at the top as their model of the future, as their concrete utopia; that this is a kind of universal law. But if we also consider the price nature had to pay for this model, a price that now increasingly affects people in the affluent societies too, it may be asked why do not these people question this myth? Because even in the North, the paradigm of unlimited growth of science and technology, goods and services—of capital—and GNP have led to an increasing deterioration in the environment, and subsequently the quality of life.

DIVIDE AND RULE: MODERN INDUSTRIAL SOCIETY'S SECRET

Most people in the affluent societies live in a kind of schizophrenic or "double-think" state. They are aware of the disasters of Bhopal and Chernobyl, of the "greenhouse" effect, the destruction of the ozone layer, the gradual poisoning of groundwater, rivers and seas by fertilizers, pesticides, herbicides, as well as industrial waste, and that they themselves increasingly suffer the effects of air pollution, allergies, stress and noise, and the health risks due to industrially produced food. They also know that responsibility for these negative impacts on their quality of life lies in their own lifestyles and an economic system based on constant growth. And yet (except for very few) they fail to act on this knowledge by modifying their lifestyles.

One reason for this collective schizophrenia is the North's stubborn hope, even belief, that they can have their cake and eat it: ever more products from the chemical industry *and* clean air and water, more and more cars and no "greenhouse" effect; an ever increasing output of commodities, more fast- and processed-foods, more fancy packaging, more exotic, imported food *and* enjoy good health and solve the waste problem.

Most people expect science and technology to provide a solution to these dilemmas, rather than taking steps to limit their own consumption and production patterns. It is not yet fully realized that a high material living standard militates against a genuinely good quality of life, especially if problems of ecological destruction are clearly understood.

The belief, however, that a high material living standard is tantamount to a good or high quality of life is the ideological support essential to uphold and legitimize the constant growth and accumulation model of modern industrial society. Unless the masses of people accept this the system cannot last and function. This equation is the real ideological-political hegemony that overlies everyday life. No political party in the industrialized countries of the North dares question this schizophrenic equation, because they fear it would affect their election prospects.

We have already shown that this double-think is based on assumptions that there are no limits to our planet's resources, no limits to technological progress, no limits to space, to growth. But as, in fact, we inhabit a limited world, this limitlessness is mythical and can be upheld only by colonial divisions: between centres and peripheries, men and women, urban and rural areas, modern industrial societies of the North and "backward," "traditional," "underdeveloped" societies of the South. The relationship between these parts is hierarchical not egalitarian, and characterized by exploitation, oppression and dominance.

The economic reason for these colonial structures is, above all, the *externalization of costs* from the space and time horizon of those who profit from these divisions. The economic, social and ecological costs of constant growth in the industrialized countries have been and are shifted to the colonized countries of the South, to those countries' environment and their peoples. Only by dividing the international work-force into workers in the colonized peripheries and workers in the industrialized centres and by maintaining these relations of dominance even after formal decolonization, is it possible for industrial countries' workers to be paid wages ten times and more higher than those paid to workers in the South.

Much of the social costs of the reproduction of the labour force within industrial societies is externalized *within* those societies themselves. This is facilitated through the patriarchal-capitalist sexual division of labour whereby women's household labour is defined as non-productive or as non-work and hence not remunerated. Women are defined as housewives and their work is omitted from GNP calculations. Women can therefore be called the internal colony of this system.

The ecological costs of the industrial production of chemical fertilizers, pesticides, atomic energy, and of cars and other commodities, and the waste and damage for which they are responsible during both the production and the consumption process, are being inflicted on nature. They manifest themselves as air-, water-, soil-pollution and poisoning that will not only affect the present, but all future generations. This applies particularly to the long-term effects of modern high technology: atomic industry, genetic engineering, computer technology and their synergic effects which nobody can either predict or control. Thus, both nature and the future have been colonized for the short-term profit motives of affluent societies and classes.

The relationship between colonized and colonizer is based not on any measure of partnership but rather on the latter's coercion and violence in its dealings with the former. This relationship is in fact the secret of unlimited growth in the centres of accumulation. If externalization of all the costs of industrial production were not possible, if they had to be borne by the industrialized countries themselves, that is if they were internalized, an immediate end to unlimited growth would be inevitable.

CATCHING-UP IMPOSSIBLE AND UNDESIRABLE

The logic of this accumulation model, based on exploitation and colonizing divisions, implies that anything like "catching-up development" is impossible for the colonies, for all colonies. This is because just as one colony may, after much effort, attain what was considered the ultimate in "development," the industrial centres themselves have

already "progressed" to a yet more "modern" stage of development; "development" here meaning technological progress. What today was the TV is tomorrow the colour TV, the day after the computer, then the ever more modern version of the "computer generation" and even later artificial intelligence machines and so forth. This catching-up policy of the colonies is therefore always a lost game. Because the very progress of the colonizers is based on the existence and the exploitation of those colonies.

These implications are usually ignored when development strategies are discussed. The aim, it is usually stated, is not a reduction in the industrialized societies' living standards but rather that all the "underdeveloped" should be enabled to attain the same level of affluence as in those societies. This sounds fine and corresponds to the values of the bourgeois revolutions: equality for all! But that such a demand is not only a logical, but also a material impossibility is ignored. The impossibility of this demand is obvious if one considers the ecological consequences of the universalization of the prevailing production system and lifestyle in the North's affluent industrial societies to everyone now living and for some further 30 years on this planet. If, for example, we note that the six per cent of the world's population who live in the USA annually consume 30 per cent of all the fossil energy produced, then, obviously, it is impossible for the rest of the world's population, of which about 80 per cent live in the poor countries of the South, to consume energy on the same scale.

According to Trainer, those living in the USA, Europe and Japan, consume three-quarters of the world's energy production. "If present world energy production were to be shared equally, Americans would have to get by on only one-fifth of the per capita amount they presently consume." Or, put differently, world population may be estimated at eleven billion people after the year 2050; if of these eleven billion people the per capita energy consumption was similar to that of Americans in the mid-1970s, conventional oil resources would be exhausted in 34–74 years; similar estimations are made for other resources.

But even if the world's resource base was un-limited it can be estimated that it would be around 500 years before the poor countries reached the living standard prevailing in the industrialized North; and then only if these countries abandoned the model of permanent economic growth, which constitutes the core of their economic philosophy. It is impossible for the South to "catch-up" with this model, not only because of the limits and in-equitable consumption of the resource base, but above all, because this growth model is based on a colonial world order in which the gap between the two poles is increasing, especially as far as economic development is concerned.

These examples show that catching-up devel-opment is not possible for all. In my opinion, the powers that dominate today's world economy are aware of this, the managers of the transnational cor-porations, the World Bank, the IMF, the banks and governments of the club of the rich countries; and in fact they do not really want this universalization, because it would end their growth model. Tacitly, they accept that the colonial structure of the so-called market economy is maintained worldwide. This structure, however, is masked by such euphe-misms as "North-South relations," "sustainable development," "threshold-countries" and so on which suggest that all poor countries can and will reach the same living standard as that of the affluent countries.

Yet, if one tries to disregard considerations of equity and of ecological concerns it may be asked if this model of the good life, pursued by the societies in the North, this paradigm of "catching-up devel-opment" has at least made people in the North happy. Has it fulfilled its promises there? Has it at least made women and children there more equal, more free, more happy? Has their quality of life improved while the GDP grew?

We read daily about an increase in homeless-ness and of poverty, particularly of women and children, of rising criminality in the big cities, of growing drug, and other addictions, including the addiction to shopping. Depression and suicides are on the increase in many of the affluent societies, and direct violence against women and children seems to be growing—both public and domestic violence as well as sexual abuse; the media are full of reports of all forms of violence. Additionally the urban centres are suffocating from motor vehicle exhaust emissions; there is barely any open space left in which to walk and breathe, the cities and highways are choked with cars. Whenever possible people try to escape from these urban centres to seek relief in the countryside or in the poor South. If, as is commonly asserted, city-dwellers' quality of life is so high, why do they not spend their vaca-tions in the cities?

It has been found that in the USA today the quality of life is lower than it was ten years ago. There seems to be an inverse relationship between GDP and the quality of life; the more GDP grows, the more the quality of life deteriorates. For exam-ple: growing market forces have led to the fact that food, which so far was still prepared in the home is now increasingly bought from fast-food restaurants; preparing food has become a service, a commodity. If more and more people buy this commodity the GDP grows. But what also grows at the same time is the erosion of community, the isolation and lone-liness of individuals, the indifference and atomiza-tion of the society. As Polanyi remarked, market forces destroy communities. Here, too, the pro-cesses are characterized by polarizations: the higher the GDP the lower the quality of life.

But "catching-up development" not only en-tails immaterial psychic and social costs and risks, which beset even the privileged in the rich coun-tries and classes. With the growing number of eco-logical catastrophes—some man-made like the Gulf War or Chernobyl—material life also deteriorates in the rich centres of the world. The affluent society is one society which in the midst of plenty of com-modities lacks the fundamental necessities of life: clean air, pure water, healthy food, space, time and quiet. What was experienced by mothers of small children after Chernobyl is now experienced by mothers in Kuwait. All the money of oil-rich Kuwait cannot buy people sunlight, fresh air, or pure water. This scarcity of basic common necessi-ties for survival affects the poor and the rich, but with greater impact on the poor.

In short, the prevailing world market system, oriented towards unending growth and profit, cannot be maintained unless it can exploit external and internal colonies: nature, women and other people, but it also needs people as consumers who never say: "IT IS ENOUGH." The consumer model of the rich countries is not generalizable worldwide, neither is it desirable for the minority of the world's population who live in the affluent societies. Moreover, it will lead increasingly to wars to secure ever-scarcer resources; the Gulf War was in large part about the control of oil resources in that region. If we want to avoid such wars in the future the only alternative is a deliberate and drastic change in lifestyle, a reduction of consumption and a radical change in the North's consumer patterns and a decisive and broad-based movement towards energy conservation....

These facts are widely known, but the myth of catching-up development is still largely the basis of development policies of the governments of the North and the South, as well as the ex-socialist countries. A TV discussion in which three heads of state participated—Robert Mugabe of Zimbabwe, Vaclav Havel of the CSFR, and Richard von Weizsacker, President of the then FRG—is a clear illustration of this. The discussion took place after a showing of the film *The March,* which depicted millions of starving Africans trying to enter rich Europe. The President of the FRG said quite clearly that the consumption patterns of the 20 per cent of the world's population who live in the affluent societies of the industrialized North are using 80 per cent of the world's resources, and that these consumption patterns would, in the long run, destroy the natural foundations of life—worldwide. When, however, he was asked, if it was not then correct to criticize and relinquish the North's consumption patterns and to warn the South against imitating the North he replied that it would be wrong to preach to people about reducing consumption. Moreover, people in the South had the right to the same living standard as those in the North. The only solution was to distribute more of "our" wealth, through development aid, to the poor in the South, to enable them to "catch-up." He did not mention

that this wealth originated as a result of the North's plundering of the colonies, as has been noted.

The President of socialist Zimbabwe was even more explicit. He said that people in the South wanted as many cars, refrigerators, TV sets, computers, videos and the same standard of living as the people in the North; that this was the aim of his politics of development. Neither he nor von Weizsacker asked whether this policy of universalizing the North's consumption patterns through a catching-up strategy was materially feasible. They also failed to question the ecological consequences of such a policy. As elected heads of state they dared not tell the truth, namely that the lifestyle of the rich in the North cannot be universalized, and that it should be ended in these countries in order to uphold the values of an egalitarian world.

Despite these insights, however, the catching-up development myth remains intact in the erstwhile socialist countries of the East. Developments in East Germany, Poland and the ex-Soviet Union clearly demonstrate the resilience of this myth; but also the disaster that follows when the true nature of the "free" market economy becomes apparent. People in East Germany, the erstwhile GDR, were anxious to participate in the consumer model of capitalist FRG and, by voting for the destruction of their own state and the unification of Germany, hoped to become "equal." Political democracy, they were told, was the key to affluence. But they now realize, that in spite of political democracy and that they live in the same nation state as the West Germans, they are *de facto* treated as a cheap labour pool or a colony for West German capital, which is interested in expanding its market to the East but hesitates to invest there because the unification of Germany means that the East German workers will demand the same wages as their counterparts in West Germany. Where, then, is the incentive to go East? Less than a year after the unification, people in East Germany were already disappointed and depressed: unemployment had risen rapidly; the economy had virtually broken down; but no benefits had accrued from the new market system. According to the politicians, however, a period of common effort will be rewarded by catching-up with the West

Germans. And, inevitably, the women in East Germany are worst affected by these processes. They who formerly had a participation rate of 90 per cent in the labour force are the first to lose their jobs, and more rapidly than men; they form the bulk of the unemployed. Simultaneously, they are losing whatever benefits the socialist state had provided for them: creches, a liberal abortion law, job security as mothers, time off for child-care, and so on.

But due to their disappointment with the socialist system people do not, yet, understand that this is the normal functioning of capitalism; that it needs colonies for its expansionism, that even democracy and formal equality do not result automatically in an equal standard of living or equal economic rewards.

In East Germany, the anger and the disappointment about what people call their betrayal by West German politicians, particularly Chancellor Kohl, has been converted into hostility towards other minorities, ethnic and racial minorities, foreign workers, other East Europeans, all of whom wanted to enter the "European House" and sit at the table of the rich.

In other parts of the world the collapse of the catching-up development myth leads to waves of fundamentalism and nationalism directed against religious, ethnic, racial, "others" within and outside their own territory. The main target of both nationalism and fundamentalism, and communalism, is women, because religious, ethnic and cultural identity are always based on a patriarchy, a patriarchal image of women, or rather control over "our" women, which, as we know from many examples, almost always amounts to more violence against women, more inequality for women. Moreover, the collapse of the myth of catching-up development results in a further militarization of men. Practically all the new nationalisms and fundamentalisms have led to virtual civil war in which young, militarized men play the key role. As unacceptable as equals by the rich men's club and unable to share their lifestyle they can only show their manhood— as it is understood in a patriarchal world—by shouldering a machine-gun.

The myth of catching-up development, therefore, eventually leads to further destruction of the environment, further exploitation of the "Third World," further violence against women and further militarization of men.

DOES CATCHING-UP DEVELOPMENT LIBERATE WOMEN?

… But more specifically let us ask why, for women, the catching-up development path even in the affluent societies of the industrialized North, is and will remain an illusion.

1. The promises of freedom, equality, self-determination of the individual, the great values of the French Revolution, proclaimed as universal rights and hence also meant for women, are betrayed for many women because all these rights depend on the possession of property, and of money. Freedom is the freedom of those who possess money. Equality is the equality of money. Self-determination is the freedom of choice in the supermarket. This freedom, equality, self-determination is always dependent on those who control the money/property. And in the industrialized societies and nations they are mostly the husbands or the capitalists' state. This at least is the relationship between men and women that is protected by law; the man as breadwinner, the woman as housewife.

Self-determination and freedom are *de facto* limited for women, not only because they themselves are treated as commodities but also because, even if they possess money, they have no say in what is to be offered as commodities on the market. Their own desires and needs are constantly manipulated by those whose aim is to sell more and more goods. Ultimately, women are also persuaded that they want what the market offers.

2. This freedom, equality and self-determination, which depend on the possession of money, on purchasing power, cannot be extended to all women in the world. In Europe or the USA the system may be able to fulfil some of women's demand for equity with men, as far as income and jobs are concerned (or wages for housework, or a guaranteed minimum income), but only as long as it can

continue the unrestricted exploitation of women as producers and consumers in the colonies. It cannot guarantee to *all* women worldwide the same standard of living as that of middle-class women in the USA or Europe. Only while women in Asia, Africa or Latin America can be forced to work for much lower wages than those in the affluent societies—and this is made possible through the debt trap—can enough capital be accumulated in the rich countries so that even unemployed women are guaranteed a minimum income, but all unemployed women in the world cannot expect this. Within a world system based on exploitation, "some are more equal than others."

3. This, however, also means that with such a structure there is no real material base for international women's solidarity. Because the core of individual freedom, equality, self-determination, linked to money and property, is the *self-interest of the individual* and not altruism or solidarity; these interests will always compete with the self-interests of others. Within an exploitative structure interests will necessarily be antagonistic. It may be in the interest of Third World women, working in the garment industry for export, to get higher wages, or even wages equivalent to those paid in the industrialized countries; but if they actually received these wages then the working-class woman in the North could hardly afford to buy those garments, or buy as many of them as she does now. In her interest the price of these garments must remain low. Hence the interests of these two sets of women who are linked through the world market are antagonistic. If we do not want to abandon the aim of international solidarity and equality we must abandon the materialistic and self-centred approach to fighting only for our own interests. The interests' approach must be replaced by an ethical one.

4. To apply the principle of self-interest to the ecological problem leads to intensified ecological degradation and destruction in other parts of the world. This became evident after Chernobyl, when many women in Germany, desperate to know what to feed to their babies demanded the importation of unpolluted food from the Third World. One example of this is the poisoning of mothers' milk in the affluent countries by DDT and other toxic substances as a result of the heavy use of fertilizers, pesticides and insecticides in industrialized agriculture. Rachel Carson had already warned that poisoning the soil would eventually have its effect on people's food, particularly mothers' milk; now that this has happened many women in the North are alarmed. Some time ago a woman phoned me and said that in Germany it was no longer safe to breastfeed a baby for longer than three months; mothers' milk was poisoned. As a solution she suggested starting a project in South India for the production of safe and wholesome baby food. There, on the dry and arid Deccan Plateau, a special millet grows, called *ragi*. It needs little water and no fertilizer and is poor people's cheap subsistence food. This millet contains all the nutrients an infant needs. The woman suggested that ragi should be processed and canned as baby food and exported to Germany. This, she said, would solve the problem of desperate mothers whose breast milk is poisoned and give the poor in South India a new source of money income. It would contribute to their development!

I tried to explain that if ragi, the subsistence food of the poor, entered the world market and became an export commodity it would no longer be available for the poor; its price would soar and that, provided the project worked, pesticides and other chemicals would soon be used to produce more ragi for the market in the North. But ragi production, she answered, would have to be controlled by people who would guarantee it was not polluted. This amounts to a new version of eco-colonialism. When I asked her, why as an alternative, she would not rather campaign in Germany for a change in the industrialized agriculture, for a ban on the use of pesticides, she said that this would take too much time, that the poisoning of mothers' milk was an emergency situation. In her anxiety and concerned only with the interests of mothers in Germany she was willing to sacrifice the interests of poor women in South India. Or rather she thought that these conflicting interests could be made compatible by an exchange of money. She did not realize that this money would never suffice to buy the same healthy food for

South Indian women's infants that they now had free of cost.

This example clearly shows that the myth of catching-up development, based on the belief of the miraculous workings of the market, particularly the world market, in fact leads to antagonistic interests even of mothers, who want only to give their infants unpolluted food.

STUDY QUESTIONS

1. Explain why Mies thinks the catch-up policy is a myth—both impossible and undesirable to obtain.

2. Evaluate the strength of Mies' arguments. Why are catch-up policies ill-conceived? Is it morally wrong for poor countries to seek a higher standard of living?

3. What is Mies' alternative to catch-up policies? Do you agree with her? Explain your answer.

53

Environmental Risks, Rights, and the Failure of Liberal Democracy: Some Possible Remedies

LAURA WESTRA

A brief biography of Laura Westra appears at the beginning of Reading 58.

In this article, Westra argues that democracies are failing to come to grips with environmental degradation. Traditional interpretations of rights, especially those of Judith Jarvis Thomson, fail to recognize the legitimate right not to be put at undue risk. Westra argues that this right can be defended and that political leaders must go beyond democracy in enforcing it. A rational risk response may require political activity that is revolutionary.

If you only have procedural democracy in a society that's exhibiting internal environmental stress and already has cleavages, say, ethnic cleavages, then procedural democracy will tend to aggravate these problems and produce societal discord, rather than social concord.

THOMASHOMER-DIXON, 1996

DEMOCRACY IS NOT ENOUGH

The list of environmental assaults on the physical integrity of ecosystems and, through them, on our physical integrity and capacities occurs equally in affluent countries of North America and Western Europe and in developing ones of Southeast Asia. The global distribution of the threats, from remote islands in the Pacific Ocean (Colborn, Dumanoski, and Myers 1996) to "pristine" areas in the Arctic (Colborn 1996; Nikiforuk, 1996), demonstrate that geographic and political boundaries are not capable of containing and limiting environmental degradation and disintegrity. A careful study of the "hot spots" and locations where the worst hazards persist, shows that they are equally global in distribution. We cannot separate democracies from—say—military regimes and other nondemocratic states on the basis of the spread and severity of the environmental threats to which their citizens are exposed.

The "toxic doughnut" area in Chicago is a persistent threat to the life and health of residents (Gaylord and Bell 1995), although it is located in a country that prides itself on its status as the "land of the free" and that routinely allows its leaders and politicians to praise its democratic institutions, in contrast with other undesirable forms of government the world over. Equally hazardous, Royal Dutch Shell Oil's operation in Ogoniland, Nigeria, uses the dictatorship of General Sani Abbacha and his military clique to enforce the acceptance of extreme health hazards on its citizens. Of course, those who oppose these hazardous corporate activities in Nigeria are brutally and violently repressed or murdered, while the Chicago residents are not.

The U.S. residents, primarily minorities in most large cities (Westra and Wenz 1995; Bullard 1994), are not imprisoned or executed, and the army is not sent in to restrain and eliminate their protests. In some sense, their plight is therefore "better": They only suffer the physical harms imposed upon them by others, and their life and health are slowly, insidiously attacked and diminished. They only suffer from "ecoviolence"; they are not imprisoned and executed if they protest, as they might have been in Nigeria. But, in some sense, their plight is even worse. Ostensibly possessed of civil rights, basic education, access to information, and constitutional guarantees about freedom of choice, life, and the pursuit of happiness, they are manipulated instead to contribute willingly (but unknowingly) to their own plight. Aggressive advertising and marketing techniques render the products of modern technology not only extremely desirable but also "necessary" as things everyone should have—"free choices," though their corporate sponsors and originators employ "trade secret" and other hard-won rules and regulations to protect themselves while keeping citizens in the dark about the effects and consequences of their choices.

At the same time, public relation (PR) departments work steadily so that questions about the risks and harms imposed, and whether they are and should be truly offset by the so-called benefits available, are raised as rarely as possible. Further, as David Korten shows, two other severe problems arise in connection with the pursuit of economic gain through techno-corporate activities. The first is a clear attack on democracy, as independent PR firms are hired at great cost to generate "public movements" and campaigns, with the double aim of "selling" their ideas and preparing the public to accept and actively pursue certain products and services. The second problem is that legislative modifications, regulations, or deregulations favorable to business, are also sought.

The result of these activities is that "free democratic choices" are neither truly free nor truly democratic. Korten (1995) cites Washington journalist William Greider:

> [The corporations'] ... tremendous financial resources, the diversity of their interests, the squads of talented professionals—all these assets and some others—are now relentlessly focused on the politics of governing. This new institutional reality is the centerpiece in the breakdown of contemporary democracy. Corporations exist to pursue their own profit maximization, not the collective aspirations of the Society.

The problem is embedded in democracy in two senses:

1. Corporations are taken to be fictitious legal persons (French 1984) and are free to pursue their aims unless it can be proven (in the legal sense) that some citizen or citizens are directly harmed by their chosen activities. Further, there is no overarching conception of "the good" for all that can be contrasted with *their* perception of the good, which is economic rather than intellectual or spiritual.

2. Moreover, because there is no "good" to guide public policy, aside from aggregate choices and preferences, and because the latter can be and in fact often is routinely manipulated and underinformed, the myth of "one man/one vote" remains a vague ideal, not a reality.

The justification often proposed to counterbalance these negative impacts centers on the "economic advantages" provided by multinational corporate giants. But, as we indicated in the Chicago example, the economic advantage is not evenly distributed or fairly apportioned among rich and poor: Moreover, if we shift to the global scene, even economic advances depend on "relative" rather than on "absolute" income. The Bruntlandt commission proposed a "3% global increase in per capita income." That would translate into a first-year per-capita increase (in U.S. dollars) of $633 for the United States and, among others, $3.60 for Ethiopia. After 10 years, the respective figures would be $7,257 for the United States and $41 for Ethiopia: a vast advantage for the "haves" over the "have nots." Korten (1995) adds, "This advantage becomes a life-and-death issue in a resource-scarce world in which the rich and the poor are locked in mortal competition for a depleting resource base" (see also Homer-Dixon 1994).

Objections may be raised about such polarized descriptions of corporate activities. For instance, David Crocker believes that "demonizing" corporations is philosophically fallacious and practically incorrect because many corporations are "good" and seek to support and implement the common good in their activities (Crocker, personal communication, 1996). This objection, however, is open to a counterobjection. The main point at issue is not that this or that corporation is "bad" and needs to be stopped, but that Western democracies and their institutions appear to have no mechanism available, at this time, to protect the public from hazards and harms, many of which are—in part—self-inflicted under conditions of public misinformation and manipulation.

In this case, to say that there is no need to institute radical changes and to implement a system of criminal charges against the corporate risk imposers is like saying that, because many of us are generally decent people who do not view physical assaults and murder as acceptable activities, there is no need for strong laws and sanctions about these crimes. Leaving the choice to either engage in harmful activities or not, within the ambit of the present loose regulative structures and unrealistic legal criteria (Brown and Lemons 1995), to corporate goodwill of individual firms is to support tacitly the status quo, thereby becoming accomplices to the crimes perpetrated.

So far, this work has addressed the operation of legitimate business, registered, licensed and—to some extent—regulated. This sort of business is global in scope, but even licenses and regulations tend to lose their force when they reach national borders. And what about business that is neither regulated, licensed, nor even *known* as such to any nation or state? The "shadow economy," as Ed Ayres (1996) terms it, represents an additional pervasive global threat. We used to think of some of those "business" activities or of their concomitant effects as "externalities" and think of others as "anomalies." Ayres says:

> These are untaxed, unregulated, unsanctioned and—often—unseen. Most of them are things we've heard about but only fleetingly; we think of them as anomalies, rather than as serious or systemic threats to our mainframe institutions. They range from black markets in illicit drugs, cheap weapons,

endangered wildlife, toxic waste, or ozone-depleting chemicals, to grey markets in unlisted securities or unapproved treatment for cancer.

Activities that fall under the heading of "shadow economy" include subsistence agricultural workers and those in other "unregistered occupations"—illegal industries, but also the work of "unlocated populations" such as migrants and refugees; it also includes "nonlocated activity" such as that arising from "electronic exchanges." Ayres (1996) lists the "three largest industries in the world" as (1) the military ($800 billion), (2) illicit drugs ($500 billion), and (3) oil ($450 billion). All three have a "shadow" side (1 and 3) or are entirely illegitimate (2). All three are among the most hazardous activities in the world because, aside from the individual hazards they involve or represent, they are in *principle* beyond the control of society in various ways.

The solution Ayres proposes might be the right one for all forms of techno-corporate enterprise. Neither national nor international databases carry accurate information about the shadow economy, hence, in the face of global threats, Ayres suggests that the "old geopolitical maps" are obsolete. Because borders no longer function as they were intended to do, because they have become impotent to contain benign and hazardous activities alike, the present maps should be superimposed with a "new kind of map"is, with "maps illuminating the kinds of phenomena that now count most: the watersheds, bioregions, climatic zones and migratory routes that are essential to the security of all future economies" (Ayres 1996).

For both the legitimate and the shadow economy, it is necessary to understand the essential nature of ecological and climate functions and related global threats. It is equally necessary for all of us to understand the natural functions of natural systems and the relation between the products we buy and these systems.

For these reasons, I propose a reexamination of environmental risks and harms from the standpoint of the ethics of integrity (Westra 1994a). I will argue that a proliferation of individual and aggregate

rights is undesirable from the environmental point of view (and this has been argued here as well, in support of limits for corporate rights). Still, the right to life, health, and personal physical integrity appear to be primary and worthy of strong support. Moreover, the latter is necessarily embedded in ecosystem integrity, as Holmes Rolston argues (Rolston 1996; Westra 1995a).

In the next section, I consider some examples of the recent literature on the topic of risks and harms, in order to place the integrity argument in context.

RISKS AND HARMS; RIGHTS AND CONSENT

In her book *The Realm of Rights,* Judith Jarvis Thomson (1990) argues that "we do not have a claim against *merely being put at risk of harm*" and that we ought to reject what she terms the "risk thesis"—that is, the thesis that "we have claims against others that they not impose risks of harm on us." In contrast, Anthony Ellis (1995) argues that the risk thesis can be defended despite Thomson's condemnation. I will argue that his position is essentially correct and that Thomson's difficulties in drawing the line between risk and harm, for instance, is no sound reason to reject the thesis, particularly in the face of diffuse global threats, which prompted the recent acceptance of a "precautionary principle" (Brown and Lemons 1995). I will also argue that, although democracy is taken to be the form of government that is the best supporter and defender of human rights, it is precisely the unquestioned acceptance of the primacy of democratic institutions that presents the major obstacle to the prevention of public harms, particularly environmentally induced risks to public health.

Hence, the problematic interface between rights, democratic institutions, and health risks needs to be reexamined because the public interest in this respect may not be best supported by democratic choices without further controls. I will propose an argument based on an analogy with biomedical ethics and the moral and legal status of "quarantines" in response to disease-engendered public health threats. If, contrary to Thomson's opinion, *we* have the right not to be "put at risk of harm," then we need to find the best way of reaching public-policy decisions that will ensure our rights will not be infringed. Notwithstanding the close links between civil rights and democracy, on both practical and theoretical grounds, democratic practices appear insufficient to protect us from endangerment caused by the reckless practices of individuals and corporate citizens. Throughout this discussion and for the purposes of this work, *liberal democracy* and *democracy* will refer to the form of democracy we can observe implemented in North America and in Western European nations. I will not enter into the debate about the various ideological variants present in the constitutions and institutions of democratic states, because my argument is concerned with the real consequences of democracy as it is practiced in North America and Western Europe.

Environmental risks and *environmental harms* in this section will be compared to such "harms" as exposure to contagious diseases. The environmental harms considered will be those that impose threats of grave physical injury to human health: They are the *indirect* counterparts of the *direct* harms arising from exposure to contagious diseases. The environmental threats considered will be those that seriously affect life-support systems that we depend on in various ways. For example, even a noncatastrophic event like the elimination of earthworms and other biomass in the soils at an agricultural location may be a contributing factor to hazardous floods, particularly in conjunction with climatic changes. The latter are also fostered and magnified by environmental degradation (e.g., ozone-layer and deforestation problems). Although at times local environmental hazards may be contained so that the functioning of the system or the human health in the area wherein they occur, may not be affected, the onus to prove that this is the case should be on the would-be polluter. In general, the repeated occurrences of seemingly small and localized threats lead to system failure and global health threats.

It may seem that precise comparison with health threats may not be possible. But one might argue that a combination of infectious diseases, malnutrition, some organ malfunction, and the lack of local hygiene, when occurring jointly to someone in a developing country, may also render the combination a lethal threat, despite the fact that each problem might be curable or open to some solution in itself. Hence, for the environmental threats that pose, singly or jointly, an indirect but severe threat to our health, the analogy with health-care issues seems an apt one from several standpoints:

1. The magnitude and gravity of the threats
2. The lack of specific intentions to harm on the part of those who endanger us
3. The lack of intention to inflict harm on specific individuals
4. The necessity to restrain individual freedoms (on the part of risk imposers), although neither "punishment" nor "retribution" may be appropriate conceptual categories to define the restraints imposed
5. The lack of precise proofs of either direct "guilt" or even of specific "harm" inflicted.

These difficulties are common to environmentally induced harms as well as health endangerments, despite the many differences between the two fields.

Finally, I will argue against the common assumption that consent to certain institutionally approved practices and corporate activities entails the consent to all possible "side effects," including consent to be put at risk of harm. Even though we might derive some individual and collective benefits from those activities, it can be argued that consent to be harmed cannot be given, on moral grounds.

Risks, Harms, and Consent

From a moral (Kantian) point of view, we can argue against consent to harm, as long as *harm* is understood in the physical sense, not simply in the sense of being wronged or not getting one's due (Simmons 1979). But the claim that somehow embracing the lifestyle existing in affluent countries

entails giving "tacit consent" to the bad consequences accompanying that way of life needs to
be examined from the standpoint of political theory
as well. Tacit consent, in the context of one's political obligation to governmental institutions, may
not be assumed simply because we are silent or
because we do not protest.

A. John Simmons (1979) argues that, although
"consent is called tacit when it is given by remaining
silent and inactive …," it must be expressed "by the
failure to do certain things" when a certain response is
required to signify disagreement. Unless this sequence
characterizes it, the "tacit consent" may simply represent "(1) a failure to grasp the nature of the situation,
(2) a lack of understanding of proper procedures, or
(3) a misunderstanding about how long one has to
decide whether or not to dissent" (Simmons 1979).

Another possibility may be that a simple failure
of communications has occurred. Thus, the conditions needed to establish the presence of tacit consent eliminate the possibility of simple, nonspecific
voting in favor of some political institutions, without the particularity required for explicit consent
to the hazardous practices in question. After citing
the problems inherent in John Locke's position on
this question, Simmons (1979) adds "calling consent
'tacit' on my account, specifies its mode of expression, not its lack of expression." Locke, Simmons
argues, was confused about "acts of enjoyment" in
one's country, such as enjoying public highways,
police protection, and the like as "signs of consent"
instead. Because of this confusion, Locke believed
that one gave tacit consent to one's government
simply because one used (and enjoyed) a country's
amenities. If the same argument is applied here—
that is, that enjoying some features of a system implies tacit consent for the system *in toto,* in all its
activities including hazardous ones—then those
who argue that by enjoying certain features of our
modern, Western, technological lifestyle, we thereby
give consent to any and all "side effects" that ensue
might have a good point. However, they do not
because this position is as "confused" as that of
Locke's, Simmons (1979) argues.

Moreover, there are certain things to which we
cannot consent in our social and political life.

Enslavement is a clear example. Humans are created
free and only acquire the obligation of a nation's
citizen through consent (explicit). But, although
consent is a powerful tool in general, its power
does not extend to relinquishing one's "inalienable"
rights, such as the right to life or to freedom itself:
The right to self-defense cannot be abdicated. Thomas
Hobbes (1958) says, "A man cannot lay down the
right of resisting them that assault him by force to
take away his life." Simmons (1979) says that Kant
argues for a similar position as well:

> Kant holds that "no contract could put a
> man into the class of domestic animals
> which we use at will for any kind of
> service"; that is because "every man has
> inalienable rights which he cannot give up
> even if he would."

Kant holds human life to have infinite value, and
he believes that humans cannot affect (or permit
others to affect) their physical integrity for any advantage or any other consideration. Hence, it may be
argued that the human rights representing and supporting these inalienable human goods—such as life,
freedom, and physical integrity—cannot be transferred or set aside, even if *explicit (tacit)* consent were
present. In this case, there is a solid historical and
theoretical basis for the somewhat novel position I
have advanced in support of criminalizing those activities that represent an attack on our physical being.

To be sure, it is permissible and not immoral
to trade off some of our freedom in exchange for
wages, provided that respect for our humanity is
present in the transaction, or for a great common
ideal (say, the defense of our common freedom
from enslavement), or to engage in warfare, that
is, in a potentially lethal activity (in our country's
defense). Not all cases are so clear-cut that they
evidently fall either in one camp (of permissible
activities) or in the other (of activities that represent
an immoral trade-off) as some, or perhaps even all
workplace activities normally entail at least some
risk of harm. Even a philosophy professor who
must drive her car, or walk to her teaching institution, exposes herself to some risk of traffic mishaps.
If she were to remain at home and teach from her

house, those risks would be avoided. But inactivity and a sedentary lifestyle are at least as hazardous to one's health as well.

We must keep in mind that the public-health threats considered here, whether they are directly posed by environmental conditions or indirectly caused by circumstances due to environmental dis-integrity and degradation, are the sort of severe threats epidemiologists document (McMichael 1995); they are not the occasional or possible chance happen-ings one may encounter in the circumstances out-lined in the previous paragraph. The health threats I have in mind are of three kinds:

1. Threats that seriously impair our natural capa-bilities (e.g., changes in our normal reproductive, intellectual, emotional, or immune systems).

2. Threats that pose an imminent danger of death to individuals or groups.

3. Threats that include long-term, delayed, and mutagenic effects: Like the reproductive effects in item 1, there are threats to *our species*, as well as to the affected individuals.

The effects named under these three headings have an undeniable negative impact on our rights, both human and legal, and we consider these fur-ther below in order to understand why the risk thesis should be rejected.

Risks, Harms, and Rights

W. N. Hohfeld (1923) described four forms of legal rights: (1) claim rights, (2) rights as privilege or lib-erty, (3) rights as power, and (4) rights as immunity. It is primarily the last form that concerns us, although where immunity rights are present, claim rights or liberty rights, for instance, may be present as well.

Hohfeld's discussion is primarily intended to clarify the meaning and scope of various judicial terms in common use and their relation to one an-other in order to understand the "deeper unity" present in the law: "In short the deeper the analysis, the greater becomes one's perception of fundamen-tal unity and harmony in the law" (Hohfeld 1923). When we turn to his discussion of "immunities,"

both the cases and the examples he cites show that the concept may not be the most appropriate for our purpose. In a section on "Immunities and Disabilities," he says:

> A right is one's affirmative claim against another, and a privilege is one's freedom from the right or claim of another. Similarly, a power is one's affirmative "control" over a given legal relation as against another, whereas an *immunity* [my italics] is one's freedom from the legal power or "control" of another, as regards some legal relation. (Hohfeld 1923)

As an example of immunity, Hohfeld cites "ex-emption from taxation" as a better and more accu-rate term than "privilege." Hence, the meaning he proposes appears somewhat different from a con-cept used to refer to the right to the freedom from bodily harm. A better way to introduce the sort of "right" appropriate to our argument may be one of the personal rights, that is, the "rights of bodily safety and freedom." Hohfeld adds that it is "the duty of all of us not to interfere with our neighbors' lawful freedom." This is one of the primitive rights; it may also be termed "the right not to be interfered with" (Hohfeld 1923).

Thomson accepts the Hohfeldian framework, which includes the correlativity between rights and duties, but she rejects the risk thesis, as stated at the outset. She may base her rejection on the problem of "thresholds" and question the limits of both probability and gravity of harms as factors of the risk thesis (DeCew 1995). As Thomson rightly argues, it is problematic to identify *the* harm in many cases. She offers an example. A log left on a highway may well present a risk of harm to some-one, but we have no certainty that a harm will happen to someone and no information about the possible gravity of such a harm. We can begin here to note the parallel between the example she offers of a log left on a highway (Thomson 1990; Ellis 1995), and that of risky environmental exposures or changes. She notes that we cannot be sure of several points, and that affects our acceptance of the risk the-sis. These uncertainties are primarily (1) who is likely to be passing by and tripping over the log and (2) the precise harm such person or persons may incur, since these may range from very minor to quite grave depending on circumstances. We might envision icy road conditions and an elderly "tripper" or, at the other extreme, a clear, empty roadway and an athletic young person who would quickly get up with little or no harm.

In the case of environmental harms, we need not specify or prove that process X producing substance Y has actually harmed someone, before claiming that corporation Z (by engaging in process X) is liable, through Y, for the harm produced, if we accept the risk thesis. This represents the major current problem for those who are harmed: The required "proof" of harm is often unavailable, unclear, or delayed. The problems of environmental harm lie in (1) science's lack of predictive capacities; (2) the synergistic and cumulative effects of other contributory causes to the harm; (3) the lack of sustained research to sufficiently support item 2; (4) the accelerated introduction of substances, products, and processes, which further reduces the availability of research (as in item 3); (5) the difficulty of establishing clear thresholds, in the face of items 1–3; (6) the existence of harms, the effects of which develop and manifest themselves slowly over time (e.g., cancers). And this list, lengthy as it is, may only represent a partial list addressing only presently acknowledged problems (Shrader-Frechette 1991; T. Colborn et al. 1996).

However, both Ellis and Thomson agree on one issue: If an agreed-on threshold of harm is reached, then the risk violates a right. The difficulties listed above (1–6) show clearly how hard it is to draw a precise dividing line between a risk of harm that is plausible or probable and one that is not. Separating a minor harm from a significant one is equally difficult. It is also hard to indicate who specifically is "put at risk." In fact, from an environmental point of view, the level of harm inflicted may vary. For instance, a fetus, pregnant women, and older people may all encounter a greater risk than adult males from exposure to the same substance(s). It is equally impossible to specify who precisely may be at risk because some environmental hazards cause harms far from the location from where they occurred.

An example of the latter can be found in some of the recent cholera pandemics. Rita Colwell (1996) showed the connection between environmental degradation (engendered by such practices as deforestation, for instance), global climatic changes, ocean warming, the extraordinary growth of plankton in the oceans, and the way the latter fosters the spread of the *E. coli* bacterium from one continent to the other: "Cholera offers an excellent example of how greater understanding of environmental factors allows us to understand the disease better, not only its virulence but … its transmission and epidemiology." In this case, it would not be possible to point to *one* perpetrator, at *one* location, much less to designate specific persons as victims. Anthony Ellis (1995) argues one aspect of these issues, in response to Thomson:

> It is merely that it is indeterminate who is put at risk. If this simply means that it is hard, perhaps impossible, to find out who is put at risk, this is true, but irrelevant. If I illegitimately drop a bomb on a city, and it is impossible to determine whom, exactly, I killed, this does not imply that I did not violate anyone's rights; I violated the rights of all those I killed, whoever they may have been.

Other conceptual problems may include the following: (1) Too many people may have claims against those who impose risks; (2) the risk exposure may not actually cause harm (i.e., I dropped the bomb, but everyone was safe in an air shelter); (3) such a thesis may commit us to "absurd consequences"—for example, the consequence that "every time you drive your automobile you violate the rights of all those whom you put at risk, no matter how small the risk" (Ellis 1995). Finally, Ellis adds, we could reject such objections as the last one, by saying that "permission, in a democratic society, has been obtained in advance."

This, of course, is the crux of the problem, from the point of view of environmental hazards. Does living in a democracy, even in a Western industrialized country, with the lifestyle common to our society, mean giving *implicit* consent to risk exposure, or to the abandonment of our rights to security from harm? It does not mean giving tacit consent, as shown in our earlier discussion. Most arguments against tacit consent also show that some rights may not be relinquished, not to one's legitimate government (except in special cases, such as self-defense on behalf of one's own country, for instance; or perhaps to save another's life through a kidney donation). It is certainly immoral and impermissible to do so for economic advancement, even for one's own economic benefit. Implausible though such a thesis may be, Ellis raises it as a question, and it is often implicit and assumed in business ethics literature (Friedman 1993), with the common understanding of many who take for granted that "hazards" (unspecified) are the price one pays for technologic advances and, in general, for modern progress (Mesthene 1990; Winner 1977).

RISKS, RIGHTS, AND DEMOCRACY

John Rawls (1993) has argued that a "law of peoples" can be drawn from his theory of justice, and that a "social contract doctrine is universal in its reach." He also argued that both are not only compatible with but also dependent on a doctrine of human rights because these represent an integral part of a society's "common good conception of justice." The law in such societies must "at least uphold such basic rights as the right to life and security, to personal property, and elements of the rule of law …" (Rawls 1993). For our purpose, the most important element mentioned here is the "right to life and security." The Canadian Charter of Rights refers to this as "the right to life and the security of persons." According to Rawls, it might seem that both human and civil rights could be supported and in fact identified with the practices and the ideals of democratic institutions. Yet in Western democracies as well as in less developed countries, it does not appear that environmental hazards and risks have been controlled or eliminated on the basis of general human rights to freedom from harm.

It is important to understand why this is so, and a good place to start is by considering a situation where democracy, civil rights, and due process are invoked in order to demonstrate the "right" way to deal with the hazards of technology transfers to third world countries. After listing statistics about deaths related to a chemical industry's operation and marketing, Kristin Shrader-Frechette (1991) argues that corporations "have an obligation to guarantee equal protection from risk across national boundaries" rather than employ what she terms the "isolationist strategy." Corporations cannot restrict their moral and legal restraints to the activities they practice in the country of origin. Yet Shrader-Frechette admits that, "indeed, a rational risk response may require political activity that is nothing less than revolutionary." But at this time, both those in developing countries and those in minority communities in Western democracies are treated in ways that infringe their rights: Both are often "isolated" from moral consideration (Westra 1995a).

The problem is that there is no proof of intent to harm on the part of corporations or other institutions involved in these practices. In fact, if questioned, they may respond with several arguments in support of their activities. These are (1) the "social progress argument," (2) the "countervailing benefit argument," (3) "the consent argument," and (4) the "reasonable-possibility argument" (Shrader-Frechette 1991). But (1) only works if we accept the subordination of individual and group rights to some (unproven) consequentialist "good" such as "progress," a doubtful notion as it stands because of the gravity of its side effects. The next argument (2) is problematic as well: Even benefits ought not to be promoted at any cost. Shrader-Frechette (1991) says, "The argument is that a bloody loaf of bread is sometimes better than no loaf at all, that a dangerous job is preferable to no job, and that food riddled with pesticides banned is better than no food at all."

This argument is hard to defend even on utilitarian grounds, and it is impossible to support on Kantian grounds and from the standpoint of human rights. The "consent argument" (3) has been discussed and will be discussed in detail in the next section. For now, it is sufficient to note that the "free, informed consent" to which corporations appeal in defense of their limited responsibility is seldom, if ever, available from those who are "financially strapped and poorly educated." The final argument (4) suggests that risks and harms imposed are not preventable without "heroic" commitments that cannot in fairness be demanded of any corporation. But if there are human rights such as the right to the nonimposition of cancer (Gewirth 1983), then it is not heroism that is required but the simple adherence to morality.

So far, only physical, quantifiable harms have been discussed, without even envisaging the possibility of "social" or "group harms" (Simon 1995). The implication of this discussion? It is necessary though not sufficient to introduce democratic procedures and due process, globally, in order to attempt to prevent the unjust imposition of harms on the vulnerable and the disempowered. Rawls (1993) also argues for the extension of constructivist principles for justice as fairness, for "the basic structure of a closed and self-contained democratic society," to extend the ideal of justice and human rights through a "law of people." His starting point is the democratic, liberal society where he supports the "egalitarian features of the fair value of political liberties, of fair equality of opportunity, and of the difference principle." On the basis of this extension, he indicates the existence of respect for human rights and views it as a *condition* for admitting any country or national state to participate in the "law of nations." These are viewed as bedrock of any conception of justice, extended, as it were, from the starting point of appropriate basic principles within a self-contained democracy. I now turn to an examination of the real import of democracy when we consider risks and harms.

Democracy entails that collective decisions be based on open acceptance of certain choices and preferences over others and that these choices be reached through majority votes. But even in the countries where democratic systems are in power, it appears that the system is powerless to prevent the infringement of human rights through the imposition of harms to human life and health, at least through environmental means. Why does this happen? First, it is clear that democracy tends to further "the

interests of the majority at the expense of the minority" (Gilbert 1995). Second, and even harder to address, is the fact that in the face of global hazards that affect everyone on Earth, there are still limits to the reach of democratic powers. For instance, in border issues that often give rise to violent conflicts, democracy is powerless because citizens on either side of the disputed border can only vote within the limits of their national area (Gilbert 1995; Westra 1994a). Further, the immense power of Western multinational corporations, which represent the source of many of these hazards, is not subject to democratic decision making, either in their country of origin or in the (less developed) host countries (Westra 1994b; Korten 1995; Donaldson 1993).

Hence, self-contained democracies are not sufficient to mitigate these risks, and it seems urgent to establish respect and accept a risk thesis that would serve to link more clearly the existence of hazardous products and practices and the clear duties of all not to infringe upon the rights to "life and security of persons," through a "law of peoples" (Rawls 1993). This would help not only those who belong to the same community and are part of the same democratic nation but also all those who might be affected by these risks anywhere else.

Yet it is unclear just how democratic systems, even if globally implemented, would help solve the problem. Now it may make sense to say that a minority who lost out on its *political* choice must, under a democracy's rule, learn to live with its loss since it occurred through fair means and a fair opportunity to change the situation exists for the future. But it would be much harder to say that all those whose preference was not on the winning side must be equally stoic in the face of unchosen, unconsented, and uncompensated harms, which a majority chose to impose upon them (Westra 1995a). As Gewirth (1983) would argue, the imposition of grave harms cannot be supported on moral grounds because it constitutes a gross infringement of human rights.

Hence, we can drive a wedge between democratic political systems and the absolute support of human rights through a reconsideration of the imposition of risks and harms. Rex Martin discusses the relation between democracy and rights in the *System of Rights* (1993), and he argues that civil rights should have priority status: "In sum, the priority of civil rights holds over aggregative considerations insofar as those considerations concern policies for civil rights directly, or concern such rights in relation to other social policy matters." Martin's argument is that, in a system of rights, "External checks over and beyond those afforded by the representative principle are required to keep majority rule from mischief. ..." Martin (1993) admits, "... representative democracy has some tendencies to the same abuse (as 'class-interested majority rule'), and therefore needs additional controls."

The example we considered earlier—of hazardous technology transfers to impoverished, uninformed, and unconsenting third world people—showed a case where the input of moral theories, utilities rights, and justice was deemed necessary to redress the injustices perpetrated because of the lack of due process and democratic procedures in those countries (Shrader-Frechette 1991). But the question now is not whether the consideration of these moral theories is necessary but whether the input of democracy is *sufficient* to ensure the presence of those moral considerations, especially the primacy of individual and group rights. The main problems with democracy seem to arise in connection with consent to the risk of harm. Should a majority have the right to consent, through their vote, to practices and activities that might impose the risk of harm upon defeated minorities? And even if we should answer this question in the affirmative, does anybody—whether in a majority or minority position within a democracy—have the right to consent even to their own harm? Both these questions need to be discussed. Speaking of environmental justice, Wigley and Shrader-Frechette (1995) say, "The doctrine of free informed consent, an important part of the traditional American value system, likewise provides a foundation for environmental justice." In this context, they proceed to analyze the concept of informed consent in the context of biomedical ethics, noting that the concept has not been used in either environmental or technological ethics. The following four criteria are suggested

to indicate the presence of informed consent: "... The risk imposers must disclose full information about the threat; potential victims must be competent to evaluate it; they must understand the danger; and they must voluntarily accept it" (Wigley and Shrader-Frechette 1995).

In the light of our earlier discussion of democratic choices and of the lack of precision in both scientific information about specific harmful effects and of the possible geographic spread of risks, several other questions may be raised. One question might be: How and from whom should consent be sought? Another problem might be: Even if we could circumscribe a specific area where all inhabitants could be polled on such a question, the provided information may not be sufficient to guarantee that the four criteria are met, as Franz Ingelfinger, for instance, argues in "Informed (but Uneducated) Consent" (1991). The doctrine of informed consent in the biomedical setting is intended to be directed at the interaction between health-care provider and one patient or, at most, a group of patients. Hence, the consent criteria cannot be readily applied to great numbers of people from whom the risk imposers are separated by geographic location, language, cultural background, and the like.

But in that case, the imposition of wide-ranging environmental risks and harms does not fit the informed-consent model because it is more like experimentation on unconsenting subjects, contrary to the Nuremberg Code (1948). The problem is that often grave environmental hazards are, by their very nature, impossible to contain.

So far, I have argued that, unless we deal with such specifics as environmental justice at a certain location, for instance, the consent criteria cannot properly be applied. But even this argument assumes that, at least in theory and in principle, people can consent to harms, provided that they are free to choose, fully informed, and that they understand the full extent of the harm to which they are exposed. But this belief is not beyond critique. For instance, we *can* object on Kantian grounds to this assumption. Moral action implies universalizability and reversibility, and it precludes the use of any autonomous person as means to anyone's ends, even their own. Hence, as it would be impermissible, on Kantian grounds, to commit suicide even for our own "good" (e.g., for the cessation of terminal, excruciating pain); so too, it would be impermissible to accept trade-offs, such as consent to cancer risks, to obtain a hazardous job. Hence, it can be argued that

> The Categorical Imperative is formulated in such a way that consent can never be relevant in informing us of what our duties to others are. Thus one is precluded from even entertaining the notion that consent would be a defeasibility condition of the Categorical Imperative. (Barnes 1996)

Although Kant's position that suicide is immoral is controversial, it is undoubtedly and clearly his position. Kant is somewhat closer to the present-day thought on not using any part of ourselves as means, even for a personally desired end. Kant is quite explicit on this point: We *cannot* consent to sales or trade-offs that would turn autonomous humans into slaves, for instance, or that might foster the exchange of bodily parts for money (Kant 1979). Hence, we can conclude that consent to harms is based on weak arguments both from the standpoint of political theory and from that of Kant's moral doctrine.

Moreover, it can also be claimed that, in general, utilitarian arguments should be considered only *after* human rights and justice principles. In that case, if consent to harm is not possible in principle, or if it is questionable even if obtained, then the introduction of truly democratic conditions and due process will not be sufficient to mitigate, let alone justify, the wide-ranging imposition of risks and harms on large numbers of unspecified persons, through environmental means. In sum, I have argued that we should accept, as Ellis suggests, the risk thesis Thomson rejects, as necessary because it can be argued that—although not all rights are primary—the right to life and freedom from harm is primary among them.

In contrast, the usually accepted connection between primary human rights and democracy can be shown to be less strong than it is generally thought to be. In that case, our next problem is:

How are we to prevent harms, and to restrain risk imposers when even the "best," most enlightened form of governance (i.e., democracy) may not be sufficient to accomplish the goal? To attempt an answer, we will return to biomedical ethics and the moral and legal categories used to remedy the possible spread of infectious diseases.

RISK, RIGHTS AND CONSENT: A LESSON FROM THE "WHITE DEATH"

I have noted that biomedical ethics may not offer the best analogy for questions of consent arising from environmental and technological hazards. We could not ensure "full disclosure," reach everyone who might be at risk, and communicate clearly and understandably the extent and gravity of the harm; moreover, neither risk imposers nor risk assessors could predict accurately the probability and gravity of the harms. Yet uncertainties—endemic to scientific discourse involving a large range of variables, added to the impredictability about location, gravity of exposure, and other specifics—ought not to force us to reject with Thomson, the risk thesis.

And if we hold fast to both (1) the primacy of rights—especially the right to life and to freedom from harm—and (2) the risk thesis itself, then we need to seek another avenue to ensure that rights be protected, given the failure of present democratic institutions to guarantee appropriate restraints to risk imposers. The resurgence of many infectious diseases, assumed to have been conquered and eliminated (e.g., tuberculosis), for instance, may indicate a possible avenue for public policy. Tuberculosis is making a comeback in North America and in other parts of the world; it is now resistant to most antibiotics, harder than ever to control because of population density and other modern conditions, and therefore brings with it threats of the "white death." Tuberculosis is highly contagious and requires very little contact to spread, unlike, for instance, sexually transmitted diseases like AIDS. It is sufficient to sit next to an infected person, to breathe the same air, to be infected. Tuberculosis is curable, but it requires a lengthy course of treatment. Many people who want to get well decide to abandon the treatment when the worst symptoms subside, despite the fact that they are still highly contagious (Davis 1995). If these persons are not prepared to persevere with their treatment and yet want to continue to lead a normal life, interacting with others, they are "endangering" not only their close associates but also the general public. The question is what to do when the disease, its course, treatment, and hazards are fully explained to contagious persons and they understand yet refuse to comply with either treatment or restraints. Some action must be taken in defense of the public interest and the public safety.

As in the case of contagious childhood diseases, what is necessary is the use of "quarantines" and other forms of involuntary restraints and treatment. The starting point is the realization that tuberculosis is a threat to public health *"par excellence"* (Davis 1995). As far as I know, however, only New York City has clear-cut legislation in this regard (at least at this time). The following course of action is supported by this new legislation:

> The City Department of Public Health may order a person removed to a hospital or detained for treatment there only if two conditions are met. First, the Department must have found the tuberculosis to be active and without treatment likely to be transmitted to others.... Second, the Department must have found the subject of the order unable or unwilling to undergo less restrictive treatment.
> (Davis 1995)

The above requirements are based on "epidemiological or clinical evidence, X-rays or laboratory tests," and the final decision to commit rests with the courts in a way parallel to that designed to ensure commitment for mental illness (Davis 1995). Note that, in order to restrain the liberty of risk imposers in this context, it is not necessary to "prove" they have harmed someone in a court of law; it is sufficient to demonstrate that they and their activities are hazardous and potentially harmful to the public. Depending on the response of the infectious person to requests to be treated, the interests of public health may be served by "civil confinement for treatment," which in turn may be justified as preventing harm to the public through "reckless endangerment" (Davis 1995). In fact, jail could justifiably be used to stop the endangerment for anyone who might resist the suggested "civil confinement for treatment."

How can this situation help us conceptualize the problem of imposing restraints on those endangering the public through environmentally hazardous practices? First, we need to note that some public threats cannot be controlled through democratic institutions, that is, through *voluntary* public choices. One may counter that even the imposition of forced restraints is embedded in a general system of individual rights and democratic institutions. That is, of course, correct. But it is important to understand that rights to life and health are primary and should be put ahead of other choices and preferences. This perspective allows us to view environmental endangerment as something that needs to be controlled directly and even by coercive means, rather than something that is simply to be limited only by cost-benefit analyses or by a counting of heads and a weighing of preferences. To explain detention in medical cases, Davis (1995) says, "The alternative to detention is the moral equivalent of letting someone, without adequate justification, walk crowded streets with a large bomb that could go off at any moment."

In the "white death" threats, we are not sure of the gravity of the harm imposed; we cannot anticipate just who is at risk from the infected person with any certainty; we cannot be sure of precise numbers of potentially affected persons; we have information about risks and harms, but we cannot present a specific infected person or persons as "proof," to justify placing the risk imposer under criminal restraints. The reason and the only reason we can offer for imposing criminal restraints or civil restraints is reckless endangerment, without being able to point to one or many persons who might have been harmed.

In fact, it is in order *not* to have "victims" that we are justified in invoking civil and criminal restraints. Contrast this preventive approach with that of corporate bodies who expose persons in their immediate vicinity of their hazardous operations to risks of harms but who *demand* not proof of endangerment but clear proof of *actual harm* before they are even prepared to compensate, let alone to consider discontinuing their hazardous activities.

Much more could be said about this topic, and it is fair to say that there are disanalogies as well as analogies between cases in biomedical ethics, allowing justification for restraints in cases of reckless endangerment, and the imposition of environmental risks and harms. Perhaps the most problematic difference is that, while one person's "restraints" will only affect her life (and provide a much greater benefit in the process), restraints of corporate activities on a grand scale might have grave repercussions for all stake-holders, not only the corporation subject to restraints. Nevertheless, it seems that there are enough parallels to make a reasonable case for considering seriously the approach I suggest, for all others employed so far appear to have met with scant success.

THE GOOD AND THE COMMUNITY: LAWS RESTRAINING CHOICE

The argument I have proposed essentially contrasts individualism with communitarianism. But the latter is viewed as a special case: the case of a community of life, whereby each individual's personal integrity and the ecological integrity of her habitat are so completely intertwined that no question can be raised about whether the value of integrity in each case is intrinsic or instrumental. Rolston (1996) makes this point eloquently in his philosophical analysis of "biological immunity":

> The organismic integrity protected by immunity has to fit into an ecosystemic integrity. An organism without a habitat is soon extinct. The immune system is zealously defending the self, but all the while the ecosystem in which this self lives is the fundamental unit of development and survival. There are no immune organisms, period; there are only immune organisms-in-ecosystems.

From the perspective of immunity, our strong individual rights to life and self-defense can easily be extended to our habitat, in line with Rolston's proposed definition of our organisms as "organisms-in-ecosystems." Hence, to invoke stronger, changed laws appears entirely defensible on grounds of self-defense. These laws must replace laws that place economically driven, unintended harms, slowly unfolding over time, in a separate category so that only clear, quickly evident and intended harms are deemed to be criminal. Attacks on our bodily integrity and our genetic capacities are also crimes; they might be defined as attacks on our capacities as a small *c*, embedded in the capital *C*, or the capacities of ecological integrity. In my previous work, the collaborative definition of integrity used the letter *C* to represent the undiminished capacities of an ecosystem in its unmanipulated state, following its natural evolutionary trajectory, free, as much as possible, from human interference or stress.

To better understand the sort of crime described in these "attacks," we may invoke the difference between premeditated murder and manslaughter. It seems intuitively true to say that pain and suffering aside, no one has the right to remove someone else's organs for their own purposes, no matter how "good" the perpetrators may perceive their purpose to be. It would seem equally intuitively true to add that it is equally impermissible to intrusively interfere with the natural functions of these organs. When the damage caused is more than damage to one individual but it becomes, as in the cases researched by Theo Colborn (Colborn et al. 1996), damage to reproductive capacities, to the next generations, hence to humanity in general, it becomes a case of attempted genocide, deserving even more than the punishment of the laws of the perpetrators' country: It requires that they be accountable to and punished by a world tribunal.

Surely, if there is a good that is not in doubt, it is the right we have to our own physical and intellectual capacities undiminished by others. This common good is neither based on the preferences of one culture or another, nor limited to any relative viewpoint, as it is compatible with a great variety of cultural "goods" and ideals. Hence, I propose our undiminished capacities c, as a basic good that permits with varying degrees of appropriateness a number of societal coercive actions, parallel to those needed to support the ecological integrity it requires to thrive C. This "good" may also be compatible with moral theories such as the Kantian respect for autonomously chosen ends and the Rawlsian emphasis on fairness and the difference principle. These possible connections need to be examined in some detail.

> What does Rawls (1975) say about the good? His understanding may raise problems:

> That we have one conception of the good rather than another is not relevant from a moral standpoint. In acquiring it we are influenced by the same sort of contingencies that leads us to rule out a knowledge of our sex and class.

The defense of life through individual and systemic integrity may not be in conflict with a variety of conceptions of the good. But the wholesale acceptance of the possibility of any and all such "conceptions of the good" may well conflict with the spirit of the principle of integrity, in the same sense that utilitarianism also does. Michael Sandel (1982) examines the "status of the good" in Rawls. He argues:

> For Rawls, utilitarianism goes wrong not in conceiving the good as the satisfaction of arbitrarily given desires, undifferentiated as to worth—for justice as fairness shares in this, but only in being indifferent to the way these consummations are spread across individuals.

Although Rawls, in Sandel's estimation, departs from utilitarianism, the remaining connection with "the satisfaction of arbitrarily given desires" is—at best—compatible with the primacy of life, as the necessary prerequisite to the existence of "desires." But it is not compatible with the nonnegotiable status of

the principle of integrity (PI). Some may argue, for instance, that the desire to accept a trade-off between diminished health, life span or genetic capacities, and economic advantage, if well understood, is legitimate for a society. Some may also argue that this is precisely what is happening in affluent democracies at this time; hence, only the *distributive* aspect of this "contract" should be scrutinized from the standpoint of morality, not its existence.

In contrast, the PI takes a strongly Kantian position in not permitting such trade-offs, whether or not they are fairly distributed across society. The basis of the principle of integrity is the value of integrity, which encompasses the infinite value of all life, of life-support systems, and of individual and systemic capacities, now and into the future. This excludes the possibility of legitimate trade-offs and places those concerns at the forefront of both morality and public policy. The primacy and the centrality of this value explains the emphasis on the need for national laws and for global regulative mechanisms to protect it as an absolute, rather than treating it as one value among many, subject to public choice or majoritarian preferences.

The holistic perspective is absolutely vital here: Life-support systems cannot be protected in piecemeal fashion. When hazards travel between continents, not only countries, clearly national policies will be insufficient. Global regulations and tight global security will also be required to prevent the present techno-hazard transfer between North American and Western European countries and Southeast Asian ones and into economically depressed minority areas in the affluent countries. An interesting parallel may be found in recent improvement in Canadian legislation directed at serial criminals of a special kind: the sexual predators.

One of the most horrible cases in Canada (1988–1994) saw Paul Bernardo and his wife Karla Homolka involved in terrible crimes over a lengthy period because of Bernardo's change of venue during his "career" as a rapist, torturer, and murderer. He was eventually found guilty of a series of viciously sadistic rapes in a Toronto suburb, which earned him the title of "Scarborough rapist." The DNA evidence that eventually implicated him, however, was neglected at one location when he moved to another, on the west side of Toronto, to St. Catharines, Ontario, about 50 kilometers away. There he met and married Homolka in a storybook wedding where the young, attractive couple, both blonde and blue-eyed, appeared to be the epitome of "nice" middle-class Canadians. But when Homolka's 15-year-old sister died under suspicious circumstances at their parents' home on Christmas Eve (with Karla and Bernardo in attendance) and two other schoolgirls 14 and 15 years old were eventually abducted, with only their remains found weeks later, it should have been clear that the Scarborough's rapist's career was not over. Because different police forces in different areas were involved in the investigations, the connection was not made in time to prevent at least the last two grisly murders.

Eventually, tapes recording the horror of the girls' sexual assaults and torture were discovered, and the wife, a full participant and assistant in the crimes and the abductions, testified against the husband (*The Globe and Mail* 1995). The similarity between the case of sexual predators, now the subject of a commissioned inquiry, and the hazardous practices described earlier in this essay is that both are cases of system failure. This can obviously occur even when the crimes committed are already in the criminal code as such; and even such cases cannot be easily stopped because of failures in coordination. We also need to take very seriously the crimes of ecoviolence that are not even properly treated as such now because they can lead to serial recurrences, with almost complete impunity to the perpetrators. According to Justice Archie Campbell, Head of the Commission reporting on serial predators, from 1988 to 1994, the name of Bernardo and a series of similar crimes kept "coming up." But lacking an investigative body capable of and charged with coordinating the findings of various jurisdictions, Bernardo was able to "throw investigations off stride by the simple act of moving from one police jurisdiction to another." Judge Campbell wrote, "When Bernardo stopped stalking, raping and killing in Toronto and started stalking, raping and killing in St. Catharines and

Burlington, he might as well have moved to another country for a fresh start" (I. Ross, *The Globe and Mail* 1996).

Justice Campbell's remarks bring to mind the legal corporate practices that are taken for granted: Corporations simply close down one operation and move out to another location, often in a less developed country, which they perceive as less demanding in their environmental regulations. Perhaps the corporation has been charged and fined for repeated environmental infractions. Unfortunately for all of us, the move does not herald an increased environmental concern or a newly found respect for human life and its habitat. The move is most often followed by practices indicating the same disregard for human and ecological safety that led to the original problems.

As long as the charges are viewed as creating economic externalities only (and moving and reorganizing expenses are tax-deductible), the immorality becomes institutionalized, simply another way of doing business. Even repeated offenses, in different venues, cause little discomfort unless the public becomes aware of the infractions through some spectacular accident; and even then, there is no extradition for noncriminal cases. Like sexual predators, corporate predators can simply move and resume the activities that forced the move with little or no fear of retribution.

If even in criminal cases (short of murder, perhaps) it is far too easy to inflict great harm repeatedly on an unprotected public, then the move to criminalize hazardous practices, as a first step, appears inevitable. Like serial predators, corporations gain confidence and ability through repeated, almost routine moves. Unlike the average predator, they possess large resources that can be mobilized and utilized in defense of their goals. Hence, it is vital to recognize that good personal or corporate morality and conscience must be encouraged and supported through laws that will force those who lack such virtues to comply.

Therefore, to affirm the urgent need for strict global regulations for the protection of public life, health, and integrity is not to commit the hasty generalization of tarring all corporations, good and bad, with the same brush. It is intended to recognize the primacy of individual and ecological integrity and to attempt to coordinate and institutionalize principles and ideals that are already, for the most part, present in global regulations and in national and international laws. In essence it is to recognize the role of a holistic perceptive in public decision making (Brown 1995).

REFERENCES

Ayres, E. "The Expanding Shadow Economy," *Worldwatch* (July/August 1996): 11–23.

Barnes, C. "Consent Theory: Can One Consent to Be Harmed?" Unpublished paper, presented at the University of Windsor, 1996.

Brown, D., and J. Lemons, eds.1995. *Sustainable Development: Science Ethics and Public Policy*. Dordrecht, The Netherlands: Kluwer, 1995.

Bullard, R. *Dumping in Dixie*. Boulder, CO: Westview Press, 1994.

Colborn, Theo. "Plenary Address" to the International Association of Great Lakes Researchers, Erindale College, Toronto, May 27, 1996.

Colborn, Theo, DianneDumanoski, and John Peterson Myers. *Our Stolen Future*. New York: Dutton, 1996.

Colwell, Rita. "Global Change: Emerging Diseases and New Epidemics." President's Lecture, American Association for the Advancement of Science (AMSIE '96), February 1996.

Davis, M. "Arresting the White Death: Involuntary Patients, Public Health, and Medical Ethics." Paper presented at the central meeting of the American Philosophical Association, April 1995.

DeCew, J. "Rights and Risks." Comments on A. Ellis's "Risks and Rights." Unpublished paper. 1995.

Donaldson, Thomas. "Moral Minimums for Multinations." In *Ethical Issues in Business*, edited by T. Donaldson and P. Werhane. Englewood Cliffs, NJ: Prentice Hall, 1993, 58–75.

Ellis, Anthony. "Risks and Rights." Paper presented at the central meeting of the American Philosophical Association, April 1995.

French, P. A. *Collective and Corporate Responsibility*. New York: Columbia University Press, 1984.

Friedman, Milton. "The Social Responsibility of Business Is to Increase Its Profits." In *Ethical Issues in Business*, edited by T. Donaldson and P. Werhane. Englewood Cliffs, NJ: Prentice Hall, 1993, 249–254.

Gaylord, C., and E. Bell, "Environmental Justice: A National Priority." In *Faces of Environmental Racism*, edited by L. Westra and P. Wenz. Lanham, MD: Rowman & Littlefield, 1995.

Gewirth, A. "Human Rights and the Prevention of Cancer." In *Human Rights*. Chicago: University of Chicago Press, 1983, 181–217.

Gilbert, Paul. *Terrorism, Security and Nationality*. London: Routledge, 1995.

Hobbes, Thomas. *Leviathan*. New York: Bobbs-Merrill, 1958.

Hohfeld, W. N. *Fundamental Legal Conceptions*. New Haven, CT: Yale University Press, 1923.

Homer-Dixon, Thomas. "On the Threshold: Environmental Changes as Causes of Acute Conflict." *International Security* 16, no. 2 (Fall 1991): 76–116.

Homer-Dixon, Thomas. "Environmental Scarcity and Violent Conflict: Evidence from Cases." *International Security* 19, No. 1 (Summer 1994): 5–40.

Homer-Dixon, Thomas, in Hurst, Lyda, "The Global Guru," *The Toronto Star*, July 20, 1996, "Insight," pp C1 and C5.

Ingelfinger, Franz L. "Informed (but Uneducated) Consent." In *Biomedical Ethics*, edited by J. Zembaty and T. Mappes. eds., 1991, 220–221.

Kant, Immanuel. *The Metaphysical Elements of Justice*. New York: Bobbs-Merrill, 1965.

Kant, Immanuel. *On the Old Saw*. Philadelphia: University of Pennsylvania Press, 1974.

Kant, Immanuel. *Lectures on Ethics*, translated by Louis Infield. Indianapolis: Hackett, 1979, pp. 116–126 ("Duties to Oneself"); and pp. 157–160 ("Duties towards the Body Itself").

Korten, David. *When Corporations Rule the World*. West Hartford, CT: Kumarian Press, Berret Koehler Publishers, 1995.

Martin, Rex. *A System of Rights*. New York: Clarendon Press/Oxford University Press, 1993.

McMichael, Anthony J. *Planetary Overload*. Cambridge, UK: Cambridge University Press, 1995.

Mesthene, Emmanuel G. "The Role of Technology in Society." In *Technology and the Future*, 5th ed., edited by A. Teich. New York: St. Martin's Press, 1990, pp. 77–99.

Nikiforuk, A. "Arctic Pollution: Poisons for a Pristine Land." *The Globe and Mail* (July 20, 1996), D8.

Rawls, J. "From Fairness to Goodness." *Philosophical Review*, 1984 (1975): 536–554.

Rawls, J. "The Law of Peoples." In *On Human Rights*. New York: Basic Books/HarperCollins, 1993, pp. 41–82.

Rolston, Holmes, III. "Immunity in Natural History." In *Perspectives in Biology and Medicine* 39, no. 3 (Spring 1996): 353–372.

Sandel, Michael. *Liberalism and the Limits of Justice*. Cambridge, MA: Cambridge University Press, 1982.

Shrader-Frechette, K. *Risk and Rationality*. Berkeley, CA: University of California Press, 1991.

Simmons, A. John. *Moral Principles and Political Obligations*. Englewood Cliffs, NJ: Princeton University Press, 1979.

Simon, Thomas. "Group Harm." *Journal of Social Philosophy* 26, no. 3 (Winter 1995): 123–139.

Thomson, J. J. *The Realm of Rights*. Cambridge, MA: Harvard University Press, 1990.

Westra, L. *An Environmental Proposal for Ethics: The Principle of Integrity*. Lanham MD: Rowman & Littlefield, 1994a.

Westra, L. "Risky Business: Corporate Responsibility and Hazardous Products." *Business Ethics Quarterly* 4, no. 1, (1994b): 97–110.

Westra, L. "Ecosystem Integrity and Sustainability: The Foundational Value of the Wild." In *Perspectives on Ecological Integrity*, edited by L. Westra and J. Lemons. Dordrecht, The Netherlands: Kluwer, 1995a, pp. 12–33.

Westra, L. "Integrity, Health and Sustainability: Environmentalism Without Racism." In *The Science of the Total Environment*. Oxford, UK: Elsevier, for the World Health Organization, 1996.

Wigley, D., and Shrader-Frechette, K. "Consent, Equity and Environmental Justice: A Louisiana Case Study." In *Faces of Environmental Racism*, edited by L. Westra and P. Wenz. 1995. *The Faces of Environmental Racism: The Global Equity Issues*, Lanham, MD: Rowman & Littlefield, 1995, pp. 135–162.

Winner, Langdon. *Autonomous Technology*. Cambridge, MA: MIT Press, 1977.

STUDY QUESTIONS

1. Is Westra correct about the failure of democracies to deal with environmental degradation and risk?

2. Are there natural rights? What are they? Do we have a right against others that they not impose risks of harm on us, as Westra argues? Or is Thomson correct in rejecting such a right?

3. Is Westra's solution threatening to democracy itself?

FOR FURTHER READING

Bullard, Robert, *Confronting Environmental Racism*. Cambridge, MA: South End Press, 1993.

Serba, James P., ed., *Earth Ethics*. Englewood Cliffs, NJ: Prentice Hall, 1995.

Wenz, Peter S., *Environmental Justice*. Albany, NY: SUNY Press, 1988.

Westra, Laura. *An Environmental Proposal for Ethics*. Lanham, MD: Rowman & Littlefield, 1994.

Westra, Laura and Peter S. Wenz, eds., *Faces of Environmental Racism*. Lanham, MD: Rowman & Littlefield, 1995.

54

All Our Relations: Native Struggles for Land and Life

WINONA LADUKE

Winona LaDuke is a Native American activist, writer, and environmentalist. She was the Green Party's vice-presidential candidate in the 2000 elections. She is the founder and director of the White Earth Land Recovery Project: www.nativeharvest.com/. This selection, from her book, All our Relations: Native Struggles for Land and Life, *portrays the struggles of indigenous peoples in North America.*

The last 150 years have seen a great holocaust. There have been more species lost in the past 150 years than since the Ice Age. During the same time, Indigenous peoples have been disappearing from the face of the Earth. More than 2,000 nations of Indigenous peoples have gone extinct in the Western Hemisphere and one nation disappears from the Amazon rainforest every year.

There is a direct relationship between the loss of cultural diversity and the loss of biodiversity. Wherever Indigenous peoples still remain, there is also a corresponding enclave of biodiversity. Trickles of rivers still running in the Northwest are home to salmon still being sung back by Native people. The last few Florida panthers remain in the presence of traditional Seminoles, hidden away in the great cypress swamps bordering the Everglades. Some of the largest patches of remaining prairie grasses sway on reservation lands. One half of all reservation lands in the United States is still forested, much of it is old-growth. Remnant pristine forest ecosystems, from the northern boreal forests to the Everglades, largely overlap Native territories.

In the Northwest, virtually every river is home to people, each as distinct as a species of salmon. The Tillamook, Siletz, Yaquina, Alsea, Siuslaw, Umpqua, Hanis, Miluk, Colville, Tututni, Shasta, Costa, and Chetco are all peoples living at the mouths of salmon rivers. One hundred and seven stocks of salmon have already become extinct in the Pacific Northwest, and 89 are endangered.

"Salmon were put here by the Creator, and it is our responsibility to harvest and protect the salmon so that the cycle if life continues," explains Pierson Mitchell of the Columbia Intertribal Fishing Commission. "Whenever we have a funeral, we mourn our loved one, yes, but we are also reminded of the loss of our salmon and other traditional foods," laments Yakama Tribal Chairman Bill Yallup, Sr.

The stories of the fish and the people are not so different. Environmental destruction threatens the existence of both. The Tygh band of the Lower Deschutes River in Oregon includes a scant five families, struggling in their traditional way of life and their relationship to the salmon. "I wanted to

"Voices from White Earth" from *A Forest of Voices: Conversations in Ecology*, 2nd Ed., ed. Chris Anderson and Lex Runciman (Mayfield Publishing, 2000).

dance the salmon, know the salmon, say goodbye to the salmon," says Susana Santos, a Tygh artist, fisherwoman, and community organizer. "Now I am looking at the completion of destruction, from the Exxon Valdez to … those dams. … Seventeen fish came down the river last year. None this year. The people are the salmon, and the salmon are the people. How do you quantify that?"

ALL OUR RELATIONS

Native American teachings describe the relations all around—animals, fish, trees, and rocks—as our brothers, sisters, uncles, and grandpas. Our relations to each other, our prayers whispered across generations to our relatives, are what bind our cultures together.

The protection, teachings, and gifts of our relatives have for generations preserved our families. These relations are honored in ceremony, song, story, and life that keep relations, close—to buffalo, sturgeon, salmon, turtles, bears, wolves, and panthers. These are our older relatives—the ones that came before and taught us to live. Their obliteration by dams, guns, and bounties is an immense loss to Native families and cultures. Their absence may mean that a people sing to a barren river, a caged bear, or a buffalo far away. It is the struggle to preserve what remains and the struggle to recover what has been lost that characterizes much of Native environmentalism. It is these relationships that industrialism seeks to disrupt. Native communities will resist with great determination.

> *Salmon was presented to me and my family through our religion as our brother. The same with deer. And our sisters are the roots and berries. And you would treat them as such. Their life to you is just as valuable as another person's would be.*
>
> —MARGARET SALUSKIN, YAKAMA

TOXIC INVASION OF NATIVE LAND

There are more than 700 Native on the North American continent. Today, Native America covers four percent of the land in the US, with over 500 federally recognized tribes.

More than 1,200 Native American reserves dot Canada. The Inuit homeland, Nunavut, formerly one-half of Canada's Northwest Territories, is an area of land and water (including Baffin Island) that is five times the size of Texas. Eighty-five percent of Nunavet's population is Native.

While native peoples have been massacred and fought, cheated and robbed of their historical lands, today their lands are subject to one the most invasive industrial interventions imaginable. According to the Worldwatch Institute, 317 reservations in the United States are threatened by environmental hazards, ranging from toxic wastes to clearcuts.

Reservations have been targeted as sites for 16 proposed nuclear waste dumps. More than 100 proposals have been floated in recent years to dump toxic waste in Indian communities. Seventy-seven sacred sites have been disturbed or desecrated through resource extraction and development activities. The federal government is proposing to use Yucca Mountain—a Nevada landmark sacred to the Shoshone—as a dumpsite for the nation's high-level nuclear waste.

More than 1,000 slag piles and tailings from abandoned uranium mines sit on Dine (Navajo) land, leaking radioactivity into the air and water. Some groups of Dine teenagers in this region now have a cancer rate 17 times the national average.

According to Tom Goldtooth, executive director of the Native Environmental Network, "Most Indigenous governments are over 22 years behind the states in infrastructure development. The EPA has consistently failed to fund tribes on an equitable basis compared with states. The EPA has a statutory responsibility to allocate financial resources that will provide an equitable allocation between tribal governments and states."

CHILDREN OF LITTLE THUNDER

In our communities, Native environmentalists sing centuries-old songs to renew life, to give thanks for strawberries, to call home fish, and to thank Mother Earth for all her blessings.

We are the descendants of Little Thunder, the Lakota Chief who witnessed the 1855 massacre in Nebraska cleared out the Great Plains to make way for the cowboys, cattle, and industrial farms. We have seen the great trees felled, the wolves taken for bounty, and the fish stacked and rotting like cordwood. Those memories compel us, and the return of the descendants of these predators provokes us to stand again—stronger and, hopefully, with more allies.

We are the ones who stand up to the land eaters, the tree eaters, the destroyers and culture eaters. We live off the beaten track, out of the mainstream in small villages, on a vast expanse of prairie, on dry deserts, or in the forests. We often drive old cars, live in old houses and mobile homes. There are usually small children and relatives around, the kids careening underfoot.

We seldom carry briefcases and we rarely wear suits. You are more likely to find us meeting in a local community center, camping outside or visiting in someone's house than at a convention center or at a $1,000-per-plate fundraiser.

We organize in small groups with names like Native Americans for a Clean Environment, Dine CARE (Citizens against Ruining Our Environment), Anishinaabe Niijii, and the Gwichin Steering Committee.

We are underfunded at best (more often not funded at all), working out of our homes with a few families or five to ten volunteers. We coalesce in national or continental organizations such as Indigenous Environmental Network, a network of 200-plus groups. IEN provides a diverse agenda of technical and political support to grassroots groups seeking to protect their land, preserve biodiversity, and sustain communities, IEN seeks ultimately to secure environmental justice.

Other Native groups include the Southwest Network for Environmental and Economic Justice, Honor the Earth, Indigenous Women's Network and the Seventh Generation Fund. In addition to numerous regional organizations, there also are groups based on a shared ecosystem or cultural practice, such as the California Indian Basketweavers

Association, Great Lakes Basketmakers, or Council of Elders.

Despite our meager resources, we are winning many hard-fought victories at the local level. We have faced down huge waste dumps and multinational mining, lumber, and oil companies. Throughout the Native nations, people continue to fight to protect Mother Earth for future generations.

Some of the victories include a moratorium on mining in the sacred hill of the Northern Cheyenne, Blackfeet, and Crow territory; an international campaign that stopped the building of mega-dams in northern Canada; the restoration of thousands of acres of White Earth land in Minnesota; and the rebuilding of a nation in Hawai'i.

Grassroots and land-based struggles characterize most of Native environmentalism. We are nations of people with distinct land areas and our leadership and direction emerge from the land on up. Our commitment and tenacity spring from our deep connection to the land. This relationship to land and water is continuously reaffirmed through prayer, deed, and our way of being—minobimaatisiiwin, the "good life."

This relationship survives in remembered phrases down through the generations. You can hear them today spoken in native homes across North America:

> This is where my grandmother's and children's umbilical cords are buried.…
>
> This is where the great giant lay down to sleep …
>
> These are the four sacred Mountains between which the Creator instructed us to live.…
>
> This is the last place our people stopped in our migration here to this village.

LIVING ON THE WHITE EARTH

I live on an Anishinaabeg reservation called White Earth in northern Minnesota, where I work on land culture, and environmental issues locally through an organization called the White Earth Land Recovery Project and nationally through a Native foundation called Honor the Earth. We, the Anishinaabeg, are a forest culture. Our creation stories, culture, and way of life are entirely base on the forest—the source of our medicinal plants, food, and birch-bark baskets.

Virtually my entire reservation was clearcut at the turn of the century.

In 1874, Anishinaabe leader Wabunoquod said, "I cried and prayed that our trees would not be taken from us, for they are as much ours as is this reservation". Our trees provided the foundation for major lumber companies, including Weyerhauser. The destruction of our forests continued for ten decades.

In 1889 and 1890, Minnesota led the country in lumber production, and the state's northwest region was the leading source of timber. Two decades later, 90 percent of White Earth land was controlled by non-Indians, and our people were riddled with disease. Many became refugees in nearby cities. Today, three-fourths of all tribal members live off the reservation. Non-Indians still control ninety percent of our land.

There is a direct link in our community between the loss of biodiversity—the loss of animal and plant life—and the loss of the material and cultural wealth of the White Earth people. But we have resisted. Today, we are in litigation against logging expansion, and the White Earth Land Recovery Project works to restore our forests, recover the land, and restore out traditional forest culture. Our experience of survival and resistance is hared with many others.

In the final analysis, the survival of Native America is fundamentally about the collective survival of all human beings. The question of who gets to determine the destiny of the land—those with the money or those who pray on the land—is a question that is alive throughout society. The question is posed eloquently by Lil'wat grandmother Loretta Pascal:

This is my reason for standing up. To protect all around us, to continue our way of life, our culture. I ask them, "Where did you get your right to destroy these forests? How does your right supersede my right?" These are our forests, these are our ancestors.

As Columbia River Tribes activist Ted Strong tells us:

"If this nation has a long way to go before all of our people are truly treated equally without regard to race, religion, or national origin, it has even farther to go before achieving anything that remotely resembles equal treatment for other creatures who called this land home before humans ever set foot upon it …

While the species themselves—fish, fowl, game, and their habitat—have given us unparalleled wealth, they live crippled in their ability to persist and in conditions of captive squalor. … This enslavement and impoverishment of nature is no more tolerable or sensible than enslavement and impoverishment of other human beings. …

"Perhaps it is because we are the messengers that not only our sovereignty as [Native] governments but our right to identify with a deity and a history—our right to hold to a set of natural laws as practiced for thousands of years—is under assault. Now more than ever, tribal people must hold onto their timeless and priceless customs and practices.

"The ceremony will continue," Strong says. "This is a testament to the faith of the Indian people. No matter how badly the salmon have been mistreated, no matter how serious the decline, it has doubled their commitment. It has rekindled the hope that today is beginning to grow in many young people."

STUDY QUESTIONS

1. LaDuke talks of resistance: what is it to be resisted?

2. What does LaDuke mean by saying "we are a forest culture"? How might you describe your culture?

55

Indigenous Knowledge and Technology: Creating Environmental Justice in the Twenty-First Century

LINDA ROBYN

As we begin to examine the relationship between American Indians and environmental justice, it is important to note that American courts have many times in the past criminalized, whether consciously or not, traditional knowledge. Indian people who have challenged multinational corporate giants and the government through political activism in an effort to halt environmentally destructive projects on their lands have been criminalized and arrested to silence their claims. Leaving traditional knowledge out of environmental policy is a grave injustice because it is socially injurious to Native peoples and, in effect, all people, not only in the United States but worldwide.

When writing about Indigenous peoples, the exclusion of environmental issues also establishes an injustice because it does not recognize the origins of social institutions among all human beings. Therefore, everything in American Indian culture is associated with an environmental perspective, even issues that filter through the American court system. As will be examined, Native peoples today are using their sophisticated traditional knowledge, combined with militant strategies in some cases, to effect change. Providing equitable justice for Indigenous people establishes an important precedent that can put social institutions like criminal justice in a context where the connection between society and the environment is recognized.

American Indian institutions originate within Native cultures in ways that associate policies with natural principles and natural laws defined by traditional cultural perspectives. The following represents a reflection of this understanding.

The Native peoples of the Americas represent a wide variety of cultures and social organization strategies. The diversity of Native cultures and kinds of social organizations which developed through time represent a high degree of social/political complexity and are varied according to the demands and necessities of the environment. For example, American Indian nations organized at the band level of social/political development have used effective strategies to take advantage of marginal habitats such as the Arctic and deserts of the Americas where resources were limited.

Winona LaDuke, a member of the Anishinabe Nation, author, activist, and scholar of environmental and Indigenous issues, writes that "sustainability in these marginal habitats did not simply rely

Linda Robyn is associate professor of criminal justice at Northern Arizona University.
Robyn, Linda, "Indigenous Knowledge and Technology: Creating Environmental Justice in the Twenty-First Century" from *The American Indian Quarterly*, Vol. 26, No. 2, pp. 198–220. Copyright © 2002. Lincoln, N.E.: The University of Nebraska Press.

placed within the whole. For any American Indians even today, their way of life revolves around the environment. One does not, and indeed cannot, own the other if a healthy balance is to be maintained. Rather, only what is necessary to survive is taken from one another.[10]

As it is with balance, the spiritual connection with the natural world is sacred. There is a balance of knowledge and power between humans, animals, all of the environment, the heavens, and earth. All these pieces tied together make up the whole. Spirituality, of The Way, guides the balance.

The incongruence in the values and in the understanding of progress between these very different cultures helps explain the lack of inclusion of Indigenous knowledge. For many American Indian people, values are expressed by the strong relationship between family members, kinship ties, the environment, and the knowledge of the unity of all these things. European values allowed land and environment to be viewed as commodities to be exploited, and these colonizers imposed their will upon the land with little thought of the consequences. The knowledge and values of the Indians from the Great Lakes region emerged from their woodland cultures and spirituality. There was a timeless value placed on all things. Native values are circular with all things being related as revealed from the outer world and their religion. This idea will be developed in the rest of the article.

An example of woodland culture spirituality comes form the Anishinabe (Chippewa) people who developed a code of ethics and a value system which guides the behavior of many in accordance with natural law—or *mino bimaatisiiwin*—translated as the good life of continuous rebirth. LaDuke writes that *mino bimaatisiiwin* "guides behavior toward others, toward animals, toward plants and the ecosystem, and it is based on tenets of reciprocity and cyclical thinking."[11]

In contrasting the value system and knowledge base of the Chippewa with capitalistic values, it is reciprocity or reciprocal relations that define responsibilities and ways of relating between humans and the world around them. This, in turn, affects the technology used by Indigenous groups, such as the Chippewa, by ensuring methods of harvesting resources that will not deplete supplies needed for survival. LaDuke writes:

> Within this act of reciprocity is also an understanding that "you take only what you need and leave the rest". Implicit in the understanding of Natural Law is also the understanding that most of what is natural is cyclical: whether our bodies, the moon, the tides, seasons, or life itself. Within this natural cycling is also a clear sense of birth and rebirth, a knowledge that what one does today will affect us in the future, on the return.

These tenets, and the overall practice of *mino bimaatisiiwin* imply a continuous inhabiting of place, and intimate understanding of the relationship between humans and the ecosystem, and the need to maintain balance. For the most part, social and economic systems based on these values are decentralized, communal, self-reliant, and very closely based on the land of that ecosystem. This way of living has enabled Indigenous communities to live for thousands of years upon their land as, quite frankly, the only examples of continuous sustainability which exist on Turtle Island (North America). We hope there will be more.[12]

The contrasting views of the value and technology system of the Chippewa versus the European-American capitalistic values of power, materialism, economic efficiency, and immediacy have led to confusion and misunderstanding about other people and their ways. European-American views toward family and religious are different than the views of many American Indians. While not all European-Americans are of the Christian religion, much of the knowledge contained in the exploitive dynamics of the Christian religion are closely tied to the concepts of our capitalistic society and are not connected to the earth or environment as is the spirituality of The Way of American Indians.[13] The result is a culture conflict in which both sides see their values and methods of looking at life as the only correct way. In this context, the unequal balance and hierarchical social structure produced by the expansionary needs of capitalism are, to many American Indian people, highly destructive to their perception of the need for balance between physical and spiritual worlds.

The sharp contrast between these two sets of cultural views is a major point of contention between dominating cultures and Indigenous peoples today. These differences could also be a contributing factor to changes that are beginning to take place in many Indigenous communities. Native peoples who have not been included in decision-making concerning the potentially environmentally devastating impact of corporate intrusion upon their lands are critically thinking about, assessing, and demanding that their voices be heard and not discounted or ignored as in times past.

In exploring the concept of critical thinking, criminologist Richard Quinney writes that "[W]ithout critical thought we are bound to the only form of social life we know—that which currently exists. We are unable to choose a better life; our only activity is in further support of the system in which we are currently a part and which continues to exploit us."[14] Nowhere is this more true than with multinational corporations who engaged in colonial-style projects on many reservations with disastrous results for the people and the environment. As the effects of these disasters emerged, Indian people on other reservations targeted for corporate exploitation began to take notice. Armed with knowledge about the environmental stability of their homelands, many tribes decide that the inevitable destruction caused by corporate exploitation was not worth the price of letting their resources be taken from the earth. By utilizing their knowledge about environmental devastation and not accepting the colonial-style offers of multinational corporations at face value, the tide on reservations is beginning to turn. Today, Native peoples are calling for inclusion in these decisions by challenging powerful corporations and governmental institutions through a critical perspective on power and control.

As Indigenous peoples continue to challenge the power structure of multinational corporations and the state, and assert their sovereignty rights as First Nations to control the natural resources within their territories according to treaties, the question of power and control over resources is beginning to change. This change can be seen in the relatively recent phenomenon of cooperation between some tribal groups and environmentalists. During the late 1960s and early 1970s, mainstream environmental groups and Indian tribes were usually at odds with each other over issues of concern such as natural resources and fishing and hunting rights.[15] When the Sokaogon Chippewa Indians began their long fight against Exxon's plans to mine next to their reservation in 1976, it was as if the death knell for the tribe had sounded with no hope of staving off this multinational giant. However, many environmentalists began to realize that "we all live downstream" and saw the importance of Indians' assertion of treaty rights as an integral part of environmental protection strategy. In 1976, the Sokaogon became engaged in a battle not only to preserve their wild rice subsistence culture and the treaty-protected waters flowing through their reservation, but for their economic and cultural survival as well. The Sokaogon's very cultural and economic survival depended on their ability to protect and defend the environment. The two could not be separated.[16]

Through this decade-long struggle against the formidable resources of Exxon and the state of Wisconsin, the Chippewa were able to garner support from some non-Indian neighbors, people in the tourist industry who also stood to lose their livelihoods if the fishing streams were hopelessly polluted by mining, and people in the environmental community. "By the time Exxon finally withdrew from the project in 1986, the Chippewa had assembled a broad-based Indian-environmentalist coalition that included every mainstream environmental organization in Wisconsin".[17] When Exxon and other multinational corporations regroup and return with other mining projects it will not be easy to get their projects underway. One important coalition known as the *Anishinaabe Niiji* (Friends of the Chippewa) that developed from then ten-year struggle between Exxon and the Sokaogon is now an established political force with powerful resources and the ability to take positive action to ensure that Indigenous voices are heard as the resource wars in Wisconsin continue into the new century.

An extremely important strategy that will continue to be used in the protection of natural resources is that of asserting treaty rights. According to LaDuke, one of the most important aspects of Indian treaty rights "is the power of the treaties to clarify issues which would otherwise be consigned to nation-state apologists to the realm of 'opinion' and 'interpretation.' The treaties lay things out clearly, and they are matters of international law."[18] Being victimized by a long history of exploitation has taught American Indian leaders new ways to defend the natural resources on their lands by using the law and trust relations with the United States as weapons in federal court.

By recognizing that a trust relationship exists between the United States and Indian tribes, and that this relationship binds the federal government to a set of responsibilities to tribes, courts and laws are being used to ensure that those responsibilities are met. Important lessons learned in the environmental battles of the 1970s include using trust status to the tribes' maximum advantage to protect their natural resources and lands, as well as reminding the federal government of its obligations as they have been established in treaties.[19]

To understand this trust relationship, the definition of "trust" must be considered. Trust is "a right in property held by one person, called the trustee, for the benefit of another, called the beneficiary, or *cestui que* trust."[20] The federal government has been active as *trustee* in this relationship by carrying out its trust responsibilities through the Bureau of Indian Affairs and the Department of the Interior. This occurred amidst criticism from the tribes for paternalism and ineffectiveness.[21]

Through battles fought over the years, tribes have some to realize that they need to acquire and apply legal expertise to effectively deal with these struggles. In bringing matters regarding resources to court, tribes have had to shift their perspective from looking at their lands in a communal "traditional" way to viewing their properties as "real estate." Imitating the capitalistic attitudes and strategies of corporations *and* demanding their legal, sovereign rights within the "white" justice system has become an effective and essential defensive tactic in defending tribal resources.[22] Through these conflicts in the U.S court system, tribes will continue to develop their own judicial and economic strengths in establishing tribal control over their own natural resources.

In society built upon hierarchical power such as the United States, however, establishing tribal control over natural resources will meet with resistance. Sociologist Stephen Pfohl has written extensively about deviant behavior, social control, and power from a critical perspective.[23] He argues that if we examine the current situation through the lens of a critical perspective, we find that the control of resources is governed by the interests of those most privileged by power. Using Pfohl's critical perspective in examining the situation of American Indians, I would argue that Indian people have been, throughout history, ritually stripped of their power, except for treaty rights. Resistance of Indian people through assertion of treaty rights to keep their land base and protect their resources threatens the privilege and control of powerful multinational corporations and the state.

In the previous example of the Sokaogon's resistance to Exxon, as they fought (and continue to fight) to hold on to their way of life, many Chippewa in Wisconsin have fiercely resisted the destruction of the environment and the destruction of their treaty rights by multinational corporations and the state. The Chippewa of Wisconsin, along with several grassroots organizations, are no longer willing to submit to the corporations' ongoing war of aggression against Native peoples and the natural world.[24] The Chippewa's unwillingness to acquiesce to the most powerful institutions on the world has been met with various institutional sanctions, including criminalizing those who dare to resist.

In order to maintain control over the land and resources of others (in this case, the Chippewa of Wisconsin), corporate/state actors must effectively neutralize the efforts of those who would oppose this control. As a tactic to mobilize public opinion in favor of corporations, American Indians who have resisted the environmentally destructive corporate mega-projects on tribal lands have been portrayed by the media as deviant and un-American because they are supposedly impeding progress. We need only to look to past examples of American Indians as victims of ethnocide and ethnoviolence.[25] American Indians, as a whole, have been systematically portrayed as deviant since first contact with Europeans, and later, European-Americans who have engaged in deculturating and redefining them as inferior beings.[26] Historic rituals of embedding in the Anglo mind images of Native peoples as "savages," "backward," "uncivilized," and "unintelligent," justified the continue repression of traditional ways and forced assimilation into the dominant culture through violence when deemed necessary.[27]

Their construction as the "deviant other" along with political and economic disempowerment provides the context for multinational corporations and the state of Wisconsin to wage a war of aggression against the Chippewa for their natural resources. This can be seen in the intense racial conflicts between the Chippewa and non-Indians experienced in Wisconsin for the past twenty years. These conflicts are a relevant political fact. Since off-reservation treaty rights allowing the Chippewa to spearfish outside reservation boundaries were reaffirmed by the Supreme Court in the 1983 *Voigt* case, many northern communities in Wisconsin have been bitterly divided.[28] Sportfishers and hunters find the traditional practices of spearing, gill-netting, and "shining" (night hunting) used by the Chippewa concerned with following their traditions rather than sport, objectionable. Opponents of the court's decision consider it "unjust" for the Chippewa to have "special privileges" denied to other Wisconsin residents—like longer hunting seasons and the right to shoot deer from vehicles—just because of some "old treaties."[29] Limited by very strict state regulations, many sportfishers were upset that the efficient Chippewa methods of harvesting fish for subsistence were not available to non-Indians. The opposition started in small groups protesting the regained Chippewa treaty rights. As the groups enlarged, the controversy turned into racial slurs and violence. Bait shops in northern towns sold "Treaty Beer" with labels protesting Indian spearfishing and claiming to be the "True Brew of the Working

Man," while many restaurants and taverns displayed and dispensed literature attacking spearfishing and called for the abrogation of Chippewa treaties.[30] Victimizing the Chippewa also included hurling rocks, insults, racial epithets like "timber niggers," waving effigies of speared Indian heads like props from a horror movie, displaying signs with slogans like "Save Two Walleye, Kill a Pregnant Squaw," and using large motorboats trailing anchors to capsize Indian boats.[31]

The intense racism experienced by the Chippewa prompted Archbishop William Wantland of the Episcopalian Diocese of Eau Clair, Wisconsin, to state that "of all the states I've lived in this Union, Wisconsin is the most racist. I grew up in the South. And I said that before the *Voigt Decision* was handed down. It's obvious—the racism, the hatred, the bitterness, the prejudice."[32] Wantland's reflection on the hostility and racism toward the Chippewa since the court's decision in 1983 is particularly telling: "I felt I was caught in a time warp this spring in Wisconsin. I thought I saw the '50s and '60s. I thought I saw Selma and Little Rock and Montgomery."[33]

None of the racism described here is unrelated to multinational corporations and the ongoing war of aggression against Native peoples and natural resources. Even though the Supreme Court made its position on the *Voigt Decision* abundantly clear when it refused to hear the state of Wisconsin's appeal, and even though the U.S. Constitution states that treaties are the supreme law of the land, Governor Tommy Thompson criticized the Chippewa for exercising their treaty rights. It is important to note that every study conducted on the impact of Chippewa spearfishing, from both the Wisconsin Department of Natural Resources and the Great Lakes Indian Fish and Wildlife Commission, to the most recent report commissioned by Congress, has failed to find any evidence to support the accusations that the Chippewa are threatening the fish resource.[34] This gives one pause to wonder why Thompson and the corporate CEOs would hide behind false hysteria.

The mass media effectively assisted the antitreaty movement by fueling the fires with sensationalism surrounding the treaty controversy and almost completely ignored the economic and political contexts of the issue.[35] Plans to institute a mining district in the ceded territory of the Wisconsin Chippewa, actively pursued by the executive branch of the state of Wisconsin, has the potential to cause serious long-term damage to the resource and economic bases of northern Wisconsin. Behind the well of the racist rhetoric of the spearfishing controversy

> lies the essential and inseparable connection between the political assault against Indian treaties and the corporate assault on the environment in the 1990s. By focusing on the issue of resource control in the ceded territory, it is possible to see the convergence between the anti-Indian movement, represented by groups like Protect Americans' Rights and Resources (PARR) and stop Treaty Abuse (STA), and the pro-mining policy of the Thompson administration in Wisconsin.[36]

Through effective use of the mass media and by using the convenient excuse that spearfishing was a drain on fish resources, it became easy for those in positions of power to portray the Chippewa as deviants who were "raping the resources," resisting mining, and therefore impeding pursuit of the capitalistic American Dream.

Criminologist Raymond Michalowski has written extensively on the subject of state-corporate crime and the political economy of crime. His work on the dynamic relationship between the capitalist economic model and the hierarchical workings of the state helps analyze resistance as deviance. Michalowski writes that "it is the political economy of a society in connection with its cultural history that determined the definition of what acts are adaptive, rebellious, or maladaptive."[37] Michalowski points out that

> to understand the "criminality" of any particular individual or group [in this case resistance by the Chippewa] requires critical examination of the objective yet dynamic connections between individual experience and the historically specific character of material and social relations.[38]

In applying Michalowski's analysis to the scenario occurring between the Chippewa and the corporate/state actors in Wisconsin, it is important to recognize that identity is always socially constructed and that relationships of power play an important role in this construction. From this perspective, being Indian in America is not merely a static condition or state defined by some constellation of perceived physical differences but is a set of social and material relations between American Indians and white Americans that extend back to the time the first treaties were made. Indigenous peoples have existed within and adapted to a set of material and controlling social relations that provides others with greater access to wealth than themselves. Resistance as deviance and social control is located in recurrent historical struggles to control material existence. A critical view of these hierarchical social structures argues that these historical creations do not exist naturally; they are synthetic. The age-old structures between powerful institutions and the Chippewa are reproduced over and over again as part of the everyday struggles of people. A critical approach to the events occurring between the Chippewa and corporate/state institutions provides a framework for challenging these recurrent historical struggles, the hierarchical structure of government, and its application of law.[39] Indigenous peoples have existed within and adapted to a set of material and controlling social relations that provides others with greater access to wealth than themselves.

Social control is always an exercise of power. Linear colonial logic argues that those who are "less civilized" (that is, Indigenous peoples who have different ways of utilizing knowledge) are unable to properly exploit the land and its resources, so therefore, those deemed to be "civilized" (the colonizers) would make decisions about the land and decide on the "who" and "why" when making the laws concerning that land and the environment. Ward Churchill is a well-known scholar, activist, and coordinator of American Indian studies with the Center for Studies of Ethnicity and Race in America at the University of Colorado at Boulder. Churchill and LaDuke have written extensively on issues of Native peoples worldwide. In discussing issues of social control and land they write,

> land has always been the issue of greatest importance to politics and economics in this country. Those who control the land are those who control the resources within and upon it. No matter what the resource issue at hand is, social control and all the other aggregate components of power are fundamentally interrelated.[40]

The many stories of resistance are not solely about Indian resistance, but involve an environmental social movement that is able to counteract corporate power as well. The assertion of Native land right takes place in the context of an environmental movement willing to accept other ways of "knowing" and "understanding" to appreciate the knowledge Native people have about the environment, and to accept Native leadership in environmental battles. As has been demonstrated in previous examples, Native peoples today are challenging the most powerful institutions of a large nation-state by using their capabilities to blend assertion of treaty with innovative forms of environmental activism.

The state and multinational corporations have consistently used their historically structured hierarchical positions of power to keep Indian people powerless and in a position of relative disadvantage in the past. Clearly, when the efforts of those privileged by power have been blocked by resistance based in treaty rights, unethical practices in dealing with the tribes have occurred which have caused them injury and harm. Those in powerful positions have countered Indian resistance by using the force of racism. Sociologist Robert Bullard argues that "[W]hether by conscious design or institutional neglect, communities of color in urban ghettos, in rural 'poverty pockets,' or on economically impoverished Native-American reservations face some of the worst environmental devastation in the nation."[41] The struggle engaged in by the Chippewa to protect their natural resources from the state of Wisconsin and huge multinational corporations is but one such example.

Environmental racism experienced by the Chippewa is evident in the systematic efforts put forth to exclude them from participation in the decision-making process. In an effort to "neutralize" the opposition, corporations have narrowly defined issues that can be raised in environmental impact statements and have ignored the objections of those opposed to the destruction caused by mining. And, as we have seen, with the increasing power of mining opponents, other methods of "neutralizing" the opposition must be found by the state and corporations. As illustrated earlier in this article, the state government and corporations have resorted to using the climate of race hatred to weaken and divide potential coalitions active against their multinational corporate vision of industrial development.

Examining these situations from a critical perspective helps facilitate an understanding of the way in which those in power are participants in creating an environmentally harmful atmosphere which maintains current hierarchical positions of power. The critical perspective presented here can be applied to deconstruct the unequal relationship between the state/corporate entities and those who are less powerful, to reconstruct a better form of balance.

As mentioned earlier, balance is a very old and important concept to almost all Indian people and affects every facet of life. Today, it is widely recognized that our environment is drastically out of balance. We are in a state of environmental deterioration that requires alternative approached to economic survival. Underneath the rhetoric of the environmental problem lies the inseparable issue of power and what Stephen Pfohl describes as powerful rituals of control, which affect human rights as a whole.[42] The point is not only to understand the problem, but also to solve it. The common denominator is direct action aimed against the status quo. With the assertion of Native rights comes a firm rejection of business-as-usual. Structured arrangements of power within our society have given us images of those who deviate from the dominant order. In a world constructed as much by symbolic action as physical behavior, being a person who has disparate political beliefs or has skin of a different color may be reason enough to call in forces of control. This "natural" or commonsensical character of a social order is really not natural at all but synthetic, artificial, and feigned.

This historically established synthetic order is now being questioned and, in the case of many American Indian tribes previous examples in this article have shown, truly challenged. This is a good start, but more is needed. No single movement or group of related movements can succeed in offsetting present situations only through a shared rejection of injustices. They must also fight for their perception of justice by putting forward a unified vision of the alternatives.

As tribes continue to challenge state and corporate power, new definitions of who they are as Indian people and the role they play economically will emerge. Circular ways of viewing profitable business by utilizing environmentally sustainable methods will assist in redefining the ways Indian people, corporations, and the state do business and will redefine relationships between these groups. New and different ways to take what is needed from the environment without causing total environmental devastation must be examined in the future. Decreasing the environmental deterioration occurring today will require alternative approaches to economic security through sustainable land use practices. Sharing the knowledge that American Indian people have in this area will place the focus on cooperation rather than on hierarchical control. Rearranging this focus will have enormous impacts in the area of policy implementation.

POLICY IMPLEMENTAIONS

Policy is built on variety of philosophical and epistemological arguments, ultimately grounded in subjective choice, and developed using the political skills of strategy and persuasion. Based on this, the central question becomes: What philosophical and epistemological frame of reference is best suited for developing and initiating policy leading to environmental justice and power relations that are based on reciprocity rather than hierarchical domination? The critical perspective used here stresses the significance of values in rethinking how environmental

policy should be dealt with and is tested by placing views about the environment into an American Indian, specifically Chippewa, way of life. In other words, there is a need top reconceptualize neocolonial values deemed to be authoritative. When making decisions, policy should be grounded in doctrines and principles that stress reciprocal power and a holistic way of viewing the environment.

For most of this century, positivist philosophies dominated social science with the belief that questions and problems posed in the social world could be understood and solved using the same techniques as those applied to the physical world. Some have come to question the ability of positivist approaches to deal with complex social issues like those considered in U.S. policy.[43] The basic problem with the positivist approach is its inability to provide a way to transcend political interest in order to obtain policy knowledge.

What is suggested here is how policy analysis might benefit from a methodology which acknowledges that scientific knowledge is dependent upon the normative assumptions and social meanings of the world it explores. John Dryzek is one of the leading political scientists in policy analysis in the United States. Dryzek suggests that policy analysis should address ethics and normative theory and then apparent normative basis of the status quo in the decision-making process; that is, the values and interests represented in the existing regime and policy process.[44]

Along the same lines, political scientist Mary Hawkesworth argues that in order to effectively examine policy, the underlying values which derive decision making must be acknowledged. Most importantly, for Hawkesworth, sources of power must be critically examined. Indeed, the critical study of any subject should take into account the hierarchies of power that are inherent in our society.[45]

The critical perspective proposed here challenges policy analysts to place themselves within an environmental justice framework which would attempt to uncover the underlying assumptions that may contribute to and produce unequal protection. A framework such as this addresses the ethical and political questions of "who gets what, why, and how much."[46] Addressing ethical and political questions such as these is important because one frame of reference by itself does not inform the whole of the problems associated with negative environmental impacts on people of color and low-income groups.

The critical perspective challenges the policy analyst to choose among social values, and, because values underlie decisions, the policy analyst should recognize that by choosing only one framework, their frame of reference is culturally bound and dependent. This point is made by critically examining the values and lifestyle of American Indians.

A critical perspective offers a new frame of reference for policy-making grounded in the doctrines and principles of many American Indian people regarding the environment. This perspective demands critical thinking about the policies of both private and public sectors developed by those privileged with power in response to environmental issues. The critical perspective questions the assumptions upon which current policies are based, examines traditional solutions, and advocates new ways of thinking about the environment. While not perfect by any means, this perspective allows for different realities and reciprocal relations of power based upon mutual respect and insists that these different realities should be reflected in decisions and policies made to include Indigenous peoples.

Formulating environmental policies from a critical perspective includes taking into consideration questions about responsibilities toward the environment and how these responsibilities ought to be reflected in the policies adopted by the government, in the private sector, and in the habits of the population as a whole.

As we begin to view our history and future as Native people from critical perspective, we can reinterpret the values and validity of our own traditions, teachings, and culture within a contemporary context. With this in mind, there are many things that are possible to shade with our global society. One of the most important of these from a Native as well as a non-Native perspective is the reestablishment of a land ethic that is based upon the sound experience of our heritage. Some of these values may be transferable to the whole of society now that we are beginning a new century. Native philosophies of the land generally demonstrate an ethic that presents the earth as vital because we are all born of the earth and require its resources for our very survival. From this perspective it is also possible to see how the relationships that we form with nature are of essential importance. This is one of the elemental teachings that originate generally from within Native culture that expresses our relatedness to nature, creation, and each other. It is important to understand that we must begin, as a global society, to realize this wholeness or relatedness.

To illustrate, for many Ojibwa/Chippewa people, the environment is not an issue. It is a way of life. As with other tribes, the Ojibwa consider themselves inseparable from the natural elements of their land, placing environmental sustainability at the forefront. Environmental sustainability is the ability of a community to utilize its natural, human, and technological resources to ensure that all members of present and future generations can attain a high degree of health and well-being, economic security, and a say in shaping their future while maintaining the integrity of the ecological systems upon which all life and production depends. The most important aspects of sustainability include economic security, ecological integrity, democracy, and community.[47]

As expressed by our ancestors, we are part of nature and must begin to express an idea of community rather than conquest. Native teachings can help us understand our relationship with lied and creation as well as expand our awareness' of nature and natural cycles. We can begin to see that the earth is a resource for all our needs, in fact, our only resource. As human beings, it becomes increasingly valuable for us to recognize this relationship so that we may benefit by using the gifts of creation effectively and efficiently. By utilizing the environment and eliminating waste in appropriate ways, we begin to establish a way of seeing the future from the perspective of generations to come; not only with respect to oil and luxury items, but by placing value on clean air, water, and soil in ways that will sustain us and our societies into the future. Such an awareness of life can begin to have a profound effect on our whole global society. As a community sharing life with then earth, we can see our dependence with, not independence from, nature.

Though the realization that holistic Indigenous knowledge concerning the environment is important and essential to our survival as a whole, the teachings that Native peoples of the Americas present to our global society can be utilized in many ways, if given the chance.

However, our history has been one in which American Indian holistic views of the environment have come into conflict with the dominant capitalistic nature of early European settlers and continue to do so today. Since the beginning of the United States republic, control of the land and natural resources had been a source of conflict between European-American settlers and Indigenous nations. Disputes over land usage and ownership have defined the totality of government-Indian relationships from the first contact to the present day. The European perspective of exploitation of land and its resources will continue into the foreseeable future. Corporate mega-projects, development proposals, and get-rich-quick schemes have been inflicted upon tribes for years. Millions of dollars are at stake with large multinational corporations and the federal government clamoring to do business on reservations. These historically-structured, powerful institutions whose sole purpose for existence is to make as much money as possible through whatever ethical and unethical means necessary, will be slow be accept philosophies other than their own.

To illustrate, the 561 federally recognized Indian reservations within the United States are the most exploited and environmentally degraded lands anywhere in rural America. Through sanctioning of certain power arrangements by the federal Bureau of Indian Affairs, corporations and federal agencies have pressured, bribes, cajoled, and enticed their way in to mine for strategic minerals that would environmentally devastate the sacred rice beds of the Sokaogon Chippewa; to strip mine coal, as on the Crow and Navajo reservations; to drill for oil, as on the Blackfeet reservation; and to site garbage dumps and medical-waste incinerators, as on the Salt River and Gila River reservations. This historically structured process of exploitation and expropriation, all in the name of progress, goes on and on.[48]

Linear concepts of progress sanctioned through laws created in a capitalistic stratified society make up the current experience of sustainability. What distinguishes the American Indian perspective on the environment from the dominant capitalistic paradigm of Euro-centric environmental exploitation is that Natural Law (all of life naturally moves in a circular fashion) is supreme law and should provide the guiding principles upon which societies and peoples function. The holistic view of sustainability for the Ojibwa people, for example, is that laws made by nations, states, and municipalities are inferior to Natural Law and should be treated in this manner.[49]

Holistic environmental paradigms stand in sharp contrast to life in an industrial society. Natural Law is preempted in industrial society as human domination over nature becomes the central way of life. In contrast to the American Indian cyclical process of thinking, this linear concept of progress dominates industrial societies. Progress is defined in terms of economic growth and technological advancement and is key to the development of dominant civilized societies. From this perspective, the natural world is seen as something that is wild and in need of taming and cultivation. Those not part of this mentality are seen as primitive and in need of being civilized. Civilizing those who are not part of the dominant paradigm is the philosophical basis of colonialism, conquest, and the view that Western knowledge is the only legitimate way of "knowing."

Even though American Indian perspectives have a greater impact today on environmental politics and policy than previously, American Indian philosophies, values, and knowledge are not included in those policy decisions that benefit large corporations and serve the interests of the state. There is a vast social distance between the parties involved in corporate land and mineral issues that causes a breakdown in communication as well as misinterpretations of each party's actions. Walter Bresett, activist and member of the Red Cliff band of Chippewa, argues that Indians and non-Indians alike are being victimized by large corporations that reduce economic options.[50]

Activist and author Al Gedicks writes, "the sooner we stop labeling 'native issues' as something separate and distinct from our own survival, the sooner we will appreciate the critical interconnections of the world's ecosystems and social systems."[51] Environmental concerns can be absolutely crucial within the context of reservation politics; even before the most hostile of tribal councils, the kind of "Mother Earth" talk that would make Anglo corporate executives or legislators roll their eyes can make all the difference.[52] In dealing with American Indian people when making important decisions, such as formulating environmental policy, corporate America and the federal government would be wise to realize that among American Indian tribes there is a growing respect and a demand for the inclusion of generations of cumulative Indigenous knowledge which is essential in balancing business practices with sustainability.

Environmental harms follow the path of least resistance and are connected to many things such as the air we breathe, our food, water, lifestyles, and legal decisions. Developing economically sustainable alternatives will depend on many variables, such as research, effective organizing and lobbying, legal representation, effective use of the media, interactive utilization of Native rights and environmental movements by Indigenous groups and state/local governments, and an essential inclusion of Native beliefs and values concerning the environment.

Including these values singularly or in combination, depending on the context, into the political deliberative and locatives process can help bring about environmentally sound, long-term, sustainable economic alternatives. With the inclusion of Indigenous knowledge and values, the socially harmful interaction between economic and political institutions that we have seen in the past can be decreased while at the same time helping restore the balance which is so important to Native peoples. Clearly, incorporating these kinds of values and beliefs into policy decisions challenges and decolonizes the harmful, wasteful projects of profit-maximizing corporations and growth-at-all-costs government policies while strengthening Indian nations as a whole.

As a global society, it is possible to examine our relationship with the earth and realize that our future lies in our ability to sustain ourselves and the developments we choose to impose on the environment. Native traditions have incorporated many ways to sustain the harvest of resources that will not destroy their future availability. For example, Menominee Tribal Enterprises, in Keshena, Wisconsin, received international recognition for achievements made toward sustainable forestry practices. Situated on 220,000 acres of forested lands, the Menominee system of intensive forest management "is now a recognized leader in shelterwood systems for uneven-aged management of white pine, and hemlock-yellow birch ecosystems."[53]

We cannot return to a pristine existence, but we can make the best possible use of what we now have. We have an opportunity as a society to integrate our ways of "doing" to match the patterns and requirements of nature and natural environment. Cooperation with the environment is one way to integrate Native traditional values and mainstream concepts of development and future survival. With the assistance of Native traditions and teachings, we as a society can begin to identify patterns of nature that do work and present us with alternatives to ecological and global crises.

Corporations and the state would have us believe there is no other way, other than their way, to survive economically. They do not want to look at other ways of knowing because those ways might be more powerful than they are. As Mander writes, the only group of people, so far, who are clear-minded on this point are Native peoples, simply because they have kept their roots alive in an older, alternative, nature-based philosophy that has remained effective for tens of thousands of years and that has nurtured dimensions of knowledge and perceptions that seem outdated to many. It is crucial that Euro-centrism be reassessed for its impacts on the environment, tradition, and Native peoples, because Native societies and their knowledge of the environment, not our own, may well hold the key to future survival.[54]

In times past, Native nations in the Americas achieved an ecological balance with their environment. The great success that Native people experienced using natural patterns and strategies for survival is available to us now. It may be time for us to begin to examine the alternatives used throughout history to achieve the survival of Native societies. For example, Gedicks suggests investing in locally owned small firms and in labor-intensive technologies such as tribal fish hatcheries, renewable energy, recycling forest products, and organic farming, which would create far more jobs than mining, while at the same time contributing to an environmentally stable economy. Gedicks also suggests encouraging utilities to buy locally-produced renewable energy rather than encouraging electric utilities to build coal-fired power plants. He cites Northern States Power, a company building a wind farm in Buffalo Ridge, Minnesota, as an example of available, cost-effective technology.[55] From an American Indian context it is important, once again, to recognize the influence of past history, cultural perspectives, and environmental relationships. The logic that led us into the problems our society faces today is not adequate to develop informed solutions to these contemporary concerns.

Traditional knowledge, in all forms, is connected to the environment from which American Indian societies emerged. The role of the environment in American Indian culture creates a holistic perspective that influences Indigenous institutions, such as criminal justice, education, religion, community and interpersonal relationships, resource use, harvest, and many other important aspects of people's lives.

Together as a whole society, cooperation, not competition, can become a driving force. It may be possible to see our relationship with nature and the earth as a community of living people who interact interdependently with all communities and institutions of the earth, allowing us to become beings, persons, and societies that are part of nature once again.

NOTES

1. Winona LaDuke, foreword to *The New Resource Wars: Native Struggles against Multinational Corporations*, ed. A1 Gedicks (Boston MA: South End Press, 1993), p. ix.

2. LaDuke, foreword, p. xi.

3. Louise Grenier, *Working with Indigenous Knowledge: A Guide for Researchers* (Ottawa ON: International Development Research Centre, 1998), p. 1.

4. Grenier, *Working with Indigenous Knowledge*, p. 2.

5. Richard Wilk, "Sustainable Development: Practical, Ethical and Social Issues in Technology Transfer in Traditional Technology for Environmental Conservation and Sustainable Development in the Asian-Pacific Region," in proceedings, UNESCO–University of Tsukuba International Seminar on Traditional Technology for Environmental Conservation and Sustainable Development in the Asian-Pacific Region, 11–14 December 1995, Tsukuba Science City, Japan, p. 21. United Nations Educational, Scientific and Cultural Organization, New York; University of Tsukuba, Tsukuba, Japan. Cited in Grenier, *Working with Indigenous Knowledge*, p. vii.

6. Massaquoi (1993), quoted in Grenier, *Working with Indigenous Knowledge*, p. 102.

7. Renier, *working with Indigenous Knowledge*, p. 2.

8. G. E. Tinker, *Missionary Conquest: The Gospel and Native American Cultural Genocide* (Minneapolis MN: Fortress Press, 1993).

9. John Bodley, *Victims of Progress*, 2nd ed. (Palo Alto CA: Mayfield Press, 1982), p. 24.

10. Odessa Ramirez, "The Year of the Indigenous Peoples," *Social Justice: A Journal of Crime, Conflict and World Order* 19:2 (1992): 78–86.

11. LaDuke, foreword, p. x.

12. LaDuke, foreword, pp. x–xi.

13. Tinker, *Missionary Conquest*, pp. 8–11.

14. Quinney (1974), quoted in Stephen Pfohl, *Images of Deviance and Social Control: A Sociological History*, 2nd ed. (New York: McGraw Hill, 1994), p. 401.

15. A. Josephy, (1975), "Indian's Odd Foes," *New York Times*, 27 November 1975, cited in Gedicks, *The New Resource Wars*, p. 189.

16. Gedicks, *The New Resource Wars*, p. 189–90.

17. Gedicks, *The New Resource Wars*, p. 190.

18. LaDuke, foreword, p. xi.

19. Donald Fixico, *The Invasion of Indian Country in the Twentieth Century: American Capitalism and Tribal Natural Resources* (Boulder: University Press of Colorado, 1998), p. 177.

20. This definition of "trust" is provided by the fifty edition of *Citron's Law Lexicon*, comp. William C. Citron (Cincinnati OH: Anderson Publishing, 1973), pp. 290–91, cited in Fixico, *The Invasion of Indian Country*, p. 178.

21. Fixico, *The Invasion of Indian Country*, p. 178.

22. Fixico, *The Invasion of Indian Country*, p. 180.

23. See Pfohl, *Images of Deviance and Social Control.*

24. A partial list of grassroots organizations includes: Anishinabe Niiji, Chequamegon Alliance, Citizens for a Better Environment, Earth First!, Environmental Defense Fund, Environmental Mining Network, Environmentally Concerned Citizens of Lakeland Areas, Friends of the Earth, Madison Treaty Rights Group, Midwest Treaty Network, Rusk County Citizens Action Group, Sinsinawa Dominican Sisters of Wisconsin, and Wolf River Conservation Club.

25. See Barbara Perry, "From Ethnocide to Ethnoviolence: Layers of Native American Victimization," *Contemporary Justice Review* 5:3 (2000): 231–47.

26. See Perry, "From Ethnocide to Ethnoviolence"; David Standard, *American Holocaust* (New York: Oxford University Press, 1992); Devon A. Mihesuah, *American Indians: Stereotypes and Realities* (Atlanta GA: Clarity Press, 1996); and M. Annette Jaimes, "Native American Identity and Survival: Indigenism and Environmental Ethics," in *Issues in Native American Cultural Identity*, ed. Michael K. Green (New York: Peter Lang, 1995), pp. 273–96.

27. See Perry, "From Ethnocide to Ethnoviolence"; and James Riding In, "Images of American Indians: American Indians in Popular Culture: A Pawnee's Experiences and Views," in *Images of Color, Images of Crime*, ed. Coramae Richey Mann and Marjorie S. Zatz (Los Angeles CA: Roxbury, 1998). pp. 15–29.

28. Gedicks, *The New Resource Wars*, p. 163.

29. Ronald N. Satz, "Chippewa Treaty Rights: The Reserved Rights of Wisconsin's Chippewa Indians in Historical Perspective," *Transactions* 79:1 (1991): 101.

30. Satz, "Chippewa Treaty Rights," p. 101.

31. Satz, "Chippewa Treaty Rights," p. 101.

32. Satz, "Chippewa Treaty Rights," p. 104.

33. Masinaigan (1990), 7–8, cited in Satz, "Chippewa Treaty Rights," p. 104.

34. Busiahn (1991); U.S. Dept. of the Interior (1991), quoted by Gedicks, *The New Resource Wars*, p. 164.

35. Gedicks, *The New Resource Wars*, p. 164.

36. Gedicks, *The New Resource Wars*, p. 164.

37. Raymond Michalowski, "A Critical Model for the Study of Crime," in *Criminal Behavior: Text and Readings in Criminology*, ed. Delos H. Kelly, 2nd ed. (New York: St. Martin's Press, 1990), 196.

38. Michalowski, "A Critical Model for the Study of Crime," p. 196.

39. Linda Robyn, "A Critical Model for the Study of Resource Colonialism and Native Resistance," in *Controversies in White-Collar Crime*, ed. Gary Potter (Cincinnati OH: Anderson, 2002), pp. 86, 96.

40. Ward Churchill and Winona LaDuke, "Native North America: The Political Economy of Radioactive Colonialism," in *The State of Native America: Genocide, Colonization, and Resistance*, ed. M. Annette Jaimes (Boston: South End Press, 1992), pp. 241–62.

41. Robert Bullard, *Confronting Environmental Racism* (Boston MA: South End Press, 1993), p. 17.

42. Pfohl, *Images of Deviance and Social Control*, pp. 7–8, 430–35.

43. Frank Fischer and John Forester, *The Argumentative Turn in Policy Analysis and Planning* (Durham NC: Duke University Press, 1993), pp. 214–15.

44. John Dryzek, "From Sciences to Argument," in *The Argumentative Turn in Policy Analysis and Planning*, ed. Frank Fischer and John Forester (Durham NC: Duke University Press, 1993), pp. 10–15.

45. Mary Hawkesworth, "Epistemology and Policy Analysis," in *Advances in Policy Studies Since 1950*, ed. William Dunn and Rita Mae Kelly (New Brunswick NJ: Transaction, 1992), pp. 295–329.

46. Robert Bullard, *Dumping in Dixie: Race, Class, and Environmental Quality*, 2nd ed. (Boulder CO: Westview Press, 1994), p. 119.

47. Anthony Cortese, Elizabeth Kline, and Jessie Smith, "Second Nature Partnership Training Manual," comp. and pub. Second Nature (manual used at Partnership Training: Education for a Sustainable Future, Northern Arizona University, 14–18 June 1994).

48. Margaret L. Knox, "Their Mother's Keepers," *Sierra Magazine* 78:2 (March/April 1993): 50.

49. LaDuke, foreword, pp. xi–xi.

50. Walter Bresett (remarks presented at A Watershed Conference on Mining and Treaty Rights, Tomahawk WI, 30–31 October 1992).

51. Gedicks, *The New Resource Wars*, p. 202.

52. Knox, "Their Mother's Keepers," p. 50.

53. Dave Bubser, "Menominee Sustainable Forestry," *Cultural Survival Quarterly* 16:3 (fall), quoted in Gedicks, *The New Resource Wars*, pp. 29, 197.

54. Jerry Mander, *In the Absence of the Sacred: The Failure of Technology and the Survival of the Indian Nations* (San Francisco CA: Sierra Club Books, 1991), p. 384.

55. Gedicks, *The New Resource Wars*, p. 197.

STUDY QUESTIONS

1. What is meant by "indigenous knowledge"?

2. Why does Robyn use the phrase *state and corporate power*? From an indigenous perspective, how are these related?

3. According to Robyn, what types of things do we all have to learn from indigenous cultures?

56

Earth Democracy

VANDANA SHIVA

Vandana Shiva is an internationally renowned scholar, feminist, and antiglobalization activist. Visit http://www.vandanashiva.org/ for further details. This brief essay links political freedom with environmental integrity.

Earth democracy is my vision, the basis of my activism.

Today, we are being ruled by terror and greed, fear and insecurity. As we face the tightening control of public space by corporate globalization and militarized police states, by an economic fascism aided by political fascism, our challenge has become to reclaim our freedom and the freedom of our fellow

Introduction to Ecofeminism, ed. Maria Mies (Zed Books, London 1993). Reprinted by permission of Zed Books.

beings. The Earth Democracy Movements takes up this challenge by advocating the creation of all-inclusive living economies that protect life on earth while providing basic needs for all.

The Earth Democracy Movement is based on two fundamental principles. The first is the continuity of all life on earth, and its right to freedom on the basis of gender, race, religion, class, and species. The second is the continuum between and indivisibility of justice, peace and sustainability—we believe that without ecological sustainability and a just division of the earth's bounties, there can be no peace.

Corporate globalization ruptures these continuities. Because corporations establish their dominance through a divide and rule policy, corporate globalization creates competition and conflict between different species and peoples, often subjugating other species to the demands of humankind. By spreading insecurity, it transforms diversity into a set opposi-tional differences, which then give rise to funda-mentalisms that diminish freedom and shift our focus from sustainability and justice and peace to ethnic and religious conflict and violence.

The Earth Democracy Movement is commit-ted to going beyond the triple crisis of economic injustice ecological non-sustainability, and the sub-jugation of people and other species brought on by the growth of global capitalism. Instead, the Earth Democracy Movement provides an alternative worldview in which humans are embedded in the earth family. In this vision, we are connected to each other through love and compassion, not hatred and violence, and ecological responsibility and economic justice replace greed, consumerism, and competition as the fundamental objectives of human life.

DIVERSITY VS. MONOCULTURE

Corporate globalization embraces exclusivist mono-cultural modes of thinking—the belief in the nec-essary dominance of one species, one race, one economy, one religion. This monoculturalism is leading to the destruction of resources; the creation of monopolies over land, biodiversity, water, and food; the deepening of poverty and the exclusion of millions from their livelihoods and economic se-curity; and the destruction of democracy, peace, and cultural diversity. It creates a negative system that provides short-run benefits to just a few. Monocultures are the result of exclusion, intoler-ance, and domination, and they support exclusion, intolerance, and domination. Their very presence indicates some dominant group or species and ex-perienced coercion and loss of freedom.

The Earth Democracy Movement counters the spread of monoculturalism by transforming our minds and actions, liberating us from this dominant pattern of thought. Earth democracy recontextua-lises human beings as one member of the earth family (Vasudhaiva Kutumbkam). When the intrin-sic worth and value of every life form and even human is recognized, biological diversity and cul-tural diversity flourish.

By replacing monocultures with diverse cul-tures, and replacing one-dimensional systems with multidimensional ones, the economics of scarcity can be replaced by the economy of mutually-shared abundance, the guaranteed provision of basic needs, and access to vital resources. Reembedding humans in the ecological matrix of biological and cultural diversity reopens spaces for sustainability, justice, and peace by reorganizing relationships. It also restructures constellations of power, revitalizing freedom and democracy. Gandhi's concept of Swadeshi—of economic freedom and economic democracy—is at the core of the vision.

THE EXCLUDED MIDDLE

Corporate globalization promotes the formation of monocultural thinking by advocating the logic of exclusion, of apartheid, of "us" and" them," of ei-ther/or. It polarizes societies and species into two camps, ignoring continuities, excluding the middle. It creates divisions and exclusions that pit the econ-omy against ecology, development against environ-ment, people against the planet, and people against one another in a new culture of hate.

be enshrined in international law and policy, and to be backed by popular democratic pressure to reform the WTO and the World Bank. A step in the right direction would be to implement the review of TRIPs (Trade Related Intellectual Property Rights), that countries of the global south are calling for, along with an exclusion of life from patentability and a review of structural adjustment programs that impose export-led agricultural strategies and promote policies of water privatization. Since sovereignty, based on the doctrine of eminent domain, has become the conduit for global usurpation of communities' resources and has undermined their sovereign rights, reclaiming biodiversity and water commons must go hand in hand with reclaiming sovereignty, and redefining a new partnership between people and governments on the basis of a public trust doctrine.

Mandates to defend water and biodiversity as commons will have democratic power and substance to the extent they recognize and strengthen local communities' rights at the global level. Global commons that are not built from, or based on the authority of, locally controlled commons would be ecologically and democratically fraudulent. The idea for global commons is merely a recognition and reinforcement of local community rights.

CONCLUSION

The economic, ecological, and social crises resulting from corporate globalization invite a new way of thinking and being on this planet. We can embrace a new worldview in which compassion not greed is globalized, a new consciousness in which we are not reduced to consumers of globally-traded commodities and to narrow, fragmented, one-dimensional identities based on color, religion, or ethnicity, but can instead experience our lives as diverse beings with planetary consciousnesses, mindful and aware of what our actions may cost other humans, other species, and future generations, and connected to each other and the world in the common fabric of life.

Beginning with people's everyday actions, Earth democracy offers us the potential for changing the way governments, intergovernmental organizations, and corporations operate. It creates a new paradigm for global conveyance while empowering local communities, and the possibility of strengthening ecological security while improving economic security. Under Earth democracy, societies would be immune to the virus of communal hatred and fear. With Earth democracy, we would be able to achieve freedom with diversity, and peace with sustainability and justice.

Vandana Shiva is an international scholar, author, and lecturer, and has served as the director of the Research Foundation for Science Technology and Natural Resource Policy in India since 1982.

STUDY QUESTIONS

1. What does Shiva mean by "earth democracy"?
2. According to Shiva, what is wrong with "privatization"?

57

The Power and the Promise of Ecological Feminism

KAREN J. WARREN

Karen Warren is the editor of several books and the author of numerous articles in environmental philosophy. She is professor of philosophy at Macalester College. In this reading she examines the connections between the domination of nature and the domination of woman, suggesting that ecofeminism, a feminist ethic of nature, holds great promise for developing humanity on both accounts.

Ecological feminism is the position that there are important connections—historical, symbolic, theoretical—between the domination of women and the domination of nonhuman nature. I argue that because the conceptual connections between the dual dominations of women and nature are located in an oppressive patriarchal conceptual framework characterized by a logic of domination, (1) the logic of traditional feminism requires the expansion of feminism to include ecological feminism and (2) ecological feminism provides a framework for developing a distinctively feminist environmental ethic. I conclude that any feminist theory and any environmental ethic which fails to take seriously the interconnected dominations of women and nature is simply inadequate.

INTRODUCTION

Ecological feminism (ecofeminism) has begun to receive a fair amount of attention lately as an alternative feminism and environmental ethic.[1] Since Francoise d'Eaubonne introduced the term *ecofeminisme* in 1974 to bring attention to women's potential for bringing about an ecological revolution[2] the term has been used in a variety of ways. As I use the term in this paper, ecological feminism is the position that there are important connections—historical, experiential, symbolic, theoretical—between the domination of women and the domination of nature, an understanding of which is crucial to both feminism and environmental ethics. I argue that the promise and power of ecological feminism is that *it provides a distinctive framework both for reconceiving feminism and for developing an environmental ethic which takes seriously connections between the domination of women and the domination of nature.* I do so by discussing the nature of a feminist ethic and the ways in which ecofeminism provides a feminist and environmental ethic. I conclude that any feminist theory *and* any environmental ethic which fails to take seriously the twin and interconnected dominations of women and nature is at best incomplete and at worst simply inadequate.

From *Environmental Ethics* (1990), pp. 125–46. Reprinted by permission of the author.

FEMINISM, ECOLOGICAL FEMINISM, AND CONCEPTUAL FRAMEWORKS

Whatever else it is, feminism is at least the movement to end sexist oppression. It involves the elimination of any and all factors that contribute to the continued and systematic domination or subordination of women. While feminists disagree about the nature of and solutions to the subordination of women, all feminists agree that sexist oppression exists, is wrong, and must be abolished.

A "feminist issue" is any issue that contributes in some way to understanding the oppression of women. Equal rights, comparable pay for comparable work, and food production are feminist issues wherever and whenever an understanding of them contributes to an understanding of the continued exploitation or subjugation of women. Carrying water and searching for firewood are feminist issues wherever and whenever women's primary responsibility for these tasks contributes to their lack of full participation in decision making, income producing, or high status positions engaged in by men. What counts as a feminist issue, then, depends largely on context, particularly the historical and material conditions of women's lives.

Environmental degradation and exploitation are feminist issues because an understanding of them contributes to an understanding of the oppression of women. In India, for example, both deforestation and reforestation through the introduction of a monoculture species tree (e.g., eucalyptus) intended for commercial production are feminist issues because the loss of indigenous forests and multiple species of trees has drastically affected rural Indian women's ability to maintain a subsistence household. Indigenous forests provide a variety of trees for food, fuel, fodder, household utensils, dyes, medicines, and income-generating uses, while monoculture-species forests do not.[3] Although I do not argue for this claim here, a look at the global impact of environmental degradation on women's lives suggests important respects in which environmental degradation is a feminist issue.

Feminist philosophers claim that some of the most important feminist issues are *conceptual* ones: these issues concern how one conceptualizes such mainstay philosophical notions as reason and rationality, ethics, and what it is to be human. Ecofeminists extend this feminist philosophical concern to nature. They argue that, ultimately, some of the most important connections between the domination of women and the domination of nature are conceptual. To see this, consider the nature of conceptual frameworks.

A *conceptual framework* is a set of *basic* beliefs, values, attitudes, and assumptions which shape and reflect how one views oneself and one's world. It is a socially constructed lens through which we perceive ourselves and others. It is affected by such factors as gender, race, class, age, affectional orientation, nationality, and religious background.

Some conceptual frameworks are oppressive. An *oppressive conceptual framework* is one that explains, justifies, and maintains relationships of domination and subordination. When an oppressive conceptual framework is *patriarchal*, it explains, justifies, and maintains the subordination of women by men.

I have argued elsewhere that there are three significant features of oppressive conceptual frameworks: (1) value-hierarchical thinking, i.e., "up-down" thinking which places higher value, status, or prestige on what is "up" rather than on what is "down"; (2) value dualisms, i.e., disjunctive pairs in which the disjuncts are seen as oppositional (rather than as complementary) and exclusive (rather than as inclusive), and which place higher value (status, prestige) on one disjunct rather than the other (e.g., dualisms which give higher value or status to that which has historically been identified as "mind," "reason," and "male" than to that which has historically been identified as "body," "emotion," and "female"); and (3) logic of domination, i.e., a structure of argumentation which leads to a justification of subordination.[4]

The third feature of oppressive conceptual frameworks is the most significant. A logic of domination is not *just* a logical structure. It also involves a substantive value system, since an ethical premise is needed to permit or sanction the "just" subordination of that which is subordinate. This justification typically is given on grounds of some alleged characteristic (e.g., rationality) which the dominant (e.g., men) have and the subordinate (e.g., women) lack.

Contrary to what many feminists and ecofeminists have said or suggested, there may be nothing *inherently* problematic about "hierarchical thinking" or even "value-hierarchical thinking" in contexts other than contexts of oppression. Hierarchical thinking is important in daily living for classifying data, comparing information, and organizing material. Taxonomies (e.g., plant taxonomies) and biological nomenclature seem to require *some* form of "hierarchical thinking." Even "value-hierarchical thinking" may be quite acceptable in certain contexts. (The same may be said of "value dualisms" in non-oppressive contexts.) For example, suppose it is true that what is unique about humans is our conscious capacity to radically reshape our social environments (or "societies"), as Murray Bookchin suggests.[5] Then one could truthfully say that humans are better equipped to radically reshape their environments than are rocks or plants—a "value-hierarchical" way of speaking.

The problem is not simply *that* value-hierarchical thinking and value dualisms are used, but *the way* in which each has been used *in oppressive conceptual frameworks* to establish inferiority and to justify subordination.[6] It is the logic of domination, *coupled with* value-hierarchical thinking and value dualisms, which "justifies" subordination. What is explanatorily basic, then, about the nature of oppressive conceptual frameworks is the logic of domination.

For ecofeminism, that a logic of domination is explanatorily basic is important for at least three reasons. First, without a logic of domination, a description of similarities and differences would be just that—a description of similarities and differences. Consider the claim, "Humans are different from plants and rocks in that humans can (and plants and rocks cannot) consciously and radically reshape the communities in which they live; humans are similar to plants and rocks in that they are both members of an ecological community." Even if humans are "better" than plants and rocks with respect to the conscious ability of humans to radically transform communities, one does not

thereby get any *morally* relevant distinction between humans and nonhumans, or an argument for the domination of plants and rocks by humans. To get *those* conclusions one needs to add at least two powerful assumptions, viz., (A2) and (A4) in argument A below:

(A1) Humans do, and plants and rocks do not, have the capacity to consciously and radically change the community in which they live.

(A2) Whatever has the capacity to consciously and radically change the community in which it lives is morally superior to whatever lacks this capacity.

(A3) Thus, humans are morally superior to plants and rocks.

(A4) For any X and Y, if X is morally superior to Y, then X is morally justified in subordinating Y.

(A5) Thus, humans are morally justified in subordinating plants and rocks.

Without the two assumptions that *humans are morally superior* to (at least some) nonhumans, (A2), and that *superiority justifies subordination*, (A4), all one has is some difference between humans and some nonhumans. This is true *even if* that difference is given in terms of superiority. Thus, it is the logic of domination, (A4), which is the bottom line in ecofeminist discussions of oppression.

Second, ecofeminists argue that, at least in Western societies, the oppressive conceptual framework which sanctions the twin dominations of women and nature is a patriarchal one characterized by all three features of an oppressive conceptual framework. Many ecofeminists claim that, historically, within at least the dominant Western culture, a patriarchal conceptual framework has sanctioned the following argument B:

(B1) Women are identified with nature and the realm of the physical; men are identified with the "human" and the realm of the mental.

(B2) Whatever is identified with nature and the realm of the physical is inferior to ("below") whatever is identified with the "human" and the realm of the mental; or, conversely, the latter is superior to ("above") the former.

(B3) Thus, women are inferior to ("below") men; or, conversely, men are superior to ("above") women.

(B4) For any X and Y, if X is superior to Y, then X is justified in subordinating Y.

(B5) Thus, men are justified in subordinating women.

If sound, argument B establishes *patriarchy*, i.e., the conclusion given at (B5) that the systematic domination of women by men is justified. But according to ecofeminists, (B5) is justified by just those three features of an oppressive conceptual framework identified earlier: value-hierarchical thinking, the assumption at (B2); value dualisms, the assumed dualism of the mental and the physical at (B1) and the assumed inferiority of the physical vis-à-vis the mental at (B2); and a logic of domination, the assumption at (B4), the same as the previous premise (A4). Hence, according to ecofeminists, insofar as an oppressive patriarchal conceptual framework has functioned historically (within at least dominant Western culture) to sanction the twin dominations of women and nature (argument B), both argument B and the patriarchal conceptual framework, from whence it comes, ought to be rejected.

Of course, the preceeding does not identify which premises of B are false. What is the status of premises (B1) and (B2)? Most, if not all, feminists claim that (B1), and many ecofeminists claim that (B2), have been assumed or asserted within the dominant Western philosophical and intellectual tradition.[7] As such, these feminists assert, as a matter of historical fact, that the dominant Western philosophical tradition has assumed the truth of (B1) and (B2). Ecofeminists, however, either deny (B2) or do not affirm (B2). Furthermore, because some ecofeminists are anxious to deny any ahistorical identification of women with nature, some ecofeminists deny (B1) when (B1) is used to support anything other than a strictly historical claim about what has been asserted or assumed to be true within patriarchal culture—e.g., when (B1) is used to assert that women properly are identified with the realm of

nature and the physical.[8] Thus, from an ecofeminist perspective, (B1) and (B2) are properly viewed as problematic though historically sanctioned claims: they are problematic precisely because of the way they have functioned historically in a patriarchal conceptual framework and culture to sanction the dominations of women and nature.

What *all* ecofeminists agree about, then, is the way in which *the logic of domination* has functioned historically within patriarchy to sustain and justify the twin dominations of women and nature.[9] Since *all* feminists (and not just ecofeminists) oppose patriarchy, the conclusion given at (B5), all feminists (including ecofeminists) must oppose at least the logic of domination, premise (B4), on which argument B rests—whatever the truth-value status of (B1) and (B2) *outside of* a patriarchal context.

That *all* feminists must oppose the logic of domination shows the breadth and depth of the ecofeminist critique of B: it is a critique not only of the three assumptions on which this argument for the domination of women and nature rests, viz., the assumptions at (B1), (B2), and (B4); it is also a critique of patriarchal conceptual frameworks generally, i.e., of those oppressive conceptual frameworks which put men "up" and women "down," allege some way in which women are morally inferior to men, and use that alleged difference to justify the subordination of women by men. Therefore, ecofeminism is necessary to *any* feminist critique of patriarchy, and, hence, necessary to feminism (a point I discuss again later).

Third, ecofeminism clarifies why the logic of domination, and any conceptual framework which gives rise to it, must be abolished in order both to make possible a meaningful notion of difference which does not breed domination and to prevent feminism from becoming a "support" movement based primarily on shared experiences. In contemporary society, there is no one "woman's voice," no *woman* (or *human*) *simpliciter*: every woman (or human) is a woman (or human) of some race, class, age, affectional orientation, marital status, regional or national background, and so forth. Because there are no "monolithic experiences" that all women share, feminism must be a "solidarity movement" based on shared beliefs and interests rather than a "unity in sameness" movement based on shared experiences and shared victimization.[10] In the words of Maria Lugones, "Unity—not to be confused with solidarity—is understood as conceptually tied to domination."[11]

Ecofeminists insist that the sort of logic of domination used to justify the domination of humans by gender, racial or ethnic, or class status is also used to justify the domination of nature. Because eliminating a logic of domination is part of a feminist critique—whether a critique of patriarchy, white supremacist culture, or imperialism— ecofeminists insist that *naturism* is properly viewed as an integral part of any feminist solidarity movement to end sexist oppression and the logic of domination which conceptually grounds it.

ECOFEMINISM RECONCEIVES FEMINISM

The discussion so far has focused on some of the oppressive conceptual features of patriarchy. As I use the phrase, the "logic of traditional feminism" refers to the location of the conceptual roots of sexist oppression, at least in Western societies, in an oppressive patriarchal conceptual framework characterized by a logic of domination. Insofar as other systems of oppression (e.g., racism, classism, ageism, heterosexism) are also conceptually maintained by a logic of domination, appeal to the logic of traditional feminism ultimately locates the basic conceptual interconnections among *all* systems of oppression in the logic of domination. It thereby explains at a *conceptual* level why the eradication of sexist oppression requires the eradication of the other forms of oppression.[12] It is by clarifying this conceptual connection between systems of oppression that a movement to end sexist oppression— traditionally the special turf of feminist theory and practice—leads to a reconceiving of feminism as *a movement to end all forms of oppression.*

Suppose one agrees that the logic of traditional feminism requires the expansion of feminism to include other social systems of domination (e.g., racism and classism). What warrants the inclusion of nature in these "social systems of domination"? Why must the logic of traditional feminism include the abolition of "naturism" (i.e., the domination or oppression of nonhuman nature) among the "isms" feminism must confront? The conceptual justification for expanding feminism to include ecofeminism is twofold. One basis has already been suggested: by showing that the conceptual connections between the dual dominations of women and nature are located in an oppressive and, at least in Western societies, patriarchal conceptual framework characterized by a logic of domination, ecofeminism explains how and why feminism, conceived as a movement to end sexist oppression, must be expanded and reconceived as also a movement to end naturism." This is made explicit by the following argument C:

(C1) Feminism is a movement to end sexism.

(C2) But Sexism is conceptually linked with naturism (through an oppressive conceptual framework characterized by a logic of domination).

(C3) Thus, Feminism is (also) a movement to end naturism.

Because, ultimately, these connections between sexism and naturism are conceptual—embedded in an oppressive conceptual framework—the logic of traditional feminism leads to the embracement of ecological feminism.[13]

The other justification for reconceiving feminism to include ecofeminism has to do with the concepts of gender and nature. Just as conceptions of gender are socially constructed, so are conceptions of nature. Of course, the claim that women and nature are social constructions does not require anyone to deny that there are actual humans and actual trees, rivers, and plants. It simply implies that *how* women and nature are conceived is a matter of historical and social reality. These conceptions vary cross-culturally and by historical time period. As a result, any discussion of the "oppression or domination of nature" involves reference to historically specific forms of social domination of nonhuman nature by humans, just as discussion of the "domination of women" refers to historically specific forms of social domination of women by men. Although I do not argue for it here, an ecofeminist defense of the historical connections between the dominations of women and of nature, claims (B1) and (B2) in argument B, involves showing that within patriarchy the feminization of nature and the naturalization of women have been crucial to the historically successful subordinations of both.[14]

If ecofeminism promises to reconceive traditional feminism in ways which include naturism as a legitimate feminist issue, does ecofeminism also promise to reconceive environmental ethics in ways which are feminist? I think so. This is the subject of the remainder of the paper.

CLIMBING FROM ECOFEMINISM TO ENVIRONMENTAL ETHICS

Many feminists and some environmental ethicists have begun to explore the use of first-person narrative as a way of raising philosophically germane issues in ethics often lost or underplayed in mainstream philosophical ethics. Why is this so? What is it about narrative which makes it a significant resource for theory and practice in feminism and environmental ethics? Even if appeal to first-person narrative is a helpful literary device for describing ineffable experience or a legitimate social science methodology for documenting personal and social history, how is first-person narrative a valuable vehicle of argumentation for ethical decision making and theory building? One fruitful way to begin answering these questions is to ask them of a particular first-person narrative.

Consider the following first-person narrative about rock climbing:

For my very first rock climbing experience, I chose a somewhat private spot, away from other climbers and onlookers. After studying "the chimney," I focused all my energy on making it to the top. I climbed with intense determination, using whatever strength and skills I had to accomplish this challenging feat. By midway I was exhausted and anxious. I couldn't see what to do next—where to put my hands or feet. Growing increasingly more weary as I clung somewhat desperately to the rock, I made a move. It didn't work. I fell. There I was, dangling midair above the rocky ground below, frightened but terribly relieved that the belay rope had held me. I knew I was safe. I took a look up at the climb that remained. I was determined to make it to the top. With renewed confidence and concentration, I finished the climb to the top.

On my second day of climbing, I rappelled down about 200 feet from the top of the Palisades at Lake Superior to just a few feet above the water level. I could see no one—not my belayer, not the other climbers, no one. I unhooked slowly from the rappel rope and took a deep cleansing breath. I looked all around me—really looked—and listened. I heard a cacophony of voices—birds, trickles of water on the rock before me, waves lapping against the rocks below. I closed my eyes and began to feel the rock with my hands—the cracks and crannies, the raised lichen and mosses, the almost imperceptible nubs that might provide a resting place for my fingers and toes when I began to climb. At that moment I was bathed in serenity. I began to talk to the rock in an almost inaudible, child-like way, as if the rock were my friend. I felt an overwhelming sense of gratitude for what it offered me—a chance to know myself and the rock differently, to appreciate unforeseen miracles like the tiny flowers growing in the even tinier cracks in the rock's surface, and to come to know a sense of *being in relationship* with the natural environment. It felt as if the rock and I were silent conversational partners in a longstanding friendship. I realized then that I had come to care about this cliff which was so different from me, so unmovable and invincible, independent and seemingly indifferent to my presence. I wanted to be with the rock as I climbed. Gone was the determination to conquer the rock, to forcefully impose my will on it; I wanted simply to work respectfully with the rock as I climbed. And as I climbed, that is what I felt. I felt myself *caring* for this rock and feeling thankful that climbing provided the opportunity for me to know it and myself in this new way.

There are at least four reasons why use of such a first-person narrative is important to feminism and environmental ethics. First, such a narrative gives voice to a felt sensitivity often lacking in traditional analytical ethical discourse, viz., a sensitivity to conceiving of oneself as fundamentally "in relationship with" others, including the nonhuman environment. It is a modality which *takes relationships themselves seriously*. It thereby stands in contrast to a strictly reductionist modality that takes relationships seriously only or primarily because of the nature of the *relators* or parties to those relationships (e.g., relators conceived as moral agents, right holders, interest carriers, or sentient beings). In the rock-climbing narrative above, it is the climber's relationship with the rock she climbs which takes on special significance—which is itself a locus of value—in addition to whatever moral status or moral considerability she or the rock or any other parties to the relationship may also have.[15]

Second, such a first-person narrative gives expression to a variety of ethical attitudes and behaviors often overlooked or underplayed in mainstream Western ethics, e.g., the difference in attitudes and behaviors toward a rock when one is "making it to the top" and when one thinks of oneself as "friends with" or "caring about" the rock one climbs.[16] These different attitudes and behaviors suggest an ethically germane contrast between two different types of relationship humans or climbers may have toward a rock: an imposed conqueror-type relationship, and an emergent caring-type relationship.

This contrast grows out of, and is faithful to, felt, lived experience.

The difference between conquering and caring attitudes and behaviors in relation to the natural environment provides a third reason why the use of first-person narrative is important to feminism and environmental ethics: it provides a way of conceiving of ethics and ethical meaning as *emerging out of* particular situations moral agents find themselves in, rather than as being *imposed on* those situations (e.g., as a derivation or instantiation of some predetermined abstract principle or rule). This emergent feature of narrative centralizes the importance of *voice*. When a multiplicity of cross-cultural *voices* are centralized, narrative is able to give expression to a range of attitudes, values, beliefs, and behaviors which may be overlooked or silenced by imposed ethical meaning and theory. As a reflection of and on felt, lived experiences, the use of narrative in ethics provides a stance from which ethical discourse can be held accountable to the historical, material, and social realities in which moral subjects find themselves.

Lastly, and for our purposes perhaps most importantly, the use of narrative has argumentative significance. Jim Cheney calls attention to this feature of narrative when he claims, "To contextualize ethical deliberation is, in some sense, to provide a narrative or story, from which the solution to the ethical dilemma emerges as the fitting conclusion."[17] Narrative has argumentative force by suggesting *what counts* as an appropriate conclusion to an ethical situation. One ethical conclusion suggested by the climbing narrative is that what counts as a proper ethical attitude toward mountains and rocks is an attitude of respect and care (whatever that turns out to be or involve), not one of domination and conquest.

In an essay entitled "In and Out of Harm's Way: Arrogance and Love," feminist philosopher Marilyn Frye distinguishes between "arrogant" and "loving" perception as one way of getting at this difference in the ethical attitudes of care and conquest.[18] Frye writes:

> The loving eye is a contrary of the arrogant eye.

The loving eye knows the independence of the other. It is the eye of a seer who knows that nature is indifferent. It is the eye of one who knows that to know the seen, one must consult something other than one's own will and interests and fears and imagination. One must look at the thing. One must look and listen and check and question.

The loving eye is one that pays a certain sort of attention. This attention can require a discipline but **not** a self-denial. The discipline is one of self-knowledge, knowledge of the scope and boundary of the self. … In particular, it is a matter of being able to tell one's own interests from those of others and of knowing where one's self leaves off and another begins.…

The loving eye does not make the object of perception into something edible, does not try to assimilate it, does not reduce it to the size of the seer's desire, fear and imagination, and hence does not have to simplify. It knows the complexity of the other as something which will forever present new things to be known. The science of the loving eye would favor The Complexity Theory of Truth [in contrast to The Simplicity Theory of Truth] and presuppose The Endless Interestingness of the Universe.[19]

According to Frye, the loving eye is not an invasive, coercive eye which annexes others to itself, but one which "knows the complexity of the other as something which will forever present new things to be known."

When one climbs a rock as a conqueror, one climbs with an arrogant eye. When one climbs with a loving eye, one constantly "must look and listen and check and question." One recognizes the rock as something very different, something perhaps totally indifferent to one's own presence, and finds in that difference joyous occasion for celebration. One knows "the boundary of the self," where the self—the "I," the climber—leaves off and the rock

begins. There is no fusion of two into one, but a complement of two entities *acknowledged* as separate, different, independent, yet *in relationship;* they are in relationship *if only* because the loving eye is perceiving it, responding to it, noticing it, attending to it.

An ecofeminist perspective about both women and nature involves this shift in attitude from "arrogant perception" to "loving perception" of the nonhuman world. Arrogant perception of nonhumans by humans presupposes and maintains *sameness* in such a way that it expands the moral community to those beings who are thought to resemble (be like, similar to, or the same as) humans in some morally significant way. Any environmental movement or ethic based on arrogant perception builds a moral hierarchy of beings and assumes some common denominator of moral considerability in virtue of which like beings deserve similar treatment or moral consideration and unlike beings do not. Such environmental ethics are or generate a "unity in sameness." In contrast, "loving perception" presupposes and maintains *difference*—a distinction between the self and other, between human and at least some nonhumans—in such a way that perception of the other as other *is* an expression of love for one who/which is recognized at the outset as independent, dissimilar, different. As Maria Lugones says, in loving perception, "Love is seen not as fusion and erasure of difference but as incompatible with them."[20] "Unity in sameness" alone is *an erasure of difference.*

"Loving perception" of the nonhuman natural world is an attempt to understand what it means *for humans* to care about the nonhuman world, a world *acknowledged* as being independent, different, perhaps even indifferent to humans. Humans *are* different from rocks in important ways, even if they are also both members of some ecological community. A moral community based on loving perception of oneself *in relationship with* a rock, or with the natural environment as a whole, is one which acknowledges and respects difference, whatever "sameness" also exists.[21] The limits of loving perception are determined only by the limits of one's (e.g., a person's, a community's) ability to respond lovingly (or with appropriate care, trust, or friendship)—whether it is to other humans or to the nonhuman world and elements of it.[22]

If what I have said so far is correct, then there are very different ways to climb a mountain and *how* one climbs it and *how* one narrates the experience of climbing it matter ethically. If one climbs with "arrogant perception," with an attitude of "conquer and control," one keeps intact the very sorts of thinking that characterize a logic of domination and an oppressive conceptual framework. Since the oppressive conceptual framework which sanctions the domination of nature is a patriarchal one, one also thereby keeps intact, even if unwittingly, a patriarchal conceptual framework. Because the dismantling of patriarchal conceptual frameworks is a feminist issue, *how* one climbs a mountain and *how* one narrates—or tells the story—about the experience of climbing also are *feminist issues*. In this way, ecofeminism makes visible why, at a conceptual level, environmental ethics is a feminist issue. I turn now to a consideration of ecofeminism as a distinctively feminist and environmental ethic.

ECOFEMINISM AS A FEMINIST AND ENVIRONMENTAL ETHIC

A feminist ethic involves a twofold commitment to critique male bias in ethics wherever it occurs, and to develop ethics which are not male-biased. Sometimes this involves articulation of values (e.g., values of care, appropriate trust, kinship, friendship) often lost or underplayed in mainstream ethics.[23] Sometimes it involves engaging in theory building by pioneering in new directions or by revamping old theories in gender sensitive ways. What makes the critiques of old theories or conceptualizations of new ones "feminist" is that they emerge out of sex-gender analyses and reflect whatever those analyses reveal about gendered experience and gendered social reality.

As I conceive feminist ethics in the pre-feminist present, it rejects attempts to conceive of ethical theory in terms of necessary and sufficient conditions, because it assumes that there is no essence (in the sense of some transhistorical, universal, absolute abstraction) of feminist ethics. While attempts to formulate joint necessary and sufficient conditions of a feminist ethic are unfruitful, nonetheless, there are some necessary conditions, what I prefer to call "boundary conditions," of a feminist ethic. These boundary conditions clarify some of the minimal conditions of a feminist ethic without suggesting that feminist ethics has some ahistorical essence. They are like the boundaries of a quilt or collage. They delimit the territory of the piece without dictating what the interior, the design, the actual pattern of the piece looks like. Because the actual design of the quilt emerges from the multiplicity of voices of women in a cross-cultural context, the design will change over time. It is not something static.

What are some of the boundary conditions of a feminist ethic? First, nothing can become part of a feminist ethic—can be part of the quilt—that promotes sexism, racism, classism, or any other "isms" of social domination. Of course, people may disagree about what counts as a sexist act, racist attitude, classist behavior. What counts as sexism, racism, or classism may vary cross-culturally. Still, because a feminist ethic aims at eliminating sexism and sexist bias, and (as I have already shown) sexism is intimately connected in conceptualization and in practice to racism, classism, and naturism, a feminist ethic must be anti-sexist, anti-racist, anti-classist, anti-naturist and opposed to any "ism" which presupposes or advances a logic of domination.

Second, a feminist ethic is a *contextualist* ethic. A contextualist ethic is one which sees ethical discourse and practice as emerging from the voices of people located in different historical circumstances. A contextualist ethic is properly viewed as a *collage* or *mosaic,* a *tapestry* of voices that emerges out of felt experiences. Like any collage or mosaic, the point is not to have *one picture* based on a unity of voices, but a *pattern* which emerges out of the very different voices of people located in different circumstances. When a contextualist ethic is *feminist,* it gives central place to the voices of women.

Third, since a feminist ethic gives central significance to the diversity of women's voices, a feminist

Lastly, an ecofeminist ethic involves a reconception of what it means to be human, and in what human ethical behavior consists. Ecofeminism denies abstract individualism. Humans are who we are in large part by virtue of the historical and social contexts and the relationships we are in, including our relationships with nonhuman nature. Relationships are not something extrinsic to who we are, not an "add on" feature of human nature; they play an essential role in shaping what it is to be human. Relationships of humans to the nonhuman environment are, in part, constitutive of what it is to be a human.

By making visible the interconnections among the dominations of women and nature, ecofeminism shows that both are feminist issues and that explicit acknowledgement of both is vital to any responsible environmental ethic. Feminism *must* embrace ecological feminism if it is to end the domination of women because the domination of women is tied conceptually and historically to the domination of nature.

A responsible environmental ethic also *must* embrace feminism. Otherwise, even the seemingly most revolutionary, liberational, and holistic ecological ethic will fail to take seriously the interconnected dominations of nature and women that are so much a part of the historical legacy and conceptual framework that sanctions the exploitation of nonhuman nature. Failure to make visible these interconnected, twin dominations results in an inaccurate account of how it is that nature has been and continues to be dominated and exploited and produces an environmental ethic that lacks the depth necessary to be truly *inclusive* of the realities of persons who at least in dominant Western culture have been intimately tied with that exploitation, viz., women. Whatever else can be said in favor of such holistic ethics, a failure to make visible ecofeminist insights into the common denominators of the twin oppressions of women and nature is to perpetuate, rather than overcome, the source of that oppression.

This last point deserves further attention. It may be objected that as long as the end result is "the same"—the development of an environmental

ethic which does not emerge out of or reinforce an oppressive conceptual framework—it does not matter whether that ethic (or the ethic endorsed in getting there) is feminist or not. Hence, it simply is *not* the case that any adequate environmental ethic must be feminist. My argument, in contrast, has been that it *does* matter, and for three important reasons. First, there is the scholarly issue of accurately representing historical reality, and that, ecofeminists claim, requires acknowledging the historical feminization of nature and naturalization of women as part of the exploitation of nature. Second, I have shown that the conceptual connections between the domination of women and the domination of nature are located in an oppressive and, at least in Western societies, patriarchal conceptual framework characterized by a logic of domination. Thus, I have shown that failure to notice the nature of this connection leaves at best an incomplete, inaccurate, and partial account of what is required of a conceptually adequate environmental ethic. An ethic which *does not* acknowledge this is simply *not* the same as one that does, whatever else the similarities between them. Third, the claim that, in contemporary culture, one can have an adequate environmental ethic which is *not* feminist assumes that, in contemporary culture, the label *feminist* does not add anything crucial to the nature or description of environmental ethics. I have shown that at least in contemporary culture this is false, for the word *feminist* currently helps to clarify just *how* the domination of nature is conceptually linked to patriarchy and, hence, how the liberation of nature, is conceptually linked to the termination of patriarchy. Thus, because it has critical bite in contemporary culture, it serves as an important reminder that in contemporary sex-gendered, raced, classed, and naturist culture, an unlabeled position functions as a privileged and "unmarked" position. That is, without the addition of the word *feminist*, one presents environmental ethics as if it has no bias, including male-gender bias, which is just what ecofeminists deny: failure to notice the connections between the twin oppressions of women and nature *is* male-gender bias.

One of the goals of feminism is the eradication of all oppressive sex-gender (and related race, class, age, affectional preference) categories and the creation of a world in which *difference does not breed domination*—say, the world of 4001. If in 4001 an "adequate environmental ethic" is a "feminist environmental ethic," the word *feminist* may then be redundant and unnecessary. However, this is *not* 4001, and in terms of the current historical and conceptual reality the dominations of nature and of women are intimately connected. Failure to notice or make visible that connection in 1990 perpetuates the mistaken (and privileged) view that "environmental ethics" is *not* a feminist issue, and that *feminist* adds nothing to environmental ethics.[37]

CONCLUSION

I have argued in this paper that ecofeminism provides a framework for a distinctively feminist and environmental ethic. Ecofeminism grows out of the felt and theorized about connections between the domination of women and the domination of nature. As a contextualist ethic, ecofeminism refocuses environmental ethics on what nature might mean, morally speaking, *for* humans, and on how the relational attitudes of humans to others—humans as well as nonhumans—sculpt both what it is to be human and the nature and ground of human responsibilities to the nonhuman environment. Part of what this refocusing does is to take seriously the voices of women and other oppressed persons in the construction of that ethic.

A Sioux elder once told me a story about his son. He sent his seven-year-old son to live with the child's grandparents on a Sioux reservation so that he could "learn the Indian ways." Part of what the grandparents taught the son was how to hunt the four leggeds of the forest. As I heard the story, the boy was taught, "to shoot your four-legged brother in his hind area, slowing it down but not killing it. Then, take the four legged's head in your hands, and look into his eyes. The eyes are where all the suffering is. Look into your brother's eyes and feel his pain. Then, take your knife and cut the four-legged under his chin, here, on his neck, so that he dies quickly. And as you do, ask your brother, the four-legged, for forgiveness for what you do. Offer also a prayer of thanks to your four-legged kin for offering his body to you just now, when you need food to eat and clothing to wear. And promise the four-legged that you will put yourself back into the earth when you die, to become nourishment for the earth, and for the sister flowers, and for the brother deer. It is appropriate that you should offer this blessing for the four-legged and, in due time, reciprocate in turn with your body in this way, as the four-legged gives life to you for your survival." As I reflect upon that story, I am struck by the power of the environmental ethic that grows out of and takes seriously narrative, context, and such values and relational attitudes as care, loving perception, and appropriate reciprocity, and doing what is appropriate in a given situation—however that notion of appropriateness eventually gets filled out. I am also struck by what one is able to see, once one begins to explore some of the historical and conceptual connections between the dominations of women and of nature. A *re-conceiving* and *re-visioning* of both feminism and environmental ethics, is, I think, the power and promise of ecofeminism.

NOTES

1. Explicit ecological feminist literature includes works from a variety of scholarly perspectives and sources. Some of these works are Leonie Caldecott and Stephanie Leland, eds., *Reclaim the Earth: Women Speak Out for Life on Earth* (London: The Women's Press, 1983); Jim Cheney, "Eco-Feminism and Deep Ecology," *Environmental Ethics* 9 (1987): 115–45; Andrée Collard with Joyce Contrucci, *Rape of the Wild: Man's Violence against Animals and the Earth* (Bloomington: Indiana University Press, 1988); Katherine Davies, "Historical Associations: Women and the Natural World," *Women & Environments* 9, no. 2 (Spring 1987): 4–6; Sharon Doubiago, "Deeper than Deep Ecology: Men Must Become Feminists," in *The New Catalyst Quarterly*, no 10. (Winter 1987/88): 10–11; Brian Easlea, *Science and Sexual Oppression: Patriarchy's Confrontation with Women and Nature* (London: Weidenfeld & Nicholson, 1981); Elizabeth Dodson Gray, *Green Paradise Lost* (Wellesley, Mass.: Roundtable Press, 1979): Susan Griffin, *Women and Nature: The Roaring Inside Her* (San Francisco: Harper and Row, 1978); Joan L. Griscom, "On Healing the Nature/History Split in Feminist Thought," in *Heresies #13: Feminism and Ecology* 4 no. 1 (1981): 4–9; Ynestra King, "The Ecology of Feminism and the Feminism of Ecology," in *Healing Our Wounds: The Power of Ecological Feminism*, ed. Judith Plant (Boston: New Society Publishers, 1989), pp. 18–28; "The Eco-feminist Imperative," in *Reclaim the Earth*, ed. Caldecott and Leland (London: The Women's Press, 1983), pp. 12–16, "Feminism and the Revolt of Nature," in *Heresies # 13: Feminism and Ecology* 4, no. 1 (1981): 12–16, and "What is Ecofeminism?" *The Nation*, 12 December 1987; Marti Kheel, "Animal Liberation Is A Feminist Issue," *The New Catalyst Quarterly*, no. 10 (Winter 1987–88): 8–9; Carolyn Merchant, *The Death of Nature: Women, Ecology and the Scientific Revolution* (San Francisco: Harper and Row, 1980); Patrick Murphy, ed., "Feminism, Ecology, and the Future of the Humanities," special issue of *Studies in the Humanities* 15, no. 2 (December 1988); Abby Peterson and Carolyn Merchant, "Peace with the Earth: Women and the Environmental Movement in Sweden," *Women's Studies International Forum* 9, no. 5–6 (1986): 465–79; Judith Plant, "Searching for Common Ground: Ecofeminism and Bioregionalism," in *The New Catalyst Quarterly*, no. 10 (Winter 1987/88): 6–7; Judith Plant, ed., *Healing Our Wounds: The Power of Ecological Feminism* (Boston: New Society Publishers, 1989); Val Plumwood, "Ecofeminism: An Overview and Discussion of Positions and Arguments," *Australasian Journal of Philosophy*, Supplement to vol. 64 (June 1986): 120–37; Rosemary Radford Ruether, *New Woman/New Earth: Sexist Ideologies & Human Liberation* (New York: Seabury Press, 1975); Kirkpatrick Sale, "Ecofeminism—A New Perspective," *The Nation*, 26 September 1987): 302–05; Ariel Kay Salleh, "Deeper than Deep Ecology: The Eco-Feminist Connection," *Environmental Ethics* 6 (1984): 339–45, and "Epistemology and the Metaphors of Production: An Eco-Feminist Reading of Critical Theory," in *Studies in the Humanities* 15 (1988): 130–39; Vandana Shiva, *Staying Alive: Women, Ecology and Development* (London: Zed Books, 1988); Charlene Spretnak, "Ecofeminism: Our Roots and Flowering," *The Elms-wood Newsletter*, Winter Solstice 1988; Karen J. Warren, "Feminism and Ecology: Making Connections," *Environmental Ethics* 9 (1987): 3–21; "Toward an Ecofeminist Ethic," *Studies in the Humanities* 15 (1988): 140–156; Miriam Wyman, "Explorations of Eco-feminism," *Women & Environments* (Spring 1987): 6–7; Iris Young, "'Feminism and Ecology' and 'Women and Life on Earth: Eco-Feminism in the 80's'," *Environmental Ethics* 5 (1983): 173–80; Michael Zimmerman, "Feminism, Deep Ecology, and Environmental Ethics," *Environmental Ethics* 9 (1987): 21–44.

2. Francoise d'Eaubonne, *Le Feminisme ou la Mort* (Paris: Pierre Horay, 1974), pp. 213–52.

3. I discuss this in my paper, "Toward An Ecofeminist Ethic."

4. The account offered here is a revision of the account given earlier in my paper "Feminism and Ecology: Making Connections." I have changed the account to be about "oppressive" rather than strictly "patriarchal" conceptual frameworks in order to leave open the possibility that there may be some patriarchal conceptual frameworks (e.g., in non-Western cultures) which are *not* properly characterized as based on value dualisms.

5. Murray Bookshin, "Social Ecology versus 'Deep Ecology'," in *Green Perspectives: Newsletter of the Green Program Project*, no. 4–5 (Summer 1987): 9.

6. It may be that in contemporary Western society, which is so thoroughly structured by categories of gender, race, class, age, and affectional orientation, that there simply is no meaningful notion of "value-hierarchical thinking" which does not function in an oppressive context. For purposes of this paper, I leave that question open.

7. Many feminists who argue for the historical point that claims (B1) and (B2) have been asserted or assumed to be true within the dominant Western philosophical tradition do so by discussion of that tradition's conceptions of reason, rationality, and science. For a sampling of the sorts of claims made within that context, see "Reason, Rationality, and Gender," ed. Nancy Tuana and Karen J. Warren, a special issue of the American Philosophical Association's *Newsletter on Feminism and Philosophy* 88, no. 2 (March 1989): 17–71. Ecofeminists who claim that (B2) has been assumed to be true within the dominant Western philosophical tradition include: Gray, *Green Paradise Lost*; Griffin, *Woman and Nature: The Roaring Inside Her*; Merchant, *The Death of Nature*; Ruether, *New Woman/New Earth*. For a discussion of some of these ecofeminist historical accounts, see Plumwood, "Ecofeminism." While I agree that the historical connections between the domination of women and the domination of nature is a crucial one, I do not argue for that claim here.

8. Ecofeminists who deny (B1) when (B1) is offered as anything other than a true, descriptive, historical claim about patriarchal culture often do so on grounds that an objectionable sort of biological determinism, or at least harmful female sex-gender stereotypes, underlie (B1). For a discussion of this "split" among those ecofeminists ("nature feminists") who assert and those ecofeminists ("social feminists") who deny (B1) as anything other than a true historical claim about how women are described in patriarchal culture, see Griscom, "On Healing the Nature/History Split."

9. I make no attempt here to defend the historically sanctioned truth of these premises.

10. See, e.g., Bell Hooks, *Feminist Theory: From Margin to Center* (Boston: South End Press, 1984), pp. 51–52.

11. Maria Lugones, "Playfulness, 'World-Travelling,' and Loving Perception," *Hypatia* 2, no. 2 (Summer 1987): 3.

12. At an *experiential* level, some women are "women of color," poor, old, lesbian, Jewish, and physically challenged. Thus, if feminism is going to liberate these women, it also needs to end the racism, classism, heterosexism, anti-Semitism, and discrimination against the handicapped that is constitutive of their oppression as black, or Latina, or poor, or older, or lesbian, or Jewish, or physically challenged women.

13. This same sort of reasoning shows that feminism is also a movement to end racism, classism, ageism, heterosexism and other "isms," which are based in oppressive conceptual frameworks characterized by a logic of domination. However, there is an important caveat: ecofeminism is *not* compatible with all feminisms and all environmentalisms. For a discussion of this point, see my article, "Feminism and Ecology: Making Connections. What it *is* compatible with is the minimal condition characterization of feminism as a movement to end sexism that is accepted by all contemporary feminisms (liberal, traditional Marxist, radical, socialist, Blacks and non-Western).

14. See, e.g., Gray, Green Paradise Lost; Griffin, Women and Nature; Merchant, The Death of Nature; and Ruether, New Woman/New Earth.

15. Suppose, as I think is the case, that a necessary condition for the existence of a moral relationship is that at least one party to the relationship is a moral being (leaving open for our purposes what counts as a "moral being"). If this is so, then the Mona Lisa cannot properly be said to have or stand in a moral relationship with the wall on which she hangs, and a wolf cannot have or properly be said to have or stand in a moral relationship with a moose. Such a necessary-condition account leaves open the question whether *both* parties to the relationship must be moral beings. My point here is simply that however one resolves *that* question, recognition of the relationships themselves as a locus of value is a recognition of a source of value that is different from and not reducible to the values of the "moral beings" in those relationships.

16. It is interesting to note that the image of being friends with the Earth is one which cytogeneticist Barbara McClintock uses when she describes the

importance of having "a feeling for the organism," "listening to the material [in this case the corn plant]," in one's work as a scientist. See Evelyn Fox Keller, "Women, Science, and Popular Mythology," in *Machina Ex Dea: Feminist Perspectives on Technology*, ed. Joan Rothschild (New York: Pergamon Press, 1983), and Evelyn Fox Keller, *A Feeling For the Organism: The Life and Work of Barbara McClintock* (San Francisco: W. H. Freeman, 1983).

17. Cheney, "Eco-Feminism and Deep Ecology," 144.

18. Marilyn Frye, "In and Out of Harm's Way: Arrogance and Love," *The Politics of Reality* (Trumansburg, New York: The Crossing Press, 1983), pp. 66–72.

19. Ibid., pp. 75–76.

20. Maria Lugones, "Playfulness," p. 3.

21. Cheney makes a similar point in "Eco-Feminism and Deep Ecology," p. 140.

22. Ibid., p. 138.

23. This account of a feminist ethic draws on my paper "Toward an Ecofeminist Ethic."

24. Marilyn Frye makes this point in her illuminating paper, "The Possibility of Feminist Theory," read at the American Philosophical Association Central Division Meetings in Chicago, 29 April–1 May 1986. My discussion of feminist theory is inspired largely by that paper and by Kathryn Addelson's paper "Moral Revolution," in *Women and Values: Reading in Recent Feminist Philosophy*, ed. Marilyn Pearsall (Belmont, Calif.: Wadsworth Publishing Co., 1986) pp. 291–309.

25. Notice that the standard of inclusiveness does not exclude the voices of men. It is just that those voices must cohere with the voices of women.

26. For a more in-depth discussion of the notions of impartiality and bias, see my paper, "Critical Thinking and Feminism," *Informal Logic* 10, no. 1 (Winter 1988): 31–44.

27. The burgeoning literature on these values is noteworthy. See, e.g., Carol Gilligan, *In a Different Voice: Psychological Theories and Women's Development* (Cambridge: Harvard University Press, 1982); *Mapping the Moral Domain: A Contribution of Women's Thinking to Psychological Theory and Education*, ed. Carol Gilligan, Janie Victoria Ward, and Jill McLean Taylor, with Betty Bardige

(Cambridge: Harvard University Press, 1988); Nel Noddings, *Caring: A Feminine Approach to Ethics and Moral Education* (Berkeley: University of California Press, 1984); Maria Lugones and Elizabeth V. Spelman, "Have We Got a Theory for You! Feminist Theory, Cultural Imperialism, and the Women's Voice," *Women's Studies International Forum* 6 (1983): 573–81; Maria Lugones, "Playfulness"; Annette C. Baier, "What Do Women Want In A Moral Theory?" *Nous* 19 (1985): 53–63.

28. Jim Cheney would claim that our fundamental relationships to one another as moral agents are not as moral agents to rights holders, and that whatever rights a person properly may be said to have are relationally defined rights, not rights possessed by atomistic individuals conceived as Robinson Crusoes who do not exist essentially in relation to others. On this view, even right talk itself is properly conceived as growing out of a relational ethic, not vice versa.

29. Alison Jaggar, *Feminist Politics and Human Nature* (Totowa, N.J.: Rowman and Allanheld, 1980), pp. 42–44.

30. Henry West has pointed out that the expression "defining relations" is ambiguous. According to West, "the "defining" as Cheney uses it is an adjective, not a principle—it is not that ethics defines relationships; it is that ethics grows out of conceiving of the relationships that one is in as defining what the individual is."

31. For example, in relationships involving contracts or promises, those relationships might be correctly described as that of moral agent to rights holders. In relationships involving mere property, those relationships might be correctly described as that of moral agent to objects having only instrumental value, "relationships of instrumentality." In comments on an earlier draft of this paper, West suggested that possessive individualism, for instance, might be recast in such a way that an individual is defined by his or her property relationships.

32. Cheney, "Eco-Feminism and Deep Ecology," p. 144.

33. One might object that such permission for change opens the door for environmental exploitation. This is not the case. An ecofeminist ethic is anti-naturist. Hence, the unjust domination and

exploitation of nature is a "boundary condition" of the ethic; no such actions are sanctioned or justified on ecofeminist grounds. What it *does* leave open is some leeway about what counts as domination and exploitation. This, I think, is a strength of the ethic, not a weakness, since it acknowledges that *that* issue cannot be resolved in any practical way in the abstract, independent of a historical and social context.

34. Nathan Hare, "Black Ecology," in *Environmental Ethics*, ed. K. S. Shrader-Frechette (Pacific Grove, Calif.: Boxwood Press, 1981), pp. 229–36.

35. For an ecofeminist discussion of the Chipko movement, see my "Toward an Ecofeminist Ethic," and Shiva's *Staying Alive*.

36. See Cheney, "Eco-Feminism and Deep Ecology," p. 122.

37. I offer the same sort of reply to critics of ecofeminism such as Warwick Fox who suggest that for the sort of ecofeminism I defend, the word *feminist* does not add anything significant to

environmental ethics and, consequently, that an ecofeminist like myself might as well call herself a deep ecologist. He asks: "Why doesn't she just call it [i.e., Warren's vision of a transformative feminism] deep ecology? Why specifically attach the label *feminist* to it ...?" (Warwick Fox, "The Deep Ecology-Ecofeminism Debate and Its Parallels," *Environmental Ethics* 11, no. 1 [1989]: 14, n. 22). Whatever the important similarities between deep ecology and ecofeminism (or, specifically, my version of ecofeminism)—and, indeed, there are many—it is precisely my point here that the word *feminist* does add something significant to the conception of environmental ethics, and that any environmental ethic (including deep ecology) that fails to make explicit the different kinds of interconnections among the domination of nature and the domination of women will be, from a feminist (and ecofeminist) perspective such as mine, inadequate.

STUDY QUESTIONS

1. What are the central connections between feminism and environmental ethics?

2. What does Warren mean by the "logic of domination"?

3. In the section "Ecofeminism as a Feminist and Environmental Ethics," Warren offers eight

criteria for a feminist ethic. Discuss two of them.

4. In the same section noted in Question 3, Warren gives eight characteristics of an ecofeminist ethic. Discuss two of them.

58

The Earth Charter: From Global Ethics to International Law Instrument

INTRODUCTION BY LAURA WESTRA

Laura Westra was, until her retirement, a professor of philosophy at the University of Windsor. A leading environmentalist, she also served as the secretary of the International Society for Environmental Ethics. She is the author of An Environmental Proposal for Ethics: The Principle of Integrity *(1994); co-editor of* Faces of Environmental Racism *(1995);* Perspectives on Ecological Integrity *(1995);* The Greeks and the Environment *(1997), and* Technology and Values *(1997). She has published more than sixty articles and chapters in books and journals.*

In 1972 the nations that were gathered at Stockholm agreed that environmental protection should be added to the core agenda of the United Nations, together with "peace, human rights, and equitable social and economic development" (Rockefeller, 2002:xi). This belief was emphasized and supported by many at the 1992 Earth Summit at Rio de Janeiro. In 1994, the Earth Charter Initiative worked to develop a document that would start by accepting the complete interdependence of humanity with global natural systems and that would involve all countries and nationalities from both the North and the South. As Rockefeller explained it,

> The product of a decade long, world-wide cross-cultural dialogue on shared values, the Earth Charter reflects an effort to build on and further develop the ethical visions in the Stockholm Declaration (1972), the World Charter for Nature (1982), the Rio Declaration (1992), and a variety of non-governmental covenants and declarations. (Rockefeller, 2002:xii)

The Earth Charter is an "ethical vision," but it is also a compendium and re-working of soft law. In addition, the International Draft Covenant of Environment and Development (2000 revision) is presently under consideration at the United Nations, and its wording is being reviewed by a UN committee to ensure that the main principles of the Earth Charter are preserved within it. After the committee's work has been completed and the Covenant manifests as much as possible of the spirit, if not the letter, of the Earth Charter in its articles, the United Nations will ensure that it is presented for ratification to all states, as it proposes to bridge the sectors of environment and development.

The Covenant is thus intended to regulate "relations between humankind and nature" (UN Secretary-General's report) and to create "an agreed single set of fundamental principles like a code of conduct ... which may guide states, inter-governmental organization and individuals" (Covenant, p. 14).

This introduction was commissioned for this work and appears here in print for the first time.

Turning now to specific provisions of the Covenant, both Objectives and Fundamental Principles repeat and support the main concerns of the Earth Charter, although the Covenant is much less detailed than the Charter, as well as less specific, thus manifesting, even in draft form, many of the same problems of vagueness and lack of prescriptive specificity of most international covenants, no matter what the topic.

This vagueness is not the result of chance: Through negotiations most international agreements are negotiated "down" from their original intent. Blocs and alliances fostered by the most powerful countries are intended to ensure that business-as-usual will prevail in the interest of those countries and that the regulatory regime under consideration does not cause too many impediments to affluent Western economies. Although the work on the Charter was done by non-governmental organizations (NGOs) and by citizens from countries all over the world, vagueness is not a problem. Consequently the Charter speaks with a strong voice, indicting harmful practices and explicitly defending life and the intrinsic value of both natural systems and processes, as well as biodiversity. It is vital to ensure that the major principles of the Earth Charter are thus preserved in the Covenant, especially those that emphasize the important connection between human health and human rights (Westra, 2000) and the interface between human rights and "ecological rights" (Taylor, 1998). The Earth Charter, Principle 2 says:

> 2: Care for the community of life with understanding, compassion and love, and
>
> 2(a): Accept that with the right to own, manage, and use natural resources comes the duty to prevent environmental harm and to protect the rights of people.

The connection between environmental harm and human rights is rendered explicit. In addition, Principle 6(c),

> Ensure that decision making addresses the cumulative, long-term, indirect, long distance, and global consequences of

human activitie sensures that the connection between environmental harms and human activities and practices is spelled out.

In contrast, the Covenant's Articles 4, 5, 6, and 7 state only the following:

> Article 4: Interdependent Values—Peace, development, environmental protection and respect for human rights and fundamental freedoms are interdependent.
>
> Article 5: Intergenerational Equity—The freedom of action of each generation in regard to the environment is qualified by the needs of future generations.
>
> Article 6: Prevention—Protection of the environment is best achieved by preventing environmental harm, rather than by attempting to remedy or compensate such harm.
>
> Article 7: Precaution—Lack of scientific certainty is no reason to postpone action to avoid potentially irreversible harm to the environment.

Some of the key concepts are preserved, but the question of long-term, long-distance, and cumulative harms resulting from human activities is not addressed, nor are duties as well as rights emphasized. Human health itself is not even mentioned, yet a number of high-level, UN-sponsored World Health Organization (WHO) meetings on environment and health, with conferences in Frankfurt (1989) and Helsinki (1994), culminated in a "Declaration of the Third Ministerial Conference on Environment and Health" (London, 1999), which clearly connected environmental harms to human health and thereby to human rights.

It is both wrong and illogical to exclude the important scientific findings of the WHO in regard to human health in general, and in relation to environmental conditions specifically, from any document that is aimed at preventing environmental harm and promoting sustainability. The spurious separation between "environment" and "humankind" militates against Articles 4 and 5 of the Draft

Covenant and against the main principles that animate the Earth Charter:

> 1: Respect Earth and life in all its diversity, and 1(a): Recognize that all beings are interdependent and every form of life has value regardless of its worth to human beings.

Hence the respect for human beings cannot be separated from respect for their habitat, one that they have in common with the rest of life. It is clear that if this connection is emphasized and made explicit, grave consequences would follow for present practices and institutions. For example, when the activities of tobacco companies were fully disclosed and the consequences of those activities were eventually scientifically documented, many business and institutional practices were severely curtailed because such rights as freedom of expression were pitted against public rights to health and *life*.

When linkages between climate-induced disasters, temperature extremes, and soil erosion that leads to desertification and famine are openly acknowledged, then state-supported but unsafe business practices and, in general, *a status quo* that gives privileges to trade over life will be brought into question. The changes required will be drastic for both institutional practices and the law, because not one industrial enterprise (e.g., tobacco companies) but all of them will have to admit their responsibility.

This Draft Covenant represents a "bridge" of sorts between the failure to protect that is so clear in most other international environmental instruments and the universal obligations that best define environmental duties. Insofar as the Draft Covenant will add the connections and the emphases that I propose and will not allow signatories to further water down and erode the underlying normative message of the Earth Charter, it may well become one of the first international legal instruments committed to the joint protection of humankind and its habitat.

It is significant that the development of the Earth Charter principles demonstrates the "bottom-up" globalization referred to earlier. From a substantive point of view, even more significant is the connection that many of its principles have with public health and hence with human rights; that emphasis helps to connect the Earth Charter to some of the strongest and most accepted international law instruments based on universal human rights, thus giving rise to universal rather than contractual obligations. Hence when the Earth Charter becomes part of an international covenant, the covenant will embody both aspects of cosmopolitanism.

The Earth Charter, as a cosmopolitan moral perspective, includes respect for the preconditions of life—a recognition of the interconnectedness of all life. It emphasizes a respect for communities and peoples that is basic to global ethics. It is a declaration of fundamental principles for creating a just, sustainable, and peaceful society in the twenty-first century.

BIBLIOGRAPHY

Rockefeller, Steven. 2002. "Foreword" to *Just Integrity*, Peter Miller and Laura Westra, eds. Lanham, MD: Rowman & Littlefield, xi–xiv.

Soskolne, Colin, and Bertollini, Roberto. 1999. *Ecological Integrity and Sustainable Development: Cornerstones of Public Health.* (www.euro.who.int/document/gch/globaleco/ecorep5.pdf)

Taylor, Prudence. 1998. "From Environmental to Ecological Human Rights: A New Dynamic in International Law?" *The Georgetown Int'l. Envtl. Law Review*, Vol. 1. 10:309.

Westra, Laura. 2000. "Institutionalized Environmental Violence and Human Rights" in *Ecological Integrity: Integrating Environment, Conservation and Health*, David Pimentel, Laura Westra, and Reed Noss, eds., Washington, DC: Island Press, pp. 279–294.

WHO European Centre for Environment and Health. 2000. "Annex B: Declaration of the Third Ministerial Conference on Environmental and Health" (signed in London on June 18, 1999), pp. 323–334.

The Earth Charter

PREAMBLE

We stand at a critical moment in Earth's history, a time when humanity must choose its future. As the world becomes increasingly interdependent and fragile, the future at once holds great peril and great promise. To move forward we must recognize that in the midst of a magnificent diversity of cultures and life forms we are one human family and one Earth community with a common destiny. We must join together to bring forth a sustainable global society founded on respect for nature, universal human rights, economic justice, and a culture of peace. Towards this end, it is imperative that we, the peoples of Earth, declare our responsibility to one another, to the greater community of life, and to future generations.

Earth, Our Home

Humanity is part of a vast evolving universe. Earth, our home, is alive with a unique community of life. The forces of nature make existence a demanding and uncertain adventure, but Earth has provided the conditions essential to life's evolution. The resilience of the community of life and the well-being of humanity depend upon preserving a healthy biosphere with all its ecological systems, a rich variety of plants and animals, fertile soils, pure waters, and clean air. The global environment with its finite resources is a common concern of all peoples. The protection of Earth's vitality, diversity, and beauty is a sacred trust.

The Global Situation

The dominant patterns of production and consumption are causing environmental devastation, the depletion of resources, and a massive extinction of species. Communities are being undermined. The benefits of development are not shared equitably and the gap between rich and poor is widening. Injustice, poverty, ignorance, and violent conflict are widespread and the cause of great suffering. An unprecedented rise in human population has overburdened ecological and social systems. The foundations of global security are threatened. These trends are perilous—but not inevitable.

The Challenges Ahead

The choice is ours: form a global partnership to care for Earth and one another or risk the destruction of ourselves and the diversity of life. Fundamental changes are needed in our values, institutions, and ways of living. We must realize that when basic needs have been met, human development is primarily about being more, not having more. We have the knowledge and technology to provide for all and to reduce our impacts on the environment. The emergence of a global civil society is creating new opportunities to build a democratic and humane world. Our environmental, economic, political, social, and spiritual challenges are interconnected, and together we can forge inclusive solutions.

Universal Responsibility

To realize these aspirations, we must decide to live with a sense of universal responsibility, identifying ourselves with the whole Earth community as well as our local communities. We are at once citizens of different nations and of one world in which the local and global are linked. Everyone shares responsibility for the present and future well-being of the human family and the larger living world. The spirit of human solidarity and kinship with all life is strengthened when we live with reverence for the mystery of being, gratitude for the gift of life, and humility regarding the human place in nature.

We urgently need a shared vision of basic values to provide an ethical foundation for the emerging world community. Therefore, together in hope we affirm the following interdependent principles for a sustainable way of life as a common standard by which the conduct of all individuals, organizations, businesses, governments, and transnational institutions is to be guided and assessed.

PRINCIPLES

I. Respect and Care for the Community of Life

1. Respect Earth and life in all its diversity.
    a. Recognize that all beings are interdependent and every form of life has value regardless of its worth to human beings.
    b. Affirm faith in the inherent dignity of all human beings and in the intellectual, artistic, ethical, and spiritual potential of humanity.
2. Care for the community of life with understanding, compassion, and love.
    a. Accept that with the right to own, manage, and use natural resources comes the duty to prevent environmental harm and to protect the rights of people.
    b. Affirm that with increased freedom, knowledge, and power comes increased responsibility to promote the common good.
3. Build democratic societies that are just, participatory, sustainable, and peaceful.
    a. Ensure that communities at all levels guarantee human rights and fundamental freedoms and provide everyone an opportunity to realize his or her full potential.
    b. Promote social and economic justice, enabling all to achieve a secure and meaningful livelihood that is ecologically responsible.

4. Secure Earth's bounty and beauty for present and future generations.
    a. Recognize that the freedom of action of each generation is qualified by the needs of future generations.
    b. Transmit to future generations values, traditions, and institutions that support the long-term flourishing of Earth's human and ecological communities.

In order to fulfill these four broad commitments, it is necessary to:

II. Ecological Integrity

5. Protect and restore the integrity of Earth's ecological systems, with special concern for biological diversity and the natural processes that sustain life.
    a. Adopt at all levels sustainable development plans and regulations that make environmental conservation and rehabilitation integral to all development initiatives.
    b. Establish and safeguard viable nature and biosphere reserves, including wild lands and marine areas, to protect Earth's life support systems, maintain biodiversity, and preserve our natural heritage.
    c. Promote the recovery of endangered species and ecosystems.
    d. Control and eradicate non-native or genetically modified organisms harmful to native species and the environment, and prevent introduction of such harmful organisms.
    e. Manage the use of renewable resources such as water, soil, forest products, and marine life in ways that do not exceed rates of regeneration and that protect the health of ecosystems.
    f. Manage the extraction and use of nonrenewable resources such as minerals and fossil fuels in ways that minimize depletion and cause no serious environmental damage.
6. Prevent harm as the best method of environmental protection and, when knowledge is limited, apply a precautionary approach.

a. Take action to avoid the possibility of serious or irreversible environmental harm even when scientific knowledge is incomplete or inconclusive.

b. Place the burden of proof on those who argue that a proposed activity will not cause significant harm, and make the responsible parties liable for environmental harm.

c. Ensure that decision making addresses the cumulative, long-term, indirect, long distance, and global consequences of human activities.

d. Prevent pollution of any part of the environment and allow no build-up of radioactive, toxic, or other hazardous substances.

e. Avoid military activities damaging to the environment.

7. Adopt patterns of production, consumption, and reproduction that safeguard Earth's regenerative capacities, human rights, and community well-being.

a. Reduce, reuse, and recycle the materials used in production and consumption systems, and ensure that residual waste can be assimilated by ecological systems.

b. Act with restraint and efficiency when using energy, and rely increasingly on renewable energy sources such as solar and wind.

c. Promote the development, adoption, and equitable transfer of environmentally sound technologies.

d. Internalize the full environmental and social costs of goods and services in the selling price, and enable consumers to identify products that meet the highest social and environmental standards.

e. Ensure universal access to health care that fosters reproductive health and responsible reproduction.

f. Adopt lifestyles that emphasize the quality of life and material sufficiency in a finite world.

8. Advance the study of ecological sustainability and promote the open exchange and wide application of the knowledge acquired.

a. Support international scientific and technical cooperation on sustainability, with special attention to the needs of developing nations.

b. Recognize and preserve the traditional knowledge and spiritual wisdom in all cultures that contribute to environmental protection and human well-being.

c. Ensure that information of vital importance to human health and environmental protection, including genetic information, remains available in the public domain.

III. Social and Economic Justice

9. Eradicate poverty as an ethical, social, and environmental imperative.

a. Guarantee the right to potable water, clean air, food security, uncontaminated soil, shelter, and safe sanitation, allocating the national and international resources required.

b. Empower every human being with the education and resources to secure a sustainable livelihood, and provide social security and safety nets for those who are unable to support themselves.

c. Recognize the ignored, protect the vulnerable, serve those who suffer, and enable them to develop their capacities and to pursue their aspirations.

10. Ensure that economic activities and institutions at all levels promote human development in an equitable and sustainable manner.

a. Promote the equitable distribution of wealth within nations and among nations.

b. Enhance the intellectual, financial, technical, and social resources of developing nations, and relieve them of onerous international debt.

c. Ensure that all trade supports sustainable resource use, environmental protection, and progressive labor standards.

d. Require multinational corporations and international financial organizations to act transparently in the public good, and hold them accountable for the consequences of their activities.

11. Affirm gender equality and equity as prerequisites to sustainable development and ensure universal access to education, health care, and economic opportunity.

 a. Secure the human rights of women and girls and end all violence against them.

 b. Promote the active participation of women in all aspects of economic, political, civil, social, and cultural life as full and equal partners, decision makers, leaders, and beneficiaries.

 c. Strengthen families and ensure the safety and loving nurture of all family members.

12. Uphold the right of all, without discrimination, to a natural and social environment supportive of human dignity, bodily health, and spiritual well-being, with special attention to the rights of indigenous peoples and minorities.

 a. Eliminate discrimination in all its forms, such as that based on race, color, sex, sexual orientation, religion, language, and national, ethnic or social origin.

 b. Affirm the right of indigenous peoples to their spirituality, knowledge, lands and resources and to their related practice of sustainable livelihoods.

 c. Honor and support the young people of our communities, enabling them to fulfill their essential role in creating sustainable societies.

 d. Protect and restore outstanding places of cultural and spiritual significance.

IV. Democracy, Nonviolence, and Peace

13. Strengthen democratic institutions at all levels, and provide transparency and accountability in governance, inclusive participation in decision making, and access to justice.

 a. Uphold the right of everyone to receive clear and timely information on environmental matters and all development plans and activities which are likely to affect them or in which they have an interest.

 b. Support local, regional and global civil society, and promote the meaningful participation of all interested individuals and organizations in decision making.

 c. Protect the rights to freedom of opinion expression, peaceful assembly, association, and dissent.

 d. Institute effective and efficient access to administrative and independent judicial procedures, including remedies and redress for environmental harm and the threat of such harm.

 e. Eliminate corruption in all public and private institutions.

 f. Strengthen local communities, enabling them to care for their environments, and assign environmental responsibilities to the levels of government where they can be carried out most effectively.

14. Integrate into formal education and life-long learning the knowledge, values, and skills needed for a sustainable way of life.

 a. Provide all, especially children and youth, with educational opportunities that empower them to contribute actively to sustainable development.

 b. Promote the contribution of the arts and humanities as well as the sciences in sustainability education.

 c. Enhance the role of the mass media in raising awareness of ecological and social challenges.

 d. Recognize the importance of moral and spiritual education for sustainable living.

15. Treat all living beings with respect and consideration.

 a. Prevent cruelty to animals kept in human societies and protect them from suffering.

 b. Protect wild animals from methods of hunting, trapping, and fishing that cause extreme, prolonged, or avoidable suffering.

c. Avoid or eliminate to the full extent possible the taking or destruction of non-targeted species.

16. Promote a culture of tolerance, nonviolence, and peace.

a. Encourage and support mutual understanding, solidarity, and cooperation among all peoples and within and among nations.

b. Implement comprehensive strategies to prevent violent conflict and use collaborative problem solving to manage and resolve environmental conflicts and other disputes.

c. Demilitarize national security systems to the level of a non-provocative defense posture, and convert military resources to peaceful purposes, including ecological restorations.

d. Eliminate nuclear, biological, and toxic weapons and other weapons of mass destruction.

e. Ensure that the use of orbital and outer space supports environmental protection and peace.

f. Recognize that peace is the wholeness created by right relationships with oneself, other persons, other cultures, other life, Earth, and the larger whole of which all are a part.

THE WAY FORWARD

As never before in history, common destiny beckons us to see a new beginning. Such renewal is the promise of these Earth Charter Principles. To fulfill this promise, we must commit ourselves to adopt and promote the values and objectives of the Charter.

This requires a change of mind and heart. It requires a new sense of global interdependence and universal responsibility. We must imaginatively develop and apply the vision of a sustainable way of life locally, nationally, regionally, and globally. Our cultural diversity is a precious heritage and different cultures will find their own distinctive ways to realize the vision. We must deepen and expand the global dialogue that generated the Earth Charter, for we have much to learn from the ongoing collaborative search for truth and wisdom.

Life often involves tensions between important values. This can mean difficult choices. However, we must find ways to harmonize diversity with unity, the exercise of freedom with the common good, short-term objectives with long-term goals. Every individual, family, organization, and community has a vital role to play. The arts, sciences, religions, educational institutions, media, businesses, nongovernmental organizations, and governments are all called to offer creative leadership. The partnership of government, civil society, and business is essential for effective governance.

In order to build a sustainable global community, the nations of the world must renew their commitment to the United Nations, fulfill their obligations under existing international agreements, and support the implementation of Earth Charter principles with an international legally binding instrument on environment and development.

Let ours be a time remembered for the awakening of a new reverence for life, the firm resolve to achieve sustainability, the quickening of the struggle for justice and peace, and the joyful celebration of life.

Chapter 10

The Greening of Spirituality

ONE OF THE VEXING QUESTIONS about the environmental movement is its connection to spirituality. Historically, it has not thrived within Judaism, Islam, and Christianity. In fact, at least in Europe, the United States and Canada, the rise of non-Christian religious movements have been tied closely to the rise of environmentalism. Whether the vegetarianism and non-violence of many Hindu and Buddhist traditions, the earth-based spirituality of Pagan traditions, the deep spiritual connection of people and culture to land and environment found in many indigenous traditions, or hosts of other metaphysical nature-based ideas, a true flourishing and reawakening of ecologically compatible spiritualities has occurred.

This has left Christianity and Judaism, in particular, reeling. Numerous connections between these traditions and environmental crisis were seen. Christianity participated actively in the colonization of indigenous peoples and many feel it is at least partly responsible for not only numerous genocides but also vast exploitation of the planet. Furthermore, these scriptures also appear to condone human domination of nature. Not surprisingly, environmentalism did not initially flourish within these traditions. Recently, however this has changed, and the different traditions within Judaism, Christianity and Islam now have developed careful responses to environmentalism, in many cases going so far as to argue that it is God's desire that we take care of this planet. Increasingly in the United States, Christian and Jewish communities are taking leadership roles, at both national and community levels, in environmental stewardship. We begin, then with readings from these traditions.

Hinduism and Buddhism have been inspiring to environmentalists for their nonviolent attitude towards animals, as well as traditions of sustainability and harmony with nature. The two essays explore some of these ideas.

Finally, we turn to modern paganism, traditions which place spirituality in the here and now, the earth, and our bodies, as much as in unseen beings. Pagans often borrow heavily from the environmental movement itself, and thus not surprisingly are highly ecologically conscious. Deep Ecology, discussed in Section 3, also has ties to paganism.

There are of course numerous other spiritual traditions on this planet; interestingly, many of them come with built-in environmental ethics.

Indigenous perspectives were taken up previously in Section 9, as well as in the introduction to this text.

59

Genesis 1–3

According to ancient Hebrew tradition, Moses (ca. 1450 BCE) wrote this account of the creation of the heavens, Earth, and all that dwells therein. While scholars dispute the authorship and date, they agree that it is a very old account and sets forth the Hebrew-Christian view of a divine Creator who creates the world as good and man and woman in his own image. Scholars often refer to the two accounts of the creation as the E and J accounts, since in the first God is referred to as Elohim and in the second as Yahweh (or Jehovah). These chapters form the basis for the Western religious view of the relationship of humanity to nature.

1. THE CREATION AND THE FALL

The First (E) Account of the Creation. [1]In the beginning God created the heavens and the earth. [2]Now the earth was a formless void, there was darkness over the deep, and God's spirit hovered over the water.

[3]God said, "Let there be light," and there was light. [4]God saw that light was good, and God divided light from darkness. [5]God called light "day," and darkness he called "night." Evening came and morning came: the first day.

[6]God said, "Let there be a vault in the waters to divide the waters in two." And so it was. [7]God made the vault, and it divided the waters above the vault from the waters under the vault. [8]God called the vault "heaven." Evening came and morning came: the second day.

[9]God said, "Let the waters under heaven come together into a single mass, and let dry land appear." And so it was. [10]God called the dry land "earth" and the mass of waters "seas," and God saw that it was good.

[11]God said, "Let the earth produce vegetation: seed-bearing plants, and fruit trees bearing fruit with their seed inside, on the earth." And so it was. [12]The earth produced vegetation: plants bearing seed in their several kinds, and trees bearing fruit with their seed inside in their several kinds. God saw that it was good. [13]Evening came and morning came: the third day.

[14]God said, "Let there be lights in the vault of heaven to divide day from night, and let them indicate festivals, days and years. [15]Let them be lights in the vault of heaven to shine on the earth." And so it was. [16]God made the two great lights: the greater light to govern the day, the smaller light to govern the night, and the stars. [17]God set them in the vault of heaven to shine on the earth, [18]to govern the day and the night and to divide light from darkness. God saw that it was good. [19]Evening came and morning came: the fourth day.

[20]God said, "Let the waters teem with living creatures, and let birds fly above the earth within the vault of heaven." And so it was. [21]God created great sea-serpents and every kind of living creature with which the waters teem, and every kind of winged creature. God saw that it was good. [22]God blessed them, saying, "Be fruitful and multiply, and fill the waters of the seas; and let the birds multiply upon the earth." [23]Evening came and morning came: the fifth day.

[24]God said, "Let the earth produce every kind of living creature: cattle, reptiles, and every kind of wild beast." And so it was. [25]God made every kind of wild beast, every kind of cattle, and every kind of land reptile. God saw that it was good.

[26]God said, "Let us make man in our own image, in the likeness of ourselves, and let them be masters of the fish of the sea, the birds of heaven, the cattle, all the wild beasts and all the reptiles that crawl upon the earth."

[27]God created man in the image of himself, in the image of God he created him, male and female he created them.

[28]God blessed them, saying to them, "Be fruitful, multiply, fill the earth and conquer it. Be masters of the fish of the sea, the birds of heaven and all living animals on the earth." [29]God said, "See, I give you all the seed-bearing plants that are upon the whole earth, and all the trees with seed-bearing fruit; this shall be your food. [30]To all wild beasts, all birds of heaven and all living reptiles on the earth I give all the foliage of plants for food." And so it was. [31]God saw all he had made, and indeed it was very good. Evening came and morning came: the sixth day....

The Second (J) Account of the Creation: Paradise
[5]At the time when Yahweh God made earth and heaven there was as yet no wild bush on the earth nor had any wild plant yet sprung up, for Yahweh God had not sent rain on the earth, nor was there any man to till the soil. [6]However, a flood was rising from the earth and watering all the surface of the soil. [7]Yahweh God fashioned man of dust from the soil. Then he breathed into his nostrils a breath of life, and thus man became a living being.

[8]Yahweh God planted a garden in Eden which is in the east, and there he put the man he had fashioned. [9]Yahweh God caused to spring up from the soil every kind of tree, enticing to look at and good to eat, with the tree of life and the tree of the knowledge of good and evil in the middle of the garden. [10]A river flowed from Eden to water the garden, and from there it divided to make four streams. [11]The first is named the Pishon, and this encircles the whole land of Havilah where there is gold. [12]The gold of this land is pure; bdellium and onyx stone are found there. [13]The second river is named the Gihon, and this encircles the whole land of Cush. [14]The third river is named the Tigris, and this flows to the east of Ashur. The fourth river is the Euphrates. [15]Yahweh God took the man and settled him in the garden of Eden to cultivate and take care of it. [16]Then Yahweh God gave the man this admonition, "You may eat indeed of all the trees in the garden. [17]Nevertheless of the tree of the knowledge of good and evil you are not to eat, for on the day you eat of it you shall most surely die."

[18]Yahweh God said, "It is not good that the man should be alone. I will make him a helpmate." [19]So from the soil Yahweh God fashioned all the wild beasts and all the birds of heaven. These he brought to the man to see what he would call them; each one was to bear the name the man would give it. [20]The man gave names to all the cattle, all the birds of heaven and all the wild beasts. But no helpmate suitable for man was found for him. [21]So Yahweh God made the man fall into a deep sleep. And while he slept, he took one of his ribs and enclosed it in flesh. [22]Yahweh God built the rib he had taken from the man into a woman, and brought her to the man. [23]The man exclaimed: "This at last is bone from my bones, and flesh from my flesh! This is to be called woman, for this was taken from man." [24]This is why a man leaves his father and mother and joins himself to his wife, and they become one body.

[25]Now both of them were naked, the man and his wife, but they felt no shame in front of each other.

The Fall. 3. [1]The serpent was the most subtle of all the wild beasts that Yahweh God had made. It asked the woman, "Did God really say you were not to eat from any of the trees in the garden?" [2]The woman answered the serpent, "We may eat the fruit of the trees in the garden. [3]But of the fruit of the tree in the middle of the garden God said, 'You must not eat it, nor touch it, under pain of death.'" [4]Then the serpent said to the woman, "No! you will not die! [5]God knows in fact that on the day you eat it your eyes will be opened and you will be like gods, knowing good and evil." [6]The woman saw that the tree was good to eat and pleasing to the eye, and that it was desirable for the knowledge that it could give. So she took some of its fruit and ate it. She gave some also to her husband who was with her, and he ate it. [7]Then the eyes of both of them were opened and they realized that they were naked. So they sewed fig leaves together to make themselves loincloths.

[8]The man and his wife heard the sound of Yahweh God walking in the garden in the cool of the day, and they hid from Yahweh God among the trees of the garden. [9]But Yahweh God called to the man. "Where are you?" he asked. [10]"I heard the sound of you in the garden," he replied. "I was afraid because I was naked, so I hid." [11]"Who told you that you were naked?" he asked. "Have you been eating of the tree I forbade you to eat?" [12]The man replied, "It was the woman you put with me; she gave me the fruit, and I ate it." [13]Then Yahweh God asked the woman, "What is this you have done?" The woman replied, "The serpent tempted me and I ate."

[14]Then Yahweh God said to the serpent, "Because you have done this, Be accursed beyond all cattle, all wild beasts. You shall crawl on your belly and eat dust every day of your life. [15]I will make you enemies of each other: you and the woman, your offspring and her offspring. It will crush your head and you will strike its heel."

[16]To the woman he said: "I will multiply your pains in childbearing, you shall give birth to your children in pain. Your yearning shall be for your husband, yet he will lord it over you."

[17]To the man he said, "Because you listened to the voice of your wife and ate from the tree of which I had forbidden you to eat, Accursed be the soil because of you. With suffering shall you get your food from it every day of your life. [18]It shall yield you brambles and thistles, and you shall eat wild plants. [19]With sweat on your brow shall you eat your bread, until you return to the soil, as you were taken from it. For dust you are and to dust you shall return."

[20]The man named his wife "Eve" because she was the mother of all those who live. [21]Yahweh God made clothes out of skins for the man and his wife, and they put them on. [22]Then Yahweh God said, "See, the man has become like one of us, with his knowledge of good and evil. He must not be allowed to stretch his hand out next and pick from the tree of life also, and eat some and live for ever." [23]So Yahweh God expelled him from the garden of Eden, to till the soil from which he had been taken. [24]He banished the man, and in front of the garden of Eden he posted the cherubs, and the flame of a flashing sword, to guard the way to the tree of life.

STUDY QUESTIONS

1. What is the proper relationship between humanity and nature according to the Genesis account? Go over Genesis 1:26–29. Then compare it with Genesis 2:15. Do you see a different message in the two accounts?

2. How is nature, after the fall, understood?

3. What type of relationship between man and nature is portrayed here?

60

Jewish Tradition, the Traditional Jew and the Environment

BARRY FREUNDEL

Dr. Barry Freundel is the rabbi of Kesher Israel congregation in Washington DC, and a professor at Towson University. He is a leading voice on environmental and biomedical ethics in the Modern Orthodox tradition. In this essay he provides a detailed account of why environmental concerns are deeply a part of Judaism. He also differentiates Judaism, which places God and man at the center of ethical considerations, from spiritual perspectives, such as many indigenous and pagan traditions, which see inherent value within the ecological relationships in nature.

"At the time that the Holy One, Blessed Be He, created the first man, He took him and had him pass before all the trees of the Garden of Eden, and said to him: See my works, how fine and excellent they are! Now all that I made was created for you. Think about this and do not harm them, there will be none to fix them after you."[1]

"One should not remove stones from his ground to public ground. A certain man was removing stones from his ground into public ground when a pious man found him doing so and said to him, 'Fool, why do you remove stones from ground which is not yours to ground which is yours?' The man laughed at him. Sometimes later he had to sell his field and when walking on that public ground he stumbled over those same stones. He then said: 'How well did the pious man say to me, why do you remove stones from ground which is not yours to ground which is yours?"[2]

These two Rabbinic sources—with grand existential scope and in pragmatic utilitarian fashion respectively—present Judaism's intrinsic concern with people's treatment of God's world, while at the same time embodying the *raison d'être* of the environmental movement that has shaped national and international agendas over the past few decades. Since the environment is such a major world issue, it is important to analyze, through traditional sources, whether and how Judaism and the Jewish community ought to share in this issue. It is with that purpose in mind—to look at Judaism's view of ecology and the environment and to assess the present environment movement through Jewish eyes—that this paper is presented.

The environment is a natural locus of concern for Judaism. Since the health of the planet first became a popular subject for discussion in secular culture in the 1960's series of important articles on the subject have been written from a Jewish perspective based on the very large number of Biblical, Rabbinic and mystical texts that deal with or touch on the issues involved.[3] in addition several Jewish environmental organizations and projects have made their mark on the community and the world.[4]

The Traditional Jew and the Environment by Barry Freundel. Printed by permission of author.

Often the discussion begins with the Biblical commandment of *bal tashhit*—not to destroy, without appropriate purpose, any object from which someone might derive legitimate benefit. The origin of this prohibition is the Torah's requirement that soldiers at war not cut down fruit trees.[5] Absent this law Jewish combatants might have taken down these trees in order to increase the pressure on their adversaries who would now lose an important source of food, or to use the wood from these trees in besieging an enemy.

War time is, clearly, a moment of overarching need, and, sadly, of great destruction. If limits are imposed on the misuse of natural resources under those circumstances, then clearly ecological concerns are well-rooted in Jewish tradition. If we remember that for Biblical era combatants a restriction such as this is tantamount to a contemporary declaration placing half the world's available petroleum resources off-limits for a modern army; we must necessarily extend the prohibition to other less extreme circumstances as well. Wanton environmental destruction is certainly prohibited for anyone if it is prohibited for soldiers under the pressure of war and battle. In fact, the great rabbinic scholar and legal codifier Maimonides (1138–1204) includes a significant number of destructive activities under this prohibitive rubric, thus indicating that the parameters of the prohibition have long been seen to be broader than the single case of fruit trees and war described in the Biblical verses.[6]

Not only direct acts of wanton destruction are prohibited, but even indirect acts, such as cutting off water sources necessary for the trees to grow, are also precluded.[7] Similarly, when normal human activity does require some destruction of natural resources, decisions must be made in favor of methods that involve less rather than greater destruction (i.e., destroy the tree that does not bear fruit before the one that does bear fruit.)[8] Further, even partial destruction or unwarranted depreciation of the momentary value of natural resources are precluded or restricted by this law.[9]

Beyond the prohibition of actual destruction, an entire series of Jewish laws deals with maintaining the general environmental quality of life. The Mishnah (edited c. 200 CE.) in the second chapter of tractate *Baba Bathra* requires that one not open a shop in a courtyard if the noise pollution of customers coming and going will disturb a neighbor's sleep;[10] that one must put a pigeon cote at least fifty cubits (approximately 75 to 100 feet) from town so that the scavenging birds do not damage people's vegetable gardens;[11] that threshing floors must also be kept at this same distance to prevent the chaff from creating an air pollution problem for the city.[12] So too carrion, graves and tanneries also have this same distance requirement because of the odors they produce.[13] In the latter case there is also an imperative that the tannery be place on the side of the city away from or directly opposite the direction of the prevailing winds in that region.[14] That will also help keep the air quality of the town within appropriate standards. This series of legislation is an obvious forerunner to and a useful precedent for *halakhic* (Jewish legal) analysis of many different aspects of contemporary environmental issues.

Environmental concerns play a role in other areas as well. When the Jewish people entered the land of Israel for the first time the Bible says that God removed the seven nations who were living there previously; but only slowly, so that the land not become barren and the environment thus be ruined. If these people had been taken away precipitously the concern was that no one would have been there to preserve the proper ecological balance while the Jews were getting settled.[15]

The Biblical Book of Jonah tells the story of God sending that prophet to Nineveh so that its populace can repent and it not be destroyed. Jonah balks at the idea and only after some dramatic and miraculous interventions by God, agrees (or more accurately, is compelled), to go.

The book ends with God's explanation to Jonah of why Nineveh was so important to Him. Part of the reason is the large number of human beings who lived there, many of whom were innocent young children. But the climatic words of the book are '*u-veheimah rabbah*—and many animals.[16] They, too, and the concern for their well-being which would be harmed if the city fell, were factored into God's considerations of how to judge Nineveh and direct its fate.

Concern for the well-being of animals is manifest in many parts of Jewish practice. Traditionally one says, "May it wear out and you acquire another one" to someone who has put on a new garment. This is, however, not said for anything made of leather as an animal must be killed for the wish to come true.[17]

In much the same vein: Normally when one performs a commandment for the first time a special blessing is recited. This blessing called *she-heheyanu* praises God for allowing the individual to reach the point in time when he or she can fulfill God's imperative. Meat can only be eaten according to traditional Jewish practice, if the animal has been killed by the correct process of ritual slaughter. Nonetheless, one who performs this ritual slaughter for the first time—even though this act fulfills an important precept—does not recite this blessing as an animal must be killed at that moment—and so there is no joyous benediction.[18]

Even simple environmental amenities that improve the quality of life are subject to *halakhic* concern. In that regard, trees must be kept 25 to 50 cubits (depending on the species of tree and the amount of shade a typical representative of that species usually has), from the city wall. In this way these trees will not block the cool breezes that might alleviate the heat that is so prevalent in the dessert climate of Israel from reaching those inside the town's limits.[19]

For this reason, as well, cities in Israel are required to be surrounded by a *migrash*—an amenities area (a park in modem parlance) of 1000 cubits on all sides of the town, left for public enjoyment, into which nothing may intrude?[20] This *migrash* stands between the city with its inhabitants, and its cultivated fields.

Further, according to the Rabbis, the *migrash* may not be turned into a field as such a change destroys the beauty of the city. Keeping things in balance, a field may also not be made into a *migrash* as doing that will diminish the crops. So, too, a *migrash* cannot be made into a part of the town because that too will destroy the city's beauty, while making a *migrash* out of the city's territory

destroys the places where people need to live. All of this is the opinion of the Rabbis. In contrast, Rabbi Eliezer argues that in order to preserve Jewish cities, the law should allow a field to become a *migrash* and a *migrash* to become part of the city as long as basic space ratio between these different areas is maintained as the town grows or shrinks.[21]

In a similar vein, what farmers call the wooly locusts, i.e., sheep and small cattle may not be raised in Israel itself, as they, with their grazing, will defoliate the land and devour its crops.[22] Intriguingly, one early Rabbi, who kept a goat because drinking its milk was Necessary for his health, is said to have diminished the entire rabbinic enterprise due to this environmentally troubling act. Even though it was only one goat, and even though he kept it tethered to his bed, the fact that he subverted the environmental rules of the Rabbis discredited him as the scholar who brought "falsehood" (*dofi*) into Jewish law.[23] It is in his generation that we first find unresolved debates about Jewish practice appearing in rabbinic texts, and that is blamed on this one decision.[24] In short, violating an environmental enactment can lead to the most far reaching consequences.

An interesting law promoting positive development of the environment in the land of Israel comes from the case of a farmer whose olive trees are swept away in a flood and are then found rooted in another person's field. Though discussion and debate surround the question of who owns what with regard to the fruit that they bear in their new location, all agree that the trees are not to be returned to their original owner. Rabbi Johanan, the author of this *halakhah*, explains his decision as emerging from his concern that Israel be well cultivated and settled. Presumably the original farmer, who almost surely gets part of his livelihood from growing olives, will replace his lost trees. The other fellow may or may not have had any interest in olive trees. Now, however, he is almost certainly going to preserve these trees and this new source of income, and two olive groves will grow in the land, where only one had existed before. Rabbi Jeremiah calls Rabbi Johanan "a great teacher" for this decision.[25]

A similar consideration led to alteration of the sacrificial service in the ancient Temple in

Jerusalem. Olive wood and wood from grape vines were precluded from use on the altar in that Temple. One sage explains that the reason for this prohibition is again concern for the settlement and cultivation of the land of Israel. "Do not cut down these types of trees that are so important to the environmental and economic well being of the land," says he. The second opinion is even more specific to environmental concerns. These kinds of wood produce a great deal of smoke when they burn, and this production of noxious air pollution is to be avoided especially when worshipping God.[26]

Returning to more general discussions of environmental issues: most nuisances, if implemented for someone's benefit and tolerated by one's neighbors when first initiated, cannot subsequently be removed because of the latter's complaints. Once the nuisance has been accepted this creates an easement that allows the activity to continue. This is not true, however, in regard to four particular types of nuisance issues. Smoke, the odor of a privy, dust and vibration are assumed to be such noxious intrusions into a human being's personal environment that no one can ever be assumed to have truly and completely accepted their presence.

Therefore, if one engages in work that produces these types of pollution, he can only protect himself by purchasing the rights to create these nuisances from those affected.[27]

The United States has implemented a number of programs that have corporations paying for the amount of environmental damage that they cause. These contemporary programs are conceptually similar to this ancient rabbinic law.

A corollary to this law is found in the case of the members of a courtyard being allowed to prevent one of their number from engaging in a profession that will bring the noise pollution of customers or other nuisances to the courtyard's environment. Only a teacher of Torah to children cannot be prevented in this way, despite the number of people who may come to the area to facilitate children or others learning from his or her wisdom. Only the study of sacred Jewish texts is considered to be a more important value and communal need than noise pollution.[28]

Jerusalem as the holiest of cities also had special legislation designed to protect its unique environment for the enjoyment of its inhabitants and visitors. In that regard all garbage was removed from the city each day[29] and no kilns were ever allowed to operate within its borders.[30] In this way vermin and smoke were kept out of the area and the quality of life for everyone in Jerusalem was improved.

Given the broad extent of Biblical and Rabbinic legislation in this area, one can reasonably ask whether any underlying principles or rationale can be found to explain the strong concern for environmental issues found in Jewish law? On analysis, several approaches seem to emerge from the sources.

Certainly the most direct and obvious answer is that the Earth is God's. Just as Adam was put in the Garden of Eden, le'avdah 'uleshomrah—"to work it and watch over it,"[31] so too, all human beings are required to watch over, preserve and protect the Almighty's creations. Perhaps the fullest treatment of this view appears in the writings of Samson Raphael Hirsch (1808–1888), who describes improper use of Earth's resources as theft from God and as reflecting an arrogant usurpation of His ownership of this world.[32]

Something closely akin to the concept of natural law may also be at work here. The Biblical prohibition against mixing diverse types of seeds and creating hybrids is explained by some as violating hukim shehakakti be'olami—"laws which I (God), have inscribed in my world."[33] By extension all environmental violations may fall into this category as they run the risk of causing harm to the natural order that the Creator built into His universe.

One interesting extension of this approach may be reflected in the numerous sources that equate at least some of the ecological sensitivity in Jewish law with maintaining the proper balance in nature. Ramban (Nahmanides, 1194–1270), in discussing Biblical Prohibitions against mixing species (kilayim),[34] slaughtering an animal and its offspring on the same day,[35] taking the mother bird when taking the eggs or young offspring,[36] and castration[37] suggests that these laws emerge from a concern that all species be preserved and not disappear from this world. This same idea appears in Sefer Hahinukh (13th century) which explains that while God's providence and mercy extend to every human being, in the animal kingdom the same attributes are directed only at entire species. This means that God is concerned that individual species be preserved.[38] Much present environmental legislation reflects the same concern.

This "preservation of species" concern is given a pragmatic rational in the *Talmud*. "Rab Judah said in Rab's name:" of all that the Holy One Blessed be He, created in His world He did not create a single thing without purpose ..." There then follows a list of medicinal uses for even the lowliest of creatures such as snails, files and mosquitos.[39] Again this suggests that the loss of a single species means the loss of something very precious.

God, too, uses this theme of balance and harmony within nature, in His statement to Job. Job, an extremely righteous man, suffers terribly though he has not sinned. He challenges God to justify why all this has happened to him. Eventually God speaks from out of the whirlwind to Job and describes the magnificence and interconnectedness of all creation. It is that interconnectedness that somehow responds to Job's challenge—though scholars have long debated precisely why this is so and how this answers Job's challenge.[40]

Perhaps, the most dramatic statement of this balance is Rabbi Haninah's (1st–2nd century CE), attempt to explain why his son died before his time. His answer: because he cut down a fig tree before its time.[41]

A mystical approach to the environment should also be mentioned here. In *Kabbalah* (Medieval Jewish mysticism) all objects, even inanimate ones—and certainly plant life and animals— contain a spark of God. As such, everything that exists has the right to be treated with the respect due to the presence of the divine. The Baal Shem Tov (c. 1698–1760), the founder of Hassidism, is recorded as having said that "The *Shehina* (the divine presence), permeates all four orders in the world: inanimate objects, plants, living things and humans. It is inherent in all creatures in the universe whether they are good or bad."[42]

A later Hassidic master Rabbi Nachman of Bratslav (1772–1810), put his approach more poetically, "Oh, that you might merit hearing the songs and praises of the grasses and plants! Every blade of grass sings a song of praise to God without any extraneous motives, without strange thoughts, without any idea of reward. How good, how lovely it is when one hears this song of the grasses; it is good to be pious among them."[43] Further, based on the verse, *ki ha' adam etz hasadeh* ...—"for man is as the tree of the field" which appears in the *bal tashhit* context[44] the Bratslaver declared the act of cutting down a tree for no appropriate purpose tantamount to murder.[45]

A more rationalistic presentation that also suggests that all of nature has an intrinsic status deserving of respect beings with God's personal covenant with the Earth, itself. After the Almighty floods the Earth in the time of Noah, He declares—by way of a sacred covenant—that He will never destroy it in this way again.[46] Since the Jewish people also see themselves as sharing in a covenantal partnership with God, they must, perforce, not only live up to their specific obligations to the Creator that is part of their compact with Him; they must also preserve and protect those entities which He has, by covenant, placed under His personal protection. It is part of their partnership with God to be concerned about those things which God has taken as precious unto Himself. In fact the Bible explicitly describes human beings who live under God's protective providence as also having formed a covenant with stones and with animals. "For your covenant shall be with the stones of the field, and the beast of the field are at peace with you."[47]

Perhaps the most individually challenging suggestion of all is that Jewish environmental teaching does not really begin as an attempt to protect the Earth, but rather it emerges out of concern for the callousness and cruelty that a human being displays when he or she is insensitive to nature and to this beautiful world that God has given to humankind. Sefer Hahinukh, in explaining the reason for the *bal tashhit* prohibition with which we began our discussion says:"... it is in order to teach our souls the good and the productive and to cleave to those qualities. As a result the good also cleave to us. Similarly, we should separate from all evil things and from every destructive element. For this is the way of the pious and people of good deeds—loving peace, and rejoicing in the God of all creation and bringing them close to Torah. They do not destroy anything—even a mustard seed—and it troubles them to encounter any destruction or harm. Further, if they can act to save from destruction, they use all their power to save ..."[48] Similar sentiments are echoed by Rabbi Samson Raphael Hirsch who describes purposeless physical damage as childish arrogance, senseless rage, and of an animal rather than that of a human being.[49]

An intriguing story in this regard is the tale of Rabbi Judah Hanasi's (late 2nd–early 3rd century) experiencing painful physical distress sent from heaven, because he told a calf that tried to hide under his robes to avoid being slaughtered, "Go, for this reason were you created." Since he showed no mercy he was made to suffer until the that his maid was going to sweep away a nest of weasels and he stopped her out of compassion for these small animals. This despite the fact that these weasels, as adults, would inevitably become destructive scavengers that would need to be destroyed. At that point his suffering ceased.[50]

The Midrash goes so far as to make ecological sensitivity a *sine qua non* for the good life of the righteous and the exact opposite for the wicked. "A wicked man while alive is thought of as dead because he sees the sun shine and does not say the blessing, 'who creates light,' the sun sets and he does not recite the blessing on food. But the righteous recite blessings on every single thing that they eat, drink, see or hear."[51] In other words the righteous live a life that sanctifies the world around them.

This teaching is in line with the Talmudic dictum that one who consumes anything from this world without saying a blessing is guilty of stealing from God.[52] That comment now carries an additional ecological message indicating that taking anything from nature must involve an act sanctification of the world, and by derivation, an act of sanctification of ourselves.

Given all the positive Rabbinic and Biblical statements regarding environmental issues that we have discussed, why then does the Jewish community and particularly the Orthodox segment of that community not take a greater role in protecting the environment? Part of the answer may be that Jews suffered a 2000 year alienation from their homeland and the natural environment in Israel when they were forced into exile and Diaspora after the destruction of the second Temple in 70 CE. This was compounded by the fact that in many places and for significant periods of time, Jews, as a persecuted minority, were not even allowed to own land.

Thought contemporary Israelis are nowhere near ecologically perfect, my experience has been that much more concern for the environment exists in that country where—because of the geography of what is a very small state and its economic realities—agriculture is an issue that is frequently part of the consciousness of the average citizen. This is different than their Diaspora co-religionists who rarely anything to do, on a personal level, with the land or with nature.

Nonetheless, this alienation is inappropriate. The Midrash says, quite correctly, "Even if a king rules from one end of the world to the other, if the fields produce he will succeed, and if not he is lost."[53] Many militarily powerful countries have fallen or struggled to survive when the strength of their armies of their weapons has not matched the output of their wheat fields.

There is one other consideration as well, and if will serve as the concluding point that this paper will explore. For the Jewish community to speak out on this issue, it must first become more comfortable with the existing ideology of ecology. For a number of reasons it has not been completely at home, and frankly, almost certainly cannot fit within all of the existing conceptual structures of the movement.

One of the founding attitudes underpinning contemporary environmental thinking is an early and frequent critique of the Hebrew Bible and its claimed insensitive treatment of this issue. This critique usually focuses on God's command to Adam to subdue or conquer the world.[54]

In ignoring all of the other sources that display ecological concern, this approach gives an exaggerated emphasis to this one verse. It then goes on to suggest a return to a type of Paganism that views every blade of grass, every tree, every animal as having a deity that protects it. This, it is suggested, will move mankind back to proper respect for nature.[55]

There are many reasons why no Jew can sign on to such an approach, not the least of which is the fact that the Jewish mystical understanding of nature described above comes very close to embracing this position, without demanding a return to a polytheistic world-view.[56] It should be noted here that Sefer Hahinukh argues that the supernatural focus of Paganism is of concern to God precisely because it tends to destroy the natural order of things. This text makes the claim that it was the practitioners of ancient Pagan magic who boasted of creating hybrid creatures with for example the head of an eagle and the body of a lion.[57] Nothing could be more disruptive to the structure of creation than this type of activity.

There is also a second concern that should be raised here. From a traditional Jewish perspective Paganism presents a problem in that it seems to diminish God Himself by positing that other deities rule along with Him. But Paganism, as traditional Judaism understands it, also diminishes humankind. God invested in human beings as the most important entities in the created universe[58] and Pagans, by placing stones, wood and animals above mankind, effectively diminish people's existential and ontological status within their belief system.

It is, therefore, no accident—Jewish tradition would argue—that some forms of Paganism came to allow unspeakable acts such as child sacrifice.[59] Diminishing the value of people can and did lead to these outrages. For those who make this argument it is, therefore, no surprise that the consequences of the "new ecological Paganism" include the murder of veterinary professors, the dangerous insertion of metal roads into trees that injure lumberjacks who cut them down, the death threats to those involved in research, even important and lifesaving research, with animals, etc.

This occurs—or so the argument goes—as a natural consequence of this "new ecological Paganism," that like its ancient predecessor diminishes the human being's place in the universe thus making acts of physical violence less reprehensible. For some Jews, therefore, as long as an ideology that endorses Paganism is present, this fact alone will serve as an excuse not to be involved in the environmental movement, even if one need not be part of these destructive activities to be fully engaged.

Closely related to this is the approach of some activists that people are no more existentially or ontologically significant than animals. The term "speciesism" that has made its way into the lexicon in some quarters, is used to refer to the human being's "inappropriate" sense of superiority to other species. Here traditional Judaism is unequivocal. From Genesis on it is humanity and, in fact, every single human being, who exists in a place that is more cosmically significant than the niche held by any animal.[60]

Similarly—for some—almost all human activity and technology is seen as intrusive and destructive. Therefore no West Side Highway was ever built in lower New York City to replace the one that collapsed many years ago, no nuclear power plants can be constructed anywhere, no new oil drilling can be allowed on United Status land or in its territorial waters and no technology or construction can be done without insuring that virtually all negative environmental impact has been vitiated—at least according to some who are most involved in the ecology movement. Further, any suggestion that environmental damage is being done, even if insufficient or contradictory evidence exists, leads to calls for legislation to radically alter how society functions to prevent this putative harm to nature.

Without specific reference to the *halakhic* reaction to any or all of these particular environmental and public policy issues, the tendency to oppose almost every project of this type is not consistent with Jewish tradition. Judaism sees man as unequivocally superior to animals, and as able to make use of this world and all it contains for any and all positive purposes. In fact, creation is considered incomplete without people to bring the potential that God has built into it into existence.

A prime example of the clash between a Jewish ecology and at least some current secular approaches is the previously cited discussion of placing tanneries on the downwind side of the city. Where Judaism recognizes the necessity of promoting these industries and places them where they will do the least harm, some modem ecologists would seek to ban them altogether. Similarly, though fruit trees, in general, may not be destroyed as discussed above, they may in fact, be cut down if the value of the wood is greater than the value of the fruit that the tree can produce.[61]

In this regard it is interesting to note Abraham Ibn Ezra's (1089-1164) explanation of why the builders of the Biblical Tower of Babel were punished.[62] The Bible describes these builders, who lived shortly after Noah and his flood came to the world, as saying that they were construction their city and their tower to "prevent people from being scattered over all the Earth."[63] In Ibn Ezra's opinion it was their attempt to limit civilization to only one location on the globe that led to God making them speak different languages which forced them to separate and populate the entire planet.[64] Their plans put them in direct opposition to the prophet Isaiah's statement of God's purpose for the world. *Lo tohu bera'ah lashevet yetzarah*—"He did not create it barren, He formed it to be settled,"[65] and of God's command to Adam and Eve—later repeated to Noah and his sons—*milu et ha 'aretz*—"fill the world."[66]

The Talmud specifically rejects the extreme ecological view in the following debate: Rav Hisda said: "When one can eat barley bread and eats wheat bread he violates *bal tashhit*—(do not destroy)," Rav Papa says: "If one can drink beer and drinks wine, he is also in violation of this verse (wheat and wine are more extravagant and cause more environmental consequences)." But this is incorrect. "Do not destroy," as applied to oneself is more important."[67] In other words, reasonable use and enjoyment of this world, even if such acts cause greater ecological consequences, is permissible.

How, then, should the Biblical command of *vekivshuhah* (subdue or conquer the Earth), that some find so objectionable, be understood? It is not to be taken as license to conquer the world by raping and destroying its resources. Its implication is assumed to be consistent with the Bible's description of how Adam and Eve are to function in the Garden of Eden, i.e., *l'ovdah u'leshomrah*—"to work it and to watch it," or perhaps idiomatically "to develop it while preserving it."[68] Responsible use mixed with sincere concern, progress with restraint, growth and technology with conservation and preservation, appear to be the agenda that the Bible and Jewish tradition have for this world of ours.

In summation, then, Judaism has a strong pro-environmental bent, but incorporates it within a positivist view of technology, industry, growth and, most importantly, of faith in the human being. If ecology is to be the issue of the twenty-first century, the Jewish community needs to be heard in favor of legitimate concern for and protection against uncontrolled ecological damage. But it also needs to create a God–human being centered environmental movement that to its most essential faith principles.

NOTES

1. Koheleth Rabba 7:28
2. Tosefta Bava Kama: chapter 2 (end), B. Bava Kama 50b.
3. A partial list includes: Gerstenfeld, Marnfred; Manna as an Environment Paradigm, in B'Or Ha'Torah 14 (2004) 123–130, Zemer, Moshe; Ecology as a Mitzvah, in Environment in Jewish Law; Essays and Responsa, Walter Jacob and Moshe Zemer, ed, New York, (2003) 24–33, Blanchard, Tsvi; Can Judaism Make Environmental Policy? Sacred and Secular Language in Jewish Ecological Discourse, in Judaism and Ecology;

Created World and Revealed Word, Hava Tirosh-Samuelson, ed, (2002) 423–448, Fishbane, Michael A; Toward a Jewish Theology of Nature, in Judaism and Ecology; Created World and Revealed Word, Hava Tirosh-Samuelson, ed, (2002) 17–24, Rosenberg Shalom; Concepts of Torah and Nature in Jewish Thought, in Judaism and Ecology; Created World and Revealed Word, Hava Tirosh-Samuelson, ed, (2002) 189–225, Schwartz, Richord; Environment Ethics and Spiritual Consciousness, In Edah 2, 1 (2002), Sokol, Moshe Z; What are the Ethical Implications of Jewish Theological Conceptions of the Natural World?, in Judaism and Ecology; Created World and Revealed Word, Hava Tirosh-Samuelson, ed, (2002) 261–282, Sperber, Daniel; Jewish Environment Ethics, in Edah 2,1 (2002), Schwartz, Eilon; "Bal Tashchit" : a Jewish Environmental Precept, in Judaism and Environmental Ethics; a Reader, Martin D. Yaffe, ed, Lanham, (2001) 230–249, Helfand, Jonathan I; The Earth is the Lord's: Judaism and Environment Ethics, in Torah of the Earth; Exploring 4,000 Years of Ecology in Jewish Thought, Arthur Waskow, ed, Woodstock, VT, (2000) v. 1, 127–140, Lamn Norman, Ecology in Jewish law and theology in Torah of the Earth, (2000), 1, 103–126, Freundel, Barry; Judaism's Environmental Laws, in Ecology & the Jewish Spirit; Where Nature and the Sacred Meet, Ellen Bernstein, ed, Woodstock, VT: (1998) 214–224, Intrator, Sam M; Sustaining the Work of Creation: an exploration of Jewish environmental education, in Journal of Jewish Education 64, 1–2 (1998) 102–114, Attia, Ilana; Jewish Environmental Law: a selected bibliography of classical sources with annotations, in B'Or Ha'Torah 10(1997) 17–23, Perelmuter, Hayim Goren; "Do not destroy": Ecology in the Fabric of Judaism, in Harvest of a Dialogue; Reflections of a Rabbi/Scholar on a Catholic Faculty, Dianne Bergant and John T. Pawalikowski, ed. Hoboken, NJ (1997) 213–226, Strikovsky, Aryeh; G-d, Man, and Tree, in B'Or HA'Torah 10 (1997) 25–29, Bleich, J. David; Judaism and Natural Law, in WCJS 8, 3 (1982) 7–11, Carmell, Aryeh; Judaism and the Quality if the Environment, in Challenge: Torah Views on Science and Its Problems, A. Carmell and C. Domb, ed New York (1976) 500–525, Belkin, Samuel; Man as a Temporary Tenant, in Judaism and Human Rights, Milton R. Konovitz, ed, New York, (1972), Freudenstein, Eric G; Ecology and the Jewish Tradition, in Judaism (1970), 409–414.

4. Adam Teva V'Din: The Israel Union for Environmental Defense, Alma—Association for Environmental Quality, The Arava Institute for Environment Studies, Canfei Nesharim, Coalition on the Environment and Jewish Life, Eco-Activist Beit Midrash, Green Zionist Alliance, Hazon, Jewish National Fund, Jewish Global Environment Network, The Noah Project, Teva Learning Center.

5. Deuteronomy 20:19–20.

6. Mishneh Torah, Laws of Kings, 6:8. Maimonides includes smashing utensils, tearing cloths, demolishing buildings, blocking springs of water and destroying food. See also Sifrei to these verses in Deuteronomy that if destroying the tree is prohibited, then destroying the fruit must also be prohibited. Many other types of wanton destruction are included in this prohibition by other authorities.

7. Sifrei loc. Cit. See also the incident involving Hezekiah and the waters of Gihon in Jerusalem, 2 Chronicles 32:2–4, 30 and Rabbinic disapproval of his actions, B. Pesahim 56a.

8. B. Baba Kamma 91b

9. Rashi (1040–1105), Kiddushin 32a s.v. *befumbayni,* but see Shiltei Giborim, Avodah Zarah, chapter 1.

10. M. Baba Bathra 2:3.

11. Ibid 2:5.

12. Ibid 2:8.

13. Ibid 2:9.

14. See discussion B. Baba Bathra 25a. See also Tosefot, ad. Loc, s.v. *ein burseki.*

15. Exodus 23:29–30. Deuteronomy 7:22.

16. Jonah 4:11. For discussion of a rabbinic text that explains the continued existence of evil people as resulting from the need for them to feed the animal in their care, see my: Of Hearts, Headlines, and Halacha, in Jewish Action, 45:3, Spring 1985.

17. Ramo (16th century), Orah Hayim 223:6.

18. Ramo, Yoreh Deah 28:2.

19. M. Baba Bathra 2:11 and B. Baba Bathra 24b.

20. Numbers 35:2–5 and Rashi ad. Loc. See also Maimonides, Laws of Shemita 13:5.

21. B. Arkhin 33b.

22. B. Baba Kamma 79b.

23. M. Sotah 9:9, Tosefta Baba Kama 8:13, B. Sotah 47a–b, B. Temurah 15b–16a.

24. M. Hagigah 2:2, Rashi, Sotah 47a Temurah ibid.

25. B. Baba Metziah 10a.

26. B. Tamid 29b.

27. Maimonides, Laws of Neighbors 11:4. In some cases other nuisances may also be included in this category, See Maimonides, ibid. 11:5 and B. Baba Bathra 23a.

28. B. Baba Bathra 21a.

29. B. Baba Kamma 82b.

30. Ibid.

31. Genesis 2:15.

32. Horeb #56, see also Belkin op.cit.

33. J. Kilayim 1:7.

34. Leviticus 19:19.

35. Leviticus 22:28.

36. Deuteronomy 22:6.

37. Leviticus 22:24.

38. Mitzvah 294 and 545.

39. B. Shabbat 77b.

40. Job chapter 40 ff. For a number of different approaches to the book to the meaning of God's response see Nahum Glatzer, The Dimensions of Job, N.Y. 1969.

41. B. Baba Kama 91b–92a.

42. Toledot Yaakov Yosef, p.25.

43. Magid Sihot p.48.

44. Deuteronomy 20:20.

45. For a full treatment of the mystical approach see Lamm op. cit.

46. Genesis 9:8–13.

47. Job 5:23.

48. Mitzvah #529

49. Horeb #56.

50. B. Baba Metziah 85a.

51. Tanhuma Deuteronomy end.

52. B. Berakhoth 35a–35b. Tosefta, Berakhoth 4:1, see Helfand op.cit.

53. Leviticus Rabba 22:1.

54. Genesis 1:26,28.

55. cf. White, Lynn, "The Historical Roots of Our Ecological Crisis," in Science, 155: 1203–1207, (1967), online at http://www.uvm.edu/~gflomenh/ENV-NGO-PA395/articles/Lynn-White.pdf.

56. Paganism in fact does not have such a wonderful environmental record. The Romans plowed salt into the ground to ruin the fertility of the Temple Mount and cf. Isaiah 37:24 for defoliation and ecological destruction by the pagans of his day. Further. Hirsch. loc. cit. argues that ecological destruction implies lack of recognition of God s ownership of the world and, therefore, is itself tantamount to paganism.

57. #62

58. Cf. Ps. 8:6 You have made him (man) but little lower than God.

59. Deuteronomy 12:31.

60. In addition to Genesis 1:28 cf. Genesis 2:19–20 and the commentaries of David Kimhi (1160–1235) and Nahmanides to Genesis 2:18.

61. B. Baba Kama 91b– 92a.

62. Genesis 11:1–9.

63. Ibid, 11:4.

64. See his commentary to Genesis 11:3.

65. Isaiah 45:18

66. Genesis 1:28, 9:1.

67. B. Shabbat 140b.

68. Genesis 2:15.

STUDY QUESTIONS

1. According to Rabbi Freundel, why is the environment a moral issue to a Jew?

2. For non-Jews, what does this perspective contribute to environmental thought?

3. Compare/contrast this perspective to one of the other religious traditions mentioned in this text.

4. How might a modern day pagan respond to Rabbi Freundel's characterizations of paganism?

61

The Judeo-Christian Stewardship Attitude to Nature

PATRICK DOBEL

Patrick Dobel is associate professor and director of the Graduate School of Public Affairs at the University of Washington in Seattle.

Dobel argues that the Judeo-Christian attitude is an ethics of stewardship and that humility toward God regarding nature, not arrogance, is enjoined by our religious heritage.

Browsing in a local bookstore recently, I took down several of the more general books from the "Ecology" shelf. Scanning the tables of contents and indexes of 13 books, I discovered that nine of them made reference to "Christianity," "the Bible" or the "Judeo-Christian tradition." Examining their contents more closely, I found that seven of these books blamed specific Christian or Bible-based values as significant "causes" of the ecology crisis.

Over half these books referenced an article by Lynn White, Jr., titled "The Historical Roots of Our Ecologic Crisis" (*Science,* March 10, 1967). In this short, undocumented and simplistic article White argues that the root of the entire problem lies in "the Christian maxim that nature has no reason for existence save to serve man." From the Christians' penchant for cutting down sacred Druidic groves to the development of "modern science from natural theology," Christianity, White argues, laid the foundations of Western "arrogance towards nature" and "limitless rule of creation."

Almost all similar statements are indebted to White; they even cite the same examples: grief over the destruction of the sacred groves; respect for Saint Francis of Assisi. Although few of the authors have read anything about him except that he talked to birds, they have raised poor Francis to the rank of first "ecological saint," while conveniently ignoring his myriad admonitions about asceticism and communal ownership of property.

DOMINION OVER THE EARTH

The ecological indictment of Christianity boils down to two somewhat contradictory assertions: that the postulated transcendence and domination of humanity over nature encourages thoughtless exploitation of the earth and that the otherworldly orientation of Christianity encourages contempt and disregard for the earth. In documenting the first indictment authors often cite Genesis 1:26: "Let us make man in our image, after our likeness; and let them have dominion over the fish of the sea, and over the birds of the air, and over the cattle, and over every creeping thing that creeps upon the earth." Some also quote Genesis 1:28: "Be fruitful and multiply, and fill the earth and subdue it; and have dominion over the fish of the sea and over the birds of the air and over every living thing that moves upon the earth."

These texts lead to the conclusion that the Bible emphasizes the absolute superiority of humanity over the rest of creation. And this relation must be primarily one of antagonism and alienation, for "cursed is the ground because of you; in toil you shall eat of it all the days of your life.... In the sweat of your face you shall eat bread" (Gen. 3:17).

Thus Christianity separates both humanity and God from the earth and destroys the inherent sacredness of the earth. This alienation is coupled with humanity's innate superiority over nature and the divine mandate to exploit nature limitlessly for human ends—a mandate that is carried out in the context of antagonism and an expectation that the earth must be treated harshly to gain the yield of human survival. Together these notions have shaped Western culture's spoliation of the earth.

In bringing the second indictment, critics point out that Christianity's otherworldly preoccupation also contributes to human abuse of the environment. Christians are instructed to "kill everything in you that belongs only to the earthly life" and to "let your thoughts be on heavenly things, not on the things that are on the earth" (Col. 3:2–5). The emphasis is upon awaiting "a new heaven and a new earth in which righteousness dwells" (II Pet. 3:13). In some ways this stress undercuts the mandates of superiority and rule since it implies that humanity rules nothing but a fallen and contemptible orb. If the contempt, however, is tied to an antagonistic human domination and the need of people to discipline their unruly bodies through work, it can provide an ethical framework to support the thoughtless and arrogant exploitation which is part of the ecology crisis. The thesis linking Calvinism with the rise of industrialization reflects this ambivalent world-hating but smug and exploitative attitude.

The critics see modern science and technology along with notions of unbridled progress and exploitation emerging from this Judeo-Christian matrix. They conclude that Christianity must accept most of the "blame" for the unique "Western" perspectives which have led to the present state of affairs. This "blame" somehow rings false when the ecologists extend the link to the later implications of a secularized technology and a liberal view of human progress.

LOOKING FOR THE ROOTS

The attempt to discover historical roots is a dubious business at best, and in this case it borders on the ludicrous. Christianity's ecological critics consistently underestimate the economic, social and political influences on modern science and economy; their approach makes for good polemics but bad history. Their thesis lacks a careful historical analysis of the intellectual and practical attitudes toward the earth and its use in the consciously Christian Middle Ages. They disregard the earth-centered ideals of the Christian Renaissance and its concern with the delicate limitations of the Great Chain of Being, and they pay little attention to the emergence of a peculiarly non-Christian deism and theism which defined God in the 17th and 18th centuries to accommodate a newly secularized nature and new developments in science and trade. These critics neglect to mention the specifically Christian prohibitions which often made religion a detriment to economic and scientific development.

They also ignore the rise of the secularized nation-state from the decay of "Christendom"; yet these new government regimes provided much of the impetus to maximize the exploitation of resources and the discovery of new lands. Most of the operative "roots" of the present crisis are to be found in the far more secularized and non-Christian world of nationalism, science and liberalism in the 16th through the 19th centuries.

Given the unsoundness of the theory that blames Christianity for the environmental crisis, it is surprising that it has gained such remarkable currency. In light of this fact there are two distinct tasks which confront the Christian community. First, this thesis should be addressed in some detail, not only to show its flaws but to discover what ideas and practices the tradition can contribute to a concrete ecological program. Second, we must use the vast ethical and conceptual resources of the

Judeo-Christian tradition to develop a God-centered ecological ethic which accounts for the sacredness of the earth without losing sight of human worth and justice. In addressing myself to this second task, I will try to develop appropriate responses to the following questions through textual exegesis of the Bible: What is the ethical status of the earth as an entity in creation? What is the proper relation of humanity to the earth and its resources?

Ecological critics have nostalgically lamented the decline of "nature worship" and have spoken wistfully of the need to import "Eastern" concepts of pantheism or quietist respect for the "equality of all life." Even some of the most secularized ecologists are calling for a rediscovery of the "sacredness" of nature.

Although it is hard to discover the enduring sacredness of anything in a totally secularized world, we must keep several points in mind about these calls. First, all cultures, regardless of religion, have abused or destroyed large areas of the world either because of economic or population pressures or from simple ignorance. Second, the ethical consequences of the new nature worship, neopantheism and the militant assertion of the equality of all creaturehood pose grave problems for establishing any prior claims of worth or inherent dignity for human beings. The more undifferentiated God and the world become, the harder it is to define individual humans as worthwhile with specific claims to social justice and care. Third, a sort of mindless ecological imperative based upon such notions is ultimately reactionary and anti-human, as well as anti-Christian. There are fundamental ethical differences between plants and animals and between animals and human beings. To resort simplistically to militantly pro-earth and antiprogress positions misses the vital Christian and humanistic point that our sojourn upon the earth is not yet completed and that we must continue to work unflaggingly toward social justice and the well-being of all people.

The unique contribution a Christian ecology can make to the earth is the assertion that we can insist on a reasonable harmony with our world without abandoning our commitment to social justice for all members of our unique and self-consciously alienated species. We can love and respect our environment without obliterating all ethical and technological distinctions, and without denying the demand that we cautiously but steadily use the earth for the benefit of all humanity.

The first question to address is the status of the earth and its resources. A different way of putting this is "Who owns the earth?" The answer of the entire Judeo-Christian tradition is clear: God. "In the beginning God created the heavens and the earth" (Gen. 1:3). In direct ethical terms God created the earth, and in distributive-justice terms it belongs to him: "The earth is the Lord's and the fullness thereof" (Ps. 24:1). As an act of pure love he created a world and he "founded the earth to endure" (Ps. 119:90–91).

What kind of world did God create? The answer has two dimensions: the physical or descriptive and the ethical. As a product of nature the world was created as a law-bound entity. The laws are derivative of God's will for all creation as "maintained by your rulings" (Ps. 119:90–91). Things coexist in intricate and regulated harmony—the basic postulate of science, mythology and reason. Although we have a world of laws, it is also a world of bounty and harmony. For it had been promised that "while the earth remains, seedtime and harvest shall not cease" (Gen. 8:22). It was arranged "in wisdom" so that in the balance of nature, "All creatures depend upon you to feed them … you provide the food with a generous hand." God's presence ultimately "holds all things in unity" (Col. 1:16–20) and constantly "renews" the world (Ps. 104:24–30). This world abounds in life and is held together in a seamless web maintained by God-willed laws.

In ethical terms, God saw that the world was "very good" (Gen. 1:31). In love and freedom he created the world and valued it as good. All the creatures of the world also share in this goodness (I Tim. 4:4). This does not mean that the world is "good for" some purpose or simply has utilitarian value to humanity. The world, in its bounty and multiplicity of life, is independently good and ought to be respected as such.

As an independent good, the earth possesses an autonomous status as an ethical and covenanted entity. In Genesis 9:8–17, God directly includes the earth and all the animals as participants in the covenant. He urges the animals to "be fruitful and multiply." Earlier in Genesis 1:30, he takes care specifically to grant the plant life of the earth to the creatures who possess "breath of life." In the great covenant with Noah and all humanity, he expressly includes all other creatures and the earth.

> And God said, "This is a sign of the covenant which I make between *me and you and every living creature* that is with you, for all future generations: I set my bow in the sky, and it shall be a sign of the *covenant between* me and the earth" [emphasis added].

The prophets, Isaiah especially, constantly address the earth and describe its independent travail. Paul describes the turmoil and travail of the earth as a midwife of all creation and redemption (Rom. 8:18–22). The earth must be regarded as an autonomous ethical entity bound not just by the restraints of physical law but also by respect for its inherent goodness and the covenanted limitations placed upon our sojourn. Perhaps we must think seriously of defining a category of "sins against the earth."

The proper relation between humanity and the bountiful earth is more complex. One fact is of outstanding moral relevance: the earth does not belong to humanity; it belongs to God. Jeremiah summarizes it quite succinctly: "I by my great power and outstretched arm made the earth, land and animals that are on the earth. And I can give them to whom I please" (Jer. 27:5). For an ecological ethic this fact cannot be ignored. The resources and environment of the earth are not ours in any sovereign or unlimited sense; they belong to someone else.

A TRUST FOR FUTURE GENERATIONS

Humanity's relation to the earth is dominated by the next fact: God "bestows" the earth upon all of humanity (Ps. 115:16). This gift does not, however, grant sovereign control. The prophets constantly remind us that God is still the "king" and the ruler/owner to whom the earth reverts. No one generation of people possesses the earth. The earth was made "to endure" and was given for all future generations. Consequently the texts constantly reaffirm that the gift comes under covenanted conditions, and that the covenant is "forever." The Bible is permeated with a careful concern for preserving the "land" and the "earth" as an "allotted heritage" (Ps. 2:7–12).

This point is central to the Judeo-Christian response to the world. The world is given to all. Its heritage is something of enduring value designed to benefit all future generations. Those who receive such a gift and benefit from it are duty-bound to conserve the resources and pass them on for future generations to enjoy. An "earth of abundance" (Judg. 18:10) provides for humanity's needs and survival (Gen. 1:26–28, 9:2–5). But the injunction "obey the covenant" (I Chron. 16:14–18) accompanies the gift.

There are some fairly clear principles that direct our covenanted responsibilities toward the earth. Each generation exists only as "sojourner" or "pilgrim." We hold the resources and the earth as a "trust" for future generations. Our covenanted relations to the earth—and for that matter, to all human beings—must be predicated upon the recognition and acceptance of the limits of reality. For there is a "limit upon all perfection" (Ps. 119:96), and we must discover and respect the limits upon ourselves, our use of resources, our consumption, our treatment of others and the environment with its delicate ecosystems. Abiding by the covenant means abiding by the laws of nature, both scientific and moral. In ecological terms the balance of nature embodies God's careful plan that the earth and its bounty shall provide for the needs and survival of all humanity of all generations.

The combined emphases upon God's ownership, our trusteeship and the limits of life call for an attitude of humility and care in dealing with the world. Only "the humble shall have the land for their own to enjoy untroubled peace" (Ps. 37:11). Knowledge of limits, especially of the intricacy of the ecosystems, makes humility and care a much more natural response. The transgression of limits usually brings either unknown or clearly dangerous consequences and ought to influence all actions with a singular sense of caution. Humility and respect do not mean simple awe, or withdrawal from all attempts to use or improve the bounty we are given. At the very least, they lead to the loss of arrogant ignorance which leads us to pursue policies in contradiction to the clear limits and laws of nature and particular ecosystems.

THE STEWARDSHIP IMPERATIVE

The New Testament distills these notions and adds a strong activist imperative with its account of stewardship. This activist element is a vital alternative to some of the more extreme ethical positions in reactionary ecological ethics. The parable of the good steward in Luke 12:41–48 and the parable of the talents in Matthew 25:14–30 summarize the concept. The preservation of what is given "in trust" demands a recognition of the owner's dictates for the resources. We must know the limits and laws of the world in order to use them wisely. Our actions must be guided, in part, by concerns for future generations. Above all, we must never knowingly exhaust or ruin what has been given to us. If doing so is absolutely necessary to sustain life, then equity demands that we must leave some equally accessible and beneficial legacy to replace what has been exhausted.

But there is more involved in being a "faithful and wise steward." Even the most conservative banker is obliged to improve the stock for the benefit of the heirs. The parable of the talents makes it abundantly clear that we who are entrusted with his property will be called to account for our obligation to improve the earth. The stewardship imperative assumes that the moral and ecological constraints are respected, and it adds the obligation to distribute the benefits justly. The steward must "give them their portion of the food at the proper time." Mistreating his charges, gorging himself on the resources in excess consumption, and not caring for the resources will all cause the stewards to be "cut off." True stewardship requires both respect

for the trusteeship and covenanted imperatives and an active effort to improve the land for the future and to use it in a manner to benefit others. Ethical proportionality applies to all those responsible for the earth, for "when a man has had a great deal given to him on trust, even more will be expected of him" (Luke 12:48–49).

AN INFORMED HUMILITY

The lessons are clear. Any ecological ethic which takes into account both God and humanity and does not reduce both to some extension of undifferentiated nature must begin with a rejection of the unbridled sovereignty of humanity over the earth. In this rejection is the recognition that all work upon the earth must be informed by a clear understanding of and respect for the earth as an autonomous and valuable entity and the laws of nature on which the bounty of the earth depends.

These are necessary but by no means sufficient within the Judeo-Christian tradition. For the earth, while it possesses its own moral autonomy, is not God and must not be confused as such. Our own relation to it must be predicated upon a careful understanding that earth and its resources are for any generation a restricted gift held in trust for future generations. We must never lose sight of the fact that a just and informed humility provides the framework for a working relationship with the earth.

Much more work remains to be done on the "ethics of stewardship"; I have merely suggested a few ethical considerations: the obligation not to exhaust nonrenewable resources, the imperative to provide accessible replacements, the necessity to improve our heritage modestly and carefully, the greater responsibility of the advantaged to improve that which exists and to share, and the obligation to refrain from excessive consumption and waste. "Each of you has received a special gift, so like good stewards responsible for all the different gifts of God, put yourselves at the service of others" (I Pet. 4:10–11).

STUDY QUESTIONS

1. Compare Dobel's understanding of a Christian environmental ethics with another tradition mentioned in this text.

2. If human beings do not own Earth, what is our role, according to Dobel? Do you agree? Explain your answer.

3. If one does not accept a theistic version of creation, does the stewardship model make any sense? A steward is one who manages the household affairs of another person. If there is no God, Earth is not God's household. But then whose is it? To whom are we stewards?

62

Islamic Environmental Ethics, Law, and Society

MAWIL Y. IZZI DEEN (SAMARRAI)

Mawil Y. Izzi Deen (Samarrai) is assistant professor, King Abdul Aziz University, Jeddah, consultant to the Saudi Arabian Center for Science and Technology, and co-author of Islamic Principles for the Conservation of the Natural Environment. Deen sets forth the Islamic view that the foundation of environmental protection is found in the idea that God created the world and set human beings in it to enjoy and carefully use it. Ecological balance and sustainable care of nature are promoted by Islam.

Islamic environmental ethics, like all other forms of ethics in Islam, is based on clear-cut legal foundations which Muslims hold to be formulated by God. Thus, in Islam, an acceptance of what is legal and what is ethical has not involved the same processes as in cultures which base their laws on humanistic philosophies.

Muslim scholars have found it difficult to accept the term "Islamic Law," since "law" implies a rigidity and dryness alien to Islam. They prefer the Arabic word *Sharī'ah* (Shariah) which literally means the "source of water." The Shariah is the source of life in that it contains both legal rules and

ethical principles. This is indicated by the division of the Shariah relevant to human action into the categories of: obligatory actions (*wājib*),—those which a Muslim is required to perform; devotional and ethical virtues (*mandūb*),—those actions a Muslim is encouraged to perform, the non-observance of which, however, incurs no liability; permissible actions (*mubāh*),—those in which a Muslim is given complete freedom of choice; abominable actions (*makrūh*),—those which are morally but not legally wrong; and prohibited actions (*haram*)—all those practices forbidden by Islam.

Reprinted from *Ethics of Environment*, ed. J. Ronald Engel and Joan Gibb Engel (London: Bellhaven Press, 1990), p. 189–98.
Reprinted by permission of John Wiley and Sons, Ltd. Notes deleted.

your dwellings lest Solomon and his armies crush you, unperceiving.

And [Solomon] smiled, laughing at her speech, and said: My Lord, arouse me to be thankful for Thy favor wherewith Thou hast favored me and my parents, and to do good that shall be pleasing unto Thee, and include me among [the number of] Thy righteous slaves. (Sūrah 27: 18–19)

Ethics in Islam is not based on a variety of separate scattered virtues, with each virtue, such as honesty or truth, standing isolated from others. Rather virtue in Islam is a part of a total, comprehensive way of life which serves to guide and control all human activity. Truthfulness is an ethical value, as are protecting life, conserving the environment, and sustaining its development within the confines of what God has ordered. When 'Āisha, the wife of the Prophet Muhammad, was asked about his ethics she replied: "His ethics are the whole Qur'ān." The Qur'ān does not contain separate scattered ethical values. Rather it contains the instructions for a complete way of life. There are political, social and economic principles side by side with instructions for the construction and preservation of the earth.

Islamic ethical values are based not on human reasoning, as Aristotle claimed values to be, nor on what society imposes on the individual, as Durkheim thought, nor on the interests of a certain class, as Marxists maintain. In each of these claims values are affected by circumstances. In Islam, ethical values are held to be based on an accurate scale which is unalterable as to time and place. Islam's values are those without which neither persons nor the natural environment can be sustained.

THE HUMAN–ENVIRONMENT RELATIONSHIP

As we have seen, within the Islamic faith, an individual's relationship with the environment is governed by certain moral precepts. These originate with God's creation of humans and the role they were given upon the Earth. Our universe, with all its diverse component elements was created by God and the human being is an essential part of His Measured and Balanced Creation. The role of humans, however, is not only to enjoy, use and benefit from their surroundings. They are expected to preserve, protect and promote their fellow creatures. The Prophet Muhammad (peace be upon him) said: "All creatures are God's dependents and the best among them is the one who is most useful to God's dependents." The Prophet of Islam looked upon himself as responsible for the trees and the animals and all natural elements. He also said: "The only reasons that God does not cause his punishment to pour over you are the elderly, the suckling babes, and the animals which graze upon your land." Muhammad prayed for rain when he was reminded that water was short, the trees suffering from drought, and animals dying. He begged for God's mercy to fall upon his creatures.

The relationship between human beings and their environment includes many features in addition to subjugation and utilization. Construction and development are primary but our relationship to nature also includes meditation, contemplation and enjoyment of its beauties. The most perfect Muslim was the Prophet Muhammad who was reported by Ibn 'Abbās to have enjoyed gazing at greenery and running water.

When reading verses about the Earth in the Holy Qur'ān, we find strong indications that the Earth was originally a place of peace and rest for humans:

Is not He [best] Who made the earth a fixed abode, and placed rivers in the folds thereof, and placed firm hills therein, and hath set a barrier between the two seas? Is there any God beside Allah? Nay, but most of them know not! (Sūrah 27:61)

The Earth is important to the concept of interrelation. Human beings are made from two components of the Earth—dust and water.

And Allah hath caused you to grow as a growth from the earth, And afterward

He maketh you return thereto, and He will bring you forth again, a [new] forthbringing. And Allah hath made the earth a wide expanse for you. That ye may thread the valleyways thereof. (Sūrah 71:17–20)

The word "earth" (ard) is mentioned twice in this short quotation and in the Qur'ān the word occurs a total of 485 times, a simple measure of its importance.

The Earth is described as being subservient to humans: "He it is Who hath made the earth subservient unto you, so walk in the paths thereof and eat of His providence" (Sūrah 67:15). The Earth is also described as a receptacle: "Have we not made the earth a receptacle both for the living and the dead" (Sūrah 77: 25–26). Even more importantly, the Earth is considered by Islam to be a source of purity and a place for the worship of God. The Prophet Muhammad said: "The earth is made for me [and Muslims] as a prayer place (masjid) and as a purifier." This means that the Earth is to be used to cleanse oneself before prayer if water is unobtainable. Ibn 'Umar reported that the Prophet of Islam said: "God is beautiful and loved everything beautiful. He is generous and loves generosity and is clean and loves cleanliness."

Thus it is not surprising that the Islamic position with regard to the environment is that humans must intervene in order to protect the Earth. They may not stand back while it is destroyed. "He brought you forth from the earth and hath made you husband it" (Sūrah 11:61). For, finally, the Earth is a source of blessedness. And the Prophet Muhammad said: "Some trees are blessed as the Muslim himself, especially palm."

THE SUSTAINABLE CARE
OF NATURE

Islam permits the utilization of the natural environment but this utilization should not involve unnecessary destruction. Squandering is rejected by God: "O Children of Adam! Look to your adornment at every place of worship, and eat and drink, but be not prodigal. Lo! He loveth not the prodigals" (Sūrah 7:31). In this Qur'ānic passage, eating and drinking refer to the utilization of the sources of life. Such utilization is not without controls. The component elements of life have to be protected so that their utilization may continue in a sustainable way. Yet even this preservation must be undertaken in an altruistic fashion, and not merely for its benefit to human beings. The Prophet Muhammad said: "Act in your life as though you are living forever and act for the Hereafter as if you are dying tomorrow."

These actions must not be restricted to those which will derive direct benefits. Even if doomsday were expected imminently, humans would be expected to continue their good behaviour, for Muhammad said: "When doomsday comes if someone has a palm shoot in his hand he should plant it." This hadīth encapsulates the principles of Islamic environmental ethics. Even when all hope is lost, planting should continue for planting is good in itself. The planting of the palm shoot continues the process of development and will sustain life even if one does not anticipate any benefit from it. In this, the Muslim is like the soldier who fights to the last bullet.

A theory of the sustainable utilization of the ecosystem may be deduced from Islam's assertion that life is maintained with due balance in everything: "Allah knoweth that which every female beareth and that which the wombs absorb and that which they grow. And everything with Him is measured" (Sūrah 13:8). Also: "He unto Whom belongeth the sovereignty of the heavens and the earth, He hath chosen no son nor hath He any partner in the sovereignty. He hath created everything and hath meted out for it a measure" (Sūrah 25:2).

Humans are not the owners, but the maintainers of the due balance and measure which God provided for them and for the animals that live with them.

And after that He spread the earth,
And produced therefrom water
thereof and the pasture thereof,

And He made fast the hills,
A provision for you and
for your cattle.
(SŪRAH 79:30–33)

The Qur'ān goes on to say:

But when the great disaster cometh,
The day when man will call
to mind his [whole] endeavor.
(SŪRAH 79:34–35)

Humans will have a different home (*ma'wā*) or place of abode, different from the Earth and what it contains. The word *ma'wā* is the same word used in modern Arabic for "environment." One cannot help but wonder if these verses are an elaboration on the concept of sustainable development, a task that humans will undertake until their home is changed.

Sayyid Qutb, commenting on these verses, observes that the Qur'ān, in referring to the origin of ultimate truth, used many correspondences (*muwāfaqāt*)—such as building the heavens, darkening the night, bringing forth human beings, spreading the earth, producing water and plants, and making the mountains fast. All these were provided for human beings and their animals as providence, and are direct signs which constitute proof as to the reality of God's measurement and calculation. Finally, Sayyid Qutb observes that every part of God's creation was carefully made to fit into the general system, a system that testifies to the Creator's existence and the existence of a day of reward and punishment.

At this point, one must ask whether it is not a person's duty to preserve the proof of the Creator's existence while developing it. Wouldn't the wholesale destruction of the environment be the destruction of much which testifies to the greatness of God?

The concept of the sustained care of all aspects of the environment also fits into Islam's concept of charity, for charity is not only for the present generation but also for those in the future. A story is told of 'Umar ibn al-Khattāb, the famous companion of the Prophet. He once saw that an old man, Khuzaymah ibn Thābit, had neglected his land. 'Umar asked what was preventing him from cultivating it. Khuzaymah explained that he was old and could be expected to die soon. Whereupon, Umar insisted that he should plant it. Khuzaymah's son, who narrated the story, added that his father and 'Umar planted the uncultivated land together.

This incident demonstrates how strongly Islam encourages the sustained cultivation of the land. Land should not be used and then abandoned just because the cultivator expects no personal benefit.

In Islam, law and ethics constitute the two interconnected elements of a unified world view. When considering the environment and its protection, this Islamic attitude may constitute a useful foundation for the formulation of a strategy throughout, at least, the Muslim world. Muslims who inhabit so much of the developing world may vary in local habits and customs but they are remarkably united in faith and in their attitude to life.

Islam is a religion of submission to God, master of all worlds. The Earth and all its inhabitants were created and are dominated by God. All Muslims begin their prayers five times a day with the same words from the Holy Qur'ān: "Praise be to Allah, Lord of the Worlds" (Sūrah 1:1). These opening words of the Qur'ān have become not only the most repeated but also the most loved and respected words for Muslims everywhere. Ibn Kathīr, like many other Qur'ānic commentators, considers that the word "worlds" (*ālamīn*) means the different kinds of creatures that inhabit the sky, the land, and the sea. Muslims submit themselves to the Creator who made them and who made all other worlds. The same author mentions that Muslims also submit themselves to the signs of the existence of the Creator and His unity. This secondary meaning exists because "worlds" comes from the same root as signs; thus the worlds are signs of the Creator.

A Muslim, therefore, has a very special relationship with those worlds which in modern times have come to be known as the environment.

Indeed, that these worlds exist and that they were made by the same Creator means that they are united and interdependent, each a part of the perfect system of creation. No conflict should exist between them; they should exist in harmony as different parts of the whole. Their coexistence could be likened to an architectural masterpiece in which every detail has been added to complete and complement the structure. Thus the details of creation serve to testify to the wisdom and perfection of the Creator.

THE PRACTICE OF ISLAMIC ENVIRONMENTAL ETHICS

Islam has always had a great influence on the formation of individual Muslim communities and the policy making of Muslim states. Environmental policy has been influenced by Islam and this influence has remained the same throughout the history of the Islamic faith.

The concept of *himā* (protection of certain zones) has existed since the time of the Prophet Muhammad. *Himā* involved the ruler or government's protection of specific unused areas. No one may build on them or develop them in any way. The Mālikī school of Islamic law described the requirements of *himā* to be the following. First, the need of the Muslim public for the maintenance of land in an unused state. Protection is not granted to satisfy an influential individual unless there is a public need. Second, the protected area should be limited in order to avoid inconvenience to the public. Third, the protected area should not be built on or cultivated. And fourth, the aim of protection (Zuhaylī 5:574) is the welfare of the people, for example, the protected area may be used for some restricted grazing by the animals of the poor.

The concept of *himā* can still be seen in many Muslim countries, such as Saudi Arabia, where it is practised by the government to protect wildlife. In a less formal way it is still practised by some bedouin tribes as a custom or tradition inherited from their ancestors.

The *harīm* is another ancient institution which can be traced back to the time of the Prophet Muhammad. It is an inviolable zone which may not be used or developed, save with the specific permission of the state. The *harīm* is usually found in association with wells, natural springs, underground water channels, rivers and trees planted on barren land or *mawāt*. There is careful administration of the *harīm* zones based on the practice of the Prophet Muhammad and the precedent of his companions as recorded in the sources of Islamic law.

At present the role of Islam in environmental protection can be seen in the formation of different Islamic organizations and the emphasis given to Islam as a motive for the protection of the environment.

Saudi Arabia has keenly sought to implement a number of projects aimed at the protection of various aspects of the environment, for example, the late King Khalid's patronage of efforts to save the Arabian ornyx from extinction.

The Meteorology and Environmental Protection Administration (MEPA) of Saudi Arabia actively promotes the principles of Islamic environmental protection. In 1983 MEPA and the International Union for the Conservation of Nature and Natural Resources commissioned a basic paper on the Islamic principles for the conservation of natural environment.

The Islamic faith has great impact on environmental issues throughout the Arab and Muslim world. The first Arab Ministerial Conference took as its theme "The Environmental Aspects of Development" and one of the topics considered was the Islamic faith and its values. The Amir of Kuwait emphasized the fundamental importance of Islam when he addressed the General Assembly of the United Nations in 1988. He explained that Islam was the basis for justice, mercy, and cooperation between all humankind; and he called for an increase in scientific and technological assistance from the North to help conserve natural and human resources, combat pollution and support sustainable development projects.

Finally, it is imperative to acknowledge that the new morality required to conserve the environment which the World Conservation Strategy emphasizes, needs to be based on a more solid foundation. It is not only necessary to involve the public in conservation policy but also to improve its morals and alter its attitudes. In Muslim countries such changes should be brought about by identifying environmental policies with Islamic teachings. To do this, the public education system will have to supplement the scientific approach to environmental education with serious attention to Islamic belief and environmental awareness.

STUDY QUESTIONS

1. Compare Deen's view of the Islamic environmental ethics with the preceding views on Hinduism and Buddhism. Then compare it with Patrick Dobel's view (Reading 61) of Christian environmental ethics.

2. What insights or practices in Islam have you found that might be helpful in developing a Western environmental ethic? How would Islam contribute toward a global ecumenical environmental ethic?

63

Satyagraha for Conservation: A Hindu View

O. P. DWIVEDI

O. P. Dwivedi is chair and professor, Department of Political Studies, University of Guelph, Canada, and has served as World Health Organization consultant to the Department of Environment, India. He is the coauthor of Hindu Religion and the Environmental Crisis.

In this essay, Dwivedi argues that a profound environmental ethics, consisting in satyagraha (the persistent quest for truth) permeates Hinduism. Hinduism holds to a strong version of the equal sanctity of all life and for thousands of years practiced sustainable agriculture and nonviolence (ahimsa) toward animals and nature. Dwivedi argues that in the last hundreds of years satyagraha lost much of its effectiveness, but there are signs that it is reasserting itself.

The World Commission on Environment and Development acknowledged that to reconcile human affairs with natural laws "our cultural and spiritual heritages can reinforce our economic interests and survival imperatives." But until very recently, the role of our cultural and spiritual

Reprinted from *Ethics of Environment and Development*, ed. J. Ronald Engel and Joan Gibb Engel (London: Bellhaven Press, 1990), by permission of John Wiley & Sons Limited the author.

heritages in environmental protection and sustainable development was ignored by international bodies, national governments, policy planners, and even environmentalists. Many fear that bringing religion into the environmental movement will threaten objectivity, scientific investigation, professionalism, or democratic values. But none of these need be displaced in order to include the spiritual dimension in environmental protection. That dimension, if introduced in the process of environmental policy planning, administration, education, and law, could help create a self-consciously moral society which would put conservation and respect for God's creation first, and relegate individualism, materialism, and our modern desire to dominate nature in a subordinate place. Thus my plea for a definite role of religion in conservation and environmental protection.

From the perspective of many world religions, the abuse and exploitation of nature for immediate gain is unjust, immoral, and unethical. For example, in the ancient past, Hindus and Buddhists were careful to observe moral teachings regarding the treatment of nature. In their cultures, not only the common person but also rulers and kings followed those ethical guidelines and tried to create an example for others. But now in the twentieth century, the materialistic orientation of the West has equally affected the cultures of the East. India, Sri Lanka, Thailand, and Japan have witnessed wanton exploitation of the environment by their own peoples, despite the strictures and injunctions inherent in their religions and cultures. Thus, no culture has remained immune from human irreverence towards nature. How can we change the attitude of human beings towards nature? Are religions the answer?

I believe that religion can evoke a kind of awareness in persons that is different from scientific or technological reasoning. Religion helps make human beings aware that there are limits to their control over the animate and inanimate world and that their arrogance and manipulative power over nature can backfire. Religion instills the recognition that human life cannot be measured by material possessions and that the ends of life go beyond conspicuous consumption.

As a matter of fact, religion can provide at least three fundamental mainstays to help human beings cope in a technological society. First, it defends the individual's existence against the depersonalizing effects of the technoindustrial process. Second, it forces the individual to recognize human fallibility and to combine realism with idealism. Third, while technology gives the individual the physical power to create or to destroy the world, religion gives the moral strength to grow in virtue by nurturing restraint, humility, and liberation from self-centredness. Directly and indirectly, religion can be a powerful source for environmental conservation and protection. Thus, we need a strategy for conservation that does not ignore the powerful influence of religions, but instead draws from all religious foundations and cultures.

World religions, each in their own way, offer a unique set of moral values and rules to guide human beings in their relationship with the environment. Religions also provide sanctions and offer stiffer penalties, such as fear of hell, for those who do not treat God's creation with respect. Although it is true that, in the recent past, religions have not been in the forefront of protecting the environment from human greed and exploitation, many are now willing to take up the challenge and help protect and conserve the environment. But their offer of help will remain purely rhetorical unless secular institutions, national governments, and international organizations are willing to acknowledge the role of religion in environmental study and education. And I believe that environmental education will remain incomplete until it includes cultural values and religious imperatives. For this, we require an ecumenical approach. While there are metaphysical, ethical, anthropological and social disagreements among world religions, a synthesis of the key concepts and precepts from each of them pertaining to conservation could become a foundation for a global environmental ethic. The world needs such an ethic.

THE RELIGION AND ENVIRONMENT DEBATE

In 1967, the historian, Lynn White, Jr., wrote an article in *Science* on the historical roots of the ecological crisis. According to White, what people do to their environment depends upon how they see themselves in relation to nature. White asserted that the exploitative view that has generated much of the environmental crisis, particularly in Europe and North America, is a result of the teachings of late medieval Latin Christianity, which conceived of humankind as superior to the rest of God's creation and everything else as created for human use and enjoyment. He suggested that the only way to address the ecological crisis was to reject the view that nature has no reason to exist except to serve humanity. White's proposition impelled scientists, theologians, and environmentalists to debate the bases of his argument that religion could be blamed for the ecological crisis.

In the course of this debate, examples from other cultures were cited to support the view that, even in countries where there is religious respect for nature, exploitation of the environment has been ruthless. Countries where Hinduism, Buddhism, Taoism and Shintoism have been practiced were cited to support the criticism of Thomas Derr, among others, that "We are simply being gullible when we take at face value the advertisement for the ecological harmony of non-Western cultures." Derr goes on to say:

> even if Christian doctrine had produced technological culture and its environmental troubles, one would be at a loss to understand the absence of the same result in equally Christian Eastern Europe. And conversely, if ecological disaster is a particularly Christian habit, how can one explain the disasters non-Christian cultures have visited upon their environments? Primitive cultures, Oriental cultures, classical cultures—all show examples of human dominance over nature which has led to ecological catastrophe. Overgrazing, deforestation and similar errors of sufficient magnitude to destroy civilizations have been committed by Egyptians, Assyrians, Romans, North Africans, Persians, Indians, Aztecs, and even Buddhists, who are foolishly supposed by some Western admirers to be immune from this sort of thing.

This chapter challenges Derr's assertion with respect to the role of the Hindu religion in the ecological crisis. We need to understand how a Hindu's attitude to nature has been shaped by his religion's view of the cosmos and creation. Such an exposition is necessary to explain the traditional values and beliefs of Hindus and hence what role Hindu religion once played with respect to human treatment of the environment. At the same time, we need to know how it is that this religion, which taught harmony with and respect for nature, and which influenced other religions such as Jainism and Buddhism, has been in recent times unable to sustain a caring attitude towards nature. What are the features of the Hindu religion which strengthen human respect for God's creation, and how were these features repressed by the modern view of the natural environment and its resources?

THE SANCTITY OF LIFE IN HINDUISM

The principle of the sanctity of life is clearly ingrained in the Hindu religion. Only God has absolute sovereignty over all creatures, thus, human beings have no dominion over their own lives or non-human life. Consequently, humanity cannot act as a viceroy of God over the planet, nor assign degrees of relative worth to other species. The idea of the Divine Being as the one underlying power of unity is beautifully expressed in the Yajurveda:

> *The loving sage beholds that Being,*
> *hidden in mystery,*
> *wherein the universe comes to*
> *have one home;*
> *Therein unites and therefrom*

emanates the whole;
The Omnipresent One pervades
souls and matter like warp and woof
in created beings.

(YAJURVEDA 32.8)

The sacredness of God's creation means no damage may be inflicted on other species without adequate justification. Therefore, all lives, human and non-human, are of equal value and all have the same right to existence. According to the Atharvaveda, the Earth is not for human beings alone, but for other creatures as well:

Born of Thee, on Thee move mortal
creatures;
Thou bearest them—the biped
and the quadruped;
Thine, O Earth, are the five races
of men, for whom
Surya (Sun), as he rises spreads with
his rays the light that is immortal.

(ATHARVAVEDA 12.1–15)

Srsti: God's Creation

Hindus contemplate divinity as the one in many and the many in one. This conceptualization resembles both monotheism and polytheism. Monotheism is the belief in a single divine Person. In monotheistic creeds that Person is God. Polytheism, on the other hand, believes in the many; and the concept of God is not monarchical. The Hindu concept of God resembles monotheism in that it portrays the divinity as one, and polytheism in that it contemplates the divinity as one in many. Although there are many gods, each one is the Supreme Being. This attitude we may call non-dualistic theism.

The earliest Sanskrit texts, the Veda and Upanishads, teach the non-dualism of the supreme power that existed before the creation. God as the efficient cause, and nature, *Prakrti,* as the material cause of the universe, are unconditionally accepted, as is their harmonious relationship. However, while these texts agree on the concept of non-dualistic theism, they differ in their theories regarding the creation of the universe. Why have different theories been elaborated in the Veda and the Upanishads? This is one of the most important and intriguing questions we can ask. A suitable reply is given in the Rigveda:

He is one, but the wise call him by different names; such as Indra, Mitra, Varuna, Agni, Divya—one who pervaded all the luminous bodies, the source of light; Suparna—the protector and preserver of the universe; whose works are perfect; Matriswa—powerful like wind; Garutman—mighty by nature. (Rigveda 1.164.46)

The Hindu concept of creation can be presented in four categories. First is the Vedic theory, which is followed by further elaboration in Vedanta and Sankhya philosophies; the second is Upanishadic theory; the third is known as Puranic theory; and the fourth is enunciated in the great Hindu epics *Ramayana* and *Mahabharata*. Although the Puranic theory differs from the other three, a single thought flows between them. This unifying theory is well stated in the Rigveda:

The Vedas and the universal laws of nature which control the universe and govern the cycles of creation and dissolution were made manifest by the All-knowing One. By His great power were produced the clouds and the vapors. After the production of the vapors, there intervened a period of darkness after which the Great Lord and Controller of the universe arranged the motions which produce days, nights, and other durations of time. The Great One then produced the sun, the moon, the earth, and all other regions as He did in previous cycles of creation. (Rigveda 10:190.1–3)

All the Hindu scriptures attest to the belief that the creation, maintenance, and annihilation of the cosmos is completely dependent on the Supreme will. In the *Gita,* Lord Krishna says to Arjuna: "Of all that is material and all that is spiritual in this world, know for certain that I am both its origin and dissolution" (*Gita* 7.6). And the Lord says: again "The whole cosmic order is under me. By my will it is manifested again and again and by my will, it is annihilated at the end" (*Gita* 9.8). Thus, for ancient Hindus, both God and *Prakriti* (nature) was to be one and the same. While the *Prajapati* (as mentioned in Regveda) is the creator of sky, the earth, oceans, and all other species, he is also their protector and eventual destroyer. He is the only Lord of creation. Human beings have no special privilege or authority over other creatures; on the other hand, they have more obligations and duties.

Duties to Animals and Birds

The most important aspect of Hindu theology pertaining to treatment of animal life is the belief that the Supreme Being was himself incarnated in the form of various species. The Lord says: "This form is the source and indestructible seed of multifarious incarnations within the universe, and from the particle and portion of this form, different living entities, like demigods, animals, human beings and others, are created" (*Srimad-Bhagavata* Book I, Discourse III: 5). Among the various incarnations of God (numbering from ten to twenty-four depending upon the source of the text), He first incarnated Himself in the form of a fish, then a tortoise, a boar, and a dwarf. His fifth incarnation was as a man-lion. As Rama he was closely associated with monkeys, and as Krishna he was always surrounded by the cows. Thus, other species are accorded reverence.

Further, the Hindu belief in the cycle of birth and rebirth where a person may come back as an animal or a bird gives these species not only respect, but also reverence. This provides a solid foundation for the doctrine of *ahimsa—non-violence* against animals and human beings alike. Hindus have a deep faith in the doctrine of non-violence. Almost all the Hindu scriptures place strong emphasis on the notion that God's grace can be received by not killing his creatures or harming his creation: "God, Kesava, is pleased with a person who does not harm or destroy other non-speaking creatures or animals"

(Visnupurana 3.8.15). To not eat meat in Hinduism is considered both an appropriate conduct and a duty. Yajnavalkya Smriti warns of hell-fire (*Ghora Naraka*) to those who are the killers of domesticated and protected animals: "The wicked person who kills animals which are protected has to live in hell-fire for the days equal to the number of hairs on the body of that animal" (*Yajnavalkyasmriti, Acaradhyayah,* v. 180). By the end of the Vedic and Upanishadic period, Buddhism and Jainism came into existence, and the protection of animals, birds and vegetation was further strengthened by the various kings practicing these religions. These religions, which arose in part as a protest against the orthodoxy and rituals of Hindu religion, continued its precepts for environmental protection. The Buddhist emperor, Ashoka (273–236 BCE), promoted through public proclamations the planting and preservation of flora and fauna. Pillar Edicts, erected at various public places, expressed his concerns about the welfare of creatures, plants and trees and prescribed various punishments for the killing of animals, including ants, squirrels, and rats.

Flora in Hindu Religion

As early as in the time of Regveda, tree worship was quite popular and universal. The tree symbolized the various attributes of God to the Regvedic seers. Regveda regarded plants as having divine powers, with one entire hymn devoted to their praise, chiefly with reference to their healing properties (Regveda 10.97). During the period of the great epics and Puranas, the Hindu respect for flora expanded further. Trees were considered as being animate and feeling happiness and sorrow. It is still popularly believed that every tree has a *Vriksadevata,* or "tree deity," who is worshipped with prayers and offerings of water, flowers, sweets, and encircled by sacred threads. Also, for Hindus, the planting of a tree is still a religious duty. Fifteen hundred years ago, the Matsya Purana described the proper ceremony for tree planting:

> Clean the soil first and water it. Decorate
> trees with garlands, burn the guggula
> perfume in front of them, and place one

pitcher filled with water by the side of each tree. Offer prayer and oblation and then sprinkle holy water on trees. Recite hymns from the Regveda, Yajur and Sama and kindle fire. After such worship the actual plantation should be celebrated. He who plants even one tree, goes directly to Heaven and obtains Moksha. (Matsya Purana 59:159)

The cutting of trees and destruction of flora were considered a sinful act. *Kautilya's Arthasastra* prescribed various punishments for destroying trees and plants:

> For cutting off the tender sprouts of fruit trees or shady trees in the parks near a city, a fine of six panas shall be imposed; for cutting off the minor branches of the same trees, twelve panas, and for cutting off the big branches, twenty four panas shall be levied. Cutting off the trunks of the same, shall be punished with the first amercement; and felling shall be punished with the middlemost amercement. (*Kautilya's Arthasastra* III 19:197)

The Hindu worship of trees and plants has been based partly on utility, but mostly on religious duty and mythology. Hindu ancestors considered it their duty to save trees; and in order to do that they attached to every tree a religious sanctity.

Pradushana: Pollution and Its Prevention in Hindu Scriptures

Hindu scriptures revealed a clear conception of the ecosystem. On this basis a discipline of environmental ethics developed which formulated codes of conduct (*dharma*) and defined humanity's relationship to nature. An important part of that conduct is maintaining proper sanitation. In the past, this was considered to be the duty of everyone and any default was a punishable offence. Hindu society did not even consider it proper to throw dirt on a public path. Kautilya wrote:

> The punishment of one-eighth of a pana should be awarded to those who throw

dirt on the roads. For muddy water one-fourth Pana, if both are thrown the punishment should be double. If latrine is thrown or caused near a temple, well, or pond, sacred place, or government building, then the punishment should increase gradually by one pana in each case. For urine the punishment should be only half. (*Kautilya's Arthasastra* II 36:145)

Hindus considered cremation of dead bodies and maintaining the sanitation of the human habitat as essential acts. When, in about 200 BCE, Caraka wrote about *Vikrti* (pollution) and diseases, he mentioned air pollution specifically as a cause of many diseases.

> The polluted air is mixed with bad elements. The air is uncharacteristic of the season, full of moisture, stormy, hard to breathe, icy cool, hot and dry, harmful, roaring, coming at the same time from all directions, badsmelling, oily, full of dirt, sand, steam, creating diseases in the body and is considered polluted. (*Caraka Samhita, Vimanastanam* III 6:1)

Similarly, about water pollution, Caraka Samhita says:

> Water is considered polluted when it is excessively smelly, unnatural in color, taste and touch, slimy, not frequented by aquatic birds, aquatic life is reduced, and the appearance is unpleasing. (*Caraka Samhita, Vimanastanam* III 6:2)

Water is considered by Hindus as a powerful media of purification and also as a source of energy. Sometimes, just by the sprinkling of pure water in religious ceremonies, it is believed purity is achieved. That is why, in Regveda, prayer is offered to the deity of water: "The waters in the sky, the waters of rivers, and water in the well whose source is the ocean, may all these sacred waters protect me" (Regveda 7.49.2). The healing property and medicinal value of water has been universally accepted, provided it is pure and free from all pollution. When polluted water and pure water were the point of discussion among ancient Indian thinkers, they were aware of the reasons for the polluted water. Therefore Manu advised: "One should not cause urine, stool, cough in the water. Anything which is mixed with these unpious objects, blood and poison, should not be thrown into water" (*Manusmrti* IV: 56).

Still today, many rivers are considered sacred. Among these, the river Ganges is considered by Hindus as the most sacred and respectable. Disposal of human waste or other pollutants has been prohibited since time immemorial:

> One should not perform these 14 acts near the holy waters of the river Ganga: i.e., remove excrement, brushing and gargling, removing cerumen from body, throwing hairs, dry garlands, playing in water, taking donations, performing sex, attachment with other sacred places, praising other holy places, washing clothes, throwing dirty clothes, thumping water and swimming. (*Pravascitta Tatva* 1.535)

Persons doing such unsocial activities and engaging in acts polluting the environment were cursed: "A person, who is engaged in killing creatures, polluting wells, and ponds, and tanks and destroying gardens, certainly goes to hell" (*Padmapurana, Bhoomikhanda* 96: 7–8).

EFFECTIVENESS OF HINDUISM IN CONSERVATION

The effectiveness of any religion in protecting the environment depends upon how much faith its believers have in its precepts and injunctions. It also depends upon how those precepts are transmitted and adapted in everyday social interactions. In the case of the Hindu religion, which is practised as *dharma*—way of life—many of its precepts became ingrained in the daily life and social institutions of the people. Three specific examples are given below to illustrate this point.

The Caste System and Sustainable Development

The Hindu religion is known for its elaborate caste system which divides individuals among four main castes and several hundred sub-castes. Over the centuries, the system degenerated into a very rigid, hereditarily determined, hierarchical, and oppressive social structure, particularly for the untouchables and lower castes. But the amazing phenomenon is that it lasted for so many millennia even with centuries of domination by Islamic and Christian cultures.

One explanation by the ecologist, Madhav Gadgil, and the anthropologist, Kailash Malhotra, is that the caste system, as continued until the early decades of the twentieth century, was actually based on an ancient concept of sustainable development which disciplined the society by partitioning the use of natural resources according to specific occupations (or castes); and "created" the right social milieu in which sustainable patterns of resource use were encouraged to emerge. The caste system regulated the occupations that individuals could undertake. Thus, an "ecological space" was created in ancient Hindu society which helped to reduce competition among various people for limited natural resources. A system of "resource partitioning" emerged whereby the primary users of natural resources did not worry about encroachment from other castes. At the same time, these users also knew that if they depleted the natural resources in their own space, they would not survive economically or physically because no one would allow them to move on to other occupations. Religious injunctions also created the psychological environment whereby each caste or sub-caste respected the occupational boundaries of the others. In a sense, the Hindu caste system can be seen as a progenitor of the concept of sustainable development.

But the system started malfunctioning during the British Raj when demands for raw materials for their fast-growing industrial economy had to be met by commercial exploitation of India's natural resources. As traditional relationships between various castes started disappearing, competition and tension grew. The trend kept on accelerating in independent India, as each caste (or sub-caste) tried to discard its traditional role and seize eagerly any opportunity to land a job. When this happened, the ancient religious injunction for doing one's pre-scribed duty within a caste system could no longer be maintained; this caused the disappearance of the concept of "ecological space" among Hindus. There is no doubt that the caste system also degenerated within and became a source of oppression; nevertheless, from an ecological spacing view point, the caste system played a key role in preserving India's natural riches for centuries.

Bishnois: Defenders of the Environment

The Bishnois are a small community in Rajasthan, India, who practise a religion of environmental conservation. They believe that cutting a tree or killing an animal or bird is blasphemy. Their religion, an offshoot of Hinduism, was founded by Guru Maharaj Jambaji, who was born in 1450 CE in the Marwar area. When he was young he witnessed how, during a severe drought, people cut down trees to feed animals but when the drought continued, nothing was left to feed the animals, so they died. Jambaji thought that if trees are protected, animal life would be sustained, and his community would survive. He gave 29 injunctions and principal among them being a ban on the cutting of any green tree and killing of any animal or bird. About 300 years later, when the King of Jodhpur wanted to build a new palace, he sent his soldiers to the Bishnois area where trees were in abundance. Villagers protested, and when soldiers would not pay any attention to the protest, the Bishnois, led by a woman, hugged the trees to protect them with their bodies. As soldiers kept on killing villagers, more and more of the Bishnois came forward to honour the religious injunction of their Guru Maharaj Jambaji. The massacre continued until 363 persons were killed defending trees. When the king heard about this human sacrifice, he stopped the operation, and gave the Bishnois state protection for their belief.

Today, the Bishnois community continues to protect trees and animals with the same fervour. Their community is the best example of a true Hindu-based ritual defense of the environment in India, and their sacrifices became the inspiration for the Chipko movement of 1973.

The Chipko Movement

In March 1973, in the town of Gopeshwar in Chamoli district (Uttar Pradesh, India), villagers formed a human chain and hugged the earmarked trees to keep them from being felled for a nearby factory producing sports equipment. The same situation later occurred in another village when forest contractors wanted to cut trees under licence from the Government Department of Forests. Again, in 1974, women from the village of Reni, near Joshimath in the Himalayas, confronted the loggers by hugging trees and forced contractors to leave. Since then, the *Chipko Andolan* (the movement to hug trees) has grown as a grassroots ecodevelopment movement.

The genesis of the Chipko movement is not only in the ecological or economic background, but in religious belief. Villagers have noted how industrial and commercial demands have denuded their forests, how they cannot sustain their livelihood in a deforested area, and how floods continually play havoc with their small agricultural communities. The religious basis of the movement is evident in the fact that it is inspired and guided by women. Women have not only seen how their men would not mind destroying nature in order to get money while they had to walk miles in search of firewood, fodder and other grazing materials, but, being more religious, they also are more sensitive to injunctions such as *ahimsa*. In a sense, the Chipko movement is a kind of feminist movement to protect nature from the greed of men. In the Himalayan areas, the pivot of the family is the woman. It is the woman who worries most about nature and its conservation in order that its resources are available for her family's sustenance. On the other hand, men go away to distant places in search of jobs, leaving women and old people behind. These women also believe that each tree has a *Vriksadevata* (tree god) and that the deity *Van Devi* (the Goddess of forests) will protect their family welfare. They also believe that each green tree is an abode of the Almighty God *Hari*.

The Chipko movement has caught the attention of others in India. For example, in Karnataka state, the Appiko movement began in September 1983, when 163 men, women, and children hugged the trees and forced the lumberjacks to leave. That movement swiftly spread to the adjoining districts. These people are against the kind of commercial felling of trees which clears the vegetation in its entirety. They do recognize the firewood needs of urban people (mostly poor) and therefore do not want a total ban on felling. However, they are against indiscriminate clearing and would like to see a consultative process established so that local people are able to participate in timber management.

These three examples are illustrative of the practical impact of Hinduism on conservation and sustainable development. While the effectiveness of the caste system to act as a resource partitioning system is no longer viable, the examples of Bishnois and Chipko/Appiko are illustrative of the fact that when appeal to secular norms fails, one can draw on the cultural and religious sources for "forest *satyagraha*." ("Satyagraha" means "insistence or persistence in search of truth." In this context, the term "forest satyagraha" means "persistence in search of truth pertaining to the rights of trees.")

LOSS OF RESPECT FOR NATURE

If such has been the tradition, philosophy, and ideology of Hindu religion, what then are the reasons behind the present state of environmental crisis? As we have seen, our ethical beliefs and religious values influence our behaviour towards others, including our relationship with all creatures and plant life. If, for some reason, these noble values become displaced by other beliefs which are either thrust upon the society or transplanted from another culture through invasion, then the faith of the masses in the earlier cultural tradition is shaken. As the foreign culture, language and system of administration slowly takes root and penetrates all levels of society, and as appropriate answers and leadership are not forthcoming from the religious leaders and Brahmans, it is only natural for the masses to become more inward-looking and self-centered. Under such circumstances, religious values which acted as sanctions against environmental destruction do not retain a high priority because people have to worry about their very survival and freedom; hence, respect for nature gets displaced by economic factors.

That, it seems, is what happened in India during the 700 years of foreign cultural domination. The ancient educational system which taught respect for nature and reasons for its preservation was no longer available. On the other hand, the imported culture was unable to replace the ancient Hindu religion; consequently, a conflict continued between the two value systems. The situation became more complex when, in addition to the Muslim culture, the British introduced Christianity and Western secular institutions and values. While it is too easy to blame these external forces for the change in attitudes of Hindus towards nature, nevertheless it is a fact that they greatly inhibited the religion from continuing to transmit ancient values which encourage respect and due regard for God's creation.

The Hindu religion teaches a renunciation of worldly goods, and preaches against materialism and consumerism. Such teachings could act as a great source of strength for Hindu societies in their struggle to achieve sustainable development. I detect in countries like India and Nepal a revival of respect for ancient cultural values. Such a revival need not turn into fundamentalism; instead it could be based on the lessons learned from environmental destruction in the West, and on the relevant precepts enshrined in the Hindu scriptures. That should not cause any damage to the secularism now practised in India. As a matter of fact, this could develop into a movement whereby spiritual guidance is made available to the secular system of governance and socioeconomic interaction.

HOPE FOR OUR COMMON FUTURE

Mahatma Gandhi warned that "nature had enough for everybody's need but not for everybody's greed." Gandhi was a great believer in drawing upon the rich variety of spiritual and cultural heritages of India. His *satyagraha* movements were the perfect example of how one could confront an unjust and uncaring though extremely superior power. Similarly, the Bishnois, Chipko, and Appiko people are engaged in a kind of "forest *satyagraha*" today. Their movements could easily be turned into a common front—"satyagraha for the environment,"—to be used against the forces of big government and big business. This could include such other movements as *Mitti Bachao Abhiyan* (save the soil movement), *Van Mahotsava* (tree planting ceremony), *Chetna March* (public awareness march), *Kalpavriksha* (voluntary organization in Delhi for environmental conservation), and many others. The Hindu people are accustomed to suffering a great level of personal and physical hardships if such suffering is directed against unjust and uncaring forces. The minds of the Hindu people are slowly being awakened through the Chipko, Appiko, Bishnois, Chetna March, and other movements. *Satyagraha* for conservation could very well be a rallying point for the awakened spirit of Hinduism.

Hindu culture, in ancient and medieval times, provided a system of moral guidelines towards environmental preservation and conservation. Environmental ethics, as propounded by ancient Hindu scriptures and seers, was practised not only by common persons, but even by rulers and kings. They observed these fundamentals sometimes as religious duties, often as rules of administration or obligation for law and order, but either way these principles were properly knitted within the Hindu way of life. In Hindu culture, a human being is authorized to use natural resources, but has no divine power of control and dominion over nature and its elements. Hence, from the perspective of Hindu culture, abuse and exploitation of nature for selfish gain is unjust and sacreligious. Against the continuation of such exploitation, the only viable strategy appears to be *satyagraha* for conservation.

STUDY QUESTIONS

1. What are the strengths and weaknesses of the Hindu doctrine of *satyagraha* toward nature? If, as Dwivedi suggests, the teachings of the world's religions could be brought together to develop an ecumenical, global environmental ethic, what would be the unique contribution of *satyagraha*?

2. Compare the Hindu view of sanctity of life with Schweitzer's Reverence for Life (Reading 22). How are they similar and different?

3. What does Dwivedi think about the caste system in Hinduism?

4. Compare the Bishnoi and Chipko movements in India to "tree huggers" in the United States and to other Western activist movements.

64

The Buddhist Attitude Towards Nature

LILY DE SILVA

Lily de Silva is professor of Buddhist studies at the University of Peradeniya, Sri Lanka. In this essay, she sets forth a Buddhist perspective on environmental ethics, arguing that Buddhism emphasizes simple, nonviolent, gentle living. In its doctrine of karma and rebirth (similar to Hinduism), it recognizes that all animals and humans are spiritual entities to be treated with loving kindness.

Buddhism strictly limits itself to the delineation of a way of life designed to eradicate human suffering. The Buddha refused to answer questions which did not directly or indirectly bear on the central problem of human suffering and its ending. Furthermore, environmental pollution is a problem of the modern age, unheard of and unsuspected during the time of the Buddha. Therefore it is difficult to find any specific discourse which deals with the topic we are interested in here. Nevertheless, as Buddhism is a full-fledged philosophy of life reflecting all aspects of experience, it is possible to find enough material in the Pali Canon to delineate the Buddhist attitude towards nature.

The word "nature" means everything in the world which is not organised and constructed by man. The Pali equivalents which come closest to "nature" are *loka* and *yathābhūta*. The former is usually translated as "world" while the latter literally means "things as they really are." The words *dhammatā* and *niyāma* are used in the Pali Canon to mean "natural law or way."

NATURE AS DYNAMIC

According to Buddhism changeability is one of the perennial principles of nature. Everything changes in nature and nothing remains static. This concept is expressed by the Pali term *anicca*. Everything formed is in a constant process of change (*sabbe sankhārā aniccā*). The world is therefore defined as that which disintegrates (*lujjatīti loko*); the world is so called because it is dynamic and kinetic, it is constantly in a process of undergoing change. In nature there are no static and stable "things"; there are only ever-changing, ever-moving processes....

MORALITY AND NATURE

The world passes through alternating cycles of evolution and dissolution, each of which endures for a long period of time. Though change is inherent in nature, Buddhism believes that natural processes are affected by the morals of man.... Buddhism believes that though change is a factor inherent in nature, man's moral deterioration accelerates the process of change and brings about changes which are adverse to human well being and happiness....

[S]everal suttas from the Pali Canon show that early Buddhism believes there to be a close relationship between human morality and the natural environment. This idea has been systematised in the

Reprinted from *The Buddhist Attitude Towards Nature*, ed. K. Sandell (Buddhist Publication Society, Sri Lanka, 1987). Notes deleted.

theory of the five natural laws in the later commentaries. According to this theory, in the cosmos there are five natural laws or forces at work, namely *utuniyāma* (lit. "season-law"), *bī⁻janiyāma* (lit. "seed-law"), *cittaniyāma, kammaniyāma* and *dhammaniyāma*. They can be translated as physical laws, biological laws, psychological laws, moral laws and causal laws, respectively. While the first four laws operate within their respective spheres, the last-mentioned law of causality operates *within* each of them as well as *among* them.

This means that the physical environment of any given area conditions the growth and development of its biological component, i.e., flora and fauna. These in turn influence the thought pattern of the people interacting with them. Modes of thinking determine moral standards. The opposite process of interaction is also possible. The morals of man influence not only the psychological make-up of the people but the biological and physical environment of the area as well. Thus the five laws demonstrate that man and nature are bound together in a reciprocal causal relationship with changes in one necessarily bringing about changes in the other.

The commentary on the *Cakkavattis ihanāda Sutta* goes on to explain the pattern of mutual interaction further. When mankind is demoralised through greed, famine is the natural outcome; when moral degeneration is due to ignorance, epidemic is the inevitable result; when hatred is the demoralising force, widespread violence is the ultimate outcome. If and when mankind realizes that large-scale devastation has taken place as a result of his moral degeneration, a change of heart takes place among the few surviving human beings. With gradual moral regeneration conditions improve through a long period of cause and effect and mankind again starts to enjoy gradually increasing prosperity and longer life. The world, including nature and mankind, stands or falls with the type of moral force at work. If immorality grips society, man and nature deteriorate; if morality reigns, the quality of human life and nature improves. Thus greed, hatred and delusion produce pollution within and without. Generosity, compassion and wisdom produce purity within and without. This is one reason the Buddha has pronounced that the world is led by the mind, *cittena niyata loko*. Thus man and nature, according to the ideas expressed in early Buddhism, are interdependent.

HUMAN USE OF NATURAL RESOURCES

For survival mankind has to depend on nature for his food, clothing, shelter, medicine and other requisites. For optimum benefits man has to understand nature so that he can utilise natural resources and live harmoniously with nature. By understanding the working of nature—for example, the seasonal rainfall pattern, methods of conserving water by irrigation, the soil types, the physical conditions required for growth of various food crops, etc.—man can learn to get better returns from his agricultural pursuits. But this learning has to be accompanied by moral restraint if he is to enjoy the benefits of natural resources for a long time. Man must learn to satisfy his needs and not feed his greeds. The resources of the world are not unlimited whereas man's greed knows neither limit nor satiation. Modern man in his unbridled voracious greed for pleasure and acquisition of wealth has exploited nature to the point of near impoverishment....

Buddhism tirelessly advocates the virtues of non-greed, non-hatred, and non-delusion in all human pursuits. Greed breeds sorrow and unhealthy consequences. Contentment (*santu.t.thi*) is a much praised virtue in Buddhism. The man leading a simple life with few wants easily satisfied is upheld and appreciated as an exemplary character. Miserliness and wastefulness are equally deplored in Buddhism as two degenerative extremes. Wealth has only instrumental value; it is to be utilised for the satisfaction of man's needs. Hoarding is a senseless antisocial habit comparable to the attitude of the dog in the manger. The vast hoarding of wealth in some countries and the methodical destruction of large quantities of agricultural produce to keep the market prices from falling, while half the world is dying of hunger and starvation, is really a sad paradox of the present affluent age.

Buddhism commends frugality as a virtue in its own right. Once Ānanda explained to King Udena the thrifty economic use of robes by the monks in the following order. When new robes are received the old robes are used as coverlets, the old coverlets as mattress covers, the old mattress covers as rugs, the old rugs as dusters, and the old tattered dusters are kneaded with clay and used to repair cracked floors and walls. Thus nothing usable is wasted. Those who waste are derided as "wood-apple eaters." A man shakes the branch of a wood-apple tree and all the fruits, ripe as well as unripe, fall. The man would collect only what he wants and walk away leaving the rest to rot. Such a wasteful attitude is certainly deplored in Buddhism as not only anti-social but criminal. The excessive exploitation of nature as is done today would certainly be condemned by Buddhism in the strongest possible terms.

Buddhism advocates a gentle non-aggressive attitude towards nature. According to the *Sigālovāda Sutta* a householder should accumulate wealth as a bee collects pollen from a flower. The bee harms neither the fragrance nor the beauty of the flower, but gathers pollen to turn it into sweet honey. Similarly, man is expected to make legitimate use of nature so that he can rise above nature and realise his innate spiritual potential.

ATTITUDE TOWARDS ANIMAL
AND PLANT LIFE

The well-known Five Precepts (*pañca s ila*) form the minimum code of ethics that every lay Buddhist is expected to adhere to. Its first precept involves abstention from injury to life. It is explained as the casting aside of all forms of weapons, being conscientious about depriving a living being of life. In its positive sense it means the cultivation of compassion and sympathy for all living beings. The Buddhist layman is expected to abstain from trading in meat too.

The Buddhist monk has to abide by an even stricter code of ethics than the layman. He has to abstain from practices which would involve even unintentional injury to living creatures. For instance, the Buddha promulgated the rule against going on a journey during the rainy season because of possible injury to worms and insects that come to the surface in wet weather. The same concern for non-violence prevents a monk from digging the ground. Once a monk who was a potter prior to ordination built for himself a clay hut and set it on fire to give it a fine finish. The Buddha strongly objected to this as so many living creatures would have been burnt in the process. The hut was broken down on the Buddha's instructions to prevent it from creating a bad precedent for later generations. The scrupulous non-violent attitude towards even the smallest living creatures prevents the monks from drinking unstrained water. It is no doubt a sound hygienic habit, but what is noteworthy is the reason which prompts the practice, namely, sympathy for living creatures.

Buddhism also prescribes the practice of *mettā*, "loving-kindness" towards all creatures of all quarters without restriction. The *Karan iyamettā Sutta* enjoins the cultivation of loving-kindness towards all creatures, timid and steady, long and short, big and small, minute and great, visible and invisible, near and far, born and awaiting birth. All quarters are to be suffused with this loving attitude. Just as one's own life is precious to oneself, so is the life of the other precious to himself. Therefore a reverential attitude must be cultivated towards all forms of life....

The understanding of karma and rebirth, too, prepares the Buddhist to adopt a sympathetic attitude towards animals. According to this belief it is possible for human beings to be reborn in subhuman states among animals. The *Kukkuravatika Sutta* can be cited as a canonical reference which substantiates this view. The *Jātakas* provide ample testimony to this view from commentarial literature. It is possible that our own close relatives have been reborn as animals. Therefore it is only right that we should treat animals with kindness and sympathy. The Buddhist notion of merit also engenders a gentle non-violent attitude towards living creatures. It is said that if one throws dish-washing water into a pool where there are insects and living creatures, intending that they feed on the tiny particles of food thus washed away, one accumulates merit even by such trivial generosity. According to the *Macchuddāna Jātaka* the Bodhisatta threw his leftover food into a river in order to feed the fish, and by the power of that merit he was saved from an impending disaster. Thus kindness to animals, be they big or small, is a source of merit—merit needed for human beings to improve their lot in the cycle of rebirths and to approach the final goal of Nibbāna.

Buddhism expresses a gentle non-violent attitude towards the vegetable kingdom as well. It is said that one should not even break the branch of a tree that has given one shelter. Plants are so helpful to us in providing us with all necessities of life that we are expected not to adopt a callous attitude towards them. The more strict monastic rules prevent monks from injuring plant life.

Prior to the rise of Buddhism people regarded natural phenomena such as mountains, forests, groves and trees with a sense of awe and reverence. They considered them as the abode of powerful non-human beings who could assist human beings at times of need. Though Buddhism gave man a far superior Triple Refuge (*tisarana*) in the Buddha, Dhamma and Sangha, these places continued to enjoy public patronage at a popular level, as the acceptance of terrestrial non-human beings such as *devatās* and *yakkhas* did not violate the belief system of Buddhism. Therefore among the Buddhists there is a reverential attitude towards specially long-standing gigantic trees. They are called *vanaspati* in Pali, meaning "lords of the forests." As huge trees such as the ironwood, the sāla and the fig are also recognised as the Bodhi trees of former Buddhas, the deferential attitude towards trees is further strengthened. It is well known that the *ficus religiosa* is held as an object of great veneration in the Buddhist world today as the tree under which the Buddha attained Enlightenment.

The construction of parks and pleasure groves for public use is considered a great meritorious deed. Sakka the lord of gods is said to have reached this status as a result of social services such as the construction of parks, pleasure groves, ponds, wells and roads.

The open air, natural habitats and forest trees have a special fascination for the Eastern mind as symbols of spiritual freedom. The home life is regarded as a fetter (*sambādha*) that keeps man in bondage and misery. Renunciation is like the open air (*abbhokāsa*), nature unhampered by man's activity…. The Buddha's constant advice to his disciples also was to resort to natural habitats such as forest groves and glades. There, undisturbed by human activity, they could zealously engage themselves in meditation.

ATTITUDE TOWARDS POLLUTION

… Cleanliness was highly commended by the Buddhists both in the person and in the environment. They were much concerned about keeping water clean, be it in the river, pond or well. These sources of water were for public use and each individual had to use them with proper public-spirited caution so that others after him could use them with the same degree of cleanliness. Rules regarding the cleanliness of green grass were prompted by ethical and aesthetic considerations. Moreover, grass is food for most animals and it is man's duty to refrain from polluting it by his activities.

Noise is today recognised as a serious personal and environmental pollutant troubling everyone to some extent….

The Buddha and his disciples revelled in the silent solitary natural habitats unencumbered by human activity. Even in the choice of monasteries the presence of undisturbed silence was an important quality they looked for. Silence invigorates those who are pure at heart and raises their efficiency for meditation. But silence overawes those who are impure with ignoble impulses of greed, hatred and delusion….

The psychological training of the monks is so advanced that they are expected to cultivate a taste not only for external silence, but for inner silence of speech, desire and thought as well. The sub-vocal

Our tradition honors the wild, and calls for service to the earth and the community. We value peace and practice non-violence, in keeping with the Rede, "Harm none, and do what you will." We work for all forms of justice: environmental, social, political, racial, gender and economic. Our feminism includes a radical analysis of power, seeing all systems of oppression as interrelated, rooted in structures of domination and control.

We welcome all genders, all races, all ages and sexual orientations and all those differences of life situation, background, and ability that increase our diversity. We strive to make our public rituals and events accessible and safe. We try to balance the need to be justly compensated for our labor with our commitment to make our work available to people of all economic levels.

All living beings are worthy of respect. All are supported by the sacred elements of air, fire, water and earth. We work to create and sustain communities and cultures that embody our values that can help to heal to heal the wounds of the earth and her peoples, and that can sustain us and nurture future generations.

Starhawk is the author of many works celebrating the Goddess movement and Earth-based, feminist spirituality. She is a peace, environmental, and global justice activist and trainer, a permaculture designer and teacher, a Pagan and Witch. http://www.starhawk.org/

THE FIVE-POINT AGENDA

Sacred Values: Peace, Community, Family

For us, the sacred is embodied in the living systems of the earth and the human community. We see all things as interconnected and interrelated, and these values inform all our political stands.

None of these values can be implemented without peace. War destroys human lives and environmental integrity. It devastates economies, wastes our precious resources, and oppose the glorification of militarism and the use of enormous resources to support military endeavors.

Our communities and families are important to us. We support a broad definition of Family, one that honors the diversity of our cultures and life choices.

Because children are the next generation, and because they are vulnerable physically, emotionally and economically, government has a special responsibility to assure the well-being of children regardless of the economic status of their parents. We favor programs that support families in all the diverse forms they take.

We place a high value on human ingenuity, creativity, intelligence and intuition. The education

of children is the responsibility of the broader community, not of biological parents alone. We recognize that we all benefit when the next generation is well-educated. We support quality public education for children that encourages their creativity and empowerment, and programs such as school lunches that ensure their well-being and further their capacity to learn. We support higher education that is available to all who want it.

Our elders are also important to us. In them, the history, experience and wisdom of our communities live. We support to right of every person to age in dignity, to continue to contribute to society, and to know that their basic economic and health needs will be provided for.

We see mutually pleasurable erotic expression in all its diverse forms as a sacred act. We believe all people, including and especially young people, have the right to information about sexuality, health, and sexual responsibility.

Freedom of religion is an inherent right of all people. We strongly support the separation of church and state, but also recognize that political discussion necessarily contains an element of the sacred. However, we oppose attempts to restrict freedom and self-determination according to religious strictures that we do not hold.

We recognize that political decisions are made out of our deep sense of what we most Value. We also recognize that many different value systems confront each other in the political arena. We do not want to legislate our values or impose them on those whose spiritual traditions differ from ours but we do uphold our right to have our values dialogue with people whose views differ from ours, and we respect the core of sacred being in those whose views oppose ours.

We encourage the building of alliances the barriers of difference.

Diversity

We embrace diversity as a positive good-we see a multiplicity of genders, races, cultures, languages, sexual orientations and lifestyles as integral to our country's strength and central to our common heritage.

We understand the vital importance of biological diversity and the need for preservation of species and habitats.

We support education that includes many viewpoints and heritages and teaches respect for differences.

We know that historically many groups of people have been kept form access to political power and economic opportunity, that these divisions are built into the very structure of our institutions, and that their legacy of inequality is still with us. We support equal access to resources and decision making power for all people. We oppose prejudice in all its forms: sexism, racism, heterosexism, anti-Semitism, classism, able-ism, ageism, etc.

Self-Determination

We stand for the right of all people to have a voice in decisions that affect them, the right of individuals to make free and informed choices regarding their bodies, their sexuality, their powers of reproduction, and their manner of life. We recognize violence, sexual violence, abuse and incest as systemic violations of these rights.

We see the debate around abortion as a question of the sacred, and uphold strongly a woman's right to act out of her own deepest values.

We recognize the right of the terminally ill to choose to end their suffering and receive medical help and assistance in doing so. We also recognize the right of medical personnel to choose not to participate in acts that contradict their own values.

Economic violence also functions as a form of coercion. All people have a right to meet their basic needs of survival, and to determine the manner in which they will work to meet those needs.

We support the right of all people to preserve their cultures, lands, heritage, and dignity, and to secure conditions which make possible sustainable and long-lasting communities.

Human beings have a right of free expression and free exchange of information. We oppose censorship. We support the right of individuals and peoples to challenge authority and engage in political struggle to gain their right.

We oppose coercion, force, threats, and torture, and refuse to subsidize or support institutions that function by instilling fear.

We recognize that individuals' goals may conflict. The right to self-determination does not include the right to harm others. We favor negotiation and mediation whenever possible as ways to resolve conflict.

We oppose war as a means of settling differences, resolving conflicts, or furthering our ends as individuals or as nations.

Environment

We recognize that the interconnected life systems of the earth, in all their diversity, have a right to be and an inherent value that goes beyond their usefulness for human ends.

We also recognize that human life and culture depends on the health of the ecosystems that sustain all life on earth, and that our understanding of their complex interrelationships is still embryonic. Therefore, our prime concern must be the health of the environment, of the earth, the air, and the waters, and the diverse matrices of biological life.

Any government that allows the despoiling of its own lands has failed in its primary responsibility to its people. We support laws and programs that further environmental preservation, conservation, habitat restoration and healing. We oppose laws that allow the exploitation of the environment for the ends of individuals or small groups of people. We oppose programs that work toward the loss of biological diversity, or that allow biological heritage.

We know that toxicity is unfairly distributed and is often foisted onto indigenous communities, communities of people of color and of poor people. We work for environment justice and for urban environment that can be safe, healthy and sustainable.

We support the creation of rural jobs in ways that work with the environment and can be sustained in the long run.

We support the absolute right of indigenous people to protect their sacred lands from despoiling and development.

We recognize that human beings have aright to live and to draw on the resources of the environment to create our livelihood.

We believe that this can and must be done in way that are compassionate, sustainable and that further the overall quality of life.

We favor solution-oriented responses to environment problems.

Human Needs and Social Justice

Human beings have a right to those things that make possible a fulfilling life; food, clothing, shelter, education, health care, and the opportunity for meaningful work, intimate relationship, and connection with future generations. A fulfilling life is not just a life of survival, but includes participation in the making of culture, of art, music, dance, and poetry the freedom and time for spiritual development, and time for nourishing recreation and fun.

Government has a responsibility to use its power and resources to assure that each person has access to the means and opportunity to pursue a fulfilling life. Because great disparities of wealth and power exist, government has the right to redress inequalities, citizens have a responsibility to care for each other, to assure the health of the whole community rather than protect the privilege of the few.

Misfortune comes to everyone in life. The cost of illness, disability, or natural disasters should not be borne by individuals alone but be shared among many.

STUDY QUESTIONS

1. Discuss the connections between spirituality, the earth, and social justice in the Reclaiming tradition.

2. Previous readings in this section have not spoken favorably of pagans; how might the Reclaiming tradition respond to them?

3. Compare or contrast this perspective to one of the other religious traditions mentioned in this text.

Chapter 11

The New Green Capitalist Order: Economics, Sustainability, and Response

Economics is concerned with the production, distribution, and consumption of goods and services. It has to do with the allocation of scarce resources in a way that maximizes efficiency—that is, material social well-being. Economics arose out of a type of moral philosophy, classical utilitarianism, which stipulates that acts are morally right if and only if they maximize social welfare. Classical economics stipulates that a policy is economically right if and only if it maximizes material social welfare. But mainstream capitalist economics is also *libertarian,* calling for laissez-faire policies. People should be completely free to make market exchanges as they see fit. Government should not interfere with market transactions unless force or fraud is occurring. The theory, going back to Adam Smith (1723–1790), is that an *invisible hand* guides individual self-interested transactions in such a way that they actually result in utilitarian outcomes. "Every individual intends only his own gain, and he is in this, as in so many other cases, led by an invisible hand to promote an end which was no part of his intention." This is almost too good to be true—it's OK to act selfishly, for it is the best way to promote universal welfare!

Mainstream economics claims to be a *science,* a pure neutral description of how the market, led by supply and demand, works. It is free from value commitments or moral prescriptions. But this is a myth. It presupposes a powerful ideology—that selfish behavior is good, that material growth is always good, and that the former leads inexorably by an invisible hand to the latter. It teaches us that poverty and the suffering of those who lose out in market competition are the lesser of evils—the price we must pay for growth and freedom. Whether or not or to what extent these claims are true, the point is that neoclassical economics is filled to the brim with values.

Thus, the prescriptions of an economic policy and those of a moral theory may conflict. A particular allocation of resources may be economically good but morally bad, or economically wrong but morally right. For example, classical economics may approve a system that results in the rich getting richer and the poor, simply through market mechanisms, becoming so poor that they suffer terribly and even starve—whereas many ethical theories would condemn this state of affairs as grossly unjust and immoral. What is economically sound may not be morally so and, vice versa, what is morally sound may not be economically so.

Perhaps the single largest shift in environmental thinking over the last few years is in economics. Whereas once mainstream economics viewed environmental degradation and disaster as "externalities," now it sees them as opportunities. Companies, even Exxon and BP, present themselves as green, and we are told of the coming "New Green Industrial Revolution." Whereas once "Green" presented a challenge to economics, "Green" is now big business.

The question is, what about our economic order needs to change in order for it to address environmental concerns? The economic system of the past says we need less regulation, and market forces will take care of it. There is broad consensus that this is insanity. Another option is to create a new green capitalism, one which understands that the environment needs protecting, for a variety of reasons.

William Rees criticizes the materialist model of economics and argues that a fundamental change in society's perceptions is a prerequisite for environmental harmony and sustainable development. He points out that the United Nations' World Commission on Environment and Development (1987) study is flawed because it lacks an innovative paradigm for economic-environmental cooperation, which treats the environment as capital.

Mark Sagoff examines the relevance of an economic model to environmental concerns. An economic model based on cost–benefit analysis is rooted in the utilitarian idea that all values are reducible to personal preferences and how much people would be willing to spend for a good. But sometimes we judge things to be good independent of our personal preferences. The Kantian model, which treats people as ends in themselves rather than placeholders for pleasure, conflicts with the economic model, which asserts that justice should override utilitarian-economic considerations. For example, even if keeping African Americans separate and unequal would yield a higher utility than integration with white Americans, integration is more just and should be chosen. Similarly, questions of pollution and the preservation of the wilderness may not adequately be decided on a standard economic model.

Essays by John Cobb and David Schweikart examine the possibility of creating a socially just and sustainable capitalism. While extremely critical of contemporary practice, they argue that a sustainable economics might be possible. In "What Every Environmentalist Needs to Know About Capitalism," Magdoff and Foster offer a socialist critique of capitalist economics, arguing that capitalism is corrupt to the core.

In Alan Thein Durning's "An Ecological Critique of Global Advertising," we have an insightful analysis of the global pressures to create consumerism through subtle and skillful marketing skills. Advertising, as one of its proponents put it, is to make people unhappy until they buy the product in question. Is your hair too thin, your nose too short? Advertising offers you hope! "It preys on the weaknesses of its host. It creates an insatiable hunger. And it leads to debilitating overconsumption. In the biological realm, things of that nature are called parasites." Advertising is the global parasite of our time! Durning argues that this parasite threatens the lifeblood of our world.

Louis Pojman's essay "The Challenge of the Future," outlines suggestions for extending ecological consciousness to the city and to the whole world.

"Strategic Monkeywrenching" by Dave Foreman advocates selective, nonviolent ecosabotage aimed at saving the wilderness, followed by Michael Martin's ethical analysis of such behavior.

Finally, in *The Coming Insurrection,* we have an even stronger critique of not just capitalism but of contemporary liberal ecological thinking in general.

66

Sustainable Development: Economic Myths and Global Realities

WILLIAM E. REES

William Rees is a bioecologist who teaches the ecological basis for planning and economic development at the University of British Columbia's School of Community and Regional Planning in Canada.

Rees responds to the 1987 United Nations' World Commission on Environment and Development report, calling for a global view of sustainable development that is both economically sound and environmentally progressive. He points out that the problem with this report is that it accepts the standard model of economics, which is fundamentally materialist. Rees argues that a new model of economics is needed if we are to do justice to environmental values. We must realize that the environment is capital, which is nonrenewable. Then we must learn to live off the interest, not depleting the capital, but holding it in perpetuity.

INTRODUCTION

This paper develops one perspective on prospects for a sustainable future in Canada and the rest of the developed world. It is inspired by the recent publication of "Our Common Future," the report of the United Nations' World Commission on Environment and Development.... The UN study has stimulated an unprecedented level of public debate on environment and development-related matters, wherever it is available, much of which focuses on the intriguingly hopeful concept of "sustainable development."

Before addressing sustainable development directly, I would like to say a few things about Western society's perceptions of "the way things are" respecting people, development, and the environment. The following reasons for doing so also provide the premises of the paper.

1. While we think we act from factual knowledge, much individual action and government policy on development and environment is based on unconscious belief, on what Stafford Beer (1981) might call our "shared illusions".

2. This collective perception of reality is the real problem. Our culturally "shared illusions" stand in the way of sustainable development.

3. It follows that a fundamental change in society's perceptions and attitudes is a prerequisite for environmental harmony.

Let us be clear that by "perception," I am not referring to the garden variety beliefs and opinions that are amenable to change with the next edition of the National News or the Globe and Mail. Rather, I mean the unconscious "facts" and unquestioned assumptions out of which we more or less automatically react in the conduct of our day-to-day affairs.

Reprinted from *Trumpeter*, Vol. 5.4 (Fall 1988) by permission. Notes deleted.

These culturally transmitted perceptions shape our social relationships, our political systems, and the nature of economic enterprise. In short, I am talking about the deep-rooted beliefs and perceptions that constitute society's common philosophy and worldview. (The academically inclined may prefer the term "cultural paradigm.")

Whatever name we give it, it is this shared experience of reality that determines where we are "coming from" as a society. Since it also influences where we are going, it is worth some reflection here.

SCIENTIFIC MATERIALISM: SHALLOW SOIL FOR SUSTAINABLE DEVELOPMENT

The worldview that presently dominates is rooted in 19th century scientific materialism.... Building on the experimental "natural philosophy" of the previous 200 years, the late 1880's saw the deep entrenchment of scientific rationality and its companion, social utilitarianism, as the primary beacons of human progress.

Descartes had set the stage in the 17th Century with his division of reality into the separate and independent realms of mind and matter. This "Cartesian" division encouraged people to see themselves as separate and distinct from a physical reality "out there," and provided the perceptual framework for all subsequent scientific inquiry. But it was Bacon who gave modern science its raison d'etre by arguing that knowledge gained through science should be put to work. "From this perspective, knowledge is regarded not as an end but as a means, expressed and applied in technology, by which humans assume power over the material world."...

The resultant flowering of science and technology made possible the industrial revolution and unprecedented levels of material production. Not surprisingly, scientific method became associated with a glowing material future, while traditional thinking and values were scorned as obsolete and reactionary. Indeed, science came to be equated with the only true knowledge. "Facts" that have no authority of science behind them, are written off "as having no epistemological status at all." ... The scientific worldview had succeeded in separating material knowledge from values, and asserted the primacy of the former over the latter....

This materialistic rational empiricism remains the dominant paradigm of Western society. To judge from economic behavior, we see the external world, the biosphere, mainly as a warehouse to be plundered in satisfaction of the material needs and wants of humankind. Certainly, too, reductionist science remains our only acceptable analytic mode. Society's prevailing ecological myth sees "the environment" in terms of isolated, individual resources or, at best, as a mechanical construction, whose component parts are bendable to human will and purpose.

Even the organization of governments reflects this analytic perspective. Environmental management is institutionally segregated into Departments of Fisheries, Forests and Land, Water, Energy and Mines, etc., with little regard to interdependent properties of the whole. Ironically, this often leaves our federal and provincial Departments of Environment with little to do!

THE ASSUMPTIONS OF ECONOMICS

Modern economics springs from similar conceptual roots. The founders of the neoclassical school, impressed with the spectacular successes of Newtonian physics, strove to create economics as a sister science, "the mechanics of utility and self-interest."... The major consequences of this mechanical analogue is a traditional view of economic process as "a self-sustaining circular flow between production and consumption within a completely closed system." By this perception, "everything ... turns out to be just a pendulum movement. One business 'cycle' follows another.... If events alter the supply and demand propensities, the economic world returns to its previous position as soon as these events fade out." In short, "complete reversibility is the general rule, just as in mechanics...."

An important corollary of this equilibrium model is that mainstream economics essentially ignores the self-evident, continuous exchange of material resources (resources and waste disposal), and the unidirectional flow of free energy, between the economic process and the biophysical environment.

A second corollary of equilibrium theory is that continuous growth becomes theoretically possible.... Indeed, latter day economists seem to believe "not only in the possibility of continuous material growth, but in its axiomatic necessity." ... This "growmania" ... "has given rise to an immense literature in which exponential growth is taken as the normal state of affairs." ... Meanwhile, any damage to environmental processes caused by this explosive human activity is assumed to be inconsequential or reversible.

That growth is entrenched as the measure of progress is evident from a glance at the business pages of any daily newspaper. The annual percent increase in gross national product (GNP) is still taken as every nation's primary indicator of national health. Rates of under 3% are considered sluggish, and most politicians and economic planners do not feel at ease until real growth in GNP tops 4% per annum. While such rates may seem modest, even a 4% increase implies a doubling of economic activity in a mere 17 years!

With its fixation on growth, the new conservatism of such countries as the US, Britain, and Canada increasingly demands that people accept the rigorous discipline of the marketplace as the primary wellspring of values and social well-being. Meanwhile, businessmen and technocrats have become the heroes of the new age and prominent role models for youth. The competitive ethic provides the accepted standard for individual self worth, with success measured in terms of conspicuous consumption and the accumulation of personal property. In some circles it is fashionable to be both socially unconcerned and aggressively oblivious to environmental destruction. While individual rights are loudly proclaimed, there is telling silence over matters of social responsibility.

It is noteworthy in this context, that capitalist states depend on the increasing size of the national economic pie to ensure that the poor receive enough of the national wealth to survive. Indeed, it is not exaggerating to say that economic growth is the major instrument of social policy. By sustaining hope for improvement, it relieves the pressure for policies aimed at more equitable distribution of wealth.

THE ECOLOGICAL REALITY

There are two ecological problems with common economic expectations. First, the expanding economic system is inextricably linked to the biosphere. Every economy draws on the physical environment for non-renewable resources and on ecosystems for renewable resources, and all the products of economic activity (i.e., both the waste products of the manufacturing process and the final consumer goods) are eventually discharged back into the biosphere as waste.

The ultimate regulator of this activity, and one that modern economic theory essentially ignores, is the second law of thermodynamics (the entropy law): **In any closed isolated system, available energy and matter are continuously and irrevocably degraded to the unavailable state....** The effect of this law is to declare that all so-called economic "production" is really "consumption"!

Since modern economies are partially dependent on stocks of non-renewable material and energy resources, the Second Law declares that they necessarily consume and degrade the very resources which sustains them. The substitution of one depleting resource for another can only be a stopgap on the road to scarcity. Even resource recycling has a net negative impact on remaining stocks of available energy and material. In short, much economic activity contributes to a constant increase in global net entropy (disorder), through the continuous dissipation of free energy and matter. Contrary to the assumptions of neoclassical theory, there is no equilibrium of any sort in the material relationship between industrial economies and the environment.

This means that the growth of many national economies (e.g., Japan, the US) can be sustained only by continuous resource imports from elsewhere, and only in the short run. The global economy, for all practical purposes, is a closed system, a reality that is little affected by shuffling resources around (world trade). Thus, contrary to the implicit assumptions of neo-classical economics, **sustainable development based on prevailing patterns of consumptive resource use is not even theoretically conceivable.**

The second ecological difficulty with the growth-dependent economy stems from the functional dynamics of ecosystems themselves. Ecosystems, like economic systems, depend on fixed stocks of material resources. However, the material resources of ecosystems are constantly being transformed and recycled throughout the system via food-webs at the local level, and biogeochemical cycles on a global scale. In addition, evolution and succession in Nature tend toward greater order and resilience.

The material cycles and developmental trends of ecosystems thus appear at first glance to defy the thermodynamic law. Ecosystems seem to be inherently self-sustaining and self-organizing, and therefore to contribute to a reduction in global net entropy. This is possible only because ecosystems, unlike economic systems, are driven by an external source of free energy, the sun. Through photosynthesis, the steady stream of solar energy sustains essentially all biological activity and makes possible the diversity of life on Earth.

Material recycling, the self-renewing property of ecosystems, is therefore the source of all renewable resources used by the human economy. Moreover, since the flow of solar radiation is constant, steady, and reliable, **resource production from the ecological sector is potentially sustainable over any time scale relevant to humankind.**

But only potentially. Even ecological productivity is ultimately limited, in part, by the rate of energy input (the "solar flux") itself. Ecosystems therefore do not grow indefinitely. Unlike our present economy, which expands through intrinsic positive feedback, ecosystems are held in "steady-state" or dynamic equilibrium, regulated by limiting factors and negative feedback.

Why is this significant? First, human beings and their economies are now a dominant component of all the world's major ecosystems. Since these economies are growing and the ecosystems within which they are embedded are not, the consumption of ecological resources everywhere threatens to exceed sustainable rates of biological production. Second, overexploitation is exacerbated by pollution, which impairs the remaining productivity of ecosystems. (Recent reports that acid rain may be reducing rates of tree growth by as much as 25% in parts of eastern Canada serve as a timely example.) In short, modern industrial economies both directly undermine the potential for sustainable development through over-harvesting, and indirectly compromise future production through residuals discharge. It takes no special genius to realize that such trends are unsustainable.

The point of all this is not to argue for abandonment of scientific rationality or even the growth paradigm. Science, technology, and the human ingenuity to use them, are among the key factors required for sustainable development. However, I do want to stress that our current worldview, however successful in the past, is a dangerously shallow perception of present reality. In fact, the foregoing analysis shows many of its basic assumptions to be wrong. While this was of little consequence when the scale of human activity was limited, it is at the heart of the environment-development conundrum today. Only when we admit this possibility will the development question shift from: how to promote growth, to: how to achieve sustainability.

SUSTAINABLE DEVELOPMENT: CAN WE GET THERE FROM HERE?

According to the World Commission on Environment and Development, sustainable development is development that meets the needs of the present without compromising the ability of future generations to meet their own needs. There is nothing very threatening—or substantial here. However, Our Common Future goes on to define needs as the "essential needs of the world's poor, to which overriding priority should be given." It also recognized the "limitations imposed by the state of technology and social organization on the environment's ability to meet those needs."... These latter considerations raise painful questions for modern society.

To expand on the issues involved, let us define sustainable development as **any form of positive change which does not erode the ecological, social, or political systems upon which society is dependent.** Planning for sustainable development must therefore explicitly acknowledge ecological limits on the economy, and to be politically viable, have the full understanding, support, and involvement of the people affected. This in turn suggests the need for political and planning processes that are informed, open, and fair.

Social equity will inevitably become a central consideration. The World Commission reported that the 26% of the world's population living in developed countries consumes 80–86% of nonrenewable resources and up to 34–53% of food products.... Emerging ecological and social constraints suggest that reducing the present gap in standards of living between the rich and poor (between and within nations) may well require that the rich reduce both present consumption and future expectations so that the poor may enjoy a fairer share of the world's resources.

Ecologically and socially concerned citizens accept such notions as self-evident, but the more profound implications of sustainable development seem invisible to the mainstream worldview. For example, Canada was the first nation to respond with its own policy initiative to the work of the World Commission. The National Task Force on Environment and Economy was established in October 1986 to initiate dialogue and recommend action on environment-economy integration in Canada. Its subsequent report ... is regarded by government and industry as a milestone document, but with suspicion by environmentalists and other critics.

Stepping to the right of the World Commission, the Task Force defined sustainable development as "development which ensures that the utilization of resources and the environment today does not damage prospects for their use by future generations." Its report goes on to state that at the core of the concept is the requirement "that current practices should not diminish the possibility of maintaining or improving living standards in the future." Also: "Sustainable development does not require the preservation of the current stock of natural resources or any particular mix of ... assets." Nor does it place "artificial" limits on economic growth, provided that such growth is "economically and environmentally sustainable."...

This definition is self-contradictory and thus difficult to interpret rationally. First, as previously emphasized, the present generation cannot use any nonrenewable energy or material resource (e.g., oil, natural gas, phosphate ore) without eliminating the prospect for its use by future generations. Thus, the main part of the definition is simply invalid. Second, the Task Force is reluctant to admit the possibility that living standards for some may have to be reduced that others might live at all. It avoids this issue entirely. Third, and consistent with the foregoing, the Task Force clings to the growth ethic, implying that an expanding economy is the preferred, if not the only solution, to social inequity. Fourth, the Task Force disallows the possibility that the preservation of certain "mixes" of ecological resource systems may well be essential to sustainability.

In the final analysis, then, the Task Force definition of sustainable development could be used to defend practically any pattern of economic activity, including the status quo (which, one suspects, was the general idea).

To be fair, the Task Force does provide numerous recommendations for improved economic planning and environmental assessment; for demonstration projects in sustainable development; for more research into ecological problems; for better government-industry cooperation in the integration of environment and economy, etc. However, in failing to recognize its own epistemological assumptions, the Task Force was constrained from stretching beyond such commonplace adjustments.

One problem is that the Task Force report (and, to a lesser extent, **Our Common Future**) was written from within the materialist growth paradigm. This paradigm is the ecological equivalent of rose-coloured glasses. With our vision pleasantly impaired, we will always ask first that Nature continue to meet our growing demands; it is literally beyond imagining that we should seriously adapt to Nature's constraints.

Now do not get me wrong. There may well be a grand idea in the Task Force that is struggling to get out. But the fact there is a struggle is my central point. The idea we need cannot be born of the prevailing worldview; it is missing too many essential elements. If we are serious about sustainable development, we cannot get there from here, at least not directly. We have to start from a different paradigm.

TOWARD A NEW PARADIGM

I would like now to sketch some of the errant elements I believe are central to any ecologically sound approach to sustainable development. To promote understanding, I will use a metaphor drawn from the current paradigm and a model we all know, capital investment.

Environment as Capital

In the simplest case, if you have money to invest and manage it wisely, you expect your capital to grow. Indeed, the objective of this form of "development" is to accumulate capital (money, equipment, physical plant), to be better off after making your investment than before. Certainly no one sets out to deliberately lose his/her financial shirt.

Try now to conceive various living species and ecosystems processes as forms of capital. It is easy to think of species we harvest this way, since we all know that a given stock of fish, trees, or cattle is capable of generating variable rates of return (growth and reproduction) depending on the goals and skills of management. But we are much less aware of the valuable hidden services performed by ecosystems' processes mainly because they are performed so well. One example would be the inherent capacity of local ecosystems and the biosphere to absorb, neutralize, and recycle organic and nutrient wastes. These are free services that we might otherwise have to pay for, and as such can be considered as a return on our "investment" in the ecological capital doing the chore.

Clearly, any human activity dependent on the consumptive use of ecological resources (forestry, fisheries, agriculture, waste disposal, urban sprawl onto agricultural land) cannot be sustained indefinitely if it consumes not only the annual production from that resource (the "interest"), but also cuts into the capital base. In this simple truth lies the essence of our environmental crisis. We have not only been living off our ecological interest but also consuming the capital, and the rate at which we are doing so is increasing year by year. This is the inevitable consequence of exponential growth. Some examples:

1. Most major world fisheries peaked far short of their potential productivity in the early 1970's, and many, including B.C. salmon and Atlantic cod, are in a continuing state of decline from over-fishing and habitat destruction.

2. Historic forestry practices in B.C. have greatly reduced the last major temperate rain-forest, and our present "economic" clearcut methods leave an ecological disaster of denuded slopes and eroded soils. Meanwhile, tropical forests, habitat to half the world's species, have been reduced by 40%, and are being cut at the rate of 10–20 million hectares (ha.) (1–2%) per year.

3. The prairie soils of the North American breadbasket have lost half their organic content and natural nutrients under mechanized agriculture. Soil erosion from cultivated land typically claims 22 metric tons/ha./year, about ten times the rate of soil building....

4. Abetted by deforestation, over-grazing, and inappropriate land use, the world's deserts claim an additional 21 million ha. of previously habitable land/year.

5. Acid rain is sterilizing thousands of lakes, destroying fisheries, and threatening forest and agricultural productivity in much of the Northern hemisphere.

6. Carbon dioxide production from the burning of fossil fuels and destruction of forests has long exceeded the capacity of the oceans and terrestrial plants to absorb the excess. Atmospheric CO_2 has risen 25% in the industrial age and is expected to double from preindustrial levels in the next century, contributing significantly to the greenhouse effect and potentially disastrous global warming.

Admittedly, interpreting such trends is difficult and their ultimate significance controversial. However, viewed in the same light as rising standards of living, the decline of the biosphere provides a novel perspective on the origins of our unprecedented wealth. These intersecting curves reveal that since the beginning of the steam age, we have been busily converting ecological capital into financial and material capital.

This means that much of our wealth is illusion. We have simply drawn down one account (the biosphere) to add to another (the bank). It might even be argued that we have been collectively impoverished in the process. Much potentially renewable environmental capital has been permanently converted into machinery, plant, and possessions that will eventually wear out and have to be replaced (at the cost of additional resources—that irritating Second Law again!).

To put it another way, we have long been enjoying a free ride for which we now have to ante up. Forest products and food are undervalued in the marketplace to the extent the prices we pay do not include the costs of resource maintenance. Our paychecks and corporate profits are excessive to the extent that the resource base which produced them has been run down. That new CD player and the family's second car represent capital that was not plowed back into agriculture, soils management, and waste control. In simplest terms, the "good life" for some humans has been subsidized at the expense of all other life, and ultimately of our children and their descendants.

Living on the Interest

This suggests that for the foreseeable future, sustainable development is only possible if we are willing to live on the interest of our remaining ecological endowment. Fortunately, this is still generous enough, and with careful husbanding it should be possible to restore and even build up our capital base.

Success in this endeavor will obviously require a rewrite of the prevailing environmental myth and humankind's role in the scheme of things. To begin, the new eco-paradigm must dissolve our separateness and reunite humankind with the biosphere.

Let us be clear that while better environmental management may be an essential interim step, we are not merely talking about tougher environmental regulation or improved impact assessment. History has shown that restrictive measures to control inappropriate activities are simply inadequate. This is because regulation must be imposed to protect some social value that is perceived as secondary if not inimical to the interests of the regulatee. Corporations oriented to maximizing profits do not voluntarily incur the costs of pollution control. Moreover, if the general interests of society (or at least the politician) are more closely associated with profit than environment, regulations are not enthusiastically enforced.

True sustainable development cannot be forced. Rather, it is the natural product of a society that "comes from" a profound sense of being in, and of, the natural world. As noted at the outset, sustainable development requires a shift in fundamental social attitudes and values, a change in worldview. People must acquire in their bones a sense that violation of the biosphere is violation of self.

From this perspective, it would be psychologically and socially unconscionable for anyone to advance a development or resource management proposal whose long-term effect would be to reduce our ecological capital. Just as today, no sane person sets out purposely to go financially bankrupt, no one would dream of launching an ecologically bankrupt scheme. On the contrary, development would be planned and implemented, without force or coercion, in ways that would maintain or increase the renewable resource base. "Return on investment" would acquire a double meaning. Both ecological and financial criteria have to be satisfied in the cost/benefit calculus.

Think for the moment how different things would be today had enhancing our ecological capital been taken for granted as the guiding principle of resource development in British Columbia for the last 100 years. There would be no concerns that sawmills in the interior may run out of timber; no fight between loggers and conservationists over the last uncut valley in the southern half of the province; South Moresby would have been declared a National Park long ago; commercial and sport fishermen would not be locked in a bitter dispute over declining shares of a diminishing resource (and the costly salmon-enhancement program would not have been necessary). It might have cost more along the way, but paradoxically, we would be richer today.

To ears conditioned by the hard-nosed rhetoric of modern business and politics, this softer path to development will sound utterly ridiculous, vaguely threatening, or merely irrelevant. But remember, from within in the current paradigm, it is difficult to recognize any vision not supported by conventional values and assumptions. The orthodox mind can only deny the evidence and insist the Earth is flat.

This is a critical point. To acknowledge it is to admit the possibility of an alternative vision and future. With self-awareness, comes the realization that there is nothing fixed or sacred about our present way of being. Materialist society, its Rambo economics, and even the compulsive consumers of the "me" generation, are all creations of malleable culture, not of any physical law. **We made them up.** If they are no longer adapted to the changing reality, we can remake them ourselves, in an image that is.

While re-education will be a long and difficult process, it may have unexpected rewards. Human beings are multidimensional creatures, at once aggressively competitive and socially cooperative. But Western society plays up the former, while suppressing the latter; a perverted liberalism idolizes the individual, while Conservative economics deprives him/her of the community necessary to make him/her whole. The new paradigm may enable us to restore the balance in a rediscovery of self. At the least, our new consciousness should catalyze a shift in emphasis from the quantitative to the qualitative, from the material to the tangible, from growth to development, in the lives of people and communities.

The eco-paradigm is an inherently cooperative one. It springs from a felt responsibility to the whole planet and can only be expressed through socio-political effort at all levels of social organization. Although there must be leadership, no region, province, or nation can go it alone for long.

Sustainable development thus gives new meaning to McLuhan's "global village." The media that made it possible may finally have a message that makes it worthwhile. We are engaged in no less an enterprise than restoring the habitat for all of humankind, and this will require no less than total commitment and unity of purpose.

Listen for a collective sigh of relief, the arms race, which we never could afford, which consumes so much of our ecological capital, can only be seen as a perverse anachronism when viewed from the eco-paradigm. Giving up on war would free no less than 6% of gross world product for the sustainable redevelopment of the planet!

Now, of course, I am really staring off to ecotopia. It simply cannot happen, right? Perhaps, but if you cannot share this vision, take a long look from where you stand and ponder the alternative.

STUDY QUESTIONS

1. Does Rees make a good case that traditional economics is materialistic and hence unable to deal with the kinds of concerns raised by environmental consciousness?

2. How might a proponent of standard economics respond to Rees's thesis that we must treat the environment as capital?

67

At the Shrine of Our Lady of Fàtima, or Why Political Questions Are Not All Economic

MARK SAGOFF

Mark Sagoff is a research scholar at the Center for Philosophy and Public Policy, University of Maryland, College Park, and the author of several works on economic and social issues, including The Economy of the Earth: Philosophy, Law and the Environment *(1988).*

Sagoff examines and rejects the standard economic notion that the cost–benefit analysis is always the proper method for deciding social and environmental issues. Contrasting utilitarian with Kantian views of the human situation, he argues that the Kantian perspective, which treats humans as ends in themselves, should override utilitarian cost–benefit assessments. Sometimes efficiency should be sacrificed for principle.

Lewiston, New York, a well-to-do community near Buffalo, is the site of the Lake Ontario Ordnance Works, where the federal government, years ago, disposed of the residues of the Manhattan Project. These radioactive wastes are buried but are not forgotten by the residents, who say that when the wind is southerly radon gas blows through the town. Several parents at a recent conference I attended there described their terror on learning that cases of leukemia had been found among area children. They feared for their own lives as well. At the other sides of the table, officials from New York State and from local corporations replied that these fears were ungrounded. People who smoke, they said, take greater risks than people who live close to waste disposal sites. One speaker talked in terms of "rational methodologies of decision making." This aggravated the parents' rage and frustration.

The speaker suggested that the townspeople, were they to make their decision in a free market, would choose to live near the hazardous waste facility, if they knew the scientific facts. He told me later they were irrational—he said, "neurotic"—because they refused to recognize or act upon their own interests. The residents of Lewiston were unimpressed with his analysis of their "willingness to pay" to avoid this risk or that. They did not see what risk-benefit analysis had to do with the issues they raised.

If you take the Military Highway (as I did) from Buffalo to Lewiston, you will pass through a formidable wasteland. Landfills stretch in all directions, where enormous trucks—tiny in that landscape—incessantly deposit sludge which great bulldozers, like yellow ants, then push into the ground. These machines are the only signs of life, for in the miasma that hangs in the air, no birds, not even scavengers, are seen. Along colossal power lines which crisscross this dismal land, the dynamos at Niagara send electric power south, where factories have fled, leaving their remains to decay.

Arizona Law Review, Vol. 23, pp. 1283–1298. Copyright © 1981 by the Arizona Board of Regents. Reprinted by permission. Notes deleted.

To drive along this road is to feel, oddly, the mystery and awe one experiences in the presence of so much power and decadence.

Henry Adams had a similar response to the dynamos on display at the Paris Exposition of 1900. To him "the dynamo became a symbol of infinity." To Adams, the dynamo functioned as the modern equivalent of the Virgin, that is, as the center and focus of power. "Before the end, one began to pray to it; inherited instinct taught the natural expression of man before silent and infinite force."

Adams asks in his essay "The Dynamo and the Virgin" how the products of modern industrial civilization will compare with those of the religious culture of the Middle Ages. If he could see the landfills and hazardous waste facilities bordering the power stations and honeymoon hotels of Niagara Falls he would know the answer. He would understand what happens when efficiency replaces infinity as the central conception of value. The dynamos at Niagara will not produce another Mont-Saint-Michel. "All the steam in the world," Adams wrote, "could not, like the Virgin, build Chartres."

At the Shrine of Our Lady of Fàtima, on a plateau north of the Military Highway, a larger than life sculpture of Mary looks into the chemical air. The original of this shrine stands in central Portugal, where in May, 1917, three children said they saw a Lady, brighter than the sun, raised on a cloud in an evergreen tree. Five months later, on a wet and chilly October day, the Lady again appeared, this time before a large crowd. Some who were skeptical did not see the miracle. Others in the crowd reported, however, that "the sun appeared and seemed to tremble, rotate violently and fall, dancing over the heads of the throng...."

The Shrine was empty when I visited it. The cult of Our Lady of Fàtima, I imagine, has only a few devotees. The cult of Pareto optimality, however, has many. Where some people see only environmental devastation, its devotees perceive efficiency, utility, and maximization of wealth. They see the satisfaction of wants. They envision the good life. As I looked over the smudged and ruined terrain I tried to share that vision. I hope that Our Lady of Fàtima, worker of miracles, might serve, at least for the moment, as the Patroness of cost-benefit analysis. I thought of all the wants and needs that are satisfied in a landscape of honeymoon cottages, commercial strips, and dumps for hazardous waste. I saw the miracle of efficiency. The prospect, however, looked only darker in that light.

I

This essay concerns the economic decisions we make about the environment. It also concerns our political decisions about the environment. Some people have suggested that ideally these should be the same, that all environmental problems are problems in distribution. According to this view there is an environmental problem only when some resource is not allocated in equitable and efficient ways.

This approach to environmental policy is pitched entirely at the level of the consumer. It is his or her values that count, and the measure of these values is the individual's willingness to pay. The problem of justice or fairness in society becomes, then, the problem of distributing goods and services so that more people get more of what they want to buy. A condo on the beach. A snowmobile for the mountains. A tank full of gas. A day of labor. The only values we have, on this view, are those which a market can price.

How much do you value open space, a stand of trees, an "unspoiled" landscape? Fifty dollars? A hundred? A thousand? This is one way to measure value. You could compare the amount consumers would pay for a townhouse or coal or a landfill and the amount they would pay to preserve an area in its "natural" state. If users would pay more for the land with the house, the coal mine, or the landfill, than without—less construction and other costs of development—then the efficient thing to do is to improve the land and thus increase its value. That is why we have so many tract developments. And pizza stands. And gas stations. And strip mines. And landfills. How much did you spend last year to preserve open space? How much for pizza and gas? "In principle, the ultimate measure of environmental quality," as one basic text assures us, "is the value people place on these ... services or their *willingness to pay.*"

Willingness to pay. What is wrong with that? The rub is this: not all of us think of ourselves simply as *consumers*. Many of us regard ourselves *as citizens* as well. We act as consumers to get what we want *for ourselves*. We act as citizens to achieve what we think is right or best *for the community*. The question arises, then, whether what we want for ourselves individually as consumers is consistent with the goals we would set for ourselves collectively as citizens. Would I vote for the sort of things I shop for? Are my preferences as a consumer consistent with my judgments as a citizen?

They are not. I am schizophrenic. Last year, I fixed a couple of tickets and was happy to do so since I saved fifty dollars. Yet, at election time, I helped to vote the corrupt judge out of office. I speed on the highway; yet I want the police to enforce laws against speeding. I used to buy mixers in returnable bottles—but who can bother to return them? I buy only disposables now, but, to soothe my conscience, I urge my state senator to outlaw one-way containers. I love my car; I hate the bus. Yet I vote for candidates who promise to tax gasoline to pay for public transportation. I send my dues to the Sierra Club to protect areas in Alaska I shall never visit. And I support the work of the American League to Abolish Capital Punishment although, personally, I have nothing to gain one way or the other. (When I hang, I will hang myself.) And of course I applaud the Endangered Species Act, although I have no earthly use for the Colorado squawfish or the Indiana bat. I support almost any political cause that I think will defeat my consumer interests. This is because I have contempt for—although I act upon—those interests. I have an "Ecology Now" sticker on a car that leaks oil everywhere it's parked.

The distinction between consumer and citizen preferences has long vexed the theory of public finance. Should the public economy serve the same goals as the household economy? May it serve, instead, goals emerging from our association as citizens? The question asks if we may collectively strive for and achieve only those items we individually compete for and consume. Should we aspire, instead, to public goals we may legislate as a nation?

The problem, insofar as it concerns public finance, is stated as follows by R. A. Musgrave, who reports a conversation he had with Gerhard Colm.

> He [Colm] holds that the individual voter dealing with political issues has a frame of reference quite distinct from that which underlies his allocation of income as a consumer. In the latter situation the voter acts as a private individual determined by self-interest and deals with his personal wants; in the former, he acts as a political being guided by his image of a good society. The two, Colm holds, are different things.

Are these two different things? Stephen Marglin suggests that they are. He writes:

> The preferences that govern one's unilateral market actions no longer govern his actions when the form of reference is shifted from the market to the political arena. The Economic Man and the Citizen are for all intents and purposes two different individuals. It is not a question, therefore, of rejecting individual … preference maps; it is, rather, that market and political preference maps are inconsistent.

Marglin observes that if this is true, social choices optimal under one set of preferences will not be optimal under another. What, then, is the meaning of "optimality"? He notices that if we take a person's true preferences to be those expressed in the market, we may, then, neglect or reject the preferences that person reveals in advocating a political cause or position. "One might argue on welfare grounds," Marglin speculates, "for authoritarian rejection of individuals' politically revealed preferences in favor of their market revealed preferences!"

II

On February 19, 1981, President Reagan published Executive Order 12,291 requiring all administrative agencies and departments to support every new major regulation with a cost-benefit analysis establishing that the benefits of the regulation to society outweigh its costs. The Order directs the Office of Management and Budget (OMB) to review every such regulation on the basis of the adequacy of the cost-benefit analysis supporting it. This is a departure from tradition. Traditionally, regulations have been reviewed not by OMB but by the courts on the basis of their relation not to cost-benefit analysis but to authorizing legislation.

A month earlier, in January 1981, the Supreme Court heard lawyers for the American Textile Manufacturers Institute argue against a proposed Occupational Safety and Health Administration (OSHA) regulation which would have severely restricted the acceptable levels of cotton dust in textile plants. The lawyers for industry argued that the benefits of the regulation would not equal the costs. The lawyers for the government contended that the law required the tough standard. OSHA, acting consistently with Executive Order 12,291, asked the Court not to decide the cotton dust case, in order to give the agency time to complete the cost-benefit analysis required by the textile industry. The Court declined to accept OSHA's request and handed down its opinion on June 17, 1981.

The Supreme Court, in a 5–3 decision, found that the actions of regulatory agencies which conform to the OSHA law need not be supported by cost-benefit analysis. In addition, the Court asserted that Congress in writing a statute, rather than the agencies in applying it, has the primary responsibility for balancing benefits and costs. The Court said:

> When Congress passed the Occupational Health and Safety Act in 1970, it chose to place preeminent value on assuring employees a safe and healthful working environment, limited only by the feasibility of achieving such an environment. We must measure the validity of the Secretary's actions against the requirements of that Act.

The opinion upheld the finding of the Appeals Court that "Congress itself struck the balance between costs and benefits in the mandate to the agency."

The Appeals Court opinion in *American Textile Manufacturers* vs. *Donovan* supports the principle that legislatures are not necessarily bound to a particular conception of regulatory policy. Agencies that apply the law, therefore, may not need to justify on cost-benefit grounds the standards they set. These standards may conflict with the goal of efficiency and still express our political will as a nation. That is, they may reflect not the personal choices of self-interested individuals, but the collective judgments we make on historical, cultural, aesthetic, moral, and ideological grounds.

The appeal of the Reagan Administration to cost-benefit analysis, however, may arise more from political than economic considerations. The intention, seen in the most favorable light, may not be to replace political or ideological goals with economic ones but to make economic goals more apparent in regulation. This is not to say that Congress should function to reveal a collective willingness-to-pay just as markets reveal an individual willingness-to-pay. It is to suggest that Congress should do more to balance economic with ideological, aesthetic, and moral goals. To think that environmental or worker safety policy can be based exclusively on aspiration for a "natural" and "safe" world is as foolish as to hold that environmental law can be reduced to cost-benefit accounting. The more we move to one extreme, as I found in Lewiston, the more likely we are to hear from the other.

III

The labor unions won an important political victory when Congress passed the Occupational Safety and Health Act of 1970. That Act, among other things, severely restricts worker exposure to toxic substances. It instructs the Secretary of Labor to set "the standard which most adequately assures, to the extent feasible … that no employee will suffer material impairment of health or functional capacity even if such employee has regular exposure to the hazard for the period of his working life."

Pursuant to this law, the Secretary of Labor, in 1977, reduced from ten to one part per million (ppm) the permissible ambient exposure level for benzene, a carcinogenic for which no safe threshold is known. The American Petroleum Institute thereupon challenged the new standard in court. It argued, with much evidence in its favor, that the benefits (to workers) of the one ppm standard did not equal the costs (to industry). The standard, therefore, did not appear to be a rational response to a market failure in that it did not strike an efficient balance between the interests of workers in safety and the interests of industry and consumers in keeping prices down.

The Secretary of Labor defended the tough safety standard on the ground that the law demanded it. An efficient standard might have required safety until it cost industry more to prevent a risk than it cost workers to accept it. Had Congress adopted this vision of public policy—one which can be found in many economic texts—it would have treated workers not as ends-in-themselves but as means for the production of overall utility. And this, as the Secretary saw it, was what Congress refused to do.

The United States Court of Appeals for the Fifth Circuit agreed with the American Petroleum Institute and invalidated the one ppm benzene standard. On July 2, 1980, the Supreme Court affirmed remanding the benzene standard back to OSHA for revision. The narrowly based Supreme Court decision was divided over the role economic considerations should play in judicial review. Justice Marshall, joined in dissent by three other justices, argued that the court had undone on the basis of its own theory of regulatory policy an act of Congress inconsistent with that theory. He concluded that the plurality decision of the Court "requires the American worker to return to the political arena to win a victory that he won before in 1970."

To reject cost-benefit analysis, as Justice Marshall would, as a basis for public policy making is not necessarily to reject cost-effectiveness analysis, which is an altogether different thing. *"Cost-benefit analysis,"* one commentator points out, "is used by the decision maker to establish societal goals as well as the means for achieving these goals, whereas *cost-effectiveness analysis* only compares alternative means for achieving 'given' goals." Justice Marshall's

dissent objects to those who would make efficiency the goal of public policy. It does not necessarily object to those who would accomplish as efficiently as possible the goals Congress sets.

IV

When efficiency is the criterion of public safety and health one tends to conceive of social relations on the model of a market, ignoring competing visions of what we as a society should be like. Yet it is obvious that there are competing conceptions of how we should relate to one another. There are some who believe, on principle, that worker safety and environmental quality ought to be protected only insofar as the benefits of protection balance the costs. On the other hand, people argue, also on principle, that neither worker safety nor environmental quality should be treated merely as a commodity, to be traded at the margin for other commodities, but should be valued for its own sake. The conflict between these two principles is logical or moral, to be resolved by argument or debate. The question whether cost-benefit analysis should play a decisive role in policymaking is not to be decided by cost-benefit analysis. A contradiction between principles—between contending visions of the good society—cannot be settled by asking how much partisans are willing to pay for their beliefs.

The role of the *legislator,* the political role, may be more important to the individual than the role of *consumer.* The person, in other words, is not to be treated as merely a bundle of preferences to be juggled in cost-benefit analyses. The individual is to be respected as an advocate of ideas which are to be judged in relation to the reasons for them. If health and environmental statutes reflect a vision of society as something other than a market by requiring protections beyond what are efficient, then this may express not legislative ineptitude but legislative responsiveness to public values. To deny this vision because it is economically inefficient is simply to replace it with another vision. It is to insist that the ideas of the citizen be sacrificed to the psychology of the consumer.

We hear on all sides that government is routinized, mechanical, entrenched, and bureaucratized; the jargon alone is enough to dissuade the most mettlesome meddler. Who can make a difference? It is plain that for many of us the idea of a national political community has an abstract and suppositious quality. We have only our private conceptions of the good, if no way exists to arrive at a public one. This is only to note the continuation, in our time, of the trend Benjamin Constant described in the essay, *De La Liberte des Anciens Comparee a Celle des Modernes.* Constant observes that the modern world, as opposed to the ancient, emphasizes civil over political liberties, the rights of privacy and property over those of community and participation. "Lost in the multitude," Constant writes, "the individual rarely perceives the influence that he exercises," and, therefore, must be content with "the peaceful enjoyment of private independence." The individual asks only to be protected by laws common to all in his pursuit of his own self-interest. The citizen has been replaced by the consumer; the tradition of Rousseau has been supplanted by that of Locke and Mill.

Nowhere are the rights of the moderns, particularly the rights of privacy and property, less helpful than in the area of the natural environment. Here the values we wish to protect—cultural, historical, aesthetic, and moral—are public values; they depend not so much upon what each person wants individually as upon what he or she believes we stand for collectively. We refuse to regard worker health and safety as commodities; we regulate hazards as a matter of right. Likewise, we refuse to treat environmental resources simply as public goods in the economist's sense. Instead, we prevent significant deterioration of air quality not only as a matter of individual self-interest but also as a matter of collective self-respect. How shall we balance efficiency against moral, cultural, and aesthetic values in policy for the workplace and the environment? No better way has been devised to do this than by legislative debate ending in a vote. This is not the same thing as a cost-benefit analysis terminating in a bottom line.

V

It is the characteristic of cost-benefit analysis that it treats all value judgments other than those made on its behalf as nothing but statements of preference, attitude, or emotion, insofar as they are value judgments. The cost-benefit analyst regards as true the judgment that we should maximize efficiency or wealth. The analyst believes that this view can be backed by reasons; the analyst does not regard it as a preference or want for which he or she must be willing to pay. The cost-benefit analyst, however, tends to treat all other normative views and recommendations as if they were nothing but subjective reports of mental states. The analyst supposes in all such cases that "this is right" and "this is what we ought to do" are equivalent to "I want this" and "this is what I prefer." Value judgments are beyond criticism if, indeed, they are nothing but expressions of personal preference; they are incorrigible since every person is in the best position to know what he or she wants. All valuation, according to this approach, happens *in foro interno,* debate *in foro publico* has no point. On this approach, the reasons that people give for their views, unless these people are welfare economists, do not count; what counts is how much they are willing to pay to satisfy their wants. Those who are willing to pay the most, for all intents and purposes, have the right view; theirs is the more informed opinion, the better aesthetic judgment, and the deeper moral insight.

The assumption that valuation is subjective, that judgments of good and evil are nothing but expressions of desire and aversion, is not unique to economic theory. There are psychotherapists—Carl Rogers is an example—who likewise deny the objectivity or cognitivity of valuation. For Rogers, there is only one criterion of worth: it lies in "the subjective world of the individual. Only he knows it fully." The therapist shows his or her client that a "value system is not necessarily something imposed from without, but is something experienced." Therapy succeeds when the client "perceives himself in such a way that no self-experience can be discriminated as more or less worthy of positive self-regard than any other...." The client then "tends to place the basis of standards within himself, recognizing that the 'goodness' or 'badness' of any experience or perceptual object is not something inherent in that object, but is a value placed in it by himself."

Rogers points out that "some clients make strenuous efforts to have the therapist exercise the valuing function, so as to provide them with guides for action." The therapist, however, "consistently keeps the locus of evaluation with the client." As long as the therapist refuses to "exercise the valuing function" and as long as he or she practices an "unconditional positive regard" for all the affective states of the client, then the therapist remains neutral among the client's values or "sensory and visceral experiences." The role of the therapist is legitimate, Rogers suggests, because of this value neutrality. The therapist accepts all felt preferences as valid and imposes none on the client.

Economists likewise argue that their role as policymakers is legitimate because they are neutral among competing values in the client society. The political economist, according to James Buchanan, "is or should be ethically neutral: the indicated results are influenced by his own value scale only insofar as this reflects his membership in a larger group." The economist might be most confident of the impartiality of his or her policy recommendations if he or she could derive them formally or mathematically from individual preferences. If theoretical difficulties make such a social welfare function impossible, however, the next best thing, to preserve neutrality, is to let markets function to transform individual preference orderings into a collective ordering of social states. The analyst is able then to base policy on preferences that exist in society and are not necessarily his own.

Economists have used this impartial approach to offer solutions to many outstanding social problems, for example, the controversy over abortion. An economist argues that "there is an optimal number of abortions, just as there is an optimal level of pollution, or purity.... Those who oppose abortion could eliminate it entirely, if their intensity of feeling were so strong as to lead to payments that were greater at the margin than the price anyone would pay to have an abortion." Likewise economists, in order to determine whether the war in Vietnam was justified, have estimated the willingness to pay of those who demonstrated against it. Likewise it should be possible, following the same line of reasoning, to decide whether Creationism should be taught in the public schools, whether black and white people should be segregated, whether the death penalty should be enforced, and whether the square root of six is three. All of these questions depend upon how much people are willing to pay for their subjective preferences or wants—or none of them do. This is the beauty of cost-benefit analysis: no matter how relevant or irrelevant, wise or stupid, informed or uninformed, responsible or silly, defensible or indefensible wants may be, the analyst is able to derive a policy from them—a policy which is legitimate because, in theory, it treats all of these preferences as equally valid and good.

VI

Consider, by way of contrast, a Kantian conception of value. The individual, for Kant, is a judge of values, not a mere haver of wants, and the individual judges not for himself or herself merely, but as a member of a relevant community or group. The central idea in a Kantian approach to ethics is that some values are more reasonable than others and therefore have a better claim upon the assent of members of the community as such. The world of obligation, like the world of mathematics or the world of empirical fact, is intersubjective, it is public not private, so that objective standards of argument and criticism apply. Kant recognizes that values, like beliefs, are subjective states of mind, but he points out that like beliefs they have an objective content as well; therefore they are either correct or mistaken. Thus Kant discusses valuation in the context not of psychology but of cognition. He believes that a person who makes a value judgment—or a policy recommendation—claims to know what is *right* and not just what is *preferred*. A value judgment is like an empirical or theoretical judgment in that it claims to be *true*, not merely to be *felt*.

We have, then, two approaches to public policy before us. The first, the approach associated with normative versions of welfare economics, asserts that the only policy recommendation that can or need be defended on objective grounds is efficiency or wealth-maximization. Every policy decision after that depends only on the preponderance of feeling or preference, as expressed in willingness to pay. The Kantian approach, on the other hand, assumes that many policy recommendations other than that one may be justified or refuted on objective grounds. It would concede that the approach of welfare economics applies adequately to some questions, e.g., those which ordinary consumer markets typically settle. How many yo-yos should be produced as compared to how many frisbees? Shall pens have black ink or blue? Matters such as these are so trivial it is plain that markets should handle them. It does not follow, however, that we should adopt a market or quasi-market approach to every public question.

A market or quasi-market approach to arithmetic, for example, is plainly inadequate. No matter how much people are willing to pay, three will never be the square root of six. Similarly, segregation is a national curse and the fact that we are willing to pay for it does not make it better but only makes us worse. Similarly, the case for abortion must stand on the merits; it cannot be priced at the margin. Similarly, the war in Vietnam was a moral debacle and this can be determined without shadow-pricing the willingness to pay of those who demonstrated against it. Similarly, we do not decide to execute murderers by asking how much bleeding hearts are willing to pay to see a person pardoned and how much hard hearts are willing to pay to see him hanged. Our failures to make the right decisions in these matters are failures in arithmetic, failures in wisdom, failures in taste, failures in morality—but not market failures. There are no relevant markets to have failed. What separates these questions from those for which markets are appropriate is this. They involve matters of knowledge, wisdom, morality, and taste that admit of better or worse, right or wrong, true or false—and these concepts differ from that of economic optimality. Surely environmental questions—the protection of wilderness, habitats, water, land, and air as well as policy toward environmental safety and health—involve moral and aesthetic principles and not just economic ones. This is consistent, of course, with cost-effectiveness and with a sensible recognition of economic constraints.

The neutrality of the economist, like the neutrality of Rogers' therapist, is legitimate if private preferences or subjective wants are the only values in question. A person should be left free to choose the color of his or her necktie or necklace—but we cannot justify a theory of public policy or private therapy on that basis. If the patient seeks moral advice or tries to find reasons to justify a choice, the therapist, according to Rogers' model, would remind him or her to trust his visceral and sensory experiences. The result of this is to deny the individual status as a cognitive being capable of responding intelligently to reasons; it reduces him or her to a bundle of affective states. What Rogers' therapist does to the patient the cost-benefit analyst does to society as a whole. The analyst is neutral among our "values"—having first imposed a theory of what value is. This is a theory that is impartial among values and for that reason fails to treat the persons who have them with respect or concern. It does not treat them even as persons but only as locations at which wants may be found. And thus we may conclude that the neutrality of economics is not a basis for its legitimacy. We recognize it as an indifference toward value—an indifference so deep, so studied, and so assured that at first one hesitates to call it by its right name.

VII

The residents of Lewiston at the conference I attended demanded to know the truth about the dangers that confronted them and the reasons for these dangers. They wanted to be convinced that the sacrifice asked of them was legitimate even if it served interests other than their own. One official from a large chemical company dumping wastes in the area told them, in reply, that corporations were people and that people could talk to people about their feelings, interests, and needs. This sent a shiver through the audience. Like Joseph K. in *The Trial,* the residents of Lewiston asked for an explanation, justice, and truth, and they were told that their wants would be taken care of. They demanded to know the reasons for what was continually happening to them. They were given a personalized response instead.

This response, that corporations are "just people serving people" is consistent with a particular view of power. This is the view that identified power with the ability to get what one wants as an individual, that is, to satisfy one's personal preferences. When people in official positions in corporations or in the government put aside their personal interests, it would follow that they put aside their power as well. Their neutrality then justifies them in directing the resources of society in ways they determine to be best. This managerial role serves not their own interests but those of their clients. Cost-benefit analysis may be seen as a pervasive form of this paternalism. Behind this paternalism, as William Simon observes of the lawyer-client relationship, lies a theory of value that tends to personalize power. "It resists understanding power as a product of class, property, or institutions and collapses power into the personal needs and dispositions of the individuals who command and obey." Once the economist, the therapist, the lawyer, or the manager abjures his own interests and acts wholly on behalf of client individuals, he appears to have no power of his own and thus justifiably manipulates and controls everything. "From this perspective it becomes difficult to distinguish the powerful from the powerless. In every case, both the exercise of power and submission to it are portrayed as a matter of personal accommodation and adjustment."

The key to the personal interest or emotive theory of value, as one commentator has rightly said, "is the fact that emotivism entails the obliteration of any genuine distinction between manipulative and non-manipulative social relations." The reason is that once the effective self is made the source of all value, the public self cannot participate in the exercise of power. As Philip Reiff remarks, "the public world is constituted as one vast stranger who appears at inconvenient times and makes demands viewed as purely external and therefore with no power to elicit a moral response." There is no way to distinguish tyranny from the legitimate authority that public values and public law create.

"At the rate of progress since 1900," Henry Adams speculates in his *Education,* "every American who lived into the year 2000 would know how to control unlimited power." Adams thought that the Dynamo would organize and release as much energy as the Virgin. Yet in the 1980s, the citizens of Lewiston, surrounded by dynamos, high tension lines, and nuclear wastes, are powerless. They do not know how to criticize power, resist power, or justify—power—for to do so depends on making distinctions between good and evil, right and wrong, innocence and guilt, justice and injustice, truth and lies. These distinctions cannot be made out and have no significance within an emotive or psychological theory of value. To adopt this theory is to imagine society as a market in which individuals trade voluntarily and without coercion. No individual, no belief, no faith has authority over them. To have power to act as a nation, however, we must be able to act, at least at times, on a public philosophy, conviction, or faith. We cannot replace with economic analysis the moral function of public law. The antinomianism [*antinomian*—the rejection of law and morality] of cost-benefit analysis is not enough.

STUDY QUESTIONS

1. Do you agree with Sagoff in his distinction between the person as *consumer* and *citizen*? Should there be a radical divide ("schizophrenia") between our economic selves and our moral-political selves?

2. Sagoff seems to hold that not all values are subjective, but some are objectively true or better. What arguments can you think of for both views of values?

3. How is the psychotherapeutic model (Carl Rogers offers an example) similar to the economic model of value preferences? Do you agree with Sagoff that psychotherapists leave out something important? What?

4. Can the standard economic analysis incorporate Sagoff's criticism, arguing that the moral-legislative aspects can be taken into account in assessing the total cost-benefits? Or is there a fundamental cleavage between these two ways of viewing things?

68

Toward a Just and Sustainable Economic Order

JOHN B. COBB, JR.

John B. Cobb, Jr., retired in 1990 from 32 years as professor of theology at the Claremont School of Theology. He continues part-time teaching in religion at the Claremont Graduate School. He is founding director of the Center for Process Studies. In 1981 he published The Liberation of Life *with Charles Birch, and in 1989,* For the Common Good *with Herman Daly (updated and expanded version in 1994). More recently he has published* Sustainability, Sustaining the Common Good *and, with Clifford W. Cobb,* The Green National Product.*

The present global system aims at economic integration for the sake of maximizing "growth" as measured by the gross national product (GNP). This leads to sustained efforts to destroy all national barriers to trade and to make all people interdependent. The results are widespread injustice and unsustainable pressures on the environment. The Brundtland Commission's proposal of "sustainable developments," which involves expanding the entire economy five-to tenfold, will not work. Increasing the GNP does not correspond well with improving economic welfare, much less with social well-being. Realizing this noncorrespondence may make it possible to develop an economic order that is geared to meeting the needs of people rather than increasing production. Such an economy would be decentralized and organized from the bottom up.

Many morally concerned people today believe we should make moderate changes in the present economic order so as to render it just and sustainable.

Others, however, and I am one of them, believe the basic principles that govern the global economy today inherently lead to increasing injustice and

---

From *Journal of Social Ideas*, Vol. 51 (1995). Reprinted by permission of the author.

unsustainability. Policies based on these principles concentrate wealth in fewer hands, leaving the poor more destitute. They transfer wealth from poorer to richer countries. And they speed the destruction of natural resources, especially in the poorer countries. Reforms within the system can moderate these tendencies, but they cannot basically change them. If we are concerned for either justice or sustainability, we must envision, and work for, a different economic system.

At present there is little discussion of alternatives. Many assume that the only options are the present global market economy, on the one hand, and the bureaucratically managed economy, on the other. The latter has shown itself, particularly in eastern Europe and China, to be inseparable from political injustice and oppression. It has also shown itself to be inefficient in its use of resources, whereas sustainability requires efficiency. To suppose that these are the only options limits us to a choice between two unjust and unsustainable systems. We need to envision ways of organizing the global economy that differ from both.

This article offers some principles and outlines of an alternative economic system that has the possibility of being both sustainable and just. After expounding the vision that now shapes our national and international policies and institutions, their achievements and limitations are addressed. The principle of "sustainable development" is analyzed, its shortcomings noted, and an alternative proposed.

THE VISION THAT NOW GUIDES US

The most important change in the global order after World War II was the shift from a primarily political world system to a primarily economic one. This shift is not manifest in the United Nations. It was clearly expressed at the 1944 meeting at Bretton Woods, where the International Monetary Fund (IMF) and the World Bank were established, and shortly thereafter with the General Agreement on Tariffs and Trade (GATT; Kock, 1969; Van Dormael, 1978). Whereas the United Nations was designed to deal with international affairs, assuming the continuing sovereignty of states, the institutions generated at Bretton Woods were designed to deal with the global economy. The most powerful nations are now cooperating for the sake of the growth of the global economy. Competition is among firms across national boundaries. Through trade agreements, the governments of even the most powerful nations have systematically given up their ability to control these economic actors by raising tariffs or other actions deemed to be in restraint of trade. They have also greatly restricted the ability of the weaker nations to do so (Raghavan, 1990).

This massive shift of power from nations to transnational corporations was long obscured by the cold war. The shift occurred within the First World, but public attention was riveted on the confrontation between the First and Second Worlds. At the deepest level this, too, was economic, and it was the vastly greater growth of the First World system that led to the collapse of the Second. But the political and military conflict was more visible. Now that this conflict has drastically diminished, and the Second World is seeking entry into the First World system, the primacy of the global economic order is apparent.

In the past the United Nations provided a forum for debate about economic issues in which the concerns of the poorer nations were voiced. But this debate had little influence on actual global economic policies, and today it has been largely silenced. Serious discussion of economic matters takes place only in those institutions created after World War II to give new shape to the planet. Political agreements needed to attain the goals of the global economic institutions are made through negotiations among the major economic powers, most visibly through the annual economic summit of leaders from the big seven economic powers.

The policies of these powers, and of the global institutions they largely control, are shaped for their economic benefit. However, one should not view this cynically. The goal of Bretton Woods was to increase the rate of economic growth globally. It has been assumed throughout that global economic growth benefits all. The enemy is not the self-interest of individual nations but is seen as policies that slow this global growth.

Economic theory from the time of Adam Smith (1776/1991) has viewed the one engine of growth as being rational, competitive behavior in the market. In this view all sell their labor and goods as dearly as possible and acquire the labor and goods of others as cheaply as possible. This brings about efficient allocation of resources, improved organization, and technological development. These, in turn, cause increased production and lower prices; in short, economic growth. The chief obstacle to such growth is viewed as imposition of restrictions by governments. Although all governments necessarily impose some restrictions, according to standard economic theory these should be kept to a minimum.

Equally important is the size of the market. The larger the market, the more specialization can be achieved within it. Increased specialization leads to "economies of scale," that is, to increased efficiency, lower prices, and more consumption. Most nations have national markets within which investments and goods flow freely and a high degree of specialization is possible. Since World War II the goal has been a global free market that allows for much greater specialization internationally.

The major obstacle to this global market is restriction placed on economic action across national boundaries. Tariffs are imposed, exports are controlled, and ownership of business by outsiders is limited. These policies cause the people of a country to produce for themselves what could be produced more cheaply by others. Total production is less than it could be.

The global economic institutions work to reduce all such barriers to trade with their accompanying inefficiencies. Ratification by all national participants of the recently completed GATT negotiations (called the Uruguay Round) will go a long way toward realizing these goals. It will establish the World Trade Organization (WTO) as the arbiter of international disputes. Meanwhile, short of global economic integration, the free market can be expanded regionally. The two most important expansions thus far have been the European Community and the North American Free Trade Agreement (NAFTA).

SUCCESS AND LIMITATIONS

The single-minded pursuit of global economic growth has achieved many of its goals. From the end of World War II until around 1980 the global economy grew at a remarkable rate (Green, 1984). Some countries moved from poverty to affluence, inspiring others to see this as a possibility for themselves as well. At the same time, the already affluent nations greatly increased their wealth. The market magic worked. The growth of some was not at the expense of others but rather facilitated the growth of others.

Nonenvironmental Issues

When one goal is pursued in this way, it is inevitable that there will be unintended side effects. Successful cases of rapid growth, such as South Korea, Taiwan, and Singapore, all had highly authoritarian governments during the important take-off stage. These were needed to maintain discipline in a laboring class that was being severely exploited (Bello & Rosenfeld, 1990). However, when growth reached a certain level, some of the prosperity was shared with the workers, and at that point the governments could become less authoritarian. Although few citizens of democracies are attracted to these methods, the promise that in time the exploited would also profit from the policies required for growth has come true to a considerable degree. Thus the general conviction that rapid economic growth makes possible the solution of other problems, including those it creates, has been reinforced.

A second problem has been that the breakdown of established communities, inherent in growth-oriented policies, has led to the moral decay of some societies. For example, in many tropical countries the displacement of peasant farms with modern agribusiness monoculture has reduced the need for farm labor and sent millions of people to the slums surrounding cities. There traditional social values are hard to maintain. This breakdown can be illustrated in the United States as well, where levels of family instability, crime, drugs, and social alienation have increased along with the urbanization associated with growth of the gross national product (GNP). This raises questions about the wisdom of our primary commitment to growth-oriented policies. The reply is often that more growth is needed in order to reintegrate alienated people into the economic system and to have the resources to deal with all social needs.

A third problem is that, alongside the success stories, there are other countries in which economic growth has not kept up with the increase of population (Brown, 1987). This is especially common in sub-Saharan Africa. In many of these countries growth-oriented policies have concentrated wealth in fewer hands, so that masses of the people are much poorer than they were before these policies were put into effect.

The response is usually that this results from imperfect implementation of market policies. Too many governments have tried to manage economic developments bureaucratically, have taxed business too much, have inhibited free trade, have yielded to political pressures (David, 1985). On this assumption the task is to overcome these restrictions on business activity and allow the economy to grow rapidly enough to absorb the unemployed and improve the standard of living of all. The restructuring agreements imposed by the IMF on debtor countries move in this direction (Cobb, 1994).

Environmental Issues

A fourth problem has been environmental. When firms compete with each other in the free market, their decisions are not guided by environmental considerations. They can produce more cheaply when they dispose of their wastes in the least expensive way—for example, in the nearest river. The loss of fish is costly to fishermen, and the loss of recreational areas diminishes the quality of life for others, but as long as competitors are also disposing of wastes in this cheap way, no manufacturer can afford to do otherwise. The cost is borne by society as a whole. Recognizing this, all advanced industrial nations have rules governing the disposal of industrial waste.

Most advocates of the free market affirm the need of such rules. They recognize that market activity has unintended side effects that transfer costs to third parties. These are called "externalities" (Daly & Cobb, 1994). In an ideal market all externalities would be internalized, so that the purchaser pays the full cost of the goods. As long as all producers within the market abide by the same rules, there is "a level playing field."

Unfortunately, the desirability of internalizing social costs through governmental regulations has not been assimilated into the thinking of most of the economists who influence policies. The problem is particularly acute as free markets are expanded beyond national boundaries. When this happens, differing regulations in the countries involved destroy the level playing field and give the advantage to industries in the country with the lowest standards.

The progressive reduction of barriers to trade between the United States and Mexico during the 1980s serves as an example of the problem. As tariffs were reduced, many U.S. companies found it more economical to relocate production across the border. One reason they could produce more cheaply there was that they did not have to spend money on expensive waste disposal. They could dump their wastes into the Rio Grande. They could ship their products back into the United States to undersell the goods of competitors who were subject to U.S. rules. Now it is recognized that the river should be cleaned up. The best proposals now being considered at the governmental level are for an expenditure of nine billion dollars for this purpose. The Sierra Club estimates that the cost for a real cleanup would be twenty-one billion dollars (Sierra Club, 1993, p. 16). In any case, these costs are to be borne primarily by the taxpayers and concerned citizens of Mexico and the United States, rather than by the polluters.

In the negotiation of NAFTA under the Bush administration, little attention was given to these environmental matters. The goal was to secure existing U.S. investments in Mexico, improve the climate for additional investment, and thus increase the total growth rate of North America. The Clinton administration is more concerned with environmental issues, but the basic problem of the lack of a level playing field is still dealt with only tangentially in a side agreement to NAFTA.

The problem is not only with regard to those plants that actually move across the border. The problem is also with legislation within the United States. If a state desires, for environmental reasons, to enact new restrictive legislation, it is told that more of its businesses will move away. In view of the number of polluting industries that have already moved across the Mexican border, it is clear that this is not always an idle threat! If the industry wishes to remain in the United States, it may still find it advantageous to move—from California to Utah, for example. The extension of the free market beyond political boundaries inherently makes it more difficult to slow environmental decay within those boundaries.

The exhaustion of resources is a somewhat different problem. With regard to pollution, the problem is that those committed to economic growth fail to pay attention to an accepted economic principle, namely, that external costs should be internalized. With regard to resources, the problem is that economic thinking has not developed the needed principle—instead, it is based on the idea that natural resources are, for practical purposes, inexhaustible.

The assumption of inexhaustible resources has gained repeated reinforcement from experience. For example, when an ore is said to be exhausted, this means only that mining the remaining inferior grades of ore is not profitable at current prices with current technology. As prices rise and new technology is developed, more ore can be extracted. Also, plastics can be devised as substitutes for scarce minerals. Thus economists typically hold that we should give technological ingenuity a free hand and allow the market to provide the needed incentives.

Unfortunately, this theory has led to blindness to the actual effects of the free market in many parts of the world. Since industry is the sector of the economy capable of continuing growth, growth-oriented policies emphasize the export of whatever is available in order to bring in the capital needed for industrialization. In many countries the available resource most desired by the global market is lumber. Accordingly, the earth as a whole is being rapidly deforested.

To understand what is happening, Alan Durning asks us to imagine a time lapse film of the earth.

Since 1950 vast tracts of forest vanish from Japan, the Philippines, and the mainland of Southeast Asia, from most of Central America and the horn of Africa, from western North America and eastern South America, from the Indian subcontinent and sub-Saharan Africa. Fires rage in the Amazon basin where they never did before. Central Europe's forests die, poisoned by the air and the rain. Southeast Asia looks like a dog with the mange. Malaysian Borneo is scalped... The clearing spreads to Siberia and the Canadian north. (Durning, 1994, p. 22)

It is almost meaningless to speak of substituting other resources for forest cover. The loss of forest cover leads to extensive erosion, which limits the possibility of reforestation. It also destroys large tracts of agricultural land. It leads to the extinction of species. It takes away the livelihood of those who have depended on this resource. It changes the weather both locally and globally. There is no way in which its costs could be adequately internalized, although, if economists had undertaken such calculations, this might have helped to slow down the process of deforestation. Technology, in the form of developing new types of trees that grow more rapidly and survive on poorer soil, can play a positive role once the devastation has occurred, but it is a small compensation for what has been permanently lost.

The global economic system is not the only cause of the reduction of forest cover, but it has been and continues to be the major factor. The growth-oriented switch from peasant farms to agribusiness displaces many lowland farmers onto forested hillsides, which they must then clear if they are to survive. Many countries export lumber on an unsustainable basis in order to get the capital for industrialization. Those governments that do wish to preserve this basic resource for use by their own people are inhibited from doing so by the need to increase their exports as part of the structural adjustment imposed by the IMF (Bello, 1994).

Advocates of growth-oriented policies sometimes argue that, however regrettable some of these environmental losses are, economic growth will offer rewards that more than compensate. Growth also enables societies to afford the luxury of setting aside selected areas for scenic and recreational enjoyment. These supporters of the growth solution point out that it is affluent nations that best protect their environment. If we pursue growth-oriented policies unflinchingly, they claim, eventually all countries will be able to give high priority to reducing the pollution of their environment and to protecting natural resources. Thus the response to issues of unsustainability is like the response to problems of social breakdown and injustice. For standard economic thinking, economic growth is the only solution.

SUSTAINABLE GROWTH

Most advocates of growth-oriented solutions now recognize that some actions taken for the sake of growth are not sustainable. For example, the extensive use of chemicals that deplete the ozone layer is recognized as unsustainable. An agreement was reached in 1987, The Montreal Protocol, to curtail the production of these chemicals (Meadows, Meadows, & Randers, 1992). Although some economists might argue that the elimination of some popular species of fish would not much matter, since others could be substituted or technology could invent substitutes for our table, most agree that it is better to aim at sustainable limits of fishing particular stocks, at least on a global basis. Accordingly, there is general consensus that some forms of economic growth are better than others—that is, economic growth that is not destructive of the natural environment (or of social order) is preferable to that which is.

This recognition is given its most influential expression in what is often called "the Brundtland Report" by the United Nations World Commission on Environment and Development headed by a former prime minister of Norway, Gro Brundtland. The official title of the report is *Our Common Future* (Brundtland, 1987).

This report describes well the multiple interrelated environmental and human problems afflicting the planet. It recognizes that economic development thus far has not led to a decrease in human misery. It shows utmost sensitivity for the suffering of the global poor. It argues that overriding priority should be given to their needs, and also that development should meet the needs of the present without compromising the ability of future generations to meet theirs.

The report points out that current practices are wasteful. It leans heavily on the sorts of insights that Hunter and Amory Lovins have so effectively highlighted—namely, that if we used our resources more efficiently, we could continue present high levels of consumption with much less pressure on the environment (Lovins, 1977).

Our Common Future proposes that the global poor need greatly increased per capita consumption in order to have a decent life. Since their numbers will also continue to increase, the report calls for a five-to tenfold increase of goods and services for them. This might appear to be threatening to those who are committed to continuing and strengthening the present global economic system, since it prepares us to think of restricting growth in the already affluent nations and concentrating it in the poorer ones, while making sure that wealth in these countries is fairly distributed.

In fact, no such proposal is made. Instead, the report assumes that the present global system will continue. In this system the poor can be benefited only as the rich grow richer, that is, only by, and in proportion to, an increase in the total economy. Hence, a five-to tenfold increase of consumption by the poor requires a similar increase in consumption by the rich. The only answer to how such growth can occur without intensifying ecological destruction is that resources can be used more efficiently and that particularly destructive channels of growth can be avoided).

Those who are primarily concerned for justice and sustainability agree that many of the poor need greatly increased consumption. The increase in total global production required to make this possible could be covered by more efficient use of resources. Care in avoiding especially dangerous types of growth might enable humanity to find its way through the current crisis, increasing the consumption by the poor and maintaining the affluence of the rich, while relating sustainably to the environment. But the proposal that the rich must grow richer by the same percentage as the poor is disastrous.

When a family with $1500 a year increases its income to $4500, this is an increase of only $3000. The family needs it and the Earth can afford it. When a family with $150,000 a year increases its income to $450,000, this is an increase of $300,000. The family does not need it, and the earth cannot afford the additional consumption.

It may be claimed, nevertheless, that this is the only realistic possibility for helping the poor. The forces that now rule the world will not accept any form of development for the poor that does not increase their own wealth and power. Any program designed to help the poor while leaving the affluent where they are would require a massive shift of power that is now unthinkable.

But is this true "realism"? Is a five-to ten-fold increase in global industrial output possible? Even if half of this increase came from greater efficiency in the use of resources, the answer is "No." Present levels of resource use and pollution are unsustainable (Postel, 1994). Tripling or quadrupling these levels is not a realistic option.

Furthermore, the policies directed to the end of increasing production have always proved costly to the poor. In some instances, as noted above, successful countries have been able to compensate their poor at later stages of development with improved living standards. But on a global basis such success is impossible. To continue policies that harm the poor now for the sake of a later improvement that cannot occur is profoundly unjust.

The disastrous consequences of the global system are already visible in many parts of the world, and especially in parts of Africa. In "The Coming Anarchy," Robert D. Kaplan (1994) describes the vast migration to the cities throughout the "developing" world and the rise of slums as major centers of population. He details the situation in West Africa, and especially Sierra Leone, as a warning of where tendencies in many other places are leading.

The exploitation of the people and resources of this part of Africa goes back to the slave trade and the colonial period. However, it was accelerated with the neocolonial system that developed after World War II with political independence. Forests covered 60% of Sierra Leone at independence in 1961. Now this area has been reduced to 6%, and the export of logs continues. Deforestation has resulted in widespread erosion of former farmland, and deforested land has become swampy, ideal breeding grounds for malarial mosquitoes. The population has continued to grow, while the basis of livelihood in the rural area declined. The result has been massive urban migration, chiefly to new slums where water supply and sewers are not distinguished.

The Sierra Leone government maintains some order in the cities during the day, none by night. Other armies roam the countryside. AIDS and tuberculosis spread rapidly. Malaria is extremely widespread, and is no longer responsive to earlier forms of treatment. Fear of malaria keeps outsiders away. In any case, with the disappearance of the forests and the end of the cold war, foreign powers have little interest in what happens.

COUNTERING THE IDEALIZATION OF GROWTH

The Brundtland Report assumes that increased consumption is a good thing, needed especially by the poor. It accepts the trickledown approach to their economic well-being as the only one available. Given these assumptions, its proposals may be as good as can be found. But since they lead to an impasse, and since policies based on this report will continue to sacrifice the poor and add to the pressure on the environment, we need to think about an alternative global economic system. This, of course, will be seen as "unrealistic," since "realism" requires that we accept the present system and only propose policies that are compatible with it. But it is better to be unrealistic than to support a global direction that has already brought catastrophe to many and will eventually lead to catastrophe for all.

Little progress can be made toward a different way of envisaging the global system as long as "growth" is viewed as a, indeed *the,* self-evident good. Demystification of growth requires recognition that increased per capita GNP, which is the standard meaning of "growth," is not identical with improvement in the economic well-being of real human beings. To promote this demystification, I have worked with others (especially Clifford W. Cobb) to develop an Index of Sustainable Economic Welfare (ISEW) for the United States (Cobb & Cobb, 1994).

Computation of the ISEW begins with personal consumption, but them adjusts this in relation to income distribution. (Our assumption is that the well-being of the society as a whole is affected by the condition of the poorest.) The index then adds for household services, chiefly the contribution of housewives. It subtracts for "defensive costs," that is, costs that result from economic growth and the social changes, such as urbanization, that accompany it. (For example, the cost of commuting to work should not be viewed as an addition to welfare just because it adds to the GNP.) This applies also to the cost of pollution. Since it is an index of *sustainable* welfare, it subtracts for the reduction of natural capital, and adds or subtracts for change in the net international position.

The index can be used to compare growth as measured by per capital GNP with economic welfare as measured by per capita ISEW. From 1951 to 1990, (in 1972 dollars) per capita GNP for the U.S. more than doubled from $3741 to $7756; per capita ISEW rose less than 15% from $2793 to $3253. This suggests that economic well-being can be improved better in other ways than by simply seeking GNP growth. This suggestion is reinforced by figures for the second half of this period. From 1971 to 1990, per capita GNP rose from $5405 to $7756, or 43%; per capita ISEW *fell* from $3425 to $3253, or 5%.

Only *economic* welfare is considered in these calculations. Other indicators of social health in the United States, such as family stability, the quality of public education, crime, alcohol and drug abuse, and citizen participation in political life, show that significant social decline has accompanied growth of production.

The disconnection between economic growth and social well-being can be illustrated by international comparisons as well. One example is infant mortality rates. In 1990, Sri Lanka, with a per capital GNP of only 1/2x that of the United States, and in the midst of ethnic strife amounting to civil war, had an infant mortality rate of 19 per 1000, only slightly more than the 17.6 figure for black citizens of the United States (Jackson, 1993). Clearly the reduction of infant mortality is not dependent on, or guaranteed by, the increase of GNP.

Over a broader front, the state of Kerala in India shows that many social needs can be met without significant economic growth. The per capita income in Kerala is about the same as that for India as a whole. But, with regard to infant mortality and life expectancy, it ranks well in comparison with highly industrialized nations. At the same time it has greatly reduced its rate of population growth without resorting to authoritarian measures. It has achieved this by educating its people, and especially its women, about health and population issues, providing inexpensive care to all, and meeting other basic needs (Alexander, 1994; Franke & Chasin, 1989).

The danger of using GNP growth as an indicator of well-being can be illustrated in another way. When peasants lose their land to multinational agribusiness, some of them are employed. Their wages show up in GNP. Their basic inability to feed and house themselves is not counted as a loss. Hence, even though they are less well fed and housed as employees than they were as independent peasants, the GNP goes up. If these large estates were broken up again into peasant holdings, the new owners would be better off. But this could not be ascertained from GNP figures.

This means that even the idealistic proposal to which the Brundtland Report *might* lead, that is, increase of per capita consumption by the poor without increasing that of the rich, is a poor guide to what is needed. Our concern should be that the poor have access to the means of production whereby they can feed, clothe, and house themselves and have an enjoyable life free from external oppression. How this would show up in GNP figures should be a secondary consideration or not one at all. The question is whether we can envision a world in which the basic needs of all, and some less basic ones as well, are met without continuing unsustainable pressures on the environment.

AN ALTERNATIVE GLOBAL ECONOMIC SYSTEM

The centerpiece of the present global economic system is the principle that the greater the specialization in production, the more efficiently workers can produce. The larger the market, the more specialization is possible. Hence the ideal is a global free market in which everyone everywhere concentrates on producing what is best produced in that location and imports everything else from other regions. The ideal is complete global interdependence.

The intended and actual consequence of present economic policy is that no community or nation feeds, or houses, or clothes itself. All of this is to depend on trade. This trade is "free" in the sense that the firms engaged in it are free from interference or restriction by governments. But the people of each region are not free *not* to trade. They cannot live without importing the necessities for their livelihood, however unfavorable the terms of trade may be.

An alternate ideal is one on which relatively small regions are relatively self-sufficient economically. People of such regions can then make basic decisions about themselves and about the rules by which they are governed. They are free to trade or not according to the terms of trade that are attractive to them. Not to trade means to deny themselves many desirable goods, but it does not threaten their healthy survival.

Within such regions the market should be as free as possible. The community should set the terms on which all firms compete, including standards dealing with minimum wages, workplace safety, and the environment. These requirements on the producers will internalize the social costs that result from inadequate wages, poor health, and pollution.

If these requirements are not to be unfair to producers, then goods produced elsewhere, where low wages, poor working conditions, and extensive pollution are tolerated, cannot be allowed to undersell local products. Tariffs at least equal to the extra costs of production within the region must be assessed. The region would establish its trading policies with its social goals in view—not for the sake of minimizing prices and maximizing global specialization and production. One of its goals would be to encourage other regions to organize their economies in similar ways, and tariffs could be used to this end.

The terms "relatively small" and "relatively self-sufficient" are intentionally vague. There may be places where this can realistically refer to a single village. In other instances it may be pointless to seek anything resembling self-sufficiency at a level smaller than a nation. In either case it requires that several competing producers can be supported in the region.

In most cases, there would be several levels of organization with different types of production involved. For example, in the United States a region the size of a country might become relatively self-sufficient with regard to most of the necessities of life. But the production of cars would make sense only in a region including several states, and aircraft production might be at the national level.

Each productive activity should take place in as small a region as is practical, with the recognition that for some purposes this region will be quite large. The smaller regions are communities, and the larger regions are communities of communities and communities of communities of communities. In all cases, the political unit will include the economic one and set conditions for competition within it. No subordination of political institutions to economic ones will be allowed.

The communities of communities would be governed by representatives of the communities governed. They should also have responsibility to ensure that the local communities function as such, that is, that they not exclude any of their residents from the rights and privileges of citizenship. They also would not allow any community to export pollution to its neighbors.

Although there is little need for production to take place at the global level, there are many problems that can only be dealt with there. The United Nations already functions as a community of nations. That is, its decisions are made by representatives of nations, which themselves should be transformed into communities of communities. The United Nations should be strengthened in order to deal with those issues that can only be confronted globally, such as the protection of local resources whose value is global, as well as countering and mitigating international conflict. On the other hand, the Bretton Woods institutions should be dismantled, since they embody the principle of the independence of economic institutions from political ones. Their necessary functions should be taken over by agencies fully responsible to the General Assembly of the United Nations. This would restore the subordination of economic institutions to political ones in which the will of the people *can* be expressed.

The primacy of the political over the economic, combined with weakening global economic institutions, would make possible economic decentralization. It would be possible for nations and even regions within nations to develop relatively self-sufficient economies. They would then trade with one another only as this did not weaken their capacity to meet their own basic needs. They would cooperate in establishing larger markets for goods that cannot be efficiently produced for smaller ones.

Since much of the unsustainability of the present economy stems from the appropriation of the resources of the poorer countries by the richer ones, the ending of the present global economic system would counter this. For example, most of the rapid deforestation of the planet is for the sake of export, either of lumber or of beef that can be raised on formerly forested land. If the focus of attention is on the local economy, the value of the standing forest counts for more. In this and other ways, in regions which were not heavily oriented to export, the people would often be concerned that their region continue to provide a habitable home to their children, and they would be more likely to adopt sustainable relations to the environment.

Nevertheless, policies that commend themselves locally may have negative consequences globally. An example is production of ozone-destroying chemicals. They may be produced in a part of the world where destruction of the ozone layer does not seem a pressing problem. The most threatened regions may have little direct political clout with those that cause the danger. Global political institutions must have the power to protect the global environment from such local infringements. Global warming may prove another problem that will require strict rules from the global level to be enforced in every region.

FANTASY OR POSSIBLE FUTURE?

I have proposed a global order that *could* be relatively just and sustainable. Economic decentralization would reduce pressure on the environment and give people more participation in the decisions that are important for their lives. It would not guarantee that those decisions would be wise, however. This is not a utopia. It *does* offer a chance for a decent survival, one that continuation of present policies precludes.

It can still be objected that this is too different from the structures and practices to which we are accustomed, that it appeals to motives that have been subordinated to profit and consumerism, that it implies a transfer of power that no one is in a position to effect, that it requires changes that would be painful. One's response to these objections will depend on the degree of one's distress about what is now taking place and the impending catastrophes. Those who are relatively content with what has been happening and are able to avoid thinking of catastrophes to come will conclude that it is better to continue muddling along, mitigating suffering where possible, and adapting to the rest. Those who are truly concerned about the suffering now occurring because of dominant policies, and those who are unable to accept continued movement toward the precipice as "realistic," will acknowledge the extreme difficulty of changing direction, but will take the first step.

That step is the acknowledgment that the redirection of efforts is urgent. Only in that context can there be serious discussion of further steps that can and should be taken. Hoping that some of my readers share with me the sense of urgency, I will describe further steps that are now possible in order to begin the shift of direction.

The next step is to raise the consciousness of those who are already deeply concerned about injustice and unsustainability. Too many of them have accepted the idea that justice and sustainability can be attained by, or in tandem with, the pursuit of growth-oriented policies, assuming that economic growth is inherently beneficial. Exposing the fallacy of this assumption may make it possible to mobilize the natural constituencies for economic policies that would make for justice and sustainability.

The environmental movement is one such constituency. A substantial part of this movement has begun to understand the close connection between environmental decay and policies aimed at economic growth. Several major environmental organizations, such as the Sierra Club and Greenpeace, opposed NAFTA, along with the Humane Society. On the other hand, many environmental organizations, including the Natural Resources Defense Council, the Environmental Defense Fund, and the National Audubon Society, supported it. They were pleased that with its side agreements it introduced environmental considerations into a trade agreement for the first time, and they see that it offers promise in dealing with specific environmental problems such as the polluted Rio Grande. They see the basic relation between economic growth and environmental protection as positive.

Rosemary Ostergen (personal communication, March 2, 1994), Director of Membership of the Environmental Defense Fund, wrote to those supporters of the Fund who had questioned its advocacy of NAFTA. She stated, "We believe that collective action and economic growth will prove to be a more effective vehicle to prevent further environmental degradation from occurring in North America." Not mentioned were the facts that it is precisely the sort of undirected economic growth promoted by the agreement that polluted the Rio Grande, that the expansion of such growth will add to pollution elsewhere, that NAFTA's promotion of agribusiness will displace millions of peasants and degrade the soil, and that it will speed up the exploitation of other resources in Mexico. In other words, like many environmentalists, the Environmental Defense Fund does not see the inherent conflict between sustaining the environment and policies directed toward increasing the GNP.

Labor is a second natural constituency for changing the direction of the global economy. In relation to the test case of NAFTA, organized labor understood its interests better than many of the environmentalists. Since the globalization of the economy has already depressed wages in the United States, and it was easy to see that NAFTA was one more step in this direction, the leaders of organized labor were united in opposition. Unfortunately, the globalization of the economy has already greatly weakened organized labor. Also, labor leaders did not articulate an alternative vision for the economic future; so they appeared to be opposing "progress" for the sake of "special interests."

The growing underclass is a third group that, if it were able to function as a constituency, would certainly have reason to support change. This underclass is created by the global economy and will continue to grow as long as the present growth-oriented, globalizing policies are in effect. Unfortunately, the underclass is poorly organized and is forced to exist on a day-by-day basis, rather than to dream dreams of a new economic order.

Communitarians constitute a fourth natural constituency of support for change. Unfortunately, many of them are also neoliberals in economic thinking, not recognizing that it is the application of standard economic principles that systematically undermines community (e.g., Etzioni, 1983). Other communitarians ignore economic issues, concentrating on social and political ones, not realizing that all the progress they make there can often be wiped out by a single decision made by a distant corporation.

Humanitarians are a fifth such constituency. The present policies are brutal in their effects of billions of people. The suffering will grow worse and will not be compensated in most countries by an eventual improvement. Nevertheless, most humanitarians are persuaded that economic growth is an essential part of the solution to human problems. Most continue to suppose that an increase in per capita GNP indicates that the lot of human beings is improving. Most do not see that the catastrophes that are coming upon humanity are the result of just these growth-oriented policies (e.g., Sherman, 1992; Weaver, 1994).

Even if all these natural constituencies for change were mobilized, could they give a different direction to the global system? Each year the transnational corporations and the elites all over the world, who profit from the present global system, grow more powerful. By supporting trade that cannot be controlled or regulated at the national level, governments are surrendering to these corporations control not only over international economic transactions but also over the laws that operate within their own countries (Nader, 1994). This surrender is now embodied in binding international agreements such as NAFTA and GATT. Billions of people have been persuaded that political institutions are inefficient and corrupt and that only business leaders can get "the job" done. Could all this be reversed?

Not easily, certainly. Probably not until more catastrophes strike and people grow more desperate. But desperation by itself is more likely to lead to acceptance of totalitarian governments than to decentralization of economic and political power, unless a vision of a livable alternative already has strong support. Otherwise, most will continue to believe the solution to the problems caused by global economic integration is more rigorous application of the policies directed to that end.

Meanwhile, in addition to raising consciousness about the incompatibility of aiming primarily at economic growth with the attainment of justice and sustainability, we can form alliances to oppose further steps in the direction now called "progress." We can also support subdominant trends that appear in many areas. Even within business there is growing recognition that highly centralized control is not efficient. Decentralization of decision making does occur. There are political movements in the same direction.

There is increasing recognition that top-down development projects do not work. For example, the World Bank, after much criticism, finally withdrew from the Narmada Project in India, the largest water project ever undertaken. Development for the sake of the people should begin instead where they are and help them attain their own goals along the lines articulated in "Another Development" (Ekins, 1992, chap. 5).

There are significant movements in agriculture away from land-exploiting agribusiness toward small scale stewardship of land by families. And there are many communities that are, as far as the present economy allows, taking more responsibility for their own lives (Fisher, 1993). Some institutions are beginning to support local farmers and business rather than tie into the national and global economies (Valen, 1992). Some colleges and universities are introducing programs of study that clarify the present functioning of the global economy and its consequences and promote thinking about alternatives. Many individuals are reordering their lives around service rather than around gaining wealth, and the New Roadmap Foundation works to encourage this decision (Dominguez & Robin, 1992). Thus, while the dominant trends at the top lead to injustice and unsustainability, there is a new ferment among the peoples of the world calling for and embodying new directions.

REFERENCES

Alexander, W. M. (1994, April). *Exceptional Kerala: Efficient and sustainable human behavior.* Paper distributed at the Seventh International Conference for Human Ecology, Michigan State University, East Lansing, MI.

Bello, W., with Cunningham, S., & Rau, B. (1994). Dark victory: The United States, structural adjustment and global poverty. London: Pluto Press.

Bello, W., & Rosenfeld, S. (1990). Dragons in distress: Asia's miracle economies in crisis. San Francisco: Food First.

Brown, L. R. (1987). Analyzing the demographic trap. In L.R. Brown (Ed.), State of the world (pp. 20–37). New York: W. W. Norton.

Brundtland, G. (Ed.). (1987). Our common future. New York: World Commission on Environment and Trade.

Cobb, C. W., & Cobb, J. B., Jr. (1994). The Green National Product: A proposed index of sustainable economic welfare. Lanham, MD: University Press of America.

Cobb, J. B., Jr. (1994). Sustaining the common good: A Christian perspective on the global economy. Cleveland, OH: Pilgrim Press.

Daly, H. F., & Cobb, J. B., Jr. (1994). For the common good: Redirection the economy toward community, the environment, and a sustainable future. Boston: Beacon Press.

David, W. L. (1985). The IMF policy paradigm: The macroeconomics of stabilization, structural adjustment, and economic development. New York: Praeger Publishers.

Dominguez, J., & Robin, V. (1992). Your money or your life. New York: Viking/Penguin.

Durning, A. T. (1994). Redesigning the forest economy. In L.R. Brown (Ed.), State of the world (pp. 22–40). New York: W. W. Norton.

Ekins, P. (1992). A new world order: Grassroots movements for global change. London: Routledge.

Etzioni, A. (1983). An immodest agenda. New York: McGraw-Hill.

Fisher, J. (1993). The road from Rio: Sustainable development and the nongovernmental movement in the Third World. Westport, CT: Praeger.

Franke, R., & Chasin, B. (1989). Kerala: Radical reform as development in an Indian state. San Francisco: Food First Institute.

Green, R. H. (Ed.). (1984). The international financial system: An ecumenical critique. Geneva World Council of Churches.

Jackson, R. L. (1993, December 16). Panel calls for U.S. to curb infant deaths. Los Angeles Times, p. A37.

Kaplan, R. D. (1994, February). The coming anarchy. The Atlantic Monthly, pp. 44–76.

Kock, K. (1969). International trade policy and the Gatt. Stockholm: Almquist & Wiksell.

Lovins, A. B. (1977). Soft energy paths: Toward a durable peace. San Francisco: Friends of the Earth.

Meadows, D. H., Meadows, D. L., & Randers, J. (1992). Beyond the limits: Confronting global collapse: Envisioning a sustainable future. Post Mills, VT: Chelsea Green.

Nader, R. (1994, May/June). GATT threatens U.S. environment, consumer protection laws. Public Citizen, pp. 18–21.

Postel, S. (1994). Carrying capacity: Earth's bottom line. In L. R. Brown (Ed.), State of the world (pp. 3–21). New York: W. W. Norton.

Raghavan, C. (1990). Recolonization: GATT, the Uruguay round, & the Third World. Penang: Third World Network.

Sherman, A. (1992, December 9). Rethinking development: A market-friendly strategy for the poor. Christian Century, pp. 1130–1134.

SierraClub. (1993, October 6). Analysis of the North American Free Trade Agreement and the North American Agreement on Environmental cooperation. Washington. DC: Author.

Smith, A. (1991). An inquiry into the nature and causes of the wealth of nations. New York: Alfred Knopf (Original work published 1776).

Valen, G. L. (1992). Hendrix College local food project. In D. J. Eagan & D. W. Orr (Eds.). The campus and environmental responsibility (pp. 77–87). San Francisco: Jossey-Bass.

Van Dormael, A. (1978). Bretton Woods: Birth of a monetary system. New York: Holmes & Meier.

Weaver, J. H. (1994, March 16). Can we achieve broad-based sustainable development? Christian Century, pp. 282–284.

STUDY QUESTIONS

1. Summarize Cobb's description of our current economic system. What are some of the nonenvironmental problems with it?

2. Why is "economic growth" potentially at odds with environmental integrity and social justice?

3. Outline Cobb's vision of a just economic future.

69

What Every Environmentalist Needs to Know About Capitalism

FRED MAGDOFF AND JOHN BELLAMY FOSTER

For those concerned with the fate of the earth, the time has come to face facts: not simply the dire reality of climate change but also the pressing need for social-system change. The failure to arrive at a world climate agreement in Copenhagen in December 2009 was not simply an abdication of world leadership, as is often suggested, but had deeper roots in the inability of the capitalist system to address the accelerating threat to life on the planet. Knowledge of the nature and limits of capitalism, and the means of transcending it, has therefore become a matter of survival. In the words of Fidel Castro in December 2009: "Until very recently, the discussion [on the future of world society] revolved around the kind of society we would have. Today, the discussion centers on whether human society will survive."[1]

1. THE PLANETARY ECOLOGICAL CRISIS

There is abundant evidence that humans have caused environmental damage for millennia. Problems with deforestation, soil erosion, and salinization of irrigated soils go back to antiquity. Plato wrote in *Critias*:

> What proof then can we offer that it [the land in the vicinity of Athens] is… now a mere remnant of what it once was?… You are left (as with little islands) with

something rather like the skeleton of a body wasted by disease; the rich, soft soil has all run away leaving the land nothing but skin and bone. But in those days the damage had not taken place, the hills had high crests, the rocky plane of Phelleus was covered with rich soil, and the mountains were covered by thick woods, of which there are some traces today. For some mountains which today will only support bees produced not so long ago trees which when cut provided roof beams for huge

From *Monthly Review*, Vol. 61, No. 10 (March 2010). Reprinted by permission.

buildings whose roofs are still standing. And there were a lot of tall cultivated trees which bore unlimited quantities of fodder for beasts. The soil benefited from an annual rainfall which did not run to waste off the bare earth as it does today, but was absorbed in large quantities and stored in retentive layers of clay, so that what was drunk down by the higher regions flowed downwards into the valleys and appeared everywhere in a multitude of rivers and springs. And the shrines which still survive at these former springs are proof of the truth of our present account of the country.[2]

What is different in our current era is that there are many more of us inhabiting more of the earth, we have technologies that can do much greater damage and do it more quickly, and we have an economic system that knows no bounds. The damage being done is so widespread that it not only degrades local and regional ecologies, but also affects the planetary environment.

There are many sound reasons that we, along with many other people, are concerned about the current rapid degradation of the earth's environment. Global warming, brought about by human-induced increases in greenhouse gases (CO_2, methane, N_2O, etc.), is in the process of destabilizing the world's climate—with horrendous effects for most species on the planet and humanity itself now increasingly probable. Each decade is warmer than the one before, with 2009 tying as the second warmest year (2005 was the warmest) in the 130 years of global instrumental temperature records.[3] Climate change does not occur in a gradual, linear way, but is non-linear, with all sorts of amplifying feedbacks and tipping points. There are already clear indications of accelerating problems that lie ahead. These include:

- Melting of the Artic Ocean ice during the summer, which reduces the reflection of sunlight as white ice is replaced by dark ocean, thereby enhancing global warming. Satellites show that end-of-summer Arctic sea ice was 40 percent less in 2007 than in the late 1970s when accurate measurements began.[4]

- Eventual disintegration of the Greenland and Antarctic ice sheets, set in motion by global warming, resulting in a rise in ocean levels. Even a sea level rise of 1–2 meters would be disastrous for hundreds of millions of people in low-lying countries such as Bangladesh and Vietnam and various island states. A sea level rise at a rate of a few meters per century is not unusual in the paleoclimatic record, and therefore has to be considered possible, given existing global warming trends. At present, more than 400 million people live within five meters above sea level, and more than one billion within twenty-five meters.[5]

- The rapid decrease of the world's mountain glaciers, many of which—if business-as-usual greenhouse gas emissions continue—could be largely gone (or gone altogether) during this century. Studies have shown that 90 percent of mountain glaciers worldwide are already visibly retreating as the planet warms. The Himalayan glaciers provide dry season water to countries with billions of people in Asia. Their shrinking will lead to floods and acute water scarcity. Already the melting of the Andean glaciers is contributing to floods in that region. But the most immediate, current, and long-term problem, associated with disappearing glaciers—visible today in Bolivia and Peru—is that of water shortages.[6]

- Devastating droughts, expanding possibly to 70 percent of the land area within several decades under business as usual; already becoming evident in northern India, northeast Africa, and Australia.[7]

- Higher levels of CO_2 in the atmosphere may increase the production of some types of crops, but they may then be harmed in future years by a destabilized climate that brings either dry or very wet conditions. Losses in rice yields have already been measured in parts of Southeast Asia, attributed to higher night temperatures that cause the plant to undergo enhanced nighttime respiration. This means losing more of what it produced by photosynthesis during the day.[8]

- Extinction of species due to changes in climate zones that are too rapid for species to move or adapt to, leading to the collapse of whole ecosystems dependent on these species, and the death of still more species. (See below for more details on species extinctions.)[9]

- Related to global warming, ocean acidification from increased carbon absorption is threatening the collapse of marine ecosystems. Recent indications suggest that ocean acidification may, in turn, reduce the carbon-absorption efficiency of the ocean. This means a potentially faster build-up of carbon dioxide in the atmosphere, accelerating global warming.[10]

While global climate change and its consequences, along with its "evil twin" of ocean acidification (also brought on by carbon emissions), present by far the greatest threats to the earth's species, including humans, there are also other severe environmental issues. These include contamination of the air and surface waters with industrial pollutants. Some of these pollutants (the metal mercury, for example) go up smoke stacks to later fall and contaminate soil and water, while others are leached into surface waters from waste storage facilities. Many ocean and fresh water fish are contaminated with mercury as well as numerous industrial organic chemicals. The oceans contain large "islands" of trash—"Light bulbs, bottle caps, toothbrushes, Popsicle sticks and tiny pieces of plastic, each the size of a grain of rice, inhabit the Pacific garbage patch, an area of widely dispersed trash that doubles in size every decade and is now believed to be roughly twice the size of Texas."[11]

In the United States, drinking water used by millions of people is polluted with pesticides such as atrazine as well as nitrates and other contaminants of industrial agriculture. Tropical forests, the areas of the greatest terrestrial biodiversity, are being destroyed at a rapid pace. Land is being converted into oil palm plantations in Southeast Asia—with the oil to be exported as a feedstock for making biodiesel fuel. In South America, rainforests are commonly first converted to extensive pastures and later into use for export crops such as soybeans. This deforestation is

causing an estimated 25 percent of all human-induced release of CO_2.[12] Soil degradation by erosion, overgrazing, and lack of organic material return threatens the productivity of large areas of the world's agricultural lands.

We are all contaminated by a variety of chemicals. A recent survey of twenty physicians and nurses tested for sixty-two chemicals in blood and urine—mostly organic chemicals such as flame retardants and plasticizers—found that

> each participant had at least 24 individual chemicals in their body, and two participants had a high of 39 chemicals detected.... All participants had bisphenol A [used to make rigid polycarbonate plastics used in water cooler bottles, baby bottles, linings of most metal food containers—and present in the foods inside these containers, kitchen appliances etc.], and some form of phthalates [found in many consumer products such as hair sprays, cosmetics, plastic products, and wood finishers], PBDEs [Polybrominated diphenyl ethers used as flame retardants in computers furniture, mattresses, and medical equipment] and PFCs [Perfluorinated compounds used in nonstick pans, protective coatings for carpets, paper coatings, etc.].[13]

Although physicians and nurses are routinely exposed to larger quantities of chemicals than the general public, we are all exposed to these and other chemicals that don't belong in our bodies, and that most likely have negative effects on human health. Of the 84,000 chemicals in commercial use in the United States, we don't even have an idea about the composition and potential harmfulness of 20 percent (close to 20,000)—their composition falls under the category of "trade secrets" and is legally withheld.[14]

Species are disappearing at an accelerated rate as their habitats are destroyed, due not only to global warming but also to direct human impact on species habitats. A recent survey estimated that over 17,000 animals and plants are at risk of extinction. "More than one in five of all known mammals, over a

but are actually good for society because they help to make our economy function "efficiently."

Let consider some of the key aspects of capitalism's conflict with environmental sustainability.

A. Capitalism Is a System that Must Continually Expand

No-growth capitalism is an oxymoron: when growth ceases, the system is in a state of crisis with considerable suffering among the unemployed. Capitalism's basic driving force and its whole reason for existence is the amassing of profits and wealth through the accumulation (savings and investment) process. It recognizes no limits to its own self-expansion—not in the economy as a whole; not in the profits desired by the wealthy; and not in the increasing consumption that people are cajoled into desiring in order to generate greater profits for corporations. The environment exists, not as a place with inherent boundaries within which human beings must live together with earth's other species, but as a realm to be exploited in a process of growing economic expansion.

Indeed, businesses, according to the inner logic of capital, which is enforced by competition, must either grow or die—as must the system itself. There is little that can be done to increase profits from production when there is slow or no growth. Under such circumstances, there is little reason to invest in new capacity, thus closing off the profits to be derived from new investment. There is also just so much increased profit that can be easily squeezed out of workers in a stagnant economy. Such measures as decreasing the number of workers and asking those remaining to "do more with less," shifting the costs of pensions and health insurance to workers, and introducing automation that reduces the number of needed workers can only go so far with out further destabilizing the system. If a corporation is large enough it can, like Wal-Mart, force suppliers, afraid of losing the business, to decrease their prices. But these means are not enough to satisfy what is, in fact, an insatiable quest for more profits, so corporations are continually engaged in struggle with their competitors (including frequently buying them out) to increase market share and gross sales.

It is true that the system can continue to move forward, to some extent, as a result of financial speculation leveraged by growing debt, even in the face of a tendency to slow growth in the underlying economy. But this means, as we have seen again and again, the growth of financial bubbles that inevitably burst.[24] There is no alternative under capitalism to the endless expansion of the "real economy" (i.e., production), irrespective of actual human needs, consumption, or the environment.

One might still imagine that it would be theoretically possible for a capitalist economy to have zero growth, and still meet all of humanity's basic needs. Let's suppose that all the profits that corporations earn (after allowing for replacing worn out equipment or buildings) are either spent by capitalists on their own consumption or given to workers as wages and benefits, and consumed. As capitalists and workers spend this money, they would purchase the goods and services produced, and the economy could stay at a steady state, no-growth level (what Marx called "simple reproduction" and has sometimes been called the "stationary state"). Since there would be no investment in new productive capacity, there would be no economic growth and accumulation, no profits generated.

There is, however, one slight problem with this "capitalist no-growth utopia": it violates the basic motive force of capitalism. What capital strives for and is the purpose of its existence is its own expansion. Why would capitalists, who in every fiber of their beings believe that they have a personal right to business profits, and who are driven to accumulate wealth, simply spend the economic surplus at their disposal on their own consumption or (less likely still) give it to workers to spend on theirs—rather than seek to expand wealth? If profits are not generated, how could economic crises be avoided under capitalism? To the contrary, it is clear that owners of capital will, as long as such ownership relations remain, do whatever they can within their power to maximize the amount of profits they accrue. A stationary state, or steady-state, economy as a stable solution is only conceivable if separated from the social relations of capital itself.

Capitalism is a system that constantly generates a reserve army of the unemployed; meaningful, full employment is a rarity that occurs only at very high rates of growth (which are correspondingly dangerous to ecological sustainability). Taking the U.S. economy as the example, let's take a look at what happens to the number of "officially" unemployed when the economy grows at different rates during a period of close to sixty years (Table 1).

For background, we should note that the U.S. population is growing by a little less than 1 percent a year, as is the net number of new entrants into the normal working age portion of the population. In current U.S. unemployment measurements, those considered to be officially unemployed must have looked for work within the last four weeks and cannot be employed in part-time jobs. Individuals without jobs, who have not looked for work during the previous four weeks (but who have looked within the last year), either because they believe there are no jobs available, or because they think there are none for which they are qualified, are classified as "discouraged" and are not counted as officially unemployed. Other "marginally attached workers," who have not recently looked for work (but have in the last year), not because they were "discouraged," but for other reasons, such as lack of affordable day care, are also excluded from the official unemployment count. In addition, those working part-time but wanting to work full-time are not considered to be officially unemployed. The

unemployment rate for the more expanded definition of unemployment (U-6) provided by the Bureau of Labor Statistics, which also includes the above categories (i.e., discouraged workers, other marginally attached workers, and part-time workers desiring full-time employment) is generally almost twice the official U.S. employment rate (U-3). In the following analysis, we focus only on the official unemployment data.

What, then, do we see in the relationship between economic growth and unemployment over the last six decades?

1. During the eleven years of very slow growth, less than 1.1 percent per year, unemployment increased in each of the years.

2. In 70 percent (nine of thirteen) of the years when GDP grew between 1.2 and 3 percent per year, unemployment also grew.

3. During the twenty-three years when the U.S. economy grew fairly rapidly (from 3.1 to 5.0 percent a year), unemployment still increased in three years and reduction in the percent unemployed was anemic in most of the others.

4. Only in the thirteen years when the GDP grew at greater than 5.0 percent annually did unemployment not increase in any of these years.

Although this table is based on calendar years and does not follow business cycles, which, of course, do not correspond neatly to the calendar, it is clear

TABLE 1   Change in Unemployment at Different Growth Rates of the Economy (1949–2008)

Change in real GDP from previous year	Average change in percent unemployment from pervious year*	Number of years	Years with growth in unemployment
<1.1	1.75	11	11
1.2–3.0	0.13	13	9
3.1–5.0	−0.25	23	3
>5.0	−1.02	13	0

*A negative number indicates a growth in employment.

Source: NIPA Table 1.1.1. Percent Change From Preceding Period in Real Gross Domestic Product.
Series Id: LNS14000000Q, Current Population Survey, Bureau of Labor Statistics, Quarterly Unemployment Rate.

that, if the GDP growth rate isn't substantially greater than the increase in population, people lose jobs. While slow or no growth is a problem for business owners trying to increase their profits, it is a disaster for working people.

What this tells us is that the capitalist system is a very crude instrument in terms of providing jobs in relation to growth—if growth is to be justified by employment. It will take a rate of growth of around 4 percent or higher, far above the average growth rate, before the unemployment problem is surmounted in U.S. capitalism today. Worth noting is the fact that, since the 1940s, such high rates of growth in the U.S. economy have hardly ever been reached except in times of wars.

B. Expansion Leads to Investing Abroad in Search of Secure Sources of Raw Materials, Cheaper Labor, and New Markets

As companies expand, they saturate, or come close to saturating, the "home" market and look for new markets abroad to sell their goods. In addition, they and their governments (working on behalf of corporate interests) help to secure entry and control over key natural resources such as oil and a variety of minerals. We are in the midst of a "land-grab," as private capital and government sovereign wealth funds strive to gain control of vast acreage throughout the world to produce food and biofuel feedstock crops for their "home" markets. It is estimated that some thirty million hectares of land (roughly equal to two-thirds of the arable land in Europe), much of them in Africa, have been recently acquired or are in the process of being acquired by rich countries and international corporations.[25]

This global land seizure (even if by "legal" means) can be regarded as part of the larger history of imperialism. The story of centuries of European plunder and expansion is well documented. The current U.S.-led wars in Iraq and Afghanistan follow the same general historical pattern, and are clearly related to U.S. attempts to control the main world sources of oil and gas.[26]

Today multinational (or transnational) corporations scour the world for resources and opportunities wherever they can find them, exploiting cheap labor in poor countries and reinforcing, rather than reducing, imperialist divisions. The result is a more rapacious global exploitation of nature and increased differentials of wealth and power. Such corporations have no loyalty to anything but their own bottom lines.

C. A System that, by Its Very Nature, Must Grow and Expand Will Eventually Come Up against the Reality of Finite Natural Resources

The irreversible exhaustion of finite natural resources will leave future generations without the possibility of having use of these resources. Natural resources are used in the process of production—oil, gas, and coal (fuel), water (in industry and agriculture), trees (for lumber and paper), a variety of mineral deposits (such as iron ore, copper, and bauxite), and so on. Some resources, such as forests and fisheries, are of a finite size, but can be renewed by natural processes if used in a planned system that is flexible enough to change as conditions warrant. Future use of other resources—oil and gas, minerals, aquifers in some desert or dryland areas (prehistorically deposited water)—are limited forever to the supply that currently exists. The water, air, and soil of the biosphere can continue to function well for the living creatures on the planet only if pollution doesn't exceed their limited capacity to assimilate and render the pollutants harmless.

Business owners and managers generally consider the short term in their operations—most take into account the coming three to five years, or, in some rare instances, up to ten years. This is the way they must function because of unpredictable business conditions (phases of the business cycle, competition from other corporations, prices of needed inputs, etc.) and demands from speculators looking for short-term returns. They therefore act in ways that are largely oblivious of the natural limits to their activities—as if there is an unlimited supply of natural resources for exploitation. Even if the reality of limitation enters their consciousness, it merely speeds up the exploitation of a given resource, which is extracted as rapidly as possible, with capital then moving on to new areas of resource exploitation. When each individual capitalist pursues the goal of making a profit and accumulating capital, decisions are made that collectively harm society as a whole.

The length of time before nonrenewable deposits are exhausted depends on the size of the deposit and the rate of extraction of the resource. While depletion of some resources may be hundreds of years away (assuming that the rate of growth of extraction remains the same), limits for some important ones—oil and some minerals—are not that far off. For example, while predictions regarding peak oil vary among energy analysts—going by the conservative estimates of oil companies themselves, at the rate at which oil is currently being used, known reserves will be exhausted within the next fifty years. The prospect of peak oil is projected in numerous corporate, government, and scientific reports. The question today is not whether peak oil is likely to arrive soon, but simply how soon.[27]

Even if usage doesn't grow, the known deposits of the critical fertilizer ingredient phosphorus that can be exploited on the basis of current technology will be exhausted in this century.[28]

Faced with limited natural resources, there is no rational way to prioritize under a modern capitalist system, in which the well-to-do with their economic leverage decide via the market how commodities are allocated. When extraction begins to decline, as is projected for oil within the near future, price increases will put even more pressure on what had been, until recently, the boast of world capitalism: the supposedly prosperous "middle-class" workers of the countries of the center.

The well-documented decline of many ocean fish species, almost to the point of extinction, is an example of how renewable resources can be exhausted. It is in the short-term individual interests of the owners of fishing boats—some of which operate at factory scale, catching, processing, and freezing fish—to maximize the take. Hence, the fish are depleted. No one protects the common interest.

In a system run generally on private self-interest and accumulation, the state is normally incapable of doing so. This is sometimes called the tragedy of the commons. But it should be called the tragedy of the private exploitation of the commons.

The situation would be very different if communities that have a stake in the continued availability of a resource managed the resource in place of the large-scale corporation. Corporations are subject to the single-minded goal of maximizing short-term profits—after which they move on, leaving devastation behind, in effect mining the earth. Although there is no natural limit to human greed, there are limits, as we are daily learning, to many resources, including "renewable" ones, such as the productivity of the seas. (The depletion of fish off the coast of Somalia because of overfishing by factory-scale fishing fleets is believed to be one of the causes for the rise of piracy that now plagues international shipping in the area. Interestingly, the neighboring Kenyan fishing industry is currently rebounding because the pirates also serve to keep large fishing fleets out of the area.)

The exploitation of renewable resources before they can be renewed is referred to as "overshooting" the resource. This is occurring not only with the major fisheries, but also with groundwater (for example, the Oglala aquifer in the United States, large areas of northwestern India, Northern China, and a number of locations in North Africa and the Middle East), with tropical forests, and even with soils.

Duke University ecologist John Terborgh described a recent trip he took to a small African nation where foreign economic exploitation is combined with a ruthless depletion of resources.

> Everywhere I went, foreign commercial interests were exploiting resources after signing contracts with the autocratic government. Prodigious logs, four and five feet in diameter, were coming out of the virgin forest, oil and natural gas were being exported from the coastal region, offshore fishing rights had been sold to foreign interests, and exploration for oil and minerals was underway in the interior.

The exploitation of resources in North America during the five-hundred-year post-discovery era followed a typical sequence—fish, furs, game, timber, farming virgin soils—but because of the hugely expanded scale of today's economy and the availability of myriad sophisticated technologies, exploitation of all the resources in poor developing countries now goes on at the same time. In a few years, the resources of this African country and others like it will be sucked dry. And what then? The people there are currently enjoying an illusion of prosperity, but it is only an illusion, for they are not preparing themselves for anything else. And neither are we.[29]

D. A System Geared to Exponential Growth in the Search for Profits Will Inevitably Transgress Planetary Boundaries

The earth system can be seen as consisting of a number of critical biogeochemical processes that, for hundreds of millions of years, have served to reproduce life. In the last 12 thousand or so years the world climate has taken the relatively benign form associated with the geological epoch known as the Holocene, during which civilization arose. Now, however, the socioeconomic system of capitalism has grown to such a scale that it overshoots fundamental planetary boundaries—the carbon cycle, the nitrogen cycle, the soil, the forests, the oceans. More and more of the terrestrial (land-based) photosynthetic product, upwards of 40 percent, is now directly accounted for by human production. All ecosystems on earth are in visible decline. With the increasing scale of the world economy, the human-generated rifts in the earth's metabolism inevitably become more severe and more multifarious. Yet, the demand for more and greater economic growth and accumulation, even in the wealthier countries, is built into the capitalist

system. As a result, the world economy is one massive bubble.

There is nothing in the nature of the current system, moreover, that will allow it to pull back before it is too late. To do that, other forces from the bottom of society will be required.

E. Capitalism Is Not Just an Economic System—It Fashions a Political, Judicial, and Social System to Support the System of Wealth and Accumulation

Under capitalism people are at the service of the economy and are viewed as needing to consume more and more to keep the economy functioning. The massive and, in the words of Joseph Schumpeter, "elaborate psychotechnics of advertising" are absolutely necessary to keep people buying.[30] Morally, the system is based on the proposition that each, following his/her own interests (greed), will promote the general interest and growth. Adam Smith famously put it: "It is not from the benevolence of the butcher, the brewer, or the baker that we expect our dinner, but from their regard to their own interest."[31] In other words, individual greed (or quest for profits) drives the system and human needs are satisfied as a mere by-product. Economist Duncan Foley has called this proposition and the economic and social irrationalities it generates "Adam's Fallacy."[32]

The attitudes and mores needed for the smooth functioning of such a system, as well as for people to thrive as members of society—greed, individualism, competitiveness, exploitation of others, and "consumerism" (the drive to purchase more and more stuff, unrelated to needs and even to happiness)—are inculcated into people by schools, the media, and the workplace. The title of Benjamin Barber's book—*Consumed: How Markets Corrupt Children, Infantilize Adults, and Swallow Citizens Whole*—says a lot.

The notion of responsibility to others and to community, which is the foundation of ethics, erodes under such a system. In the words of Gordon Gekko—the fictional corporate takeover artist in Oliver Stone's film *Wall Street*—"Greed is Good." Today, in the face of wide-spread public outrage, with financial capital walking off with big bonuses derived from government bailouts, capitalists have turned to preaching self-interest as the bedrock of society from the very pulpits. On November 4, 2009, Barclay's Plc Chief Executive Officer John Varley declared from a wooden lectern in St. Martin-in-the-Fields at London's Trafalgar Square that "Profit is not Satanic." Weeks earlier, on October 20, 2009, Goldman Sachs International adviser Brian Griffiths declared before the congregation at St. Paul's Cathedral in London that "The injunction of Jesus to love others so ourselves is a recognition of self-interest."[33]

Wealthy people come to believe that they deserve their wealth because of hard work (theirs of their forbearers) and possibly luck. The ways in which their wealth and prosperity arose out of the social labor of innumerable other people are downplayed. They see the poor—and the poor frequently agree—as having something wrong with them, such as laziness or not getting a sufficient education. The structural obstacles that prevent most people from significantly bettering their conditions are also downplayed. This view of each individual as a separate economic entity concerned primarily with one's (and one's family's) own well-being, obscures our common humanity and needs. People are not inherently selfish but are encouraged to become so in response to the pressures and characteristics of the system. After all, if each person doesn't look out for "Number One" in a dog-eat-dog system, who will?

Traits fostered by capitalism are commonly viewed as being innate "human nature," thus making a society organized along other goals than the profit motive unthinkable. But humans are clearly capable of a wide range of characteristics, extending from great cruelty to great sacrifice for a cause to caring for non-related others, to true altruism. The "killer instinct" that we supposedly inherited from evolutionary ancestors—the "evidence" being chimpanzees' killing the babies of other chimps—is being questioned by reference to the peaceful characteristics of other hominids such as gorillas and bonobos (as closely related to humans as chimpanzees).[34] Studies of human babies have also shown that, while selfishness is a human trait, so are cooperation, empathy, altruism, and helpfulness.[35] Regardless of what traits we may have inherited from our hominid ancestors, research on pre-capitalist societies indicates that very different norms from those in capitalist societies are encouraged and expressed. As Karl Polanyi summarized the studies: "The outstanding discovery of recent historical and anthropological research is that man's economy, as a rule, is submerged in his social relationships. He does not act so as to safeguard his individual interest in the possession of material goods; he acts so as to safeguard his social standing, his social claims, his social assets."[36] In his 1937 article on "Human Nature" for the *Encyclopedia of the Social Sciences*, John Dewey concluded—in terms that have been verified by all subsequent social science—that:

> The present controversies between those who assert the essential fixity of human nature and those who believe in a greater measure of modifiability center chiefly around the future of war and the future of a competitive economic system motivated by private profit. It is justifiable to say without dogmatism that both anthropology and history give support to those who wish to change these institutions. It is demonstrable that many of the obstacles to change which have been attributed to human nature are in fact due to the inertia of institutions and to the voluntary desire of powerful classes to maintain the existing status.[37]

Capitalism is unique among social systems in its active, extreme cultivation of individual self-interest or "possessive-individualism."[38] Yet the reality is that non-capitalist human societies have thrived over a long period—for more than 99 percent of the time since the emergence of anatomically modern humans—while encouraging other traits such as sharing and responsibility to the group. There is no reason to doubt that this can happen again.[39]

The incestuous connection that exists today between business interests, politics, and law is reasonably apparent to most observers.[40] These include outright bribery, to the more subtle sorts of buying access, friendship, and influence through campaign contributions and lobbying efforts. In addition, a culture develops among political leaders based on the precept that what is good for capitalist business is good for the country. Hence, political leaders increasingly see themselves as political entrepreneurs, or the counterparts of economic entrepreneurs, and regularly convince themselves that what they do for corporations to obtain the funds that will help them get reelected is actually in the public interest. Within the legal system, the interests of capitalists and their businesses are given almost every benefit.

Given the power exercised by business interests over the economy, state and media, it is extremely difficult to effect fundamental changes that they oppose. It therefore makes it next to impossible to have a rational all ecologically sound energy policy, health care system, agricultural and food system, industrial policy, trade policy, education, etc.

IV. CHARACTERISTICS OF CAPITALISM IN CONFLICT WITH SOCIAL JUSTICE

The characteristics of capitalism discussed above—the necessity to grow; the pushing of people to purchase more and more; expansion abroad; use of resources without concern for future generations; the crossing of planetary boundaries; and the predominant role often exercised by the economic system over the moral, legal, political, cultural forms of society—are probably the characteristics of capitalism that are most harmful for the *environment*. But there are other characteristics of the system that greatly impact the issue of *social justice*. It is important to look more closely at these social contradictions imbedded in the system.

A. As the System Naturally Functions, a Great Disparity Arises in Both Wealth and Income

There is a logical connection between capitalism's successes and its failures. The poverty and misery of a large mass of the world's people is not an accident, some inadvertent byproduct of the system, one that can be eliminated with a little tinkering here or there. The fabulous accumulation of wealth—as a direct consequence of the way capitalism works nationally and internationally—has simultaneously produced persistent hunger, malnutrition, health problems, lack of water, lack of sanitation, and general misery for a large portion of the people of the world. The wealthy few resort to the mythology that the grand disparities are actually necessary. For example, as Brian Griffiths, the advisor to Goldman Sachs International, quoted above, put it: "We have to tolerate the inequality as a way to achieving greater prosperity and opportunity for all."[41] What's good for the rich also—according to them—coincidentally happens to be what's good for society as a whole, even though many remain mired in a perpetual state of poverty.

Most people need to work in order to earn wages to purchase the necessities of life. But, due to the way the system functions, there is a large number of people precariously connected to jobs, existing on the bottom rungs of the ladder. They are hired during times of growth and fired as growth slows or as their labor is no longer needed for other reasons—Marx referred to this group as the "reserve army of labor."[42] Given a system with booms and busts, and one in which profits are the highest priority, it is not merely convenient to have a group of people in the reserve army; it is absolutely essential to the smooth workings of the system. It serves, above all, to hold down wages. The system, without significant intervention by government (through large inheritance taxes and substantial progressive income taxes), produces a huge inequality of both income and wealth that passes from generation to generation. The production of great wealth and, at the same time great poverty, within and between countries is not coincidental—wealth and poverty are likely two sides of the same coin.

In 2007, the top 1 percent of wealth holders in the United States controlled 33.8 percent of the wealth of the country, while the bottom 50 percent of the population owned a mere 2.5 percent. Indeed, the richest *400 individuals* had a combined net worth of $1.54 trillion in 2007—approaching that of the bottom *150 million people* (with an aggregate net worth of $1.6 trillion). On a global scale, the wealth of the world's 793 billionaires is, at present, more than $3 trillion—equivalent to about 5 percent of total world income ($60.3 trillion in 2008). A mere 9 million people worldwide (around one-tenth of 1 percent of world population) designated as "high net worth individuals" currently hold a combined $35 trillion in wealth—equivalent to more than 50 percent of world income.[43] As wealth becomes more concentrated, the wealthy gain more political power, and they will do what they can to hold on to all the money they can—at the expense of those in lower economic strata. Most of the productive forces of society, such as factories, machinery, raw materials, and land, are controlled by a relatively small percentage of the population. And, of course, most people see nothing wrong with this seemingly natural order of things.

B. Goods and Services Are Rationed According to Ability to Pay

The poor do not have access to good homes or adequate food supplies because they do not have "effective" demand—although they certainly have biologically based demands. All goods are commodities. People without sufficient effective demand (money) have no right in the capitalist system to any particular type of commodity—whether it is a luxury such as a diamond bracelet of a huge McMansion, or whether it is a necessity of life such as a healthy physical environment, reliable food supplies, or quality medical care. Access to all commodities is determined, not by desire or need, but by having sufficient money or credit to purchase them. Thus, a system that, by its very workings produces inequality and holds back workers' wages, ensures that many (in some societies, most) will not have access to even the basic necessities or to what we might consider a decent human existence.

It should be noted that, during periods when workers' unions and political parties were strong, some of the advanced capitalist countries of Europe instituted a more generous safety net of programs, such as universal health care, than those in the United States. This occurred as a result of a struggle by people who demanded that the government provide what the market cannot—equal access to some of life's basic needs.

C. Capitalism Is a System Marked by Recurrent Economic Downturns

In the ordinary business cycle, factories and whole industries produce more and more during a bloom—assuming it will never end and not wanting to miss out on the "good times"—resulting in overproduction and overcapacity, leading to a recession. In other words, the system is prone to crises, during which the poor and near poor suffer the most.

Recessions occur with some regularity, while depressions are much less frequent. Right now, we are in a deep recession or mini-depression (with 10 percent official unemployment), and many think we've averted a full-scale depression by the skin of our teeth. All told, since the mid-1850s there have been thirty-two recessions or depressions in the United States (not including the current one)—with the average contraction since 1945 lasting around ten months and the average expansion between contractions lasting about six years.[44] Ironically, from the ecological point of view, major recessions—although causing great harm to many people—are actually a benefit, as lower production leads to less pollution of the atmosphere, water, and land.

V. PROPOSALS FOR THE ECOLOGICAL REFORMATION OF CAPITALISM

There are some people who fully understand the ecological and social problems that capitalism brings, but think that capitalism can and should be reformed. According to Benjamin Barber: "The struggle for the soul of capitalism is…a struggle between the nation's economic body and its civic soul: a struggle to put capitalism in its proper place, where it serves our nature and needs rather than manipulating and fabricating whims and wants. Saving capitalism means bringing it into harmony with spirit—with prudence, pluralism and those 'things of the public'… that define our civic souls. A revolution of the spirit."[45] William Greider has written a book titled *The Soul of Capitalism: Opening Paths to a Moral Economy*. And there are books that tout the potential of "green capitalism" and the "natural capitalism" of Paul Hawken, Amory Lovins, and L. Hunter Lovins.[46] Here, we are told that we can get rich, continue growing the economy, and increase consumption without end—and save the planet, all at the same time! How good can it get? There is a slight problem—a system that has only one goal, the maximization of profits, has no soul, can never have a soul, can never be green, and, by its very nature, it must manipulate and fabricate whims and wants.

There are a number of important "out of the box" ecological and environmental thinkers and doers. They are genuinely good and well-meaning people who are concerned with the health of the planet, and most are also concerned with issues of social justice. However, there is one box from which they cannot escape—the capitalist economic system. Even the increasing numbers of individuals who criticize the system and its "market failures" frequently end up with "solutions" aimed at a tightly controlled "humane" and non-corporate capitalism, instead of actually getting outside the box of capitalism. They are unable even to think about, let alone promote, an economic system that has different goals and decision-making processes—one that places primary emphasis on human and environmental needs, as opposed to profits.

Corporations are outdoing each other to portray themselves as "green." You can buy and wear your Gucci clothes with a clean conscience because the company is helping to protect rainforests by using less paper.[47] *Newsweek* claims that corporate giants such as Dell, Hewlett-Packard, Johnson & Johnson, Intel, and IBM are the top five green companies of 2009 because of their use of "renewable" sources of energy, reporting greenhouse gas emissions (or lowering them), and implementing formal environmental policies and good reputations.[48] You can travel wherever you want, guilt-free, by purchasing carbon "off-sets" that supposedly cancel out the environmental effects of your trip.

Let's take a look at some of the proposed devices for dealing with the ecological havoc without disturbing capitalism.

A. Better Technologies That Are More Energy Efficient and Use Fewer Material Inputs

Some proposals to enhance energy efficiency—such as those to help people tighten up their old homes so that less fuel is required to heat in the winter—are just plain common sense. The efficiency of machinery, including household appliances and automobiles, has been going up continually, and is a normal part of the system. Although much more can be accomplished in this area, increased efficiency usually leads to lower costs and increased use (and often increased size as well, as in automobiles), so that the energy used is actually increased. The misguided push to "green" agrofuels has been enormously detrimental to the environment. Not only has it put food and auto fuel in direct competition, at the expense of the former, but it has also sometimes actually decreased overall energy efficiency.[49]

B. Nuclear Power

Some scientists concerned with climate change, including James Lovelock and James Hansen, see nuclear power as an energy alternative, and as a partial technological answer to the use of fossil fuels; one that is much preferable to the growing use of coal. However, although the technology of nuclear energy has improved somewhat, with third-generation nuclear plants, and with the possibility (still not a reality) of fourth-generation nuclear energy, the dangers of nuclear power are still enormous—given radioactive waste lasting hundreds and thousands of years, the social management of complex systems, and the sheer level of risk involved. Moreover, nuclear plants take about ten years to build and are extremely costly and uneconomic. There are all sorts of reasons, therefore (not least of all, future generations), to be extremely wary of nuclear power as any kind of solution. To go in that direction would almost certainly be a Faustian bargain. [50]

C. Large-Scale Engineering Solutions

A number of vast engineering schemes have been proposed either to take CO_2 out of the atmosphere or to increase the reflectance of sunlight back into space, away from earth. These include: *Carbon sequestration schemes* such as capturing CO_2 from power plants and injecting it deep into the earth, and fertilizing the oceans with iron so as to stimulate algal growth to absorb carbon; and *enhanced sunlight reflection schemes* such as deploying huge white islands in the oceans, creating large satellites to reflect incoming sunlight, and contaminating the stratosphere with particles that reflect light.

No one knows, of course, what detrimental side effects might occur from such schemes. For example, more carbon absorption by the oceans could increase acidification, while dumping sulphur dioxide into the stratosphere to block sunlight could reduce photosynthesis.

Also proposed are a number of low-tech ways to sequester carbon such as increasing reforestation of low-tech ways to sequester carbon such as increasing reforestation and using ecological soil management to increase soil organic matter (which is composed mainly of carbon). Most of these should be done for their own sake (organic material helps to improve soils in many ways). Some could help to reduce the carbon concentration in the atmosphere. Thus reforestation, by pulling carbon from the atmosphere, is sometimes thought of as constituting negative emissions. But low-tech solutions cannot solve the problem given an expanding system—especially considering that trees planted now can be cut down later, and carbon stored as soil organic matter may later be converted to CO_2 if practices are changed.

D. Cap and Trade (Market Trading) Schemes

The favorite economic device of the system is what are called "cap and trade" schemes for limiting carbon emissions. This involves placing a cap on the allowable level of greenhouse gas emissions and then distributing (either by fee or by auction) permits that allow industries to emit carbon dioxide and other greenhouse gases. Those corporations that have more permits than they need may sell them to other firms wanting additional permits to pollute. Such schemes invariably include "offsets" that act like medieval indulgences, allowing corporations to continue to pollute while buying good grace by helping to curtail pollution somewhere else—say, in the third world.

In theory, cap and trade is supposed to stimulate technological innovation to increase carbon efficiency. In practice, it has not led to carbon dioxide emission reductions in those areas where it has been introduced, such as in Europe. The main result of carbon trading has been enormous profits for some corporations and individuals, and the creation of a sub-prime carbon market. [51] There are no meaningful checks of the effectiveness of the "offsets," nor prohibitions for changing conditions sometime later that will result in carbon dioxide release to the atmosphere.

VI. WHAT CAN BE DONE NOW?

In the absence of systemic change, there certainly are things that have been done and more can be done in the future to lesson capitalism's negative effects on the environment and people. There is no particular reason why the United States can't have a better social welfare system, including universal health care, as is the case in many other advanced capitalist countries. Governments can pass laws and implement regulations to curb the worst environmental problems. The same goes for the environment or for building affordable houses. A carbon tax of the kind proposed by James Hansen, in which 100 percent of the dividends go back to the public, thereby encouraging conservation while placing the burden on those with the largest carbon footprints and the most wealth, could be instituted. New coal-fired plants (without sequestration) could be blocked and existing ones close down.[52] At the world level, contraction and convergence in carbon emissions could be promoted, moving to uniform world per capita emissions, with cutbacks far deeper in the rich countries with large per capita carbon footprints.[53] The problem is that very powerful forces are strongly opposed to these measures. Hence, such reforms remain at best limited, allowed a marginal existence only insofar as they do not interfere with the basic accumulation drive of the system.

Indeed, the problem with all these approaches is they allow the economy to continue on the same disastrous course it is currently following. We can go on consuming all we want (or as much as our income and wealth allow), using up resources, driving greater distances in our more fuel-efficient cars, consuming all sorts of new products made by "green" corporations, and so on. All we need to do is support the new "green" technologies (some of which, such as using agricultural crops to make fuels, are actually not green!) and be "good" about separating out waste that can be composted or reused in some form, and we can go on living pretty much as before—in an economy of perpetual growth and profits.

The very seriousness of the climate change problem arising from human-generated carbon dioxide and other greenhouse gas emissions has led to notions that it is merely necessary to reduce carbon footprints (a difficult problem in itself). The reality, though, is that there are numerous, interrelated, and growing ecological problems arising from a system geared to the infinitely expanding accumulation of capital. what needs to be reduced is not just *carbon footprints*, but *ecological footprints*, which means that economic expansion on the world level and especially in the rich countries needs to be reduced, even cease. At the same time, many poor countries need to expand their economies. The new principles that we could promote, therefore, are ones of sustainable human development. This means *enough* for everyone and no more. Human development

would certainly not be hindered, and could even be considerably enhanced for the benefit of all, by an emphasis on sustainable human, rather than unsustainable economic, development.

VII. ANOTHER ECONOMIC SYSTEM IS NOT JUST POSSIBLE—IT'S ESSENTIAL

The foregoing analysis, if correct, points in the fact that the ecological crisis cannot be solved within the logic of the present system. The various suggestions for doing so have no hope of success. The system of world capitalism is clearly unsustainable in: (1) its quest for never ending accumulation of capital leading to production that must continually expand to provide profits; (2) its agriculture and food system that pollutes the environment and still does not allow universal access to a sufficient quantity and quality of food; (3) its rampant destruction of the environment; (4) its continually recreating and enhancing of the stratification of wealth within and between countries; and (5) its search for technological magic bullets as a way of avoiding the growing social and ecological problems arising from its own operations.

The transition to an ecological—which be believe must also be a socialist—economy will be a steep ascent and will not occur overnight. This is not a question of "storming the Winter Palace." Rather, it is a dynamic, multifaceted struggle for a new cultural compact and a new productive system. The struggle is ultimately against the *system of capital*. It must begin, however, by opposing the *logic of capital*, endeavoring in the here and now to create in the interstices of the system a new social metabolism rooted in egalitarianism, community, and a sustainable relation to the earth. The basis for the creation of sustainable human development must arise *from within* the system dominated by capital, *without being part of it*, just as the bourgeoisie itself arose in the "pores" of feudal society.[54] Eventually, these initiatives can become powerful enough to constitute the basis of a revolutionary new movement and society.

All over the world, such struggles in the interstices of capitalist society are now taking place, and are too numerous and too complex to be dealt with fully here. Indigenous peoples today, given a new basis as a result of the ongoing revolutionary struggle in Bolivia, are reinforcing a new ethic of responsibility to the earth. La Via Campesina, a global peasant-farmer organization, is promoting new forms of ecological agriculture, as is Brazil's MST (Movimento dos Trabalhadores Rurais Sem Terra), as are Cuba and Venezuela, Recently, Venezulean President Hugo Chavez stressed the social and environmental reasons to work to get rid of the oil-rentier model in Venezuela, a major oil exporter.[55] The climate justice movement is demanding egalitarian and anti-capitalist solutions to the climate crisis. Everywhere radical, essentially anti-capitalist, strategies are emerging, based on other ethics and forms of organization, rather than the profit motive: ecovillages; the new urban environment promoted in Curitiba in Brazil and elsewhere; experiments in permaculture, and community-supported agriculture, farming and industrial cooperatives in Venezuela, etc. The World Social Forum has given voice to many of these aspirations. As leading U.S. environmentalist James Gustave Speth has stated: "The international social movement for change—which refers to itself as 'the irresistible rise of global anti-capitalism'—is stronger than many may imagine and will grow stronger."[56]

The reason that the opposition to the logic of capitalism—ultimately seeking to displace the system altogether—will grow more imposing is that there is no alternative, if the earth as we know it, and humanity itself, are to survive. Here, the, aims of ecology and socialism will necessarily meet. It will become increasingly clear that the distribution of land as well as food, health care, housing, etc. should be based on fulfilling human needs and not market forces. This is, of course, easier said than done. But it means making economic decisions through democratic processes occurring at local, regional, and multiregional levels. We must face such issues as: (1) How can we supply everyone with basic human needs of food, water, shelter, clothing, health care, educational and cultural opportunities? (2) How much of the economic production should be consumed and how much invested? and (3) How should the investments be directed? In the process, people must find the best ways to carry on these activities with positive interactions with nature—to improve the ecosystem. New forms of democracy will be needed, with emphasis on our responsibilities to each other, to one's own community as well as to communities around the world. Accomplishing this will, of course, require social planning at every level: local, regional, national, and international—which can only be successful to the extent that it is *of and by*, and not just ostensibly for, the people.[57]

An economic system that is democratic, reasonably egalitarian, and able to set limits on consumption will undoubtedly mean that people will live at a significantly lower level of consumption that what is sometimes referred to in the wealthy countries as a "middle class" lifestyle (which has never been universalized even in these societies). A simpler way of life, though "poorer" in gadgets and ultra-large luxury homes, can be richer culturally and in reconnecting with other people and nature, with people working the shorter hours needed to provide life's essentials. A large number of jobs in the wealthy capitalist countries are nonproductive and can be eliminated, indicating that the workweek can be considerably shortened in a more rationally organized economy. The slogan, sometimes seen on bumper stickers, "Live Simply so that Others May Simply Live," has little meaning in a capitalist society. Living a simple life, such as Helen and Scott Nearing did, demonstrating that it is possible to live a rewarding and interesting life while living simply, doesn't help the poor under present circumstances.[58] However, the slogan will have real importance in a society under social (rather than private) control, trying to satisfy the basic needs for all people.

Perhaps the Community Councils of Venezuela—where local people decide the priorities for social investment in their communities and receive the resources to implement them—are an example of planning for human needs at the local level. This is the way that such important needs as schools, clinics, roads, electricity, and running water can be met. In a truly transformed society, community councils can interact with regional and multiregional efforts. And the use of the surplus of society, after accounting for peoples' central needs, must be based on their decisions.[59]

The very purpose of the new sustainable system, which is the necessary outcome of these innumerable struggles (necessary in term of survival and the fulfillment of human potential), must be to satisfy the basic material and non-material needs of all the people, while protecting the global environment as well as local and regional ecosystems. The environment is not something "external" to the human economy, as our present ideology tells us; it constitutes the essential life support systems for all living creatures. To heal the "metabolic rift" between the economy and the environment means new ways of living, manufacturing, growing food, transportation and so forth.[60] Such a society must be sustainable; and sustainability requires substantive equality, rooted in an egalitarian mode of production and consumption.

Concretely, people need to live closer to where they work, in ecologically designed housing built for energy efficiency as well as comfort, and in communities designed for public engagement, with sufficient places, such as parks and community centers, for coming together and recreation opportunities. Better mass transit within and between cities is needed to lessen the dependence on the use of the cars and trucks. Rail and significantly more energy efficient than trucks in moving freight (413 miles per gallon fuel per ton versus 155 miles for trucks) and causes fewer fatalities, while emitting lower amounts of greenhouse gases. One train can carry the freight of between 280 to 500 trucks. And it is estimated that one rail line can carry the same amount of people as numerous highway lanes.[61] Industrial production needs to be based on ecological design principles of "cradle-to-cradle," where products and buildings are designed for lower energy input, relying to as great degree as possible on natural lighting and heating/cooling, ease of construction as well as easy reuse, and ensuring that the manufacturing process produces little to no waste.[62]

Agriculture based on ecological principles and carried out by family farmers working on their own, or in cooperatives and with animals, reunited with the land that grows their food has been demonstrated to be not only as productive or more so than large-scale industrial production, but also to have less negative impact on local ecologies. In fact, the mosaic created by small farms interspersed with native vegetation is needed to preserve endangered species.[63]

A better existence for slum dwellers, approximately one-sixth of humanity, must be found. For the start, a system that requires a "plant of slums," as Mike Davis has put it, has to be replaced by a system that has room for food, water, homes, and employment for all.[64] For many, this may mean returning to farming, with adequate land and housing and other support provided.

Smaller cities may be needed, with people living closer to where their food is produced and industry more dispersed, and smaller scale.

Evo Morales, President of Bolivia, has captured the essence of the situation in his comments about changing from capitalism to a system that promotes "living well" instead of "living better." As he put it at the Copenhagen Climate Conference in December 2009: "Living better is to exploit human beings. It's plundering natural resources, It's egoism and individualism. Therefore, in those promises of capitalism, there is no solidarity or complementarity. There's no reciprocity. So that's why we're trying to think about other ways of living lives and living well, not living better. Living better is always at someone else's expense. Living better is at the expense of destroying the environment."[65]

The earlier experiences of transition to noncapitalist systems, especially in Soviet-type societies, indicate that this will not be easy, and that we need new conceptions of what constitutes socialism, sharply distinguished from those early abortive attempts. Twentieth-century revolutions typically arose in relatively poor, underdeveloped countries, which were quickly isolated and continually threatened from abroad. Such post-revolutionary societies usually ended up being heavily bureaucratic, which a minority in change of the state effectively ruling over the remainder of the society. Many of the same hierarchical relations of production that characterize capitalism were reproduced. Workers remained proletarianized, while production was expanded for the sake of production itself. Real social improvements all too often existed side by side with extreme forms of social repression.[66]

Today we must strive to construct a genuine socialist system; one in which bureaucracy is kept in check, and power over production and politics truly resides with the people. Just as new challenges that confront us are changing in our time, so are the possibilities for the development of freedom and sustainability.

When Reverend Jeremiah Wright spoke to *Monthly Review*'s sixtieth anniversary gathering in September 2009, he kept coming back to the refrain "What about the people?" If there is to be any hope of significantly improving the conditions of the vast number of the world's inhabitants—many of whom are living hopelessly under the most severe conditions—while also preserving the earth as a livable planet, we need a system that constantly asks: "What about the people?" instead of "How much money can I make?" This is necessary, not only for humans, but for all the other species that share the planet with us and whose fortunes are intimately tied to ours.

NOTES

1. Fidel Castro Ruz, "The Truth of What Happened at the Summit," December 19, 2009, http://monthlyreview.org.

2. Plato, *Timaeus and Critias* (London: Penguin, 1977), 133–34.

3. James Hansen, Reto Ruedy, Makiko Sato, and Ken Lo, "If It's That Warm, How Come It's So Damned Cold?" http://columbia.edu/-jeh1/.

4. Hansen, *Storms of My Grandchildren* (New York: Bloomsbury, 2009), 164.

5. Hansen, *Storms of My Grandchildren*, 82–85; Richard S. J. Tol, et al., "Adaptation to Five Meters of Sea Level Rise," *Journal of Risk Research*, no. 5 (July 2006), 469.

6. World Glacier Monitoring Service/United Nations Environment Programme, *Global Glacier Change: Facts and Figures* (2008), http://grid.unep.ch/glaciers; Baiqing Xu, et al., "Black Soot and the Survival of Tibetan Glaciers," *Proceedings of the National Academy of Sciences,* December 8, 2009, http://pnas.org: Carolyn Kormann, "Retreat of Andean Glaciers Foretells Water Woes," *Environment 360*, http://e360.yale.edu/; David Biello, "Climate Change is Ridding the World's Tropical Mountain Ranges of Ice," *Scientific American Observations,* December 15, 2009, http://scientificamerican.com; Union of Concerned Scientists, "Contrarians Attack IPCC Over Glacial Findings,

But Glaciers are Still Melting," January 19, 2010, ucsusa.org.

7. Agence France Presse (AFP), "UN Warns of 70 Percent Desertification by 2025," October 4, 2005.

8. Shaobing Peng, et al., "Rice Yields Decline with Higher Night Temperature from Global Warming," *Proceedings of the National Academy of Sciences* 101 no. 27 (2005), 9971–75.

9. James Hansen, "Strategies to Address Global Warming" (July 13, 2009), http//Columbia.edu; Hansen, *Storms of My Grandchildren*, 145–47.

10. "Arctic Seas Turn to Acid, Putting Vital Food Chain at Risk," *Guardian,* October 4; 2009; The Earth Institute, Columbia University, "Ocean's Uptake of Manmade Carbon May be Slowing," November 18, 2009, http://earth.columbia.edu; "Seas Grow Less Effective at Absorbing Emissions," *New York Times,* November 19, 2009; S. Khatiwal, F. Primeau, and T. Hall, "Reconstruction of the History of Anthropogenic CO2 Concentrations in the Ocean," *Nature* 462, no. 9 (November 2009), 346–50.

11. Lindsey Hoshaw, "Afloat in the Ocean, Expanding Islands of Trash," *New York Times*, November 10, 2009.

12. United Nations Food and Agricultural Organization, http://fao.org.

13. Bobbi Chase Wilding, Kathy Curtis, Kirsten Welker-Hood, 2009. *Hazardous Chemicals in Health Care: A Snapshot of Chemicals in Doctors and Nurses,* Physicians for Social Responsibility, http://psr.org.

14. Lyndsey Layton, "Use of potentially harmful chemicals kept secret under law," *Washington Post,* January 4, 2010.

15. Frank Jordans, "17,000 Species Threatened by Extinction," *Associated Press,* November 3, 2009.

16. Monitra Pongsiri, et al., "Biodiversity Loss Affects Global Disease Ecology," *Bioscience* 59, no. 11 (2009), 945–54.

17. James Hansen, Storms of My Grandchildren, ix.

18. Johan Rockström, et al., "A Safe Operating Space for Humanity," *Nature,* 461 (September 24, 2009), 472–75.

19. Donella H. Meadows, Dennis L. Meadows, Jorgen Randers, and William W. Behrens. *The Limits to Growth: A Report for the Club of Rome's Project on the Predicament of Mankind* (New York: Universe Books, 1972); Donella H. Meadows, Jorgen Randers, and Dennis L. Meadows, *The Limits to Growth: The 30-Year Update* (White River Junction, VI: Chelsea Green Publishing Company, 2004).

20. Erik Assadourian, "The Rise and Fall of Consumer Cultures," in Worldwatch Institute, *State of World, 2010* (New York: W. Norton, 2010), 6.

21. Epicurus, "The Vatican Collection," *The Epicurus Reader* (Indianapolis: Haskett, 1994), 39.

22. "Poverty Facts and Statistics," *Global Issues,* http://globalissues.org.

23. Curtis White, "Barbaric Heart: Capitalism and the Crisis of Nature," *Orion* (May-June 2009), http://orionmagazine.org/index.php/articles/article/4680.

24. For treatments of the role of speculation and debt in the U.S. economy, see John Bellamy Foster and Fred Magdoff, *The Great Financial Crisis* (New York: Monthly Review Press, 2009) and Fred Magdoff and Michael Yates, *The ABCs of the Economic Crisis* (New York: Monthly Review Press, 2009).

25. "Fears for the World's Poor Countries as the Rich Grab Land to Grow Food," *Guardian,* July 3, 2009; "The Food Rush: Rising Demand in China and West Sparks African Land Grab," *Guardian,* July 3, 2009.

26. For a brief discussion of European expansion, see Harry Magdoff and Fred Magdoff, "Approaching Socialism," *Monthly Review* 57, no. 3 (July-August 2005), 19–61. On the relation of oil and gas to the wars in Iraq and Afghanistan; see Michael T. Klare, *Rising Powers, Shrinking Planet* (New York: Metropolitan Books, 2008).

27. British Petroleum, *BP Statistical Review of World Energy,* June 2009, http://bp.com; John Bellamy Foster, *The Ecological Revolution* (New York: Monthly Review Press, 2009), 85–105.

28. David A. Vaccari, "Phosphorus Famine: A Looming Crisis," *Scientific American,* June 2009:54–59.

29. John Terborgh, "The World is in Overshoot," *New York Review of Books* 56, no. 19 (December 3, 2009), 45–57.

30. Joseph A. Schumpeter, *Business Cycles* (New York: McGraw Hill, 1939), vol. 1, 73.

31. Adam Smith, *The Wealth of Nations* (New York: Modern Library, 1937), 14.

32. Duncan K. Foley, *Adam's Fallacy* (Cambridge, MA: Harvard University Press, 2006).

33. "Profit 'Is Not Satanic' Barclays Says, after Goldman Invokes Jesus," Bloomberg.com, November 4, 2009.

34. Frans de Waal. "Our Kinder, Gentler Ancestors," *Wall Street Journal,* October 3, 2009.

35. J. Kiley Hamlin, Karen Wynn, and Paul Bloom, "Social Evaluation by Preverbal Infants," *Nature* 50, no. 2 (November 22, 2007), 557–59; Nicholas Wade. "We may be Born with an Urge to Help," *New York Times,* December 1, 2009. Some recent research in this regard is usefully summarized in Jeremy Rifkin, *The Empathic Civilization* (New York: Penguin, 2009), 128–34.

36. Karl Polanyi, *The Great Transformation* (Boston: Beacon, 1944), 46.

37. John Dewey, Selections from the Encyclopedia of the Social Sciences (New York: Macmillan, 197), 536.

38. See C. B. Macpherson, *The Political Theory of Possessive Individualism* (Oxford: Oxford University Press, 1962).

39. For a fuller discussion of these issues see Magdoff and Magdoff, "Approaching Socialism," 19–23.

40. For a discussion of the power of finance in the U.S. political system, see Simon Johnson, "The Quiet Coup," *Atlantic Monthly*, May 2009.

41. Julia Werdigier, "British Bankers Defend Their Pay and Bonuses," *New York Times*, November 7, 2009.

42. For a contemporary view of the reserve army, see Fred Magdoff and Harry Magdoff, "Disposable Workers," *Monthly Review* 55, no. 11 (April 2005), 18–35.

43. Matthew Miller and Duncan Greenberg, ed., "The Richest People In America" (2009), Forbes, http://forbes.com; Arthur B. Kennickell, "Ponds and Streams: Wealth and Income in the U,S,, 1989 to 2007." Federal Reserve Board Working Paper 2009-13, 2009, 55, 63; "World GDP," http://economywatch.com, accessed January 16, 2010; "World's Billionaires," Forbes.com, March 8, 2007; Capgemini and Merrill Lynch Wealth Management, *World Wealth Report, 2009,* http://us.capgemini.com, introduction.

44. "How Many Recessions Have Occurred in the U.S. Economy?" *Federal Reserve Board of San Francisco*, January 2008, http://frbsf.org; National Bureau of Economic Research, Business Cycle Expansions and "Contractions, January 17, 2010," http://nber.org.

45. Benjamin Barber, "A Revolution in Spirit," *The Nation,* February 9, 2009, http://thenation.com/doc/20090209/barber.

46. Paul Hawken, Amory Lovins, and L. Hunter Lovins, *Natural Capitalism* (Boston: Little, Brown and Co., 1999). For a detailed critique of the ideology of "natural capitalism," see F.E. Trainer, "Natural Capitalism Cannot Overcome Resource Limits," http://mnforsustain.org.

47. "Gucci Joins Other Fashion Players in Committing to Protect Rainforests," *Financial Times*, November 5, 2009.

48. Daniel McGinn, "The Greenest Big Companies In America," *Newsweek,* September 21, 2009. http://newsweek.com.

49. Fred Magdoff, "The Political Economy and Ecology of Biofuels," Monthly Review 60, no. 3 (July-August 2008), 34–50.

50. James Lovelock, *The Revenge of Gaia* (New York: Perseus, 2006), 87–105, Hansen, *Storms of My Grandchildren,* 198–204. On the continuing dangers of nuclear power, even in its latest incarnations, see Rebert D. Furber, James C. Warf, and Sheldon C. Plotkin, "The Future of Nuclear Power," *Monthly Review* 59, no. 9 (February 2008), 38–48.

51. Friends of the Earth, "Subprime Carbon?" (March 2009), http://foe.org/suprime carbon, and *A Dangerous Obsession* (November 2009), http://columbia.edu; Larry Lohman, "Climate Crisis: Social Science Crisis," forthcoming in M. Voss, ed., *Kimawandel* (Wiesbaden: Vs-Verlag), http://tni.org//archives/archives/lohmann/sciencecrisis.pdf.

52. See Hansen, *Storms of My Grandchildren,* 172–77, 193–94, 208–22.

53. See Aubrey Meyer, *Contraction and Convergence* (Devon: Schumacher Society, 2000); Tom Athansiou and Paul Baer, *Dead Heat* (New York: Seven Stories Press, 2002).

54. Karl Mark and Frederick Engels, *Collected Works* (New York: International Publishers, 1975), vol. 6, 327; Karl Marx, *Capital,* vol. 3 (London: Penguin, 1981), 447–48.

55. "Chàvez Stresses the Importance of Getting Rid of the Oil Rentier Model in Venezuela," MRzine, http://mrzine.org (January 11, 2010).

56. James Gustave Speth, *The Bridge at the Edge of the World* (New Haven: Yale University Press, 2008), 195.

57. On Planning, see Magdoff and Magdoff, "Approaching Socialism," 36–61.

58. See Helen and Scott Nearing, *Living the Good Life* (New York: Schocken, 1970). Scott Nearing was for many years the author of life "World Events" column in *Monthly Review.*

59. See lain Bruce, *The Real Venezuela* (London: Pluto Press, 2008), 139–75.

60. On the metabolic rift, see Foster, *The Ecological Revolution,* 161–200.

61. C. James Kruse, et al., "A Modal Comparison of Domestic Freight Transportation Effects on the General Public, Center for Ports and Waterways," *Texas Transportation Institute*, 2007; http://americanwaterways.com; Mechanical Database website, Rail vs. Truck Industry, accessed; http://mechdb.com January 17, 2010.

62. William McDonough and Michael Braungart, *Cradle to Cradle* (New York: North Point Press, 2002).

63. See Miguel A. Altieri, "Agroecology, Small Farms, and Food Sovereignty," *Monthly Review* 61, no. 3 (July–August 2009), 102–13.

64. Mike Davis, *Planet of the Slums* (London: Verso, 2007).

65. Interview of Evo Morales by Amy Goodman, *Democracy Now,* December 17, 2009, http://democracynow.org/2009/12/17/bolivian-president-evo-morales-on-climate.

66. See Paul M. Sweezy, *Post-Revolutionary Society* (New York: Monthly Review Press, 1980).

STUDY QUESTIONS

1. Why do the authors blame capitalism for the environmental crisis?

2. How does capitalism alter our social systems to meet its ends? Is this criticism fair?

3. Why do the authors think capitalism cannot be reformed?

70

Is Sustainable Capitalism an Oxymoron?

DAVID SCHWEICKART

Is Joel Kovel right that it is either "the end of capitalism or the end of the world:? Or are Paul Hawken, Amory and Hunter Lovins right that we are on the brink of a "natural capitalism" that can usher in an ecological and social utopia, "a world where cities have become peaceful and serene because cars and buses are whisper quiet, vehicles exhaust only water vapor, and parks and greenways have replaced unneeded urban freeways…. . Living standards for all people have dramatically improved, particularly for the poor and those in developing countries. Involuntary unemployment no longer exists… ." I argue that while Hunter-Lovins" have much to offer and Kovel overstates his case, a sustainable capitalism is highly unlikely. I sketch an alternative to both "natural capitalism" and Kovel's non-market socialism that is more promising than either.

From *Perspectives on Global Development and Technology,* Vol. 8, No. 2–3: 559–80(22) (2009). Copyright © 2008. Reprinted by permission.

> *Marx says that revolutions are the*
> *locomotives of world history. But the situation*
> *may be quite*
> *different. Perhaps revolutions are not the train*
> *ride, but the*
> *human race grabbing for the emergency brake.*
> **Walter Benjamin**

The subtitle of Joel Kovel's The Enemy of Nature (originally published in 2002, revised edition 2007) states his thesis bluntly: The End of Capitalism or the End of the World? Kovel thinks we need a revolution—although he is fully cognizant as to how remote that prospect seems.

> Growing numbers of people are beginning
> to realize that capitalism is the
> uncontrollable force driving our ecological
> crisis, only to become frozen in their
> tracks by the awesome implications of this
> insight. (Kovel 2007:xi)

Paul Hawken, Amory Lovbins and Hunter Lovins also think we need a revolution, but of a different sort than the one envisaged by Kovel. Their book, *Natural Capitalism* (published in 1999), is subtitled *Creating the Next Industrial Revolution.* Then-President Clinton is reported to have called it one of the five most important books in the world today.

Hawken and the Lovins' agree with Kovel that the current model of capitalism is problematic. "Capitalism, as practiced, is a financially profitable, non-sustainable aberration in human development" (Hawken, Lovins, and Lovins 1999:5). "But they do not see the problem as residing in capitalism itself. They distinguish among four kinds of capital, all necessary for production: human capital, financial capital, manufactured capital and natural capital. The problem with the current from of capitalism, they argue, is its radical mispricing of these factors. Current market prices woefully undervalue—and often do not value at all—the fourth factor: the natural resources and ecological systems "that make life possible and worth living on this planet (*Ibid.* 2)."

All economists, liberal, Left and Right, recognize that market transactions can involve "externalities"—costs (or benefits) not paid for by the transacting parties. all agree that there is a role for governments to play in rectifying these defects. The standard remedies involve taxation (for negative externalities) and subsidies (for positive externalities). More recently, "cap and trade" schemes for carbon emission have been added to the list.

Hawken and the Lovins' argue that these remedies—properly applied—can work. The first step, they say, is to eliminate the *perverse* incentives now in place. They document the massive subsidies that governments currently provide for ecologically destructive behavior, e.g. highway construction and repair, which encourages suburban sprawl and the shift away from more efficient modes of transportation, agricultural subsidies that encourage soil degradation and wasteful use of water, subsidies to mining, oil, fishing and forest industries, etc.

Second step: impose resource and pollution taxes so as to reflect the true costs of "natural capital." Sweeten the pie by phasing out all taxes on labor—the payroll tax, which increases unemployment, and income taxes as well. The point is to level the playing field so that more sustainable technologies and more energy-efficient processes can compete fairly with the destructive practices of "industrial capitalism." We might even want to go further, and subsidize—at least initially—the technologies that reduce the negative environmental impact of our production and consumption choices.

Natural Capitalism is chock full of examples of the shocking waste pervasive in our current system and of the existing technologies and procedures that could reduce our impact on the environment to a small fraction of what it is now. Many of these changes are already underway. Many more will follow if appropriate government policies are adopted. Hawken and the Lovin's envisage a bright future:

> Imagine for a moment a world where cities
> have been peaceful and serene because cars
> and buses are whisper quiet, vehicles
> exhaust only water vapor, and parks and
> greenways have replaced unneeded urban
> freeways. OPEC has ceased to function
> because the price of oil has fallen to five

dollars a barrel, but there are few buyers for it because cheaper and better ways now exist to get the services people once turned to oil to provide. Living standards for all people have dramatically improved, particularly for the poor and those in developing countries. Involuntary unemployment no longer exists, and income taxes have been largely eliminated. Houses, even low-income housing units, can pay part of their mortgage costs by the energy they *produce*. (*Ibid*[1])

Such a future will come about if we harness the creative energy of capitalism and let the markets work.

Let us examine these two contrasting perspectives. Let us think first about ethics and energy. Consider the ethical commitments that underlie their respective analyses. Kovel cites Marx directly and with full approval:

From the standpoint of a higher form of society the private ownership of the globe by single individuals will appear quite as absurd as private ownership of one man by another. Even a whole society, a nation, or even all simultaneously existing societies taken together, are not the owners of the globe. They are only possessors, its usufructuaries, and like *boni patres familias*, they must hand it down to succeeding generations in an improved condition.[1]

Hawken and the Lovins' might not agree that private ownership is absurd, but they would certainly embrace the ethical clause: We "are only possessors [of the earth], its usufructuaries, and like *boni patres familias*, [we] must hand it down to succeeding generations in an improved condition." There is no real disagreement here about ethics.

Kovel, although cataloguing at length the environmental destruction taking place on our planet, says very little about energy policy, *per se*. He is confident than an "ecosocialist" movement, based on "ecosocialist" values, if victorious, will be able to solve our concrete problems.

Hawken and the Lovins have much to say about energy. They argue that vast amounts of energy are currently wasted—and that is much profit to be made in reducing this waste. They are convinced that technologies already exist that, if properly implemented, could drastically reduce, and eventually eliminate, fossil fuel consumption—without relying on nuclear power. Many of these are already profitable. Others would be, if sensible governmental policies were put in place.

Kovel would object here, not to the technologies *per se* or to the proposals for eliminating the vast amounts of energy wasted due to faulty building or production design, but to the Hawken-Lovins' faith that the "capitalist market" can be successfully employed to get us to the promised land.

In essence there are two fundamental differences between the "ecosocialism" of Kovel and the "natural capitalism" of Hawken-Lovins.

- Kovel is deeply distrustful of the profit motive. He does not think greed can serve the good. Hawken-Lovins' think that the profit motive can be harnessed so as to provide powerful incentives to develop sustainable sources of energy and to eliminate the energy waste so rampant today.

- Kovel is convinced that "grow or die" is an imperative of capitalism that renders "sustainable capitalism" impossible. Hawken and the Lovins' do not confront this argument directly, but appear to believe that either a) capitalism is compatible with a steady-state, non-growing economy or b) an economy can grow indefinitely without consuming more energy and natural resources than it can sustainably reproduce.

Let us examine the "grow or die" issue first.

CAPITALISM: GROW OR DIE?

Anti-capitalist ecologists always say this. In Kovel's (2007) words, "capital must expand without end in order to exist (p. 38)." But is this true? It would seem not to be. Individual small businesses sometimes survive for long periods of time. Marx's prediction that the "petty bourgeois" sector would disappear has turned our not to be true. (The tendency toward monopoly/oligopoly, which he correctly identified, has been offset by the continual rise of new entrepreneurial businesses.)

Capitalism itself has survived prolonged depression—the Great One of 1929 lasted a decade. Periods of stagnation have been even more common—witness Japan throughout the 1990s. To be sure, capitalism incentivizes growth, but it is not at all clear that thwarted growth leads to death. We can point to lots of counterexamples.

It is not true either that the various ecological crises we are facing will bring about "the end of the world." Consider the recently-released Stern Review, commissioned by the British government, which has been applauded by environmentalists for its strong recommendation that urgent action be taken. If nothing is done, we risk "major disruption to economic and social activity, later in this century and the next, on a scale similar to those associated with the great wars and economic depression of the first half of the 20th century."[2]

This is serious. Some sixty million people died of World War Two. The Stern Review estimates as many as two hundred million people could be permanently displaced by rising sea level and drought. But this is not "the end of the world." Even if the effects are far worse, resulting in billions of deaths, there would still be lots of us left. If three-quarters of the present population perished, that would still leave us with 1.6 billion people—the population of the planet in 1900.

I say this not to minimize the potentially horrific impact of relentless environmental destruction, but to caution against exaggeration. We are not talking about thermonuclear war—which *could have* extinguished us as a species. (It still might.) And we shouldn't lose sight of the fact that millions of people on the planet right now, caught up in savage civil wars or living beneath those US bombers currently devastating Iraq, are faced with conditions more terrible than anyone reading this article is likely to face in his or her lifetime due to environmental degradation.[3] Nor will readers suffer more than most of the three billion people alive now who survive on less than $2/day.

We may not be facing the end of the world—but still, Kovel has a point. He may have overstated the case, but from an ecological point of view there is something, at least prima facie, *crazy* about capitalism. An ecological world-view tends to emphasize harmony, sustainability, moderation—rather like that of the ancient Greeks, for whom a constant striving for *more* was regarded as a mark of an unbalanced, deranged soul. Yet every capitalist enterprise is motivated to grow, and to grow without limit. For reasons of greed and fear.

There is no mystery here. We all know how it works. Under conditions of constant or increasing returns to scale, expanding production brings increased profits, which accrue to the firm's owners. For almost everyone, more money is better than less money—even if one wants to give much of it away to the charity of one's choice. It is an idiosyncratic businessman indeed, who does not want his business to grow. (Classical political economist used to invoke the law of diminishing returns to argue that successful businesses would be self-limiting in size—but no one makes that argument anymore.)

The feat factor is at least as important. Failure to take the steps that will, if successful, "grow the company," puts the company at risk. The big fish tend to eat the little fish. Capitalist market competition is cut-throat competition.

(It is worth nothing that not all competition is like this. Athletic competition typically is not. Losers don't lose *everything*. Losing teams aren't driven from the league. Indeed, steps are usually taken in professional sports, e.g., giving the teams with the worst records priority in drafting new players, to prevent the strong teams from getting over stronger at the expense of the weaker teams. No such corrective mechanisms exist in capitalist economies—apart from rather feeble anti-trust laws.)

There is a deeper structural issue that we must consider. It may well be the case that all capitalist firms want to grow—but wanting doesn't make it so. Obviously many firms do not get what they want. Many firms fail.

The root problem with capitalism is not that individual firms are incentivized to grow, but that *the economy as a whole* must grow—not to survive, but to remain *healthy*. As we have noted failed to grow but did not collapse. However, none of those periods—recession, stagnation, depression—can be regarded as happy times.

Why should it be the case that a capitalist economy must grow to be healthy? The answer to this question is rather peculiar. A capitalist economy must grow to be healthy because *capitalism relies on private investor* for its investment funds. These investors are free to invest or not as they see fit. (It is, after all, *their* money.) But this makes economic health dependent on "investor confidence," dependent on, as Keynes put it, "the animal spirits" of the investors. If investors do not foresee a healthy return on their investments, commensurate with the risks they are taking, then they *won't* invest. Or they 'II invest abroad.

But if investors don't invest domestically, their pessimism becomes a self-fulfilling prophesy. Lack of investment translates into layoffs, first in the construction industry, machine-tools industries and the countless others dependent on orders for capital goods, and then, since layoffs lead to a decline in consumer-goods consumption, in other sectors as well. Aggregate demand drops further; the economy slides toward recession.

As we all know, a slumping economy is not just bad for capitalist investors; it is bad for almost everyone. Unemployment rises, which adds stress to almost all workers, even those who retain their jobs. Government revenues fall, adding pressure to cut both government employment and government services. Indeed, public funds for environmental programs are jeopardized—as mainstream economists are quick to point out, impatient as they are with "antigrowth" ecologists. Growth is necessary, they insist, to give us the means to clean up the messes we have made. (It might be noted that in some ways recessions are good for the environment. People consume less, waste less. CO_2 emissions dropped drastically in the US during the Great Depression and even more dramatically in Russia during its post-Communist collapse. But no political

movement anywhere is going to come to power promising to confront the environmental crisis by engineering a depression—nor can a party be expected to remain in power if its policies provoke one.)

So we see: a healthy capitalism requires a steady expansion of consumption. If sales decline, investors lose confidence—as well they should. To be sure, *some* profitable investments can be made in a slumping economy (defined in the business press—correctly—as a declining rate of growth, or worse, a negative rate of growth), but far fewer investors are willing to play a zero-sum or negative-sum game than will play the positive-sum game that investors play in an expanding economy. (Environmentalists and other often point out that GDP growth is not an accurate indicator of human happiness or human development—which is certainly true—but these critics rarely, if ever, point out that GDP growth is *precisely* what is important to investors, who must, at all costs, be kept happy.)[4]

For a capitalist economy to remain healthy, sales must be kept up. Which means that a healthy capitalism requires what would doubtless strike a visitor from another planet (or from a pre-capitalist society) as exceedingly strange—a massive, privately-financed effort to persuade people to consume what they might otherwise find unnecessary. Advertising is but the tip of the iceberg. John Kenneth Galbraith's account, articulated more than forty years ago, remains apt:

> The control or management of demand is, in fact, a vast and rapidly growing industry in itself. It embraces a huge network of communications, a great array of merchandising and selling organizations, nearly the entire advertising industry, numerous ancillary research, training and other related services and much more. In everyday parlance this great machine, and the demanding, and varied talents that it employs, are said to be engaged in selling goods. In less ambiguous language, it means that it is engaged in the management of those who buy goods. (Galbraith 1967:200)

Government also has a key role to play. Governments must be prepared to go into debt to stimulate the economy when an economy slows down. "Fiscal responsibility" goes out the window, no matter how conservative the government, when people stop buying—as well it should. Those recent checks sent to all US taxpayers, courtesy of President Bush and a Democratic congress, aimed at containing the gathering financial storm triggered by the sub-prime mortgage debacle, should remind us all how vitally a capitalist economy depends on what so many environmentalists and other social critics deride as "consumerism."

The problem is not simply "growth." A healthy capitalism depends, not simply on ever-increasing consumption, but on a steady *rate* of growth. When the growth *rate* declines, investors pull back. But a steady rate of growth, so essential to healthy capitalism, implies *exponential* growth, and exponential growth, to anyone with mathematical sensibilities, is deeply disturbing. If an economy grows 3 percent/year—the U.S. average growth rate during the twentieth century—consumption doubles every twenty-four years—which translates into a 16-*fold* increase in consumption over the course of a century. (Of course we did not have *steady* growth during the twentieth century. On the contrary, we had many ups and downs, among them a Great Depression—and fascism, World War II, etc. Still, the *average* rate of growth for the century was 3 percent/year, giving us a 16-fold increase in inflation-adjusted (GDP).)

Needless to say, exponential growth tends to stress the environment. Even a much lower growth rate, say the 1.2 percent/year that the Stern Report assumes, entails a doubling of global consumption every sixty years. As Kenneth Boulding (himself an economist) has noted, "Only a madman or an economist thinks exponential growth can go on forever in a finite world."[5]

We don't have to imagine "forever." Simply note that if our economy were to continue to grow at 3 percent/year throughout the twenty-first century, we will be consuming sixteen times more in 2100 than we are now. Not sixteen *percent* more. Sixteen *times* more.

OBJECTION

There is an important rejoinder to be made to his argument. Growth *need not* add to resource depletion or pollution. GDP is a quantitative figure that doesn't pretend to correlate with general well-being. An oil spill that puts lots of people to work cleaning it up enhances GDP; when harried couples eat out more often, no longer having time to cook at home, GDP goes up. By the same logic, if unemployed people are put to work planting trees, GDO goes up. If there is a shift from capital-intensive factory farming to labor-intensive organic farming in such a way that the market value of the latter exceeds the market value of the former, GDP goes up.

Consider the effect of a green tax—say raising the gasoline tax from its current forty cents to $4/gallon (a third of what is needed to capture the externalities in involved, according to Lester Brown's (2008) latest calculation (p. 268))—bringing the pump price up to $7/gallon. In and of itself, this need not effect overall spending (i.e. GDP) at all. People would presumably drive less—which is the point of the tax. Their overall expenditures on gasoline likely would go up, which means they could consume less of other things. Bur their *total* expenditures would not be affected. Of curse their cutback in consumption else-where would trigger layoffs in those industries, and hence a decease in overall demand. But the government could counter that effect by using the gasoline-tax revenues in such a way as to compensate. If they are used to employ people engage in environmentally constructive work (either directly or by awarding contracts to private businesses engaged in environment-enhancing endeavors), than overall demand will not be impaired, and society will be better off.

Consider a variation on this model—the one suggested by Hawken and the Lovins' and heartily endorsed by (conservative) economist, Gregory Mankiw (head of George W. Bush's Council of Economic Advisors for a number of years). Instead of the government involving itself directly in employing people to restore the environment, suppose it just cuts income taxes instead, by precisely the amount that it would garner from the gasoline tax. Here's Mankiw's assessment:

> Cutting income taxes while increasing gasoline taxes would lead to more rapid economic growth, less traffic congestion, safer roads and reduced risk of global warming—all without jeopardizing long-term fiscal solvency. This may be the closest thing to a free lung that economics has to offer. (Quoted by Brown, 2008, p. 270)

REPLY TO THE OBJECTION

How should we evaluate this rejoinder? The reader will recall that in evaluating the Hawken-Lovins' case for "natural capitalism," I pointed out that they do not confront the "grow or die" argument directly, but that they must believe that either a) capitalism *is* compatible with a steady-state, non-growing economy or b) an economy can grow indefinitely without consuming more energy and natural resources than it can sustainably reproduce. My argument thus far has been directed at a). The rejoinder claims b).

Notice the assumption tucked away in the Mankiw endorsement of a heavy gasoline tax paired with an income tax cut. If we are to have our cake and eat it too, it must be assumed that the *negative* effect on the environment of the "more rapid economic growth" he asserts will be forthcoming *will be more than offset* by the decrease in carbon emissions resulting in the gasoline tax.

Is the wrong? I can't say that he is. But it should be noted that we are no longer talking economic *science* anymore. We are talking about *faith*—the economists' faith that exponential growth *can* go on forever in a finite world.

Is this a rational faith? One is reminded of Pascal's Wager. Blaise Pascal (1623-1662) was a mathematician-philosopher deeply concerned with the question of God's existence. His argument is simple. Does God exist? Maybe yes, maybe no. What is the rational response to this hugely important, highly contentious question? Pascal's answer: do

what any good mathematician would do—calculate expected gains and losses. Consider: If you bet yes, that God exists, and are right, and live your life accordingly, the rewards are infinite—an eternity in heaven. If you bet yes, and are wrong—how much will you lose? In fact very little. The time you will have spent going to church or in prayer. Feelings of guilt from time to time. The gains you might have obtained from taking advantage of certain situations in ways that an existing God might disapprove. But if you bet no and are wrong? An eternity of hellfire. An open and shut case, no: the possibility of infinite happiness set against a life that may or may not prove to be a bit happier now and infinite horror afterwards.

Can exponential growth go on forever (or at least for a long, long time)? If we decide to stick with capitalism, betting that it can—well, here's the Pascalian kicker: we can be almost certain it won't make us happier—at least not those of us who are doing most of the consuming and polluting right now. There is a large literature on happiness. We *know* that increased consumption, once we get beyond a certain point, does not translate into increased happiness. Bill McKibben cites some of the evidence:

> Compared to 1950, the average American family now owns twice as many cars, uses 21 times as much plastic, and travels 25 times farther by air. Gross Domestic Product has tripled since 1950 in the US. We obviously eat more calories. And yet—the satisfaction meter seems not to have budged. More Americans say their marriages are unhappy, their jobs are hideous, and they don't like the place where they live. The number who, all things considered, say they are "very happy" with their lives has slid steadily over that period...In the United Kingdom per capita gross domestic product grew 66 per cent between 1973 and 2001, and yet people's satisfaction with their lives changed not a whit. Nor did it budge in Japan, despite a fivefold increase in income in the postwar years.[6]

Thus, if we put our trust in a regulated capitalism, and it delivers the wise governance and technological innovation that keep the economy growing steadily without inducing environmental havoc, the expected gain is slight at best. But if we place our faith in capitalism and are wrong? Not hellfire or the end of the world—but massive planetary misery.

This Pascalian argument has been a bit too quick. There are some implicit assumptions that needs to be examined. Growth may not make those of us in the "developed" world any happier, but what about the bottom half of humanity? What about the 1.2 billion who live on less than a dollar a day? Would not steady growth make *them* happier?

Certainly growth of a certain kind would increase well-being in large parts of the planet—increased access to healthy food, clean water, effective waste disposal, health care, education, and to employment. But do we have any good reason to think that *capitalist* growth will provide these things? Certainly the historical record suggests the contrary. Angus Maddison's (1995) careful studies show that the gap between rich countries and poor countries has steadily widened from 3 to 1 in 1820 to 70 to 1 in 1990, and still more since then. Immanuel Wallerstein (1995) goes so far as to argue that the basic well-being of the lower half of humanity is significantly worse now than it was five hundred years ago. (To be sure people live longer now and there are many more of us, but compare the life of a median-income person today, living in a desolate, crime-ridden, drug-infested slum in one of the Third World's mega-cities with a peasant living in an intact community five centuries ago (p. 115 ff).)

One can still *hope* that things will change, but the evidence in support of such hope is meager. Indeed, capitalism's desperate drive to grow is deeply implicated in the persistence of global poverty. The argument is straightforward. As Marx and Keynes have emphasized, capitalist stability is constantly threatened by the specter of overproduction (deficient effective demand), leading to economic crises unlike those of any preceding epoch, deriving not from scarcity caused by war, pestilence or bad weather, but from the expansionary dynamic of the system. Too much leads to too little. If more goods are produced than people of the inclination or money to buy, prices fall, workers are laid off, demand slumps further—recession.

Hence capitalist economies must continually seek new markets, at home and also abroad. But poor-country domestic industry and agriculture cannot compete with their rich-country counter parts, and there are no forces intrinsic to capitalism that insure that people displaced by more productive technology will find employment elsewhere. So poverty increases. (The phenomenon of free trade devastating poor-country economies is as old as capitalism itself. Marx (1967) quotes from the Governor-General's report of 1834-35 on the effects of British textile imports on domestic cloth production in their crown-jewel colony: "The misery hardly finds parallel in the history of commerce. The bones of the cotton weavers are bleaching the plains of India" (p. 406).)

Of course there have been many, many schemes proposed to address the stark fact that globalizing capitalism, 160 years after Marx and Engels issued their *Manifesto,* has left eighty percent or so of the world's population deeply mired in poverty, some 47 percent subsisting on less that $2/day (purchasing power parity). None of these have put much of a dent in the global disparity, nor are they likely too. I have argued this point in more detail elsewhere.[7] Let me simply note here that to counter that Pascalian argument, one must assume that the capitalist growth one bets on must not only be sustainable but must trickle down substantially to the bottom segments of humanity.

Given the historical record to date, and the structural features of capitalism causally implicated in this record, a bet on capitalism would be, surely, a very long sot.

AN ALTERNATIVE?

There is an even deeper assumption built into my Pascalian argument. Pascal's wager is not just about belief. It is about restructuring one's life. My Pascalian wager is also about restructuring. But if there is no viable *alternative* to capitalism, then what?

We might as well assume that growth can go on forever in a finite world. A belief that allows for hope is surely better than one that counsels despair.

Can we conceive of a economic alternative to capitalism that is a) economically viable, b) *not* dependent on growth for its stability, yet c) conducive to the entrepreneurial innovation we will need to get though the current crisis? It will probably come as a surprise to many readers, but the answer is clearly *yes*. In my view theoretical analysis, well supported by empirical evidence, strongly supports the thesis that a truly democratic economy could satisfy the above criteria. Let me sketch the basic institutions of a democratic economy, one that retains competitive markets, but extends democracy to both the workplace and to the financial system. (Needles to say, I will have to paint with a broad brush. In practice a democratic economy would be more complex than what I present here.)[8]

DEMOCRATIZED WORK

Imagine an economy as technologically developed as our own in which each workplace is run as a democratically. Suppose businesses are regarded as communities, not legal entities that can be bought and sold. Management is appointed by a worker council elected by the workforce, one-person, one-vote—just as, in some localities today, city managers are appointed by an elected city council. These enterprises compete with one another in the market.

Such enterprises can be expected to be efficient. Workers do not receive wages but a specified share of the firm's profit. Hence *everyone* has a direct, tangible financial stake in the company's performing well. Everyone is motivated, not only to work efficiently, but to monitor co-workers—thus reducing the need for external supervision. It is not surprising, then, that empirical studies that compare democratic firms to comparable capitalist firms consistently find the former performing at least as well as the latter, and often better.[9]

But here is something interesting. Although democratic and capitalist firms are both motivated to produce efficiently and to satisfy consumer desires,

they are strikingly different in their orientation toward growth. Under conditions of constant returns to scale, capitalist firms expand, whereas democratic firms do not. For capitalist firms aim at maximizing total profits, whereas democratic firms aim (roughly) at maximizing profit-per-worker. That is to say, if the owners of a capitalist firm can make \$X under present conditions, they can make \$2X by doubling the size of their operation. But if a democratic firm doubles its size, it doubles its workforce, leaving its per-capita income unchanged.

This is an enormously important structural difference, with implications that go well beyond environmental concerns. Let us focus on those that bear on the question at hand.

One implication: democratic competition is less intense than capitalist competition. Firms compete for market share, but not for market dominance.

This means that democratic firms—when competing with other democratic firms—do not face the same "grow or die" imperative that capitalist firms face. Neither greed nor fear works the same way. However greedy workers may be, they cannot increase their incomes by expanding, unless economies of scale are significant. At the same time, they do not have to worry much about being driven out of business by a more innovative or efficient rival. They have more time to adjust, to copy whatever successful innovation their rival has introduced. (Non-profit institutions are similar to democratic firms in this regard. Successful universities, for example, do not keep expanding. They compete for students, but they don not drive their competitors out of business. When educational innovations occur, they are not used to dominate their competitors. Innovations tend to spread, administrators coming under pressure to adopt "best practices.")

A second implication: When innovation brings about a productivity gain, workers are free to choose leisure over increased consumption. This option is virtually non-existent in a capitalist firm. Owners do not increase their profits by allowing their workforce to work less. To the contrary, increases in productivity often lead to workers working more or harder than before—since productivity-enhancing innovations often put their jobs at risk. As economist Juliet Schor (1992) has documented, per capita consumption doubled in the United States since post-World War Two, while the number of hours of work—for those who had work—went up, not down. Suppose, sixty years ago we in the US, happy with our standard of living (which was the envy of the world) had opted to take our productivity gains in leisure instead increased consumption:

> We could now produce our 1948 standard of living (measured in terms of marketed goods and services) in less than half the time it took that year. We actually could have chosen the four-hour day. Or a working year of six months. Or, *every worker in the United States could now be taking every other year off from work—with pay* [emphasis hers] (p. 2)

We should remember that 1948 was not the Dark Ages. Families had washing machines, refrigerators, cars (not as many as today, but there were more buses and trams), telephones, record players, TVs (admittedly black and white), typewriters. There were lots of movie theaters, bowling alleys, community swimming pools. True, people didn't have cell phones or CDs or PCs or DVDs, but life was hardly uncomfortable. (I'm thinking here of middle-class life. Life for poor people was miserable—as it still is.)

If excess consumption (consumerism) is a serious environmental threat, and if market competition is essential to an efficiently functioning economy, then it is vital to have an system that offers non-consumption incentives to its businesses. Increased leisure is a readily available option in a democratic firm. But not in a capitalist firm. (As Marx so vividly documented in *Capital,* the struggle over the length of the working day has been on-going from the inception of capitalism. The struggle for shorter hours, more vacation time, more leisure has *always* been resisted by capital—and for good reason. All else equal, firms do not make more money by giving workers more time off.)

It follows that, unlike a capitalist economy, an economy of democratic firms can be innovative, but non-growing (in terms of consumption). Workers may well be content to live on steady incomes, choosing to take the benefits of innovation as leisure rather than increased consumption. Of course this choice is not *guaranteed* by the democratic structure. An environmental consciousness—or at least a consciousness as to what actually makes people happy—matters. But such a consciousness does not conflict with the structural imperatives of a democratic economy, as it does with the imperatives of a healthy capitalism.

The reader will notice that the alternative to capitalism being sketched here might seem to be more in line with the "natural capitalism" of Hawken-Lovins' than with the ecosocialism of Kovel. As indicated above, Kovel disagrees with Hawken, Lovins and Lovins as to the utility of the profit motive. The "Economic Democracy" that I am sketching here embraces market competition. However, it should be noted that "profit" under Economic Democracy is conceptually distinct from capitalist profit. In both cases the desire for profit motivates production. In both cases, profit is defined as the difference between sales revenue *and* costs. *But in a capitalist firm, labor is a cost; in a democratic firm, it is not.* In a democratic firm profit is the difference between sales revenues and non-labor costs. Profit is the residual that goes to the workers as income. This difference accounts for fundamental motivational differences. Workers are incentivized to use their non-labor materials efficiently and to marshal their work-time effectively, but they have no interest in relentless expansion, no interest in replacing skilled labor by unskilled, no interest in driving down the "cost" of labor. Nor do they have the slightest interest in moving their facilities abroad, where labor costs are lower and environmental regulations less strict.

DEMOCRATIZED INVESTMENT

I have said that Economic Democracy democratizes both the workplace and the financial markets. Thus far we have considered the democratization of work. Enterprises are regarded as communities, not entities to be bought or sold. Let us turn our attention now to finance.

Capitalist financial institutions, for all their ever-increasing, mind-boggling complexity, exist for one fundamental purpose: to mobilize the private savings of individuals and make them available to individuals wanting to start new businesses, or to existing enterprises wanting to expand production, upgrade their technologies, introduce new products, etc.

Suppose we decide not to rely on the private savings of private individuals for investment. Suppose we don't want to be hostage to the "animal spirits" of investors. A substitute mechanism for generating investment capital is readily available: taxation. For technical reasons, the most appropriate tax is a flat-rate tax on the value of each enterprise's capital assets. (This tax is a surrogate interest rate—the charge enterprises and entrepreneurs pay for their use of capital. It can also be thought of as a "leasing fee," the charge workers in a democratic enterprise must pay for the capital assets they employ.)

These tax revenues will fund the bulk of the new investment our society decides to undertake, both private and public. How will they be allocated? There are various possibilities. The most transparent, and in many ways the fairest is to allocate these revenues to regions and communities on a per capita basis. That is to say, if region A has X percent of the nation's population, it gets X percent of the investment funds. These funds are then distributed to local and regional investment banks—public banks—charged with loaning them out to individuals and enterprises needing funds to start up, upgrade or expand business operations. Loan applications are judged in terms of projected profitability, employment creation, and, if the community so desires, environment enhancement. Bank managers are public officials, charged with allocating effectively the funds entrusted to them. Since all records are open to public inspection, the task of monitoring their performance should not be unduly difficult.

This democratization of investment has two consequences of importance to environmental sustainability. First, and most importantly, economic stability and economic health, regional as well as national, no longer depend on economic growth, since investment no longer depends on the "animal spirits" of investors. Every year funds flow into each region. If there is insufficient demand for these funds, they can be rebated to the taxpayers, thus keeping up effective demand. If the problem persists, the capital-assets tax rate can be cut. There is no longer any danger of investors deciding not to invest or to move their funds abroad. The investment fund is tax-generated. All of it stays in country.

The second important consequence: every year regions receive funds that can be used as they see fit, so long as they involve capital expenditure. This means that every year funds are available that can be used for environmental experimentation—for the construction of local mass transit or bike paths or community gardens, whatever. Communities can learn from the experiences of other communities what works and what doesn't. Funds are available for "public entrepreneurial projects" that might otherwise by difficult to come by. With democratic finance, regions do not compete for capital as they do under capitalism. Capital flows in each year as a matter of right. Regions do not have to entice businesses to their areas by offering subsidies, tax holidays, lax environmental regulations, etc., as they commonly do under capitalism.

The "natural capitalists" might object at this point. They are eager to harness the entrepreneurial spirit to ecological ends. They like to point out the many opportunities that currently exist to make good by doing good—more energy efficient manufacturing, green buildings, leasing rather than selling (to promote recycling), efficient water management, organic agriculture—the list goes on. They may be right—although it is striking, when one surveys the concrete proposals for dealing with environmental issues being put forth in the flood of books now on the market, how large a role almost all assign to local and national *governments*. No serious thinker thinks *laissez-faire* will save us.[10]

Be that as it may, a good case can be made for maintaining an entrepreneurial capitalist sector in a democratic economy. We need entrepreneurs (capitalist or socialist) to respond to the environment-enhancing incentives put in place. Workplaces in the capitalist sector will not (by definition) be democratic, but given the fact that these capitalist enterprises must compete with democratic enterprises for qualified workers, abuses are unlikely. Indeed, most capitalist firms will likely set up some participatory structures to keep morale high (though they are not required to do so.)

Where would private entrepreneurs get their capital? From private sources, if they want, but also from the public banks. There is no reason to restrict the loans these banks make to democratic firms only. However, to prevent an entrepreneurial firm from becoming a permanent, eternal capitalist firm, paying dividends forever to passive shareholders, a simple provision can be enacted. To set up a capitalist firm, (i.e., one in which workers who do not elect the firms management), a firm must obtain a license, which is good for a finite period of time, say twenty or thirty years. When the license expires, the enterprise must be sold to the state and turned over to its workers to be run democratically. (Its originators may sell it earlier, to the state or to private individuals, but it remains a private firm only for the number of years specified on the initial license.)

I have argued at length in both *Against Capitalism* and *After Capitalism* that such an "economic democracy" would work, and would be more ecologically sustainable than even best-case forms of capitalism. It would also be far more egalitarian than capitalism and far more democratic. It could be a full-employment economy with the government serving as an employer-of-last-resort. It could (therefore) be a society without domestic poverty.[11]

There is one final feature that should be explicated. The economic democracy I advocate practices "socialist protectionism." It practices "free trade" with countries of comparable levels of development and comparable environmental regulations, but it blocks both wage and environmental competition by imposing tariffs on goods coming from countries with low wages and or weak environmental standards, so that the price to consumers of an imported commodity is what it would be if the exporting country paid comparable wages and had comparable environmental regulations. (Economic Democracy embraces competition based on efficiency and consumer satisfaction, but *not* "race-to-the-bottom" competition.)

The tariff is the "protectionist" part of socialist protectionism. The "socialist" part is the rebating of the collected tariffs to the countries that produced the items upon which the tariffs were leveled. These funds are targeted to governmental or non-governmental agencies that are working to improve labor and environmental conditions in that country.

One further note: Our Economic Democracy relinquishes all claims to "intellectual property rights" with regard to poor countries, and with regard to all publicly-funded environmental research. Since workers do not face the threat of low-wage competition from poor countries, and since the per-capita benefits from squeezing poor people are slight, they can be expected to generous with their intellectual "property."

CONCLUSION

I have argued that Kovel, although excessively apocalyptic and too dismissive of market competition, is essentially right. A sustainable capitalism *is* an oxy-moron—if "sustainable" means more than the survival of the human species, with perhaps a relatively small global middle class continuing to live in relative comfort and affluence behind whatever walls are necessary to keep out the desperate multitude. Our species cannot *flourish* under capitalism.

I have also argued that Hawken, the Lovins's and other "natural capitalists," while doing excellent work in proposing creative solutions to concrete problems, have not confronted two fundamental questions: Does a healthy capitalism require a steady rate of growth? Can exponential growth go on forever in a finite world? I have argued that the answer to the first question is "yes," but that it is foolish to the point of irrational to base one's hope for the future on a positive answer to the latter.

I am inclined to say that too many environmentalists aren't "ecological" enough. An ecological consciousness entails an awareness of thee interconnectedness of things. The fact of the matter is, the massive environmental problems we face are not unrelated to other social problems: national and global unemployment, national and global poverty, political dominance by an immensely wealthy capitalist class that undercuts genuinely democratic governance, an increasingly harried and increasingly insecure "middle class" that finds its opportunities for self-, family- and community-enhancing leisure time ever more restricted.[12]

We need to recognize that institutional reforms are possible that address, simultaneously, *all* of these problems, including the environmental ones—and that these reforms must take us "beyond capitalism." Of course I am not the only one who believes this. All the "watermelons" do (the derisive term the anti-environmental right applies to those who are "green on the outside, red on the inside.") But so does at least one Nobel laureate in economics. Let me call your attention to a little noted, almost off-handed, remark made by Amartya Sen in this 1999 treatise, *Development as Freedom*—a work based on, interestingly enough, a series of presentations given to the World Bank.

> The solutions to these problems—inequality (especially that of grinding poverty in a world of unprecedented prosperity) and of public goods (that is, goods people share together, such as the environment) will almost certainly call for institutions *that take us beyond the capitalist market economy.* (Sen 1999:267)

I think we are in position now to see what those institutions might be.

CODA

My argument is not meant to imply that nothing can be done so long as global capitalism dominates our world, or that all our efforts should be directed at delegitimizing this deeply destructive yet deeply rooted system. Kovel is right that people can become "frozen in their tracks by the awesome implications of the insight" that capitalism must go.

But as the proponents of *Natural Capitalism* make clear, there are *many* things that can be done right now—things which are good in and of themselves, things, the struggle for which help to develop further an environmental consciousness—fertile ground for the "watermelon consciousness" that must ultimately prevail if our species is to flourish.

My argument should make it clear, moreover, that neither "the market" nor "the corporation" nor "the entrepreneur" is the fundamental structural barrier to ecological and social sanity. A sensible socialism will be an "ecosocialism." It will also be a *market socialism*. Corporations need not be abolished. They should be democratized. Entrepreneurs ought not be scorned. Entrepreneurial creativity—properly incentivized—has a vital role to play in getting us to a rational, sustainable, human social order.

There are intelligent people on the Left who disagree with the conciliatory approach I seem to be taking here. Radical physicist-environmental researcher, Denis Rancourt (2007) insists that reformism

> avoids root causes, it does not challenge the relevant power structures, it entices us into collaboration, it seduces us into personal consumption responsibility as a substitute for effective political action, it turns our attention toward learning about atmospheric chemistry rather than about the relevant major human-controlled planetary forces, and it gives us something we relate to (the weather) rather than sensitizing us to real world problems and all the exploited people outside of our class rather than creating meaningful occasions for empathy and solidarity.

I think this is wrong—although I feel the force of the argument. To be sure, one should be wary of environmental initiatives funded by major corporations (of which there are now many)—but being wary does not imply automatic rejection. It is here that having a concrete, viable alternative in mind is helpful in evaluating which initiatives to support and which to reject. We must keep in mind that should we get to Economic Democracy, our democratic corporations will face many of the same hard issues that rapacious capitalist corporations now face, e.g., how to produce efficiently, minimizing waste, how to shift from a reliance on oil, how to recycle effectively, etc. The more we learn now, the better—including what does not work and why not.

Will we get there? One can take heart from Paul Hawken's latest book, mentioned above. The subtitle lifts the spirit: *How the Largest Movement in the World Came into Being and Why No One Saw it Coming.* Hawken argues that three great currents have begun to converge: organizations concerned with environmental issues, those with social justice and those with preserving indigenous cultures. His data base points to the existence [of] at least a million organizations involving tens of millions of people. There exists enormous discontent with the existing world order, and the discontented are organizing. There is enormous distrust of corporations. There is a deep suspicion, especially now that global financial markets are in turmoil, that the masters of the universe are not as smart as so many thought they were. Clearly the global economic order is in the midst of a legitimation crisis. Might this crisis open up some space for thinking the unthinkable, i.e., that there exists a viable, desirable, sustainable economic perhaps within reach? If so, where might this thinking take us?

BIBLIOGRAPHY

Brown, Lester. 2008. *Plan B 3.0: Mobilizing to Save Civilization.* New York: Norton. Galbraith, John Kenneth. 1967. *The New Industrial State.* Boston: Houghton-Mifflin. Hargroves, Karlson and Michael Smith, eds. 2006. *The Natural Advantage of Nations: Business Opportunities, Innovation and Governance in the 21st Century.* Earthscan 2006.

Hart, Stuart. 2007. *Capitalism at the Crossroads: Aligning Business, Earth and Humanity* Philadelphia: Wharton School Publishing.

Hawken, Paul. 2005. *The Ecology of Commerce: A Declaration of Sustainability.* New York: Harper Collins.

———. 2007. *Blessed Unrest: How the Largest Movement in the World Came into Being and Why No One Saw it Coming.* New York: Viking.

Hawken, Paul, Amory Lovins and L. Hunter Lovins. 1999. *Natural Capitalism: Creating the Next Industrial Revolution.* Boston: Little, Brown.

Kovel, Joel. 2007. *The Enemy of Nature: The End of Capitalism or the End of the World?* New York: Zed Books.

Maddison, Angus. 1995. *Monitoring the World Economy, 1820–1992.* Paris: OECD.

Marx, Karl. 1967. *Capital* v. 1. New York: International Publishers.

McKibben, Bill. 2007. "Happiness Is…" *The Ecologist.* January 2, 2007.

Olsen, Mancer and Hans-Martin Landsberg (eds). 1973. *The No-Growth Society.* New York: Norton.

Rancourt, Denis. 2007. "Global Warming: Truth or Dare?" Activistteacher.blogspot.com/2007/02/global_warming_truth_or_dare.html.

Schor, Juliet. *The Overworked American: The Unexpected Decline of Leisure.* New York: Basic Books.

Schweickart, David. 1993. *Against Capitalism.* Cambridge University Press.

———. 2002. *After Capitalism.* Lanham, MD: Rowman and Littlefield.

———. 2008. "Global Poverty: Alternative Perspectives on What We Should Do—and Why." *Journal of Social Philosophy*

Sen, Amartya. 1999. *Development as Freedom.* New York: Anchor Books.

Speth, James Gustave. 2008. *The Bridge at the Edge of the World: Capitalism, the Environment, and Crossing from Crisis to Sustainability.* New Haven: Yale University Press.

Stern, Nicolas. 2007. *The Economics of Climate Change.* Cambridge: Cambridge University Press.

Wallerstein, Immanuel. 1995. *Historical Capitalism with Capitalist Civilization.* London: Verso.

NOTES

1. Kovel, p. 268, citing *Capital,* v.3.

2. Sir Nicholas Stern. 2007. *The Economics of Climate Change*. Cambridge: Cambridge University Press: ii.

3. During one ten-day period in January 2008, some 100,000 lbs. of explosives were dropped on a Baghdad neighborhood. For a vivid account, see Tom Engelhardt, "Bombs Away over Iraq," January 29, 2008, at Tomdispatch.com. Engelhardt points out that was the same quantity of explosives dropped by German airforce on the ancient Basque city of Guernica in 1937, provoking an international outcry that included Pablo Picasso's famous depiction.

4. A recent survey of alternative indices—Human Development Index, Index of Sustainable Economic Welfare (ISEW), Genuine Progress Indictor (GPI), Index of Social Health, and the Happy Planet Index)—and their relationship to GDP, see James Gustave Speth, *The Bridge at the Edge of the World: Capitalism, the Environment, and Crossing from Crisis to Sustainability* (Yale University Press, 2008), pp. 138–142. I'm pleased to report that Speth, Dean of Yale University's School of Forestry and Environmental Studies, who served at Jimmy Carter's White House environmental advisor and as head of the United Nation's largest agency on international development, has come to essentially the same conclusion this paper purports to demonstrate.

5. Quoted in Mancer Olsen and Hans-Martin Landsberg (eds). *The No-Growth Society*. New York: Norton. 1973: 97.

6. Bill McKibben, "Happiness Is…" *The Ecologist.* January 2, 2007: 36. See also the reference cited in note 9.

7. See my "Global Poverty: Alternative Perspectives on What We Should Do—and Why" *Journal of Social Philosophy* (Winter 2008): 471–91.

8. For more details and a fuller presentation of the arguments to be set out in this section, see my *After Capitalism*. Lanham, MD: Rowman and Littlefield. 2002. A more extensive treatment of essentially the same model, oriented more toward professional philosophers and economists, can be found in my *Against Capitalism*. Cambridge University Press. 1993.

9. See my *After Capitalism,* Chapter Three for references.

10. See for example, Paul Hawken, The Ecology of Commerce: A Declaration of Sustainability. Harper Collins 1993, 2005, Karlson Hargroves and Michael Smith, eds., The Natural Advantage of Nations: Business Opportunities, Innovation and Governance in the 21st Century. Earthscan 2006, Stuart Hart Capitalism at the Crossroads: Aligning Business. Earth and Humanity. Wharton School publishing 2007 and well as Lester Brown, Plan B 3.0.

11. Genuine full employment is impossible under capitalism, since unemployment is the essential disciplinary stick to keep the workforce in line. Democratic firms do not need this stick, since the conflict between the interests of owners and the interests of workers that lies at the heart of every capitalist enterprise—more work for less money/ less work for more money—does not exist in a democratic firm. Domestic poverty is also essential to a healthy capitalism, since unemployment, to be disciplinarily effective, must be degrading.

12. Hawken and the Lovins are not guilty of this charge. Hawken, for example, in his most recent book, explicitly links the fate of the environmental movement with that of the social justice movement. Cf. *Blessed Unrest: How the Largest Movement in the World Came into Being and Why No One Saw it Coming*. Viking 2007.

STUDY QUESTIONS

1. Compare and contrast Kovel's to Hawken, Lovins, and Lovins's claims about the future of global economics.

2. Why does capitalism depend upon a steady rate of growth?

3. Why, and under what conditions, is Schweickart capitalism potentially sustainable?

4. What does Schweickart mean by 'Democratized work'?

71

An Ecological Critique of Global Advertising

ALAN THEIN DURNING

Alan Thein Durning is a senior researcher at Worldwatch Institute in Washington, D.C., and the author of How Much Is Enough? The Consumer Society and the Future of the Earth. *In this essay, he argues that advertising promotes consumerism, which creates artificial needs in such a way as to undermine a sustainable society. While Durning does not condemn the idea of advertising itself, as a means of providing useful information, he argues that today's Madison Avenue experts have gone far beyond the limits of that function and instead are promoting a dangerous false consciousness.*

Last January a single message was broadcast simultaneously in every inhabited part of the globe. The message was not "love thy neighbor" or "thou shalt not kill." It was "Drink Coke."

This first global advertisement was, on the face of it, simply a piece of technical showmanship—an inevitable one, considering the pace of change in telecommunications. On a symbolic level, however, it was something more. It was a neat encapsulation of the main trend in human communications worldwide: commercialization.

For better or for worse, almost all of humanity's 5.5 billion individuals, divided among 6,000 distinct cultures, are now soaking in the same gentle bath of advertising. The unctuous voices of the marketplace are insinuating themselves into ever more remote quarters of the globe and ever more private realms of human life.

Advertising has become one of the world's premier cultural forces. Almost every living person knew the word "Coke," for example, long before the global ad. Two years ago, the trade journal *Adweek* published a two-page spread depicting Hitler, Lenin, Napoleon, and a Coke bottle. "Only one," read the caption, "launched a campaign that conquered the world. How did Coke succeed when history's most ambitious leaders failed? By choosing the right weapon. Advertising."

Aside from the arrogance of that statement, what is disturbing about it is its truth. Owing to skillful and persistent marketing, Coke is sold in virtually every place people live. Go to the end of a rural road on any Third World continent, walk a day up a donkey trail to a hardscrabble village, and ask for a Coke. Odds are you'll get one. This state of affairs—development workers call it "Coca-Colonization"—means that Coke's secret formula has probably reached more villages and slums than has clean drinking water or oral rehydration formula.

The point here is not to single out Coca-Cola—others would have circum-advertised the globe soon if the soft drink empire hadn't—but rather to question whether advertising has outgrown its legitimate role in human affairs. Advertisers maintain that their craft, far from being too widely practiced, is just beginning to achieve its destiny: to stimulate business growth, create jobs, and to unify humanity by eroding the ancient

Reprinted from *Worldwatch*, Vol. 6.3 (May–June, 1993) by permission of the Worldwatch Institute.

hatreds that divide us and joining us together in the universal fellowship of a Coke.

But from the perspective of the Earth's long-term health, the advertising industry looks somewhat different. Stripped to its essentials, contemporary advertising has three salient characteristics. It preys on the weaknesses of its host. It creates an insatiable hunger. And it leads to debilitating over-consumption. In the biological realm, things of that nature are called parasites.

If that rather pointed metaphor is apt, we are left with the sticky problem doctors face in treating any parasite: finding a medicine and a dosage that will kill the worm without poisoning the patient. How can we restrain the excesses of advertising without resorting to poisonous state censorship or curtailing the flow of information in society? Actions that are too heavy-handed, for example, could bankrupt the free—but advertising-dependent—press.

THE MANUFACTURE OF NEEDS

The purpose of advertising, according to orthodox economic theory, is to provide us with information about the goods and services offered in the marketplace. Without that stream of information we consumers won't make informed choices, and Adam Smith's invisible hand will be not only invisible but also blind. We won't know when a better frozen dinner comes along, nor will we know where to get the best deal on a new car.

The contents of marketing messages themselves, however, show the simplemindedness of that explanation. Classified ads and yellow page telephone directories would suffice if advertising were only about telling people who already want something where to get it and what it costs. Rather, advertising is intended to expand the pool of desires, awakening wants that would lie dormant otherwise—or, as critics say, manufacturing wants that would not otherwise exist.

Entire industries have manufactured a need for themselves. Writes one advertising executive, ads can serve "to make [people] self-conscious about matter of course things such as enlarged nose pores [and]

bad breath." Historically, advertisers have especially targeted women, playing on personal insecurities and self-doubt by projecting impossible ideals of feminine beauty.

As B. Earl Puckett, then head of the department store chain Allied Stores Corporation, put it 40 years ago, "It is our job to make women unhappy with what they have." Thus for those born with short, skinny eyelashes, the message mongers offer hope. For those whose hair is too straight, or too curly, or grows in the wrong places, for those whose skin is too dark or too light, for those whose body weight is distributed in anything but this year's fashion, advertising assures that synthetic salvation is close at hand.

Ads are stitched together from the eternal cravings of the human psyche. Their ingredients are images of sexual virility, eternal youth, social belonging, individual freedom, and existential fulfillment. Advertisers sell not artifacts but lifestyles, attitudes, and fantasies, hitching their wares to the infinite yearnings of the soul.

They also exploit the desire individuals in mass societies feel to define a distinctive identity. Peter Kim, director of research and consumer behavior for the advertising agency J. Walter Thompson, says the role of brands in consumer society is "much akin to the role of myth in traditional societies. Choosing a brand becomes a way for one group of consumers to differentiate themselves from another."

Advertisers are extraordinarily sophisticated in the pursuit of these ends. The most finely wrought ads are masterpieces—combining stunning imagery, bracing speed, and compelling language to touch our innermost fears and fancies. Prime-time television commercials in the industrial countries pack more suggestion into a minute than anything previously devised.

From an anthropological perspective, ads are among the supreme creations of this era, standing in relation to our technological, consumer culture as the pyramids did to the ancients and the Gothic cathedrals to the medievals. Those structures embodied faith in the transcendent, acted out a quest for immortality, and manifested hierarchical social rankings. Advertisements, like our age, are mercurial, hedonistic, image-laden, and fashion-driven; they glorify the individual, idealize consumption as the route to personal fulfillment, and affirm technological progress as the motive force of destiny.

ADVERTISING AND THE EARTH

Of course, advertising is not the only force to promote consumption in today's world. That point is amply evident in the recent history of Eastern Europe. There, where most advertising was illegal under the communist regimes of the past, popular desires for the Western consumer lifestyle were pervasive—indeed, they were among the forces that overthrew socialism. Communism had failed to deliver the goods.

Other forces driving the earth-threatening consumption levels of the world's affluent societies include everything from human nature's acquisitive streak to the erosion of informal, neighborhood sharing networks that has accompanied the rising mobility of our time. They include social pressures to keep up with the Joneses, the proliferation of "convenience" goods to meet the time-crunch created by rising working hours, national economic policies that favor consumption over savings and raw materials production over efficiency and recycling, and the prevailing trend in urban design—away from compact, human-scale cities toward anonymous, auto-scale mall and sprawl.

All these things—plus the weight of sheer purchasing power—define one of the world's most pressing environmental challenges: to trim resource consumption in industrial countries. Citizens of these nations typically consume 10 times as much energy as their developing country counterparts, along with 10 times the timber, 13 times the iron and steel, 14 times the paper, 18 times the synthetic chemicals, and 19 times the aluminum.

The consumer societies take the lion's share of the output of the world's mines, logging operations, petroleum refineries, metal smelters, paper mills, and other high-impact industrial plants. These enterprises, in turn, account for a disproportionate share of the resource depletion, environmental pollution, and habitat degradation that humans have caused worldwide. A world full of consumer societies is an ecological impossibility.

And even if advertising is not the sole force driving up consumption, it is an important one. It is a powerful champion of the consumer lifestyle, and is spreading its influence widely.

COMMERCIALIZING THE GLOBE

"Fifty years ago," wrote philosopher Ivan Illich in 1977, "most of the words an American heard were personally spoken to him as an individual, or to someone standing nearby." That certainly isn't true today. Most of the words an American—or a citizen of any industrial country—hears are sales pitches broadcast over the airwaves to us as members of a mass market. The text we read, the images we see, and the public places we visit are all dominated by commercial messages.

Take the example of commercial television, long the premier advertising medium. Aside from sleeping and working, watching television is the leading activity in most consumer societies, from the United States and the United Kingdom to Japan and Singapore.

Commercial TV is advancing around the world, and everywhere it has proved exceptionally effective at stimulating buying urges. As Anthony J. F. Reilly, chief executive of the food conglomerate H. J. Heinz, told *Fortune* magazine, "Once television is there, people of whatever shade, culture, or origin want roughly the same things." Harnessed as an educational tool, TV can be powerful and effective, as in India and Africa, where lessons are beamed to teacher-less villages. But the overwhelming trend in broadcasting almost everywhere is commercialization.

In 1985, the International Advertising Association rhapsodized: "The magical marketing tool of television has been bound with the chains of laws and regulations in much of the world, and it has not been free to exercise more than a tiny fraction of its potential as a conduit of the consumer information and economic stimulation provided by advertising. Those chains are at last being chiseled off."

During the 1980s, governments deregulated or privatized television programming in most of Western Europe. Public broadcasting monopolies splintered in Belgium, France, Italy, Germany, Norway, Portugal, Spain, and Switzerland—allowing advertising on a scale previously witnessed only in the United States. As the European Community became both a single market and a common broadcasting region this year, advertising time on European TV became a hot commodity, providing access to the region's 330 million consumers and $4 trillion of disposable income.

Meanwhile, commercial television is quickly spreading outside the industrial countries. In India, declares Gurcharan Das, chairman of Procter & Gamble India, "an advertiser can reach 200 million people every night" through television. India has gone from 3 million TVs in 1983 to more than 14 million today. Latin America has built or imported 60 million sets, almost one per family, since the early 1950s. All told, perhaps half the world's people have access to commercial television broadcasts.

The commercialization of television is just one part of the general expansion of advertising worldwide, an expansion that includes magazines and newspapers, billboards and displays, catalogs, and other media. The overall growth stands out starkly in historical trends.

Total global advertising expenditures multiplied nearly sevenfold from 1950 to 1990; they grew one-third faster than the world economy and three times faster than world population. They rose—in real, inflation-adjusted terms—from $39 billion in 1950 to $256 billion in 1990. (For comparison, the gross national product of India, the world's second most populous state, was just $253 billion that year.) In 1950, advertisers spent $16 for each person on the planet, in 1970 they spent $27, and in 1990, $48 (see Figure 1).

Americans are the most advertised-to people on Earth. U.S. marketers account for nearly half

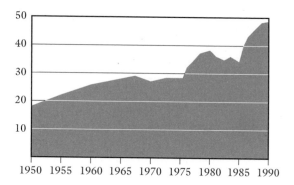

FIGURE 1 World Advertising Expenditures, Per Capita, 1950–90

of the world's ad budget, according to the International Advertising Association in New York, spending $468 per American in 1991. Among the industrial countries, Japan is second in the advertising league, dedicating more than $300 per citizen to sales pitches each year. Western Europe is close behind. A typical European is the target of more than $200 worth of ads a year. The latest boom is underway in Eastern Europe, a region that John Lindquist of the Boston Consulting Group calls "an advertising executive's dream—people actually remember advertisements."

Advertising is growing fast in developing countries as well, though it remains small scale by Western standards. South Korea's advertising industry grew 35 to 40 percent annually in the late 1980s, and yearly ad billings in India jumped fivefold in the 1980s, surpassing one dollar per person for the first time.

AD-ING LIFE

The sheer magnitude of the advertising barrage in consumer societies has some ironic results. For one thing, the clamor for people's attention means relatively few advertisements stick. Typical Americans are exposed to some 3,000 commercial messages a day, according to *Business Week*. Amid such a din, who notices what any one ad says?

To lend their messages greater influence, marketers are forced to deliver ever higher quality pitches—and to seek new places to make them. They are constantly on the lookout for new routes into people's consciousness.

With the advent of the remote control, the mute button, and the video cassette recorder during the 1980s, people could easily avoid TV commercials, and advertisers had to seek out consumers elsewhere. Expanding on the traditional print and broadcast media, advertisers began piping messages into classrooms and doctors' offices, weaving them into the plots of feature films, posting them on chair-lift poles, printing them on postage stamps and board games, stitching them on Boy Scout merit badges and professional athletes' jerseys, mounting them in bathroom stalls, and playing them back between rings on public phones.

Marketers hired telephone solicitors, both human and computerized, to call people directly in their homes. They commissioned essays from well-known authors, packaged them between full-page ads fore and aft, and mailed them to opinion leaders to polish the sponsors' images. And they created ad-packed television programming for use at airports, bus stops, subway stations, exercise clubs, ski resorts, and supermarket checkout lines.

This creeping commercialization of life has a certain inevitability to it. As the novelty of each medium wears off, advertisers invent another one, relentlessly expanding the share of our collective attention span that they occupy with sales spiels.

Next, they will meet us at the mall, follow us to the dinner table, and shine down on us from the heavens. In shopping centers, they have begun erecting wall-sized video screens to heighten the frenzy of the shopping experience. Food engineers are turning the food supply into an advertising medium. The Viskase company of Chicago prints edible ad slogans on hot dogs, and Eggverts International is using a similar technique to advertise on thousands of eggs in Israel. Lighting engineers are hard at work on featherweight ways to turn blimps into giant airborne neon signs, and, demonstrating that not even the sky is the limit, Coca-Cola convinced orbiting Soviet cosmonauts to sip their soda on camera a couple of years ago.

The main outcome of this deadening commercialization is to sell not particular products, but consumerism itself. The implicit message of all advertising is the idea that there is a product to solve each of life's problems. Every commercial teaches that existence would be satisfying and complete if only we bought the right things. As religious historian Robert Bellah put it, "That happiness is to be attained through limitless material acquisition is denied by every religion and philosophy known to humankind, but is preached incessantly by every American television set."

GET 'EM WHILE THEY'RE YOUNG

The commercialization of space and time has been accompanied by the commercialization of youth. Marketers are increasingly targeting the young. One specialist in marketing to children told the *Wall Street Journal,* "Even two-year-olds are concerned about their brand of clothes, and by the age of six are full-out consumers." American children and teenagers sit through about three hours of television commercials each week—20,000 ads a year, translating to 360,000 by the time they graduate from high school.

The children's market in the United States is so valuable—topping $75 billion in 1990—that American companies spent $500 million marketing to kids in 1990, five times more than they spent a decade earlier. They started cartoons centered around toys and began direct-mail marketing to youngsters enrolled in their company-sponsored "clubs."

Such saturation advertising has allowed some firms to stake huge claims in the children's market. Mattel vice president Meryl Friedman brags, "Mattel has achieved a stunning 95 percent penetration with Barbie [dolls] among girls 3 to 11 in the United States."

Predictably, major retailers have opened Barbie departments to compete for the loyalty of doll-doting future consumers, and marketers pay premium prices to employ the dolls as an advertising medium. Barbies come equipped with Reebok shoes and Benetton clothes.

MADISON AVENUE'S PAPER TRAIL

Advertising's main ecological danger may be the consumption it inspires, but it also consumes heavily itself. Advertisers use a substantial share of the world's paper, particularly its heavily-processed high-quality paper. Paper production involves not only forest damage but also large energy inputs and pollution outputs.

Ads pack the daily mail: 14 billion glossy, difficult-to-recycle mail-order catalogs plus 38 billion other assorted ads clog the post office each year in the United States. Most of those items go straight into the trash—including 98 percent of advertising letters sent in direct-mail campaigns, according to the marketing journal *American Demographics.*

Ads fill periodicals: most American magazines reserve 60 percent of their pages for advertising, and some devote far more. *Bride's* was so proud of its February/March 1990 edition that it submitted the issue to the *Guinness Book of World Records* and boasted in *Advertising Age,* "The Biggest Magazine in History.... It contains 1,040 pages—including 798 advertising pages."

Newspapers are no different; in the United States, they typically contain 65 percent, up from 40 percent half a century ago. Every year, Canada cuts 42,000 acres of its primeval forests—an area the size of the District of Columbia—just to provide American dailies with newsprint on which to run advertisements.

For big and immediate paper savings, newspapers could shift classified advertising—and telephone companies their directories—onto pay-per-use electronic data bases accessible through phone lines. Still, advertising remains heavy in nonclassified sections of newspapers. Trim out all the ads and most of the text would fit in a single section.

The problem in reducing the scale of advertising in the print media is that the financial viability of newspapers and magazines is linked to the number of advertising pages they sell. In the past two years of economic recession, for example, advertising pages have been harder to sell, and many periodicals have been forced to publish fewer articles. That is not good for the flow of information in democratic societies. To get less-commercialized information sources, subscribers may have to accept higher prices, as have the readers of *Ms.*, which dropped advertising three years ago.

THE INDUSTRY OF NEEDS

The needs industry—advertising—defends itself, ultimately, by claiming that advertising, whatever its social and cultural demerits, is an indispensable component of a healthy economy. As one Madison Avenue axiom counsels, "A terrible thing happens when you don't advertise: Nothing." Advertising, in this view, isn't the trim on the industrial economy, it's the fuel. Take out the ads, and the economy sputters to a halt; put in more ads, and the economy zooms. More ads equal more wants, more wants make more spending, and more spending makes more jobs.

Some promoters even call for governments to foster more advertising. The American Advertising Federation took out a full page in *Time* magazine last March to write, "Dear Mr. President ... We respectfully remind you of advertising's role as an engine of economic growth. It raises capital, creates jobs, and spurs production.... It increases government revenues since jobs produce taxable income, and greater sales increase sales taxes ... Incentives to advertise are incentives for growth."

The validity of such claims is dubious, of course, but they cut to the heart of a critical issue. Even if advertising does promote growth, the question remains as to what kind of growth. Growth in numbers of second mortgages and third cars and fourth televisions may increase the money flowing around the economy without making us one bit happier. If much advertising is an exercise in generating dissatisfaction so that people will spend more and work harder, the entire process appears morally questionable. Several generations ago, Catholic theologian John Ryan dubbed this treadmill "squirrel cage progress."

Many of the areas in which the world needs growth most desperately—environmental literacy, racial and sexual equality, and political participation, for example—are not the stuff of advertising campaigns. "Civilization, in the real sense of the term," advised Gandhi, "consists not in the multiplication, but in the deliberate and voluntary reduction of wants."

RE-CHANNELING ADVERTISING

What legitimate role is there for advertising, then? In a sustainable society, how much advertising would there be?

None! say some, as E. F. Schumacher commented in 1979: "What is the great bulk of advertising other than the stimulation of greed, envy and avarice ... at least three of the seven deadly sins?" More succinctly, reader Charlotte Burrowes of Penacook, New Hampshire, wrote to *Worldwatch* a year ago, "There'll be a special hell for advertisers."

In fairness, though, some advertising does provide useful information about products and services. The task for democratic societies struggling to restore balance between themselves and their ecosystems is to decide how much advertising to tolerate, and while respecting the rights of individuals to speak their minds, to place appropriate limits on marketing.

The precise limits cannot yet be identified, but it may help define the issue to consider whether there are spaces that should be free of advertising. Churches? Schools? Hospitals? Funeral homes? Parks? Homes? Work places? Books? Public libraries? Public swimming pools? Public buildings? Public buses? Public streets? Mail boxes? Newspapers? Television broadcasts? What about times of day, days of the week, and times of life? Early morning? Sundays? Childhood?

Restraining the excesses of marketers and limiting commercials to their legitimate role of informing consumers would require fundamental reforms in the industry, changes that will not come about without a well-organized grassroots movement. The advertising industry is a formidable foe on the march around the world, and advertisers are masters at the slippery art of public relations. Madison Avenue can buy the best talents available to counter and circumvent reformers' campaigns, unless those campaigns are carefully focused and begin with the industry's vulnerabilities.

Advertising's Achilles heel is its willingness to push products demonstrably dangerous to human health, and this is the area where activists have been most successful and best organized. Tobacco ads are or soon will be banished from television throughout the Western democracies, and alcohol commercials are under attack as never before.

Another ready target for advertising reform activists is the assault that marketers make on children. Public sentiment runs strongly against marketing campaigns that prey on youngsters. Action for Children's Television, a citizens' group based in Boston, won a victory in late 1990 when the U.S. Congress limited television commercials aimed at children. The same year, public interest organizations in the European Community pushed through standards for European television that will put strict limits on some types of ads.

The Australian Consumers' Association is attacking junk food ads, calling for a ban or tough restrictions on hawking unhealthful fare to youngsters. Of food ads aired during children's television programs, the association's research shows that 80 percent are for high-fat, high-salt, excessively packaged snacks. The American Academy of Pediatrics is similarly concerned. Noting the high proportion of advertisements for products that violate nutrition guidelines, the organization is urging Congress to ban food ads that target the young.

Alternatively, consumers could take aim at trumped-up corporate environmental claims. Since 1989, marketers have been painting their products "green" in an attempt to defuse citizen anger at corporate ecological transgressions. In 1990, for example, the oil company Texaco offered Americans "free" tree seedlings to plant for the good of the environment; to qualify, a customer had to buy eight or more gallons of gasoline. Unmentioned in the marketing literature was the fact that it takes a typical tree about four years to store as much carbon dioxide as is released in refining and burning eight gallons of fuel, and that most tree seedlings planted by amateurs promptly die.

In the United States, one fourth of all new household products introduced in 1990 advertised themselves as "ozone-friendly," "biodegradable," "recyclable," "compostable," or something similar—claims that half of all Americans recognize as "gimmickry." Environmentalists in the Netherlands and France have attempted to cut away such misinformation by introducing a 12-point environmental advertising code in their national legislatures. Ten state attorneys general are pushing for similar national standards in the United States. Meanwhile, official and unofficial organizations throughout Europe, North America, and Japan have initiated "green labeling" programs, aiming to steer consumers to environmentally preferable products.

Efforts to restrict advertising of tobacco and alcohol, to curtail advertising to children, and to regulate environmental claims of marketers are parts of a broader agenda. The nonprofit Center for the Study of Commercialism in Washington, D.C., is calling for an end to brand-name plugs in feature films, for schools to declare themselves advertising-free zones, and for revision of the tax code so that money spent on advertising is taxable.

Just as the expanding reach of advertising is not going unchallenged, small networks of citizens everywhere are beginning to confront commercial television. In Vancouver, British Columbia, English teacher Michael Maser gets secondary students to study television production so they will be able to recognize techniques used to manipulate viewers' sentiments. Millions of young people could benefit from such a course, considering how many products are pitched to them on TV. Along the same lines as Maser's teaching, the Center for Media and Values in Los Angeles has been promoting media literacy since 1989, by furnishing parents throughout North America with tips on teaching their children to watch with a critical eye.

More boldly, some attempt to fight fire with fire. The Vancouver-based Media Foundation is building a movement aimed at using the same cleverness and humor evident in much commercial advertising to promote sustainable ends. Local groups raise funds to show the group's products on commercial television and in commercial magazines. TV spots have run in California, Ontario, and a half-dozen other states and provinces. Their "Tube Head" series of ads tell viewers to shut off the set. In one magazine ad, above a photo of a dark, sleek sports car, a caption purrs, "At this price, it will surely take your breath away." And below: "$250,000." In fine print, it explains, "U.S. sticker price based on individual share of social costs associated with automobiles in U.S. over average car life of 10 years. Does not include … oil spills at sea and on land; acid rain from auto emissions … environmental and health costs from global warming."

The premier spot in the Media Foundation's "High on the Hog" campaign shows a gigantic animated pig frolicking on a map of North America while a narrator intones: "Five percent of the people in the world consume *one-third* of the planet's resources…. Those people are us." The pig belches.

Imagine a message like *that* broadcast simultaneously to every inhabited part of the globe!

STUDY QUESTIONS

1. Do you agree with Durning that advertising poses a dangerous threat to society? Provide illustrations from your experience to support your views on the matter.

2. How, according to Durning, is advertising like a parasite? Do you agree with him?

3. How can we ensure that advertising serves good purposes rather than environmentally bad purposes? Could the cure for advertising be worse than the parasite itself?

72

The Challenge of the Future: Private Property, the City, the Globe, and a Sustainable Society

LOUIS P. POJMAN

Louis P. Pojman was professor of philosophy at the United States Military Academy at West Point and the editor of this volume. He is the author of numerous books and articles. In this essay Pojman argues that we cannot rest content with saving the wilderness; we must also apply environmental ethics to city life. He outlines a theory of a global sustainable society and suggests some examples of working toward that goal.

Much of this book has been about the wilderness or natural habitats, as though the cities were anti-environmental. I want to correct this impression, focusing on sustainable city life. Then, I will bring together many of the themes in this anthology, pointing toward a universal environmental ethic and law that requires regulation by an international body. Finally, I want briefly to suggest some practical things we all can do to live responsibly toward the environment. First, I turn to the matter of the uses of private property.

1. PRIVATE PROPERTY AND ENVIRONMENTAL ETHICS

"Nor shall private property be taken for public use without just compensation." (From the Fifth Amendment of the Constitution of the United States of America, commonly known as the Taking Clause)

In January 1986 David Lucas purchased two beachfront lots on South Carolina's Isle of Palm for $975,000, planning to build a house on one lot and sell the other lot to a home builder. In 1988 the state subsequently passed the Beachfront Management Act, which prohibited building in the area, arguing that the proposed building projects would harm the dunes and hence were a nuisance. Lucas brought the case to a local court, which awarded him $1.2 million in compensation. However, the South Carolina Supreme Court reversed the decision, citing a rule that where property is taken to prevent public harm, no compensation is required. Lucas appealed to the U.S. Supreme Court, which heard his arguments on March 2, 1992. Justice John Scalia wrote the Court's decision, which reversed the South Carolina Supreme Court decision, remanding the case back to the court to produce an equitable settlement. A strong component in majority decision was the *Taking Clause* of the Fifth Amendment (quoted above). Justice Scalia also quoted from Justice Oliver Wendell Holmes's exposition in *Pennsylvania Coal Co. v. Mahon* (1922) that "while property may be regulated to a certain

This essay is adapted from Louis P. Pojman, *Global Environmental Ethics* (McGraw-Hill, 2000).

extent, if regulation goes too far it will be recognized as a taking." And if it is a taking, then compensation is required. Justice Scalia conceded that the operative phrase "if regulation goes too far" was vague and relative to custom, but in *Agins v. Tiburon* the Court explained that a regulation goes "too far" if it "denies an owner [all] economically viable use of his land." Justice Scalia thought that this was occurring in Lucas's case.

Justice Harry Blackmun wrote a spirited minority dissent in which he defended the South Carolina Supreme Court's decision because it rested "on two premises that until today were unassailable—that the State has the power to prevent any use of property it finds to be harmful to its citizens, and that a state statute is entitled to a presumption of constitutionality."

> If the state legislature is correct that the prohibition on building in front of the setback line prevents serious harm, then, under this Court's prior cases, the Act is constitutional. "Long ago it was recognized that all property in this country is held under the implied obligation that the owner's use of it shall not be injurious to the community, and the Takings Clause did not transform that principle to one that requires compensation whenever the State asserts its power to enforce it." (*Keystone Bituminous Coal Assn. v. DeBenedictis*). The Court consistently has upheld regulations imposed to arrest a significant threat to the common welfare, whatever their economic effect on the owner.[1]

Blackmun's argument rests on the same reasoning as zoning laws (e.g., prohibiting pornography from being sold openly in stores or taverns from being opened in certain residential communities). Just because I buy a piece of land with the intention of building a liquor store on it does not automatically mean that I'm entitled to compensation when a zoning law rules out my endeavor. However, if no law exists and I start to build my liquor store, then, if the state zones against liquor stores, I am entitled to compensation. The fact that Lucas had

not actually started to construct his buildings before the law was passed seems to weigh against compensation. On the other hand, the state should probably offer to buy the property from him at a fair price. Or perhaps an environmental organization should purchase Lucas's land at a fair price.

But the larger issues are (1) whether the state has the right to prohibit what it considers harmful use of the land and (2) whether it has to compensate anyone when it prohibits ecological degradation from occurring on the land. If land is valuable for the common good and posterity, environmentalists argue, we are doing harm by depleting its quality. The ramifications of this idea are far reaching. Many artificial lakes and reservoirs in the Southwest are used mainly for recreation and cover precious bottomland with good topsoil. We are running out of good topsoil. So should we prohibit interest groups from constructing these artificial lakes? Dammed-up lakes also affect the natural environment in deleterious ways. Should this reason be good enough to prohibit their construction? Even if the land is privately owned? Golf courses often take up similarly good land and typically require enormous quantities of water and fertilizer, the latter of which seeps into the underground water supply. Should we prevent private country clubs from creating golf courses? What about highways and parking lots and shopping malls that are constructed on land that will one day be needed for farming and whose waste seeps into the underground water supply? And should owners be compensated for the restrictions we put upon them? Similarly, suppose I want to fill in wetlands I own in order to construct a shopping mall. The courts have ruled that the state may forbid me from filling in these wetlands because wetlands provide natural habitats for wildlife, help reduce flooding by slowing the runoff of heavy rains, and promote the cycling of nutrients. Should the state be made to compensate me for not filling in the wetlands? This would be very costly and probably strain the state's coffers.

Taking the environment seriously certainly limits our freedom to do what we want with land. Private property no longer has the same meaning. Until recently we thought that the owner had virtually absolute control of his or her private property, absolute discretion in what uses he or she saw fit for the land—just as long as no one else was being harmed. But if environmentalists are right, there is no absolute right to do what you want with your land. Rather, we have to extend the notion of harm to include future use—even to future people. Joseph Sax calls such protections of nature "public rights" because their infringement need not harm any identifiable person, but whose harm may be diffuse and affect future people or existing people in the future. We now have to say that property rights have been severely constricted because the land is precious, a common good that must remain in good condition for future use in perpetuity. We are not absolute owners of the land, but stewards of it.

This thinking is not new. Suppose a pharmaceutical company, at great cost, produces a powerful drug that it believes will be a cure for some malady, but then it turns out that the drug has unanticipated harmful side effects. The company has no claim to compensation from the state, which has prohibited the use of the drug, but must swallow the loss itself. Similarly, when we discover that a use of the land, hitherto thought to be benign, is harmful, the state has a right to prohibit such use without having to compensate the owner. Or take the fact that refrigerators and air conditioners used chlorofluorocarbons (CFCs). In our ignorance we thought that such use was benign. Now we have evidence that CFCs are depleting the ozone layer, causing cancer. Aren't we within our rights to pass legislation demanding that a substitute be found for harmful CFCs? Just because they were allowed in a previous time of ignorance is no reason for thinking that the companies should now be compensated for being required to stop using such chemicals.[2] Whether the state should help in the research and development of substitutes is another matter. Perhaps it should.

Environmental considerations seem to require that we amend our understanding of *land* property rights. Once thought to be absolute—as long as we were not directly using our property to unjustly harm others—we now see that some uses of land, formerly thought benign, may well harm others, including those who will live after us. Or, if not harm them directly, at least prohibit them from using the land for optimal purposes (e.g., if I fill in the wetlands, species may be lost and we may be unable to restore them to their original state). We must see the land not as our inalienable, absolute property, but as an entrustment—that is, a stewardship model must replace the ownership model. The land is on loan to us to use and develop as long as we do not make it significantly worse.

The Wise Use Movement

I hope the preceding discussion sounds rational, even commonsensical to you. One might say that what environmentalists are advocating is wise use of the land, as well as the wilderness, the forests, and the waterways. Unfortunately, words are cheap and names misleading. Alas, anti-environmentalists have coopted the good phrase "wise use" to defeat many of the programs necessary to maintain and preserve the environment. In 1979 Ron Arnold wrote a series of articles for *Logging Management* in which he called for a coalition to counter the environmental movement. Alan Gottlieb followed up on his call and together they organized what has become known as the Wise Use Movement, a phrase borrowed from Teddy Roosevelt's chief of the Forestry Service, Gifford Pinchot. It has become an umbrella organization for more than 200 organizations dedicated to fight environmentalist agenda—e.g., from promoting the cutting of old growths in national forests, removing protection from endangered species, allowing private development of public lands and strip mining, to mandating compensation for any *takings* by the government—when they are taken for environmental causes.

I regard the Wise Use Movement as a fearful reaction to the radical changes that are occurring in our understanding of humanity's relationship to its environment. It is hard to change old ways of thinking, and sometimes environmentalists are not patient, understanding, or ready to negotiate with those who haven't developed a sufficiently progressive attitude toward nature. Indeed, some environmentalists seem fanatical, resorting to ecosabotage (see Reading 80). Although the Wise Use Movement must be exposed and resisted, more work probably needs to be done to find intermediate solutions for those who stand to lose their jobs, investments, and property as we pursue the quest for ecological wholeness.[3]

Let me now turn to another difficult issue on which more work needs to be done.

2. THE CITY

In 1800 about 2% of the world's population lived in urban areas; by 1900 the figure had doubled to 4%; in 1950 it had reached 30%. Since 1950 the number has jumped from 750 million to 2.64 billion—projected to reach 3.3 billion by 2005. In 1975 about one-third of the world's population lived in cities. In 1997, 2.64 billion people, or 46% of the world's population, lived in cities and, according to UN estimates, that figure will soon reach 53.7%. The projection is that almost two-thirds of humanity will live in cities by 2015. The 61 million people being added to cities each year come mainly through rural to urban migration. The most dramatic shifts are taking place in the developing nations, where urban population growth is 3.5% per annum, as opposed to 1% in the more developed nations. In 1800 about 6% of the U.S. population lived in cities. By 1900 the figure was 40%, and by 1997 it was 75%. Until a few generations ago most Americans lived on farms, produced their own food and clothes, educated their children at home, and lived a simple life, far from urban problems of overcrowding and crime. They rode horses and fished in nearby streams and rivers.

The number of urban areas is also increasing. In 1800 London was the only city with more than one million people. Today 326 cities have more than one million people, and 14 are megacities, urban areas with populations of more than 10 million. Tokyo is currently the most populous city with 27 million people in its densely populated urban area, about one-quarter of Japan's entire population.

Lagos, Nigeria, growing at a rate of 5.4%, has increased from 10.3 million people in 1995 to more than 13.5 million in 2001, heading toward 25 million by 2015.

Our founding fathers were committed to small town, rural America. The first antiurban tract, *Notes on the State of Virginia* (1781), written by Thomas Jefferson, deplored urbanity as being opposed to good government.

> The mobs of the great cities add just as much to the support of pure government as sores do to the strength of the human body.[4]

In a letter to Benjamin Rush, Jefferson wrote, "I view great cities as pestilential to the morals, the health and the liberties of man."[5] He envisioned the simple living, citizen farmer, uncorrupted by urban luxury and sophistication, as the ideal democrat, the morally righteous man who had a stake in good government and who had no need for the unnecessary frills of urban society.

Nineteenth-century Americans shared Jefferson's faith in the farmer. Essayist Ralph Waldo Emerson thought that only farmers created wealth and that all trade depended on their endeavors. He shared Jefferson's views on the moral superiority of farmers:

> The uncorrupted behavior which we admire in animals and in young children belongs to [the farmer], to the hunter, the sailor—the man who lives in the presence of Nature. Cities force growth and make men talkative and entertaining, but they make them artificial.[6]

Similar sentiments are found in the writings of Plato (in Book II of the *Republic*), Henry Thoreau, Herman Melville, Nathaniel Hawthorne, and Edgar Allan Poe, who compared the city to a sewer of evil and wickedness. William James (1842–1910) deplored the "hollowness" and "brutality" of large cities and advocated their decentralization. James's colleague at Harvard, Josiah Royce (1855–1916), offered three criticisms of urbanity. (1) Cities were so overwhelmed with large numbers of alienated and unassimilated people that the essential fabric of society was stretched to the breaking point; (2) the centralization of culture produced mass conformity and intellectual stagnation; and (3) cities promoted the "spirit of the mob," which is the enemy of individualism and liberty.

These criticisms, though debatable, have continued throughout the twentieth century and seem likely to trouble us as we enter into the twenty-first century. Counterculture critic Ted Roszak sums up the present criticism—cities are decadent.

> ... the problem posed by the city as an imperialistic cultural force that carries the disease of colossalism in its most virulent form.... At the same time, the city is a compendium of our society's ecological bad habits. It is the most incorrigible of wasters and polluters; its economic style is the major burden weighing upon the planetary environment. Of all the hypertrophic institutions our society has inflicted upon both the person and the planet, the industrial city is the most oppressive.[7]

The case against cities goes like this: Cities are parasites on the agricultural base located in the country. They take in resources—water from the mountains, food from the farms, oil from other nations, coffee and tea and other products from the developing countries. Although they take advantage of concentrated labor and produce important goods and services, which rural areas are unable to do, they also create expensive luxury items, which no one really needs and which may actually weaken society's moral fiber—like indulgent department stores for the rich, neon light districts, the compressed trees called the Sunday *New York Times,* and energy-inefficient buildings—and they typically are filled with vehicles which pollute the atmosphere. Advertising creates false consciousness and a craving for the spoils of splendor. The city is often a cesspool of pollution, a sewer of vice, violence, crime, corruption, poor schools, poverty, unemployment, high taxes, suffering, and alienation. Typically dense with the anonymous homeless, panhandlers, muggers, and drug addicts, pungent with the smell of decay, the ugly sights of gaudy graffiti and garish advertisements, and the noise of boomboxes, garbage trucks, and ambulances, the urban ulcer ubiquitously bombards our senses and crowds out our thoughts, alienating us from our selves. The barrage of sensory stimulation overwhelms us, suffocating the inner voice within, so that we become alienated individuals in the lonely crowd. A common, superficial media culture informs our ideas and dictates our tastes and fashions. These unnatural conditions close people off from the realities of the wilderness and agriculture—children and some adults actually suppose that food naturally comes wrapped in clean cellophane packages. Sheltered from the killings, from the blood and stench of the slaughterhouse, from the screams of the cattle and sheep and pigs, from the chickens *tortured* by our modern death chambers, the people of the city live in ignorance—not blissful ignorance, however, for decadence, disease, and death haunt their lives and render all too many of them meaningless.

Yet cities offer civilization:[8] culture and convenience, commerce and industry, employment and job-training, business headquarters and research centers, libraries and universities, music and theater, and a wide range of diverse ideas and attitudes. Its standards of sanitation and health care are usually better than those in rural areas. For the prosperous, city life can be liberating. The concentration of people, wealth, culture, and business offers enormous opportunities for those equipped to take advantage of them.

Cities like Minneapolis, Minnesota; Vancouver, Canada; and Melbourne, Australia—with their public parks, lakes, walking trails, bicycle paths, open spaces, low crime rates, and children's playgrounds—stand out as models for the future. Every home in Minneapolis is within six blocks of green spaces. Melbourne reduced land taxes to attract the middle class to its environs, restricted the height of buildings to 131 feet (about 12 stories), and successfully renovated the decrepit structures of its inner city. Some 50,000 people now live in the central business district, a fivefold increase from a decade ago. But only time will tell what difference the recent addition of a mammoth casino will make.[9]

In 1993, Cajamarca, Peru, one of the poorest communities in the world, was racked by disease, unemployment, and water problems. Its infant mortality rate of 94.7 per 1,000 live births was 82% higher than the Peruvian national average. The Kilish River, a source of drinking water for the poor, had been contaminated by mining operations and untreated sewage. Overgrazing in nearby rural areas and clear-cutting of forests for fuel had caused severe soil erosion, exacerbating flooding problems and contributing to a depressed economy. In 1993 nongovernmental organizations (NGOs), in cooperation with businesses and local unions, organized communities in the urban and nearby rural areas into 76 "minor population centers," each with its own mayor and council. This dramatic decentralization of government power enabled the people to deal with local issues while communicating with an area-wide, overarching authority. Together they set up carpentry schools, an efficient water delivery system, refuse collection, health services, and park improvements. In the rural areas outside the city they terraced the steep hillsides and put into operation a plan to reduce mining pollution.[10]

In 1980 an NGO developed the Orangi Pilot Project (OPP) in the poverty-stricken, ethnically diverse city of Karachi, Pakistan. The residents were organized into groups of 20 to 40 families living along the same lane and taught to use appropriate technology to construct low-cost sanitation facilities. After this four-year project was successful, OPP developed basic health and family planning programs, including immunization programs for children. Next it created a credit program to fund loans for small family enterprises, a low-cost housing upgrade program, a program to assist in improving educational facilities, a women's work center program, and a rural development program. Each house received a sanitary latrine. The Karachi government contributed to the construction costs of health and sanitation facilities, but by simplifying design and standardizing parts, these costs were greatly reduced, in some cases to as low as one-fifth of similar improvements elsewhere in the city. Within a decade 95% of the children were being immunized, 44% of the families were practicing birth control, epidemic disease was under control, and hygiene and nutrition had improved. Infant mortality fell from 130 per 1,000 live births in 1982 to 37 in 1991. Through the work center women learned to stitch clothing, enabling them to do piecework bound for international export at higher wages than they had ever earned, thus contributing to the overall wealth of the community.[11]

Such examples of sustainable urbanization, often in conjunction with nearby rural development, are impressive and offer models of a better future, but success stories are still too few and far between. Accessible clean water, sanitation systems, decentralized government, local empowerment to men and women, education, job training, and inexpensive basic health care—all seem necessary but not sufficient for sustainable city life. A moral consciousness must exist to energize and synthesize a community. People must believe in environmental goals and commit themselves to them.

The evils of cities, mentioned earlier, tend to compete with and even outweigh these possible environmental virtues, causing many people to fear urban existence, treating the city as a nice place to visit but a bad place to live. Because most of us want the benefits of city life, the question is, How can we restructure our cities so that they are environmentally sustainable centers of human flourishing?

This is the big question, and in answer I can only point to some attempts that have been made. We need to solve this problem. When we visit cities, we see children growing up without trees to climb or rivers in which to swim. In their place are urban jungles where skyscrapers replace redwoods on the near horizon. Comparing that with my own edge-of-the-town, semi-rural upbringing, where I spent summers playing barefoot in the woods, swimming in ponds and rivers, sadness overcomes me because urban children are missing these simple joys. I see children who are over-socialized, programmed from the nursery school to the university, never feeling the call of the wild or imbibing the wide open spaces of the prairie or the flow of the river, captives of too much repressive civilization, their watches mechanically dictating their schedules from their earliest years.

There are too many people in the cities. Every week one million people are added to these urban centers. Poor people are lured from the countryside of other countries by the promise of a better life, only to add to the malaise of urban poverty. Cities are densely populated, and the friction of our encounters ruffles our nerves and leaves us yearning for clean open spaces, for freedom of movement. We need more parks in our cities—much on the European model—and fewer cars and trucks. New York City, with its ban on motor vehicles in Central Park on weekends, has taken a step in the right direction. The ban should be extended to the other five days of the week and to other parts of our cities, because motor vehicles are the main air polluters in New York City and elsewhere. Affordable public transportation should replace cars wherever feasible. Recycling of aluminum cans, glass, and paper is cumbersome but is an environmental necessity. We must make it both natural and economical.

People in cities need more places to plant trees and gardens where they can grow flowers and vegetables. Tall buildings should not dominate the skyline, but smaller ones that allow the light to shine on its inhabitants. Political decentralization is necessary in order to afford people a greater opportunity to participate in the political process. An efficient government, a streamlined court system, and a sense of fairness must bind people to each other—promoting the commonweal. But this sense of a common life and a common cause is difficult to create, especially when politicians and intellectuals emphasize differences rather than commonality, where ethnic and cultural diversity are allowed to divide people. Neither a nation, nor a city divided against itself, can long survive, let alone flourish, and a political structure that allows unjust discrimination will sink in the quicksand of the swamps of exaggerated racial identity, ethnicity, and hate. Diversity may be enriching and has a legitimate place—diversity of ideas—as long as people adhere to a common core morality, an agreed-upon political process that brings us together as a moral community—*e pluribus unum*. But where we do approach that common culture—in TV programs and films, for example—it is often shallow and amoral.

Because we prize freedom so much and depend on an unplanned free market economy to such a remarkable degree, it is difficult to solve these seemingly intractable environmental and social problems. Capitalism, our economic system, is like a powerful machine that is under no one's control, satisfying short-term wants and offering wealth, but threatening to uproot our traditions and all those spiritual bonds that tie us together. The truth is that we are not dealing with it successfully; we are allowing it to proceed unchecked in a manner dangerous to our future—as the rich get richer and the poor get prison.

Environmentalists have focused virtually all of their attention on the wilderness, on pristine nature. But in doing so, they may have missed something equally important, the urban environment. The challenge of the twenty-first century will be not only to preserve the wilderness but also to reinvigorate our urban centers with simple dignity and natural beauty.

3. GLOBALISM: ONE WORLD, ONE ETHIC

In the last section we saw that part of the solution to urban crises lay in decentralized authority combined with a supporting, enlightened government. Reducing the locus of power to the smallest possible group, down to the individual, makes sense, because each individual or small group is a better authority on where the shoe pinches than a distant bureaucracy is. On the other hand, individuals and communities often lack resources to lift themselves from poverty or environmental degradation without help, so an overarching umbrella authority is necessary to distribute goods and services. Moreover, there is the problem of the tragedy of the commons to contend with, which leads to the necessity of an overarching regulatory system. My business or community or country is likely to reason that it is in our interest to use CFCs (or burn fossil fuels) because the benefits we reap are solely ours, whereas we share the harms, a depleted ozone layer (or enhanced greenhouse effect), with others. But if everyone thinks this way, the ozone layer is likely to be destroyed and everyone will suffer a cataclysmic global disaster. Similarly, with regard to emitting greenhouse gases, if we all act in our perceived immediate interest, we are bound to reap total and global ruin. Thus it is in all our interests to give up some of our autonomy and accept "mutually agreed-upon, mutually coercive regulations" which, if followed by the majority, will result in mutual benefit. Recently, I was in North Carolina and heard about the problem of disposing of pig waste (a pig, I was told, discharges an enormous amount of waste—five times the amount of an average human). The sanitation facilities were inadequate, and pig waste was seeping into the water supply in parts of the state, but the state government was reluctant to force the pig industry to invest in better waste disposal systems lest it move out of North Carolina to a state with more relaxed regulations. The solution in such cases is for a federal standard, nationally enforced. Similarly, I was told that Switzerland had imposed strict safety regulations on the pig industry. The result? All pig industries have moved out of Switzerland to less demanding countries. The Swiss still eat the same amount of pork but pay more for it. The solution is obvious: For the health of all people, we should have an international regulatory commission monitoring and enforcing safety standards.

Many of our most intractable environmental problems are international in nature. Radiation from Chernobyl was experienced as far west as Sweden and Switzerland; air pollution from Poland's factories drifts to neighboring countries; greenhouse gases effect climate patterns all over the globe; the depletion of the ozone layer affects the health of people in many nations; and we all will suffer from the loss of biodiversity. Rivers and underground water tables—aquifers—do not respect national boundaries, so that if country A depletes its water table, country B, frugal though it may be, will also experience a loss of water. The recent conferences on the environment in Stockholm (1972), Rio de Janeiro (1992), and Kyoto, Japan (December 1997), fragmented and seemingly fraught with

controversy and national self-interest though they were, are a fledgling step in the right direction. At least, we're talking with each other about global environmental degradation and solutions to that degradation, seeking to work out a set of universal rights from which global environmental law will arise. Principles 7 and 8 of the Rio Declaration put the matter this way:

> Principle 7: States shall cooperate in a spirit of global partnership to conserve, protect and restore the health and integrity of the Earth's ecosystem. In view of the different contributions to global environmental degradation, States have common but differentiated responsibilities. The developed countries acknowledge the responsibility that they bear in the international pursuit of sustainable development in view of the pressures their societies place on the global environment and of the technologies and financial resources they command.

> Principle 8: To achieve sustainable development and a higher quality of life for all people, States should reduce and eliminate unsustainable patterns of production and consumption and promote appropriate demographic policies.

Other principles call for compensation of victims of pollution (13), a prohibition of reallocation of toxic substances to poorer countries (14), the internalization of the environmental costs of pollution (16), and the ecological protection of weaker countries from oppression and domination by the wealthier corporations and nations (23). The Charter of the United Nations will be the "appropriate means" for resolving "all their environmental disputes."[12]

As international body, such as the United Nations, will be needed to regulate and enforce these environmental laws. This will not be easy for nationalists to swallow, but we are gradually moving toward universal government to complement and qualify national autonomy. The world is shrinking. Already, several multinational corporations are among the wealthiest bodies in the world, richer than most nations.[13] Even as the capitalist economy has became global, the regulation of the environment must become more global. The road to an enforceable global environmental law will be fraught with obstacles, but in the end we must realize our common humanity, a common objective morality, and a common commitment to ecological wholeness and sustainable living.

4. WORKING FOR A SUSTAINABLE SOCIETY

On May 14, 1998, Marjory Stoneman Douglas died at the age of 108. The author of many short stories, novels, and works of nonfiction, she is best known for her influential 1947 call to arms, *The Everglades: River of Grass*, a natural and political history of the wetlands of southern Florida. Mrs. Douglas protested against the poor land management that was imperiling the Everglades' ecosystem, opposed state and local policies that encouraged overdevelopment, and led the campaign to have the central core of the Everglades preserved as a national park. The Everglades has shrunk from more than 4,000 square miles to less than half that size, the result of over-drainage, urban sprawl, and pollution from government-supported sugar cane and diary farming. Many environmentalists believe that its fate is still in doubt. Regarding the apathy of the people of South Florida to the plight of the Everglades, Mrs. Douglas said, "They could not get it through their heads that they had produced some of the worst conditions themselves, by their lack of cooperation, their selfishness, their mutual distrust and their willful refusal to consider the truth of the whole situation." Unless people act responsibly "over-drainage will go on … and the soil will shrink and burn and be wasted and destroyed, in a continuing ruin." In 1969 she helped to found Friends of the Everglades, a conservation organization that now has 5,000 members. Joe Podgor, the former executive director, called her "the giant on whose shoulders we all stand." In 1990, on her 100th

birthday—blind, hearing impaired, and frail—she continued to speak out against those who plundered the Everglades. Roderick J. Jude, a longtime leader of the Florida chapter of the Sierra Club, said, "The Everglades wouldn't be there for us to continue to save if not for her work through the years." Finally, in 1996, after decades of struggle, the voters of Florida approved a constitutional amendment for cleaning up of the Everglades. In 1997, hoping to rescue the endangered ecosystem from polluted run-off from the sugar cane industry, the Clinton administration and the state of Florida agreed to buy more than 50,000 acres of sugar cane fields on the outskirts of the Everglades National Park. In 1993 President Clinton awarded her the Presidential Medal of Freedom and said, "Long before there was an Earth Day, Mrs. Douglas was a passionate steward of our nation's natural resources, and particularly her Florida Everglades."[14]

Marjory Douglas deserves to be ranked with Henry Thoreau, John Muir, President Theodore Roosevelt, Aldo Leopold, Herman Daly, Rachel Carson, Chico Mendes, and Lois Gibbs—all mentioned earlier in this work—as one of the friends of the Earth, people, who by their integrity, courage, and commitment, made important contributions toward preserving and promoting ecological well-being. They all attest to the fact that citizens can make a difference in making this a better world. These are our present-day heroes, our much needed role models for simple living, local acting, and global thinking.

The fate of the Earth is still in doubt. Many questions about the state of the environment remain. Good and honest people can differ on their reading of the evidence regarding the best energy policy, the best ways to limit pollution, the prognosis of the greenhouse effect, the implications of population growth, and so forth. Some of you, reading this book, will opt for radical action to save the planet, others for a more conservative policy, and still other for mixed strategies. We live in a democracy, which is sometimes dull and sluggish in promoting the common good, but which affords opportunity for open debate about these important and difficult environmental issues. But although the democratic processes are often painfully slow, they seem the most moral—or least dangerous—processes at our disposal. Those who become impatient with these processes may engage in nonviolent protest to get their point across, but certainly, if history has taught us anything, it is that violence—whether it be perpetrated in the name of the Palestinian cause on the West Bank or that of Catholic freedom in Northern Ireland, and including eco-sabotage—is counterproductive. Violence begets more violence, destroying even the good that exists. Concerned citizens, then, must engage in a peaceful political process, working for a raised consciousness about environmental concerns in the public domain. We must also live out our ecological philosophy because, to a remarkable degree, the personal is the political. Your actions speak louder than your words.

UNITED STATES: THE BIGGEST CONSUMER IN THE WORLD

In one lifetime (70 years) each person in the United States consumes and wastes:

Resource Consumption	Waste
623 tons of fossil fue	840 tons of agricultural waste
613 tons of sand, gravel & stone	823 tons of garbage & industrial waste
26 million gallons of water	7 million gallons of polluted water
21,000 gallons of gasoline	70 tons of air pollution
50 tons of food	19,250 bottles
48 tons of wood	7 automobiles
19 tons of paper	

Each person in the United States uses 70 times as much energy as a Bangladeshi, 50 times as much as a Malagasy, and 20 times as much as a Costa Rican.

Because we typically live longer, the effect of each of us is further multiplied. In a year each person in the United States uses 300 times as much energy as a Malian; over a lifetime the total is 500 times as much.

Even if all such effects as the clearing of forests and burning of grasslands are factored in and attributed to poor people, those who live in the poor parts of the world are typically responsible for the annual release of one-tenth of a ton of carbon each, whereas the average for residents of the Western nations is 3.5 tons. The richest one-tenth of those in the United States annually emit 11 tons of carbon apiece.

Much has been accomplished since the 1960s, but much has yet to be done. On the plus side, a growing number of citizens have become conscious of environmental concerns, as the membership in environmental organizations such as the Sierra Club, the Wilderness Society, the Nature Conservancy, and others indicates. The celebration of Earth Day each April 22 since 1990 represents a heightened awareness of the environmental crisis. Many school systems, such as those of Wisconsin, incorporate environmental education into the curriculum. In the United States we've seen the passing of the Federal Water Pollution Control Act; the Clean Air Act; the Wilderness Act, setting aside or protecting several ecosystems; the Endangered Species Act, protecting species from harm; and the Toxic Substance Control Act, requiring the screening of new substances before they are widely used. These and the recent international conferences on environmental concerns, such as global warming and biodiversity, already discussed, are steps in the right direction.

On the negative side, the greenhouse effect is getting worse; carbon dioxide in the atmosphere has increased from 280 ppm at the beginning of the Industrial Revolution to 360 ppm, and it threatens to reach 500 ppm by the middle of the twenty-first century.[15] The great glaciers on Antarctica are breaking up, and climate patterns may be changing dangerously. The ozone layer continues to be depleted, and acid rain and other pollutants continue their destructive effect on lakes and forests. The world's rivers and underground aquifers are increasingly polluted, and rich topsoil continues to be eroded. The destruction of the rain forests and the forests everywhere continues at a menacing pace. The future of the Earth is in jeopardy.

The Earth's population, which has passed 6.4 billion, continues to grow exponentially. People in the developing countries seek to increase their living standards and consumption in a manner similar to those of the developed countries, depleting resources and producing enormous pollution. Add to this the fact that we're losing much of our topsoil and our food production is declining. In 1981 Julian Simon, in his book *The Ultimate Resource*, showed how global food production had continued to rise, and thus become cheaper, for several decades. He wrote, "The obvious implication of this historical trend toward cheaper food—a trend that probably extends back to the beginning of agriculture—is that real prices for food will continue to drop.... It is a fact that portends more drops in price and even less scarcity in the future."[16]

A few years later, however, the sharp growth rates in food production began to level off. Now the gains in grain production are coming in smaller increments, too small to keep pace with the world's population growth. Bill McKibben points out that "The world reaped its largest harvest of grain per capita in 1984; since then the amount of corn and wheat and rice per person has fallen by six percent. Grain stockpiles have shrunk to less than two month's supply."[17]

Why Recycle Paper?

1. To save forests: Recycling one ton of office paper saves seventeen trees.

2. To save energy: It takes 60% less energy to manufacture paper from recycled stock than from virgin materials. Every ton of recycled paper saves 4,200 kilowatts of energy, enough to meet the energy needs of at least 4,000 people.

3. To save water: Making paper from recycled paper stock uses 15% less water than making paper "from scratch." Recycling one ton of paper saves 7,000 gallons of water, enough to supply the daily water needs of almost 30 households.

4. To reduce garbage overload: Every ton of paper not landfilled saves 3 cubit yards of landfill space.

What can we do? If the thoughts set forth in this work have any validity, we can and ought to live more simply. We in the West must lower our consumption levels and reduce the pollution we cause, at the same time encouraging people everywhere to deal with exponential population growth and resource consumption. We can use less and more efficient electricity, recycle paper, plastics, glass and metal, use fluorescent lights, incline toward a vegetarian diet, walk and cycle for short distances, and use public transportation wherever possible, instead of using cars. We can keep in good physical condition and decrease energy use by walking up stairs instead of using elevators. Instead of turning up the thermostat, put on an extra sweater. Wherever possible, we should install solar panels in our buildings. We can strive to make our cities more environmentally wholesome and, at the same time, promote organic farming and local gardens. We can increase our appreciation of the wilderness and spend time camping and hiking, observing wildlife, and appreciating the beauty and stillness of forests and canyonlands. We can join and support an environmental organization that best identifies our values and concerns. We can support political leaders who promote environmental integrity. We can share our ideas and vision of a better world with others, encouraging them to join the environmental movement for a better world. We can become informed citizens and then educate the media, newspapers, radio, and television personnel to the significance of environmental concerns. Our hope is in the young. If we can instill an environmental consciousness in the children, in our homes, churches, and schools, we may be able to save our global home—our planet.

In sum: Live simply so that others may simply live.

NOTES

1. Lucas v. South Carolina Coastal Council (Blackmun, J. dissenting).

2. I am indebted for this illustration to Gary Varner, "The Eclipse of Land as Private Property" in Ethics and Environmental Policy, eds. F. Ferre and P. Hartel (Athens, GA: The University of Georgia Press, 1994). Varner's article contains a helpful discussion of these matters.

3. For a good discussion of the "Wise Use Movement" see Lisa Newton and Catherine Dillingham, Watersheds 2 (Wadsworth, 1997), Ch. 10.

4. Thomas Jefferson, Notes on the State of Virginia (New York: Harper & Row, 1964), 158.

5. Thomas Jefferson, Works of Thomas Jefferson, Vol. 4, ed. P. Ford (New York: Putnam, 1905), 146–7.

6. Ralph Waldo Emerson, Society and Solitude (Boston: Houghton Mifflin, 1883), 148.

7. Theodore Roszak, Person/Planet (London: Gollancz, 1979), pp. 253–4.

8. Webster's Dictionary defines civilization as "(1) a relatively high level of culture and technological development; specifically, the stage of cultural development at which writing and the keeping of written records is attained; (2) refinement of thought; (3) a situation of urban comforts.

9. "Cities at Work" by Brendan I. Koerner, U.S. News & World Report, June 8, 1998.

10. "Cities Take Action: Local Environmental Initiatives" by Jeb Brugmann, World Resources: The Urban Environment 1996–97 (New York: Oxford University Press, 1996), pp. 128–9.

11. "The Orangi Pilot Project, Karachi, Pakistan," by Akhtar Badshah, World Resources: The Urban Environment 1996–97 (New York: Oxford University Press, 1996), pp. 132–3.

12. The Rio Declaration, approved by the United Nations Conference on Environment and Development (Rio de Janeiro, Brazil, June 3–14, 1992) and later endorsed by the 47th session of the United Nations General Assembly on December 22, 1992. Reprinted in L. Pojman, ed. Environmental Ethics, 3rd ed. (Wadsworth, 2001).

13. For a good discussion of the coming global economy, see William Greider, One World, Ready or Not (New York: Simon & Schuster, 1997).

14. "Marjory Douglas, Champion of Everglades, Dies at 108," New York Times, May 15, 1998, p. A23.

15. "Climate Is an Angry Beast, and We Are Poking It with Sticks" (Wallace Broecker in McKibben, "A Special Moment in History," Atlantic Monthly, May 1998, p. 70).

16. Julian Simon, The Ultimate Resource (Princeton University Press, 1981).

17. Bill McKibben, "A Special Moment in History," Atlantic Monthly, May 1998, p. 62.

STUDY QUESTIONS

1. What should be done in cases like the one of David Lucas's property rights? Was the Supreme Court wrong in stating that he was entitled to compensation? Could such a policy bankrupt governments?

2. Why are cities crucial to environmental ethics? Do you agree that a major challenge of the twenty-first century will be to produce sustainable cities? Explain your answer.

3. What are the most important features in a sustainable city?

4. Assess the argument that the development of a global environmental ethic requires international environmental law. Will we need a global regulating body to enforce such law? Or is there a more effective way of dealing with environmental problems? Explain your answer.

5. What else can be done to produce a sustainable society?

6. What can you do to promote environmental well-being?

7. Imagine an ideal ecologically sustainable country. What would it look like?

73

Strategic Monkeywrenching

DAVE FOREMAN

Dave Foreman is the founder of Earth First!, an activist environmental organization that advocates "monkeywrenching." Monkeywrenching is the name coined for the destruction of machines or property that is used to destroy the natural world. It includes wrecking heavy equipment like bulldozers; hammering spikes into trees, which will later damage saw blades; and punching holes into whaling ships.

… Only one hundred and fifty years ago, the Great Plains were a vast, waving sea of grass stretching from the Chihuahuan Desert of Mexico to the boreal forest of Canada, from the oak-hickory forests of the Ozarks to the Rocky Mountains. Bison blanketed the plains—it has been estimated that 60 million of the huge, shaggy beasts moved across the grass. Great herds of pronghorn and elk also filled this Pleistocene landscape. Packs of wolves and numerous grizzly bears followed the immense herds.

One hundred and fifty years ago, John James Audubon estimated that there were several *billion* birds in a flock of passenger pigeons that flew past him for several days on the Ohio River. It has been said that a squirrel could travel from the Atlantic seaboard to the Mississippi River without touching the ground, so dense was the deciduous forest of the East.

At the time of the Lewis and Clark Expedition, an estimated 100,000 grizzlies roamed the western half of what is now the United States. The howl of the wolf was ubiquitous. The condor dominated the sky from the Pacific Coast to the Great Plains. Salmon and sturgeon filled the rivers. Ocelots,

jaguars, margay cats and jaguarundis roamed the Texas brush and Southwestern deserts and mesas. Bighorn sheep in great numbers ranged the mountains of the Rockies, Great Basin, Southwest and Pacific Coast. Ivory-billed woodpeckers and Carolina parakeets filled the steamy forests of the Deep South. The land was alive.

East of the Mississippi, giant tulip poplars, chestnuts, oaks, hickories and other trees formed the most diverse temperate deciduous forest in the world. On the Pacific Coast, redwood, hemlock, Douglas fir, spruce, cedar, fir and pine formed the grandest forest on Earth.

In the space of a few generations we have laid waste to paradise. The tall grass prairie has been transformed into a corn factory where wildlife means the exotic pheasant. The short grass prairie is a grid of carefully fenced cow pastures and wheat fields. The passenger pigeon is no more. The last died in the Cincinnati Zoo in 1914. The endless forests of the East are tame woodlots. The only virgin deciduous forest there is in tiny museum pieces of hundreds of acres. Six hundred grizzlies remain, and they are going fast. There are only three condors left in the wild and they are

From *Ecodefense: A Field Guide to Monkeywrenching*, by Dave Foreman (Tucson, A.Z.: Ned Ludd, 1987), pp. 10–17. Reprinted by permission of the author.

scheduled for capture and imprisonment in the Los Angeles Zoo. Except in northern Minnesota and Isle Royale, wolves are known merely as scattered individuals drifting across the Canadian and Mexican borders (a pack has recently formed in Glacier National Park). Four percent of the peerless Redwood Forest remains and the monumental old growth forest cathedrals of Oregon are all but gone. The tropical cats have been shot and poisoned from our southwestern borderlands. The subtropical Eden of Florida has been transformed into hotels and citrus orchards. Domestic cattle have grazed bare and radically altered the composition of the grassland communities of the West, displacing elk, moose, bighorn sheep and pronghorn and leading to the virtual extermination of grizzly, wolf, cougar, bobcat and other "varmints." Dams choke the rivers and streams of the land.

Nonetheless, wildness and natural diversity remain. There are a few scattered grasslands ungrazed, stretches of free-flowing river undammed and undiverted, thousand-year-old forests, Eastern woodlands growing back to forest and reclaiming past roads, grizzlies and wolves and lions and wolverines and bighorn and moose roaming the backcountry; hundreds of square miles that have never known the imprint of a tire, the bite of a drill, the rip of a 'dozer, the cut of a saw, the smell of gasoline.

These are the places that hold North America together, that contain the genetic information of life, that represent sanity in a whirlwind of madness.

In January of 1979, the Forest Service announced the results of RARE II [its Roadless Area Review and Evaluation]: of the 80 million acres of undeveloped lands on the National Forests, only 15 million acres were recommended for protection against logging, road building and other "developments." In the big tree state of Oregon, for example, only 370,000 acres were proposed for Wilderness protection out of 4.5 million acres of roadless, uncut forest lands. Of the areas nationally slated for protection, most were too high, too dry, too cold, too steep to offer much in the way of "resources" to the loggers, miners and grazers. Those roadless areas with critical old growth forest values were allocated for the sawmill. Important

grizzly habitat in the Northern Rockies was tossed to the oil industry and the loggers. Off-road-vehicle fanatics and the landed gentry of the livestock industry won out in the Southwest and Great Basin....

The BLM [Bureau of Land Management] wilderness review has been a similar process of attrition. It is unlikely that more than 9 million acres will be recommended for Wilderness out of the 60 million with which the review began. Again, it is the more spectacular but biologically less rich areas that will be proposed for protection.

During 1984, Congress passed legislation designating minimal National Forest Wilderness acreages for most states (generally only slightly larger than the pitiful RARE II recommendations and concentrating on "rocks and ice" instead of crucial forested lands). In the next few years, similar picayune legislation for National Forest Wilderness in the remaining states and for BLM Wilderness will probably be enacted. The other roadless areas will be eliminated from consideration. National Forest Management Plans emphasizing industrial logging, grazing, mineral and energy development, road building, and motorized recreation will be implemented. Conventional means of protecting these millions of acres of wild country will largely dissipate. Judicial and administrative appeals for their protection will be closed off. Congress will turn a deaf ear to requests for additional Wildernesses so soon after disposing of the thorny issue. The effectiveness of conventional political lobbying by conservation groups to protect endangered wild lands will evaporate. And in half a decade, the saw, "dozer" and drill will devastate most of what is unprotected. The battle for wilderness will be over. Perhaps 3% of the United States will be more or less protected and it will be open season on the rest. Unless ...

Many of the projects that will destroy roadless areas are economically marginal. It is costly for the Forest Service, BLM, timber companies, oil companies, mining companies and others to scratch out the "resources" in these last wild areas. It is expensive to maintain the necessary infrastructure of roads for the exploitation of wild lands. The cost of repairs, the hassle, the delay, the down-time may just be too much for the bureaucrats and exploiters to accept if there is a widely-dispersed, unorganized, *strategic* movement of resistance across the land.

It is time for women and men, individually and in small groups, to act heroically and admittedly illegally in defense of the wild, to put a monkeywrench into the gears of the machine destroying natural diversity. This strategic monkeywrenching can be safe, it can be easy, it can be fun, and—most importantly—it can be effective in stopping timber cutting, road building, overgrazing, oil and gas exploration, mining, dam building, powerline construction, off-road-vehicle use, trapping, ski area development and other forms of destruction of the wilderness, as well as cancerous suburban sprawl.

But it must be strategic, it must be thoughtful, it must be deliberate in order to succeed. Such a campaign of resistance would follow these principles:

Monkeywrenching Is Non-Violent

Monkeywrenching is non-violent resistance to the destruction of natural diversity and wilderness. It is not directed toward harming human beings or other forms of life. It is aimed at inanimate machines and tools. Care is always taken to minimize any possible threat to other people (and to the monkeywrenchers themselves).

Monkeywrenching Is Not Organized

There can be no central direction or organization to monkeywrenching. Any type of network would invite infiltration, *agents provocateurs* and repression. It is truly individual action. Because of this, communication among monkeywrenchers is difficult and dangerous. Anonymous discussion through this book and its future editions, and through the Dear Ned Ludd section of the *Earth First! Journal*, seems to be the safest avenue of communication to refine techniques, security procedures and strategy.

Monkeywrenching Is Individual

Monkeywrenching is done by individuals or very small groups of people who have known each other for years. There is trust and a good working relationship in such groups. The more people involved, the greater are the dangers of infiltration or a loose mouth. Earth defenders avoid working with people they haven't known for a long time, those who can't keep their mouths closed, and those with grandiose or violent ideas (they may be police agents or dangerous crackpots).

Monkeywrenching Is Targeted

Ecodefenders pick their targets. Mindless, erratic vandalism is counterproductive. Monkeywrenchers know that they do not stop a specific logging sale by destroying any piece of logging equipment which they come across. They make sure it belongs to the proper culprit. They ask themselves what is the most vulnerable point of a wilderness-destroying project and strike there. Senseless vandalism leads to loss of popular sympathy.

Monkeywrenching Is Timely

There is a proper time and place for monkeywrenching. There are also times when monkeywrenching may be counterproductive. Monkeywrenchers generally should not act when there is a non-violent civil disobedience action (a blockade, etc.) taking place against the opposed project. Monkeywrenching may cloud the issue of direct action and the blockaders could be blamed for the ecotage and be put in danger from the work crew or police. Blockades and monkeywrenching usually do not mix. Monkeywrenching may also not be appropriate when delicate political negotiations are taking place for the protection of a certain area. There are, of course, exceptions to this rule. The Earth warrior always thinks: Will monkeywrenching help or hinder the protection of this place?

Monkeywrenching Is Dispersed

Monkeywrenching is a wide-spread movement across the United States. Government agencies and wilderness despoilers from Maine to Hawaii know that their destruction of natural diversity may be met with resistance. Nation-wide monkeywrenching is what will hasten overall industrial retreat from wild areas.

Monkeywrenching Is Diverse

All kinds of people in all kinds of situations can be monkeywrenchers. Some pick a large area of wild country, declare it wilderness in their own minds, and resist any intrusion against it. Others specialize against logging or ORV's [off-road vehicles] in a variety of areas. Certain monkeywrenchers may target a specific project, such as a giant powerline, construction of a road, or an oil operation. Some operate in their backyards, others lie low at home and plan their ecotage a thousand miles away. Some are loners, others operate in small groups.

Monkeywrenching Is Fun

Although it is serious and potentially dangerous activity, monkeywrenching is also fun. There is a rush of excitement, a sense of accomplishment, and unparalleled camaraderie from creeping about in the night resisting those "alien forces from Houston, Tokyo, Washington, DC, and the Pentagon." As Ed Abbey says, "Enjoy, shipmates, enjoy."

Monkeywrenching Is Not Revolutionary

It does *not* aim to overthrow any social, political or economic system. It is merely nonviolent self-defense of the wild. It is aimed at keeping industrial "civilization" out of natural areas and causing its retreat from areas that should be wild. It is not major industrial sabotage. Explosives, firearms and other dangerous tools are usually avoided. They invite greater scrutiny from law enforcement agencies, repression and loss of public support. (The Direct Action group in Canada is a good example of what monkeywrenching is *not*.) Even Republicans monkeywrench.

Monkeywrenching Is Simple

The simplest possible tool is used. The safest tactic is employed. Except when necessary, elaborate commando operations are avoided. The most effective means for stopping the destruction of the wild are generally the simplest: spiking trees and spiking roads. There are obviously times when more detailed and complicated operations are called for. But the monkeywrencher thinks: What is the simplest way to do this?

Monkeywrenching Is Deliberate and Ethical

Monkeywrenching is not something to do cavalierly. Monkeywrenchers are very conscious of the gravity of what they do. They are deliberate about taking such a serious step. They are thoughtful. Monkeywrenchers, although nonviolent—are warriors. They are exposing themselves to possible arrest or injury. It is not a casual or flippant affair. They keep a pure heart and mind about it. They remember that they are engaged in the most moral of all actions: protecting life, defending the Earth.

A movement based on these principles could protect millions of acres of wilderness more stringently than any Congressional act, could insure the propagation of the grizzly and other threatened life forms better than an army of game wardens, and could lead to the retreat of industrial civilization from large areas of forest, mountain, desert, plain, seashore, swamp, tundra and woodland that are better suited to the maintenance of natural diversity than to the production of raw materials for overconsumptive technological human society.

If loggers know that a timber sale is spiked, they won't bid on the timber. If a Forest Supervisor knows that a road will be continually destroyed, he won't try to build it. If seismographers know that they will be constantly harassed in an area, they'll go elsewhere. If ORVers know that they'll get flat tires miles from nowhere, they won't drive in such areas.

John Muir said that if it ever came to a war between the races, he would side with the bears. That day has arrived.

STUDY QUESTIONS

1. What is the significance of the widespread destruction of the wilderness and animals described in the first part of Foreman's essay?

2. Why, according to Foreman, is monkey-wrenching necessary for saving the environment?

3. What are the principles of monkeywrenching? Evaluate them.

74

Ecosabotage and Civil Disobedience

MICHAEL MARTIN

Michael Martin is emeritus professor of philosophy at Boston University. Here he asks if eco-sabotage (sabotaging the mechanisms of environmental destruction, but causing no physical harm to humans) can be considered a form of civil disobedience. The question is important for legal reasons, because currently ecosabotage is essentially considered a form of terrorism. In fact, ecosabotage is often called ecoterrorism.

I define ecosabotage and relate this definition to several well-known analyses of civil disobedience. I show that ecosabotage cannot be reduced to a form of civil disobedience unless the definition of civil disobedience is expanded.

I suggest that ecosabotage and civil disobedience are special cases of the more general concept of conscientious wrongdoing. Although ecosabotage cannot be considered a form of civil disobedience on the basis of the standard analysis of this concept, the civil disobedience literature can provide important insights into the justification of ecosabotage. First, traditional appeals to a higher law in justifying ecosabotage are no more successful than they are in justifying civil disobedience. Second, utilitarian justifications of ecosabotage are promising. At present there is no a priori reason to suppose that some acts of ecosabotage could not be justified on utilitarian grounds, although such ecosaboteurs as Dave Foreman have not provided a full justification of its use in concrete cases.

INTRODUCTION

The recent arrest by the FBI of Dave Foreman, founder of the radical environmental group Earth First!, for conspiracy to sabotage two nuclear power plants and a facility that manufactures triggers for nuclear bombs[1] raises anew the issue of the morality of breaking the law for ethical purposes. In this paper I explore a number of analytic and moral

From *Environmental Ethics*, Vol. 12 (Winter 1990). Reprinted by permission.

questions connected with what has been called eco-sabotage: sabotage for the purpose of ecological protection. What is ecosabotage? Is it a form of civil disobedience? Can it be morally justified? Have advocates of ecosabotage such as Foreman in fact provided an ethically acceptable justification for what they sometimes advocate? Although ecosabotage has received wide coverage in popular magazines[2] and other periodicals,[3] these important and difficult questions have been in large part neglected by environmental ethicists.[4]

ECOSABOTAGE DEFINED

Sabotage in the name of environmental protection not only has occurred in real life but has also been detailed in field guides and in fiction. In their book *Ecodefense: A Field Guide to Monkey Wrenching*, Dave Foreman and Bill Haywood describe a number of techniques that can be used to stop, or at least slow down, the destruction of the environment by lumber companies, land developers, and similar organizations.[5] These include how to spike trees with nails in order to break saw blades, use cutting torches on power lines, puncture tires of road construction equipment, disable bulldozers, and burn billboards Edward Abbey's novel, *The Monkey Wrench Gang*, which influenced the leaders of Earth First!,[6] tells the story of a small group of environmental activists in the southwestern United States who, among other things, blow up railroad bridges, destroy construction machinery, and pull up survey stakes to frustrate land development and road construction.[7] Field guides and fictional accounts aside, environmental activists such as Margaret K. Millet, Mark L. Davis, and Marc A. Baker have reportedly actually tried to cut down a tower that carries power to pump water to the Central Arizona Project, a massive irrigation canal, Earth First! cofounder Howie Wolke is reported to have spent six months in jail for pulling up survey stakes that marked a road into a site where an oil well was being drilled,[8] Paul Watson, leader of the radical environment group the Sea Shepherds has claimed responsibility for sinking two of Iceland's four whaling ships by opening key valves in the ships,[9] and the Sea Shepherds also reportedly sank two Spanish whalers and one Cypriot whaling ship by attaching mines to the hulls.[10]

Can this great variety of acts of ecosabotage be subsumed under one definition? Perhaps, but the construction of such a definition is not easy. I approach the analytic task by first considering some of the elements that such a definition must include. First, any definition of ecosabotage must distinguish it from legal protests concerning environmental issues. Clearly this cannot be done merely in terms of the goals of the two kinds of activities, since an act of ecosabotage and a lawful ecological demonstration can have the same long-range goal, viz., the protection of the environment. Second, a definition of ecosabotage must distinguish it from sabotage for nonecological purposes, for example, wartime sabotage. This distinction cannot be made on purely behavioral grounds, since externally considered, some wartime sabotage might be indistinguishable from ecosabotage. For example, sabotaging a nuclear munitions plant might be either an act of wartime sabotage or an act of ecosabotage depending on what the act is supposed to achieve. Third, the definition must not restrict ecosabotage to the destruction of property. Even some acts of wartime sabotage do not involve this, for example, the removal of essential parts of machinery in a munitions factory. In ecosabotage, the removal of survey stakes from road construction sites might more appropriately be called obstruction rather the destruction.[11] Fourth, ecosabotage should be distinguished from the typical acts of civil disobedience that have been adapted by environmental organizations such as Greenpeace.[12] Fifth, ecosabotage must be distinguished from vandalism, the destruction of property or other mischief that is motivated by malice or spite.

It is also important to recognize that an adequate definition of ecosabotage must be as ethically neutral as possible—that is, the moral justification of ecosabotage must not be built into its definition. In other words, the question of what ecosabotage *means* must be separated as much as possible from the question of whether ecosabotage is *morally justified*. To be sure, these two questions are difficult to separate when, for example, it is unclear whether some criteria are relevant to the definitional or the moral issues. For example, it could be argued that part of the definition of ecosabotage is that it does not aim at harming human beings or other animal forms. On the other hand, it could be maintained that this is not part of the definition of ecosabotage and that an act of ecosabotage that aims at harming human or animal forms is simply not morally justified. An adequate definition of ecosabotage must decide such issues in a principled way.

Taking these elements into account, I suggest the following definition:

> Person P's act A is an act of ecosabotage iff (if and only if) (1) in doing A, P has as P's aim to stop, frustrate, or slow down some process or act that P believes will harm or damage the environment, (2) P's act A is motivated by a sense of religious or moral concern, (3) A is illegal, and (4) A is not a public act.

Condition (1) seems essential if ecosabotage is to be distinguished from other forms of sabotage. Condition (2) also appears essential because it distinguishes ecosabotage from vandalism. Foreman, for example, argues that destroying the technology that is polluting the Earth is a moral responsibility. He also goes so far as to claim that "it's a form of worship toward the Earth. It's really a very spiritual thing to go out and do."[13] These remarks suggest that ecosaboteurs can be motivated by religious as well as moral considerations. Thus, we need not claim that an act of ecosabotage *must* be morally motivated, for it can be religiously inspired. Condition (3) also seems essential for any definition of ecosabotage. Without it, a private act of prayer aimed at petitioning the deity to stop the destruction of the environment would be an act of ecosabotage because such an act would otherwise meet conditions (1), (2), and (4). Condition (4) is the most controversial condition in the definition, for it is certainly not clear that it needs to be part of the definition and the vagueness of ordinary language makes it uncertain whether it should be a necessary condition for the correct application of the term.[14] However, I see no other way to distinguish a typical act of civil disobedience used by environmental activists, for example, placing one's body in front of road construction equipment, from an act of

ecosabotage, such as pulling up survey stakes. As I have already noted, the crucial difference between these two acts is not that the latter destroys property and the former does not. The difference can best be seen when one compares the typical acts of civil disobedience practiced by organizations such as Greenpeace and the acts of ecosabotage that are allegedly practiced by members of Earth First!.[15] In a typical Greenpeace action, arrests are expected. Indeed, Greenpeace activists may want to be arrested as a way of advertising their cause. This is not to say that Greenpeace always publicizes its plans in advance. Surprise is essential for some of its actions. Nevertheless, once an action is completed—once the entrance to the incinerator is blocked or the whalers are frustrated—Greenpeace activists do not try to escape; they stay and accept their arrest, hoping that it will be reported in the media. On the other hand, an act of ecosabotage is done in secret. Even when ecosaboteurs do not destroy property but merely disturb operations, they do not intend to be caught. Indeed, part of Foreman and Haywood's field guide to monkey wrenching is devoted to instructing potential ecosaboteurs on how not to get arrested.[16] This is not to say that if ecosaboteurs are caught, they will not use their own arrests to their own advantage in the media, but getting caught is not typically part of their plan.

This definition is value neutral in the sense that it does not assume that act A is either religiously or morally justified or unjustified. Although it can be assumed that the ecosaboteur *believes* that his or her act is justified either morally or religiously, the ecosaboteur could be mistaken. Moreover, the definition is neutral about whether A is effective or not in stopping, frustrating, or slowing down some process that is believed to be damaging the environment. The ecosaboteur believes that the act will be effective, but, again, he or she could be mistaken.

I have chosen not to include the condition that P believes that A will not injure any human beings or living things in the *definition* of ecosabotage. To be sure, ecosaboteurs typically maintain that they intend no such injury. Foreman is reported to have said that his philosophy "is nonviolent because it is directed toward inanimate machinery."[17]

Paul Watson, the leader of the Sea Shepherds, waited until after the crew had left to sink the Icelandic whaling ships. Doc Sarvis, the philosophical spokesperson for "the monkey wrench gang" in Abbey's novel, is also opposed to violence against human beings. However, it is doubtful that this condition should be part of the definition of ecosabotage. Consider the analogous case of wartime sabotage. A worker who, in order to help the enemy, intentionally caused damage to a munitions plant although he or she knew other workers would be injured, would not for that reason alone have failed to perform an act of sabotage. On analogy with this example, I am inclined to maintain that although considerations of intentional noninjury to human beings or other animals are relevant in determining the morality of an act of ecosabotage, they are irrelevant when we are simply considering whether some act is or is not one of ecosabotage.

ECOSABOTAGE AND CIVIL DISOBEDIENCE

Is ecosabotage as defined above a type of civil disobedience? On the standard account of civil disobedience, the answer seems to be "No." Consider these typical definitions of civil disobedience taken from discussions of the topic by leading contemporary philosophical theorists.[18] According to Hugo Bedau, an act A is an act of civil disobedience iff A is illegal, done publicly, nonviolently and conscientiously with the intent to frustrate (one of) the laws, policies or decisions of the government.[19] According to Jeffrie Murphy, an act A is an act of civil disobedience iff (i) there is some law L according to which A is illegal, (ii) L is believed by the agent to be immoral or unconstitutional or irreligious or ideologically objectionable, and (iii) this belief motivates or explains A.[20] According to Christian Bay, an act is an act of civil disobedience iff A is an act or process of public defiance of a law or policy enforced by established government authorities insofar as the action is premeditated, understood by the actor(s) to be illegal or contested legally,

carried out and persisted in for limited public ends and by way of carefully chosen and limited means.[21] Finally, according to Carl Cohen, an act A is an act of civil disobedience iff A is an act of protest, deliberately unlawful, and conscientiously and publicly performed.[22]

On three of these definitions, an act of ecosabotage is clearly not an act of civil disobedience. For Bedau, Bay, and Cohen, it is a necessary condition of civil disobedience that it be publicly performed. Ecosabotage, however, by the definition proposed above is not publicly performed. In addition, Bedau's definition rules out many acts of ecosabotage as acts of civil disobedience by requiring that an act of civil disobedience be nonviolent. Furthermore, Bedau's and Bay's definitions rule out many acts of ecosabotage as acts of civil disobedience because acts of ecosabotage are often aimed at frustrating the actions or policies of private companies and not the government.

Murphy's definition does not seem to apply to the typical act of ecosabotage for a different reason. An ecosaboteur who breaks some law L by destroying construction equipment probably does not object on either moral or constitutional or religious grounds to the law L insofar as it states that it is illegal to knowingly destroy someone else's property. What he or she objects to is the use to which the construction equipment is being put. Murphy, however, in a footnote qualifies his definition by saying that "the agent may have no objection to L per se but may violate L because he views it as symbolic for or instrumentally involved with some other law L^0 ... to which he does object. In my view, such a person (Thoreau for example) is also to be regarded as civilly disobedient."[23] Taken by itself this seems to allow a typical act of ecosabotage to be an act of civil disobedience because, for example, the ecosaboteur objects to some law L^0 that allows the timber company to clear-cut the forest. Law L, the law that the ecosaboteur is breaking, is in some sense "instrumentally involved with L^0." However, later on in the same footnote Murphy adds: "What is most important is that motives of this sort be distinguished from the typical criminal motive:

self-interest. We do not think of a criminal act as a *public* act of *protest:* but these features *do* typically characterize acts of civil disobedience."[24] If we take this qualification seriously, then ecosabotage is not civil disobedience for it is certainly not a *public* act of protest. In the end, then, these four definitions of civil disobedience exclude ecosabotage because of the requirement that acts of civil disobedience must be done publicly.

Some general category is surely needed that includes both morally and religiously motivated illegal acts whether they are done publicly or not. One could accomplish this by expanding the concept of civil disobedience to include nonpublic acts. This, in fact, is the approach taken by Howard Zinn when he defines an act of civil disobedience "broadly" as a deliberate violation of the law for a vital social purpose.[25] Interestingly enough, from the standpoint of ordinary usage, Zinn's definition seems be more correct than the others so far considered. Certainly people who ran the underground railroad before the Civil War were said to have engaged in acts of civil disobedience, but these acts were not publicly performed.[26] In accordance with Zinn's definition, an act of ecosabotage *could* be an act of civil disobedience on the grounds that by definition ecosaboteurs are motivated by a sense of religious or moral duty and that a least some ecosaboteurs do deliberately violate the law for a vital social, i.e., moral purpose. However, it is unclear if all acts of ecosabotage fall under Zinn's definition. Would an ecosaboteur who pulled up survey stakes or destroyed construction equipment because of a mystical-religious feeling of unity with nature be described as breaking the law for a vital *social* purpose?

I suggest taking a different approach. Let us allow that civil disobedience must be public, or at least that it must be done for a social purpose, and introduce the concept of *conscientious wrongdoing* to cover either public *or* nonpublic law breaking for either religious *or* moral purposes. In this context, we can then specify that an act *A* is an act of conscientious wrongdoing iff it is an act of breaking a law for some moral or religious purpose. In this way, acts of civil disobedience on both the standard

account and Zinn's expanded version as well as acts of ecosabotage can be considered special cases of conscientious wrongdoing.

CAN ECOSABOTAGE BE GIVEN A CONSEQUENTIALIST JUSTIFICATION?

As I have just shown, without an expanded analysis of civil disobedience, ecosabotage cannot be viewed as a form of civil disobedience. Nevertheless, the civil disobedience literature can still provide insight into ecosabotage's possible justification. Most theorists of civil disobedience maintain that because acts of civil disobedience break the law and conflict with accepted modes of social conduct, they require some special justification to overcome what seems to be their prima facie wrongness. The same could be said about acts of ecosabotage.

If one follows this line of argument, the burden of justification is clearly on the civil disobedient person or the ecosaboteur. This burden is thought to be especially difficult to meet in a democracy because when laws are made by the people's representatives, they seem to have a legitimate claim to the obedience of all citizens. Yet this claim is never absolute. Democratic processes do not work perfectly: unjust and evil laws can be enacted; shortsighted and destructive policies can be pursued; it can either be impossible or can take too much time to change laws by lawful means. Thus, concerned citizens may sometimes legitimately entertain illegal means of changing the status quo and educating and arousing their fellow citizens. Before they become civil disobedients or ecosaboteurs, however, they need to have a clear rational justification for their actions.[27]

Carl Cohen, in his comprehensive study of civil disobedience, reports that historically there have been two basic ways to justify civil disobedience: the appeal to higher law and the appeal to teleological or consequentialist considerations.[28] Although both approaches are relevant to the justification of ecosabotage, I focus on the consequentialist justification in detail in this eassay.[29] This emphasis is in no way intended to suggest, however, that there are no limits to consequentialist justification.[30]

As Cohen maintains, a consequentialist justification need not be restricted to a specific calculus of goods or evils:

> It simply indicates that the justification will rely upon some intelligent weighing of consequences of the disobedient act. The protester here argues, in effect, that his particular disobedience of a particular law, at a particular time, under given circumstances, … is likely to lead in the long run to a better or more just society than would his compliance, under those circumstances, with the law in question.[31]

According to Cohen, the disobedient person appeals to two sorts of factors to justify his or her actions: moral principles that specify the goal of the disobedient act and factual considerations that specify the means to achieving this goal. The goals of the disobedient act, Cohen argues, are usually not in question but are shared by the vast majority of the citizens of the community. In the rare cases that they are not in harmony with the community, their justification "is almost certain to fail."[32] On the other hand, the means of achieving the goals are controversial and their justification involves a delicate and often inconclusive balancing of conflicting considerations. The person who is contemplating a disobedient act must consider the *background* of the case at hand and ask questions such as: "How serious is the injustice whose remedy is the aim of disobedient protest? How pressing is the need for that remedy? Have extraordinary but lawful means—assemblies of protests, letter-writing campaigns, etc.—been given full trial?"[33] The potentially disobedient person must also consider the *negative* effects of the disobedience and ask questions such as:

> How great is the expense incurred by the community as a consequence of the disobedience? … Is any violence entailed or threatened by the disobedient act? And if so, to property or to persons? … Has a bad example been set, a spirit of defiance or hooliganism been encouraged? Has respect for law been decreased in the community, or the fundamental order to society disturbed?[34]

Finally, the potential disobedient must estimate the *positive* results from the contemplated action and ask questions such as: how much influence will the disobedient act have in accomplishing change? Will it bring significant pressure to bear on legislatures that can bring about change? Can it attract public attention to some wrong or evil? Will the public put pressure on lawmakers? Or will the action of the disobedient be misunderstood and cause resentment? Will there be a backlash against the protesters?

These considerations are surely relevant to any consequentialist justification of acts of ecosabotage. Further, there seems to be no reason why a successful justification could not be given for at least some such acts. On a general level, the environmental goal of the public seems to be very similar to the goal of the ecosaboteurs: saving the environment from destruction and pollution. Recent polls indicate that the public is extremely concerned about environmental problems and is willing to go far in affording it protection.[35] Whether the more specific goals of radical environmental groups would be approved by the public is less clear: for example, Earth First!'s goal of saving the grizzly bears or the Sea Shepherds' goal of saving the whales. Nevertheless, it is not implausible to suppose that most people are sympathetic with these specific goals to some degree.

Whether members of environmental groups who use ecosabotage can justify their means in relation to the goal of saving the environment is, of course, the crucial issue. Unless strong general arguments can be raised against *any* use of ecosabotage, the justification of each proposed act of ecosabotage must be decided individually. A consideration of some of the most obvious general arguments against ecosabotage suggests that such arguments are in fact weak and cannot therefore be used to undermine all ecosabotage.

First, it may be objected that ecosabotage is beyond the pale of moral legitimacy because it involves violence. However, since there is no plausible general argument against the use of violence in civil disobedience, it hardly seems likely that ecosabotage can be faulted simply on this ground. Even Thoreau[36] and Gandhi[37] allowed that violence is sometimes an appropriate action and history points to cases in which violence in civil disobedience has had a beneficial effect. As Zinn points out:

> Violent labor struggles of the 1930's brought significant gains for labor. Not until Negro demonstrations resulted in violence did the national government begin to work seriously on civil rights legislation. No public statement on race relations has had as much impact as the Kerner Commission report, the direct result of outbreaks of violence in the ghettos.[38]

In any case, the distinction between violence against people and violence against property that both Zinn[39] and Cohen[40] stress in the context of justifying civil disobedience is relevant here. Violence directed against property is much less difficult to justify than violence against people.[41] Zinn has emphasized that violence in the context of civil disobedience should "be guarded, limited, aimed carefully at the source of injustice."[42] Advocates of ecosabotage in Earth First! say that violence should be directed only against property: they advocate destroying only equipment and facilities that are themselves used to destroy, deface, and pollute the environment.[43] Ecosaboteurs in the Sea Shepards also attempt to limit and focus their violence: they wreck equipment that is used to destroy whales.

A second possible objection to ecosabotage is that it erodes respect for the law, thus deteriorating the social fabric of civilized society. However, as a general argument against ecosabotage, this has no greater weight than it does against traditional civil disobedience. As Cohen notes, the allegation that civil disobedience erodes the social fabric is "essentially factual, not philosophical, but the facts are exceedingly complex and difficult to determine accurately.... The evidence available from the American experience of the 1950s and 1960s does not seem to support the allegation."[44] The same counterargument applies to ecosabotage. To be sure, there is a great amount of disrespect for the law in our country and in the world: murder, massacre, terrorism, rape, governmental corruption, and white collar crimes are rife. But it is pure conjecture to suppose that ecosabotage with its carefully circumscribed scope and targets has contributed or will significantly contribute to this disrespect.

In any case, one might argue that respect for the law is not the highest value. As Cohen points out: "It is possible, of course, that the wrong against which the civil disobedient protests is more serious than the alleged deleterious consequence to the social fabric."[45] Foreman and others would surely argue that what they are fighting for is more important than respect for the law. Indeed, they might maintain that respect for the law will be of little importance in a world with polluted air and water, devoid of natural wildernesses, and depleted of most of its natural variety. This value assessment is controversial, but it is not obviously wrong or absurd.

One important difference between civil disobedience and ecosabotage provides the basis for another objection. It could be argued that although civil disobedients disobey the law on one level, they show respect for it on another level by acting publicly—thus inviting arrest—and by accepting the result of the punishment. Ecosaboteurs, on the other hand, show their contempt for the law by acting secretly, thus attempting to avoid arrest and punishment. Although the standard accounts of civil disobedience that require publicly performed acts would not allow secret acts to be acts of civil disobedience, these same accounts provide a rationale for such secret acts. As Cohen argues in defense of the operation that helped runaway slaves escape to Canada, "To continue this practice in the interests of other, later runaways, it was essential for the managers of the underground railways to conceal their repeated violations of the fugitive slave laws. Concealment in such cases is a pressing tactical need, stemming from concern for the welfare of specific human beings, not from shame or remorse for the disobedient conduct."[46] Surely the same sort of argument could be used to defend ecosaboteurs: to continue protecting the environment, they must conceal their identity.[47] Concealment in such cases is a pressing tactical need, stemming from concern for the welfare of the environment, not from shame or remorse for unlawful conduct. There is no *a priori* reason to suppose that ecosaboteurs have less personal integrity than the managers of the underground railroad or that they consider their cause less morally significant than the managers of the underground railway considered theirs.

There are, of course, other general arguments that can be used against ecosabotage, but because they parallel the general ones that have been raised against civil disobedience and can be answered in a similar way, we need not consider them here.[48]

HAVE ADVOCATES OF ECOSABO-
TAGE SUCCESSFULLY JUSTIFIED
ECOSABOTAGE?

One might reasonably conclude from the above that although ecosabotage can be morally justified on consequentialist grounds in some contexts and although there are no general arguments standing in the way of such justification, the case for particular acts of ecosabotage has yet to be made. Although it is beyond the scope of this paper to provide such a justification, I consider critically how in fact advocates of ecosabotage such as Foreman have attempted to justify ecosabotage. In some cases where there is a gap in the justification, I fill in what I believe is a reasonable extrapolation or reconstruction of what a rational ecosaboteur might say. I show that the rationales given by advocates of ecosabotage follow in outline the sort of argument that, according to Cohen, a consequentialist justification of civil disobedience should take.

In a consequentialist justification, the moral goals of the civil disobedient are usually shared by the community. When they are not, they are likely to fail to persuade the community and not succeed politically. I have argued above that the general goals of ecosabotage are probably shared by most members of the community and that even the particular ones may be. However, Foreman explicitly interprets these goals in a nonanthropocentric way. Advocating the environmental philosophy of deep ecology, he argues:

> Deep ecology says that every living thing in the ecosystem has intrinsic worth and a nature-given right to be there. The grizzly bear, for example, has a right to exist for its own sake—not just for material or entertainment value to human beings. Wilderness has a right to exist for its own sake, and for the sake of the diversity of life-forms it shelters; we shouldn't have to justify the existence of the wilderness area by saying, "Well, it protects the watershed, and it's a nice place to backpack and hunt, and its pretty…. Furthermore, deep ecology goes beyond the individual and says that it's the species that's important. And more important yet is the community of species that makes up a given biosystem. And ultimately, our concern should be with the community of communities—the ecosystem.[49]

Whether Foreman's biocentrism and holism is philosophically justified, we cannot decide here.[50] But what does seem likely is that these points of view are not widely shared by the vast majority of the moral community and would be considered by the majority of the community to be rather eccentric. Given his biocentric and holistic interpretation of the goals of Earth First!, therefore, the means as well as the goals of the organization become controversial. As Cohen points out: "Even if the community is wrong [about the goals], and the eccentrics right, deliberate disobedient pursuit of their special objectives, as long as they are in the moral minority, is not likely to advance the protesters' goals and not likely to be defensible on utilitarian grounds."[51] However, the ecosaboteur need not pursue what the moral community will perceive as eccentric goals. There are good anthropocentric reasons why natural diversity should be preserved,[52] why tropical forest should be safeguarded,[53] why whales should be saved,[54] and so on.

According to Cohen, a civil disobedient must consider the background of the case at hand and evaluate both the importance of the goals and whether legal means have been given a fair trial. Foreman's statement certainly suggests that he advocates deliberating on the background of acts of ecosabotage very carefully and has considered the importance of the goals of ecosabotage and legal alternatives to it. Thus, he maintains:

> Species are going under everday.
> Old-growth forests are disappearing.
> Overgrazing continues to ruin our western public lands. Off-road vehicles are cutting up the countryside everywhere. Poisons are continually and increasingly being injected into the environment. Rain forests are being clear-cut. In short, the environment is *losing* … everywhere. And to try to fight such an essential battle with less than every weapon we have available to us is foolish and, in the long run, suicidal.[55]

One need not just take Foreman's word for this bleak picture of environmental devastation. Many environmentalists have painted a similar picture, albeit in more scholarly and less colorful tones.[56]

But are there not legal means of stopping the destruction? Foreman at one time certainly thought there were. At the beginning of his environmental career he was a Washington lobbyist for the conventional environmental group, the Wilderness Society. However, personal experience quickly led to his disillusionment with the effectiveness of such groups in bringing about change and stopping the devastation.[57] Now as a member of Earth First! he has had personal experience of illegal actions being effective. He cites one example in which the legal action of the Sierra Club, a conventional environmental organization, failed to stop the destruction of a wilderness while Earth First!'s blockage of road construction by civil disobedience provided enough public awareness to be successful.[58]

One wonders, of course, if Foreman's experience is typical and if he has reported the facts accurately. Are there cases not mentioned by Foreman where legal means have succeeded and where illegal ones have not? To give a more adequate justification, one would have to consider in a systematic way a wider range of cases than Foreman considers in which legal and illegal methods have been tried in order to see their relative effectiveness. His anecdotal evidence at most makes a prima facie case that illegal means are sometimes more effective than legal means for affording environmental protection.[59]

Cohen also suggests that in any utilitarian justification of civil disobedience it is important to consider the possible negative consequences of one's action. Foreman gives evidence of having done this. When asked whether monkey wrenching—his term for ecosabotage—is counterproductive to the environmental cause and serves only to make environmentalists look bad, Foreman had this to say:

> On the surface, this argument seems worth considering. But the fact is, there's already an awful lot of monkey wrenching going on, and such a backlash hasn't come about. The Forest Service tries to keep it quiet, industry tries to keep it quiet, and I think that there has even been an effort in the media to downplay the extent and effectiveness of monkey wrenching in America today…. It's easy to be cowed into compromising and being overly moderate by the charge that you are going to cause a negative reaction, going to tarnish the whole environmental movement. But in my opinion, the argument itself is a more fearsome anti-environmental weapon than any actual backlash could ever hope to be, because it keeps many of us from using all the tools we have available to slow down the destruction.[60]

Again independent evidence for a negative reaction should be sought. For example, do Greenpeace's door-to-door canvassers find it harder than a few years ago to obtain contributions because of the negative publicity occasioned by Earth First!? Do polls show that the public is becoming less sympathetic to environmental causes than it was before news of ecosabotage? Until evidence such as this is obtained we will not know if ecosabotage is having a negative impact. But Foreman is certainly justified in remaining skeptical about the purported negative impact until such evidence is produced.

Another possible negative consequence of ecosabotage is the unintentional injury to human beings. This problem is considered to be especially worrisome in the case of tree spiking. The main danger is that a saw blade can break and cause injury to the saw operator or to other people involved in the milling process. Ecosaboteurs respond to this problem in at least three different ways. Some tree spikers mark the trees they have spiked. For example, it is reported that after Mike Roselle, a member of Earth First!, spiked trees in Cathedral Forest, he painted a large *S* on them.[61] Thus, the recommended procedure is the notification of all parties who would be involved in cutting and milling trees. Consequently, only those who defied the warning were in jeopardy.[62] Other spikers, however, try to keep their spikes from being detected,[63] arguing that automation places most mill operators in control booths out of danger.[64] Although this might be true, it would not protect the sawyers cutting down the tree. The chain on the sawyer's chain saw can break upon hitting a spike, whip back into the sawyer and cause serious injuries. Moreover, some ecosaboteurs may argue that although they should take care not to injure people, "nothing is more dangerous to the long-term health of the people of this planet than the large scale destruction of the environment, and we have to stop that."[65] Consequently, any potential danger to the mill workers must be weighed against the greater danger to the world's population through environmental damage.

Whether these answers are completely adequate is a difficult issue that we cannot pursue here.[66]

Cohen also maintains that a potential civil disobedient must estimate the positive results from the contemplated action. Does ecosabotage have positive results? For example, does it accomplish the goal of slowing or stopping the destruction of the environment? Foreman says:

> I'm convinced that monkey wrenching can be one of the most effective ways of protecting our few remaining wild places. If a sufficient number of sincere individuals and small groups around the country were to launch a serious campaign of strategic monkey wrenching—a totally defensive effort to halt the continued destruction of wilderness—it would in fact cause the retreat of industrial civilization from millions of acres of wildlands.
>
> For example, if a logging company knows that the trees are going to be consistently spiked with large nails—which plays hell with expensive saw blades at the mills—or that roads will be repeatedly blocked by having rocks dumped onto them, it quickly becomes impractical to try to maintain a profitable operation ... so industrialization will retreat, leaving more land for the grizzly bear, for elk, for old-growth forests....
>
> For these reasons, along with the fact that conventional efforts to save the environment are not working, I believe that monkey wrenching is probably the single most effective thing that can be done to save natural diversity.[67]

It is important to notice that in this quotation Foreman argues only that ecosabotage *could* work, not that it *has* worked or *will* work. However, Foreman does cite actual cases in which conventional civil disobedience methods, for example, blockage of a road by human beings, have been successful in getting public sympathy and attention. An ecosaboteur might argue by analogy: because conventional methods of civil disobedience have worked, it is likely that methods of ecosabotage will work as well. However, this analogy is far from perfect. Human beings blocking a road may make good press and create favorable publicity whereas tree spiking and rock dumping may not. Foreman's argument, in any case, is not based on the favorable publicity that monkey wrenching will cause. He maintains that ecosabotage will make it economically unfeasible for industry to continue to destroy the wilderness. In principle, this may be true. But does the use of ecosabotage in fact work in this way? Until evidence is cited of industrialization *actually* retreating, "leaving more land for the grizzly bear, for elk, for old-growth forest" as a result of tree spiking and other acts of ecosabotage, one should leave as an open question whether ecosabotage is justified in terms of Cohen's utilitarian model of justification.

It is also important to note that in the passage just cited Foreman argues that ecosabotage can be effective if "a sufficient number" of individuals and groups engage in it. If it is not successful now, Foreman might argue, it is because not enough people are trained and devoted ecosaboteurs. This may or may not be true, but a similar argument could be invoked by environmentalists who are opposed to ecosabotage. After all, it might be argued, if enough people marched on Washington, wrote letters to their government representatives, and performed public acts of conscientious wrongdoing, that is, engaged in conventional civil disobedience, it would "cause the retreat of industrial civilization from millions of acres of wildlands." The number of people needed is unclear. But it is plausible to suppose that public outrage would have to be extensive—as, for example, it ultimately was in relation to the Vietnam War—to have the sort of impact that Foreman desires.

Foreman argues simultaneously that ecosabotage is already widespread, but that its presence is being covered up by government, industry, and the media, that the environment is losing, and that a sufficient number of ecosaboteurs would save the environment. Although there is no inconsistency in these remarks, they do raise the question of just how much more ecosabotage would have to occur to prevent the environment from losing and to save the environment from destruction. In response, it might argued that the number of ecosaboteurs that would be necessary for making a significant impact on environmental protection is several orders of magnitude less than the number of legal protesters, letter writers, public acts of civil disobedience, and

so on that would produce the same impact. For this reason at least, it may be said, ecosabotage is to be recommended over conventional strategies. On the other hand, the training and dedication that is involved in leading the life of an ecosaboteur would surely limit the number of potential candidates. Indeed, it is not clear that there are enough potential ecosaboteurs to make the difference that Foreman wants. Furthermore, in view of probable arrests it would seem that their ranks would have to be constantly replenished. There are then indirect considerations suggesting that ecosabotage is not likely in practice to have the impact that Foreman anticipates in theory.

Although Foreman does not cite evidence that ecosabotage actually works, a very recent article by C.M. does.[68] C.M. maintains that monkey wrenching is probably costing the government and industry about 20 to 25 million dollars per year in terms of damaged equipment, lost time, and legislative and law enforcement expenses. "This represents money industry is not able to use to deforest public lands, sink oil wells in the backcountry, invest in more destructive equipment, influence politicians with campaign contribution ..."[69] Even if corporations pass on these costs to their customers, according to C.M., monkey wrenching will cause the price of wood products to increase and thus indirectly decrease their consumption.

C.M. supplements this theoretical argument by citing actual cases in which ecosabotage has worked. For example, C.M. claims that there have been two cases in which the Forest Service withdrew timber sales after learning that trees were spiked. Moreover, C.M. argues that the firebombing of a $250,000 wood chipper in Hawaii, which "was grinding rainforest into fuel for sugar mills (without a permit and in violation of a court order)," left the company bankrupt. Finally, he or she argues that the controversial nature of ecosabotage has publicity value by taking "seemingly obscure environmental issues out the dark of scientific calculations into the limelight of individual passion and commitment."[70]

C.M.'s arguments for ecosabotage, nevertheless, are not enough to justify its use on utilitarian grounds. For this, C.M. would also have to show that typical acts of civil disobedience, that is, public acts of conscientious wrongdoing, were ineffective, for surely these are more desirable otherwise on utilitarian grounds than acts of ecosabotage if only because they are less likely to be interpreted as showing contempt for the law. In general, nonpublic acts of conscientious wrongdoing can be justified only when public nonviolent acts of conscientious wrongdoing cannot be utilized. Presumably there was no public way to help runaway slaves.[71] In the case of ecosabotage, however, public illegal means seem to be available. Road construction can be halted, for example, by lying down in front of the equipment, as well as by monkey wrenching the engines that run the equipment; trees can be protected by climbing them as well as by spiking. These nonviolent acts of conscientious wrongdoing also cost the government and industry a large amount of money, and have publicity value. In order to make their case, ecosaboteurs must show that public nonviolent acts of conscientious wrongdoing cannot work *and* that acts of ecosabotage can. To my knowledge they have not done so.[72]

CONCLUSION

In this paper I have defined ecosabotage and related this definition to several well-known analyses of civil disobedience. The comparison shows that ecosabotage cannot be assimilated to civil disobedience unless one expands the definition of the latter. The standard analyses of civil disobedience simply exclude it. I have suggested that ecosabotage and civil disobedience be considered special cases of the more general concept of conscientious wrongdoing. I have argued that although ecosabotage cannot be considered a form of civil disobedience on the standard analysis of this concept, the civil disobedience literature can provide important insights into the justification of ecosabotage.

Although other types of justification are possible, only a consequentialist one was considered in this paper. At present, there is no reason to suppose that some acts of ecosabotage could not be justified on consequentialist grounds, but I have concluded that advocates of ecosabotage such as Dave Foreman have not provided a full consequentialist justification of its use in concrete cases.

Evidence has been cited by C.M. showing that it does actually work in practice, but evidence is lacking that acts of civil disobedience would not be preferable. Nevertheless, Foreman and other advocates of ecosaboteurs such as C.M. have come further along in giving an adequate consequentialist justification of ecosabotage than is often realized and they have also met many of the objections against its use.

NOTES

1. Jim Robbins, "For Environmentalist, Illegal Acts are Acts of Love," *Boston Globe*, 2 June 1989, p. 3.

2. See for example, John J. Berger, "Tree Shakers," *Omni* 9 (1987): 20–22; Jamie Malanowski, "Monkey-Wrenching Around," *The Nation*, 2 May 1987, pp. 568–70; Joe Kane, "Mother Nature's Army," *Esquire*, February 1987, pp. 98–106.

3. J. A. Savage, "Radical Environmentalists: Sabotage in the Name of Ecology," *Business and Society Review 56–59* (Summer 1986): 35–37; David Peterson, "The Plowboy Interview: Dave Foreman: No Compromise in Defense of Mother Earth," *Mother Earth, News*, January–February 1985, pp. 16–22.

4. Two notable exceptions are Eugene C. Hargrove, "Ecological Sabotage: Pranks or Terrorism?" *Environmental Ethics* 4 (1982): 291–92, and Roderick Nash, *The Rights of Nature: A History of Environmental Ethics* (Madison: University of Wisconsin Press, 1989), pp. 189–98.

5. Dave Foreman and Bill Haywood, eds., *Ecodefense: A Field Guide to Monkeywrenching*, 2d ed. (Tucson, Arizona: A Ned Ludd Book, 1987).

6. See Kane, "Mother Nature's Army," p. 100.

7. Edward Abbey, *The Monkey Wrench Gang* (New York: Avon Books, 1975).

8. Robbins, "For Environmentalists, Illegal Acts are Acts of Love," p. 3.

9. *New York Times*, 10 November 1986, p. A1; November 13, p. A21. Cited by Sissela Bok, *A Strategy for Peace* (New York: Pantheon Press, 1989), pp. 179–80, n. 12.

10. *New York Times*, 10 November 1986, p. A10. Cited by Bok, *A Strategy for Peace*, pp. 179–80, n. 12.

11. The point here is not whether the parts of the machinery or the survey stakes are property, but that no property needs to be destroyed. Of course, survey stakes might be destroyed by being burned, but this need not happen in order for an act of ecosabotage to occur. One might, of course, argue that a survey itself is a type of property, because it costs money to construct, and that pulling up the stakes destroys it, because it costs money to do the survey again. Nevertheless, in this broad sense of property, acts of civil disobedience, e.g., sit-ins and blockades, also destroy property in this sense because they cost money. On grounds of clarity I do not use property in this broad sense.

12. See Jan Knippers Black, "Greenpeace: The Eco-logical Warriors," *USA Today*. November 1986, pp. 26–29; Michael Harwood, "Daredevils for the Environment," *New York Times Magazine*, 2 October 1988, pp. 72–75.

13. Robbins, "For Environmentalist, Illegal Acts are Acts of Love," p. 3.

14. It may be objected that this definition has a mistaken implication, namely, that a public act cannot be an act of ecosabotage. Suppose that as members of the road construction crew watch in amazement an environmental activist disables a bulldozer in order to prevent road construction and suppose this act was motivated by a moral concern for the environment. Surely, it may be said, this would be a case of ecosabotage. However, the concept of sabotage is vague and in some cases people's linguistic intuitions may differ over what is a correct application of the term. I personally would hesitate to call this an act of sabotage. At the very least, most people would agree that it is a marginal or borderline case. My definition can be understood as an *explication* of the concept of ecosabotage—that is, as an attempt to reconstruct the meaning of ecosabotage by eliminating vagueness and thus exclude certain borderline cases. For an account of explication see Michael Martin, *Concepts of Science Education* (Glenview, Ill.: Scott, Foresman and Company, 1972), pp. 77–79.

15. It should be noted that Earth First! does not *officially* advocate ecosabotage, but unlike Greenpeace it does not reject it.

16. Foreman and Haywood, *Ecodefense*, chap. 9.

17. Robbins, "For Environmentalist, Illegal Acts are Acts of Love," p. 3; see also Dave Foreman, "Strategic Monkeywrenching," in Foreman and Haywood, *Ecodefense*, p. 14.

18. It should be noted that except for Bedau's, these definitions do not include nonviolence as part of the *meaning* of civil disobedience. However, one should recall that nonviolent methods have been a crucial part of civil disobedience practice from Gandhi to King. See Gene Sharp, *The Politics of Nonviolent Action*, part 3, *The Dynamics of Nonviolent Action* (Boston: Porter Sargent Publisher, 1973), p. 608. Nevertheless, it is doubtful that nonviolent methods should be built into the meaning of civil disobedience. One may imagine circumstances in which a person honestly believes that he or she is justified in using violence to make his or her protest effective. To say that such a person's act could not be an act of civil disobedience seems arbitrary. See Carl Cohen, *Civil Disobedience: Conscience. Tactics, and the Law* (New York: Columbia University Press, 1971), pp. 22–36.

19. H. A. Bedau, "On Civil Disobedience," *Journal of Philosophy*, 53 (1961): 661. Quoted in Hugo Adam Bedau, ed., *Civil Disobedience: Theory and Practice* (New York: Pegasus, 1969), p. 218.

20. Jeffrie Murphy, "Introduction," *Civil Disobedience and Violence*, ed. Jeffrie Murphy (Belmont, Calif.: Wadsworth Publishing Co., 1971), p. 1.

21. Christian Bay, "Civil Disobedience: Prerequisite for Democracy in Mass Society," in *Civil Disobedience and Violence*, p. 76.

22. Cohen, *Civil Disobedience*, p. 39.

23. Murphy, "Introduction," *Civil Disobedience and Violence*, p. 1, n. 1.

24. Ibid.

25. Howard Zinn, "A Fallacy on Law and Order: That Disobedience must be Absolutely Nonviolent," in *Civil Disobedience and Violence*, p. 103.

26. See Cohen, *Civil Disobedience*, p. 18, who claims that such examples constitute "a marginal category."

27. In order to apply this argument to ecosabotage in the United States, certain assumptions must be made that might well be challenged. For example, it must be assumed that the laws that facilitate environmental destruction are democratically established and that it is prima facie wrong to disobey a democratically established law.

28. Cohen, Civil Disobedience, chap. 5.

29. According to Cohen, civil disobedients have often attempted to justify their conduct by appeals to a law higher than human law. This higher law justification has taken two major forms: an appeal to commands of God that are revealed to human beings in the Bible or other allegedly divinely inspired works or an appeal to nontheological higher laws that are discerned by the light of natural reason. There are three serious problems with both types of justifications. First, there seems to be no objective way to decide what these higher laws are. Second, principles of higher law are usually stated vaguely and abstractly. Consequently, it seems impossible to reach any objective decision on how they apply to concrete cases. Third, such justification would at best justify *direct* civil disobedience, that is, the breaking of a law that is itself morally objectionable in terms of higher law principles. But many acts of civil disobedience are indirect—that is, the civil disobedient disobeys some law that he or she has no objection to because the disobedience is a means to eliminate some serious injustice in a related area. It could be argued that these same problems are found in any attempt to justify ecosabotage by appeal to higher law principles. However, Cohen is mistaken in limiting nonconsequentialist justifications of civil disobedience to the higher law tradition. A complete account of nonconsequentialist justifications of civil disobedience would also have to take into account deontological theories of justification ranging from Kant to Rawls.

30. For a review of some recent literature see Hugo Bedau, "The Limits of Utilitarianism and Beyond," *Ethics* 95 (1985): 333–41. For a standard criticism of utilitarianism see William Frankena, *Ethics*, 2d ed. (Englewood Cliffs: Prentice-Hall, 1973), chap. 3. See also G. E. Moore, *Principia Ethica* (Cambridge: Cambridge University Press, 1903), chap. 5, secs. 91–93.

31. Cohen, *Civil Disobedience*, p. 120. If Cohen means that the goal must be shared by the vast majority to be *morally* justified, he is mistaken. I do not interpret him in this way, however. It is correct, nevertheless, that unless the goal is shared by the majority, the civil disobedient will not be practically successful—that is, the disobedient will have failed to justify his or her action to the community, and thus the disobedient will not be politically effective.

32. Ibid., p. 123.

33. Ibid., p. 125.

34. Ibid., pp. 125–26.

35. A recent national opinion survey indicates that eighty percent of Americans agree with the following statement: "Protecting the environment is so important that requirements and standards cannot be too high, and continuing environmental improvement must be made regardless of cost." Cited by Martin and Kathleen Feldstein. "In Defense of Pollution," *Boston Globe*, 1 August 1989, p. 24.

36. Thoreau defended John Brown in "A Plea for Captain John Brown," delivered in Concord and Boston a month before his execution. See Zinn, "A Fallacy on Law and Order," p. 105.

37. Gandhi wrote in *Young India*, "No rules can tell us how this disobedience may be done and by whom, when and where, nor can they tell us which laws foster in truth. It is only experience that can guide us." And "I do believe that where there is only a choice between cowardice and violence I would advise violence." See Zinn, "A Fallacy on Law and Order," p. 105.

38. Zinn, "A Fallacy on Law and Order," p. 110.

39. Ibid., p. 108.

40. Cohen, Civil Disobedience, p. 125.

41. Hargrove calls our attention to the fact that our society is "dedicated to the protection of property (including construction equipment and bridges)." See Hargrove, "Ecological Sabotage," p. 291. Even so there is a clear moral distinction to be drawn between violence against people and violence against property.

42. Zinn, "A Fallacy on Law and Order," p. 109.

43. See Foreman, "Strategic Monkeywrenching," *Ecodefense,* p. 15.

44. Cohen, *Civil Disobedience,* pp. 150–51.

45. Ibid., p. 150.

46. Ibid., pp. 19–20. On Cohen's own definition the managers of underground railways did not perform acts of civil disobedience. Cohen (p. 39) defines civil disobedience in terms of acts that are publicly performed.

47. T. O. Hellenbach, "The Future of Monkey-wrenching," in Foreman and Haywood, *Ecodefense,* p. 19.

48. See Cohen, *Civil Disobedience,* chap. 6.

49. Peterson, "The Plowboy Interview," p. 18.

50. For a recent critique of these points of view see Bryan G. Norton, *Why Preserve Natural Variety?* (Princeton: Princeton University Press, 1989), chaps. 8 and 9.

51. Cohen, *Civil* Disobedience, p. 123.

52. See Norton, Why Preserve Natural Variety? chap. 11.

53. Norman Myers, *The Primary Source: Tropical Forests and Our Future* (New York: W. W. Norton & Company, 1985), chaps. 10–15.

54. Peter M. Dora, "Cataceans: A Litany of Cain," *People, Penguins, and Plastic Tree*, ed. Donald VanDeVeer and Christine Pierce (Belmont, Calif.: Wadsworth Publishing Co., 1986), pp. 127–34.

55. Peterson, "The Plowboy Interview," p. 22; see also Foreman, "Strategic Monkeywrenching," *Ecodefense,* pp. 10–14.

56. See, for example, Lester R. Brown, Christopher Flavin, and Sandra Postel, "A World at Risk," *The State of the World: 1989,* ed. L. Brown et al. (New York: W. W. Norton & Company, 1989), pp. 3–20; Myers, *The Primary Source,* chaps. 5–9; Norman Myers, "The Sinking Ark," *People, Penguins, and Plastic Tree,* pp. 111–119.

57. Kane, "Mother Nature's Army," p. 100.

58. Peterson, "The Plowboy Interview," p. 19. It should be noted that this was not an act of ecosabotage.

59. However, the independent evidence provided by the effectiveness of the illegal actions of Greenpeace in protecting whales and seals confirms Foreman's contention. See Black, "Greenpeace: The Ecological Warriors," p. 29.

60. Peterson, "The Plowboy Interview," pp. 21–22.

61. Kane, "Mother Nature's Army," p. 980.

62. Savage, "Radical Environmentalists," p. 35.

63. See Foreman and Haywood, *Ecodefense,* pp. 24–51.

64. Malanowski, "Monkey-Wrenching Around," p. 569. But whether all employees of the mills, for example, the head rig offbearers who guide the logs, are safe is another question.

65. Ibid.

66. It should be noted that according to defenders of ecosabotage there has never been a documented case of anyone being seriously injured from its practice. See C.M., "An Appraisal of Monkey-wrenching." *Earth First!,* 2 February 1990.

67. Peterson, "The Plowboy Interview," p. 21.

68. See C.M., "An Appraisal of Monkeywrenching." According to *Earth First!* C.M. "is a widely published writer and scholar whose career dictates anonymity."

69. Ibid.

70. Ibid.

71. See Lester Rhodes, "Carrying on a Venerable Tradition," *Earth First!,* 2 February 1990. Rhodes compares ecosaboteurs to those who ran the underground railroad.

72. To be sure, Foreman has argued that monkey wrenching should not be used when there is a non-violent civil disobedience action such as blockages taking place. But what must be shown is that blockages and the like cannot bring about the same results as ecosabotage. See Foreman, "Strategic Monkeywrenching," *Ecodefense,* p. 15.

STUDY QUESTIONS

1. What are the different kinds of ecosabotage? Which of them should be called ecoterrorism, and which should not? Explain.

2. Summarize and criticize Martin's conclusion concerning the permissibility of ecosabotage.

75

The Coming Insurrection

Sixth Circle: "The Environment Is an Industrial Challenge"

THE INVISIBLE COMMITTEE

This reading is from The Coming Insurrection, *a controversial insurrectionary text.*
The authors are unknown; the French police believe the authors to be the Tarnac 9.
This selection critiques contemporary ecological thinking, seeing environmentalism as the
"new morality of capitalism."

Ecology is the discovery of the decade. For the last thirty years we've left it up to the environmentalists, joking about it on Sunday so that we can act concerned again on Monday. And now it's caught up to us, invading the airwaves like a hit song in Summertime, because it's 68 degrees in December.

One quarter of the fish species have disappeared from the ocean. The rest won't last much longer.

Bird flu alert; we are given assurances that hundreds of migrating birds will be shot from the sky.

Mercury levels in human breast milk are ten times higher than the legal level for cows. And these lips which swell up after I bite the apple—but it came from the farmer's market. The simplest gestures have become toxic. One dies at the age of 35 from "a prolonged illness" that's to be managed just like one manages everything else. We should've seen it coming before we got to this place, to pavilion B of the palliative care center.

You have to admit: this whole "catastrophe," which they so noisily inform us about, it doesn't really touch us. At least not until we are hit by one of its foreseeable consequences. It may concern us, but it doesn't *touch* us. And that is the real catastrophe.

There is no "environment catastrophe." The catastrophe is the environment itself. The environment is what's left to man after he's lost everything. Those who live in a neighborhood, a street, a valley, a war zone, a workshop—they don't have an "environment;" they move through a *world* peopled by presences, dangers, friends, enemies, moments of life and death, all kinds of beings. Such a world has its own consistency, which varies according to the intensity and quality of the ties attaching us to all of these beings, to all of these places. It's only us, the children of the final dispossession, exiles of the final hour-the ones who come into the world in concrete cubes, pick our fruits at the supermarket, and watch for an echo of the world on television—only we get to *have an environment.* And there's no one but us to witness our own annihilation, as if it were just a simple change of scenery, to get indignant about the latest progress of the disaster, to patiently compile its encyclopedia.

What has congealed as an environment is a relationship to the world based on management, which is to say, on estrangement. A relationship to the world wherein we're not made up *just as much* of the rustling trees, the smell of frying oil in the building, running water, the hubbub of schoolrooms, the mugginess of summer evenings. A relationship to the world where there is me and then my environment, surrounding me but never really constituting me. We have become neighbors in a planetary co-op owners' board meeting. It's difficult to imagine a more complete hell.

No material habitat has ever deserved the name "environment," except perhaps the Metropolis of day. The digitized voices making announcements, tramways with such a 21st century whistle, bluish streetlamps shaped like giant matchsticks, pedestrians done up like failed fashion models, the silent rotation of a video surveillance camera, the lucid clicking of the subway turnstiles supermarket checkouts, office time-clocks, the electronic ambiance of the cyber café, the profusion of plasma screens, express lanes and latex. Never has a setting been so able to do without the souls traversing it. Never has a surrounding been more automatic. Never has a context been so indifferent, and demanded in return—as the price of survival—such equal indifference from us. Ultimately the environment is nothing more than the relationship to the world that is proper to the metropolis, and that projects itself onto everything that would escape it.

It goes like this; they hired our parents to destroy this world, now they'd like to put us to work rebuilding it, and—to top it all off—at a profit. The morbid excitement that animates journalists and advertisers these days as they report each new proof of global warming reveals the steely smile of the new green capitalism, in the making since the 70s, which we waited for at the turn of the century but which never came. Well, here it is! It's sustainability! Alternative solutions, that's it too! The health of the planet demands it! No doubt about it anymore, it's a green scene; the environment will be the crux of the Political economy of the 21st century. A new volley of "industrial solutions" comes with each new catastrophic possibility.

The inventor of the H-bomb, Edward Teller, proposes shooting millions of tons of metallic dust into the stratosphere to stop global warming. NASA, frustrated at having to shelve its idea of an anti-missile shield in the museum of cold war horrors, suggests installing a gigantic mirror beyond the moon's orbit to protect us from the sun's now- fatal rays. Another vision of the future: a motorized humanity, driving on bio-ethanol from Sao Paulo to Stockholm; the dream of cereal growers the world over, for it only means converting all of the planet's arable lands into soy and sugar beet fields. eco-friendly cars, clean energy, and environmental consulting coexist painlessly with the latest Chancel ad in the pages of glossy magazines.

We are told that the environment has the incomparable merit of being the first truly global problem presented to humanity. A global problem, which is to problem that only those who are organized on a global level will be able to solve. And we know who they are. These are the very same groups that for close to a century have been the vanguard of disaster, and certainly intend to remain as such, for the small price of a change of logo. That EDF had the impudence to bring back its nuclear program as the new solution to the global energy crisis says plenty about how much the new solutions resemble the old problems.

From Secretaries of State to the back rooms of alternative cafes, concerns are always expressed in the same words, the same as they've always been. We have to get *mobilized*. This time it's not to rebuild the county like in the post war era not for the Ethiopians like in the 1980s, not for employment like in the 1990s. No, this time it's for the environment. It will thank you for it. Al Gore and degrowth movement stand side by side with the eternal great souls of the Republic to do their part in resuscitating the little people of the Left and the well-known idealism of youth. Voluntary austerity writ large on their banner, they work benevolently to make us compliant with the "coming ecological state of emergency." "The round and stick mass of their guilt lands on our tired shoulders, coddling us to cultivate our garden, sort out our trash, and eco-compost the leftovers of this macabre feast."

Managing the phasing out of unclear power, excess CO_2 in the atmosphere melting glaciers, hurricanes, epidemics, global over-population, erosion of the soil, mass extinction of living species… this will be our burden. They tell us, "everyone must do their part," if we want to save our beautiful model of civilization. We have to consume a little less *in order to be able to keep consuming*. We have to produce organically *in order to keep producing*. We have to control ourselves *in order to go on controlling*. This is the logic of a world straining to maintain itself whilst giving itself an air of historical rupture. This is how they would like to convince us to participate in the great industrial challenges of this century. And in our bewilderment we're ready to leap into the arms of the very same ones who presided over the devastation, in the hope that they will get us out of it.

Ecology isn't simply the logic of a total economy; it's the new morality of capital. The system's internal state of crisis and the rigorous screening that's underway demand a new criterion in the name of which this screening and selection will be carried out. From one era to the next, the idea of virtue has never been anything but and invention of vice. Without ecology, how could we justify the existence of two different food regimes, one "healthy and organic" for the rich and their children, and the other notoriously toxic for the plebes, whose offspring are damned to obesity. The planetary hyper-bourgeoisie wouldn't be able make their normal lifestyle seem respectable if its latest caprices weren't so scrupulously "respectful of the environment." Without ecology, nothing would have enough authority to gag any and all objections to the exorbitant progress of control.

Tracking, transparency certification, eco-taxes, environmental excellence, and the policing of water, all give us an idea of the coming state of ecological emergency. Everything is permitted to a power structure that bases its authority in Nature, in health and in well-being.

"Once the new economic and behavioral culture has become common practice, coercive measures will doubtless fall into disuse of their own accord," You'd have to have all the ridiculous aplomb of a TV crusader to maintain such a frozen perspective and in the same breath incite us to feel sufficiently "sorry for the planet" to get mobilized, whilst remaining anesthetized enough to watch the whole thing with restraint and civility. The new green-asceticism is precisely the self-control that is required of us all in order to negotiate a rescue operation where the system has taken itself hostage. From now on, it's in the name of environmentalism that we must all tighten our belts, just as we did yesterday in the name of the economy. The roads could certainly be transformed into bicycle paths, we ourselves could perhaps, to a certain degree, be grateful one day for a guaranteed income, but

only at the price of an entirely therapeutic existence. Those who claim that generalized self-control will spare us form an environmental dictatorship are lying: the one will prepare the way other, and we'll end up with both.

A long as there is Man and Environment, the police will be there between them.

Everything about the environmentalist's discourse must be turned upside-down. Where they talk of" catastrophes" to label the present system's mismanagement of beings and things, we only see the catastrophe of its all too perfect operation. The greatest wave of famine ever known in tropics (1876-1879) coincided with a global drought, but more significantly, it also coincided with the apogee of colonization. The destruction of the peasant's world and of local alimentary practices meant the disappearance of the means for dealing with scarcity. More than the lack of water, it was the effect of the rapidly expanding colonial economy that littered the Tropics with millions of emaciated corpses. What presents itself everywhere as an ecological catastrophe has never stopped being, above all, the manifestation of a disastrous relationship to the world. Inhabiting a nowhere makes us vulnerable to the slightest jolt in the system, to the slightest climactic risk. As the latest tsunami approached and the tourists continued to frolic in the waves, environmentalism's present paradox is that under the pretext of saving the planet from desolation it merely saves the causes of its desolation.

The normal functioning of the world usually serves to hide our state of truly catastrophic dispossession. What is called "catastrophe" is no more than the forced suspension of this state, one of those rare moments when we regain some sort of presence in the world. Let the petroleum reserves run out earlier than expected; let the suffer some great social disruption and some great "return to savagery of the population," a "planetary threat," the "end of civilization!" Either way, any loss of control would be preferable to all the crisis management scenarios they envision. When this comes, the specialists in sustainable development won't be the ones with the best advice. It's within the malfunction and short-circuits of the system that we find the elements of a response whose logic would be to abolish the problems themselves. Among the signatory nations to the Kyoto Protocol, the only countries that have fulfilled their commitments, in spite of themselves, are the Ukraine and Romania. Guess why. The most advanced experimentation with "organic" Agriculture on a global level has taken place since 1989 on the island of Cuba. Guess why. And it's along the African highways, and no-where else, that auto mechanics has been elevated to a form popular art. Guess how.

What makes the crisis desirable is that in the crisis the environment cases to be the environment. We are forced to reestablish contact, albeit a potentially fatal one, with what's there, to rediscover the rhythms of reality. What surrounds us is no longer a landscape, a panorama, a theater, but something to inhabit, something we need to come to terms with, something we can learn from, We won't let ourselves be led astray by the one's who've brought about the contents of the "catastrophe." Where the managers platonically discuss among themselves how they might decrease emissions" without breaking the bank," the only realistic option we can see is to "break the bank" as soon as possible and, in the meantime, take advantage of every collapse in the system to increase our own strength.

New Orleans, a few days after Hurricane Katrina. In this apocalyptic atmosphere, here and there, life is reorganizing itself. In the face of the inaction of the public authorities, who were too busy cleaning up the tourist areas of the French Quarter and protecting shops to help the poorer city dwellers, forgotten forms are reborn. In spite of occasionally strong-armed attempts to evacuate the area, in spite of white supremacist lynch mobs, a lot of people refused to leave the terrain. For the latter, who refused to be deported like "environmental refugees" all over the country, and for those who came from all around to join them in solidarity, responding to a call form a former Black Panther, self-organization came back to the fore. In a few weeks time, the Common Ground Clinic was set up. From the very first days, this veritable "country hospital" provided free and effective treatment to those who needed it, thanks to the constant influx of volunteers. For more than a year now, the clinic is still the base of a daily resistance to the clean—sweep operation of government bulldozers, which are trying to turn that part of the city into a pasture for property developers. Popular kitchens, supplies, street medicine, illegal takeovers, the construction of emergency housing, all this practical knowledge accumulated here and there in the course of a life, has now found a space where it can be deployed. Far from the uniforms and sirens.

Whoever knew the penniless joy of these New Orleans neighborhoods before the catastrophe, their defiance towards the state and the widespread practice of making do with what's available wouldn't be at all surprised by what became possible there. On the other hand, anyone trapped in the anemic and atomized everyday routine of our residential deserts might doubt that such determination could be found anywhere anymore. Reconnecting with such gestures, buried under years of normalized life, is the only practicable means of not sinking down with the world. The time will come when we take these up once more.

STUDY QUESTIONS

1. Discuss the statement: "Ecology isn't just the logic of total economy, it's also the new morality of Capital."

2. How is this essay similar and different from other critiques of green capitalism?

3. This book is one of the most controversial books of the last decades. Glenn Beck has featured it, many anarchists are offended by it, and the French police think it was written by terrorists. Why is this?